FIFTH EDITION

World Politics

Interests, Interactions, Institutions

FIFTH EDITION

World Politics

Interests, Interactions, Institutions

Jeffry A. Frieden
Harvard University

David A. Lake
University of California, San Diego

Kenneth A. Schultz
Stanford University

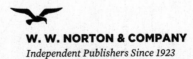

W. W. NORTON & COMPANY
Independent Publishers Since 1923

W. W. Norton & Company has been independent since its founding in 1923, when William Warder Norton and Mary D. Herter Norton first published lectures delivered at the People's Institute, the adult education division of New York City's Cooper Union. The firm soon expanded its program beyond the Institute, publishing books by celebrated academics from America and abroad. By midcentury, the two major pillars of Norton's publishing program—trade books and college texts—were firmly established. In the 1950s, the Norton family transferred control of the company to its employees, and today—with a staff of four hundred and a comparable number of trade, college, and professional titles published each year—W. W. Norton & Company stands as the largest and oldest publishing house owned wholly by its employees.

Editor: Laura Wilk

Assistant Editor: Catherine Lillie

Project Editor: Caitlin Moran

Managing Editor, College: Marian Johnson

Managing Editor, College Digital Media: Kim Yi

Production Manager: Eric Pier-Hocking

Media Editor: Spencer Richardson-Jones

Associate Media Editor: Alexandra Malakhoff

Media Project Editor: Marcus Van Harpen

Assistant Media Editor: Lena Nowak-Laird

Ebook Production Manager: Mateus Manço Teixeira

Ebook Production Coordinator: Lizz Thabet

Marketing Manager, Political Science: Ashley Sherwood

Design Director: Rubina Yeh

Photo Editor: Catherine Abelman

Permissions Manager: Bethany Salminen

Permissions Consultant: Elizabeth Trammell

Composition: Graphic World

Manufacturing: Transcontinental Interglobe, Inc.

Permission to use copyrighted material is included on p. A-9.

W. W. Norton & Company, Inc., 500 5th Avenue, New York, NY 10110

wwnorton.com

W. W. Norton & Company Ltd., 15 Carlisle Street, London W1D 3BS

1 2 3 4 5 6 7 8 9 0

Contents in Brief

Contents

Part 1: Foundations

Chapter 2: Understanding Interests, Interactions, and Institutions 42

Part 2: War and Peace

Part 3: International Political Economy

Chapter 7: International Trade   306

Chapter 8: International Financial Relations   364

Chapter 9: International Monetary Relations   406

Chapter 10: Development: Causes of the Wealth and Poverty of Nations

446

Part 4: Transnational Politics

Part 5: Looking Ahead

Preface

As this textbook has evolved over the course of five editions, we have been guided throughout by two principles that spurred our enthusiasm for the project and that, we believe, make this textbook special. First, this text is organized around substantive puzzles that draw scholars and students alike to the study of world politics. This is a field that grapples with some of the most interesting and important questions in political science: Why are there wars? Why do countries have a hard time cooperating to prevent genocides or global environmental problems? Why are some countries rich while others are poor? This book gives students the tools they need to start thinking analytically about the answers to such questions. Second, we have sought to bridge the gap between how scholars of international relations conduct their research and how they teach their students. The text draws from the insights and findings of contemporary international relations scholarship and presents them in a way that is accessible to undergraduates who are just starting out in this field. Our ambition is to provide students with a "toolbox" of analytic concepts common to many theories of world politics that can be applied to a wide variety of topics. We hope to lay a solid foundation on which students can build their own understanding of the continually evolving world of international politics.

The core concepts in this toolbox are interests, interactions, and institutions. Chapter 2 presents the framework, and the remaining chapters apply it. The book is organized around the principle that problems in world politics can be analyzed using these key concepts:

- Who are the relevant actors and what are their interests?

- What is the nature of their interactions? What strategies can they be expected to pursue? When are their choices likely to bring about cooperation or conflict?

- How do institutions constrain and affect interactions? How might they impede or facilitate cooperation? When and how do institutions favor different actors and their interests?

Different problems and issues will emphasize interests, interactions, or institutions to varying degrees. There is no single model of world politics that applies equally to war, trade and international financial relations, and the struggles for improved human rights and a cleaner global environment. Nonetheless, any complete understanding of world politics must include all three key concepts. Although we do not refer extensively to the traditional paradigms based on realism, liberalism, and constructivism in the book, we show briefly in the Introduction how each of these major "-isms" of international relations theory can be understood as a different set of assumptions about interests, interactions, and institutions in world politics.

We were fortunate to work with two contributors on this edition: Stephanie Rickard at the London School of Economics revised Chapter 7, International Trade, and Susan Hyde at the University of California, Berkeley, revised Chapter 11, International Law and Norms. Their contemporary perspectives on the scholarship and their commitment to the needs of today's students helped us further sharpen the tool kit we provide in these foundational chapters. We're grateful for their fresh perspectives.

Plan of the Book

This book has five parts. The first part (Chapters 1 and 2) introduces the broad patterns of conflict and cooperation in international history and lays out the text's framework. Part 2 (Chapters 3 through 6) deals with the central puzzles in the study of war and political violence:

- War is an extremely costly way for states to settle their disputes. Given the human and material costs of military conflict, why do states sometimes wage war rather than resolve their disputes through negotiation? (Chapter 3)

- War is costly for states, but what if there are actors within the state—such as politicians, businesses, or the military—who see war as beneficial and who expect to pay few or none of its costs? Do states fight wars to satisfy influential domestic interests? (Chapter 4)

- In a well-governed country, the police prevent and punish acts of violence between individuals. Where are the police in international politics? Why is it so hard for the international community to prevent and punish acts of aggression? (Chapter 5)

- A great deal of politically motivated violence in the contemporary world is committed by or directed against nonstate actors, particularly rebel groups engaged in civil wars or terrorist networks. Why do some individuals and groups resort to violence against their governments or unarmed civilians? (Chapter 6)

Part 3 (Chapters 7 through 10) discusses the main puzzles in international economic relations:

- Virtually all economic analysis concludes that trade is economically beneficial. Why, then, does every country restrict trade in some way? Why have policies toward trade varied so much from country to country and over time? (Chapter 7)

- Every year, approximately $5 trillion is invested abroad. Why is so much money invested in foreign countries? And why do relations between foreign investors and the countries in which they invest often become hostile and politically controversial? (Chapter 8)

- In the absence of global government and a global currency, how are goods and services traded among countries? (Chapter 9)

- Why are some countries rich and others poor? How do international politics and economics affect development? (Chapter 10)

Part 3 (Chapters 11 through 13) considers relatively new issues associated with global governance:

- In a world of sovereign states, how can the international community constrain states' actions? When and why do states do what is "right"? (Chapter 11)

- Why do states undertake costly actions to protect the human rights of people outside their borders? In light of the widespread support for the principle of human rights, why has the movement to protect those rights not been even more successful? (Chapter 12)

- Nearly everyone wants a cleaner and healthier environment. Why, then, is it so hard to cooperate internationally to protect the environment? (Chapter 13)

Part 5 presents the concluding chapter (Chapter 14), which considers a variety of challenges to the international system in the coming decades, including the spread of both weapons of mass destruction and cyberweapons, the rising power of China, and the growing backlash against globalization.

Pedagogical Features: Applying the Concepts

Our approach to the study of international relations is problem-oriented. Each chapter begins with a puzzle about world politics: a question or set of questions that lack obvious answers. We then use the concepts of interests, interactions, and institutions—along with known empirical regularities, current research results, and illustrative cases—to "solve" the puzzle and lead students to a deeper understanding of world politics. Each chapter includes numerous pedagogical features intended to helps students learn—and apply—the concepts.

- **"Thinking Analytically"** sections at the start of each chapter preview how the concepts of interests, interactions, and institutions are used in the chapter's analysis.

- **"What Shaped Our World?"** boxes apply the interests, interactions, and institutions framework to explain historical events that continue to shape contemporary world politics and illustrate the analytic theme of the chapter.

- **"Controversy"** boxes probe ethical issues to stimulate classroom discussion and show how interests, interactions, and institutions can help us understand—if not necessarily resolve—the difficult normative trade-offs involved.

- **"How Do We Know?"** boxes survey published research findings and describe empirical facts or regularities that are important for understanding the larger puzzle discussed in the chapter.

- **"Study Tool Kit"** sections at the end of each chapter include key terms, further readings, and "Interests, Interactions, and Institutions in Context" sections that review key analytic insights in the chapter.

Innovative Online Resources for Students and Instructors

This Fifth Edition of *World Politics* is accompanied by an innovative formative assessment package to support teaching and learning both online and face-to-face:

For Students

InQuizitive   Developed by a team of *World Politics* users directed by Dustin Tingley (Harvard University) in close collaboration with the textbook authors, InQuizitive for *World Politics* helps students get the most out of their reading assignments. After students work through basic questions on key concepts and definitions, InQuizitive asks them to try their hand at applying the concepts from the text to alternative examples and cases. The result is deeper engagement with the text and a clear sense of how concepts from the reading can be applied to real-world situations. See the back cover for more information.

New "Check Your Understanding" Ebook Quizzes   The newly enhanced *World Politics* ebook, which comes free with each new copy of the text, helps students confirm their understanding as they read and prepares them for graded assignments such as InQuizitive. New "Check Your Understanding" quizzes tied to each section of the text provide opportunities for students to identify concepts they have mastered and those that they need to further review. When assigned alongside InQuizitive, the ebook gives students a seamless experience that gets them learning and applying in one place.

New Bargaining Model Activities   New activities provide step-by-step guides to the complex processes introduced in Chapter 2's Primer on Game Theory. The three-part structure of each tutorial first introduces a concept with an animation, then checks students' understanding with a quiz, and finally challenges them to apply what they've learned in a final application activity. Bargaining model and game theory activities cover the following topics:

- The Prisoner's Dilemma
- Comparative advantage

- The Stag Hunt
- Chicken
- Baseline bargaining
- Bargaining with shifting power
- Bargaining and first-strike advantage

News Analysis Activities   These new biweekly exercises help students apply the main concepts of *World Politics* to current issues. Each News Analysis Activity includes a link to a contemporary news story and an assessment that invites students to apply the interests, interactions, and institutions framework to make sense of events happening right now. Instructors can also use the News Analysis Activities as a way of bringing current events into the course. Each News Analysis Activity offers a great way to ensure that students know how to apply what they are learning and affords instructors a common perspective on a contemporary issue in world politics.

For Instructors

An extensive set of additional materials for instructors supports this book's goal of making an analytical approach to world politics accessible to introductory-level students. Norton offers a Test Bank, an Instructor's Manual, and sets of lecture and art PowerPoint slides—all of which have been developed specifically to accompany *World Politics*. Also available to instructors as a resource is W. W. Norton's Teaching Political Science Online Guide. Student resources and activities such as the ebook, InQuizitive, Bargaining Model Activities, and News Analysis Activities can be found on the *World Politics* Digital Landing Page at digital.wwnorton.com/worldpol5.

Resources for Your LMS include links to the Test Bank, the News Analysis Activities, the Bargaining Model Activities, and InQuizitive. Grades from InQuizitive can be set up to automatically populate your LMS gradebook, and sign-on is simple for your students. Speak with your Norton representative to integrate InQuizitive in your LMS.

Acknowledgments

We owe many debts in preparing this text. Roby Harrington at Norton brought us together and encouraged us to write this book. His vision, judgment, and steady editorial hand are reflected throughout. Ann Shin at Norton expertly guided the project from first draft to finished product and educated us in the art of writing and revising a textbook. The final form and content of this book reflect her efforts to keep three sometimes over-committed academics on track, on theme, and on time. We are grateful also to the rest of the Norton team that worked on this Fifth Edition, including editor Laura Wilk, project editor Caitlin Moran, and Samantha Held, for her thorough copyediting. Assistant editor Catherine Lillie helped keep the many pieces of the manuscript moving throughout the process, and production manager Eric Pier-Hocking kept a close eye on the quality of the printed book as all those pieces came together. Spencer Richardson-Jones, Lena Nowak-Laird, and Alexandra Malakhoff brought creativity and order to the development of the ancillary resources. We owe thanks to all of them.

We are enormously grateful to the many reviewers and class-testers who provided guidance and helpful comments at many different stages of this project. For their advice on the First Edition, we would like to thank:

Rodwan Abouharb, *Louisiana State University*

Karen Adams, *University of Montana*

Todd Allee, *University of Illinois, Urbana-Champaign*

Juliann Allison, *University of California, Riverside*

Claire Apodaca, *Florida International University*

Alan Arwine, *Texas Tech University*

Robert Brown, *Temple University*

Renato Corbetta, *University of Alabama, Birmingham*

Andrew Cortell, *Lewis & Clark College*

Benjamin Fordham, *Binghamton University*

Giovanna Gismondi, *Ohio University*

Darren Hawkins, *Brigham Young University*

Paul Hensel, *Florida State University*

Uk Heo, *University of Wisconsin, Marathon*

Tobias Hofmann, *College of William & Mary*

Elizabeth Hurd, *Northwestern University*

Michael Kanner, *University of Colorado, Boulder*

Scott Kastner, *University of Maryland*

Jonathan Keller, *James Madison University*

Alan Kessler, *University of Texas*

Andy Konitzer, *Samford University*

David Leblang, *University of Virginia*

Ashley Leeds, *Rice University*

Lisa Martin, *University of Wisconsin*

Ronald Mitchell, *University of Oregon*

Will H. Moore, *Florida State University*

Layna Mosely, *University of North Carolina*

Robert Packer, *Pennsylvania State University*

Robert Pahre, *University of Illinois, Urbana-Champaign*

Glenn Palmer, *Pennsylvania State University*

Leanne Powner, *College of Wooster*

Tonya Putnam, *Columbia University*

Stephen Quackenbush, *University of Missouri*

John Quinn, *Truman State University*

Robert Rauchhaus, *University of California, Santa Barbara*

Chad Rector, *George Washington University*

Dan Reiter, *Emory University*

Stephen Saideman, *McGill University*

Idean Salehyan, *University of North Texas*

Todd Sechser, *University of Virginia*

Megan Shannon, *University of Mississippi*

Randolph Siverson, *University of California, Davis*

Oleg Smirnov, *Stony Brook University*

Mark Souva, *Florida State University*

Patricia Sullivan, *University of Georgia*

Hiroki Takeuchi, *Southern Methodist University*

Aleksandra Thurman, *University of Michigan*

Kelly Wurtz, *Trinity College*

For the Second Edition, we received helpful advice from the following reviewers:

David Andersen, *CSU Sacramento*

Philip Barker, *Austin College*

Marijke Breuning, *University of North Texas*

Tom Brister, *Wake Forest University*

Terry Chapman, *University of Texas at Austin*

John Conybeare, *University of Iowa*

Michaelene Cox, *Illinois State University*

Monti Datta, *University of Richmond*

David Dreyer, *Lenoir-Rhyne University*

Sean Ehrlich, *Florida State University*

Traci Fahimi, *Irvine Valley College*

David Grondin, *University of Ottawa*

Surupa Gupta, *University of Mary Washington*

Tamar Gutner, *American University*

Yoram Haftel, *University of Illinois at Chicago*

Phil Kelly, *Emporia State University*

Robert S. Kravchuk, *University of North Carolina at Charlotte*

Ashley Leeds, *Rice University*

Anika Leithner, *California Polytechnic State University*

Doug Lemke, *Pennsylvania State University*

Lisa Martin, *University of Wisconsin, Madison*

Molly Melin, *Loyola University Chicago*

Amanda Murdie, *Kansas State University*

Rusty Nichols, *Southwestern College*

Richard Nolan, *University of Florida*

Ausra Park, *Davidson College*

Mark Pollack, *Temple University*

Kathy Powers, *University of New Mexico*

Melanie Ram, *California State University, Fresno*

Dan Reiter, *Emory University*

Kirsten Rodine Hardy, *Northeastern University*

Stephen Saideman, *McGill University*

Chris Saladino, *Virginia Commonwealth University*

Susan Sell, *George Washington University*

Megan Shannon, *University of Mississippi*

Nicole Simonelli, *Purdue University*

Oleg Smirnov, *Stony Brook University*

Mark Souva, *Florida State University*

Allan Stam, *University of Michigan*

Richard Stoll, *Rice University*

Jelena Subotic, *Georgia State University*

Joel Trachtman, *Tufts University*

James Walsh, *University of North Carolina at Charlotte*

Jesse Wasson, *Rochester Institute of Technology*

Jeremy Youde, *University of Minnesota Duluth*

For their valuable suggestions for the Third Edition, we thank:

Klint Alexander, *Vanderbilt University*

Sarah Bush, *Temple University*

Jennifer De Maio, *California State University, Northridge*

Erik Gartzke, *University of California, San Diego*

Amy Gurowitz, *University of California, Berkeley*

Marcus Holmes, *Fordham University*

Jesse Johnson, *Kansas State University*

Joon Kil, *Irvine Valley College*

Jenn Larson, *New York University*

Kyle M. Lascurettes, *Lewis & Clark College*

Brooke Miller, *Middle Georgia State College*

Paul Musgrave, *Georgetown University*

Simon Nicholson, *American University*

Dave Ohls, *American University, School of International Service*

Andrew Owsiak, *University of Georgia*

Tonya Putnam, *Columbia University*

Ryan Salzman, *Northern Kentucky University*

Randolph Siverson, *University of California, Davis*

Adam Van Liere, *University of Wisconsin, La Crosse*

Byungwon Woo, *Oakland University*

For their advice on the Fourth Edition, we would like to thank:

Michael Allen, *Boise State University*

Juliann Emmons Allison, *University of California, Riverside*

Thomas Ambrosio, *North Dakota State University*

Constantine Boussalis, *Trinity College Dublin*

Marissa Brookes, *University of California, Riverside*

Thomas Chadefaux, *Trinity College Dublin*

Stephen Chaudoin, *University of Illinois, Urbana-Champaign*

Olga Chyzh, *Iowa State University*

Jennifer Clemens, *University of Wisconsin, Milwaukee*

David Dreyer, *Lenoir-Rhyne University*

Imad El-Anis, *Nottingham Trent University*

Henry Esparza, *University of Texas at San Antonio*

Songying Fang, *Rice University*

Richard Frank, *Australian National University*

Arman Grigoryan, *Lehigh University*

Jillienne Haglund, *University of Kentucky*

Anjo G. Harryvan, *University of Groningen*

Jeff Kaplow, *College of William & Mary*

Barbara Koremenos, *University of Michigan*

Jenn Larson, *New York University*

Dirk Leuffen, *University of Konstanz*

Yonatan Lupu, *George Washington University*

Elizabeth Menninga, *University of Iowa*

Amanda Murdie, *University of Georgia*

João Nunes, *University of York*

Andrew Owsiak, *University of Georgia*

Lindsay Reid, *University of California, Davis*

Cynthia Roberts, *Hunter College*

Megan Shannon, *University of Colorado*

Carolyn Somerville, *Hunter College*

Feng Sun, *Troy University*

Taku Tamaki, *Loughborough University*

Daniel Thomas, *Leiden University*

Jakana Thomas, *Michigan State University*

Matt Wahlert, *Miami University*

Geoffrey Wallace, *University of Washington*

Neil Winn, *University of Leeds*

We're grateful to the following instructors for their insights on the text and media components for this Fifth Edition:

Geoff Allen, *University of Utah*

Dwight Alvis, *West Virginia State University*

Thomas Ambrosio, *North Dakota State University*

Celeste Beesley, *Brigham Young University*

Christopher Day, *College of Charleston*

Manochehr Dorraj, *Texas Christian University*

Stacie Goddard, *Wellesley College*

Paul Holman, *University of Maine*

Anne Holthoefer, *Saint Anselm College*

Michael Kenwick, *Rutgers University*

Brandon Kinne, *University of California, Davis*

Shanna Kirschner, *Allegheny College*

Stephen Kocs, *College of the Holy Cross*

Sarah Lischer, *Wake Forest University*

Shawna K. Metzger, *University of Virginia*

Daniel Nagashima, *University of Illinois, Urbana-Champaign*

Ivana Stradner, *University of California, Berkeley*
Hiroki Takeuchi, *Southern Methodist University*
Dale Walton, *Lindenwood University*
Elizabeth Wheat, *University of Wisconsin, Green Bay*
Carol Wise, *University of Southern California*

For research assistance, we thank Austin Beacham, Jonathan Chu, Cynthia Mei Balloch, Eric Belz, Jeffrey Bengel, Charles Frentz, Lonjezo Hamisi, Oliver Kaplan, Aila Matanock, Brandon Merrell, Allison Myren, Alexander Noonan, Priya Rajdev, Rachel Schoner, and Stephanie Young. Deborah Seligsohn assisted with extensive revisions to Chapter 13 on the environment for the Fourth Edition, many of which carry over to this Fifth Edition. We also thank Helena de Bres of Wellesley College for her thoughtful ideas and hard work on the "Controversy" boxes in the First Edition and David Singer of MIT for his work on the figures and boxes in the international political economy chapters in previous editions, some of which carry over into this Fifth Edition. Nancy Frieden graciously hosted an authors' meeting. Robert Trager of the University of California, Los Angeles, developed simulations and interactive bargaining models to accompany the text. Susan Sell of Australian National University revised the PowerPoint set that accompanies the book. Daniel Fusterman of State College of Florida, Steven Hall of Ball State University, and Nina Kollars of U.S. Naval War College spent many hours working on the Test Bank for the Fifth Edition. James Igoe Walsh of the University of North Carolina at Charlotte brought his experience as a teacher to the Instructor's Manual for the Fifth Edition. Dustin Tingley of Harvard University and Lisa McKay helped develop the InQuizitive course that accompanies the book, which was executed by the talented author team of Celeste Beesley of Brigham Young University, Daniel Fuerstman of the State College of Florida, Steven Hall of Ball State University, and Robert Shum of SUNY Brockport. We are grateful for their contributions to the project.

Introduction

What Is World Politics and Why Do We Study It?

On May 1, 1921, a storm of violence broke out between Arabs and Jews living in Palestine.[1] Tensions between the communities were already high because Arabs resented the influx of Jewish migrants into the area and the encroachment of Jewish neighborhoods onto Arab-owned land. But the violence that began that day started from a misunderstanding. When a May Day demonstration by Jewish Marxists in Tel Aviv got out of control, police shot into the air to disperse the crowd. Arabs in nearby Jaffa interpreted the gunfire as the start of an attack and started killing Jews and smashing their shops. When Jews rushed out to confront them, a battle broke out.

In the midst of the violence, a rabbi named Ben-Zion Uziel donned his rabbinical robes, walked out between the two sides, and implored them to go back to their homes. The rabbi urged both sides to forswear war and instead focus on creating prosperity that all could enjoy: "We say to you that the land can bear all of us, can sustain all of us. Let us stop the battles among ourselves, for we are brothers."[2]

Chroniclers of this episode suggest that the appeal worked: the gunfire stopped, and the armed bands went home.[3] If so, the effect was at best temporary. The turmoil of 1921 continued for several days and spread to other parts of the country. Fighting between Arabs and Jews would begin anew only eight years later. In 1948, the state of Israel was created on that land, and that state has since seen frequent clashes with neighboring Arab states and with the stateless Palestinian people who once lived there. The Arab-Israeli conflict is one of the most intractable and dangerous rivalries in the world today. Still, as one scholar notes, "on that day in 1921, some men who otherwise would have died went home to enjoy life with their families."[4]

Though little more than a footnote in history, this anecdote illustrates what we study when we study world politics, and why we study it. The field of world politics—also called *international relations*—seeks to understand how the peoples

---

1. For a discussion of the violence and its causes, see Mark Levine, *Overthrowing Geography: Jaffa, Tel Aviv, and the Struggle for Palestine 1880–1948* (Berkeley: University of California Press, 2005), 110–11.
2. Marc D. Angel, "The Grand Religious View of Rabbi Benzion Uziel," *Tradition* 30, no. 1 (1995): 47.
3. Abraham Joshua Heschel, *Israel: An Echo of Eternity* (New York: Farrar, Straus and Giroux, 1969), 175–78; Angel, "Grand Religious View," 47.
4. Arthur A. Stein, *Why Nations Cooperate* (Ithaca, NY: Cornell University Press, 1990), 210.

and countries of the world get along. As this account from May 1921 suggests, international relations can span the continuum from open warfare to peaceful cooperation. Some countries fight wars against one another and, when they are not fighting, spend significant resources preparing to fight, while other countries have managed to live in peace for long periods. Sometimes countries engage in lucrative economic dealings, selling each other goods and services and investing in one another's economies. These interactions can make some people and nations very rich, while others stay mired in poverty.

Like the people in the anecdote, the countries of the world are also increasingly aware of the natural resources they share and depend on: the atmosphere, the water, the land. The common threat of environmental degradation creates a need for international cooperation; in some cases governments have responded to this need, and in other cases they have not. And, as the story of Rabbi Uziel suggests, small groups—even individuals—can sometimes make a difference, whether through the work of a mediator, the lobbying of human rights groups, or more ominously, the activities of terrorist organizations. Understanding this varied landscape of conflict and cooperation is the task of those who study world politics. Getting you started down this path is the task of this book.

Why study world politics? The nineteenth-century Scottish historian Thomas Carlyle once wrote of economics that it was not a happy science, but rather a "dreary, desolate, and, indeed, quite abject and distressing one; what we might call. . . . the dismal science."[5] Those who study world politics often think that Carlyle's criticism applies equally well to the field of international relations. The history of world politics, in fact, offers its fair share of distressing observations: international wars have claimed millions of lives, civil wars and genocides have claimed millions more, and in most cases, outsiders who might have prevented these deaths have chosen not to get involved. Since 1945, international politics has taken place under the threat of nuclear war and fears about the potential use of nuclear weapons have intensified as countries like North Korea and Iran and terrorist groups like Al Qaeda have actively sought to acquire them.

International economic relations have in some cases been harmonious and have generated enormous wealth for some countries. Global income and living standards improved dramatically over the last century, making this the most prosperous time in world history. And yet, as one looks around the globe today, the inequality in living standards is also stark. In 2017, the most recent year for which comprehensive data are available, about 10 percent of the world's population—just under 700 million people—lived on less than $1.90 a day, the international standard for extreme poverty. Although this figure had been improving for decades, the global pandemic that started in 2020 was expected to push another 100 million people into extreme poverty.[6] Meanwhile, the richest 1 percent of the world's population owns about

---

5. Carlyle used this phrase in an article defending slavery in the West Indies; see Thomas Carlyle, "Occasional Discourse on the Negro Question," *Fraser's Magazine* 40 (December 1848): 672.

6. World Bank, *Poverty and Shared Prosperity 2020: Reversals of Fortune* (Washington, DC: World Bank, 2020), p. 28, https://openknowledge.worldbank.org/bitstream/handle/10986/34496/9781464816024.pdf (accessed 4/12/21).

43 percent of total global wealth.[7] Concerns about the effects of *globalization*—the dramatic expansion of cross-border flows—have spurred resistance in both poor and rich countries, fueling the rise of nationalist and populist movements seeking to reverse this trend.

Countries have also struggled to act on common interests and values. While most states have signed treaties promising to protect the basic human rights of their citizens, many governments still kill, arrest, and torture their people, and outsiders usually do little to stop these violations. The COVID-19 pandemic created common interests in preventing transmission of the virus and ensuring that everyone could have access to a vaccine that would bring the global crisis to an end. States often reacted selfishly, however, with China concealing information about the early stages of the outbreak and wealthy nations holding onto vaccine doses to ensure that their citizens got them first. And despite the increasing awareness of threats to the global environment, international efforts to do something about them often fall short of what is needed.

Still, the picture is not entirely bleak. One can point to a number of ways in which the world has changed for the better. For hundreds of years, the continent of Europe experienced horrific warfare, culminating in the first half of the twentieth century in two world wars that claimed tens of millions of lives. Today, most of Europe is at peace, and a war between, say, Germany and France in the foreseeable future is inconceivable.

After World War II, many countries emerged economically shattered or destitute after years of colonial rule, but some have experienced extraordinary prosperity in the decades since. For example, in the 1950s, South Korea had one of the world's poorest economies, with a per capita national income of about $1,000 a year. Today, South Korea boasts the twelfth-largest economy in the world, with a per capita national income of over $40,000 a year.[8]

At the beginning of the twentieth century, only a handful of countries worldwide had political systems that guaranteed the civil rights of their citizens and gave people a say in their government through free and fair elections. By the beginning of the twenty-first century, more than half of the world's population lived in democratic countries. And despite the uneven track record of efforts to protect the global environment, cooperation in this area was virtually unknown a few decades ago. In recent years, the number of international environmental treaties and organizations has grown dramatically, as has awareness of the common challenges we face.

We study world politics because the bad things that happen in the world distress us and because the good things give us hope that, through understanding and effort, the world could be a better place.

---

7. Credit Suisse Research Institute, *Global Wealth Report 2020*, https://www.credit-suisse.com/media/assets/corporate/docs/about-us/research/publications/global-wealth-report-2020-en.pdf (accessed 4/12/21).

8. Gross domestic product (GDP) per capita is measured in 2017 U.S. dollars. Data are from Robert C. Feenstra, Robert Inklaar, and Marcel P. Timmer, "The Next Generation of the Penn World Table," *American Economic Review* 105 (2015): 3150–82, available for download at www.ggdc.net/pwt, version 10.0. Current figures and ranking are from 2019.

Puzzles in Search of Explanations

This book is organized around what we consider to be the most compelling and pressing puzzles in the study of world politics. Puzzles are observations about the world that demand an explanation. In some cases they arise because the world does not work in the way we might expect. Some things that happen seem like they should not, and some things that don't happen seem like they should.

War, for example, is a puzzling phenomenon. Given the enormous human and material costs that wars impose on the countries that fight them, one might wonder why countries do not settle their conflicts in other, more reasonable ways. The difficulty of achieving international cooperation to end genocides or to protect the environment presents another such puzzle: Given the widespread agreement that genocide is horrific and that the environment needs protecting, why is it so hard for countries to do something about these issues?

Other puzzles arise because of variations that need to be explained. Some countries today are enormously wealthy, with living standards more opulent than ever experienced in world history; in many other countries, people scrape by on meager incomes and suffer from malnutrition, poor health, and inadequate schooling. What accounts for these vastly different outcomes? The study of world politics is the effort to make sense of these puzzles.

Each chapter of this book poses one of these puzzles and then shows how we can build theories to make sense of it. A **theory** is a logically consistent set of statements that explains a phenomenon of interest. When we confront the puzzle "Why did this happen?" theories provide an answer. They specify the factors that play a role in causing the events we are trying to understand, and they show how these pieces fit together, thus helping us make sense of the puzzle. A theory of war explains why wars happen and identifies the conditions that make war between countries more or less likely. A theory of trade explains why countries sometimes choose to trade with one another and identifies the factors that increase or decrease the amount of that trade. A theory of international environmental policy identifies the factors that foster or impede cooperation in this area.

In addition to this primary role of explanation, theories help us to describe, predict, and prescribe. They help us to *describe* events by identifying which factors are important and which are not. Since it would be impossible to catalog all of the events that precede, say, the outbreak of a war, we need theories to filter the events that are worth including from those that are not. Theories help us to *predict* by offering a sense of how the world works and suggesting how a change in one factor will lead to changes in behavior and outcomes. And theories may help *prescribe* policy responses by identifying what must be changed to foster better outcomes. Once a good understanding has been established of why wars happen, it might be possible to take steps to prevent them. Knowing which factors help countries emerge from poverty makes it possible to advocate policies that have a chance of helping. Just as an understanding of how the human body works is important for curing diseases, developing theories of how the world works is the first step in the quest to make it better.

theory

A logically consistent set of statements that explains a phenomenon of interest.

Theories also provide manageable explanations for complex phenomena. Given how complicated the world is, simplifying it in this way may seem like a misguided pursuit. Whereas the movement of a falling object may be characterized by mathematical equations dictated by the laws of physics, the decisions of individuals and groups are influenced by factors too numerous to list, let alone predict. Any theory, therefore, is doomed to oversimplify. But this is precisely the point of theorizing. We do not build theories because we believe the world is simple or mechanical. Rather, we build them because we know that the world is extraordinarily complex and that the only way to understand important phenomena is to cut away some of the complexity and identify the most important factors. As a result, any general explanation will not be right in every single case.

Given this outlook, we generally aspire for probabilistic claims. A *probabilistic claim* is an argument about the factors that increase or decrease the likelihood that a particular outcome will occur. For example, while we cannot predict with certainty whether a given conflict will end in war or peace, we can identify conditions that increase or decrease the danger of war. Similarly, we use theories to identify factors that make trade protection, or international investment, or cooperation to protect human rights or the environment, more or less likely. Given the world's complexity, developing a compelling probabilistic argument is no small feat.

The Framework: Interests, Interactions, and Institutions

No single theory adequately answers all the puzzles posed in this book. Instead, we offer a framework—a way of thinking about world politics that will be useful in building theories to shed light on these puzzles. The framework rests on three core concepts: interests, interactions, and institutions.

Interests are the goals that actors have, the outcomes they hope to obtain through political action. A state may have an interest in protecting its citizens or acquiring more territory; businesses generally have an interest in maximizing profits; an environmental activist has an interest in protecting the atmosphere, the oceans, or whales.

Interactions are the ways in which two or more actors' choices combine to produce political outcomes. The outcomes that we observe—wars, or trade and financial exchanges, or cooperation to protect human rights or the environment—reflect the choices of many actors, each looking out for its own interests, but also taking into account the interests and likely actions of others. War is the product of an interaction because it requires at least two sides: one side must attack, and the other must decide to resist. Similarly, efforts at international cooperation require multiple states to coordinate their policy choices toward a common goal.

Institutions are sets of rules, known and shared by the relevant community, that structure political interactions. Institutions define the "rules of the game,"

interests

What actors want to achieve through political action; their preferences among the possible outcomes that might result from their political choices.

interactions

The ways in which the choices of two or more actors combine to produce political outcomes.

institutions

Sets of rules (known and shared by the relevant community) that structure interactions in specific ways.

often embodied in formal treaties and laws or in organizations like the United Nations (UN). Institutions create procedures for making joint decisions, such as voting rules; they also lay out standards of acceptable behavior, and they often include provisions for monitoring compliance and punishing those who violate the rules.

Applying this framework to any particular puzzle is straightforward. We first think about who the relevant political actors are and what interests they may have. We think about the choices, or strategies, available to each actor; how those choices interact to produce outcomes; and how the strategic interaction influences what the actors actually decide to do. And we think about what institutions, if any, might exist to govern their behavior.

The framework is intentionally flexible, pragmatic, and open to a variety of assumptions about which interests, interactions, and institutions matter. A theory emerges when we identify the specific interests, interactions, and institutions that work together to account for the events or pattern of events we hope to explain.

In building explanations, we do not precommit to any single set of actors or interests as being the most important, regardless of the issue area. Sometimes it is useful to think about states as actors pursuing goals such as power, security, or territorial expansion. In other situations we get more leverage thinking about politicians concerned with holding on to office, or businesses interested in maximizing profits, or labor unions interested in protecting their members' jobs, or groups of like-minded individuals with strong ideological interests in, say, protecting human rights or extending the dominion of a particular religion.

We cannot judge whether any particular assumption about actors and interests is right or wrong; rather, we judge whether that assumption is useful in explaining the puzzle in question. Indeed, assumptions are simplifying devices, which means that, strictly speaking, none captures the exact, entire truth. Since not all decisions are made by individuals, it is not precisely accurate to say that a state or an interest group or an institution is an actor; yet sometimes it is quite useful to assume precisely that. Similarly, ascribing interests to individuals—such as assuming that politicians care primarily about holding on to office—is a sweeping generalization that cannot be right 100 percent of the time, yet very powerful insights can be drawn from this assumption.

We focus on two broad types of interactions that arise to one degree or another in all aspects of politics: bargaining and cooperation. **Bargaining** describes situations in which two or more actors try to divide something they both want. States may bargain over the allocation of a disputed territory; finance ministers may bargain over how high or how low to set the exchange rate between their currencies; rich countries may bargain with poor countries over how much aid the former will give and what the recipients will do in return; governments may bargain over how much each will pay to alleviate some environmental harm.

Cooperation occurs when actors have common interests and need to act in a coordinated way to achieve those interests. Governments that want to stop one country from invading another may try to act collectively to impose military or economic sanctions on the aggressor. Governments that share an interest in preventing

bargaining
An interaction in which two or more actors must decide how to distribute something of value. In bargaining, increasing one actor's share of the good decreases the share available to others.

cooperation
An interaction in which two or more actors adopt policies that make at least one actor better off relative to the status quo without making others worse off.

climate change, the spread of a contagious virus, or degradation of the ozone layer need to cooperate in restraining their countries' emissions of the offending pollutants. Individuals who want to lobby for a particular trade policy or an environmental regulation have to pool their time, money, and effort to achieve their common aim. In short, bargaining and cooperation are everywhere in political life.

The institutional setting can vary considerably depending on the issues at stake. In some areas of world politics, there are well-established rules and mechanisms for enforcing those rules. International trade, for example, is governed by the World Trade Organization (WTO), which sets out rules that determine what kinds of trade policies member countries can and cannot have and provides a dispute resolution mechanism that allows countries to challenge one another's policies.

Other areas of world politics have weaker institutions. As we will see in Chapter 5, the UN theoretically governs the use of military force by states, but in practice it has had a hard time enforcing these rules on its strongest members. As we will see in Chapter 12, an extensive body of international human rights law sets out standards for how governments should treat their citizens; unfortunately, noncompliance is common, and offenders are rarely punished.

We will also at times focus on institutions at the domestic level—that is, the rules that determine who governs within countries and how leaders make decisions. Domestic political institutions determine which actors have access to and influence on the policy-making process. In some cases, differences in domestic political institutions can have profound effects on world politics. In Chapter 4, for example, we will encounter a phenomenon known as the *democratic peace*, the observation that mature democratic states have rarely, if ever, engaged in war against one another.

Levels of Analysis

The variety of actors and institutions that play a role in world politics means that we will see important interactions at three levels:

- At the *international level*, representatives of states with different interests interact with one another, sometimes in the context of international institutions, such as the UN or WTO.

- At the *domestic level*, subnational actors with different interests—politicians, bureaucrats, business and labor groups, voters—interact within domestic institutions to determine a country's foreign policy choices.

- At the *transnational level*, groups whose members span borders—such as multinational corporations, transnational advocacy networks, and terrorist organizations—pursue their interests by trying to influence both domestic and international politics.

These levels are interconnected. The interests that states pursue at the international level often emerge from their domestic politics. For example, whether a country's representatives push for liberalizing trade agreements with other countries depends on whether the interests within that country that support freer trade prevail over those who oppose it. Similarly, the relative influence of actors within domestic politics may depend on international conditions. Leaders may be able to use militarized conflict with other states to enhance their hold on power at home. International institutions that promote trade liberalization enhance the power of domestic interests that benefit from trade. Finally, transnational actors operate at all levels. Transnational networks like Amnesty International or Greenpeace try to change national policies by lobbying governments or mobilizing public opinion within key countries, and they try to change international outcomes by working with (or against) international institutions.

Because of these interconnections, we do not automatically privilege one level of analysis over others. Although international relations scholarship has experienced vigorous debate over which level of analysis is the "right" or the "best" one,[9] we find that no single level is always superior to others in making sense of the puzzles. In some cases it is possible to build useful explanations from the bottom up in a two-step process: (1) domestic interests, interactions, and institutions determine the interests that state representatives bring to the international level, and then (2) these interests combine in international interactions and institutions to determine the final outcome. Chapters 7–10 on international political economy generally rely on this two-step logic.

In other cases, however, it is more useful to start elsewhere. In Chapters 3–6 we start our analysis of war on the international level. Given that states have conflicting interests over things like territory or one another's policies or regime composition, why does the bargaining interaction sometimes lead to war? Only after laying out this basic logic do we turn to some of the domestic factors that push states toward more or less belligerent policies. In Chapters 11–13, transnational actors play a central role, and we show how they pursue their goals by altering domestic interests and changing the prospects for international cooperation.

Integrating Insights from Realism, Liberalism, and Constructivism

In adopting a flexible framework based on interests, interactions, and institutions, we depart from the way the field of world politics is often organized. Many textbooks and courses on world politics emphasize the contrasts among three schools of thought: realism, liberalism, and constructivism. Unlike our framework, which holds few preconceptions about how the world works, these three "-isms" represent different worldviews about the nature of international politics. Much ink has been spilled over the years by proponents arguing for the superiority of their preferred approach.

We can understand the differences among realism, liberalism, and constructivism by mapping them into our framework (see Table A). Each school of thought is

---

9. For a classic statement of this debate, see J. David Singer, "The Levels-of-Analysis Problem in International Relations," *World Politics* 14, no. 1 (October 1961): 77–92.

TABLE A *Realism, Liberalism, and Constructivism*

	INTERESTS	INTERACTIONS	INSTITUTIONS
Realism	The state is the dominant actor. States seek security and/or power. States' interests are generally in conflict.	International politics is primarily about bargaining, in which coercion always remains a possibility.	The international system is anarchic, and institutions exert little independent effect. International institutions reflect the interests of powerful states.
Liberalism	Many types of actors are important, and no single interest dominates. Wealth is a common goal for many actors. Actors often have common interests, which can serve as the basis for cooperation.	International politics has an extensive scope for cooperation. Conflict is not inevitable but occurs when actors fail to recognize or act on common interests.	International institutions facilitate cooperation by setting out rules, providing information, and creating procedures for collective decision making. Democratic political institutions increase the scope for international politics to reflect the common interests of individuals.
Constructivism	Many types of actors are important. Actors' interests are influenced by culture, identity, and prevailing ideas. Actors' choices often reflect norms of appropriate behavior rather than interests.	Interactions socialize actors to hold particular interests, but transformations in patterns of interaction can occur as actors come to understand their interests differently.	International institutions define identities and shape action through the norms of just and appropriate behavior that they prescribe.

defined by a cluster of assumptions about which interests, interactions, and institutions are most important to understanding world politics.

Realism Realist ideas can be found in the writings of Thucydides (ca. 460–400 B.C.E.), Niccolò Machiavelli (1469–1527), Thomas Hobbes (1588–1679), and Jean-Jacques Rousseau (1712–1778). Realism was most forcefully introduced to Americans by Hans Morgenthau, a German expatriate whose 1948 book *Politics among Nations* remains a classic statement of the realist approach.[10] Realism was given its modern and scientific guise by the contemporary scholar Kenneth Waltz.[11]

Realism starts with two key assumptions: that states are the dominant actors—indeed, some would say the only relevant actors—on the international stage, and that the institutional setting of world politics is characterized by anarchy.

---

10. Hans Morgenthau, *Politics among Nations: The Struggle for Power and Peace* (New York: Knopf). First published in 1948, this book has been released in many editions since then.

11. Kenneth N. Waltz, *Theory of International Politics* (Reading, MA: Addison-Wesley, 1979).

Anarchy, a term we will revisit in Chapter 2, refers in this context to the absence of a central authority in the international system—the fact that there is no world government ruling over states the way that countries have governments to rule over their citizens.

anarchy

The absence of a central authority with the ability to make and enforce laws that bind all actors.

Realists assume that anarchy profoundly shapes the interests and interactions that matter in world politics. Because there is no central government and there is no international police force, states must live in constant fear of one another. With no external restraint on the use of military force, every state must first and foremost look out for its own survival and security. Hence, all states have an interest in security, and this interest dominates other possible interests because no other goal can be realized unless the state is secure.

In practice, the interest in security leads to an interest in acquiring power—primarily military capabilities. By accumulating power and ensuring that potential enemies do not become more powerful, states can reduce their vulnerability to attack and conquest. Unfortunately, the quest for power inevitably brings states' interests into conflict with one another: when one state improves its military capabilities to enhance its own security, it typically undermines the security of its now comparatively weaker neighbors—a problem known as the "security dilemma." For realists, then, international politics is, as Hobbes described, the "state of nature": a war of "every man, against every man" in which life is "nasty, brutish, and short."[12]

Because states are concerned with security and power, nearly all interactions involve bargaining and coercion. Each state tries to get a bigger share for itself, one state's gain is another state's loss, and the threat of war looms over everything. Even when the potential gains from cooperation are large, realists argue, states worry more about the division of the benefits than about the overall gain. Each must fear that the state gaining the most will be able to exploit its gains for some future advantage. As a result, states may forgo mutually beneficial exchanges if they expect to be left at a disadvantage. Cooperation, realists conclude, is difficult and rare.

Finally, realists assert that because of the anarchic nature of the international system, international institutions are weak and exert little independent effect on world politics. Institutions like the UN and the WTO merely reflect the interests and power of the dominant countries, which had the most say in their creation and design. Although realists may recognize that institutions can matter at the margin, they conclude that rules are unlikely to be followed and that states will always bow to interests and power in the end.

In short, realism sees a rather bleak world of states jockeying for power under the shadow of war, and many of the unpleasant features of world politics mentioned earlier flow from this understanding. War is a permanent fixture of international relations because there is nothing to stop states from waging war when it is in their interests to do so. The risk of war can be managed by careful diplomacy and temporary alliances between states that face common threats, but neither domestic nor international institutions can deliver lasting peace.

---

12. These famous quotes are from Thomas Hobbes's *Leviathan*, originally published in 1651.

Even the realm of international economic relations is colored by the struggle for power. Economists tell us that unfettered commerce makes all countries collectively better off, but realists understand that restrictions on trade and capital flows are often sensible measures to increase or preserve a state's relative power. Finally, cooperation is hard because states look out for themselves, and international institutions are generally too weak to compel desirable behaviors. As a result, realists are not surprised that many of the world's collective needs, such as the protection of human rights and the global environment, go unmet.

Liberalism An equally venerable tradition, liberalism is rooted in the writings of philosophers John Locke (1632–1704) and Immanuel Kant (1724–1804) and economists Adam Smith (1723–1790) and David Ricardo (1772–1823). Contemporary advocates include Bruce Russett and John R. Oneal, who make the modern case for the pacifying effects of democracy, international commerce, and international law,[13] and Robert O. Keohane and Joseph S. Nye, whose work helped bring the study of international institutions to the fore.[14]

Analytically, liberalism is the school of thought that most closely resembles the approach taken in this book. Liberal theorists accept many different types of actors as important in world politics: individuals, firms, nongovernmental organizations, and states. Unlike realism, liberalism does not require that any one interest dominate all others. Instead, liberal theory, like the framework presented here, is quite flexible in ascribing goals to actors. While realism assumes that states' interests in security and power derive from external imperatives (the need to survive in an anarchic world), liberals are more likely to see governments' interests as coming from within (from the interplay of different domestic actors operating within domestic political institutions). Moreover, since wealth can be used to purchase the means to accommodate many different desires, liberals assume that, for many practical purposes, actors can be treated as if they wish to maximize wealth.

Liberals are generally optimistic about the possibilities for cooperation in world politics. Whereas realists see most situations as involving conflicting interests over relative power, liberals see many areas in which actors have common interests that can serve as the basis for cooperation. The costs of war mean that states have common interests in avoiding conflict. The potential for profitable exchanges creates a common interest in lowering barriers to allow the flow of goods and money across borders and in creating institutions to facilitate international transactions. The common interest in clean air and clean water creates a basis for cooperating to protect these shared resources. Although liberals acknowledge that world politics is often wracked by conflict, they do not believe that conflict is inevitable; rather, conflict arises when actors fail to recognize or act on common interests.

---

13. Bruce Russett and John R. Oneal, *Triangulating Peace: Democracy, Interdependence, and International Organizations* (New York: Norton, 2001).

14. Robert O. Keohane and Joseph S. Nye, *Power and Interdependence: World Politics in Transition* (New York: Longman); first published in 1977, this volume is now available in a fourth edition, published in 2012. Robert O. Keohane, *After Hegemony: Cooperation and Discord in the World Political Economy* (Princeton, NJ: Princeton University Press, 1984).

Whether actors can cooperate to further their common interests depends a great deal on institutions, both domestic and international. At the domestic level, liberals believe that democracy is the best way to ensure that governments' foreign policies reflect the underlying harmony of interests among individuals. In this view, which we will revisit in Chapter 4, conflict and war are the fault of selfish politicians, voracious militaries, and greedy interest groups, whose influence can be tamed only by empowering the people through democratic institutions. At the international level, the scope for cooperation gives rise to a demand for institutions. Liberals posit that international institutions facilitate cooperation by resolving a host of dilemmas that arise in strategic interactions and by making it easier for states to make collective decisions. In Chapter 2 we will consider these dilemmas and the ways in which institutions might resolve them.

Thus, while liberalism does not see a perfect world, it envisions a world in which progress is possible. The danger of war can be reduced by spreading democracy, strengthening global institutions, and fostering economic interdependence so that every country's welfare will be linked to that of others. Economic activity also has the potential to create great wealth, making it possible to lift countries and people out of poverty. And global challenges can give rise to international institutions that can make cooperation possible. While this optimistic view makes liberalism a more appealing theory than realism, theories must be judged by how closely they describe the world in which we actually live, not the world in which we would like to live.

Constructivism A relatively new approach, constructivism has roots in critical theory and sociology, and its most forceful proponents in world politics have been Peter J. Katzenstein, John G. Ruggie, and Alexander Wendt.[15] Like liberals, constructivists focus on a wide variety of actors and interests in world politics, and they believe that international institutions can be effective, even transformative. Constructivists depart from liberals, however, by de-emphasizing the material sources of interests (for example, wealth) and instead focusing on the role of nonmaterial factors, such as ideas, culture, and norms.

What actors want is not fixed and predetermined but is instead a function of their culture, prevailing ideas, and identity, or their conception of who they are. Whether states perceive common or conflicting interests depends not only on their relative military power or economic ties but also on whether they share a common political or cultural identity (for example, "we are all democracies" or "we are all Western") or identify each other as foes ("you are not like us").

One prominent strand of constructivist thought emphasizes the role of norms, or standards of behavior defined in terms of rights and obligations (see Chapter 11). Whereas the other schools of thought assume that actors are purposive, selecting among possible alternatives according to their anticipated effects, constructivists

---

15. Peter J. Katzenstein, ed., *The Culture of National Security: Norms and Identity in World Politics* (New York: Columbia University Press, 1996); John Gerard Ruggie, *Constructing the World Polity: Essays on International Institutionalization* (New York: Routledge, 1998); Alexander Wendt, *Social Theory of International Politics* (New York: Cambridge University Press, 1999).

assume that social actors pursue what they believe is right and proper, as based on their conceptions of who they are and how they wish others to view them. So, for example, if a large number of countries decide that using a certain kind of weapon is barbaric, then states that wish to be seen as civilized may decide to forgo those weapons—even if using them would enhance their security. Thus, a desire to conform to certain standards of behavior can trump other interests.

Institutions, in turn, embody the rules appropriate for behavior and thereby exert a profound effect on actions and observed outcomes. For example, once an international agreement or institution proscribes a behavior as illegal or illegitimate, states that care about how others view them will have an incentive to conform. Thus, compliance with international institutions depends not only on the institutions' ability to monitor and enforce their terms but also on their members' desire to be seen as compliant.

Because ideas about right or appropriate behaviors can change, constructivists see significant potential for change, even fundamental transformation, in world politics. The rough-and-tumble international system described by realists is not, according to constructivists, foreordained by the condition of anarchy. If actors come to understand their interests differently, their conception of appropriate behavior could change dramatically. More concretely, state behavior can be altered by the conscious efforts of activists to promote new norms, such as norms against the use of certain weapons (see Chapter 11), norms promoting intervention in genocidal conflicts (see Chapters 5 and 11), and norms favoring the protection of human rights (see Chapter 12). For this reason, constructivists place particular emphasis on the role of transnational actors, such as advocacy networks of human rights or environmental activists, who try to spread norms around the world.

All three approaches—realism, liberalism, constructivism—offer insights into important problems of world politics. Nonetheless, each tends to emphasize particular aspects of our framework at the expense of others, and all make strong assumptions about which interests, interactions, and institutions matter the most. As a result, each approach sacrifices explanatory power and flexibility for the sake of intellectual purity.

Not surprisingly, most international relations scholarship in recent years has moved away from arguments based on a single approach, instead borrowing insights from more than one. Indeed, as the field progresses, it has become harder to pigeonhole scholars and their work into any one category. For example, many contemporary scholars believe that coercive power plays a fundamental role in international politics (realism) but argue that this power is often used in pursuit of goals that arise from the interplay of domestic interests (liberalism) and ideas (constructivism).[16] Hence, rather than trying to promote one school of thought over others, our goal is to answer important puzzles of international politics and, in the process, use the tools developed in this book to help us understand today's complex world.

---

16. See, for example, Jeffrey W. Legro and Andrew Moravcsik, "Is Anybody Still a Realist?" *International Security* 24, no. 2 (Autumn 1999): 5–55.

Thinking Analytically about World Politics

By the end of the course, you should not only know a lot about international politics—you should also know how to *think* about international politics. When bad or puzzling things happen, you should be able to ask: "Whose interests did that outcome serve? Why were the people or countries involved not able to cooperate to achieve something better? How might new institutions be created, or existing institutions reformed, so that this does not happen again?"

Ultimately, we study world politics because doing so lets us grapple with important and interesting questions about ourselves and our world. This book cannot provide definitive answers to all the questions. After all, while we are confident in our understanding of certain phenomena, for others our understanding is still evolving and our theories are tentative—perhaps waiting to be overturned by the next generation. Instead, this book seeks to equip you with the tools you need to develop your own understanding. In the "information age," in which facts (and assertions masquerading as facts) are cheap and plentiful, the most valuable skill is the ability to think critically and analytically about what shapes our world.

Study Tool Kit

Interests, Interactions, and Institutions in Context

- We can develop theories to explain behavior and outcomes in world politics by considering the interests of the main actors involved, the strategies available to them and how their choices interact to produce outcomes, and the institutions that govern their behavior.

- World politics reflects the interactions of a variety of actors—including states, politicians, business groups, terrorist organizations, transnational advocacy networks, and individuals—as they pursue their interests.

- Most interactions involve either cooperation (which happens when actors with similar interests try to coordinate their behavior toward a common goal) or bargaining (which happens when actors with different interests try to achieve a favorable outcome at the expense of other actors).

- Institutions, both domestic and international, are the rules that can alter the costs and benefits of some strategies and determine how actors arrive at collective decisions.

- The main theoretical traditions in international relations—realism, liberalism, and constructivism—make different assumptions about which interests, interactions, and institutions are most important for building explanations.

Key Terms

theory, p. xxix

interests, p. xxx

interactions, p. xxx

institutions, p. xxx

bargaining, p. xxxi

cooperation, p. xxxi

anarchy, p. xxxv

For Further Reading

Finnemore, Martha. *The Purpose of Intervention: Changing Beliefs about the Use of Force.* **Cornell Studies in Security Affairs. Ithaca, NY: Cornell University Press, 2004.** Develops a constructivist argument that patterns of military intervention have changed over the last two centuries because of changing norms about the appropriate purposes for using force.

Katzenstein, Peter J., ed. *The Culture of National Security: Norms and Identity in World Politics.* **New Directions in World Politics. New York: Columbia University Press, 1996.** Presents a collection of essays showing how constructivism uses norms, culture, and identity to answer fundamental questions about international security.

Keohane, Robert O., and Joseph S. Nye. *Power and Interdependence.* **4th ed. Boston: Longman, 2012.** Presents a liberal argument that economic and political interdependence between states complicates the exercise of power in international relations.

Morgenthau, Hans J., Kenneth W. Thompson, and W. David Clinton. *Politics among Nations: The Struggle for Power and Peace.* **7th ed. Boston: McGraw-Hill Higher Education, 2006.** Presents an updated and abridged version of Morgenthau's classic statement of realist theory.

Russett, Bruce M., and John R. Oneal. *Triangulating Peace: Democracy, Interdependence, and International Organizations.* **New York: Norton, 2001.** Presents theory and evidence that three key pillars of liberalism—democracy, economic interdependence, and international institutions—can reduce the risk of war.

Waltz, Kenneth N. *Theory of International Politics.* **Long Grove, IL: Waveland Press, 2010.** Articulates a realist theory emphasizing the importance of power and anarchy in explaining recurring patterns of international politics.

FIFTH EDITION

World Politics

Interests, Interactions, Institutions

1

What Shaped Our World?
A Historical Introduction

THE PUZZLE *How has conflict among nations ebbed and flowed over the centuries? When and how have war or peace, prosperity or stagnation, prevailed?*

Above: During the nineteenth century, global trade grew at a rapid rate. While the increase in international trade was most pronounced among the advanced economies of Europe, many people in Asia also found themselves integrated into the global economy in new ways during this period. By the time of this painting, around 1840, Canton, China (present-day Guangzhou), had become a significant international trading port.

Most western Europeans and North Americans born around 1800 spent their adult lives in an atmosphere of peace and economic growth. So too did their children, and their children's children, and their children's children's children. Between the end of the Napoleonic Wars in 1815 and the start of World War I in 1914, peace and prosperity by and large reigned in western Europe and North America. There were periodic wars among the European great powers, but they were relatively short; there were brutal conflicts with the indigenous peoples of the Americas, but they were on sparsely inhabited frontiers; there was a bloody civil war in the United States, but it was confined to one country. There were occasional financial panics and recessions, but between 1815 and 1914 the advanced economies of western Europe and North America grew more than eightfold while output per person quadrupled.[1] This was the fastest growth in world history by a very long shot; it roughly equaled in a hundred years what had been achieved in the previous thousand.

Europeans and North Americans born around 1900 had a very different experience. While they were in their teens, the world plunged into a horrific, protracted war that wiped out the better part of a generation of young men. If those born around 1900 were fortunate enough to survive World War I, they and their children spent the next 10 years being subjected to postwar violence, economic uncertainty, fragile democracy, and ethnic conflict. Despite a brief recovery in the 1920s, in 1929 the world spiraled downward into economic depression, mass unemployment, dictatorship, trade wars, and eventually another global war. If they, and their children and their children's children, were again lucky and survived World War II, their world was then divided into two hostile camps—one led by the United States, the other by the Soviet Union. These two contending alliances carried on a cold war that included the deployment of enough nuclear weapons to annihilate life on earth several times over.

International relations profoundly affected these many generations of Europeans and North Americans— as they did, in different ways, generations of people in Africa, Asia, and Latin America. During the nineteenth century, the inhabitants of many poor countries found

---

1. Angus Maddison, *The World Economy: A Millennial Perspective* (Paris: OECD Publications, 2001).

themselves absorbed into a world economy for the first time. Some prospered; others struggled. Latin Americans achieved independence from their colonial masters, while many areas of Africa and Asia were subjected to new colonial rule and domination by Europeans. The twentieth century brought industrialization and urbanization to much of the developing world and eventually saw the end of colonialism. For people north and south, east and west, global events beyond their control—great-power war, international financial crises, colonial expansion, the division of the world into warring camps—changed their lives profoundly, as they continue to change ours, and as they have changed lives for centuries.

Thinking Analytically about What Shaped Our World

Whether in the military realm or in the realm of international economics, interactions among countries around the world have ranged from deadly conflict to fruitful cooperation. At times, when national interests have clashed, countries have engaged in bitter armed battles over everything from territory to theology and in equally bitter commercial conflicts over markets and money. At other times, the same countries have found common ground upon which to base harmonious interactions on everything from geopolitics to trade, investment, and finance.

What will the future bring for today's youngest generations? Will they experience general peace and prosperity, or war and deprivation? Will those born in the world's poor nations come closer to the living standards of the rich, or fall further behind? Will governments tie their economies more closely together, or pull them apart? Will the world remain peaceful, or collapse into military conflict and war? Whose interests and which institutions will shape these interactions? The study of international politics hopes to illuminate the answers to these kinds of questions. We do not aspire to predict the future, but we do seek to gain a fuller understanding of the past and present by providing guidelines for analyzing the choices available to people and governments and how they decide among those choices.

Much of the rest of this book provides and applies analytical tools for understanding international relations. This chapter sets the stage for what follows by reviewing the course of international political and economic relations in modern times, since about 1500. With this grounding, we move in subsequent chapters to providing theoretical principles with which to understand international relations, and then we apply them to a wide variety of contemporary topics.

The Emergence of International Relations: The Mercantilist Era

The world as a meaningful political and economic unit emerged only after 1500. Before then, most major societies existed in practical or complete isolation from all but those on their immediate borders. To be sure, there was some trade among societies: China to Constantinople, Central Africa to North Africa, Constantinople to Europe. But this trade was extraordinarily difficult and expensive, and therefore it involved only the most valuable and easily transported goods.

All that changed after 1492, as wave upon wave of explorers, conquerors, traders, and settlers went forth from Europe's Atlantic nations. First Spain and Portugal, then England, France, and the Netherlands, sent soldiers and traders all over the New World, Africa, and Asia in search of possessions and profit. By 1700, the world was unquestionably controlled by western Europeans. They exercised direct rule over vast colonial possessions in the Western Hemisphere, India, Southeast Asia, and elsewhere, and they used their military might to impose their will on local rulers even where they did not establish colonial domain. European influence was rarely welcomed by local populations, and its effects were often disastrous for local societies. Nonetheless, western Europe's influence was global and dictated economics and politics on every continent.

For centuries after 1492, the Europeans used their military prowess to control much of the rest of the world, with formal empires or without them. Europe dominated world politics, and the European economies were the world center of economic activity. Important as developments outside Europe may have been for the people living there, the analysis of world politics after 1492 necessarily has Europe at its core. This would change only in the twentieth century, with the rise of militarily and economically important non-European powers: the United States, Japan, Russia, and eventually China.

For several hundred years beginning in the 1500s, however, it was the rulers of western Europe who held sway over the rest of the world. These governments, almost all of them absolute monarchies, had two main interests. First, they wanted to ensure their own political and military power, a desire that led them to seek control over ever-greater territories and ever-greater resources. Second, the European governments wanted access to markets in other parts of the world. European societies had thriving commercial classes, typically strongly allied with their respective monarchies, and each crown was hungry for revenue. There were rich natural treasures to be had abroad—precious metals, spices, tropical crops—and customers for the products of Europe's growing industries.

Western Europeans' economic and military interests were reflected in the colonial order they established, known as mercantilism. **Mercantilism** was a system by which imperial governments used military power to enrich themselves and their supporters, then used those riches to enhance their military power. Mercantilism's principal mechanism was the establishment of monopolies that

mercantilism

An economic doctrine based on a belief that military power and economic influence complement each other; applied especially to colonial empires in the sixteenth through eighteenth centuries. Monopolies at the center of mercantilist trade policies favored the mother country over its colonies and over its competitors.

controlled and manipulated trade and other economic activities to direct money into the coffers of the government and its business supporters.

Some mercantilist monopolies were held directly by colonial governments, such as the Spanish crown's control over many of its colonies' gold and silver mines. Other mercantilist monopolies were granted by governments to private businesses, such as the Dutch East India Company and the Hudson's Bay Company. These private enterprises held exclusive rights to economic activities in vast areas of the colonial world.

The mercantilist powers' most important controls were those used to manipulate the terms of trade. The mercantilists' goal was to turn the terms of trade against the colonies and in favor of the mother country—to reduce the prices that the mother country paid its colonists for what it bought and to raise the prices that the mother country charged its colonists for what it sold. One common way of achieving this effect was to require colonies to buy and sell certain goods only from and to the colonial power. In colonial Virginia, for example, farmers could sell their tobacco only to England—a restriction that artificially reduced demand for their tobacco and, therefore, its price. And Virginians could buy many manufactured goods only from England, which meant that the supply of manufactures was artificially reduced and their prices raised. Subjects received less for what they produced and paid more for what they consumed, but in return, they obtained the protection of a powerful empire. Supporters of mercantilism argued that it benefited both the empire, which became richer and more powerful, and its subjects, who were protected. Not all colonial subjects agreed, as the "How Do We Know?" section explains.

The mercantilist powers' international political and economic interests were closely intertwined. For mercantilism's proponents, this was one of its great attractions. The English philosopher Thomas Hobbes wrote: "Wealth is power, and power is wealth." One of his fellow mercantilist thinkers drew out the connections: "Foreign trade produces riches, riches power, power preserves our trade and religion." And a French mercantilist was even more explicit: "Our colonies depend on our navy, our trade depends on our colonies, and our trade allows the state to maintain armies, increase the population, and provide for ever more glorious and useful functions."[2]

As the countries of western Europe took control of ever-larger portions of the world, they also battled with one another over wealth and power. The struggle for supremacy in Europe was inextricably linked to the battle for possessions elsewhere,

The British imposed mercantilist policies on their colonies in North America. For example, the tobacco being loaded onto these ships in the Virginia colony could be exported only to Britain, where the American producers received a lower price for their crops than they otherwise would on world markets.

2. All cited in Jacob Viner, "Power versus Plenty as Objectives of Foreign Policy in the Seventeenth and Eighteenth Centuries," *World Politics* 1, no. 1 (October 1948): 15–16.

Mercantilism and the 13 Colonies

British colonialism in North America followed the patterns of mercantilism, the system adopted by European colonial powers after about 1500. How did mercantilism work? Whom did it help and hurt? Why did many colonies come to oppose it? Economic historian Robert Paul Thomas estimated the cost to the colonies of mercantilist economic restrictions in 1770, a representative year in the decade leading up to the outbreak of the American Revolution (Table A).

The costliest restriction was the "enumeration" of certain goods, which meant they could be exported only to Britain. This measure artificially increased the supply of the enumerated goods to the British market, which caused their prices to drop, and it kept American producers from selling in markets where their goods could command higher prices. There were also restrictions on what could be imported to the colonies, and certain goods were available only if they were bought from Britain—at higher prices than those available elsewhere.

The principal cost to the 13 colonies was the lower price they received for enumerated goods, especially the tobacco and rice that made up most of their exports. Thomas calculated that without enumeration, the colonists would have been able to sell their tobacco at a price 49 percent higher than what they actually received, and their rice for more than double. If prices had been higher, we can also assume that the colonists would have produced more of the goods, so Thomas factors in forgone production as well. In 1770, the total cost of these export controls, almost all due to the constraints on tobacco and rice, was $2.4 million. Thomas further estimated that the restrictions on imports raised the prices of goods that the colonists bought from abroad by more than one-third—a total burden of $560,000. Thomas then took into account rewards ("bounties") that the colonists earned for producing favored goods. The total net cost in 1770 was about $2.7 million, approximately $1.24 per person.

However, the 13 colonies received benefits from being in the British Empire. Most important was the protection of the British army and navy. Thomas calculated the economic value of these benefits in two ways. First, he estimated the cost to the British government of stationing its troops in the region, along with how much American shippers would have had to pay for private insurance if they had not had the protection of the world's greatest navy. Second, Thomas calculated how much the American government spent to provide these services itself after independence. The lower of the two estimates was $1,775,000 in 1770. Subtracting the benefits from the costs, Thomas figured that the colonies' net burden from imperial rule in 1770 was about $885,000—or 42 cents per person, less than 0.5 percent of a colonist's average annual income. (When he calculated the average from 1763 to 1772, the net burden on the colonists was even lower: 26 cents per person per year.)

It hardly seems worth fighting a revolution over 42 cents a year. Even in today's money, the net burden (costs minus benefits) would come to about $200. It is important to note that the burden of mercantilism did not fall evenly on all colonists. The principal losers were the tobacco and rice planters of Virginia and South Carolina, as well as the merchants and craftsmen of New England. The former lost owing to export controls; the latter owing to restrictions on shipping and manufacturing. Thus, it is perhaps not surprising that the principal supporters of independence were in these regions where the costs of colonialism were highest.

TABLE A *Mercantilism: Costs and Benefits*	1770	1763–72 (AVERAGE/YEAR)
Burdens		
Burden on colonial foreign commerce	$2,660,000	$2,255,000
Burden per capita	$1.24	$1.20
Benefits		
Benefit of British protection	$1,775,000	$1,775,000
Benefit per capita	$.82	$.94
Balance per capita	−$.42	−$.26

Source: Robert Paul Thomas, "A Quantitative Approach to the Study of the Effects of British Imperial Policy on Colonial Welfare," *Journal of Economic History* 25, no. 4 (December 1965).

and the search for military advantage was closely tied to economic competition. International politics and markets were battlegrounds on which the major powers contended.

First the Spanish and Portuguese fought for predominance in the New World and elsewhere. After the Spaniards emerged victorious, they faced new contenders. Beginning in the 1560s, the Spanish possessions in the Netherlands revolted and eventually formed the new Dutch Republic. The British challenged Spain continually from the 1580s onward, defeating the Spanish Armada in 1588. Finally, in the Thirty Years' War (1618–48), the French, Dutch, and other allies sealed the decline of Spain. This war ended with the **Peace of Westphalia**, which stabilized the borders of the belligerents and attempted to resolve some of the religious conflicts that had complicated their relations. Because the peace treaties called on governments not to interfere in the internal affairs of other countries, some scholars regard this as the beginning of the modern system of states, which are expected to respect one another's **sovereignty** within their borders (see the "What Shaped Our World?" box in Chapter 2, p. 49, for details on the state system and Westphalia).

Once the anti-Spanish alliance had defeated Spain, its members turned on one another. The English and the Dutch fought each other in a series of wars, which, combined with rapid English commercial growth, meant that by the 1660s the English had surpassed the Dutch as the world's leading trading and maritime power. This shift in power launched a 150-year conflict that pitted England and its allies, on the one hand, against France and its allies, on the other. Anglo-French rivalry culminated with the Seven Years' War (1756–63, also called the French and Indian War in North America), which effectively ended the French presence in the New World and established British predominance. The French challenge to Britain resurged during the French Revolution, which began in 1789 and led to the Napoleonic Wars (1804–15). The British and their supporters finally defeated Napoleon at Waterloo in 1815, sealing British international **hegemony**.

For three centuries after 1492, world politics was dominated by the efforts of the principal European states to overpower one another and to control the non-European parts of the world (see "What Shaped Our World?"). They pursued their economic and military interests by creating formal mercantilist colonial empires in some areas while exercising less formal military and economic dominion elsewhere. Meanwhile, they battled one another for their possessions and for global predominance. The rulers of western Europe fought on two fronts—to subdue the populations of their empires and to expand at the expense of other European rulers.

By the end of the Napoleonic Wars in 1815, however, both central organizing principles of the mercantilist era were being challenged. With the defeat of France by the anti-Napoleon coalition, conflict among the principal powers in Europe subsided and their security interests evolved. Meanwhile, the Industrial Revolution gathered force in Britain and in continental Europe, thus starting to alter the economic interests of the industrializing nations.

Peace of Westphalia
The settlement that ended the Thirty Years' War in 1648; often said to have created the modern state system because it included a general recognition of the principles of sovereignty and nonintervention.

sovereignty
The expectation that states have legal and political supremacy—or ultimate authority—within their territorial boundaries.

hegemony
The predominance of one nation-state over others.

Colonialists and the Colonized

Most of the Europeans who came to dominate the world after 1500 viewed Africa, Asia, and Latin America as full of primitive peoples who were centuries behind the civilizations of Europe. The reality was quite different. In 1500, as the first European colonial surge began, only one of the world's 10 largest cities was in Europe: the world's most populous city, Peking (now Beijing), was more than three times the size of Europe's largest city, Paris. When Spanish explorers arrived in Tenochtitlán, the capital city of the Aztecs—what is now Mexico City—they were amazed. One of the Spaniards wrote: "These great towns and temple-pyramids and buildings rising from the water, all made of stone, seemed like an enchanted vision."[a] The gap between Europe and the regions the Europeans colonized was often small; most of these regions had well-developed economies, social systems, and governments. How, then, did Europe come to rule the world so quickly and so completely?

Interests The causes of European imperialism remain hotly contested. At a minimum, European states were interested in securing access to the precious metals and trade of the lands they had newly "discovered." Rulers sponsoring the transoceanic expeditions wanted to enhance their own wealth and that of their merchants. They also wanted to strengthen their economies and societies against other European states, which they feared might gain riches abroad that would give them an advantage within Europe. These political interests overlapped with a religious motive, pushed by a still-powerful church and missionaries who sought new converts and strove to "uplift" supposedly primitive peoples to the standards of Christian civilization.

Interactions Imperialism was facilitated by industrialization in Europe, which quickly widened the wealth gap between it and the rest of the world: by 1870, income per person in the United Kingdom was five or six times what it was in Africa or Asia.[b] As the wealth gap grew, technological developments in transportation and communications

Spanish invaders in Tenochtitlán, 1520.

gave Europeans a tremendous edge: the steamship, the railroad, and the telegraph were crucial to imperial expansion. The Europeans' technological advantages meant that they largely controlled their interactions with people elsewhere. Perhaps the most important European advances were related to the development of new weapons—such as long-distance artillery, accurate rifles, and the Maxim self-powered machine gun—that enabled relatively small numbers of Europeans to defeat large military forces in the rest of the world.

Institutions The institutional arrangements that resulted from these increasingly one-sided and violent interactions were colonial empires. Empire was an institution that transferred political authority from local rulers to an imperialist home country. The European colonial powers typically ruled their colonies so as to further their own interests. Valuable resources were controlled by the colonialists, while the imperial powers usually gave the colonies only as much authority as was in the interests of the imperial center. Although local elites often retained some measure of autonomy, it existed only at the discretion of the imperial state. The lack of political rights and self-rule is what eventually gave rise to demands for independence, from the American Revolution of 1776 against the British, to the revolts against Spain and Portugal by Latin American states in the early eighteenth century, and finally to the collapse of nearly all remaining European empires after World War II.

---

a. Quoted in Michael E. Smith, *The Aztecs* (Oxford: Blackwell, 1996), 2.

b. Angus Maddison, *The World Economy: A Millennial Perspective* (Paris: OECD Publications, 2001), 264.

The Hundred Years' Peace

The century from 1815 to 1914 was remarkably different from those that preceded it and the one that followed. The major powers were far more interested than they had been before in trading and investing worldwide, including with one another. Instead of imposing strict restraints on the movement of goods and money around the world, most governments welcomed ever-greater links among their economies. Their economic interactions became more cooperative as they pursued a common interest in global economic integration.

This cooperation contributed to the accelerated economic growth that much of the world experienced during this period (Figure 1.1). On the military front, global conflicts among the major powers gave way to generally peaceful ties among the countries of Europe (and, eventually, North America and Japan). To be sure, Europeans continued to use military and economic means to tighten and expand their control over people in their colonies and other poor countries. But interactions among the industrialized nations were generally pacific, and the world economy became very tightly integrated.

The Pax Britannica

Figure source: Adapted from Esteban Ortiz-Ospina and Diana Beltekian, "Trade and Globalization," Our World in Data, October 2018, https://ourworldindata.org/trade-and-globalization (accessed 10/20/20) based on data from Fouquin and Hugot (CEPII 2016).

Between 1815 and 1914, relations among the European powers—and such rising non-European powers as the United States and Japan—were far calmer than they had been for the previous 300 years. While powerful nations certainly continued to care about their security interests, their relations became much more stable and cooperative.

Several sources contributed to the greater cooperation among European powers. The first was a common interest in protecting ruling regimes from new

---

FIGURE 1.1 *Global Value of Exported Goods as a Share of GDP, 1840–1938*

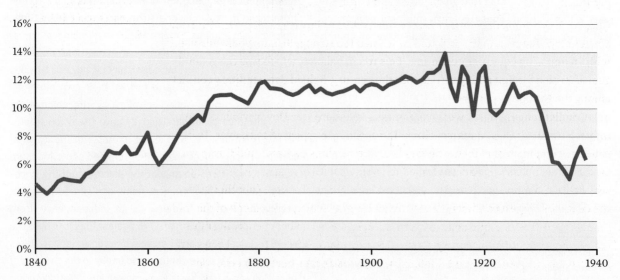

---

political pressures. The French Revolution and the ensuing wars had, among other things, pitted democratic revolutionaries against absolutist and autocratic governments, and the autocrats had won. Few European nations were at all democratic, and those that were democratic were very partially so: in 1830, barely 2 percent of the British population was permitted to vote, and even then the disproportionate allocation of seats meant that those city dwellers who could vote were unlikely to have much influence. All through the nineteenth century, however, movements for greater representation of the middle classes, farmers, and working classes grew in strength. Sometimes rulers gave in to these demands. But throughout Europe there was a common fear of revolution—by democratic forces originally, and eventually by the growing socialist and communist movements.

The common interest of the European rulers in suppressing revolution helped them overcome their political differences. The monarchies that ruled Prussia, Russia, and Austria, in fact, established a formal Holy Alliance in 1815 that was aimed largely at facing the revolutionary threat. Eventually, cooperation extended to most of Europe in what came to be called the Concert of Europe, a system under which the major powers consulted one another on important diplomatic affairs. At the same time, the growing integration of the markets of the European powers gave them some common economic interests, as we will discuss in the next section.

In addition to the convergence of interests among the principal powers, their interactions were stabilized by the reality of British diplomatic, military, and economic predominance. In fact, the period is sometimes called the **Pax Britannica** (Latin for "British peace," by analogy with the Pax Romana that Rome was said to have created within its classical empire). British hegemony proved to be a stabilizing force among European nations. British military power was important—the British navy "ruled the waves" with few challengers—but the country's significance rested also on its role in affecting interactions among European countries that had long been in conflict. Britain tried to prevent the supremacy of any one country on the European continent, acting to maintain a balance of power. (As we will see in Chapter 5, countries may form alliances in an effort to balance the power of a stronger country.) If one country or coalition seemed too strong, Britain would ally itself with an opposing country or coalition. This rough balance, which was the general goal of British foreign policy throughout the century, helped deter military conflict among the European powers.

Conflicts among the powers were muted, and there were few periods of open military strife. The age of massive intra-European war appeared to be over. To be sure, the power balance did not always keep interactions peaceful, and European (and non-European) powers continued to compete with one another for military advantage and influence. The decline of one empire and the rise of another led to the century's biggest conflicts. The Ottoman Empire, which ruled much of the Middle East, North Africa, and southeastern Europe, weakened continually over the course of the nineteenth century. As the Ottoman state tottered, Russia attempted to expand its influence in the Middle East, and when other European countries

Pax Britannica
"British Peace," a century-long period, beginning with Napoleon's defeat at Waterloo in 1815 and ending with the outbreak of World War I in 1914, during which Britain's economic and diplomatic influence contributed to economic openness and relative peace.

sought to restrain Russia, the Crimean War (1853–56) and Russian defeat were the result. Meanwhile, Prussia gradually unified a new German empire under its control. The French tried to discourage this process, but Prussia's victory in the Franco-Prussian War (1870–71) settled the matter. The finalization of German unification indicated the arrival of a new power in Europe. Despite these conflicts, the century from 1815 to 1914 was one of relative peace among the world's principal diplomatic and military powers.

Free Trade

Just as the absolutist European rulers—monarchs or others—could agree on a common opposition to democratic and other revolutionaries, they could also agree on the desirability of ending the mercantilist economic controls of the earlier imperial period. To some extent, the reduction of barriers to trade among nations reflected the more peaceful nature of relations among them. But the reversal of mercantilism also came from changes in the economic interests of the major powers themselves.

British desires for more open trade first displaced mercantilist interests. In the late eighteenth century, British inventors and industrialists introduced a flurry of technological innovations that revolutionized production. Employers brought workers together in large factories to use new machinery, new energy sources, and new forms of organization. Power looms and mechanical spinners transformed the textile industry. Improvements in the use of water power, and eventually the development of steam power, made the machinery more powerful still. By the 1820s, British industry was producing cotton fabric and other textiles, iron, chemicals, and machinery at an unprecedented rate and at extremely low prices.

The economic interests created by Britain's Industrial Revolution saw mercantilist barriers to trade as irrelevant or harmful. Allowing foreigners to sell their products freely to Britain promised several positive effects. British manufacturers could lower their costs both directly, by importing cheaper raw materials, and indirectly, because cheaper imported food would allow factory owners to pay lower wages without reducing workers' standard of living. And if foreigners earned more by selling to Britain, they would be able to buy more British goods. For these reasons, Britain's manufacturing classes and regions developed a dislike of mercantilism and a desire for free trade.

The City of London, which had become the world's financial center, added its influence to that of other free-trade interests. After all, Britain's international bankers had a powerful reason to open up the British market to foreigners: the foreigners were their customers. American or Argentine access to the thriving British market would make it easier for the Americans and Argentines to pay their debts to London. Of course, there were supporters of mercantilism and of barriers to trade more generally. Foremost among them were British farmers, who were protected by the Corn Laws. These were taxes, or tariffs, on imported grain. For 20 years, protectionist British farmers squared off against industrialists and other city dwellers. Eventually, over the course of the 1840s, Parliament repealed most of the previous British mercantile controls on foreign trade.

After Britain, the world's most important economy, discarded mercantilism, many of the nation's customers and suppliers followed suit. In 1860, France joined Great Britain in a sweeping commercial treaty that freed trade between them and subsequently drew most of the rest of Europe in this direction. As the German states moved toward unification in 1871, they created a free-trade area among themselves and then opened trade with the rest of the world. Many New World governments also reduced trade barriers, as did the remaining colonial possessions of the free-trading European powers.

Mercantilism was dead, and integration into world markets—trade liberalization— was the order of the day. Over the course of the 1800s, trade as a percentage of the advanced countries' economies grew two to three times faster than their economies as a whole. By the end of the century, trade was seven or eight times as large a share of the world's economy as it had been at the beginning of the century.[3]

The opening of world trade was encouraged by, and itself encouraged, major advances in transportation and communications. The railroad fundamentally changed the speed and cost of carrying cargo overland. The steamship revolutionized oceangoing shipping, reducing the Atlantic crossing from over a month in 1816 to less than a week in 1896. By the late 1800s, telegraphs, telephones, steamships, and railroads had replaced horses, carrier pigeons, couriers, and sails. The transportation revolution led to a 20-fold increase in the world's shipping capacity during the nineteenth century.[4]

The Gold Standard

The **gold standard** organized monetary relations in this global economic order. When a country's government went "on gold," it promised to exchange its currency for gold at a preestablished rate. The country's currency became equivalent to gold, interchangeable at a fixed rate with the money of any other gold-standard country. Britain had had a gold-backed currency since 1717. As international trade and investment grew, more countries were drawn away from silver and other monetary metals and toward gold, the traditional international medium of exchange. Great Britain's status as the global market leader attracted other countries to use the same monetary system.

By the 1870s, most of the industrial world had adopted the gold standard. With all major currencies directly convertible into gold at fixed rates, the industrial world essentially shared one international currency. The predictability of the gold standard facilitated world trade, lending, investment, migration, and payments (which we will examine in more detail in Chapter 9 on international monetary relations).

International trade, investment, and immigration grew dramatically. Citizens of rich countries invested huge portions of their savings abroad. In the 75 years before

gold standard
The monetary system that prevailed between about 1870 and 1914, in which countries tied their currencies to gold at a legally fixed price.

---

3. Angus Maddison, *Monitoring the World Economy, 1820–1992* (Paris: Development Centre of the OECD, 1995), 38. For an excellent survey of the period, see Peter T. Marsh, *Bargaining on Europe: Britain and the First Common Market, 1860–1892* (New Haven, CT: Yale University Press, 1999).

4. Peter Mathias and Sidney Pollard, eds. *The Cambridge Economic History of Europe*, vol. 8, *The Industrial Economics: The Development of Economic and Social Policies* (Cambridge: Cambridge University Press, 1989), 56; and Maddison, *World Economy: A Millennial Perspective*, 95.

1914, 50 million people left Europe for other continents, and another 50 million left their homelands in Asia to live elsewhere. Free trade, the gold standard, and the new technologies of transportation and communications linked world markets for goods, labor, and capital more tightly than ever before. In short, the world entered its first era of what we now call globalization.

Colonial Imperialism

However peaceful their diplomatic and economic relations may have been in Europe, the principal powers continued to use military force and economic controls on countries in the rest of the world. After a lull in the early part of the century, there was a burst of territorial expansion after 1870 that left most of Africa and Asia part of colonial empires.

The European powers, and eventually non-European powers such as the United States and Japan, were interested in the poor countries of Latin America, Africa, and Asia for both security and economic reasons. The rich nations were interested in extracting the resources and accessing the markets of the poor countries, in many cases wanting to secure them for themselves (rather than sharing them with others). The major powers also saw the rest of the world as a sort of chessboard on which they could fight battles among themselves in their quest for military supremacy. The European (and American and Japanese) presence in the rest of the world expanded, contracted, and adjusted in accordance with the shifting goals of the major powers and changes in the interactions among them.

The colonies had been central to the mercantilist system, but as mercantilism declined, the economic benefits of colonialism faded. For a hundred years after 1760, in fact, the European empires shrank dramatically. Many in the colonies who had previously supported colonialism began to favor independence, and many people in Europe (such as the father of modern economics, Adam Smith, along with other free traders in Britain) came to see the colonies as unnecessarily burdensome. Eventually, Britain, France, Spain, and Portugal lost almost all their New World colonies, and by 1850 the only major colonial possessions remaining were British India, the Dutch East Indies (now Indonesia), and French Algeria.[5]

In the 1870s, however, colonial expansion started anew. The new powers that arose inside and outside Europe—Germany, Italy, Japan, the United States—saw colonial possessions as a way of improving their military position. The established powers, especially Britain and France, did not want their newer rivals accumulating colonial power and wealth at their expense. At the same time, the growth of industry in the developed world increased the desire for overseas markets and resources. And there was an upsurge in nationalist sentiment, especially in such

---

5. Britain's Canadian and Australian possessions had obtained effective autonomy by the 1850s, although they were still formally colonies. Within the British Empire, certain colonial areas were given extensive grants of self-government; for all intents and purposes, by the late nineteenth century, Canada, Australia, and New Zealand acted as if they were independent.

newly important nations as Germany, Italy, and Japan, which spurred governments to satisfy nationalistic demands for expansion.

The result was a scramble for new colonies. From a few scattered outposts in Africa, Europeans quickly spread out to occupy and rule the entire continent, leaving only Ethiopia and Liberia independent by 1890. Britain consolidated and extended its control of South Asia, while it, France, the Netherlands, Germany, Japan, and the United States took over almost all the rest of Southeast and East Asia (Map 1.1). Within the space of a few decades, the industrialized nations had subjected most of the poor regions of the world to direct colonial control. The only major exceptions were Latin America, Persia (Iran), Siam (Thailand), and China, and even they had their sovereignty restricted by military and economic constraints imposed by the European nations, Japan, and the United States.

The Thirty Years' Crisis

A century of relative peace and prosperity in Europe ended with the most devastating military and economic conflicts in modern history. Generations of people in the advanced industrial world had their expectations of stability and security shattered by two terrible world wars and a catastrophic worldwide economic depression. The collapse of Europe's diplomatic balance led to three decades of global conflicts on the military, diplomatic, economic, and political fronts.

Tension in Europe

Contention among the principal powers had grown after 1900. One source of renewed conflict was the changing European power balance. On the one hand, the Ottoman, Austro-Hungarian, and Russian empires were weakening under the weight of socioeconomic stagnation, political instability, and ethnic conflict. On the other hand, new economic and political actors were joining the world stage: the United States, after decades of avoiding foreign entanglements, was becoming more engaged with the rest of the world both politically and economically, and Japan had become a serious international force, as reflected in its decisive victory in the Russo-Japanese War of 1904–5.

The most striking change in the European power balance was the rise of Germany. In 1870, the French and German populations and economies were of roughly similar size, and their economies were substantially smaller than Britain's, but by 1900, Germany's population and economy were the largest in Europe, larger even than those of Britain. This shift created frictions among European nations. The Germans, who had come late onto the world scene, felt that they had fallen behind in the race for colonies. Frustrated with their meager colonial possessions, they focused on Europe and appeared to have designs on neighboring lands with large German populations. These neighbors feared German expansionism and domination. For decades, the major European

MAP 1.1 *The Colonial Empires, 1914*

After 1870, European countries, Japan, and the United States dramatically expanded their colonial possessions. By 1914, almost all of Asia and Africa had been taken over by the colonial powers. In the poorer regions of the world, only Latin America, China, and a handful of countries in Africa and Asia remained independent.

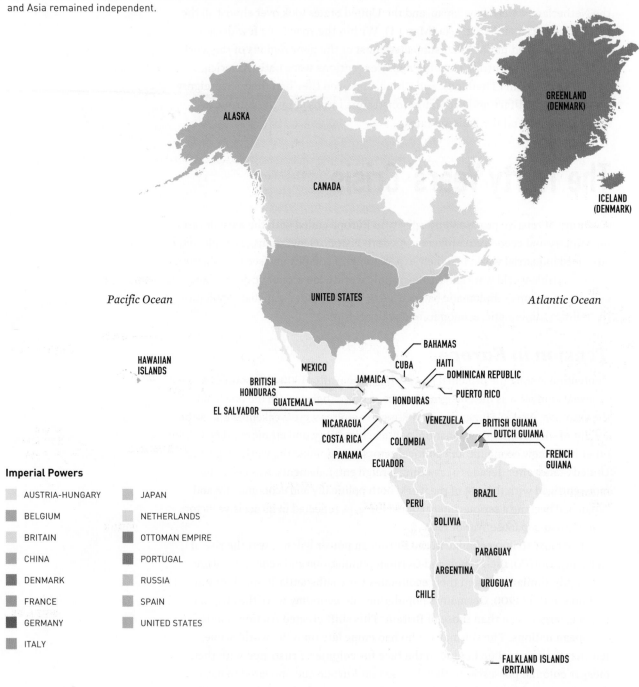

Pacific Ocean

Atlantic Ocean

GREENLAND (DENMARK)

ICELAND (DENMARK)

ALASKA

CANADA

UNITED STATES

HAWAIIAN ISLANDS

BAHAMAS
CUBA
HAITI
DOMINICAN REPUBLIC
MEXICO
JAMAICA
PUERTO RICO
BRITISH HONDURAS
HONDURAS
GUATEMALA
EL SALVADOR
NICARAGUA
VENEZUELA
BRITISH GUIANA
COSTA RICA
DUTCH GUIANA
COLOMBIA
PANAMA
FRENCH GUIANA
ECUADOR

BRAZIL
PERU
BOLIVIA
PARAGUAY
ARGENTINA
URUGUAY
CHILE

FALKLAND ISLANDS (BRITAIN)

Imperial Powers

AUSTRIA-HUNGARY	JAPAN
BELGIUM	NETHERLANDS
BRITAIN	OTTOMAN EMPIRE
CHINA	PORTUGAL
DENMARK	RUSSIA
FRANCE	SPAIN
GERMANY	UNITED STATES
ITALY	

Arctic Ocean

NORWAY
SWEDEN
BRITAIN
IRELAND
NETH.
DENMARK
BEL.
GER.
FRANCE
AUSTRIA-HUNGARY
RUSSIAN EMPIRE

SPAIN
ITALY
PORTUGAL
GREECE
OTTOMAN EMPIRE
AFGHANISTAN
MONGOLIA
KOREA
JAPAN
FRENCH MOROCCO
SPANISH MOROCCO
PERSIA
CHINA
RIO DE ORO
ALGERIA
CYRENAICA
EGYPT
QATAR
TRUCIAL OMAN
INDIA
TIBET
NEPAL
TAIWAN

Pacific Ocean

GAMBIA
FRENCH WEST AFRICA
ERITREA
OMAN
BURMA
GHANA
NIGERIA
FR. EQUATORIAL AFRICA
SUDAN
ADEN
FRENCH SOMALILAND
SIAM
FRENCH INDOCHINA
PHILIPPINES
LIBERIA
TOGO
CAMEROON
ETHIOPIA
BRITISH SOMALILAND
CEYLON
SIERRA LEONE
RIO MUNI
UGANDA
ITALIAN SOMALILAND
MALAY STATES
FR. EQUATORIAL GUINEA
BELGIAN CONGO
GERMAN EAST AFRICA
BRITISH EAST AFRICA
DUTCH EAST INDIES
GERMAN NEW GUINEA
PAPUA
ANGOLA
MOZAMBIQUE
PORTUGUESE GUINEA
N. RHODESIA
NYASALAND
Indian Ocean
GER. SW AFR.
BECHUANA-LAND
S. RHODESIA
MADAGASCAR
SWAZILAND
BASUTOLAND
UNION OF SOUTH AFRICA

AUSTRALIA

NEW ZEALAND

nations had had generally cooperative political and economic relations; now, the prospect of a challenge to the previous arrangements made governments wary and suspicious.

Eventually, Europe divided into two hostile camps. On the one side were the central and southern European powers of Germany, Austria-Hungary, and the Ottoman Empire; on the other were Britain and France to the west and Russia to the east. Crises, whether in Morocco or the Caribbean, the Balkans or Africa, aggravated tensions until war erupted in the summer of 1914. The Central powers—Germany, Austria-Hungary, the Ottoman Empire, and Bulgaria—were arrayed against the Allied powers: most of the rest of Europe (Map 1.2).

MAP 1.2 *Europe, 1914*

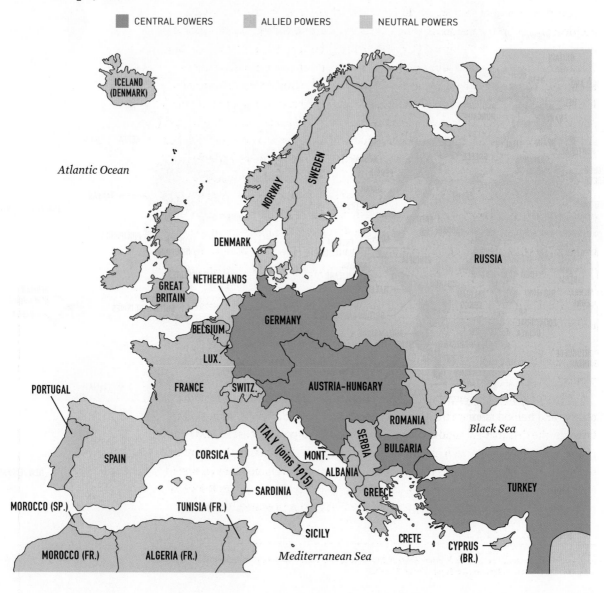

World War I and Its Effects

All participants expected the war to be short and decisive, but it turned out to be long and largely inconclusive—and extraordinarily bloody. Especially on the western front, in Belgium and northern France, huge armies settled into entrenched positions. Trench warfare was punctuated by attempts to break through enemy lines that typically led only to massive losses in dead, wounded, and captured troops on both sides. The first battle of the Marne, in September 1916, cost each side about a quarter million dead and wounded in a week. The entry of the United States in April 1917 on the side of the Allies, and the failure of German submarine warfare to cut Britain off from its supplies, guaranteed the defeat of the Central powers, but the victors had little to show for their success. The war was far longer and far costlier than anyone had imagined it would be; it took the lives of at least 15 million people, including about 7 million civilians.

Despite its immense cost, World War I did little to resolve the underlying political and military tensions that had unsettled Europe; indeed, it exacerbated them. The war utterly disrupted European politics both among and within nations. It led to the collapse of the four great empires of central, eastern, and southern Europe. In the territory from Finland to Yugoslavia, the Austro-Hungarian and Russian empires shattered into pieces, and central and eastern Europe suddenly had a dozen new successor states. The Ottoman Empire, which before the war had stretched from the Persian Gulf to Libya and from Albania to Yemen, was reduced to the far smaller country of Turkey. The German Empire lost what few colonies it had along with large portions of its European territory and population (Map 1.3).

In addition to changing the political map of Europe, the war fundamentally altered domestic social and economic conditions. For most of Europe, economic recovery was slow and partial; many central and eastern European countries went through debilitating bouts of hyperinflation, with prices rising by thousands or millions of percentages. In the most dramatic case, that of Germany, prices rose to a level *1 million million times*—that is, a trillion times—their immediate postwar level. The German mark, previously traded at 4.2 to the dollar, was eventually valued at 4,200,000,000,000—that is, 4.2 trillion—to the dollar. In the final months of the German hyperinflation, the central bank had to print so much currency that it used more than 30 dedicated paper mills, 29 plate manufacturers, and 132 printing plants.[6]

This terrible experience bankrupted much of the central European middle classes and helped alienate them from the new democratic systems. Along with farmers, the dissatisfied middle classes grew to be an important base for extreme right-wing movements, such as the Fascists in Italy and the Nazis in Germany. At the same time, the war and its aftermath increased the power and organization of European labor movements and the socialist parties they supported. In Russia, a radical socialist movement took power, and soon there were communist parties

---

6. Gerald D. Feldman, *The Great Disorder: Politics, Economics, and Society in the German Inflation, 1914–1924* (New York: Oxford University Press, 1993), 782–85.

MAP 1.3 *Europe after World War I, 1920*

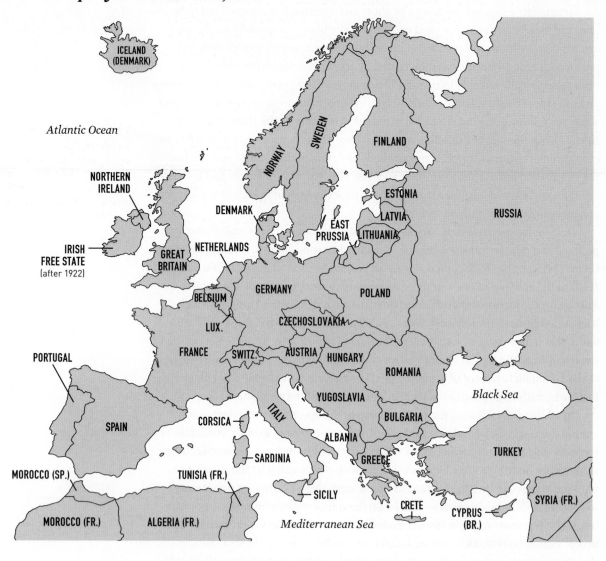

everywhere, representing a revolutionary left-wing challenge to capitalism. The communists favored government ownership of the means of production, rather than capitalist private property, and a planned economy rather than a market system. Politics was polarized and nationalist sentiments inflamed, promoting tensions among European nations.

While it further weakened the bases of peace in Europe, the war demonstrated the international economic and military predominance of the United States. The entry of the United States into the war in 1917, both with its millions of troops and its billions of dollars in loans to the Allies, effectively guaranteed the Allied victory. President Woodrow Wilson guided the negotiations that led to the **Treaty of Versailles**, which ended the war. Economically, while the Europeans were engulfed in war, the United States rushed into the vacuum they left in the rest of the world

Treaty of Versailles

The peace treaty between the Allies and Germany that formally ended World War I on June 28, 1919.

and seized a dramatically increased share of global trade and investment. In fact, the United States became the principal source of war loans to the Allies, such that between 1914 and 1919, America changed from being the world's biggest debtor to its biggest lender. The European powers were dependent on the United States for financial, commercial, and diplomatic leadership to rebuild from the most destructive war the world had ever known.

After this flurry of involvement in European politics and economics, however, the United States drew back. President Wilson could not convince the U.S. Senate to approve American entry into the **League of Nations**. Ironically, this was an international institution created, largely along lines defined by Wilson at Versailles, to bring the world's nations together to increase cooperation and guarantee the peace. In 1920, the Republican Party swept the presidency and both houses of Congress on a platform opposed to Wilson's internationalism and committed to an isolationist foreign policy that would insulate the United States from the uncertainties of intra-European conflict.

Interwar Instability

Europe was left to its own devices, without even the semblance of the pre-1914 balance. The French and British were weak in victory, Germany was bitter in defeat, Russia was isolated in its communist experiment, and the Ottoman and Austro-Hungarian empires had dissolved into a series of small states beset by constant diplomatic and economic tensions. Economic conditions were unsettled, political systems were unstable, and diplomatic relations were tense when not downright hostile.

The French and Germans, in particular, continued to clash diplomatically over issues left unsettled on the battlefield. These included control of the border regions of Alsace, Lorraine, and the Saar—the former two of which went to France, the latter to Germany. Another issue was Germany's commitment not to militarize the Rhineland, a region of Germany bordering France. Germany objected to this restriction on its sovereignty, while France regarded the movement of troops into the border region as a threat.

French and German interests also conflicted over the so-called war debts–reparations tangle. The Treaty of Versailles imposed payments of reparations, a fine levied on the losers for having started the war. This demand created great resentment in Germany, especially given the country's troubled economic conditions. The French argued, among other things, that they needed reparations to pay their debts to the United States. They would, they said, reduce demands on Germany if the United States would forgive some or all of these war debts; after all, the European Allies had paid a high price in lives and property. But the Americans were in no mood to give away billions of dollars to further their involvement with Europe. And so, all throughout the 1920s and 1930s, the principals in World War I continued their battles in the diplomatic and economic realms.

The worst was yet to come: in 1929, the world spiraled downward toward further conflict. The global Great Depression that began in that year was more severe, lasted longer, and caused more hardship than any other economic downturn in

League of Nations

A collective security organization founded in 1919 after World War I. The League ended in 1946 and was replaced by the United Nations.

After World War I ended, continuing tensions prevented cooperation on economic issues. Germany suffered hyperinflation that made its currency, the mark, virtually worthless. Here, children play next to a tower of marks representing the equivalent of one American dollar.

modern history. Industrial production dropped by half in the United States, and by 1932, one-quarter of the country's workers were unemployed. In Germany, unemployment topped one-third of the labor force. No country was untouched.

The economic catastrophe deepened political polarization within nations, in many cases bringing extreme right-wing, highly nationalistic, often militaristic governments to power. By the late 1930s, the Nazis and their fascist allies controlled central, eastern, and southern Europe, as well as Japan. All these countries were hostile to the international economy and to the rich nations of western Europe and North America. In Latin America and in the colonial world, the collapse of the world economy drove nations to turn inward, strengthening the hand of nationalist and anticolonial forces.

World War II

Europe descended once again into war. World War II largely pitted the fascist governments that had turned against the global economy, on the one hand, against the democratic powers that remained committed to some form of international economic cooperation (along with the Soviet Union), on the other. The three major fascist powers—Germany, Italy, and Japan—sought to restore and increase their military might and territory through war, and in 1940 they established a formal alliance, the Axis.

An expansionist Nazi Germany annexed Austria in 1938 and occupied Czechoslovakia in 1939. Also in 1939, Germany attacked Poland and quickly overpowered it, leading Britain and France to declare war on Germany in support of their Polish ally. But in May 1940, Germany invaded France, which it defeated and occupied within six weeks. Through invasion, coercion, and persuasion, the Axis powers built a network of followers, protectorates, and colonies that extended throughout virtually all of Europe, Asia, and North Africa, excluding Britain and the Soviet Union. The democratic Allies were restricted to Britain, North America, Australia, and New Zealand. In June 1941, Germany invaded the Soviet Union, and soon German troops were on the outskirts of Moscow. In December, Japan—which had already come to occupy most of China and Indochina—attacked the American naval base at Pearl Harbor.

The United States had been supporting the British with supplies, but the Japanese attack on Pearl Harbor in 1941 overcame any lingering American reluctance to get involved in another world war. From then on, the war pitted the Axis against the three major Allies—the United States, Britain, and the Soviet Union. The bulk of the war in Europe was fought along the eastern front, between the Germans and the Soviets, where millions of troops faced each other over thousands of miles of territory. After an initial frenzied retreat, the Soviets battled back and turned the tide at Stalingrad in early 1943. Meanwhile, the British and Americans carried out operations in North Africa before invading Italy in 1943 and France in 1944, while American forces advanced against Japan in the Pacific. In May 1945, Germany surrendered unconditionally. In August, in an attempt to force a Japanese surrender, the United States dropped nuclear weapons on the cities of Hiroshima and Nagasaki; the Japanese surrendered several days later.

The human and economic costs of World War II were unimaginably large. About 110 million people served in the combined armed forces, of whom 25 million were killed. Approximately 30 million civilians were killed by the war directly, and this number does not include the 7 million or more people, mostly Jews, whom the Germans and their allies murdered in a planned genocide. Four-fifths of the dead were from Allied nations, including some 20 million from the Soviet Union (13 million military, 7 million civilian). Most of Europe and Japan were left in ruins.

The Cold War

The impact of World War II on international politics was profound. Unlike in 1918, the results of the war were conclusive, and they fundamentally altered international power relations. Germany, Japan, Italy, France, and Britain, which had defined great-power politics before the war, were effectively finished as world powers; the only two nations with the ability to project significant military force were the United States and the Soviet Union. The question that remained was how this two-power world would be ordered. On the one hand, the two principal wartime allies had cooperated in defeating the Axis powers. On the other hand, they represented fundamentally different socioeconomic systems and had divergent interests in the organization of the postwar world.

The Superpowers Emerge

At war's end, the United States, the Soviet Union, Great Britain, and France were united in victory. The Allies defined the terms of the peace, carved up Germany into zones of occupation, and divided Europe into spheres of influence. Many people, including in the United States, felt that the four principal victors could, should, and would cooperate under the auspices of the new United Nations (UN) to manage international relations peacefully.

But within months, conflicts grew between the United States and the Soviet Union. Perhaps disagreements were inevitable between a capitalist democracy and a communist one-party system. It may be that the two superpowers were driven toward discord by the very structure of their power relations as they struggled for influence in Europe. Scholars continue to debate whether the source of the division was the inherently different economic or military interests of the two superpowers, or rather some failure in their attempts to interact productively.

By 1949, the two superpowers were consolidating control over their respective blocs. The United States drew together its new allies—including the defeated Axis nations—into a Western system. The Americans worked to solidify their coalition as a common military alliance (the North Atlantic Treaty Organization, or NATO) and as a collaborative economic order (the Bretton Woods System). The Soviet Union, for its part, now led a communist alliance that stretched from central Europe to the Pacific, including China, North Korea, and North Vietnam. The international order divided into communist and capitalist parts, and the Cold War between them was the defining characteristic of international politics from the late 1940s until the late 1980s.

The Blocs Consolidate

The Cold War pitted the two superpowers against each other. Their military and economic interests were almost diametrically opposed. The United States favored market-based, capitalist economic activities, while the Soviet Union rejected markets and capitalism in favor of a centrally planned socialism. In the geopolitical sphere, the Soviets regarded a pro-American Western Europe as a threat to their western borders, and a pro-American Japan as a threat to the east; the Americans saw the Soviets and their communist allies as a military menace to their own European and Asian allies. In an atmosphere of trust and stability, it might have been possible for the two superpowers to work out an amicable understanding, but as it turned out, interactions between them quickly turned hostile and suspicious, and they devoted their efforts to fortifying themselves against each other.

Each superpower went about building up its respective coalition. The United States provided $14 billion in Marshall Plan and other aid to Western Europe and Japan in order to speed postwar reconstruction. It also led the Western world in creating a system of military alliances in the North Atlantic, Southeast Asia, Latin America, and elsewhere. The most important of these, the **North Atlantic Treaty Organization (NATO)**, brought together North America and most of Western Europe in a collective military institution united against the Soviet Union and its allies (see Chapter 5 for more details on NATO and other military alliances).

The United States also guided its allies toward a newly integrated and strongly institutionalized Western economic order. The **Bretton Woods System**, so called because its founding documents were negotiated at the Bretton Woods resort in New Hampshire, included institutions intended to encourage the freer movement of goods and capital around the world. In trade relations, the General Agreement on Tariffs and Trade (GATT) oversaw a substantial reduction in trade barriers.[7] In monetary affairs, the International Monetary Fund (IMF) supervised a restored but reformed gold-dollar standard, in which the U.S. dollar was tied to gold and all

North Atlantic Treaty Organization (NATO)

An alliance formed in 1949 among the United States, Canada, and most of the states of Western Europe in response to the threat posed by the Soviet Union. The alliance requires its members to consider an attack on any one of them as an attack on all.

Bretton Woods System

The economic order negotiated among allied nations at Bretton Woods, New Hampshire, in 1944, which led to a series of cooperative arrangements involving a commitment to relatively low barriers to international trade and investment.

---

7. The original institution was to be the International Trade Organization, but it encountered opposition in the United States. As a result, an "interim" institution, the GATT, was established.

other currencies were tied to the dollar. The International Bank for Reconstruction and Development (also called the World Bank) worked to encourage a resumption of private investment, especially in the developing nations (these economic institutions are discussed in more detail in Part 3).

By the early 1960s, the Western world had rebuilt an integrated international economy—not a copy of the pre-1914 age of free trade and the gold standard, but something new. The commitment to economic integration was now combined with social welfare programs such as unemployment insurance and the widespread public provision of health care, pensions, housing, and other social benefits. This extensive social safety net helped cushion workers from the harshest effects of global competition, and the Bretton Woods System thus represented a compromise between economic integration and national commitments to social reform and the welfare state.

The Soviet Union also consolidated its bloc. It created a military alliance with its European allies, the **Warsaw Pact**. It strengthened military ties with the communist government that took power in China in 1949. In the economic realm, the Soviet bloc developed a socialist variant of economic integration in which different nations specialized in different products. This economic cooperation was overseen by an institution called the Council for Mutual Economic Assistance, which brought together the communist nations and some of their supporters in the developing world. The Cold War, indeed, extended to competition over the support of many newly independent countries in Africa, Asia, and the Caribbean. Eventually, there was a rough division of the world between countries that tended to ally with the United States and those that tended to ally with the Soviet Union (Map 1.4).

The defining feature of military relations between the two superpowers was the development of nuclear weapons. By 1954, both the United States and the Soviet Union had atomic and hydrogen bombs, possessing a destructive power far beyond anything previously possible. With the development of long-distance bombers and missiles, eventually both superpowers had the ability to destroy each other (and their allies) many times over. The potent American and Soviet weapon stockpiles led to a real fear that war between the two superpowers would be unimaginably devastating and might threaten all humanity.

However, the roughly equal arsenals of nuclear weapons created something of a standoff: each side's destructive capacity was sufficient to deter an attack on its homeland or its close allies. Since neither the United States nor the Soviet Union could really hope to conquer the other or its principal friends, their competition was limited to other regions of the globe.

Indeed, despite the absence of direct warfare between the superpowers, the Cold War was by no means a peaceful time for people in much of the world. On several occasions, crises between the Americans and the Soviets came to the brink of war, such as the 1949 Berlin airlift.

In the aftermath of the German surrender, Germany was divided into four zones, controlled respectively by the Americans, British, French, and Soviets. The country's traditional capital, Berlin, which was located deep inside the Soviet zone, was also divided in four. Over time, the Western allies came to work together in

Warsaw Pact

A military alliance formed in 1955 to bring together the Soviet Union and its Cold War allies in Eastern Europe and elsewhere; dissolved on March 31, 1991, as the Cold War ended.

MAP 1.4 *The Cold War and Its Alliances, 1980*

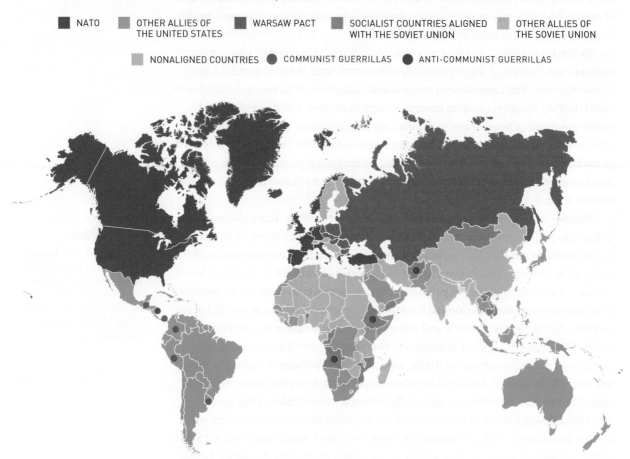

NATO OTHER ALLIES OF THE UNITED STATES WARSAW PACT SOCIALIST COUNTRIES ALIGNED WITH THE SOVIET UNION OTHER ALLIES OF THE SOVIET UNION

NONALIGNED COUNTRIES COMMUNIST GUERRILLAS ANTI-COMMUNIST GUERRILLAS

their zones, but there was constant friction between them and the Soviets. In June 1948, the Soviet Union blockaded land and rail routes into Berlin from the Western zones. This action cut West Berlin off from supplies of everything from food to coal. The Soviets clearly expected the Western allies to either withdraw or give in to several Soviet demands about the occupation. But the allies quickly organized a massive airlift that lasted nearly a year and involved almost 300,000 flights, providing millions of tons of supplies to the residents of West Berlin. In May 1949, the Soviets finally backed down and once again permitted transport between the Western occupation zones and West Berlin. However, the level of tension between East and West remained high. It was only heightened in 1961, when the East Germans built a wall between East and West Berlin, cutting the city in half.

Perhaps the most dramatic confrontation of the Cold War took place soon after the Berlin Wall went up, several thousand miles away, in Cuba. In 1959, a left-wing nationalist movement headed by Fidel Castro succeeded in ousting pro-American dictator Fulgencio Batista. Over the next several years, the new revolutionary government of Cuba moved quickly leftward and allied itself with the Soviet Union. An American-sponsored invasion in April 1961 failed, but the Cuban government was deeply fearful of American attempts to undermine it. Meanwhile, the Soviet government under Nikita Khrushchev was concerned that it was losing the nuclear arms race to the United States. In the summer of 1962, the Soviets secretly began installing nuclear missiles in Cuba; these were intended both to help protect the pro-Soviet Cuban government and, more important, to help even out the nuclear balance by putting Soviet missiles within easy striking distance of the United States.

In October 1962, American spy planes spotted the missile installations, which the U.S. government regarded as a clear and present danger to American national security. American ships encircled the island, prepared to prevent Soviet naval vessels from reaching it, and plans for an American invasion were developed, even though many of the participants realized that such an action might lead to a nuclear war between the two sides. For about a week, the U.S. and Soviet governments bargained over the missiles amid widespread expectation that war would break out. Finally, the two sides agreed to a deal: the Soviets would dismantle their missiles in Cuba if the United States withdrew its nuclear missiles from Turkey.[8]

In addition to the threat of war between the two nations, each superpower routinely used military force to prevent other countries from falling into the sphere of its rival. U.S. military and intelligence services undermined governments that were communist or seen as likely to come under communist influence: Iran in 1953, Guatemala in 1954, the Congo and Cuba in 1961, the Dominican Republic in 1962, Chile in 1971, and Nicaragua from 1979 to 1988. The Soviet Union similarly used military power to extend or preserve its own influence. Its forces invaded Hungary in 1956 and Czechoslovakia in 1968, when these allies seemed likely to leave the Soviet orbit. The Soviet Union also invaded Afghanistan in 1979, leading to a decade-long war that sapped the Soviets' military might.

In the colonial and postcolonial world, especially, the two superpowers constantly jockeyed for influence. Wars in Korea and Vietnam were the most obvious instances. In both cases, the Soviets supported one side of a civil conflict while the Americans supported the other side. The United States and some of its allies sent troops to both South Korea and South Vietnam; the Soviet Union and some of its allies sent supplies to both North Korea and North Vietnam. Similar "proxy wars" were fought in many regions and over many decades. Much of the developing world became a Cold War battleground between pro-American and pro-Soviet forces.

Decolonization

The involvement of the two superpowers in the affairs of Africa, Asia, and Latin America accompanied a broader emergence of these regions to a prominent place in world politics. This was a relatively new phenomenon in the modern era: between 1914 and the mid-1950s, the developing world remained largely at the margins of world politics. Europe, North America, and Japan were preoccupied with two world wars, the Great Depression, postwar reconstruction, and the Cold War.

---

8. The literature on the crisis is enormous; for an example, see Michael Dobbs, *One Minute to Midnight: Kennedy, Khrushchev, and Castro on the Brink of Nuclear War* (New York: Knopf, 2008). The tense showdown during the crisis is an example of brinksmanship, which we will discuss in Chapter 3.

Under these conditions, relations with the colonies and the independent developing nations were of less importance. The economic implications were particularly striking. For decades, Africa, Asia, and Latin America had supported themselves by exporting agricultural products and raw materials to the industrial world and importing manufactured products. But for much of the time between 1914 and 1955, the rich nations were unwilling or unable to continue normal trade relations; they were absorbed in war, devastated by economic crisis, or rebuilding after war.

The developing world thus was forced to rely less on its economic ties with the industrial nations and more on its own markets and products. While in the early stages it was external events—depression and war—that cut off the developing world, eventually the governments of many countries, and even some colonies, began to encourage and undertake substantial efforts at industrial development, providing at home what had previously been imported from Europe or North America. For example, by the early 1960s Brazil's industries supplied 99 percent of the country's consumer goods, 91 percent of its intermediate inputs (such as steel and chemicals), and 87 percent of its capital goods (such as machinery and equipment).[9] At that point the Brazilian economy, which was roughly the size of the Dutch economy, was close to self-sufficient in manufactured goods.

This economic turn inward was accompanied by an upsurge in nationalist sentiment. In Latin America, China, and Turkey, this trend brought to power governments that were unfavorable—even hostile—to foreign trade, foreign investment, and foreign finance. In many colonies, the rise in nationalism fed into dissatisfaction with continued colonial rule.

After World War II ended, the colonial clamor for greater autonomy, and even independence, increased. The European empires had been weakened by the war, and their ability to sustain colonialism by force had diminished. Meanwhile, the nationalist movements had grown in strength and resolve, and they demanded autonomy and even independence more insistently. Many in the developing world looked to the experiences of the United States and the Latin American republics, which had gained their independence in the late eighteenth and early nineteenth centuries. Now **decolonization** was on the agenda again, as another group of colonial subjects fought to leave the colonial empires. In some instances, such as in British India, the colonial powers gave in to these demands, albeit reluctantly, recognizing that they had little alternative. But in other instances, such as British Kenya, French Algeria, and the Dutch East Indies (Indonesia), independence came only after violent conflict between the colonialists and the colonized.

Pressure on the colonial powers did not come only from the nationalist independence movements. In many instances, the United States encouraged its European allies to release their subjects. American anticolonialism had moral sources but also more material motivations. For example, American businesses welcomed a decolonization that would allow them fuller access to the markets of the developing world. And in the context of the Cold War, the United States was particularly concerned that colonialism would undermine American influence in the developing

decolonization

The process of colonial possessions winning independence, especially during the rapid end of the European empires in Africa, Asia, and the Caribbean between the 1940s and the 1960s.

---

9. Werner Baer, *The Brazilian Economy: Growth and Development*, 3rd ed. (New York: Praeger, 1989), 70.

ЖИЗНЬ И СВОБОДУ ГИЗЕНГЕ!

СМЕРТЬ КОЛОНИАЛИЗМУ!

During the Cold War, both superpowers sought the support of newly independent African countries. This Soviet poster calls for "Death to Colonialism!" and the liberation of Antoine Gizenga, a political prisoner in the Congo.

world. With so much of the world under European colonial control, it was hard for the United States to make a case for the evils of Soviet domination. The Americans feared that colonialism would push independence-minded Africans and Asians toward the communists in their search for allies.

Developments within the colonies, within the imperial nations, and in international politics brought the end of colonialism more quickly than anyone had imagined possible. Within a few years of the end of World War II, almost all of colonial Asia and the Middle East were independent; North Africa gained its independence over the course of the 1950s, and by 1965 almost all of Africa was free. Colonialism was finished, and the world was made up of sovereign states.

The Rise of the Developing World

Many of the newly independent nations of Africa, Asia, and the Caribbean resisted involvement in the battle between the American and Soviet blocs. They concentrated on problems inherent in the relationship between rich industrialized nations and poor developing countries—the divide between North and South rather than East and West. In the late 1950s and early 1960s, leaders of such countries as India, Egypt, Ghana, and the Philippines came together to form a nonaligned movement of nations that professed independence from both blocs. These countries were variously known as developing countries, less developed countries, and members of the third world—this last moniker used to distinguish them from the capitalist "first" and communist "second" worlds. They organized themselves to redress perceived inequities in their relationship with the advanced industrial world, especially in the nature of their economic ties.

Most developing-country attempts to reform the international economy were ineffectual, as these countries lacked the power to make their points any more than rhetorically. But in 1973, the success of the major oil-producing developing nations in manipulating world oil markets and dramatically increasing oil prices sparked hope for more balance in North-South economic relations. The resulting oil shocks, or fluctuations in the price of oil, had mixed success. The developing nations had raw materials that the industrialized world wanted, and if they could organize themselves as effectively as had the members of the Organization of the Petroleum Exporting Countries (OPEC), they might be able to extract more resources from the rich nations. Some producers of raw materials (copper, bauxite, and bananas, for example) followed OPEC in organizing cartels to try to raise prices, with mixed success. But the developing world also agitated more generally for what it called the New International Economic Order, which would be more favorable to developing nations.

The Cold War Thaws

Even as the developing world organized itself in ways that did not fit the East-West dimension, by the mid-1960s the two superpower alliances were themselves beginning to show signs of strain. France withdrew from NATO, and the United States got bogged down in a war in Vietnam that was unpopular both abroad and at home. The Soviet Union lost its most important ally when China broke with the rest of the Soviet bloc, while dissatisfaction in Eastern Europe and at home put pressure on the Soviet government to provide greater political and economic freedoms.

Although conflict persisted in relations between the United States and the Soviet Union, in the 1970s both sides warily attempted a relaxation of tensions. The two blocs built more political, economic, and cultural ties, and they negotiated a series of agreements to limit the arms race between them. This reduction in hostility, or détente, was set back by continued competition in the third world and Europe, but the threat of armed conflict seemed to recede.

Globalization and Its Discontents

The relaxation of U.S.-Soviet tensions reduced the threat of superpower war. Two decades of upheaval fundamentally altered the postwar patterns of international politics and gave rise to new diplomatic and security challenges. The world economy became more globalized, but international economic relations were increasingly contested.[10]

The Cold War Ends

Relations between the United States and the Soviet Union had been improving since the mid-1960s, but in 1979 they took a turn toward greater hostility. In December of that year, Soviet troops entered Afghanistan to support a fragile

---

10. With apologies to Joseph E. Stiglitz, *Globalization and Its Discontents* (New York: Norton, 2002).

pro-Soviet government. The United States and its allies responded vigorously to this first direct use of Soviet troops outside of the Warsaw Pact, imposing trade sanctions, financing Afghan insurgents, and boycotting the 1980 Olympic Games in Moscow. Soviet troops were soon bogged down in a guerrilla war that many observers compared to the American experience in Vietnam.

Ronald Reagan took office as U.S. president in 1981, committed to a strongly anti-Soviet stance. The Reagan administration substantially increased military spending, especially spending connected to the U.S.-Soviet rivalry. In reaction, the Soviets attempted to increase their own military spending.

The renewed tension put great strains both on international relations and on the Soviet economic and political order. The Soviet economy was falling increasingly behind that of the West, and the faltering Soviet system was finding it more difficult to keep up militarily. In 1988, the Soviets relaxed their control over their Eastern European allies; in 1989, Soviet troops withdrew from Afghanistan, the Berlin Wall came down, and communists began loosening their grip on governments all over central and Eastern Europe. By 1991, the Soviet Union had dissolved into 15 new, independent, non-communist countries, and the communist governments of the Soviet Union's European allies were out of power. The Cold War was over, and only one superpower was left standing.

Worldwide Economic Developments

The international economy also experienced disruption and change in the 1970s and 1980s. After the OPEC oil shocks of 1973–74, the industrialized capitalist world entered a decade of recession, high unemployment, and high inflation. In the early 1980s, austerity measures to cut government spending and restrain wages helped bring inflation under control, but many economies remained stagnant. The developing nations too ran into trouble as a global debt crisis erupted in 1982 and drove many heavily indebted poor nations into crisis.

Over the course of the 1980s, supporters and opponents of increasing the role of market forces in economic activity faced off in developed, developing, and communist countries. In almost all instances, the crisis eventually led to a turn toward the market. In the West, cross-border trade and investment increased very substantially (see Figure 1.2 for the growth of world trade since World War II). Regional trade agreements proliferated and were strengthened (see Chapter 7 for details). The European Union, first created as the European Coal and Steel Community by Belgium, France, West Germany, Italy, the Netherlands, and Luxembourg in 1951, grew to include almost all of western Europe by 1995 (only Norway, Iceland, and Switzerland refrained from joining), removed all barriers to the movement of goods and capital among member states in 1991, and eventually replaced most of the members' national currencies, such as the French franc and the German mark, with a common currency, the euro, in 1999. The United States, Canada, and Mexico created the North American Free Trade Agreement (NAFTA) in 1994, which similarly removed many economic barriers among those three countries.

Most developing countries responded to the difficulties of the 1980s by removing previous barriers to international economic involvement, instead welcoming

FIGURE 1.2   *Global Value of Exported Goods as a Share of GDP, 1945–2014*

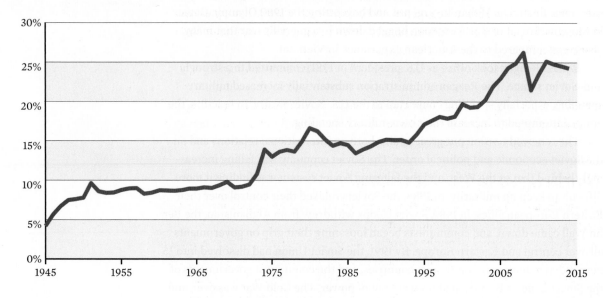

Figure source: Esteban Ortiz-Ospina and Diana Beltekian, "Trade and Globalization," Our World in Data, October 2018, https://ourworldindata.org/trade-and-globalization (accessed 10/20/20).

foreign trade and investment. The watchword became *globalization*, with a level of international economic integration that had not been seen since 1914.

The most stunning changes took place in the communist world. China and Vietnam embraced capitalist economic reform in the early 1980s but maintained their one-party systems. Attempts to reform the Soviet system and maintain communist control failed, and the Soviet Union broke up into 15 separate independent states. Some of them, along with many of the former communist-run countries of central and Eastern Europe, joined the European Union, and some also adopted the euro. Russia, however, remained somewhat aloof from Europe, preferring to try to build ties with some of the other former component parts of the Soviet Union.

Military conflict did not disappear. The first major sign that the post-Cold War age would not be entirely peaceful came when a crisis erupted in the Persian Gulf. In August 1990, Iraq, led by President Saddam Hussein, invaded its small, oil-rich neighbor Kuwait (for more on these events, see the discussion in Chapter 3). Almost immediately, the UN Security Council and the Arab League, a regional organization of Arab states in Africa and West Asia, condemned the invasion and called on Iraq to withdraw from Kuwait. When Iraq refused, an American-led coalition of 34 countries began a month of massive air attacks on Iraq, followed by a ground assault that defeated Iraqi forces within three days.

The global response to the Iraqi invasion seemed to demonstrate that the world community, acting through the UN, might be able to act collectively to resolve diplomatic problems of general concern. The record of the next few years was mixed. In 1992, a UN mission that went to Somalia with the intent of ensuring that humanitarian supplies would reach the civilian population as the country descended into a state of lawlessness was a qualified success. A year later, another UN mission, sent to Rwanda to try to mediate a resolution of that country's civil war, was unable to halt a horrific genocide in which the Rwandan government orchestrated the murder of as many as a million Rwandan citizens, most of them from the minority Tutsi ethnic group. Despite the mixed record, UN involvement in these and other conflicts raised hopes of further international collaboration to resolve difficult diplomatic and military problems.

By the 1990s it was widely believed that the world had entered a new era of relaxed military tension, enhanced global cooperation, and heightened economic integration. The Cold War was over and Western capitalism had triumphed, spearheaded by a strong American-led alliance. Globalization and American dominance seemed to presage a new era in world politics.

Challenges to the New Order

Events since 2000 have called the expectation of a new era into question, on both the military-diplomatic and economic fronts.

The first major shock was the terror attacks of September 11, 2001, which made horribly clear that military conflicts would continue and alerted the world to a new kind of international threat. On that day, 19 members of the Islamist network Al Qaeda hijacked four passenger airplanes and flew two into the World Trade Center in New York City and one into the Pentagon outside Washington; the fourth crashed in rural Pennsylvania. Some 3,000 people were killed in the attacks. Within a month, the United States and its NATO allies launched an invasion of Afghanistan, whose extremist government harbored Al Qaeda's leader Osama bin Laden and refused to hand him over to American authorities. The regime fell quickly, but conflict continued between Islamists and the new American-backed government. The Security Council eventually provided a UN force to help enforce peace in the country in the face of a continued extremist insurgency.

Military and diplomatic tensions rose as the major powers debated how to deal with the Iraqi government of Saddam Hussein, which had flouted previous UN decisions. Tensions between the United States and Iraq had been high since the early 1990s, when the United States led a multinational coalition to war in response to Iraq's invasion of Kuwait. As a condition of the ceasefire that ended that war, Iraq agreed to eliminate its programs to develop nuclear, chemical, and biological weapons and to permit UN inspectors to monitor its compliance. For most of the next decade, the Iraqi government attempted to undermine the inspections regime and its economic sanctions. In 2002, the administration of U.S. president George W. Bush argued that Iraq's weapons of mass destruction programs were rapidly reaching fruition. Concerned that Iraq might use its new weapons to act aggressively in the region, the Bush administration decided to remove Iraq's dictator, Saddam Hussein, from power—by force if necessary. Bush may also have wanted to assert American power to demonstrate a new, more forceful foreign policy; to secure supplies of oil from the Persian Gulf; and to transform the Middle East by building an effective democracy in an important country.

The United States turned to the UN Security Council to support its efforts toward regime change in Iraq, but it faced determined opposition from France, Russia, and China, each of which can veto any substantive resolution within the Security Council. Although these states shared concerns about the Iraqi regime and its suspected weapons programs, they were reluctant to endorse military action. Though the United States failed to obtain authorization from the Security Council for the war, it claimed sufficient authority under past UN resolutions on Iraq and under the right of self-defense in the UN Charter. After Hussein rejected an ultimatum to step down, the United States led a "coalition of the willing" to a rapid initial military victory in 2003.

Yet the war turned out to be one of the longest and most inconclusive in U.S. history. To the surprise of many, the United States did not find the stockpiles of chemical and biological weapons it had claimed existed. This embarrassment helped turn sentiment at home against the war. The Bush administration also did not adequately anticipate the damage that the decade of sanctions had wreaked on Iraq's social and physical infrastructure, and it found itself leading a "failed state" and embroiled in a broad-based insurgency. American troops eventually tamped down the violence, but tensions between the Shiite majority and the Sunni minority remained high, and the Kurds established an essentially autonomous enclave in the north of the country. U.S. forces first withdrew in 2011, but only three years later they were back in Iraq to prop up the failing state and help battle a new insurgency. Eventually the military situation stabilized, but it remains to be seen how history will evaluate the impact of the war in Iraq.

The second Iraq war was only the beginning of turmoil in the Middle and Near East. In 2010 anti-authoritarian uprisings that began in Tunisia spread throughout North Africa and much of the rest of the Muslim world. In Syria, opposition to the country's regime turned into a bloody civil war that fueled regional conflicts that appeared to pit, variously, Sunnis against Shiites, Kurds against Arabs, Islamists against secularists, and extremists against moderates. The Middle and Near Eastern conflicts spilled over into neighboring countries and drew in nations from outside the region, often pitting the United States and its allies against Russia and Iran (as in Libya in 2011).

In 2014 the picture was complicated further by the emergence of a movement calling itself the Islamic State of Iraq and Syria (ISIS), commonly known as simply

Syrians fleeing bombings in the southern region drive toward the Syrian-Turkish border. Opposition to the country's regime turned into a bloody civil war that fueled regional conflicts and contributed to the flood of refugees into Europe, provoking bitter debates between those who welcomed them and those who saw them as an unwanted economic burden.

the Islamic State.[11] This movement appeared even more extreme than Al Qaeda: it declared its intent to establish a worldwide caliphate, seized substantial territory in Iraq and Syria, built alliances with other Islamist extremists, and sponsored or endorsed a barrage of terrorist attacks in Western countries. While the Islamic State was eventually uprooted several years later from the territory it had seized, it has remained an active terrorist force.

Although the Islamic State faded somewhat from view, tensions in the Middle and Near East remained high. The United States and most of its allies were increasingly concerned about Iranian influence, as the Islamic Republic of Iran built up a network of supporters around the Middle East. There was also concern that the Iranian government was planning to develop nuclear weapons. After long negotiations, the Iranians signed the Joint Comprehensive Plan of Action with the United States, the European Union, Russia, and China in 2015. The deal committed Iran to measures intended to ensure that it would not develop nuclear weapons, and Iran's compliance was monitored by the International Atomic Energy Agency.

Continued military conflict in the Middle East, along with difficult economic and political conditions throughout the region, drove millions of refugees and migrants out of their native lands beginning in 2010. As unprecedented millions of people from the Middle East and North Africa sought refuge in Europe, it provoked bitter debates between Europeans who welcomed the refugees and those who saw them as an unwanted immigrant burden.

In Asia, an economically and politically resurgent China confronted several of its neighbors, especially Japan and Vietnam, over long-standing territorial disputes (see Chapter 2 for more on these conflicts). China's ally North Korea joined the nuclear club and set about expanding its military capabilities, ignoring the condemnation and

The recent influx of refugees and migrants into Europe, triggered by unrest in the Middle East, has emboldened nationalist groups in many European countries. Riding a wave of anti-immigrant sentiment, the Alternative for Germany political party won seats in the lower house of the German legislature after the 2017 elections, making it the first far-right party to do so since World War II.

---

11. The movement's full Arabic name is al-Dawlah al-Islamiyah fil Iraq wa al-Sham. Variants include "Daesh," an acronym of the Arabic name, the "Islamic State of Iraq and al-Sham" (ISIS), and the "Islamic State of Iraq and the Levant" (ISIL), based on an alternative translation of the Arabic.

sanctions of the United States and its allies. The administrations of U.S. presidents Barack Obama and Donald J. Trump attempted to limit and contain the expansion of Chinese diplomatic and military influence in Asia, but it was clear that China was now a world power and would play a major—perhaps dominant—role in the region's politics.

Conflict between Russia and the West also accelerated into the most serious disagreement since the Cold War. In February 2014, popular demonstrations forced the pro-Russian government of Ukraine out of office, and it was replaced by a pro-European coalition. The Russian government responded by annexing the Crimean Peninsula, a largely Russian-speaking region that had been ceded to Ukraine under Soviet rule in the 1950s. Soon after, Russian-backed separatists in eastern Ukraine launched military operations that created separatist enclaves on Ukrainian territory. The West imposed escalating economic sanctions against Russia, but the military standoff remained a continuing source of antagonism between Russia on the one hand, and Europe and the United States on the other.

The administration of U.S. president Donald Trump, which took office in January 2017, shifted course on a number of diplomatic dimensions. The administration was wary of many of the United States' multilateral commitments and allies, often preferring to take unilateral measures rather than work through existing international institutions. As an example, the Trump administration denounced and eventually withdrew from the Joint Comprehensive Plan of Action, to the distress of America's European allies. More directly, President Trump assailed the country's NATO allies for contributing too little to the common defense, eventually withdrawing some troops from Germany as a signal of his displeasure. The Trump administration, however, cultivated close ties with ideologically similar governments in central and eastern Europe, many of which were antagonistic toward America's traditional western European allies.

Meanwhile, Chinese foreign policy took an increasingly assertive tone (see Chapter 2). The country, now the second-largest economy in the world, worked to expand its diplomatic and economic influence in Asia and Africa. While there had always been some friction between China and the United States, U.S-China relations became increasingly confrontational as the Trump administration increased restrictions on Chinese companies in the United States, and as China tightened its controls on Hong Kong and pursued other aggressive measures widely seen as expansionist.

As relations between the United States and China deteriorated and as the traditional ties between the United States and its NATO allies appeared to fray, questions proliferated about how the global diplomatic scene was going to evolve. The rise of China—and of a more nationalist Trump administration—seemed to presage future conflict.

Challenges to the post–Cold War diplomatic order were followed by serious challenges to its economic order as well. Enthusiasm for economic globalization began to wane in the first decades of the 2000s. This trend was accelerated by the 2008–9 global financial crisis and the economic dislocation caused by the COVID-19 pandemic that began late in 2019.

Between the global financial crisis and the global pandemic, skepticism grew about economic integration: globalization no longer seemed appealing to many people. In the European Union, the backlash against globalization largely took the form of left-wing opposition to the austerity measures provoked by the eurozone's debt crisis and right-wing hostility to the European Union. In June 2016 British voters shocked the world by choosing by referendum to leave the European Union—the first time a member state left the union. In the United States, strong antiglobalization sentiment emerged among both Democrats and Republicans, and Republican Donald Trump won the presidency in 2016 after a campaign that was more hostile to international trade, international investment, and immigration than any major-party candidate had been since the 1930s.

As what came to be called "populism" grew on both the left and the right, previous commitments to international economic cooperation were called into question. Thus, just as international diplomatic affairs were taking a more combative turn, international economic relations were also heading toward more troubled waters. Although Trump was defeated in the 2020 election and his successor, Joseph Biden, was more sympathetic to multilateral military and economic cooperation, many of the underlying tensions that animated Trump's foreign policy outlook remain. As the Biden administration moved to rebuild frayed diplomatic ties, it also expressed concerns about looming competition with China and the nature of America's trade relations. Major questions remain on both diplomatic and economic fronts about how world politics will evolve over the coming decades.

What Will Shape Our World in the Future?

Today, the two overriding questions in international affairs have to do with the future of great-power politics and the future of globalization. On the military and diplomatic front, the United States remains predominant: its military spending is almost equal to that of the 10 next-largest spenders combined. However, China is the dominant power in Asia, Russia is resurgent, and other powers are on the horizon. Meanwhile, questions have been raised about the future of long-standing ties between the United States and its allies. Economically, hostility to globalization appears to be strong and growing, although the world remains more tightly linked than it has been since 1914. There are important uncertainties about both the security and the economic dimensions of world politics. To understand where the world is likely to head, we need to identify the interests of the major actors in contemporary world politics and to analyze how these interests interact as they work themselves out on the world stage.

The Great Powers and the World

The United States is likely to play a major role in the international political order for the foreseeable future. Nonetheless, other major powers are on the rise. China and Russia are increasingly flexing their military and diplomatic might in their regions and globally. While the European Union is not cohesive enough to constitute a major foreign-policy actor, there are pressures pushing in that direction. Even such developing countries as India and Brazil have expanded their international political influence.

As centers of military and diplomatic power proliferate, the relationship among the current and future great powers is in question. Since the end of World War II, one anchor of world politics has been the alliance between the United States, on the one hand, and its traditional friends in Europe and Asia, on the other. These ties were strained by the Trump administration's embrace of a less globalist, more unilateralist attitude toward international politics. Meanwhile, American relations with Russia remain antagonistic, and there are many sources of tension between the United States and China. A whole range of new and evolving alliance patterns seem conceivable—all of which would change power balances around the world.

In this context, one important set of questions is about the security and economic goals the United States will pursue. Will it recommit to multilateral military and diplomatic cooperation, within the institutional framework built after World War II (NATO and the United Nations, for example)? Or will it put distance between itself and its European and Asian allies, and loosen its ties to the existing multilateral institutions? These questions, still unanswered within the United States, will have a powerful impact on world politics.

The second set of questions has to do with how other major countries interact with each other, and with the United States, in the international arena. How will the European Union, individual European countries, and Japan react to the rising power of China and Russia? How will they respond to potential changes in America's military and diplomatic orientation? How will China and Russia deal with each other? Will they focus on attempting to collaborate with other major powers in pursuit of any common goals that remain, or will they attempt to establish dominant positions—perhaps as a challenge to the United States' position—in particular regions or issue areas? How will the West deal with the continuing challenges from Islamist extremists whose influence in the Muslim world seems to remain strong and whose resources—including military might—appear substantial?

Globalization

The future of globalization similarly appears in question. The world's major nations no longer seem to agree on the desirability of further international economic integration.

Skepticism about globalization was undoubtedly spurred by the economic crisis that began in 2008 (for details, see Chapter 8). That crisis led to major upheavals in global financial markets, a serious drop in world trade, and costly debt crises in a succession of countries. Questions proliferated in the aftermath of the worldwide pandemic that began late in 2019. The pandemic affected economic activity around the world and disrupted global supply chains that had previously tied many of the world's economies together. Countries found that the pandemic-induced dislocations complicated their access to essential medical equipment and interfered with their companies' supplies of important inputs to production. Both the financial crisis and the pandemic led many people to question the desirability of such high levels of dependence on international economic connections.

Although the general structure of international economic institutions and interactions survived the crisis and the pandemic, these events raised questions about the extent to which countries were interested in closer integration with the global economy. While most governments continue to profess an interest in economic integration, ongoing trends may indicate that these goals are not so clear-cut. The Trump administration expressed grave doubts about the way the United

The coronavirus pandemic of 2020 demonstrated the challenges of globalization. While the virus required people to maintain social distance to limit its spread, the interconnected nature of global markets made procuring the equipment necessary to fight the virus—including personal protective equipment and medical supplies—extremely difficult.

States' international trade and investment ties had developed, most Americans appear uninterested in any expansion of trade agreements, and the Biden administration shows no appetite for major new trade policy initiatives. Russia shows little interest in opening its borders more fully to international trade, finance, and investment. Some developing countries, similarly, appear to be pulling away from the world economy as economic openness proves less effective, and more costly, than anticipated. Almost every member of the European Union has a political movement that is skeptical about European integration—or downright opposed to it. The United Kingdom left the EU. Did enthusiasm for international economic engagement peak in the 1990s? Are countries (and regional groups such as the European Union) now more concerned with their own affairs than with global cooperation?

There is also growing concern that international economic trends may pose a threat to social and environmental goals. Certainly, rapid growth in the developing world challenges the planet's ability to support more industry, more cities, more automobiles—more of the features of modern life that billions of poor people hope for but that may not be compatible with environmental sustainability. Is there enough interest among governments to deal with the problem? Is there an ability to work together to address the issues?

Looking Ahead

What will the lives of today's youngest generations be like in the future? Will there be serious military threats, and will these threats come from conflicts among the major powers—the United States, Europe, Russia, China—or from religiously motivated terrorists? Will the industrialized world collaborate in diplomatic affairs, or will it splinter into contending blocs? For those born in the poor nations of Asia, Africa, and Latin America, will the next 50 years bring prosperity and a hope of catching up with the West, or will poverty persist and spread? Will the international economic order remain open and relations among the major economic centers remain collaborative, or will countries and regions turn toward self-sufficiency?

Our best hope for understanding the future of world politics is to develop analytical tools that accurately reflect the basic forces at play. This brief overview of the historical processes and events that created today's world shows how the interests of people and countries affect how they interact with one another, as well as how their interactions influence and are influenced by the institutions of international politics. The chapters that follow suggest ways of thinking about the interests, interactions, and institutions that have shaped the world we live in and that will continue to shape it for us, our children, and our children's children.

Study Tool Kit

Interests, Interactions, and Institutions in Context

- Conflict and cooperation among nations have ebbed and flowed over time. Individual countries have also varied in their own relations with other nations. Explaining the ebbs and flows, and the differences among countries, is the principal purpose of the study of international relations.

- Our explanations focus on understanding how the interests of the world's countries, and of the people in them, lead the world's nations to interact with one another, and to what effect.

- We also study the kinds of international institutions that arise from and mediate these interactions.

Key Terms

mercantilism, p. 5

Peace of Westphalia, p. 8

sovereignty, p. 8

hegemony, p. 8

Pax Britannica, p. 11

gold standard, p. 13

Treaty of Versailles, p. 20

League of Nations, p. 21

North Atlantic Treaty Organization (NATO), p. 24

Bretton Woods System, p. 24

Warsaw Pact, p. 25

decolonization, p. 28

For Further Reading

Burbank, Jane, and Frederick Cooper. *Empires in World History: Power and the Politics of Difference.* **Princeton, NJ: Princeton University Press, 2010.** Surveys the role of empires and imperialism from Roman times to the present.

Carr, E. H. *The Twenty Years' Crisis, 1919–1939.* **New York: Harper & Row, 1964.** Originally published in 1939, serves as a classic analysis of how and why the world collapsed into conflict during the decades after World War I.

Findlay, Ronald, and Kevin H. O'Rourke. *Power and Plenty: Trade, War, and the World Economy in the Second Millennium.* **Princeton, NJ: Princeton University Press, 2007.** Surveys the interrelated development of international trade and international power politics since early medieval times.

Frieden, Jeffry. *Global Capitalism: Its Fall and Rise in the Twentieth Century and Its Stumbles in the Twenty-first.* **New York: Norton, 2020.** Presents an overview of the development of the modern world economy from the 1890s to the present.

Lauren, Paul Gordon, Gordon A. Craig, and Alexander L. George. *Force and Statecraft: Diplomatic Challenges of Our Time.* **6th ed. Oxford: Oxford University Press, 2020.** Gives an overview of modern diplomatic history, with an analysis of basic concepts in diplomacy.

Williamson, Jeffrey G. *Trade and Poverty: When the Third World Fell Behind.* **Cambridge, MA: MIT Press, 2011.** Analyzes the history of economic growth and development worldwide, showing how trade affected the development process of non-European regions of the world.

2

Understanding Interests, Interactions, and Institutions

THE PUZZLE *What explains the patterns of world politics? Why do interests, interactions, and institutions matter in international relations?*

Above: China's naval maneuvers in the South China Sea have led to confrontations with neighboring states over competing claims to the sea and the resources within it. States' interests in power and wealth often bring them into conflicts that lead to bargaining over how to divide objects of value, such as territory. Although an international court has ruled that China's expansive claims in this region are unjustified, international institutions have only limited ability to resolve these disputes.

On April 2, 2020, a Vietnamese fishing vessel operating in the South China Sea collided with a Chinese surveillance ship and sank. All eight fishermen on board were rescued and transferred to another Vietnamese boat, but the incident sparked a diplomatic storm in the region and beyond. Vietnam lodged an official protest with the United Nations (UN), claiming that the Chinese ship rammed the boat as it was fishing in Vietnamese waters around the Paracel Islands. China, which claims the same collection of coral islands and reefs and calls them the Xisha Islands, accused the men of illegally fishing in Chinese waters and said that the collision was due to reckless maneuvers on the Vietnamese side. The Philippine government joined Vietnam in protesting the sinking of the vessel, recalling that its own fishermen had faced similar harassment in waters disputed with China.

A few weeks later, U.S. secretary of state Mike Pompeo condemned the incident in an address to members of the Association of Southeast Asian Nations (ASEAN), calling it part of a pattern of "continuing provocative behavior."[1] Beijing reacted angrily to the criticism, declaring that it was prepared to take "all necessary measures to firmly safeguard its sovereignty, rights and interests in the South China Sea."[2] Around the same time, Chinese vessels began patrolling around a ship authorized by the Malaysian government to survey for oil and gas in waters claimed by both countries. U.S. warships, already in the region conducting exercises, moved in to protect the Malaysian ship, which left the area peacefully after completing its task.[3]

These were not the first maritime standoffs in this region, which has been the subject of competing claims since the 1930s. But the escalating tensions came at a particularly fraught moment in relations between China

1. Sofia Tomacruz, "Pompeo Urges ASEAN to Call Out Beijing's Moves in South China Sea during Pandemic," Rappler, April 23, 2020, www.rappler.com/nation/258824-us-urges-countries-oppose-china-moves-south-china-sea-coronavirus-pandemic (accessed 10/21/20).

2. Associated Press, "Recent Developments Surrounding the South China Sea," ABC News, April 26, 2020, https://abcnews.go.com/International/wireStory/recent-developments-surrounding-south-china-sea-70356913 (accessed 10/21/20).

3. Niharika Mandhana, "U.S. Warships Support Malaysia against China Pressure in South China Sea, Wall Street Journal, May 13, 2020, www.wsj.com/articles/u-s-sends-warships-to-support-malaysia-in-south-china-sea-amid-china-pressure-11589382717 (accessed 10/21/20).

and the United States. Pompeo charged that Beijing was seeking to extend its control of the contested sea while other countries were preoccupied with the COVID-19 pandemic. At the time, the disease was contained in China but still spreading rapidly around the globe and in the United States. Indeed, anti-Chinese rhetoric went on to play a large role in the 2020 U.S. presidential election, as President Donald Trump sought to deflect anger at the virus's death toll away from his administration.

But even before the pandemic, the United States and China were on a collision course. The two countries have had tense relations since 1949, when communists prevailed in China's long-running civil war and established the People's Republic of China (PRC) on the mainland. The PRC became a major adversary during the early Cold War, intervening against U.S. forces in the Korean War (1950–53), supporting communist North Vietnam in the Vietnam War (1965–73), and sparking crises with Taiwan, where Nationalist Chinese forces allied with the United States had fled after 1949.

The more recent rivalry, however, has its roots in China's impressive economic growth over the last 40 years, which has propelled it to become the world's second-largest economy. This growth has fueled an increase in military spending, which has greatly improved the quality and quantity of China's military force. Since the 1990s, when projections started showing that China's economy would surpass that of the United States in the mid-2000s, U.S. foreign policy has grappled with the "rise of China" and the question of how to manage the threat China poses to U.S. global leadership.

The United States' initial response to China's rise was a policy known as "engagement," which sought to bring China into the U.S.-led international economic institutions, such as the World Trade Organization (WTO). The hope was that as China came to play a larger role in these institutions, it would have a stake in their success and become a partner with the United States, rather than a competitor.

By the time President Trump came into office in 2016, these hopes were waning. China's behavior in the South China Sea had become more aggressive, not less. President Xi Jinping, who came into office in 2012, embarked on a project of "national revival," including a more ambitious foreign policy that seeks to expand Chinese global influence and crack down on domestic dissent.

In response, the United States has taken a number of actions designed to counter China's ambitions and reverse the integration of the two countries' economies. On the military side, the United States has maintained alliances with South Korea, Japan, and the Philippines while pursuing closer partnerships with other countries in the region, including India and Vietnam. President Trump, who had labeled China an "economic enemy" during the 2016 campaign, imposed tariffs to compel China to purchase more U.S. exports. The resulting trade war threatened a decoupling of the two countries' economies, a process that the COVID-19 pandemic could accelerate.

These events lead us to consider several questions. Why has China's rise led to increasing tensions with the United States? What do they hope to achieve through maritime confrontations with fishing boats and survey ships? What role can institutions like the UN, ASEAN, and the WTO play in helping ensure that these conflicts do not escalate to war and/or disrupt global economic relations?

Thinking Analytically about Interests, Interactions, and Institutions

We study international relations in order to gain insight into such questions of conflict and cooperation. We seek to understand why states and their leaders make certain choices and why we observe certain outcomes. To help in our task, this chapter takes a closer look at three core concepts that enable us to think analytically about world politics: interests, interactions, and institutions.

Interests are the fundamental building blocks of politics. Explanations of international political events begin by specifying the relevant actors (such as China or the president of the United States) and their interests (such as power, security, or wealth). As actors pursue their interests, they interact with other actors; the nature of these *interactions* affects the outcomes and whether actors can get what they want. *Institutions* (such as the UN, WTO, and ASEAN) may also influence the outcomes of interactions by providing rules that facilitate cooperation. This framework can be used to analyze and understand not only the growing tensions between the United States and China but also the puzzles described in the chapters that follow and, equally important, others that will arise in the future.

Interests: What Do Actors Want from Politics?

Interests are what actors want to achieve through political action. For example, in international relations we often assume that states have an interest in security—that is, in preventing attacks on their territories and citizens. This interest prompts states to confront potential enemies and to protect friends whose security is linked to their own. An interest in security helps explain why Vietnam and the Philippines reacted against China's actions toward their fishermen and why the United States has backed them in this dispute. As the primary motivations behind actors' choices, interests are the fundamental building blocks of any political analysis.[4]

More precisely, interests are the preferences of actors over the possible outcomes that might result from their political choices. Interests determine how actors rank the desirability of different outcomes, from most to least preferred. An actor motivated by an interest in money prefers outcomes that give it more money over those that give it less. A state interested in security prefers outcomes that strengthen it and weaken its adversaries over outcomes that have the opposite effect. For example, given the United States' general interest in security, it might prefer a democratic China that is friendly toward American allies in the region and restrains its military growth. If this best outcome were to prove impossible, the United States' second-best result might be a contained China that is too weak to pose a threat to U.S. allies in the region. This outcome would be preferable to an aggressive China that seeks to expand its territory and increase its military might in ways that could threaten the United States and its regional partners. Between each of these broad alternatives, of course, are many intermediate outcomes that can be similarly rank-ordered.

Interests can be many and varied, depending on the specific policy or event under examination. In identifying the interests of an actor, analysts sometimes draw on prior theories of human nature or behavior; at other times, they rely on the statements or actions of the actors themselves; and at other times still, they simply assume that actors have a particular interest. At the most general level, analysts often group interests into three categories: power or security, economic or material welfare, and ideological goals.

In the first category, all political actors are understood to require a degree of security as a prerequisite to all of their other goals—whatever else they want, actors must first be safe from threats to their existence and independence. This interest in security can also induce an interest in power: that is, the political, military, and economic resources that actors can use to ward off threats and get others to do their bidding. The desire for power may be rooted in an urge to dominate other people,

interests
What actors want to achieve through political action; their preferences among the possible outcomes that might result from their political choices.

---

4. For a more extensive treatment of the theoretical and methodological issues in studying interests, see Jeffry A. Frieden, "Actors and Preferences in International Relations," in *Strategic Choice and International Relations*, ed. David A. Lake and Robert Powell (Princeton, NJ: Princeton University Press, 1999): 39–76.

FIGURE 2.1 **The Rise of China in Economic and Military Power, 1992–2019**

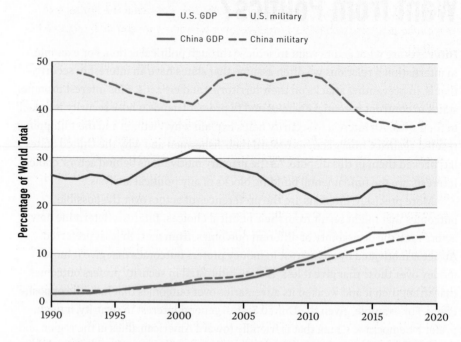

Figure sources: Military spending from the Stockholm International Peace Research Institute, Military Expenditure Database, www.sipri.org /databases/milex (accessed 8/23/20). GDP from World Bank, https://data.worldbank .org/indicator/NY.GDP.MKTP .CD (accessed 8/23/20).

but it also arises because power is useful for all other goals, particularly in the competitive environment of international politics. Thus, China's rising military and economic power poses a potential threat to the United States and China's neighbors because that power can be used to threaten their security, their territory, and other interests they hold dear (see Figure 2.1).

In the second category, political actors are presumed to desire a higher standard of living or quality of life, defined largely in terms of greater income, more consumable goods and services, or more leisure time (less work). For Vietnamese fishermen, the question of which country controls the rich fisheries of the South China Sea has a direct impact on their livelihood; for the countries that border on that sea, oil and gas deposits lying under the seafloor promise a source of income; for American workers and companies, trade with China brings both the hope of increased income from exports but also the danger of losing out domestically to Chinese imports. The interest in wealth is not incompatible with the interest in power: economic growth can be invested in military resources that enhance security, while security is a prerequisite to economic growth. As noted earlier, China's rising military power is rooted in impressive economic growth that has also greatly improved living standards for its people and lifted millions out of poverty.

Finally, political actors may also be motivated to achieve moral, religious, or other ideological goals, including democracy, human equality and dignity, the glory of a particular god, and so on. In this category, ideas often play a key role in shaping what actors want or believe to be good and desirable, even including what it means to be secure or wealthy. Again, there is not necessarily a conflict between these interests and others, as power or wealth may be a means toward ideological ends.

Scholars have long debated whether one conception of interest is more universal, true, or useful than others. Indeed, the three sets of general interests roughly divide the three schools of realism, liberalism, and constructivism identified in this book's Introduction. In turn, various debates over what the interests of actors *should be* are often tied to debates over what policies should be pursued in specific contexts.

Our approach in this book is agnostic; that is, we do not assume that one set of interests is always better in helping unravel puzzles of world politics. Rather, for some puzzles it may be sufficient to specify a general interest in security, increased wealth, or protecting the environment. For other puzzles, it may be necessary to move beyond general assumptions and specify preferences over narrow sets of outcomes—say, between deploying 100,000 versus 200,000 troops or between negotiating a multilateral international environmental treaty versus following a unilateral policy. Whichever level of detail is relevant depends on the purpose of the analysis, the questions being asked, and the puzzle under consideration.

We should add that the challenge of identifying what interests motivate an actor is not just one confronted by scholars, since policymakers may also be uncertain what their adversaries or partners want. Debates over U.S. policy toward China have centered on the extent to which Chinese leaders prioritize economic development or regional power and influence. Although the two interests can reinforce one another, they can also come into tension. If China places a higher priority on economic growth, then it might avoid risky confrontations with neighbors that could destabilize markets and lead other states to stop trading with it. On the other hand, to the extent that Chinese leaders prioritize territorial ambitions and regional influence, they would be motivated to take more aggressive actions, even at the expense of economic repercussions. The relative balance of these interests matters not only for Chinese foreign policy choices but also for U.S. responses. If China's leaders primarily value economic growth, then it would make sense for the United States to help integrate the country into the world economy; if, on the other hand, China is primarily interested in power and influence, then encouraging its economic development would only lead to a stronger adversary.

Actors and Interests

Many different types of actors participate in international relations. In the story of U.S.-China relations, we have already encountered *states* (the United States, China, Vietnam, and the Philippines), *governments* (the Trump administration and the regime of Xi Jinping), *private actors* within countries (firms, Vietnamese fishermen), and *international organizations* (the UN, ASEAN, the WTO).

Individuals are always the most basic political actors, as they cannot be divided into smaller political units. And in some cases, particular individuals, such as Trump and Xi, are crucial actors in their own right. But it is often convenient to group individuals into larger categories of people who share common interests (states) or who somehow combine their conflicting desires into a joint or collective interest (the election of a government, for example). We call both individuals and these composite groups **actors**.

actors
The basic unit for the analysis of international politics; can be either individuals or groups of people with common interests.

state

A central authority that has the ability to make and enforce laws, rules, and decisions within a specified territory.

sovereignty

The expectation that states have legal and political supremacy—or ultimate authority—within their territorial boundaries.

anarchy

The absence of a central authority with the ability to make and enforce laws that bind all actors.

national interests

Interests attributed to the state itself, usually security and power.

Of these composite actors, one that has particular prominence in international relations is the state. A **state** is a central authority that has the ability to make and enforce laws, rules, and decisions within a specified territory. Most countries are governed by states, though some may experience a breakdown of central authority and become what are sometimes called failed states.[5] The concept of sovereignty is a key part of the definition of the state. **Sovereignty** refers to the expectation that states have legal and political supremacy within their territorial boundaries. To say that states are sovereign means that they have ultimate authority over their own policies and political processes, such as the maintenance of domestic order and the provision of governance (see "What Shaped Our World?"). State sovereignty also means that there is no central authority in the international system that can make and enforce rules that bind states in the same way that states make and enforce rules that bind their citizens. This condition of **anarchy** is often assumed to be a defining feature of international politics.

When discussing states as actors, we may use the concept of the *state* in two different ways that are important to distinguish. Scholars sometimes assume that states are motivated by an interest in security—that is, safety from external and internal threats—and in accumulating power as a means to ensure security. These goals are said to be **national interests**, or interests that belong to the state itself. In this usage, the states-as-actors assumption sees international politics as driven by states' quest for security and power.

Alternatively, the states-as-actors concept serves as a convenient shorthand for sets of national leaders acting in the name of their countries. This use of the term reflects the fact that many actions in international politics are taken by individuals who represent the state: political leaders, diplomats, members of the armed forces, or others acting in an official capacity. Hence, we often lapse into language like "the United States threatened China," when in fact it was certain representatives of the United States who threatened representatives of China. When using the concept of the state as a shorthand for a set of composite interests, we make no prior assumption about where the interests pursued by those agents originate. Sometimes the state's representatives act on behalf of a particular domestic interest group—for example, when negotiating a trade agreement that is in the interest of exporting industries. Alternatively, state leaders might act to further their own personal or political agendas. In such cases, the interests that matter are those of the interest group or politician, but when those interests play out at the international level, they are pursued by people acting in the name of the state (see Chapter 4).

As this discussion suggests, there is no fixed or permanent set of actors in international relations. Like interests, actors are an analytical concept that is imposed on explanations by observers seeking to understand why events happen in a certain way. Identifying any set of individuals as the actors in an explanation is a choice we make to help account for observed outcomes. There is no right or wrong way to specify the actors in any event or set of events. As with interests, we judge different

---

5. On failed states and state building, see Timothy Sisk, *Statebuilding: War and Conflict in the Modern World* (Malden, MA: Polity, 2013).

The Rise of the State

We currently live in a world of nearly 200 states. States are some of the most important actors in world politics. How did an international system of states come to be?

Interests All political systems involve a relationship between the rulers and the ruled. The rulers aim to satisfy their interests in wealth and power, whereas the ruled hope to obtain physical security, basic needs, and public amenities such as education and roads. Thus, the rulers and the ruled make an exchange: the rulers are supposed to provide the goods that their citizens want, and the ruled provide military manpower, money (usually in the form of taxes), and perhaps other kinds of services. The nature of the bargain is not always fair, and one of the core dilemmas of politics is how to structure the relationship so that the rulers actually act in the interests of the ruled.

Institutions The modern state is just one, relatively recent, way of organizing politics. Sociologist Max Weber (1864–1920) defined the state as "a human community that (successfully) claims the monopoly of the legitimate use of physical force within a given territory."[a] This means that states are territorially bounded political units in which a central governing authority is the only actor that can legitimately use force, both against its own citizens and against other states.

Yet things were not always this way. In 1000 C.E., Europe was fractured into an uncounted number of political units, all enmeshed in often crosscutting lines of authority. Under feudalism, kings granted landholdings to the aristocracy, who in turn owed obligations to the king, including supplying military manpower. Nobles in one realm could acquire lands in another, thereby owing obligations to two or more kings. There were also self-governing "free cities," which owed allegiance to no king. The Catholic Church wielded political authority through entities like the Holy Roman Empire (962–1806). Prior to the emergence of the state, many rulers shared and competed for authority over any particular area.

Over time, an informal international institution emerged to ensure the state's exclusive control within its own boundaries: sovereignty. Sovereignty is composed of four core elements: (1) the sovereign possesses ultimate authority over the people and territory of a given realm, (2) other states and religious bodies are excluded from exercising political authority over a sovereign people or territory, (3) sovereignty is indivisible, and (4) all sovereign units are formally equal or have the same legal status. The core principles of sovereignty are often violated in practice, but the concept has had a profound impact on world politics.

Interactions How did a system of sovereign states come about? One prominent argument comes from Charles Tilly, who contended that "states make wars, and wars make the state."[b] As they bargained and fought over territory and wealth, small units either merged or were absorbed by larger ones. Polities that managed to raise money and manpower effectively outcompeted those that did not.

The institution of sovereignty also emerged out of competitive interactions. The Thirty Years' War (1618–48) was a bloody, Europe-wide affair that stemmed in part from emerging states' efforts to meddle in one another's internal affairs. The Peace of Westphalia, which ended that conflict, enshrined (even if it did not invent) the concept of sovereignty as a way to constrain this destructive behavior.

As we will see in later chapters, new actors and interactions have challenged the nature of sovereignty. Although the future remains uncertain, what is clear is that states as political units will continue to evolve.

The signing of the Peace of Westphalia.

a. Max Weber, *From Max Weber: Essays in Sociology*, ed. and trans. H.H. Gerth and C. Wright Mills (New York: Oxford University Press, 1946): 77–128.

b. Charles Tilly, "Reflections on the History of European State Making," in *The Formation of National States in Western Europe*, ed. Charles Tilly (Princeton: Princeton University Press, 1975): 42.

conceptualizations of actors only by whether they are useful in helping us understand world politics.

For example, how might we explain the tensions that arose between China and the United States over the course of 2020? At one level, it might be useful to think in terms of the leaders of the two countries and their political interests. For President Trump, 2020 was an election year, and he worried that the effects of the pandemic and resulting economic downturn would sink his chances of reelection. Thus, he hoped that stoking tensions with China would help deflect blame from his administration. Trump had also drawn support from workers who feared losing their jobs due to Chinese imports, so escalating tensions over trade served the interests of an important bloc of supporters. Similarly, within China, the pandemic led to criticism of the Communist Party for how it handled the outbreak. The government also faced pro-democracy protests in Hong Kong. A more aggressive foreign policy might have been useful for rallying the nation behind the regime. Not only did China clash repeatedly with its neighbors in the South China Sea, but it also sparked a conflict with India over a long-running territorial dispute and took steps to increase central control over Hong Kong. Thus, we could see these events as the product of American and Chinese leaders (the main actors) seeking to maintain domestic political power (their main interests) through aggressive foreign policies. (For more on how insecure leaders might use conflict to improve their hold on power at home, see Chapter 4.)

However, this explanation must be incomplete, since tensions between the United States and China and disputes over the South China Sea have been growing for decades, spanning multiple Chinese and American leaders. The political interests of two individual leaders at a particular moment in 2020 cannot explain this longer pattern. For that, we need to think about more enduring actors, such as the states, pursuing more enduring interests, such as security and influence in Asia. Ever since the creation of the PRC in 1949, the United States has worried about the threat that China poses to American allies in the region, who are also important trading partners. For its part, China has seen the United States' military presence in the region as an impediment to its territorial aspirations—including control over the South China Sea and unification with Taiwan—as well as its influence in its own neighborhood. Thus, the long-term pattern can be understood as the product of states (the main actors) pursuing security, power, and, in the case of China, sovereignty over what they see as their national territory (the main interests).

While it is tempting to ask which of these two explanations is correct, another way to think about them is that they answer different questions. The explanation that focuses on states helps us understand why China and the United States are engaged in long-running conflicts that sparked confrontations even before 2020 and will likely continue to do so under the administration of President Joseph Biden. The explanation that focuses on leaders may help us understand why relations flared up the way they did in that particular year. Moreover, there is no rule that says that a decision or event can only further one interest. In confronting China, Trump was acting on long-standing interests in containing Chinese power as well as short-term interests in reelection. For any given policy choice, it may be difficult to know for sure which interests are being pursued. In these cases, we judge any assumption about actors by how useful it is in explaining the overall pattern of events we observe.

Thus, any analysis starts with the question: Who are the actors, and what are their interests? This is very much a subjective decision by the analyst. In general, we prefer explanations that are simpler over those that are more complex, but how simple a good explanation must be is never defined in the abstract. Moreover, as we will see in the rest of this chapter, the question of which actors and their interests to include cannot be answered by itself; it requires attention to the interactions and institutions in which those actors are embedded. All three concepts—interests, interactions, and institutions—are necessary for a sufficient explanation of any particular event.

Table 2.1 lists key categories of actors in world politics, the interests commonly ascribed to these actors by analysts, and specific examples. The list, of course, is not exhaustive. Any of the actors can be broken down into smaller sets of individuals for explanatory purposes. But we will encounter these actors again and again throughout this book. In the following chapters, we specify different sets of actors and their interests as needed to explain the puzzles being addressed.

TABLE 2.1 *Key Categories of Actors and Interests in World Politics*

ACTOR	COMMONLY ASCRIBED INTERESTS	EXAMPLES
States	Security, power, territory, wealth, ideology	United States, Canada, China, Switzerland, India, Uruguay
Politicians	Reelection/retention of office, ideology, policy goals	President of the United States, prime minister of India, Speaker of the U.S. House of Representatives
Firms, industries, or business associations	Wealth, profit	General Motors, Sony, the pharmaceutical industry, National Association of Manufacturers, Business Roundtable
Classes or factors of production	Material well-being, wealth	Capital, labor, land, human capital
Bureaucracies	Budget maximization, influence, policy preferences; often summarized by the adage of "where you stand depends on where you sit"	Department of Defense, Department of Commerce, National Security Council, Ministry of Foreign Affairs
International organizations	As composites of states, they reflect the interests of member states according to their voting power. As organizations, they are assumed to be similar to domestic bureaucracies.	United Nations, International Monetary Fund, Universal Postal Union, Organisation for Economic Co-operation and Development
Nongovernmental organizations, often transnational or international in scope and membership	Moral, ideological, or policy goals; human rights; the environment; religion	Red Cross, Amnesty International, Greenpeace, the Catholic Church

Interactions: Why Can't Actors Always Get What They Want?

Actors make choices in order to further their interests. Yet political outcomes depend not just on the choices of one actor, but on the choices of others as well. China might prefer that Vietnam, Malaysia, and other countries give up their claims to the South China Sea, but those countries have refused to do so, leading to recurrent naval clashes in the region. The United States might prefer that China make concessions to buy more American products, but China did not agree to purchase as much as the Trump administration demanded. Interests are essential in analyzing any event in international relations because they represent how actors rank alternative outcomes. But to account for the actual outcomes, we must examine the choices of all the relevant actors and how those choices interact to produce a particular result. As we use the term here, **interactions** are the ways in which the choices of two or more actors combine to produce political outcomes.

When outcomes result from an interaction, actors have to anticipate the likely choices of others and take those choices into account when making their own decisions. Let's start small and consider the collision between the Vietnamese fishing boat and the Chinese vessel mentioned at the outset. Since each side claimed the waters they were in, each wanted the other side to leave the area and recognize its right to be there. From the perspective of the Vietnamese fishermen, their interests in income and personal well-being might have led to the following ordering of possible outcomes: (1) the Chinese boat leaves the area and allows them to fish there; (2) they leave the area unharmed and fish somewhere else; (3) they collide with the Chinese vessel, risking injury, death, and imprisonment. If so, their only chance of getting their best possible outcome required staying put and refusing Chinese demands that they leave. But doing so risked bringing about their worst possible outcome: getting sunk.

Whether staying put would lead to the Vietnamese fishermen's best or worst outcome depended on what the Chinese would do in response. Would their ship ram the boat, risking an international incident, or would they back down? Whether it made sense for the Vietnamese to resist or leave depended crucially on the answer to this question. If they expected China to back down, then resisting the demand to leave would secure their best outcome; if they expected the Chinese ship to carry out its threat, then resistance would lead to their worst outcome, and it would be better to leave. Hence, in making their choice, the Vietnamese side had to consider not only what they themselves wanted but also what they expected the other side to do. In this case, a collision occurred, apparently because the Vietnamese boat decided to risk a confrontation. Had they been certain that this would be the outcome, they might have chosen differently, even though their underlying interests were the same.

Although this showdown took place on a small scale, it is an example of an interaction that happens regularly in international politics as actors maneuver to

interactions

The ways in which the choices of two or more actors combine to produce political outcomes.

get their way while trying to avoid costly collisions, whether those be trade wars or shooting wars. We call such situations *strategic* interactions because each actor's strategy, or plan of action, depends on the anticipated strategy of others. Many of the most intriguing puzzles of international politics derive from such interactions.

We make two assumptions in studying interactions. First, we assume that actors behave with the intention of producing a desired result. That is, actors are assumed to choose among available options with due regard for their consequences and with the aim of bringing about outcomes they prefer. Second, in cases of strategic interaction, we assume that actors adopt strategies according to what they believe to be the interests and likely actions of others. That is, actors develop strategies that they believe are their best response to the anticipated strategies of others. In the preceding example, if the Vietnamese fishermen believed that China would back down from its threat, the best response was to resist the demand to leave; if they believed that the Chinese ship would ram them, then the best response was to comply with China's demand, even though doing so would have meant accepting a second-best outcome. A best-response strategy is the actor's plan to do as well as possible in light of the interests and likely strategies of the other relevant actors. Together, these assumptions link interests to choices and, through the interaction of choices, to outcomes.

Formulating a strategy as a best response, of course, does not guarantee that the actor will obtain its most preferred or even a desirable outcome. Sometimes the choices made by others leave actors facing a highly unwelcome outcome, one that may leave them far worse off than the status quo. If one state chooses to initiate a war, for instance, the other state must respond by either giving in to its demands or fighting back, and both options may leave the second state worse off than before the attack. A strategy is a plan to do as well as possible, given one's expectations about the interests and actions of others. It is not a guarantee of obtaining one's most preferred result.

Understanding the outcomes produced by the often complex interplay of the strategies of two or more actors can be difficult. A specialized form of theory, called game theory, has been invented to study strategic interactions. We offer a brief introduction to game theory in the "Special Topic" appendix to this chapter (p. 86), focusing on relatively simple games to communicate the core ideas behind strategic interaction.

Cooperation and Bargaining

Interactions can take various forms, but most can be grouped into two broad categories: cooperation and bargaining. Political interactions usually involve both forms in varying degrees.

Interactions are cooperative when actors have a shared interest in achieving an outcome and must work together to do so. **Cooperation** occurs when two or more actors adopt policies that make at least one actor better off without making any other actor worse off. Opportunities for cooperation arise all the time in social and political life. For example, when a group of friends wants to throw a party, they may find that none of them can spare the time or money to do so alone. But if they all contribute a little, they can each enjoy the benefits of throwing the party. The

cooperation

An interaction in which two or more actors adopt policies that make at least one actor better off relative to the status quo without making others worse off.

MAP 2.1 *Maritime Claims in the South China Sea*

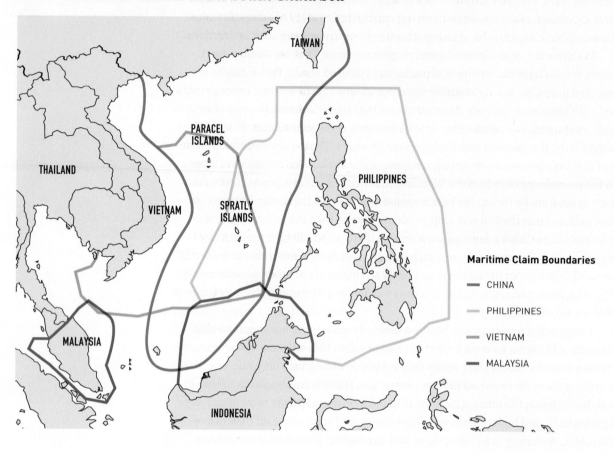

TAIWAN

THAILAND

VIETNAM

PARACEL ISLANDS

SPRATLY ISLANDS

PHILIPPINES

MALAYSIA

INDONESIA

Maritime Claim Boundaries

— CHINA

— PHILIPPINES

— VIETNAM

— MALAYSIA

Note: This map shows how China's maritime claims have created disputes with its neighbors. To simplify the illustration, some countries' claims are not depicted. For a complete map of maritime claims in East Asia, see Stratfor, "Cooperation as a Means to All Ends in the South China Sea," RealClearDefense, September 26, 2016, www.realcleardefense .com/articles/2016/09/27/ cooperation_as_a_means_to_ all_ends_in_the_south_china_ sea_110133.html.

members of a community all benefit if there are good roads to drive on and clean water to drink, but again, most likely no individual alone is able to provide these. If they all agree to pay taxes to a central agency that will provide roads and water, then they can all be better off. A group of firms may share an interest in lobbying Congress for trade protection from foreign imports. By pooling their resources and acting together, they may be more effective at getting their way than each individual firm would be on its own. In the international system, states may have opportunities to cooperate to defend one another from attack, to further a shared interest in free trade or stable monetary relations, to protect the global environment, or to uphold human rights.

We will look more closely at each of these types of situations in the following chapters. In the case of the South China Sea, China's expansive maritime claims threaten those of every state bordering on that body of water (see Map 2.1), but particularly Vietnam, the Philippines, and Malaysia. Thus, all of these states share an interest in resisting China's demands. Although they are all individually weak relative to China, they are in a stronger position to resist Chinese demands by working together, especially with the support of the United States, which opposes Chinese control of the waterway for security and economic reasons. These common interests provide a possible basis for cooperation.

There are also possibilities for cooperation between China and the United States. China has benefited greatly from an international economic system that has few barriers to trade. Its growth in recent decades has been fueled by its ability to export low-cost manufactured goods to the rest of the world. The United States has also benefited from the openness of the trading system, which has been a boon to U.S. exporters, multinational companies, and consumers. Although job losses in sectors hurt by imports have provoked opposition to free trade in recent years—and particularly trade with China—economists estimate that, overall, trade increases employment in the United States.[6] (For more on the distributional consequences of international trade, see Chapter 7.) To the extent that the open trading system benefits both countries, they have a common interest in sustaining it.

Cooperation is defined from the perspectives of the two or more actors who are interacting. Even though cooperation may benefit the actors who are directly involved, it may hurt other parties. The friends agreeing to throw a party together may disrupt their neighbors by making noise late into the night. Firms that cooperate to lobby Congress for trade protection may impose higher prices on consumers. Cooperation to oppose China's demands in the South China Sea would obviously harm Beijing's interest in the territory. Cooperation between the United States and China on trade could come at the expense of workers in some sectors who might lose their jobs. Indeed, cooperation is not always an unmitigated good; its benefits exist only for those who adjust their policies to bring about an outcome they prefer.

Figure 2.2 depicts in simple terms the problem of cooperation between two actors. Imagine that two actors can enact policies that have the potential to increase their overall income or welfare. The income of the actors is plotted along two dimensions, with Actor A's income increasing along the horizontal axis and Actor B's income increasing along the vertical axis. Since the concept is easier to illustrate with a divisible good like money, we use dollars in the example, but welfare is the more general concept, which includes not only income but other desired goods or outcomes. All points within the graph represent possible outcomes produced by different combinations of policies chosen by the two actors.

Assume that by cooperating, the two actors can make as much as $1,000, a limit determined in this case by the available technology and resources. This limit is depicted by the downward-sloping line in Figure 2.2, which shows all the different ways $1,000 can be divided between the two actors. The point at which the line touches the horizontal axis depicts a situation in which Actor A gets $1,000 and Actor B gets nothing, the point at which the line touches the vertical axis depicts a situation in which Actor B gets all the money, and every point in between represents

---

6. Robert C. Feenstra and Akira Sasahara, "The 'China Shock,' Exports and U.S. Employment: A Global Input–Output Analysis," *Review of International Economics* 26, no. 5 (November 2018): 1053–83, https://doi.org/10.1111/roie.12370.

FIGURE 2.2 *Cooperation*

In this world, there is $1,000 worth of a good that can be captured by State A and State B. In the status quo, State A gets $200 and State B gets $200. Through cooperation, both states can improve their outcomes by capturing and sharing the remaining $600. The green-shaded triangle—defined by the points *q*, *a*, and *b*—outlines all possible superior outcomes.

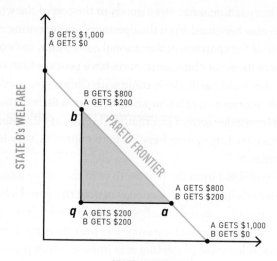

different divisions of the maximum feasible income. For example, if the two actors cooperate to make the maximum income in such a way that State A gets $600, then State B gets $400; if State A gets $200, then State B gets $800. This line representing the possible divisions of the maximum feasible benefit is called the *Pareto frontier*, after the Italian economist Vilfredo Pareto (1848–1923), who developed these ideas.

However, the actors may have chosen policies that do not result in the maximum possible benefit. Let's assume that past policy combinations have produced an outcome referred to as the status quo (*q*). As *q* is depicted in Figure 2.2, the actors are not doing as well as they could, with each making $200, for a total of $400 rather than $1,000. This means that they could potentially benefit by changing their policies to get closer to the Pareto frontier line and thus to the maximum feasible income. Any policy combination that leads to an outcome in the shaded area *qba* would make both actors better off than they are under the status quo. Moving outward from *q*, into the shaded area, represents cooperation, or an improvement in the welfare of at least one actor.

We can see that policies along the line segment between *q* and *a* improve A's welfare at no loss to B, while policies along the line segment between *q* and *b* improve B's welfare at no loss to A. Any movement into the shaded area defined by points *q*, *b*, and *a* represents an improvement in the welfare of both actors, and any policy combination on the Pareto frontier between *b* and *a* makes the actors as well off as possible, given available resources and technology. Cooperation consists of mutual policy adjustments that move actors toward or onto the Pareto frontier, increasing the welfare of some or all partners without diminishing the welfare of any one actor. Because it makes at least one party better off than otherwise, we refer to cooperation as a *positive-sum game*.

Bargaining describes interactions in which actors must decide how to distribute, or divide, something of value. For example, two states may want the same piece of territory, just as Vietnam and China both want the Paracel/Xisha Islands and the surrounding waters. Bargaining describes the process by which they come to divide the territory. They may negotiate, impose sanctions on one another, engage in threats or displays of force, or fight. All these tactics are different forms of bargaining. Given the nature of the situation, the more territory one side gets, the less the other gets.

Bargaining is illustrated in Figure 2.3. When actors bargain, they move along the Pareto frontier, as represented by the green arrow. On the frontier line, any improvement in A's welfare comes strictly at the expense of B's welfare. For

bargaining

An interaction in which two or more actors must decide how to distribute something of value. In bargaining, increasing one actor's share of the good decreases the share available to others.

FIGURE 2.3 *Bargaining*

State A and State B are bargaining over the division of $1,000. Each point along the line is a possible division. For every $1 that State A gains, State B loses $1, and vice versa.

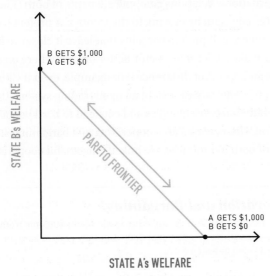

The horizontal bar below is a different representation of the same concept as the diagonal line above. The bar represents a good that States A and B both want. The more State A gets, the less State B gets (possible deal 1); the more State B gets, the less State A gets (possible deal 2).

example, if Actor A gains 100 percent of a contested piece of territory under a given bargain, that means Actor B gets 0 percent of the territory; if Actor A gives up 20 percent of the territory through bargaining, Actor B gains that 20 percent of the territory.

Bargaining interactions are characterized by distributional conflict, as each actor seeks a greater share of the good at the expense of the other; however, to reach a bargain, both sides must decide that a deal is better than the alternative. A car buyer and a car seller may haggle over the price of the car, but ultimately they will agree to a price only if both prefer that price to making no deal. Similarly, while two states may bargain hard over how to divide a piece of territory, they will agree to a deal only if each believes that the alternative, which may involve fighting a war, is worse. Indeed, we typically represent war as the outcome of a bargaining interaction in which the adversaries are unable to agree to a peaceful deal (see Chapter 3). While bargaining interactions are defined by their redistributive nature, bargains generally create value for both sides relative to the alternative of no deal.

Thus, while we treat cooperation and bargaining as distinct phenomena, most interactions in international relations combine elements of both (Figure 2.4). Although both states may gain by moving to the frontier, A prefers bargains that leave it closer to *a*, whereas B prefers bargains that leave it closer to *b*. Movement toward the frontier makes at least one actor better off, but where on the frontier they end up makes an important difference. For example, even if China and the United States want to cooperate to sustain an open trading system, their policy choices have distributional consequences and can lead to hard bargaining over the terms of cooperation. Often, actors are cooperating and bargaining simultaneously, and the outcomes of both interactions are linked. Successful cooperation generates

---

FIGURE 2.4 *Cooperation and Bargaining*

Through cooperation, State A and State B can improve their joint outcome from the starting point—the status quo—to capture an additional $600. But they have to bargain over exactly how that $600 will be divided between them.

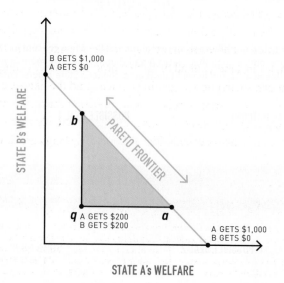

gains worth bargaining over. And if the actors cannot reach a bargain over the division of gains, they may end up failing to cooperate.[7]

Cooperation and bargaining can succeed or fail for many reasons. Just because actors might benefit from cooperation does not mean they will actually change their policies to realize the possible gains. And even though bargaining might seem doomed to fail—after all, why would one actor agree to reduce its welfare?—actors often do succeed in redistributing valuable goods between themselves. We now turn to some of the primary factors that influence the success or failure of cooperation and, later, of bargaining.

When Can Actors Cooperate?

If cooperation makes actors better off, why do they sometimes fail to cooperate? By far the most important factor is each actor's interests. Even when actors have a collective interest in cooperating, situations exist in which their individual interests lead them to "defect"—that is, to adopt an uncooperative strategy that undermines the collective goal. The strength of the incentives to defect goes a long way toward determining the prospects for cooperation.[8]

Consider the easiest kind of cooperative interaction, what we call a problem of **coordination**. This kind of situation arises when actors need only coordinate their actions with one another, and once their actions are coordinated, none receive any benefit from defecting. A classic example is deciding which side of the road cars should drive on. Drivers have a shared interest in avoiding crashes, so they are always better off if all drive on the right or on the left, rather than some driving on each side of the road. It does not matter which side of the road is selected. Indeed, different countries have different rules: cars drive on the right side of the road in the United States and continental Europe and on the left side in Great Britain, South Africa, and Japan. What matters is that all drivers in the region make the same choice. Moreover, no driver would intentionally deviate from that choice, since doing so would be very dangerous. In short, there is no incentive to defect from the coordinated arrangement.

In the international economy, firms, industries, and even governments face coordination problems all the time, as suggested by the numerous agreements on international standards. There are many ways to encode information to be sent over the Internet, for instance, but all firms that produce devices connected to the Internet—computers, smartphones, gaming devices, and the like—are better off coordinating on a single format. Similarly, it is important that international airline pilots speak a single language so as to communicate effectively with one another and with air traffic controllers worldwide; although any language could in principle

coordination

A type of cooperative interaction in which actors benefit from all making the same choices and subsequently have no incentive not to comply.

---

7. On bargaining and cooperating simultaneously, see James D. Fearon, "Bargaining, Enforcement, and International Cooperation," *International Organization* 52, no. 2 (1998): 269–305.

8. On the general forms of cooperation reviewed here, see Arthur A. Stein, "Coordination and Collaboration Regimes in an Anarchic World," *International Organization* 36, no. 2 (1982): 299–324; Duncan Snidal, "Coordination versus Prisoners' Dilemma: Implications for International Cooperation and Regimes," *American Political Science Review* 79, no. 4 (December 1985): 923–42; and Lisa L. Martin, "Interests, Power, and Multilateralism," *International Organization* 46, no. 4 (1992): 765–92.

serve this role, English became the standard due to the dominance of the United States. In coordination situations, cooperation is self-sustaining because once coordination is achieved, no one can benefit by unilaterally defecting.

A more serious barrier to cooperation arises if the actors have an individual incentive to defect from cooperation, even though cooperation could make everyone better off. Cooperative interactions in which actors have a unilateral incentive to defect are called problems of **collaboration**. This kind of problem is often illustrated by a simple game called the Prisoner's Dilemma. Imagine that two criminals have been detained by the police for committing a crime together. The district attorney does not have enough evidence to convict them on felony charges but can convict each suspect of a misdemeanor. She confines the prisoners separately and presents each with the following offer: "If neither of you is willing to testify, I will charge both of you with a misdemeanor and sentence you each to one year in prison. If you defect on your accomplice by providing evidence against him, I will let you go free and will put him in prison for ten years. However, he has been offered the same deal. If he provides evidence against you, you'll be the one behind bars. Finally, if you both squeal on one another, you'll each be charged with a felony, but your sentences will be reduced to five years in exchange for testifying."

Collectively, the prisoners would do best by cooperating with each other and refusing to testify; they would, together, serve a total of only two years behind bars. However, the prisoners are motivated not by the collective outcome but rather by the desire to shorten their own individual sentences. Thus, each has an incentive to rat out the other. Each prisoner reasons as follows: "Suppose my partner stays quiet. In that case, I should defect on him so that I will be released immediately rather than remain quiet and spend a year behind bars. On the other hand, suppose that my accomplice plans to defect on me. In that case, I should also defect on him, because giving testimony will reduce my sentence to five years rather than the ten I will face if I stay quiet."

Because both prisoners reason the same way, both will end up providing evidence against the other and both will be imprisoned for five years. This outcome, of course, is worse for each of them than the outcome they could achieve if they cooperated with one another and remained silent; the dilemma is that each individual's incentive to defect against the other undermines their collective interest in cooperation. For a more formal and complete discussion of this dilemma, see the "Special Topic" appendix to this chapter (p. 86), a discussion of game theory that includes the Prisoner's Dilemma.

Although the dilemma of fictional prisoners may seem remote from the subject matter of this book, analogous situations often arise in international relations. Consider the nuclear arms race between the United States and the Soviet Union during the Cold War. Both countries built costly nuclear weapons at a furious pace, such that by the late 1980s the United States had about 23,000 nuclear weapons, while the Soviet Union had about 42,000 (Figure 2.5).

One might ask, Why not agree to stop building when the United States had 2,300 warheads and the Soviet Union had 4,200? Stopping at that point would have kept the same ratio of forces but at a much lower cost. Both states might

collaboration

A type of cooperative interaction in which actors gain from working together but nonetheless have incentives not to comply with any agreement.

FIGURE 2.5 *U.S. and USSR/Russian Strategic Nuclear Weapons Inventories, 1945–2019*

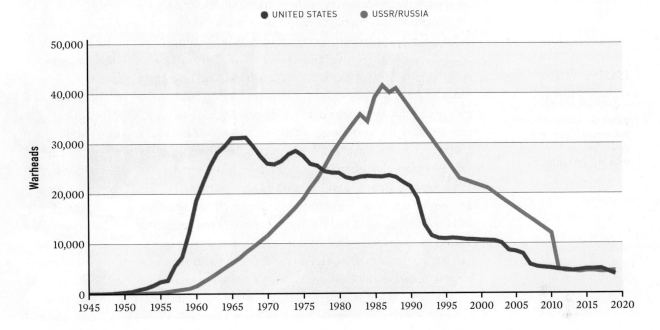

● UNITED STATES   ● USSR/RUSSIA

have been better off with such an agreement. The problem, however, is that each state had an incentive to cheat on such a deal in order to attain (or maintain) superiority over the other. If one stopped building, the other would be tempted to keep going. Therefore, each feared that its own restraint in building weapons would be exploited, leaving it vulnerable. Given these incentives and fears, the best strategy for each state was to go on amassing weapons. As a result, both countries ended up worse off than if they could have cooperated to limit their arms competition.[9]

A specific type of collaboration problem arises in providing **public goods**, which are products such as national defense, clean air and water, and the eradication of communicable diseases. Public goods are defined by two qualities. First, if the good is provided to one person, others cannot be excluded from enjoying it as well (formally, the good is *nonexcludable*). If one person in a country is protected from foreign invasion, for instance, all other citizens are also protected. Second, if one person consumes or benefits from the public good, the quantity available to others is not diminished (formally, the good is *nonrival in consumption*). Again using the example of national defense, one person's enjoyment of protection from foreign invasion does not diminish the quantity of security available to others. Many global environmental issues, such as ozone depletion and climate change, are also public goods (as we will discuss in more detail in Chapter 13).

Figure source: Hans M. Kristensen and Robert S. Norris, "Global Nuclear Weapons Inventories, 1945–2013," *Bulletin of the Atomic Scientists* 69 (2013): 75–81. Updated through 2019 through the *Bulletin of the Atomic Scientists* Nuclear Notebook series, available at http://explore.tandfonline.com/page/pgas/rbul-nuclear-notebooks (accessed 10/20/20).

public goods

Products that are nonexcludable and nonrival in consumption, such as national defense.

---

9. In fact, the United States and the Soviet Union did sign several arms control agreements, which may have prevented the arms race from being even worse. It was not until the collapse of the Soviet Union in 1991 that serious reductions in nuclear armaments took place.

The North Atlantic Treaty Organization (NATO) provides a public good for its members by bolstering their security from external threats. At a December 2019 NATO meeting, U.S. president Donald Trump reiterated his criticism that other countries were free-riding on the contributions of the United States and demanded that they increase defense spending.

collective action problems

Obstacles to cooperation that occur when actors have incentives to collaborate but each acts with the expectation that others will pay the costs of cooperation.

free ride

To fail to contribute to a public good while benefiting from the contributions of others.

Public goods are contrasted with purely private goods, which are products that only one person can possess and consume. Your sandwich for lunch is a private good: if it's available to you, it is not automatically available to all others, and if you eat it, it is not available to be eaten by any others.

Efforts to produce public goods always face **collective action problems**, which we will encounter many times in this book. Given that actors can enjoy public goods whether or not they contribute to the provision of those goods, each prefers that others pay to produce the good while it gets to enjoy the good for free. That is, each actor aims to benefit from the contributions of others without bearing the costs itself. For example, individuals would prefer to benefit from national security without paying taxes or volunteering for military service. Similarly, all states might want a genocide to be stopped, but each would prefer that others assume the risks of the necessary military intervention. In such situations, even though everyone wants the public good to be provided, each individual has an incentive to **free ride** by not contributing while benefiting from the efforts of others. When contributions are voluntary, free riding leads public goods to be provided at a lower level than that desired by the actors.

This is why public goods are often provided by governments, which have the power to tax citizens or otherwise mandate their contributions. Free riding is no longer so attractive if, say, the failure to contribute taxes can lead to steep fines or imprisonment. This is also why collaboration among governments on global issues can prove so difficult, as there is no international authority that can force countries to contribute to the provision of global public goods.

As this discussion suggests, some of the problems associated with cooperation are addressed by institutions, which might be able to alter actors' incentives so that their individual interests line up with the collective interest. The role of institutions in promoting cooperation is discussed later in this chapter. Even in the absence of institutions, though, we can identify several factors that facilitate cooperation.

Numbers and Relative Sizes of Actors It is easier for a small number of actors to cooperate and, if necessary, to monitor each other's behavior than for a larger number of actors to do so. Two actors can communicate more readily and observe each other's actions better than a thousand actors can. Thus, the smaller the number of actors, the more likely they are to cooperate successfully. As we will see in Chapter 7, firms can organize more easily to lobby their governments for trade protection than can consumers, who are typically more numerous. Environmental agreements are easier to monitor and enforce—thus, more likely to be agreed upon—among small groups of countries.

In the case of public goods, moreover, some groups may have a single member or a small coalition of members willing to pay for the entire public good. This could happen if these members receive benefits from the public good sufficient to offset the entire costs of providing it. In such *privileged groups*, the single member or small coalition of members provides the public good despite free riding by others.[10]

As we will see in Chapter 5, international efforts to reverse acts of aggression generally require that a very powerful state, such as the United States, be motivated to conduct a military operation largely on its own. Similarly, success in limiting ozone emissions (see Chapter 13) stemmed in part from the disproportionately large role of the United States, Russia, and Japan in the industries responsible for the emissions. Some analysts attribute the economic openness of the international economy in the mid-nineteenth and mid-twentieth centuries to public goods like the international monetary regime provided unilaterally by Britain and the United States, which were the largest powers in those eras, respectively.

Iteration, Linkage, and Strategies of Reciprocal Punishment Cooperation is more likely when actors have opportunities to cooperate over time and across issues. The incentive to defect or free ride in any given interaction can be overcome if actors expect to be involved in multiple, repeated interactions with the same partners.[11] In this situation—commonly known as **iteration**—actors can prevent one another from cheating by threatening to withhold cooperation in the future. Even when an actor has incentives to defect in the current interaction, knowing that the other actor will refuse to cooperate with it in the future can offset those temptations. Thus, "good behavior" can be induced today by the fear of losing the benefits of cooperation tomorrow. Countries are less likely to cheat on a trade agreement with a country they trade with often and expect to trade with again in the future

iteration
Repeated interactions with the same partners.

---

10. On privileged groups, see Mancur Olson, *The Logic of Collective Action: Public Goods and the Theory of Groups* (Cambridge, MA: Harvard University Press, 1965).

11. On iteration and international cooperation, see Robert Axelrod, *The Evolution of Cooperation* (New York: Basic Books, 1984). The trench warfare example mentioned in the following text is described in Chapter 4.

(see Chapter 7). The threat of reciprocal punishment can be a powerful tool for enforcing cooperation even when actors are tempted to cheat.[12] You are more likely to leave a generous tip for the waiter at a local restaurant that you think you'll frequent in the future—lest you get poor service on another visit—than you are in a restaurant you don't expect ever to visit again.

In one particularly telling example of how frequent interaction can generate cooperation, a system of "live and let live" emerged during the trench warfare of World War I. After an initial period of rapid gains, troops on both sides of the war bogged down in fixed trenches within rifle range of one another. Despite incentives to kill the enemy whenever possible, lest he kill you, many areas along the trenches developed a form of restrained cooperation in which, even in the absence of any communication, the troops stationed there did not fire upon one another. Occasional failures of cooperation, when shooting began for some reason, were punished by two-for-one or three-for-one retaliation by the other side. This response usually led back to restraint and renewed cooperation. What made cooperation possible even in this most unlikely of circumstances was the long-term deployment of troops in the same area, creating iteration and reciprocity in action.

Closely related to iteration is the concept of **linkage**, which ties cooperation on one policy dimension to cooperation on other dimensions. Whereas iteration enables victims to punish cheaters by withholding the gains from future cooperation, linkage enables victims to retaliate by withholding cooperation on other issues. Defection on military affairs, for instance, might be punished by withdrawing cooperation on economic matters. If actors know the failure of cooperation on one dimension puts cooperation on other issues at risk, then they have more incentive to cooperate on all.

Information   One final factor that affects the likelihood of cooperation is the availability of information. In some cases, it is easy to observe whether a partner has cooperated or defected, such as when cooperation entails a public act like participating in a military operation. In other cases, however, cooperative and uncooperative acts may be hard to observe or distinguish from one another. If cooperation involves reducing armaments, for example, the fact that states can build weapons in secret means that defection may go unobserved.

When actors lack information about the actions taken by another party, cooperation may fail because of uncertainty and misperception.[13] A state might defect under the mistaken belief that it can get away with it or because it doubts other parties will abide by the terms of cooperation. Alternatively, cooperation might unravel if cooperative acts are mistaken for defection. Suppose one party mistakenly

12. For the expectation of future punishment to induce current cooperation, however, actors must value the future enough that future gains matter. Everyone discounts the future; that is, they value it somewhat less than the present. A dollar today is worth more to us than a dollar next year, and much more than a dollar received in 20 years. The more actors discount the future, the less likely the threat of future punishment will encourage them to cooperate today. Conversely, the more actors value the future, the more likely the threat of future punishment will encourage cooperation now.

13. On the consequences of misperception, see Robert Jervis, *Perception and Misperception in International Relations* (Princeton, NJ: Princeton University Press, 1976).

linkage

The linking of cooperation on one issue to interactions on a second issue.

believes that the other has defected and cuts off cooperation as punishment; the other party, which has been cooperating all along, then perceives the first actor's punishment as a new defection and cuts off cooperation in retaliation. Simple misperceptions can lead to hostile punishments and the breakdown of cooperation, even though all actors thought they were acting cooperatively.[14]

Who Wins and Who Loses in Bargaining?

Whereas cooperation has the potential to make actors collectively better off, bargaining creates winners and losers: the more one actor gets from a bargain, the less others can have. When two or more actors desire the same good—for example, a sum of money or a piece of territory—it is impossible for all of them to get their best possible outcome at the same time. Why, then, are bargains ever reached? Why do actors consent to losses? What determines who wins and who loses?

Considering these questions introduces a core concept in international politics: power. In the standard definition, which we owe to the political scientist Robert Dahl, **power** is the ability of Actor A to get Actor B to do something that B would otherwise not do.[15] In the context of bargaining, power is most usefully seen as the ability to get the other side to make concessions and to avoid having to make concessions oneself. The more power an actor has, the more it can expect to get from others in the final outcome of bargaining.

Power is one of the most frequently used yet ambiguous terms in the study of international relations. Sometimes it is understood as an end in itself—an interest, as we have defined that concept—and sometimes as a means toward other ends. Other times power is conceived as a reality or set of circumstances created by past interactions that structure or constrain the choices currently available to actors. Their large economies, past investments in military forces, and large stockpiles of nuclear weapons, for instance, gave the United States and the Soviet Union enormous political advantages over other countries during the Cold War, deterring other states from even contemplating challenging the core interests of either superpower.

Our focus here, in the context of explaining bargaining outcomes, is what is sometimes called compulsory power, or the ability of one actor to compel another to act in certain ways.[16] Understood in this way, the outcome of any bargaining interaction is fundamentally influenced by what would happen in the event that no bargain was reached. The outcome that occurs when no bargain is achieved is often called the *reversion outcome*. In some cases, the reversion outcome is the same as the status quo. For example, if a car buyer and a prospective seller cannot agree on a price, then the seller is left with his car and the buyer keeps her money. What is lost is a chance to make a potentially profitable deal.

power

The ability of Actor A to get Actor B to do something that B would otherwise not do; the ability to get the other side to make concessions and to avoid having to make concessions oneself.

---

14. George W. Downs, David M. Rocke, and Randolph M. Siverson, "Arms Race and Cooperation," in *Cooperation under Anarchy*, ed. Kenneth Oye (Princeton, NJ: Princeton University Press, 1986): 118–46.

15. Robert A. Dahl, "The Concept of Power," *Systems Research and Behavioral Science* 2, no. 3 (July 1957): 201–15.

16. See Michael Barnett and Raymond Duvall, eds., *Power in Global Governance* (New York: Cambridge University Press, 2005).

When actors bargain over the terms of cooperation, a failure to agree can prevent the collective benefits from being enjoyed. For example, if states contemplating intervention in a civil war or negotiating an environmental treaty cannot agree on how to divide the costs, then the civil conflict will rage on or the environmental harm will continue. In other cases, the consequences of disagreement are more severe: the reversion outcome may be a war or some other kind of conflict, such as economic sanctions, that leaves one or even both actors worse off than they were before the dispute began.

The actor that would be more satisfied with the reversion outcome generally has less incentive to make concessions in order to reach a successful bargain. Conversely, the actor that would be less satisfied with the reversion outcome becomes desperate to reach an agreement and thus offers relatively bigger concessions in the hopes of inducing the more satisfied actor to agree. In short, bargaining power belongs to those actors who would be most satisfied with, or most willing to endure, the reversion outcome. In the car-buying example, if the seller needs money and is anxious to sell the car quickly, a more patient buyer can extract a better deal.

Internationally, in negotiations over global climate change, the United States has been less willing to go along with other countries in part because the expected costs of climate change to the United States are lower. Given its geography and economic resources, the United States is better equipped than many other states to weather the effects of a warming planet and rising sea levels. Lower vulnerability to these harms has helped sustain opposition in the United States to complying with greenhouse gas limitations mandated in international environmental agreements, effectively shifting the burden of cuts onto other countries (see Chapter 13).

Because bargaining outcomes are determined largely by how each actor evaluates the reversion outcome, power derives from the ability to make the reversion outcome better for oneself and/or worse for the other side. To shift the reversion outcome in their favor, actors have three basic ways of exercising power: coercion, outside options, and agenda setting.

coercion

A strategy of imposing or threatening to impose costs on other actors in order to induce a change in their behavior.

Coercion The most obvious strategy for exercising power is coercion. **Coercion** is the threat or imposition of costs on other actors to reduce the value of the reversion outcome (no agreement) and change their behavior. Thus, states can use their ability to impose costs on others to demand a more favorable bargain than they would otherwise receive. China's harassment of fishing boats and survey vessels in the South China Sea seeks to make those activities costlier for other states in the hope that they will concede their rights to the disputed waters. President Trump's decision in 2018 to enact tariffs on Chinese imports was an attempt to impose costs on the Chinese economy in order to compel concessions on trade. The target of coercion, of course, can itself try to impose costs in response, and indeed China's retaliatory tariffs against the United States hurt farmers who depend on exports into the Chinese market.[17]

---

17. For an analysis of how China used retaliatory tariffs to impose political costs on Trump, see Sung Eun Kim and Yotam Margalit, "Tariffs As Electoral Weapons: The Political Geography of the US–China Trade War." *International Organization* 75, no. 1 (2021): 1–38.

Means of international coercion include military force and economic sanctions. The ability to impose costs on others and to defend against costs that others would seek to impose derives in large part from material capabilities—the physical resources that enable an actor to inflict harm and/or withstand the infliction of harm. In coercive interactions among states, these capabilities are often measured in terms of military resources—such as the number of military personnel or level of military spending—as well as measures of economic strength, since economic resources can be converted into military power. The balance of such capabilities among states is a strong predictor (though not the only one) of who wins and who loses in warfare.[18] Similarly, the size of a country's economy has an impact on its ability to impose and/or withstand economic sanctions, which cut off a country's access to international trade.

In coercive bargaining, the side with the larger and more capable military has an advantage. In 2017, China launched its first domestically built aircraft carrier with much fanfare, in a demonstration of its might relative to that of potential enemies.

Simply being able to impose higher material costs than the other side is not enough ensure successful coercion, however. In determining whether to give in to another's demands, an actor has to compare the costs it will incur from no agreement to the value of whatever concessions are being demanded. If both sides value the issue in question equally, then the side that can impose higher costs is likely to prevail. But if one side cares more intensely about whatever is in dispute, it may be willing to withstand much higher costs without giving in.

This helps explain why weak states can at times defeat great powers. When France tried to reassert colonial control over Vietnam after World War II, the leader of the Vietnamese resistance, Ho Chi Minh, warned the French that their superior military power would not matter: "You will kill ten of our men, and we will kill one of yours, and in the end it will be you who tire of it."[19] The Vietnamese leader's optimism sprang from the belief that, while the French were fighting for an overseas colony, his people were fighting for their homeland, and they were thus willing to bear higher costs of war. His bargaining power stemmed not from military capabilities but from what we will refer to in Chapter 3 as resolve.

Outside Options Actors can also get a better deal when they have attractive **outside options**, or alternatives to reaching a bargain with a particular partner that are more attractive than the status quo. In this case, the reversion outcome is

outside options
The alternatives to bargaining with a specific actor.

---

18. See, for example, Dan Reiter and Allan C. Stam, *Democracies at War* (Princeton, NJ: Princeton University Press, 2002).

19. This quotation is often cited, and the exact wording sometimes varies. The original source is Jean Sainteny, *L'histoire d'une paix manquée: Indochine, 1945–47* (Paris: Amiot-Dumont, 1953): 231.

the next-best alternative for the party with the outside option. An actor with an attractive alternative can walk away from the bargaining table more easily than can an actor without such an option.

The actor with the better outside option can use its leverage to get a better deal or resist pressure to concede. For example, during U.S.-China trade negotiations, China restricted soybean imports from American farmers in order to pressure the Trump administration to back down. In order to meet its people's strong demand for soybeans, China turned to alternative suppliers, particularly Brazil.[20] The availability of this outside option allowed China to continue resisting American trade pressure without forgoing a key food product. By contrast, the United States lost leverage over China due to the fact that China supplies key products on which the United States depends, such as surgical masks and other personal protective equipment necessary for combating the COVID-19 pandemic and products that American companies require as part of their production processes. Some in the United States called for a "decoupling" of the two economies precisely to reduce this dependence and create more outside options.

As with coercion, the relative attractiveness of each actor's outside options is what matters. Both actors may have alternatives, but the one with the more attractive outside option can more credibly threaten to walk away and, therefore, can get the better deal. In competitive economic markets with many buyers and sellers, for instance, little power is exercised by any given actor, since every buyer and seller has equally attractive outside options.

agenda setting

Actions taken before or during bargaining that make the reversion outcome more favorable for one party.

Agenda Setting Finally, actors might gain leverage in bargaining through **agenda setting**. Agenda setting consists of actions taken before or during bargaining that make the reversion outcome more favorable for one party. A party that can act first to set the agenda transforms the choices available to others. For example, by sponsoring legislative proposals, calling public attention to issues, and cajoling individual legislators, the president of the United States has important agenda-setting power in Congress. Faced with a presidential proposal or a presidentially inspired public outcry, legislators often have little choice but to respond to the president's initiative; they do not necessarily have to agree with the president's proposal, but they must respond to an issue they might otherwise have preferred to avoid.[21]

Agenda-setting power exists between countries when states can take unilateral actions that alter the options available to others. When the United States deregulated its airline industry to capitalize on its market position and benefit its domestic consumers, other countries were forced to deregulate their industries as well in order to remain competitive, often over the opposition of their national air carriers. In territorial disputes, agenda setting can take the form of a "fait accompli," a French term that means "accomplished fact," which in this context refers to seizing

---

20. Yusuf Khan, "China Is Sourcing More of Its Farm Goods from Other Countries, and That's a Bad Sign for the US," Business Insider, July 31, 2019, https://markets.businessinsider.com/news/stocks/china -sources-more-farm-goods-brazil-us-trade-war-2019-7-1028403926 (accessed 10/21/20).

21. John W. Kingdon, *Agendas, Alternatives, and Public Policies*, 2nd ed. (New York: HarperCollins, 1995).

a disputed piece of territory before the other state can react.[22] By taking a piece of territory and fortifying it against attack, a state can move the reversion point to its most preferred outcome and make it hard for its adversaries to undo the act. For example, China has bolstered its leverage in the South China Sea by building military fortifications on some of the larger islands. In doing so, the Chinese have not only taken possession of those islands but also made it harder for other countries to dislodge them.

Even though bargaining creates winners and losers, bargains can be made as long as they give all parties more than (or at least as much as) they can expect to get in the reversion outcome. In other words, actors consent to painful concessions when the consequences of not agreeing are even more painful. As we will see in Chapter 3, the fact that bargains exist that all sides prefer over war does not guarantee that those bargains will always be reached. A host of problems can prevent actors from finding or agreeing to mutually beneficial deals. For example, uncertainty about how each side evaluates its prospects in a war can make it hard to know which bargains are preferable to war. There may also be situations in which states cannot credibly promise to abide by an agreement that has already been made. Bargaining may also be complicated if the good being bargained over is hard to divide. (Since this is a broad topic, we leave fuller consideration of these issues for Chapter 3.)

In sum, both interests and interactions matter in politics. Political outcomes depend on the choices of two or more actors. Since political outcomes are contingent on the choices of multiple actors, any given actor does not always or even most of the time obtain its most preferred outcome. Indeed, in bargaining, an actor may be worse off afterward than it would be if it had never entered the interaction. Interactions are often quite complex, but they are critical to understanding how interests are transformed into outcomes—often in paradoxical ways.

Institutions: Do Rules Matter in World Politics?

Institutions play a major role in social and political life, domestically and internationally. We typically define **institutions** as sets of rules, known and shared by the relevant community, that structure interactions in specific ways. Many political institutions are embodied in laws or organizations. The U.S. Congress is an institution that, under the Constitution, has the power to makes laws for the country. Congress in turn has rules that determine how members can propose and approve new laws. The UN is an institution in which states make collective decisions about military actions or economic sanctions; the UN has rules that determine which states have a say over these matters and how their votes are counted. International economic institutions include the International Monetary Fund, the WTO, and the

institutions
Sets of rules (known and shared by the relevant community) that structure interactions in specific ways.

---

22. Dan Altman, "By Fait Accompli, Not Coercion: How States Wrest Territory from Their Adversaries," *International Studies Quarterly* 61, no. 4 (December 2017): 881–91.

World Bank. Other institutions are more informal and exist only as shared understandings of principles and norms. These informal institutions, such as the widespread international norm against slavery, can also be important (see Chapter 11).

Institutions vary in their goals and rules, but they generally serve to facilitate cooperation among their members.[23] As discussed in the previous section, even when actors have common interests, certain factors may make cooperation difficult. Cooperation can flounder if the problems identified earlier—incentives to defect, large numbers of actors, nonrepeated interactions, and imperfect information—are not successfully resolved. Institutions can provide solutions to these problems. Indeed, it is precisely to facilitate cooperation that actors first create and subsequently comply with the rules embodied in institutions.

How Do Institutions Affect Cooperation?

In much of political and social life, the primary way that institutions promote cooperation is through enforcement, or the imposing of punishments on actors who fail to cooperate. Imagine, for example, that the prisoners in the Prisoner's Dilemma game described earlier were both members of an organized crime group, and it was understood that members who rat each other out would find themselves at the bottom of a river wearing cement shoes. In that case, the prisoners would no longer have an individual incentive to defect on each other; the external enforcement by the organization would change the way they rank-ordered the possible outcomes, and cooperation between them now would make sense both individually and collectively.

Similarly, governments provide public goods by compelling individuals to pay for them in the form of taxes; the threat of fines or jail time for failing to pay weakens the incentive to free ride on the contributions of others. Cooperation among private actors within a country may also be enforced by institutions. For example, a sales contract between a customer and a firm can be enforced by courts, whose rulings are backed by the police powers of the state. In short, when institutions have means of imposing punishments for defection, they can effectively enforce cooperation.

Institutions at the international level generally lack the capacity to impose punishments on states. The international system is characterized by anarchy, as explained earlier. Whereas most countries are governed by a state—a central authority with the ability to make and enforce laws within its boundaries—there is no such central authority at the global level. Some people think the UN is a world government, but as we will see in Chapters 5 and 11, this is not the case. Even poor, weak states have more enforcement power over their citizens than the UN has over actors in the international system. It cannot tax its members, raise its own military, or field its own police force.

The condition of anarchy means that international institutions do not generally enforce cooperation among their members. Instead, cooperation at the international level has to be self-enforcing; that is, the members have to police themselves

---

23. See Robert O. Keohane, *After Hegemony: Cooperation and Discord in the World Political Economy* (Princeton, NJ: Princeton University Press, 1984).

and assume responsibility for punishing defectors. The fact that countries are largely dependent on self-help does not mean that international institutions are useless, but it does shape our understanding of the role they play. In general, international institutions, even informal ones, facilitate cooperation by making self-enforcement easier. They do so in at least four ways: by setting standards of behavior, verifying compliance, reducing the costs of joint decision making, and resolving disputes. Different institutions may emphasize one or another of these tasks, but all are important.

Setting Standards of Behavior Clear standards of behavior reduce ambiguity and enhance cooperation. For example, parents who tell a teenager, "Don't stay out too late—or else," invite continuing conflict. What does "too late" mean? "Or else" is also ambiguous. If the parent grounds the teenager for a week, is this "unfair," as the aggrieved youth will likely claim, or "letting her off easy," as the parent might retort? The costs of such a conflict could be avoided with a clear statement: "Be home by midnight, or you'll be grounded for a week." The teenager might still choose to stay out later, but the standard for evaluating lateness and the consequences would no longer be in dispute.

International institutions set standards of behavior in similar ways. The dispute in the South China Sea provides a useful example. China claims almost the entire sea, as well as the islands, rocks, and reefs within it, on the grounds that it has historically ruled over the body of water. The other states, by contrast, claim maritime boundaries that extend 200 nautical miles from their coastlines, on the basis of an international agreement called the UN Convention on the Law of the Sea (UNCLOS).[24] UNCLOS, which has 168 signatories, has been in effect since 1994, but it codified a body of laws, customs, and practices that had accrued in the decades leading up to its negotiation in the early 1980s. The agreement spells out in great detail countries' rights to different parts of the seas, including how those rights are affected by the presence of islands, even drawing legal distinctions between islands, rocks, and "low-tide elevations" (features that are above the water only at low tide). Not surprisingly, the English text of the agreement runs for 200 pages.[25] Arms control agreements between the United States and the Soviet Union during the Cold War similarly ran to hundreds of pages, detailing precise numbers for different types of weapons systems and limits on their capabilities.

Clear standards of behavior enable others to determine whether an actor is violating an agreement. The aggrieved parties can call violators to account and, if the violations are not corrected, can withdraw from cooperation entirely or impose sanctions. Clear standards are especially important for international agreements, which must be enforced by participants (as opposed to third parties,

---

24. For a good discussion of the historical, political, and legal considerations surrounding this dispute, see Bill Hayton, *The South China Sea: The Struggle for Power in Asia* (New Haven, CT: Yale University Press, 2014).

25. United Nations, "United Nations Convention on the Law of the Sea," https://www.un.org/depts/los /convention_agreements/texts/unclos/unclos_e.pdf (accessed 10/21/20).

as in domestic affairs). Without an authoritative third-party enforcement mechanism, such as the courts or the police, there is a real potential for disputes to escalate on account of incomplete or inaccurate information. By accurately identifying violations and violators, international institutions can help defuse potentially costly cycles of reciprocal punishments set off by misperceived violations.

Clear standards of behavior cannot eliminate all disputes. Rules can never address all possible circumstances, and there may well be ambiguous situations that those looking to evade the rules can exploit. When President Trump imposed tariffs on China and other countries in order to compel them to make concessions on trade, this act may have violated the terms of the WTO, which does not permit countries to raise tariffs above negotiated levels on particular countries. However, these rules include an exception for actions taken to protect "essential security interests," and the Trump administration argued that the tariffs were legitimate on those grounds. This interpretation would likely not have held up in a court, but the ambiguity created space for the policy to proceed.

Verifying Compliance In addition to standards against which actors can judge compliance, institutions often provide ways to acquire information on compliance. President Ronald Reagan famously said about arms control agreements with the Soviet Union: "Trust, but verify"—a rough translation of an old Russian proverb.

In many international institutions, self-reporting is common practice: countries are required to submit reports documenting their compliance. Such a procedure might appear weak, but it allows other parties of the agreement to inspect the self-reporting of others, assess those reports against their private knowledge of others' compliance, and publicize and criticize any inconsistencies. Discrepancies between self-reports and later-verified accounts open the country to further disrepute and possible sanctions.

At the other extreme, some international agreements permit on-site inspections. The International Atomic Energy Agency (IAEA), for instance, inspects declared nuclear material facilities in over 70 countries under the Treaty on the Non-Proliferation of Nuclear Weapons (NPT). This treaty, adopted in 1968, prohibits most countries from diverting fissionable material from civilian nuclear reactors for use in making nuclear weapons. The IAEA inspectors help to monitor compliance with this prohibition. As an example of highly intrusive inspections, drilling down deeply in what used to be considered the domestic affairs of states, the international monitoring of elections in newly democratizing countries has recently become an international norm (see "How Do We Know?" section).

Regularly inspecting nuclear power facilities to promote safe and peaceful use of nuclear technology is one way that international institutions verify compliance with standards. Here, International Atomic Energy Agency officials examine uranium enrichment in Iran.

The International Diffusion of Election Monitoring

Before 1962, no national election was ever monitored by international observers. Today, nearly 80 percent of all elections are observed by a variety of organizations, including other national governments, international organizations, and private entities. This growing trend is illustrated in Figure A. International election monitoring challenges the norm of international sovereignty, which, in principle, gives states wide latitude in how they choose their leaders. Incumbent governments must invite international monitors, and most now do so seemingly voluntarily. How did this new international institution of election monitoring get established?

In original research, Susan Hyde theorizes that election monitoring grew from the need for "true" democrats to signal their commitment to free and fair elections in the face of international skepticism and from the desire of established democratic states to promote new democracies. Hyde begins from the supposition that some leaders—like the first U.S. president, George Washington, who intentionally stepped down after two terms in office to set a precedent of limited executive rule—are sincere in their commitment to democracy. Other leaders, she argues, are pseudo-democrats who will cheat to obtain or remain in office. In elections in countries that have reestablished democracy after periods of authoritarian rule or that have recently gained independence, true democrats must find some way of identifying themselves to voters at home and supporters abroad as sincerely committed to democracy.

Inviting observers to monitor elections and certify the results as "free and fair" is one way of doing this. Thus, the first leaders to invite international monitors were trying to distinguish themselves from the potentially larger set of leaders who were not necessarily committed to democracy. It was in the interests of these true democrats to invite election monitors, and as Figure A demonstrates, few early cases of monitoring were criticized for significant electoral fraud. True democrats do not cheat.

As the practice of monitoring began to spread, established democracies in North America and Europe started to reward leaders that both invited monitors and held honest elections. Greater foreign aid was one of a range of benefits provided. This change in their interactions with donor states reinforced the desire of true democrats to invite election monitors. Yet this same interaction prompted some pseudo-democrats also to invite international election monitors in the hopes that (1) their cheating would go undetected and (2) they could receive the benefits provided by the international community as well. In short, the pseudo-democrats had an interest in mimicking the behavior of true democrats. The result of this now broader set of interactions, however, was to spread the institution of election monitoring to nearly all countries. At present, any new democracy that does not invite election monitors is immediately suspected of engaging in election fraud.

Ironically, as the practice of election monitoring spread, more and more cases of electoral fraud were discovered. Pseudo-democrats both invite monitors and cheat, and their efforts to manipulate elections are sometimes uncovered. Hyde finds that true democrats respond by inviting larger and more professional observer missions, further institutionalizing the practice of election monitoring. In turn, pseudo-democrats once again copy their true democratic cousins and invite larger missions as well. The effect has been to expand and institutionalize the practice of election monitoring. Whether or not total electoral fraud has decreased as a result of this uptick in monitoring remains an open question that is very difficult to answer.

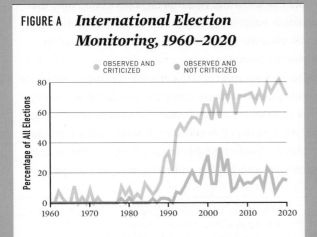

FIGURE A *International Election Monitoring, 1960–2020*

Source: Susan D. Hyde, *The Pseudo-Democrat's Dilemma: Why Election Observation Became an International Norm* (Ithaca, NY: Cornell University Press, 2011). We are grateful to Hyde for providing data updated to 2020.

Finally, institutions protect the ability of countries to verify compliance independently. Rules specifying the status of embassies and the treatment of embassy personnel allow for diplomatic representation of one country on the territory of another, but they also permit embassy officials on-site access to collect information and track developments in the foreign state. Similarly, the Treaty on Open Skies, signed in 1992 and ratified by the United States and 34 other countries, formally permits states to use "national technical means," including satellites and high-flying spy planes, to observe developments on the ground below in foreign territories. Such tools were important in verifying the arms control agreements between the United States and the Soviet Union during the Cold War. The treaty, which was negotiated just as the Cold War was ending, formally acknowledged and ratified what had been long-standing practice.[26]

Reducing the Costs of Joint Decision Making

Institutions make it easier for actors to make decisions collectively. Recall the example of the "rules of the road" from the discussion of coordination earlier in this chapter. In a society where the side-of-the-road rule had not been established, each driver would have to negotiate with each oncoming car over who would drive on the left and who would drive on the right. Stops would be frequent, and crashes would be inevitable. The time lost in travel as a result of negotiating these individual encounters, as well as the crashes, would be the costs of joint decision making. Given the huge costs, societies establish institutions—rules of the road—to routinize decision making, avoid conflicts, and reduce the costs of driving. Smoother traffic flow and faster commutes are the benefits of the institution.

Domestic political institutions similarly operate to reduce the costs of joint decision making. Imagine that a society needed to decide collectively on all matters of policy in the absence of any agreed-upon rules. Every time someone wanted to propose a new policy, he or she would have to consult all citizens to figure out how they would decide whether to enact the policy or not. Should the policy be passed by popular referendum? If so, who could vote? Would it pass by a simple majority (50 percent plus one vote), by a supermajority (greater than 50 percent, usually two-thirds), or by unanimous consent? Alternatively, would the policy be decided by a subgroup of society? Would this subgroup be a representative body, only the most highly affected individuals, or a single individual? What powers would this subgroup have? Would it be able not only to establish the policy, but also to tax others if necessary to implement the policy?

The list of possible decision-making rules and the alternatives to be considered for each policy are virtually endless. In the absence of some agreed-upon rules on collective decision making, the costs of any policy initiative would be enormous. They might be so large, in fact, that no policy would ever generate sufficient benefits to offset the costs of enacting it. Nothing would ever get done. For this reason, societies create political institutions—rules of the political game—that define how

---

26. At the time of this writing, the Open Skies Treaty was in jeopardy, as the Trump administration withdrew the United States in November 2020, and Russia announced a few months later that it would withdraw. Biden opposed the withdrawal, but it was unclear if the United States would rejoin the treaty.

joint political decisions will be made. These institutions are useful because they reduce the costs of joint decision making.

International institutions serve to reduce the costs of joint decision making among nations in the same way. The UN was created as a permanent forum where countries could come together to deliberate and attempt to resolve disagreements. Since its founding, the UN and its associated agencies have undertaken 71 peace-keeping operations, fought the Korean War, authorized the 1991 Persian Gulf War, rewritten the law of the sea, managed refugee problems worldwide, fed people displaced by conflict or famine, helped eliminate smallpox globally, and undertaken a host of other activities. A relatively clear set of rules determines which issues get referred to the General Assembly and which to the Security Council, and each body has specific voting rules. These rules reduce the costs of joint decision making among member states just as they do in other social settings. A large number of other international institutions help reduce the costs of joint decision making on a broad range of issues.

Resolving Disputes   International institutions also facilitate cooperation by providing mechanisms for resolving disputes. When parties disagree about whether one or more of them have violated an agreement or how to interpret the terms of an agreement, it can be helpful to have determined in advance how to handle such differences. Domestically, disputes are routinely referred to courts for authoritative resolution; in fact, courts are the default forum for dispute resolution, unless the parties to an agreement have specifically consented to other provisions, such as arbitration.

Most international agreements do not contain explicit dispute resolution procedures, and each party may seek to interpret the agreement according to its own interests and be limited only by its desire for a reputation as a "good partner." Nonetheless, some international agreements do provide mechanisms for dispute resolution. Many international economic transactions regularly delegate dispute resolution to national courts—for instance, agreeing in advance that disputes will be decided according to the laws of the state of New York—or to one of many international arbitration boards. UNCLOS has provisions for maritime disputes to go to an arbitration panel or standing court, a mechanism that has been used successfully to resolve dozens of cases.[27] In 2013, the Philippines invoked this provision and brought its dispute with China over the South China Sea to the Permanent Court of Arbitration (PCA). The court ruled in 2016 that China's expansive claims, based on historical rights, had no legal force, and it upheld the Philippines' position in the dispute.[28]

---

27. Stephen C. Nemeth, Sara McLaughlin Mitchell, Elizabeth A. Nyman, and Paul R. Hensel, "Ruling the Sea: Managing Maritime Conflicts through UNCLOS and Exclusive Economic Zones," *International Interactions* 40, no. 5 (October 2014): 711–36. See also Sara McLaughlin Mitchell and Andrew P. Owsiak, "Judicialization of the Sea: Bargaining under the UNCLOS Regime," *American Journal of International Law*, forthcoming.

28. For information on this case, see Permanent Court of Arbitration, "The South China Sea Arbitration (The Republic of Philippines v. The People's Republic of China)," https://pca-cpa.org/en/cases/7 (accessed 11/2/20).

What happened next is instructive about what dispute resolution mechanisms can and cannot do. China rejected the jurisdiction of the court and refused to acknowledge the validity of the ruling. The court has no enforcement powers, meaning that it could give the Philippine position the blessing of international law, but it could not compel China to comply with its decision. And since China has vastly more military and economic power, Manila has limited ability to force China to withdraw its claims or to remove its ships from waters claimed by the Philippines. Recognizing this reality, Chinese vice foreign minister Liu Zhenmin dismissed the ruling as "nothing more than a piece of waste paper," one that "will not be enforced by anyone." Even so, China has taken some modest steps in the direction of compliance, including letting Filipino fishermen operate around Scarborough Shoal, the main island feature in the disputed area, and experimenting with new ways to articulate its claim in a manner that is more consistent with international law.[29] Moreover, in July 2020, the United States relied on the PCA's ruling to declare that it views Chinese claims in the South China Sea to be illegal, reiterating its commitment to defending allies in the region.[30]

Thus, by ruling on whether a given action is allowed or not according to the standards of the institution, dispute resolution mechanisms resolve ambiguities in agreements, increase the expectation that violations will be called out, and bestow legitimacy on efforts to sanction violators. In principle, these functions permit states to enforce the rules of the institution, thereby enabling mutually beneficial cooperation. But dispute resolution bodies do not have enforcement powers. While they identify violators and victims and may even suggest remedies, they do not impose punishments. Instead, any efforts to sanction violators come from the victimized states and any that wish to help them. Below, we will return to this point to understand why compliance with these mechanisms is nonetheless generally quite high.

In sum, institutions facilitate international cooperation in important ways. International institutions do not, however, directly enforce cooperation, except in extremely rare cases when they are empowered to punish defectors directly. Rather, despite a well-developed infrastructure of institutions, international politics remains largely a realm of self-help in which states alone must choose whether and how to penalize those who fail to cooperate. What international institutions do, however, is make compliance more likely by clarifying the terms of cooperation, providing information, and lowering the costs of joint decision making—including the costs of deciding when to punish states that choose not to follow the rules.

---

29. Bill Hayton, "Denounce but Comply: China's Response to the South China Sea Arbitration Ruling," *Georgetown Journal of International Affairs* 18, no. 2 (2017): 104–11. See also Asia Maritime Transparency Initiative, "Failing or Incomplete? Grading the South China Sea Arbitration," July 19, 2019, https://amti.csis.org/failing-or-incomplete-grading-the-south-china-sea-arbitration (accessed 6/25/20).

30. Michael R. Pompeo, "U.S. Position on Maritime Claims in the South China Sea," U.S. Department of State, July 13, 2020, www.state.gov/u-s-position-on-maritime-claims-in-the-south-china-sea (accessed 8/3/20).

Whom Do Institutions Benefit?

Institutions may help states cooperate, and in that sense they can make all their members better off. But institutions rarely benefit everyone equally. Institutions are themselves a product of the cooperation and bargaining that brought them into being. They reflect past political bargains, with the winners getting to write the rules or, at least, having a disproportionate say over the rules. As a result, rules are never neutral; instead, they embody the bargaining strength of the actors at the time the rules were written or amended. Thus, all institutions contain what we describe as a policy bias.[31]

Institutions bias outcomes in many ways. In the United States, for instance, citizens' interests are represented at the national level through different electoral institutions. These institutions themselves are a reflection of bargaining within the constitutional convention of 1787. The more populous states at the time sought a legislature in which representatives were allocated by population, which would give them a larger voice. The less populous states, knowing they would be routinely outvoted, wanted some form of guaranteed representation. The result was a compromise, with seats in the House of Representatives being determined by population and seats in the Senate being reserved two for each state. The larger states were forced to compromise by the unwillingness of the smaller states to agree to the Constitution without this provision.

These rules matter. Since they are elected by and responsive to different subsets of the national population, it is hardly surprising that the majority of the House of Representatives, the majority of the Senate, and the president—with the largest constituency—often differ in their interests. Indeed, the framers of the Constitution explicitly intended to create competing branches of government with different constituencies and policy preferences. Institutions that represent many smaller constituencies are likely to produce policies that favor particular groups in society through large, omnibus "logrolls" that contain something for everyone. Institutions that represent larger constituencies are more likely to enact policies meant to benefit society as a whole. For this reason, Congress is often thought to be more beholden to "special interests," whereas the president is expected to act more in the national interest.

International institutions differ widely in their rules and in their policy bias. Some institutions, including the General Assembly of the UN, have a one country–one vote rule. China, with a population of nearly 1.4 billion, has the same official weight as Tuvalu, whose population is around 11,600.[32] This rule gives each citizen of Tuvalu the same voice in the General Assembly as about 120,000 Chinese. The Security Council, by contrast, has voting rules that privilege five particular states—the United States, Great Britain, France, Russia, and China—by giving them a veto over any action the council might take. This means that even if a majority of states

---

31. For a review of the effects of institutions, including policy bias, see Ronald Rogowski, "Institutions as Constraints on Strategic Choice," in Lake and Powell, *Strategic Choice*, 115–36.

32. World Bank, "Population, Total – China," https://data.worldbank.org/indicator/SP.POP.TOTL?locations==CN; World Bank, "Population, Total – Tuvalu," https://data.worldbank.org/indicator/SP.POP.TOTL?locations ==TV (accessed 12/21/20).

on the Security Council, or around the world, want the UN to enact a particular policy, it can be blocked by any one of these five states.

Why these particular states? They were the five major victors of World War II, and hence they were in a position to write the rules when the UN was created in the aftermath of that war. That they continue to have this privileged position now, almost 80 years since the end of the war, attests to the way institutions can crystallize certain bargains, making them persist over time, even long after the conditions that brought them into being have passed. The effects are considerable, however, as we will discuss further in Chapter 5. For example, the fact that China has a veto in the Security Council means that Vietnam's protest to the UN after the sinking of its fishing boat landed in a body that cannot act without China's consent.

Other organizations have weighted voting rules, which give the largest contributors the most influence. In the IMF, for example, the United States contributes about 17 percent of the fund's resources, and consequently it gets 17 percent of the votes on the organization's Board of Governors—by far the largest vote share of any individual country. The weights have been periodically renegotiated to reflect changes in the contributions and bargaining power of states, but the United States and the European Union still retain large enough shares of the votes to each block any important decision within the organization.

Still other institutions operate by unanimous consent, permitting any member to veto an action. ASEAN is one such body. Formed in 1967 to promote regional cooperation on a variety of political and economic issues, the organization now has 10 member states: Brunei, Cambodia, Indonesia, Laos, Malaysia, Myanmar, the Philippines, Singapore, Thailand, and Vietnam. Since it formed at the time of the Vietnam War, a period of intense conflict in the region, the member states prioritized the principle of sovereign equality and consensus so that it could make no decision unless all members were in accord. Although this rule prevents the organization from taking actions that are counter to the interests of any member, it can also hamstring collective responses. For example, in 2012, when Chinese actions in the South China Sea spurred demands from some members to issue a tough response, the action was blocked by Cambodia, whose support China had wooed with financial and commercial concessions.[33]

Because institutions matter and bias policy in consequential ways, states struggle over their rules. These struggles are likely to loom large in U.S.-China relations. The main institutions that govern the global economy—the WTO, IMF, and World Bank—were constructed in the aftermath of World War II by the United States and its allies. China, like the rest of the communist bloc at the time, was excluded from these institutions and had no say in their design. China did not join the IMF and World Bank until 1980, and it would wait another 20 years to join the WTO. In recent decades, China's growing economic clout has caused it to seek greater influence in those bodies. And reforms to the voting rules of the

---

33. Hayton, *South China Sea*, 192–200.

OPENING CEREMONY
35th ASEAN SUMMIT
and Related Summits
3 November 2019, Bangkok/Nonthaburi, Thailand

ASEAN
THAILAND 2019
ENHANCING PARTNERSHIP
FOR SUSTAINABILITY

Leaders of the ten countries that make up the Association of Southeast Asian Nations meet annually to discuss issues of economic, political, and developmental importance to the region. Unlike the UN and IMF, ASEAN operates by unanimous consent, permitting any member to veto an action.

World Bank and IMF have increased China's share of voting power. For example, China's share of voting power in the IMF increased from 2.6 percent in 1990 to 6.1 percent in 2021, making it the third most influential country after the United States and Japan.

Going forward, China might also seek to change the rules of these institutions or promote alternative institutions in which it has greater clout. For example, developing countries, including China, have complained that development loans from the World Bank often come with painful conditions pushed by Western governments, including demands for policy changes and governance reforms. China supported the creation of the Asian Infrastructure Investment Bank (AIIB) in 2016, which had 102 members at the time of this writing.[34] Like the World Bank and other Western-dominated lending institutions, the AIIB provides loans for development projects. Unlike the World Bank, in which the United States holds 15.8 percent of the voting power and China only 4.7 percent, China is the single largest vote holder in the AIIB, with 26.7 percent.[35] Although it is too soon to know how important this new institution will be, in principle, the AIIB could serve as an alternative source of loans for borrowers who want to avoid the politically intrusive conditions often demanded by U.S.-led institutions.[36]

---

34. Information on members, prospective members, and voting power in the AIIB can be found at Asian Infrastructure Investment Bank, "Members and Prospective Members of the Bank," October 13, 2020, www.aiib.org/en/about-aiib/governance/members-of-bank/index.html (accessed 10/21/20).

35. Information on voting power in the World Bank can be found at World Bank, "International Bank for Reconstruction and Development: Subscriptions and Voting Power of Member Countries," October 20, 2020, http://pubdocs.worldbank.org/en/795101541106471736/IBRDCountryVotingTable.pdf (accessed 11/2/20).

36. For a variety of views on the importance of the AIIB, see "Should Washington Fear the AIIB?" *Foreign Affairs*, June 11, 2015, www.foreignaffairs.com/articles/china/2015-06-11/should-washington-fear-aiib (accessed 10/21/20).

Institutions are both the shapers of politics (by facilitating cooperation) and the products of political action. Given the relative consistency in the basic institutions of government in the United States and many other countries, we often attribute a "taken for granted" or natural quality to political institutions. But it is important to understand that all institutions reflect particular policy biases and, as a result, are always the object of continuing political debate and struggle.

Why Follow the Rules?

Why do actors follow rules? If they have incentives to defect from rules and ignore institutions, why do they not always do so? If the rules are biased against them, why would they go along with them anyway? These have been key questions for many scholars of international relations. Some analysts argue that states ignore institutions whenever those institutions do not serve their interests, so the institutions we see merely reflect the current bargaining strength of states and do not affect policy.[37] Others argue that if institutions did not matter, states would not devote so much energy to writing the extensive rules we observe. In this view, rates of compliance in international politics are surprisingly high. Indeed, although this finding remains contested, international lawyers argue that when states do violate international rules, the reason is more often a lack of capacity to live up to their obligations than an attempt to seize an advantage over others.[38]

Actors comply with institutions for two reasons. First, since many problems in international relations combine both cooperation and bargaining, actors may agree to comply with rules for the broader cooperation they facilitate, even though the outcome of those particular rules is biased against them. In these situations, the value of the cooperation created by the institution outweighs the costs of a relatively disadvantageous bargain. States observe the rules of the WTO not just because other countries might be authorized to punish them for violations, but also because the wider system of free trade that the WTO supports and promotes is of great benefit to them. They fear that defiance of its mandates would place at risk the whole system of trade rules and the gains from trade.

Thus, even the United States, the world's largest trader, often complies with the findings of the WTO dispute settlement process. In 1995, the small country of Costa Rica brought suit against the United States in the WTO to lift U.S. restrictions on the cotton and synthetic-fiber underwear that Costa Rica exported to the United States. The United States tried to defend its restrictions as necessary to prevent serious damage to its domestic industry, but it was repeatedly found to be in violation of WTO rules. Washington eventually complied, in spite of the protests of domestic producers, even though retaliation from Costa Rica itself would have been but a minor irritant. Similarly, countries abide by the NPT not just because

---

37. For a skeptical view of international institutions, see John J. Mearsheimer, "The False Promise of International Institutions," *International Security* 19, no. 3 (1994): 5–49.

38. See Abram Chayes and Antonia Handler Chayes, "On Compliance," *International Organization* 47, no. 2 (1993): 175–205. This view is criticized in George W. Downs, David M. Rocke, and Peter N. Barsoom, "Is the Good News about Compliance Good News about Cooperation?" *International Organization* 50, no. 3 (1996): 397–406.

the inspections of the IAEA may reveal cheating that could then be referred to the UN Security Council for possible sanctioning, but also because the restraints on all countries make the world a safer place. In such cases, the prospect of continued, mutually beneficial cooperation restrains the short-run temptation for countries to ignore rules they do not like.

The second reason actors comply with institutions is that they are already in place and often cheaper to use, even if they are biased, than are the costs of creating a brand-new institution that might more fully reflect the actors' interests.[39] Creating new institutions is not easy. As we've discussed, actors must agree on the members, voting rules, and many other procedures that together constitute the institution. Since those rules will affect the cooperation and bargains reached, actors will struggle over which rules should be adopted. In the negotiations that eventually led to the end of the Vietnam War, the parties spent more than six months just wrangling over the shape of the table at which they would sit.

The time and effort spent negotiating new rules can be considerable. In the case of an existing institution, the costs of creating a set of rules have already been paid. The costs of any new institution, however better suited to the matter under discussion, would have to be paid anew. If the policy bias of an institution is small enough, actors may choose to work within the existing rules rather than create new ones from scratch. If the policy bias is too large, actors will choose to disband the institution, ignore it, or reform it.[40] In many circumstances, however, they recognize that maintaining the institution, though far from ideal, is less costly than creating a new one.

Institutions are the rules of the political game. Valued and respected for the cooperation they facilitate, institutions are not, however, a panacea for problems of international cooperation. When the temptation to defect becomes too large, or the fear of being taken advantage of grows too severe, countries will violate the rules—just as actors within countries choose at times to disobey the law. Yet institutions do make international cooperation more likely, and countries that desire cooperation follow the rules more often than we might otherwise expect.

Conclusion: Explaining World Politics

This chapter has outlined the basic concepts of interests, interactions, and institutions that serve throughout the book to unravel a variety of puzzles of international politics.

---

39. For an exploration of how the difficulty of setting up new institutions limits actors' ability to change the rules of existing institutions, see Phillip Y. Lipscy, *Renegotiating the World Order: Institutional Change in International Relations* (New York: Cambridge University Press, 2017).

40. Joseph Jupille, Walter Mattli, and Duncan Snidal, *Institutional Choice and Global Commerce* (New York: Cambridge University Press, 2013).

To illustrate how this analytical framework can be used in concrete ways, we return to the example that opened this chapter. Competition between the United States and China is rooted in a mix of security and economic interests. The United States fears that a rising China will pursue more aggressive policies in Asia at the expense of American allies and long-term influence. At the same time, trade with China, while benefiting U.S. consumers, has not only led to domestic job losses in sectors that compete with Chinese imports but also fueled China's impressive economic growth. The Chinese government, for its part, has pursued rapid economic development both to improve the living standards of its people and to increase its power and influence. In the process, it has pressed a variety of territorial claims on its neighbors, especially in the South China Sea, possession of which might yield economic and strategic benefits.

These longer-term sources of conflict were exacerbated in 2020 by the outbreak of the COVID-19 pandemic. This disease threatened the health of people in both the United States and China and disrupted their economies, jeopardizing the political interests of their leaders. Both Trump and Xi responded with policies that intensified the conflict.

These clashing interests have led to hard bargaining between the United States and China on a variety of issues. In the South China Sea, China has used coercion in order to make it costly for its neighbors to maintain their claims to the waterway. Although China's enormous power gives it leverage over these small states, the United States has pledged to support those countries in order to blunt China's bargaining advantage. As of this writing, there have been small-scale clashes and shows of military force, but neither side has been able to impose its most preferred outcome on the other, and the conflict has not escalated to war. On the economic front, President Trump sought to change the balance of trade between the United States and China by imposing tariffs on Chinese imports and bargaining for greater access to the Chinese market.

This broad pattern of competition is likely to continue under the Biden administration. In his first major address on foreign policy, the new secretary of state, Antony Blinken, identified China as "the only country with the economic, diplomatic, military, and technological power to seriously challenge . . . all the rules, values, and relationships that make the world work the way we want it to."[41] A week earlier, Xi similarly declared that "The United States is the biggest threat to our country's development and security."[42] Thus, conflicts between the world's two most powerful states are poised to be a central feature of international politics in this century.

At the same time, the two countries share some common interests. A war between them would be devastatingly costly. The costs of fighting mean that states have a shared interest in reaching some bargain that allows them to avoid war. Whether or not that is possible, as well as the factors that make peaceful bargains

---

41. Blinken's speech can be found at https://www.state.gov/a-foreign-policy-for-the-american-people/ (accessed 3/3/21).

42. Chris Buckley, "'The East Is Rising': Xi Maps Out China's Post-Covid Ascent," The *New York Times*, March 3, 2021, https://www.nytimes.com/2021/03/03/world/asia/xi-china-congress.html (accessed 3/3/21).

more or less likely, is the subject of the next chapter. The two countries also have a shared interest in the continuation of the international trading system, which is a source of economic growth. Thus, while they are likely to engage in hard bargaining over the terms of trade, both would prefer to avoid a collapse of international trade, as happened in the 1930s.

Finally, international institutions play a role in determining whether these conflicts can be contained. A host of organizations and agreements (for example, the UN, ASEAN, UNCLOS) exist to create standards by which to judge contentious issues like the maritime dispute in the South China Sea and to facilitate cooperation by states with shared interests. Similarly, a number of institutions (such as the WTO and the IMF) provide rules and dispute resolution mechanisms for managing crises in trade and international finance. As we have seen, however, though institutions may facilitate cooperation, they can rarely compel or enforce it. Their procedures tend to privilege the interests of powerful states, as with the veto rule in the UN Security Council, or raise high hurdles for action, as with the unanimity rule in ASEAN. The looming competition between the United States and China is likely to test existing institutions and create conflicts over their rules and standards going forward.

Study Tool Kit

Interests, Interactions, and Institutions in Context

- Interests are the fundamental building blocks of politics. Explanations of international political events begin by specifying the relevant actors and their interests.

- Cooperation is a type of interaction involving two or more actors working together to achieve a preferred outcome. Successful cooperation depends on the number and relative sizes of actors involved, the number of interactions among the actors, and the accuracy of the information they possess.

- Bargaining is a type of interaction involving the distribution of something of value: if one actor gets "more," someone else necessarily gets "less." In bargaining, outcomes depend on what will happen in the event that no agreement is reached. Actors derive power from their ability to make the consequences of no agreement less attractive for the other side.

- Institutions are sets of rules. Actors comply with institutions because they facilitate cooperation and lower the cost of joint decision making in the pursuit of valued goals.

- Institutions also bias policy outcomes. Rules restrain what actors can and cannot do, and thus they make some outcomes more or less likely. Actors struggle over institutions in an effort to shift policy toward outcomes they prefer.

Key Terms

interests, p. 45

actors, p. 47

state, p. 48

sovereignty, p. 48

anarchy, p. 48

national interests, p. 48

interactions, p. 52

cooperation, p. 53

bargaining, p. 57

coordination, p. 59

collaboration, p. 60

public goods, p. 61

collective action problems, p. 62

free ride, p. 62

iteration, p. 63

linkage, p. 64

power, p. 65

coercion, p. 66

outside options, p. 67

agenda setting, p. 68

institutions, p. 69

For Further Reading

Avant, Deborah D., Martha Finnemore, and Susan K. Sell, eds. *Who Governs the Globe?* **New York: Cambridge University Press, 2010.** Explores new patterns of governance within the otherwise anarchic international system.

Bueno de Mesquita, Bruce, Alastair Smith, Randolph M. Siverson, and James D. Morrow. *The Logic of Political Survival.* **Cambridge, MA: MIT Press, 2003.** Integrates interests, interactions, and institutions to explain a wide range of behaviors in domestic and international politics.

Economy, Elizabeth. *The Third Revolution: Xi Jinping and the New Chinese State.* **New York, NY: Oxford University Press, 2018.** A valuable introduction to developments in China that shape its foreign and domestic policy.

Enloe, Cynthia. *Bananas, Beaches, and Bases: Making Feminist Sense of International Politics.* **2nd ed. Berkeley: University of California Press, 2014.** Updated edition of a pathbreaking feminist analysis of international politics.

Hayton, Bill. *The South China Sea: The Struggle for Power in Asia.* **New Haven, CT: Yale University Press, 2014.** An accessible account of the origins and recent history of the conflict over the South China Sea.

Keohane, Robert O. *After Hegemony: Cooperation and Discord in the World Political Economy.* **Princeton, NJ: Princeton University Press, 1984.** Classic statement on the role and importance of international institutions.

Kydd, Andrew H. *International Relations Theory: The Game-Theoretic Approach.* **New York: Cambridge University Press, 2015.** Introduction to game theory with applications to world politics.

Lake, David A., and Robert Powell, eds. *Strategic Choice and International Relations.* **Princeton, NJ: Princeton University Press, 1999.** Examines interests, interactions, and institutions in detail within the context of international relations theory.

Milner, Helen V., and Dustin Tingley. *Sailing the Water's Edge: The Domestic Politics of American Foreign Policy.* **Princeton, NJ: Princeton University Press, 2015.** Explores how the interactions of the president, Congress, interest groups, bureaucracies, and the public have influenced U.S. foreign policy since 1945.

A Primer on Game Theory

Game theory is a tool for analyzing strategic interactions. Over the last 50 years, it has been developed and applied broadly in nearly all the social sciences, as well as in biology and other physical sciences—and it is even making inroads in the humanities. Among its earliest and most useful applications was international politics. We provide here a brief overview of game theory to introduce strategic thinking and illustrate concepts discussed in the text.

Imagine two actors, Actor 1 (A1) and Actor 2 (A2), with only two choices, which we call cooperation (C) and defection (D). Since each actor has two choices, there are four possible outcomes to this "game": both might cooperate (CC), both might defect (DD), A1 might cooperate while A2 defects (CD), and A1 might defect while A2 cooperates (DC). The mapping of choices into outcomes is best depicted using a 2 × 2 matrix, as shown in Figure A.1.[a] As defined in the chapter text, the actors' interests determine how they rank the four possible outcomes from best (4) to worst (1), with higher "payoffs" representing more preferred outcomes. A1's payoffs are given first in each cell; A2's are given second.

Both actors choose simultaneously without knowledge of the other's choices but with knowledge of their own preferences and those of the other actor.[b] The outcome we observe is a function of the interaction—that is, the choices of both actors. Each actor can choose only C or D, but their payoffs differ across the four possible outcomes. Suppose A1 chooses C and ranks CC (mutual cooperation) over CD. In choosing C, A1 only partially controls which outcome arises; A1's actual payoff depends crucially on whether A2 chooses C (creating CC) or D (creating CD). This scenario highlights a key point: that *strategic interaction depends on the choices of all relevant actors*, and a strategic interaction framework is thus most useful in explaining situations in which outcomes are contingent on the choices of all parties.

In such a setting, purposive actors—that is, actors who seek their highest expected payoff—choose strategies, or plans of action, that are a best response to the anticipated actions of the other. Sometimes it makes sense for an actor to make the same choice (C or D) regardless of what the opponent does; in these cases, the actor is said to have a *dominant strategy*. In other cases, each player's best choice depends on what the opponent does. For example, a player's best response might be to cooperate when the other side cooperates and defect when the other side defects.

Since each actor is trying to play its best response, and since each expects the other to play its own best response, the outcome of the game is determined by the

---

a. The same games can be represented in extensive form as a "game tree." Both are common in the larger literature.

b. In some of the games discussed here, the outcome does not depend on the assumption that the actors move simultaneously.

A Game Matrix

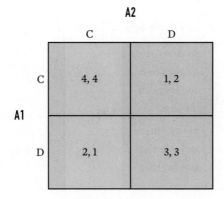

combination of the two actors' strategies, each of which is perceived to be a best response to the other. An outcome that arises from each side choosing best-response strategies is called an *equilibrium*. An equilibrium outcome is stable because the actors have no incentive to alter their choices; since, in equilibrium, both are playing their best responses, by definition they cannot do better by changing their choices. In the game illustrations that follow, the equilibrium (or *equilibria*, when there is more than one) is denoted by an asterisk (*) in the appropriate cell.

The Prisoner's Dilemma

As described in the text (pp. 59–60), the Prisoner's Dilemma is a commonly cited game in international relations because it captures problems of collaboration, such as arms races and the provision of public goods. Reread the full text on pp. 59–60, and keep in mind that each prisoner can either *cooperate with his accomplice* and refuse to provide evidence to the district attorney or *defect on his accomplice* by ratting him out. Therefore, four different outcomes are possible for each player, ranked as follows:

- **Best outcome (ranked 4):** The prisoner defects while his partner cooperates (DC), meaning that he is freed immediately, while his partner is jailed for 10 years.

- **Second-best outcome (3):** The prisoner and his partner both cooperate (CC), and therefore each spends only 1 year in prison.

- **Third-best outcome (2):** The prisoner and his partner both defect (DD), and each is imprisoned for 5 years.

- **Worst outcome (1):** The prisoner cooperates while his partner defects (CD), meaning that he goes to prison for 10 years while his partner goes free.

In short, each prisoner has identical interests and ranks the four possible outcomes as DC > CC > DD > CD (the "greater than" symbol should be read in each case as

FIGURE A.2 *The Prisoner's Dilemma*

		A2	
		C	D
A1	C	Both prisoners get out and split the loot.	A1 goes to jail; A2 goes free and keeps all the loot.
	D	A1 goes free and keeps all the loot; A2 goes to jail.	Both go to jail and split the loot later.

		A2	
		C	D
A1	C	3, 3	1, 4
	D	4, 1	2, 2*

meaning that the first outcome is "preferred over" the second), as depicted in Figure A.2.

What each prisoner should do is unclear at this point, but here is where the techniques of game theory help. As close examination of the matrix reveals, each criminal's dominant strategy is to defect, regardless of his partner's actions. If his partner cooperates (that is, stays quiet), he is better off defecting (that is, talking to the district attorney) (DC > CC). If his partner defects, he is also better off defecting (DD > CD). The equilibrium that results from each prisoner playing his best response is DD, or mutual defection. The paradox, or dilemma, arises because both criminals would in fact be better off if they remained silent and got released relatively quickly than if they both provided evidence and went to jail (CC > DD). But despite knowing this, each still has incentives to defect in order to get off easy (DC) or at least safeguard against his partner's defection (DD). The only actor who wins in this contrived situation is the district attorney, who sends both criminals to jail.

Although it is a considerable simplification, many analysts have used the Prisoner's Dilemma to capture the essential strategic dilemma at the core of the collective action problem. Each individual prefers free riding while others contribute to the public good of, say, national defense, (DC) over contributing if everyone else does and receiving the good (CC), over not contributing if no one else does (DD), and finally over contributing if no one else contributes (CD). As with the prisoners, each individual has a dominant strategy of not contributing (that is, defecting); thus, the public good of national defense is not provided voluntarily. The dilemma is solved only by the imposition of taxes by an authoritative state.

Chicken

The game of Chicken represents a second strategic dilemma. The animating story here is the game played by teenagers in the 1950s (and perhaps today by teenagers not yet familiar with game theory!). Two drivers speed down the middle of the road toward one another. The first to turn aside, the "chicken," earns the derision

FIGURE A.3 *Chicken*

		A2				A2	
		C	D			C	D
A1	C	Both drivers swerve; neither is humiliated or harmed.	A1 is "chicken"; A2 "wins."	**A1**	C	3, 3	2, 4*
	D	A1 "wins"; A2 is "chicken."	Both drivers are killed in a serious wreck.		D	4, 2*	1, 1

of his or her peers. The other driver wins. If both swerve simultaneously, neither is humiliated. If neither turns aside, both risk death in a serious wreck. If turning aside is understood as cooperation and continuing down the middle of the road as defection, the actors' interests are DC > CC > CD > DD, as shown in Figure A.3 (note that this is the same order of preferences as in the Prisoner's Dilemma, except for the reversal of the last two outcomes).

Lacking a dominant strategy, the key to one's strategy in Chicken is to do the opposite of what you think the other driver is likely to do. If you think your opponent will stand tough (D), you should turn aside (C). If you think your opponent will turn aside (C), you should stand tough (D). Two equilibria exist (DC and CD). The winner is the driver who by bluster, swagger, or past reputation convinces the other that she is more willing to risk a crash.

Chicken is often taken as a metaphor for coercive bargaining (see p. 67 in the text). Nuclear crises are usually thought of as Chicken games. Both sides want to avoid nuclear disaster (DD), but each has incentives to stand tough and get the other to back down (DC). The state willing to take the greatest risk of nuclear war is therefore likely to force the other to capitulate. The danger, of course, is that if both sides are willing to run high risks of nuclear war to win, small mistakes in judgment or calculation can have horrific consequences.

The Stag Hunt

A final game, which is often taken as a metaphor for problems of coordination in international relations (see p. 59 in the chapter text), is the Stag Hunt. This is one of a larger class of what are known as assurance games.[c] The motivating parable was

---

c. Another common assurance game captures situations in which two actors want to coordinate on the same action, but they have different preferences. For example, two friends want to spend the evening together, but one wants to attend a sporting event and the other a movie. The worst outcome for each is to spend the evening alone. Interested readers should model this game and describe its dynamics in terms similar to those for the Stag Hunt and the other games in this appendix.

told by political philosopher Jean-Jacques Rousseau. Only by working together can two hunters kill a stag and feed their families well. One must flush the deer from the forest, and the other must be ready to fire his arrow as the animal emerges. In the midst of the hunt, a lone rabbit wanders by. Each hunter now faces a decision: he could capture the rabbit alone, but to do so he must abandon the stag, ensuring that it will get away.

A rabbit is good sustenance but not as fine as the hunter's expected share of the stag. In this game, both hunters are best off cooperating (CC) and sharing the stag. The next-best outcome is to get a rabbit while the other tries for the stag (DC); however, if both go for the rabbit (DD), they then split the rabbit. The worst outcome for each hunter is to spend time and energy hunting the stag while the other hunts the rabbit (CD), leaving him and his family with nothing. Thus, each hunter's interests create the ranking CC > DC > DD > CD, as depicted in Figure A.4.

Despite the clear superiority of mutual cooperation, a coordination dilemma arises. If each hunter expects that the other will cooperate and help bring down the stag, each is best off cooperating in the hunt. But if each expects that the other will be tempted to defect and grab the rabbit, thereby letting the stag get away, he will also defect and try to grab the rabbit. Lacking a dominant strategy, each can do no better than what he expects the other to do—creating two equilibria (CC and DD).

The Stag Hunt captures situations in which the primary barrier to cooperation is not an individual incentive to defect but a lack of trust. If we define trust in this context as an expectation that the partner will cooperate, then trust leads to mutual cooperation while a lack of trust leads to mutual defection. (By contrast, in the Prisoner's Dilemma it never makes sense to trust an accomplice, and if one accomplice expects the other accomplice to cooperate, the best response is to defect.) Imagine, for example, two states have placed their military forces at their border in order to defend against a possible attack from the other side. Since having troops close to the border creates a risk of an accident, the states could cooperate by withdrawing their forces some distance from the border. If neither state wants to attack, then reducing

FIGURE A.4   *The Stag Hunt*

		A2	
		C	D
A1	C	Both hunters split the stag.	A1 goes hungry; A2 eats the rabbit.
	D	A1 eats the rabbit; A2 goes hungry.	Both hunters split the rabbit.

		A2	
		C	D
A1	C	4, 4*	1, 3
	D	3, 1	2, 2*

the risk of accident through mutual withdrawals (CC) is better than leaving forces at the border, even unilaterally (DC). But neither state wants to be the only one to withdraw (CD < DD). In this scenario, each state will withdraw if it trusts that the other will withdraw, and each will keep its forces in place if it does not trust that the other will withdraw.

As this brief survey suggests, game theory helps clarify the core dilemmas in certain types of strategic situations. Many games are far more complex than the examples described here, with more possible actions than "cooperate" or "defect," information asymmetries, random chance, and many more devices to capture elements of real-world strategic situations. The games presented here are more like metaphors than accurate representations of actual situations in international relations. But they illustrate how thinking systematically about strategic interaction helps us understand why actors cannot always get what they want—and, in fact, often get rather disappointing outcomes, even though all actors might prefer other results. In both the Prisoner's Dilemma and the Stag Hunt, for instance, all actors prefer CC over DD, and this mutual preference is known in advance. Nonetheless, in the Prisoner's Dilemma mutual defection is the equilibrium result, and in the Stag Hunt it is one of two expected outcomes. In all three games, outcomes are the result of the choices not of one actor, but of all.

3

Why Are There Wars?

THE PUZZLE *War is an extremely costly way for states to settle their disputes. Given the human and material costs of military conflict, why do states sometimes wage war rather than resolve their disputes through negotiation?*

Above: States may go to war over territory that they consider integral to their nation. In 2020, Indian and Chinese soldiers clashed along the Line of Control in Ladakh, a disputed territory that lies between the two countries. The conflict resulted in 20 Indian casualties. Could tensions over the region lead to war?

In August 1914, the major countries of Europe embarked on a war the likes of which the world had never before seen. Convinced that the war would be over by Christmas, European leaders sent a generation of young men into a fight that would last four years and claim more than 15 million lives. The fighting was so intense that in one battle the British army lost 20,000 soldiers in a single day, as wave after wave of attacking infantry were cut down by German machine guns. At the time, it was called the Great War. Those who could never imagine another such horrific event dubbed it the "war to end all wars." Today, we know this event as the First World War, or World War I, because 20 years later the countries of Europe were at it once again. World War II (1939–45) claimed 30–50 million lives.

There is no puzzle in the study of international politics more pressing and important than the question of why states go to war. It is the most tragic and costly phenomenon that we observe in social and political life. The costs of war can be counted on a number of dimensions. The most obvious cost is the loss of human life. By one estimate, wars among states in the twentieth century led to 40 million deaths directly from combat, plus tens of millions more deaths linked to war-related hardships.[1] In addition, wars have left untold millions injured, displaced from their homes and countries, impoverished, and diseased.

War has economic and material costs as well. Since 2001, the United States has spent over $2 trillion on military operations in Iraq, Afghanistan, and Syria.[2] Nations also routinely spend large sums of money to prepare for the possibility of war. In 2020, military expenditures by all countries amounted to just under $2 trillion—or about $250 per person.[3] Wars can also disrupt the international economy. Conflicts in the oil-rich Middle East, including the Iran-Iraq War (1980–88), the Persian Gulf War

1. Bethany Ann Lacina and Nils Petter Gleditsch, "Monitoring Trends in Global Combat: A New Dataset of Battle Deaths," *European Journal of Population* 21 (2005): 145–66.

2. Neta C. Crawford, "United States Budgetary Costs and Obligations of Post-9/11 Wars through FY2020: $6.4 Trillion," Watson Institute for International and Public Affairs, Boston University, November 13, 2019, https://watson.brown.edu/costsofwar/figures/2019/budgetary-costs-post-911-wars-through-fy2020-64-trillion (accessed 12/16/20). The $2 trillion number in the text is military spending and does not include additional expenses associated with homeland defense against terrorism and commitments to veterans' health care.

3. Diego Lopes da Silva, Nan Tian, and Alexandra Marksteiner, "Trends in World Military Expenditure, 2020," Stockholm International Peace Research Institute, April 2021, https://www.sipri.org/publications/2021/sipri-fact-sheets/trends-world-military-expenditure-2020 (accessed 5/23/2021).

(1990–91), and the Iraq War (2003–10), contributed to spikes in world oil prices. In short, as U.S. Civil War general William Sherman famously declared, "War is hell."

But if everyone recognizes that war is hell, why do wars happen? The costs that make the puzzle of war so pressing also make the phenomenon so perplexing. Given the enormous costs associated with war, why would states sometimes choose this course?

At first glance, the answer might seem straightforward: states fight wars because they have conflicting interests over important issues. Often, for instance, two states desire the same piece of territory. Nazi Germany wanted to expand into Central Europe; World War II started when the Poles, who did not want to give up their land, fought back. In 1980, Iraq invaded Iran, in part, to seize the latter's southern oil fields, leading to the Iran-Iraq War. Alternatively, one state might object to the policies or ideology of another. World War I grew out of Austria-Hungary's demand that Serbia end its support for nationalist movements that threatened to tear the multiethnic Austro-Hungarian Empire apart. War between the United States and Afghanistan broke out in 2001 because the United States wanted Afghanistan to hand over Osama bin Laden and dismantle terrorist training camps on its territory, something that the Afghans refused to do. Clearly, part of the explanation for any war requires that we identify the conflicting interests that motivated the combatants.

While such interest-based explanations are correct, they are also incomplete. By identifying the object or issue over which a war was fought, they neglect the key question of why states resorted to war in order to resolve their dispute. In each case, the conflicts were disastrously costly to at least one and, in some cases, all the states involved. In addition to the millions of dead mentioned earlier, World War I led to the ouster of three of the leaders who brought their countries into the war, and it hastened the breakup of the Austro-Hungarian, Russian, and Ottoman empires. World War II brought about the defeat and occupation of its main instigators, Germany and Japan. The Nazi leader Adolf Hitler committed suicide, and his Italian ally Benito Mussolini was hung by his own people. Iran and Iraq fought for eight years only to end their conflict in a stalemate, causing 1–2 million casualties and leaving Iraq on the brink of economic collapse. The Afghan government's refusal of U.S. demands led to its removal from power and, 10 years later, to bin Laden's death at the hands of American soldiers. Given these grave consequences, it makes sense to wonder whether all participants would have been better off if they could have come to a settlement beforehand that allowed them to avoid the costs of war. Explaining war thus requires us to explain why its participants fail to reach such agreements.

Thinking Analytically about Why Wars Happen

Most disputes between states are settled without the parties resorting to war. Although wars tend to capture our attention, it is important to remember that war is an exceedingly rare phenomenon; most countries are at peace with one another most of the time. Figure 3.1 shows the number of states involved in interstate wars in each year from 1820 to 2020, expressed as a percentage of the total number of states in existence at the time. As the figure indicates, war is a recurrent feature of international politics in the sense that it fluctuates in frequency but never disappears completely. Yet war is the exception rather than the rule: in most years, the percentage of states involved in war is quite low. All this peace cannot be explained by an absence of issues to fight over.

Hence, when seeking to explain war, we need to ask not only "What are these parties fighting over?" but also "Why are they fighting?"[4] In terms of the framework laid out in Chapter 2, answering the first question requires us to understand how states' interests can give rise to conflicts over things like territory, policies, and the composition or character of each other's governments. The answer to the second question lies in the strategic interactions that determine whether or how these conflicts are resolved. As we saw in the previous chapter, the international system lacks institutions—such as legislatures, courts, or international police forces—that can resolve conflicts between states through legal, judicial, or electoral mechanisms. As a result, interstate conflicts have to be settled through bargaining. Understanding why wars occur requires us to identify the factors that sometimes prevent states from settling their conflicts through peaceful bargains that would permit them to avoid the costs of war.

---

4. The theory of war developed in this chapter relies extensively on James D. Fearon, "Rationalist Explanations for War," *International Organization* 49, no. 3 (Summer 1995): 379–414.

FIGURE 3.1 **The Percentage of States Involved in Interstate War per Year, 1820–2020**

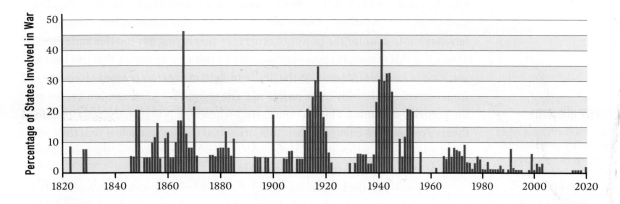

What Is the Purpose of War?

Figure sources: Meredith Reid Sarkees and Frank Wayman, *Resort to War: 1816–2007* (Washington, DC: CQ Press, 2010). Updated to 2020 by author.

A **war** is an event involving the organized use of military force by at least two parties that reaches a minimum threshold of severity.[5] Every component of this definition is important. The requirement that force be *organized* rules out spontaneous, disorganized violence, such as large-scale rioting. The requirement that force be used by *at least two parties* distinguishes war from mass killings perpetrated by a government against some group that does not fight back. The *minimum threshold*—scholars often require that a war cause at least 1,000 battle deaths—excludes cases in which military force is used at low levels, such as brief skirmishes or minor clashes. If the main adversaries in the conflict are states, then we refer to the event as an **interstate war**; if the main parties to the conflict are actors within a state—such as a government fighting a rebel group—then the event is a **civil war**.[6] This chapter focuses on understanding interstate wars. Chapter 6 covers conflicts involving nonstate actors, including civil wars.

Given that scholars have been trying to understand war for millennia, the number of theories and explanations that have been proposed over the years is naturally quite large, and the bargaining model that we lay out in this chapter is only one approach. At least three other broad schools of thought have been influential in modern scholarship. While these approaches contribute important insights, they also have gaps that are filled by the bargaining approach.

The first, described in this book's Introduction as realism, argues that war is the inevitable result of international anarchy (pp. xxxiv–xxxvi). The absence of a

war

An event involving the organized use of military force by at least two parties that reaches a minimum threshold of severity.

interstate war

A war in which the main participants are states.

civil war

A war in which the main participants are within the same state, such as the government and a rebel group.

---

5. See, for example, J. David Singer and Melvin Small, *The Wages of War, 1816–1965: A Statistical Handbook* (New York: Wiley, 1972).

6. There are also cases that have elements of both kinds of wars. In the Vietnam War, South Vietnam, with the support of the United States, fought a civil war against a communist insurgency while at the same time fighting an interstate war against communist North Vietnam, which supported the rebel factions in the south. See Chapter 6 for more on the international dimensions of civil wars.

central authority capable of policing interstate relations means that wars can happen because there is nothing to stop states from using force to get their way.[7] Moreover, anarchy creates insecurity and motivates states to compete for power. In this view, states fight wars either to increase their own power (for instance, by enlarging their territory) or to counter the power of others (by destroying adversaries and their allies). For this reason, realism emphasizes two primary dynamics that can lead to war. One is a preventive motive: the desire to fight in order to prevent an enemy from becoming relatively more powerful.[8] The second is a phenomenon known as the **security dilemma**. This dilemma arises when efforts that states make to defend themselves, such as enlarging their militaries, make other states fear that they will be attacked. If these threatened states arm themselves in response, the result is a spiral of fear and insecurity that may end in war.[9]

As we will see, the bargaining model of war shares realism's presumption that anarchy leads to a world in which states often use or threaten to use military force to further their interests and that states address conflicts through bargaining rather than institutions like courts. The bargaining model also anticipates prevention and the fear of attack as two of several motives that can lead to war. Its main departure from realism is in recognizing that the use of military power imposes costs on states, so even if threatening force is useful to get a better deal, states are generally better off if they do not have to actually use force—creating the puzzle that is at the heart of this chapter.

A second alternative to the bargaining model emphasizes the role of misperceptions or mistakes. Starting from the observation that the costs of war often far exceed any potential benefits, scholars in this tradition conclude that wars must occur because decision makers inaccurately estimate their chances of winning or the costs that they will have to pay. When European leaders sent their armies to war in August 1914, most were convinced that the troops would be home by Christmas—a prediction that turned out to be off by four years. Both sides also expected to win the war, meaning that at least one side was being overly optimistic. This kind of argument rests either on research in cognitive psychology—which shows that people are bad at weighing risks and often fall prey to wishful thinking—or on organizational approaches that emphasize how the ideology and interests of political and military elites can lead to incorrect and overly optimistic assessments of war.[10]

A concern about such theories is that while perceptual pitfalls are universal, war is quite rare, and these theories have a hard time explaining why wars happen at some points in time but not others. As we will see, uncertainty about the likely

7. Kenneth N. Waltz, *Theory of International Politics* (1979; repr., Long Grove, IL: Waveland Press, 2010).

8. See, for example, Dale C. Copeland, *The Origins of Major War* (Ithaca, NY: Cornell University Press, 2000); and Stephen Van Evera, *Causes of War* (Ithaca, NY: Cornell University Press, 1999).

9. Robert Jervis, "Cooperation under the Security Dilemma," *World Politics* 30, no. 2 (January 1978): 167–214.

10. The classic work applying cognitive psychology to international relations is Robert Jervis, *Perception and Misperception in International Politics* (Princeton, NJ: Princeton University Press, 1976). For an argument that military ideologies can lead to incorrect and overly optimistic assessments, see Stephen Van Evera, "The Cult of the Offensive and the Origins of the First World War," *International Security* 9, no. 1 (Summer 1984): 58–107. The effect of military biases may depend on domestic institutions that influence the degree to which civilians control the military; this argument is taken up in Chapter 4.

security dilemma

A dilemma that arises when efforts that states make to defend themselves cause other states to feel less secure; can lead to arms races and war because of the fear of being attacked.

outcome and costs of war plays an important role in the bargaining model approach developed here. However, we emphasize not the psychological or organizational origins of potential mistakes but rather the difficulties of gathering necessary information in the strategic context of bargaining.

Finally, a long tradition of scholarship argues that wars are fought not because they serve the interests of states but because they serve the interests of influential groups within states, such as corporations, arms merchants, and the military.[11] In this view, the puzzle of war has an easy answer: Wars are fought in spite of their costs because those costs do not fall on the actors who call the shots. Although this chapter introduces the bargaining model by treating states as the main actors, we will see in Chapter 4 that the potential role of internal politics and domestic interests can be incorporated quite easily.

Interests at War: What Do States Fight Over?

At the root of every war lies a conflict over something that states value. The purpose of warfare is not to fight but rather to obtain, through fighting or the threat of fighting, something the state wants. Hence, we should think about the problem of war as a problem of bargaining over objects or issues that are of value to more than one state. Using the framework developed in Chapter 2, we focus on situations in which states' interests conflict, giving rise to a strategic interaction that involves bargaining over the distribution of whatever is in dispute. The analysis thus starts by assuming that there is an object of value—what we will sometimes refer to as a "good"—and that each state prefers more of the good over less.

What kinds of goods do states fight over? *Territory* has historically been the most common source of trouble. Indeed, a study of 155 wars over the last three centuries found that over half (83) involved conflicts over territory—more than any other single issue.[12] States come into conflict if more than one wants the same piece of territory. There are a number of reasons why a piece of territory may be valuable to more than one state. First, it might contribute to the wealth of the state, particularly if it contains valuable resources such as oil, natural gas, or minerals. For instance, the lengthy Iran-Iraq War stemmed in part from the fact that Iraq coveted Iran's southern oil fields. Territory can also be economically valuable simply because it would add to the industrial or agricultural resources at the state's disposal.

Territory may also cause conflict between two states because of its military or strategic value. For example, the Golan Heights, on the border between Israel and Syria, has a commanding position over northern Israel from which it is possible to launch devastating attacks on the towns below. Israel seized the Golan Heights from Syria in the 1967 Six Day War, and this territory has been a source of conflict between the two states ever since.

Finally, a piece of territory might be valuable for ethnic, cultural, or historical reasons. The long-standing conflict between Israel and its Arab neighbors stems

---

11. See citations to this literature in Chapter 4.

12. Kalevi J. Holsti, *Peace and War: Armed Conflicts and International Order, 1648–1989* (Cambridge: Cambridge University Press, 1991).

MAP 3.1 *Territorial Claims in the Kashmir Region*

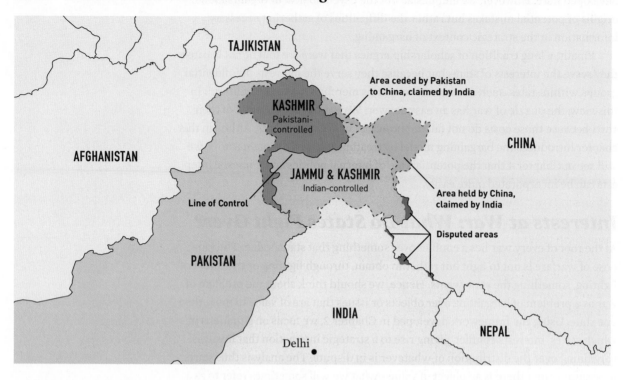

Map note: The Line of Control, which originated as a cease-fire line after the First Kashmir War (1947–48), divides the region into Indian- and Pakistani-administered areas.

from the latter's resistance to the creation of a Jewish state on land where many Arabs had lived. In this case, the dispute goes beyond simply the location of a border, as some Arab states have refused to recognize Israel's right to exist.[13]

Similarly, the long-running conflict between India and Pakistan over the Kashmir region is driven by the fact that both have historical and ethnic claims to the land. When the two countries gained their independence from Britain in 1947, India pressured Kashmir's Hindu leader to join with India, which is predominantly Hindu. However, because the people of Kashmir, like the people of Pakistan, are predominantly Muslim, Pakistan has claimed the territory on the basis of religious ties. Map 3.1 illustrates the current boundaries of the disputed area, which are further complicated by China's claims to neighboring portions of Tibet. In territorial disputes, states threaten or use military force to compel concessions and/or to seize and hold disputed land.

Wars can also arise out of conflicts over states' *policies*. Such conflicts come about when one state enacts a policy that benefits it but harms the interests of another state. The conflict that led to the 2003 Iraq War centered on Iraq's alleged pursuit of weapons of mass destruction, which the United States saw as a threat to its broader interests in the region. Ongoing U.S. conflicts with North Korea and Iran have similar sources. The armed conflict between Russia and Ukraine that began in 2014 revolved around the latter's decision to pursue closer economic ties to the

---

13. Egypt recognized Israel in 1979, and Jordan did likewise in 1994.

West, which, according to Russia, harmed the interests of ethnic Russians living in the country. A state's mistreatment of its own citizens can also spark international conflict. For example, the United States and its allies waged war against Serbia in 1999 for its repressive treatment of civilians in the Kosovo region. Similarly, the United States launched cruise missiles against Syria in 2017 after the government deployed chemical weapons on its own people.

When states have policy disputes, war, or the threat of war, may be a mechanism for compelling policy change. In the case of Kosovo, two months of bombing by the United States and its allies led the Serbian government to end its military campaign against the Kosovars. Alternatively, war may be used to replace an offending regime with a friendlier one that will pursue different policies. This was the United States' goal in Iraq and Afghanistan, though its efforts to install more pliant regimes in those countries ultimately embroiled American forces in civil wars that lasted much longer than the initial operations to oust the former, hostile regimes (see Chapter 6).

The possibility of using military force to change regimes suggests a third kind of conflict between states: conflicts over *regime type*, or the composition of another country's government. In its conflict with Ukraine, Russia sought to pressure the Ukrainian government to adopt reforms that would give Ukraine's Russian minority greater autonomy and influence. During the Cold War, the United States saw communist regimes as natural allies of the Soviet Union, and hence it sought to prevent other countries from establishing such regimes. The United States' desire to protect the pro-American South Vietnamese government from internal and external

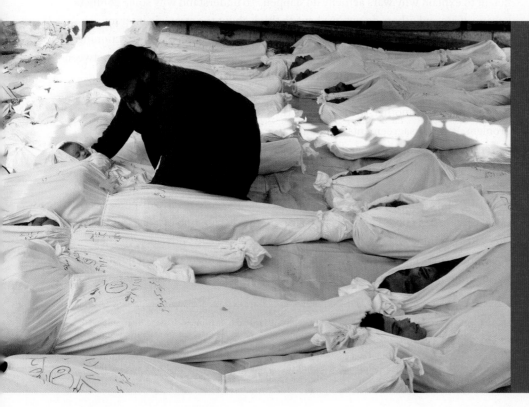

States sometimes threaten or use military force to influence the policies of foreign governments. The Syrian government attacked rebel-held villages with chemical weapons in August 2013 (pictured here), and April 2017. After the second attack, the United States carried out an air strike on a Syrian air base that it believed to be the source.

pro-communist forces motivated the country to involve itself in Vietnam's civil war. During this period, both the United States and the Soviet Union intervened regularly in the affairs of other states to prop up friendly governments or to remove unfriendly ones. The role of outside powers in civil wars, such as in Vietnam, will be addressed in Chapter 6.

As the example of Vietnam suggests, conflicts over territory, policy, and/or regime may spring from deeper conflicts that give rise to concerns about relative power. The specific conflict that started World War II was a dispute between Germany and Poland over a small strip of territory that lay between them. However, Britain and France were concerned that a victory over Poland would further strengthen and embolden Germany, making it a more formidable foe in their ongoing struggle for influence and territory in Europe. Hence, they had a stake in the outcome of the German-Polish territorial dispute because of its potential to affect their relative power with respect to Germany. The Cold War rivalry between the United States and the Soviet Union similarly imbued many local conflicts with global importance because of their perceived potential to change the balance of power between the two nations. And, as discussed in Chapter 2, today's tensions between the United States and China over the latter's claims in the South China Sea stem in part from the fact that control over that waterway would give China strategic advantages in any future conflict.

Bargaining and War

Conflicting interests are clearly necessary for wars to happen, but they are not sufficient to explain why wars actually do happen. To understand why some conflicts become wars and others do not, we have to think about the strategic interactions that states engage in when they seek to settle their disputes. In a well-functioning domestic political system, disputes over the kinds of issues that lead to war between states are often settled through institutional mechanisms. Property disputes can be resolved by courts backed by effective police powers. If one person engages in actions that harm another, the latter may turn to the legal system to solve the problem. Policy disagreements and conflicting ideas over who should govern can be settled by elections. As noted in Chapter 2, however, the international system lacks reliable legal, judicial, and electoral institutions. For this reason, states must generally try to settle conflicts with one another through bargaining.[14]

Bargaining describes interactions in which actors try to resolve disputes over the allocation of a good. They may bargain over the distribution of a disputed territory to determine whether there is a division acceptable to both sides. Or they may bargain over each other's policies so that objectionable ones might be modified or eliminated. Although we often think of bargaining as entailing compromise

---

14. Although some interstate disputes have been adjudicated through institutions like the International Court of Justice (ICJ), these institutions lack strong enforcement mechanisms to guarantee compliance with their rulings, and disputants often engage in bargaining after an ICJ ruling to determine whether and how its terms will be implemented. Hence, these rulings are a part of, rather than a substitute for, the bargaining process. See, for example, Colter Paulson, "Compliance with Final Judgments of the International Court of Justice since 1987," *American Journal of International Law* 98, no. 3 (2004): 434–61.

or give-and-take, the bargaining process does not always imply that differences will be split. Indeed, in many cases, states assume all-or-nothing bargaining positions. For example, when President George W. Bush demanded in October 2001 that the Afghan government hand over Al Qaeda leaders responsible for the 9/11 terrorist attacks, he declared that "these demands are not open to negotiation or discussion."[15]

A crisis occurs when at least one state invokes a threat of military force in an attempt to influence the outcome of bargaining. At this point, we enter the domain of **crisis bargaining**, a bargaining interaction in which the consequences of not reaching an agreement can involve the use of force, including war. In such interactions, at least one state sends the message "Satisfy my demands, or else"—where the "or else" involves imposing costs on the other side through military action. The use of threats in this manner is often referred to as **coercive diplomacy**.

In some cases, this message takes the form of an explicit ultimatum, such as President Bush's March 2003 pronouncement that Iraqi leader Saddam Hussein had 48 hours to leave the country or face an invasion. In other cases, the threat is conveyed implicitly through menacing actions such as military maneuvers or the mobilization of troops. For instance, Russia prefaced its August 2014 military incursion into Ukraine by massing troops on the border and running military exercises, but it did not issue an explicit ultimatum or set of demands (at least not publicly). Whether explicit or implicit, the purpose of such actions is clear: they seek to wrest concessions from the other side by making the alternative seem unacceptably costly.

The costs and likely outcome of a war determine which deals each side will consider acceptable in crisis bargaining. We can generally assume that the best possible outcome for a state in a crisis is to get the entire good without having to fight. If the other side gives in, the state gets its most preferred settlement of the underlying issue and avoids paying the costs associated with war. It is quite likely, though, that a state would also accept something less than its most preferred settlement, given that the alternative of fighting is costly.

For example, imagine a conflict over a piece of territory worth $100 million. Assume a state believes that in the event of a war, it is certain to win the territory; however, the costs of war, if put in monetary terms, would amount to $30 million. In that case, the expected value of going to war for that state is $100 million – $30 million = $70 million. Hence, the state should be willing to accept any deal that gives it at least $70 million worth of the territory. Since a state has the option to wage war if it determines that doing so is in its interests, the state will accept a bargain only if that bargain gives it at least as much as it can expect to get from war. And for any deal to prevent a war, it must satisfy all sides in this way: each state must decide that it prefers the deal over fighting a war. Hence, in our simple example, war can be averted only if the other state is willing to settle for the remaining $30 million worth of territory or less.

The discussion at the outset of this chapter implies a very simple proposition: Because war is costly, a settlement that all sides prefer over war generally exists.[16]

crisis bargaining

A bargaining interaction in which at least one actor threatens to use force in the event that its demands are not met.

coercive diplomacy

The use of threats to advance specific demands in a bargaining interaction.

---

15. Elisabeth Bumiller, "Bush Pledges Attack on Afghanistan Unless It Surrenders bin Laden Now," *New York Times*, September 21, 2001, A1.

16. See Fearon, "Rationalist Explanations for War."

The graphic on pp. 104–105 illustrates the logic behind this proposition. Assume that two states—call them State A and State B—have conflicting interests over the division of a particular good, represented by the green bar in each diagram on the left-hand page. To make this concrete, think of this good as a piece of territory, as in the example on the right-hand page. Any line dividing the bar, such as the dotted line labeled *Possible deal* in panel 1, represents a possible division of the good, such as a border drawn through the territory. State A receives the share of the good to the left of that line, and State B receives the share of the good to the right. Since both states prefer more of the good over less, State A wants to get a deal as far to the right as possible, and State B wants to get a deal as far to the left as possible. Put another way, State A's most preferred outcome, or ideal point, is at the far right of the bar, which would mean State A gets the entire good, and State B's ideal point is on the far left, which would mean State B gets the entire good. (Hence, this horizontal bar is identical to the diagonal line used to illustrate bargaining in Figure 2.3 on p. 57).

Now consider what happens if the two states go to war. Moving to panel 2, the line labeled *War outcome* indicates the actual, or expected, outcome of a violent conflict. In the case of a conflict over territory, we can think of this line as indicating how much territory each state would control after a war. The farther that line is to the right, the better State A is expected to fare in the event of war; the farther it is to the left, the better State B is expected to fare.

Crucially, fighting entails costs. These costs diminish the value of the expected war outcome to each state. As shown in panel 3, the value of war to each state is the share of the good it expects to win, minus the costs it expects to incur. Notice that the value of war to State A (which corresponds to the portion of the bar to the left of the dotted red line) is smaller than the share of the good that it expects to get from war (the portion of the bar to the left of the *War outcome* line). Indeed, as the figure is constructed, State A expects to win more of the good in a war than it would get from the possible deal in the first panel, but once the costs of war are taken into account, the possible deal is actually preferable to war.

To understand how the costs affect the value of war for each state, we have to think about those costs as they relate to the value of the good. Looking at the corresponding example on the right-hand page of the graphic, imagine that State A expects to win 70 percent of the territory, at the cost of 5,000 lives. State A's war value hinges on how much State A values those lost lives relative to the value of the territory. If State A thinks that losing those soldiers is equivalent to losing 30 percent of the entire territory, then its value for war is 70 – 30 = 40 percent of the value of the territory. State B would make a similar calculation. For both states, the costs of war would effectively increase if either the number of lives lost went up or the value attached to the territory went down.

As panel 4 shows, State A prefers over war any deal that gives it more than its value for war (deals that fall to the right of the dotted red line). Deals in this range give State A more than it expects to get through war, once the costs are taken into account. Similarly, State B prefers over war any deal that gives it more than its value for war (deals that fall to the left of the dotted blue line). Notice that the set of deals that State A prefers to war overlaps with the set of deals that State B prefers to war, creating a region called the **bargaining range**. Any division of the good in this bargaining range gives both states more than they expect to get from fighting a war. As this exercise demonstrates, the fact that war imposes costs on both sides means that such a range of deals always exists. Hence, in theory, there are bargains that both sides would prefer over war.

Although the preceding exercise treated the good in dispute as a piece of territory, this general framework and insight can be applied to any kind of issue over which states have conflicting interests. For example, consider the conflict between North Korea and the United States over the former's nuclear arsenal. In this case, the United States' ideal outcome, which we could put at one end of the bar, is for North Korea to disarm completely and become a democratic state. North Korea's ideal outcome, which would be located at the opposite end of the bar, is for the United States to accept North Korea's status as a nuclear power and recognize its existing regime.

In between are various compromise alternatives that neither considers ideal, including the current status quo, in which North Korea has a modest number of nuclear devices but the United States refuses to recognize its right to them. This point is close to North Korea's ideal point. Another point on the bar, closer to the United States' ideal point than to the status quo, would be for North Korea to dismantle some of its nuclear weapons and admit international inspectors. Though the substantive meaning of any location on the bar depends on the exact issue in dispute, the basic argument for the existence of a bargaining range holds across issues.

Clearly, this simple model does not accurately describe the complexity of real-world bargaining interactions. Nevertheless, it is useful because it forces us to think about all the ways in which bargaining could go wrong. Understanding why wars happen even though a peaceful bargain theoretically exists for virtually any conflict is the main purpose of this chapter.

Compellence and Deterrence: Varieties of Coercive Bargaining

The model is also useful for thinking about the conditions under which states might have an interest in initiating a crisis in the first place. The pre-crisis distribution, or status quo, can be represented as a line dividing the bar (see Figure 3.2). Where the status quo is located relative to the states' values for war determines which state, if any, might have an interest in changing the status quo through a threat of force. If a state is already getting from the status quo at least as much as it expects to get through war, then it generally cannot gain by threatening war to change the status quo. However, if a state expects to get more through war than it has in the status quo, then it has an interest in making a challenge.

bargaining range
The set of deals that both parties in a bargaining interaction prefer over the reversion outcome. When the reversion outcome is war, the bargaining range is the set of deals that both sides prefer over war.

The Model: Bargaining and War

1. A possible deal: Two states, A and B, have conflicting interests over a good (represented by the green bar). Both states want as much of the good as possible. The dotted line represents the distribution of the good based on *one* possible deal. Any deal determines A's and B's shares.

STATE B's IDEAL OUTCOME

STATE B's SHARE

A

B

STATE A's SHARE

POSSIBLE DEAL

STATE A's IDEAL OUTCOME

2. The expected outcome of war: As they bargain, each state evaluates how much it can expect to get as a result of war. The dotted line shows the expected outcome of war. Here, A would get more by going to war than by accepting the above deal.

B's SHARE AFTER WAR

A

B

A's SHARE AFTER WAR

WAR OUTCOME

3. Costs of war: However, war also involves costs, and these costs must be subtracted from what each state hopes to gain. So, although war would give A more of the good than it would get under the deal in panel 1, the costs incurred reduce the value of war to A.

COSTS TO B

VALUE OF WAR TO B

A

B

VALUE OF WAR TO A

COSTS TO A

WAR OUTCOME

4. The bargaining range: Each state prefers any deal that gives it more than its expected value of war, once costs are subtracted. Because war inflicts costs on both sides, there is a range of possible deals that both sides would prefer over war.

DEALS B PREFERS TO WAR

WAR OUTCOME

VALUE OF WAR TO B

A

BARGAINING RANGE

B

VALUE OF WAR TO A

DEALS A PREFERS TO WAR

An Example: Bargaining over Territory

POSSIBLE DEAL

1. A conflict over territory: Imagine two states have a conflict of interest over a piece of territory. State A would like to have the whole territory, as would State B. A deal is proposed to divide the territory at the dotted line.

WAR OUTCOME

2. The expected outcome of war: Based on the strength of their respective armies and other resources, a war over the territory is expected to result in State A winning the portion of the territory to the left of the dotted line.

WAR OUTCOME

COSTS OF WAR

3. Costs of war: Each side also considers the costs of war. Imagine that State A values the territory it would win as a result of war at $100 million but values the costs of war (both financial and human) at $30 million. These costs would reduce the value of war to A by 30 percent.

WAR OUTCOME

BARGAINING RANGE

4. The bargaining range: Each side should prefer any deal that gives it more territory than what it expects from war, once the costs of war are subtracted from the territory it wins. Any border drawn through the shaded range divides the territory into shares that both sides prefer over war.

The top panel of Figure 3.2 depicts such a situation: in the status quo, State A's share of the good is less than what A would expect to gain from war, even when the costs of war are taken into account. This does not mean that there will be a war, since, after all, a bargaining range still exists. But in this situation, the dissatisfied state can profit by threatening war in order to get a better deal. As the lower panel in Figure 3.2 shows, this logic divides the bar into three segments. If the status quo is to the left of the red dotted line indicating State A's value for war, then State A has an interest in threatening war to try to get a better outcome. Similarly, if the status quo is to the right of the blue dotted line indicating State B's value for war, then State B prefers war over the status quo and thus has an interest in sparking a crisis. Finally, if the status quo is in the bargaining range, then both prefer the current situation over war, and neither can expect to gain by waging war.

We often classify threats according to whether they are intended to preserve or change the existing relationship between states. An effort to change the status quo through the threat of force is called **compellence**. A compellent threat is intended to coerce the target state into making a concession or changing a current policy. Compellent threats take the form of "Give me y, or else" (where y is something that the threatener values) or "Stop doing x, or else" (where x is an objectionable policy). The United States' demand that Afghanistan hand over Osama bin Laden and stop harboring the Al Qaeda terrorist network after the 9/11 attacks is an example of compellence.

compellence

An effort to change the status quo through the threat of force.

deterrence

An effort to preserve the status quo through the threat of force.

A strategy of **deterrence**, by contrast, seeks to preserve the status quo by threatening the other side with unacceptable costs if it engages in some undesirable behavior. A deterrent threat takes the form of "Don't do x, or else" (where x is some possible future action that the threatener finds objectionable). The most common deterrent threat is one that all states make implicitly all the time: "Don't attack me, or I'll fight back." This effort to deter attacks on one's own country is referred to as *general deterrence*. Another form of deterrence occurs when a state seeks to protect a friend. In this case, the deterrent message takes the form of "Don't attack my ally x, or else." This kind of threat is generally referred to as *extended deterrence* because in this case the threatener attempts to extend protection to another state. Extended deterrence is crucial in the context of alliances, a subject that we will consider in Chapter 5.

In general, crises may involve a combination of deterrent and compellent threats. When one side tries to compel another, the target may issue deterrent threats, or some third state may issue a deterrent threat on the target's behalf. Crises often involve such threats and counterthreats, as each side tries to improve its bargaining position by bringing to bear its capability to

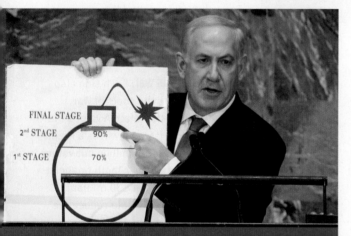

In a 2012 speech to the United Nations, Israeli prime minister Benjamin Netanyahu declared that Israel would not permit Iran to reach the final stage of acquiring a nuclear weapon. He argued that a credible threat of military action was needed to deter Iran from crossing that "red line." In 2020, the killing of top Iranian nuclear scientist Mohsen Fakhrizadeh was attributed to Israel as evidence of its continued determination to prevent Iran from developing nuclear warheads.

FIGURE 3.2 *Bargaining and the Status Quo*

Here, the status quo clearly gives State A less than war would (the value of war equals the war outcome minus costs).

State A has an incentive to challenge any status quo that gives it less than war would, because it could do better by going to war. The same holds for State B. If the status quo is within the bargaining range, however, neither State A nor State B could improve its outcome by going to war, so neither state will challenge the status quo.

harm the other. In many cases, threats alone will succeed in bringing about an outcome that both sides find acceptable. Indeed, the most effective threats never need to be carried out, since they coerce the target into making desired concessions or refraining from objectionable actions. If this contest of threats fails to generate an outcome that both sides prefer over fighting, we then observe the descent into war. This brings us back to the core puzzle: Given the costs associated with war, why does crisis bargaining sometimes fail to achieve a peaceful solution? The following sections elaborate several possible answers.

Do Wars Happen by Mistake? War from Incomplete Information

In July 1990, Iraq was engaged in coercive diplomacy with its small neighbor to the south, Kuwait. Two years earlier, Iraq had emerged from a disastrous eight-year war with Iran, and Iraqi leader Saddam Hussein desperately needed to rebuild his

MAP 3.2 *Oil Fields in Iran, Iraq, Kuwait, and Saudi Arabia*

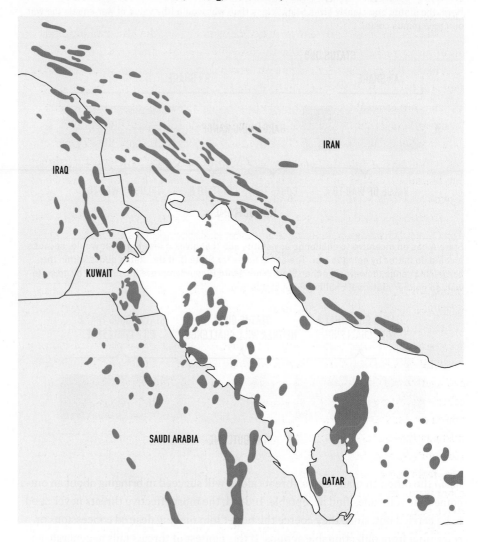

Source: A.S. Alsharhan, "Petroleum Systems in the Middle East," Geological Society, London, Special Publications, 392, 361–408, 1 January 2014, https://doi .org/10.1144/SP392.19.

country's shattered economy. Given that Iraq was sitting on oil deposits containing an estimated 112 billion barrels of oil, it was not hard to imagine where money for reconstruction would come from. But Hussein was not content simply to pump and sell Iraq's own oil, and he quickly turned his gun sights on Kuwait.

Kuwait's 95 billion barrels of recoverable oil reserves made a tempting target, and moreover, Hussein felt that his neighbor was standing in the way of his plans for economic recovery. For one thing, Kuwait was pumping more oil than it had previously agreed to. This extra supply meant that the price of oil was lower than it would otherwise be, depriving Iraq of needed revenue. Iraq also charged that Kuwait was stealing oil from oil fields that straddled the countries' shared border, as shown in Map 3.2. Finally, Kuwait had lent Iraq substantial sums of money during the war, and Saddam Hussein hoped to get this debt forgiven. When Kuwait refused demands to reduce its oil production, reimburse Iraq for the "stolen" oil, and forgive the debts, Iraq flexed its military muscle. Beginning in mid-July, Iraq started moving its forces closer to the border with Kuwait, at one point moving an entire division per day. By the end of the month, 100,000 Iraqi troops, supported by thousands of tanks, were in position near the border.

With the help of spy satellites, American officials watched the buildup, and they passed on their intelligence to the Kuwaitis. Despite their concern, most officials in the U.S. government did not anticipate that Iraq would invade, nor did the Kuwaitis bow to Hussein's demands. To many observers, the Iraqi moves looked like an effort to intimidate, not a prelude to invasion. According to reporter Bob Woodward's account, "Everything Saddam had to do to prepare for an invasion was exactly what he also had to do if his intention was simply to scare the Kuwaitis. There was no way to distinguish the two."[17] On August 2, with Kuwait still holding out, Hussein revealed that he had not simply been bluffing: Iraqi forces swept into Kuwait and fully occupied the country in a matter of hours.

In retrospect, it is clear that Iraq was willing and able to wage war against Kuwait if its demands were not met. At the time, however, key decision makers in Kuwait and Washington were not sure of Hussein's intentions. Would he really risk the wrath of the world by gobbling up his small neighbor? Would he be willing to put his military and his country through another war so soon after the previous one? The invasion of Kuwait happened in part because, unsure of the answers to these questions, the Kuwaitis decided that calling Hussein's bluff was preferable to giving in to his demands. When it became apparent that the threat was not, in fact, a bluff, war was already upon them.

This episode illustrates one reason that bargaining can fail to resolve disputes and avert war. When states have poor and incomplete information about each other's willingness and ability to wage war, two mistakes are possible, both of which can lead to armed conflict. First, a state confronted by demands may mistakenly yield too little or not at all—just as Kuwait failed to budge in the face of Hussein's threats. In these cases, bargaining can break down because at least one state feels that it can achieve more through fighting (in this case, Iraq) than the other is willing to offer in the negotiations (Kuwait). The second, related danger is that a state may demand too much (Iraq in this example) under the mistaken belief that the other side will cave in (Kuwait, and its protector, the United States). In this event, the state may not realize its mistake until war is already upon it. In either case, even though there might be a way to settle the issue that both sides would prefer to war, uncertainty about each other's willingness to wage war can prevent such a settlement from being reached.

Where does this uncertainty come from? Recall that the main issue in crisis bargaining is how each state evaluates its prospects in a war. How likely is it that the state will be able to win the war? What will the human, financial, and political costs be? These assessments are important because each state's value for war determines what bargains it prefers over fighting. If one state is uncertain of how much its adversary values war, then it is also uncertain of how much it must concede in order to prevent a war. This uncertainty will arise whenever a state lacks information about any of the myriad factors that determine its adversary's evaluation of war.

---

17. Bob Woodward, *The Commanders* (New York: Simon & Schuster, 1991), 200.

In September 2016, Russia initiated massive military drills off the coast of Crimea, showcasing the country's ships, cruise missiles, and antiaircraft system. The degree to which a country will mobilize its capabilities for war can be a source of uncertainty in bargaining.

A poker analogy is useful here. In poker, the fact that at least some cards are hidden from view means that players know more about the strength of their own hand than do their opponents. The hidden cards are what might be called private information: important facts that are known only to the player who observes those cards. Because no player sees all the cards, the game is played under a condition known as **incomplete information**. All players lack information about their opponents' hands and have private access to information about their own hands.

Incomplete information arises in crisis bargaining when states cannot readily observe or measure the key political and military factors that determine their adversaries' expected value for war. The hidden cards in this context can be many and varied, and we typically differentiate between two broad classes of unknowns: capabilities and resolve. *Capabilities* are factors that determine the state's physical ability to prevail in war: the number of troops it can mobilize, the number and quality of its armaments, the economic resources it has to sustain the war effort. We might also include in this list the quality of the country's military leadership and military strategies. In addition, since third parties sometimes join wars on one or both sides, any uncertainty about what those third parties will do can lead to uncertainty about the capabilities that each side will bring to bear in the event of war (see Chapter 5).

Resolve, a more abstract concept, refers to a state's willingness to bear the costs of fighting and how much the state values the object of dispute relative to those costs.[18] How many people is the country willing to lose in order to obtain, say, a given piece of territory? How much is it willing to pay in blood and money in order to win policy concessions or change another country's regime? Resolve

incomplete information

A situation in which actors in a strategic interaction lack information about other actors' interests and/or capabilities.

resolve

The willingness of an actor to endure costs in order to acquire a particular good.

---

18. Resolve is a widely used concept in international relations, but scholars often differ in their views of what it means and how it is determined. See, for example, Joshua D. Kertzer, *Resolve in International Politics* (Princeton, NJ: Princeton University Press, 2016).

determines not only whether a state is willing to fight but also the degree to which its potential capabilities would actually be mobilized in the event of war. We frequently make the distinction between *total wars* (in which states mobilize their entire military and economic resources) and *limited wars* (in which states fight with something less than their full potential, often because their aims are limited or of relatively low value).

How a state evaluates the stakes of conflict determines where on this continuum its effort will fall. The combatants in World War II saw the conflict as a war of national survival, and during the height of the war (1943–45) the United States spent about 37 percent of its gross domestic product (GDP) on defense. Other belligerents spent half of their GDP or more. By contrast, total U.S. defense spending in 2008, in the midst of wars in Iraq and Afghanistan, amounted to about 4 percent of GDP, and only a portion of that paid for those wars. Resolve is obviously a difficult quality to measure, as it hinges on a variety of political, ideological, and psychological factors. Indeed, it may be difficult for a leader to accurately assess his or her own country's resolve, much less the resolve of its adversary.

How could such uncertainty lead to war? When states have incomplete information about the capabilities and/or resolve of their opponents, bargaining over goods that they both desire may fail to achieve peaceful settlements. A central dynamic of bargaining under this kind of uncertainty is a phenomenon known as a **risk-return trade-off**: essentially, there is a trade-off between trying to get a good deal and trying to minimize the possibility that war will break out.

At one extreme, a state can generally ensure peace by capitulating to all of its adversary's demands. "Peace at any price" might not be a very attractive outcome, however. Kuwait, for example, could have given in to all of Iraq's demands and would likely have avoided war. At the other extreme, a state can hold firm and yield nothing to its adversary. This strategy promises a good deal if it works, but doing so runs a risk that the adversary will decide to fight rather than settle for nothing—as Iraq did when Kuwait refused to give in. Between these extremes, a state will generally find that it can reduce the risk of war only by making more generous offers, moving away from its ideal outcome. Put another way, a state can improve the bargaining outcome for itself only by embracing a higher risk of war. Although war is costly and regrettable in retrospect, bargaining strategies that entail a risk of war can be perfectly rational, given the uncertainty that states face.

Incentives to Misrepresent and the Problem of Credibility

Given that incomplete information can lead to war, why can't states simply tell each other how capable and resolved they are and thereby avoid conflict? Actually, a large part of what goes on in a crisis consists precisely of such efforts at communication. Crises are generally characterized by diplomatic exchanges, threats and counterthreats, mobilization of forces, movement of troops, and positioning of weaponry. These actions, in part, have a military purpose: one cannot wage war, after all, without first mobilizing the necessary forces and putting them in place.

risk-return trade-off
In crisis bargaining, the trade-off between trying to get a better deal and trying to avoid a war.

But these actions also have a political purpose: they are the language of coercive diplomacy, the vocabulary that states use to convince one another that they are willing to back their bargaining positions with the threat of force.

The problem that arises in this context is that, as much as states may have an interest in communicating their hidden information, they may not always be able to do so effectively. A crucial question that arises in crisis bargaining is whether the messages a state sends have **credibility**. A credible threat is a threat that the target believes will be carried out, and a threat lacks credibility if its target has reason to doubt that it will be executed. The credibility of a threat refers not only to the belief that the threatener will start a war; the target must also believe that the threatener is willing to fight long enough and hard enough that giving in to its demands is a better option than a costly war. In the case of the U.S. war against Afghanistan, the Taliban government probably had little doubt that President Bush would implement his threat to invade, but it may have doubted that the United States would be willing and able to bear the costs of a long war. In other words, the threat to start a war was credible, but the threat to remove Taliban leaders from power was, in their eyes, not.

Note that the credibility of a threat refers to the target's beliefs, not the actual intentions of the state issuing the threat. A state may fully intend to follow through on a threat, but it may have a hard time convincing its adversaries that it will in fact do so. Saddam Hussein genuinely intended to invade Kuwait if his demands were not met; observers in the United States and Kuwait, however, did not see the threat conveyed by his mobilization as credible. Similarly, a state may have no intention of carrying out its threat, but the target may mistakenly believe otherwise. In such cases, the bluff can succeed.

Why is credibility hard to achieve? There are two interrelated reasons. First, following through on threats is costly. A state may say that it will wage war if its demands are not met, but the costs of war might be so high that it would not make sense for the state to fulfill this threat if it were called on to do so. This concern about credibility was particularly pronounced during the Cold War between the United States and the Soviet Union. With both sides in possession of large arsenals of nuclear weapons, it was well understood that war could quickly escalate into total annihilation. Given this situation, officials in the United States worried about how they could deter the Soviet Union from attacking Western Europe. Would the United States really risk New York to save London or Paris? If the Soviets believed the answer to this question was no, then the United States' commitment to defend Western Europe would lack credibility. It was precisely these kinds of concerns that led Great Britain and France to develop their own nuclear capabilities in order to deter the Soviets; after all, it was much more credible that France would risk Paris to save Paris.

Even without the prospect of nuclear annihilation, threats may lack credibility because their targets appreciate the costs of carrying them out. In the midst of the crisis between Iraq and Kuwait in 1990, the United States announced joint naval exercises with the United Arab Emirates. On the same day, a spokesperson for the State Department issued an extended deterrent threat by reaffirming the United

credibility

Believability. A credible threat is a threat that the target believes will be carried out. A credible commitment is a commitment or promise that the recipient believes will be honored.

States' commitment to protecting its friends in the Persian Gulf. Iraq's response was contemptuous. Hussein called the U.S. ambassador to his office the next day and told her that he was not scared by American threats. After all, he reportedly said, "Yours is a society which cannot accept 10,000 dead in one battle."[19] Thus, the United States' deterrent threat had little credibility in Hussein's eyes because he believed that the United States would be unwilling to bear the costs of war.

The second reason that credibility is hard to achieve stems from the conflicting interests at the heart of the bargaining interaction. Even though states have a common interest in avoiding war, each also wants the best possible deal for itself; states thus have incentives to hide or misrepresent their information.

In some cases, this incentive means that states will conceal information about their true strength. After Iraq invaded Kuwait, the United States massed a large force in Saudi Arabia and threatened war unless Iraq retreated. It was widely assumed that if war came, U.S. forces would attack Iraqi positions in Kuwait head-on. Such a strategy would have provided the most direct route to the objective, but there were clear costs involved: the Iraqi forces in Kuwait were dug in behind strong defenses, including trenches filled with oil that could be lit on fire as soon as U.S. troops tried to cross. Saddam Hussein's resistance to U.S. pressure stemmed in part from his belief that his defenses would make the liberation of Kuwait very costly.

In fact, war planners in the United States decided early on that they would not attack directly at the strength of the Iraqi positions. Instead, they secretly shifted the bulk of the U.S. force into the desert west of the Kuwaiti border. The military plan called for a "left hook": U.S. tanks would enter Iraq on the western flank of Iraqi forces in Kuwait and then swoop around behind them, thereby outflanking the enemy's fortifications. This tactical decision meant that the United States expected to incur lower casualties than Iraq expected it would be able to inflict.[20]

Theoretically, if the United States could have communicated these expectations to Iraq, its threat would have been more credible and perhaps Hussein would have decided to back down. But it is easy to see why the United States could not say to Hussein: "You think that war will be too costly for us, but you are mistaken. Rather than attack your forces head-on, we will go around them on the western flank." Had the United States sent such a message, Iraq could have taken measures to counter the tactic, such as by repositioning its forces to the west. Hence, any bargaining advantage that the United States might have reaped by revealing its strength would have been nullified. In the strategic context of the crisis, it made sense for the United States to hide its strongest cards.

In other cases, states misrepresent in order to hide their weakest cards. Anyone who has played poker knows that it sometimes makes sense to bluff—that is, to act as if one has a strong hand in the hopes that others will fold. A similar incentive

---

19. A transcript of this meeting was published in the *New York Times* on September 22, 1990. Hussein may also have been encouraged to ignore U.S. threats because American ambassador April Glaspie seemed to indicate that the United States had no strong interest in the outcome of the Iraq-Kuwait dispute.

20. For a discussion of Persian Gulf War strategy, see Lawrence Freedman and Efraim Karsh, "How Kuwait Was Won: Strategy in the Gulf War," *International Security* 16, no. 2 (Autumn 1991): 5–41.

exists in international crises. In this context, a bluff is a threat to use force that the sender does not intend to carry out. In a crisis, a successful bluff could reap large rewards. In 1936, Germany marched its military forces into a region on its border with France known as the Rhineland—a region that, according to the 1919 treaty that ended World War I, Germany was required to keep demilitarized. Hitler sent his forces in anyway, daring the Western powers to stop him. Though alarmed by this move, both France and Great Britain chose not to risk a full-scale war over the issue, and Germany was thus able to remilitarize the Rhineland unopposed. Interestingly, there is good reason to believe that Hitler's move was a bluff. Although this point is somewhat controversial, some evidence suggests that German troops were under orders to retreat if confronted.[21] If so, then one of the key moments in the lead-up to World War II was a well-executed bluff.

This observation raises a dilemma: How can states credibly convey their information in order to diminish the risk of war due to uncertainty? Given a strategic environment that sometimes rewards misrepresentation, how can a genuine threat be made believable?

Communicating Resolve: The Language of Coercion

To help us answer these questions, another example will be helpful. On June 25, 1950, without any warning, North Korea invaded South Korea. The Korean peninsula had been split in two after World War II, divided at the 38th parallel between the communist North and the non-communist and pro-Western South. North Korea's attack was a bold attempt to reunify the country under communist rule, and the United States quickly joined the South in repelling the attack. After three months, the United States' efforts were largely successful, and North Korean forces began to retreat to their side of the 38th parallel. At this point, the United States decided to press the attack, cross into North Korea, and topple the communist regime there.

This possibility raised grave concerns in neighboring China, which had only the previous year been taken over by a communist government. On October 3, 1950, Chinese diplomats conveyed a message through the Indian ambassador that a move across the 38th parallel would trigger Chinese intervention.[22] Nonetheless, the threat went unheeded. The U.S. operation had been planned and authorized under the assumption that the Chinese would not intervene, and the October 3 warning did nothing to change any minds.[23] U.S. forces crossed into North Korea on October 7 and advanced rapidly. In response, 600,000 Chinese troops poured into the Korean peninsula, leading to three more years of fighting and a costly stalemate.

---

21. James Thomas Emmerson, *The Rhineland Crisis, 7 March 1936: A Study in Multilateral Diplomacy* (Ames: Iowa State University Press, 1977), 98–100.

22. The United States did not recognize the People's Republic of China as a legitimate government, so the two countries did not have direct diplomatic contacts.

23. See, for example, William Stueck, *Rethinking the Korean War: A New Diplomatic and Strategic History* (Princeton, NJ: Princeton University Press, 2002), chap. 4.

Why was China's threat dismissed, in the words of Secretary of State Dean Acheson, as "a Chinese Communist bluff"? An October 4 memorandum describes Acheson's rationale:

> The Secretary pointed out that the Chinese Communists were themselves taking no risk in as much as their private talks to the Indian Ambassador could be disavowed. . . . if they wanted to take part in the "poker game" they would have to put more on the table than they had up to the present.[24]

Acheson's reasoning for downplaying China's threat is instructive. The Chinese government was making an extended deterrent threat: "Don't invade North Korea, or we will intervene to defend it." From the U.S. perspective, it was possible that China would actually make good on this threat, but it was also possible that China was simply trying to bluff the United States into staying out of North Korea. Regardless of which possibility was true, the message conveyed through the Indian ambassador was cheap and easy to send. There was nothing in the message or the way it was sent that would give American decision makers reason to think that China was not simply bluffing. Unless the Chinese were willing to pay some costs—"to put more on the table"—there was little reason to take their threat seriously.

This example suggests a more general insight: For threats to be credible, they must be costly in such a way that the sender would make the threat only if it really intended to carry the threat out. Consider the problem that the United States faced in October 1950 in these, admittedly oversimplified, terms:

> *It is possible that the Chinese government is resolved to intervene if we attack North Korea, and it is possible that it is not so resolved. How can we know if we are facing a "resolute" China or an "irresolute" China? What would we look for to distinguish these two "types" of adversaries? The answer is this: We would want to look for actions that a resolute China be willing to take but an irresolute China would be unwilling (or, at least, less likely) to take. If we see such actions, then we are more likely to be facing a resolute China, and we have to take its threat seriously. If we do not see such actions, then there may be reason to doubt China's resolve.*

The message that the Chinese actually sent did not have much credibility because an irresolute China could just as easily have made the same claim.

What kinds of actions can help an opponent distinguish whether its adversary is resolved? In general, the literature has identified three mechanisms that states use to make their threats credible: brinksmanship, tying hands, and paying for power.

Brinksmanship: The "Slippery Slope" Some of the earliest scholarship on the question of how to make threats credible took place in the 1950s, when policy makers and academics were preoccupied by the credibility of threats in the nuclear age. If

---

24. U.S. Department of State, *Foreign Relations of the United States, 1950*, vol. 7, *Korea* (Washington, DC: U.S. Government Printing Office, 1976), 868–69.

everyone understood that nuclear war would bring total annihilation to each side, then under what conditions could threats between nuclear powers ever be credible? Since no state would ever intentionally "pull the trigger" and bring about Armageddon, the threat to do so was not credible. This observation raised the question of whether nuclear weapons had any utility at all in the emerging Cold War between the United States and the Soviet Union.

The most important insight into this issue came from Thomas Schelling, an early theorist of the strategy of crisis bargaining. In Schelling's view, although it was understood that no state would intentionally bring about its own destruction by starting a total nuclear war, these weapons could nonetheless be wielded for diplomatic effect through a strategy known as **brinksmanship**. The basic idea was that states could signal their resolve in the crisis by approaching the "brink" of war through provocative actions. Schelling describes this concept:

> The brink is not, in this view, the sharp edge of a cliff where one can stand firmly, look down, and decide whether or not to plunge. The brink is a curved slope that one can stand on with some risk of slipping, the slope gets steeper and the risk of slipping greater as one moves toward the chasm.[25]

The costs of war are such that, if faced with a simple choice of whether to jump or not, no sane decision maker would jump. But rational leaders might decide to step out onto the "slippery slope" and thereby increase the risk that war would start inadvertently. Schelling famously referred to such an act as a "threat that leaves something to chance."[26] The willingness to take such a chance separates resolute from irresolute adversaries. After all, the less a state values the good in dispute, and the more it fears a war over that issue, the less willing it will be to step onto the slope and embrace a risk of war.

In a brinksmanship crisis, each side bids up the risk of war—moving further and further down the slippery slope—until either one side decides to give in or both sides fall together into the precipice (as in the game of Chicken discussed in the "Special Topic" appendix to Chapter 2, on pp. 86–91). Exactly how a war might start "inadvertently" is not always clear; fortunately, in the case of nuclear war, we do not know the answer to that question. Absent a computer glitch, it still takes a human hand to pull the trigger.

Schelling's general idea was that as tensions rose in an international crisis, the risk of accidents would increase. A limited skirmish between forces could inadvertently escalate if a nervous local commander thought his position was about to be overrun and decided to launch his tactical nuclear weapons in order not to lose them to the enemy. Or, in the midst of a tense crisis, a flock of geese might be mistaken on the radar for incoming bombers (as actually happened in the 1950s), leading to a decision to launch rather than risk being disarmed by a first strike (which, fortunately, did not happen in this incident). Alternatively, the tension of

brinksmanship

A strategy in which adversaries take actions that increase the risk of accidental war, with the hope that the other will "blink" (lose its nerve) first and make concessions.

---

25. Thomas C. Schelling, *The Strategy of Conflict* (Cambridge, MA: Harvard University Press, 1960), 199.
26. Schelling, *Strategy of Conflict*, 187.

Leaders may use brinksmanship to make the threat of nuclear war credible. In the 1962 Cuban missile crisis, U.S. president John F. Kennedy took steps toward nuclear war—for example, putting missile crews on alert—in order to pressure the Soviets to dismantle nuclear missile sites in Cuba.

a nerve-wracking crisis might cause leaders to give in to passion and fury and lose their cool, rational heads. In any event, it was precisely the willingness to court this risk that would credibly separate the genuinely resolved opponents from the bluffers.

Tying Hands   A second way in which states can send credible signals of their willingness to fight is by making threats in ways that would make backing down difficult. For example, after Iraq invaded Kuwait in August 1990, President Bush repeatedly and publicly stated that the conquest would "not stand." He made this commitment first on August 5, 1990, and reiterated it throughout the crisis, including during his State of the Union address on January 29, 1991. The United States matched Bush's words with deeds, particularly the deployment of over 500,000 U.S. troops to the region and an extensive diplomatic effort to build international consensus for an attack. Unlike the case with China's threat to fight in support of North Korea, which Acheson felt could be disavowed, Bush was clearly on record as asserting that the policy of his administration was to reverse the Iraqi invasion.

By taking such clear, public statements and actions, Bush put his reputation, and that of the country, on the line. It was not unreasonable to expect that in doing so, he had made it quite costly to retreat from this position—to decide, in the face of Iraqi resistance, that the invasion would be allowed to stand after all. Doing so would have been embarrassing for him as a leader and for the country as a whole. It would have called into question the credibility of future U.S. threats, and Bush could expect his political opponents to use such a retreat against him in the next election.

The general insight here is that under some conditions, threats can generate what are known as **audience costs**—that is, negative repercussions that arise if a

audience costs
Negative repercussions for failing to follow through on a threat or to honor a commitment.

leader does not follow through on a threat.[27] Two audiences might impose these costs. The first is the international audience—other states that might doubt future threats made by the leader or by the country. Once a country fails to fulfill a threat, the international audience costs might impede that country's ability to convince future adversaries of its resolve. For example, one of the reasons that U.S. decision makers were skeptical of China's threat to intervene in the Korean War was that it came in the wake of a series of unfulfilled threats over a different issue: Taiwan. As early as March 1949, the Chinese communist government began issuing threats to "liberate" Taiwan from the Nationalist Chinese forces that had fled there. These threats, repeated several times over the course of the next year and a half, combined with China's failure to carry them out, led some analysts in the United States to discount the threats over Korea as similarly empty bluster.[28] International audience costs might also arise if allies come to doubt the trustworthiness of the country's threats, which may lead them to seek other protectors (see Chapter 5).

A second audience that might punish a leader for backing down from a threat is in the leader's own country: voters and political opponents who might seek to reprimand a leader who has tarnished the country's honor and reputation by making empty threats. For example, in 2012 U.S. president Barack Obama declared that any use of chemical weapons by the Syrian regime against its people would cross a "red line" and compel a forceful response. His decision the following year not to strike Syria after it deployed the banned weapons was widely criticized by domestic opponents and used to foster the perception that Obama was weak on foreign policy.

If threats expose state leaders to audience costs, whether international or domestic, they can have the effect of "tying their hands." This phrase comes from a famous scene in Homer's *Odyssey* in which the main character, Odysseus, asks to have his hands tied to the mast of his ship as it sails past the sirens. The call of the sirens was so beautiful that sailors who heard it were bewitched into steering their ship into the rocks. By tying his hands to the mast, Odysseus hoped to experience the sirens' call without succumbing to this enchantment. State leaders in a crisis tie their hands for similar reasons: because threats are costly to carry out, they know that they might choose not to follow through if faced with that decision. By exposing themselves to audience costs, they blunt the temptation to back down from their threats and thereby tie their own hands.

In the process of tying their hands, of course, state leaders also send a powerful message to their opponents: "I cannot back down; hence, my threat is completely credible." As with acts of brinksmanship, engaging in actions that incur audience costs separates the resolute from the irresolute. Those most likely to back down from a threat are less willing to take steps that will make backing down costly.

---

27. James D. Fearon, "Domestic Political Audiences and the Escalation of International Disputes," *American Political Science Review* 88, no. 3 (September 1994): 577–92. For recent arguments that audience costs do not play a major role in crises, see Marc Trachtenberg, "Audience Costs: An Historical Analysis," *Security Studies* 21, no. 1 (2012): 3–42; and Jack Snyder and Erica D. Borghard, "The Cost of Empty Threats: A Penny, Not a Pound," *American Political Science Review* 105, no. 3 (August 2011): 437–56.

28. Anne Sartori, *Deterrence by Diplomacy* (Princeton, NJ: Princeton University Press, 2005), 33–39.

Paying for Power   A final mechanism that states use to signal their resolve in a crisis involves taking costly steps to increase their capabilities, such as by mobilizing and deploying a large military force, increasing military manpower, and/or spending large sums of money. For example, during a 1961 crisis between the United States and the Soviet Union over Berlin, President Kennedy asked Congress to increase the army's strength by 350,000 troops, with much of the growth coming from an increase in the number of people drafted and a call-up of reserve forces. This last step was particularly costly, in a political sense, because reservists are people who have finished their military service and have families and regular jobs. As a result, calling up 150,000 reservists led to political resistance. There was also a concrete monetary cost to these actions.

As already noted, military mobilizations play an important role in crises because they give states the material capabilities needed to back up their threats. Even the most credible threat is not going to be effective unless the threatened action promises to be very costly to the adversary. Thus, one purpose of military mobilization is to put force behind diplomatic maneuvers. At the same time, costly actions of this sort can affect the opponent's estimate of the state's resolve through several mechanisms.[29] First, increasing the state's military capabilities may decrease the costs associated with carrying out a threat. Since these costs are what call credibility into question in the first place, visible steps taken to reduce them can make it more believable that the threatener will do what it says. Second, the threatening state's willingness to pay the costs associated with these actions can signal that it cares a great deal about the issue in question. By calling up the reserves, Kennedy was trying to send the message that he cared so much about the fate of Berlin that he was willing to pay the political costs associated with this action.

We started this section by noting that a condition of incomplete information is dangerous because states might miscalculate in bargaining, such as by mistakenly resisting threats that turn out to be genuine. Such mistakes played a role in the Iraqi invasion of Kuwait in 1990 and in the onset of war between the United States and China in 1950. Brinksmanship, tying hands, and paying for power are strategies for communicating a willingness to fight; they are mechanisms that help states figure out which threats are genuine and which are not. Interestingly, though, these cures for incomplete information entail risks that can be just as dangerous as the underlying problem they address.

This danger is clearest in the case of brinksmanship strategies, through which states bid up the risk of accidental war in order to prove their resolve. The hope in doing so is that the adversary will blink, and thus war will be averted. But there is no guarantee that the states will not lose control and fall into the precipice. Ironically, then, to avoid a war driven by uncertainty, states have to embrace some risk of accidental war. Hand-tying strategies can have similar risks. Although actions that raise the costs of backing down can convince the other side to give in, there is also a risk that both sides will tie their hands in a contest of threats and counterthreats.

---

29. Branislav L. Slantchev, *Military Threats: The Costs of Coercion and the Price of Peace* (Cambridge: Cambridge University Press, 2011).

Both sides can then become locked into intransigent and incompatible bargaining positions from which it is too costly to retreat. Once each side has eliminated its ability to compromise, war may be inevitable—even if the initial uncertainty that led to the crisis has been removed. Finally, while military mobilizations might persuade an adversary to yield, they can also provoke the other side to strike first—a possibility that we will revisit shortly.

In the case of the Persian Gulf War, it is quite possible that President Bush's hand-tying actions between August 1990 and January 1991 eventually convinced Saddam Hussein that the United States was willing to fight, in spite of his original belief to the contrary. He may have resisted nonetheless because his own pattern of defiance and counterthreats in those months had tied his own hands as well. Hussein may have feared domestic repercussions for a retreat in the face of American threats, or he may have been concerned that such a retreat would embolden Iraq's neighbor and long-standing enemy, Iran. By January 15, 1991, neither side was willing to compromise, and the U.S.-led war to liberate Kuwait began. We thus see that incomplete information can cause war both directly, through miscalculation, and indirectly, by forcing states to communicate their resolve in ways that can foreclose successful bargaining.

This discussion generates several predictions about the conditions that make war more or less likely. In general, the harder it is for states to learn about each other's capabilities and resolve, the more severe the problem of incomplete information will be. When states are relatively opaque, in the sense that it is hard for outsiders to observe their military capabilities or their political decision-making processes, it is more likely that uncertainties of this kind will arise and bedevil the quest for negotiated settlements. The strategic situation might also influence the degree of uncertainty that states face. For example, as the number of states that might potentially get involved in a particular crisis increases, the number and importance of the "hidden cards" grows dramatically: in the event of a war, who will join and who will not? Finally, this discussion sensitizes us to the question of whether states can find ways to signal their intentions in a credible manner. Problems of incomplete information are more likely to be overcome when states can find costly ways to signal their intentions and thereby convince their adversaries to make concessions.

Can an Adversary Be Trusted to Honor a Deal? War from Commitment Problems

Incomplete information provides one compelling answer to the puzzle of war: uncertainty about capabilities or resolve can make it difficult for states to agree on a settlement that all sides prefer over war. The ability to identify such a settlement, however, does not always guarantee that war will be avoided. What happens if the states do not trust one another to abide by that settlement in the future?

In this section we develop a second set of explanations for why bargaining may fail. The causes of war considered here all arise from a common underlying challenge: the difficulty that states can have making credible promises *not* to use force to revise a settlement at a later date. In this context, credibility has the same meaning as before, but we use it here to describe a pledge to avoid force rather than a threat to use it. In order for states to successfully reach an agreement that avoids armed conflict, they must assure each other that they will not later use force to revise the terms of the deal. A commitment problem arises when a state cannot make such a promise in a credible manner.

The Prisoner's Dilemma introduced in Chapter 2 is a quintessential example of such a problem. Although the prisoners in this game would like to commit to cooperating with each other, their incentives are such that a commitment to do so is not credible: when given the choice, they will prefer to defect. Commitment problems are particularly common in the absence of any enforcement mechanism, such as a court, that can hold people to their commitments. In the international system, external enforcement of commitments can be difficult to arrange (though not impossible, as we will see in the concluding section of this chapter). Next we consider three ways in which an inability to make credible commitments to a bargain might undermine the search for a peaceful settlement of international disputes.[30]

Bargaining over Goods That Are a Source of Future Bargaining Power

Commitment problems are clearest in disputes over goods that can serve as a source of future bargaining power. The best examples of such goods are strategically important pieces of territory and weapons programs. States bargain over territory all the time, but in some cases the territory in question has military significance, perhaps because it contains high ground from which one could launch an effective attack or islands that sit astride strategically important sea routes. For example, China and Japan have in recent years been locked in dispute over eight uninhabited islands in the East China Sea, known as the Senkaku to Japan and the Diaoyu to China. Not only are the surrounding waters rich in fish and in oil and gas deposits, but the islands are also close to strategically important sea routes that are vital for naval movements in the region. As a result, control over the islands potentially affects the countries' relative military power.

Bargaining over weapons programs has a similar quality. In recent years, the United States has sought to pressure several states—including Iraq (prior to 2003), Libya, Iran, and North Korea—into abandoning the development of weapons of mass destruction. These efforts have met with varying levels of success. Libya agreed to dismantle its weapons programs in December 2003. North Korea agreed several times to freeze its nuclear program, but these deals unraveled, and North Korea effectively entered the nuclear club in 2006. In 2015, the United States and its partners reached a deal with Iran to freeze its nuclear program, but President

---

30. The ideas are introduced in Fearon, "Rationalist Explanations for War," and are further elaborated in Robert Powell, "War as a Commitment Problem," *International Organization* 60, no. 1 (Winter 2006): 169–203.

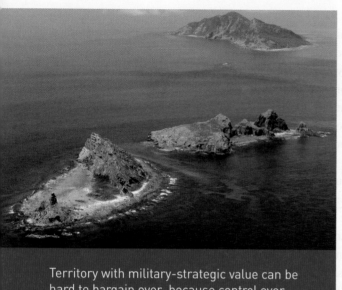

Territory with military-strategic value can be hard to bargain over, because control over the good affects the relative military power of the states involved in the negotiations. The uninhabited Senkaku/Diaoyu Islands have been a source of conflict between Japan and China partly because they sit astride strategically important sea routes.

Donald Trump pulled out of that agreement in 2018 and sought to pressure Iran into making further concessions. As with strategically important territory, a deal on this matter does not simply resolve a dispute; it also directly affects the military capabilities of the participants. A country that agrees to give up a weapons program makes itself weaker by doing so.

The difficulty in bargaining over such objects is that a state will be reluctant to render itself more vulnerable to attack without credible promises that the other side will not exploit that vulnerability in the future. The state may be able to avoid war now by making concessions, but doing so entails a risk that its adversary, made stronger by the deal, will then press new claims. Unless there is some way for the other side to credibly commit *not* to use its newfound power, a threatened state may decide that it would rather fight today than face a future in which it is considerably weaker. Thus, even if there is some deal that is preferable to war now, if this deal will lead to a change in capabilities that can be exploited later, the state that would be rendered weaker may decide to forgo that deal and gamble on a war.

This strategic dilemma has presented an important obstacle to the United States' efforts to convince countries like North Korea and Iran to give up their nuclear programs peacefully. It is important to remember that the United States had hostile relations with these countries before they sought to acquire nuclear weapons. As we already saw, the United States fought a war against North Korea from 1950 to 1953. That war ended with a cease-fire but not a peace treaty, and ever since, around 30,000 U.S. troops have been stationed in South Korea. U.S. hostility toward the North is driven not only by the lingering issue of Korea's division but also by the nature of its regime, which is one of the most repressive systems in the world. Similarly, hostility between the United States and Iran dates back to the 1979 revolution, which toppled Iran's pro-American leader and installed an Islamic fundamentalist government. (See "Controversy" on pp. 124–125 for an extended discussion of negotiations between the United States and Iran over the latter's nuclear program.)

To the extent that these states see their nuclear programs as a counterweight against American (and, in the case of Iran, also Israeli) power, they would be reluctant to give up those programs if, by doing so, they rendered themselves more vulnerable to U.S. demands on other issues. The experience of Libya is instructive in this respect. As noted earlier, Libya agreed in December 2003 to end its chemical and nuclear weapons programs and to submit to international inspections. In return, the United States and Britain promised to normalize relations with the country and not to press for fundamental changes in the regime of Libyan leader

Mu'ammar Qaddafi—even though he ran a brutal dictatorship. In March 2011, however, Qaddafi faced a rebellion against his rule, and his attacks on civilians triggered military action by the United States, Britain, and other European countries. Qaddafi was ousted and then killed by rebel forces seven months later.

Whether or not Libya would have deterred this intervention had it continued its weapons programs, the lesson was clear: a promise by the United States to forswear regime change is not necessarily a credible or lasting guarantee. The success of any effort to end these programs peacefully requires the United States to find a way to commit credibly not to exploit the power shift brought about by disarmament.

When the United States and its allies intervened in March 2011 to support the rebellion against Libyan leader Mu'ammar Qaddafi, his military forces were targeted by NATO planes, and Qaddafi was captured and killed. Leaders who agree to give up weapons programs, as Qaddafi had done in 2003, make themselves more vulnerable to subsequent pressure.

Prevention: War in Response to Changing Power

A second, related problem arises if the balance of military capabilities is anticipated to change because of factors external to the bargaining process. A common source of this kind of power shift is different rates of economic growth. As noted in Chapter 1, uneven economic development has led to the relative rise and decline of states over time. The growth of Germany's power in the late nineteenth and early twentieth centuries had a dramatic impact on that country's ability to challenge its neighbors. Similarly, as we saw in Chapter 2, China's impressive economic growth since 1980 has increased its influence in international politics and led to growing competition with the United States. If a state is growing much more rapidly than its adversary, then the military capabilities that it can bring to bear in future disputes will be greater than those it can bring to bear today. A second important source of large shifts in military capabilities is the development and acquisition of new technologies, such as nuclear weapons. The acquisition of nuclear weapons can cause an abrupt and profound shift in a state's capacity to impose costs on its adversaries.

Regardless of their exact source, anticipated changes in military capabilities can present an insurmountable dilemma in crisis bargaining. To see this, we revisit the bargaining model introduced earlier. Figure 3.3 illustrates what happens to the bargaining interaction when the power of one state, in this case State A, is expected to increase. In the top panel, the expected outcome of the war is initially close to State B's ideal point (or the far left of the bar, where State B would get all of the good). Let's assume, however, that State A's power is expected to grow so that, at some time in the future, the new war outcome will be closer to State A's ideal point (or the far right of the bar), as in the lower panel.

In the initial period, the states can agree to some distribution inside the bargaining range. But both sides can anticipate that, in the future, State A will no longer be satisfied with this deal and will demand a new deal in the new bargaining range.

Should the United States Make a Nuclear Deal with Iran?

The United States and Iran have been in conflict since 1979, when a pro-American government in Tehran was overthrown by an Islamic revolutionary movement deeply hostile to the United States, the West, and Israel. In addition to taking U.S. embassy workers hostage and holding them for 444 days, the new Iranian regime set its foreign policy on a collision course with the United States. It has sponsored terrorist attacks in the region, supplied arms and training to militant groups, including those fighting U.S. forces in Iraq (2003-present); and threatened U.S. allies, such as Israel and Saudi Arabia. Iran has also, since the 1990s, been working to create enriched uranium and weapons grade plutonium: the fuel that powers nuclear weapons. This quest, and efforts to roll back Iran's program, have been a key source of conflict in the region and a lightning rod for debate within the West and in American domestic politics.

Although Iran denies that it wants to build nuclear weapons, its nuclear activities have alarmed the United States and much of the international community since they came to light in 2002. At the urging of the United States, the United Nations and European Union imposed strict economic sanctions on Iran, including restricting its ability to export oil. These sanctions were bolstered by threats of military action, with both the United States and Israel indicating that they would use force to prevent Iran from getting the bomb, if necessary. In 2015, this pressure led to the signing of the Joint Comprehensive Plan of Action (JCPOA), an agreement whereby Iran would roll back and freeze its nuclear program in exchange for the relaxation of sanctions. In 2018, however, U.S. president Donald Trump withdrew from the deal and reimposed sanctions in order to negotiate terms more favorable to the United States. But Trump failed to secure a better deal before leaving office, and at the time of this writing in spring 2021, President Joseph Biden was seeking to rejoin the agreement despite criticism from Republicans.

Although bargaining provides a way for states to settle disputes and avoid the costs of war, the question of whether to negotiate with Iran over its nuclear ambitions has been

Applying the Concepts

fraught with controversy. While there is widespread agreement that an Iranian nuclear weapon would threaten the security of U.S. allies in the region and beyond, disagreements revolve around whether the United States has the ability to shape the bargaining **interaction** in a way that will get Iran to make concessions or whether the U.S. policy should instead seek to change Iran's domestic **institutions** in order to empower actors with different **interests**, thereby fundamentally changing that country's foreign policy.

Trump withdrew from the JCPOA not because Iran was cheating on the deal—in fact, the administration conceded that Iran was complying with its terms—but because he believed those terms did not go far enough. Core criticisms of the JCPOA were that (1) some of the restrictions expired after 10 or 15 years, potentially allowing Iran to restart its program; (2) the deal did not cover other Iranian activities, including its support for militant groups and development of ballistic missiles; and (3) the relaxation of sanctions would give the regime renewed resources to finance those activities and hold on to power. Thus, the United States' withdrawal from the JCPOA was accompanied by an expansive list of demands that touched

Hostilities between Iran and the United States date back to 1979, when an Islamic revolution in Iran brought to power a hostile regime.

not only Iran's nuclear activities but also its broader foreign policy behavior.[a]

Of course, a deal in which your adversary gives you everything you want is always better than a deal in which you have to compromise. The key stumbling block is whether your adversary is willing to concede that much. In a bargaining interaction, a state will only agree to extensive demands if it believes that the alternative is even worse. Thus, Trump's demands were coupled with a campaign of "maximum pressure": efforts to reimpose and even tighten economic sanctions while beefing up the U.S. military presence in the region to pose a credible threat of force. In January 2020, U.S. forces assassinated a top Iranian military commander in Iraq as a way to signal the country's willingness to take tough action. Nevertheless, this pressure did not yield Iranian concessions. Instead, Iran restarted some previously frozen nuclear activities and increased its stocks of enriched uranium.

The argument against reviving the JCPOA is that maximum pressure must continue until either Iran gives in or economic stress causes the regime to collapse. In either case, the hope is that the regime, or its successor, would prioritize its interest in survival over the interest in regional influence that fuels its nuclear program and other activities. Advocates of this position see the problem with Iran as rooted in its domestic institutions, which empower a narrow group of elites strongly motivated by interests and ideology that put them in conflict with the West. By contrast, many Iranians would like to see greater democracy at home, a better standard of living, and more integration with the world. These demands for political liberalization have been repressed. In this view, sanctions or military action could pave the way for regime change, and a more democratic Iran would be willing to give up the country's nuclear ambitions in exchange for an end to its international isolation. If so, then a change in domestic institutions would effectively alter the country's interests, making a more comprehensive deal possible.

The alternative view is that this strategy is unlikely to work and risks substantial costs. The JCPOA was negotiated at a time when Iran was under comprehensive, multilateral sanctions from not just the United States but also the United Nations and the European Union. The support of other countries was important because the United States has not traded with Iran since the 1979 revolution. While the United States could impose financial sanctions due to its enormous influence in international financial markets, restrictions on Iranian exports required the participation of other nations. After withdrawing from the JCPOA, Trump failed to reassemble that international support and instead faced resistance among European partners and in the United Nations. Thus, maximum pressure required the United States to pressure reluctant allies and partners, worsening already-strained relations under the Trump administration (see Chapter 5). Ending that policy would further Biden's goal of mending those ties.

Moreover, while the Trump administration threatened military escalation, the costs of a war with Iran would be very high due to the country's size, terrain, and ability to strike back via terrorist groups in the region. The United States' experience with regime change in Iraq, where post-invasion turmoil bogged down U.S. forces in an extended counter-insurgency effort and destabilized the neighborhood, do not bode well for a similar operation in Iran. Thus, it is not clear that the United States has the ability to compel the extensive concessions it has demanded, nor that it can count on regime change to solve the problem. In this view, restoring the JCPOA may be the best that can be realistically achieved.

At the same time, Iranians have doubts about re-entering a deal after the United States withdrew the first time. When states agree to give up a weapons program, they make themselves weaker, potentially exposing them to future demands. Negotiated disarmament requires a credible commitment from the United States that it will abide by any deal and not exploit Iran's restraint. The fate of the JCPOA could give Iranian leaders reason to doubt any such commitment. Thus, while Americans debate whether or not it makes sense to negotiate with Iran, Iranians have similar questions about America.

Thinking Analytically

1. How might the United States credibly commit not to push for regime change if Iran were to agree to give up its weapons? What are the obstacles that make such a commitment difficult?

2. Should countries that value human rights negotiate with nondemocratic regimes that repress their own people? What are the costs and benefits of engaging a regime like Iran?

---

a. See Michael Pompeo, "Confronting Iran: The Trump Administration's Strategy," *Foreign Affairs* 97 (November/December 2018): 60–71.

As this example is constructed, State B prefers the war outcome it could obtain under the initial power distribution (labeled in blue in the top panel of Figure 3.3) over any outcome that falls in the future bargaining range. Even the best deal that State B can hope to get in the future (the red dotted line in the lower panel), gives State B less than it expects to get from war today. Hence, State B would rather fight a war now than face worse terms in the future.

Thus, even if states can locate a deal that they prefer over war today, the state that is getting stronger will face a strong temptation to use its future power to try to revise the deal later. Unless there is some way for the growing state to make a credible commitment not to do that, then its adversary may decide that it is better to gamble on war today in order to stop or slow the anticipated shift. A war that is fought with the intention of preventing an adversary from becoming relatively stronger in the future is a **preventive war**.

preventive war

A war fought with the intention of preventing an adversary from becoming stronger in the future. Preventive wars arise because a state whose power is increasing cannot commit not to exploit that power in future bargaining interactions.

FIGURE 3.3 *Bargaining and Shifting Power*

Initial power distribution: Today, State B is more powerful than State A, so fighting a war favors State B, as indicated by the fact that the war outcome is close to State B's ideal point.

Future power distribution: Tomorrow, after State A's power increases, fighting a war will favor State A, as indicated by the fact that the war outcome is now close to State A's ideal point. The best possible deal that State B can get after the power shift is indicated by the red dotted line. Because this deal gives State B less than it can expect to get from war today (the blue dotted line in the top panel), State B has an incentive to wage war now in order to prevent the power shift.

Notice that this logic is compelling only if it is believed that war will halt, or significantly delay, the anticipated change in power, which might happen if war could successfully disarm the other state or cripple its economic growth. If the shift in power will happen anyway, then there is nothing to be gained by fighting now, only to have the outcome revised later in the rising state's favor. The need to destroy the source of the adversary's rise means that wars fought in the context of shifting power tend to be especially long and costly (see "How Do We Know?" on p. 129).

The U.S. war against Iraq in 2003 had a preventive logic, even if much of the motivating intelligence turned out to be flawed. Saddam Hussein's regime was believed to have some minimal capability—and a demonstrated intention—to develop weapons of mass destruction. The preventive argument for attacking was that it would be easier to oust Hussein before he had fully developed these capabilities than to do so after he had succeeded in deploying them in his arsenal. Of course, the uncertainties surrounding Iraq's weapons program illustrate a major risk of engaging in preventive war, since the rationale for doing so is only as strong as the evidence that a disadvantageous shift in relative capabilities is coming. In Chapter 14, we will revisit the case of U.S.-China relations and consider the risks of war due to China's rise.

Preemption: War in Response to Fear of Attack

A final commitment problem that can prevent states from reaching negotiated settlements of their disputes arises from fear of attack by an opponent with a first-strike advantage. A **first-strike advantage** exists when there is a considerable benefit to being the first to launch an attack. It arises when military technology, strategies, and/or geography give an advantage to offensive actions over defensive ones. When defense is relatively effective, a state can afford to wait to see whether its opponent is going to attack because a first strike can be defeated or absorbed. When offense is relatively effective, a first strike is potentially devastating, and fear of attack creates incentives to abandon the bargaining table and rush to the battlefield.[31]

For example, if one state could launch its nuclear missiles and destroy all of its adversary's missiles on the ground before they could be launched, then that state would enjoy a first-strike advantage. A state that can land a disarming blow may be tempted to do so, and a state that is vulnerable to such a blow may feel a "use it or lose it" imperative to strike first rather than be disarmed.

First-strike advantages can create a potentially insurmountable commitment problem: unless each state can credibly promise the other that it will not attack first, there is a danger that bargaining will break down as each side hurries to land the first blow. Each side may be confident that if it manages to strike first, it can do better in war than if it accepts the deal currently on offer. Indeed, there may be no deal that both sides prefer over a war that they start.

> ### first-strike advantage
> The situation that arises when military technology, military strategies, and/or geography give a significant advantage to whichever state attacks first in a war.

---

31. There is a considerable literature on the "offense-defense balance" and its effect on the likelihood of war; see, for example, Keir Lieber, "Grasping the Technological Peace: The Offense-Defense Balance and International Security," *International Security* 25, no. 1 (Summer 2000): 71–104. A related literature emphasizes that what matters is not the actual offense-defense balance but rather the balance that is perceived by military and political leaders; see Van Evera, "Cult of the Offensive."

An example of this situation is depicted in Figure 3.4. Here, we assume that there are two different war outcomes, depending on which state lands the first blow. The expected outcome of a war started by State A is depicted in the top panel, and the expected outcome of a war started by State B is depicted in the lower panel. The first-strike advantage is captured by the assumption that each side expects to do better in a war that it starts than in a war started by its adversary (that is, the war outcome in the top panel is closer to State A's ideal point than the war outcome in the lower panel, and the opposite is true for State B). As a result, although there is a set of deals that both states prefer over a war started by either State A or State B, no deal is preferable to *both* of these possible wars. A deal within the lower bargaining range would satisfy State B but give State A less than it expects to get by attacking first (the area labeled in red in the top panel). Similarly, a deal within the upper bargaining range would satisfy State A but give State B less than it expects to get by striking first (the area labeled in blue in the lower panel).

FIGURE 3.4 *Bargaining and First-Strike Advantages*

State A attacks first: State A enjoys a significant advantage in war if it attacks first, and the war outcome will be close to its ideal point.

State B attacks first: Here, the war outcome heavily favors State B. Because the bargaining ranges in the top and lower panels do not overlap, there is no deal that both sides prefer over a war that they initiate.

Bargaining and the Duration of War

The duration of interstate wars varies a good deal. Figure A shows the distribution of war durations for 125 interstate wars over the last two centuries. About 10 wars have lasted three years or more, and they account for most of the combat deaths from wars in this period. However, most wars are relatively brief.

What determines how long a war will last? A number of factors might explain why some wars are longer than others, including the power of the adversaries and what they are fighting over. But, at a more general level, how long a war lasts is related to the strategic problem that caused the war in the first place. Once the adversaries go to war, the incentive to reach a deal that spares each side the costs of fighting does not disappear. Indeed, relatively few wars are fought until one of the states is completely occupied or unable to mount further operations; most end with some kind of bargain. This observation raises a puzzle: How does war make it possible for states to reach a settlement when they could not do so beforehand?

In a recent book, Alex Weisiger argues that if bargaining fails because of incomplete information about each adversary's relative capabilities and resolve, then war can bring about a deal by revealing the hidden information.[a] As states compete on the battlefield, features that were hard to observe beforehand—the power of each state, the effectiveness of military technologies and strategies, the willingness of the populace to bear the burdens of war—become observable. In this case, war lasts as long as is necessary for uncertainties to be resolved.

Alternatively, if the war came about because of a commitment problem, then the war can end only when the source of that problem is removed. A preventive war fought in response to the rising power of an opponent can end when either the declining power is unable to keep fighting or the rising power is crippled to the point that its rise has been forestalled.

To test these propositions, Weisiger collected data on 103 cases of interstate war since 1816 and estimated the effect of different factors on how long each war lasted. He found that one of the strongest predictors of long and severe wars was whether the war was preceded by a large shift in the adversaries' relative military capabilities, as measured not only by the size of their militaries but also by their population size and level of economic development. In particular, the typical duration of a war preceded by a large power shift is three times that of war preceded by little or no such shift. Thus, as expected, the longest wars tend to be those fought between declining and rising states, when preventive motivations loom largest. On the other hand, among wars that were not preceded by a shift in power—and were therefore more likely to be rooted in an information problem—those that experienced relatively frequent and intense battles tended to end more quickly. This finding is consistent with the idea that battles serve to resolve uncertainty, permitting the adversaries to find a settlement that both prefer over continued bloodshed.

FIGURE A *The Duration of Interstate Wars, 1816–2014*

Source: Meredith Reid Sarkees and Frank Wayman, *Resort to War: 1816–2007* (Washington, DC: Congressional Quarterly Press, 2010).

a. Alex Weisiger, *Logics of War: Explanations for Limited and Unlimited Conflicts* (Ithaca, NY: Cornell University Press, 2013). For another important study along these lines, see Branislav Slantchev, "How Initiators End Their Wars: The Duration of Warfare and the Terms of Peace," *American Political Science Review* 48, no. 4 (September 2004): 813–29.

Under these conditions, neither state will make concessions to the other at the bargaining table; instead, both will likely rush to the exits, each trying to beat the other to the punch. Negotiations in this context may be seen as nothing more than a ploy to delay the other side from mobilizing. A war that arises in this way is a **preemptive war.**[32]

The 1967 Six Day War between Israel and four Arab states (Egypt, Syria, Jordan, and Iraq) is a classic case of a preemptive war. In May 1967, Egypt responded to border skirmishes between Israel and Syria by massing troops on the Israeli border and imposing a partial blockade. On June 5, fearing that war was likely, Israel launched a surprise attack on the Egyptian air force, destroying 300 aircraft while they were still on the ground. With Egypt's main offensive threat crippled, the ensuing war lasted six days and left Israel in control of large swaths of formerly Arab-held territory.

This dynamic forms an important component of what we referred to earlier as the security dilemma. When military technology favors offensive action, a state that builds arms, even out of purely defensive motives, inevitably makes other states worry about a possible attack. If threatened states arm themselves in response, the original state will, in turn, feel less secure, feeding a self-reinforcing cycle of fear. In addition to causing arms races and hampering international cooperation, the commitment problem created by this fear fuels a risk of war.

Both preemption and prevention arise from the difficulty states can have in making credible commitments not to use their military power. The difference between the two concepts revolves around timing. Preemption is a response to an imminent threat when there is an existing first-strike advantage. Prevention is a response to anticipated changes in the distribution of power that might result in an increased threat sometime in the future. (For a discussion of how such considerations contributed to the outbreak of World War I, see the "What Shaped Our World?" section.)

We have seen, then, that even if states can locate a deal that both prefer over war at the moment of negotiation, concerns about their willingness to abide by the deal in the future can cause bargaining failure and war. Although these concerns can arise for different reasons, all the paths to war discussed in this section have at their root a common commitment problem: the difficulty of committing not to use one's power to one's advantage in the future.

In addition to shedding light on the general problem of war, this discussion generates a number of predictions about the conditions under which war is more or less likely to occur. First, war is more likely to occur when the good in dispute is a source of strategic or military power to those who possess it. For example, it is harder to strike bargains over strategically important territory than over territory that is valuable for economic reasons.[33] Second, preventive incentives arise when

---

32. It should be emphasized that this example assumes a very large first-strike advantage relative to the costs of war, so it is possible that this kind of situation arises only rarely. For a historical overview of preemptive war, which finds that very few wars start this way, see Dan Reiter, "Exploding the Powder Keg Myth: Preemptive Wars Almost Never Happen," *International Security* 20, no. 2 (Autumn 1995): 5–34.

33. Paul K. Huth, *Standing Your Ground: Territorial Disputes and International Conflict* (Ann Arbor: University of Michigan Press, 1996).

Prevention and Preemption in World War I

World War I redrew the maps of Europe, the Middle East, and Africa. It decimated a generation of young people, and the postwar settlement contributed to World War II 20 years later, as well as to more recent conflicts.

For all its far-reaching consequences, the First World War had relatively modest origins. On June 28, 1914, Archduke Franz Ferdinand, heir to the throne of the Austro-Hungarian Empire, was assassinated during a visit to neighboring Serbia. How could this event lead to a war that would ultimately involve 32 states fighting on three continents?

Interests Europe in 1914 was rife with conflicting interests. Germany's growing power brought it into competition with Britain and provoked fear in its neighbors. France hoped to reclaim territory from Germany, which in turn had designs on territory in Russia and overseas. Austria-Hungary and Russia were competing for influence in the Balkan region. The Ottoman Empire was in decline, and outsiders sought to expand at its expense.

Institutions States with compatible interests often form alliances, institutions that help them to cooperate militarily (see Chapter 5). By 1914, the major powers were divided into two hostile camps: Germany, Austria-Hungary, and Italy formed the Triple Alliance against Great Britain, France, and Russia in the Triple Entente. This alliance system meant that any conflict had the potential to expand throughout Europe. It also posed a problem for German military planners, who knew that, in the event of a war, they would face foes to the east and west.

Interactions In this combustible atmosphere, the assassination of the archduke by Serb terrorists created a dangerous spark. Austria-Hungary had a substantial Serb minority, and agitation by Serb nationalists threatened to tear the multiethnic empire apart. Thus, Austria-Hungary issued a tough ultimatum, threatening war unless Serbia clamped down on terrorist groups and anti-Austrian propaganda. This threat brought a deterrent response from the Russians. Germany then promised to protect the Austrians. Though, in principle, the conflict could have been defused by a negotiated bargain, preventive and preemptive considerations loomed large.

Although German leaders did not relish a war with Russia, they feared Russia's growing power. In the decades prior to the war, Russia had made great economic strides, building its heavy industries and railroad network. Germany's leaders watched these developments with concern and came to believe that they had a short "window of opportunity" in which to prevent future Russian domination.

In contemplating war with Russia, however, there was a significant obstacle: France. To deal with the possibility of a two-front war, the Germans came up with an audacious solution. The Schlieffen Plan took advantage of the fact that Russia's vast size made its military machine very slow. After the Russians started mobilizing, it would take six weeks before their forces could join the fight. The Germans hoped to exploit this delay to invade and quickly defeat France. German troops could then be shifted to the east in time to meet the Russian advance.

Planners believed that the strategic situation gave an advantage to whoever struck first. By acting quickly, Germany could seize key bridges and tunnels in Belgium, roll onward into Paris, and then turn their attention to Russia. If they waited, the Belgians could fortify or destroy the bridges, causing the German army to bog down in the west while the Russian "steamroller" bore down from the east. Under these conditions, negotiations threatened an intolerable delay. Preemptive incentives also meant that military mobilizations were not a useful instrument of crisis diplomacy. When the Russians mobilized on July 30, they hoped that signaling their resolve would lead the Austrians to reduce their demands. Instead, Russia's mobilization spurred the adversaries to the battlefield.

By August 3, Europe was at war. When the Russian army mobilized, Germany invaded Belgium and France. Great Britain joined the fray. Other states were tempted by one side or the other to pile on, and the battlefield expanded across and beyond Europe.

there are relatively rapid and dramatic changes in the military balance between two countries. Hence, war is more likely when such changes are anticipated or under way. Finally, bargaining failures are more common when the military-strategic situation creates substantial advantages for striking first. These advantages generally arise from the nature of military technology, which sometimes imparts large advantages to the actor who goes on the offensive first—although, as we saw in the case of World War I, particular military strategies can also create pressure to act preemptively.

Is Compromise Always Possible? War from Indivisibility

Finally, we consider a third kind of problem: sometimes, states cannot reach mutually beneficial settlements of their disputes because the disputed good cannot be divided. A good is divisible if there are ways to split it into smaller shares; an **indivisible good** cannot be divided without destroying its value. Imagine, for example, the difference between having 100 pennies and having one dollar bill. Although the amount of money available is the same in both cases, the pennies can be divided up between two people in many different ways, while the dollar bill cannot be split without ruining it. When the good in question is indivisible, compromise solutions are impossible to reach, and the bargaining becomes "all or nothing."

It is easy to see how indivisible goods could create an insurmountable obstacle in crisis bargaining. Consider a situation in which each state would prefer to fight a war rather than get none of the good. Even though there might be deals that both sides prefer over war—such as, say, a 50-50 split—an inability to divide the good into the necessary shares renders such a deal unattainable. In an all-or-nothing bargaining situation, one state must get nothing. And if both states prefer war over getting nothing, then war becomes inevitable.

Although the logic of indivisibility is quite clear, what is less clear is whether or how often indivisibility is actually a problem in international politics. What goods are truly indivisible? A key point is that indivisibility is not a physical property of a good; rather, it has to do with how a good is valued. This point is made most dramatically by the biblical story in which King Solomon, confronted by two women claiming to be the mother of the same baby, decides that the only fair solution in the face of these incompatible claims is to cut the baby in half. This solution seems odd not because it cannot be physically implemented but because doing so would kill the baby. (Fortunately, in King Solomon's case, the decision did not have to be carried out, since one woman insisted that she would rather let the other woman have her child than see it killed—whereupon Solomon decided that this woman must be the true mother.) Similarly, in a dispute over a valuable painting, one could slice the painting in two, but doing so would destroy the object's value.

indivisible good

A good that cannot be divided without destroying its value.

Hence, when we say that a good cannot be divided, we generally do not mean this literally. Rather, we mean that the good loses much, if not all, of its value when it is divided.[34] This can be the case with core values that cannot be compromised or with divisible goods that are closely linked to such core values.

A commonly cited example of an indivisible good in international relations is the city of Jerusalem.[35] Jerusalem contains some of the holiest sites of Christianity, Islam, and Judaism and has historical, cultural, and religious significance unlike any other piece of territory in the world. As a result, the status of Jerusalem is a major stumbling block in efforts to bring about peace in the Middle East.

For many Jews, Jerusalem is the focal point of the desire—sometimes symbolic, sometimes literal—to return to the promised land of Zion. Every year at Passover, Jews all over the world utter the words "Next year in Jerusalem," underscoring the city's role in forging a connection between the land of Israel and the Jewish identity. The centrality of this city has been given political expression as well: a Basic Law passed by Israel in 1980 declares that "Jerusalem, complete and united, is the capital of Israel."

In Jerusalem, the Dome of the Rock, one of Islam's holiest shrines, sits on top of the Temple Mount, the site of the original Jewish temple until 70 C.E. The concentration of holy sites in Jerusalem complicates negotiations between Israelis and Palestinians over whether and how to divide or share the city, which both sides claim as their capital.

For Muslims, East Jerusalem, or Al-Quds, is the third-holiest city (after Mecca and Medina in Saudi Arabia) and the site of the Dome of the Rock, where the prophet Mohammed is believed to have ascended to Paradise. Palestinians claim East Jerusalem, which Israel annexed after the 1967 Six Day War, as the capital of an eventual Palestinian state. This claim clearly clashes with the Israeli position that the city is indivisible and the capital of the Jewish state. Moreover, the holiest sites for both faiths sit literally on top of each other. The Dome of the Rock and Al-Aqsa Mosque were built (1,300 years ago) directly on the Temple Mount—the site of the original Jewish temple—whose Western Wall is an important place of worship for Jews. The question of whether or how to divide the city, and how to ensure that people of all faiths have access to their holy sites, is one that has so far defied resolution.

It is important, however, not to place undue emphasis on indivisibility as a source of bargaining failures. First, some of the difficulty of dealing with indivisible goods arises not from indivisibility per se, but from weak enforcement mechanisms. King Solomon's quandary is one that divorcing parents routinely face when each wants custody of their children. These disputes are settled not by dividing

---

34. H. Peyton Young, "Dividing the Indivisible," *American Behavioral Scientist* 38, no. 6 (1995): 904–20.

35. See, for example, Cecilia Albin, "Negotiating Indivisible Goods: The Case of Jerusalem," *Jerusalem Journal of International Relations* 13, no. 1 (1991): 45–76.

the children physically, but by dividing the time they spend with each parent. This kind of alternating possession would generally fail in international politics, however, because a state would not trust its adversary to hand over the good when the time came to do so. In child-custody cases, the deal is enforced by courts and police, which are generally lacking in the international context. Thus, the main obstacle to striking such a deal lies not in the nature of the good but in the difficulty of making a credible commitment to share that good over time.[36]

A second reason to be skeptical of claims of indivisibility is that states may have strategic incentives to claim that they cannot compromise on a particular issue, even if they actually could. Recall that one of the strategies that states employ in crisis bargaining is to tie their hands through public pronouncements from which it would be costly to back down. It is quite possible that claims of indivisibility—such as the Israeli Basic Law pronouncing Jerusalem the capital of Israel—have a strategic quality: they represent an effort to tie the government's hands so that compromise will become difficult, if not impossible. The hope in making such claims is that the other side will realize that it has no choice but to give in entirely. In this sense, the public positions that states take may lend objects the appearance of indivisibility in the course of the bargaining process.[37]

The point of this discussion is not to suggest that indivisible goods do not exist in international politics. Rather, it is to suggest that we should be appropriately skeptical when the participants in a dispute claim that the good in question is indivisible and hence no compromise is possible. Such a claim may reflect a bargaining position adopted for strategic reasons rather than a true description of the fundamental nature of the good in question.

In any event, there may be ways to allocate apparently indivisible goods that do not involve physical division. One possible mechanism is shared control. It has been proposed, for example, that Israelis and Palestinians jointly control certain portions of Jerusalem to ensure that all people have access to the sacred sites. Indeed, this already happens to some degree at the Temple Mount: though the site falls under Israeli sovereignty, the area on top, including the Dome of the Rock and the Al-Aqsa Mosque, is administered by Islamic authorities.

A second mechanism for dealing with indivisible goods is compensation on another issue. Although a rare painting cannot be physically divided, a dispute over it can be resolved by having one party compensate the other in exchange for the good. In this case, the object is made divisible by adding a new dimension to the deal: rather than arguing about who gets the painting, the issue becomes how much money one is willing to pay the other to get it. Since money is generally divisible, adding this new dimension creates the possibility for compromise where none previously existed. Hence, disputants may be able to find a second issue dimension on which the loser in the main issue can be compensated. The strategy of making one

36. See Powell, "War as a Commitment Problem," for a discussion of how indivisibility leads to commitment problems.

37. See Stacie E. Goddard, "Uncommon Ground: Indivisible Territory and the Politics of Legitimacy," *International Organization* 60, no. 1 (Winter 2006): 35–68.

dispute easier to solve by bringing in a second issue is known as linkage, as we saw in Chapter 2.

Has War Become Obsolete?

War arises from a variety of factors that can prevent states from reaching peaceful settlements of their disputes. Of course, the reason we study war is not just to understand why it happens, but also to identify factors that might reduce or eliminate its occurrence. On this front, there is some room for optimism. One striking observation from Figure 3.1 is that the incidence of interstate war seems to have dropped since 1950. Moreover, there has not been a war between two great powers since the Korean War ended in 1953—the longest such streak in modern history.[38]

This apparent decline in interstate war over the last seven decades has been the subject of considerable attention among political scientists.[39] However, we must approach this trend carefully. As Figure 3.1 shows, earlier periods in history experienced dips in the frequency of war that turned out to be temporary. And there are certainly contemporary disputes—involving the United States, Russia, China, North Korea, and Iran—that have the potential to escalate. Still, the observation that the past seven decades have seen a decline in interstate war is striking and important enough to motivate the following questions: Have there been changes in world politics that could explain a decline in the incidence of interstate war since World War II? To what extent can the framework offered in this chapter guide our thinking about this development?

The logic developed in this chapter has three main components: (1) war becomes possible when states have conflicting interests over a contentious issue, (2) the costs of war ensure that there exists a peaceful deal that both states prefer over fighting, but (3) bargaining may fail because of information or commitment problems or because of an inability to divide the good at stake. It follows that a decline in war could arise from (1) changing interests that lead to a decrease in the value of goods that have historically driven conflict, (2) an increase in the costs of war that leads to changing interactions, or (3) the growth of institutions that help states solve the information or commitment problems associated with uncertainty and changing power, or the problem of the indivisibility of a good. There is reason to think that all three of these factors have changed in ways that have made war less likely overall.

---

38. Scholars typically identify the following states as great powers in the post–World War II period: the United States, the Soviet Union/Russia, Great Britain, France, China (after 1950), Germany (after 1991), and Japan (after 1991).

39. See, for example, John E. Mueller, *Retreat from Doomsday: The Obsolescence of Major War* (New York: Basic Books, 1989); Joshua S. Goldstein, *Winning the War on War: The Decline of Armed Conflict Worldwide* (New York: Dutton, 2011); and Steven Pinker, *The Better Angels of Our Nature: Why Violence Has Declined* (New York: Viking, 2011). For a skeptical view, see Tanisha M. Fazal, "Dead Wrong? Battle Deaths, Military Medicine, and Exaggerated Reports of War's Demise," *International Security* 39, no. 1 (Summer 2014): 95–125; and Bear F. Braumoeller, *Only the Dead: The Persistence of War in the Modern Age* (New York: Oxford University Press, 2019).

Changing Interests: Declining Conflict over Territory

A striking feature of world politics since 1945 has been the declining role of territory in driving interstate conflicts. Not only has there been a drop in the frequency of interstate wars over territory, but there have also been fewer instances of successful conquest or annexation of territory since World War II.[40] Explanations for this observation abound, but any understanding has to start with changes in the value of possessing territory in the modern era. Whereas control of territory and population was historically an important source of state power, technological changes have weakened this link. In an age of nuclear weapons, precision-guided missiles, and increasing reliance on unmanned aerial vehicles (popularly known as drones), military power no longer depends on how large an army a state can field. Moreover, the growth of international trade and investment (see Chapters 7 and 8) means that it is generally easier to acquire resources through markets than through conquest.[41] At the same time, the spread of nationalism has made it harder for foreign states to control conquered populations, thereby raising the costs of taking territory. Thus, some of the interests that drove states to contest territory have become less potent.

The interests of key states also changed after World War II. Whereas previously the rival territorial ambitions of the European great powers had cast that continent into frequent warfare, leadership of the international system after 1945 passed to two states—the United States and the Soviet Union—that had little interest in further territorial expansion. The United States had satisfied all of its ambitions by the early twentieth century, with the end of westward expansion and the seizure of land from Native American tribes and the final settlement of the Canadian boundary in 1902. The Soviet Union used its military success in World War II to restore its dominance over lands that it had historically controlled. Thus, the most powerful states in the system had an interest in stabilizing the territorial order rather than changing it. The United States, in particular, played a role in advancing and defending a norm of "territorial integrity"—the idea that borders should not be changed through force—a norm that became enshrined in international institutions like the United Nations (for more on the role of norms, see Chapter 11).[42]

Many newly decolonized countries also embraced this norm, even though their borders often made little sense, having been drawn in European capitals by imperial powers with scant knowledge of local conditions. Leaders in these new states decided that it was generally in their interests to respect the inherited borders and consolidate power within them, rather than open up a Pandora's box by calling all of

---

40. See, for example, Mark W. Zacher, "The Territorial Integrity Norm: International Boundaries and the Use of Force," *International Organization* 55, no. 2 (Spring 2001): 215–50; Tanisha M. Fazal, *State Death: The Politics and Geography of Conquest, Occupation, and Annexation* (Princeton, NJ: Princeton University Press, 2007); and Gary Goertz, Paul F. Diehl, and Alexandru Balas, *The Puzzle of Peace: The Evolution of Peace in the International System* (New York: Oxford University Press, 2016).

41. Stephen G. Brooks, *Producing Security: Multinational Corporations, Globalization, and the Changing Calculus of Conflict* (Princeton, NJ: Princeton University Press, 2005).

42. Zacher, "Territorial Integrity Norm"; Fazal, *State Death*, 47–52.

the colonial borders into question.[43] In sum, changes in the international system after 1945 reduced states' interest in fighting over territory—reducing the value of territory as a good—which has historically been a major cause of interstate war.

Changing Interactions: The Rising Costs of War

The human, economic, material, and psychological costs of war are all major disincentives for engaging in armed conflict. Indeed, the costs of war generally ensure that states can do better by finding a negotiated settlement of their disputes. As war becomes less attractive, states are more willing to make compromises in order to avoid it. In addition, increasing the costs of war increases the range of status quo distributions that neither state has an incentive to challenge (see Figure 3.2).

Although recent decades have been relatively free of interstate war, disputes involving nuclear-armed states, such as North Korea, persist. The high expected costs of nuclear war have contributed to peace among these states, since the threat of "mutually assured destruction" makes them cautious to escalate conflicts.

At least two major developments since 1945 have increased the expected costs of war. One is the advent of nuclear weapons, which gave states the ability to completely obliterate one another. As a result, the expected costs of nuclear war are so large that they swamp the value of whatever good is at stake. The threat of "mutually assured destruction" in the event of war engenders caution among nuclear-armed states, reducing the attractiveness of taking risks in a crisis. Indeed, it is striking that despite five decades of intense hostility between the United States and the Soviet Union during the Cold War, the two superpowers never waged war directly against each other. Although there are many theories about the cause of this so-called long peace, both states' possession of nuclear weapons certainly played a stabilizing role.[44] We will return to this topic in Chapter 14, when we consider the implications of the spread of nuclear weapons.

The second major development since 1945 has been the explosive growth of international trade and financial transactions (see Figure 14.2 on p. 617). Scholars have long thought that, as countries became more economically interdependent, the costs of war between them would grow. The more two countries value each other as trading partners, the more incentives they have to avoid conflicts that could disrupt those profitable exchanges.[45] Whether this theory is right has been a subject of vigorous academic debate.[46]

---

43. Jeffrey Herbst, *States and Power in Africa: Comparative Lessons in Authority and Control,* rev. ed. (Princeton, NJ: Princeton University Press, 2014).

44. See, for example, John Lewis Gaddis, "The Long Peace: Elements of Stability in the Postwar International System," *International Security* 10, no. 4 (Spring 1986): 99–142.

45. For a good discussion of some of the intellectual origins of this view, see Michael W. Doyle, *Ways of War and Peace: Realism, Liberalism, and Socialism* (New York: Norton, 1997), chap. 7.

46. For a recent review, see Erik Gartzke and Jiakun Jack Zhang, "Trade and War," in *The Oxford Handbook of the Political Economy of International Trade,* ed. Lisa L. Martin (Oxford: Oxford University Press, 2015).

Part of the challenge is that while it is plausible that increased trade makes countries less likely to fight one another, the reverse could also be true: peaceful relations create the conditions for greater interdependence through trade. So, although countries that trade more do fight less, figuring out the degree to which that relationship is due to trade causing peace—rather than peace causing trade—is difficult. On balance, though, most scholars consider growing commercial and financial interdependence since 1945 as a contributor to peaceful relations, particularly among the advanced industrial countries.[47]

Changing Institutions: Democracy and International Organizations

Finally, the decline in interstate conflict may be due to the growth of institutions that have helped states overcome information and commitment problems that can cause bargaining to fail. Two kinds of institutions could play a role in this regard: domestic and international.

On the domestic front, the major trend since World War II has been the expansion in the number of democratic countries (see Figure 4.5 on p. 177). This development is striking when paired with the observation that there are few, if any, clear cases of war between democratic states. This means that the spread of democratic institutions might account for some of the overall decline in interstate war in the past seven decades. Why democracy might have this effect is the subject of a larger discussion in the next chapter.

The post-1945 world has also seen a dramatic expansion in the number and activity of international organizations (see Figure 14.1 on p. 614). This period witnessed the emergence and growing assertiveness of the United Nations as well as the development of numerous regional organizations devoted to promoting peace and security.[48] A fuller examination of the role and track record of these organizations will come in Chapter 5, but we can anticipate some of the ways these institutions may have improved states' abilities to solve informational and commitment problems.

First, international organizations may enhance transparency by providing neutral observers of a state's military activities. The International Atomic Energy Agency (IAEA), for example, inspects members' nuclear energy programs in order to determine whether nuclear fuel has been diverted to produce weapons. Similarly, the United Nations often provides monitors to help observe whether parties to a conflict are fulfilling their pledges to withdraw troops or disarm, thereby reducing uncertainty among adversaries about what the other side is up to.[49]

International organizations may also make it easier to resolve commitment problems. As discussed earlier, it is difficult for nations to credibly promise not to

---

47. See, for example, Håvard Hegre, John R. Oneal, and Bruce Russett, "Trade Does Promote Peace: New Simultaneous Estimates of the Reciprocal Effects of Trade and Conflict," *Journal of Peace Research* 47, no. 6 (November 2010): 763–74.

48. Goldstein, *Winning the War on War*.

49. See, for example, Virginia Page Fortna, *Peace Time: Cease-Fire Agreements and the Durability of Peace* (Princeton, NJ: Princeton University Press, 2004).

use their power to their advantage, largely because states cannot generally rely on repeated interaction to hold one another to such a promise. Repeated interaction can help make promises credible if the prospect of future dealings motivates a state to resist the temptation to break a promise today because it fears retaliation by the other state tomorrow. Under conditions of shifting power, however, the state that is becoming more powerful has less to fear from the other side's retaliation. Furthermore, if a state can use its increased power to destroy the other state, then there may be no "shadow of the future" to stay the growing state's hand. The same holds true in situations involving first-strike advantages: the temptation to deliver a crippling blow is hard to blunt if the other side's retaliatory capability will be rendered ineffective in the process.

Because adversaries generally cannot solve this commitment problem on their own, any solutions are most likely to come from third parties—that is, a state or group of states, including international organizations, that are not directly involved in the bargaining game between the opponents. In some cases, such outsiders may be able to help build credibility for the opposing states' commitments not to exploit power or first-strike advantages. Third parties can play this role by monitoring and enforcing agreements, by providing security guarantees to one or both sides, and sometimes by interposing their forces directly between two potential combatants—all roles that the United Nations performs, as we will see in Chapter 5.

In sum, changes in interests, interactions, and institutions since 1945 have contributed to conditions that make peace a more likely outcome of international disputes than before. It is too strong to declare war obsolete or a thing of the past. But even incremental reductions in the risk of war give reason for optimism and opportunities for greater understanding of this phenomenon.

Conclusion: Why War?

We started this chapter with a puzzle: Why do states fight wars in spite of the enormous costs associated with fighting? The answer involves two ingredients: (1) a conflict of states' interests and (2) some factor or factors that prevent states from reaching a peaceful solution to that conflict. States' underlying interests in power, security, wealth, and/or national identities can give rise to disputes over territory, policy, and the composition of one another's governments. In the absence of authoritative institutions that resolve interstate disputes, states engage in bargaining interactions over these issues, sometimes invoking the threat of military force to enhance their leverage. War occurs when features of this strategic interaction prevent states from reaching a settlement that both prefer over war, with all its uncertainties and costs.

Three kinds of problems can prevent states from settling their disputes in ways that enable them to avoid the costs of war: incomplete information, difficulty in committing to honor a deal, and goods that are hard to divide. Since these obstacles occur in different degrees and in different combinations from one crisis to the next, there is no single answer to the puzzle at the heart of this chapter. Instead, our discussion has sought to identify and explore a set of mechanisms that can stymie efforts to resolve disputes peacefully. Having considered these mechanisms, we are in a better position to understand and interpret behavior and outcomes in international crises. The concepts introduced here highlight some of the key factors that determine whether a dispute can be settled without resorting to war.

In particular, we need to pay attention to (1) what the adversaries in a dispute believe about one another's willingness and ability to wage war and how uncertain those beliefs are; (2) how each side seeks to communicate its resolve, whether those efforts are credible, and to what extent they either entail a danger of accidental war or "lock in" incompatible bargaining positions; (3) whether the good in the dispute is a source of future bargaining power; (4) whether the distribution of power between the adversaries is expected to change in the future as a result of different economic growth rates or technological progress; (5) whether the military technologies and strategies of the adversaries generate sizable first-strike advantages; and (6) whether the good in question is indivisible because of its close connection to core values, such as religious identity.

In spite of the many things that can go wrong and prevent a peaceful solution, it is important to remember this point: Wars are rare and appear to have become rarer over time. Even though information is often incomplete, credible commitments are difficult to make, and core values are hard to compromise, most states most of the time are at peace with one another. The costs of war mean that not every disagreement is worth fighting over or even threatening to fight over. Hence, the very costs that make war hell also ensure that war is not the most common way that states settle their disputes.

Study Tool Kit

Interests, Interactions, and Institutions in Context

- States may have conflicting interests over goods like territory, policy, or the composition of one another's governments. However, because war is costly, a peaceful settlement that all sides would prefer over war generally exists. War occurs when the bargaining interaction fails to reach such a deal.

- In the bargaining interaction, states may be unable to reach negotiated settlements when they are uncertain about one another's willingness and ability to wage war.

- Even if states can find a mutually acceptable bargain, peace can break down if they cannot credibly commit to abiding by the terms of the agreement.

- Bargaining may also fail if the disputed good is hard to divide, which makes compromise agreements impossible to reach.

- The apparent decline in interstate war since 1945 coincides with a decrease in states' interest in territorial conquest, an increase in the costs of war due to nuclear weapons and economic interdependence that leads to a change in interactions between states, and the spread of domestic and international institutions that help resolve information and commitment problems.

Key Terms

war, p. 95

interstate war, p. 95

civil war, p. 95

security dilemma, p. 96

crisis bargaining, p. 101

coercive diplomacy, p. 101

bargaining range, p. 103

compellence, p. 106

deterrence, p. 106

incomplete information, p. 110

resolve, p. 110

risk-return trade-off, p. 111

credibility, p. 112

brinksmanship, p. 116

audience costs, p. 117

preventive war, p. 126

first-strike advantage, p. 127

preemptive war, p. 130

indivisible good, p. 132

For Further Reading

Blainey, Geoffrey. *The Causes of War*. 3rd ed. New York: Free Press, 1988. Presents a historical examination of war informed by bargaining theory.

Braumoeller, Bear F. *Only the Dead: The Persistence of War in the Modern Age*. New York: Oxford University Press, 2019. Critically examines the thesis that war has become obsolete with careful attention to the challenges of assessing this claim.

Fazal, Tanisha M. *State Death: The Politics and Geography of Conquest, Occupation, and Annexation*. Princeton: Princeton University Press, 2007. Examines how changing norms of territorial conquest affect the survival of states.

Fearon, James D. "Rationalist Explanations for War." *International Organization* 49, no. 3 (Summer 1995): 379–414. Serves as the seminal statement of the theory of war developed in this chapter.

Goddard, Stacie E. *Indivisible Territory and the Politics of Legitimacy: Jerusalem and Northern Ireland*. Cambridge: Cambridge University Press, 2010. Argues that territories can become indivisible because of the way states try to legitimize their claims.

McManus, Roseanne W. *Statements of Resolve: Achieving Coercive Credibility in International Conflict*. Cambridge: Cambridge University Press, 2017. Examines the conditions under which leaders can convey resolve through public threats and statements.

Reiter, Dan. "Exploring the Bargaining Model of War." *Perspectives on Politics* 1, no. 1 (2003): 27–43. Evaluates the argument that war is a product, as well as a continuation, of interstate bargaining.

Schelling, Thomas C. *Arms and Influence*. New Haven, CT: Yale University Press, 1966. Serves as an accessible introduction to the strategic problems that arise in coercive interactions, including problems of credibility and commitment.

Van Evera, Stephen. *Causes of War*. Ithaca, NY: Cornell University Press, 1999. Explores how power shifts and first-strike advantages contributed to major wars throughout history.

Weisiger, Alex. *Logics of War: Explanations for Limited and Unlimited Conflicts*. Ithaca, NY: Cornell University Press, 2013. Uses insights from the bargaining model of war to understand why some wars last much longer than others.

4

Domestic Politics and War

THE PUZZLE *War is costly for states, but what if there are actors within the state—such as politicians, businesses, or the military—who see war as beneficial and who expect to pay few or none of its costs? Do states fight wars to satisfy influential domestic interests?*

Above: In democratic countries, representative institutions make political leaders sensitive to voters' preferences over issues like war and peace. Here, protesters demonstrate against the possibility of war between the United States and Iran in January 2020 after clashes between the two countries' forces in Iraq.

On March 30, 1982, thousands of demonstrators marched in the streets of Buenos Aires, the capital of Argentina, denouncing the country's military government for its harsh economic policies and oppressive rule. Riot police used tear gas, rubber bullets, and water cannons to break up the protests, and over 2,000 people were arrested. A week later, the streets of Buenos Aires filled with demonstrators once more, but this time the demonstrations voiced enthusiastic support for the military regime, as many of those who had earlier called for the government's ouster now joined in the outpouring of praise. What changed in the course of a week? On April 2, the country's naval forces had invaded a small group of islands 300 miles off the coast that were the subject of a long-standing dispute between Argentina and Britain. Is there any connection between these events? Did the Argentine government provoke a war with Britain in order to revive its popularity among its people?

In 1954, representatives of the United Fruit Company went to Washington, D.C., to voice concerns about the leader of Guatemala, a man named Jacobo Arbenz. Arbenz had enacted a land reform program that led to the seizure of almost 400,000 acres belonging to the

American company. Arbenz offered to compensate United Fruit to the tune of $1.2 million, the value of the land that the company claimed for tax purposes, but the U.S. government insisted on behalf of United Fruit that the company be paid almost $16 million. In June of that year, rebels armed and trained by the U.S. Central Intelligence Agency (CIA) invaded Guatemala. Fearing a full-scale American invasion, parts of the Guatemalan military revolted, Arbenz resigned from office and fled the country, and a pro-American leader was installed. The operation cost the CIA just under $3 million.[1] Did the United States overthrow a foreign leader to benefit a single company at the expense of American taxpayers?

Our first look at the puzzle of war in Chapter 3 considered this problem from the perspective of states. We considered the interactions of two states in conflict over a particular good, such as a piece of territory, as they try to arrive at a settlement that would avoid the costs

---

1. U.S. Central Intelligence Agency, "CIA's Role in the Overthrow of Arbenz," Job 79-01025A, Box 153, Folder 3, https://history.state.gov/historicaldocuments/frus1952-54Guat/d287 (accessed 12/16/20).

of war. This kind of analysis is very common in international relations scholarship, where it is often referred to as the *unitary state assumption*: the treatment of states as coherent actors with a set of interests that belong to the state. While this assumption can be a useful starting place for analysis, we must remember that states are legal and political constructs, not beings capable of taking actions. The choices and actions of states are made by people. Decisions about waging war are made by a state's political leaders. Military plans are drawn up by military officials and carried out by soldiers.

Others within the country may also be able to influence foreign policy choices, even if they have no direct say over them. There may be interest groups such as business or ethnic lobbies that influence decision making through their organizational and financial resources. In democratic systems, voters influence policy decisions because of their ability to remove leaders who make unpopular choices. Looking inside the state reveals new actors with varied interests, as well as variation across states in the political institutions that determine who affects decision making.

How does our understanding of the causes of war change when we look inside the state and consider the interests, interactions, and institutions within it? In Chapter 3, we argued that to understand why wars happen, we need to understand why states at times cannot solve their conflicts peacefully in ways that avoid the costs associated with fighting. This argument rested on the assumption that war is costly to both states engaged in an interaction. These costs create a bargaining range, or a set of deals that both parties prefer over fighting. The assumption that war is costly makes sense when we think of the state as a unitary actor, but once we look inside the state, it is clear that the costs and benefits of war are not distributed equally within it.

Different actors within the state may place more or less value on the issue in dispute. A disputed territory might represent a source of livelihood, profit, or national pride to some but a tract of worthless land to others. The persecution of a minority group in a foreign country might arouse outrage in some, perhaps owing to ethnic attachment to the victims, while others may greet it with indifference. Most Americans in 1954 had little or no stake in the land reform policies of the Guatemalan government; to the United Fruit Company, however, millions of dollars' worth of land were at risk.

The costs of war are also distributed unevenly. Some people, such as those who might be drafted to serve in the military, can expect to pay very high and direct costs from war. Others may see the costs of war in economic terms if the need to finance the conflict leads to higher taxes. In contrast, there are some groups within a country that may profit from war financially or professionally: arms manufacturers benefit from increased purchases of their products; for military officers, combat experience leads to opportunities for medals and promotions; and for unpopular governments, such as the Argentine junta in 1982, war can build domestic support and solidify their hold on power.

These observations raise a number of questions: To what extent is war rooted not in the information and commitment problems discussed in Chapter 3 but rather in the interests of domestic actors who see personal benefit and little or no cost to war? Do wars serve the national interest or the narrow interests of office-hungry politicians, multinational companies, and/or a "military-industrial complex" composed of glory-seeking militaries and profit-seeking arms merchants? How do domestic institutions, such as democracy, influence a government's decisions and the likelihood of war between states?

Thinking Analytically about Domestic Politics and War

To answer the questions posed here, we must consider the different interests that domestic actors have in terms of war and peace. Simply identifying these interests is not enough, however, since not all actors within the state have equal say over foreign policy choices and hence not all interests are represented equally. Two factors determine which domestic interests have sway over foreign policy: the strategic interactions between actors, which determine which individuals and groups can exert effective influence and which cannot, and the institutions within the state, which determine how different actors have access to the decision-making process. Further, we must recall that war is not the choice of a single state, but rather an outcome of interactions between or among multiple states. Hence, as we consider domestic influences on foreign policy, we need to examine how these factors shape bargaining at the international level.

Why Doesn't "Politics Stop at the Water's Edge"?

If this were a course on, say, American or French or Chinese politics, the idea that policy outcomes are influenced by politicians, interest groups, bureaucrats, and (at least in the first two countries) voters would be the starting point for analysis. When studying choices about taxes and spending, social issues, environmental regulations—or any of the issues that governments regularly deal with—it is natural to examine how these various actors pursue their interests in the context of the country's political institutions. It may seem odd, then, that when studying international politics, especially the issue of war and peace, the role of domestic actors and institutions usually comes secondary and is, in fact, the subject of some controversy. Explanations of international phenomena often start by treating states as unitary actors, as we did in the last chapter, rather than as complex entities composed of individuals and groups with different interests.

Why would this be? To some extent, this choice is made to simplify the analysis: start by considering the interaction between states at the international level before complicating things by opening up the states and considering interests, interactions, and institutions within them. But the emphasis on states also reflects important intellectual traditions within the study of international politics that downplay the importance of domestic considerations.

One perspective, referred to in this book's Introduction as realism, is that states' choices are largely dictated by external factors. In an anarchic world, states face constant threats to their sovereignty and territorial integrity. To meet these threats, they need power—primarily military power. Hence, they seek opportunities to expand their own power and/or to diminish the power of those that threaten them. In this view, states' interests are fixed, determined largely by their material resources and geographic position, and are not shaped by domestic factors. Moreover, because everyone within the state shares an interest in protection from foreign threats, these common interests override other considerations that otherwise divide people on domestic issues like tax policy. The adage that "politics stops at the water's edge" captures the idea that political struggles at home should cease when dealing with matters beyond the country's borders.[2]

Nationalism could also play a role in reducing domestic political conflicts over foreign policy. **Nationalism** is a political ideology that prioritizes attachment to one's nation, where nations are groups defined by common origin, ethnicity, language, or cultural ties.[3] It motivates individuals to act in support of the nation and

nationalism
A political ideology that prioritizes attachment to one's nation, where nations are groups defined by common origin, ethnicity, language, or cultural ties.

---

2. The phrase is attributed to U.S. senator Arthur Vandenberg, who exhorted his colleagues to pursue a bipartisan foreign policy in the early years of the Cold War.

3. Key works on nationalism include Ernest Gellner, *Nations and Nationalism* (Ithaca, NY: Cornell University Press, 1983); and Benedict R. Anderson, *Imagined Communities: Reflections on the Origin and Spread of Nationalism*, rev. ed. (New York: Verso, 2006).

its interests, often to defend the nation against external threats to its territory and political sovereignty. As such, states can harness nationalism to dampen domestic divisions over foreign policy. Indeed, states often invest in building national identity through education, monuments, public events, and holidays in order to encourage national unity and justify sacrifice on behalf of the nation. In doing so, they seek to elevate national interests over personal interests, making an otherwise diverse set of individuals and groups into a more cohesive whole.

These arguments are important, but they are also not the full picture. Although international threats can inspire domestic unity, people may also have different interests that shape their views about how the nation can best respond to the threats. For example, as we saw in Chapter 2, the United States has been concerned about the rise of China for the last three decades. Most Americans agree that a hostile and militarily powerful China would be a threat to U.S. interests. But individuals and groups have disagreed over the right policy response, with some arguing that the United States should confront China militarily and others arguing for closer trade relations that would reduce the hostility in the relationship.

These policy disagreements reflect a mix of beliefs and interests. People vary in their views about the usefulness of military force in pursuing a state's foreign policy and the appropriate balance between military, diplomatic, and economic tools.[4] We usually distinguish between "hawks," who tend to favor military action, and "doves," who do not. These differences may be rooted in basic moral values, as some people are more predisposed than others to see violence as an appropriate response to threats.[5]

Differences can also arise from economic interests. People's attitudes toward U.S.-China policy differ according to whether they are likely to benefit from trade with China or be hurt by it, with the latter group tending to support more confrontational policies.[6] For instance, U.S. multinational companies hoping to trade with and invest in China have been strong advocates for closer relations, but labor unions representing workers who fear job and income losses due to competition from Chinese imports have taken a harder line. Both groups have used their access to the political system to influence the direction of U.S. policy, and political leaders can cater to these groups in order to build public support. President Donald Trump appealed to voters in industries and regions of the country heavily affected by Chinese imports by advocating a more confrontational policy toward the communist nation.

There are also limits to the argument that nationalism reduces the impact of domestic politics. Nationalism can have different effects in different countries at different times. While some countries have been successful in building a unified

---

4. For a classic study of variation in Americans' foreign policy attitudes, see Eugene R. Wittkopf, *Faces of Internationalism: Public Opinion and American Foreign Policy* (Durham, NC: Duke University Press, 1990).

5. Brian C. Rathbun, Joshua D. Kertzer, Jason Reifler, Paul Goren, and Thomas J. Scotto, "Taking Foreign Policy Personally: Personal Values and Foreign Policy Attitudes," *International Studies Quarterly* 60, no. 1 (March 2016): 124–37.

6. Benjamin O. Fordham and Katja B. Kleinberg, "International Trade and US Relations with China," *Foreign Policy Analysis* 7, no. 3 (2011): 217–36.

national identity, others have struggled to do so, particularly where there are competing ethnic, religious, or linguistic loyalties.[7] Indeed, when countries contain many nations, nationalism can be a source of division and domestic political conflict over foreign policy.

For example, the population of Ukraine is divided linguistically between Russian speakers, who live primarily in the east of the country near its border with Russia, and Ukrainian speakers, who are more prevalent in the west. This divide has sparked significant domestic conflict over Ukrainian foreign policy, particularly over the question of whether the country should align more with Russia or with western Europe. Thus, the foreign policy interests pursued by the Ukrainian government would swing depending on which party controlled power at any given time. Since 2014, this divide has fueled a civil war in which the Russian-speaking regions have sought greater autonomy or independence (see Chapter 6).

Even in countries without competing national identities, the salience of nationalism can vary. Some people prioritize national identity more than others. In recent years, parties espousing nationalism have gained ground in Europe, and nationalism was a central element of President Trump's "America First" ideology (see Chapter 14). On the other side are parties that place less emphasis on national identity and embrace values that might be described as "internationalist" or "cosmopolitan." These differences can translate into different preferences when it comes to war and peace.

Nationalists tend to place a high value on the acquisition of territory considered integral to national identity and on foreign intervention to defend the welfare of conationals living in other countries. They may downplay the costs of pursuing these interests by force.[8] Russian nationalists, for example, have supported giving aid to Russian speakers in eastern Ukraine and cheered on the Russian government's decision in 2014 to seize and annex the territory of Crimea, a part of Ukraine that is overwhelmingly Russian and which used to be part of Russia. Similarly, the Chinese government harnesses nationalist sentiment when asserting its historical ownership over the South China Sea and in other territorial disputes with its neighbors (see Chapter 2).[9] Internationalists, by contrast, may be more sensitive to the costs of using military force and less interested in pursuing "lost" territories.

In sum, countries are filled with individuals and groups that have divergent preferences for war or peace, either because they place different values on the issues in dispute with other countries or because they experience and evaluate the costs of war differently. As in other areas of politics, we can expect these actors to

---

7. Amanda Lea Robinson, "National Versus Ethnic Identification in Africa: Modernization, Colonial Legacy, and the Origins of Territorial Nationalism," *World Politics* 66, no. 4 (2014): 709–46.

8. See, for example, R. J. Johnston, David B. Knight, and Eleonore Kofman, eds., *Nationalism, Self-Determination and Political Geography* (London: Croom Helm, 1988); Stephen M. Saideman and R. William Ayres, *For Kin or Country: Xenophobia, Nationalism, and War* (New York: Columbia University Press, 2008); David R. Davis and Will H. Moore, "Ethnicity Matters: Transnational Ethnic Alliances and Foreign Policy Behavior," *International Studies Quarterly* 41, no. 1 (1997): 171–84; and Lars-Erik Cederman, Kristian Skrede Gleditsch, Idean Salehyan, and Julian Wucherpfennig, "Transborder Ethnic Kin and Civil War," *International Organization* 67, no. 2 (2013): 389–410.

9. Jessica Chen Weiss, *Powerful Patriots: Nationalist Protest in China's Foreign Relations* (Oxford: Oxford University Press, 2014).

seek to influence the state's policy choices at the international level. "Politics stops at the water's edge" is more aspiration than fact.

Whose Interests Matter?: Interactions, Institutions, and Influence

When we drop the unitary actor assumption and look within states, myriad individuals and groups with a variety of interests come into focus. Which actors matter, and which interests are likely to influence foreign policy decisions? The answer lies in institutions and interactions.

Recall from Chapter 2 that institutions are sets of rules and decision-making procedures. Within each country, domestic institutions help determine who runs the government, how decisions are made, and how disputes are resolved. In a monarchy, for example, the ruler is determined through a system of succession often based on birth order. In other systems, the leader is the person who commands the greatest support within the military and therefore can repress challengers with force. In democratic political systems, leaders are selected through regular elections in which winners are decided by the amount of popular support they can muster. Domestic institutions also determine how much decision-making power individual leaders have. In some political systems, rulers can dictate the state's policies independently or with the support of a relatively small number of key actors. In other systems, the institutions of government may distribute decision-making power among more than one body—for instance, between an executive and a legislature.

By shaping how leaders obtain power and make decisions, domestic institutions determine which actors' interests are taken into account. Leaders whose hold on power is unchallenged may not have to consider the interests of anyone else, and they can act on the basis of their personal interests or whims. More commonly, a ruler may only have to worry about maintaining the loyalty of the military by catering to that organization's interests.

In democratic political institutions, by contrast, the need to win elections forces leaders to think about how the voting public will respond to their policy choices. It also makes them dependent on organized groups that are willing to donate money and time to election campaigns. Although voters and organized interest groups are not literally in the room when decisions are made, democratic institutions force those who *are* in the room to take those actors' interests into account. Thus, institutions determine which actors and interests have a (figurative) seat at the table.

Some domestic actors may also have strategic advantages that magnify their influence. In Chapter 2 we introduced a strategic dilemma known as the collective action problem, which arises when a group of individuals with common interests seeks to act collectively to further those interests. As we saw, such efforts can fall short if each individual prefers to free ride on the efforts of others. One implication of this insight is that relatively small groups can be more effective than large groups at cooperating to further common interests. Indeed, small groups of highly motivated and informed individuals are better able to organize and coordinate their activities and prevent others from free riding. By contrast, large, dispersed groups in which each individual has only a small stake in or knowledge about a relevant policy decision are generally very hard to organize. For example, as discussed at the start of the chapter, whereas United Fruit stood to lose millions of dollars of property in Guatemala, the intervention cost each U.S. taxpayer only a few pennies. Had taxpayers been opposed to having their money spent this way, they would have had a hard time cooperating, since no individual had any incentive to spend time and money on such an effort. To the extent that a group's political influence depends on the ability of its members to cooperate, this strategic problem favors the few over the many. Thus, a relatively narrow interest group can successfully demand a policy that benefits that group at the expense of everyone else.

Appreciating the role of institutions and interactions, we can organize our discussion of domestic interests around four different types of actors, depicted in Figure 4.1. The first type consists of the leaders who make foreign policy decisions. State leaders choose when to make threats, what demands to issue, and ultimately, whether to wage war. These individuals matter the most because, by whatever rules of politics operate in their country, they have the authority to make these decisions. The next two types are bureaucracies and interest groups—both of which are organizations that have substantial resources and information to influence the decisions made by political leaders.

When the Guatemalan government seized property belonging to the United Fruit Company in the 1950s, arguing that it belonged to the workers of Guatemala, United Fruit asked the U.S. government to intervene. Here, a banner by Guatemala's General Confederation of Workers hangs in front of a United Fruit hiring hall.

The state apparatus is made up of a variety of different organizations collectively known as the **bureaucracy**. These organizations—which include the military, diplomatic corps, and intelligence agencies—may wield considerable influence because of their institutional resources and knowledge. The military in particular, by virtue of its coercive power, organizational discipline, and expertise in war fighting, can shape decisions about the use of force through both its role in implementation and its influence over political leaders.

Interest groups are groups of individuals with common interests that organize in order to push for policies that benefit their members. Of particular importance in the present context are economic interest groups, such as companies or groups of companies, and ethnic lobbies, which bring together people with similar policy interests owing to their common ethnic background. In later chapters, when we turn to issues like human rights (Chapter 12) and the environment (Chapter 13), interest groups that organize around other principles will come to the fore.

The final type of actor to consider is the most populous but rarely the most powerful: the general public. As already suggested, the influence of ordinary citizens varies considerably based on a country's domestic institutions. In democratic

bureaucracy

The collection of organizations—including the military, diplomatic corps, and intelligence agencies— that carry out most tasks of governance within a state.

interest groups

Groups of individuals with common interests that organize to influence public policy in a manner that benefits their members.

FIGURE 4.1 *Key Domestic Actors in Foreign Policy*

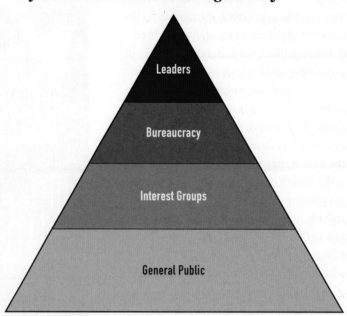

countries, free and fair elections provide individuals with a low-cost way to participate in deciding who governs. In other kinds of countries, it is harder for individual citizens to have much influence, since political leaders do not depend on their support. As long as a regime can count on the repressive power of the police and military, it can ignore the interests of ordinary people. Given this situation, understanding how the general public matters requires us to consider how democracy matters.

As we proceed through this chapter, we will walk down the pyramid in Figure 4.1 and consider arguments and evidence about the behavior of actors at each level.

Do Politicians Spark Wars Abroad in Order to Hold On to Power at Home?

As noted earlier in this chapter, Argentina sparked a war with Great Britain in 1982 when it invaded a set of nearby islands—known as the Falkland Islands to the British, the Malvinas to Argentines—that had been in dispute for a century and a half. This war was surprising in a number of respects. First, the islands were not particularly valuable pieces of territory. At the time of the war, the islands had a population of less than 2,000, and inhabitants' primary source of income was sheep farming. Indeed, just prior to the war, Britain had taken steps to weaken its hold over the islands. In 1981, Britain readied plans to withdraw the last of its naval vessels in the region and passed an act that stripped the islanders of full British citizenship.

Second, the war was surprising because of the imbalance in military power between the two states involved. Though separated from the islands by a larger distance, Britain had a far superior naval force. After Argentina invaded and occupied the Falklands on April 2, 1982, it took only 74 days for British forces to retake the islands. There were 255 dead on the British side, 635 on the Argentine side. So why did Argentina pick a fight with such a formidable foe, and why did Britain react so strongly to defend its right to islands that seemed to be of diminishing importance?

A large part of the answer to this puzzle lies not in international considerations, but in the domestic political interests of both countries' governments. At the time, British and Argentine leaders had pressing domestic problems to which military conflict may have seemed the perfect solution. The Argentine government—a group of military officers known as

An Argentine army soldier stands guard at an air base in Puerto Argentino during the Falklands War (Guerra de Las Malvinas) between Argentina and Britain. After Argentina invaded and occupied the Falklands on April 2, 1982, it took only 74 days for British forces to retake the islands.

a junta—had seized power in 1976, and its rule had become increasingly repressive and unpopular over time. In the early 1980s, Argentina suffered a severe economic downturn, which led to civil unrest and splits within the ruling group. Facing a dire threat to junta rule, the junta leader, General Leopoldo Galtieri, decided that an attack on the Malvinas might help solve the government's problem.

Knowing that most Argentines resented British control of the islands, Galtieri hoped that a bold move to seize the islands would stir up nationalist sentiment, distract people from their economic hardships, and give the military government a popular achievement that would bolster its prestige and legitimacy. Indeed, the invasion of the Malvinas had precisely this effect. Hence, Galtieri was seeking more than just territory when he seized the islands; he was also looking to solidify his hold on power.[10]

On the British side, Prime Minister Margaret Thatcher also had to worry about her political survival. Like Argentina, Britain in 1982 was in the midst of a severe recession. With unemployment soaring, Thatcher's popularity dropped precipitously. In February 1982, the month before the invasion, only 29 percent of Britons said that they approved of the job she was doing. Thatcher's firm response to the Falkland Islands crisis caused her poll numbers to soar. By May, with British operations to retake the Falklands under way, Thatcher's approval rating jumped to 44 percent. By the end of the war, her approval stood at 51 percent. The British prime minister rode this wave of popularity to electoral victory a year later. Hence, Thatcher's unexpectedly strong response to the Argentine

---

10. Jack Levy and Lily Vakily, "External Scapegoating in Authoritarian Regimes: Argentina in the Falklands/Malvinas Case," in *The Internationalization of Communal Strife*, ed. Manus I. Midlarski, 118–46 (London: Routledge, 1992).

British prime minister Margaret Thatcher, here visiting troops in the Falkland Islands, benefited politically from the Falklands War. Before the war, poor economic conditions in Britain had helped bring Thatcher's public approval rating down to just 29 percent. Once the war began, the British public rallied behind their leader, improving her approval rating to 51 percent.

invasion not only restored British control over the Falklands but also revived her political fortunes.[11]

What Do Leaders Want?

The leaders of states are not solely, if at all, statesmen or stateswomen looking out for the best interests of their nation; they are also individuals with many varied interests of their own. Some may have strong ideological beliefs that increase their willingness to pay costs or run risks in foreign policy. It is hard to understand World War II, for example, without reference to German leader Adolf Hitler's extreme ideology, which motivated him to seek out *Lebensraum* ("living space") for the German people by attacking Poland and then the Soviet Union.[12] Even in the absence of such extreme motivations, different leaders may come into office with varied ideas, personality traits, or prior life experiences that shape how they think about foreign policy, including the desirability of using military force (see "How Do We Know?").[13]

State leaders may also have more prosaic personal motivations. As the story of the Falklands War reminds us, leaders are also politicians, people who benefit from holding political office. Being in office confers all manner of benefits: the ego boost of having power, opportunities to enrich oneself and one's friends, the ability to shape policy in desired ways. As a result, politicians think a lot about how to obtain office and, once in power, how to secure their hold on it. This means that political leaders make choices with an eye toward how those choices will influence their chances of staying in power.

How might these motivations affect leaders' decisions about war and peace? At the most general level, leaders' desire to stay in power means that they must be responsive to the interests of those who control their political fate, whether voters, organized interest groups, the military, or others. As a result, the assumption that political leaders want to remain in office plays a key role in almost every aspect of this chapter: it helps account for the influence of special interest groups that can

11. Approval figures are from David Butler and Gareth Butler, eds., *British Political Facts, 1900–1994*, 7th ed. (London: Macmillan, 1994), 256. There is some controversy over how much the Falklands War contributed to the Conservative victory in 1983. See Harold D. Clarke, William Mishler, and Paul Whiteley, "Recapturing the Falklands: Models of Conservative Popularity, 1979–83," *British Journal of Political Science* 20, no 1. (January 1990): 63–81.

12. There is a debate among historians about how much of Hitler's foreign policy can be explained by his personal ideology. For a balanced view, which ultimately concludes that ideology played an important role, see Allan Bullock, "Hitler and the Origins of the Second World War," in *The Origins of the Second World War: A. J. P. Taylor and His Critics*, ed. William Roger Louis, 117–45 (New York: Wiley, 1972).

13. See, for example, Elizabeth N. Saunders, *Leaders at War: How Presidents Shape Military Interventions* (Ithaca, NY: Cornell University Press, 2011); and Michael C. Horowitz, Allan C. Stam, and Cali M. Ellis, *Why Leaders Fight* (New York: Cambridge University Press, 2015).

Are Women Leaders More Peaceful than Men?

A remarkable global trend in recent decades has been the increasing number of countries led by women. While history provides examples of queens and empresses, female heads of state have been rare in the modern era, with the numbers taking off only since the 1980s (see Figure A). The figures are still low in absolute terms—in 2020, only 15 of the 193 countries in the world had a woman chief executive—but the recent growth is part of a broader trend that has also seen increased representation of women in legislatures and militaries. How does the gender of a state's leader affect its foreign policy?

A wealth of research shows that, on average, women are less aggressive than men and more likely to seek compromise solutions to disputes. Particularly in Western countries, women are less likely than men to support the use of military force. Evidence also suggests that states with more domestic gender equality, including more women in the legislature, use less violence in international crises and spend less on their militaries, and the extension of the right to vote to women has been associated with a decrease in conflict initiated by democracies.[a]

So, are female leaders less likely to wage war? Recent research suggests a surprising answer. In one study, Michael Horowitz, Allan Stam, and Cali Ellis collected information on all heads of state from 1875 to 2004 and examined the relationship between leaders' propensity to threaten or use military force against other states and a variety of personal characteristics. The authors found that, on average, gender has little effect on dispute behavior, and if anything, women are more conflict-prone than men. While 30 percent of male leaders initiated at least one militarized conflict during their tenure, 36 percent of female leaders did.[b] This finding replicates earlier work, focused on democratic countries, indicating that female presidents and prime ministers engage in *more* conflictual behavior internationally than men do.[c]

What might explain this result? One explanation is that, even if there are differences across men and women in the general population, those differences do not hold among the subset of individuals who become heads of state. The domestic political process of gaining and holding elected office may penalize women who are seen as insufficiently "tough." Particularly in societies with low levels of women's empowerment, female leaders have an incentive to compensate by acting in a manner that runs counter to the gender stereotype, leading them to initiate more conflicts.[d]

A second explanation hinges on the beliefs and behavior of other states when confronting a female leader. Military conflict is the outcome of a strategic interaction between at least two states, not the choice of a single individual. If adversaries expect female leaders to be more dovish, then they will make greater demands on them, thus increasing the risk of conflict. Male leaders may also feel an additional incentive not to back down to a woman adversary.[e]

Overall, then, while the literature suggests that increasing gender equality has a number of beneficial effects, the rising prevalence of female heads of state does not necessarily portend a more peaceful world.

---

a. For a review of findings on gender effects on international relations, see Dan Reiter, "The Positivist Study of Gender and International Relations," *Journal of Conflict Resolution* 59, no. 7 (2015): 1301–26. On the effects of female suffrage, see Joslyn N. Barnhart, Robert F. Trager, Elizabeth N. Saunders, and Allen Dafoe, "The Suffragist Peace," *International Organization* 74, no. 4 (Fall 2020): 633–70.

b. Michael C. Horowitz, Allan C. Stam, and Cali M. Ellis, *Why Leaders Fight* (New York: Cambridge University Press, 2015), 158–77.

c. Michael T. Koch and Sarah A. Fulton, "In the Defense of Women: Gender, Office Holding, and National Security Policy in Established Democracies," *Journal of Politics* 73, no. 1 (2001): 1–16; see also Mary Caprioli and Mark A. Boyer, "Gender, Violence, and International Crisis," *Journal of Conflict Resolution* 45, no. 4 (2001): 503–18.

d. Madison Schramm and Alexandra Stark, "Peacemakers or Iron Ladies? A Cross-National Study of Gender and International Conflict," *Security Studies* 29, no. 3 (2020): 515–48.

e. Joshua A. Schwartz and Christopher W. Blair, "Do Women Make More Credible Threats? Gender Stereotypes, Audience Costs, and Crisis Bargaining," *International Organization* 74, no. 4 (Fall 2020): 872–95.

FIGURE A *Number of States with Female Leaders, 1900–2020*

Figure sources: Archigos: A Database of Political Leaders, version 4.1; Henk E. Goemans, Kristian Skrede Gleditsch, and Giacomo Chiozza, "Introducing *Archigos*: A Data Set of Political Leaders," *Journal of Peace Research* 49 (2009): 269–83. Updated to 2020 by Curtis Bell, *The Rulers, Elections, and Irregular Governance Dataset (REIGN)* (Broomfield, CO: OEF Research, 2020), available at www.oefresearch.org.

provide resources useful for maintaining power; it contributes to an understanding of the role of the military, whose support is often necessary for a government to stay in power; and it is a necessary element of arguments about the effects of accountability in democratic political systems. In short, leaders' desire to hold office explains how the interests of other domestic actors can matter at the level of policy making.

But an interest in holding on to power does not turn political leaders into mere instruments of other actors. Strategic politicians can use their control of policy to shape their political environment rather than just respond to it. In the case of war and peace, a common argument is that leaders sometimes use force abroad not to further any national interest but rather to enhance their personal hold on power at home.

The Rally Effect and the Diversionary Incentive

The idea that leaders can further their own political interests by fighting a war flows from the rally-'round-the-flag effect, or rally effect for short. The term **rally effect** refers to people's tendency to become more supportive of their country's government when it experiences dramatic international events, such as wars. This effect is most apparent in countries in which public opinion polling regularly measures popular levels of support for a leader.

Often, approval ratings jump up at the onset of a war or some other international crisis, as was the case with Thatcher's approval ratings at the outset of the Falklands War. The most dramatic rally event ever recorded followed the terrorist attacks of September 11, 2001, which caused President George W. Bush's approval rating to jump immediately from 51 to 86 percent, eventually reaching as high as 90 percent. Even in countries without opinion polls and approval ratings, we see cases in which the start of war caused an upsurge of national unity and support for the government. As we noted at the outset of this chapter, Argentina's military government reversed a tide of public discontent by invading the Falkland Islands.

Why do people rally around the flag at times of international crisis? There are a number of explanations. Social psychologists have shown that members of a group often feel greater attachment and loyalty to the group when they experience conflict with outsiders.[14] Hence, international conflict can cause an upwelling of national sentiment, and a leader can, in turn, derive increased support as the protector of the group's interests. At the same time, political opponents may decide to dampen their criticism of the government at a time of national crisis, and the government may use the emergency to crack down on dissent. This means that the government dominates the political discourse and can frame the public's evaluation of its policies without fear that opposing voices will split public opinion.[15]

rally effect

People's tendency to become more supportive of their country's government in times of dramatic international events, such as crises or wars.

---

14. See, for example, Lewis A. Coser, *The Functions of Social Conflict* (New York: Free Press, 1956). The pioneering work of the rally effect in the United States is John E. Mueller, *War, Presidents, and Public Opinion* (New York: Wiley, 1973).

15. Richard A. Brody and Catherine R. Shapiro, "A Reconsideration of the Rally Phenomenon in Public Opinion," in *Political Behavior Annual*, ed. Samuel Long, 77–102 (Boulder, CO: Westview Press, 1989).

Just a few days before invading the Falkland Islands, the Argentine government faced massive protests and calls for the overthrow of the ruling junta. Rioters confronted police, and thousands were arrested. The war with Britain provided the Argentine junta a (temporary) reprieve from these problems by shifting the public's attention away from domestic issues.

International conflict can also create a diversion from problems that might otherwise drag down a leader's popularity, such as economic troubles or scandals. Foreign policy crises tend to drive other issues out of news headlines, directing people's attention away from the domestic issues that divide and disappoint them and toward the more unifying challenge of meeting a foreign threat. Finally, international conflict may give embattled leaders an opportunity to blame foreigners for the country's problems—a phenomenon known as scapegoating.

The existence of rally effects suggests that political leaders may at times face a **diversionary incentive**: a temptation to spark an international crisis in order to rally public support at home. This idea was popularized in the 1997 movie *Wag the Dog*, in which a scandal-plagued national leader hires a movie director to produce news footage of a fake war in order to boost his approval ratings. The logic, however, long precedes Hollywood. In William Shakespeare's *Henry IV, Part II*, a dying King Henry advises his son, Prince Hal, that to prevent plots against him he needs to "busy giddy minds / With foreign quarrels." This advice echoes in the words of a Russian minister who, during a 1904 dispute with Japan, reportedly told the tsar: "What this country needs is a short, victorious war to stem the tide of revolution."[16] Whether the tsar found this argument persuasive or not, Russia and Japan declared war on each other on February 10, 1904.

diversionary incentive
The incentive that state leaders have to start international crises in order to rally public support at home.

---

16. This quotation is attributed to Russian interior minister Vladimir Plehve. However, the authenticity of the quotation is unclear, and it has been suggested that it was attributed to Plehve only later by his political enemies.

The danger posed by the rally effect should be clear from the discussion in Chapter 3. There, we assumed that a state's first-best outcome in a crisis is to get its way without having to fight. Fighting, after all, imposes costs that the state should prefer to avoid. A diversionary temptation could alter the balance of costs and benefits. If those who control the state's foreign policy think that using force abroad would greatly improve their chances of staying in power, then they may prefer war over a negotiated settlement, even one that gives them most of what they want.

These benefits may be particularly tempting to leaders who are insecure domestically because of public discontent with their policies or hard economic times. Such a leader may decide that doing nothing would mean losing office, so waging war and invoking the rally effect may be an appealing gamble. This phenomenon has been called gambling for resurrection: taking a risky action, such as starting a war, when the alternative is certain to be very bad.

A sports analogy is useful here. Hockey teams trailing in the final minutes of a game sometimes pull their goalie in order to substitute in an additional attacker. Doing so increases the chances that they can even the score, but it also makes it easier for the other team to score against their undefended net. The gamble makes sense because a loss is a loss regardless of whether a team loses by one goal or by many. Consequently, the downside risk of pulling the goalie is small compared to the upside potential of tying the game. Political leaders who think it is very likely that they will lose office because of poor economic conditions, such as the Argentine junta in 1982, might similarly see a large upside to starting a war and gambling that the outcome will be positive.

Do Leaders "Wag the Dog"?

Do leaders routinely gamble for resurrection by starting wars abroad at times of political need? To answer this question, numerous studies have sought to determine whether the likelihood that a state will get involved in military conflict increases when the leader is unpopular, the country is in a recession, citizens face high unemployment or inflation, or, in the case of democratic countries, when a well-timed rally shortly before an election could be particularly useful. Overall, these studies have found some evidence of diversionary effects, but only in particular circumstances. The relationship between, say, economic problems and international conflict is not straightforward but instead depends on a number of factors. For example, there is evidence that autocratic governments respond to inflation by starting conflicts against states with which they have historical rivalries—as in the case of the Argentine junta initiating the conflict with Great Britain. But the same study showed that this effect does not hold for democratic countries, nor does it motivate conflicts against adversaries with which the country has no history of hostility.[17] In democracies, evidence suggests that bad economic conditions have

---

17. Sara McLaughlin Mitchell and Brandon C. Prins, "Rivalry and Diversionary Uses of Force," *Journal of Conflict Resolution* 48, no. 6 (December 2004): 937–61.

different effects depending on whether government is from the left or right end of the political spectrum.[18]

At the same time, some research suggests that the relationship between international conflict and leaders' political security is the opposite of what diversionary theory suggests: international conflict is more likely to be initiated by leaders whose hold on office is relatively strong.[19] For example, in democratic systems, leaders are more likely to start wars right *after* elections, not right before them as diversionary theory would suggest. A democratic leader is most secure just after an election, since the next election is, at that point, several years away.[20]

And just as there are examples in which leaders may have "wagged the dog," there are also "dogs that didn't bark":[21] instances where politically vulnerable officials might have been tempted to use force in a diversionary manner but did not. For example, in the run-up to the 2020 U.S. presidential election, there was some speculation that President Trump might use force against Iran in order to deflect attention from the COVID-19 pandemic and the United States' ensuing economic problems. He did not do so, however, and reporting suggests that he most seriously considered escalation against Iran after the election, not before.[22]

This is not to say that diversionary incentives never play a role in particular cases; in fact, historians cite many examples in which such logic contributed to the onset of war. What these results do suggest, however, is that leaders do not *systematically* use international conflict for diversionary purposes or to gamble for resurrection. In other words, even if diversionary incentives have contributed to war in some cases, they account for only a portion of the conflict behavior we observe.

Why might this be the case? If sparking international conflict serves leaders' political interests, why do we not see more consistent evidence of this effect? One possible answer is that most political leaders are not as cynical as we assume and they would not actually start a war simply to maintain their hold on power. Although we cannot rule out this possibility, there are other conceivable explanations for why even cynical leaders might not start a war to further their own political interests.

The first explanation is that the domestic political benefits of war relative to peace have to be large—perhaps unrealistically large—in order to eliminate the possibility of a peaceful bargain. Recall the simple bargaining framework we illustrated in the previous chapter, now depicted in Figure 4.2. As shown in the top panel, the size of the bargaining range is determined by the sum of the war costs to both

18. See, for example, Philip Arena and Glenn Palmer, "Politics or the Economy? Domestic Correlates of Dispute Involvement in Developed Democracies," *International Studies Quarterly* 53, no. 4 (December 2009): 955–75; and Benjamin Fordham, "Partisanship, Macroeconomic Policy, and U.S. Uses of Force, 1949-1994," *Journal of Conflict Resolution* 42, no. 4 (1998): 418–439.

19. See Giacomo Chiozza and H. E. Goemans, "Peace through Insecurity: Tenure and International Conflict," *Journal of Conflict Resolution* 47, no. 4 (August 2003): 443–67.

20. Kurt Taylor Gaubatz, "Election Cycles and War," *Journal of Conflict Resolution* 35, no. 2 (June 1991): 212–44.

21. This phrase comes from Sir Arthur Conan Doyle's "The Adventure of Silver Blaze," a Sherlock Holmes story in which the key piece of evidence was something that did not happen. A dog not barking when a crime was being committed suggested that the perpetrator was known to the dog.

22. Eric Schmitt, Maggie Haberman, David E. Sanger, Helene Cooper, et al., "Trump Sought Options for Attacking Iran to Stop Its Growing Nuclear Program," *New York Times*, November 16, 2020, www.nytimes.com/2020/11/16/us/politics/trump-iran-nuclear.html (accessed 12/16/20).

FIGURE 4.2 *Rally Effects and the Bargaining Range*

The top panel shows the expected outcome of a war between State A and State B as well as the resulting bargaining range. The lower panel shows how the bargaining range shrinks if the leader of State A expects political benefits, in the form of a rally, as a result of war. This benefit increases the value of war to A, offsetting some or all of its costs, but as long as the benefit does not exceed the costs of war to *both* states, a bargaining range still exists.

sides. Now imagine that the leader of State A expects to reap political benefits from waging war. This benefit increases the value of war to the leader as indicated in the lower panel. This added benefit shrinks the bargaining range, but even if this benefit is greater than the expected costs to State A—so that the leader sees a net benefit rather than a net cost to war—a bargaining range could still exist, as shown.

The size of this new bargaining range is given by the sum of the net costs (the total costs to both states minus the additional political benefit). Only if this benefit exceeds the sum of the war costs to both states does the bargaining range vanish, making war inevitable. Hence, even if the leader of one state expected large political benefits from waging war, these benefits would be sufficient to cause war only if they outweighed the war costs to *both* sides. This condition becomes more likely if the leaders of both states expect political benefits from war, as was the case in the Falklands War. Notice also that the political benefits from war mean that State A can demand a better deal from State B than it otherwise could. Knowing this, potential targets might avoid picking fights with politically vulnerable leaders, thereby depriving them of the opportunity to use force opportunistically.[23] These

23. See, for example, Benjamin O. Fordham, "Strategic Conflict Avoidance and the Diversionary Use of Force," *Journal of Politics* 67, no. 1 (February 2005): 132–53; and Brett Ashley Leeds and David R. Davis, "Domestic Political Vulnerability and International Disputes," *Journal of Conflict Resolution* 41, no. 6 (December 1997): 814–34.

observations remind us that war is the product of an interaction between at least two actors and not the choice of a single actor.

The Political Costs of War

A second reason why diversionary effects might be weak is that war can impose domestic political costs in addition to promising benefits. This is evident from the Falklands case as well. While Thatcher rode her postwar wave of support to a resounding electoral victory in Britain, the Argentine junta that lost the war met a very different fate. Following Argentina's defeat, angry protesters once again filled the streets. Galtieri and other members of the junta resigned or were stripped of their posts, and several went to prison.

The story of the Russo-Japanese War has a similar ending. Far from the short, victorious war the Russians hoped for, the war actually lasted almost two years, and the Russians suffered a humiliating defeat at the hands of the Japanese. Rather than stemming the tide of domestic revolution, as the Russian minister reportedly hoped, successive defeats on the battlefield increased the public's unhappiness with the tsar's regime and helped usher in the revolution of 1905, when the tsar was forced to make political concessions to his opponents. Full-scale revolution would hit Russia in 1917, in the midst of yet more battlefield defeats in World War I. Indeed, the initial surge of patriotism that generally accompanies the onset of war can quickly give way to discontent and rebellion if the war goes badly.

One way to measure the relationship between the costs of war and its domestic political repercussions is to consider how public support for war changes as the costs mount. Figure 4.3 shows the relationship between public support and battle deaths for major U.S. military operations since and including World War II. As the graph shows, most operations started with very high levels of public support, but this support generally fell off as the number of U.S. battle deaths mounted. The only wars that remained popular throughout were World War II—a war of national

Figure sources: Numbers for World War II, Korea, Vietnam, the Gulf War, and Somalia come from Eric V. Larson, *Casualties and Consensus* (Santa Monica, CA: RAND, 1996). Other poll numbers come from Gallup, www.gallup.com/file/poll/183590/Mistake_Going_into_Iraq_and_Afghanistan_150612.pdf (accessed 11/22/17). Casualty figures for Iraq and Afghanistan are from www.icasualties.org (accessed 1/20/15).

FIGURE 4.3 *U.S. Battle Deaths and Public Support for War*

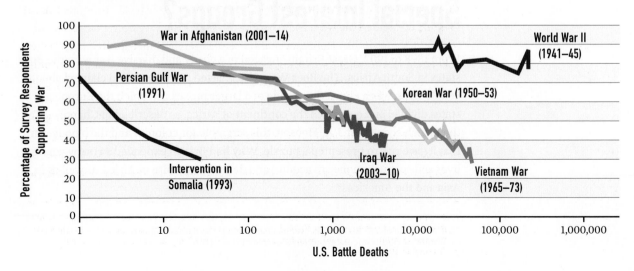

survival that followed Japan's attack on the U.S. homeland—and the Persian Gulf War, which caused relatively few deaths on the American side.

Moreover, in cases in which public support for war collapsed, presidents' approval ratings also suffered. During the Korean War, President Harry S. Truman saw his approval rating fall to as low as 22 percent, and he declined to run for reelection in 1952. The unpopularity of the Vietnam War similarly doomed the presidency of Lyndon Johnson, who dropped his bid for reelection in March 1968. The Iraq War dragged down President Bush's approval ratings, causing his Republican Party to lose control of Congress in 2006 and contributing to the election of Democrat Barack Obama in 2008. More generally, research has shown that leaders who fight losing or costly wars are more likely to be removed from office than those who win wars.[24] Such concerns about the costs of war likely figured into President Trump's decision not to escalate force against Iran before the 2020 election.

The evidence suggests that in terms of their political interests, leaders should see war not as a pure opportunity but as a gamble—and one that has a downside risk. Hence, in thinking about how reelection incentives influence the way leaders think about war and peace, we need to set the costs of losing a war against the potential benefits of the rally effect. These costs may explain why we do not see strong or systematic evidence that politically insecure politicians engage in diversionary conflict.

In light of this observation, it is worth recalling that the scandal-plagued leader in the movie *Wag the Dog* does not start an actual war; instead, he hires a movie producer to stage a fake war for public consumption. The attraction of doing this is clear: when you script the war yourself, you can make sure the right side wins. In the real world, war is a risky gamble—not just for the state but also for the political interests of its leaders.

Do Countries Fight Wars to Satisfy the Military or Special Interest Groups?

From 1898 to 1902, Great Britain engaged in a costly and divisive war with the Boer states in South Africa. The Boer War, which lasted three years and claimed about 50,000 lives, was a climactic episode of a larger process in which the European states divided and colonized the continent of Africa, as described in Chapter 1. To the British economist J. A. Hobson, this scramble for colonies and the bloody wars that it gave rise to presented a puzzle. Why had Britain expended so many young lives and so much money to acquire and defend an empire in Africa, as well as in Asia and the Americas?

---

24. See, for example, H. E. Goemans, *War and Punishment: The Causes of War Termination and the First World War* (Princeton, NJ: Princeton University Press, 2000).

The answer that Hobson arrived at was unsettling. He calculated that although imperialism did not benefit the British nation as a whole, it was extremely profitable for a few small groups within the country. The primary beneficiaries, he argued, were wealthy people with the ability to invest overseas. With colonial possessions came many opportunities for profitable investments in railroads, mines, and other properties. Investors could lend money to colonial governments at favorable interest rates and expect a high rate of return. In pushing for colonial possessions, Hobson argued, financial interests found allies in military leaders, who sought glory and larger budgets, and arms manufacturers, who sought profits. In his view, these groups used their power and influence to force British governments to pursue a policy that benefited them at the expense of the greater good.[25]

Hobson's theory of imperialism is not without critics, but the general thesis—that wars are fought to benefit military and business interests—is a familiar one. It echoes famously in the words of U.S. president Dwight Eisenhower, who warned of the influence of a **military-industrial complex**, an alliance of military leaders and arms manufacturers that presumably have an interest in an aggressive foreign policy.

In this section we consider the influence of the military and interest groups with respect to questions of war and peace. As we will see, there are times when these actors might be expected to have hawkish interests, because they anticipate benefits from war and/or pay few of the costs. These two sets of actors also have strategic advantages that they can exploit in their interactions with political leaders and others within the country. That said, we will see that the primary effect of hawkish actors is not to cause wars per se—by eliminating the bargaining range— but rather to expand the scope of a state's ambitions and to increase the conditions under which the state would consider fighting a war. Hence, hawkish domestic interests do not lead directly to the breakdown of bargaining, but they do create more opportunities for such failures to occur.

Bureaucratic Politics and the Military

Although the ultimate decision to wage war may lie in the hands of a few individuals, the actual machinery of government that deals with matters of war and peace is much larger and more complex. The leader of a modern state sits atop a large bureaucratic apparatus: a collection of organizations that manage many of the details of governance. Wars are planned and implemented by the state's military— usually a massive organization with thousands and, in some cases, millions of individuals. Negotiations with other countries are conducted by a host of diplomats around the world, typically overseen by a ministry of foreign affairs (known in the United States as the State Department). Information about other countries' military capabilities and intentions is collected and analyzed by intelligence organizations such as the United States' CIA, Britain's MI6 (Military Intelligence, Section 6), and Russia's SVR (Foreign Intelligence Service). Given all the tasks that governments

military-industrial complex

An alliance between military leaders and the industries that benefit from international conflict, such as arms manufacturers.

---

25. J. A. Hobson, *Imperialism: A Study* (London: James Nisbet, 1902).

must perform and all the individuals that are needed to carry out those tasks, bureaucracy is a necessary part of any modern state.

This observation opens up the possibility that decisions about war and peace are shaped not only by state leaders but also by the interests of the bureaucratic organizations involved in decision-making processes.[26] While such organizations care about what is best for the country, they may also care about the resources that they control and the influence that they themselves wield. They generally seek bigger budgets, more policy-making input, and opportunities for personal promotion. As a result, they may press for policies that boost their own status or fit their own worldview.

For example, prior to the 2003 Iraq War there were serious disagreements within the U.S. government between the Defense Department and the State Department. Civilian leaders at the Pentagon generally expected war with Iraq to be easy, while those at the State Department were more cautious and emphasized the need for international diplomacy. The departments also disagreed over which agency should take the lead role in rebuilding Iraq politically and economically in the aftermath of the conflict. These debates reflect a common aphorism about bureaucratic politics that "where you stand depends on where you sit"—that is, the leaders of bureaucratic agencies often take policy stands that reflect their own organizations' needs. In the end, the Defense Department won these scuffles.[27]

As this example suggests, the military is usually the most influential bureaucratic actor in matters of war and peace. Up to now, our discussion has treated the military as an instrument of the state—a tool that states use to increase their leverage in international bargaining. What happens when we think about the military as an actor in its own right?

There is a compelling—although, as we will see, incomplete—argument to be made that the more influence the military has over foreign policy decision making, the more aggressive the state will be. This argument rests on the assumption that members of the military have ideological, organizational, and professional interests in policies that make war more likely. Ideologically, leaders in the armed forces may be predisposed to see military solutions to foreign policy problems, overestimating the effectiveness of force relative to other alternatives. As an organization, the military can demand larger budgets and more personnel when the state is frequently engaged in international conflict than it can when the state is at peace. And professionally, military officers find that combat experience is crucial to being promoted to the highest ranks. All these considerations suggest that the military sees benefits to war that other actors may not.

Perhaps the most dramatic example of how military influence can lead to aggressive foreign policy is the case of Japan in the 1930s. During this period, Japan pursued a relentless campaign of expansion against its neighbors, ultimately bringing the country into war with China, France, Britain, the Netherlands,

---

26. The classic investigation of bureaucratic politics is Graham Allison and Philip Zelikow, *Essence of Decision: Explaining the Cuban Missile Crisis*, 2nd ed. (New York: Longman, 1999).

27. See, for example, Bob Woodward, *Plan of Attack* (New York: Simon & Schuster, 2004).

and the United States. This aggressive turn in foreign policy coincided with a creeping takeover by the military, which undermined the country's nascent democratic system.

In 1931, elements of the Japanese military provoked a war with China and seized the region of Manchuria, which military leaders prized for its coal and iron. A year later, the prime minister of Japan was assassinated by a group of naval officers—an event that ushered in the end of civilian control of Japanese politics. The military thus became the main instigator of Japan's expansionist policies. This case is an extreme example, but there is broader evidence to suggest that countries governed by the military, or in which civilian leadership has weak control of the military, are more likely to initiate militarized conflicts.[28] (See "What Shaped Our World?" on p. 166 for another example.)

Nevertheless, it is important not to automatically equate the military with militarism. One study examined the advice that military leaders gave U.S. decision makers in about 20 key crises during the Cold War, comparing how aggressive the officers were relative to the president's civilian advisers. The study found that military advisers were no more likely than civilians to advocate the use of force in a crisis; rather, the main difference between the two groups was over the level of force that should be used in the event of an operation, with military advisers consistently preferring larger deployments. The author concluded that the "stereotype of a belligerent chorus of generals and admirals intimidating a pacific civilian establishment is not supported by the evidence."[29]

Similarly, a study of elite opinion in the United States shows that military leaders are inclined to advocate the use of force in a narrower set of cases than are civilian leaders without any military experience.[30] Indeed, by all accounts, U.S. military officers were much more reluctant to go to war against Iraq in 2003 than were civilian leaders at the Pentagon and White House. Many top commanders thought that war with Iraq would be costly and that conducting it successfully would require larger commitments of manpower and money than the civilian leadership was willing to make.[31] Such observations suggest that, in some contexts at least, the military's interests push in a conservative direction—more appreciative of the limits of what can be achieved through force and more sensitive to the human costs of war, which are, after all, borne by its personnel.

---

28. Todd S. Sechser, "Are Soldiers Less War-Prone than Statesmen?" *Journal of Conflict Resolution* 48, no. 5 (2004): 746–74; Jessica L. Weeks, "Strongmen and Straw Men: Authoritarian Regimes and the Initiation of International Conflict," *American Political Science Review* 106, no. 2 (2012): 326–347. The idea that civilians can lose control of the military also plays a large role in explanations of World War I. See Stephen Van Evera, "The Cult of the Offensive and the Origins of the First World War," *International Security* 9, no. 1 (Summer 1984): 58–107; and Samuel R. Williamson Jr. and Russel Van Wyk, *July 1914: Soldiers, Statesmen, and the Coming of the Great War: A Brief Documentary History* (Boston: Bedford/St. Martin's, 2003).

29. Richard K. Betts, *Soldiers, Statesmen, and Cold War Crises* (New York: Columbia University Press, 1991), 4; see also David H. Petraeus, "Military Influence and the Post-Vietnam Use of Force," *Armed Forces & Society* 15, no. 4 (July 1, 1989): 489–505.

30. See Peter D. Feaver and Christopher Gelpi, *Choosing Your Battles: American Civil-Military Relations and the Use of Force* (Princeton, NJ: Princeton University Press, 2004).

31. See, for example, Michael R. Gordon and Bernard E. Trainor, *Cobra II: The Inside Story of the Invasion and Occupation of Iraq* (New York: Pantheon, 2006).

The Kargil War and Military Influence in War

One of the more dangerous episodes in modern history started rather quietly in April 1999, when Pakistani military forces secretly infiltrated across the Line of Control (LoC) that separates the Pakistani- and Indian-controlled areas of the disputed Kashmir region. When India discovered Pakistan's incursion, it mobilized to repel the attack. Over the next several weeks, the two countries fought a war in the high mountains near the town of Kargil. This was neither the first nor the bloodiest war between the two countries, but it was the first that took place under the specter of nuclear war. Only a year earlier, the two countries had openly tested nuclear devices. It was also a rare example of war between two democratic countries. How can we explain this episode?

Interests At the root of the conflict is a long-standing territorial dispute over the region of Kashmir, which both India and Pakistan claim on historical and religious grounds (see Map 3.1 on p. 98). But even while both states want to possess the entire region, actors within each country place different values on it and are willing to pay different costs to obtain it. In particular, the military in Pakistan has generally been more willing than the country's civilian leaders to run a risk of war with India.

Interactions The conflict over Kashmir has led to repeated episodes of bargaining in which force has been threatened and used, including full-scale wars in 1947, 1965, and 1971. Even so, only weeks before the Kargil War broke out, the countries' leaders had met to affirm their desire for a peaceful resolution. The infiltration of Pakistani forces across the LoC thus represented an unexpected escalation, designed to bolster Pakistan's bargaining power. Once India responded, the subsequent fighting took place in the shadow of deterrent threats. Pakistan put its nuclear forces on alert and threatened to use every weapon in its arsenal if India invaded; India responded by putting its own missiles on alert. With the risks so high and foreign pressure mounting, Pakistan had little choice but to pull its forces back behind the LoC. So why did Pakistan initiate such a dangerous gamble?

Institutions The answer lies in the country's domestic political institutions. Even though Pakistan has a democratically elected government, its military is very powerful and has on several occasions ousted civilian leaders that it did not like. Indeed, shortly after the Kargil War, the prime minister, Nawaz Sharif, was deposed and replaced by the army's chief of staff, General Pervez Musharraf. The danger of removal by the military has led to weak civilian control and oversight of the armed forces.

Although there are many unknowns about Pakistan's decision making in the lead-up to the war, there is good reason to believe that the military command manipulated Sharif into starting a conflict he did not fully understand.[a] When India accused Pakistan of crossing the LoC in May 1999, Sharif claimed that the invaders were local Kashmiri insurgents operating on their own initiative. Sharif and others claim that when he was briefed on the plan to support the insurgency, he was not told that Pakistani military forces would cross the LoC in large numbers. In addition, U.S. officials reportedly believed that the move to put Pakistani nuclear forces on alert during the war was done without Sharif's knowledge.

As this episode suggests, military organizations are sometimes willing to run greater risks than are the civilian authorities whom they are supposed to serve. When the military wields enormous influence and civilian control is weak, this behavior can have dangerous consequences for the country, its neighbors, and the world.

---

a. This discussion is based on Owen Bennett Jones, *Pakistan: Eye of the Storm* (New Haven, CT: Yale University Press, 2003), 87–109.

Interest Groups: Economic and Ethnic Lobbies

Most people are familiar with the possibility that special interest groups can influence foreign policy to further their particular interests. In the wake of the 2003 U.S. invasion of Iraq, Vice President Richard Cheney's former company, Halliburton, was awarded contracts worth billions of dollars to rebuild Iraq's infrastructure and supply American troops. By the end of 2006, the company's stock was worth four times what it had been valued at the start of the war. Considering, too, that President Bush himself had once been an oil industry executive, some observers speculated that the Iraq War was fought at the behest of oil companies interested in Iraq's oil and of military contractors interested in taxpayer dollars.

Such charges are not new. U.S. interventions in Latin American countries have often been ascribed to the influence of American businesses whose properties in those countries were at risk. The previously mentioned case of Guatemala, where United Fruit feared a major loss at the hands of an unfriendly government, was by no means unique. The United States also intervened in Cuba (1961), the Dominican Republic (1965), and Chile (1973)—all places where American investors had substantial assets.

Although economic actors such as companies and industries figure most prominently in stories of interest-group influence, not all groups organize around economic motives. Interest groups that organize around ethnic ties can also influence foreign policy. For example, governments may respond to pressure from politically powerful ethnic groups to intervene in neighbors' civil wars on behalf of ethnic kin who live across the border.[32]

In the United States, two particularly influential groups stand out. One is the pro-Israel lobby: a collection of individuals and groups who want the U.S. government to support and defend the state of Israel—a stance that often brings the United States into conflict with Israel's adversaries in the region. The main lobbying arm of this group is the American Israel Public Affairs Committee (AIPAC), which is considered one of the most effective lobbying groups in Washington.[33]

The second standout is the anti-Castro lobby—groups that represent Cuban Americans opposed to the communist regime in Cuba. A large number of Cubans fled after Fidel Castro took over in 1959 and seized their property. Cuban American groups have lobbied the U.S. government to take strong actions to contain and undermine the Castro regime, actions that have included sponsoring a failed invasion by exiles in 1961 and imposing a strict economic embargo on the country. In 2014, President Barack Obama announced that he would restore some diplomatic and economic ties with Cuba, arguing that more than five decades of isolation had

---

32. Stephen M. Saideman, *The Ties that Divide: Ethnic Politics, Foreign Policy, and International Conflict* (New York: Columbia University Press, 2001).

33. For a recent study arguing that the pro-Israel lobby wields a great deal of influence on U.S. foreign policy, see John J. Mearsheimer and Stephen M. Walt, *The Israel Lobby and U.S. Foreign Policy* (New York: Farrar, Straus & Giroux, 2007). This book generated a great deal of controversy not only because of the content of the claims but also because of concerns about the quality of the evidence. For a sample of the dispute, see Robert C. Lieberman, "The 'Israel Lobby' and American Politics," *Perspectives on Politics* 7, no. 2 (2009): 235–57, as well as the response by Mearsheimer and Walt in the same issue.

failed to change the regime. Nonetheless, the effort to lift the embargo faced resistance from the Cuban American lobby and its supporters in the U.S. Congress, and President Donald Trump reversed the opening of relations during his term.

Why do interest groups care about the state's foreign policy? In cases like the pro-Israel and anti-Castro lobbies, group members are motivated by ethnic attachment or ideological interests to support or oppose a particular country or regime. In the case of economic actors, foreign policy preferences arise whenever an actor's income depends on events in other countries or on the relationship between countries. A multinational company like United Fruit may have production facilities in numerous countries. If those countries experience political instability that threatens to disrupt the company's business, or if they are governed by unfriendly regimes that might confiscate the company's property, then the company might lobby for some form of intervention to protect its interests.

Similarly, an investor that owns stock in a foreign company or a bank that has lent money to a foreign government might lobby its own government to use military force to ensure the return on its investment or the repayment of its loan. Such lobbying could lead governments to intervene against unstable or unfriendly regimes. In the extreme case that Hobson considered, economic actors with international investments might even lobby their governments to extend direct imperial control over other countries. Although establishing and maintaining such control was costly, imperialism made it safer to invest overseas, since there was less danger that investments would be wiped out by instability or hostile governments. A smaller set of economic actors, primarily those that make and sell military armaments, also have a direct interest in their country's foreign policy, since a belligerent foreign policy keeps them in business.

However, aggressive policies may not always benefit economic actors, and these actors may instead press their governments to pursue friendly relations or even formal alliances with profitable partners. For example, American banks and companies that had important trade, financial, and investment interests in Western Europe played a significant role in lobbying for a strong U.S. commitment to defend Western Europe at the outset of the Cold War. Similarly, U.S. banks that depended heavily on loans to Asia lobbied for strong alliance commitments to Japan and South Korea.[34]

As noted earlier, U.S. corporations interested in selling goods to China have been a political force lobbying for more cooperative relations with that country. In fact, an extensive literature suggests that trade between countries decreases the likelihood of war between them, in part because businesses that profit from the trade lobby against policies that could lead to conflict.[35] In sum, depending on where and how they do business, economic actors can have an interest in peaceful relations with some countries and/or hostile relations with others.

---

34. Benjamin O. Fordham, *Building the Cold War Consensus: The Political Economy of U.S. National Security Policy, 1949–51* (Ann Arbor: University of Michigan Press, 1998).

35. Stephen G. Brooks, "Economic Actors' Lobbying Influence on the Prospects for War and Peace," *International Organization* 67, no. 4 (Fall 2013): 863–88.

How Can Small Groups Have a Big Influence on Policy?

We have seen that militaries seeking budgets and prestige, businesses seeking profits, and ethnic groups looking out for their kin may all, at times, see particular benefits to war. What is remarkable about each of these actors is how small they are relative to those who pay the costs of war. The generals and admirals who run military organizations are greatly outnumbered both by the enlisted personnel who bear the brunt of the fighting and by the rest of the population. Multinational companies and ethnic lobbies tend to make up a small fraction of society. Given how extensively they are outnumbered, when and how can these narrow interests prevail? The answer lies in the nature of the interactions between these different actors and the institutions that regulate them.

The military's influence on foreign policy decision making derives from the fact that it controls a large number of guns and people trained to use them. While militaries are generally created in order to defend a state from foreign threats, their capabilities inevitably make them key players domestically as well. In many states, the military plays a direct role in ensuring the continuation of the government. This role can either be very explicit (as with military dictatorships, in which military officers take direct control of executive power) or more subtle but no less potent.

In many countries, the military is able and willing to intervene in politics to ensure that the government is to its liking; as a result, a civilian government may have to cater to the military's interests in order to avoid being ousted in a coup d'état. In a number of countries in Latin America, Africa, the Middle East, and Asia, governments have frequently alternated between direct military rule and civilian rule—albeit under the constant threat of a coup. Moreover, authoritarian regimes that actively suppress popular dissent may rely heavily on the military to subdue challenges to their rule. In such systems, the regime's dependence on the armed forces for its continued survival gives military leaders a prominent role in decision making.

Even when the government does not depend so heavily on the military to stay in power, the military can have strong influence over foreign policy decision making. All political leaders rely on the information and expertise of bureaucratic actors within the state. No political leader is an expert in every policy area; even if that were possible, there would not be enough time for the leader to focus on every task of government. Instead, the job of making policy proposals and analyzing the implications of different decisions rests with the specialists who staff the bureaucratic agencies.

When making decisions about war, a leader has to rely on experts within the military and other agencies (such as those dealing with intelligence and diplomacy) to provide key pieces of information—what the country's capabilities are, what the capabilities of potential adversaries are, what plans there are to wage war with a given country—and deal with any contingencies that might arise. The political leader's dependence on the military for this kind of information gives military leaders the opportunity to shape decisions to their liking. A military bent on war could, for example, give the leader skewed advice about how easily the war could be won and

In 2019, Sudanese authoritarian president Omar Hassan al-Bashir (center) was ousted in an military coup d'état. He had been wanted by the International Criminal Court for his role in genocide in Darfur, among other crimes, and was largely disliked by citizens for his domestic policies. Although the military has promised a transition to democracy, it is likely to retain a prominent role in decision making in the country.

how low the costs would be. Conversely, military officials opposed to war could give conservative estimates of the likelihood of success and magnify the potential costs. In this way, the military would shape the outcome by manipulating the information that the leader uses to calculate the expected value of war and its alternatives.

Organized interest groups also rely on their superior resources and access to information in order to exert influence over policy. Consider an intervention like the one in Guatemala mentioned at the outset of this chapter. In that case, intervention cost U.S. taxpayers about $3 million, and it protected property for which United Fruit Company demanded $16 million. Given that the taxpayers who footed the bill vastly outnumbered the stockholders of the company that benefited, it is useful to think about why the latter would get their way at the expense of the former. How could economic interest groups "hijack" a state's foreign policy for their own narrow interests?

As suggested earlier, much of the answer lies in how the costs and benefits of international conflict are distributed in such situations. Precisely because taxpayers are more numerous, the costs of intervention to any individual are quite low. As a result, no individual citizen has much incentive to become informed about the situation, to call a member of Congress to weigh in on the policy, to go to Washington to bang on the doors of the State Department, and so on. Indeed, in the case of Guatemala and United Fruit Company, most U.S. citizens were likely unaware of what the CIA was up to (arming and training Guatemalan rebels) and how much taxpayer money was being spent. By contrast, the company that stands to benefit from intervention has a very large stake in the outcome. Company representatives have every incentive to become informed, to lobby representatives, and to exploit contacts within the government. Hence, in the interaction between the many who pay the costs and the few who stand to benefit, the latter have a significant advantage.

Organized interest groups can prevail because they can supply political leaders with things they need and want in exchange for favored policies. Sometimes what interest groups provide is money, which leaders can use to line their pockets or, if that is prohibited, to finance political campaigns. Concerns about the military-industrial complex center around the flow of money: industries give money to elected officials, who then allocate taxpayer money to the military, which then spends the money in ways that benefit the industries—for instance, by purchasing their arms or intervening to protect their foreign assets.[36]

In democracies, interest groups can also gain influence by promising elected officials the support of motivated voters. For example, the Cuban American lobby does not give large sums of money relative to the contributions of big economic interest groups like companies, labor unions, and professional organizations. When representatives of this lobby go to Washington, they primarily remind politicians that 1 million Cuban Americans care enough about U.S. policy toward Cuba that they vote on the basis of that issue. Moreover, these voters are concentrated in Florida, a crucial state in U.S. presidential elections. By contrast, most other voters pay little attention to this issue and do not base their votes on it. Hence, when representatives of the Cuban American or pro-Israel lobbies say, "This is an issue our voters care about," politicians tend to listen.

Limits to Interest Group Influence

In principle, then, interest groups can wield considerable influence over government policies, even if those policies come at the expense of broader national interests. So, to what extent does this mechanism explain foreign policy choices? Can the puzzle of war be resolved by finding some group within the state that actually benefits from the conflict? Though it can be tempting to see causal connections between policies and the groups those policies benefit, there are at least three reasons why we need to be cautious in jumping too hastily to interest-group explanations for wars.

The first reason has to do with evidence: How can we know that a particular policy was caused by interest-group lobbying? To put it another way, how can we be sure that the government would have behaved differently if the interest group did not exist? The challenge here is significant. Just because Halliburton benefited from the invasion of Iraq, we cannot automatically infer that the company actively lobbied for the invasion or that President Bush chose to invade in order to benefit the company.

Most foreign policy decisions that bestow benefits on narrow groups can be justified in alternative ways based on national interests. Hobson's theory of nineteenth-century imperialism has been disputed by scholars who argue that imperialism was a product of military-strategic competition among the principal powers.[37]

---

36. This is an example of a larger phenomenon known in the American politics literature as an "iron triangle": the mutual dependence that arises among members of Congress, interest groups, and government agencies.

37. See, for example, Benjamin J. Cohen, *The Question of Imperialism: The Political Economy of Dominance and Dependence* (London: Macmillan, 1974).

U.S. interventions in Latin America during the Cold War were part of a larger pattern in which the United States sought to prevent the spread of communism, sometimes in countries in which U.S. investors had no significant assets. Thus, even though United Fruit benefited from the ouster of Arbenz, fears about his association with communism might have provoked U.S. intervention even without the company's lobbying efforts.[38]

Charges that the United States intervened in the Middle East to benefit oil companies, including the 2003 invasion of Iraq, suffer similar weaknesses. Although toppling the regime of Saddam Hussein could have theoretically opened up the country's oil resources to U.S. companies, in actuality, most of the contracts went to firms from other countries, including Russia, China, and France, all of which had opposed the invasion.[39]

Moreover, U.S. interests in the Middle East reflect broader concerns. Oil is vital to U.S. power because a modern military of tanks and airplanes consumes large quantities of fuel, and the U.S. economy has long depended on oil—to fuel cars, to transport goods around the country, to heat homes and power businesses. Thus, the U.S. government has consistently sought to prevent hostile states from controlling the vast oil reserves in the region. The protection of Saudi Arabia, the single largest producer of oil, has been a keystone of U.S. policy since World War II, and the liberation of Kuwait from Iraq in 1991 (see Chapters 3 and 5) followed this pattern. Thus, the presence of oil in the Middle East plausibly feeds a national interest in wielding influence there—an interest that goes beyond a narrow concern for the profits of oil companies.

A second consideration to keep in mind is that in many issue areas there are multiple groups pushing in different directions. We already saw that economic considerations can just as readily motivate groups to pursue peace as they can encourage groups to lobby for war or intervention. Arms manufacturers spend more political effort competing with each other for government contracts than they do banding together to promote general foreign policy objectives. In the case of U.S. policy toward the Middle East, pro-Israel sentiments sometimes compete with oil interests that favor closer relations with oil-rich Arab states. The United States has regularly sold advanced military technology to Saudi Arabia, even over the objections of the pro-Israel lobby. The existence of opposing groups and demands can make it much harder for any one group to "capture" the state's foreign policy.

The final important consideration is to recall that war is the product of a bargaining interaction between or among multiple states, not a choice made by a single leader or group. Thus, to evaluate the potential influence of groups that have hawkish interests, we need to revisit the bargaining model.

---

38. For an argument against the interest-group interpretation of these cases, see Stephen D. Krasner, *Defending the National Interest: Raw Materials Investments and U.S. Foreign Policy* (Princeton, NJ: Princeton University Press, 1978), esp. chap. 8.

39. Vivienne Walt, "U.S. Companies Shut Out as Iraq Auctions Its Oil Fields," *Time*, December 19, 2009, http://content.time.com/time/world/article/0,8599,1948787,00.html (accessed 11/11/20).

How Do Domestic Interests Affect International Bargaining?

How could hawkish actors within a state affect the likelihood of war? The general answer is that domestic interests affect the likelihood of international conflict primarily by determining the extent of the state's ambitions. By influencing the costs and benefits of conflict, such interests can widen or narrow the scope of goods over which the state's leaders might be willing to wage war. They affect when and how often the state's foreign policy interests will come into conflict with those of other states, and they determine the size of the demands that the state will make and the risks that it is willing to run.

In short, variation in the nature of domestic interests that influence policy making will increase or decrease the opportunities for conflict. Except in rare circumstances, however, these interests will not be sufficient to cause war in any given interaction. Thus, the influence of hawkish interests gives states more things they might consider worth fighting over, but these interests are generally not sufficient to explain why bargaining over those goods fails in some cases but not in others.

To illustrate this point, we return in Figure 4.4 to the bargaining model and ask what would happen if the interests of State A changed in response to the influence of hawkish actors. For example, imagine that the object in dispute is a piece of territory rich with oil reserves. In the interaction depicted in the top panel, the government in State A is led by a party whose core supporters are pacifists. As a result, the government considers the costs of war over this territory to be rather high, as shown by the fact that State A's value for war (the portion of the bar to the left of the red dotted line) is far smaller than the share of territory it expects from the outcome of the war.

Recall that the costs of war are measured relative to the value of the good in dispute, so they are large when the human and economic costs of war loom large and/or when the benefit associated with possessing the territory is low. Because the dovish interests that control the state see war as very unattractive, they are highly unlikely to start a crisis over this territory. Only if the status quo distribution of the territory was located at the far left of the line—very far from State A's ideal point—would the government in State A see any potential benefit from sparking a crisis.

What happens to the international interaction if the dovish leader in State A is replaced by a leader of a party that draws support from oil companies that would profit from State A's control of the territory? Because of the influence of these actors, the new leader places more weight on the value of the land and less on the costs of war. In terms of our model, the costs of war relative to the value of the good are smaller. The lower panel shows how the value of war changes in the eyes of this hawkish government. Since the costs of war have gone down, State A's value for war shifts to the right.

Notice two things about the lower panel in Figure 4.4. First, status quo distributions that would have been tolerated by the dovish leader are unacceptable to the hawk. As a result, State A becomes more likely to initiate a crisis, and it will make larger demands of its adversary. Second, even after this shift, a bargaining range,

FIGURE 4.4   *Domestic Interests and International Bargaining*

In the top panel, State A is led by a dovish government and considers the costs of war to be high relative to the value of the good in dispute. In the lower panel, State A is led by a hawkish government and sees the costs of war as less significant, placing more value on the good in dispute. Under hawkish leaders, State A is more likely to challenge the status quo, but a bargaining range still exists.

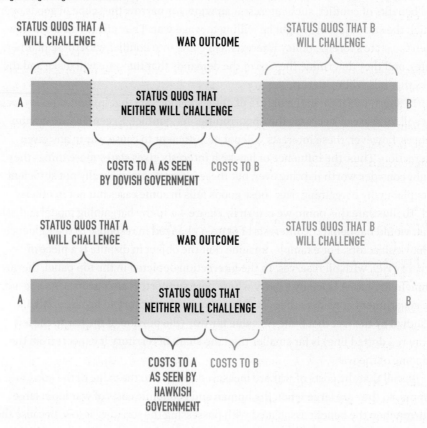

shown in light green, still exists. As before, the costs of war ensure the existence of a set of mutually acceptable bargains.

This means that absent the information, commitment, or divisibility problems discussed in Chapter 3, there is no reason why the shift from a dovish to a hawkish government should, on its own, lead to a war. However, the shift does create a danger of war that did not exist before. The new government in State A is more willing to threaten force to change the status quo. The change in governance increases the state's demands and creates a risk of conflict where none previously existed. Whether or not this potential conflict will lead to an actual war depends on features of the bargaining interaction, such as how information is distributed and whether the states can credibly commit to live by any deal they reach.

The one exception to this claim arises if there are actors who derive benefits from war that cannot be part of a negotiated settlement. For example, assume that the leader of State A represents arms manufacturers. If there is a war, they get paid to build weapons and to replace those that are destroyed. Since they get these profits only if there is a war, then it is peace rather than war that these actors find costly. Would the influence of such interests change the logic we just outlined? As we saw when considering the diversionary incentive, which is also a benefit that is only obtained by fighting, the answer is yes—but only if the net benefits from war are high enough to offset *both* states' costs of war (see Figure 4.2).

Hence, except in rare circumstances, the influence of groups that would gain much and lose little in war does not itself ensure that war will happen. When such interests hold sway, they will make the state's foreign policy more belligerent in the sense that the state will make larger demands and come into conflict with more states. However, such interests alone are not sufficient to cause war in the absence of the strategic dilemmas discussed in Chapter 3. Thus, when we think about how oil interests influence U.S. policy in the Middle East, it is reasonable to say that they explain why there are issues in the region that American leaders are willing to fight over. It is harder to argue that these interests alone explain why crises over them sometimes become wars.

Why Don't Democracies Fight One Another?

For much of the nineteenth and early twentieth centuries, France and Germany were bitter rivals. France resisted the creation of a unified German state in 1870, and the two countries fought three major wars over the next century: the Franco-Prussian War (1870–71), World War I (1914–18), and World War II (1939–45). Millions died in these wars, and cemeteries in both countries are filled with those who fell in this rivalry. Today, however, France and Germany are close allies, and while they have differences of interest and opinion on important issues, it is almost inconceivable that there could be another war between them.

The turnaround in this relationship coincided with changes in the countries' political systems that made them more democratic. France went into the Franco-Prussian War a monarchy, but it emerged with a more democratic system, which has become stronger over time. The change in Germany was even more dramatic. Ruled by a hereditary emperor in the nineteenth century, Germany devolved into a murderous dictatorship under Adolf Hitler in the 1930s. After World War II, however, Germany was divided and occupied by the victorious Allies, and what became West Germany was remade into a democratic country. When East and West Germany were reunified in the 1990s, the reborn German state inherited this democratic constitution.

There were, of course, a number of factors that helped solidify the relationship between these former adversaries after 1945, including the existence of a shared enemy in the Soviet Union; the reassuring presence of a common ally, the United States; and growing economic and financial ties that would make the two states central partners in a European Union. Nevertheless, the emergence of shared

democratic peace

The observation that there are few, if any, clear cases of war between mature democratic states.

democracy helped pave the way for a dramatic shift in how these countries dealt with each other, to the point that war between the two is now unthinkable.

Far from being an isolated example, this case is part of a larger phenomenon that scholars and policy makers call the **democratic peace**. The term refers to a well-established observation that there are few, if any, clear cases of war between mature democratic states. Our choice of words reflects some caveats about this observation. We say "few, if any, clear cases of war" because the strength of the claim depends in part on how one defines democracy and what events one considers to be wars. Since there are some ambiguous cases, there is not a universal consensus on whether wars between democratic states are nonexistent or simply rare.[40] We say "mature democratic states" because some studies have suggested that countries in the process of becoming democracies do not fit this overall pattern.[41] Even taking these qualifications into account, this is still a remarkable observation: over the 200 or so years in which democracies have existed in their modern form, they seem not to have engaged in war with one another—or, at least, they have done so less frequently than we might expect, given the overall frequency of war.

Another noteworthy aspect of this observation is that democracies are not, overall, less war prone than other kinds of states. That is, while they rarely, if ever, fight wars against other democratic states, their overall rate of war participation is roughly the same as that of nondemocratic states.[42] This means that although democracies seldom find themselves at war with one another, they are more frequently at war with nondemocratic states. Hence, there is something special about the relationships among democracies that does not carry over to their relationships with other kinds of states.

This observation is so striking and important that it has entered into policy discussions in the United States and elsewhere. President George W. Bush argued that democracy promotion should be a central aspect of American policy in the Middle East because "democracies don't go to war with each other."[43] And during his 2009 speech accepting the Nobel Peace Prize, President Barack Obama emphasized the connection between peace and democracy in Europe and pointed out that "America has never fought a war against a democracy."[44] This interest in democratic peace has been particularly salient in recent decades, which have seen a remarkable growth in the number of democracies worldwide, as Figure 4.5 shows.

Is this absence of wars among democracies a coincidence, or is there something about democratic institutions that facilitates peaceful relations among states that have them? In what ways might shared democracy influence interstate bargaining?

---

40. For a discussion of the democratic peace finding, definitional issues, and some cases that raise questions, see Bruce Russett, *Grasping the Democratic Peace: Principles for a Post–Cold War World* (Princeton, NJ: Princeton University Press, 1993), chap. 1.

41. Edward D. Mansfield and Jack Snyder, *Electing to Fight: Why Emerging Democracies Go to War* (Cambridge, MA: MIT Press, 2005).

42. Although there has been some controversy over the issue, this statement reflects the general consensus in the literature. See, for example, Nils Petter Gleditsch and Håvard Hegre, "Peace and Democracy: Three Levels of Analysis," *Journal of Conflict Resolution* 41, no. 2 (1997): 283–310.

43. White House, Office of the Press Secretary, "President and Prime Minister Blair Discussed Iraq, Middle East," White House Press Conference, November 12, 2004, https://georgewbush-whitehouse.archives. gov/news/releases/2004/11/20041112-5.html (accessed 12/16/20).

44. Barack H. Obama, "A Just and Lasting Peace," Nobel lecture, December 10, 2009, www.nobelprize.org/ prizes/peace/2009/obama/lecture (accessed 12/16/20).

FIGURE 4.5 **The Spread of Democracy, 1800–2018**

What Is Democracy?

To answer these questions, we turn to the third leg of our framework: institutions. Domestic institutions determine the rules of political decision making within a state. They govern the relationship between the leadership and the people, and they help determine the extent to which citizens' interests matter when it comes to war and peace. Although there are many different kinds of political systems, the distinction that has attracted the most attention is that between democratic and nondemocratic systems.

A **democracy** is a political system in which candidates compete for political office through frequent, fair elections in which a sizable portion of the adult population can vote. This definition encompasses two major aspects of democracy: the ability of different individuals and groups to compete for political office and the ability of a significant percentage of the people to participate in the selection process through voting.

Nondemocratic countries, also known as **autocracies**, fall short of this definition in a variety of ways.[45] In some, leaders obtain office through hereditary succession, as in Saudi Arabia, or on the back of a military coup, as happened in Myanmar in 2021. In others, such as China, only one political party is permitted to hold power, and competition from other parties is outlawed. Still others might hold elections among multiple parties but restrict competition so that the ruling party is all but certain to win. Such multiparty or electoral authoritarianism is the most common form of nondemocratic system in the world today; examples include Venezuela, Russia, and Ethiopia.[46] Map 4.1 on p. 178 shows the type of regime in each country at the beginning of 2021.

Figure source: Monty G. Marshall, Ted Robert Gurr, and Keith Jaggers, "Polity V Project: Political Regime Characteristics and Transitions, 1800–2018," Center for Systemic Peace, www.systemicpeace.org/inscrdata.html (accessed 11/17/20).

democracy

A political system in which candidates compete for political office through frequent, fair elections in which a sizable portion of the adult population can vote.

autocracy

A political system in which an individual or small group exercises power with few constraints and no meaningful competition or participation by the general public.

---

45. Indeed, recent research in international relations has explored the effects of different kinds of nondemocratic governments; see, for example, Jessica L. P. Weeks, *Dictators at War and Peace* (Ithaca, NY: Cornell University Press, 2014).

46. There is an extensive literature on the nature and role of elections in authoritarian countries; see, for example, Jennifer Gandhi and Ellen Lust-Okar, "Elections under Authoritarianism," *Annual Review of Political Science* 12 (June 2009): 403–22.

MAP 4.1 *Regime Types*

This map shows the type of government in each country at the start of 2021. While democracy can be found on every continent, it is widespread in the Americas and Europe, present in parts of Asia, and scarce in Africa and the Middle East. Monarchies and military regimes are quite rare, while most autocratic regimes have limited multiparty competition.

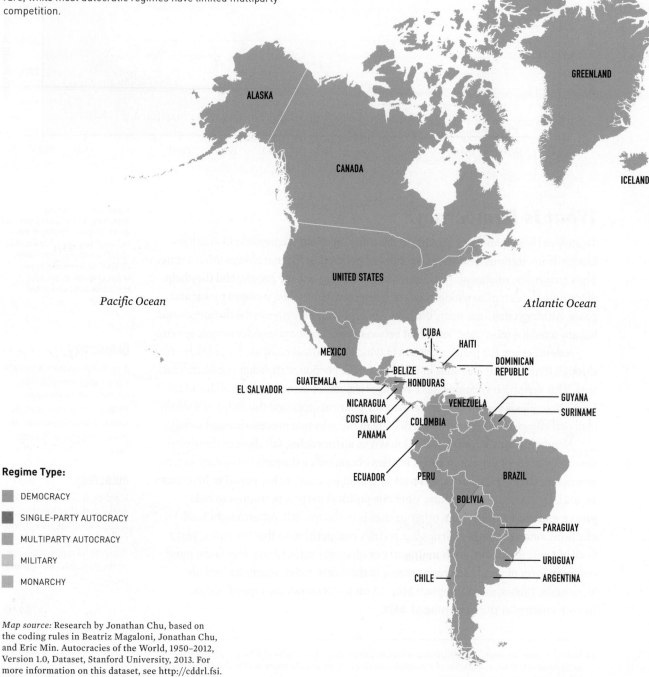

Regime Type:

- DEMOCRACY
- SINGLE-PARTY AUTOCRACY
- MULTIPARTY AUTOCRACY
- MILITARY
- MONARCHY

Map source: Research by Jonathan Chu, based on the coding rules in Beatriz Magaloni, Jonathan Chu, and Eric Min. Autocracies of the World, 1950–2012, Version 1.0, Dataset, Stanford University, 2013. For more information on this dataset, see http://cddrl.fsi. stanford.edu/povgov/research/autocracies_of_the_ world_dataset (accessed 1/26/21).

Arctic Ocean

Pacific Ocean

Indian Ocean

RUSSIA

SWEDEN
FINLAND
NORWAY
UNITED
KINGDOM
GERMANY
BELARUS
IRELAND
UKRAINE
FRANCE
SWITZERLAND
ITALY
SPAIN
GREECE
MOROCCO
ALGERIA
LIBYA
MAURITANIA
MALI
NIGER
CHAD
SENEGAL
GUINEA
NIGERIA
CEN.
AFR.
REP.
CAMEROON
GHANA
D.R.
CONGO
IVORY COAST

BOSNIA
GEORGIA
TURKEY
SYRIA
ISRAEL LEB.
JORDAN
IRAQ
EGYPT
SAUDI
ARABIA
ERITREA
S.SUDAN
SUDAN
ETHIOPIA
UGANDA
KENYA
SOMALIA
YEMEN
OMAN
U.A.E.

KAZAKHSTAN
UZBEKISTAN
TURKMENISTAN
IRAN
KUWAIT
KYRGYZSTAN
TAJIKISTAN
MONGOLIA
N. KOREA
S. KOREA
JAPAN
CHINA
TAIWAN
NEPAL
PAKISTAN
INDIA
MYANMAR (BURMA)
AFGHANISTAN
BANGLADESH
THAILAND
VIETNAM
PHILIPPINES
LAOS
CAMBODIA
MALAYSIA
SRI LANKA

TANZANIA
ANGOLA
MALAWI
ZAMBIA
MADAGASCAR
NAMIBIA
MOZAMBIQUE
ZIMBABWE
SOUTH
AFRICA
SWAZILAND
BOTSWANA

INDONESIA
PAPUA NEW GUINEA
FIJI
AUSTRALIA
NEW
ZEALAND

Another term often used to describe democracies is the word *liberal*, which we use here in its classic sense to refer to a philosophy that emphasizes the value of individual liberty. Most modern democracies are also liberal democracies, because in addition to allowing competition and voting, they have numerous protections for individuals' civil liberties and political rights, such as rights to free speech, religion, political association, and a free press. Hence, liberal democracies not only choose their leaders by democratic means, but they also impose restrictions on what those elected governments can do by giving citizens rights that the government cannot transgress. We should note that not all democratic countries are liberal; some restrict religious or press freedoms or give rights to ethnic or religious groups at the expense of individual rights. Indonesia, for example, has competitive and free elections, but it also has laws restricting the activities of civic and religious organizations, including a ban on the advocacy of certain ideas.[47]

With these definitions in place, we turn to the central question: How could democracies—especially mature, liberal democracies—be different when it comes to war and peace? Not surprisingly, the democratic peace observation has generated a great deal of scholarly interest in this question, and there is no single, settled answer. But the framework of this book suggests two broad ways in which domestic institutions can affect the likelihood of war: either by influencing the interests of states and their leaders or by influencing the bargaining interactions between and among countries.

Representation, Accountability, and Interests in War and Peace

A common argument for the distinctiveness of democracy is rooted in the idea that domestic institutions shape leaders' interests in war and peace. This argument starts with the observation that the costs of war are paid by society at large but generally not by the leader who makes the decision to wage war. It is the people who lose lives or loved ones on the battlefield, who suffer the economic hardship of wars, and who may have to pay higher taxes to support a war effort. The leader, by contrast, rarely has such direct exposure to the costs of war. This disjunction between the ruler and the ruled is humorously illustrated in the 2001 movie *Shrek*, when evil Lord Farquaad tells his knights that he is going to send them on a mission to rescue from a fire-breathing dragon a princess whom he wants to marry. Exhorting his men to combat, Lord Farquaad declares, "Some of you may die, but it's a sacrifice I am willing to make."

Over 200 years earlier, the German philosopher Immanuel Kant noted a similar dilemma. Kant wrote in the late eighteenth century, when most countries were ruled by monarchs. For such rulers, he noted, "The easiest thing in the world to do is to declare war." Kant reasoned:

> War does not affect [the ruler's] table, his hunt, his places of pleasure, his court festivals, and so on. Thus, he can decide to go to war for the most meaningless of reasons, as if it

---

47. For an assessment of political and civil rights in Indonesia, see Freedom House, "Freedom in the World 2014 - Indonesia," June 26, 2014, www.refworld.org/docid/53b2b8c23e4.html (accessed 12/16/20).

were a kind of pleasure party, and he can blithely leave its justification (which decency requires) to his diplomatic corps, who are always prepared for such exercises.[48]

In other words, a basic problem in such political systems was that the interests of the ruler and the ruled were not aligned: the ruler enjoyed the benefit of war, while the people paid its costs. In Kant's view, the solution to this problem was to establish a representative government, one in which the ruler would be accountable to the people: if "the consent of the citizenry is required in order to determine whether or not there will be war, it is natural that they consider all its calamities before committing themselves to so risky a game."[49] In this view, political institutions that foster broad representation would serve to align the interests of the ruler and the ruled, making those with the power to decide on war sensitive to the costs that their decisions impose on others.

The primary mechanism through which political institutions influence decisions about war and peace is **accountability**: the ability to punish or reward leaders for their decisions. Even if political leaders do not directly bear the costs of war, they can suffer politically if they make decisions that harm the people or groups on whom they rely to stay in power. In a democratic system, elections and other practices allow citizens to punish leaders for unpopular policies. Democratic leaders thus have to take into account the possibility that failed or costly wars can undermine their political support, jeopardizing their hold on office. At the same time, by making it easier for voters to make their collective voice heard, electoral institutions weaken the potential influence of small groups that may see concentrated benefits but few costs from waging war. Thus, accountability to voters can raise the political risks of war to an elected leader and ensure representation of broader rather than particularistic interests.

Autocratic leaders may also be held accountable for their actions, but the key actors are different, so the interests that are represented in decision making are different. Though these leaders do not face an electorate with real power to replace them, they may still be subject to removal by a "selectorate," the set of individuals and groups whose support is necessary for a leader to retain office. In nondemocratic systems, this selectorate can be quite small, often involving military, economic, or ethnic elites. Staying in power thus requires autocrats to prioritize policies that satisfy these particularistic interests over the public good. Autocrats are also protected by the fact that the actions needed to remove them, such as a revolution or coup, are risky to undertake. Thus, as long as members of the selectorate are sufficiently protected, paid off, or afraid, the leader can be politically insulated from the costs of war.[50] For example, after losing the first Persian Gulf War in 1991, Saddam Hussein was able to hold on to power, even in the face of popular revolts, because he was able to retain the loyalty of his elite military units and core supporters.

accountability

The ability to punish or reward leaders for the decisions they make, as when frequent, fair elections enable voters to hold elected officials responsible for their actions by granting or withholding access to political office.

---

48. Immanuel Kant, "To Perpetual Peace: A Philosophical Sketch," in *Perpetual Peace and Other Essays on Politics, History, and Morals*, trans. Ted Humphrey (Indianapolis, IN: Hackett, 1983), 113.

49. Kant, "To Perpetual Peace," 113.

50. See Bruce Bueno de Mesquita, Alastair Smith, Randolph M. Siverson, and James D. Morrow, *The Logic of Political Survival* (Cambridge, MA: MIT Press, 2003).

In this view, then, democracies are different because their leaders face systematically higher costs from war than do nondemocratic leaders. Given an equal probability of victory in war, a democratic leader values war less than the nondemocratic leader does, because the political implications of losing are worse for the former. Given equal human and material costs of war, a democratic leader values war less, because that leader is more likely to be held accountable for those costs.

Although this logic is compelling, we must point out that losing office is not the worst or only consequence of losing a war. When democratic leaders lose an election, they can generally retire in good comfort, collect their pension, perhaps go on the lecture circuit, and even continue to participate in politics if they want. Nondemocratic leaders, by contrast, often find that life after losing office is not so pleasant. Because their removal often occurs through violent means, such as a coup or revolution, nondemocratic leaders often suffer additional punishment above and beyond simply losing office.

For the Russian tsar in 1917, Russia's disastrous showing in World War I contributed to his removal from office and subsequent execution. The German emperor similarly faced popular uprisings in the wake of his country's defeat in that war, prompting him to abdicate his throne and flee into exile. And the leader of the military junta that led Argentina into the Falklands War was later tried for mishandling the war and spent five years in prison. Indeed, death, exile, and imprisonment are common punishments meted out to autocratic leaders who run afoul of their people. This suggests that the relationship between a country's political institutions and the costs its leader faces upon losing a war may not be as straightforward as Kant's logic suggests.[51]

How would this argument about accountability explain the democratic peace? If, in fact, war is costlier for democratic leaders, the likelihood of war could be influenced in several ways. As we have seen, an increase in the costs of war diminishes a state's willingness to contest the status quo, reducing the opportunities for conflict. If there are fewer things that a state is willing to fight for, the chance that it will come into violent conflict with other states decreases. Moreover, the logic of political accountability suggests that democratic leaders should be more selective about starting wars; that is, they should only be willing to wage war when their chances of victory are sufficiently high. Leaders in nondemocratic political systems may be more willing to gamble on wars that they have a low chance of winning. This logic would lower the probability of war between two democratic states, because in such interactions it is unlikely that both leaders would simultaneously judge their chances in war to be high enough.[52]

But how could this argument explain the fact that, overall, democracies are just as war prone as other states, meaning that they are particularly likely to fight wars against nondemocratic states? A possible answer lies in the observation that constraints on the use of force can make democratic states tempting targets to their nondemocratic foes. Recall how Saddam Hussein dismissed U.S. deterrent threats

---

51. Goemans, *War and Punishment*.

52. See Bruce Bueno de Mesquita, James D. Morrow, Randolph M. Siverson, and Alastair Smith, "An Institutional Explanation of the Democratic Peace," *American Political Science Review* 93, no. 4 (December 1999): 791–807.

prior to the Persian Gulf War: "Yours is a society which cannot accept 10,000 dead in one battle."[53] Although Hussein did not say so explicitly, this statement seems to reflect a sense that American leaders would find war politically too costly to fight. This belief made Hussein more likely to resist U.S. efforts to coerce him out of Kuwait.

Similarly, Japanese leaders who decided to bomb Pearl Harbor in 1941 did so, in part, under the mistaken impression that the American public would respond by opposing a war and would therefore constrain President Franklin Roosevelt's ability to retaliate. In this view, the constraints that make democracies peaceful in their relations with one another can have the opposite effect when they square off against less constrained adversaries, who may seek to exploit democracies by making larger demands and discounting their threats, thereby increasing the risk of war.[54]

Democracy and the Bargaining Interaction

Another explanation for democratic peace focuses on how democracy influences bargaining interactions between states, increasing the chances that a peaceful settlement will be found. One version of this argument focuses on the ability of democratic states to overcome information problems. Recall from Chapter 3 that states may fail to find mutually beneficial bargains if they have incomplete information about the military and political factors that determine their value for war. Resolving this informational problem is challenging because states have an incentive to conceal or misrepresent their information in the hopes of getting a better deal.

There are several reasons to think that democratic institutions and processes make it easier to overcome informational problems. First, democratic political systems are much more transparent than nondemocratic systems because democratic processes are more open and observable. For example, major policy decisions are frequently subject to public and/or legislative debate. A relatively free press can disseminate information about what decision makers are thinking, the level of popular support for war, and even details about the state's military capabilities. Opposition parties can freely voice approval of or dissent from the government's actions, thereby revealing the strength (or weakness) of the government's political support within the country. Such practices exist primarily to ensure that the public can scrutinize

Autocratic leaders, like President Putin of Russia, may also be held accountable for their actions, but the key actors are different, so the interests that are represented in decision making are different. Though these leaders do not face an electorate with real power to replace them, they may still be subject to removal by a "selectorate," the set of individuals and groups whose support is necessary for a leader to retain office. In nondemocratic systems, this selectorate can be quite small, often involving military, economic, or ethnic elites. Staying in power thus requires autocrats to prioritize policies that satisfy these particularistic interests over the public good. Autocrats are also protected by the fact that the actions needed to remove them, such as a revolution or coup, are risky to undertake.

---

53. See Chapter 3, footnote 19.

54. Indeed, evidence suggests that conflicts between democracies and dictators are usually initiated by the latter; see Dan Reiter and Allan C. Stam, "Identifying the Culprit: Democracy, Dictatorship, and Dispute Initiation," *American Political Science Review* 97, no. 2 (May 2003): 333–37.

Policy making in democratic states, like Canada, often involves public and legislative debate, resulting in a more open and observable process. Here, Prime Minister Justin Trudeau takes questions from legislators in Parliament. This greater transparency makes it easier for other states to accurately assess the democratic state's capabilities and resolve.

what its leaders are doing—an essential element of democratic accountability. A by-product of such openness is that foreign states can also glean relevant information about a democratic state's capabilities and resolve.

This is not to suggest that democratic states hide nothing—either from their own people or from outside eyes. Rather, the point is that democratic states are *relatively* more transparent than most nondemocratic systems, in which decision making occurs without broad participation, governments restrict what can be reported in the media and suppress opposition groups, and disagreements within the governing group are rarely aired in public. Thus, all other things being equal, there is less uncertainty about the capabilities and resolve of democratic states.[55]

In addition, democracies may be better able to send credible signals in crises. Recall from Chapter 3 that when states have private information, communicating their resolve in a credible manner often requires that they take costly actions—actions that a resolute state would be willing to take but an irresolute one would not. One way they can do so is by making statements or taking actions from which it would be difficult to back down. As we have seen, such threats are costly if leaders expect to lose domestic political support for failing to follow through on them.

A study of U.S. public opinion demonstrates this effect. One group of survey respondents was presented with a hypothetical scenario in which a president threatened to defend another country from invasion and then failed to do so. Another group was presented with a similar scenario in which the president failed to defend another country but had never threatened to do so. When asked to assess the president's actions, respondents in the first group gave the president a lower approval rating than the rating given by those in the second group—a result that is consistent with the idea that it is politically costly to back down from a threat.[56]

If backing down creates public disapproval, then there is reason to think that democracy magnifies the political importance of this effect. Mechanisms of accountability mean that public disapproval is more likely to result in some kind of punishment, in the form of either diminished support for the leader's agenda or a greater chance of losing office in the next election. Nondemocratic leaders, by

---

55. Kenneth A. Schultz, *Democracy and Coercive Diplomacy* (Cambridge: Cambridge University Press, 2001). For a dissenting view on the effects of democratic transparency, see Bernard I. Finel and Kristin M. Lord, "The Surprising Logic of Transparency," *International Studies Quarterly* 43, no. 2 (1999): 315–39.

56. Michael Tomz, "Domestic Audience Costs in International Relations: An Experimental Approach," *International Organization* 61, no. 4 (Fall 2007): 821–40.

contrast, are more politically insulated from whatever disapproval their actions might engender. Thus, public threats made by democratic leaders are more informative because they are costlier to make. This suggests that institutions of accountability make it easier for democratic leaders to credibly communicate their resolve with lower levels of escalation.[57]

While the previous argument suggests that democracies can make threats more effectively when they bargain, many scholars subscribe to a more ambitious argument that shared democracy changes the nature of the bargaining interaction altogether. In this view, democratic countries are unlikely to fight wars because they adhere to norms of mutual respect and nonviolence in their dealings with one another.[58] Relations among democratic states are fundamentally different from those among other kinds of countries because they regard each other as part of a community of states that share liberal values. This identity leads to greater levels of trust and more emphasis on resolving disputes through peaceful concessions rather than through threats of violence. By contrast, this courtesy is not extended to autocracies, which are seen as threatening and untrustworthy.

Several observations are consistent with this view. First, this logic helps explain why democratic states are peaceful with each other but are not more peaceful in general. While fellow democracies enjoy a presumption of friendship, autocrats are treated with suspicion and mistrust. In the extreme, autocrats may be seen as legitimate targets for regime change, as the United States argued in the case of Iraq under Saddam Hussein. Second, there is evidence that when democratic states get into disputes with one another, they are more likely to find a compromise solution and to bring in third parties to help manage the conflict peacefully.[59]

Finally, there is evidence that the publics in at least some democracies are less likely to support war against fellow democratic states. A survey of people in the United States and the United Kingdom showed that support for a hypothetical military strike against a state pursuing nuclear weapons was significantly lower if respondents were told that the target was a democracy. People in these countries

57. James D. Fearon, "Domestic Political Audiences and the Escalation of International Disputes," *American Political Science Review* 88, no. 3 (September 1994): 577–92. There is some controversy over whether democracies are really special in this respect or whether some kinds of autocrats may also be able to tie their hands by invoking audience costs. For example, Jessica Chen Weiss argues that China manipulates nationalist protests as a way to signal its resolve in crises with Japan and the United States; see Weiss, *Powerful Patriots*. There is also a robust debate about whether domestic audience costs play an important role in the outcomes of international crises. For a critical view, see Jack Snyder and Erica D. Borghard, "The Cost of Empty Threats: A Penny, Not a Pound," *American Political Science Review* 105, no. 3 (August 2011): 437–56. For evidence that democracies are not particularly effective at making credible threats, see Alexander B. Downes and Todd S. Sechser, "The Illusion of Democratic Credibility," *International Organization* 66, no. 3 (2012): 457–89.

58. This discussion synthesizes several subtly different articulations of this idea. Main ones include Russett, *Grasping the Democratic Peace*, 30–38; Michael W. Doyle, "Liberalism and World Politics," *American Political Science Review* 80, no. 4 (December 1986): 1151–69; and Thomas Risse-Kappen, "Democratic Peace—Warlike Democracies? A Social Constructivist Interpretation of the Liberal Argument," *European Journal of Political Science* 1, no. 4 (1995): 491–517.

59. See, for example, Michael Mousseau, "Democracy and Compromise in Militarized Interstate Conflicts, 1816–1992," *Journal of Conflict Resolution* 42, no. 2 (1998): 210–30; and William J. Dixon, "Democracy and the Management of International Conflict," *Journal of Conflict Resolution* 37, no. 1 (1993): 42–68.

tended to view other democracies as less threatening and had greater moral reservations about attacking them.[60]

All of this evidence is consistent with the idea that bargaining among democratic states is guided by norms that favor compromise over the use of force, which could explain the marked absence of war between such states.

Does Democracy Cause Peace?

The preceding arguments all suggest that democratic institutions can explain the peace that has prevailed among states that possess them, either by altering leaders' incentives to wage war or by facilitating the bargaining interaction. There is a well-known adage, however, that correlation does not imply causation: in this context, just because democracy and peace go together, we cannot automatically conclude that democracy *causes* peace. Why might that be? First, there could be some other factor that both causes states to become democratic and causes them not to fight. Second, it could be that the reverse is true—that is, that peace causes democracy. And third, there could be some other factor that causes peace among states that just so happen to be democracies. All three of these arguments have been made in the scholarly literature, and we briefly introduce them here both to show the richness of the debate and to stimulate thinking about what might actually be going on.

The relationship between democracy and peace could be a product of the fact that both democracy and peace share a common cause. What could this common cause be? One possibility is economic development. There is a strong tendency for democracy to emerge and survive in states that are relatively wealthy; in poorer countries, by contrast, democratic institutions are more likely to break down. While there is no general tendency for wealth alone to promote peace between countries, there is evidence consistent with a "capitalist peace" among countries with free-market economies.[61]

Another possibility is that peace causes democracy—that democracy is more likely to emerge in regions where countries already have peaceful relations with one another.[62] A menacing international environment and threats to a state's territory tend to empower its central government and military, making it hard for democracy to take root. Thus, democracy is more likely to emerge after states have settled outstanding rivalries and territorial disputes with their neighbors. If so, then it is peaceful borders that make democracies, not vice versa.[63]

Finally, it has been argued that democratic peace is really a product of shared strategic interests among democratic states that have nothing to do with their

---

60. Michael R. Tomz and Jessica L. P. Weeks, "Public Opinion and the Democratic Peace," *American Political Science Review* 107, no. 4 (November 2013): 849–65.

61. Erik Gartzke, "The Capitalist Peace," *American Journal of Political Science* 51, no. 1 (2007): 166–91; Michael Mousseau, "The Democratic Peace Unraveled: It's the Economy," *International Studies Quarterly* 57, no. 1 (March 2013): 186–97.

62. William R. Thompson, "Democracy and Peace: Putting the Cart before the Horse?" *International Organization* 50, no. 1 (Winter 1996): 141–74.

63. Douglas M. Gibler, *The Territorial Peace: Borders, State Development, and International Conflict* (Cambridge: Cambridge University Press, 2012).

domestic institutions.[64] From the late nineteenth century on, the main democratic countries were united against common threats, first against Germany and then against the Soviet Union. During the Cold War, most democracies had similar strategic interests because of a common perceived threat from the Soviet Union and the communist bloc (see Chapter 5). Especially in this latter period, the United States both bolstered democracy and worked to dampen conflict within its bloc.[65]

In this view, common interests reduced the opportunities for conflict between democratic states and provided a strong incentive to resolve peacefully any conflicts that did arise. In addition to fighting with each other less often, democratic states in these periods also tended to form alliances with each other—an indication that they perceived common strategic interests. In this view, then, the bonds among democratic states arise not from their institutions or sense of shared identity but from shared threats that produce common interests. Note that, to be compelling, this argument requires that the perception that two states share interests is independent of their political institutions, rather than being shaped by them. However, the survey evidence cited earlier suggests that people in the United States and the United Kingdom view a hypothetical democratic country as less threatening than a hypothetical autocracy.

In short, the democratic peace raises tantalizing questions for both scholars and policy makers, and we are likely to be debating this issue for some time. (See "Controversy" on p. 188.)

Conclusion: What if All the World Were Democratic?

When diplomats and state leaders come to the bargaining table with one another, they inevitably bring a great deal of baggage from their home countries. The interests that state representatives advance in international negotiations are themselves a function of interests, interactions, and institutions within their state. Political leaders may care about what is best for their country, but they also care about staying in office. As a result, they must think about how their foreign policy choices will affect the interests of important domestic constituents such as the military, organized interest groups, and in some cases, the general public.

When these domestic actors have a stake in the outcome of international bargaining, and when they have the strategic and/or institutional resources to punish or reward the leader, then their interests will be represented at the bargaining table. In particular, when groups with hawkish interests have superior

---

64. Joanne Gowa, *Ballots and Bullets: The Elusive Democratic Peace* (Princeton, NJ: Princeton University Press, 1999).

65. Patrick J. McDonald, "Great Powers, Hierarchy, and Endogenous Regimes: Rethinking the Domestic Causes of Peace," *International Organization* 69, no. 3 (2015): 557–88.

Should We Prefer a Friendly Dictator or a Hostile Democracy?

On June 30, 2012, Mohamed Morsi (below right) was sworn in as the first democratically elected leader in Egypt's 5,000-year history. The emergence of a democratic government in Egypt followed a succession of demonstrations and protest movements throughout the Middle East starting in January 2011, which brought down or challenged long-standing authoritarian governments not only in Egypt but also in Tunisia, Libya, Yemen, Syria, Jordan, and Bahrain. But hopes that this so-called Arab Spring would lead to more democratic and less repressive governments in the region were disappointed, as fundamental political reform in Egypt and other countries largely failed to materialize. After a year in power, Morsi faced a renewed wave of popular protest, and the Egyptian military took over in a coup d'état in July 2013. A year later, General Abdel Fattah al-Sisi, who had led the coup, was elected president in an election lacking real competition, and his government has clamped down on dissent, jailing political opponents and journalists.

Applying the Concepts

For the United States and other Western powers, the swing in Egypt from authoritarianism to democracy and back to authoritarianism created a foreign policy dilemma. On the one hand, American and other Western policy makers often stress the importance of promoting democratic **institutions** around the world, because doing so leads to governments that are responsive to their citizens' needs and respectful of their human rights. Moreover, the democratic peace observation suggests that democratic states have more peaceful **interactions**. On the other hand, the majority of people in a country may have **interests** that are hostile to or incompatible with those of the United States and its allies. In such cases, it can be easier to deal with an autocratic leader who is free to ignore those views. In other words, policy makers can be

torn between liking democratic institutions and disliking the interests of those empowered by such institutions.

In the case of Egypt, this tension arises from the fact that many Egyptians do not like the United States and are hostile to Israel, a key U.S. ally. Under President Hosni Mubarak, Morsi's predecessor, Egypt had good relations with both countries on the basis of a 1979 peace treaty with Israel. In the ensuing years, Egypt became a strategic partner of the United States and a major recipient of U.S. aid. But the treaty was never popular among Egyptians, and American aid was seen as propping up a repressive government. Under the autocratic Mubarak, this public opposition could be ignored or suppressed. The transition to democracy and the election of Morsi threatened this arrangement.

A poll taken in May 2013 showed that 63 percent of Egyptians wanted to annul the treaty with Israel and only 16 percent had a positive view of the United States.[a] Not only was there a danger that a more responsive government under Morsi would be more hostile to Israel, but Morsi was also the leader of a party, the Muslim Brotherhood, that seeks to eliminate Western influences from

Mohamed Morsi speaks at a rally in Cairo.

the Arab world. During the Muslim Brotherhood's brief period of rule, Egyptian relations with Israel were strained. By contrast, the Sisi government has largely restored the strategic partnership.

How should countries that espouse democratic values manage this dilemma between institutions that are attractive but interests that are hostile? Should the United States continue to send military and economic aid to Egypt's military government, or should it push for the restoration of democracy?

One view is that a country's security interests must outweigh any commitment that it might have to democracy. From the perspective of U.S. policy makers, democratic institutions are desirable in parts of the world where people have interests similar to those of the United States, but they are dangerous where they empower people with very different interests and ideas. While this is not an ethically appealing argument, it is the position that has historically shaped U.S. policy. In the case of Egypt, President Obama initially held back aid and military sales after the coup but later released them. President Trump also closely embraced the Sisi government and resisted calls to push for liberalization in Saudi Arabia, another longtime ally in the region.

These decisions to prioritize security interests over democracy did not represent a new strategy for the United States. During the Cold War, the United States feared that elections in other countries would empower communist parties that would in turn become allies of the Soviet Union; military dictatorships, though brutal to their own people, made more reliable partners. Thus, in several countries— Iran (1953), Guatemala (1954), Chile (1973)—the United States conspired in the overthrow of democratic governments by military dictators. Supporters of this strategy also argue that the elected leaders who were overthrown were likely to become dictators themselves. Morsi's opponents, for example, questioned whether the Muslim Brotherhood was committed to democracy or human rights. In fact, the military coup enjoyed a great deal of popular support because of dissatisfaction with the Morsi government and constitutional reforms that it had pushed.

The most common argument against placing security interests above democracy is based on moral considerations: people have a right to a government that is responsive to their interests and respects their civil liberties. By installing or supporting dictators, the United States is complicit in the human rights abuses committed by those regimes. In addition, one could argue that U.S. interests are best served by promoting democracy in the long run, even where it is inconvenient to do so in the short run.

By supporting authoritarian regimes like Egypt under Mubarak, the United States has stoked anti-American sentiment and contributed to the hostility of Egypt's people. In some cases, this hostility has fed the ranks of terrorist organizations like Al Qaeda that have targeted the United States and its interests. In this view, the United States would be safer in the long term if it did not prop up autocratic regimes in the region and instead supported the self-determination of people there.

A woman casts her ballot in the 2014 Egyptian presidential election that brought Abdel Fattah al-Sisi into office.

Thinking Analytically

1. Why might the United States care what kind of government Egypt has? Do democratic states have an interest in promoting democracy abroad, or does the preference for democracy only reflect a certain kind of values?

2. What are the risks of pressuring an allied government to make democratic reforms?

a. Pew Research Center, "Egyptians Increasingly Glum," May 16, 2013, www.pewglobal.org/2013/05/16/egyptians-increasingly-glum (accessed 3/24/2021).

organization and resources, they can push the state toward greater international ambition and thus a greater risk of war. As we have seen, there are times when military organizations and economic or ethnic interest groups have both the interests and the ability to push foreign policy in such a direction.

In contrast, when interactions and institutions empower those who bear the costs of war, they can exert a pacifying effect at the international level. Economic actors that benefit from international commerce and investment may lobby for peaceful relations with profitable partners. Representative institutions give voice to the people who bear the costs of war, thereby weakening the influence of concentrated interests that might promote conflict for their own reasons. Free, fair, and frequent elections provide a relatively low-cost mechanism for people to punish leaders who engage in failed or costly wars. The relative openness and transparency of democratic political processes can reduce informational and commitment problems that can cause bargaining to fail. Although these features may make democracies tempting targets for autocratic foes, they also help account for the relative rarity of war among democratic states.

Does this mean that a world full of democratic states would be a world without war? Certainly, the evidence to date is encouraging, although not definitive. There are at least two reasons to be cautious. First, although the number of democracies in the world has generally increased over time, the spread of democracy has experienced reversals. There have been several periods during which democracy has broken down, particularly the 1930s (leading to the low point in 1940) and the 1970s. During these periods, economic and international upheaval caused some democratic systems to fail. The last decade has also witnessed a number of cases of "democratic backsliding"—countries in which democratically elected leaders have undermined essential features of democracy, such as in Hungary, Poland, and Turkey.[66] Democratic institutions have also come under stress in the United States, where President Trump tried to overturn his loss in the 2020 election.[67]

It is worth remembering that Adolf Hitler came to power in Germany through relatively democratic institutions—which he then subverted before embarking on his campaign of foreign expansion. Hence, democratic systems have given birth to forces that undermined democracy and engaged in aggressive foreign policies. Even if there are no cases of war between two democratic states, there have been wars between democracies and states that were once democratic.

A second reason for caution centers on the interests that will come to be represented by the spread of democracy. Recall that democratic institutions make leaders more sensitive to the interests of the citizenry. Kant, and those who follow in his tradition, assumed that citizens are generally cautious, since it is they who bear the costs of war. But what if the public is motivated by nationalist, ethnocentric, or even genocidal ideas? If fear and hatred of a rival are intense, accountability may induce

66. Nancy Bermeo, "On Democratic Backsliding," *Journal of Democracy* 27, no. 1 (2016): 5–19.
67. Pippa Norris, "It Happened in America," *Foreign Affairs*, January 7, 2021, www.foreignaffairs.com/articles/united-states/2021-01-07/it-happened-america (accessed 2/1/21).

belligerence rather than caution, and leaders may fear domestic political retribution for being overly "soft" toward the nation's ethnic or religious enemies.[68] The costs of war might, as a result, actually be less than the political costs of compromise.

We already saw in the case of India and Pakistan that the fact that both were democracies in the spring of 1999 did not prevent a war from breaking out between them. (See "What Shaped Our World?" on p. 166.) A history of conflict and bloodshed, fueled by religious differences, has created a great deal of enmity between not just the governments but also the people in these states. Indeed, the Kargil War was popular on both sides; in Pakistan, people were disappointed only that their country did not prevail.

Hence, the international effects of democracy's spread may very well depend not only on the institutions that take root but also on the interests of those they empower.

---

68. For evidence that leaders may be punished for making concessions to a rival, see Michael Colaresi, "When Doves Cry: International Rivalry, Unreciprocated Cooperation, and Leadership Turnover," *American Journal of Political Science* 48, no. 3 (2004): 555–70.

Study Tool Kit

Interests, Interactions, and Institutions in Context

- There may be actors within a state who perceive significant benefits from war and expect to pay little or none of its costs. In particular, there are conditions under which political leaders, business and ethnic lobbies, and the military will see conflict as furthering their narrow interests.

- These actors have a variety of institutional and organizational advantages that make it possible for them to exert more influence on foreign policy decision making than the general population can.

- Except in rare circumstances, these hawkish interests are not sufficient to cause war on their own. Rather, their main effect is to increase the aggressiveness of the state's foreign policy and the scope of its ambitions, thereby creating more opportunities for conflict.

- Democratic political institutions—in particular, free and fair elections, party competition, and free media—can diminish the influence of hawkish interests, increase the costs of war for political leaders, or change the bargaining interaction in a way that makes a peaceful settlement more likely.

Key Terms

nationalism, p. 147

bureaucracy, p. 151

interest groups, p. 151

rally effect, p. 156

diversionary incentive, p. 157

military-industrial complex, p. 163

democratic peace, p. 176

democracy, p. 177

autocracy, p. 177

accountability, p. 181

For Further Reading

Allison, Graham, and Philip Zelikow. *Essence of Decision: Explaining the Cuban Missile Crisis*. **2nd ed. New York: Longman, 1999.** Presents a classic study of the effects of bureaucratic politics on foreign policy making in one of the most dramatic crises of the Cold War.

Chiozza, Giacomo, and H. E. Goemans. *Leaders and International Conflict.* **Cambridge: Cambridge University Press, 2011.** Explores how democratic and autocratic leaders make decisions about international conflict with an eye toward staying in office and staying alive.

Doyle, Michael W. "Liberalism and World Politics." *American Political Science Review* **80, no. 4 (December 1986): 1151–69.** Offers an influential discussion of how liberal political systems might affect foreign policy choices; this analysis brought the study of the democratic peace to the forefront of political science.

Feaver, Peter D., and Christopher Gelpi. *Choosing Your Battles: American Civil-Military Relations and the Use of Force.* **Princeton, NJ: Princeton University Press, 2004.** Presents a systematic study of how civilians and military officers differ in their views about the use of force.

Fordham, Benjamin O. *Building the Cold War Consensus: The Political Economy of U.S. National Security Policy, 1949–51.* **Ann Arbor: University of Michigan Press, 1998.** Examines how different economic interests came together to underpin the United States' international commitments during the Cold War.

Russett, Bruce, and John Oneal. *Triangulating Peace: Democracy, Interdependence, and International Organizations.* **New York: Norton, 2001.** Gives a comprehensive review and analysis of the effects of democracy, trade, and international institutions on violent conflict between states.

Saunders, Elizabeth N. *Leaders at War: How Presidents Shape Military Interventions.* **Ithaca, NY: Cornell University Press, 2011.** Shows how the beliefs that U.S. presidents bring into office can shape the ways they respond to foreign crises.

Snyder, Jack. *Myths of Empire: Domestic Politics and International Ambition.* **Ithaca, NY: Cornell University Press, 1991.** Explores how domestic interest groups and military organizations can push great powers to adopt expansionist foreign policies—often with disastrous consequences for the state as a whole.

Weeks, Jessica L. P. *Dictators at War and Peace.* **Ithaca, NY: Cornell University Press, 2014.** Explores the variation among autocratic governments and how different kinds of nondemocratic leaders weigh decisions about war and peace.

Weiss, Jessica Chen. *Powerful Patriots: Nationalist Protest in China's Foreign Relations.* **New York, NY: Oxford University Press, 2014.** Shows how the Chinese government harnesses nationalism at home to gain leverage in disputes with the United States and Japan.

5

International Institutions and War

THE PUZZLE *In a well-governed country, the police prevent and punish acts of violence between individuals. Where are the police in international politics? Why is it so hard for the international community to prevent and punish acts of aggression?*

Above: Collective security organizations like the United Nations can influence interactions between adversaries in ways that promote peaceful outcomes. However, these institutions face significant challenges in achieving their goals.

When North Korea invaded South Korea in June 1950, the United Nations (UN) responded by authorizing member states to use military force to resist this act of aggression. Although North Korea had some influential supporters, including the Soviet Union and China, a coalition of 20 nations led by the United States successfully expelled the North Koreans from South Korea by October 1950. At that point, the UN expanded the forces' mandate, and they pushed into North Korea. This act provoked China to intervene in order to save its ally, and the Korean War dragged on for another three years.

Around the same time, Chinese forces also invaded Tibet, a region to China's west. China had long claimed sovereignty over this vast, mountainous territory, but Tibet had declared independence from China in 1911. Although China never recognized this declaration, Tibet was, in practice, an independent state for the next several decades as China, distracted by civil war and the Japanese invasion in the 1930s, was unable to resist. Not long after the Communists gained control of mainland China in 1949, they sought to reassert the country's historic claim over Tibet. Units of the People's Liberation Army swept into the region in October 1950, quickly defeating the Tibetan army and forcing Tibet's leaders to accept Chinese rule. Tibet's political and religious leader, the Dalai Lama, appealed to the UN to meet China's attack on Tibet with the same kind of response that it had mustered against North Korea. But in this case, the UN took no action, and China's conquest of Tibet was allowed to stand.

Although aggression and theft are not unique to international politics, they pose a particular problem in relations between countries. Within countries, governments have tools to deter and punish acts of violence that occur between people. Police forces and courts exist to enforce order domestically. Even if the police cannot always stop a crime in progress, they can investigate and try to bring the perpetrator to justice. The existence of a police force has a deterrent effect on would-be criminals, who can be dissuaded from committing crimes by the expectation that they might be caught and punished. Although total security is rarely possible, people who live in societies with well-functioning police and judicial systems rarely have to commit acts of violence to defend themselves.[1] The same cannot be said of actors in the international system.

Where are the police in world politics? The short answer is that the international system has no police force analogous to what exists in most countries. While each state possesses its own police and its own military, there is no authoritative institution above states with an independent force that can police relations among them. As suggested by the Korean and Tibetan examples just described, this condition of anarchy means that there is variation in how the international community responds to acts of aggression. And this variation has real consequences for people living in the states where such aggression occurs. Thanks to the international efforts that kept it independent, South Korea is today a thriving and prosperous country, with a standard of living that far exceeds that of the impoverished North. Tibet, on the other hand, remains a part of China in spite of the fact that an active movement for Tibetan independence continues to this day.

Understanding this variation in international responses requires that we explore the institutions that govern whether and how outside actors respond to acts of violence in the international system. The most obvious of these outside actors are bodies like the UN or its predecessor, the League of Nations (1919–46). Formally known as collective security organizations, these institutions are the closest approximation to a world government that we have. Collective security organizations try to govern relations among their members, providing them with tools for peaceful conflict resolution and mechanisms for organizing collective responses to acts of aggression. Collective security organizations are thus a natural first place to look for the police in international politics.

For much longer than such organizations have existed, however, states have used alternative institutions to arrange for help from others: alliances. If collective security organizations are like governments, alliances more closely resemble neighborhood associations: relatively small groups of actors that work together to meet common threats or address common needs. Alliances are institutions that help states cooperate militarily, for instance, by coming to one another's defense in the event of war. In the absence of an effective world police force, alliances represent attempts by small numbers of like-minded states to look out for one another.

This chapter continues our inquiry into the puzzle of war by examining how international institutions affect interactions between states as they try to cooperate to prevent or stop international and civil conflict.

Thinking Analytically about International Institutions and War

Alliances and collective security organizations both influence whether or not outsiders will intervene in the event that war breaks out. As a result, they play a role in the bargaining that precedes a war, the bargaining that seeks to end an ongoing war, and the bargaining that takes place in the aftermath of fighting. But, despite these common features, these two types of institutions also differ greatly in how they operate. They form in response to different kinds of interests that third parties may have in international disputes. And while both try to facilitate cooperation among states, they address different aspects of the strategic interactions that surround third-party involvement in international conflict. Hence, the factors that predict their success or failure are quite different.

Alliances form when states have compatible interests that motivate them to cooperate militarily. Allies often seek to influence bargaining interactions with a potentially hostile third party by convincing the adversary that they are willing to fight together in the event of war. A core function of alliances is to strengthen the commitment that member countries make to one another and to signal that commitment to nonmember countries in a credible manner.

By contrast, collective security organizations like the UN form around a common interest, which all states are presumed to share, in reducing violence within and between countries. Their primary challenge is to facilitate collective action by the international community to deter, end, and prevent the recurrence of international and civil wars. The task is a daunting one, and international efforts can be stymied either by the opposition of leading states or by their unwillingness to pay the costs of intervention. As a result, collective efforts to keep the peace are uneven but certainly better than if these organizations did not exist at all.

---

1. To be sure, the police can themselves be a cause of violence either because the state uses them as an instrument of repression or because of poor oversight and control. How governments control or encourage violence by police is an important area of inquiry outside of the scope of an international relations class.

Alliances: Why Promise to Fight Someone Else's War?

World War II in Europe started as a territorial dispute between Germa[ny and] Poland but quickly grew into something much larger. After Germany i[nvaded] Poland on September 1, 1939, Britain and France responded two days la[ter by] declaring war on Germany. On September 17, the Soviet Union joined t[he war] invading Poland from the east, and Poland was quickly swallowed up b[y its] neighbors. Several months later, in June 1940, Italy joined the war on G[ermany's] side and launched an invasion of southern France as German forces at[tacked] France in the north.

In each case, states that joined the war were carrying out the term[s of] treaties that they had signed in the preceding decades. France and Poland had long-standing promises, codified in treaties from 1921 and 1925, to help each other in the event of war with Germany. Britain made a similar commitment to Poland in March 1939. Italy and the Soviet Union, for their parts, had each sig[ned trea]ties pledging support for German military activities. Italy and German[y signed the] so-called Pact of Steel in May 1939. Germany and the Soviet Union unv[eiled the] Molotov-Ribbentrop Pact (so named for the two countries' foreign mi[nisters)] days before the invasion of Poland. In that treaty, the two countries ple[dged not to] attack each other and agreed to divide Poland between them; in additi[on, Germany] promised the Soviets control over Finland, Estonia, Latvia, and Lithua[nia.]

Alliances are institutions that help their members cooperate mili[tarily in] the event of a war. Like all institutions, alliances specify standards of b[ehavior, or] expectations about how states are to behave under certain conditions. [They may] include procedures for joint decision making and provisions for moni[toring and] verifying each member's compliance. Alliances also codify bargains be[tween] members that settle distributional issues; for instance, they might pre[empt or] resolve conflicts that could get in the way of cooperation or specify ho[w each] member will contribute to the common cause.[2] Alliances may also be l[inked to other] forms of cooperation, such as increased trade.[3]

These provisions vary depending on the interests of the allies. Some alliances are offensive, while others are defensive. An *offensive alliance* is an agreement between states to join one another in attacking a third state. The Molotov-Ribbentrop Pact is a classic example of such an agreement. It not only specified the nature of Soviet-German military cooperation, but it also spelled out how the spoils of conquest would be divided. More commonly, alliances are *defensive*: states pledge to come to one another's defense in the event that one of them is attacked. The

---

2. The role of alliances in settling territorial conflicts among allies is noted by Douglas M. Gibler, "Control the Issues, Control the Conflict: The Effects of Alliances That Settle Territorial Issues on Interstate Rivalries," *International Interactions* 22, no. 4 (1997): 341–68.

3. Paul Poast, "Does Issue Linkage Work? Evidence from European Alliance Negotiations, 1860 to 1945," *International Organization* 66, no. 2 (2012): 277–310.

British and French pledges to Poland had this character. Defensive alliances may be open-ended in the sense that allies pledge to defend one another against any and all attackers, or they may be targeted only at specific countries. Alliances may also differ in what they require member states to do in the event of attack. A typical defensive alliance requires states to come to one another's aid militarily—that is, to treat an attack on an ally as an attack on oneself. Other alliance agreements specify merely that the states will consult one another in the event of war.

The most comprehensive effort to collect and code information on alliances through history, the Alliance Treaty Obligation and Provision (ATOP) project, provides us with a sense of how common these different kinds of provisions are. ATOP researchers identified 573 alliance treaties between states in the period from 1815 to 2016.[4] Of these, just over half (289) included promises of active military support in the event that one of the allies became involved in a conflict. The vast majority of such alliances (72 percent) were purely defensive in character, only 5 percent were purely offensive, and the rest (23 percent) had both offensive and defensive provisions. Of the agreements that did not provide for active military assistance, most (233) provided for consultation between the allies if either member became involved in military conflict. About a fifth of all alliances included a neutrality clause, which required that each member promise not to join in any attack against an ally.

The United States currently has defensive alliances with a number of countries. The most prominent of these is the North Atlantic Treaty Organization (NATO), which allies the United States with Canada and 28 countries in Europe. The United States also has long-standing defense pacts with Japan, South Korea, the Philippines, and Australia. If any of these states comes under attack, it can invoke the U.S. alliance commitment and ask the United States to come to its aid. In turn, the United States can appeal to others if it is attacked. NATO invoked its mutual defense provision for the first time in the alliance's history after the terrorist attack on the United States in September 2001. European NATO members assisted in flying aircraft equipped with the Airborne Warning and Control System (AWACS) over U.S. skies from October 2001 to May 2002.

In addition to spelling out their offensive or defensive character, alliances may codify bargains over how much and what each state will contribute to the common defense. Some alliances are symmetrical, meaning that the members have similar responsibilities and contribute in roughly equal amounts. Other alliances are highly asymmetrical, typically because one of the members is much more powerful than the others. For example, while the United States has pledged to defend South Korea, there is little expectation that South Korea would be in a position to return the favor if the U.S. homeland were attacked. In exchange for protection, South Korea provides bases for American troops in East Asia, has contributed to U.S. military efforts in the region, and generally supports U.S. foreign policy diplomatically

---

4. The data collection is described in Brett Ashley Leeds, Jeffrey M. Ritter, Sara McLaughlin Mitchell, and Andrew G. Long, "Alliance Treaty Obligations and Provisions, 1815–1944," *International Interactions* 28 (2002): 237–60. The data and codebook are available at http://atopdata.org (accessed 12/27/20). The figures reported here do not include nonaggression pacts (that is, agreements to refrain from using force), since these do not meet the definition of an alliance.

Burden sharing - how much each state in an alliance contributes to the common cause - can be a source of hard bargaining within alliances

interests that motivate them to cooperate.

and economically.[5] The issue of burden sharing—that is, how much each state in an alliance contributes to the common cause—can be a source of hard bargaining within alliances, as tensions between the United States and its allies in recent years attest (See "What Shaped our World?" on p. 214).

Interests and Alliances

Given that alliances can drag a country into other countries' wars, why do states sign them? Alliances form when states have compatible interests that provide the basis for cooperation. In some cases, states share a common interest in achieving the same outcome. In the lead-up to World War II, the leaders of Britain and France did not agree to defend Poland out of the goodness of their hearts; they did so because they feared that, were Germany to conquer Poland, Germany would become militarily stronger, economically more self-sufficient, and therefore a greater threat to their own security. Thus, Britain and France shared Poland's interest in its own survival. Similarly, the United States formed the NATO alliance after World War II because it believed that securing countries like Britain, France, and West Germany from Soviet domination was crucial to its own security. Indeed, having shared enemies is a strong predictor of whether alliance negotiations succeed.[6]

In other cases, alliance partners might have complementary interests that serve as the basis for a deal. The alliance between the United States and South Korea rests on the fact that South Korea wants protection from North Korea and China, while the United States wants military bases and partners in projecting its power in East Asia. Thus, each partner can provide something that the other values.

5. For an analysis of costs and benefits of the U.S. alliance system, see Mira Rapp-Hooper, *Shields of the Republic: The Triumph and Peril of America's Alliances* (Cambridge, MA: Harvard University Press, 2020).
6. Paul Poast, *Arguing about Alliances: The Art of Agreement in Military-Pact Negotiations* (Ithaca, NY: Cornell University Press, 2019).

Whatever the specific interests are that bring states together into alliances, allies generally have aligned interests in the context of bargaining with third-party states. Figure 5.1 shows how we can depict such an alignment in our bargaining framework. As before, the disputed good is shown as a horizontal bar, and any possible deal separates this good into shares enjoyed by States A and B. We now assume that there is some third state, State C, that also has a stake in the outcome of bargaining between States A and B. If, say, State C has aligned interests with State A, then State C's ideal point is, like State A's ideal point, at the far right end of the bar. This means that the more of the good State A gets, the happier State C is. Thus, their interests are aligned, at least when it comes to this dispute with State B.

How these alignments arise is a complicated question without a single answer. A long tradition in the study of international relations holds that alliances form to create or preserve a **balance of power**—that is, a situation in which the military capabilities of two states or groups of states are roughly equal.[7] When a balance of power exists, no state or bloc has a clear military advantage over the other. A power imbalance, in contrast, is considered threatening to the weaker side's interests. According to balance of power theory, alliances form when it is in the interest of two or more states to combine their capabilities in order to match the capabilities of another, stronger state or bloc that poses a threat to their security.

For example, after World War II, the Soviet Union kept substantial military forces stationed in Eastern European countries that it had occupied during the war. The United States feared that these forces gave the Soviet Union a military advantage that could be used to threaten the West. This fear aligned U.S. interests with those of states in Western Europe who were directly threatened by the proximity of Soviet power. The NATO alliance thus formed in large part to enable cooperation that would balance the power of the Soviet Union.

FIGURE 5.1 *Alignment of Interests*

If State C shares common interests with State A, then both State A and State C prefer a deal as far to the right as possible. The more of the good State A gets, the happier State C is.

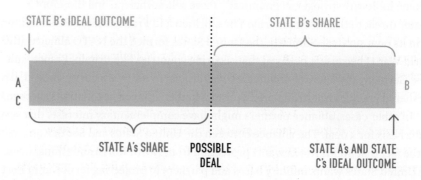

---

7. See, for example, Edward Vose Gulick, *Europe's Classical Balance of Power: A Case History of the Theory and Practice of One of the Great Concepts of European Statecraft* (New York: Norton, 1955). For an influential statement of the theory, see Kenneth N. Waltz, *Theory of International Politics* (1979; repr., Long Grove, IL: Waveland Press, 2010). For a historical analysis of balancing and its alternatives, see Paul Schroeder, "Alliances, 1815–1945: Weapons of Power and Tools of Management," in *Historical Dimensions of National Security Problems*, ed. Klaus Knorr (Lawrence: University Press of Kansas, 1976), 247–86.

Red paint defacing a monument to Russian soldiers in Warsaw, Poland, testifies to the anger many Poles feel toward Russia, which kept military forces stationed in that country from 1945-1993. Poland sought to join NATO after the Cold War to counter the threat it perceives from Russia due to geographic proximity and this history of occupation.

Although this dynamic can explain some aspects of alliance formation, balance of power theory does not fully account for all alliance decisions. First, not all alliances form with the intent of balancing a stronger state. When the Soviet Union allied with Nazi Germany against Poland, it joined the stronger state, exacerbating rather than alleviating the imbalance of power in Central Europe. We refer to such behavior as bandwagoning.[8] **Bandwagoning** occurs when states team up with the more powerful side in a dispute. Often, bandwagoning alliances are offensive. The shared interests that underlie them arise not from a common fear but from a desire to cooperate for a common gain at some other state's expense, just as Germany and the Soviet Union cooperated to carve up Poland.

But states may also side with a stronger state because they perceive a greater threat from a weaker one. After the collapse of the Soviet Union in 1991, many central and Eastern European countries sought to join NATO, even though NATO was objectively more powerful than any other state or bloc around. The United States, NATO's largest member, has alone accounted for 40–50 percent of all world military spending in the decades since the Cold War. Nonetheless, many countries in the region saw Russia, the largest republic of the former Soviet Union, as the greater threat due to geographic proximity and the countries' histories of Soviet occupation. The expansion of NATO to include these states—with 14 members added from 1999–2020—led to a significant *imbalance* of power in Europe.

As this example suggests, states may form or join alliances not simply to balance power but to counter threats, and the most threatening state may not be the most powerful one.[9] Which states are perceived as threatening depends on a constellation of factors, including such considerations as geographic proximity,

bandwagoning

A strategy in which states join forces with the stronger side in a conflict.

---

8. Randall L. Schweller, "Bandwagoning for Profit: Bringing the Revisionist State Back In," *International Security* 19, no. 1 (1994): 72–107.

9. Stephen M. Walt, *The Origins of Alliances* (Ithaca, NY: Cornell University Press, 1987).

historical experiences, the existence (or not) of high-value disputes, and commercial, ideological, or cultural ties.

These factors may also explain why certain countries see some alliance partners as more desirable than others. For example, when Saudi Arabia sought allies against Egypt in 1957, why did it choose to ally with fellow Arab monarchies Jordan and Iraq rather than with Israel, a state with much more impressive military capabilities and also reason to fear Egypt? The answer lies not in the balance of power but rather in the ideological and religious incompatibility between Saudi Arabia and the Jewish state, which made an alliance between the two unthinkable.[10]

Conversely, shared cultural or religious identity can help explain why some pairs of states see each other as particularly attractive allies. Strategic cooperation between the United States and Israel, for example, is partly rooted in the perception that Israel is an outpost of Western cultural and democratic values in the Middle East and hence more "like" the United States than are other states in the region.[11] Thus, in thinking about the conditions that give rise to common interests that form the bases of alliances, the need to balance power is an important consideration, but it exists alongside many others.

Alliances and Interstate Bargaining

The possibility of intervention by an ally influences interstate bargaining by changing the likely outcome and costs of war for each side. Returning to the three-state example introduced in Figure 5.1, imagine that if States A and B were to fight a war, the expected outcome would be as shown in the top panel of Figure 5.2. In this interaction, State B is assumed to be more powerful, so the war outcome is close to its ideal point. This means that State B can extract a favorable bargain from State A and is likely to challenge State A to try to realize that bargain (in other words, there is a large range of status quo outcomes in which State B will make a demand of State A). If State C is expected to join State A in this war, however, the outcome and costs will be quite different, as shown in the lower panel. With State C's power added to that of State A, the expected outcome shifts to the right, in State A's favor. Moreover, State B is likely to suffer higher costs in a war against two adversaries, whereas State A is likely to incur lower costs now that State C is carrying some of the burden.

As before, the bargaining range is the set of deals that are preferred to war by both sides. Because of the change in the likely war outcome, the bargaining range has shifted to the right in the lower panel, benefiting States A and C. War is less attractive to State B, which can no longer extract a lopsided deal. State B's incentive to challenge State A also declines. By shrinking the range of status quos that State B can profitably challenge, the prospect of State C's participation deters State B from initiating crises in the first place. Hence, State C's willingness to intervene influences the bargaining interaction between States A and B by shifting each side's evaluation of war.

---

10. Walt, *Origins of Alliances*, 204–6.

11. See, for example, Michael N. Barnett, "Identity and Alliances in the Middle East," in *The Culture of National Security*, ed. Peter J. Katzenstein (Ithaca, NY: Cornell University Press, 1996), 400–417.

FIGURE 5.2 *Alignments, Alliances, and Interstate Bargaining*

The bargaining interaction between State A and State B is determined by the expected outcome of a war between the two states.

However, this interaction changes when State C is expected to join State A in the event of a war. As shown below, when State C's power is added to State A's, the expected war outcome shifts to the right, and State B's costs of war increase. As a result, the set of deals that are preferable to war shifts closer to the ideal point of States A and C, and the range of status quo distributions that State B will challenge shrinks.

In addition, the possibility of intervention can affect whether the opposing sides reach a bargain. In the example just given, the shift in the bargaining range was based on the assumption that both States A and B believe that State C would intervene in the event of war. In other words, it is assumed that the two sides form their expectations on the basis of the same information about State C's intentions. What would happen if this was not the case? For example, what if State A expected State C to join a war, but State B did not?

When the parties to a dispute have different information about what third parties will do, the uncertainty can heighten the probability that a bargaining failure will lead to war, for reasons discussed in Chapter 3. As we have seen, Iraq in August 1990 did not know whether the United States would defend Kuwait, and its doubts about U.S. threats to intervene helped bring about the Persian Gulf War. Similarly, we saw in the case of the Korean War that the United States was uncertain about whether China would come to the aid of North Korea if U.S. troops crossed the 38th parallel. In the lead-up to World War I, Germany was unsure until the last moment whether Britain would join its allies, France and Russia, in the event of war.

Allies may perform joint military exercises in order to improve their ability to fight together and to publicize their commitment to do so. Here, American and South Korean soldiers engage in an exercise near the border with North Korea.

This observation suggests that alliances influence the bargaining interaction between states by influencing the states' beliefs about what third parties will do. While aligned interests are necessary for alliances to form, a key reason that states sign alliances is to signal those interests to others. After all, if it were completely obvious to everyone which states would come to the defense of others, there would be little need to negotiate and sign treaties to this effect.[12]

Because of their role as signals, alliances face the same challenge of credibility discussed in Chapter 3 with respect to threats. Indeed, an alliance entails an implied threat: "If you attack my ally, I will fight you." However, just because a state has an interest in the outcome of its ally's bargaining interactions does not ensure that the state will actually fight alongside its ally in the event of war. An alliance commitment may be questionable for the same reasons that threats are questionable: they are costly to carry out, and there can be incentives to bluff. Alliances are not, after all, binding contracts. There is no external mechanism to compel states to fulfill their treaty obligations. Rather, the promise to come to another's defense in the event of war is precisely that: a promise, which may or may not be fulfilled. In fact, there are many instances in which allies have not lived up to their commitments. In June 1941, for example, less than two years after signing the Molotov-Ribbentrop Pact, Germany broke its side of the agreement by invading the Soviet Union and grabbing all of Poland for itself.

This observation suggests that when we talk about alliances, we should be clear to treat them as institutions and not as actors in their own right. It sometimes serves as a useful shorthand to talk about alliances as cohesive actors; for example, we might say: "NATO intervened in Libya." However, we must remember that

---

12. James D. Morrow, "Alliances: Why Write Them Down?" *Annual Review of Political Science* 3 (2000): 63–83.

alliances are institutions formed by states in response to common interests. These institutions may shape states' interests in a way that helps them to act as a cohesive group, but at all times decision-making power rests with the states, not with the alliance itself.[13]

How Alliances Establish Credibility

Whether an alliance can successfully further the interests of allied states depends on the states' willingness to fight on one another's behalf and on their ability to signal this willingness in a credible manner. Therefore, alliances must accomplish two key tasks in order to enhance their chances of success. First, they must make it more likely that allies will fight on one another's behalf than they would in the absence of an alliance. This can be accomplished by decreasing the costs of fighting, increasing the benefits of fighting, and/or increasing the costs of not fighting—that is, of abandoning an ally. Second, alliances must do these things in a way that leads adversaries to believe that the allies will indeed fight together. Hence, the goal is both to heighten the allies' interests in aiding one another and to influence interactions with rival states by shaping their expectations.

Alliances typically have a number of features designed to further these goals. First, while alliances form in response to compatible interests, they can strengthen the alignment of interests by settling preexisting conflicts or encouraging deeper ties between their members, such as through increased trade.[14] These effects can increase the benefits of coming to an ally's aid. For example, while the U.S.-Japan alliance formed as a way to counter Soviet and Chinese influence in East Asia, the two countries became close trading partners over the ensuing decades, so that threats to Japan indirectly threaten U.S. economic interests. Deep diplomatic ties can also help allies negotiate side payments, additional benefits or concessions to induce partner states to join their coalitions.[15]

Second, alliances can increase the probability of prevailing in a war and reduce the costs of war by improving the member countries' ability to fight effectively together. Allies put significant effort into improving their war-fighting capabilities; they may engage in joint military planning and exercises, coordinate arms production and acquisition to ensure that their systems are compatible, and, in some cases, station troops on one another's soil.[16] For example, the United States has more than

---

13. This characteristic distinguishes alliances from empires and more hierarchical relationships between states in which the capabilities of two or more actors are combined but decision-making power rests in a dominant state. On security hierarchies, see David A. Lake, *Entangling Relations: American Foreign Policy in Its Century* (Princeton, NJ: Princeton University Press, 1999).

14. Gibler, "Control the Issues, Control the Conflict"; Poast, "Does Issue Linkage Work?"; and Joanne Gowa, *Allies, Adversaries, and International Trade* (Princeton, NJ: Princeton University Press, 1994).

15. Marina E. Henke, *Constructing Allied Cooperation: Diplomacy, Payments, and Power in Multilateral Military Coalitions* (Ithaca, NY: Cornell University Press, 2019).

16. For a discussion of different ways major powers signal resolve to protect allies, see Roseanne W. McManus and Mark David Nieman, "Identifying the Level of Major Power Support Signaled for Protégés: A Latent Measure Approach," *Journal of Peace Research* 56, no. 3 (2019): 364–78. For an analysis of the effects of stationing U.S. troops in other countries, see Carla Martinez Machain and T. Clifton Morgan, "The Effect of US Troop Deployment on Host States' Foreign Policy," *Armed Forces & Society* 39, no. 1 (January 2013): 102–23.

25,000 troops stationed in South Korea and routinely performs joint military exercises with the South Korean military. By doing so, it makes the expected value of the two states fighting together higher than it would be in the absence of an alliance. This coordination is publicly revealed (even if actual war-fighting strategies are not), which serves to put potential adversaries on notice. Some alliances also contain provisions for joint decision making that further enhance their members' collective war-fighting abilities. For instance, NATO appoints a Supreme Allied Commander Europe which is responsible for all troops under the organization's authority.

Third, alliances can increase the costs of abandonment—that is, of failing to fight on an ally's behalf. Prior to the nineteenth century, it was common to cement alliances through a marriage between royal families under the theory that a king would have special motivation to defend an ally if his daughter were married to that ally's monarch. More commonly, the fact that alliance treaties are generally made public— often accompanied by public signing ceremonies and, in some countries, open ratification processes—can bring states' reputations into play.[17] States may fear that their failure to come to an ally's defense after making such a public commitment would hurt their credibility in future conflicts.[18] Such hand-tying strategies seek to bolster the credibility of alliances just as they do the credibility of other threats.

So do alliances actually work? As we have seen, alliances have two tasks: to increase the likelihood that two states will cooperate militarily in the event of war and to signal this willingness to other states in a way that influences the outcome of bargaining. With respect to the second task, evidence suggests that alliances are generally successful in deterring attacks on their members. On average, states with defensive alliances are less likely to be targeted by militarized actions than are states that lack allies.[19] This does not mean, of course, that alliances always succeed in deterring attacks, as the historical review in the next section will attest.

The fact that alliances primarily work by preventing attacks on their members complicates our ability to assess the first task—that is, whether alliances increase member states' willingness to fight together. Research suggests that historically, states have honored alliance agreements in wartime about 60–70 percent of the time, although this figure appears to be markedly lower (close to 20 percent) in the second half of the twentieth century.[20] Crucially, however, we can only observe

---

17. This is generally true of defensive alliances. Offensive alliances, in contrast, may be kept secret if the intended target would otherwise take countermeasures to blunt the effectiveness of the alliance.

18. For research on how violating agreements can make it harder for states to make new alliances, see Mark J. C. Crescenzi, Jacob D. Kathman, Katja B. Kleinberg, and Reed M. Wood, "Reliability, Reputation, and Alliance Formation," *International Studies Quarterly* 56, no. 2 (2012): 259–74; and Brad L. LeVeck and Neil Narang, "How International Reputation Matters: Revisiting Alliance Violations in Context," *International Interactions* 43, no. 5 (2017): 797–821.

19. Brett Ashley Leeds, "Do Alliances Deter Aggression? The Influence of Military Alliances on the Initiation of Militarized Interstate Disputes," *American Journal of Political Science* 47, no. 3 (2003): 427–39; see also Matthew Fuhrmann and Todd S. Sechser, "Signaling Alliance Commitments: Hand-Tying and Sunk Costs in Extended Nuclear Deterrence," *American Journal of Political Science* 58, no. 4 (October 2014): 919–35.

20. Brett Ashley Leeds and Sezi Anac, "Alliance Institutionalization and Alliance Performance," *International Interactions* 31, no. 3 (2005): 192. For a different analysis, which suggests that this rate decreased significantly after 1945, see Molly Berkemeier and Matthew Fuhrmann, "Reassessing the Fulfillment of Alliance Commitments in War," *Research & Politics* 5, no. 2 (2018): 1–5.

whether an alliance is honored if a member is attacked—that is, if deterrence fails. Absent such a challenge, we do not know whether the allies would have fought together in the event of an attack. But if third parties are most likely to challenge the alliances that are least credible, then the reliability of the alliances that are challenged is lower than the overall reliability of all alliances. Put another way, the allies that are most likely to fight together are unlikely to be called on to do so. Thus, estimates of alliance reliability risk underestimating how effective they actually are.[21]

It is worth noting that this same problem bedevils contemporary debates in the United States about whether to maintain existing alliance commitments in Europe and East Asia. The main effect of these alliances is to preserve stability in these regions and prevent allies from being attacked. When the alliances succeed, they prevent bad things from happening. Thus, while the costs in terms of military spending and the commitment of troops are tangible, the benefits—that is, potential wars that did not occur—can be harder to perceive.[22]

Why Aren't Alliance Commitments Ironclad?

If states have compatible interests that lead them to form alliances and signal their commitments to one another, why is there often uncertainty about whether members will actually fulfill their obligations? Why do allies and other states that are the targets of alliances sometimes have different expectations about whether allies will actually come to one another's aid? To answer these questions, we need to think about the choices facing all parties to a strategic interaction.

While ironclad alliance guarantees can deter challenges to an ally, they also increase the risk that the ally will become more adventurous, making larger and riskier demands on other states. To see this, return to Figure 5.2 (p. 203). Alliances have two effects. As emphasized earlier, an alliance between States A and C deters a challenger, State B, by reducing the probability that it will win a war against the combined might of the two allies. This is why States A and C are interested in forging the alliance in the first place.

At the same time, the alliance strengthens State A in its bargaining with State B. As the expected war outcome moves to the right, the range of status quo outcomes in which State A has an incentive to challenge State B expands. As a result, State A is likely to demand a better bargain from State B and, following the risk-return trade-off explained in Chapter 3, run a risk of war to obtain its demands. In other words, while the alliance between States A and C weakens State B and deters it from challenging State A, the same alliance strengthens State A and gives it an incentive to demand more of State B.

Why might this situation pose a dilemma? A problem occurs if State C expects to pay greater costs of war than its ally, State A, perhaps because State C cares less about the good in dispute. In this case, there are some status quos that State C would prefer to war but that State A has an incentive to challenge. If State A were

---

21. Alastair Smith, "To Intervene or Not to Intervene: A Biased Decision," *Journal of Conflict Resolution* 40, no. 1 (1996): 16–40.

22. Rapp-Hooper, *Shields of the Republic*.

to start a crisis under these conditions, then State C would be put in the undesirable position of having to either abandon its ally or risk being dragged into a war that it values less than the status quo. Thus, while State C wants to defend State A from challenges, it must also worry about becoming "entrapped" in a costly war by a reckless ally.[23]

entrapment

The condition of being dragged into an unwanted war because of the opportunistic actions of an ally.

In response to this dilemma, states attempt to avoid **entrapment** by limiting their commitments or leaving those commitments purposely ambiguous. In other words, in order to protect themselves from opportunism by their allies, states rarely forge ironclad agreements that they must fulfill. Rather, states attempt to reserve a measure of discretion for themselves on when, how, and to what extent they will meet their alliance obligations.

An important example of this challenge can be found in U.S. relations with China and Taiwan. Since 1949, the United States has sought to defend Taiwan from mainland China, which regards the island as a renegade province. China has repeatedly warned that if Taiwan officially declares independence, that act will be cause for war. The dilemma for the United States has been this: how to deter China from attacking without, at the same time, making Taiwan feel that it could declare and win its independence with the help of the United States. On the one hand, China might attack if it believes the United States would abandon Taiwan. On the other hand, an ironclad promise to defend Taiwan might encourage pro-independence politicians there to take the fateful step that would risk a war. In order to navigate this dilemma, the United States has at times pursued a policy of "strategic ambiguity": making its intentions less than fully clear in the hopes that China will be deterred from attacking while Taiwan will act with restraint.

This dilemma shows that there can be a trade-off between the *credibility* of alliances (which requires ironclad promises) and efforts to *control* alliance partners (which can require ambiguity and flexibility). There is seldom any way to avoid this trade-off. The more credible the guarantee to an ally, the greater the incentive for that ally to behave opportunistically. But the greater the discretion that the state retains in an effort to limit the risk of entrapment, the less credible is the alliance and the less successful it will be in deterring challengers.

Analyzing the European Alliance System, 1879–1990

As we have seen, alliances are institutions that states create in order to facilitate cooperation in support of common interests. They form when states' interests are aligned to an extent that they may be willing to fight on one another's behalf. They work by making it more likely that the states will, in fact, fight together in the event of war and by signaling this willingness to potential adversaries. As a result, the success or failure of an alliance depends on (1) the strength of the interests that brought the allies together; (2) the ability of the alliance to alter its members'

23. On entrapment and other forms of opportunism by allies, see Glenn H. Snyder, "The Security Dilemma in Alliance Politics," *World Politics* 36, no. 4 (1984): 461–95.

preferences so that in the event of war, fighting is preferable to abandonment; (3) the effectiveness of the alliance in convincing the adversary of this fact; and (4) the ability of the members to limit the risk of entrapment.

We can now use these concepts to analyze some of the major events of the last century through the lens of alliance politics. As noted in Chapter 1, the first and second halves of the twentieth century were markedly different in terms of warfare between the world's major powers. In both periods, international politics was shaped by conflicts in Europe among the world's large, industrialized countries. In both periods, states that felt threatened formed alliances in the hopes of protecting themselves from rivals. Yet the outcomes in these two periods were quite different. The first half of the century witnessed two world wars of unprecedented destructiveness; the second half was remarkable for the absence of war between the two superpowers, in spite of the intense hostility between them. Although a number of factors help explain these developments, part of the answer is that alliances played a stabilizing role in the second period, but not in the first. The logic developed here can help explain why.

Pre–World War I: Two Armed Camps
In the lead-up to the First World War, the major powers of Europe divided themselves into two competing alliance blocs. On one side was the Triple Alliance, composed of Germany, Austria-Hungary, and Italy; on the other side were Britain, France, and Russia, bound by an agreement that came to be known as the Triple Entente. An entente, which comes from the French word for "understanding," is generally seen as a weak form of alliance, requiring consultation and coordination but not necessarily a strict commitment of military assistance. In Europe, the polarization into two blocs had been decades in the making and reflected the ambitions of a rising Germany, the fears of Germany's neighbors to the east and west, and specific conflicts over territory and colonies.

Although the apparent symmetry between the two alliances might theoretically have created a stable balance, the system was, in fact, fraught with danger. The alliance network created the possibility that any small conflict could drag all the European powers into war. Of course, since European decision makers understood these risks, this system did foster some caution and mutual deterrence by raising the expected costs of war for each side. And indeed, several crises in the first decade of the twentieth century were resolved peacefully, in spite of much saber rattling.

Nonetheless, the system had several features that made it unstable. First, as we saw in Chapter 3, the strategic situation created a number of preventive and preemptive incentives. Germany feared the rise of Russian power, causing some strategists to argue that war with Russia would be better sooner than later. In addition, Germany's need to plan for a two-front war—against France to the west and Russia to the east—gave rise to the Schlieffen Plan, Germany's war plan with precise timetables and preemptive logic (see the "What Shaped Our World?" box in Chapter 3, p. 131).

Second, this delicate balance made each of the major powers highly dependent on its allies for security; the prospect of losing an ally was seen as particularly dangerous. Hence, when Austrian archduke Franz Ferdinand was assassinated by a

Serb extremist on June 28, 1914, the threat that Serb nationalism could rip the Austro-Hungarian Empire apart was also felt keenly in Germany. In the ensuing crisis, Germany gave its ally a blank check, promising to back Austria-Hungary in whatever the latter chose to do. This commitment, however, emboldened Austria-Hungary, leading it to issue a harsh ultimatum to Serbia.[24]

When Russia decided to back Serbia, the interconnected alliances turned a local crisis into a Europe-wide war: Austria-Hungary attacked Serbia; Russia mobilized against Austria-Hungary; Germany declared war on Russia, Belgium, and France; and Britain declared war on Germany and Austria-Hungary. This process, whereby the actions of a small number of states drag all their allies to war, has been referred to as "chain-ganging," evoking the image of convicts chained together, forced to move in the same direction.[25]

Finally, the sheer number of states involved magnified the possibility of miscalculations. Whether an ally would actually fight in the event of war was a crucial question in determining how hard a state could push or how much it should give. Uncertainty about which countries would join a prospective war created considerable scope for errors.

Probably the most important source of uncertainty was how Great Britain would react in the event of war. Because it had the most powerful navy in the world—larger, in fact, than the next-three-largest navies combined—whether Britain would join a continental war was a crucially important question, and one over which there was a good deal of doubt until the very last minute. Although the Triple Entente committed Britain to consult with France and Russia in the event of war, the British public and many policy makers in government were not keen to shed British blood over what appeared to be a distant matter.

This uncertainty led German decision makers to believe for some time that Britain might stand aside while Germany took on France and Russia. Moreover, suggestions by British leaders that Britain would join its allies in war were discounted by German leaders as bluffs. It is unclear whether German leaders would have backed off from war had they been certain that Britain would intervene; it is clear, however, that Germany was encouraged by British wavering to take an aggressive position in the crisis. When Britain belatedly made clear that it would join in the fight, the military actions and diplomatic commitments already made by Germany and Austria were hard to reverse. Once war started, the network of alliances brought all of Europe into the conflict.[26]

The Coming of World War II, 1919–1939 Germany was defeated in World War I, but with Adolf Hitler's ascension to power in 1933, Germany once more posed a

---

24. Some historians argue that Germany issued the blank check precisely to incite Austro-Hungarian stubbornness and thus provoke war. Among others, see Fritz Fischer, *Germany's Aims in the First World War* (New York: Norton, 1967).

25. Thomas J. Christensen and Jack Snyder, "Chain Gangs and Passed Bucks: Predicting Alliance Patterns in Multipolarity," *International Organization* 44, no. 2 (Spring 1990): 137–68.

26. In a final example of how the alliance system failed, Italy refused to join its allies (Germany and Austria) when war broke out. After sitting on the sidelines for several months, Italy decided that the Triple Entente powers were more likely to win. Hence, Italy decided to side with the Triple Entente and, in May 1915, attacked its former ally, Austria-Hungary, with whom it had a long-standing territorial dispute.

challenge to its neighbors. Although European powers again sought to contain the German threat through alliances, the effort was too little and too late to prevent another devastating war.

Until the eve of war in 1939, the alliance system that formed to contain Germany rested on a few thin reeds, which easily snapped under Hitler's pressure. Under the terms of the Treaty of Locarno (1925), Britain pledged to defend Belgium and France in the event that either was attacked by Germany and to ensure that Germany respected the demilitarization of the Rhineland region, which bordered those countries. France also signed alliances with several of Germany's neighbors to the east: Poland, Czechoslovakia, Yugoslavia, and Romania. The first of these treaties was tested, and failed, in 1936 when Hitler remilitarized the Rhineland and Britain refused to support France in taking any action to stop the move.

France's guarantees to the eastern European countries lacked credibility because of the geographic separation between them. With most of the French forces positioned to defend a fortified line on the German frontier, France was in a weak position to defend its distant allies from the German threat. The weakness became all too clear in September 1938, when France and Britain acquiesced to German demands for a section of Czechoslovakia called the Sudetenland. Six months later, in March 1939, Germany invaded and conquered the rest of Czechoslovakia, and France did not lift a finger to save its ally. Not until Germany attacked Poland in September 1939 did France and Britain, which had pledged to defend Poland only days earlier, find the resolve to fulfill their commitments.

In August 1939, Britain formed a defensive alliance with Poland. One month later, Germany invaded Poland, Britain stepped in to defend its ally, and World War II began.

Hence, rather than being deterred by the states that sought to contain him, Hitler exploited weak alliances that were not backed up by sufficient resolve or capabilities, highlighting the lack of common interests and credible commitments among the allies. Bandwagoning by Italy, the Soviet Union, and eventually Japan only strengthened his hand. The resulting imbalance between a bloc of revisionist powers and a fragmented group of buck-passing allies, combined with a leader ideologically bent on conquest, cast the world into war once more.

The Cold War: The "Long Peace" in Europe, 1945–1990
After the Second World War, European politics came to be dominated by the competition between two superpowers: the United States, which emerged from the war an unmatched industrial powerhouse, and the Soviet Union, whose large army sat astride much of Eastern and Central Europe. Once again, the countries of Europe sorted into

alliances in response to this emerging rivalry. But this time, in the five decades that followed the end of World War II, there were no wars among the major European powers.[27] How did alliances contribute to stability in this period, when they had failed to keep the peace before?

Within 10 years after the end of World War II, most countries in Europe belonged to either the **North Atlantic Treaty Organization (NATO)** or the **Warsaw Pact**. NATO covered most of the states of Western Europe and bound them in a collective defense treaty with the United States. Its core provision was in Article 5 of the North Atlantic Treaty, which specified that each member would consider an attack against one or more members to be an attack against them all. The Warsaw Pact covered the states of Eastern Europe and the Soviet Union. Germany, which was split after the war into two countries, was also split between the blocs, with West Germany in NATO and East Germany in the Warsaw Pact.

Each bloc formed in response to a perceived threat from the other. NATO was established in 1949 in response to the Soviet military presence in Eastern Europe—a presence that the Soviets used to install puppet governments in those countries. The Warsaw Pact formed in 1955 after West Germany was admitted into NATO, raising the fear in Moscow that its enemy in the two world wars would again be rearmed and active on the European stage.

Although the experience of World War I would seem to suggest that two alliance blocs, roughly evenly divided, can be a cause of war, the Cold War alliance system had a number of features that made it different, and more stable, than what came before. First, the diplomatic landscape was much more complicated in 1914 than it was at mid-century, with several major powers in competition and highly dependent on their allies for security. During the Cold War, by contrast, the system was dominated by the two superpowers. This meant that there was less scope for miscalculation, since the outcome of any conflict depended on the choices of fewer key actors.

A second major feature of the Cold War alliances was their highly institutionalized nature. Both NATO and the Warsaw Pact were more than just pieces of paper promising mutual aid in the event of war. Rather, they included a dense set of military, political, and economic relationships. The United States, in particular, needed to demonstrate that it would uphold its promise to defend its allies an ocean away, since any uncertainty about the U.S. commitment was seen as inviting Soviet aggression against Western Europe.

As a result, the NATO alliance provided for close integration of the American and European militaries, a joint command led by an American officer, and the basing of more than a quarter-million U.S. troops on European soil, primarily in West Germany. This forward deployment of U.S. forces served both military and political purposes. It ensured that the United States had capabilities in place to slow a Soviet offensive until much larger reinforcements could come across the sea. It also served

North Atlantic Treaty Organization (NATO)

An alliance formed in 1949 among the United States, Canada, and most of the states of Western Europe in response to the threat posed by the Soviet Union. The alliance requires the members to consider an attack on any one of them as an attack on all.

Warsaw Pact

A military alliance formed in 1955 to bring together the Soviet Union and its Cold War allies in Eastern Europe and elsewhere; dissolved on March 31, 1991, as the Cold War ended.

---

27. John Lewis Gaddis, "The Long Peace: Elements of Stability in the Postwar International System," *International Security* 10, no. 4 (Spring 1986): 99–142.

to signal the United States' commitment to the region. In the event of a Soviet attack, U.S. troops would have been quickly involved in the fighting, ensuring that the United States could not remain indifferent.

This political aspect of the American presence in Europe was most clearly evident in the Berlin Brigade, a garrison of about 7,000 troops in West Berlin. Like the rest of Germany, the capital city of Berlin had been divided into western and eastern portions after the war. The city sat in the midst of Communist East Germany, however, so West Berlin was a small island of Western and American influence surrounded by a "red" sea. Given its geographic isolation, the American garrison would have been quickly overrun in the event of a war.

Nonetheless, its presence was seen as a crucial signal of the U.S. commitment to defend Western Europe. The theorist Thomas Schelling described its role vividly:

> The garrison in Berlin is as fine a collection of soldiers as has ever been assembled, but excruciatingly small. What can 7,000 American troops do . . . ? Bluntly, they can die. They can die heroically, dramatically, and in a manner that guarantees that the action cannot stop there. They represent the pride, the honor, and the reputation of the United States government and its armed forces; and they can apparently hold the entire Red Army at bay.[28]

Hence, the military presence was a kind of hand-tying strategy (see Chapter 3): an effort to ensure that if the American commitment to NATO was triggered by a Soviet attack, the United States would have little choice but to fulfill that commitment. The strength of this pledge, clearly signaled to the Soviet Union, had a deterrent effect that contributed to the relative stability of Europe during the Cold War. ("What Shaped Our World?" on p. 214 examines questions about NATO's future since the Cold War.)

As this historical overview suggests, alliances were used frequently in twentieth-century Europe by states looking for partners in defense or conquest. Measured in terms of whether allies fought together when war came, many (but not all) of these alliances were successful. Measured in terms of whether they were able to prevent war in the first place, the track record is more uneven. By far the most successful alliances on this score were the Cold War alliance blocs. Anchored by two strong powers, held together by common security interests, and institutionalized through a variety of military, political, and economic ties, NATO and the Warsaw Pact contributed to a period of relative peace in Europe after World War II. By contrast, the alliances in the first half of the twentieth century either abetted aggression—in the case of the Japanese, Italian, and Russian alliances with Hitler's Germany—or failed to contain it, contributing to the outbreak of two catastrophic wars. The inability of alliances to keep the peace would propel the search for a different kind of institution to serve this end: collective security organizations.

---

28. Thomas C. Schelling, *Arms and Influence* (New Haven, CT: Yale University Press, 1966), 47.

The Future of NATO

Ever since the end of the Cold War, analysts and policy makers have wondered whether NATO's days were numbered. The Soviet Union lost control of its Eastern European satellites in the late 1980s, its military forces withdrew from their territory, and the Warsaw Pact collapsed. When the Soviet Union disintegrated in December 1991, it seemed plausible that the NATO alliance would crumble as well. Since then, the alliance has experienced additional crises. The U.S. decision to invade Iraq in 2003 caused a serious rift. Under the Trump administration, long-standing concerns about burden sharing came to the fore, generating tensions that once again called the alliance's future into question.

In spite of these crises, NATO has proven to be quite resilient. While the United States has reduced its troop presence in Europe from Cold War levels, 74,000 U.S. military personnel remain stationed there today. Rather than withering away, NATO expanded eastward, adding 14 states, many of which had once been allies or republics of the former Soviet Union (see the map).

The alliance also expanded its mission. In the 1990s, NATO intervened with air strikes in the wars that accompanied the breakup of Yugoslavia—not because a NATO member had been attacked, but to address the humanitarian crises those wars created. After the September 11, 2001, terrorist attacks on the United States, the alliance invoked Article 5 of the North Atlantic Treaty, declaring that the entire alliance had been attacked. NATO subsequently played an important role in efforts to stabilize Afghanistan after the U.S. invasion in 2001. In March 2011, NATO initiated a military campaign against Libya in response to that regime's violent crackdown against domestic opponents. How do we explain these developments?

Interests Those who expected NATO to perish believed that the common interests and fears that originally brought the alliance into being had vanished.[a] Subsequent events suggest that its members still share interests in common. These include a basic concern for security, with an expanded conception of where the main threats

lie—particularly, terrorism and the ability of terrorists to take root in chaotic, war-torn regions. NATO operations in the former Yugoslavia and Libya showed that the alliance could act on a common commitment to stop massive violations of human rights. NATO members also had an interest in ensuring that former Soviet satellites in Eastern Europe developed stable, democratic, pro-Western regimes; for their part, many of those states wanted the protection of NATO to guard against a resurgent Russia.

Institutions NATO's persistence also reminds us that institutions often adapt to changing environments rather than die. In the 1990s, those worried about the future of the alliance argued that NATO had to go "out of area, or out of business"—meaning that it had to take new missions not necessarily confined to the territory of the member states. In extending its reach to the former Yugoslavia, Afghanistan, and Libya, NATO transformed from a purely defensive alliance into an institution that facilitates cooperation on a broader set of goals.

Interactions Common interests and institutional adaptation do not preclude tough bargaining within the alliance. NATO faces a collective action problem: although all members benefit from its activities, they may prefer that others bear the costs. Concerns about free riding by alliance members go back to NATO's earliest days. During the Cold War, the United States, by far the largest member, was willing to bear a disproportionate share of the costs of collective defense. In return, Washington dominated alliance decision making.

In the last two decades, this bargain has come under strain. American leadership was questioned during the lead-up to the 2003 Iraq War, when key NATO allies, particularly France and Germany, refused to endorse the Bush administration's case for preventive war. Conflicting views and interests divided the alliance, preventing it from reaching a common policy toward Iraq. In 2011, Germany refused to take part in the operation in Libya.

More recently, the United States has pressured European partners to increase their defense contributions. In 2014, the alliance agreed that members should spend at least 2 percent of their GDP on defense by 2024—a benchmark that, in 2019, only 6 of the 28 members reached. When he came into office, Trump demanded a faster

---

a. For an example of this argument, see John J. Mearsheimer, "Back to the Future: Instability in Europe after the Cold War," *International Security* 15, no. 1 (Summer 1990): 5–56.

timetable and suggested that the U.S. commitment to NATO might depend on whether countries met this target. He directed particular scorn at Germany and threatened to relocate 12,000 of the 36,000 U.S. troops stationed there. Many European governments have responded that military spending is a poor indicator of what they contribute to the common defense; still, a number have taken steps to meet the target. Even though President Joseph Biden promised to mend ties with NATO, tensions over burden sharing are unlikely to go away.

Russia has tried to exacerbate conflicts within the alliance. Military advances into Georgia (2008) and Ukraine (2014)—both countries that at times courted NATO membership—have raised the costs of further alliance expansion. Russia has also supported domestic actors in the West who are skeptical of NATO membership. Whether the institution and the common but fraying interests of its members will remain sufficiently robust to overcome the recent rounds of more intense bargaining, both within the alliance and with Russia, remains an open question.

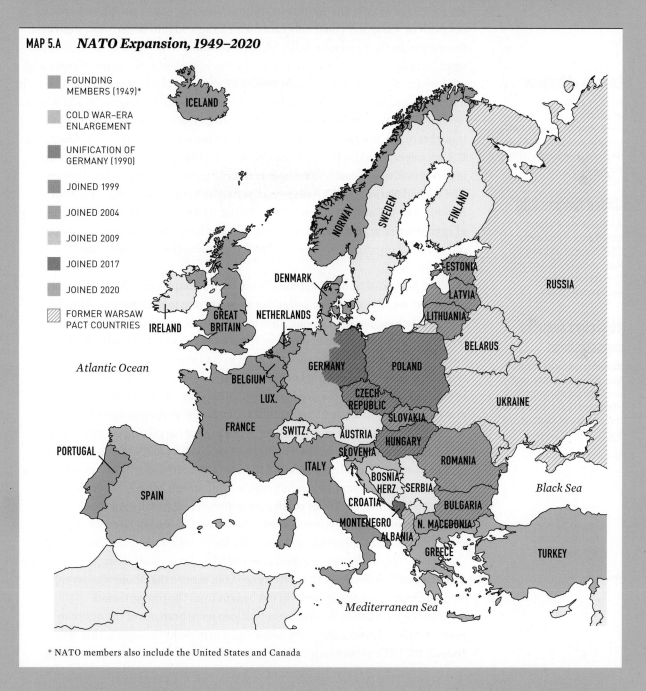

MAP 5.A *NATO Expansion, 1949–2020*

FOUNDING MEMBERS (1949)*

COLD WAR–ERA ENLARGEMENT

UNIFICATION OF GERMANY (1990)

JOINED 1999

JOINED 2004

JOINED 2009

JOINED 2017

JOINED 2020

FORMER WARSAW PACT COUNTRIES

* NATO members also include the United States and Canada

Collective Security: When Can the UN Keep the Peace?

As World War I was coming to a close, world leaders began to think about what the postwar world should look like. U.S. president Woodrow Wilson argued that the only way to prevent another such war was to change the nature of world politics. Wilson was convinced that the prewar pattern, in which major powers jockeyed for advantage against one another in shifting alliances, had to go. Alliances could not prevent wars; they could only cause wars to spread into larger, more destructive events. In their place, he believed, there should be a permanent institution that would enable countries to police the international system in the name of peace and security for all. From this vision, in 1919, the **League of Nations** was born. Although it limped along until 1946, it effectively died in 1939 with the onset of World War II.

As World War II was coming to a close, world leaders once again turned their thoughts to the question of how to prevent another such war. Like his predecessor, U.S. president Franklin D. Roosevelt championed the idea of a permanent governing body that would enable the major powers to police the international system. The **United Nations (UN)** was created in 1945 as a successor to the League of Nations. The UN still functions to this day, but its track record in responding to acts of aggression is, at best, mixed. Why is this? Why have efforts to build an effective international organization capable of policing international politics failed to create a lasting peace?

The League of Nations and the UN are both examples of collective security organizations. Like alliances, **collective security organizations** are institutions that facilitate cooperation among their members. These two kinds of institutions, however, form in response to different kinds of interests. Alliances form when two or more states have a common interest in the outcome of bargaining interactions with an adversary or a set of adversaries. Collective security organizations, by contrast, form under the presumption that all states have a common interest in preventing war and aggression, regardless of who the perpetrator and victim are. Unlike alliances, their primary purpose is not to alter bargaining outcomes in favor of one state or another but rather to ensure that changes to the status quo, if they occur, happen peacefully. They forbid the use of military force by one member state against another, and they generally provide mechanisms, such as mediators or arbitrators, to help member states resolve their disputes peacefully. An attack by one member against another is considered to be a threat to the whole community. As a result, the entire membership is responsible for coming to the aid of the victims of aggression. This collective response is intended to deter would-be aggressors in the first place and, in the event that deterrence fails, ensure that those who wrong the community by engaging in war will not benefit from the transgression.

Although collective security organizations were born out of the desire to prevent interstate wars, they have also sought to prevent violence within states. Indeed, the UN has been quite active in dealing with civil wars and maintaining

League of Nations

A collective security organization founded in 1919 after World War I. The League ended in 1946 and was replaced by the United Nations.

United Nations (UN)

A collective security organization founded in 1945 after World War II. With over 190 members, the UN includes all recognized states.

collective security organizations

Broad-based institutions that promote peace and security among their members. Examples include the League of Nations and the United Nations.

peace in their aftermath. In recent decades, there also has been pressure to expand the UN's scope to deal with gross violations of human rights, such as cases of **genocide**, the systematic slaughter of an identifiable group of people, such as an ethnic or religious group. In fact, genocidal conflicts have led to the sharpest criticism of the UN in recent years: for inaction in such places as Rwanda (1994), Bosnia (1992–95), and Darfur (2003–present; more on these cases will follow). In 2016, the UN condemned a nonstate terrorist organization, the Islamic State, for committing genocide against religious minorities in Iraq and Syria (see Chapter 6 for more on the Islamic State).

Unlike alliances, whose membership is restricted to a small number of states with common interests, the membership of collective security organizations is generally universal, or nearly universal. The UN, for example, includes all internationally recognized states. Universal membership reflects the presumption of a community with universally shared interests in international peace and security. There are also numerous regional security organizations—such as the Organization of American States, the African Union, and the Organization for Security and Co-operation in Europe—that include all or most of the states in each relevant region.

How Does Collective Security Work?

In theory, collective security works as follows. The mechanism is triggered when one state attacks or threatens to attack another. If it is determined that these events constitute an act of aggression—or, in the language of the UN, a "threat to international peace and security"—then all members of the organization are called on to act against the state that has committed the offending action. Depending on the circumstances, the prescribed action can range from economic sanctions to full-scale military intervention. This threat of intervention is intended primarily to deter actors from making aggressive demands against or attacking one another in the first place. A state that knows its actions will be opposed by the full weight of the international community should be reluctant to engage in aggression.

While intervention in interstate conflicts reflects the classic view of collective security, in practice the tool kit of collective security organizations has evolved and expanded in at least two important respects. First, largely because of the difficulties of mounting unified responses to international aggression (see "The Dilemmas of Collective Security" on p. 219), the UN and regional collective security organizations have developed alternative strategies that are intended to foster peaceful conflict resolution without requiring costly interventions. The UN secretary-general, who leads the organization, plays an active role in mediating conflicts and thereby helping states identify mutually beneficial bargains.[29] The UN also authorizes the deployment of peacekeeping forces—troops from neutral third parties—to

genocide
Intentional and systematic killing aimed at eliminating an identifiable group of people, such as an ethnic or religious group.

---

29. Kjell Skjelsbaek and Gunnar Fermann, "The UN Secretary-General and the Mediation of International Disputes," in *Resolving International Conflicts*, ed. Jacob Bercovitch (Boulder, CO: Lynne Rienner, 1996), 75–104.

The United Nations deploys neutral peacekeeping forces from third parties to help monitor areas of conflict and enforce peace agreements. Here, UN peacekeeping troops patrol the border between Lebanon and Israel shortly after the Lebanese militant group Hezbollah fired missiles across the border into Israel, resulting in return fire.

humanitarian interventions

Interventions designed to relieve humanitarian crises stemming from civil conflicts or large-scale human rights abuses, including genocide.

help monitor and enforce peace agreements. We will say more about the theory and practice of peacekeeping in the discussion that follows.

Second, collective security organizations have in recent decades extended their mandate to include stopping or preventing civil conflicts and large-scale human rights abuses. Civil wars and genocides have at times been labeled as "threats to international peace and security," giving rise to **humanitarian interventions**, or collective interventions designed to relieve humanitarian crises. Ironically, while peacekeeping and humanitarian intervention do not fit the original view of collective security, they are, in practice, the bulk of what collective security organizations have done in recent decades.

Collective security organizations can influence the bargaining interaction between adversaries in at least three ways, all of them intended to foster peaceful outcomes. First, as with alliances, the prospect of outside involvement makes war less attractive by changing the likely outcome of the interaction between states or, in the case of civil wars, between groups. At the extreme, the combined weight of the entire international community means that the defeat of the challenger is virtually certain. (Consider what Figure 5.2 would look like if State C were replaced with every country in the world.) The status quo is stable if both sides know that they will surely lose if they attempt to change the status quo by force. Under such conditions, neither side can shift the bargain in its favor by threatening war.

Second, outsiders can help resolve the commitment problems identified in Chapter 3 by promising to enforce what would otherwise be an unbelievable commitment by one state not to exploit its power against another. A shift in relative power between two states might be rendered less dangerous if the weakened state can count on others to defend it, thus diminishing any incentive it might have to wage war preventively. Likewise, a state may feel secure handing over a piece of strategic territory if it knows that others will come to its aid in the event that its adversary exploits this territory to attack or press further claims. In other words, the state that is made more powerful by the deal can more credibly commit not to exploit its newfound power if it knows that any attempt to do so will be countered by the international community.

For example, as noted in Chapter 3, Israel and Syria have a conflict over the strategically valuable Golan Heights, which Israel seized from Syria in 1967. Since control of this territory imparts a military advantage to its owner, Israel has refused to return any land to Syria without guarantees that it (Israel) will remain safe from attack. In 1974, however, the two states agreed to withdraw their forces from the Golan Heights, and the UN inserted over 1,000 peacekeeping troops into observation posts in the hills between the two sides' positions.[30] For four decades, those troops helped ensure that neither side would deploy forces to the area, thereby easing a source of tension in the region. Starting in 2014, the peacekeepers came under attack by militant groups engaged in the Syrian Civil War (see Chapter 6), but the mission has continued in spite of the risks.

Third, collective security organizations may play a positive role in promoting peace not by threatening direct intervention for or against any particular side but by serving as neutral observers and peacekeepers. Peacekeepers diminish first-strike advantages by interposing themselves between two adversarial factions, as in the Golan Heights. Such operations are particularly useful in cases in which previously warring parties have each pledged to disarm and demobilize, but each fears that if it disarms and the other does not, it will be at a dangerous disadvantage. As we will see in Chapter 6, the commitment problem associated with disarmament is a major obstacle to preventing and ending civil wars. The UN often deploys peacekeeping missions into these situations in order to make sure that both sides uphold their promises. For example, following the end of the civil war in Liberia, which claimed almost 150,000 lives from 1989 to 2003, the UN inserted 15,000 peacekeepers to facilitate disarmament and demobilization of former rebels.

The Dilemmas of Collective Security

Regardless of where and how a collective security organization chooses to intervene, it faces two major challenges: a collective action problem and a joint decision-making problem. The collective action problem arises from the fact that collective security organizations, unlike their members, do not have the power to tax anyone or to raise and field military forces. As a result, the organizations are wholly dependent on their members to provide troops, funds, and military equipment for any operation. The member states that contribute then face the costs and risks associated with sending troops into combat or forgoing trade because of economic sanctions.

Crucially, the international peace and stability that these actions are intended to provide is a public good. Recall from Chapter 2 that a public good can be enjoyed whether or not one actually contributed to its creation. If the international

---

30. For more information on the UN peacekeeping mission in the Golan Heights, see https://peacekeeping.un.org/en/mission/undof (accessed 12/23/20).

While the UN Security Council has the authority to identify and dictate the organization's response to international security threats, it is sometimes difficult for members with competing interests to agree on the best course of action. Since 2011, Russia has vetoed 16 resolutions related to human rights abuses and chemical weapons attacks by the Syrian government in Syria's long-running civil war.

community succeeds in preventing or reversing an act of aggression, all members of the community enjoy the benefit—whether or not they took costly action. After all, even if all states have an interest in seeing aggression halted, their first preference will often be to have the aggression halted by someone other than themselves.

Hence, collective security organizations necessarily face a free-rider problem: the temptation that member states face to let the burden of maintaining peace—a public good—fall on others. Because of this problem, even if all states share an interest in cooperating to stop or prevent a war, their collective effort may fall well short of what is required to do so. Indeed, UN peacekeeping missions are often underfunded and undermanned relative to their mandates; the temptation to free ride, to pass the costs to other states, leads to lower levels of cooperation than is desirable.

The challenges of joint decision making are also severe. Members of the organization need to be able to determine which acts constitute a threat to the community, which states are aggressors, and what actions to take in response. These determinations are not always straightforward. Since collective security organizations permit states to use force in self-defense, and states generally justify their military actions as defensive ones, determining which acts are acts of aggression and which are legitimate self-defense is necessary for the organization to function. Otherwise, the entire system can collapse, as each side accuses the other of being at fault. A finding that a particular act constitutes a threat to international peace and security not only delegitimizes that act as a violation of community interests but also grants legitimacy to those who use force to reverse it. As we will see, this grant of legitimacy can be an asset to states that operate under the organization's seal of approval.[31]

31. On the UN's legitimacy role, see Ian Hurd, *After Anarchy: Legitimacy and Power in the United Nations Security Council* (Princeton, NJ: Princeton University Press, 2007); and Alexander Thompson, *Channels of Power: The UN Security Council and U.S. Statecraft in Iraq* (Ithaca, NY: Cornell University Press, 2009).

Determining whether a given act merits an international response is complicated by the mix of interests that member states have. Although they may share a general interest in halting aggression and promoting the peaceful settlement of disputes, they may also have specific interests that diverge in any particular conflict. Recall that collective security organizations, because of their universal membership, often include states with varying, even opposing, interests.

Whereas NATO during the Cold War included only states that perceived a common threat from the Soviet Union, the UN during this period included not only the United States and its NATO allies, but also the Soviet Union and its allies, as well as states that were neutral in the superpower rivalry. This mix of interests means that in many situations, the members of a collective security organization may not all be neutral outsiders to a particular military action. Some may have reasons to favor one side or the other in a dispute, meaning that some will be motivated to see aggression where others will not. Collective security works best when all states are satisfied with the current status quo—a condition that is rarely met.

Institutional Responses to the Challenges of Collective Security

The design of collective security organizations reflects the challenges posed by the dilemmas of collective action and joint decision making. Recall that institutions facilitate cooperation in situations that arise repeatedly. Rather than treating each new crisis in an ad hoc manner, requiring renegotiation of standards and rules each time, institutions embody a lasting set of standards and decision-making rules.

In the two most ambitious collective security organizations attempted in the last century—the League of Nations and the UN—these two major problems were addressed by vesting the main decision-making power in the hands of relatively small councils dominated by the strongest states in the system. These councils were given the authority to determine whether a particular action was a threat to international peace and security and to prescribe the organization's response. The League Council began with 4 permanent members—Great Britain, France, Italy, and Japan—and 4 nonpermanent members who were elected every three years. Germany later joined as a fifth permanent member,[32] and the council was expanded to 15.

When the UN replaced the League in 1946, its **Security Council (UNSC)** had a similar structure: 5 permanent members and 6 (later 10) nonpermanent members. The **permanent five (P5)** are the United States, Great Britain, France, Russia (formerly the Soviet Union), and China. In both cases, the privileged few shared a common trait: with the exception of Germany, which was admitted to the League only belatedly, they were the victors of the global wars that gave birth to these organizations.

The voting rules of both councils amplified the influence of these permanent members. In the case of the League Council, all decisions had to be unanimously

UN Security Council (UNSC)

The main governing body of the UN, which has the authority to identify threats to international peace and security and to prescribe the organization's response, including military and/or economic sanctions.

permanent five (P5)

The five permanent members of the UN Security Council: the United States, Great Britain, France, Russia (formerly the Soviet Union), and China.

---

32. Originally, the United States was intended to be the fifth permanent member, but the United States never joined the League, because of congressional opposition.

approved by all 15 members. As a result, any member of the council could block the organization from acting by withholding its support. In other words, every member of the council had **veto power**, and permanent members had permanent veto power. This voting rule was modified in the UN Security Council. Enacting a substantive resolution in the Security Council requires a "yes" vote from at least 9 of the 15 council members *and* the support of every one of the P5. This change was intended to make decisive action easier—by eliminating the requirement that all members agree—but it also magnified the asymmetrical role of the P5, each of which can veto a resolution it does not like.

These arrangements have several virtues. First, vesting decision-making power with a relatively small group of states means that decisions are not subject to consensus within the entire membership (which, in the case of the UN, now numbers 193). This both reduces the costs of coming to an agreement and, in theory at least, makes it possible for the organization to respond to crises quickly. Second, these rules ensure that when the organization acts, it does so with the consent of the strongest powers in the international system. This arrangement can help address the collective action problem by ensuring that any operation that is approved will enjoy cooperation and contributions from those members with the greatest resources and capabilities. Moreover, the veto ensures that at a minimum, the organization's actions will not be forcibly opposed by any of these powerful members.

As with all institutions, however, the effects of these rules are not neutral; rather, they bias policy outcomes in a direction that favors the states that were in a position to dictate the rules at the outset. The organization cannot act without unanimity among the most powerful states in the system, any one of which can exercise its veto. Such unanimity can be difficult to achieve. When the major powers disagree among themselves, the permanent-member veto introduces a bias toward inaction. The veto also ensures that the organization cannot act in ways that harm the interests of any of the permanent members.

As a result, the organization wields its policing powers unevenly: it may respond to the crimes of those who are weak or who have no friends among the permanent members, while the crimes of the strong, or those with friends in high places, may go unpunished. In the case of Tibet, mentioned at the outset of this chapter, any effective action by the UN

Because of its institutional rules, the UN is unlikely to undertake missions that harm the interests of any of its most powerful members. For example, China blocked UN efforts to impose economic sanctions on the government of Sudan in response to the genocide in the Darfur region. As a big buyer of Sudanese oil, China has an interest in sparing Sudan from punishment.

against China could have been blocked by China's ally, the Soviet Union.[33] More recently, Russia has blocked efforts to sanction the government of Syria, a long-time Russian ally, for indiscriminate killing of civilians during the civil war that has raged in that country since 2011.

In sum, collective security organizations help states cooperate to further their collective interests in international peace by providing rules and standards to address challenges that complicate collective action and joint decision making. Nonetheless, these institutions operate under constraints that limit their ability to act effectively. Collective security organizations are most likely to succeed when two conditions are met. First, the powerful member states that are central to their decision-making processes must all agree on the desirability of collective action. At a minimum, none of these states can be sufficiently opposed that it will block such action.

Second, at least some members must value the collective good highly enough that they are willing to pay the costs in lives and money to ensure that the good is provided. This is most likely when the anticipated costs of intervention are low or when states have some private interest in contributing above and beyond the public interest in stopping aggression. In other words, collective security institutions are useful at promoting cooperation when their key members have strong common interests in protecting the peace; unfortunately, the existence of such common interests is not guaranteed.

The Experience of Collective Security: The United Nations

To see how these predictions have been borne out historically, we consider the experience of the most ambitious collective security organization ever created: the UN. This organization arose from the ashes of World War II with the aspiration, articulated in its founding charter, to "save succeeding generations from the scourge of war"—a goal that had become all the more pressing with the development of nuclear weapons, which have the capacity to kill millions in the blink of an eye.

Although the world has not since seen a repetition of global warfare or the nightmare of nuclear war, the role of the UN in preventing these outcomes is not clear. Indeed, the UN has had uneven success in fulfilling its creators' aspirations. In this section, we briefly review the experience of the UN. As we will see, the challenges facing collective security organizations described in the preceding discussion play a large role in accounting for this organization's limited success historically.

What Does the UN Do?   When countries join the UN, they sign on to the organization's charter.[34] Members pledge not to use force in disputes with one another and to seek assistance from the organization in resolving their conflicts peacefully.

---

33. Communist China was not, at that time, on the Security Council. Until 1971, China's seat on the council was held by Taiwan.

34 The entire UN Charter can be viewed at www.un.org/en/charter-united-nations/index.html (accessed 12/23/20).

Chapter VII of the UN Charter authorizes the Security Council to identify acts of aggression and threats to peace and to determine what measures should be taken in response. The charter first provides for economic and diplomatic sanctions to be applied against aggressor states, but it also authorizes the Security Council to "take such action by air, sea, or land forces as may be necessary to maintain or restore international peace and security."

In practice, the Security Council can authorize two different kinds of military operations: peace-enforcement and peacekeeping. A **peace-enforcement operation** is intended to impose peace upon warring parties by intervening with force in an ongoing conflict, consistent with the traditional vision of collective security. The Security Council can authorize such an operation under Chapter VII of the charter after finding that a particular situation is a threat to international peace and security. The invasion of one state by another is a classic example of the kind of act that was intended to trigger intervention under Chapter VII. In recent years, the Security Council has also authorized action under Chapter VII for purely civil conflicts when the state in question could not or did not request intervention. These interventions are usually intended to protect civilians in the midst of an ongoing conflict while working to bring that conflict to an end.

Because peace-enforcement operations are generally targeted against one or more sides that are viewed as aggressors, they are not impartial, and the expectation is that troops involved in such operations will engage in combat. Hence, peace-enforcement operations tend to be heavily armed, and one or more P5 members may be centrally involved in providing the necessary resources.

A **peacekeeping operation**, by contrast, typically follows the conclusion of an interstate or civil war. The combatants have agreed to end the fighting but consider it valuable to have an impartial force in place to make sure that war does not resume. In such instances, the UN may assemble a multinational peacekeeping force with the mandate to verify that the terms of the peace agreement are kept: that the cease-fire holds; that any temporary cease-fire lines are respected; that troops are withdrawn or demobilized, if there are provisions to that effect; and so on. In the aftermath of civil conflict, peacekeeping forces have also helped to administer elections and ensure their fairness, reform police and security forces, and reintegrate demobilized rebels into society.

The deployment of peacekeeping forces typically requires that the parties to the conflict agree to invite them in—a requirement known as *host nation agreement*. Hence, except in rare cases, peacekeepers are not imposed on warring parties; rather, they deploy only with those parties' consent, a condition that lowers their expected cost. Interestingly, peacekeeping operations are not explicitly envisioned by the UN Charter. The difficulties of organizing peace-enforcement operations during the Cold War led the UN to innovate this less costly and less controversial strategy for conflict management. When authorizing peacekeeping operations, the UN Security Council typically invokes Chapter VI of the charter, which provides for steps to peacefully resolve disputes that have the potential to threaten international peace and security; however, it has also invoked Chapter VII for peacekeeping operations that might require a more forceful approach.

Although peacekeepers may be physically interposed between the adversaries or may patrol in areas where fighting could recur, they are typically lightly armed. Their purpose is not to fight a war, but to make sure that a war does not restart. For this reason, their main resource is not military power, but rather their perceived impartiality; that is, they are neutral brokers, favoring neither side in the dispute. As a result, peacekeepers are often drawn from distant countries with only weak interests in the conflict, and rarely from the P5 (although China has recently increased its contributions). To illustrate, Table 5.1 provides a list of the top 10 contributors to peacekeeping missions in January 2021, only one of which is a permanent member; the ranking of the permanent members is also shown.

TABLE 5.1 *Top Contributors to UN Peacekeeping Operations, January 2021*

RANK	COUNTRY	NUMBER OF PERSONNEL
1	Bangladesh	6,711
2	Rwanda	6,378
3	Ethiopia	6,297
4	Nepal	5,711
5	India	5,429
6	Pakistan	4,761
7	Egypt	3,154
8	Indonesia	2,825
9	China	2,465
10	Ghana	2,297

Contributions of Peacekeepers from the P5

RANK	COUNTRY	NUMBER OF PERSONNEL
9	China	2,465
34	France	623
36	Great Britain	529
71	Russia	62
80	United States	30

Source: United Nations Department of Peacekeeping Operations, "Summary of Troops Contributing Countries by Ranking," https://peacekeeping.un.org/sites/default/files/02-country_ranking_34_jan2021.pdf (accessed 3/18/2021).

TABLE 5.2 *Examples of United Nations Operations*

	PEACE ENFORCEMENT	PEACEKEEPING
Interstate	Korean War (1950–53): Repel invasion of South Korea by North Korea. Persian Gulf War (1991): Reverse invasion of Kuwait by Iraq.	India–Pakistan (1949–present): Monitor cease-fire in Jammu and Kashmir in the aftermath of the first India-Pakistan War. Israel–Syria (1974–present): Monitor the cease-fire and disengagement of forces in the Golan Heights.
Intrastate	Sudan (2007–present): Protect civilians and humanitarian aid workers amid ongoing conflict in Darfur. Intervention in Libya (2011): End threat of violence to civilians by the Libyan regime.	El Salvador (1991–95): Monitor cease-fire and political reforms in the aftermath of civil war. Liberia (2003–18): Support the implementation of a cease-fire and assist with reform of the police and military.

Table 5.2 gives some examples of peace-enforcement and peacekeeping operations approved by the UN, indicating whether they took place in the context of interstate or intrastate conflicts.

Cold War Paralysis   The UN was born with high hopes but soon found its ambitious aspirations frustrated by conflict among the most powerful states in the international system. The Cold War between the United States and the Soviet Union, which lasted from approximately 1946 to 1989, meant that the Security Council was largely incapable of dealing with issues that cut across this key divide. On many matters that came before the council, one side or the other had an interest in blocking effective action.

Figure 5.3 shows the numbers of vetoes cast in the Security Council in five-year increments. As the figure shows, the Soviet Union wielded the veto prolifically during the early years of the institution. For example, when the United States put forward proposals in 1947 to help Greece in its civil war against communist rebels, the Soviet Union exercised its veto. The United States, for its part, wielded its veto quite frequently to stop resolutions that it saw as harmful to its allies, including a number of resolutions censuring Israel for its treatment of Palestinians in the occupied territories. France, Great Britain, and China also exercised their vetoes, though on significantly fewer occasions. All in all, from 1946 to 1989, there were 192 vetoes cast on substantive issues before the council. This compares to 646 resolutions passed in the same period.[35] The UN was most active in cases that did not cut across the Cold War divide—that is, cases in which one or both superpowers had little direct interest.

The major exception to this generalization, the UN-sponsored intervention in the Korean War, is the one that proves the rule. Two days after North Korea invaded

---

35. Although the overall pattern of vetoes over time is instructive, observed vetoes can understate the degree of deadlock in the UNSC since many issues never come to a vote if everyone anticipates a veto. Thus, the threat of a veto alone can block action, even if the veto is never cast.

FIGURE 5.3 *Vetoes Cast in the UN Security Council, 1946–2020*

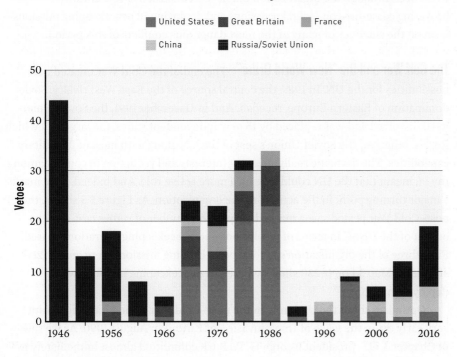

Legend: United States, Great Britain, France, China, Russia/Soviet Union

Figure source: Dag Hammarskjöld Library, "Security Council – Veto List," http://research.un.org/en/docs/sc/quick (accessed 10/27/20).

South Korea, the Security Council passed Resolution 83, authorizing member states to assist South Korea in repelling the attack. While the United States provided the bulk of the forces for this operation, it was joined by 19 other states. Given that North Korea was an ally of the Soviet Union, the latter should have been expected to veto the Security Council resolution. This act would not have prevented American intervention, but it would have denied the operation the blessing of the UN and perhaps some multilateral support.

The veto failed to materialize because, at the time, the Soviet Union was boycotting meetings of the Security Council due to a dispute over China's representation in the body. When the UN was created, mainland China was ruled by a pro-American Nationalist government. In 1949, however, Communist forces defeated the Nationalists in a civil war, and the latter fled to the island of Taiwan. A year later, when the Korean War broke out, China's seat on the Security Council was held by a representative of the Nationalist government in Taiwan. The Soviet Union argued that China's seat should be filled by a representative of the Communist government on the mainland, and it refused to attend meetings of the Security Council until that demand was met. Hence, when Resolution 83 came to a vote on June 27, 1950, the Soviet representative was not present to cast a veto. The Soviet Union ended its boycott of the Security Council not long afterward.[36]

36. China's seat on the Security Council remained in the hands of Taiwan until 1971, when warming relations between the United States and the People's Republic of China paved the way for the seat to be transferred to the mainland's control.

The Cold War divide thus hampered the UN for the first five decades of its existence. Although the organization did have a constructive role at times—brokering cease-fires on several occasions and deploying 18 peacekeeping missions—it sat on the sidelines of many of the most dangerous conflicts of this period.

The Gulf War and the "New World Order"

The end of the Cold War created new possibilities for the UN. In 1989, the central source of the East-West rivalry, Soviet domination of Eastern Europe, receded. And in December 1991, the Soviet Union itself dissolved and was replaced by 15 new independent states, the largest of which, Russia, inherited the Soviet Union's seat in the UN along with most of its military capabilities. The dramatic realignment of interests and reduction in conflict among the P5 meant that the UN could take on a more active role. And indeed, 1990 marks a major turning point in the activity of the organization. As Figure 5.3 shows, the post–Cold War period saw a marked drop in the number of vetoes cast, and the output of the UNSC in terms of resolutions and peacekeeping operations soared. Fifty-three of the organization's 71 total peacekeeping missions were authorized after 1989. Map 5.1 on p. 230 shows where UN peacekeeping missions were deployed in 2020.

Optimism about the UN's role in the post–Cold War period hit a high point very early on, in the wake of Iraq's invasion of Kuwait in August 1990. As we saw in Chapter 3, U.S. president George H. W. Bush committed almost immediately to ensuring that the conquest of Kuwait would not stand. Bush also made a concerted effort to line up UN support at every step of the way. Between Iraq's invasion of Kuwait and the U.S.-led military operation to reverse it, the Security Council passed 12 resolutions on the crisis. The most important of these, Resolution 678, authorized member states to use "all necessary means" to bring about the unconditional withdrawal of Iraqi forces from Kuwait if Iraq did not comply voluntarily by January 15, 1991.

The Security Council's approval of this resolution owed a great deal to the reduction of conflict in the international system with the end of the Cold War. The Soviet Union had long been an ally of Iraq, and in an earlier period it might have been expected to veto a resolution like 678. In the post–Cold War environment, however, when the Soviet Union desired better relations with the West, it was relatively easy to overcome the Soviet Union's reluctance to approve the use of force against its former ally.

The blessing of the UN meant that the United States had substantial international assistance in the ensuing war. The coalition that fought Iraq included troops from 35 nations. As shown in Figure 5.4, the United States supplied the vast majority of the troops for the operation, but the multinational cast and UN blessing had political, if not much military, significance. The participation of a number of Arab and Muslim states was seen as important in blunting Iraq's argument that the United States was waging a war against Islam. The limited mandate of the operation—to liberate Kuwait and not to occupy Iraq—was intended to reassure states in the region that the United States did not have expansionist objectives. International support also reduced the financial costs of the conflict. Contributions from other

FIGURE 5.4 **Allied Troop Contributions to the Persian Gulf War, 1990–91**

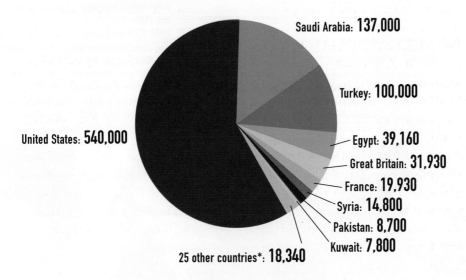

Saudi Arabia: **137,000**

Turkey: **100,000**

Egypt: **39,160**

Great Britain: **31,930**

France: **19,930**

Syria: **14,800**

Pakistan: **8,700**

Kuwait: **7,800**

United States: **540,000**

25 other countries*: **18,340**

Figure source: U.S. General Accounting Office, *Persian Gulf: Allied Burden Sharing Efforts*, GAO/NSIAD-92-71, Appendix II, 16-7, www.gao.gov/products/NSIAD-92-71 (accessed 1/11/21).

*Bangladesh, Morocco, Qatar, United Arab Emirates, Canada, Italy, Australia, Netherlands, Oman, Spain, Bahrain, Belgium, Senegal, Niger, Argentina, Philippines, Greece, Poland, South Korea, Czechoslovakia, Denmark, Norway, New Zealand, Hungary.

countries covered about 90 percent of the $61 billion the United States spent fighting the war—making the Persian Gulf War the least expensive war in America's history on a per capita basis.

The successful operation of the UN machinery in this case led to great optimism about the role the organization could play in the new international environment. Bush, in his State of the Union address just before the war, spoke of the opportunity to create "a new world order, a world where the rule of law, not the law of the jungle, governs the conduct of nations"—a world in which "a credible United Nations can use its peacekeeping role to fulfill the promise and vision of the UN's founders." Indeed, the UN had seemed to meet the first challenge of this new era quite successfully.

The optimism would turn out to be overblown. The Iraqi invasion of Kuwait was, in many respects, an easy case for effective international action. By invading a weak neighbor, Iraq had committed a flagrant violation of international law. More important, the attack was seen as directly threatening the interests of the United States and its allies. After gobbling up Kuwait, Iraq was in possession of 20 percent of the world's known oil reserves. Furthermore, the attack put Iraq in a position to threaten Saudi Arabia, home to another 25 percent of the world's oil. All told, the Persian Gulf region contained two-thirds of this valuable natural resource. The possibility that so much of the world's oil could come under the control of a hostile power was seen as threatening to vital American interests. As a result, the United States was strongly motivated to take forceful action to reverse the Iraqi invasion. In all likelihood, it would have done so even if it had been unable to secure UN approval.

Hence, the success of the UN in this case owed a great deal to the fact that the United States, the most powerful actor in the international system, perceived a direct threat to its own interests. The international community was, in this instance,

MAP 5.1 *UN Peacekeeping Operations Active in 2020*

UNFICYP
United Nations Peacekeeping Force in Cyprus (Est. 1964)
UNFICYP was established to prevent the recurrence of violence between the Greek Cypriot and Turkish Cypriot communities on the island of Cyprus. The mission currently maintains a buffer zone, supervises the cease-fire, and undertakes humanitarian activities.

UNMIK
United Nations Interim Administration Mission in Kosovo (Est. 1999)
UNMIK supports self-governance in Kosovo in the wake of the conflict between Kosovar ethnic Albanians and the Serbian government, which claims the Kosovo Province.

MINURSO
United Nations Mission for the Referendum in Western Sahara (Est. 1991)
Created to safeguard a transitional period to prepare a referendum through which the people of Western Sahara could choose between independence and integration with Morocco, MINURSO continues to monitor the cease-fire, reduce the threat of mines and unexploded ammunition, and facilitate communication between Saharans in Western Sahara and in Algerian refugee camps.

MINUSMA
United Nations Multidimensional Integrated Stabilization Mission in Mali (Est. 2013)
MINUSMA assists in providing security and supporting political reconciliation in Mali, where civil unrest led to advances by Al Qaeda–affiliated militants.

MINUSCA
United Nations Multidimensional Integrated Stabilization Mission in the Central African Republic (Est. 2014)
MINUSCA protects civilians, facilitates humanitarian assistance, and promotes human rights in response to conflict in the Central African Republic.

MONUSCO
United Nations Organization Stabilization Mission in the Democratic Republic of the Congo (Est. 2010)
MONUSCO took over from an earlier mission (MONUC) to focus on the protection of civilians, humanitarian personnel, and human rights defenders under imminent threat of physical violence and to support the government of the DRC in its stabilization and peace consolidation efforts.

Atlantic Ocean

Pacific Ocean

UNIFIL

United Nations Interim Force in Lebanon (Est. 1978)

Initially established to monitor the withdrawal of Israeli forces from Lebanon, UNIFIL now oversees the cease-fire, supports the deployment of Lebanese forces into southern Lebanon, and supports humanitarian services and the return of refugees and displaced persons to Lebanon.

UNDOF

United Nations Disengagement Observer Force (Est. 1974)

UNDOF supervised the withdrawal of Israeli and Syrian forces from the Golan Heights and maintains a cease-fire between them.

UNTSO

United Nations Truce Supervision Organization (Est. 1948)

The UN's first peacekeeping mission, UNTSO supervised the cease-fire between Israel and its Arab neighbors following their 1948 war.

UNMOGIP

United Nations Military Observer Group in India and Pakistan (Est. 1949)

UNMOGIP maintains the cease-fire between India and Pakistan in their dispute over Kashmir.

UNAMID

African Union/United Nations Hybrid Operation in Darfur (Est. 2007)

With ongoing strife in Darfur between the government of Sudan and rebel militias, UNAMID protects civilians, facilitates the provision of humanitarian aid, and supports implementation of a peace agreement. While its mandate ended December 31, 2020, it is not expected to fully withdraw from the country until summer 2021.

UNISFA

United Nations Interim Security Force for Abyei (Est. 2011)

UNISFA exists to oversee demilitarization and monitor peace in the disputed Abyei area of Sudan. The operation will monitor the flashpoint border between north and south and is authorized to use force in protecting civilians and humanitarian workers in Abyei.

UNMISS

United Nations Mission in the Republic of South Sudan (Est. 2011)

In 2011, South Sudan became the newest country in the world. UNMISS is on the ground to consolidate peace and security and to help establish conditions for development.

WESTERN SAHARA (MOR.)

SERBIA

CYPRUS

LEBANON

SYRIA

ISRAEL

PAKISTAN

EGYPT

MALI

INDIA

SUDAN

CEN. AFR. REP.

S. SUDAN

D. R. CONGO

Indian Ocean

Map source: https://peacekeeping.un.org/en.

what we called in Chapter 2 a *privileged group*, since a single member was motivated strongly enough to provide the public good. The next several years would provide ample evidence that when such incentives are lacking, the community's collective interests in stopping aggression and/or ending gross violations of human rights are generally not enough to compel effective international intervention.

The "Triumph of the Lack of Will": Bosnia, Rwanda, and Darfur

The hard tests of the new world order came only a few years after the victory in the Persian Gulf. The decades that followed witnessed a number of bloody and heartrending crises that transfixed the international community but also exposed the limits of that community's willingness to do much about them.[37]

One visible example of the limited will of the international community played out in the former Yugoslav republic of Bosnia-Herzegovina. The civil conflict in Bosnia was the bloodiest of several violent acts in the breakup of Yugoslavia. Originally composed of five republics—Serbia, Slovenia, Croatia, Bosnia-Herzegovina, and Macedonia—the Yugoslav federation began to dissolve in 1991. While Slovenia, Croatia, and Bosnia sought independence, Serbia, the largest republic, tried to hold the multiethnic state together by force.

The conflict in Bosnia was the most complicated and bloody because this republic was home to three ethnic groups: Serbs (comprising 31 percent of the prewar population), Croats (25 percent), and Bosnian Muslims (44 percent). Many Serbs did not want to live in an independent Bosnia; rather, they wanted to carve out portions of that republic and join with Serbia. The more radical Croats had similar thoughts of joining Croatia. When Bosnia declared its independence from Yugoslavia in March 1992, militant Serbs and Croats rebelled, triggering a three-way war.

The ensuing conflict, which lasted three years, was incredibly brutal, with 300,000 killed, mostly civilians, and at least 2 million refugees displaced from their homes. In addition, the combatants engaged in widespread atrocities against civilians: shelling cities, herding men and boys into detention camps where they were malnourished and mistreated, raping women and girls in order to terrorize the population. While crimes were committed by all sides, the greatest offenders were the Serbs, who engaged in a systematic campaign of what became known as "ethnic cleansing": clearing coveted territory of all non-Serbs by either killing them or scaring them into flight.

The international response to these events was feeble and at times counterproductive. Although there was unanimous condemnation of the violence, no one was willing to exert on behalf of Bosnia the kind of effort that had been marshaled to save Kuwait only one year earlier. Without compelling interests, such as securing an important natural resource (like oil), the UN, at the behest of the United States and European powers, responded in a half-hearted way. A peacekeeping force of mostly European troops was deployed to the area—despite the fact that there was no peace to keep.

---

37. We take our heading for this section from the title phrase of an insightful analysis of this period; see James Gow, *Triumph of the Lack of Will: International Diplomacy and the Yugoslav War* (New York: Columbia University Press, 1997).

Pressed into the war zone under Chapter VII, the UN Protection Force (UNPROFOR) nonetheless had many of the qualities of a traditional peacekeeping force: it was lightly armed, dispersed throughout the country, required to be neutral, and ordered to fire only in self-defense. Its main mission was to distribute food and medicine to civilians and to help keep them out of harm's way. Hence, UNPROFOR sought to treat the symptoms of the war, but it had neither a mandate nor the requisite capabilities to end the war itself. On several occasions Serb forces took peacekeepers hostage and chained them to artillery pieces in order to deter air strikes against their positions.

The UN declared several Bosnian cities to be "safe havens" where civilians could find refuge from the war under its protection. The hollowness of this promise became evident in the worst atrocity of the war. In July 1995, Serb forces overran the safe haven of Srebrenica and proceeded to massacre 8,000 Muslim men and boys. The 600 Dutch peacekeepers charged with defending the city could do little to resist. When Serb forces threatened to kill some Dutch hostages, the Dutch government and the UN commanders on the ground decided to negotiate their troops' surrender.[38]

The massacre at Srebrenica did finally spark tougher international intervention. In August–September 1995, the United States and NATO conducted sustained air strikes against Serb forces. These attacks helped bring about a peace conference in Dayton, Ohio, that led to the Bosnian war's end in December 1995. Now with a peace to keep, U.S. and NATO forces were deployed as peacekeepers, with the blessing of the UN and alongside international police forces organized by the UN. In a pattern repeated elsewhere (see "The Quiet Successes" on p. 236), the UN mechanism had more success in maintaining a peace already achieved than in ending aggression and gross violations of human rights.

A similar lack of international will was apparent in Rwanda in 1994 and in the ongoing conflict in the Darfur region of Sudan. In Rwanda, conflict between the country's principal ethnic groups, the Hutus and the Tutsis, erupted in genocide in April 1994. In the course of three months, an estimated 800,000 people were killed—many hacked to death by machetes—including 75 percent of the Tutsi population. The international response to this tragedy was very weak. A small UN peacekeeping force already on the ground was overwhelmed. After 10 of its peacekeepers were killed on the first day of the conflict, Belgium withdrew its forces, and other nations followed suit. As the death toll rose, the international community stood by and watched. The killing stopped only after a Tutsi rebel force succeeded in defeating the Hutu forces responsible for much of the slaughter.

The case of Darfur is similarly tragic. A bloody conflict has raged in western Sudan since 2003, where government-supported militias have carried out systematic killings of the people there. In another widely acknowledged genocide, it is estimated that 200,000–400,000 people have died, and up to 3 million have been displaced from their homes. In spite of widespread outrage, the response of the UN has been weak. Although the UN and African Union deployed a joint peacekeeping force to the region

---

38. Samantha Power, *"A Problem from Hell": America and the Age of Genocide*, rev. ed. (New York: Basic Books, 2013), 399–400.

Should Outsiders Intervene Militarily to Stop Humanitarian Crises?

In 2011, Libyans revolted against the dictatorial rule of leader Mu'ammar Qaddafi. After initial successes by the rebels, Qaddafi's forces began to reclaim control as they moved east along the coast. The prospect of a bloodbath in Benghazi, Libya's second-largest city, spurred the international community to action. The Security Council passed a resolution authorizing member states to "take all necessary measures" to protect civilians in Libya, which allowed NATO to begin air operations and a naval blockade against Qaddafi's forces. With NATO support, the rebels beat back the loyalists at Benghazi. Qaddafi was captured and killed two months later.

The Libya operation is an example of armed humanitarian intervention: the use of military force by outsiders to stop mass killing or genocide within a country. Other notable examples include the UN-sponsored intervention to relieve a famine caused by civil war in Somalia in 1991–93 and, on a smaller scale, U.S. air strikes against Syria in 2017 and 2018 to punish the regime's use of chemical weapons.

Applying the Concepts

The main argument for armed humanitarian intervention rests on the idea that everyone shares an **interest** in preventing suffering and death due to civil wars or murderous governments. But the practice remains controversial. Critics argue that (1) claims of humanitarianism disguise the self-interested reasons that actually motivate intervention, (2) military force is a poor instrument for influencing the strategic **interaction** between governments and civilians, and (3) existing **institutions** are not up to the task of deciding whether and when to intervene.

The case for armed humanitarian intervention rests on the moral imperative to protect unarmed civilians facing death at the hands of their government. When a state has failed in its basic obligation to protect its citizens from massacre, genocide, and other crimes against humanity, it has been argued that other states have a responsibility to intervene, by force if necessary (for more on the emergence of the "responsibility to protect" norm, see Chapter 11).

In the case of Libya, the looming attack on Benghazi reminded Western decision makers of their countries' failure to act under similar circumstances in July 1995, when Serb forces overran the city of Srebrenica in Bosnia and massacred 8,000 men and boys. If given the chance to prevent another such atrocity, why not act? A policy of intervention can not only save lives that are at immediate risk but also deter governments from committing atrocities in the first place.

While this argument seems compelling, the uncomfortable fact is that most humanitarian crises do not trigger this kind of response. Genocidal killings in Rwanda (1994), in the Darfur region of Sudan (starting in 2003), and against the Rohingya in Myanmar (starting in 2016) met international condemnation but not concerted military action. In Syria, where a civil war has claimed hundreds of thousands of lives, U.S. air strikes in 2017 and 2018 were an exception to a policy that otherwise avoided direct confrontation with the Syrian regime as it bombed and starved civilian populations.

Because the international community cannot possibly protect everyone everywhere in the world, the application of this policy is bound to be inconsistent and influenced by interests other than humanitarianism. The fact that Qaddafi was a hostile and unpredictable leader with enormous oil wealth suggests that other interests contributed to the decision to support the rebellion. No comparable interests compelled intervention in Rwanda, Sudan, or Myanmar, and Russia's interest in preserving a friendly regime in Syria motivated it to block intervention efforts there.

Humanitarian intervention also threatens the interests that states have in exercising sovereign control over internal matters. While atrocities committed against civilians are unacceptable, states have a legitimate interest in maintaining order domestically and preserving their territorial integrity. Indeed, to some critics, the West's recent willingness to intervene looks a good deal like another, older practice: imperialism. Just as imperial powers claimed to bring "civilization" to the lands they conquered,

Benghazi, Libya

humanitarianism may be used to disguise self-interested efforts to undermine or take over unfriendly states.

Another concern about these operations is that military force is a blunt and costly instrument for influencing the interaction between governments and their citizens. Although the most direct way to protect civilians is to deploy troops to shield them from the government's security forces, outsiders are usually reluctant to put their own people in harm's way. For this reason, the Libya campaign was conducted entirely from the air, relying on bombs and cruise missiles. While this strategy was effective at preventing NATO casualties, it also limited NATO's ability to influence events on the ground. Even if an intervention succeeds in easing a crisis, an enduring solution requires a long-term commitment by outside actors that may not be credible. When the foreigners go home, conflict may erupt again. Indeed, Libya has fallen back into civil war as different factions vie to rule that country.

Finally, humanitarian intervention raises the institutional question of who should decide when the international community can get involved. The UN is the natural venue for such a determination. Even so, for the Security Council to authorize intervention in purely domestic conflicts requires an expansive interpretation of what constitutes a "threat to international peace and security." Two members of the Security Council—China and Russia— have been loath to endorse humanitarian intervention, in part because their own human rights records are spotty. Because of the threat of their veto, the Security Council could not act against Sudan or Syria. In the case of Libya, the Security Council (with China and Russia abstaining) approved an operation to protect civilians but did not endorse the goal of ousting Qaddafi.

Supporters of humanitarian intervention have argued that NATO, as an alliance of democracies, is well qualified to act in support of human rights. But under international law, the alliance does not have the authority to undertake such an operation on its own, nor is it universally seen as an impartial force. Thus, while the international community has at times taken steps to protect people in harm's way, it still grapples with the question of how to perform this responsibility well.

Thinking Analytically

1. When do humanitarian interests override a state's interests in exercising sovereign control over its internal policies? Are there good criteria for deciding the answer to this question?

2. What are the advantages and disadvantages of vesting decisions about the legality of humanitarian intervention in the Security Council? If you could design an alternative institution to make this decision, what would its membership and voting rules be?

Weak support from member states can lead to UN operations that lack the personnel and mandate needed to end a conflict. The UN deployed a peacekeeping force to Sudan in response to fighting in the Darfur region, but troop contributions fell below authorized levels, and it was unable to halt the fighting.

(UNAMID), it could not end the violence. Member states were unwilling to support or contribute troops to a more robust military operation, and deployed troop levels consistently fell below the level authorized by the Security Council. A change of government in Sudan paved the way for a peace agreement in October 2020, and UNAMID ended its mission. It remains to be seen whether this deal will halt the conflict.

This discussion is not meant to imply that the UN mechanism never works. Rather, it suggests that absent compelling national interests, member states are reluctant to pay heavy costs or embrace high risks to further the community's interest in stopping aggression or ending humanitarian crises. In all these cases, the member states cared about the suffering, but they did not care enough to undertake the kind of military operation that would have been needed to end the conflicts that caused the suffering. The "Controversy" section on p. 234 discusses the NATO-led intervention in Libya (2011) and the challenges that international organizations face when it comes to such interventions.

The Quiet Successes In other cases, the costs of intervention are seen as relatively low, and the UN's track record in these situations has been more impressive. These cases generally fall under the category of traditional peacekeeping: monitoring and assisting in the implementation of peace agreements. Because the existence of a peace agreement indicates that the opposing parties are ready to stop fighting and resolve their differences, the risks associated with getting involved are not that high. Keeping peace after a war is generally easier than making peace during a war.

For this reason, UN efforts have been most successful in the area of post-conflict reconstruction.[39] In the case of El Salvador, for example, a UN peacekeeping

39. See Michael W. Doyle and Nicholas Sambanis, *Making War and Building Peace: United Nations Peace Operations* (Princeton, NJ: Princeton University Press, 2006).

operation played an important role in that country's recovery from a 12-year civil war that claimed 75,000 lives. The UN Observer Mission in El Salvador (ONUSAL) comprised about 700 military observers and civilian police from 17 countries, but it had an expansive mandate to help rebuild the country. ONUSAL not only helped to monitor the demobilization of the warring factions after a 1992 peace agreement, but it also assisted in implementing political reforms designed to address the root causes of the conflict, such as reforming the judiciary, forming and training a new civilian police force, and redistributing land to former combatants. ONUSAL also monitored an election in 1994 to ensure that it was free and fair and that all sides would respect the result. The mission's mandate ended in April 1995, leaving a country that was, until a recent growth in criminal violence, free and democratic.

Similar stories of success in post-conflict reconstruction can be found in Mozambique, Liberia, Sierra Leone, East Timor, Cambodia, and even Bosnia, where a NATO-led peacekeeping force with the United Nations' blessing went in after the 1995 peace deal. It was deemed to have fulfilled its mission and departed in December 2004.[40]

People following the news likely heard much more about the UN's failings in Bosnia, Rwanda, and Darfur than about the quieter victories in places like El Salvador and Bosnia after 1995. Bloodshed naturally draws more attention than do peace and reconciliation, so the failures of the UN get more publicity than do its successes. (See "How Do We Know?" on p. 238 for more evidence on the success of peacekeeping operations.)

From 9/11 to Iraq and After: Consensus Lost

During the 1990s, civil conflicts such as the ones in Bosnia and Rwanda were much more prominent on the UN agenda than were cases of international aggression like the Persian Gulf War. As we have seen, the main impediment to effective action in these cases was a lack of will—the absence of compelling national interests that could have justified committing resources and taking risks. The September 11, 2001, terrorist attacks against the United States changed this focus, exposing a threat that many UN member states, including all of the P5, had reason to fear. The unanimous condemnation of the terrorist attacks and international support for the United States' war in Afghanistan suggested that once again the UN mechanism could work effectively in the new international environment.

This optimism would prove short-lived, however. Just over a year after the 9/11 attacks, the U.S. effort to mount a war against Iraq divided the Security Council and left the organization alienated from its most powerful member. Although all members were on record demanding that Iraq fully account for its past weapons programs, they parted ways on the desirability of using military force to enforce this demand. A majority of the Security Council members, including France, Russia, and China, refused to back a proposed resolution in January 2003 authorizing the use of force against Iraq, in part because many members of the council were reluctant to endorse the U.S. doctrine of preventive war (defined in Chapter 3), which they saw as contrary to the UN Charter's rules on the use of force. Claiming authorization

---

40. The UN force was replaced by a European Union force (EUFOR Althea, named after the Greek goddess of healing).

Does Peacekeeping Keep the Peace?

Since its creation in 1946, the UN has undertaken 71 peacekeeping missions. Around 4,000 peacekeepers have died in the course of these operations, whose total cost has been about $100 billion. At the time of this writing, over 94,000 personnel from 121 countries were deployed in 13 ongoing operations around the globe.[a] Given this expenditure of time, blood, and treasure, it is reasonable to ask: Do peacekeeping operations actually work?

A number of studies have sought to answer this question. Virginia Page Fortna collected information on cease-fires in interstate and civil wars since 1946. There is a good deal of variation in how long cease-fires last. Some break down almost immediately, others last for years, and still others form the basis for a permanent peace between the adversaries. To determine whether peacekeepers can affect how long a cease-fire will last, Fortna recorded, for each case, whether a peacekeeping force was sent in to monitor and/or enforce the agreement.

Even when other factors that influence the durability of peace are taken into account, the presence of a peacekeeping operation has a substantial effect on the likelihood that a cease-fire will endure. Looking at the 48 cease-fires in interstate wars that ended between 1946 and 1998, Fortna found that the presence of peacekeepers reduced by 85 percent the probability that a cease-fire would break down in any given year.[b] Similarly, in an analysis of 94 cease-fires in 60 civil wars in the period 1989–99, Fortna found that the presence of peacekeepers reduced the risk of renewed fighting in any given year by about 60 percent.[c]

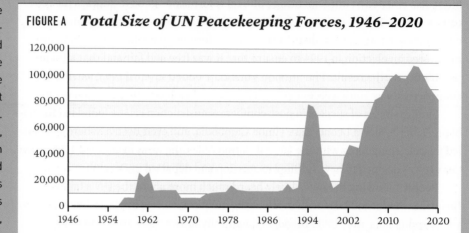

FIGURE A *Total Size of UN Peacekeeping Forces, 1946–2020*

Note: Highest month for each year. Figures include troops, military observers, and police.

Figure sources: Global Policy Forum, "Size of UN Peacekeeping Forces, 1947-2009," www.globalpolicy.org/component/content/article/102-tables-and-charts/40734-size-of-un-peacekeeping-forces-1947-2009.html (accessed 03/19/18). Updated through August 2020 using data from https://peacekeeping.un.org/sites/default/files/0_front_page_august_2020.pdf (accessed 10/27/20).

In addition to preventing wars from recurring, UN peacekeepers can also reduce violence in the midst of fighting. By analyzing data on the size of peacekeeping missions and the number of casualties, Lisa Hultman, Jacob Kathman, and Megan Shannon show that a larger UN presence reduces battlefield violence and lowers civilian deaths. By their estimate, increasing UN military personnel in a country from zero to 10,000 reduces the predicted number of civilian deaths due to fighting from about 25 per month to 4 per month. The deployment of UN police forces has similar effects.[d] Given that civil wars can last for many years, these deployments can potentially save thousands of lives. This suggests that prominent failures to protect civilians, such as in Bosnia, Rwanda, and Darfur, do not occur because peacekeepers are ineffective, but because the international community has committed too few of them. Considering the enormous human and economic costs associated with warfare, peacekeeping operations appear to be well worth their price.

a. Data are from www.un.org/en/peacekeeping/resources/statistics/factsheet.shtml (accessed 10/16/20).

b. Virginia Page Fortna, "Interstate Peacekeeping: Causal Mechanisms and Empirical Effects," *World Politics* 56 (July 2004): 481–519. See also Virginia Page Fortna, *Peace Time: Cease-Fire Agreements and the Durability of Peace* (Princeton, NJ: Princeton University Press, 2004).

c. Virginia Page Fortna, *Does Peacekeeping Work? Shaping Belligerents' Choices after Civil War* (Princeton, NJ: Princeton University Press, 2008), 105.

d. Lisa Hultman, Jacob D. Kathman, and Megan Shannon, *Peacekeeping in the Midst of War* (New York: Oxford University Press, 2019), 123–24.

under prior UN resolutions and Article 51 of the UN Charter permitting self-defense, the United States went ahead with the invasion without explicit UN support.

More recently, conflicts among the P5 have threatened to once again sideline the UN. As noted earlier, Russia has wielded its veto to prevent the UN from imposing economic or military sanctions on Syria, a longtime Russian ally. Between the start of the Syrian Civil War in 2011 and December 2019, Russia had vetoed sixteen resolutions condemning the mass killing of civilians and the use of chemical weapons. Similarly, in the spring of 2014, when Russian tanks and troops moved into Ukraine and annexed Crimea, the Security Council debated the matter, but there was no chance that the institution would act against one of its permanent members. The two draft resolutions on Ukraine that came to a vote both fell victim to Russia's veto.[41]

In addition, there is little prospect of the Security Council getting involved in conflicts between China and its neighbors over disputed islands in the South China Sea—disputes that have the potential to become flashpoints for conflict between the United States and China (see Chapter 2). As a result of these rising tensions among the P5, the UN will once again find itself unable to act on key matters of international security. Indeed, the number of vetoes cast in recent years is climbing back to levels seen during the Cold War (see Figure 5.3).

As this overview suggests, the UN faces two essential requirements if it is to work as intended. First, none of the veto-wielding members can see a potential operation as threatening to its interests. If this requirement is not met—as was true through much of the Cold War and in the case of Iraq—then action can be blocked thanks to the voting rule. Second, member states, particularly the powerful member states, must care enough about the conflicts in question to devote the necessary resources and take the necessary risks. If those risks are low, as in the case of post-conflict peacekeeping, this requirement may not be hard to satisfy. In the more costly cases of reversing aggression or stopping genocides, a strong interest, such as existed in the Gulf War case, is necessary to ensure that sufficient resources are brought to bear. Thus, effective action can be thwarted in two ways: by self-interest, as in the case of Ukraine, or by apathy, as in the case of Rwanda.

One might draw the cynical conclusion that the UN mechanism is most likely to be effective precisely when it is needed least—that is, when the powerful states agree enough and care enough to take action. In a case like the Gulf War, one could argue, the UN served simply to give a stamp of approval to actions that the United States would have taken anyway. Moreover, it is also clear from the experience of the Iraq War that the failure to get UN approval will not always stop a great power from taking actions that it wants to take.

In light of this conclusion, one might question whether the UN matters at all when it comes to war and peace. The answer is that although the UN matters less than one might hope, the organization does indeed make a difference. First, as already noted, it has played a constructive role in organizing peacekeeping missions to help countries reconstruct in the wake of conflict. In these cases, the UN's perceived impartiality bestows a legitimacy on peacekeepers' efforts that is needed for them to play the role of an honest broker.

---

41. An excellent resource on vetoed resolutions can be found at http://research.un.org/en/docs/sc/quick (accessed 10/16/20).

Second, the United States' experience in its two wars against Iraq, in 1991 and 2003, shows that the UN's blessing can be a valuable resource. In the Gulf War, UN support helped build both domestic and international support for the war effort, which contributed to the United States' ability to prevail at a low cost to itself. In the case of the Iraq War, the absence of UN support had important implications for the United States' ability to stabilize the country after toppling Hussein's regime. One study of post-conflict reconstruction showed that in order to implement a nation-building effort in Iraq that was the same size per capita as the one that was deployed in Bosnia in 1995, the United States would have needed 480,000 combat troops and 12,600 international police.[42] The absence of UN backing, however, meant that some countries that often contribute peacekeeping or police forces to these kinds of missions, such as Pakistan and India, refused to do so in this case. As a result, the U.S.-led coalition had, in March 2004, 154,000 total combat troops, 85 percent of whom were American. And those troops had to serve double duty as an international police force, because there was no separate deployment of police. Hence, there are costs to going to war without the backing of the UN—even if these costs are not always sufficient to prevent a great power from doing so.

Finally, although cooperation is uneven, the UN facilitates joint decision making. Its rules of procedure in the Security Council and established mechanisms for fielding peacekeeping and peace-enforcement operations keep countries from having to "reinvent the wheel" each time a crisis arises. Vetoes may interfere with decision making, but without clearly established rules, decisions would be harder to reach even in those instances where cooperation would otherwise be successful. Indeed, if the UN did not exist, states would need to create an organization very similar to the one we already have.

Conclusion: Are Poor Police Better than None?

At the outset of this chapter, we asked whether and when international institutions can prevent or stop wars between and within states. The track record of both alliances and collective security organizations has been uneven, at best, in this regard. Both are imperfect substitutes for an effective police force of the kind that we take for granted in a well-governed country.

Alliances form in response to common interests—generally, the perception of a common threat. For this reason, allies are often better able to work together in concert than are the more fractious members of, say, the UN. However, the existence of alliances does not ensure that allies will fight together, nor does it ensure that other states will be deterred from making threats. Not all alliances are created equally, as the capabilities and resolve underlying the commitment to defend an ally can vary

---

42. James Dobbins, John G. McGinn, Keith Crane, Seth G. Jones, et al., *America's Role in Nation-Building: From Germany to Iraq* (Santa Monica, CA: RAND, 2003).

quite considerably. When these are in doubt, as in the case of France's alliance with Czechoslovakia in the interwar period, the alliance can fail to both deter threats and defend against them. When member states are strongly resolved and take the necessary steps to lock in and demonstrate that commitment, as in the case of NATO, then the alliance can be a source of peace through credible deterrence.

For collective security organizations, like the UN, the primary challenge involves providing a public good in an environment in which private interests often compete and the costs of providing the good may be more than anyone is willing to pay. Moreover, the joint decision-making rules set down by the organizations' founding members gave those states important privileges to block actions that they do not like. Hence, these organizations have been most effective only when there has been relatively strong agreement among the most powerful states, and they have been crippled when those states are in conflict. They have had their greatest successes when at least one powerful state had a sufficient interest that it was willing to pay costs and take risks to provide the public good for everyone. They have also had more quiet successes when those costs and risks were relatively low, such as in cases of post-conflict reconstruction.

Former UN secretary-general Dag Hammarskjöld reportedly said, "The UN was not created to take humanity to heaven but to save it from hell."[43] This statement reflects a pragmatic understanding of the limits of governance in the international system. States have conflicts of interests that they are willing to fight over, as do people within states. In the absence of an impartial police force, the ability of third parties to enforce peace depends on whether those parties are willing and able to step in.

Do outsiders have an interest in intervening? Do the available institutions promote intervention by lowering the costs of getting involved or by increasing the costs of staying out? Does intervention influence the interaction between combatants in a way that resolves the information and commitment problems that can lead to violence? All these questions have to be answered in the affirmative for outside intervention to have a chance at preventing or reversing acts of violence. In cases like the wars in Korea and the Persian Gulf, these conditions were met, and South Korea and Kuwait owe their continued existence to this fact. Similarly, in places like El Salvador and Liberia, effective outside assistance has helped these countries rebuild after decades of civil conflict. But in many other cases these conditions are not met, and the results can be disastrous, as in Bosnia, Rwanda, and Darfur.

And yet, as we survey this uneven record, Hammarskjöld's statement reminds us that even an imperfect police force may be better than none. Although the international system has no central authority analogous to that of a well-governed domestic system, the institutions that have developed in its place have a beneficial—albeit imperfect and uneven—impact on world politics. Alliances and collective security organizations are poor substitutes for an effective and neutral police, but it is likely that the world would be an even more violent place in their absence.

---

43. The original source of this well-known quotation is unclear, and slight variations in wording can be found in the secondary literature, possibly because Hammarskjöld said something to this effect more than once. For a speech in which he made this point, see Andrew W. Cordier and Wilder Foote, eds., *Public Papers of the Secretaries-General of the United Nations*, vol. 2, *Dag Hammarskjöld* (New York: Columbia University Press, 1972), 301.

Study Tool Kit

Interests, Interactions, and Institutions in Context

- Alliances form when states have compatible interests that lead them to cooperate militarily. They are institutions created between or among states to facilitate cooperation for the purpose of influencing the outcomes of disputes with outsiders.

- Alliances are successful at deterring or fighting off challenges when allies have a strong interest in coming to one another's aid in the event of war and when they are able to signal this interest to their adversaries in a credible manner.

- Collective security organizations form around a common interest, which all states are presumed to share, in promoting peace. As broad-based institutions, their primary role is to facilitate collective action within the international community so that states can respond effectively to prevent or stop outbreaks of violence whenever and wherever they may occur.

- Collective security organizations are successful when leading states perceive a common and compelling interest in stopping an act of aggression. They fail when leading states have conflicting interests in the outcome of a particular dispute or when they have too little interest in the matter to justify the costs of intervention.

Key Terms

alliances, p. 197

balance of power, p. 200

bandwagoning, p. 201

entrapment, p. 208

North Atlantic Treaty Organization (NATO), p. 212

Warsaw Pact, p. 212

League of Nations, p. 216

United Nations (UN), p. 216

collective security organizations, p. 216

genocide, p. 217

humanitarian interventions, p. 218

UN Security Council (UNSC), p. 221

permanent five (P5), p. 221

veto power, p. 222

peace–enforcement operation, p. 224

peacekeeping operation, p. 224

For Further Reading

Doyle, Michael W., and Nicholas Sambanis. *Making War and Building Peace: United Nations Peace Operations.* **Princeton, NJ: Princeton University Press, 2006.** Examines the track record of UN peacekeeping and peace-enforcement operations in civil wars; finds that while the UN is not well equipped to end wars, it has been helpful in peacekeeping and post-conflict reconstruction.

Henke, Marina E. *Constructing Allied Cooperation: Diplomacy, Payments, and Power in Multilateral Military Coalitions.* **Ithaca, NY: Cornell University Press, 2019.** Explores how countries like the United States use diplomacy and side payments to build coalitions for military operations.

Hultman, Lisa, Jacob D. Kathman, and Megan Shannon. *Peacekeeping in the Midst of War.* **New York: Oxford University Press, 2019.** A rigorous examination of the effectiveness of peacekeepers in reducing battlefield violence and violence against civilians during civil wars.

Lake, David A. *Entangling Relations: American Foreign Policy in Its Century.* **Princeton, NJ: Princeton University Press, 1999.** Considers the different ways that states can institutionalize their relationships with other countries, from empire to informal alignments.

Poast, Paul. *Arguing about Alliances: The Art of Agreement in Military-Pact Negotiations.* **Ithaca, NY: Cornell University Press, 2019.** Examines the bargaining that goes into forging alliances, with an eye toward the conditions that cause negotiations to succeed or fail.

Power, Samantha. *"A Problem from Hell": America and the Age of Genocide,* **rev. ed. New York: Basic Books, 2013.** Graphically details the failings of the United States and the UN in the face of genocide, including the cases of Bosnia and Rwanda.

Snyder, Glenn H. *Alliance Politics.* **Ithaca, NY: Cornell University Press, 1997.** Offers a comprehensive presentation of theory and historical evidence on the origins and maintenance of alliances.

Voeten, Erik. "The Political Origins of the UN Security Council's Ability to Legitimize the Use of Force." *International Organization* **59, no. 3 (Summer 2005): 527–57.** Seeks to explain why people care whether or not the UN authorizes a military operation.

Walt, Stephen M. *The Origins of Alliances*. **Ithaca, NY: Cornell University Press, 1987.** Tests balance of power theory and offers a reformulation that hinges on perceptions of threat, not just power.

Waltz, Kenneth N. *Theory of International Politics*. **1979; repr., Long Grove, IL: Waveland Press, 2010, esp. chaps. 6 and 8.** Presents a modern formulation of balance of power theory and argues that it explains the relative stability of the pre-1945 and Cold War international systems.

Weiss, Thomas G. *What's Wrong with the United Nations (and How to Fix It)*. **Cambridge: Polity, 2008.** An accessible and balanced survey of the strengths and weaknesses of the UN, with suggestions for how the institution could be improved.

6

Violence by Nonstate Actors: Civil War and Terrorism

THE PUZZLE *A great deal of politically motivated violence in the contemporary world is committed by or directed against nonstate actors, particularly rebel groups engaged in civil wars or terrorist networks. Why do some individuals and groups resort to violence against their governments or unarmed civilians?*

Above: Transnational terrorist networks such as the Islamic State use violence to advance their political goals. In March 2017, the Islamic State claimed responsibility for an attack in London, England, in which an assailant drove a car into a crowd of pedestrians along Westminster Bridge, killing four people and wounding more than 50 others before fatally stabbing a police officer.

On September 11, 2001, the United States experienced the worst attack on its homeland since the Japanese bombing of Pearl Harbor. On that day, the threat came not from the naval and air forces of a rival state but from 19 individuals armed with box cutters. This small group of men, affiliated with the terrorist network known as Al Qaeda, hijacked four airplanes and crashed them into the World Trade Center in New York City and the Pentagon in Washington, D.C. Thanks to the heroic efforts of its passengers, a plane likely headed for the White House went down in a western Pennsylvania field. Nearly 3,000 people died in the attacks. In response, the United States launched a "global war on terror," a series of military operations around the world that included the invasion of Afghanistan, whose government had hosted Al Qaeda. The administration of President George W. Bush then made the case for war against Iraq based partly on the argument (now largely discredited) that the regime there could transfer chemical, biological, or nuclear weapons to terrorists.

The wars in Afghanistan and Iraq both had two major phases. In the first, the United States and its allies quickly defeated the armed forces of the opposing states.

The Taliban regime in Afghanistan collapsed after two months; the Iraqi regime fell after six weeks. In both cases, however, victory in the interstate phase of the conflict was followed by a much longer conflict against a different kind of enemy. Both countries descended into civil war as rebellious factions, including elements of the previous regimes, took up arms against one another and the U.S.-installed governments. The United States' role thus shifted from trying to defeat the Iraqi and Afghan militaries to trying to quell two domestic rebellions.

The civil phase of these conflicts lasted much longer and claimed more lives—American, Afghan, and Iraqi—than did the initial invasions. U.S. troops left Iraq in 2011, but the lingering conflict there gave birth to a new militant group—the Islamic State (IS)—whose activities drew the U.S. military back to the region only three years later. Since then, the Islamic State and related groups have organized or inspired terrorist attacks throughout the world, including Africa, Asia, Europe, and the United States. In short, the United States has spent much of the twenty-first century engaged in deadly conflict not with other states but with nonstate actors—transnational terrorist networks and rebel groups within Afghanistan and Iraq.

The U.S. experience is representative of broader developments in world politics. While violence by and against nonstate actors has long been a prominent feature of international politics, its importance has increased in recent years. A great deal of armed conflict in the contemporary world takes place not between states but *within* them (see Figure 6.1 on p. 254). Terrorism has also been a growing international concern, particularly since September 11, 2001, which ushered in a period of increased terrorist violence (see Figure 6.3 on p. 280). How do we explain political violence by nonstate actors?

As a first cut, the tools we use to understand interstate war are quite useful in helping us understand civil war and terrorism. Both phenomena arise when nonstate actors, such as rebel groups or terrorist organizations, have *interests* that bring them into conflict with states. These disputes can lead to conflict when these actors lack access to political *institutions* that could address their demands through peaceful means, leading to a bargaining *interaction* that can bring about violence owing to information problems, commitment problems, and/or issue indivisibility. While some of the specifics may change, we can learn a great deal simply by taking the models from earlier chapters and relabeling State A as "government" and State B as "rebel group" or "terrorist organization."

That said, there is a crucial difference between nonstate actors and states. To understand the problem that nonstate actors face, think of a cause that you care about, such as immigration or the quality of the food in your school's dining halls. Imagine that you wanted to form a group that would lobby the government or university administrators to enact policies that further your cause. To do so, you would have to convince people to volunteer their time and raise money to support your activities. It may be hard to find people who are committed to the same cause, and some may sympathize with your goals but not have spare time or money to donate. This challenge can be daunting, and many would-be activists give up.

Now imagine that pursuing your cause will require your supporters to take up arms against the police or military, plant bombs in shopping malls, or blow themselves up on crowded buses. Finding people to contribute is likely to become quite a bit harder. You will also have to figure out how to buy guns, explosives, and other tools of rebellion. Along the way, there is the danger that people you approach will alert the police to your activities. What circumstances would lead you to take these risks? And how could you get others to follow you? This dilemma is the central challenge faced by rebel groups and terrorist organizations.

Thinking Analytically about Civil War and Terrorism

Rebel groups and terrorist organizations bring together individuals whose interests put them in conflict with either their own or some foreign government. If dissatisfied groups lack access to political institutions that could address their interests peacefully—or if their goals are too extreme to be accommodated by existing institutions—then they may resort to violence against the government and its citizens. But common interests alone are not enough to ensure that individuals will be able to act collectively to produce violence.

Actors who want to fight together face a collective action problem (see Chapter 2). For groups seeking to rebel against a government, or for terrorist organizations seeking to enlist people in dangerous, possibly suicidal, missions, getting support from like-minded individuals is an enduring challenge. Whatever substantive interests they seek to further, all such groups have an organizational interest in finding sympathizers and motivating them to participate in the fight. And governments in conflict with such groups have to implement strategies that diminish the pool of potential supporters and/or encourage free riding. These imperatives profoundly affect the likelihood, conduct, and outcome of violence involving nonstate actors.

Thus, we can understand both civil war and terrorism through a two-step process. In the first step, we consider what factors bring together groups of individuals who are able and willing to use violence to further their interests. In the second step, we ask why the interactions between these groups and their target states sometimes lead to costly, protracted conflicts. Understanding these processes can then help us identify how different strategies and institutions may be able to prevent or defuse this kind of violence.

The Relationship between Civil War and Terrorism

A **civil war** is an armed conflict that occurs between organized actors within a state and that meets some minimum threshold for severity. In most cases, civil wars pit the government of the state against one or more rebel groups, who may also fight among themselves. In some cases, such as Somalia for much of the 1990s, there is no functioning central government to speak of, and conflict arises among several groups, each trying to assume that role. Scholars conventionally require a conflict to cause at least 1,000 battle-related deaths in order to qualify as a civil war, though lower thresholds are sometimes used.[1] Map 6.1 shows countries that experienced a civil war in the period 2010–18 (dark blue) as well as those that experienced a lower-level civil conflict that caused at least 25 battle-related deaths (light blue).

Terrorism is the use or threatened use of violence against noncombatant targets by individuals or nonstate groups for political ends. Terrorism generally consists of attacks by individuals or small groups on civilian targets such as airplanes, trains, schools, or restaurants. The purpose of these acts is not simply to kill the targets but to create widespread fear in the hopes of achieving a particular goal. (We will expand on the definition of terrorism later in the chapter.) The orange dots on Map 6.1 show the location of each terrorist attack in the period 2010–18 that claimed at least one life.

As these definitions make clear, civil war is a kind of armed conflict that is distinguished by the nature of its participants, while terrorism is a strategy for using violence that is distinguished primarily by the nature of its targets. Thus, *civil war* and *terrorism* should not be equated or treated as synonymous. Nevertheless, we study civil war and terrorism in a single chapter for three main reasons.

First, they share a common underlying quality: the use of violence by nonstate actors to achieve political goals. This pairing gives us the opportunity to think about the similarities and differences between these kinds of violence and violence that takes place between states—that is, interstate war. Many of the same tools and concepts used to explain interstate war in Chapter 3 will reappear here, though with some key differences.

More important, as nonstate actors, both rebel groups and terrorist organizations face the same fundamental problem: how to organize individuals and mobilize resources in order to engage in violence. States, almost by definition, have solved this problem. States generally have some capacity to raise money and to enlist or conscript people to fight their wars. Thus, when we consider bargaining between states, we typically take it for granted that the participants have some ability to mobilize resources in order to wield power internationally. We cannot make the same assumption when dealing with nonstate actors. This challenge influences why

civil war
A war in which the main participants are within the same state, such as the government and a rebel group.

terrorism
The use or threatened use of violence against noncombatant targets by individuals or nonstate groups for political ends.

---

1. In addition, for a conflict to be considered a civil war, casualties must be incurred by all sides. One-sided killings—such as when a government massacres civilians—are thus not considered in this category.

MAP 6.1 *Civil War and Terrorist Attacks, 2010–18*

This map depicts the countries that experienced a civil conflict (causing at least 25 battle-related deaths) or a civil war (causing at least 1,000 battle-related deaths) in the period from 2010 to 2018. Each dot represents the location of a terrorist attack against a civilian target (that is, excluding all attacks against military installations) that killed at least one person in that same period.

Aims of Rebel Groups:

- ◼ EXPERIENCED A CIVIL WAR
- ◼ EXPERIENCED CIVIL CONFLICT
- ● FATAL TERRORIST ATTACK

Map sources: Data on civil wars are from UCDP/PRIO Armed Conflict Dataset version 20.1. Therése Pettersson and Magnus Öberg, "Organized Violence, 1989–2019," *Journal of Peace Research* 57, no. 4 (2020): 597–613. Data on terrorist attacks are from National Consortium for the Study of Terrorism and Responses to Terrorism (START), Global Terrorism Database [Data file], 2019, www.start.umd.edu/gtd (accessed 1/14/21).

Arctic Ocean

UNITED KINGDOM
NORWAY
IRELAND
FRANCE
SWEDEN
FINLAND
GERMANY
BELARUS
UKRAINE
SPAIN
ITALY
BOSNIA
GREECE
TUNISIA
MOROCCO
ALGERIA
LIBYA
EGYPT
TURKEY
SYRIA
ISRAEL
LEB.
IRAQ
IRAN
KAZAKHSTAN
UZBEKISTAN
TURKMENISTAN
KYRGYZSTAN
TAJIKISTAN
MONGOLIA
RUSSIA
N. KOREA
S. KOREA
JAPAN
CHINA
NEPAL
SAUDI ARABIA
PAKISTAN
INDIA
MYANMAR (BURMA)
TAIWAN
Pacific Ocean
MAURITANIA
SENEGAL
GUINEA
MALI
NIGER
CHAD
SUDAN
YEMEN
AFGHANISTAN
THAILAND
BANGLADESH
VIETNAM
LAOS
CAMBODIA
PHILIPPINES
NIGERIA
CEN. AFR. REP.
S. SUDAN
ETHIOPIA
SOMALIA
MALAYSIA
BURKINA FASO
CAMEROON
UGANDA
KENYA
RWANDA
BURUNDI
PAPUA NEW GUINEA
IVORY COAST
D. R. CONGO
TANZANIA
INDONESIA
Indian Ocean
ANGOLA
ZAMBIA
MALAWI
MADAGASCAR
NAMIBIA
MOZAMBIQUE
ZIMBABWE
AUSTRALIA
SOUTH AFRICA
BOTSWANA
NEW ZEALAND

some dissatisfied groups end up leading rebellions or terrorist campaigns while others do not.

The second reason for studying these topics together is that the strategies rebel groups and terrorists employ for using violence share some similarities. Both types of groups are, more often than not, weaker than the states they confront, and their strategies have to adjust to this fact. As we will see, rebel groups often use a tactic known as insurgency or "guerrilla warfare," which involves hit-and-run attacks against military, government, and civilian targets. Though not identical, both insurgency and terrorism are forms of **asymmetrical warfare**, or conflict between actors with highly unequal capabilities, that seek to circumvent the superior military strength of the target. These strategies share similarities in terms of how they are intended to work and the challenges they pose to states confronted by them.

Third, there is a very close empirical relationship between civil wars and the incidence of terrorism. As Map 6.1 shows, the overlap between the two kinds of events is striking. Every country that is coded as having a civil conflict or war from 2010 to 2018 also has had at least one terrorist attack. Of the 37,583 recorded terrorist attacks in those years, 82 percent occurred in a country that had a civil war; another 16 percent occurred in a country that had a civil conflict. Only 2 percent occurred in a country that had no civil conflict. Thus, while neither is a necessary ingredient for the other, civil violence and terrorism go hand in hand.

Indeed, many violent nonstate actors are both rebel groups in a civil war and terrorist organizations. Virtually all rebel groups attack civilians to some degree, primarily to dissuade them from collaborating with the government or to coerce them into aiding the rebellion. Beyond that, a significant number of rebel groups systematically use violence against civilians as a strategy for coercing domestic or foreign governments to give in to their demands.[2]

The Islamic State, for example, is one of many rebel groups involved in the Syrian Civil War that broke out in 2011, and it has used conventional means of warfare to seize and hold territory in both Syria and Iraq (for more on the origins of the Islamic State, see "What Shaped Our World?" on p. 276). At the same time, the Islamic State has planned and executed terrorist attacks not only in those countries but also in other parts of the world, such as France, Belgium, and Britain. In addition, it has inspired terrorist attacks by individuals with no formal connection to the group, including mass shootings in San Bernardino, California (December 2015), and Orlando, Florida (June 2016). Similarly, Boko Haram is a rebel group that has sought to control large swaths of northern Nigeria. It also engages extensively in terrorist attacks throughout the country.

Given these observations, recent scholarship has moved away from an earlier tendency to study civil war and terrorism separately and more frequently focuses

---

asymmetrical warfare
Armed conflict between actors with highly unequal military capabilities, such as when rebel groups or terrorists fight strong states.

---

2. Two studies, with somewhat different criteria, estimate that 25–30 percent of rebel groups use terrorism systematically. See Jessica A. Stanton, "Terrorism in the Context of Civil War," *Journal of Politics* 75, no. 4 (2013): 1009–22; and Virginia Page Fortna, "Do Terrorists Win? Rebels' Use of Terrorism and Civil War Outcomes," *International Organization* 69, no. 3 (2015): 519–56.

on the relationship between these kinds of violence.[3] This chapter is guided by that view.

Why Does War Occur within States?

Figure 6.1 shows the number of states involved in interstate and civil wars in each year from 1816 to 2019. Except during periods of large, multilateral wars, in any given year generally more states are involved in civil war than in interstate war. The gap is even more pronounced in the most recent four decades, when civil wars have been much more numerous and have killed millions more people than interstate wars in the same period.[4]

Given that civil wars occur between a government and one or more rebel groups within the same country, why is this topic appropriate to study in a class on international relations, which typically deals with phenomena that cross state borders? There are two main reasons. First, as we will see in this chapter, the theoretical tools that we have developed to explain interstate wars are also very useful in explaining their intrastate counterparts. By examining them side by side, we start to see these two kinds of conflict as instances of a single, broader phenomenon: the use of violence by organized actors to pursue political interests. Seeing interstate and intrastate conflict in this way permits useful comparisons that deepen our understanding of both.

Moreover, civil war is an appropriate topic within the scope of international relations because, while the primary conflict occurs within a single country, the determinants and effects of a civil war are rarely so contained. External actors often play a significant role in the onset, duration, and outcome of civil conflict. Foreign states with an interest in the victory of either the government or the rebels often give money, arms, training, and/or sanctuary to their preferred side. Indeed, some governments intentionally support rebels in an effort to subvert their regional rivals.[5] This aid can be critical in determining whether a rebel group forms in the first place, how long it can sustain its operations against the government, and which side wins. Indeed, most civil wars involve some outside assistance to the rebels, the government, or both.[6]

In addition, civil wars can have spillover effects beyond their borders. As Map 6.1 shows, civil wars often cluster together geographically. By one estimate, a state is twice as likely to experience a civil conflict if one or more of its neighbors is experiencing one.[7] To some extent, this clustering is due to the fact that some of the

---

3. See, for example, Stanton, "Terrorism in the Context of Civil War"; Fortna, "Do Terrorists Win?"; Michael G. Findley and Joseph K. Young, "Terrorism and Civil War: A Spatial and Temporal Approach to a Conceptual Problem," *Perspectives on Politics* 10, no. 2 (June 2012): 285–305; and Jakana Thomas, "Rewarding Bad Behavior: How Governments Respond to Terrorism in Civil War," *American Journal of Political Science* 58, no. 4 (October 2014): 804–18.

4. See, for example, James D. Fearon and David D. Laitin, "Ethnicity, Insurgency, and Civil War," *American Political Science Review* 97, no. 1 (2003): 75–90.

5. Melissa M. Lee, *Crippling Leviathan: How Foreign Subversion Weakens the State* (Ithaca, NY: Cornell University Press, 2020).

6. See, for example, Patrick M. Regan, *Civil Wars and Foreign Powers: Outside Intervention in Intrastate Conflict* (Ann Arbor: University of Michigan Press, 2000).

7. Halvard Buhaug and Kristian Skrede Gleditsch, "Contagion or Confusion? Why Conflicts Cluster in Space," *International Studies Quarterly* 52, no. 2 (2008): 215–33.

FIGURE 6.1 *Interstate and Civil Wars, 1816–2019*

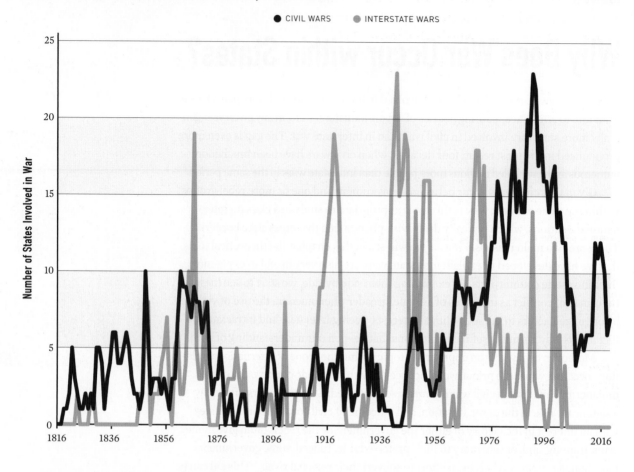

● CIVIL WARS   ● INTERSTATE WARS

Figure sources: For 1816–2007, data are from the Correlates of War project version 4.0; see Meredith Reid Sarkees and Frank Wayman, *Resort to War: 1816–2007* (Washington, DC: CQ Press, 2010). For 2008–19, data are from the UCDP/PRIO Armed Conflict Dataset version 20.1; see Therése Pettersson and Magnus Öberg, "Organized Violence, 1989–2019," *Journal of Peace Research* 57, no. 4 (2020): 597–613.

risk factors of civil war, such as low economic development, also cluster together: poor states tend to have poor neighbors. But there is also reason to believe that civil wars, like diseases, can be contagious, particularly when the groups participating in a conflict straddle an international border. Civil wars also create refugee flows that can burden neighboring states, and they may involve widespread crimes against humanity that shock the consciences of those far away from the actual fighting.

These harms have motivated greater international efforts to intervene in civil wars, with the United Nations (UN) increasingly citing purely domestic conflicts as "threats to international peace and security." Indeed, of the 71 peacekeeping operations undertaken by the UN from 1948 to 2019, 41 were deployed to conflicts within a single state and another 12 dealt with conflicts having both international and civil dimensions.[8]

The long-running war in the Democratic Republic of the Congo (DRC) is an extreme but illustrative example of the interdependence between interstate and intrastate violence. The conflict that started in 1996 had its roots in the civil war and genocide that took place in neighboring Rwanda two years earlier (see Chapter 5).

---

8. Descriptions of UN peacekeeping operations can be found at https://peacekeeping.un.org/en (accessed 9/14/20).

The genocide ended when the Tutsi-dominated Rwandan Patriotic Front ousted the Hutu-led government that had perpetrated the killings. Large numbers of Hutu militants then fled across the border into the DRC (then called Zaire) and started carrying out raids against their former homeland. In an example of cross-border contagion, the Rwandan government responded by arming Tutsis living in eastern Zaire, who then joined with other groups to form a broader resistance movement against the Zairian regime. Sensing a chance to rid themselves of a hostile neighbor, Rwanda, Uganda, and Angola openly intervened on the side of the rebels, who unseated Zaire's government in May 1997, at which point the country was renamed the DRC.

Conflict resumed the following year when the new Congolese government turned on its former allies and asked them to leave. The ensuing war, which officially ended in 2003 but has continued to smolder to this day, involved 25 different rebel groups supported directly or indirectly by eight different countries. In addition to claiming millions of lives, the war has led to massive atrocities, including horrific levels of rape. The resulting humanitarian crisis spurred the deployment of 20,000 UN peacekeepers in 1999, but these forces have been unable to stop the violence entirely. Given the scale and number of countries involved, this conflict has sometimes been called "Africa's World War,"[9] and it stands as a stark example of how civil conflicts can originate in international events and have effects that resonate beyond the borders of a single state.

The civil war in the Democratic Republic of the Congo was fueled by the intervention of neighboring states. The war, which began in 1996, has claimed millions of lives, led to atrocities such as widespread rape and torture, and involved the forcible recruitment of thousands of child soldiers.

Why Rebel?

At the root of all civil wars is some conflict of interests between the government and a subset of the population. The literature on civil wars generally classifies these conflicts as stemming from two different sources: grievances and greed.[10] Grievances can arise when government policies discriminate against members of a particular group, whether by repressing their language or culture, blocking their access to jobs or political office, or denying them government services, such as education, health care, and public infrastructure. These kinds of policies can lead to vast inequalities in wealth and quality of life among groups. Greed is a group's desire to control more of the country's economic resources. For instance, groups may want a greater share of the profits from natural resource extraction (such as oil or minerals) or privileged access to jobs and government largesse.

---

9. Gérard Prunier, *Africa's World War: Congo, the Rwandan Genocide, and the Making of a Continental Catastrophe* (New York: Oxford University Press, 2009).

10. Paul Collier and Anke Hoeffler, "Greed and Grievance in Civil War," *Oxford Economic Papers* 56, no. 4 (2004): 563–95.

In either case, conflicts are rooted in individuals' and groups' basic interests in their own economic and social well-being, autonomy, and power. When these interests bring them into conflict with their government, dissatisfied groups have three options: they can try to leave the state, they can try to alter its policies, or they can try to take over the state altogether. Thus, intrastate conflicts give rise to demands that involve the same kinds of issues that we saw in interstate conflicts: territory, policy, and regime.

Territorial conflict in this context takes the form of separatism or irredentism. Both arise when a rebel group seeks to carve out a piece of the state's territory. A group is **separatist** if it wants to create its own independent state in the territory. Separatism generally arises when a group that is concentrated in a particular region of the country has grievances with the central government and expects to fare better under its own governance.

The newest state in the international system, South Sudan, achieved its independence from Sudan in 2011 after decades of separatist conflict that claimed more than 2 million lives (see "Controversy" on p. 258). Separatist conflicts also gave rise to East Timor, which separated from Indonesia in 2002; Kosovo, which declared its independence from Serbia in 2008; and Eritrea, which won its independence from Ethiopia in 1993. Most separatist conflicts are not as successful. Rebels in Chechnya have been fighting for that region's independence from Russia for over two decades, to no avail. The Liberation Tigers of Tamil Eelam (or Tamil Tigers) fought for a separate state in northern Sri Lanka from 1983 until their defeat in 2009. The United States also experienced a failed separatist movement when the Confederate states seceded in 1861 and were defeated in the ensuing civil war.

A rebel group is **irredentist** if members seek to attach their territory to a country next door. Irredentism usually arises when people of one state share ethnic or religious ties with the people in the neighboring state and therefore expect that their interests will be better served under its governance. For example, for much of the twentieth century, the government of Great Britain clashed with Catholics in Northern Ireland who wanted to join that region with the rest of Ireland, which is majority Catholic. The ongoing civil war in Ukraine is fueled by Russian speakers in the eastern portion of the country who would like to join Russia.

If leaving is impractical, a group motivated by grievances or greed may threaten civil war in order to change the policies pursued by the central government. Some minority groups in India, for example, have resorted to violence in order to win official recognition of their language—an act that confers a variety of political and social benefits. The civil war in Iraq pitted a variety of groups against each other and against the U.S.-led occupation in order to influence the policies of the new state. Members of the Sunni Arab minority fought to preserve the privileges that they had enjoyed under Saddam Hussein (himself Sunni), secure their share of Iraq's oil revenue, and protect their political, civil, and religious rights. Kurds, concentrated in the northern regions, sought to make sure that the new state would be highly decentralized, giving them autonomy in their region as well as influence over its oil.

Finally, dissatisfied groups might seek to seize control of the central government and establish a new regime. The civil war in Syria broke out in 2011 because of dissatisfaction with the repressive rule of President Bashar al-Assad. The Assad

separatist

An actor that seeks to create an independent state on territory carved from an existing state.

irredentist

An actor that seeks to detach a region from one country and attach it to another, usually because of shared ethnic or religious ties.

family, which has run Syria since 1970, comes from the Alawite sect of Islam, which makes up about 11 percent of the Syrian population but receives a vastly disproportionate share of influence and benefits. The numerous rebel factions that are seeking to oust Assad come from other, more populous groups that have been excluded from power. During the 1970s and 1980s, White-minority governments in Rhodesia (now Zimbabwe) and South Africa fought civil wars against groups pushing for democratic systems that would lead to Black-majority rule. Political exclusion of a significant group is a common reason why rebels seek to overturn the existing polity.[11] Clashes over control of the central government are also common in newly independent states when the retreat of the colonial power creates a space for groups to fight over control of the new state.

It should be apparent from this discussion that rebel groups often form on the basis of ethnic and/or religious divisions: Catholic versus Protestant, Hutu versus Tutsi, Sunni versus Shiite, and so on. Indeed, the majority of civil wars have an ethnic or religious component to them. As a result, it might be tempting to assume that civil wars are caused by ethnic or religious differences and that countries divided in this way have a higher risk of conflict. In fact, this is not the case, and there are many diverse countries that do not experience internal violence.[12] Ethnic or religious differences alone do not cause the conflicts of interest that underlie civil wars. It is when these differences give rise to discriminatory economic and social policies, inequality, political exclusion, and/or intolerance that demands for territory, policy change, or regime change can arise.[13]

Members of the Kashmiri separatist group Hizbul Mujahideen have used terrorism to impose costs on India with the goal of ending Indian rule in Kashmir so that the region can join Pakistan. Here, supporters of the separatist movement mourn the death of Burhan Wani, a commander of Hizbul Mujahideen who was killed in a confrontation with Indian forces.

When Does Dissatisfaction Lead to Armed Opposition?

Of course, most countries have dissatisfied people who would like greater control over their territory, more influence over policy, privileged status for their language and culture, a bigger share of the country's wealth, a larger role in

11. Lars-Erik Cederman, Andreas Wimmer, and Brian Min, "Why Do Ethnic Groups Rebel? New Data and Analysis," *World Politics* 62, no. 1 (2010): 87–119.

12. Fearon and Laitin, "Ethnicity, Insurgency, and Civil War."

13. See Donald L. Horowitz, *Ethnic Groups in Conflict*, 2nd ed. (Berkeley: University of California Press, 2000); and Lars-Erik Cederman, Nils B. Weidmann, and Kristian Skrede Gleditsch, "Horizontal Inequalities and Ethnonationalist Civil War: A Global Comparison," *American Political Science Review* 105, no. 3 (2011): 478–95. The danger associated with excluding ethnic groups from power raises the intriguing question of why some leaders do it anyway. For an interesting analysis of this question, see Philip Roessler, *Ethnic Politics and State Power in Africa: The Logic of the Coup-Civil War Trap* (Cambridge: Cambridge University Press, 2016).

Should Every Group Have a State of Its Own?

On July 9, 2011, tens of thousands of people gathered in Freedom Square in Juba, South Sudan, to witness the birth of the international community's newest state. As the joyous crowd looked on, the flag of the Republic of Sudan came down, and the flag of the Republic of South Sudan was raised to the sound of the new national anthem. The country's first president signed its constitution and took the oath of office. Though the mood was jubilant, it was tinged with sadness, since the road to South Sudan's independence had been long and bloody.

South Sudan was the twenty-fifth state to join the international system since 1990, and in still many other places around the world, people are struggling for states of their own to no avail. The Israeli-held West Bank and Gaza Strip, South Ossetia and Abkhazia in Georgia, majority-Russian areas in eastern Ukraine, Tibet in China, Aceh in Indonesia, Chechnya in Russia, Catalonia in Spain—all are regions whose people are seeking independence and that, in some cases, exercise de facto statehood that is not internationally recognized.

Applying the Concepts

Should all these regions get states of their own? The main argument in favor of statehood rests on the principle of self-determination: the idea that communities have the right to choose how they are governed and to which authority they are subject. Proponents argue that members of minority groups are more likely to have their **interests** met by a state whose boundaries conform to those of their group than by a state whose boundaries were imposed by outsiders. The argument against statehood is that it is rarely possible to carve out new states in a way that protects everyone's interests; that allowing secession can set off a chain reaction of conflictual **interactions**; and that groups' interests can instead be better met through **institutions** that protect minority rights.

The principle of self-determination stands in opposition to the practice of imperialism, whereby foreign powers exercise control over conquered lands, and self-determination movements were instrumental in bringing about the end of formal imperialism after World War II. Although few colonies remain in the world, the aftereffects of the imperial era are still ubiquitous—particularly in the existence of states whose boundaries were drawn by foreigners without much regard to the interests of the people living there. Such was the case with South Sudan. Originally colonized and jointly ruled by the British and the Egyptians, the region was joined with northern Sudan prior to gaining independence as the Republic of Sudan in 1956.

The union of the two Sudans was fraught with tension from the outset. Most northerners are Arabic-speaking Muslims, while most southerners either are Christian or practice indigenous religions. Home to the bulk of Sudan's population and urban centers, the northern region dominated the country's political and economic life and enjoyed the lion's share of its oil revenues. Despite the south's desire for greater autonomy, the north wanted to hold on to the southern region, which contains about 80 percent of the country's oil reserves.

As a result of these conflicting interests, rebellion broke out in the south in 1955, shortly before Sudan became independent, and the country experienced civil war for all but 10 of the next 50 years. A deal struck in 2005 provided for a popular vote on South Sudan's future, and in a referendum held in January 2011, 98.8 percent of the region's inhabitants voted for independence. Thus, the people of South Sudan had a very compelling case for independence. Indeed, granting their demand earlier would have prevented a great deal of suffering and death.

A woman in Juba encourages people to vote in the January 2011 separation referendum.

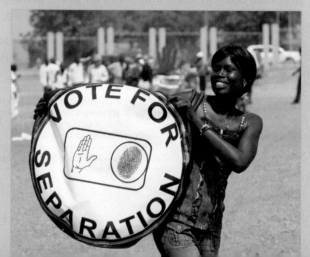

For this reason, some have advocated partition into separate states as a practical solution to ethnic civil wars.[a]

But what should be done if not evereryone living in the secessionist region would have their interests served by a new state? In the case of South Sudan, opposition to independence was minimal, but in Kosovo, which declared independence from Serbia in 2008, a significant minority of ethnic Serbs do not want separation and worry about their fate. In such cases, secession may give rise to further conflict as newly created minorities struggle within the new state. Even if possible, a "clean" partition—that is, one in which no minorities are left on either side—may require large population transfers, which can themselves be quite brutal. South Sudan's border with Sudan is also contested in places, leading to militarized threats and violence.

Another concern is that allowing groups to secede can set off a cascade of further demands for secession. The principle of self-determination is silent with respect to what criteria a group should meet in order to merit its own state. Does everyone need to have the same religion, speak the same language, or have the same skin color? Can any collection of people, no matter how small, proclaim themselves a nation and seek recognition? In the absence of clear principles for drawing lines, the potential for violent conflict is high.

South Sudan is a case in point, since the new country is as much an artificial creation as the state it left. The people come from more than a dozen different ethnic groups, speak many different languages, and follow different religious faiths. Indeed, less than two years after independence was achieved, a political struggle between leaders representing the two largest ethnic groups cast the country into a civil war that by some estimates killed 400,000, displaced 4 million people, and cast 6 million into starvation. Given these differences, there could be an argument for breaking South Sudan into ever-smaller units. But where does the process end? The international community's hesitation to recognize new states rests in large part on similar concerns about a slippery slope that could lead to the splintering of the entire system. Thus, partition may set off a chain of conflictual interactions, both within newly created states and between them.[b] Fortunately, South Sudanese president Salva Kiir and his main rival, Riek Machar, signed an agreement in February 2020 aimed at ending the country's civil war, though disagreements remain.[c]

In the end, those sympathetic to the plight of "trapped" minorities might argue instead for institutions that protect those groups' interests without redrawing borders.

Countries with heterogeneous populations have fostered civil peace through democracy, rules protecting minority rights, and institutions that give autonomy to regions where such groups are the majority. While partition may be necessary and desirable in some cases, it can be more practical instead to promote institutions that make it possible for diverse people to live together rather than granting every request to live apart.

Thinking Analytically

1. What criteria should the international community use to decide when it should support the creation of a new state like South Sudan?

2. What are some alternatives to partition that might have addressed the interests of the people of South Sudan?

a. Chaim Kaufmann, "Possible and Impossible Solutions to Ethnic Civil Wars," *International Security* 20, no. 4 (1996): 136–75.

b. Nicholas Sambanis, "Partition as a Solution to Ethnic War: An Empirical Critique of the Theoretical Literature," *World Politics* 52, no. 4 (2000): 437–83.

c. "South Sudan rivals Salva Kiir and Riek Machar strike unity deal," BBC News, February 22, 2020, www.bbc.com/news/world-africa-51562367 (accessed 10/12/20).

government, or a different kind of government altogether. And yet, civil wars are relatively rare. Grievances and greed are necessary to fuel the emergence of armed opposition groups, but they are clearly not sufficient. Why do some dissatisfied groups organize to further their interests through the threat or use of violence while others, indeed most, do not?

We can illustrate this question more concretely by considering the uprisings that spread across the Middle East and North Africa in the winter and spring of 2011. The Arab Spring (so named not only because of the season in which it occurred, but also because spring denotes an awakening) involved mass protests in various countries, including Tunisia, Libya, Egypt, Syria, Yemen, and Bahrain. Though local circumstances varied, all the protests were driven to some degree by the same set of factors: a large number of unemployed young men, an increase in food prices, and long-standing dissatisfaction with corrupt and repressive governments. In all cases, the protesters demanded the removal of government officials and/or liberalization of the regimes.

In spite of these similarities, the outcomes varied quite significantly. In Tunisia and Egypt, leaders stepped down in response to largely peaceful mass protests. In Bahrain, protests were swiftly put down by the government. The opposition movement in Libya organized into an armed rebel group that waged open war against the Libyan regime and ultimately succeeded in ousting it; in the power vacuum that ensued, the country then fell back into civil war. In Syria, a violent crackdown led to the emergence of a full-scale civil war that has claimed hundreds of thousands of lives, caused violence to spread into neighboring states, and, at the time

Not all conflicts between dissatisfied groups and the government result in civil war. Mass protests in Tunisia led to the resignation of President Zine al-Abidine Ben Ali in January 2011 and the establishment of a new government without large-scale violence.

of this writing, showed little sign of ending anytime soon. What might explain this variation?

In general, three sets of factors help explain the emergence of organized, armed opposition groups: features of the group and its interests, features of the country in which the group resides, and features of the international system that influence the possibilities for external support.

Group-Level Explanations In some cases, the nature of a group's interests facilitates its ability to organize. Individuals' religious or ideological beliefs may motivate them to see contributing to the cause as beneficial in its own right. In a study of why individuals participated in El Salvador's civil war, Elisabeth Wood found that many peasants were motivated by a sense of justice and a desire to do something meaningful with their lives.[14] When this is the case, there is no incentive to free ride and the collective action problem does not arise.

Similarly, individuals from the same ethnic or religious group may have higher levels of trust or collective solidarity and feel a stronger social disincentive to free ride when working with one another. Indeed, the majority of civil wars involve mobilization along ethnic lines, meaning that the rebels and the government tend to draw support from different ethnic groups.[15] As we already saw, this pattern may reflect interethnic tensions over the division of wealth and political power or the status of a particular religion, language, or culture. But even if ethnicity does not give rise to a grievance, it can be a resource for mobilizing people for or against the government. Because people of the same ethnic group tend to trust one another, it is easier to recruit fighters and raise funds from people of the same ethnicity than from outsiders. Indeed, when people trust their ethnic or religious kin more than they trust others, elites can strategically highlight and manipulate group differences in order to build a base of support.

Particularly when accompanied by violence, this strategy can cause a society to polarize along ethnic or religious lines, as individuals seek protection among their "own kind." This process of polarization played out rapidly and with tragic consequences in Iraq's capital city, Baghdad, following the American invasion. Before that, Baghdad was home to both Shiites and Sunnis, many living in mixed neighborhoods. In the aftermath of the invasion, radicals on each side started targeting those from the other group. Even if you were, say, a moderate Shiite who preferred to live in peace with your Sunni neighbors, the insecurity of knowing that you and your family might be attacked simply because of your religious identity would lead you to seek protection from other Shiites. This dynamic caused people to fill the ranks of Sunni or Shiite militias, thereby increasing the power bases of the militia leaders

---

14. Elisabeth Jean Wood, *Insurgent Collective Action and Civil War in El Salvador* (Cambridge: Cambridge University Press, 2003).

15. Fearon and Laitin, in "Ethnicity, Insurgency, and Civil War," report that 51 percent of civil wars between 1945 and 1999 were fought along ethnic lines, and another 18 percent were mixed or ambiguous. Using different data and criteria, Nicholas Sambanis reports that 77 out of 109 civil wars from 1960 to 1999 were ethnic in nature; see Nicholas Sambanis, "Do Ethnic and Nonethnic Civil Wars Have the Same Causes? A Theoretical and Empirical Inquiry (Part 1)," *Journal of Conflict Resolution* 45, no. 3 (2001): 259–82.

who had sparked the violence in the first place. People also fled areas controlled by the other sect, causing mixed neighborhoods to all but vanish from the map.[16] This process of polarization is akin to the security dilemma in conflicts between states, in which conflicts can escalate simply out of each side's fear that the other side may escalate (see Chapter 3).

In addition, some traditional societies may be organized into tribes, which are substate groups with familial or ethnic ties. Tribes generally have their own systems of formal or informal governance, which facilitate collective action. If a tribal leader chooses to join a rebellion, the leader can bring along other members of the tribe. The civil war in Libya stemmed in large part from the decision of several key tribes to withdraw their support from the government.

In the absence of strong ethnic ties or ideological motivations, groups that seek to mobilize against the government have to find other ways to encourage participation. One way is to compensate supporters materially. Rebel groups operating in areas of Africa with easy access to diamonds or other precious minerals can sell these goods on international markets, sometimes illegally, and funnel the proceeds to their fighters. The sale of so-called blood diamonds enriched rebels fighting in Sierra Leone (1996–99), while the long-running civil conflict in Colombia was fueled by the cocaine trade. Indeed, some rebel groups are essentially criminal gangs deeply engaged in smuggling, human trafficking, and extortion.[17]

Another way rebel groups may amass fighters is through forcible recruitment, or kidnapping. Men, women, and children may be taken from their homes at gunpoint and used as fighters, porters, messengers, spies, or sexual slaves. This practice was shockingly illustrated in April 2014, when nearly 300 Nigerian schoolgirls were kidnapped and forced to marry members of the rebel group Boko Haram. The UN estimates that tens of thousands of children under the age of 18 are participating in civil conflicts around the world.[18]

Country-Level Factors
Certain features of a country can also contribute to the risk that armed opposition will emerge. Three in particular are important to note. The first has to do with the country's political institutions or regime type. The incentive to threaten or use violence depends in part on whether the country's normal political processes provide for peaceful methods of redressing grievances. After all, fighting is very costly, so it makes sense to seek policy change or influence through existing political channels, if possible. If groups can pursue their goals by running candidates in elections or securing their rights through courts, then they have an alternative to taking up arms. This suggests that democratic countries should have a lower risk of experiencing civil wars, a hypothesis for which there is some evidence.[19]

---

16. For some detailed maps showing the changes in the ethnic distribution in Baghdad from 2003 to 2009, see http://gulf2000.columbia.edu/maps.shtml (accessed 9/14/20).

17. See, for example, John Mueller, "The Banality of 'Ethnic War'," *International Security* 25, no. 1 (2000): 42–70.

18. For the UN program on children and armed conflict, see https://childrenandarmedconflict.un.org (accessed 9/14/20).

19. Håvard Hegre, Tanja Ellingsen, Scott Gates, and Nils Petter Gleditsch, "Toward a Democratic Civil Peace? Democracy, Political Change, and Civil War, 1816–1992," *American Political Science Review* 95, no. 1 (2001): 33–48.

Nevertheless, the relationship between a country's political institutions and the possibility of civil war is complicated by another consideration: the ability of a rebel group to form depends in part on the government's repressive capacity—that is, how easily it can prevent, deter, or eliminate armed opposition. In this respect, authoritarian governments can have an advantage, owing to extensive police and surveillance activities, a greater willingness to use violence against their own citizens, and the absence of civil liberties. As a result of these competing considerations, there is reason to believe that the risk of civil war is highest in countries that are neither fully democratic nor strongly autocratic, because they lack both effective channels of peaceful participation and an effective apparatus of repression.[20]

A second factor that is known to influence a country's civil war risk is its wealth. That poor countries are much more likely to experience civil wars than rich countries is the strongest and most consistent finding in the scholarly literature. There is some disagreement, however, as to the mechanism underlying this relationship. One natural interpretation is that people in poor countries have greater reason to be unhappy with their lot. Poverty breeds desperation, and a lack of economic opportunities can also lead to a large pool of unemployed young men who can be recruited as fighters. By contrast, people in rich countries may find that their lives are too comfortable to undertake the risks associated with violent strategies.[21]

An alternative interpretation hinges on the government's capacity to prevent and defeat rebellions. Richer states tend to have better and stronger police and military forces as well as the capacity to project their authority throughout the country. They may also have greater resources with which to compensate disaffected groups. By contrast, poorer countries often have police and militaries that are not much better trained or equipped than their domestic opponents. With more limited resources, they may also have a hard time exerting their authority outside of one or two main cities. The inability to project forces throughout the country makes it possible for rebel groups to organize in places that are beyond the government's effective reach.[22]

This last insight has led scholars to think about a third set of country-level factors that can affect civil wars: those that make it easier or harder for governments to find and defeat rebels. Civil wars are more likely to occur in populous countries, since rebels can more easily recruit from and hide in large populations. They are also more likely in countries that cover large areas, which are hard to police. Some scholarship has also suggested that civil war risk is higher in countries with rugged terrain, such as jungles and mountains. The difficulty of rooting rebels out of

---

20. There is some controversy on this point. Hegre et al., "Toward a Democratic Civil Peace?" and Fearon and Laitin, "Ethnicity, Insurgency, and Civil War," both showed a high risk of civil war in "anocracies"— that is, states that are neither fully democratic nor fully autocratic. This view was called into question by James Raymond Vreeland in "The Effect of Political Regime on Civil War: Unpacking Anocracy," *Journal of Conflict Resolution* 52, no. 3 (2008): 401–25. It may be that this relationship holds for some kinds of civil wars and not others. For example, Halvard Buhaug argues that "semi-democracies" have the highest risk of civil wars over government or policy, while democracies have a higher risk of territorial conflict; see Halvard Buhaug, "Relative Capability and Rebel Objective in Civil War," *Journal of Peace Research* 43, no. 6 (2006): 691–708. For a recent review of this literature, see Håvard Hegre, "Democracy and Armed Conflict," *Journal of Peace Research* 51, no. 2 (2014): 159–72.

21. Collier and Hoeffler, "Greed and Grievance in Civil War."

22. Fearon and Laitin, "Ethnicity, Insurgency, and Civil War."

Russia has been supporting separatists in eastern Ukraine directly and indirectly since unrest broke out in 2014. Ukraine and Western supporters of the government believe that Russian "volunteers" often fight with the secessionists. Here, suspected Russian soldiers take cover in the trenches outside Shyrokyne.

mountainous terrain explains why the English spent considerable effort during the thirteenth and fourteenth centuries incorporating the rebellious Welsh into their kingdom and why the United States in the twenty-first century has had such a hard time eliminating the Taliban from the mountains that straddle the Afghanistan-Pakistan border. Nevertheless, there is some debate among scholars about whether these kinds of examples generalize to a broader pattern.[23]

International Factors Finally, rebel groups may be able to obtain resources if there are foreign countries that have an interest in their cause. Though civil wars pit rebels against the government of their own state, most civil wars witness some meddling by other countries. Foreign states may intervene directly by sending their forces across the border to assist one side or the other; more commonly, sympathetic states may give arms, money, or training to rebel groups. Rebels may also operate from bases in neighboring countries, allowing them to organize and train in sanctuaries that are hard for the government to reach.[24]

There are several reasons why foreign governments might have an interest in supporting or hosting rebels. One possibility is that they share the interests of the rebel group. Just as two states with aligned interests may seek to cooperate militarily to improve the bargaining outcome (see Chapter 5), a state whose interests are aligned with those of a rebel group may look for ways to increase the group's fighting capabilities. Irredentist groups—that is, rebel groups seeking to join their land

---

23. Fearon and Laitin, in "Ethnicity, Insurgency, and Civil War," show that more mountainous countries experience higher civil war risk. But studies that look at variation within countries have found that mountainous regions are not necessarily more likely to be the site of civil conflict than nonmountainous regions; see, for example, Halvard Buhaug and Jan Ketil Rød, "Local Determinants of African Civil Wars, 1970–2001," *Political Geography* 25, no. 3 (March 2006): 315–35.

24. Idean Salehyan, *Rebels without Borders: Transnational Insurgencies in World Politics* (Ithaca, NY: Cornell University Press, 2009).

to that of a neighboring state—are likely to receive such support from the state they hope to join. During the civil war in the former Yugoslavia (see Chapter 5), Serbia gave aid to ethnic Serbs living in Bosnia and Croatia who wanted to carve out a "Greater Serbia" from these lands. Russia has given military support to ethnic Russians in eastern Ukraine who started a separatist war in 2014 with the goal of either joining Russia or creating a new Russian majority state.

More broadly, states or individuals may support rebellions that involve ethnic kin in other states.[25] For example, Irish rebels fighting British rule in Northern Ireland received money from Irish Americans who sympathized with their cause. Rebel groups may also attract foreign support because of their ideology. During the Cold War, movements espousing communist ideals often received support from the Soviet Union or China. Similarly, Iran has, since its Islamic revolution in 1979, been active in supporting militant Islamist groups such as Hamas, a Palestinian group, and Hezbollah, which operates in Lebanon.

By supporting groups with aligned interests, a foreign state can force the government to make greater concessions, or it can improve the chances that the rebels will replace the government altogether and implement policies closer to the foreign state's ideal point. This may be a particularly attractive strategy when the foreign state is weak relative to the target. In the 1970s, Somalia built up a separatist movement in Ethiopia after several attempts to seize Somali-inhabited territory through more conventional means failed. Thus, supporting rebels was seen as a way around Somalia's military weakness (though this strategy ultimately failed as well).

A second possibility is that outsiders may support rebels not because they care about the rebels' goals, per se, but because they have other conflicts of interest with the government. In these cases, support for rebels can be a relatively low-cost way for one state to impose costs on another in the hopes of gaining concessions, tying down some of the opponent's resources at home, or hastening the ouster of a hostile government. For example, after Eritrea won its independence from Ethiopia, the Eritrean government gave support to other rebel movements in Ethiopia in order to strengthen its hand in a border dispute that arose after the separation. More generally, states that have long-standing disputes with their neighbors have a high likelihood of supporting and/or hosting rebel groups against their rivals.[26]

In some cases, the interests of outside parties can cause civil wars to become **proxy wars**, or conflicts in which two opposing states support opposite sides in a civil war within some third state. Such proxy wars were common during the Cold War, when the dangers of a direct confrontation between the superpowers were so great that conflict was often channeled through other actors. Thus, the Soviet Union and China supported communist rebels in South Vietnam, Laos, and Cambodia, while the United States supported the governments of those states. For its

proxy wars
Conflicts in which two opposing states "fight" by supporting opposite sides in a war, such as the government and rebels in a third state.

25. Stephen M. Saideman, *The Ties That Divide: Ethnic Politics, Foreign Policy, and International Conflict* (New York: Columbia University Press, 2001). See also Lars-Erik Cederman, Luc Girardin, and Kristian Skrede Gleditsch, "Ethnonationalist Triads: Assessing the Influence of Kin Groups on Civil Wars," *World Politics* 61, no. 3 (2009): 403–37.

26. Idean Salehyan, Kristian Skrede Gleditsch, and David E. Cunningham, "Explaining External Support for Insurgent Groups," *International Organization* 65, no. 4 (October 2011): 709–44.

part, the United States supported rebels in countries with pro-Soviet governments like Nicaragua, Afghanistan, and Angola. The civil war that started in Yemen in 2015 has similarly become a battleground in a proxy war between Saudi Arabia and Iran. Unfortunately for the inhabitants of these countries, there is a significant cost to being a pawn in other states' conflicts: civil wars in which both the rebels and the government receive external support tend to last longer, thanks to additional fuel that outsiders bring to the fire.[27]

All these factors contribute in some measure to explaining why Libya, of all the countries that experienced protests during the 2011 Arab Spring, had the most successful armed rebellion. The Libyan rebels benefited from the country's large size and the regime's relatively weak grip on its eastern regions, where the rebellion took hold before the government could stamp it out. The strong tribal structure in Libya also facilitated collective action, since tribal leaders who went into opposition brought with them the resources and manpower of their tribes. Rebels also profited, literally, from their ability to seize oil production and exporting facilities. Sales of oil from rebel-controlled ports helped to finance arms purchases. Finally, and most notably, the Libyan rebels benefited from Western intervention on their behalf, which came in the form of air strikes against pro-government forces, arms, and training. Though intervention was justified primarily as a humanitarian act, the United States had long seen Libyan leader Mu'ammar Qaddafi as a hostile and unpredictable influence in the region and seized the opportunity to oust him. In other Arab-Spring countries, by contrast, rebels were less likely to oust governments backed by powerful foreign governments. The United States looked the other way when Bahrain, a key strategic ally, cracked down on its protesters, and Russia's support for the Syrian regime constrained the prospects of intervention in support of the rebellion there.

Civil War as a Bargaining Failure

We have seen that the potential for civil violence arises when (1) there are groups of people within a country motivated by greed or grievances that put their interests in conflict with those of the government; (2) those people cannot pursue their grievances through regular political institutions; and (3) those people can, owing to their own resources, foreign support, and/or the state's weakness, overcome the collective action problem to recruit enough fighters and purchase enough weaponry to pose a threat. Once these conditions are met, the interaction between the rebels and the government can start to look like the bargaining interaction introduced in the interstate context in Chapter 3: two actors with opposing interests bargaining in the shadow of threats to use force.

As with interstate conflicts, civil conflicts can, in theory, be resolved through compromises that would allow the actors to avoid the horrendous costs associated with war. A territorial dispute could lead to a negotiated secession or, more likely, a grant of autonomy that would give the rebel group many of the benefits of self-rule

---

27. See, for example, Dylan Balch-Lindsay, Andrew J. Enterline, and Kyle A. Joyce, "Third-Party Intervention and the Civil War Process," *Journal of Peace Research* 45, no. 3 (2008): 345–63.

in its region.[28] Regime and policy disputes can be defused through policy concessions or power-sharing arrangements that give rebels greater representation in the government. Thus, once a capable opposition group has emerged, the puzzle of civil war is the same as the puzzle of international war: Why do the actors sometimes fail to reach bargains that would permit them to avoid the costs of war?

The three mechanisms discussed in Chapter 3—information problems, commitment problems, and indivisibilities—are all relevant in answering this question, though, as we will see, commitment problems loom particularly large in this context.[29]

Civil War from Incomplete Information As in international bargaining, incomplete information can arise if the capabilities and resolve of each side are hard to observe. In the context of civil conflicts, it can be particularly difficult to gauge the size and effectiveness of rebel groups, which often organize covertly and take steps to hide their strength (or weakness) in order to avoid government crackdowns. Moreover, there may be less of an opportunity for prewar communication and diplomacy between the government and rebel leaders, since rebels do not enjoy the same protection from arrest or execution that international diplomats enjoy.

Some scholars find informational arguments to be less convincing as explanations for most civil wars because these conflicts tend to last so long. While the median duration of interstate wars since 1945 is three months, the corresponding figure for civil wars is six years.[30] Recalling the argument from Chapter 3 that wars can remove uncertainty about relative strength and resolve (see the "How Do We Know?" box on p. 129), it seems unlikely that these conflicts would last years, even decades, if the underlying problem was simply a lack of information.

Nonetheless, much recent research has emphasized the importance of information that the general public can provide about either the government or insurgents. Many civil wars are guerrilla wars, where the battle, so to speak, is really for the "hearts and minds" of the people. With insurgents operating in the countryside or hiding in areas difficult for the government to access, the government needs information from the public about the rebels—how strong they are, what they appear to be planning, and so on. However, people will provide this information only if they support the government, are protected from reprisals by the insurgents, or are otherwise induced to do so by community- or individual-level benefits. The rebels, in turn, typically seek to earn the loyalty of the local populace to prevent them from sharing information with the government. How to win this contest for hearts and minds remains controversial (see "Insurgency and Counterinsurgency: The Strategies of Civil War" on p. 271), but information from the public is now understood to be critical for both governments and rebels.[31]

---

28. For evidence that granting autonomy can prevent the outbreak of violence, see Lars-Erik Cederman, Simon Hug, Andreas Schädel, and Julian Wucherpfennig, "Territorial Autonomy in the Shadow of Conflict: Too Little, Too Late?" *American Political Science Review* 109, no. 2 (2015): 354–70.

29. For a review of how bargaining theory applies to civil wars, see Barbara F. Walter, "Bargaining Failures and Civil War," *Annual Review of Political Science* 12 (June 2009): 243–61.

30. Fearon and Laitin, "Ethnicity, Insurgency, and Civil War," 75.

31. See Eli Berman, Joseph H. Felter, and Jacob N. Shapiro, *Small Wars, Big Data: The Information Revolution in Modern Conflict* (Princeton, NJ: Princeton University Press, 2018).

Civil War from Commitment Problems A more likely explanation for long civil wars is that they are rooted in commitment problems that are particularly difficult to resolve.[32] Several kinds of commitment problems are prevalent in civil conflicts. First, as we have seen, anticipated changes to the relative power of two sides can generate incentives for preventive war. When power dynamics are changing, the rising actor cannot credibly commit to not exploiting its power in the future to revise any deal made today; as a result, the actor that expects to grow weaker may prefer war now to a less desirable deal in the future.

In the context of civil conflicts, changes in the relative power of rebels and the government arise regularly because of the ups and downs of the state's economy. When the economy falters, the government's tax revenue falls, depriving it of resources that could be used to combat a rebellion; at the same time, popular discontent associated with a poor economy makes it easier for rebels to attract new recruits. As a result, a downturn in the economy creates a window in which rebels are relatively strong and have incentives to press demands. And the government, facing a strong rebellion, has incentives to make concessions.

In addition, economic downturns are generally temporary, often driven by short-term shocks such as a change in the price of oil or, in countries that depend heavily on agriculture, too little or too much rainfall in a given year. If everyone expects the economy to recover in the near future, then the rebels' newfound strength (and the government's relative weakness) is known to be temporary. As with a rising state, the government may not be able to commit credibly to abiding by any concessions it makes to the rebel camps once economic conditions improve. Hence, the anticipated economic recovery creates incentives for rebels to fight now in the hopes of obtaining an irreversible victory while they are relatively strong. This logic suggests that economic downturns should be associated with a higher risk of civil wars, and that is exactly what researchers have found.[33]

A second commitment problem results from the fact that the combatants in a civil war generally have to live together, in the same country, once their conflict is settled. When two states seek to settle a dispute or end a war, their armies can remain intact and retreat behind their respective borders. As a result, both sides retain the coercive power needed to sustain a deal. In the case of civil conflicts, however, this is usually not an option. Say a rebel group mobilizes and arms its members in order to make demands on the government. The government, hoping to avoid war, decides to make concessions but also requires, as part of the deal, that the rebels demobilize and disarm. This is a sensible demand to ensure civil peace and order; unless a new state is created through secession, rebel forces will have to be integrated into the existing state.

This demand, however, gives rise to a severe commitment problem: Once the rebels have disarmed, how can they be sure that the government will continue to abide by the deal? The government might simply exploit the rebels' disarmament to

---

32. James D. Fearon, "Why Do Some Civil Wars Last So Much Longer than Others?" *Journal of Peace Research* 41, no. 3 (May 2004): 275–301.

33. See, for example, Edward Miguel, Shanker Satyanath, and Ernest Sergenti, "Economic Shocks and Civil Conflict: An Instrumental Variables Approach," *Journal of Political Economy* 122, no. 4 (2004): 725–53.

crack down and eliminate them as a threat altogether. Hence, any deal that requires rebel groups to disarm directly affects the future bargaining power of the actors. As we saw in the case of interstate conflict, this dynamic can create an insurmountable obstacle to reaching a negotiated settlement, either before or during conflict.[34]

Partly for this reason, civil wars rarely end with negotiated settlements. Indeed, the majority of civil wars end only when one side achieves an outright military victory or when the rebel group simply peters out from a loss of support. One study found that only a quarter of civil conflicts since 1945 have ended with a peace agreement or cease-fire, compared to 50 percent of interstate conflicts that ended in one of those ways.[35]

Reaching an agreement either before or during fighting requires some mechanism to ensure that the government will live by the deal once the rebels lay down their arms. In some cases, it might be possible to craft power-sharing agreements that give all sides some control over the military after the conflict so that none can unilaterally exploit the others.[36] A more likely mechanism for these purposes, however, is the presence of some third party, such as peacekeepers from the UN, that can monitor and enforce the terms of the deal. We will revisit this issue shortly.

Just as the government may have a hard time committing to a deal, there can be commitment problems on the rebel side as well. Rebel organizations, unlike states, often have a hard time controlling all their members. Even if the leaders are willing to accept some deal, they may not be able to guarantee that all members of the group will lay down their arms. Within any group, there may be some members with extreme, even fanatical, views, who are unwilling to accept a compromise and will continue fighting. Unless the rebels can credibly commit to reining in their extreme factions, the government may be unwilling to cut a deal, or bargains may be struck that will not hold. As long as each faction can, on its own, decide to reject a deal and keep fighting, war will continue until there is a deal that is acceptable to the most extreme faction—or until one side or the other is decisively defeated. For this reason, rebellions that have more factions tend to generate longer wars.[37]

An example of this problem comes from the civil war that has raged since 2003 in the Darfur region of Sudan, a conflict that gained a great deal of international attention because of the genocide carried out by pro-government Arab militias against the non-Arab people of that region (see Chapter 5). Fighting on behalf of the latter were two main rebel groups, the Sudan Liberation Movement (SLM) and the Justice and Equality Movement (JEM), along with a number of smaller groups. Though both SLM and JEM purported to speak for the same people, they disagreed over the terms of any peace deal, and factions within each group had different preferences.

---

34. Barbara F. Walter, *Committing to Peace: The Successful Settlement of Civil Wars* (Princeton, NJ: Princeton University Press, 2002).

35. Joakim Kreutz, "How and When Armed Conflicts End: Introducing the UCDP Conflict Termination Dataset," *Journal of Peace Research* 47, no. 2 (2010): 243–50.

36. See, for example, Caroline Hartzell and Matthew Hoddie, "Institutionalizing Peace: Power Sharing and Post–Civil War Conflict Management," *American Journal of Political Science* 47, no. 2 (April 2003): 318–32.

37. David E. Cunningham, "Veto Players and Civil War Duration," *American Journal of Political Science* 50, no. 4 (2006): 875–92.

The major parties in the civil war in Sudan signed a peace agreement in August 2020. Rebellions that involve more factions tend to generate longer wars, as it is more difficult to get all to agree to a deal. After many failed attempts, the recent agreement appears to be holding.

The government of Sudan signed an agreement in 2006 with the SLM, but the JEM rejected the deal and continued fighting. The SLM withdrew from the deal in 2010. A tentative peace deal was signed by the government, SLM, JEM, and other groups in August 2020, though two small factions refused to take part in the agreement. In the end, the government largely capitulated to the demands of the rebels, but even then efforts to end the war have been complicated by the multitude of factions within the rebel movement.[38] As of early 2021, it appears that this agreement is holding.

Civil War from Indivisibilities   Finally, conflict might be unavoidable if the issue in dispute is valued in such a way that it is difficult to divide. As we saw in Chapter 3, governments and separatist groups might find it hard to compromise over pieces of territory that are imbued with religious or ethnic significance. The more common problem, though, is that the state may have incentives to treat its *entire territory* as indivisible, particularly if there are many possible groups with separatist interests. Consider the case of Russia, which has fought two bloody civil wars in the breakaway region of Chechnya since the Chechen republic's predominantly Muslim inhabitants declared independence in 1993. Given the costs of this war, which claimed tens of thousands of lives and sparked terrorist attacks by Islamist militants, Russia might have been better off letting the Chechens take their land and go.

If Russia faced a single possible separatist group, the dangers of such a concession might not be too large. But in a large, multiethnic country, concession to one group might encourage others to mobilize for similar reasons. Russia is home to more than 100 different ethnic groups, many of whom seek separation or greater autonomy from the central government in Moscow. If the government appears

---

38. "Sudan Signs Peace Deal with Rebel Groups from Darfur," Al Jazeera, August 31, 2020, www.aljazeera.com/news/2020/08/31/sudan-signs-peace-deal-with-rebel-groups-from-darfur (accessed 10/12/20).

willing to let one group go, then all other potential claimants have incentives to make their own demands. Although any one set of concessions might not be too painful, the collective costs of making concessions to multiple groups could be quite large.

This dynamic means that a state might reasonably see its entire territory as an indivisible good, since the loss of a little can bring about a loss of enormous value. In such cases, a state has an incentive to resist making concessions to any challenger in order to convince all potential challengers that they will face similar resistance. This suggests that the more potential separatist groups a government faces, the less likely it is to make concessions to any single group—a prediction that has been confirmed in recent research.[39]

Insurgency and Counterinsurgency: The Strategies of Civil War

If a civil war breaks out, how is it fought? To what extent do strategies of using violence differ when they are employed by nonstate actors? For most Americans, the term *civil war* evokes memorable battles between Union and Confederate soldiers, blue uniforms against gray, marching against each other in formation—in other words, a conventional war that happened to be fought by people who previously considered themselves citizens of the same country. The majority of civil wars worldwide bear no resemblance to this image. Most rebel armies do not engage in direct combat with government forces. Instead, most rebellions take the form of insurgencies.[40]

Insurgency is a military strategy in which small, often lightly armed units engage in hit-and-run attacks against military, government, and civilian targets. Unlike conventional military strategies, insurgency does not rely on capturing and holding territory. Instead, insurgents usually attack military bases, government buildings, or population centers and then melt back into rural areas, jungles, mountains, civilian populations, or across borders to take sanctuary in neighboring states. In order to blend into their surroundings, insurgents rarely wear distinctive uniforms. Indeed, the Chinese Communist leader Mao Tse-tung argued that insurgents should "swim" among the people just as fish swim in the sea—that is, hidden among the multitude.

insurgency
A military strategy in which small, often lightly armed units engage in hit-and-run attacks against military, government, and civilian targets.

---

39. Monica Duffy Toft, *The Geography of Ethnic Violence: Identity, Interests, and the Indivisibility of Territory* (Princeton, NJ: Princeton University Press, 2005), esp. chap. 5 on Russia and Chechnya; and Barbara F. Walter, *Reputation and Civil War: Why Separatist Conflicts Are So Violent* (Cambridge: Cambridge University Press, 2009). Technically, the dynamic described here is, at root, an information problem arising from uncertainty about the government's resolve to fight separatists. Treating the state's territory as indivisible is a strategy that the government employs to build a reputation for toughness, and not something intrinsic to the nature of the good. As we saw in Chapter 3, apparent indivisibilities are often rooted in strategic considerations.

40. A recent study classified 147 civil wars that occurred between 1944 and 2004 into three types, depending on whether the government, rebels, or both used heavy weapons such as tanks and artillery. Conventional wars, in which both sides used heavy weapons, accounted for 34 percent of the cases. Insurgencies, in which the government used heavy weapons but the rebels did not, accounted for 54 percent. The remaining 12 percent were cases in which both sides lacked heavy weapons. See Stathis N. Kalyvas and Laia Balcells, "International System and Technologies of Rebellion: How the End of the Cold War Shaped Internal Conflict," *American Political Science Review* 104, no. 3 (Autumn 2010): 423.

Many of the small armed groups involved in the Syrian Civil War, including the Al-Rahman Corps, have used insurgent strategies in their fight against the Syrian government.

The resort to insurgency is a direct response to the collective action problem facing rebel organizations. First and foremost, insurgency is well suited for groups that are small and weak relative to their adversary. Insurgency is a form of asymmetrical warfare, or conflict between actors with highly unequal military capabilities. Generally lacking the ability to raise a large fighting force or acquire sophisticated weaponry, rebels resort to tactics that avoid direct confrontations with usually larger and better-armed government forces. The purpose of insurgency is not to defeat the military but rather to impose costs on the government in order to induce concessions. The hit-and-run strategy means that rebels rarely score decisive victories; at the same time, they are hard to defeat because they are hard to find. This elusiveness helps explain why civil wars often endure for years or decades, even when the rebel forces number only in the hundreds or low thousands.

The strategy of insurgency can also help address the collective action problem by increasing the pool of individuals who may be willing to side with the rebels. By attacking civilians or police stations, courts, and other official sites, insurgents seek to undermine confidence in the government and encourage people to join them for protection. The Taliban insurgency in Afghanistan, for example, has sought to undermine faith in the U.S.-backed government by making people feel insecure and then offering to provide protection in exchange for support.

Insurgents also, by hiding among the noncombatant population, seek to provoke government forces into attacking civilians, with the hope that these attacks will radicalize people into joining their cause. For example, Taliban fighters often fire on U.S. and Afghan government forces from populated areas in the hopes that the retaliation will mistakenly kill civilians. The large number of Afghan civilians killed by U.S. air strikes has helped fuel opposition to the Western presence and has increased recruitment of new rebels. Far more Afghan civilians have been killed by the Taliban than by the United States and its allies, but the Taliban have been better able to exploit deaths caused by outsiders. This strategy of provocation is also used by terrorists and will be discussed further later in the chapter.

The nature of insurgency means that these kinds of rebellions can be hard to defeat through the conventional military strategies that characterize interstate combat. Highly mechanized modern forces with tanks, jet planes, and heavy artillery are effective for confronting an opposing force that operates out in the open, but they are not useful for dealing with a stealthy adversary that hides in the shadows and among civilian populations.[41] One way a government might respond to this challenge would be to engage in indiscriminate attacks against the civilian populations that might be sympathetic to the rebels' cause. Recalling Mao's fish analogy, the purpose of such a policy is to "drain the sea" within which the rebels hide. Not surprisingly, when pro-government forces engage in this kind of strategy, civilian casualties are very high.[42]

Whether this approach can actually be effective at defeating an insurgency has been the subject of mixed findings in the literature. On the one hand, indiscriminate attacks have been shown in some cases to decisively defeat militants or at least hinder their ability to operate; for example, the Sri Lankan government eliminated the Liberation Tigers of Tamil Eelam (LTTE) in 2009 in the course of an unrestrained offensive that killed as many as 40,000 civilians trapped in the war zone.[43] On the other hand, there is also evidence that attacks on civilians can be counterproductive, spurring people to join the rebellion out of revenge or decreasing the willingness of civilians to cooperate with government forces.[44]

An alternative response to insurgency is one that focuses on winning the support of noncombatant populations in order to undercut the insurgency politically. The basic idea of this strategy is to provide security and support to civilians so that they will not be tempted or coerced into joining the rebellion. To the extent that people see their interests as aligned with the government's, rebels have a harder time recruiting fighters. In addition, greater confidence in the pro-government forces creates incentives for civilians to help identify militants who are hiding among them, thereby neutralizing one of the insurgents' key advantages. Civilians often fear that if they were to "rat out" militants, the government would not be able to protect them from reprisals. Counterinsurgency (COIN) operations are intended to ease this fear by making the government's commitment to defend civilians credible.

---

41. Jason Lyall and Isaiah Wilson III, "Rage against the Machines: Explaining Outcomes in Counterinsurgency Wars," *International Organization* 63, no. 1 (2009): 67–106.

42. Benjamin Valentino, Paul Huth, and Dylan Balch-Lindsay, "'Draining the Sea': Mass Killing and Guerrilla Warfare," *International Organization* 58, no. 2 (2004): 375–407.

43. Jason Lyall, "Does Indiscriminate Violence Incite Insurgent Attacks? Evidence from Chechnya," *Journal of Conflict Resolution* 53, no. 3 (June 2009): 331–62; Jacqueline L. Hazelton, "The 'Hearts and Minds' Fallacy: Violence, Coercion, and Success in Counterinsurgency Warfare," *International Security* 42, no. 1 (2017): 80–113; and Lionel Beehner, "What Sri Lanka Can Teach Us about COIN," *Small Wars Journal* 6 (August 2010): 1–8.

44. Luke N. Condra and Jacob N. Shapiro, "Who Takes the Blame? The Strategic Effects of Collateral Damage," *American Journal of Political Science* 56, no. 1 (January 2012): 167–87; Matthew Adam Kocher, Thomas B. Pepinsky, and Stathis N. Kalyvas, "Aerial Bombing and Counterinsurgency in the Vietnam War," *American Journal of Political Science* 55, no. 2 (April 2011): 201–18.

Though not a new approach, this idea inspired a major rethinking of U.S. military strategy in Iraq and Afghanistan. Facing persistent insurgencies in both countries, the military articulated a COIN doctrine in 2006 that focuses on using military forces to protect the civilian populations and to create a secure space for economic reconstruction. Rather than emphasizing search-and-destroy missions against insurgent forces, the COIN doctrine prioritizes deploying troops within towns and cities alongside national army and police forces to provide security and create confidence in the governments on behalf of which the United States is fighting. The strategy also calls for steps to reduce the danger of accidentally killing civilians—for example, by relying more on ground forces and less on bombs and missiles launched from airplanes, which are responsible for a large share of civilian deaths. In addition, COIN operations involve an injection of economic resources to help jump-start development and undercut rebels' efforts to "buy" new fighters and supporters.

In short, the COIN doctrine is an attempt to defeat an insurgency by giving the population an interest in the survival of the government, thereby exacerbating the rebels' collective action problem and eliminating their informational advantages. This model had success in Iraq in 2007, when the deployment of more U.S. troops and the shift to the new COIN strategy helped bring about a dramatic reduction in insurgent activity and civilian deaths. This "surge" coincided with a split among the rebellious Sunnis, as some local leaders decided to assist the government in combating extremists who were responsible for much of the violence.

Though the United States was not primarily responsible for this turn, the surge made credible the American commitment not to abandon the government and enabled closer cooperation with local groups. The resulting reduction in violence paved the way for a significant withdrawal of American forces in Iraq, as well as their transition out of a combat role.[45] Figure 6.2 shows the trend in Iraqi civilian

Figure source: The Iraq Body Count project, www.iraqbodycount.org/database (accessed 10/24/20).

FIGURE 6.2 *Estimated Civilian Deaths Due to Violence in Iraq, 2003–2020*

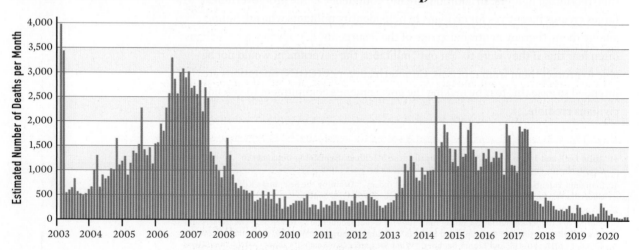

45. For an analysis of the various factors that reduced violence in Iraq, see Stephen Biddle, Jeffrey A. Friedman, and Jacob N. Shapiro, "Testing the Surge: Why Did Violence Decline in Iraq in 2007?" *International Security* 37, no. 1 (Summer 2012): 7–40.

deaths due to the conflict, including the dramatic reduction after 2007. Taking advantage of this relative calm, U.S. forces left the country at the end of 2011. In the fall of 2009, President Barack Obama decided to try the same model against the Taliban insurgency in Afghanistan, increasing the U.S. troop presence there to 100,000 (together with roughly 40,000 troops from other countries) and implementing the COIN strategy.

Neither of these efforts brought about lasting solutions to those conflicts. As Figure 6.2 shows, only two years after U.S. forces left Iraq, the civil war there reignited, fed by the emergence of the militant Islamic State in neighboring Syria (see "What Shaped Our World?" on p. 276). In Afghanistan, the increased troop presence and new strategy had some successes, but there was no marked reduction in violence nor much prospect that the Taliban could be defeated militarily. Despite limited progress, most U.S. and allied forces withdrew by the end of 2014, and those that remained transitioned away from combat roles. In 2017, President Donald Trump announced that he was sending as many as 5,000 additional troops to Afghanistan to reverse worsening conditions there. And while President Trump claimed in 2019 and 2020 to be winding down the conflict, troop levels remained similar to their pre-2017 levels. The frustrations experienced in these countries by the world's most powerful state are a testament to the effectiveness of the strategy of insurgency.

What Can Be Done about Civil War?

Given the enormous human toll of civil wars, it is natural to ask whether there are steps that outside actors can take to reduce the risk of this kind of violence. As mentioned earlier, there is already a great deal of outside interference in civil wars, but much of it takes the form of support for one side or the other; indeed, this support is often responsible for the onset and long duration of these wars. Can outside actors play a more positive role? In terms of our framework, we have seen how domestic groups whose interests conflict with those of the government may engage in a bargaining interaction that sometimes leads to the outbreak of violence. To what extent can the third leg of the framework—institutions—help resolve this problem?

In principle, international institutions can help in several respects. First, international efforts could influence the bargaining interaction between the government and domestic opponents in a way that increases the chances for a peaceful outcome. One such intervention would be to impose costs on actors that resort to force, much as collective security is intended to raise the costs of international aggression. As we saw in the previous chapter, collective security organizations like the UN have become increasingly active in intrastate conflicts. The track record has been, at best, uneven. Efforts to end ongoing conflicts in the former Yugoslavia, Rwanda, and elsewhere were ultimately hampered by the fact that few states had interests strong enough to motivate them to intervene, leading to half-hearted, ineffectual measures. In other cases, such as in Syria, powerful states had conflicting interests that prevented collective action among the international community.

External efforts can play a much more positive role in keeping the peace once the combatants decide to stop fighting. As we have seen, agreements that require

The Rise of the Islamic State

The Islamic State burst onto the world stage in the summer of 2014, when it launched a dramatic invasion into Iraq from its strongholds in Syria. The crisis prompted the United States to initiate air strikes against IS positions and to coordinate a counterattack with Iraqi forces. How did this group arise?[a]

Interests The Islamic State is the latest iteration of a group that first formed during the civil war that erupted following the 2003 U.S. invasion of Iraq. The U.S. occupation met resistance from a variety of actors. Most important were members of the Sunni sect, who enjoyed a privileged position under the ousted regime of Saddam Hussein. Sunnis had a political interest in spoiling the consolidation of a new regime that would be dominated by the majority Shiite sect.

In addition, groups like Al Qaeda, which orchestrated the 9/11 attacks, aspired to create an Islamic "caliphate"—a territory under the rule of a Muslim religious leader—and they saw the removal of Western influence as a precondition to that end. The U.S. occupation of Iraq created an opportunity for individuals who shared that goal to fight Americans close to home. In 2004, a violent insurgent group of Sunnis and foreign fighters pledged allegiance to Osama bin Laden and became known as Al Qaeda in Iraq (AQI). In 2006, AQI joined with other militant groups to form the Islamic State of Iraq (ISI).

Interactions AQI and ISI employed violence for two main purposes. First, attacks on U.S. forces were intended to increase the costs of occupation and coerce an American withdrawal. Second, attacks on the Shiite population were intended to provoke conflict between Shiites and Sunnis and thereby make any political reconciliation impossible. While the second part of the strategy succeeded in feeding a bloody sectarian war, the United States responded to the violence by increasing its forces in 2007. Combined with resistance from Sunni tribes who were repelled by AQI's harsh tactics, this troop surge decimated the group by 2008. ISI got a new lease on life, however, thanks to the United States' withdrawal of its forces in 2011 and the outbreak of civil war in neighboring Syria.

Institutions Syria's descent into civil war led to a dramatic contraction of the Syrian regime's reach and authority. The government increasingly relied on Islamist groups allied with the regime and supported by Iran to fight rebels in central and eastern Syria. ISI took advantage of this political vacuum and sent forces to Syria.

While the group's initial activity in Syria involved terrorist attacks against the regime and rival groups, growing strength allowed it to turn to a more ambitious goal: carving out a state in the Sunni regions straddling Syria and Iraq. In 2013, the group rebranded itself as the Islamic State of Iraq and Syria (ISIS) and focused its violence against other Sunni groups, including Al Qaeda affiliates.

ISIS also started to perform the tasks of a state within the areas it controlled: taxing and conscripting its inhabitants, providing services, issuing currency, and regulating people's behavior. In addition, it developed conventional military capabilities designed to conquer territory. This process of state building culminated in the 2014 offensive into Iraq. With large swaths of territory and several major cities under its control, the group declared itself the head of a new caliphate, the Islamic State.

Over the next several years, the United States and its allies fought to expel the Islamic State from lands it occupied. In 2017, U.S.-backed forces ousted the Islamic State from its self-declared capital in Raqqa, Syria, and in March 2019 Syrian rebels drove the group from its last stronghold. With its state apparently defeated, the Islamic State seemed likely to return to its roots as an insurgent group, sponsoring and inspiring terrorist attacks in the region and beyond.

---

a. Much of this history is based on William McCants, *The ISIS Apocalypse: The History, Strategy, and Doomsday Vision of the Islamic State* (New York: St. Martin's, 2015).

rebels to disarm create a severe commitment problem because of the government's incentives to renege on the deal once the rebels have complied. Peacekeepers may help alleviate this problem if they can credibly guarantee the safety of disarmed and demobilized rebels and help them reintegrate into society. International peace-building efforts may also help with the economic and political reconstruction of the country, which is important to long-term stability. For example, many peacekeeping missions after civil wars help organize and monitor elections, train the civilian police force, and bolster the judicial system. If successful, these efforts can lead to new political institutions through which future disputes can be handled without recourse to coercive bargaining. Evidence suggests that strong international efforts at peace building can not only prevent the resumption of violence but also encourage the emergence of more democratic countries.[46] We should note, however, that peacekeepers may not always play a beneficial role in the societies in which they operate. In poor, unstable, and uncertain countries just recovering from conflict, peacekeepers have been shown to exploit their superior positions and resources to engage in transactional sex with local women, despite prohibitions on such behavior by the United Nations and other supervising organizations.[47]

There have also been some international efforts to reduce the ability of rebel groups to finance themselves through sales of drugs or minerals. For example, the Kimberley Process, initiated in 2003 (and named after the town in South Africa where the idea was hatched), is an international process that certifies rough diamonds that did not come from conflict zones. The hope is that if consumers purchase only diamonds that have the certification, the ability of rebels to finance themselves with so-called blood diamonds will be choked off.

Of course, most of these efforts are designed to end civil wars and prevent them from restarting after a peace deal; ideally, international intervention could reduce the likelihood that bloody and destructive civil wars will break out in the first place. There are several challenges to this aspiration. As already noted, there are dissatisfied groups and individuals within most countries that could provide the basis for armed opposition to the government. Although we know some of the factors that increase the risks of civil war, these conflicts are very hard to forecast with much certainty. As a result, it can be hard to correctly anticipate where the next civil war will break out and to target conflict management efforts appropriately. Moreover, there are truly repressive regimes that deserve the opposition of their people. In these cases, reducing the risk of armed rebellion can have the unintended effect of diminishing the government's incentives to liberalize.

---

46. Walter, *Committing to Peace*; Virginia Page Fortna, *Does Peacekeeping Work? Shaping Belligerents' Choices after Civil War* (Princeton, NJ: Princeton University Press, 2008); and Michael W. Doyle and Nicholas Sambanis, "International Peacebuilding: A Theoretical and Quantitative Analysis," *American Political Science Review* 94 (2000): 779–801.

47. See Bernd Beber, Michael J. Gilligan, Jenny Guardado, and Sabrina Karim, "Peacekeeping, Compliance with International Norms, and Transactional Sex in Monrovia, Liberia," *International Organization* 71, no. 1 (2017): 1–30; for a brief summary, see Bernd Beber, Michael Gilligan, Jenny Guardado, and Sabrina Karim, "U.N. Peacekeeping and Transactional Sex," *Washington Post*, June 16, 2015, www.washingtonpost.com/news/monkey-cage/wp/2015/06/16/u-n-peacekeeping-and-transactional-sex (accessed 11/9/20).

In the long run, the best chance for reducing civil conflict hinges on changing interests and institutions within a country, particularly through economic development and democratization. Relatively wealthy countries have the lowest risk of civil war because their people have less to gain and more to lose by taking up arms and because wealthy governments are better able to buy off dissatisfied groups and/or deter the emergence of armed opposition. Well-functioning democracies provide institutions that enable groups and individuals to pursue their interests through peaceful political processes. Even so, these are long-run developments over which outsiders have only limited influence. Though states and international organizations constantly seek ways to promote development and democratization, these efforts, at best, support internal processes.

Moreover, the route to development and democracy can be rocky and dangerous. Though economic growth is good, it can have uneven effects as some groups within a country grow wealthy while others remain mired in poverty. This kind of inequality can become a grievance that feeds civil conflict. Transitions to democracy can also be risky. During the period of transition, the regime may be too weak to deter violence, and nascent democratic institutions may not be strong enough to channel political demands in peaceful ways. There is some evidence to suggest that periods of democratization are associated with an increased risk of civil war.[48]

The promotion of democracy by third parties also must be done carefully. Some evidence suggests that foreign aid given for purposes of democracy building can reduce the risk of civil war in countries that are already democratizing.[49] Bringing democracy to countries that are currently autocratic, on the other hand, requires some effort to destabilize the existing regime or, as in the case of the U.S. invasion of Iraq, remove it forcibly. As the U.S. experience vividly shows, however, the weakening or destruction of an autocratic regime can itself precipitate civil war.[50] The civil conflict in Iraq that followed the invasion is estimated to have claimed tens of thousands, if not hundreds of thousands, of lives. And, as we have seen, while U.S. forces helped bring about a reduction in violence after 2007, Iraq's civil war reignited only a few years after those troops left, dimming the prospects that Iraq will emerge prosperous and democratic.

Terrorism: Why Kill Civilians?

Though definitions abound, terrorism is conventionally defined as the premeditated threat or use of violence against noncombatant targets by individuals or subnational groups to obtain a political or social objective through intimidation of a larger

---

48. See, for example, Lars-Erik Cederman, Simon Hug, and Lutz F. Krebs, "Democratization and Civil War: Empirical Evidence," *Journal of Peace Research* 47, no. 4 (2010): 377–94.

49. Burcu Savun and Daniel C. Tirone, "Foreign Aid, Democratization, and Civil Conflict: How Does Democracy Aid Affect Civil Conflict?" *American Journal of Political Science* 55, no. 2 (2011): 233–46.

50. For a general finding to this effect, see Goran Peic and Dan Reiter, "Foreign-Imposed Regime Change, State Power, and Civil War Onset, 1920–2004," *British Journal of Political Science* 41, no. 3 (2010): 453–75.

audience.[51] Unlike conventional warfare, terrorism attempts to win concessions not by defeating the armed forces of another actor but by attacking civilians, civilian police forces, or military units not engaged in combat. Terrorists hope that these attacks will sow fear among some target population and, in turn, induce that population to concede to the terrorists' political or social demands. The existence of such demands is crucial, as otherwise terrorism is no different from simple criminality.

Terrorism is transnational, and thus the subject of international relations, when it involves a perpetrator and victim from different countries or when it aims to alter the behavior of a foreign government. Figure 6.3 shows the number of transnational terrorist attacks per year from 1970 to 2014, along with their estimated fatalities. Though terrorism rose to high levels in the 1970s and 1980s, it has increased considerably in the decade and a half since September 11, 2001, which marked the single bloodiest terrorist attack in this time period. Most terrorism, however, is purely domestic and does not cross national borders. Indeed, by one estimate, 89 percent of terrorist attacks since 1970 have been domestic.[52]

How can we understand people who hijack airliners and fly them into skyscrapers or blow themselves up on crowded trains and buses? A common explanation for terrorism is that terrorists are hate-filled, irrational extremists who win glory by taking the lives of others. This is too simplistic. Rather, terrorism is a product of a strategic interaction between the terrorists and the governments they hope to influence. As such, violence can be understood as a bargaining failure prompted by incomplete information, commitment problems, and indivisibilities. At the same time, terrorists, like the rebel groups considered in the previous section, face challenges in finding resources and recruits willing to undertake dangerous, possibly even suicidal, missions and in organizing collective action without being detected or ratted out. These organizational imperatives affect the nature of terrorist groups and the strategies they select.

Are Terrorists Rational?

Our framework usually starts by asking what interests motivate the relevant actors. In the context of terrorism, this immediately raises the question of whether terrorists can be thought of as actors who rationally pursue some interest. In popular discussions, it is often implied that terrorists are irrational, crazed "fanatics." If this were true, it would significantly complicate our ability to analyze their behavior within the analytical framework developed in this textbook. At least three reasons for this perception must be examined before we turn to an explanation of terrorism.

---

51. This definition, used by scholars, is similar to that in the *United States Code*, title 22, chap. 38, sec. 2656f(d). Any definition of terrorism is itself a political statement. *Terrorist* is a term of opprobrium intended to delegitimize the action and, in turn, the cause for which violence is used. Thus, who is and is not a terrorist is often contested. State terrorism, which we do not consider here, involves the targeting of noncombatants by the government with the intent of influencing an audience. State-*sponsored* terrorism involves government funding or support of terrorists.

52. Kirssa Cline Ryckman and Mike Ryckman, "All Politics Is Local: The Domestic Agenda of Terror Groups and the Study of Transnational Attacks," *Journal of Global Security Studies* 2, no. 1 (2017): 55–73. This estimate counts only attacks by known groups that conducted more than one attack.

FIGURE 6.3 *Transnational Terrorist Attacks and Fatalities, 1970–2014**

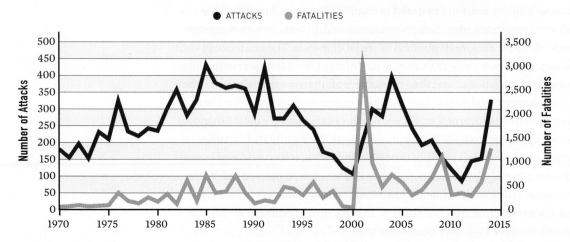

● ATTACKS   ● FATALITIES

Figure sources: Attack data are from the National Consortium for the Study of Terrorism and Responses to Terrorism (START), Global Terrorism Database [Data file], 2017, www.start.umd.edu/gtd. Transnational attacks were identified using Kirssa Ryckman, "GTD Add-On: Terror Groups' Home," https//doi.org/10.7910/DVN/F6MTML, Harvard Dataverse, V1 (2016), UNF:6:1wXz57cxaKoR1/tmURSgdA== (accessed 4/7/21). More recent data are not available.

*The figure reports attacks directed against civilian targets (that is, not police or military) conducted by known groups that carried out more than one attack. Figures for 1993 are interpolated.

First, groups that resort to terrorism often possess interests that are not widely shared, especially by the target audience. Describing terrorists as irrational may simply mean that terrorists rank alternative outcomes in ways that seem "unreasonable," at least from the broader population's perspective. *Rationality* refers to purposive behavior or the strategies by which individuals or groups pursue their interests; the term *rational* is not a statement about the substance of an individual's or group's preferences. We may not agree with the preferences of terrorists and their supporters, but the fact that we disagree does not necessarily mean that the strategy they choose in pursuit of their interests is irrational. Indeed, there is substantial evidence that, given their interests, terrorist networks choose targets, respond to risk, and adjust to counterterrorist efforts in quite purposeful or rational ways.[53]

One common explanation for the expanding number of suicide attacks in recent years, for instance, is that as sites have become harder to destroy using more conventional methods, terrorists have upgraded from "dumb bombs" controlled by a timer to "smart bombs" in the form of well-trained suicide bombers who can adapt to countermeasures and react to events at the scene.[54] Reflecting a highly rational calculus, terrorists appear to select targets according to how well they are defended, the chances of a successful attack, and the targets' political impact.

A second reason why many perceive terrorists to be irrational is that the choice to become a terrorist—especially to become a suicide bomber—may entail costs larger than the potential gains and thus appears not to be an effective strategy for obtaining one's goals. Currently, we have no good explanations for why any particular individual chooses to become a terrorist or a suicide bomber. After all, the sacrifice of one's own life seems a high price to pay for any cause. However, we also lack complete explanations for why individuals would voluntarily choose to join a national military and go into battle to risk death for their country. For any

---

53. See, for example, Charlinda Santifort, Todd Sandler, and Patrick T. Brandt, "Terrorist Attack and Target Diversity: Changepoints and Their Drivers," *Journal of Peace Research* 50, no. 1 (2012): 75–90.

54. Eli Berman and David Laitin, "Hard Targets: Theory and Evidence on Suicide Attacks," NBER Working Paper W11740, National Bureau of Economic Research, Cambridge, MA, November 2005.

individual, such choices may be irrational in that the personal costs (the risk of death) exceed the personal gains. Moreover, individuals may be motivated by goals that have nothing to do with the organization's political agenda, such as a desire for adventure, a feeling of belonging, or loyalty to a community.[55] Acknowledging this point, however, does not imply that a terrorist organization lacks purpose and careful strategizing in how it deploys its forces.

A third reason for the perception of irrationality is that terrorist attacks sometimes appear to be random. In some cases, it is clear why terrorists choose a certain target. The World Trade Center and the Pentagon, for instance, were deliberately chosen as targets on 9/11 because they represent the core of America's international power—business and the military. More generally, terrorists most frequently target businesses and diplomatic missions, which also serve as emblems of the target state's power. But certainly, some terrorist attacks are random, as when a suicide bomber selects one crowded pizzeria rather than another.

Random selection of targets and times, however, is often part of a terrorist's strategy. After all, one objective of terrorism is to strike fear into the target population. If terrorist attacks are systematic and predictable, the population will adjust accordingly and avoid likely targets when an attack is anticipated. By selecting random times and places, terrorists can make people feel unsafe everywhere and greatly magnify the threat they pose and the fear they instill. In other words, randomness can be quite rational.

Why Terrorism?

A key point in understanding terrorism is that terrorist organizations are weak in two important senses: they are weak relative to the states they seek to coerce, and they are weak relative to the extensive demands they make.[56] This weakness arises from the nature of the interests that motivate them.

People and groups that use terrorism may be motivated by any number of interests. They may seek to overthrow a government, expel a foreign power from their homeland, or carve out a new utopian society based on some economic or religious ideology. Al Qaeda seeks to eradicate Western influence from the Middle East in order to bring about Islamist governments in the region. Palestinian terrorist groups like Hamas have sought the destruction of the state of Israel. The Shining Path is a Marxist terrorist group that has operated in Peru since the 1980s and sought to destabilize the government and bring about a communist revolution. White nationalism organizations in the United States, often linked to at least ideologically similar organizations abroad, have attempted to start race wars in order to transform the United States into a White ethnostate.

---

55. See, for example, Max Abrahms, "What Terrorists Really Want: Terrorist Motives and Counterterrorism Strategy," *International Security* 32, no. 4 (2008): 78–105.

56. That terrorism is a "weapon of the weak" is conventional wisdom in academic and policy discussions, but we have to be precise about what this phrase means. Terrorism is an attractive strategy when relatively small groups confront powerful states with sophisticated militaries; see, for example, Cullen S. Hendrix and Joseph K. Young, "State Capacity and Terrorism: A Two-Dimensional Approach," *Security Studies* 23, no. 2 (2014): 329–63. Among groups that are fighting a state, however, weaker groups are not necessarily more likely to resort to terrorism than stronger groups are; see Fortna, "Do Terrorists Win?"

Extremists come from both the left and right of the political spectrum. White nationalist groups have become more prominent in the United States in recent years.

extremists

Actors whose interests are not widely shared by others; individuals or groups that are politically weak relative to the demands they make.

Whatever interests they seek to promote, terrorists are typically **extremists** in the sense that their interests are not widely shared by others, or, at least, their willingness to pay costs to achieve those interests is not widely shared. In any population, individual interests in a given issue—for instance, the most appropriate political system, the distribution of resources, proper religious beliefs, and so on—can usually be arrayed along a spectrum. For most issues, this range of interests is distributed in a bell-shaped curve, with most people being "moderate" and clustered in the middle of the distribution (Figure 6.4).

When we call someone extreme, we typically mean that an individual's interests are significantly different from those of the majority. In the curve illustrated in Figure 6.4, extremists exist in the "tails" of the distribution to either the left or the right of the moderate majority. In fact, what it means to be an extremist is relative: someone who is an extremist in one society might not be so extreme in another. For example, moderates in Britain may have very different interests from moderates in Pakistan. But extremism implies that relatively few other individuals in the relevant population share the extremists' political preferences. And even if other people share terrorists' ultimate objectives—for example, many peaceful individuals in the Middle East resent Western influence there and would like to see it end—they may not care so intensely that they are willing to kill or die for that goal.

Because extremist groups are small and the majority of the population is unsympathetic to their goals or methods, they tend to be weak politically relative to the demands they make. The problem of recruitment is particularly acute, since the pool of motivated individuals is relatively small and extremists have difficulty convincing others to share their interests and join their causes. Moreover, their fringe status means that they will seldom be able to further their interests by participating in normal political processes or making use of existing institutions, even in a democracy. Instead, their hope lies in using violence to coerce concessions or somehow alter the status quo in their favor.

FIGURE 6.4 *Extremist Interests*

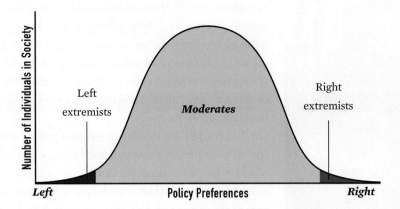

The resort to violence is further complicated by the fact that terrorists are weak not only relative to their demands but also relative to their targets. States are nearly always stronger politically and militarily than the terrorist networks they face.[57] Whereas states have populations and economies they can tax for resources and standing militaries they can deploy, terrorist organizations are often starved for resources, quite small in numbers, and poorly armed, especially in their formative stages, when they are most vulnerable to government countermeasures. Like rebel groups, they often must resort to such criminal activities as drug running or bank robbery to acquire their initial funding, although some grow out of legitimate religious and service activities (such as Hamas) or depend on the personal wealth of their founders (such as Al Qaeda, which was founded by millionaire Osama bin Laden).

This weakness is central to understanding why terrorism involves attacks on civilians, businesses, government embassies, and other official buildings. The object of terrorism is to bypass the other side's military and inflict pain and suffering on the target population so as to induce political change. In this sense, because it avoids a direct confrontation that would result in certain defeat, terrorism is like insurgency. As we will see, terrorism can also be used, like insurgency, to provoke government repression that increases the group's support base. The main difference between terrorism and insurgency is that the latter more commonly involves hit-and-run attacks on military units, whereas terrorism targets civilians or nonmilitary aspects of the government.

The relative weakness of terrorists also influences how they choose to organize. Terrorists adopt organizational forms that make it difficult for traditional military forces to defeat them. Unlike states, which have internal hierarchies, terrorists typically form networks of small, self-contained cells that are loosely connected to one another and, in some cases, to a central directorate. While these cells of individuals and groups cooperate to achieve common aims, they do not routinely

---

57. This is particularly true with transnational terrorism. Terrorism in the context of civil wars is often directed at weak states or takes place in the context of state failure.

Terrorists sometimes carry out seemingly random attacks on public places as a purposeful strategy to strike fear into the target population, as in the 2020 attack on the campus of Kabul University in Afghanistan, which killed 35 people.

share information within the network; each cell is largely responsible for its own activities and acquires resources and information from other cells or the central directorate only as necessary. This loose network insulates the individual cells and allows the organization to survive when penetrated or attacked. If the potential target state successfully infiltrates or destroys one cell, the rest of the network remains largely intact.[58]

In addition, transnational terrorist groups may spread their message through publications and social media in an effort to inspire "lone wolf" attacks—that is, attacks by individuals who are not actually members of the group but who share its goals. The April 2013 attack on the Boston Marathon, which killed 3 people and injured over 250, was committed by two brothers who were allegedly radicalized by extremist propaganda and learned bomb-making skills from an online Al Qaeda publication. Similarly, the Islamic State has encouraged supporters in the West to drive vehicles into crowds of people—a tactic that has led to mass casualty attacks in a number of European countries. Such lone wolf attacks are rarely as lethal as those planned by an organization, but they are very hard to prevent because the perpetrators have no observable connection to a terrorist group.

Another way that terrorists make it hard for traditional military forces to defeat them is by hiding within sympathetic populations, just as rebels take refuge in jungles, mountains, and cities. In cases where the group is not too extreme and thus has affiliated individuals who share its interests, or in which the local population has been radicalized to share the extremists' beliefs, terrorists can live within a larger population that protects and supports them. Palestinian extremists, for example, can blend into the wider Palestinian community, which supports many of their goals if not always their methods. In other cases, terrorist groups can buy support from a corrupt, failed, or sympathetic state to gain refuge, as Al Qaeda did in Afghanistan prior to 9/11. Hidden within larger populations, terrorists are difficult to identify. Attempts to eliminate them, in turn, are likely to cause collateral damage to the larger population, raising the costs of any retaliatory or preemptive attack by the target state. Indeed, networks of loosely connected cells hidden in sympathetic populations make terrorist groups hard to eradicate.

Terrorism as a Bargaining Failure

Like states, terrorist organizations use or threaten to use violence to raise the costs to—and, hopefully, elicit concessions from—the other side. In this way, terrorism and threats of terrorism are forms of bargaining. But if the target state has an

---

58. For an interesting analysis of how terrorists manage their organizations that draws on captured internal communications, see Jacob N. Shapiro, *The Terrorist's Dilemma: Managing Violent Covert Organizations* (Princeton, NJ: Princeton University Press, 2013).

The Islamic State has released numerous online propaganda and training videos designed to inspire lone wolf attacks by people who are sympathetic to, but not members of, the organization.

idea of the costs that terrorists can inflict on it, and if the terrorists know that they are unlikely to defeat the state but can extract some concessions by threatening violence, why can't the two sides reach a compromise that reflects their relative bargaining positions? If such a bargain were possible, then the terrorists would be spared the costs of carrying out attacks and the target would not incur the damage and subsequent widespread fear. Given that the costs of violence theoretically make a mutually preferable deal available, can we understand terrorism, like international and civil war, as the result of a bargaining failure?

One natural answer to these questions is that terrorists' goals may be so extreme that compromise is simply not possible. If terrorists want everyone in the target population to convert to a different religion, or if they seek to eliminate the target state, then it may be difficult to imagine some compromise settlement that would be acceptable to both sides. In the extreme case where the adversary seeks your death or the obliteration of your identity, the costs of concessions and the costs of conflict may be indistinguishable, and there is little choice but to fight. But while we do not rule out the possibility of this extreme case—for example, Hamas and other Palestinian terrorist groups have called for the destruction of Israel— what separates terrorists from mass murderers is that they kill in order to advance a political objective, not as an end in its own right. Therefore, a mutually beneficial bargain generally exists in theory, even if there are significant barriers to identifying and achieving such a bargain in practice. As in the cases of international and civil war, we can group these barriers in terms of information problems, commitment problems, and indivisibility.

Terrorism and Incomplete Information Like states in conflict, terrorists have private information and incentives to misrepresent that information to targets. Precisely because terrorist networks are small, weak, and often shadowy organizations that hide within sympathetic populations or in fragile states, targets usually possess incomplete information about their size, capabilities, and resolve. Often, the first time anyone learns of a new terrorist group is after it claims credit for an attack. Even when targets have intelligence sources within the terrorist group, they may acquire relatively little information because the cell that is infiltrated or monitored may know little about other cells. Terrorist networks, in turn, have incentives to misrepresent their capabilities and resolve. By exaggerating claims of strength and commitment, these organizations seek to negotiate more favorable deals with their targets.

As we now know, there were numerous hints about the impending 9/11 attacks before they happened, and bin Laden made no secret of the fact that he considered himself to be at war with the United States.[59] The U.S. government ignored these warning signals, in part, because its separate agencies were not able to put together the disparate pieces of the puzzle before them and because officials saw other threats as more important. But the government also downplayed the warning signs because they could be interpreted as the normal blustering of terrorists whose aspirations seemed to far exceed their reach. The same can be said about the Islamic State. Few took Abu Bakr al-Baghdadi's ambition to form a new caliphate seriously until his group conquered nearly one-third of Iraq in 2014.

As we saw in Chapter 3, overcoming information problems requires actors to communicate their capabilities and resolve in a credible manner. But the nature of terrorist organizations makes credible communication particularly difficult. Since their ability to carry out attacks against militarily superior targets typically hinges on the element of surprise, terrorists cannot reveal their true capabilities or strategies in advance without undermining their effectiveness. If Al Qaeda had announced before 9/11 that it would fly hijacked airliners into the World Trade Center and the Pentagon unless the U.S. government conceded to its demands, the United States would have quickly responded by grounding all airplanes (which it did immediately after the attacks) and surrounding New York and Washington, D.C., with constant air patrols. By tipping its hand in advance, Al Qaeda would have lost the ability to implement those very attacks on the United States.

The use of attacks to signal capability and resolve distinguishes terrorist organizations from states engaged in coercive diplomacy. States often communicate by using strategies short of force, such as public statements and mobilizations. Terrorist organizations cannot engage in the same kind of public displays without exposing themselves to the authorities and risking a crackdown. Instead, they tend to mobilize their efforts in secret, and attacks become the public signals.[60] Thus, unlike in interstate relations, there may be no bargaining between terrorists and states before the violence starts.

Terrorism and Commitment Problems

The difficulty of making commitments credible also looms large in this context.[61] As part of any agreement reached before or after a terrorist attack, the target will insist that the offending organization promise

---

59. See *The 9/11 Commission Report: Final Report of the National Commission on Terrorist Attacks upon the United States* (New York: Norton, 2004), 254–77.

60. Harvey E. Lapan and Todd Sandler, "Terrorism and Signalling," *European Journal of Political Economy* 9, no. 3 (1993): 383–97.

61. Ethan Bueno de Mesquita, "Conciliation, Counterterrorism, and Patterns of Terrorist Violence," *International Organization* 59, no. 1 (2005): 145–76; and Navin A. Bapat, "State Bargaining with Transnational Terrorist Groups," *International Studies Quarterly* 50, no. 1 (2006): 213–29.

For decades, the separatist group Euskadi Ta Azkatasuna (ETA) carried out terrorist attacks throughout Spain in an effort to gain independence for the Basque Country. Bombings such as that depicted here were common. In 2011 ETA announced the cessation of its armed activity, and in 2018 it declared that it had dissolved as an organization and ceased its political action.

not to employ violence in the future. After all, the whole point of making concessions is to reduce the threat and fear of future attacks. If the terrorists' commitment to refrain from further attacks is not credible, however, this can prevent the conclusion of an agreement that both sides prefer. It can be particularly hard for terrorist organizations to achieve credibility in this context, since the target must judge both the trustworthiness of the terrorist leadership and its ability to exert control over potential defectors within the group's ranks. Given the loosely connected nature of most terrorist organizations, centralized control is often difficult for terrorists to achieve. Even if the group's leadership is willing to make a deal, it may not be able to rein in all the "loose cannons" that might want to continue the fight.

Terrorists can most credibly demonstrate their commitment to peace by publicly renouncing terror, disarming, and giving the target or some neutral third party full access to the network so as to alleviate any lingering information problems. This approach has been key to the still-fragile peace between Catholics and Protestants in Northern Ireland, where the Irish Republican Army (IRA) has disavowed terrorism, disarmed, and joined the political process.

As in the case of civil wars, however, the need for disarmament creates another commitment problem: If the terrorists disarm, how can they be certain that the target will honor its side of the agreement? After all, it is the target's fear of continuing attacks that gives terrorists their power over the target in the first place. Once the terrorists give up their ability to attack, the target no longer has any incentive to compromise with them, and it may choose to subsequently defect from the agreement and crush any lingering opposition. For both terrorists and targets, credibly agreeing not to fight may be very difficult. Indeed, the difficulties of committing to peace have been a source of continued fighting in many terrorist conflicts—including that between the Basque separatist group Euskadi Ta Azkatasuna (ETA) and

Spain, where both sides wanted peace for a long time before ETA finally dissolved in 2018.[62]

States may also see fighting terrorists, rather than compromising with them, as a solution to a different commitment problem. A common argument for not negotiating with terrorists is that even if it makes sense to compromise with any one group, doing so will simply encourage others to emerge with new demands. After all, if any individual or group that threatens to detonate a bomb can wrest concessions from the target government, then the government faces a potentially endless list of demands from an ever-increasing set of adversaries. This is similar to the problem, mentioned earlier, of governments that face many potential separatist groups: though making concessions to any one might make sense, buying off every group would be too costly. When faced with a large number of potential adversaries, the government would like to commit itself not to negotiate with any of them. Resisting any single group's demands, even at the risk of experiencing new attacks, signals this commitment and may thereby deter the emergence of new challengers.

Terrorism and Indivisibilities

Finally, bargaining may fail if the goods in dispute cannot readily be divided or subject to compromise. The view that it is not possible to negotiate with terrorists often derives from the perception that the goals of terrorist organizations are nonnegotiable. The connection between religion and terrorism furthers this perception, since goods that are connected to religious identities may be particularly hard to split.

Hamas and other Palestinian terrorist groups do not want a Jewish state on the land between the Jordan Valley and the Mediterranean Sea; if given the choice, they would institute an Islamic regime in what is now Israel. Most Israelis want their state to be a Jewish state, though one that permits citizens to practice other religions openly. In principle, there are middle positions between a Jewish state and an Islamic state on this land. One could imagine a state with no officially sanctioned religion in which all faiths could be freely practiced or a state that officially sanctioned both religions. But while such compromises exist both in principle and practice, there are those on both sides who see the state's religious identity as an all-or-nothing issue.

The connection between religion and terrorism is real, but it should not be overstated. Although many are more likely to describe violence as terrorism when it is carried out by religious groups and individuals, most acts of terrorism are not religiously motivated.[63] Figure 6.5 breaks down international terrorist groups by their type of goal and shows the number of attacks and casualties (killed and wounded) perpetrated by each type of group between 1968 and 2005 (the only period in which data are broken down in this way). According to these figures, religious groups committed only 13 percent of terrorist attacks in this period. However, these attacks were particularly lethal, accounting for 42 percent of all casualties. Religion also plays a pronounced role in suicide terrorism, as the belief that a reward is waiting

62. "ETA's Bloody History: 853 Killings in 60 Years of Violence," Associated Press, May 16, 2019, https://apnews.com/article/62a64037ca0e47358c771947ace133b8 (accessed 11/9/20).

63. Connor Huff and Joshua D. Kertzer, "How the Public Defines Terrorism," *American Journal of Political Science* 66, no. 1 (2018): 55–71.

FIGURE 6.5 **The Number of Attacks and Fatalities by Group Goal, 1968–2005**

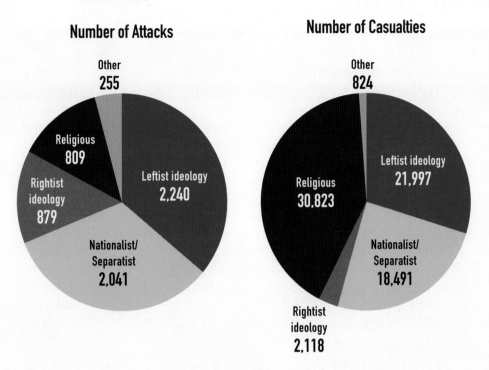

in the afterlife seems important in motivating this kind of behavior. Though not all groups that use suicide terrorism draw on explicitly religious ideologies, most do, and the vast majority of suicide attacks involve perpetrators and targets from different religions.[64] If the individuals engaged in terrorism believe that the ideals they are pursuing cannot be compromised, then there may be little scope for bargaining.

How Can Terrorists Hope to Win? Strategies of Violence

We have already seen that terrorist organizations are generally weak relative to their adversaries, particularly those engaged in transnational terrorism against militarily powerful states. Given that they cannot defeat their target in any conventional sense, how can they hope to succeed? What purpose does killing people serve? (For more on whether terrorism is an effective strategy, see "How Do We Know?" on p. 290.)

When a group turns to terrorism, there are four principal strategies by which it may use violence to further its interests: coercion, provocation, spoiling, and outbidding.[65] These strategies are not mutually exclusive; any particular attack can

Figure source: James A. Piazza, "Is Islamist Terrorism More Dangerous? An Empirical Study of Group Ideology, Organization, and Goal Structure," *Terrorism and Political Violence* 21, no. 1 (2009): 63. Leftist ideology includes groups whose goals were characterized as anarchist, antiglobalization, communist, socialist, and environmental. Rightist ideology includes groups whose goals were characterized as racist, right-wing conservative, and reactionary.

64. Eli Berman and David D. Laitin, "Religion, Terrorism, and Public Goods: Testing the Club Model," *Journal of Public Economics* 92, no. 10–11 (2008): 1942–67. See also Robert A. Pape, *Dying to Win: The Strategic Logic of Suicide Terrorism* (New York: Random House, 2005).

65. Andrew H. Kydd and Barbara F. Walter, "The Strategies of Terrorism," *International Security* 31, no. 1 (Summer 2006): 49–80. We combine their strategies of attrition and intimidation into a single strategy of coercion.

Does Terrorism Work?

Terrorism is effective at killing and maiming people and at creating fear within targeted populations. However, the purpose of terrorism is not simply to kill and terrorize but to achieve some political or social objective. Is terrorism an effective strategy for advancing a group's interests?

A number of scholars have explored this question, and the results have been contradictory.[a] Among the many challenges in answering this question is properly specifying the alternative—that is, is terrorism effective compared to what? Even if terrorist groups rarely get their way, terrorism may be more effective for achieving some goals than doing nothing, mobilizing peacefully, or pursuing other strategies. There is also a concern that groups use terrorism because they are too small and weak to take on their target with more conventional means. If so, then it is the group's weakness, not the nature of its strategy, that would explain its failure.

In a recent study, Virginia Page Fortna sought to tackle these problems by taking advantage of the fact that some rebel groups engaged in civil wars use terrorism and others do not.[b] Civil wars provide a sample of groups that had severe conflicts of interest with the government and engaged in violent rebellion using different strategies. This observation permits a relatively clean comparison of the success rates of groups that relied on terrorism and those that did not. Fortna collected data on 104 rebel groups in the period 1989–2004. Of these, she estimated that 24 (about a quarter) routinely engaged in the deliberate and indiscriminate killing of civilians. Moreover, she found that there was no evidence within this population that relatively weaker groups used terrorism while relatively stronger ones did not.

Each conflict had one of five possible outcomes: (1) the rebels were defeated, (2) the rebellion fizzled out because of low activity, (3) the war was still ongoing at the time of the study, (4) the war ended with a peace agreement, or (5) the rebels defeated the government. Figure A shows the distribution of outcomes for rebel groups that did and did not use terrorism. The evidence suggests that rebel groups that used terrorism were significantly *less* successful than those that did not. In particular, terrorist groups were more likely to be defeated by the government, had less chance of getting a peace agreement, and never won an outright victory.

Terrorism does seem to help organizations sustain their demands. Civil wars that involve terrorism are more likely to continue or fester, and they last significantly longer than those that do not. This suggests that terrorism, by avoiding the state's military capacity, can be an effective method for prolonging a struggle. In doing so, terrorism may be good for preventing outcomes that a group dislikes rather than compelling outcomes that it wants.

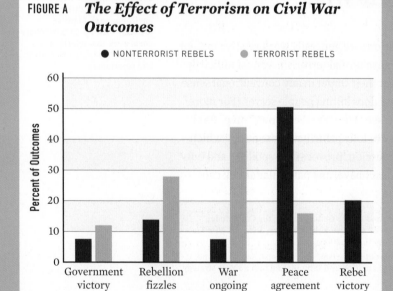

FIGURE A *The Effect of Terrorism on Civil War Outcomes*

● NONTERRORIST REBELS   ● TERRORIST REBELS

Percent of Outcomes

Government victory · Rebellion fizzles · War ongoing · Peace agreement · Rebel victory

a. See, for example, Robert A. Pape, *Dying to Win* (New York: Random House, 2005); Andrew H. Kydd and Barbara F. Walter, "The Strategies of Terrorism," *International Security* 31, no. 1 (Summer 2006): 49–80; Jakana Thomas, "Rewarding Bad Behavior: How Governments Respond to Terrorism in Civil War," *American Journal of Political Science* 58, no. 4 (October 2014): 804–18; Max Abrahms, "Why Terrorism Does Not Work," *International Security* 31, no. 2 (Fall 2006): 42–78; and Seth G. Jones and Martin C. Libicki, *How Terrorist Groups End* (Santa Monica, CA: Rand, 2008).

b. Virginia Page Fortna, "Do Terrorists Win? Rebels' Use of Terrorism and Civil War Outcomes," *International Organization* 69, no. 3 (2015): 519–56.

involve elements of more than one. The key to understanding them is to recognize that terrorists act in front of at least two audiences: (1) the government and population of the target state and (2) the "home" population—that is, the people on whose behalf they claim to act. The different strategies of terrorism seek to impress these audiences in order to advance the organization's twin interests in wresting concessions from the target and winning supporters among the home population. In particular, coercion and spoiling are intended to influence the beliefs of the target, while provocation and outbidding are intended to influence the beliefs of the home population.

Coercion Terrorists may attack or threaten to attack in order to coerce a target into making concessions. **Coercion** attempts to induce policy change by imposing costs—usually civilian deaths and injuries—on the target. More specifically, coercion works through the threat of future costs. The purpose of a terrorist attack is not simply to kill people or destroy buildings; rather, it is to create fear among the target population that there will be future attacks unless the terrorists' demands are met. By threatening to inflict harm on the target, terrorists aim to intimidate potential victims, thereby motivating individuals to press their own government to change its policy.

coercion

A strategy of imposing or threatening to impose costs on other actors in order to induce a change in their behavior.

Since coercive strategies rely heavily on civilians' fear of future attacks, it follows that actual attacks occur primarily to make threats of future violence credible. As we saw earlier, attacks are usually the most effective way for terrorist organizations to signal their capabilities and resolve. Thus, attacks are a form of costly signaling intended to make credible the terrorists' threats of future violence unless their demands are met. This type of signaling can entail small demonstration attacks, such as bomb scares, which are designed not to kill people or destroy property but rather to call attention to the terrorist network and signal its ability to kill and destroy in the future.

In a form of pure signaling, the Basque separatist group ETA often warned the public about its attacks so that people would not be killed. More spectacularly, Al Qaeda's attacks on 9/11 were meant to coerce the United States into withdrawing its troops from the Arabian Peninsula and ending its support for the Saudi regime. The simultaneous hijacking of four airliners and the ensuing destruction were intended to demonstrate Al Qaeda's ability to carry out great violence at the core of America's centers of power.

Provocation Terrorists may attack in order to provoke the target government into a disproportionate response that alienates moderates in the terrorists' home society or in other sympathetic audiences. Particularly dramatic and heinous terrorist attacks often leave the target government with little political choice but to respond with a vigorous counterstrike. After 9/11, there was significant domestic support—even pressure—for the administration of President George W. Bush to strike back forcefully against Al Qaeda. The Israeli government has long maintained a policy of at least "an eye for an eye," responding aggressively to all terrorist attacks on its soil or citizens.

When terrorists are hiding within their home population, any counterstrike is likely to inflict collateral damage—that is, deaths and injuries to innocent bystanders. If the terrorists' home population already fears the target government, such forceful retaliation can further radicalize that population and increase its support for the terrorists. Other audiences outside the terrorists' home society may also be alienated and possibly threatened by what they regard as the target's overly aggressive responses. Thus, this strategy helps address the terrorist organization's collective action problem by creating a larger pool of extremists or sympathetic moderates from which they can draw fighters.

For **provocation** strategies to be effective, the terrorists' home population must have some degree of uncertainty about the target's interests.[66] For example, many people in the Middle East fear that the United States is an imperialist state aligned with Israel to impose its will on their countries, with little regard for Muslim lives. This is precisely the message that groups like Al Qaeda and the Islamic State use to mobilize people to their cause, and they hope that a disproportionate U.S. response that kills innocent civilians will essentially confirm this narrative.

After 9/11, the United States' invasion of Afghanistan and overthrow of the Taliban regime received generally broad support because the war could be understood as a response to the attacks; however, the subsequent invasion of Iraq, which had no role in the 9/11 attacks, was widely seen internationally as unjustified. In the words of a U.S. national intelligence estimate released in 2006, Iraq became a "'cause célèbre' for jihadists, breeding a deep resentment of U.S. involvement in the Muslim world and cultivating supporters for the global jihadist movement."[67] (For more on how this contributed to the emergence of the Islamic State, see "What Shaped Our World?" on p. 276.) The war also inspired increased anti-American sentiment around the world, complicating the United States' relationships with other countries.

Disproportionate responses may lead the terrorists' home society to believe that it has more to fear from the target than from the extremists. Terrorist organizations thus continue to provoke their targets in the hopes that the targets' retaliations will drive new supporters to the terrorists' cause and increase their political power over time.

Spoiling

Terrorists may also attack to spoil, or sabotage, a prospective peace between their target and the moderate leadership from their home society.[68] Target states are often uncertain whether the home state of their terrorist opponents, even if led by moderates, wants to settle the conflict and can control its extremists. Targets want to negotiate with trustworthy and capable moderates who want to

---

66. On provocation strategies, see Ethan Bueno de Mesquita and Eric S. Dickson, "The Propaganda of the Deed: Terrorism, Counterterrorism, and Mobilization," *American Journal of Political Science* 51, no. 2 (2007): 364–81.

67. Office of the Director of National Intelligence, "Trends in Global Terrorism: Implications for the United States," National Intelligence Estimate, April 2006, www.dni.gov/files/documents/Special%20Report_Global%20Terrorism%20NIE%20Key%20Judgments.pdf (accessed 09/16/20).

68. Andrew Kydd and Barbara F. Walter, "Sabotaging the Peace: The Politics of Extremist Violence," *International Organization* 56, no. 2 (2002): 263–96.

and can make peace; they do not want to negotiate with untrustworthy or incapable moderates who cannot or will not prevent further terrorist attacks. Unable to judge the sincerity or capability of their opponent's leadership, target governments watch for terrorist attacks to occur and break off negotiations when they do. By attacking, the terrorists can thus scuttle an agreement they oppose and hold out for terms they hope will be more favorable.

The purpose of this **spoiling** strategy is not to apply pressure on the target per se but to play on doubts in the target state about whether the opponent can be trusted to implement a peace agreement and abide by it in the future. When terrorists attack the target, the latter learns that the terrorists' home government either does not want to or cannot control its extremists, and thus the target is more likely to reject agreements as not credible. Attacks motivated by this logic are most likely to occur during or shortly after peace negotiations.

spoiling
A strategy of terrorist attacks intended to sabotage a prospective peace between the target and moderate leadership from the terrorists' home society.

Outbidding

Finally, terrorist organizations may use violence to outbid potential rivals for support among their home populations. In poker, a player may raise the bet to convince others that she is holding a stronger hand. Likewise, when two or more terrorist networks or factions compete for support within their home populations, one may attack a target in an effort to outbid the others and demonstrate its capability for leadership and commitment to the cause for which all the groups are fighting. **Outbidding** arises when the home population is uncertain about which of several organizations is best able to represent and further its interests. In these cases, an organization may mount dramatic attacks not simply to coerce the target but also to impress the audience at home.

outbidding
A strategy of terrorist attacks designed to demonstrate superior capability and commitment relative to other groups devoted to the same cause.

Rivalries among different factions of the Palestinian movement have created this kind of dynamic. Since the early 1990s, a number of groups—most prominently Fatah and Hamas—have competed for the support of the Palestinian people. Though originally a terrorist group, Fatah renounced violence and is no longer considered a terrorist organization; it has argued instead for a process of negotiation leading to the creation of a Palestinian state. Hamas has continued to engage in terrorist attacks, as have Islamic Jihad and other militant factions, some of which spun off from Fatah. For these groups, attacks against Israel are intended to demonstrate their credentials for leadership among Palestinians who are uncertain about which group best serves their interests. These rivalries have generated cycles of escalation wherein attacks by one group inspire others to attack so as not to be outdone; in some cases, multiple groups would claim credit for the same attack.[69] Similarly, when Peru returned to democratic rule in 1980, the Shining Path group turned to violence to distinguish itself from rival groups with similar goals that chose instead to participate in the electoral process.

The actors we call *target*, *terrorist*, and *home population* are convenient abstractions but obvious simplifications. Within any particular case, these actors may need to be disaggregated further to reveal internal divisions. Likewise, the four strategies of terror are not exclusive. Terrorist networks can attack simultaneously to coerce a

---

69. Mia M. Bloom, "Palestinian Suicide Bombing: Public Support, Market Share, and Outbidding," *Political Science Quarterly* 119, no. 1 (2004): 61–88.

target into making concessions, provoke the target into a disproportionate response that radicalizes their home population, undermine prospective peace agreements, and build support for their factions over others within their home populations. In any long-term struggle (such as that between Israel and the Palestinians or between the Tamil Tigers and the government of Sri Lanka), all four strategies are likely to be employed at some point. We isolate the strategies here merely to highlight their different logics. Understanding the multiple strategies of terrorism is also important in designing effective counterterrorist responses.

Can Terrorism Be Prevented?

Like the war on drugs, the war on poverty, or the war on crime, the "global war on terror" is likely to be a struggle without any clear end. As long as actors have different interests, and as long as individuals retain the ingenuity and ruthlessness that enabled 19 terrorists with simple box cutters to transform airplanes into maneuverable kerosene-filled bombs, terrorism will remain a possibility. Extremism, combined with problems of incomplete information and credible commitment, will continue to inspire terrorist organizations to launch attacks simply to demonstrate that they can.

As with civil wars, economic development and political liberalization might, in the long run, diffuse some of the grievances that fuel or enable terrorist violence, but there is actually little evidence that poverty on its own breeds extremism or drives people to join terrorist organizations.[70] Since ideological, religious, and nationalist extremists can arise in a variety of political and economic contexts, promoting development, while no doubt desirable, is also unlikely to be a magic bullet. Nonetheless, states can adopt certain counterterrorist strategies to make future attacks less likely and, perhaps, less destructive. The same strategies also allow states to make smaller concessions to terrorists even when bargaining works and violence is avoided.

Can Terrorists Be Deterred?　As discussed in Chapter 3, deterrence is a strategy that aims to preserve the status quo by threatening challengers with unacceptable costs. In principle, potential targets can deter terrorism by threatening massive retaliation against terrorist organizations should attacks occur. Although deterrence allowed the Cold War–era superpowers to avoid nuclear war, and although it may operate on a daily basis between states that might otherwise challenge each other if they thought the other would not fight back, many analysts are skeptical that, in practice, deterrence can work against terrorist networks.

Unlike states, terrorists do not possess a clearly identifiable territory against which targets can respond. If a terrorist organization believes it can escape retaliation by hiding in clandestine locations, it is less likely to be deterred from attacking. This consideration is real. However, target states can often find trails leading back

---

70. See, for example, Alan B. Krueger and Jitka Malečková, "Education, Poverty and Terrorism: Is There a Causal Connection?" *Journal of Economic Perspectives* 17, no. 4 (Fall 2003): 119–44; and James A. Piazza, "Do Democracy and Free Markets Protect Us from Terrorism?" *International Politics* 45 (2008): 72–91.

to a terrorist organization. For example, in the event that terrorists turn to weapons of mass destruction, such as nuclear, chemical, biological, or radiological weapons, the materials may be traceable, and large nuclear processing facilities are hard to hide. Thus, it is not the absence of a location against which to retaliate that undermines deterrence as much as two, more subtle, problems.

First, when terrorists use a strategy of provocation, retaliation by the target may simply play into their hands. Retaliating against a terrorist stronghold will likely kill a significant number of civilians, confirming for previously undecided moderates that the target really is a threat to their own security. Unless the retaliating target succeeds in eradicating the terrorist network, a cycle of attacks and counterattacks may, over time, serve only to increase political support for the terrorists.

Second, and closely related, deterrent threats by the potential target may not be credible. Since terrorists hide in larger populations and massive retaliation would likely kill many individuals who are unrelated to the terrorist network, a target state may be reluctant to attack. If a terrorist set off a nuclear explosion in New York, would the United States be willing to annihilate hundreds of thousands of likely innocent people to destroy a terrorist cell operating in, say, Somalia? Or in a country allied with the United States in the global war on terror, such as Pakistan? Or perhaps even in another advanced democratic country, like Germany (where much of the planning for the 9/11 attacks took place)?

Nuclear deterrence in the Cold War—especially extended deterrence, in which the United States promised to launch a retaliatory attack against the Soviet Union's civilian population if the Soviets invaded West Berlin or Paris—always rested on the possibility that the deterrent threats would be carried out. Although the United States might not have started another world war in response to a limited Soviet incursion in Europe, the risk that it might do so was sufficient to deter Russia. The risk that the United States or any other target would retaliate massively against terrorist attacks is not as likely or as clear. Knowing this, terrorists are less likely to be deterred than states are.

Preemption If the threat of retaliation after an attack cannot deter terrorists, states may instead take the initiative and attempt to disrupt or destroy terrorists and their networks before they attack. This strategy of preemption was the Bush administration's most distinctive response to the attacks of 9/11. In his *National Security Strategy for the United States of America* outlined in September 2002, President Bush emphasized, for the first time, preempting attacks from terrorists and states that may possess weapons of mass destruction.

The United States invaded Afghanistan not only to retaliate for the 9/11 attacks but also to prevent future attacks. The goals of the war included capturing or killing Al Qaeda's leadership and foot soldiers and dismantling the infrastructure that had been used to plot and train for attacks. Although Afghanistan was the main theater of "Operation Enduring Freedom," this operation led to the killing and detention of suspected terrorists across the globe. The United States has also made extensive use of drones—remote-controlled aircraft armed with missiles—to kill suspected

Countries can attempt to stop terrorists before they strike—a strategy known as preemption. The United States has used remotely piloted drones to kill suspected terrorists in Pakistan, among other countries. This practice has bred resentment because of collateral damage from the missile strikes.

terrorists in a variety of countries, including Pakistan, Yemen, and Somalia. And, of course, the war in Iraq was justified by President Bush, in part, as a preemptive war on terror.

Preemption can also take nonmilitary forms. Surveillance—monitoring phone calls, e-mail, international financial transactions, and other communication channels—can be used to identify terrorist networks and predict future attacks. Intelligence agencies may also detain and interrogate terrorism suspects in order to unravel plots or identify other members of an organization. A report released by the U.S. Senate in 2014 detailed an extensive program of detention and torturous interrogation methods enacted after 9/11.[71] In resorting to such methods, the United States is not alone. The use of torture, as well as other violations of civil rights, such as imprisonment without due process and extrajudicial killings, is not uncommon among states that are targeted by terrorism.[72]

Preemption is costly in many ways. The wars in Afghanistan and Iraq came at very high prices. By the end of 2019, the United States had spent over $5 trillion on costs related to these wars, which claimed the lives of over 7,000 Americans, more than 1,500 from allied countries, and hundreds of thousands of people in both Afghanistan and Iraq.[73]

Even less forceful measures entail costs. Surveillance, for instance, is expensive relative to the number of attacks it prevents. Surveillance must be continuous and comprehensive to catch attacks while they are being planned. Monitoring possible terrorist activities is akin to looking for the proverbial needle in the haystack, but in this case a potential terrorist attack is a well-hidden needle that we are not even sure exists. Moreover, surveillance is likely to infringe on the civil liberties of innocent civilians.

Preemption can also impose political costs by playing into terrorists' provocation strategies. Foreign populations may perceive preemptive actions as disproportionate responses that pose them a threat. U.S. drone attacks in Pakistan, Yemen, Somalia, and Libya have killed hundreds of noncombatants, breeding resentment

71. Senate Select Committee on Intelligence, *The Senate Intelligence Committee Report on Torture* (New York: Melville House, 2014).

72. James A. Piazza and James Igoe Walsh, "Transnational Terror and Human Rights," *International Studies Quarterly* 53, no. 1 (2009): 125–48. The authors find that terrorist attacks are associated with increased use of "disappearances" and extrajudicial killings but not necessarily torture. They note, however, that the challenge of detecting and confirming torture complicates any analysis of this relationship.

73. Neta C. Crawford, "United States Budgetary Costs and Obligations of Post-9/11 Wars through FY2020: $6.4 Trillion," Watson Institute for International and Public Affairs, Boston University, November 13, 2019, https://watson.brown.edu/costsofwar/files/cow/imce/papers/2019/US%20Budgetary%20 Costs%20of%20Wars%20November%202019.pdf (accessed 1/13/21).

that can feed terrorist recruitment.[74] There is also evidence that the systematic use of torture, extrajudicial killings, and imprisonment without due process can increase, rather than decrease, the number of attacks a country experiences.[75] Thus, in considering preemptive action, targets must balance the probability that they will make themselves safer in the short term against the risk that they will increase terrorist recruitment in the long run.

Defensive Measures As an alternative to offensive or retaliatory military operations, states can and do employ defensive measures to guard against attacks. For instance, after a rash of airplane hijackings in the 1970s, airports around the world installed metal detectors, leading to a dramatic drop in this kind of attack.[76] Even more elaborate security procedures were put in place after 9/11. In addition to implementing enhanced screening at airports, the United States has fortified its embassies abroad, protected its national monuments with barrier defenses and sometimes armed guards, and expanded its border security forces and inspection regimes. Numerous sites remain vulnerable, including the nation's shipping ports, but the country has significantly increased its homeland security efforts overall. Similarly, after a campaign of suicide bombings, Israel constructed a wall separating it from Palestinian-controlled areas of the West Bank, which dramatically reduced the number of attacks.

Defensive measures work to reduce terrorism by raising the costs of carrying out terrorist attacks. As it becomes more expensive to strike a target, whether in terms of resources deployed or time and effort consumed to evade security procedures, terrorism becomes less likely overall. Defensive measures also often have the advantage of not inflicting collateral damage on the terrorists' home population, though the Israeli security barrier in the West Bank has caused a great deal of hardship and resentment among Palestinians.

Defensive measures are not cheap. The United States has spent over a trillion dollars on homeland security since 2001.[77] Indirectly, such measures may impose even greater costs on society. Passengers must now arrive at airports earlier to clear security before boarding their planes, making air travel less efficient and more unpleasant than before. Trucks are subject to longer delays at the nation's borders. Measured by hours of productivity lost, these indirect costs may well dwarf the direct costs. That said, when measured relative to the costs of the Iraq and Afghanistan wars, these costs may seem like a bargain.

---

74. The actual number of civilian deaths from drone attacks is subject to controversy, and government-issued statistics have been challenged by nongovernmental and media organizations; see, for example, Jack Serle, "Obama Drone Casualty Numbers a Fraction of Those Recorded by the Bureau," Bureau of Investigative Journalism, July 1, 2016, www.thebureauinvestigates.com/stories/2016-07-01/obama-drone-casualty-numbers-a-fraction-of-those-recorded-by-the-bureau (accessed 1/12/21).

75. James A. Piazza and James Igoe Walsh, "Physical Integrity Rights and Terrorism," *PS: Political Science and Politics* 43, no. 3 (July 2010): 411–14.

76. See, for example, Walter Enders and Todd Sandler, "The Effectiveness of Antiterrorism Policies: A Vector-Autoregression-Intervention Analysis," *American Political Science Review* 87, no. 4 (1993): 829–44.

77. Crawford, "United States Budgetary Costs and Obligations."

Still, defensive measures will never be totally effective.[78] Terrorists select their targets based on the difficulty of penetrating defenses and the likelihood that their attacks will be successful. When the United States stepped up its internal security measures after 9/11, Al Qaeda shifted its attacks to embassies abroad and American troops in Iraq. The Islamic State encourages supporters to drive cars and trucks into crowds precisely because it is impossible to secure every market or busy street from such an attack. Given the many possible sites, it is prohibitively expensive to protect them all equally. And protecting some may only divert attacks to the next, less fortified target.

Criminalization States can criminalize terrorism and pursue specific individuals and groups for the attacks they have planned or carried out. Along with airport security measures, this was the primary response to the airplane hijackings that occurred in the late 1960s and early 1970s. By 1973, a series of international conventions on skyjackings had been put into place through which states agreed not to harbor hijackers and to turn them over to appropriate authorities. Individual terrorists and groups were pursued and brought to justice in criminal proceedings. Combined with the use of metal detectors at airports, this strategy led to a sharp decline in the number of airplane hijackings.

Criminalization is mostly reactive, seeking to arrest terrorists for attacks after they have been committed. By bringing individuals and groups to justice, states hope not only to disrupt terrorist groups but also to deter others from carrying out attacks. For transnational terrorism, this strategy hinges on effective international cooperation. Nearly all countries would agree that airplane hijackings are odious and against their interests. Even the United States and Cuba, which cooperate in few other areas, have been able to work together to effectively capture and prosecute hijackers; the two nations signed a bilateral pact in 1973 in which they agreed to return immediately any planes, passengers, crew members, and hijackers to their country of origin. The growth of transnational networks may require the development of new international institutions to combat terrorism in the future.

Yet countries do not always share such clearly compatible interests. States that sympathize with terrorists' goals and grant them safe haven, as Afghanistan did for the Taliban, or states that are too weak internally to prevent terrorist groups from operating from within their territory, like Somalia, can effectively undermine the ability of other countries to capture indicted terrorists. Even Pakistan, a country that is nominally allied with the United States in the war on terror, chafed at U.S. efforts to track down Al Qaeda leaders there. The killing of bin Laden on Pakistani soil in 2011 added to tensions in the U.S.-Pakistan relationship.

The same forces of globalization that allow terrorists to attack anywhere around the world also permit terrorists to hide anywhere. To limit terrorism, states need to share intelligence and coordinate their counterattacks. While there has been progress in expanding efforts to track and prosecute terrorists, there are still

---

78. On the limits of defensive measures, see Robert Powell, "Defending against Terrorist Attacks with Limited Resources," *American Political Science Review* 101, no. 3 (2007): 527–41.

few effective international institutions to secure compliance with antiterrorist efforts.

Negotiation and Compromise

Finally, states can attempt to negotiate and compromise with terrorist groups.[79] As explained earlier, bargaining failures are likely to be inevitable, and thus negotiations will not eliminate the problem of terrorism. Most states today maintain a policy of not negotiating with terrorists for fear of recognizing the legitimacy of their demands and tactics—and for fear of being charged with appeasement by domestic critics. Another reason countries are reluctant to negotiate with terrorists is that they do not want to spur other groups into making greater demands. Thus, few explicit negotiations occur between states and terrorists.

Nonetheless, states do talk to terrorists and have at times conceded to the demands of some of the less extreme groups.[80] In the wake of terrorist campaigns, American and French military forces withdrew from Lebanon in 1983, and Israel withdrew from occupied portions of southern Lebanon in 2000 and from the Palestinian-controlled Gaza Strip in 2005.

In 2021, Britain finally withdrew from the European Union. One particularly difficult point in the negotiations over Brexit was the border between the Republic of Ireland, which remained part of the EU, and Northern Ireland, which as part of the United Kingdom withdrew from the EU. The free movement of goods and people between Ireland and Northern Ireland was crucial to the Good Friday Agreement signed in 1998, which ended over three decades of violence between Catholics and Protestants in the latter.

In other cases, peace agreements have successfully stemmed terrorist violence. In the so-called Good Friday Agreement, signed in 1998, Britain made concessions favored by the IRA, granting Northern Ireland a great deal more autonomy and ensuring an influential role for republicans (that is, those seeking a united Ireland) in the region's governance. While some splinter groups continue to threaten violence to spoil the accords, the number of terrorist attacks by Irish nationalist groups dropped dramatically after the agreement. This accord is now in doubt, however, given Britain's exit from the European Union and the new need to regulate flows of goods and people between Ireland and Northern Ireland. Soon after Britain's exit from the EU, loyalists rioted in fear that London was giving priority to Irish nationalists and undermining commitments to keep Northern Ireland part of the United Kingdom.

More recently, a 2016 peace deal between the Colombian government and the Revolutionary Armed Forces of Colombia (FARC) ended more than five decades of conflict. A rebel group that had made systematic use of terrorist attacks, FARC disarmed in 2017 under UN supervision and re-formed as a nonviolent political party.

---

79. On bargaining, see Harvey E. Lapan and Todd Sandler, "To Bargain or Not to Bargain: That Is the Question," *American Economic Review* 78, no. 2 (1988): 16–21.

80. See Jonathan Powell, *Terrorists at the Table: Why Negotiating is the Only Way to Peace* (New York: St. Martin's Press, 2015) and Mark Perry, *Talking to Terrorists: Why America Must Engage with Its Enemies* (New York: Basic Books, 2010).

Although it can be painful reconciling with people who have committed atrocities against innocent civilians (the first version of the Colombian peace deal was rejected by voters who thought it too lenient on FARC), allowing militant groups to enter the political process and compete for power through existing institutions can be an effective route to ending the violence.[81]

Conclusion: A Challenge to States?

Violence pursued by rebel groups and terrorist organizations represents a challenge to states in several respects. For the states that are targeted by these actors, insurgency and terrorism represent threats to their people and to their ability to govern. Civil wars, in particular, exact a very high toll on the countries that suffer them—in terms of lives lost, resources spent and destroyed, and even death and disease, which linger long after the fighting stops.[82] Terrorism kills many fewer people but, by design, can lead whole nations to live in fear. Though in some cases we might share or sympathize with the interests that compel these groups to violence, the enormous costs involved are always tragic.

Rebellion and terrorism also pose challenges to states in a more fundamental sense. Many models of international relations start with the assumption that states are the main actors in world politics. This assumption is sometimes made only to simplify the analysis, as we did in Chapter 3 when we used states as actors—a simplification that allowed us to focus on bargaining dynamics. In other theoretical approaches, however, particularly those derived from the realist school, the state-centric view represents a substantive claim about which actors really matter and, by implication, which do not. The pride of place given to states usually rests on two assertions: (1) that interactions in international politics are dominated by the threat and use of force, and (2) that states, particularly large states, are the main actors capable of mobilizing and wielding military power. In this view, then, the world stage is dominated by the clash of great powers.

The importance of rebellion and terrorism call this view into question. As we have seen, nonstate actors, while lacking the size and organizational advantages of states, have developed strategies of violence that can be quite effective. Insurgency and terrorism, the main weapons of asymmetrical warfare, seek to neutralize a state's power in several ways: by evading the target state's conventional military power; exploiting vulnerabilities, such as civilians and other "soft" targets; and, at times, provoking counterattacks that may swell the ranks of the rebel or terrorist group's supporters. We have also seen that states often wield nonstate actors as weapons against one another. When direct confrontation with another state is likely to be too costly (as during the Cold War) or ineffective (as when a weak state

---

81. See, for example, Aila M. Matanock, *Electing Peace: From Civil Conflict to Political Participation* (Cambridge: Cambridge University Press, 2017).

82. On this last point, see Hazem Adam Ghobarah, Paul Huth, and Bruce Russett, "Civil Wars Kill and Maim People—Long after the Shooting Stops," *American Political Science Review* 97, no. 2 (2003): 189–202.

confronts a stronger one), sponsoring a rebel group or terrorist organization may be an effective alternative. Thus, even the bargaining interaction between states can be fundamentally influenced by the presence of nonstate actors willing to use violence.

In short, rebel groups and terrorist organizations violate the view that states monopolize the means of coercion in international politics. What strong states have is an institutional structure capable of overcoming the collective action problem inherent in wielding coercive power. This is no small matter, since many dissatisfied groups and extremist individuals will never mobilize the people, arms, and money necessary to make an impact. But those that have found a way to do so have managed to kill large numbers of people, consume vast resources, overthrow governments, and, at times, dominate the foreign policy agendas of even the most powerful states.

Study Tool Kit

Interests, Interactions, and Institutions in Context

- Civil conflict can arise when individuals have interests that conflict with those of the central government, leading to demands that involve territory, policy, or government composition. Whether a rebel group can overcome the collective action problem depends on its own resources, the capacity of the government, and the willingness of foreign states to lend support.

- Bargaining between a government and a rebel group can lead to war as a result of information problems, commitment problems, and issue indivisibilities. Particularly severe commitment problems often make civil wars hard to resolve without the outright victory of one side or the other.

- Domestic institutions that provide peaceful mechanisms for addressing groups' interests and international institutions that facilitate collective efforts to stabilize conflict-ridden countries both hold some promise for preventing civil conflicts from starting or reigniting.

- International terrorist organizations are composed of relatively small numbers of individuals with extreme preferences. Because of their weakness relative to their targets and relative to their goals, terrorists rely on a strategy of attacking civilians and organize into loose networks that are hard to root out.

- Rebel groups and terrorists employ strategies of violence that are intended both to coerce their targets and to address their collective action problem by attracting supporters. For this reason, efforts to defeat these groups often require strategies that take account of effects on noncombatants.

Key Terms

For Further Reading

Ahmad, Aisha. *Jihad & Co.: Black Markets and Islamist Power.* **New York: Oxford University Press, 2017.** An explanation of how Islamist extremists and local businesses depend on one another for success.

Berman, Eli, Joseph H. Felter, and Jacob N. Shapiro. *Small Wars, Big Data: The Information Revolution in Modern Conflict.* **Princeton, NJ: Princeton University Press, 2018.** An examination of the critical role of information in counterinsurgency warfare.

Cohen, Dara Kay. *Rape During Civil War.* **Ithaca, NY: Cornell University Press, 2016.** A detailed investigation of a common yet misunderstood tactic in civil conflicts.

Enders, Walter, and Todd Sandler. *The Political Economy of Terrorism.* **New York: Cambridge University Press, 2005.** An excellent introduction to research on terrorism.

English, Richard. *Does Terrorism Work? A History.* **New York: Oxford University Press, 2016.** A nuanced and subtle evaluation of the question posed in the title by one of the world's foremost historians of the subject.

Fazal, Tanisha M., and Margarita Konaev. "**Homelands versus Minelands: Why Do Armed Groups Commit to the Laws of War?**" *Journal of Global Security Studies* **4, no. 2 (April 2019): 149–68.** An examination of why the Geneva Conventions are only recognized by some rebel groups, even though these same laws have done much to regulate armed conflict between states.

Hultman, Lisa, Jacob D. Kathman, and Megan Shannon. *Peacekeeping in the Midst of War.* **New York: Oxford University Press, 2020.** An examination of how UN peacekeepers reduce battlefield violence and violence against civilians in civil wars.

Kilcullen, David. *The Accidental Guerrilla: Fighting Small Wars in the Midst of a Big One.* **New York: Oxford University Press, 2009.** An examination of counterterrorism and counterinsurgency doctrine as applied to the "war on terror."

Kydd, Andrew H., and Barbara F. Walter. "**The Strategies of Terrorism.**" *International Security* **31, no. 1 (Summer 2006): 49–80.** Develops the four strategies of terrorism explained in this text.

Mason, T. David, and Sara McLaughlin Mitchell, eds. *What Do We Know about Civil Wars?* Lanham, MD: Rowman & Littlefield, 2016. A collection of essays by leading scholars summarizing current scholarly understanding of the causes and outcomes of civil wars.

Shapiro, Jacob N. *The Terrorist's Dilemma: Managing Violent Covert Organizations.* Princeton, NJ: Princeton University Press, 2013. An examination of how terrorist organizations try to control their members while balancing their needs for secrecy and control.

7

International Trade

THE PUZZLE *Virtually all economic analysis concludes that trade is economically beneficial. Why, then, does every country restrict trade in some way? Why have policies toward trade varied so much from country to country and over time?*

Above: U.S. president Donald Trump implemented steel tariffs to protect American jobs, but these trade barriers ultimately increased the cost of goods made with steel for American consumers and sparked economic conflict with China.

The American steel industry employed fewer than 140,000 people in 2018. Yet this relatively small industry has received massive economic assistance from the U.S. government, primarily in the form of protection from foreign competition. A 25 percent tariff on imported steel sparked the U.S.-China trade war that erupted in 2018. This trade protection has raised the cost of steel in the United States and increased the prices that American consumers pay for goods made with steel. By one estimate, since 1970, protection and other aid to the U.S. steel industry has cost American consumers and taxpayers between $145 billion and $230 billion—a staggering amount for an industry that employs less than 0.05 percent of the total U.S. labor force.[1] The Trump administration's 2018 tariffs alone cost U.S. steel buyers $5.6 billion, and purchasers paid an extra $650,000 for each job created by the tariffs.[2]

The steel industry is hardly alone in being protected from imports, to the benefit of producers and the detriment of consumers. Footwear, dairy products, motorcycles, clothing, cotton, lumber, automobiles, and sugar are among the many other goods whose import has been restricted by the U.S. government. One group of scholars estimated that if all barriers to international trade were removed, the U.S. economy would gain some $540 billion by 2025, amounting to over $4,000 for each U.S. household per year.[3] And the United States is hardly alone in erecting obstacles to international commerce; to varying degrees, every country has such trade barriers.

People have traded across borders for as long as borders have existed. In the modern world, international trade has become one of the two most important types of

1. William H. Barringer and Kenneth J. Pierce, *Paying the Price for Big Steel* (Washington, DC: American Institute for International Steel, 2000); and William H. Barringer, Kenneth J. Pierce, and Matthew P. McCullough, *Still Paying the Price* (Washington, DC: American Institute for International Steel, 2007).

2. Gary Clyde Hufbauer and Euijin Jung, "Steel Profits Gain, but Steel Users Pay, under Trump's Protectionism," *Peterson Institute for International Economics*, December 20, 2018, www.piie.com/blogs/trade-investment-policy-watch/steel-profits-gain-steel-users-pay-under-trumps-protectionism (accessed 9/1/20).

3. Gary Clyde Hufbauer and Zhiyao (Lucy) Lu, "The Payoff to America from Globalization: A Fresh Look with a Focus on Costs to Workers," Peterson Institute for International Economics, Policy Brief 17-16, May 2017, https://www.piie.com/publications/policy-briefs/payoff-america-globalization-fresh-look-focus-costs-workers (accessed 4/14/21). It should be noted that these numbers have been questioned by other scholars, who think they are either too high or too low.

economic exchange among countries (the other is international investment, which we will examine in Chapter 8). Dramatic reductions in trade barriers and dramatic increases in international trade itself have influenced the evolution of the world economy since World War II. Yet governments have always attempted to control trade across their borders. In fact, trade policy—the restriction of imports and the promotion of exports—has long been one of the most important economic policies, foreign or domestic, that governments undertake. Those who sell or buy from abroad have a great deal at stake in international trade; so too do those who face competition from foreigners, which can threaten their jobs or businesses. Today's heated debates over the costs and benefits of international trade serve as the basis for this chapter's discussion.

We first ask why international trade takes the form it does. Most of the poorest countries export almost exclusively farm products and raw materials, and they import manufactured goods. Most rich countries, in contrast, import much of their food and raw materials and export mainly manufactured goods. Those poor countries that do export industrial products typically sell simpler goods, such as clothing, footwear, and furniture; rich countries primarily export more sophisticated manufactured goods, such as commercial aircraft and elaborate machinery. How can we explain these patterns of international trade?

Our exploration of this question raises the additional question of why international trade is so commonly restricted. Although many of us take for granted that protecting national products is good, why should a government purposely raise the prices that domestic consumers pay?

Another question arises from the fact that barriers to international trade vary a great deal. Some countries restrict trade very little, while others come close to prohibiting it. Sometimes governments cooperate closely to maintain and expand their trade relations; at other times, bargaining among governments over trade policy is conflictual and even hostile—as is the case with the United States and China. In addition, trade barriers have changed dramatically over time: both globally and in individual countries, trade has gone from generally unhindered to tightly regulated over relatively short periods. International trade became freer (that is, more unrestricted) between the 1950s and the 1990s, but since then trade has become increasingly controversial. Finally, government trade policies themselves often differ among industries, with some goods being strongly protected and others not at all.

Thinking Analytically about International Trade

Because trade policy stands at the intersection of international and domestic politics, it involves powerful interests, important interactions, and influential institutions at both the domestic and international levels. Foreign trade has major effects on domestic producers, consumers, and others. Domestically, supporters and opponents of freer trade—those who want access to world markets and those who want protection from foreign competition, respectively—square off according to their economic interests and interact in a battle over national trade policy. These interactions are mediated through the national political institutions of trade policy making: parties, legislatures, executives, and bureaucracies.

In addition, a given nation's trade policies affect other nations' trade, such that all national policies are made in interaction with those of other governments. Indeed, international trade interactions often spill into broader interstate relations—sometimes in a positive way, sometimes negatively.

A network of global and regional institutions has evolved to facilitate bargaining over trade policies. These institutions include treaties among countries as well as regional and global trade agreements. The most prominent trade institutions have been the two international organizations that have governed world trade for 60 years: first the General Agreement on Tariffs and Trade (GATT) and, since 1995, the World Trade Organization (WTO). At the regional level, trade-based institutions include the European Union (EU), which addresses many other issues in addition to trade; the North American Free Trade Agreement (NAFTA) and its successor the United States-Mexico-Canada Agreement (USMCA); and the Southern Common Market (Mercosur). All these factors help determine how open a country will be to trade and which domestic industries it will likely protect. When we consider global networks, these factors affect how open or closed international trade as a whole will be.

What's So Good about Trade?

Actors engage in foreign trade for the same reason that they trade with each other within countries: to realize the benefits of specialization. Only a household that produces everything it wants to consume, at a lower cost than it could find elsewhere, would have no reason to trade. But such a household is unlikely to exist. For example, a family that owns a farm could make its own tractor, but it is better off expending its energy on farming and using the proceeds to buy or rent a tractor. Modern societies are based on specialization—some people farm or manufacture, others transport or build—and on trade among people with different specialties. The division of labor permits diverse segments of society to focus on different economic activities in ways that benefit society as a whole. After all, if all households or all villages had to be self-sufficient, they would produce only a fraction of what they could make if they specialized.

Specialization—the division of labor—was central to Adam Smith's argument in his 1776 founding text of classical economics, *The Wealth of Nations*. Smith and his fellow economic liberals argued, against the then dominant mercantilists, that self-sufficiency was foolish because a greater division of labor made societies wealthier. In a famous example, Smith pointed out that an individual pin maker working alone could make at best 20 pins a day. In the workshops of Smith's time, however, pin making was divided into about 18 steps, with each worker specializing in 1 or 2 steps. In this way, a pin factory with 10 workers produced 48,000 pins a day—making each individual some 240 times more productive than he would be if he were working alone.[4] Smith thus argued that specialization increases productivity, and productivity fuels economic growth.[5]

The classical economists, in turn, emphasized that specialization requires access to large markets; after all, a single village could hardly use 48,000 pins a day. They argued that restricting market size slows economic growth. A village cut off from the rest of the world and forced into self-sufficiency would have to produce everything it needed, but if that village was part of a larger national or global market, it could specialize in what it did best. Producers need ample markets in order to specialize; the division of labor depends on the size of the market.

The division of labor allows gains from international trade. In farming, temperate countries like the United States and Argentina specialize in temperate crops, such as wheat, while tropical countries like Brazil and the Philippines specialize in tropical crops, such as sugarcane. The nations around the Persian Gulf, with their rich oil deposits, base their economies on oil, while countries with plentiful iron ore gain economic advantages by mining

The Scottish thinker Adam Smith's ideas about the division of labor help explain the benefits of trade.

---

4. Adam Smith, *An Inquiry into the Nature and Causes of the Wealth of Nations* (1776; repr., New York: Modern Library, 1937), 4–5.

5. *Productivity* in this context refers to the amount produced by one unit of labor with the other factors of production—especially land and capital—at its disposal. In farming, for example, the same amount of labor is more productive on good soil than on poor soil, more productive with machinery, fertilizer, and irrigation than without.

it. Similarly, countries with many unskilled laborers, such as Bangladesh and Egypt, produce goods that require lots of unskilled labor, including clothing, footwear, and furniture. Countries with many skilled technicians, such as the European nations, produce goods such as complex machinery and aircraft that require sophisticated technical knowledge. Such specialization among countries leads to economic gains based on trade.

Comparative advantage is the core concept of the economics of trade. (See the "Special Topic" appendix to this chapter, on p. 358.) It applies the principle of specialization to countries: like people, they should do what they do best. Thus, comparative advantage implies that a nation gains most by specializing in producing and exporting what it produces most efficiently. By doing so, it can earn as much as possible in order to pay to import the best products of other countries. The principle of comparative advantage leads to the conclusion that each country will be best off if it produces what it is best at producing and exchanges its products with other countries in return for things it is not so good at producing.

The word *comparative* in the term *comparative advantage* refers to a comparison among the things a country could potentially do—not between one country and another. Just as personal specialization implies that all individuals should do what they do best—not what they do better than everyone else—the specialization involved in comparative advantage implies that countries should produce what they can make most cost-effectively. In other words, it is not necessary for a country to have an **absolute advantage** (the ability to do something better than others) in producing something for it to be profitable to produce and export that thing; all that is necessary is a comparative advantage.

The principle of comparative advantage has clear implications for free trade. Since a country gains from following its comparative advantage and engaging in exchange with other nations for goods in which it does not have a comparative advantage, and since barriers to trade impede its ability to do so, trade protection is harmful to the economy as a whole. Government policies that keep out imports force the country to produce goods that are not to its comparative advantage to produce. Indeed, trade protection raises the price of imports and reduces the efficiency of domestic production. Were national governments to follow the principle of comparative advantage, they would unilaterally remove trade barriers and implement free trade. In this situation, trade policy would be fundamentally cooperative in that all countries would gain from the elimination of obstacles to international trade.

Many people find the economic argument for free trade counterintuitive. Policy makers often argue that exports are good because they create jobs, that imports are bad because they take away jobs, and that governments should stimulate the national economy by restricting imports and encouraging exports. This argument is often referred to as **neo-mercantilism**, so called because of its likeness to the classical mercantilism of the colonial powers, which aimed to run trade surpluses with their colonies. Today, politicians have once again returned to this argument to justify raising barriers to foreign imports. But economic logic insists the opposite: that imports are the gains from trade, while exports are its costs.

comparative advantage

The ability of a country or firm to produce a particular good or service more efficiently than it can produce other goods or services, such that its resources are most efficiently employed in this activity. The comparison is to the efficiency of other economic activities that the actor might undertake given all the products it can produce—not to the efficiency of other countries or firms.

absolute advantage

The ability of a country or firm to produce more of a particular good or service than other countries or firms can produce with the same amount of effort and resources.

neo-mercantilism

A belief that national economic policy should encourage exports and discourage imports, and that the country should aim to run a trade surplus. So called in relationship to the classical mercantilism of the colonial powers, which aimed at running trade surpluses with their colonies (see Chapter 1).

Free trade induces a country to follow its comparative advantage, and economic logic implies that free trade is the ideal policy. This is true, according to economic thinking, even if free trade is pursued unilaterally. Protection serves only to raise costs to consumers. The fact that other countries impose trade barriers that raise prices to their own consumers is no reason for one country to harm its own consumers in response. Countries should undertake open trade policies regardless of what other countries do.

There is a clear parallel, from this perspective, between the comparative-advantage argument and the choices available to a household. A family that owns a farm, for example, "exports" (sells its crops) in order to "import" (buy the goods and services it wants). Because the farm family wants to maximize the imports it can buy, it needs to earn more; the best way to do so is to produce more of what it produces best. The principle of comparative advantage thus illustrates how farmers, workers, and firms gain by specializing and trading, just as countries do.

Why Do Countries Trade What They Trade?

The principle of comparative advantage suggests that countries should produce and export what they do best. But how can we know what a country does best, other than by observing what it exports? And if the only way to predict a country's exports is to observe them, the theory is not of much value—especially given that trade flows are affected by many noneconomic factors, such as trade barriers. In the 1920s, Swedish economists Eli Heckscher and Bertil Ohlin addressed this puzzle and extended the classical view.

The Heckscher-Ohlin approach tries to explain national comparative advantage and therefore national trading patterns. The two economists recognized that comparative advantage is not simply a result of effort. For example, the productivity of farmers depends primarily on characteristics of their land, not on how hard they work. In countries where land is in short supply and expensive, farming is costly; where it is plentiful and cheap, farming is low in cost.

Heckscher-Ohlin trade theory describes the basic economic characteristics of a country in terms of the material and human resources it possesses. Typically, these economic features are summarized according to basic factors of production, or the resources essential for economic activity. Such factors of production include:

- Land, an essential factor in agricultural production

- Labor, usually meaning unskilled labor

- Capital for investment, which refers both to the machinery and equipment with which goods are produced and to the financial assets necessary to employ this machinery and equipment

- Human capital, which refers to skilled labor, so called because the labor has been enhanced by investment in training and education

Countries differ greatly in the degree to which they are endowed with each of these factors of production. Some are rich in land, others have abundant unskilled

Heckscher-Ohlin trade theory

The theory that a country will export goods that make intensive use of the factors of production in which it is well endowed. For example, a labor-rich country will export goods that make intensive use of labor.

labor, others have abundant human capital, and still others are wealthy in investment capital. Heckscher-Ohlin trade theory relies on these "factor endowments" to explain what determines national comparative advantage and, in turn, what countries produce and export. For example, a country with a large population and poor farmland is likely to have a comparative disadvantage in farming, but a country with few people and vast supplies of farmland is likely to have a comparative advantage in agriculture. Different products too require different mixes of resources: typically, farm goods require a lot of land, simple manufactured goods require a lot of unskilled labor, and complex machinery requires a lot of investment capital.

Heckscher-Ohlin trade theory argues that a country will export goods that make intensive use of the resources the country has in abundance, and it will import goods that make intensive use of the country's scarce resources. Countries with lots of cheap land specialize in producing farm goods; for example, the United States in the nineteenth century was relatively sparsely populated but was rich in very fertile land and exported massive quantities of cotton, tobacco, and wheat. In contrast, countries with very little arable land import many farm goods—such as Great Britain in the nineteenth century, which relied heavily on imports for its food. Countries rich in investment capital focus on making goods whose production requires a great deal of capital; for example, most North American and western European nations' industries today specialize in sophisticated manufactured goods, such as complex machinery, construction equipment, and commercial aircraft. Regions with abundant labor produce labor-intensive goods: China and other rapidly developing labor-rich nations concentrate on making products that require a great deal of labor, such as clothing, toys, furniture, and other relatively simple manufactures.

According to the Heckscher-Ohlin trade theory, developing countries that are rich in less skilled labor should export labor-intensive manufactured goods. For example, Indonesia's primary exports are textiles and clothing.

This pattern of specialization leads to analogous trade patterns. Poor countries with little capital import the capital-intensive products they need. Today, for example, poor agricultural nations tend to import their farm machinery from capital-rich industrialized nations, just as the United States did in the early nineteenth century. China and India export their labor-intensive manufactures to North America and western Europe and import capital-intensive industrial goods—including the complex machinery needed to operate their domestic factories.[6] Within North America, the capital-rich United States exports capital-intensive machinery (and capital) to Mexico, while labor-rich Mexico sends labor-intensive manufactured products (and labor) to the United States.

Each of these factors of production can be associated with different socioeconomic actors. A country abundant in land will also, typically, have many farmers. Unskilled or skilled laborers have unskilled and skilled labor, respectively, to sell on the labor market. Investors hold much of the investment capital of a country. Therefore, when we say that a country that is abundant in land will export products that make great use of land, we are saying that farmers and farmworkers will be heavily engaged in producing goods for export. The relative abundance or scarcity of factors of production has a powerful impact on the economic activities of actors within a society.

The Heckscher-Ohlin theory helps explain the broad outlines of international trade. The industrial countries are rich in capital and human capital, and they export manufactured goods that make intensive use of these resources. Most developing countries are rich in land, raw materials, or unskilled labor (or some combination of the three), and they export agricultural products, minerals, or labor-intensive manufactures.

The theory also helps explain changes over time in a country's trade relations. A poor country with abundant land and labor but little capital will export farm goods and simple labor-intensive manufactures. As the country develops, it accumulates capital and its workers become more skilled, such that its endowments change and, with them, its export patterns. This explains, for example, why the United States in the nineteenth century exported primarily raw materials and farm goods, yet today it exports almost exclusively goods and services that require large amounts of capital and skilled labor to produce. In addition to explaining aspects of world trade patterns, Heckscher-Ohlin trade theory has important implications for the domestic politics of trade policy, as we discuss later in this chapter.

There are other potential economic explanations for the patterns we observe in international trade. A great deal of modern international trade is related to the activities of multinational corporations, such as Ford Motor Company. These companies sell goods among their subsidiaries (companies they own or control) located in different countries. It has been estimated that about one-third of all American trade actually takes place *within* companies, from one of a firm's branches or

---

6. This argument applies to movements of capital and people as well as to trade. Countries rich in capital should export capital, and countries rich in labor should export labor. (Land, of course, cannot be traded across borders without changing the borders!)

Much international trade is in goods with internationally known and desirable brand names. Coca-Cola employs a global network of 225 bottling partners and sells to consumers in more than 200 countries and territories.

subsidiaries to another—say, from a Ford engine factory in Mexico to a Ford assembly plant in the United States.[7]

This sort of "intrafirm" trade may not be due primarily to the forces that Heckscher-Ohlin theory suggests but rather to production and distribution networks within companies. Companies increasingly use global supply chains to make and sell products to customers around the world. Coca-Cola employs a global network of 225 bottling partners in order to efficiently sell to consumers in more than 200 countries and territories. Footwear manufacturer Nike has more than 470 factories located in 41 countries.[8]

These kinds of global production and distribution networks also tie different companies together. Indeed, much of world trade is now carried out within global supply chains where parts and components are made in many locations around the world by various companies, to be bought, assembled, and sold by a single firm. Phone manufacturer Apple bought products from 200 different firms in 2018, and these firms were located in more than 18 countries.[9] Many of these products were used to make the company's flagship product, the iPhone. In this way, much of the manufacturing and production that was once carried out in a single location or at least in a single country has been outsourced to suppliers all over the world.

In addition, a great deal of international trade is in goods whose attraction to consumers has to do as much with brand name, reputation, or other related

---

7. Kim J. Ruhl, "How Well Is US Intrafirm Trade Measured?" *American Economic Review* 105, no. 5 (May 2015): 524–29.

8. Nike, "Nike Manufacturing Map," August 2020, http://manufacturingmap.nikeinc.com (accessed 1/25/21).

9. Apple, "Supplier List," 2019, www.apple.com/supplier-responsibility/pdf/Apple-Supplier-List.pdf (accessed 1/25/21).

considerations as it does with price. North America, for example, both imports automobiles from Europe and exports automobiles to Europe. This sort of trade is not the result of fundamentally different factor endowments (and prices) between Europe and North America—both regions are rich in capital and skilled labor and poor in unskilled labor—but rather of European consumer interest in American car brands and American consumer interest in European car brands. One estimate is that more than two-thirds of all the trade of advanced industrial countries is actually this sort of "intra-industry" trade.[10]

Other economic links among countries encourage trade. Countries that share a currency, such as those in the European Union that use the euro, trade with one another more frequently than those that do not. Countries that invest heavily in one another's economies also tend to trade heavily with one another.

Noneconomic factors also affect both what and with whom countries trade. Countries that are geographically close together trade more, since transport costs are lower. Diplomatic and military relations between nations also influence their trade patterns. Countries whose governments are hostile to one another are likely to trade little, whereas those on friendly terms are likely to trade more. There are two reasons for this. First, trade between hostile nations is riskier than trade between friendly nations: businesses avoid engaging in trade that may very well be disrupted by the outbreak of hostilities. Second, governments often pursue close economic ties with their allies in order to cement the alliance and support friendly nations. By the same token, if trade is good for a country's economy, a government might shy away from trade with an unfriendly nation in order to keep from strengthening a potential enemy. During the Cold War, as we mentioned in Chapter 5 in our discussion of the North Atlantic Treaty Organization (NATO), the United States and its allies purposely limited their economic ties with the Soviet Union even as they encouraged ties among themselves.

Some analysts believe that trade encourages friendly relations as much as friendly relations encourage trade. For example, Cordell Hull, U.S. secretary of state before and during World War II, wrote: "It is a fact that war did not break out between the United States and any country with which we had been able to negotiate a trade agreement. It is also a fact that, with very few exceptions, the countries with which we signed trade agreements joined together in resisting the Axis. The political line-up followed the economic line-up."[11]

After World War II, the two superpowers used their trade relations to reinforce their alliances: the United States and the Soviet Union encouraged their respective allies to build a common trading order that excluded members of the other alliance. After the Cold War ended, many policy makers in Europe wanted to encourage trade with the former communist countries of Eastern and Central Europe as a way

10. Organisation for Economic Co-operation and Development, "Measuring Globalisation: OECD Economic Globalisation Indicators 2010," September 2010, www.oecd.org/sti/ind/measuringglobalisationoecdeconomicglobalisationindicators2010.htm (accessed 1/25/21).

11. Quoted in Richard N. Gardner, *Sterling-Dollar Diplomacy in Current Perspective: The Origins and the Prospects of Our International Economic Order*, expanded ed. (New York: Columbia University Press, 1980), 9.

protectionism

The imposition of barriers to restrict imports.

trade barriers

Government limitations on the international exchange of goods. Examples include tariffs, quantitative restrictions (quotas), import licenses, requirements that governments buy only domestically produced goods, and health and safety standards that discriminate against foreign goods.

tariff

A tax imposed on imports. Tariffs raise the domestic price of the imported good and may be applied for the purpose of protecting domestic producers from foreign competition.

quantitative restriction (quota)

A limit placed on the amount of a particular good that is allowed to be imported and sold domestically.

nontariff barriers to trade

Obstacles to imports other than tariffs (trade taxes). Examples include restrictions on the number of products that can be imported (quantitative restrictions, or quotas); regulations that favor domestic over imported products; and other measures that discriminate against foreign goods or services. "Buy American" laws that govern what state and local governments can buy, for example, are an implicit—but nontariff— obstacle to the purchase of imports.

to encourage cooperative diplomatic relations with them. Regardless of the pattern of cause and effect, international diplomatic realities and international trade are closely related.

But the most important noneconomic source of international trade patterns is national trade policy undertaken to address the interests of domestic constituencies. Discussions of international trade often overlook the fact that while such trade takes place among countries, it really involves individuals and firms with well-defined interests. We say that "Mexico" exports a million tons of steel to "the United States," but in fact, companies in Mexico sell the steel to companies in the United States. Companies in one country profit from the sale, and companies in the other profit from the purchase. For trade is the stuff of domestic politics, as governments attempt to respond to the interests of corporations and consumers, farmers and workers, all of whom have something at stake in their countries' policies toward foreign trade.

We now consider how domestic political and economic factors affect trade policy and trade itself. In this context we examine the interests, institutions, and interactions that shape national trade policies.

Trade Restrictions Are the Rule, Not the Exception

Despite the powerful economic arguments for free trade, every country currently has at least some restrictions on trade with the rest of the world. Some countries have very high barriers to trade; others have much lower ones. Yet government policies to control and contain trade are the norm today as they have been in the past. **Protectionism**, the use of specific measures to shield domestic producers from imports, has long been one of the most common government policies worldwide. Most of today's rich countries were strongly protectionist at some point in their history.

Virtually all governments restrict at least some imports. For hundreds of years, governments have imposed a wide variety of **trade barriers**, or impediments to the importation of foreign goods. Historically, the most common barriers have been **tariffs**: taxes on imports levied at the border and paid by the importer. A tariff raises the price of the import directly, so a consumer of the imported good has to pay more for it. Another common form of trade barrier is a **quantitative restriction**, or **quota**, which limits the quantity of a foreign good that can be sold domestically. Because the reduced quantity of the good typically increases its domestic price, quantitative restrictions have the same effect as tariffs: they make the imported goods more expensive to domestic consumers. There are many other **nontariff barriers to trade**, such as regulations targeted at foreign goods or requirements that governments purchase from domestic producers. In all instances, the effect of these policies is to shelter domestic producers from foreign competition. Before we analyze the effects of these policies, it is important to emphasize how common they have been and continue to be.

The degree to which the world's major nations have been open to trade has varied greatly over time and among countries. As we saw in Chapter 1, for more than 300 years after 1492 the major European nations followed the trade policies of mercantilism, a system by which great powers used their military might to control trade with and extract wealth from their colonial possessions. The colonial powers' mercantilist regulations kept foreign goods out of their markets and reserved their colonies' markets for themselves.

Around the middle of the nineteenth century, however, Great Britain and other leading industrial countries moved in the direction of trade liberalization: they pursued policies that involved fewer restrictions on trade. Great Britain adopted free trade, permitting foreigners to sell anything to Britain without tax or restriction. More generally, from the 1860s until 1914, international trade among the principal industrialized nations was quite free. There were tariffs and other barriers, to be sure, and some countries were very protectionist—especially such industrializing nations as the United States, which had some of the world's highest trade barriers at the time. Nonetheless, most of the world's major economies were open, and world trade grew at a very rapid rate.

With the outbreak of World War I in 1914, however, international trade relations entered 30 years of crisis and closure. Efforts to rebuild the trading system after the war were not very successful, especially once the Great Depression hit in 1929. The major powers divided up the world into more or less hostile trading blocs: the British, French, Italian, Japanese, and other empires, along with the less formal German and American spheres of influence.

After 1945, the Western world under American leadership moved gradually to reduce trade barriers among the developed nations. The communist countries and most developing countries protected themselves from world markets, but the industrialized world significantly liberalized its trade. As Figure 7.1 shows, trade has become an increasingly large part of the global economy since the 1970s. Although the reduction of trade barriers remained controversial, by the 1980s the rich countries had become very open to world trade as part of the broader march toward economic globalization. Eventually, most developing and formerly communist countries joined the liberalizing and globalizing trend. Since the early 1990s, international trade has once more—as it was before 1914—been quite open. Thus, in terms of global trade relations over time, we see a pattern in which mercantilist closure gave way to freer trade, then to interwar closure, then to liberalization after 1945, and then to further liberalization leading to globalization after 1980. In 2019, total world trade—measured by the sum of exports and imports of goods and services—constituted 60 percent of GDP.

Many nations have, at some point, gone from very closed to very open to trade or vice versa. Great Britain jettisoned mercantilism in the 1840s. The United States, one of the most protectionist nations in the world through most of the nineteenth and early twentieth centuries, started moving toward freer trade in the 1930s and was leading the charge for trade liberalization by the 1950s and 1960s. The United States traded more and more with other countries starting in earnest after World War II. Developing nations such as Brazil and India were among the world's most closed economies until the 1980s, after which they reduced their barriers dramatically. Trade among European countries was quite free from the 1860s until

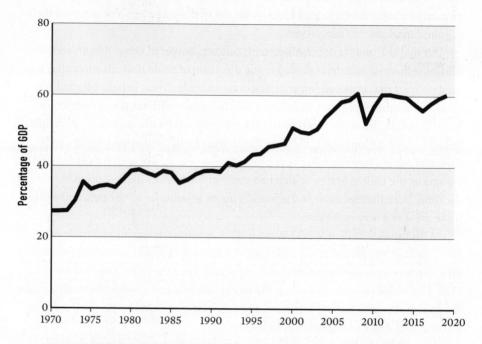

FIGURE 7.1 *Importance of Trade to the Global Economy, 1970–2019*

Figure source: World Bank, "Trade (% of GDP)," https://data.worldbank.org/indicator/NE.TRD.GNFS.ZS?end=2019&start=1960&view=chart (accessed 9/1/20).

Note: Trade is the sum of exports and imports of goods and services measured as a share of gross domestic product.

1914, but in the 1920s and 1930s, the region's nations erected very strict barriers to trade among themselves; today, trade among the 27 EU members is completely unrestricted.

Even within a single country, there can be significant differences among policies toward trade in different goods, with some goods more protected than others. Almost all developed nations protect agricultural producers much more heavily than they protect manufacturers. Developing nations, meanwhile, tend to protect manufactured products more than farm products. The United States, as well as many other industrial nations, generally protects the steel industry more than most other industries. And despite most industrial countries' rhetoric in favor of freer trade, they have imposed restrictions on many goods that might be imported from developing nations. Why are some producers—farmers, or certain kinds of farmers; industries, or certain kinds of industries—more favored by trade policy than others? Why do different countries' trade policies vary so much? Why has the world's general openness to trade changed so dramatically over time? And, perhaps most central, why have governments almost always, and almost everywhere, ignored economic analysis and advice and imposed restrictions on foreign trade?

Why Do Governments Restrict Trade? The Domestic Political Economy of Protection

For over 200 years, economic analysis has been unambiguous about the benefits of trade for national income, output, and efficiency. This perspective is reflected in the opinions of professional economists, more than 90 percent of whom believe that barriers to trade reduce national well-being (according to one survey of American economists).[12] Yet most people do not share economists' confidence in the benefits of trade. In another survey, 60 percent of Americans favored trade protection, as opposed to less than 5 percent of economists.[13] Indeed, many people seem wary of openness to international trade—a wariness evident in the fact that almost all countries, almost all the time, have substantial barriers to trade that protect their own producers. And in many developed countries, hostility to international trade has grown. In the United States, for example, the share of people who said trade with other countries was bad for America rose by 11 percentage points between 2002 and 2011.[14] However, in more recent years, support for trade has increased. A 2019 Gallup poll found that nearly three in four U.S. adults (74 percent) believe that trade represents "an opportunity for economic growth," while only one in five (21 percent) sees trade as "a threat to the economy" (see Figure 7.2).[15]

Trade barriers usually reflect domestic concerns, despite the fact that they implicate foreign relations. William McKinley, a leading protectionist member of the U.S. Congress before he became president, once said of a tariff he was shepherding through the House of Representatives: "This is a domestic bill; it is not a foreign bill."[16] This statement remains a common view of protection for domestic interests.

Trade policy typically reaches the public consciousness, and the media, when some national producers complain that there is too much or too little trade in the goods they produce. Often, producers are concerned because imported goods cut into their profits or cost them their jobs. Other producers may complain that foreign barriers to their goods keep them out of markets abroad and similarly cut into profits and cost jobs at home. To understand the domestic politics of trade, we need to know the interests in question, the institutions through which these interests are expressed, and how competing interests interact with one another.

---

12. Cletus C. Coughlin, "The Controversy over Free Trade: The Gap between Economists and the General Public," *Federal Reserve Bank of St. Louis Review* 84, no. 1 (January/February 2002): 1.

13. Coughlin, "Controversy over Free Trade," 1.

14. Pew Global Attitudes & Trends Question Database, "Question 1011," www.pewresearch.org/global/question-search/?qid=1011&cntIDs=&stdIDs= (accessed 1/25/21).

15. Lydia Saad, "Americans' Views on Trade in the Trump Era," Gallup, October 25, 2019, https://news.gallup.com/opinion/gallup/267770/americans-views-trade-trump-era.aspx (accessed 1/25/21).

16. Cited in David A. Lake, *Power, Protection, and Free Trade: International Sources of U.S. Commercial Strategy, 1887–1939* (Ithaca, NY: Cornell University Press, 1988), 111.

FIGURE 7.2 *Americans' Feelings about Trade*

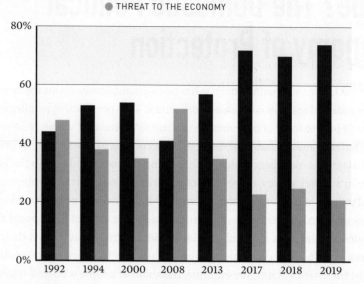

Figure source: Lydia Saad, "Americans' Views on Trade in the Trump Era," Gallup, October 25, 2019, https://news.gallup.com/opinion/gallup/267770/americans-views-trade-trump-era.aspx (accessed 1/25/21).

There are both benefits and costs to trade barriers. Virtually all tools of trade protection—tariffs, quotas, and other restrictions—make imports more expensive, which allows domestic producers to sell more of their products, to raise their prices, or both. For instance, when tariffs are imposed on foreign steel imported into the United States, American steelmakers can expand sales at higher prices. As a result, they may be able to increase their profits, raise wages, and hire more workers. Quotas, which restrict the quantity of foreign goods sold in the domestic market, ultimately have a similar impact in that the reduction in imports reduces supply, thus raising prices. So, trade barriers assist national producers. What could be wrong with that?

Consumers of the protected good most directly bear the cost of trade barriers. Tariffs and quotas raise the domestic price of imported goods and may lead to price increases for similar domestically produced goods: for example, a barrier to steel imports makes imported steel more expensive and allows domestic steelmakers to raise their prices too. Higher steel prices overall raise the costs of domestic goods that are made using steel, such as automobiles and motorcycles. Producers gain and consumers lose from protection; the *redistributive effect* is such that income is redistributed from domestic consumers to the protected domestic industry. But there is another cost as well: a trade barrier introduces economic inefficiencies. It leads domestic producers to make more goods that they are not particularly good at making (otherwise, they would not need protection), and it leads consumers to consume less of those goods that protection has made artificially expensive.

Trade protection also leads to an allocation of domestic resources—labor, capital, land, skills—that is not to the country's comparative advantage. Protection of European wheat leads European farmers to use their land for wheat farming when it might make more sense, from the standpoint of the region's overall economy, to use that land for dairy or vegetable farming or to build houses. (For more on the economic effects of trade restrictions, see the "Special Topic" appendix to this chapter, on p. 358.)

Winners and Losers in International Trade

The domestic politics of trade is infused with battles between the winners and losers created by protectionist policies and debates over the inefficiencies that these policies promote. The potential winners and losers usually constitute the principal actors in national debates over trade policy.

The United States, Canada, and Mexico—the three members of the North American Free Trade Agreement—signed a new trade agreement known as the United States-Mexico-Canada Agreement (USMCA) at the 2018 G20 Summit in Buenos Aires. Negotiations focused on trade barriers in industries like dairy and automobiles.

Domestic industries protected by trade barriers receive clear and concentrated benefits. Protection creates returns above the normal rate of profit by artificially restricting competition and supply. However, at least three groups of actors stand to lose from trade protection. First are consumers of the imported good. This group includes consuming industries, which—unlike average consumers—may be powerful and well organized. When the U.S. government imposed tariffs on imported steel in 2002, the American users of this steel—especially in the automobile industry—mobilized strongly against it (as did foreign governments), and the policy was eventually reversed. Industrial consumers of steel also opposed Trump's steel tariffs. More than 800 U.S. manufacturers petitioned the Trump administration for exemptions from the tariffs, including California Steel Industries.[17] California Steel employs more than 900 workers. It buys steel from abroad, often from Brazil, to convert into finished steel coils that it then sells to the construction industry. Although the company requested exemptions from the Trump tariff, their requests were denied.[18] Trump's steel tariffs cost this firm more than $20 million in 2018 and the company imposed a hiring freeze.

A second group that tends to oppose protection is exporters, who worry that their country's protective barriers might provoke retaliation in foreign markets. American farmers, for example, opposed the tariffs the Trump administration imposed on Chinese goods, including steel and aluminum, because they feared that China would retaliate with tariffs on American farm products. When China in fact responded exactly how farmers had anticipated, U.S. agricultural products became

17. Bani Sapra and Paul Wiseman, "Why Trump Tariffs Haven't Revitalized American Steelmakers," PBS, November 4, 2019, www.pbs.org/newshour/economy/why-trump-tariffs-havent-revitalized-american-steelmakers (accessed 1/25/21).

18. Don Lee, "Trump's Steel Tariffs Were Supposed to Save the Industry. They Made Things Worse," *Los Angeles Times*, October 29, 2019, www.latimes.com/politics/story/2019-10-29/steel-industry-faces-a-bleaker-future-than-when-trump-moved-to-rescue-it (accessed 1/25/21).

International trade involves buying and selling goods and services from foreign countries. Some people may question why it is necessary to buy goods and services from abroad, particularly if they believe in the superiority of their own country's goods.

more expensive to consumers in China and U.S. exports to China declined. With fewer sales to China, American farmers made less money and farm bankruptcies rose sharply, particularly in the upper Midwest.[19]

Third, citizens in general may be willing and able to punish politicians for the costs that protection imposes on them, especially if the connection is clear and the issue is prominent. In the 1980s, many people in Soviet-bloc (communist) countries blamed the stagnation of their economies on their governments' pervasive trade controls, and this perception may have created popular sympathy for the subsequent opening of these nations to international trade. In addition, there is evidence that consumers in developing countries favor freer trade because they understand that it will lead to reduced prices for themselves.[20] Consumers' support for free trade in developing countries may help to explain why, as these countries become more democratic, they increasingly open up their economies to international commerce.[21]

Because of the diverse interests of industries that compete with imports, use imports, and sell exports, as well as the range of interests that motivate producers and consumers, trade is politically controversial. The controversy surrounding trade goes beyond just economic interests to encompass noneconomic issues. One such issue is nationalism, which refers to the belief that one's own country is culturally superior to other countries. Because international trade involves buying and

19. Ron Wirtz, "Chapter 12 Bankruptcies on the Rise in the Ninth District," Federal Reserve Bank of Minneapolis, November 14, 2018, www.minneapolisfed.org/article/2018/chapter-12-bankruptcies-on-the-rise-in-the-ninth-district (accessed 1/25/21).

20. See, for example, Andy Baker, "Who Wants to Globalize? Consumer Tastes and Labor Markets in a Theory of Trade Policy Beliefs," *American Journal of Political Science* 49, no. 4 (October 2005): 924–38.

21. See also Helen V. Milner and Keiko Kubota, "Why the Move to Free Trade? Democracy and Trade Policy in the Developing Countries," *International Organization* 59, no. 1 (Winter 2005): 107–43.

selling goods and services from other countries, it may elicit nationalist attitudes. People who believe in the superiority of their own country may question why it is necessary to buy goods and services from abroad. Studies show that individuals who hold more nationalist views tend to be more opposed to international trade.[22]

In summary, different groups within a country hold different views on international trade. Which actors do we expect to have an interest in supporting and opposing trade protection within national political systems? And whose interests will ultimately prevail?

Economic Interests and Trade Policy

The economic characteristics of a country and of particular groups within it help explain who might be in favor of and against trade. There are two leading theories of trade-policy interests; each predicts different sets of actors that will support or oppose trade protection.

The first theory, the Stolper-Samuelson approach, emphasizes the interests of broad factors of production—land, labor, capital. Remember that the Heckscher-Ohlin approach expects that a country's exports will make intensive use of resources that the country has in abundance. A labor-rich country will export labor-intensive goods; a capital-rich country will export capital-intensive goods. This pattern, in turn, affects which groups trade will help or hurt. If the country exports labor-intensive goods, for example, the demand for labor goes up, and so do wages. This first theory argues that trade affects primarily broad factors of production: labor, capital, land, and skilled labor.

The second theory, the Ricardo-Viner approach, emphasizes specific sectors of the economy, such as the steel industry or cotton farmers. Both help us think analytically about support for and opposition to trade.

The Stolper-Samuelson Approach

The **Stolper-Samuelson theorem** provides one explanation of who will support and who will oppose trade protection; it predicts that protection benefits the scarce factor of production in the country that imposes the trade restrictions. This is simply the counterpart of the argument that more trade helps the abundant factor: as discussed already, in a labor-rich country, labor benefits most from trade. The logical implication is that reducing trade in a labor-rich country will harm labor.

Consider Bangladesh, a poor country with lots of unskilled labor and very little capital. Bangladesh exports mainly clothing and leather goods, which make intensive use of its abundant unskilled labor; it imports such capital-intensive products as machinery, equipment, and chemicals. Trade barriers artificially make imported capital-intensive goods more expensive or harder to buy, which means that at least some of them will have to be produced in Bangladesh. Some Bangladeshi capital will have to be diverted from labor-intensive production in order to produce these capital-intensive goods (from garment factories to chemical plants, for example), which

Stolper-Samuelson theorem

The theorem that trade protection benefits the scarce factor of production. This view flows from the Heckscher-Ohlin theory: if a country imports goods that make intensive use of its scarce factor, then limiting imports will help that factor. So in a labor-scarce country, labor benefits from protection and loses from trade liberalization.

---

22. Edward D. Mansfield and Diana C. Mutz, "US versus Them: Mass Attitudes toward Offshore Outsourcing," *World Politics* 65, no. 4 (2013): 571–608.

raises the domestic demand for capital and reduces the local demand for labor. This, in turn, raises the return on Bangladeshi capital (profits) and reduces Bangladeshi wages. Protection in a capital-scarce country helps owners of capital and hurts workers; therefore, we expect investors to support protection and workers to oppose it.

We can also apply the Stolper-Samuelson theorem to a labor-scarce country, such as the United States. The opposite of Bangladesh, the United States has abundant capital but scarce unskilled labor. The United States imports labor-intensive goods, such as clothing and furniture, and exports capital-intensive goods, such as airplanes. Protection restricts the imported supply of labor-intensive products and raises their price. This, in turn, increases American production of these labor-intensive products, raises the American demand for unskilled labor, and boosts the wages of American unskilled workers. By the same token, protection in land-scarce countries (such as those of western Europe, as well as Japan) helps farmers and hurts workers and owners of capital.

So, which actors would we expect to support and oppose trade barriers? We expect owners of the scarce factors of production in a country to be protectionist and owners of the abundant factors to favor free trade. In rich societies, which typically have abundant capital and skilled labor but are scarce in unskilled labor, capitalists and skilled workers should be free traders, while unskilled workers should be protectionists. In countries with abundant land, farmers should support trade; in countries where land is scarce, farmers should support protection. In poor societies, which typically have abundant unskilled labor and scarce capital, workers should support trade while capitalists should be protectionists. An important feature of the model is that actors' attitudes toward trade are not fixed but vary with the country's resources of land, labor, capital, and human capital. Thus, the model expects farmers to be protectionists in land-poor Japan but free traders in land-rich Argentina.

There is a great deal of evidence to support this model. Labor movements in the United States and other rich countries do seem to be relatively protectionist, while people with a lot of capital appear to find free trade more favorable. Japan and Europe have relatively little land, and their farmers are strongly protectionist; Australia and Canada are rich in land, and their farmers usually favor free trade. Notice that the Stolper-Samuelson predictions are about very broad groups or actors—owners of production factors (roughly the same as social classes) such as laborers, investors, and farmers.

But observers of economic policy making in the United States and elsewhere note that many demands for protection come from specific *industries*—the steel industry, sugar growers, shoe manufacturers. Often, everyone in an industrial sector—skilled and unskilled workers, managers, and owners of firms—works together to ask for trade barriers or support for their exports. For example, we tend to think of the American steel industry as relatively protectionist because we group together everyone associated with the industry. This assessment flies in the face of the Stolper-Samuelson focus on labor as a class or investors (capital) as a class. Many detailed studies of trade policy and of attitudes toward trade confirm the idea that the industry in which people work has a powerful impact on their trade-policy opinions.[23]

---

23. See especially Anna Maria Mayda and Dani Rodrik, "Why Are Some People (and Countries) More Protectionist Than Others?" *European Economic Review* 49 (2005): 1393–1430.

The U.S. steel industry, whose capital equipment is specific to the production of steel, often urges the U.S. government to provide protection from what it views as unfair "dumping"—that is, selling steel in the United States below the true cost of production. Cheap steel benefits consumers but hurts the steel industry.

The Ricardo-Viner (Specific-Factors) Approach A second approach to predicting trade-policy preferences focuses on why whole industries often act together. The **Ricardo-Viner**, or **specific-factors**, **model** has one key feature that differentiates it from Stolper-Samuelson: some factors of production are tied to their industry; that is, they are *industry-specific*. The relevant actors thus are not classes but industrial sectors. This approach is based on the principle that the factors of production are not very mobile, meaning that it is difficult for labor or capital to move from use to use.

For example, capital in the steel industry largely takes the form of steel factories and machinery; it cannot simply be turned into capital in the food-processing industry. Since they are "stuck" in the steel industry, steel manufacturers care not about the profits of capital in general or in the country as a whole but rather about the profits available only in steel. The same may be true of workers or farmers, whose job skills or land can be inherently "specific to" (some might say "trapped in") a particular industry or crop. This gives the owners, workers, or farmers a strong incentive to safeguard their current use—for example, by obtaining government protection from foreign competition.

In this model, the interests of individuals flow from the sectors of the economy in which they are employed. Given the limited mobility of labor and capital, actors associate their interests with the sector in which they are employed. A worker or manager in an industry that faces stiff import competition will be protectionist; a worker or manager in an exporting industry will want free trade. Unlike in the Stolper-Samuelson approach, people's interests are tightly bound up with the interests of others in their sector of the economy, and the pertinent actors in domestic trade-policy debates are economic sectors, not factors.

Ricardo-Viner (specific-factors) model

A model of trade relations that emphasizes the sector in which factors of production are employed rather than the nature of the factor itself. This differentiates it from the Heckscher-Ohlin theory, in which the nature of the factor—labor, land, capital—is the principal consideration.

A Firm–Based Trade Theory A third approach to trade has gained theoretical and empirical support in recent years, motivated by the observation that international trade is dominated by a very few companies. Of the more than 5 million firms in the United States, for example, only 4 percent are exporters. Even in exporting industries, a small number of companies are responsible for most of the exports: the top 1 percent of all exporting firms account for more than 80 percent of all American exports.[24] This pattern extends beyond the United States. Among 32 developing countries from different regions of the world, a given country's single top firm on average accounts for 14 percent of its total (non-oil) exports, and the top five firms make up 30 percent.[25]

This observation leads to an approach to trade and trade policy that focuses on firms. The most productive firms in an exporting industry—typically also the largest—may be most likely to benefit from trade liberalization and to be politically active in the trade arena. Certainly, we are used to seeing very large firms—General Motors, Walmart, General Electric, Google—play a major role on all sides of trade-policy debates.

There is evidence for all three of these approaches in the politics of trade protection. Broad classes—farmers, workers—sometimes mobilize for or against protection. But at the same time, much lobbying for protection is industry-based, consistent with the view that the benefits of protection accrue to industries, not to broad classes or factors. And within industries, it is typically the largest firms that dominate debate. The accuracy of each view may vary among industries and countries and over time. One study found, for example, that in the late nineteenth century, American labor was quite interchangeable, which contributed to the working class having a clear, distinctive interest in trade policy; in contrast, today's American working class is much more differentiated, so industry-based sectoral interests predominate.[26]

Groups may also support trade policies because they believe those policies help make possible other outcomes that they favor. The economist John Maynard Keynes wrote that protectionism "rests on the principle of making things relatively scarce. To those who are concerned with making these things, this is no doubt advantageous. But it causes an amount of distress more than equivalent elsewhere. The community as a whole cannot hope to gain by making artificially scarce what the country wants."[27]

This is a powerful argument; but later, in the midst of the Great Depression of the 1930s, Keynes came to believe that there could be equally powerful political

24. Andrew B. Bernard, J. Bradford Jensen, and Peter K. Schott, "Importers, Exporters and Multinationals: A Portrait of Firms in the US That Trade Goods," in *Producer Dynamics: New Evidence from Micro Data*, ed. Timothy Dunne, J. Bradford Jensen, and Mark J. Roberts (Chicago: University of Chicago Press, 2009), 513–52; and Andrew B. Bernard, J. Bradford Jensen, Stephen J. Redding, and Peter K. Schott, "Firms in International Trade," *Journal of Economic Perspectives* 21, no. 3 (2007): 105–30.

25. Caroline Freund and Martha Denisse Pierola, "The Origins and Dynamics of Export Superstars," *World Bank Economic Review* 34, no. 1 (February 2020): 28–47.

26. Michael J. Hiscox, "Commerce, Coalitions, and Factor Mobility: Evidence from Congressional Votes on Trade Legislation," *American Political Science Review* 96, no. 3 (September 2002): 593–608.

27. Cited in Robert Skidelsky, *John Maynard Keynes*, vol. 1, *Hopes Betrayed 1883–1920* (New York: Penguin, 1983), 227.

arguments against free trade. In 1933, in fact, Keynes spoke in favor of "the policy of an increased national self-sufficiency . . . not as an ideal in itself, but as directed to the creation of an environment in which other ideals can be safely and conveniently pursued." Keynes had come to believe that trade barriers might usefully give national governments breathing space as they attempted to combat mass unemployment and economic collapse. Keynes felt that protectionism might permit governments to implement other policy measures to alleviate the social and economic distress of the Great Depression.[28]

Understanding the economic interests that compete over trade is only a start to understanding national trade politics and policies. While economic interests are important, so too are other factors such as nationalism, mentioned above. If a person believes that their own country is culturally superior to other countries, they may oppose buying goods and services from foreign sources. Taken together, both economic and noneconomic interests can tell us which actors want more or less protection. But what determines who wins and who loses in the battles among supporters and opponents of trade liberalization?

Domestic Institutions and Trade Policy

Since there are always supporters and opponents of protection in any country, how are trade-policy decisions made? Why are some countries more open to trade than others? Why do governments protect some industries and not others? There are many steps between raw economic interests and the actual economic policies that result. Most of them have to do with the institutions of national politics, including the organization and representation of interests, and how policy decisions are made.

National political institutions are of stunning variety and complexity, but a general rule of thumb can help orient our understanding of their implications for trade policy. A common view starts with the observation that trade protection tends to help relatively narrow and concentrated groups—the steel industry, skilled workers—but tends to harm the economy and consumers as a whole. It follows that those political institutional forms that are particularly responsive to the interests of more concentrated groups—a particular class, a particular industry—will be more favorable to protection, while those that respond especially to broad national pressures will be less favorable. So, an important question about domestic institutions has to do with whether they favor particularistic interests (in which case they would incline toward protectionism) or broad economic and consumer interests (in which case they would incline toward less protectionist policies).

The Organization of Interests Trade protection affects large groups both positively and negatively. This raises the possibility of free riding, a concept we introduced in Chapter 2. If a trade barrier is imposed, it helps all the beneficiaries of trade protection—whether a factor of production or an industry—regardless of whether they lobbied for the policy or not. This means that some members of the winning group—some companies, some individuals—have reasons to sit back and wait for

---

28. John Maynard Keynes, "National Self-Sufficiency," *Yale Review* 22, no. 4 (June 1933): 755–69.

others to fight for them. But if all the actors in a class or industry attempt to free ride, nothing will get done. In other words, both supporters and opponents of trade protection face problems of collective action.

As we've discussed in previous chapters, the logic of collective action implies that smaller groups can organize more easily than larger groups can. We saw in Chapter 4 how smaller, highly motivated groups were better able to influence foreign policy in matters of war and peace. The same principle applies in matters of trade policy. There are typically relatively few producers and a great many consumers, which leads to the expectation that producers will win over consumers in many circumstances. This helps explain, for example, how a relatively small number of steelworkers can obtain a policy that benefits them at the expense of the vast mass of American consumers of goods that are made with steel.

Economic interests organize themselves very differently in different societies. In some western European countries, for example, most workers are members of a centralized labor federation that devises policies for virtually the entire labor movement. Even where workers in different industries might disagree, the existence of a class-wide labor federation helps create a common working-class political position and overcome collective action problems. In the United States, by contrast, labor unions tend to be organized by industry; even if there were common trade-policy interests among American workers, it might be difficult for them to express those interests in a common way.

The implication is that an organization reflecting the concerns of broad groups—such as all workers—is more likely to ignore the demands of specific groups or industries. In contrast, interests that are organized into narrower groups are more likely to pursue the particular goals of such special interests.

The Representation of Interests through Political Institutions

Just as narrowly based social groups are more likely to favor protection than broader ones are, political institutions that are more closely tied to narrow interests are more likely to favor trade protection than are institutions that reflect broader interests. This is an example of the sort of bias that political institutions can create or intensify. Generally, to the extent that democracies reflect broad interests while dictatorships are restrictive, we would expect the former to be less protectionist than the latter. Indeed, scholars have found that democratic developing countries are much more likely to liberalize their trade than dictatorships are.[29]

Apart from such broad institutional features as democracy, societies differ in how their partisan, electoral, and legislative institutions represent the interests of their citizens, and these differences are likely to affect the way trade policy is made. For example, many European countries have strong class-based parties: the working class traditionally votes for the socialist parties, and other parties associate themselves more or less explicitly with farmers or business. Although the American

---

29. Milner and Kubota, "Why the Move to Free Trade?" See also Daniel Y. Kono, "Optimal Obfuscation: Democracy and Trade Policy Transparency," *American Political Science Review* 100, no. 3 (August 2006): 369–84; Soubhik Barari and In Song Kim, "Democracy and Trade Policy at the Product Level," Working Paper, Massachusetts Institute of Technology, October 27, 2020.

labor movement has ties to the Democrats, working-class voters in the United States are less strongly connected to the Democratic Party as compared with working-class voters and left-leaning parties in Europe. This affects the parties' expression of interests and their bias toward special or general interests, and thus toward protection or freer trade. (See "How Do We Know?" on p. 330 for a discussion of how trade shapes partisanship in the United States.)

National electoral systems vary greatly, and they may cause differences among national party structures. Most industrial countries are parliamentary, with a legislature elected on a proportional basis in which voters choose the party they prefer rather than an individual local candidate. American voters elect the president on a national basis but elect individual local candidates for the House of Representatives and the Senate, whose ties to the national party may be weak. And there are systems in between, such as the Westminster system (in Great Britain) and hybrid presidential-parliamentary systems (in much of Latin America).

How might these institutions affect trade policy? Politicians with local political constituencies tend to be more responsive to local interest groups, while nationally elected politicians have less reason to cater to particular local concerns. Consider two otherwise identical countries: one with strong national parties and a powerful national executive and the other with weak national parties and a weak national executive. Politicians in the former are more likely to focus on national effects of policy and favor free trade, while politicians in the latter are more likely to emphasize local concerns and thus favor trade protection that benefits local special interests.

The same holds within a country where one branch of government may be more sensitive to local pressures than another. The American president, elected nationally, has a strong incentive to consider the impact of trade policies on the country as a whole. Members of Congress, however, have little reason to think about anything other than the effects of trade policies on their district. Traditionally, then, Congress is more protectionist than the president—although this relationship has changed in important ways more recently.

In recent years, presidential candidates have focused on winning "swing states"—states in which the vote could go either way—rather than trying to win over as many voters as possible across the country. Swing states matter because of an important national institution: the Electoral College. Each state has a certain number of Electoral College votes roughly proportional to the size of its population, and in order to become president of the United States, a candidate needs to win a majority of these votes across the country. States generally award all their Electoral College votes to the candidate that wins the popular vote in the state. Because most of the states today are solidly Democratic or Republican, a significant premium exists on winning the states that remain in play—that is, the so-called swing states.

In swing states, both parties' candidates have a realistic chance of winning the popular vote. Candidates consequently work hard to tip these states into their win column. Trade protection may be an effective way to win over voters in swing states because these states suffer disproportionately from the negative economic

Has Trade Contributed to the Polarization of Politics?

Political polarization increasingly defines American politics. Today Republicans and Democrats find themselves further apart ideologically than they have at any point in recent history. A 2020 poll found that the share of adults who see strong partisan conflicts is much higher than in 2016 or 2012.[a] In Congress, a sizable rightward shift among Republican legislators and a modest leftward shift among Democrats has left few centrists in either party and shrunk the possibilities for bipartisan cooperation. Trump's election in 2016 was itself seen as an indication of partisan polarization.[b]

The growth of partisan polarization puzzles political scientists. What factors triggered the recent rise? Why have politics become so much more polarized in recent years? Researchers David Autor, David Dorn, Gordon Hanson, and Kaveh Majlesi tackled this important question in a 2020 paper.[c] They argue that political divisions have widened because of the expansion of international trade. Foreign imports affect specific regions in a country in different ways. While regions where domestic manufacturers primarily produce the same goods as those imported from abroad generally lose out from increased trade, at the same time, other regions—such as big cities with large service sectors—gain from globalization. As the authors write, "The geographically concentrated impact of foreign imports on specific industries and regions makes the economic consequences of trade acutely recognizable and therefore politically salient." They argue that the trade-induced changes in regions' economic fortunes have inspired systematic political reactions.

Testing this argument was no easy task. First, Autor, Dorn, Hanson, and Majlesi needed to find a way to measure areas' exposure to foreign trade. To do this, they collected data on imports from China—one of the United States' largest trading partners. They then identified where domestic manufacturers of similar products were located in the United States (Figure A). For example, the furniture industry is one of the industries hardest hit by Chinese imports. U.S. furniture manufacturers generally cluster together in the mid-Atlantic region, particularly North Carolina. As Chinese furniture imports grew, these regions increasingly found themselves in economic difficulty. Furniture producers struggled to compete with lower-cost imports and, as a result, cut wages and fired workers.

Second, the authors needed to find reliable measures of political polarization. Rather than relying on just one measure, the authors used several, including Nielsen data on the ratings of cable news networks to examine the news viewing habits of households. They also explored data on campaign contributions to uncover how donor support for candidates shifted along the ideological spectrum. Finally, they examined the results of congressional and presidential elections spanning the period from 2000 through 2016.

Using these measures and a series of statistical models, the authors found evidence of ideological realignment in areas exposed to trade. From 2004 to 2016, regions more exposed to import competition shifted their consumption of TV news to the right-leaning Fox News Channel, and districts in these regions were more likely to elect a

a. Katherine Schaeffer, "Far More Americans See 'Very Strong' Partisan Conflict Now than in the Last Two Presidential Election Years," Pew Research Center, March 4, 2020, https://www.pewresearch.org/fact-tank/2020/03/04/far-more-americans-see-very-strong-partisan-conflicts-now-than-in-the-last-two-presidential-election-years/ (accessed 4/19/21).

b. Kenneth A. Schultz, "Perils of Polarization for U.S. Foreign Policy," *Washington Quarterly* 40, no. 4 (December 2017): 7–28.

c. David Autor, David Dorn, Gordon Hanson, and Kaveh Majlesi, "Importing Political Polarization? The Electoral Consequences of Rising Trade Exposure," *American Economic Review* 110, no. 10 (October 2020): 3139–83.

FIGURE A   Areas in the United States Hit Hardest by Chinese Imports

Most-affected 20%   Second-highest 20%   Middle 20%   Second-lowest 20%   Least-affected 20%

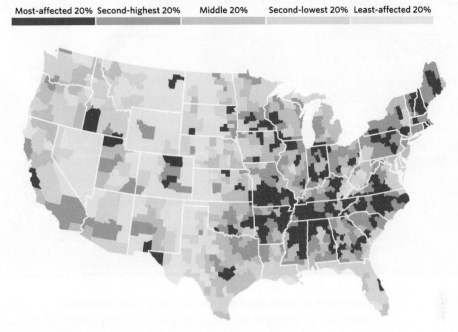

Source: Andrew Van Dam and Jessia Ma of the *Wall Street Journal,* based on data collected by the China Shock research team. From Bob Davis and Jon Hilsenrath, "How the China Shock, Deep and Swift, Spurred the Rise of Trump," *Wall Street Journal,* August 11, 2016, www.wsj.com/articles/how-the-china-shock-deep-and-swift-spurred-the-rise-of-trump-1470929543 (accessed 1/20/21).

Republican legislator in each election from 2010 to 2016 (and more conservative Republicans generally fared better). In presidential elections, counties with greater exposure to trade exhibited increased support for the Republican candidate.

These patterns suggest that exposure to international trade increases political polarization. Researchers find similar patterns in other countries including France, where regions more exposed to trade with low-wage countries exhibit increased vote shares for far-right political parties.[d]

---

d.   Clément Malgouyres, "Trade Shocks and Far-right Voting: Evidence from French Presidential Elections," Working Paper RSCAS 21, Robert Schuman Centre for Advanced Studies, 2017, https://cadmus. eui.eu/handle/1814/45886 (accessed 1/25/21).

Increasingly, presidential candidates make campaign promises to "swing states"— where the vote could go either way—rather than trying to win over as many voters as possible across the country. Candidates focused on winning swing states can promise trade protection to industries located in these states without being overly concerned about the cost of such protection for the nation as a whole.

Text **UNITED** to **30330**
BUY AMERICAN
★ ★ ★

consequences of foreign trade due to their unique economic characteristics.[30] Steel producers, for example, tend to be geographically concentrated in a handful of states, and at least two of these states—Ohio and Pennsylvania—are generally considered swing states. In order to curry favor with swing-state voters, candidates may promise to provide trade protection to businesses in those states once in office. For example, to fulfill a campaign promise to steelworkers in Ohio and Pennsylvania—both of which he won in 2016—President Donald Trump imposed tariffs on foreign steel imports in 2018.

Partisan features of government can also affect trade policy, especially if parties are associated with well-defined social groups that have preferences for particular approaches to trade. For example, in the Stolper-Samuelson framework, labor has well-defined interests in trade: if labor is scarce, laborers will be protectionist; if labor is abundant, laborers will support free trade. In most of the world, labor typically supports left-wing parties. Given this observation, governments of the Left in labor-rich countries (mainly poor nations) should be more open to trade than are governments of the Left in labor-scarce countries (mainly rich nations). Similarly, because business typically is associated with right-wing parties, governments of the Right in capital-rich countries (usually rich nations) should be more open, while in capital-poor countries (usually poor nations) they should be more protectionist.

Thus, leftist governments should support free trade in poor countries and protection in rich countries; rightist governments should support free trade in rich countries and protection in poor countries. One study of a large number of countries indeed found strong support for this joint impact of partisan politics and Stolper-Samuelson interests. For example, Bangladesh and Senegal are similarly labor-rich and capital-poor, but in the 1980s, Bangladesh's right-wing (presumably

---

30. J. Bradford Jensen, Dennis P. Quinn, and Stephen Weymouth, "Winners and Losers in International Trade: The Effects on US Presidential Voting," *International Organization* 71, no. 3 (Summer 2017): 423–57.

On the campaign trail, Donald Trump promised to stop manufacturing operations and business functions from moving abroad. Within days of winning the 2016 election, he persuaded the company Carrier to keep most of the more than 1,000 jobs it had planned to ship to Mexico in the United States in return for $7 million in economic incentives.

anti-labor) government had tariffs twice as high as Senegal's left-wing (presumably pro-labor) government.[31]

Although theory and history tend to support these explanations of trade politics, a new mass politics of trade has emerged in many advanced industrial countries in the past decade. This trend is part of a broader backlash against globalization, which has entered mass and electoral politics in very striking ways. In the 2016 presidential campaign in the United States, for example, both political parties had candidates for their nomination who were strongly and explicitly hostile to international trade. Democrat Bernie Sanders and Republican Donald Trump both criticized American trade policies, arguing that they had cost the country valuable manufacturing jobs and served primarily to enrich a corporate elite.

Donald Trump was elected president after a campaign that was more hostile to existing trade policy than any U.S. presidential campaign had been since the 1930s. Once in office, Trump's administration pursued more protectionist trade policies than any of its modern predecessors. He rejected multilateralism and severely weakened the World Trade Organization while embracing the use of tariffs. The new American politics of trade is reflected in the rise of similarly populist movements, on both the Right and the Left, in other countries. In Europe, antiglobalization sentiment tends to take the form of skepticism about the European Union, and these antiglobalization feelings have been a powerful electoral force in countries from France to Poland. These attitudes clearly contributed to Britain's vote in June 2016 to leave the European Union.

It is probably too early to know whether the recent emergence of powerful mass and electoral pressures for trade protection presages a fundamental change in

---

31. Pushan Dutt and Devashish Mitra, "Endogenous Trade Policy through Majority Voting: An Empirical Investigation," *Journal of International Economics* 58, no. 1 (October 2002): 107–33.

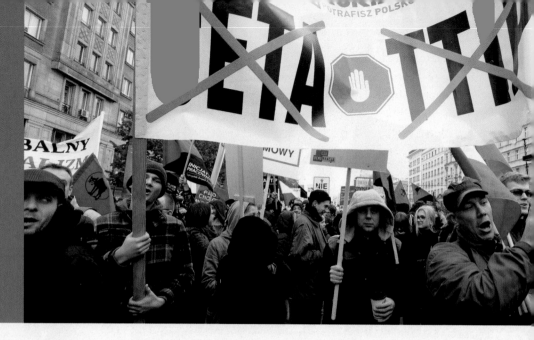

Proposed trade deals between the European Union and Canada (CETA) and between the European Union and the United States (TTIP) provoked demonstrations in Poland among citizens who were concerned about the deals' potential impact on domestic agriculture and consumer rights.

the politics of trade. Concentrated special interests remain very powerful and continue to play a central role in trade policy. But it may be, at least in some rich countries, that large segments of the electorate now have strong enough views in favor of trade protection to have a significant impact on trade policy. Indeed, between 2017 and 2019, governments worldwide introduced 2,723 new barriers to trade.[32]

Costs, Benefits, and Compensation in National Trade Policies

Even if trade liberalization makes a country's economy as a whole better off, it can seriously harm groups within the country. Concentrated groups of potential losers with a lot at stake could conceivably block policy changes that would improve conditions for the nation overall. Indeed, the electoral success of candidates hostile to trade suggests that there is a widespread sentiment in some nations that many citizens have been harmed by freer trade. For those who believe that trade benefits the national economy as a whole, one implication is that a country could be better off if it "bought off" the actors whose interests would be harmed to give them a reason to cooperate with trade policies that would benefit society at large. Such an approach would represent a movement toward the Pareto frontier in the model presented in Chapter 2.

Movement toward the Pareto frontier, called a Pareto improvement, makes everyone better off (or at least unharmed) and nobody worse off. While trade liberalization might hurt some people, the overall gains to the national economy are large enough that the losers can be fully compensated for their losses and the benefits will still remain for the rest of society. Indeed, it is not uncommon for a government to arrange compensation for people who lose from trade liberalization

---

32. Simon J. Evenett and Johannes Fritz, "The 25th Global Trade Alert Report: Going It Alone? Trade Policy after Three Years of Populism," Centre for Economic Policy Research, December 22, 2019, www.globaltradealert.org/reports/48 (accessed 1/25/21).

in order to diminish their opposition to the removal of trade barriers. The United States, for example, provides Trade Adjustment Assistance to workers harmed by the country's foreign trade; the assistance ranges from tax credits, to money for retraining, to outright grants.

More generally, the very structure of the post-1945 political economy of most Western societies has, to some extent, been based on the logic of compensation. As the industrialized world substantially reduced trade barriers after World War II, its governments implemented sweeping social policies that provided a safety net to workers, farmers, and others who might be negatively affected by the reopening of world trade. This strategy reflects a kind of compromise between supporters of economic integration on the one hand and defenders of the welfare state on the other.[33] The Bretton Woods System (introduced in Chapter 1) permitted, even encouraged, this compromise, and it was quite successful at achieving its goal of an integrated world economy and extensive social welfare policies in the industrialized nations.

The issue of compensation has attracted recent attention because many observers believe that trade has led to reduced wages for many workers in the industrial countries (see "Controversy" on p. 352). Trade puts unskilled and semi-skilled American workers in direct competition with unskilled and semi-skilled workers in poor countries with much lower wages, which may depress the wages of the former. This is a clear implication of the Heckscher-Ohlin approach: trade will tend to make the prices of factors of production (the wages of labor, the profits of capital, the returns to land) more equal across countries. Trade leads countries to export goods that use factors of production in which they are well endowed: labor-rich countries export labor-intensive goods. This increases the demand for labor and raises wages. At the same time, labor-scarce countries import labor-intensive goods rather than producing them at home, thus reducing the demand for labor and lowering wages. Consequently, wages in poor countries will rise toward the levels of those in rich countries, while wages in rich countries will fall toward the levels of those in poor countries.

For example, the wages of unskilled workers in the United States have, in fact, been stagnant or declining since the early 1970s, and trade with developing countries may have contributed to this process. The issue is controversial; some analysts think that this decline is due largely to technological changes that have made computer-based skills more valuable in the workplace. Nonetheless, there is little doubt that globalization has created winners and losers in rich countries and that working people are more likely to be on the losing side. This observation has led some analysts to suggest that rich countries will continue to face social and political conflict over economic openness that will be mitigated only if they develop more extensive social safety nets to reduce the negative impact of the world economy on some groups in society.

Clearly, the interests, interactions, and institutions that characterize different national political economies have a powerful impact on national trade policies.

---

33. John Ruggie called this compromise "embedded liberalism." See John Gerard Ruggie, "International Regimes, Transactions, and Change: Embedded Liberalism in the Postwar Economic Order," *International Organization* 36, no. 2 (Spring 1982): 379–415.

Nonetheless, focusing only on the *domestic* sources of trade policies misses an important part of the story, because each country's trade relations are part of a broader international environment. While trends in French or Indian trade depend on French and Indian domestic politics, they also depend on the global economic and political situation.

It would be difficult to understand France's turn toward protectionism in the 1930s without the context of the Great Depression, its embrace of openness after 1950 without situating it within the Cold War, or its current trade policies without knowing France's place in the single market of the European Union. Similarly, it would be difficult to explain India's protectionism upon independence in 1947 or its turn toward freer trade in the 1990s without knowing that in both instances it was enacting policies shared by most other developing countries. The *international* environment—especially the global strategic and institutional setting—has a profound effect on national trade policies and patterns.

How Do Countries Get What They Want? The International Political Economy of Trade

What a national government wants from trade is only a starting point, for every country's commercial relations depend on the international environment. Certainly, a country can pursue a unilateral trade policy; it can open its borders or close them, regardless of what other countries do. But what a country achieves depends on the actions of others. How can governments get what their constituents want out of the world economy? How do issues abroad, including the policies of other countries, affect the ability of a national government to deliver goods to its people? What is the international political economy of trade?

International economic conditions, for example, have a powerful impact on both the policies a country might like to pursue and their likely effects. The collapse of the world economy in the 1930s drove many countries inward; foreign markets were small and shrinking, and the benefits of openness shrank with them. The rapid expansion of world trade since 1945 has given many countries strong incentives to link their economies to dynamic world markets. The global financial crisis that began in 2008, however, inspired an upsurge in protectionist sentiment that continues to affect world trade today. Following the crisis, world trade plunged, and since 2009 it has only managed to keep pace with GDP growth rather than comfortably exceed it, as it did for many years previously.[34] In addition to global market conditions, the policies of other governments can have an enormous impact: for example,

---

34. World Trade Organization, "World Trade Statistical Review 2018," www.wto.org/english/res_e/statis_e/wts2018_e/wts18_toc_e.htm (accessed 1/25/21).

the opening of China and India to world trade has profoundly affected other developed and developing nations. How, then, can we understand the national politics of trade within the broader international context? How does the strategic and institutional environment affect whether countries get what they want from world trade?

Strategic Interaction in International Trade Relations

When governments enact national trade policies, they often take into account how other governments are likely to respond. A government that raises tariffs dramatically, for example, might find that other countries retaliate with even higher barriers to its exports—so that the benefits to domestic producers sheltered from imports might be canceled out by costs to exporters frozen out of foreign markets. In 2018, for example, the Trump administration attempted to help the U.S. steel industry by raising tariffs on foreign steel imports to 25 percent. The Chinese government reacted to these new tariffs by raising their own tariffs on U.S. agricultural products, and exports from U.S. farms to China subsequently declined. Exports of soybeans to China fell 94 percent, and soybean prices dropped to a 10-year low, reflecting the weaker demand. China's response meant that while U.S. tariffs may have helped some domestic steel producers, they harmed U.S. farmers and others who produced goods subject to China's retaliatory tariffs.

Attempts to create regional trading areas, such as the European Union or the USMCA, or to affect the international commercial order, such as the United States did after World War II, rely on the joint behavior of different nation-states. One government cannot achieve many of its trade-policy goals without considering the actions of other governments. (See "What Shaped Our World?" on p. 338 for a discussion on the evolution of the European Union.)

Two or more governments involved in bargaining over trade policy are engaged in strategic interaction and must anticipate the behavior of the other governments in the negotiation, who are trying to do the best for their producers (or businesses). For example, suppose that American farmers decide they would be better off if they had access to Europe's market for farm goods and are willing to reduce American agricultural trade barriers in return. American trade negotiators offer the Europeans a joint reduction of farm trade protection, and the Europeans agree.

But the Americans are wary: the Europeans might indirectly maintain their barriers, such as by imposing regulations that apply only to American crops. In fact, some American farmers argue that Europe's import bans on genetically modified food and meat from animals that have been fed hormones are trade barriers in disguise. In other words, the Europeans might find ways to "cheat" on the agreement and gain greater access to the American market without providing anything substantial in return. The Europeans, for their part, have similar concerns: the United States, they fear, will promise them open markets but find devious ways to keep European goods out.

Given this threat, both the United States and the European Union decide not to take the chance, farm trade is not liberalized, and both sides are left worse off than they would have been with an agreement. This scenario is an example of how

The Single European Market: From Creation to Crisis and Beyond

In 1945, Europe emerged from the most devastating war in history, a conflict that tore the continent apart. Today, the countries of the European Union (EU) constitute a single market for goods, services, capital, and people, yet opposition to European integration has increased in recent years and the United Kingdom has become the first member state to withdraw from the EU. How did the single European market emerge from such a troubled past? Why has it become controversial?

Interests European integration was based on common interests among the states of Western Europe and the United States in the wake of World War II, as all countries looked for a way to rebuild from the war's devastation. At the same time, the Soviet Union had taken advantage of its control of Eastern Europe to install communist regimes throughout the region. Threats of unrest from within and attack from without created shared interests among the Western European states in security and economic growth. Although these immediate threats dissipated with time, cooperation continued to rest on common interests, particularly the joint gains available through the free flow of goods, money, and people.

Interactions Although common interests are necessary for cooperation, they by no means ensure that cooperation will happen. In the aftermath of war, distrust among the states of Western Europe, particularly toward West Germany, complicated their interactions. The United States played a major role by providing security in the form of U.S. troops and injecting money through the famous Marshall Plan. The Europeans had to cooperate among themselves to distribute U.S. aid, and this spirit of cooperation continued into the next decade. Given the emerging Cold War competition with the Soviet Union, these early cooperative efforts prioritized the production of coal and steel, which were vital to both the economic development and the military might of the West.

Institutions From these modest beginnings, institutional growth took off. Six original countries moved toward greater integration with the creation of the European Economic Community (EEC) in 1957, a customs union whose members allowed free trade among themselves and imposed a common external tariff on imported goods. However, trade in services remained outside the scope of the EEC, as did many informal barriers to trade in goods, such as product standards and regulatory differences. The next institutional steps created a single European market for goods and services, along with capital and people. Today, the European Union is effectively free of barriers to trade, investment, and migration among its members. And 19 members of the EU share a common currency, the euro, with a common central bank, the European Central Bank (ECB).

Over the past decade, however, European integration has become more controversial. Many countries have political parties that are skeptical about or even opposed to their country's membership in the EU. The most striking demonstration of this was the June 2016 referendum in the United Kingdom in which British voters chose to leave the EU.

Some Europeans feel that their interests are not taken into consideration by EU officials, who are not directly accountable to national political movements. This feeling has combined with a loss of confidence in EU institutions, which was intensified by the economic crisis that began in 2008. The eurozone debt crisis, along with an upsurge of immigration from the Middle East and North Africa, fed concerns that the EU's institutions were inadequate to the task of managing the complex conflicts of interest among and within member states.

The European Union remains a singular achievement—the first time in modern history that a large number of sovereign states have created a truly integrated single market for the movement of goods, capital, and people. Nonetheless, the EU today confronts many difficult conflicts of interest that will tax its institutions over the coming decades.

The European single market allows produce from Spain to be sold alongside local produce in France without restrictions.

international trade bargaining problems can resemble a Prisoner's Dilemma (see the "Special Topic" appendix to Chapter 2, on p. 86): both sides would be better off cooperating to reduce trade barriers, but concern that the other side will cheat leads both sides to act noncooperatively to their common detriment.

This sort of cooperation problem is common in trade relations among countries. To be sure, the logic of comparative advantage discussed earlier implies that countries would maximize their overall economic welfare by unilaterally liberalizing trade. However, governments respond to pressures other than that of the economy as a whole. For this reason, a government's first-choice trade policy is almost never to remove its trade barriers unilaterally; typically, it wants to get concessions from other countries in return for its own.

However, as the example of the Prisoner's Dilemma shows (see Chapter 2), it can be difficult for political actors to arrive at a mutually beneficial accord when there is no way to guarantee that all parties to the agreement will cooperate. Just as in the security relations among countries discussed in Chapters 3–5, in the international trade realm governments that want to collaborate may be hampered by the fear that they will be taken advantage of in a high-stakes interaction. No government can take lightly the possibility that its farmers, companies, or workers might lose money or jobs because the government mismanaged an international trade negotiation. Countries face inherent difficulties in making credible commitments to abide by the terms of trade agreements; as in military matters, this can lead to a breakdown of trust and, eventually, an inability to cooperate.

Strategic problems can also develop when countries try to work out a common approach to a problem, such as when they collaborate to decide which legal rules to use to govern trade. Difficulties commonly arise when one country accuses another of unfairly subsidizing its exports with grants, loans, and other programs to raise profits artificially. Disputes in world trade often involve accusations that one country's exporters are *dumping* their goods—that is, selling them below the true cost of production in order to drive out competitors. Dumping is widely accepted to be an unfair trading practice, but it is extremely hard to define, let alone measure. Similarly, government subsidies to exporters encounter widespread disapproval from other countries. But such subsidies can take many indirect forms (such as regulation of shipping costs, complicated accounting or tax rules, or manipulation of the exchange rate), and there is often no easy way to determine whether, in fact, actual subsidies are being given. In these cases, even when countries would like to work out their conflicts amicably, there may be serious disagreements about the standards that should be used to govern fair trading relations.

For example, one of the longest-standing disputes in world trade has been between the United States and Canada, two countries with generally very friendly relations. Starting in the early 1980s, the U.S. government argued that the Canadian federal and provincial governments, which own most of the country's timber-bearing land, were charging lumber producers artificially low prices to harvest wood. This would constitute an unfair subsidy to the country's exports of softwood lumber. The Canadians, however, reject this charge. Both countries wanted to maintain their cooperative trade relations, but this cooperation was threatened by conflicting interpretations of trade rules. In these cases of coordination problems, the parties typically want to find a common position or standard but have trouble deciding which one is best.

Overcoming Problems of Strategic Interaction

The international politics of trade is full of examples of cooperation and coordination problems; it is also full of attempts to make it easier for governments to overcome these problems. In Chapter 2, we saw that several factors can facilitate cooperation and coordination: small numbers, information, repeated interaction, and linkage politics. These factors all affect international trade relations.

Small numbers make it easier for governments to monitor each other's behavior; there is likely to be less free riding among small groups of countries than in the world at large. An extreme version of this observation is the theory of *hegemonic stability*, which argues that the existence of a single very powerful nation can solve problems of collective action and free riding if the hegemonic power is large and strong enough to be both willing and able to solve these problems for the world as a whole. In terms of economic affairs, this approach argues that when there has been such a hegemonic power over the past two centuries (Great Britain after 1860 and the United States after 1945) it has facilitated trade liberalization.

Less extreme versions of the approach suggest, more modestly, that smaller numbers of countries—privileged groups (see Chapter 2)—will find it easier to monitor and enforce trade agreements than will very large groups of nations or the world as a whole. Because of the greater ease of monitoring and enforcement, small groups are more likely to succeed at liberalizing trade.[35] This might help explain why so many trade agreements take the form of regional accords among a few neighboring nations, such as the European Union and Mercosur.

Small numbers might also help explain why the United States and Canada have often been able to negotiate successfully even in the bitter dispute over softwood lumber, which involved billions of dollars and one of Canada's more important industries. In 1986 and again in 1996, despite long-standing conflict over whether Canada was, in fact, subsidizing its lumber industry, the two countries reached compromise agreements. In the first instance, the United States agreed to reduce its tariff on Canadian imports; in the second instance, Canada agreed to limit its exports to the United States.

Information can also be an important consideration in trade negotiations. Many failures of cooperation are due to fears of hidden actions—such as the fear that one government might use its superior knowledge of its own domestic conditions to take advantage of other governments. In the case of dumping and subsidies, foreigners may know very little about the national bureaucratic agencies that make decisions related to these policies.

For example, in 2001 the United States and Canada were unable to negotiate a renewal of the 1996 Softwood Lumber Agreement. Immediately after the agreement

---

35. For a reasoned summary, see David A. Lake, "Leadership, Hegemony, and the International Economy: Naked Emperor or Tattered Monarch with Potential?" *International Studies Quarterly* 37, no. 4 (December 1993): 459–89.

Mercosur (also known as Mercosul in Portuguese) began as a regional trade agreement among Argentina, Brazil, Paraguay, and Uruguay in 1991. However, it has not achieved the same level of success as the European Union has in the freer movement of goods, capital, and people.

expired, the U.S. International Trade Commission and the Department of Commerce found that Canadian lumber was being subsidized, so the United States unilaterally imposed a 27 percent tariff on Canadian imports. This retaliation triggered a new round of acrimonious conflict. If the Canadians had known about this finding, perhaps they might have reached an agreement with the Americans. They did not, however, have access to advance information about the American government's decision. This example suggests that transparency may lead to trade cooperation. It also suggests that trading partners may facilitate cooperative relations by finding ways to provide information to one another.

Repeated interaction (iteration) between governments on a continuing basis provides a reason to avoid cheating, or even the appearance of cheating, on trade deals. The possibility that the collapse of a current deal might sour future deals can impose powerful discipline on government behavior and can encourage greater efforts to cooperate. This is especially the case in a trading relationship, which is likely to go on indefinitely. By the same token, governments with a long history of dealing with one another are likely to have more information about each other—and, in good circumstances, more reason to trust one another.

Linking concessions granted in one arena to concessions received in another may also facilitate cooperation on trade. A government that would otherwise be uninterested in negotiating lower barriers to, say, trade in steel might be willing to exchange concessions in steel if its trading partner gives it concessions in some other industry. Governments can, in other words, trade among trade policies—"giving" in an area they care less about in return for "getting" in an area they care more about. These exchanges can benefit governments and their citizens. Countries might link agreements in trade (steel for apparel, for example), or they might link trade agreements with agreements on something else, such as foreign aid or military cooperation.

All these considerations help explain why countries are more likely to have friendly, collaborative trade relations in some circumstances than they are in others. This is true of pairs or groups of countries: bilateral or regional trade agreements are more likely among a small number of members, where information about the partners is readily available, where the partners have a long history of interaction, and where trade relations are linked to other economic or noneconomic relations. It may also be true for the world as a whole: when these conditions are met, at least for the leading countries in the international trading system, trade cooperation is more likely. But when there is great uncertainty about the true intentions of some of the major powers (such as Germany and Japan in the 1920s and 1930s), coupled with a real concern for the short term and the absence of a dense network of other relationships among the major powers, international trade cooperation is difficult or impossible.

Because it can be inherently difficult for governments to ensure cooperative trade relations among themselves, they have created international institutions to help overcome the variety of collective action and other strategic problems that have beset international trade relations. International institutions may indeed be the most powerful factor in affecting whether trade relations among countries are collaborative or conflictual. They run the gamut from global organizations, such as the WTO, to regional agreements, such as the USMCA, to bilateral treaties between countries. Most such institutional arrangements have the goal of facilitating trade cooperation among their member states.

International Institutions and Trade Policy

reciprocity

In international trade relations, a mutual agreement to lower tariffs and other barriers to trade. Reciprocity involves an implicit or explicit arrangement for one government to exchange trade-policy concessions with another.

most-favored-nation (MFN) status

A status established by most modern trade agreements guaranteeing that the signatories will extend to each other any favorable trading terms offered in agreements with third parties.

International organizations represent the principal systematic attempts to bring order to contemporary international trade policy. As we saw in Chapter 2, institutions can play an important part by facilitating cooperation. They can help mitigate the problems that stand in the way of interstate cooperation on trade by setting standards of behavior that governments are expected to follow. They can also gather information to assist member states in monitoring and enforcing compliance with their agreements. By providing an expectation of repeated interaction, they can restrain defection. International institutions can reduce the costs to governments of making joint decisions—a real problem in the very complex trade realm—and can help governments resolve disputes.

For all these reasons, over the years countries have developed institutional arrangements to facilitate their trade negotiations. One is the concept of **reciprocity**, according to which a concession granted by one government is met by another—a sort of linkage politics that helps bind agreements. A more general provision of this nature has developed over the course of more than 100 years to serve a similar purpose: **most-favored-nation (MFN) status**. Countries that grant one another MFN status agree to extend to each other the same concessions that they provide to all other nations with that status; for example, a tariff reduction given to one country with MFN status is automatically given to all other countries with MFN status. This system, called normal trade relations in the United States, serves to link negotiations between two countries to all their multilateral trade relations.

The World Trade Organization The most important international institution in the realm of commercial relations has a global reach: the **World Trade Organization (WTO)**, which superseded the **General Agreement on Tariffs and Trade (GATT)**. The GATT was created in 1947 as one of the original Bretton Woods institutions, and it oversaw a dramatic liberalization of trade relations, particularly among developed countries, for more than 40 years.[36] By the early 1990s, GATT members had come to believe that the GATT's somewhat loose structure was insufficient in an environment in which almost all countries—developed, developing, and formerly centrally planned—were joining the international trading system. The WTO, which opened its doors in 1995, is more structured, more formal, and more encompassing than the GATT, although its goal is very similar: to encourage the expansion of an open international trading system.

Both the GATT and the WTO have been enormously successful in their stated purpose of reducing barriers to trade among member nations, with world trade growing faster than world output for virtually the entire postwar period. The principal achievement of both organizations has been to arrange a series of "rounds" during which member states negotiate multilateral reductions in trade barriers. The negotiations take place under a loose rule of reciprocity that balances the dollar value of concessions, which are then automatically extended to all other member states under the MFN rule. There are also rules about when and how countries can use safeguards to temporarily protect domestic industries.

Although all members of the WTO have a formally equal vote, in practice the largest trading states dominate the negotiations—in particular, the United States, the European Union (which negotiates as a single actor in the WTO), Japan, and in more recent years, China. The power of the largest members comes in part from their ability to set the agenda for negotiations. It also flows from the fact that they have more attractive outside options: they can more easily contemplate "going it alone" without the WTO. For all these reasons, developing countries have often found it difficult to get their concerns onto the international trade agenda, especially before the rise of China. China's economic strength enables it to "go it alone," and it often champions the interests of developing countries, making it a powerful ally for nations with less developed economies.

Conflicts between developed and developing nations pervaded the last series of WTO negotiations, which began with a meeting in Doha, Qatar, in 2001. Developing nations accused the rich world of ignoring their concerns during the "Doha Round" of negotiations. Their principal demand was for the liberalization of agricultural trade, as many developing countries would benefit from greater access to developed countries' markets for food. Such liberalization was blocked, however, by politically

World Trade Organization (WTO)

An institution created in 1995 to succeed the GATT and to govern international trade relations. The WTO encourages and polices the multilateral reduction of barriers to trade, and it oversees the resolution of trade disputes.

General Agreement on Tariffs and Trade (GATT)

An international institution created in 1947 in which member countries committed to reducing barriers to trade and providing similar trading conditions to all other members. In 1995, the GATT was replaced by the WTO.

---

36. To be entirely accurate, the original Bretton Woods institution for trade was to be an "International Trade Organization," but it foundered and was never created; the GATT was an interim replacement that lasted far longer than its initiators expected.

Although the WTO has lowered barriers to international trade, it has often provoked opposition from actors whose interests may be harmed by trade liberalization. The 1999 demonstrations against the WTO in Seattle, Washington turned violent as angry protesters torched trash cans and other debris.

powerful farmers in the developed countries. For their part, developed countries would have liked greater liberalization of trade in services—most developed countries are major exporters of such services as finance and telecommunications—and stricter rules to protect intellectual property. After more than a decade of negotiations, no solution was found to resolve the conflict between developed and developing countries. Negotiations collapsed in July 2008 and in 2015 WTO members declared the Doha Round dead.

During the 14 years of Doha Round negotiations, China transformed beyond recognition to become a powerful global exporter. It became a member of the WTO in December 2001 after a lengthy process of negotiations. As a condition of its acceptance into the WTO, China promised to reform its economy and trade policies. Many of these reforms have not happened, however, and the structure of China's economy sometimes makes it challenging to hold the government accountable to WTO rules. For example, WTO members can, under certain circumstances, retaliate against the trade practice of dumping. As we described earlier, dumping occurs when a company exports a product at a price lower than the price it normally charges in its own home market. But in China's economy, where prices are not determined by market forces and are sometimes set by the government, it can be tough to prove dumping by Chinese companies. The United States, Europe, and Japan use prices in other countries, such as Singapore, for comparison to help determine whether China is dumping. But this imperfect solution illustrates just one of the many challenges that China's non-market economy presents for the WTO's rulebook.

While the WTO isn't perfect—China's non-market economy raises issues for its rules, the Doha Round was a disappointment, and unequal power among countries has been an ongoing source of conflict—most WTO member states nonetheless accept that the WTO, like the GATT before it, facilitates international cooperation. It helps to set standards of behavior, verify compliance, ease joint decision making, and resolve disputes. The WTO makes available a great deal of information about trade and trade policies, and it monitors national compliance with international agreements.

The WTO monitors the compliance of its member countries in two primary ways. First, members must report actions they have taken to restrict trade as well as any regional trade agreements they may enter into (such as the USMCA). Second, countries that believe that foreign exporters or importers are not complying with the rules of various regional trade agreements can file a complaint with the WTO. Complaints are referred to the Dispute Settlement Body, composed of all member states, which then appoints a panel of experts in consultation with all parties to the dispute. The panel investigates the alleged rule violation and issues a report that becomes a ruling within 60 days.

Canada turned to the WTO for help with its ongoing dispute with the United States over softwood lumber. In 2017, the most recent agreement between the two countries regarding softwood lumber trade expired, and the Trump administration subsequently imposed an 18 percent tariff on Canadian lumber imports to compensate for what it charged was dumping of the product. In response, Canada filed a complaint with the WTO arguing that it was not dumping softwood in the United States, and therefore the tariffs were unjustified. In 2020, a WTO panel determined that the U.S. tariffs breached global trading rules because Washington had not proven that Canadian firms paid artificially low prices for timber on government-owned lands. The panel asked the United States to remove the tariff.

Canada expects the United States to comply with the panel's ruling and bring its policy into line with WTO rules. Historically, the United States has usually abided by WTO rules and rulings in WTO disputes, even when the complainants were small countries that the United States could have easily ignored. The United States' reason for doing so is probably that it wants to set a favorable precedent for any future complaints it might file with the WTO: the United States wants other nations to obey rulings in its favor (as the world's largest trader, it is the most frequent defendant at the WTO), so it has itself respected WTO rulings that have not gone its way. Under the Trump administration, however, the United States was less willing to comply with WTO rulings. U.S. Trade Representative Robert Lighthizer criticized the WTO's ruling in the case of U.S. tariffs on Canadian lumber, saying that it prevented the United States from taking legitimate action against Canadian subsidies. If the United States decides not to retract the lumber tariffs, there is little the WTO itself can do to force it to comply. However, the WTO may allow Canada to take retaliatory action against the United States.

In normal times, the United States would likely appeal the WTO panel's ruling. Each side in a WTO dispute can appeal (but not block) a panel's ruling to the WTO's standing seven-member Appellate Body, which acts like a supreme court, or final court of appeal, for international trade. If the Appellate Body does not overturn the panel's ruling, it becomes binding. But at the moment, the WTO Appellate Body is effectively defunct because the Trump administration refused to appoint new members to it. The Biden administration continues to block the appointment of new members. There are too few arbiters to hear an appeal, and as a result, the United States has no recourse in its dispute with Canada over softwood lumber.

Donald Trump was highly critical of the WTO and other trade agreements and institutions in his presidential campaign, and his administration expressed a desire to renegotiate American involvement in these organizations. The Trump administration also indicated that it would like to see the WTO agreements reworked, and it believed that the WTO dispute settlement system has not, in fact, worked in America's best interests. While the United States has generally supported the dispute process and complied with rulings that have gone against it, the Trump administration's refusal to appoint new members to the Appellate Body has hampered the WTO's ability to resolve disputes. Because the Appellate Body remains without the quorum necessary to hear appeals, it can not resolve international trade disputes.

Some countries share the United States' substantive concerns about the Appellate Body, namely that it oversteps its originally prescribed role and creates law rather than interprets WTO agreements. But even these countries generally objected to Trump's tactics, which have left WTO members without a functioning Appellate Body. Without a final court of appeal, the WTO dispute settlement system threatens to unravel, which could undermine the whole system of trade rules and the gains from trade. These fears have led some countries—the European Union and 16 other WTO members, including China—to work together to create a provisional alternative to the Appellate Body for settling disputes. These countries have thus ensured that a dispute settlement process remains in place and that a crucial component of the WTO will continue to function. China's participation in the new system is especially striking and may signal its willingness to support a continuation of the multilateral trading system.

Regional Trade Agreements   In addition to the WTO—and perhaps in reaction to concerns about its organization and progress in achieving further liberalization— many similar institutions have arisen at the regional level. In fact, the number and range of **regional trade agreements (RTAs)** has grown very rapidly in the past 20 years, and by 2011 the WTO counted 489 RTAs in force (see Map 7.1 on p. 348 for select examples). The three most prominent are the European Union, which started in 1958 as a customs union of 6 countries and now encompasses 27 nations in a single market; the USMCA (formerly NAFTA), made up of the United States, Canada, and Mexico; and Mercosur, originally comprising Argentina, Brazil, Paraguay, and Uruguay. There are many other such RTAs, of varying size and involving varying degrees of commitment to openness among their members. Many are bilateral, involving only two countries; others involve dozens of countries.[37]

Some observers applaud these regional agreements, arguing that they, like the WTO, constitute institutional structures that help countries mediate or avoid divisive trade-policy conflicts. Others see them more negatively, believing that they may serve to limit member countries' trade with nonmembers. In the words of economist Robert Lawrence, the question is whether the RTAs will be "building blocks" or "stumbling blocks" on the road to an integrated world economy.[38] While questions remain, most observers today regard such regional institutions as complementary to the WTO.

To state that the WTO (or the European Union or the USMCA) facilitates cooperation among governments on trade policy is not to pass judgment on whether its actions are good or bad—ethically, economically, or otherwise. Governments may cooperate for purposes that leave some consumers, workers, or businesses worse off. Antiglobalization critics complain that the WTO is too pro-business and that it privileges

regional trade agreements (RTAs)

Agreements among three or more countries in a region to reduce barriers to trade among themselves.

---

37. For more information on RTAs, see the WTO's RTA website at www.wto.org/english/tratop_e/region_e/region_e.htm (accessed 1/25/21).

38. Robert Z. Lawrence, "Emerging Regional Arrangements: Building Blocks or Stumbling Blocks?" in *Finance and the International Economy*, vol. 5, *The AMEX Bank Review Prize Essays*, ed. Richard O'Brien (New York: Oxford University Press, 1991), 25–35.

international corporations over other interests. Those on the Left often charge that WTO rules and procedures are biased, especially in their disregard for environmental, health and safety, labor, and social policies. Indeed, WTO rules do tend to focus on trade itself and exclude other concerns that many analysts regard as important.

Other critics of globalization, such as Donald Trump, argue that the WTO and organizations like it—such as NAFTA before its transition into the USMCA—do not serve American interests. Nonetheless, the most common view around the world remains that cooperation among governments is preferable to conflict among them and that the international institutions of trade contribute to this cooperation.

Explaining Trends and Patterns in International Trade

We can now return to some of the questions about international trade relations with which we began, bringing together what we have learned from the preceding sections to try to explain them. Let's recall the major ways in which trade policies vary.

Why, within a Country, Are Some Industries Protected and Some Not?

Governments often favor some industries over others, some regions over others, some groups over others—and this is certainly true of trade policy. Perhaps the most striking such difference is that virtually all developed countries protect agriculture, whereas they have relatively open trade in manufactured products. Why are U.S. farmers (in particular, its sugar producers) strongly protected, while so many other producers are not?

We can look at the actors involved and their interests to determine which groups or industries are most likely to benefit from protection. Land is scarce in most developed countries, certainly relative to capital and skilled labor; this explains why their farmers are protectionist. We can then explore how well the actors are able to overcome their collective action problems; the more cohesive and powerful interests are likely to get more government support. Farmers are well organized, whereas consumers of food are rarely organized at all. Perhaps the country's political institutions are biased for or against some regions, classes, or industries. Many nations' electoral institutions favor farm regions over cities, as does the U.S. Senate, which allots a sparsely populated farm state the same number of senators (two) as it allots a densely populated, mostly urban state. Farmers and their parties are often pivotal in parliamentary systems, as they occupy the crucial center of the political spectrum.

All these considerations help explain why some sectors receive more trade protection than others and, in particular, why farmers in rich countries are so commonly favored. In the case of American sugar producers, they have very high stakes

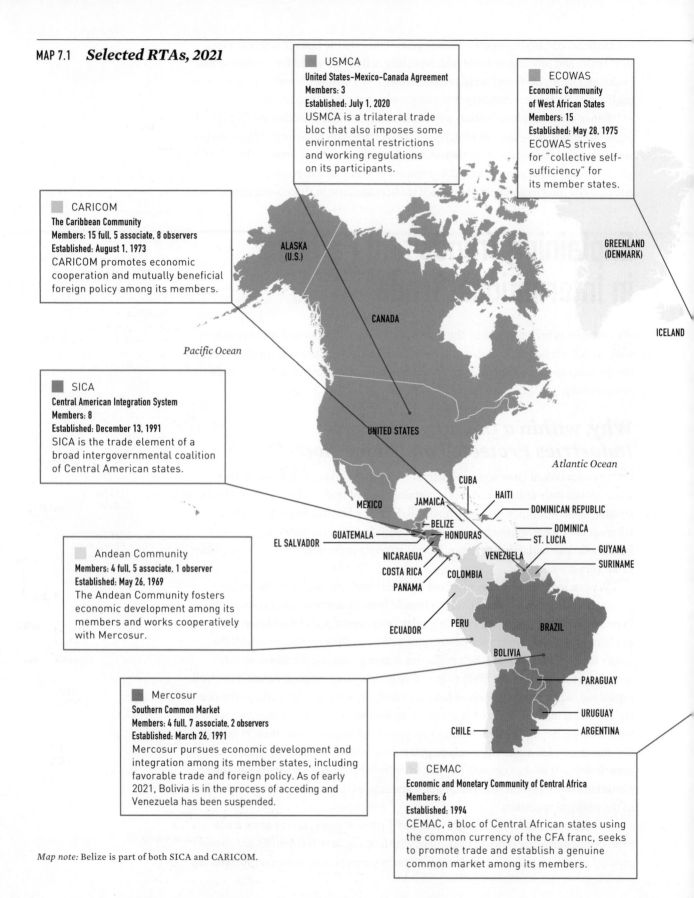

MAP 7.1 *Selected RTAs, 2021*

USMCA
United States–Mexico–Canada Agreement
Members: 3
Established: July 1, 2020
USMCA is a trilateral trade bloc that also imposes some environmental restrictions and working regulations on its participants.

ECOWAS
Economic Community of West African States
Members: 15
Established: May 28, 1975
ECOWAS strives for "collective self-sufficiency" for its member states.

CARICOM
The Caribbean Community
Members: 15 full, 5 associate, 8 observers
Established: August 1, 1973
CARICOM promotes economic cooperation and mutually beneficial foreign policy among its members.

SICA
Central American Integration System
Members: 8
Established: December 13, 1991
SICA is the trade element of a broad intergovernmental coalition of Central American states.

Andean Community
Members: 4 full, 5 associate, 1 observer
Established: May 26, 1969
The Andean Community fosters economic development among its members and works cooperatively with Mercosur.

Mercosur
Southern Common Market
Members: 4 full, 7 associate, 2 observers
Established: March 26, 1991
Mercosur pursues economic development and integration among its member states, including favorable trade and foreign policy. As of early 2021, Bolivia is in the process of acceding and Venezuela has been suspended.

CEMAC
Economic and Monetary Community of Central Africa
Members: 6
Established: 1994
CEMAC, a bloc of Central African states using the common currency of the CFA franc, seeks to promote trade and establish a genuine common market among its members.

Map note: Belize is part of both SICA and CARICOM.

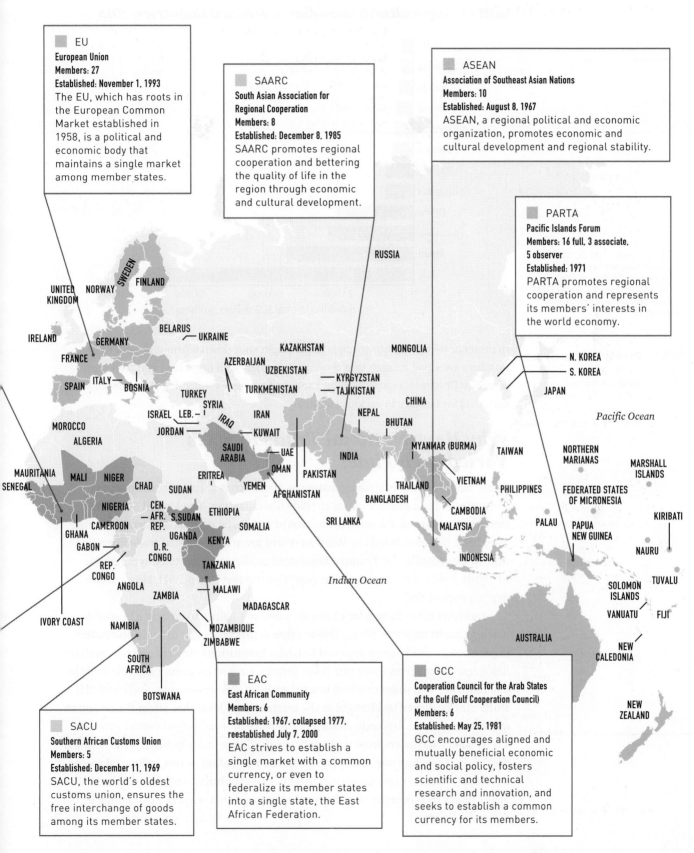

EU
European Union
Members: 27
Established: November 1, 1993
The EU, which has roots in the European Common Market established in 1958, is a political and economic body that maintains a single market among member states.

SAARC
South Asian Association for Regional Cooperation
Members: 8
Established: December 8, 1985
SAARC promotes regional cooperation and bettering the quality of life in the region through economic and cultural development.

ASEAN
Association of Southeast Asian Nations
Members: 10
Established: August 8, 1967
ASEAN, a regional political and economic organization, promotes economic and cultural development and regional stability.

PARTA
Pacific Islands Forum
Members: 16 full, 3 associate, 5 observer
Established: 1971
PARTA promotes regional cooperation and represents its members' interests in the world economy.

SACU
Southern African Customs Union
Members: 5
Established: December 11, 1969
SACU, the world's oldest customs union, ensures the free interchange of goods among its member states.

EAC
East African Community
Members: 6
Established: 1967, collapsed 1977, reestablished July 7, 2000
EAC strives to establish a single market with a common currency, or even to federalize its member states into a single state, the East African Federation.

GCC
Cooperation Council for the Arab States of the Gulf (Gulf Cooperation Council)
Members: 6
Established: May 25, 1981
GCC encourages aligned and mutually beneficial economic and social policy, fosters scientific and technical research and innovation, and seeks to establish a common currency for its members.

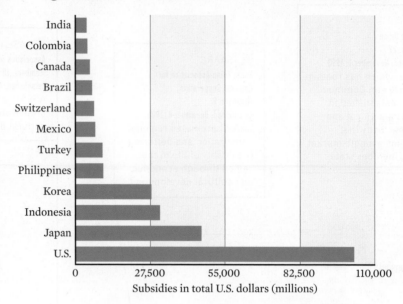

FIGURE 7.3 *Agricultural Subsidies in Selected Countries, 2018*

Figure source: OECD, "Producer and Consumer Support Estimates," OECD Agriculture Statistics, https://doi.org/10.1787/agr-pcse-data-en (accessed 2/17/21).

in protection—the country's sugar farms might shut down without it—and their numbers are small enough that they are extremely well organized and well represented in Congress. Figure 7.3 shows selected examples reflecting government subsidies for farmers in various countries.

Why Have National Trade Policies Varied over Time?

There have been many striking instances of countries shifting from openness to closure or from protectionism to trade liberalization. The United States in the 1920s was one of the most protectionist industrial nations on earth; starting after 1945, however, it led the Western world toward substantial trade liberalization. More recently, the Trump administration showed itself to be sympathetic to higher levels of trade protection (see "Controversy" on p. 352). How can we explain such shifts?

Interests may change; for example, a nation's ability to compete in world markets might improve, giving rise to more actors favorable to trade and reducing the concerns of actors opposed to trade. Institutions may change too: perhaps democratization gives more pro-trade groups, such as consumers, access to political influence and reduces a bias toward protectionist producers. Such national shifts may be driven by changes at the international level that affect the nation in question, such as a dramatic change in the price of its principal export product. The winners and losers from trade policy may change in a way that affects national policy, such as when one factor becomes more abundant or one industrial sector develops powerful export interests. And national political institutions can affect policy by strengthening the hands of groups that want to push policy in a certain direction.

Research has shown that democratization in developing countries is often associated with trade liberalization. Bolivia, which transitioned to democracy in the 1980s, has seen a significant increase in its exports of zinc and other mined minerals.

The American experience is an example of how a country's policies can shift from very high levels of trade protection to support for liberalization—and how they might be shifting back. The turn away from protection after World War II was undoubtedly assisted by the wartime destruction of foreign economies: the United States faced very little serious industrial competition, which made it relatively easy for the country to opt for trade liberalization.

As the Cold War began, the geopolitical concerns associated with binding together a pro-American Western alliance reinforced support for an open Western trading system. At the same time, the rise of powerful American manufacturing industries interested in exporting and investing overseas increased the range of actors in support of economic integration. This too was encouraged by institutional changes in the making of American trade policy in the 1930s, which gave the generally more trade-friendly president greater influence than the relatively protectionist Congress. All these factors and more may have affected American policy.

Why might trade protection have become more popular in the United States since 2000? Interests may have changed or become more intense: the rise of China as a trading power has certainly put major new pressures on many American industries and workers. Institutions play a role as well, since many of those most harmed by trade competition are in swing states in the American Midwest that play a major role in presidential elections. It remains to be seen whether these trends will lead to a thoroughgoing and lasting reorientation of American trade policy and of the United States' place in the world trading order.

Scholars continue to present arguments and evidence for and against these hypotheses. They may not, in fact, be mutually exclusive. National policy changes may be better explained in some cases by the global context, in others by the domestic interests engaged, and in still others by domestic institutions.

What Should Be Done When International Trade Harms Workers?

Applying the Concepts

Trade sparks debate because it divides actors in society: while some powerful groups have a strong **interest** in international trade and its benefits, there are many others who are harmed by foreign competition. These groups' domestic **interactions** have recently become especially bitter. The precise nature of the interactions often depends on the **institutions** that determine whether policy is made by the legislature, the bureaucracy, or the executive. People hurt by foreign trade have often found powerful political allies. One such ally is former U.S. president Donald Trump, who called NAFTA "the worst trade deal in history" and argued that "China's entrance into the World Trade Organization . . . enabled the greatest job theft in the history of our country."[a]

While some workers have lost their jobs because of trade, many people, including many American workers, have an interest in maintaining or expanding trade. A government study found that exports created nearly 12 million American jobs in 2015.[b] How should a society weigh the positive effects of trade on some workers against its negative effects on others?

Tariffs could be used selectively to protect only those industries in which workers stand to lose from trade. For instance, shoes coming into the United States from China and Vietnam have been hit with tariffs of as much as 20 percent or more for decades. Tariffs raise the price of foreign-made shoes, and the higher price helps offset the costs of higher U.S. wages. But tariffs have not stopped many U.S. footwear producers from closing their doors. Nike closed its last significant plant in the United States in Saco, Maine, in the mid-1980s.[c] Today, all of the Nike shoes sold in the United States are made abroad.

If tariffs raise prices for consumers and fail to protect workers' jobs, is there a better option? Compensation for people made worse off by trade provides one potential alternative. If trade makes a country as a whole better off—as most economists believe—then the government can tax the winnings of the beneficiaries and use the revenue to compensate the victims. In this way, the country gains from trade, while individuals who are hurt by it receive help to overcome its negative effects. In the United States, a national program called Trade Adjustment Assistance (TAA) aims to help workers who lose their jobs because of globalization. The program pays for two years of college tuition and extends unemployment benefits. However, TAA does not guarantee workers a salary similar to their previous one. An evaluation by the Labor Department found that TAA participants, especially those older than 50, generally made less money four years after starting the program than those who did not sign up.[d]

One reason why TAA fails to fully compensate workers may be trade's regional effects. Trade affects not just individuals but regions, because a single large employer often dominates a local economy. When that employer faces increased competition from foreign imports, it may cut jobs and/or reduce wages, developments that may spread beyond the single employer to affect the entire region. Consider Stuttgart, Arkansas—one of the areas of the United

States most affected by Chinese imports. This region was hit particularly hard by imports of Chinese-made footwear, and estimates suggest that the effects of these footwear imports on the region's average resident equaled a loss of $7,920. While the region also hosts a Lennox air conditioner factory, workers fired from the footwear industry could not pin their hopes on finding a new job at Lennox, as it, too, faced competition from Chinese imports. Estimates suggest that Chinese imports of refrigeration equipment cost the average resident in the region $1060.

Hickory, North Carolina—another area hit hard by Chinese imports—saw job losses in the furniture making industry. Estimates suggest that the effect of Chinese furniture imports on the average resident in the region equaled $8,100. Many workers fired from the furniture manufacturing industry went to community college using TAA benefits, but they often came away without jobs in other industries simply because there were so few jobs remaining in the area.

The regional effects of trade raise questions about how governments can best help workers while pursuing open trade policies. Most compensation programs, including TAA, assist individuals rather than entire communities. Programs that focus on communities may be better positioned to offset the costs of trade.

Ultimately, trade policy and compensation will reflect the interests of groups endowed with the greatest political influence by a country's political institutions. Because countries' institutions vary, the identity of these groups differs between countries, which helps to explain why different countries have varied trade policies and compensation programs.

a. "Full Transcript: Donald Trump's Jobs Plan Speech," Politico, June 28, 2016, www.politico.com/story/2016/06/full-transcript-trump-job-plan-speech-224891 (accessed 1/25/21).

b. Chris Rasmussen and Susan Xu, "Jobs Supported by Export Destination 2015," Department of Commerce, Office of Trade and Economic Analysis, November 8, 2016, www.trade.gov/sites/default/files/2020-12/Jobs%20Supported%20by%20Export%20Destination%202015.pdf (accessed 1/25/21).

c. Peter Whoriskey, "New Balance Struggles to Keep U.S. Shoe Factories Going," Seattle Times, August 1, 2011, www.seattletimes.com/business/new-balance-struggles-to-keep-us-shoe-factories-going (accessed 1/25/21).

d. Bob Davis and Jon Hilsenrath, "How the China Shock, Deep and Swift, Spurred the Rise of Trump," Wall Street Journal, August 11, 2016, www.wsj.com/articles/how-the-china-shock-deep-and-swift-spurred-the-rise-of-trump-1470929543 (accessed 1/20/21).

Thinking Analytically

1. Why does international trade benefit some groups within a country more than others? Which groups tend to have an interest in protectionism, and which tend to have an interest in freer trade?

2. In what way do programs that mitigate the negative impacts of trade create a Pareto improvement? Why have such programs failed to curtail the growing backlash against globalization?

Why Do Some Countries Have Higher Trade Barriers than Others?

Even within a common international trading system, national policies can differ. In the late 1930s, as the United States and some western European nations began moving away from trade protection and toward liberalization, most other industrial countries—especially Germany, Italy, and Japan—erected extremely high barriers to trade. In the 1980s, China became a global exporting powerhouse while many other developing nations remained very closed to trade.

Again, actors and their interests matter: these differences among nations may be driven by different factor endowments or sectoral features. In line with the Stolper-Samuelson approach, for example, the interests of landowners in two countries might be diametrically opposed: in favor of trade in a land-rich country, opposed to it in a land-poor country. If identical pro-farmer parties were in power in the two nations, one would reduce trade barriers while the other would raise them. A country whose economy is dominated by well-organized exporters will tend to be less protectionist than one that has very few exporters. In today's world, in which major portions of world trade are managed by huge international corporations, the role of individual firms can also have an impact on national trade policies.

The source of these differences, however, might be in national institutions, such as a party system or legislative structures biased in favor of the protectionist class (scarce factor), protectionist sectors and regions, or—on the other hand—in favor of powerful exporting companies. A democracy might give labor or consumers more influence than a dictatorship would. Anything that affects the domestic interests, institutions, or interactions of a country may well affect its trade policies.

Why Has the World Trading Order Been More or Less Open at Different Times?

Global trends are usually best explained by international factors, and trade is no exception. Three causes of the ebb and flow of open trade relations are most prominent: international economic conditions, the role of one or a few very large countries, and the creation of international institutions. Forbidding world economic conditions in the 1930s were a major source of the protectionist turn taken by many countries' trade policies, just as global economic growth in the 1990s encouraged trade liberalization among developing and formerly communist countries. The global economic crisis that began in 2008, in turn, led to an upsurge in protectionist sentiment in many nations. The ability of one or a few large countries to organize a leadership role in international trade relations—Britain and France in the late nineteenth century, the United States and its principal allies after World War II— also appears to have been important in affecting global trade, which means that recent changes in American policies may remake the trading system. Institutions such as the WTO help countries overcome some of the problems of cooperation that bedevil international trade relations, encouraging and facilitating collaborative trade ties among governments. Current challenges to these institutions may lead to an erosion of these collaborative ties.

Conclusion: Trade and Politics

International trade is the centerpiece of international economic relations, and government policies toward trade have long been among the most hotly contested. They are controversial *within countries*, as supporters and opponents of freer trade clash. Trade policies can also be controversial *among countries*, as governments come into conflict over their respective policies. This contention often breeds further discord; as the American statesman Cordell Hull said of the 1930s: "The political line-up followed the economic line-up."[39]

National policies toward foreign trade have been important to the development of the world economy and to international politics more generally. How open a nation is to trade affects its pattern of economic and social development as well as its relations with other nations. In turn, a country's trade policies are determined by the nature of its prevailing economic interests and political institutions and by its interactions with other nations. Today, international trade has become one of the more contentious issues in many nations—including, prominently, the United States—and the future of the international trading system is very much an open question.

---

39. Quoted in Gardner, *Sterling-Dollar Diplomacy*, 9.

Study Tool Kit

Interests, Interactions, and Institutions in Context

- Economists are virtually unanimous in concluding that international trade brings important benefits and that reducing trade barriers—trade liberalization—is good for a nation's economy.

- While trade may be beneficial for a country as a whole, it can harm the interests of groups and individuals in the society. Trade can create both winners and losers.

- The nature of a country's economy determines which groups have an interest in expanding or restricting trade with the rest of the world. National political institutions shape the outcomes when these interests come into conflict.

- The politics of international trade also involves strategic interaction among national governments. Governments can face difficult problems of bargaining and cooperation, which sometimes lead to trade conflicts among nations.

- The institutions of the international trading system can facilitate cooperation among governments as they confront the demands of both their own constituents and their foreign counterparts.

Key Terms

comparative advantage, p. 310

absolute advantage, p. 310

neo-mercantilism, p. 310

Heckscher-Ohlin trade theory, p. 311

protectionism, p. 316

trade barriers, p. 316

tariff, p. 316

quantitative restriction (quota), p. 316

nontariff barriers to trade, p. 316

Stolper-Samuelson theorem, p. 323

Ricardo-Viner (specific-factors) model, p. 325

reciprocity, p. 342

most-favored nation (MFN) status, p. 342

World Trade Organization (WTO), p. 343

General Agreement on Tariffs and Trade (GATT), p. 343

regional trade agreements (RTAs), p. 346

For Further Reading

Davis, Christina L. *Why Adjudicate? Enforcing Trade Rules in the WTO.* **Princeton, NJ: Princeton University Press, 2012.** Analyzes why countries tend to obey the WTO's dispute settlements and, more generally, how international institutions contribute to more cooperative trade relations.

Destler, I. M. *American Trade Politics.* **4th ed. Washington, DC: Peterson Institute for International Economics, 2005.** Surveys and analyzes the political economy of trade policy in the United States.

Guisinger, Alexandra. *American Opinion on Trade: Preferences without Politics.* **Oxford: Oxford University Press, 2017.** An innovative look at how to understand the contradictory nature of American public opinion on trade relations, particularly relevant in light of current debates.

Hiscox, Michael J. *International Trade and Political Conflict: Commerce, Coalitions, and Mobility.* **Princeton, NJ: Princeton University Press, 2002.** Evaluates the relative importance of factoral (class) and sectoral (industry) demands for protection and of variations among these considerations over time.

Hoekman, Bernard M., and Michel M. Kostecki. *The Political Economy of the World Trading System: The WTO and Beyond.* **3rd ed. New York: Oxford University Press, 2009.** Comprehensive overview of the structure and functioning of the WTO and international institutions in the international trade arena.

Irwin, Douglas A. *Free Trade under Fire.* **4th ed. Princeton, NJ: Princeton University Press, 2015.** Makes a strong argument for trade liberalization, addressing many common sources of opposition.

Krueger, Anne. *International Trade: What Everyone Needs to Know.* Oxford: Oxford University Press, 2020. Discusses how international trade policies affect workers, consumers, and the overall economy and highlights the costs and benefits of international trade.

Mansfield, Edward D., and Helen V. Milner. *Votes, Vetoes, and the Political Economy of International Trade Agreements.* Princeton, NJ: Princeton University Press, 2012. Analyzes the domestic political forces that lead countries to undertake RTAs.

Rodrik, Dani. *Straight Talk on Trade: Ideas for a Sane World Economy.* **Princeton, NJ: Princeton University Press, 2018.** A leading economist assesses current debates over world trade and the best ways policies might address them.

Rogowski, Ronald. *Commerce and Coalitions: How Trade Affects Domestic Political Alignments.* Princeton, NJ: Princeton University Press, 1989. Develops an analysis based on the Stolper-Samuelson theorem of how trade affects politics within nations.

Comparative Advantage and the Political Economy of Trade

Economists generally agree that international trade is good for the aggregate welfare of societies. Where does this consensus come from? In this appendix we introduce the concept of comparative advantage, which for centuries has been the backbone of economic thinking on international trade. We also illustrate the redistributive and welfare effects of opening a domestic economy to international trade and the countervailing effects of imposing a tariff.

Comparative Advantage

At the heart of economic analyses of international trade is the idea of *comparative advantage*. In short, comparative advantage implies that all countries benefit from trade if each country specializes in the production of certain goods. Which goods should countries produce? Economist David Ricardo provided the straightforward answer in the early 1800s: countries should focus their production only on goods that they can produce most efficiently relative to other goods.[a] If a country is good at mining copper, growing coffee beans, or producing steel, then it should focus its productive capacities on producing these goods and rely on international trade to obtain all the other goods that it needs.

What if a country is not very good at producing anything? To answer this question, it is important to distinguish between *absolute advantage* and comparative advantage. A country has an absolute advantage if it can produce a good more efficiently than any other country can. Comparative advantage, on the other hand, is determined within a country: of all the possible goods that a country might produce, it can produce some more efficiently than others. This means that *all* countries have a comparative advantage in something. A country might not be the most efficient in the world at producing coffee, but it still has a comparative advantage in coffee if it can produce coffee more efficiently than it can make steel, airplanes, or any other good.

Consider the following example used by Ricardo himself to explain the concept of comparative advantage. Assume that there are two countries in the world, Portugal and England, and that these two countries can produce only cloth and wine. Further assume that the only input in the production process is labor, such that one unit of each good (a bolt of cloth or a barrel of wine) has a cost in man-hours. For example, in England it takes 15 man-hours to produce a bolt of cloth and 30 man-hours to produce a barrel of wine. In Portugal, it takes 10 man-hours to

---

a. The idea of comparative advantage—not the term itself—was introduced by David Ricardo in Chapter 7 of his *On the Principles of Political Economy and Taxation*, www.econlib.org/library/Ricardo/ricPCover. html (accessed 1/25/21).

TABLE A.1

COUNTRY	CLOTH	WINE
	Cost in Man-Hours per Bolt	Cost in Man-Hours per Barrel
England	15	30
Portugal	10	15

produce a bolt of cloth and 15 man-hours to produce a barrel of wine. Note that it takes fewer man-hours to produce both cloth and wine in Portugal than it does in England; indeed, in this example, Portugal has an absolute advantage in the production of both goods, cloth and wine (Table A.1).

To understand the impact of each country's choice of which goods to produce, it is helpful to examine the *opportunity cost of production*. This is the value that a country forgoes in order to make one product rather than another. The resources (in this example, labor) that each nation uses to make cloth are unavailable to make wine, so the country must forgo a certain amount of wine in order to make cloth. How many bolts of cloth must a country give up to produce a barrel of wine, and vice versa?

England must give up two bolts of cloth to produce an additional barrel of wine (30 ÷ 15); alternatively, it can give up a half barrel of wine to produce a bolt of cloth (15 ÷ 30). In contrast, Portugal must give up one and a half bolts of cloth to produce an additional barrel of wine (15 ÷ 10); alternatively, it can give up two-thirds of a barrel of wine to produce an additional bolt of cloth (10 ÷ 15). Table A.2 presents these results.

Note that the opportunity cost of producing cloth is lower in England than in Portugal, whereas the opportunity cost of producing wine is lower in Portugal than in England. From these figures we can conclude that England has a comparative advantage in the production of cloth, and Portugal has a comparative advantage in the production of wine.

What happens if these two countries engage in international trade? If England focuses all its man-hours on producing cloth, and Portugal does the same for wine, then the total world production of cloth and wine will be considerably higher than

TABLE A.2

COUNTRY	OPPORTUNITY COST OF PRODUCING . . .	
	One Bolt of Cloth	One Barrel of Wine
England	$\frac{1}{2}$ barrel of wine	2 bolts of cloth
Portugal	$\frac{2}{3}$ barrel of wine	$1\frac{1}{2}$ bolts of cloth

if the two countries did not specialize or engage in trade. Ricardo's simple model tells us that international trade based on comparative advantage increases aggregate welfare, measured by the total amount of goods produced in this two-country world. The increase in aggregate welfare occurs even though England does not have an absolute advantage in the production of either good.

Distributional and Welfare Effects of Trade

Economists largely agree that international trade makes society as a whole better off, whereas tariffs and other forms of trade protection are inefficient and costly for societies. A few simple graphs can illustrate the logic behind these claims. Consider first a country in a state of autarky, in which there is no international trade. The domestic price of any good is therefore determined by the intersection of the two lines of domestic supply and domestic demand. All else being equal, producers will supply more of a good as its price increases, and consumers will demand more of a good as its price falls. Therefore, the supply line slopes upward and the demand line slopes downward. The intersection indicates the good's domestic price (P) and quantity demanded (Q), as shown in Figure A.1.

The effects of the production of the good in autarky are measured by the concepts of *consumer surplus* and *producer surplus*. Consider first the fate of consumers. The downward-sloping demand line means that the lower the price, the more people demand the good. The shaded region represents the aggregate welfare benefit for consumers; it is called a surplus because it represents the gains to consumers who would be willing to pay more than P for the good but instead purchase it for the lower price of P. Similarly, there are some producers in the country who would happily supply the good at a lower price than P. The region beneath P and bounded by the two lines represents the producer surplus. This region captures the gains to

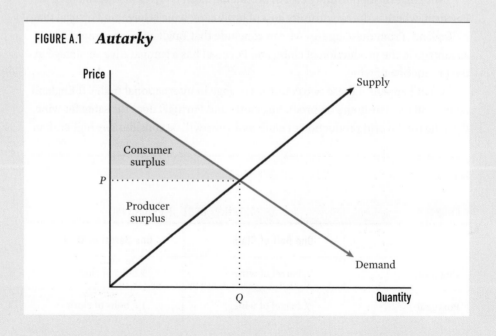

FIGURE A.1 *Autarky*

producers who benefit from a higher price than they would otherwise tolerate for selling the good.

Now consider how the price and quantity of the good change as the country begins to trade freely with other countries. Note that the world price of the good will be lower than the domestic price in autarky. The world price is determined by the intersection of global, not domestic, supply and demand. For simplicity, we assume that the country in this example is small relative to the world economy. In other words, it is a "price taker": its own domestic supply and demand of the good will not appreciably affect global supply or demand.

Figure A.2 indicates that the new domestic price declines to the (lower) world price (P_w) after the country moves from autarky to international trade openness. At this lower price, domestic consumer demand increases to Q_d because more people can enjoy the good at the new lower price. Domestic supply of the good decreases to Q_s because fewer producers are willing to produce the good at the lower price. The larger consumer demand is satisfied by imports from the rest of the world (equal to the distance between Q_s and Q_d).

Note that under free trade, the consumer surplus increases considerably because consumers are better off with the lower price. The regions labeled A and B represent the additions to consumer surplus that result from free trade. The producer surplus declines as a result of the lower world price. However, note that the combination of consumer and producer surplus—an overall measure of aggregate welfare—is larger under free trade than in autarky. There are two important implications: opening to trade redistributes income from producers to consumers, and opening to trade makes society as a whole better off.

As a final exercise, consider the implications to redistribution and to aggregate welfare of a tariff on the good. The tariff—which is a tax levied by the government on the imported good—increases the domestic price of the good to P_t, as shown in

FIGURE A.2 *Free Trade*

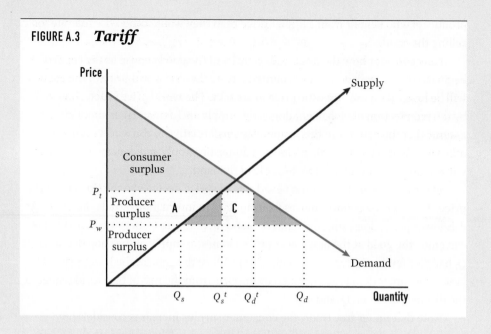

FIGURE A.3 *Tariff*

Figure A.3. The quantity demanded by consumers falls to Q_d^t because of the higher price, whereas the quantity supplied by domestic suppliers increases to Q_s^t. As expected, the consumer surplus declines, because many consumers who wish to purchase the good cannot afford the higher price. The producer surplus increases by the amount represented by Region A, as more producers benefit from a higher price than what they would normally receive. What of the remaining regions? The amount represented by Region C accrues to the government as a result of the tariff revenue. But the two dark triangular regions on either side of Region C do not benefit anyone! Known as the *deadweight loss* of the tariff, they represent the efficiency losses that trade protection imposes on society.

Where does the deadweight loss come from? The best way to understand this loss is to reflect on the concept of comparative advantage. The tariff causes an artificially higher price, which leads domestic producers to shift their production away from whatever they were previously producing and toward the higher-priced good. Suppose the country in question is England, which has a comparative advantage in the production of cloth. If England imposes a tariff on imported wine, then more English producers will shift their production away from cloth and toward wine to take advantage of the higher price, even though they are relatively inefficient in producing wine. In other words, a tariff interferes with the efficient allocation of production and works against the concept of comparative advantage.

By the same token, the artificially high price of the protected good leads consumers to reallocate their consumption away from it and toward a good they would not otherwise purchase, which is another loss to society. The losses to efficiency are represented by the dark triangles in Figure A.3. When we combine these efficiency losses with the decline in domestic consumption caused by the higher price, we can see why economists are generally in agreement that tariffs cause society as a whole to be worse off compared to free trade.

This simple set of graphs captures the essence of the political economy of trade policy. First, international trade improves aggregate welfare. However, certain producers who previously produced exclusively for the domestic market can be harmed when the country moves toward free trade. Trade tariffs lead to a decline in aggregate welfare and cause deadweight losses to society. They also result in an increased producer surplus and a reduced consumer surplus. If producer groups can successfully lobby the government for protection, they can reap great benefits. These benefits come at a cost to consumers, however, in the form of a reduced consumer surplus (owing to higher prices), and at the expense of the country as a whole in the form of an efficiency loss.

8

International Financial Relations

THE PUZZLE *Every year, approximately $5 trillion is invested abroad. Why is so much money invested in foreign countries? And why do relations between foreign investors and the countries in which they invest often become hostile and politically controversial?*

Above: Financial crises often have wide-reaching economic consequences, affecting businesses and private citizens alike. Citizens stood in long lines at unemployment agencies in Spain as a result of the worldwide Great Recession in 2008.

The global financial crisis that began in 2008 hit Europe almost immediately with a major debt crisis. Borrowers in a number of eurozone countries had built up large debts and appeared to be unable to service them. The crisis eventually came to be known as the European sovereign debt crisis (sovereign debt is debt owed by governments), and it was the most serious such crisis since the 1930s, endangering the international financial system and the world economy.

The four principal eurozone debtors were Greece, Ireland, Portugal, and Spain. In Spain and Ireland, households had borrowed hundreds of billions of dollars to finance a major housing and construction boom. When housing prices collapsed and homeowners had trouble repaying their mortgages, the two national governments started borrowing heavily from abroad to finance national bank bailouts and to stimulate their economies. Greece, however, had been running budget deficits ever since the creation of the eurozone, with the government relying greatly on foreign borrowing to cover its shortfalls. Portugal was somewhere in between: both households and the government were major borrowers.

The difficulties of the eurozone debtors were not just a problem for them, since major northern European financial institutions and investors were the ones that had loaned them most of the money. If the debtors defaulted, trillions of dollars in loans on the books of northern European banks, investors, and pension funds would go bad. The weight of so many bad loans and investments endangered the financial integrity of even the richest European countries, especially Germany and France. The sovereign debt crisis thus threatened both the sovereign debtors and their creditors—and, in fact, the entire European economy.

Faced with this looming catastrophe, leaders of the eurozone member states put together a trillion-euro package to shore up the finances of the major debtors and the region's financial system. In return, they insisted that the debtor countries impose severe austerity measures, including raising taxes, cutting government spending, and selling off public enterprises. Mass protests rocked the debtor nations, and some even entertained the idea of leaving the euro.

It took ten years for the eurozone's economic output to return to what it had been before the crisis. In the meantime the region's unemployment soared; in Greece and Spain, unemployment peaked at over 25 percent. The result was widespread dissatisfaction with both national governments and, more generally, the European Union (EU).

Political movements and parties hostile to or skeptical of European integration gained strength, culminating in Britain's June 2016 vote to leave the European Union. All over Europe, it seemed, 50 years of consensus in favor of European integration and a centrist vision of society had collapsed.

The eurozone crisis exemplifies how international finance can become a highly political issue. Today, capital flows around the world in unimaginably large quantities. Nearly half of all the world's investment—about $5 trillion annually—goes across borders. In 2020, the sum total of all international investment holdings was about $150 trillion, and every day more than $5 trillion in foreign currencies are traded. Even the United States has financed large trade and budget deficits with money from abroad, borrowing more than $8 trillion between 2005 and 2020—increasing its debt to foreigners in those years by more than $65,000 for every American household.[1]

International finance has long been the leading edge of global economic integration. Massive investment flows drove the integrated world economy of the nineteenth and early twentieth centuries, and they dried up during the years between World Wars I and II, when the world's nations turned inward. Since 1960, international finance has revived and is once again the most globalized component of the world economy, dwarfing international trade and migration.

Some analysts regard the emergence of a worldwide market for capital as one of globalization's main attractions. Companies, investors, and borrowers around the world now can tap into an enormous pool of capital. Home buyers in Arkansas can have their mortgages underwritten by investors in Germany; start-ups in India can be financed by Canadian pension funds; shopkeepers in South Africa can borrow money that comes from small savers in Japan.

Yet international finance is also extremely controversial, and critics of global economic integration have long targeted international bankers. Many policy makers in the developing world see international finance as a source of economic and political problems and as a potential threat to their nations' sovereignty.

A series of financial crises, culminating in the global economic crisis, has focused attention on how financial developments in one country can affect others. Problems that started in the U.S. market for housing finance in 2007 ended up causing the most serious international financial panic since the 1930s. Meanwhile, loans gone similarly bad in Europe threatened to tear the European Union apart. Even the world's largest and richest economies seem highly susceptible to the volatility of international financial markets.

Thinking Analytically about International Finance

Governments, firms, and individuals sometimes pursue international finance avidly and sometimes attack it mercilessly. Why is international finance so controversial? As we will see, within borrowing nations, some actors value access to foreign funds, while others resent the constraints and burdens that foreign investments sometimes impose on them. Similar conflicting interests exist within lending nations.

At the international level, lenders and borrowers have a shared interest in sustaining capital flows, but they may disagree about how the benefits from loans should be divided. For example, most Europeans favor allowing capital to flow among EU member countries, but they disagreed profoundly about which countries should have been asked to make the sacrifices necessary to resolve the region's debt crisis. Similarly, international investors and the recipients of investment may clash. These interactions frequently involve bargaining over the investments, as each side tries to get the best deal.

International institutions, such as the International Monetary Fund (IMF), structure interactions in the international financial and investment realm. Like international finance generally, however, the role of the IMF is very controversial: some analysts think it contributes to the cooperative resolution of financial problems, while others think it takes unfair advantage of struggling debtor nations. In this chapter we take a closer look at these questions.

---

1. Except where otherwise noted, all data in this section are from M. Ayhan Kose, Eswar Prasad, Kenneth Rogoff, and Shang-Jin Wei, "Financial Globalization: A Reappraisal," *IMF Staff Papers* 56, no. 1 (2009): 8–62; and the Updated and Extended External Wealth of Nations Dataset, 1970–2011, from Philip Lane and Gian Maria Milesi-Ferretti, "The External Wealth of Nations Mark II: Revised and Extended Estimates of Foreign Assets and Liabilities, 1970–2004," *Journal of International Economics* 73, no. 2 (2007), supplemented and updated from the IMF's International Financial Statistics, the Bank for International Settlements, and the U.S. Department of the Treasury.

How and Why Do People Invest Overseas?

There are many ways in which those with capital can invest in foreign lands. There are two broad categories of foreign investment: portfolio and direct. A **portfolio investment** gives the investor a claim on some income but no role in managing the investment. Loans are portfolio investments. So are shares of a company's stock (equities), for each share represents a minuscule portion of ownership in the corporation.[2]

If, for example, an investor buys bonds from an Indian corporation or from the Indian government, or if a bank lends money to an Indian corporation or the Indian government, the Indian debtor commits itself to making interest and principal payments but has no obligation to involve the creditor in figuring out how or when to use the borrowed money. Even if the Indian corporation or Indian government has a bad year, it is obligated to pay off its creditors at the preestablished interest rate.[3] Portfolio investors take little or no part in running their investment; their interest is simply in the rate of return.

A substantial portion of the portfolio investment that goes to developing countries is **sovereign lending**—that is, loans from private financial institutions to sovereign governments. Loans by European or American financial institutions to the governments of Indonesia or Brazil—or to government-owned or -controlled companies or agencies in those countries—are sovereign loans. So too are purchases by foreigners of French or American government bonds. If a private firm's government guarantees borrowing by the firm, this can also be considered a sovereign loan.

Foreign direct investment (FDI) is made by a company that owns and controls facilities in another country. For example, a Toyota truck factory in Thailand or a Disney theme park in France is an instance of FDI. FDI differs most significantly from foreign portfolio investment in that the investor maintains managerial control of—and also bears the risk of—the investment. If the Toyota factory in Thailand is not profitable, Toyota loses money. Direct investors have full authority to run their investments, but they take most of the associated risks as well.

Sovereign lending has typically been the most politically fraught component of international investment. It has led to debt crises that pit national governments against powerful private bankers, resulting in bitter domestic and international conflicts. FDI, while sometimes controversial, has been less likely to lead to these sorts of crisis-induced political upheavals, although tough negotiations often occur between governments and foreign direct investors.

portfolio investment
Investment in a foreign country via the purchase of stocks (equities), bonds, or other financial instruments. Portfolio investors do not exercise managerial control of the foreign operation.

sovereign lending
Loans from private financial institutions in one country to sovereign governments of other countries.

foreign direct investment (FDI)
Investment in a foreign country via the acquisition of a local facility or the establishment of a new facility. Direct investors maintain managerial control of the foreign operation.

---

2. Equities (stocks) can be ambiguous; an investor who owns enough of the company's shares might, in fact, take control of the company, making the investment direct. But almost all international equity investment is of the portfolio variety, meaning that it does not involve actual managerial control of the firm.

3. This distinction is blurred when foreigners buy large quantities of corporate equities—so at some point they could, in fact, exercise control over the corporation. Traditional portfolio investors, as discussed here, are not interested in control; they buy equities solely as financial instruments.

In this chapter, we will also take a preliminary look at the international flow of another factor of production: labor. Migration has been a hot political topic in many countries. Here, we concentrate on its economic dimensions; we turn to the important noneconomic sources and implications of immigration in Chapter 14.

Why Invest Abroad? Why Borrow Abroad?

Banks, corporations, and individuals invest overseas with a clear goal: to make money. Those with capital want to move their money from where profits are lower to where profits are higher. Thus, many international investors want to move money from capital-rich developed countries to capital-poor developing ones. Banks, corporations, and individuals in rich countries invest nearly a trillion dollars every year in developing- and emerging-market nations. About two-thirds of this money comes in the form of direct investment from multinational corporations (MNCs), the other third is in loans and investments in equities.[4] Figure 8.1 illustrates the rapid growth of foreign investment in emerging markets over recent decades.

The Heckscher-Ohlin theory presented in Chapter 7 explains why. A country's average profit rate depends on how plentiful capital is. Where land or labor is scarce, it is expensive; where it is plentiful, it is cheap. The same is true of capital, recognizing that the interest rate is the "price" of capital: more expensive capital means a higher rate of return. In a poor country, capital is scarce and therefore expensive, so borrowers pay higher interest rates for something in short supply. In a rich country, capital is abundant, so interest rates and profit rates are much lower. For example, in 2020 the prevailing rate of interest on long-term loans in most developed countries was 2 percent or lower, while in Latin America it was typically between 7 and 10 percent, sometimes higher.

Figure source: World Bank, "World Development Indicators," https://databank .worldbank.org/reports .aspx?source=2&series=BX .KLT.DINV.CD.WD,BX.KLT .DINV.WD.GD.ZS,BX.PEF .TOTL.CD.WD,DT.NFL.BOND .CD,DT.NFL.PCBO.CD# (accessed 1/12/21).

Note: Measures are "net inflows" in current U.S. dollars for low- and middle-income countries as defined by the World Bank. See http://data. worldbank.org/income-level/ LMY for countries included.

FIGURE 8.1 **Foreign Investment in Emerging Markets, 1970–2019**

4. This is an annual average for 2007–2019 based on the data in Figure 8.1.

The greater scarcity of capital and the higher interest rates in developing versus developed countries encourage capital to flow from richer to poorer nations. For example, Mexico is poor in capital, while the United States is rich in capital. Thus, profits and interest rates are higher in Mexico, which helps explain why American investors have, over time, accumulated investments worth over $300 billion there.

If the only considerations in international investment were differential rates of return, as in this simple Heckscher-Ohlin discussion, then all foreign investment would flow from capital-rich countries to capital-poor countries. But it decidedly does not. In fact, most international investment occurs among rich countries, and only a relatively small (but growing) fraction of international investment has gone to the developing world in the past couple of decades. Why is this the case? Cross-border investments in rich countries are simply less risky. International banks, corporations, and other investors care not just about the promised interest or profit rate on foreign investments but also about the likelihood that they will actually get the money. See Figure 8.2 for a breakdown of FDI by region in recent years.

Although all investment is risky, international investment involves a very specific risk: that a foreign government over which the investor has no influence may do things that reduce the value of the investment. This is especially true when it comes to sovereign lending, which involves a government's promise to pay debt service (interest and principal). Unlike in domestic lending, this promise cannot be enforced by the threat of foreclosure or bankruptcy. For foreign direct investors, the concern is that the local government will enact policies that devalue the investment—up to and including taking over the investment itself.

Investment among rich countries is much less risky than investment in poor countries. After all, the industrialized nations are more economically and politically stable, and they have a longer and more reliable history of treating foreign investors well. For investors to be willing to take a chance on the greater risk in the

Figure source: United Nations Conference on Trade and Development, *World Investment Report 2020: International Production Beyond the Pandemic*, Annex Table 2, https://unctad.org/system/files/official-document/wir2020_en.pdf (accessed 1/13/21).

Note: Measures are "FDI inward stock" in current U.S. dollars.

FIGURE 8.2 *Stock of Foreign Direct Investment by Region, 2000–2019*

The United Kingdom presents a low-risk environment for foreign investors because it is stable and rich. Many British brands and landmarks are owned by corporations based overseas, such as the London Taxi Company, owned by Chinese automotive manufacturer Geely.

developing world, they need either higher interest rates and profits or some reason to think that they can effectively manage the investment risks. This need can lead to negotiations—between lenders or investors on the one hand and developing countries on the other—to try to ensure a more reliable investment environment. This effort, in turn, draws international investment into international politics.

What's the Problem with Foreign Investment?

International investment is controversial because its results are often mixed: although it sometimes provides great benefits to both investors and the countries they invest in, it can also impose real costs on both sides of the relationship. This is yet another example, as we discussed in Chapter 2, of how many issues in international politics contain elements of both cooperation and bargaining. Both sets of actors stand to gain by amicably resolving their differences, so they have an interest in cooperating, but each side wants to get as much as possible out of the relationship, which leads their interaction down the path to bargaining.

In international investment, borrowers and lenders, investors and the countries they invest in, share many common interests. Both sides of the interaction gain from successful international investments and loans. The receiving country gets capital it would not otherwise have. Companies that borrow from abroad can expand their businesses, and governments that borrow from abroad can finance projects that spur development, such as roads and power plants. An inflow of foreign funds can increase the availability of credit to small business owners and homeowners. Meanwhile, the foreign investor who has sent the money overseas gets higher profits than are available at home. Borrowing and lending nations alike gain from the ability of capital to flow across borders.

But there may also be major conflicts of interest between the two sides of the relationship. Each party wants to get as much as possible from the other and to give as little as possible. Lenders want their debts repaid in full, and corporations want to bring home high profits from their foreign investments. Debtor nations, however, would rather pay less of what they owe, and host countries would rather that foreign corporations have less to take away. This situation creates both a commonality of interests in maintaining a flow of capital and a conflict of interests in distributing the benefits of the flow.

Domestic politics may also contribute to conflict between capital-sending and capital-receiving nations. In most countries, there is little disagreement when money is flowing in. Foreign capital allows the country to consume more than it produces and allows the government to spend more than it takes in through taxes; the foreign capital increases domestic consumption, investment, and economic activity, and this outcome tends to be popular. Eventually, however, lenders must be repaid and profits taken out—an outcome that is less universally popular.

Making debt service payments can require raising taxes, reducing government services, restraining wages and consumption, importing less while exporting more, and generally imposing austerity on the national economy. Debt crises throughout history—including recent ones in both developing and developed countries—have been associated with slow growth, unemployment, cuts in social spending, and general economic hardship. And there is no guarantee that the people and groups who are asked to bear the greatest burden of austerity will be those who benefited most from the capital inflow. Even if foreign borrowing and foreign investment are unambiguously good for a nation, the benefits and costs do not accrue equally to all people in the country. This fact has made international finance a contentious issue within developing—and many developed—countries.

Overseas loans and investments can be controversial within lending and investing nations too. While those making the foreign investments stand to gain, domestic workers and firms may resent money going abroad that could be lent or invested at home. And when debt crises erupt, it is common for creditor-country governments to expend time, energy, and money to try to resolve them, partly because a crisis abroad can have grave repercussions at home.

In the midst of the debt crisis of the 1980s, for instance, many Americans were shocked to learn that U.S. banks had lent more money to Latin American governments than the value of the capital base of the entire American banking system. This meant that the Latin American debt crisis could conceivably have bankrupted many of America's largest banks and caused a more general financial and economic crisis in the United States itself. Similarly, northern Europeans were startled to find out after 2008 that their banks, and often pension funds, had invested trillions of dollars in American, Spanish, and Irish mortgages and in Greek and Portuguese government bonds—and that because these investments had gone bad, their financial systems were under serious threat.

But even if it is in the general interest of creditor nations as a whole to "bail out" their troubled banks and their borrowers, it may not be in the interests of everyone in these nations. So, international investment gives rise to plenty of potential sources of conflict, and these conflicts of interest give rise to complex interactions among the sources and targets of global capital movements.

Concessional Finance

There is another, smaller and somewhat less controversial, part of international finance: money lent to developing countries by government agencies and intergovernmental organizations. Rich countries give to poor countries, or lend to them at below-market interest rates, something on the order of $150 billion a year. Such concessional finance differs from that discussed in the preceding section because it is typically lent at interest rates well below those available in the marketplace; World Bank loans to the poorest nations, in fact, bear no interest.

Many of the countries that borrow these concessional funds would not be able to borrow from private creditors, who are wary of particularly poor and unstable nations. Most countries in sub-Saharan Africa and South Asia have little access to private loans; to the extent that they can borrow, it is from North American, European, and Japanese governments or from such institutions as the World Bank and the African Development Bank.

Concessional loans from foreign governments are more a form of aid than of finance. They reflect, as does aid generally, both the economic and political motivations of the donors and lenders. The international development banks and related agencies—the World Bank, Inter-American Development Bank, Asian Development Bank, and so on—are somewhat less directly political, as they are controlled by a number of rich countries. Their lending programs emphasize basic development projects, such as economic infrastructure (power plants, dams, highways) and social infrastructure (schools, housing).

As we saw in Chapter 1, the two major international economic institutions established at Bretton Woods after World War II were the World Bank and the IMF. The **World Bank** (officially, the International Bank for Reconstruction and Development) was charged with making loans to promote economic development. The IMF was originally focused primarily on exchange rates and monetary relations, but, as we will see later in this chapter, its focus has shifted to international finance in recent decades.

Like the IMF, the World Bank is headquartered in Washington, D.C.; in fact, the two international financial institutions are across the street from each other. The World Bank gets most of its money by borrowing on major financial markets—typically at very low rates, as its bonds are guaranteed by the governments of the markets in which it borrows. Funds raised in this way are lent out to developing countries to help them build major infrastructural and other development projects. Because the World Bank can borrow at much lower interest rates than developing countries can, it can relend to them at very attractive rates. The World Bank also receives some money from developed member states that it lends out at extremely low or no interest to the poorest nations. The World Bank is oriented primarily toward financing long-term investments in such things as roads, dams, and power plants, all of which are considered essential for broader economic growth and development.

Concessional finance has been less politically controversial, as loans from individual governments are negotiated directly and, like loans from the World Bank and its related institutions, are relatively cheap. Nonetheless, countries with severe economic problems often complain about the cost of these loans, and for extremely poor nations concessional debt can be a heavy burden—despite the loans' lower interest rates.

This situation has led to calls for debt forgiveness, a measure that would alleviate some problems in very poor nations but that would come at the expense of rich nations' taxpayers. These issues, ethically important as they may be, do not have much impact on private international finance. The amounts at stake are relatively small, and private investors are typically not involved. In any case, much

World Bank
An important international institution that provides loans at below-market interest rates to developing countries, typically to enable them to carry out development projects.

government-to-government concessional debt has been canceled, and the World Bank and IMF have written off most of the debt of the most heavily indebted poor countries.[5]

Concessional finance has sometimes been criticized as politically motivated, driven by the desire of major powers to draw poor countries into their geopolitical sphere of influence. Certainly, lending governments are much more likely to make concessional finance available to their allies—and to use such finance as a "carrot" to attract support. The rise of Chinese government–owned development banks as lenders to poor countries has highlighted the geopolitical implications of concessional finance. Since 2008, indeed, these banks have averaged over $30 billion a year in loans to poor countries, beginning to rival even the World Bank in size.

The Belt and Road Initiative is a global infrastructure strategy developed by the Chinese government in 2013. The goal of the initiative is to bring massive growth to economies in Asia and throughout the world. Here, representatives from China Railway Construction Corporation oversee the building of rail lines in Nigeria.

The Chinese government also spearheaded the development of the Asian Infrastructure Investment Bank (AIIB), an intergovernmental institution that opened its doors in 2016. This multilateral institution is headquartered in Beijing and led by China. It lends money to developing countries specifically, as the name implies, for infrastructure. Although it started slowly, the AIIB intends to become a significant source of funds for development.

For some, China's initiatives are a welcome contribution to global development efforts. Most developed nations have joined the AIIB, including almost all European Union members, Canada, Australia, and New Zealand. Others, however, have been warier. The United States decided not to join the AIIB during the Obama administration, and Japan followed suit. The Trump administration continued this stance and warned about the economic and geopolitical consequences of Chinese lending.[6] It is likely that geopolitical factors—in particular, the rise of China—will play an increasingly important, and perhaps increasingly controversial, part in concessional finance. Nonetheless, the major economic and political issues related to international investment have to do with other, nonconcessional, types of finance.

---

5. For further information on the reduction of debts owed by the heavily indebted poor countries (HIPC), see International Monetary Fund, "Debt Relief under the Heavily Indebted Poor Countries (HIPC) Initiative," March 25, 2020, www.imf.org/en/About/Factsheets/Sheets/2016/08/01/16/11/Debt-Relief-Under-the-Heavily-Indebted-Poor-Countries-Initiative (accessed 1/19/21).

6. Jonathan Wheatley and James Kynge, "China Curtails Overseas Lending in Face of Geopolitical Backlash," *Financial Times*, December 7, 2020, www.ft.com/content/1cb3e33b-e2c2-4743-ae41-d3fffffa4259 (accessed 12/23/20); and Saleha Mohsin, "Trump Balks Over Billions in Secret Chinese Loans to Poor Nations," *Bloomberg*, May 21, 2018, www.bloomberg.com/news/articles/2018-05-21/trump-targets-chinese-loans-to-poor-nations-amid-trade-tensions (accessed 12/23/20).

Why Is International Finance Controversial?

Historically the most important—and most politically conflictual—component of international investment has been private lending to foreign governments. Shakespeare may have been right about the pitfalls of borrowing and lending when he wrote:

> Neither a borrower nor a lender be;
> For loan oft loses both itself and friend,
> And borrowing dulls the edge of husbandry.
> —Polonius, in Shakespeare's *Hamlet*

Indeed, the parties might end up enemies, and the borrowers could have little incentive to use the money wisely. However, there is nothing economically suspect about borrowing or lending, in principle. In the case of a private corporation, it makes sense to borrow if the borrowed funds are used in ways that increase the firm's earnings by more than the money costs. If General Motors borrows at an interest rate of 10 percent but uses the money to make investments that pay out only 5 percent, it will suffer a loss; but if the investments pay out 15 percent, both the borrower and the lender can benefit. The logic is similar for a government.

Debtor Interests and Creditor Interests

From the standpoint of the economy as a whole, it generally makes sense for a country to borrow if it uses the borrowed funds productively—that is, in ways that increase the country's output by more than it will take to repay the debt. A country might use loans to raise its national output directly; for example, it might make productive use of a government-owned natural resource (such as oil or copper). The money could also be used to increase national output indirectly, such as by building new roads that allow for the opening or improvement of agricultural lands or by building a hydroelectric power plant that makes national industry more efficient. As national output rises, the government gets more tax revenue and can service its debts more easily. If borrowed funds are used to increase the productivity of the national economy, they can pay for themselves.

Because developing countries are by definition short on capital, most of their governments are eager to borrow from abroad. The prospect of using borrowed money to speed growth and increase national output gives developing economies today a powerful interest in attracting loans from international investors, and it makes borrowing relatively uncontroversial within debtor countries—as long as times are good.

But sovereign debts can quickly become a burden to debtor nations, which makes them much less popular. A government attempting to service its debts will often impose unpopular measures. It may cut spending and raise taxes in order to earn the money it needs to pay off loans. It may raise interest rates to restrain wages, profits, and consumption, which in turn reduces imports, increases exports, and helps the country earn more foreign currency to pay its creditors. These austerity measures typically weaken the domestic economy in order to allow the government to continue paying debt service to foreign creditors.

Such measures can cause a **recession** and or even **depression**, incurring the wrath of labor, business, and other groups. For example, in the wake of the 2008–9 debt crisis, the Latvian government pushed interest rates above 20 percent, cut government spending, and raised taxes dramatically. The economy collapsed, shrinking by 25 percent in two years, and unemployment tripled to over 20 percent.[7] In Latvia, as in many such cases, some citizens regarded debt-driven austerity as doubly unfair: they were being asked to sacrifice to repay borrowed money that did not help them, and their sacrifice was going to enrich foreign banks.

One potential source of debt difficulties is international conditions, which can change in ways that make it harder for governments to pay their debts. Between 1980 and 1982, for example, American interest rates rose by 10 percent as the Federal Reserve attempted to reduce inflation. Most of the debts owed by developing countries to international banks had floating interest rates, adjusted every six months in line with American interest rates. Therefore, as American rates went up, so did the cost of outstanding loans. This was, in fact, one of the causes of the debt crisis of the 1980s.

Similarly, an international recession that reduces demand for debtors' exports can make it hard to service loans: when the Great Depression of the 1930s drove down prices and demand for debtors' products, it caused almost every debtor nation to **default**. When circumstances, especially conditions beyond a debtor nation's control, make it harder for the government to keep up its payments, some people prefer that their government simply default in order to force a reduction in the debt burden. There are, then, contending interests within debtor countries over whether to service foreign debt. Those who expect to benefit from maintaining access to international loans will disagree with those who have more to lose from the economic sacrifices required to maintain good relations with foreign creditors.

Within lending countries, when foreign debts are performing well there is usually little conflict over them. Some local companies and individuals may resent the fact that money that could be lent to them is instead being sent abroad, but the profits being brought home generally counterbalance this concern. Overall, creditor countries and their governments tend to support their lenders.

Domestic conflict within creditor nations over foreign debts arises most commonly when the loans run into trouble. In these conditions, creditors and their governments often step in with billions of dollars in new loans and aid to alleviate a debtor country's financial crisis. They do so in the belief that if such a crisis were allowed to broaden and deepen, it could spread to other nations and eventually hurt the creditor nation itself. But many people in North America, Europe, and Japan

recession
A sharp slowdown in the rate of economic growth and economic activity.

depression
A severe downturn in the business cycle, typically associated with major declines in economic activity, production, and investment; a severe contraction of credit; and sustained high unemployment.

default
To fail to make payments on a debt.

---

7. Olivier J. Blanchard, Mark Griffiths, and Bertrand Gruss, "Boom, Bust, Recovery: Forensics of the Latvia Crisis," *Brookings Papers on Economic Activity* 44, No. 2 (Fall 2013): 325–88.

resent the fact that their governments spend billions to "bail out" debtors and creditors whose plight may be the self-inflicted result of greed, venality, and bad judgment.

For example, in 1994, in the aftermath of a financial crisis in Mexico, the U.S. government provided many billions of dollars to the beleaguered Mexican government to try to keep the crisis from spreading and affecting American domestic finances. In reaction, conservative Republican political activist Patrick Buchanan charged: "What's going down is not just a bailout of Mexico, but a bailout of Wall Street. [President] Clinton and Congress are rushing to recoup for Wall Street bankers and brokers their enormous losses from the plunderings of [Mexican] ex-President Carlos Salinas and friends."[8] From the Left, the liberal magazine the *Progressive* observed: "It's amazing how our government can find money for . . . bailing out some banks or shoring up some brutal regimes, but not for solving the pressing social needs of our own country, like health care, housing, and jobs at a living wage."[9]

Many people in creditor nations regard the trillions of dollars spent in financial rescue packages over the past 30 years as money doled out to undeserving banks and investors who benefited from their ability to put pressure on policy makers. In the aftermath of the Mexican and East Asian financial rescues, the U.S. Congress enacted a number of measures that limited the executive branch's authority to use taxpayer money for such bailouts. Supporters of the bills presented the response to these crises as a clear case of Wall Street versus Main Street: bailing out banks while many small farms and businesses were allowed to go under.[10] Many American and European taxpayers were similarly angry with the financial rescues mounted by the governments of the United States and the European Union in the context of the global financial crisis that began in 2008.

Attitudes toward the IMF and other international financial institutions are often related to broader attitudes toward global economic integration. Both supporters and opponents of globalization tend to think of the IMF and its allies as important pillars of the contemporary international economy. Those wary of globalization distrust global finance and the IMF; those who favor globalization support them.

Whatever domestic disagreements there may be, in general the interests of debtor and creditor countries are clear. Both sides of the relationship stand to benefit from continued lending: borrowers get access to foreign money, and lenders get profits. But each side would prefer to gain more from the relationship. Thus, there are incentives to cooperate to keep the lending going and to bargain for the best possible deal. This sets the stage for complex interactions between debtors and creditors.

---

8. From Patrick J. Buchanan, "Congress Saves Wall Street's Bacon," Buchanan.org (blog), April 20, 1995, https://buchanan.org/blog/congress-saves-wall-streets-bacon-172 (accessed 1/19/21).

9. "Bailout for Whom?" *Progressive* 62, no. 2 (February 1998): 9–10.

10. J. Lawrence Broz, "Congressional Politics of International Financial Rescues," *American Journal of Political Science* 49, no. 3 (July 2005): 479–96.

Debtor-Creditor Interactions

In the modern era, there have been many cycles of lending and debt crises. All through the nineteenth and early twentieth centuries, rapidly growing countries borrowed heavily from the major European financial centers—primarily London, but also Paris, Amsterdam, and Berlin. Foreign borrowing was, in fact, important to the economic growth of the principal developing regions of the day: the United States, Canada, Australia, Argentina, Brazil, and others.

In most instances, debts appear to have contributed to economic development, but that did not diminish the attendant crises and political disputes. The United States, the world's largest borrower throughout the nineteenth century, was not immune: many of its state governments defaulted in the 1840s, and the state of Mississippi, whose banks borrowed heavily from London financiers in the 1830s and defaulted in 1841, has ever since continued to refuse to make payments on its London debt.

Concern about getting embroiled in debt disputes helps explain why today's private international financial flows to the developing world go primarily to the more advanced and successful developing countries. Countries facing severe developmental difficulties, or about which there is little reliable information, are simply unattractive to private creditors. For example, the governments of Burkina Faso, Nepal, and Yemen must rely overwhelmingly on concessional lending from the World Bank and other aid agencies.[11] Even in the case of well-known debtor countries, however, the debtor-creditor relationship is inherently complicated by strategic interactions.

When debtors and creditors enter into conflict, each side in the interaction has clear interests at stake. On the one hand, for debtor nations in crisis, making prompt and full debt service payments can mean restraining consumption, increasing taxes, reducing government spending, and cutting wages—in a word, **austerity**. So, debtor governments want to reduce the amounts they have to pay so as to reduce the demands on their citizens. On the other hand, creditors' profits depend on the debt service payments they receive. So, they want to be paid in full for the loans they have extended. The two sets of interests are, of course, in conflict.

As we have seen, when two actors have conflicting interests, they engage in a bargaining interaction to determine whether a mutually acceptable deal is possible. Each side has tools in its arsenal that it can use to extract favorable terms. The principal bargaining weapon available to the debtor government is the threat of default, or suspension of payment on the debt.[12] In August 1998, the Russian government responded to national economic difficulties with a default that affected as much as $80 billion in foreign debt; in December 2001, the Argentine government defaulted on $93 billion in foreign debt, and controversy over its repayment continued for the

austerity
The application of policies to reduce consumption, typically by cutting government spending, raising taxes, and restricting wages.

---

11. World Bank, "World Development Indicators," http://data.worldbank.org/data-catalog/world-development-indicators (accessed 12/23/20).

12. Legally, a *default* is invoked by the creditor when the debtor misses payments, but the term is used more generally to describe a suspension of debt service.

next fifteen years. The height of the eurozone debt crisis came when it appeared that Greece might default on some $300 billion of sovereign debt.[13]

Any sensible creditor would prefer to get some money rather than to get no money at all and therefore has an incentive to reduce the burden of debt. But creditors also have financial weapons available: they can cut off debtor governments from future lending, and they may be able to retaliate in related areas, such as freezing debtor governments' bank accounts or taking other government-owned properties. Creditors can also try to get their home governments to use broader foreign policy considerations to induce compliance, such as threatening a cutoff of aid or even military action. In short, each side can threaten to impose costs on the other in order to extract a better deal at the bargaining table. The ability of each side to get concessions from the other depends on how powerful and credible these threats are.

The bargaining between creditors and debtors over existing debt is analogous to the bargaining between countries that we described in Chapter 3, which can sometimes lead to war. Because of the costs associated with default and retaliation, there is usually a bargaining solution to their interaction that makes both sides better off than financial warfare. Both sides would prefer to restructure the debt so that the debtor can continue to make payments; this is what negotiators, arbitrators, and bankruptcy courts do in the case of domestic debt problems.

13. The amounts involved are unclear, especially for Russia. See International Monetary Fund, *World Economic Outlook* (Washington, DC: International Monetary Fund, 1998), chap. 2. On Argentina's most recent default controversy, see Matt O'Brien, "Everything You Need to Know about Argentina's Weird Default," *Washington Post*, August 3, 2014, www.washingtonpost.com/blogs/wonkblog/wp/2014/08/03/everything-you-need-to-know-about-argentinas-weird-default (accessed 1/19/21).

This graffiti in Lisbon, Portugal, depicts German chancellor Angela Merkel manipulating the strings of Portuguese leaders. Many Portuguese blamed Merkel for the austerity measures that the government enacted in order to receive an emergency loan from eurozone partners during the crisis.

However, as in the case of security relations, international debtor-creditor interactions are characterized by incomplete information. The debtor may claim that it cannot make payments, but the creditor does not know if this claim is true. Creditors cannot know whether a debtor's threat to default is, in fact, meant to avoid potentially dire consequences; the debtor may simply be bluffing in order to get a better deal. The creditor, for its part, may threaten to retaliate, but the debtor cannot know whether the threat will be carried out.

In these circumstances, cooperative relations between debtors and creditors can collapse into bitter conflict. Many debt conflicts drag on for years or even decades and can have a powerful impact on other dimensions of interstate interaction. Debt-related conflicts have even been blamed for invasions, wars, and colonialism. In some instances, the issue is resolved amicably with a negotiated settlement; in other instances, the parties remain far apart.

Of course, cooperation between debtors and creditors is not necessarily a good thing for everyone involved. This is especially the case when debtor or creditor governments pursue policies that impose major costs on domestic groups. Whether an amicable resolution of debtor-creditor interactions is a good thing or a bad thing, it is important to try to understand this type of conflict and how it develops. One prominent aspect of international debt interactions is that they have come to involve international institutions that can play an important part in debtor-creditor relations.

Institutions of International Finance

During the twentieth century, many institutions were created to regulate and mediate debtor-creditor interactions and perhaps facilitate mutually acceptable outcomes. These institutions have, to a certain extent, helped alleviate the problems that can make lending difficult or impossible and that cause conflict when debtors run into trouble. In the interwar period, the League of Nations' Economic and Financial Committee attempted to work with debtors and creditors to manage the financial difficulties of troubled nations in central and eastern Europe, with mixed results.

The **Bank for International Settlements** was established in 1930 explicitly to help oversee relations between one of the world's most problematic debtor nations, Germany, and its international creditors. It too met with mixed results. Nonetheless, by the 1940s there was consensus that some form of international financial institution might be beneficial to the resolution of sovereign debt problems.

The International Monetary Fund
Today, many aspects of international financial affairs are overseen by one of the world's most powerful international organizations, the **International Monetary Fund (IMF)**. The parties to the Bretton Woods agreement (see Chapter 1) agreed to establish the IMF in order to manage the international monetary system. After the Bretton Woods monetary regime collapsed in the early 1970s (as we will see in Chapter 9), the IMF gradually took on a more directly financial role. Today, its principal concern is financial crises in developing nations, although it has also played a role during crisis periods in developed countries.

The IMF's membership includes both borrowing and lending countries. All member states may vote on its activities, but the number of votes is allocated in

Bank for International Settlements
One of the oldest international financial organizations, created in 1930. Its members include the world's principal central banks, and under its auspices they attempt to cooperate in the financial realm.

International Monetary Fund (IMF)
A major international economic institution established in 1944 to manage international monetary relations. It has gradually reoriented itself to focus on the international financial system, especially debt and currency crises.

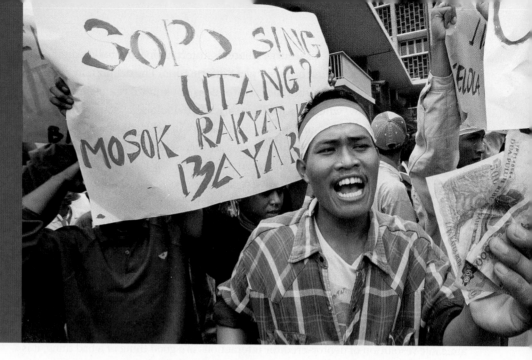

When the Indonesian government sought the IMF's help during the 1997–98 Asian financial crisis, it was forced to cut spending on popular programs, and poor Indonesians suffered. These protesters in Jakarta hold a sign asking: "The country's debt—why should the people pay?"

proportion to each member's financial contribution to the IMF's resources—its "quota." These financial contributions are, in turn, a function of the size of each country's economy and its importance to world trade and payments. As a result, the United States provides over 17 percent of the IMF's total resources; the member states of the European Union provide another 26 percent. Because IMF decisions require an 85 percent supermajority, the United States and the European Union (acting as a group) can veto fund actions. This arrangement has led to complaints that the IMF is largely a tool of its richer and most powerful members—to which those members sometimes respond that this is appropriate inasmuch as they are the ones footing most of the bills.

The IMF, indeed, needs substantial funds to carry out its activities. The total of quotas from its members is currently about $650 billion, and the fund can call upon pledges from its members of another $1 trillion. This gives the IMF, in theory, access to over $1.5 trillion dollars, although it has never come close to using all these resources. Nonetheless, many regard the IMF as the most important and most powerful international economic institution because it can mobilize an extraordinary amount of money in a relatively short time. And because debt crises often erupt suddenly, and often involve vast amounts of money, the IMF is uniquely suited to intervene in such crises.

Typically, a country facing debt difficulties turns to the IMF to negotiate a program of economic policies intended to address the sources of the problems. The conditions that the IMF demands are often economically and politically difficult for the debtor government to enact, but in return for implementing a program that meets the IMF's standards, the debtor government receives relatively inexpensive loans from the fund. Probably more important, the debtor country is "certified" as being in compliance with IMF norms, which makes it more attractive to creditors. This certification is meant to encourage private lenders to renegotiate with the debtor government and perhaps to extend it new loans to help it overcome temporary difficulties.

For example, during the debt crisis of the 1980s, the IMF signed dozens of agreements with troubled debtors, typically requiring policies of economic austerity and adjustment in return for assistance with working out their debt problems. The IMF's agreement with Indonesia in the midst of the 1997–98 Asian financial crisis obliged the Indonesian government to cut subsidies to—and therefore raise the prices of—sugar, wheat flour, corn, soybeans, fuel, and electricity. All these factors imposed hardships on Indonesia's poor and working people. The IMF also required Indonesia to shut down 16 banks controlled by relatives or cronies of the country's dictatorial president, Suharto. This move may have been less objectionable to ordinary people, but it was, of course, unpopular with the Indonesian government.[14]

While the IMF dealt mainly with developing debtor nations from the 1970s until the 2000s, the financial crisis that began in 2008 drove many industrialized countries to the fund. Over the course of the crisis, the IMF negotiated very large loans and austerity programs with Greece, Ireland, and Portugal, as well as with Ukraine, which experienced a severe crisis in 2014–15. The IMF's operations in these instances were similar to those in other debt crises, although in the European cases it worked in concert with EU authorities.

The IMF, like other international institutions, can facilitate cooperative interactions among actors in a variety of ways. It provides a set of financial and macroeconomic standards and a wealth of other information that can be used to assess the behavior of debtor nations. By increasing the likelihood that debtor-creditor relations will be iterated (repeated), the fund can make cooperation more attractive. The IMF can also help verify a debtor government's compliance with commitments to pursue economic policies that creditors want to see. And the IMF can act on behalf of the collectivity of creditor nations, which might otherwise have difficulties working out common decisions about how to deal with financial crises.

In one sense, though, the IMF is unusual. While many international institutions primarily facilitate bargaining among nation-states, the IMF negotiates agreements directly with an individual country's government. And, perhaps even more unusual, the IMF's involvement is typically closely tied to relations between the debtor government and private international creditors. While the IMF does not represent foreign creditors, there is normally an understanding that an agreement with the IMF will facilitate agreement with private lenders, and sometimes the IMF, member governments, and private creditors make this connection explicit. In this sense, the IMF plays a major part, directly or indirectly, in negotiations between sovereign governments and private financiers. This unusual relationship has also led some to charge that the IMF is biased in favor of creditors and against debtors (see "Controversy" on p. 382).

Supporters of the IMF believe that it plays an important role in managing the international financial system by allowing for orderly resolutions of debtor-creditor problems. They focus on the informational difficulties endemic in sovereign debt, as well as the need for reliable monitoring of compliance with agreements.

---

14. Stephan Haggard, *The Political Economy of the Asian Financial Crisis* (Washington, DC: Institute for International Economics, 2000).

Is the IMF Biased against Developing Countries?

In February 1989, facing a protracted fiscal crisis, Venezuela's president, Carlos Andrés Pérez, negotiated a loan with the IMF. Going back on preelection promises he had made only weeks earlier, Pérez adopted market-based reforms recommended by the IMF as part of the loan deal: liberalizing trade, privatizing state companies, restricting state spending, relaxing price controls, and deregulating exchange and interest rates. Almost immediately, Caracas erupted in violent protests that eventually led to two failed coups, the impeachment of Pérez, and the rise of coup leader Hugo Chávez to the presidency. Chávez and the supporters of his "Bolivarian Revolution" became some of the strongest critics of the IMF, and in 2007 Venezuela pulled out of the IMF and the World Bank.

The IMF's supporters argue that its actions are in the interests of developing countries like Venezuela: the IMF assists nations in financial difficulty and helps them maintain access to foreign capital that is vital to their development. But this claim is controversial. Why?

Applying the Concepts

The IMF typically is called upon when a country runs into debt trouble. These situations inevitably involve a conflict of **interests** between debtors (who want debt relief) and creditors (who want to be paid back). As an international **institution**, the IMF is charged with safeguarding global financial stability, a task that often compels it to demand substantial economic reforms from debtor nations. Many people in the debtor nations see these demands as a threat to the important institution of national sovereignty. The **interactions** among the IMF, debtor countries, and creditors vary greatly: in some cases, they are cooperative and therefore not controversial; in other cases, they collapse into acrimonious conflicts. The IMF may facilitate international financial cooperation, but critics claim that it distributes the benefits and burdens of that cooperation unevenly across member nations.

The chief criticisms that Chávez leveled at the IMF reflect both conflicts of interest and institutional concerns. Chávez's first main criticism derived from the "conditionalities" routinely attached to IMF loans. For decades, the IMF has required that countries requesting financial assistance commit to "structural adjustment programs" and economic austerity measures designed to address debtor nations' fiscal and financial problems. Critics argue that these conditions are not in the interests of debtor nations and often impose hardship on their poorest citizens, who face higher taxes, wage cuts, unemployment, and reduced social services.

The second charge is that the IMF as an international organization violates the institutional integrity of sovereign nations. This charge stems from the fact that IMF programs may include conditions associated not only with economic reforms but also with changes to specific national political institutions. The IMF asked Pérez, for instance, to institute direct elections of state governors in Venezuela in place of presidential appointments.

The IMF's critics also point out that the interactions between the IMF and debtor nations are highly unequal. Acceptance of IMF conditions is supposedly voluntary, but the high price of refusal—ineligibility for an IMF program—creates an impression of coercion. Indeed, debtor countries that turn to the IMF are typically in very weak bargaining positions; they are desperate for the IMF's financial assistance and the access to private loans it can help ensure.

Defenders of the IMF respond to these criticisms by stressing that both debtors and creditors have an interest in mutual gains from cooperation. The IMF's policy recommendations help debtor nations ensure economic recovery and restore access to foreign credit, and the benefits over the long term outweigh the temporary costs to the nation's citizens and the diminishment of a nation's sovereignty. Once these longer-term effects are taken into

Riots overtook Caracas in 1989 after the Venezuelan government imposed austerity measures recommended by the IMF. Here, people stand in line to buy food, looking on toward a victim of the violence.

account, it becomes clear that it is in the interest of debtor nations to participate in the IMF.

Supporters further argue that the IMF provides essential institutional support to the international financial system, whose smooth functioning is equally in the interests of both debtor nations and creditors. If the IMF were not there to help guarantee creditors of good debtor behavior, creditors would not lend. Member states voluntarily go to the IMF because they want its seal of approval in order to gain access to global financial markets. Typically, governments have gotten into trouble because they pursued unsustainable policies, and the IMF can help them get back on track and regain access to international finance. Without the IMF, there would be little or no international lending, and poor nations would be far worse off.

Critics counter that the IMF worries primarily about the interests of creditors, even at the expense of social progress, economic growth, and equity. There is little moral justification for subjecting the people of a country to terrible austerity measures solely to pay billions to foreign banks and investors. Many IMF programs fail even on their own terms, providing little economic relief. The allegedly "voluntary" nature of IMF programs is a fiction; a developing country that does not "voluntarily" subject itself to IMF dictates will be punished. As a result, critics argue that the IMF is a tool of the creditor nations and their investors, and its policies benefit only the rich and powerful.

The plausibility of these arguments depends on how well the IMF, in fact, delivers on its promises. If standard IMF measures actually rectify debtor nations' economic problems and contribute to economic growth, and this growth benefits the poor, then its operations may be regarded as fair and the bargains worth the cost. At this point, the evidence is mixed: while IMF programs may improve a nation's balance of payments, their record on economic growth and poverty reduction is unclear.

Thinking Analytically

1. How and why do the IMF's activities in the developing world lead to conflicts of interest?

2. As an international institution, what is the goal of the IMF? How does it try to achieve this goal?

3. Why might interactions between the IMF and debtor nations sometimes go smoothly and other times end up in acrimonious disputes?

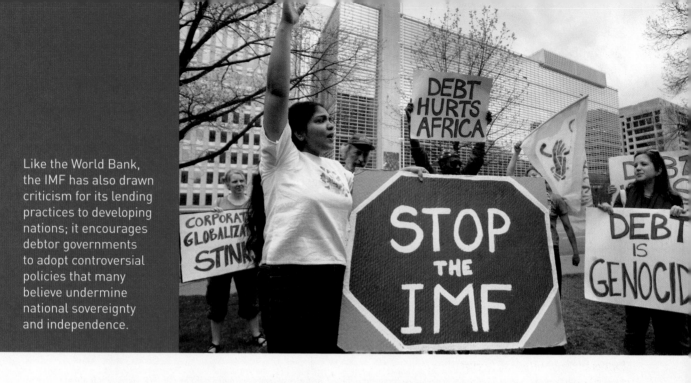

Like the World Bank, the IMF has also drawn criticism for its lending practices to developing nations; it encourages debtor governments to adopt controversial policies that many believe undermine national sovereignty and independence.

Supporters emphasize how the IMF can help debtors and creditors arrive at cooperative arrangements. They believe that the IMF's power comes from its central role in resolving financial problems in ways that are beneficial to both debtors and creditors.

However, opponents see the IMF as a tool of international financiers. They regard the IMF as a biased agency whose actions reinforce the subordinate position of debtor nations and do little to help them achieve economic growth and development. Critics argue that powerful member countries, such as the United States, use their influence to ensure that the fund imposes market-oriented policies and austerity measures on countries that have little choice in the matter. Detractors also criticize the involvement of the home governments of creditors, primarily from North America, Europe, and Japan, which they regard as unduly concerned with ensuring that "their" bankers get repaid. Creditors can be politically influential at home, and defaults abroad can threaten to bankrupt major financial institutions in industrial nations, which would, in turn, destabilize their own financial markets. This situation leads creditor governments and the IMF, in the eyes of many opponents, to serve as debt collectors for international banks, imposing policies that are not in the best interests of the debtor countries and their people.

Borrowing and Debt Crises

Lending to developing nations has been an important part of the international economy since the mid-1960s. At the same time, there have been many debt crises since international financial markets reopened to developing countries. The first such crisis started in 1982, when the government of Mexico announced that it could not service its foreign debts and went into default. Like most financial crises, this one had a self-reinforcing nature. As in a bank panic, because lenders worried that developing-country governments might not repay them, they stopped lending. This left developing-country governments without a financial cushion, and in desperation they stopped making payments to their creditors—thereby scaring international bankers even further. The more the developing countries ran out of money, the less bankers lent; the less bankers lent, the more the developing countries ran out of money. In the space of weeks, some of the most rapidly growing economies in the world were suddenly cut off from the bank lending they had relied on for 15 years.

One after another, the major debtor governments struggled to generate the foreign currency and government revenue needed to pay their creditors, until eventually their economies collapsed. By 1983, as many as 34 developing and socialist countries were formally renegotiating their debts, and a dozen more were in serious trouble. Latin America was spending nearly half of its export earnings to pay interest and principal on its foreign debt, leaving little to buy the imports it needed. Most debtor economies remained depressed for years, and the crises were not fully resolved until 1990. Austerity programs and economic reforms in debtor nations, coupled with concessions from lenders to reduce the debt burden, gradually allowed the problems to be worked out. (See "What Shaped Our World?" on p. 386 for details about this debt crisis.)

Eventually, lending resumed, but debt crises continued to occur. In 1994, Mexican finances once again collapsed. In 1997–98, combined debt and currency crises hit a series of East Asian countries, from Indonesia and Thailand to the Philippines and South Korea. This was a particularly startling shock, as these nations had long been regarded as models of developmental success. Their apparently endless potential had drawn in considerable amounts of foreign money: Thailand's foreign debt tripled from $30 billion to $90 billion in the three years leading up to 1996, while Indonesia's doubled from $25 billion to $50 billion. During the early 1990s, about $50 billion a year flowed into East Asia from global financial markets, with tens of billions more in direct investment from multinational corporations.

Once the crisis hit in the summer of 1997, however, money ran out of the East Asian debtor countries as fast as it had run in. The $50 billion annual inflow of the early 1990s turned into an outflow of over $230 billion between 1997 and 1999. After years of extraordinary growth—10 percent a year was common—the economies of Indonesia, Thailand, and Malaysia contracted by 15, 12, and 8 percent, respectively, in a matter of months. It would be years before they would recover their pre-crisis levels.

The East Asian crisis was followed by crises in Russia and Brazil in 1998–99, Argentina in 2000–1, and others since then. In all these cases, intervention by the IMF alone was not sufficient; the debt problems were so large that creditor governments also stepped in, to the tune of over $50 billion for Mexico, almost $120 billion for the three principal Asian crisis nations (Indonesia, South Korea, and Thailand), and another $70 billion for Russia and Brazil. Critics charged that taxpayers were being forced to bail out foolish investors and dissolute governments, but financial leaders insisted on the need for quick responses to avoid financial contagion.

The international politics of developing-country debt is a striking example of how actors with different interests interact strategically in a highly institutionalized

The Latin American Debt Crisis

In the 1960s, the governments of Latin America discovered a valuable resource: foreign loans. International investors had not lent money to developing countries since 1929, having been burned during the Great Depression when most countries stopped paying their debts. But by 1965 memories had faded, and international banks resumed lending to governments in the developing world.

Interests Latin American governments needed the money to build factories and roads, power plants and steel mills, schools and houses. For 15 years loans poured in, public and private projects lined up for money, and economies expanded. In the 10 years from 1973 to 1982, the region's total debt grew from $40 billion to $330 billion—almost $1 trillion in 2020 money. This borrowing boom came to a crashing halt late in the summer of 1982. In August, the Mexican government announced that it could not pay the interest and principal on its $100 billion debt to foreign banks, and international banks panicked. If Mexico, a major oil producer, couldn't or wouldn't pay its debts, perhaps other nations couldn't or wouldn't either. Investors stopped lending within weeks, and heavily indebted developing nations around the world were thrown into crisis. Within four months, about 40 countries had fallen behind on their debt payments.

Institutions The debt crisis that began in 1982 led to an economic collapse that was, for many countries, the most catastrophic in modern history. The crisis had dire effects on domestic political institutions. Latin America spiraled downward into recession and depression, unemployment, and hyperinflation (price increases of more than 50 percent a month). Governments collapsed all over the region.

At the international level, the governments of creditor and debtor nations, as well as the world's principal international financial institution, the IMF, all were important. The IMF orchestrated a multibillion-dollar bailout package even as it played an intermediary role between the creditor banks and the debtor nations. Debtor countries typically found themselves forced to enter an IMF program if they wanted to work out a better deal with their bank creditors.

Interactions The interplay among creditor governments, creditor banks, debtor governments, and the IMF made the politics of the debt crisis particularly complex. Lengthy and often bitter negotiations ensued over who would make the major sacrifices needed to address the accumulated debt burden. Most of the costs were borne by debtor nations. After decades of rapid growth, income per person in Latin America declined over the 1980s by 10 percent, real wages fell by at least 30 percent, and investment fell even further; inflation in many nations rose above 1,000 percent.[a] The 1980s became known in the region as the lost decade. Eventually, in 1989, creditor governments and banks offered some debt relief, governments began adopting new policies, and the region began growing again.

Domestically, throughout the developing world, protests erupted over the debt crisis and the unemployment, inflation, and government cutbacks it had wrought. The economic and political crisis eventually drove most of Latin America's military dictatorships from power. But this advance was overshadowed by the fact that the debtor nations had fallen even further behind economically as they struggled to shoulder their debt. What had originally seemed a golden opportunity—readily available foreign loans—now seemed a terrible burden.

Banco de México, Mexico's central bank.

a. Eliana Cardoso and Ann Helwege, *Latin America's Economy: Diversity, Trends, and Conflicts* (Cambridge, MA: MIT Press, 1995).

context. The parties have both clear conflicting interests and clear interests in common. Even though creditors want to be repaid and debtors want to pay as little as possible, both sides have an interest in continuing their relationship: the creditors want to earn profits, while the debtors want to maintain access to foreign finance. This mix of cooperative and conflictual motives leads to complicated strategic interactions. And the IMF exemplifies the role of international institutions—seen by some as effective at helping resolve conflicts, by others as tools of the powerful.

These debt crises in developing and transitional economies were dwarfed by a financial collapse that hit the advanced industrial economies in 2008. Some of the aspects of this crisis were familiar from previous debt crises—although it had been decades since an industrialized country had been so affected—while other features were very novel. Together, they plunged the world into the most serious economic downturn since the Great Depression of the 1930s.

A New Crisis Hits the United States—and the World

The 2008 financial crisis originated in the United States, the world's largest economy and most developed financial system. In 2001, the country embarked on a major foreign borrowing spree: substantial tax cuts had driven the U.S. federal government into a large deficit, much of which was financed by borrowing from abroad. Government borrowing spurred the economy, reinforced by a monetary policy of very low interest rates, and in turn, these low interest rates encouraged American households to borrow heavily. Much of the borrowing went for housing, as many Americans refinanced their homes or bought new homes. Foreigners eager to buy American investments that they regarded as safe and profitable provided large portions of the lending directly or indirectly.

From 2001 to 2007, the United States experienced a traditional borrowing boom. Every year, the country borrowed between a half-trillion and a trillion dollars from the rest of the world. A significant portion of the debt went to finance the government budget deficit; much of the rest went into the flourishing housing market. As financial markets grew at a dizzying pace, banks developed ever-more-complex ways of investing, borrowing, and lending.

Some observers warned that not enough of the new debt was going into productive investments that would increase the efficiency of the U.S. economy, such as new factories or new technologies. Other observers were concerned that American regulators were inadequately supervising the freewheeling, increasingly complex financial system. However, the U.S. government resisted stricter financial oversight, especially given its general commitment to deregulation. Meanwhile, most Americans were happy to enjoy a dramatic expansion in consumption, reduced taxes, increased government spending, and a striking increase in housing prices—all made possible by foreign borrowing.

America's debt-fed expansion eventually became an unsustainable bubble, especially in the housing market. In some parts of the country, housing prices doubled in the space of four or five years. Much of the lending was predicated on

Between 2001 and 2007, Americans enjoyed increased consumption, reduced taxes, and more government spending, all made possible by foreign borrowing. But when the debt-fueled expansion became unsustainable, the economy went into recession.

the unrealistic expectation that housing prices would continue to rise at this pace. For example, financial institutions extended mortgages to borrowers who would otherwise not have qualified, because they expected that the homes being bought would rise in value. Both borrowers and lenders were thus gambling that housing prices would continue to go up.

Eventually, housing prices stopped soaring and began to fall. Overextended mortgage holders could not pay their debts; overextended lenders faced massive losses. During 2007 and 2008, financial difficulties spread, as hundreds of billions of dollars' worth of mortgages and related financial assets went bad. Fear spread from bank to bank, culminating in September 2008, when Lehman Brothers, one of the world's leading investment banks, collapsed. This was the largest bankruptcy in American history, and it caused near panic in financial markets.

Within a few months, the crisis was transmitted around the world, eventually coming to be known as the *global financial crisis*. Soon, virtually every economy was in decline. Some countries—the United Kingdom, Spain, Portugal, and Greece—faced circumstances much like those of the United States. Also hard-hit were some developing and transition economies that had borrowed funds over the course of the decade. When the U.S. spiraled downward into crisis, so did the other debtor nations. But the damage was even more widespread, because the collapse of the debtor economies affected the creditors who had extended trillions of dollars in loans to them. As the crisis spread from debtor to debtor, and from debtor to creditor, it became the first truly international financial crisis since the 1930s, resulting in the deepest global economic downturn since that decade.

Individual governments attempted to stem the decline. The U.S. government stepped in with trillions of dollars to bail out affected financial institutions and to try to get financial markets working again, taking over some of the country's largest financial corporations in order to avoid their collapse. And the U.S. government enacted a large deficit-funded spending package to attempt to stimulate an economy in its steepest recession since the 1930s.

Within the United States, political battles broke out over the response to the financial crisis. The principal question confronting the nation was who would pay for the country's financial follies. Many Americans were furious that the government was spending taxpayer dollars to bail out imprudent banks and corporations. Others argued that attempts to stimulate the economy were simply throwing taxpayer money at the problem without any guarantee that it would work. As in other debt crises, many felt that the interests of working-class and middle-class Americans were being sacrificed to address problems created by wealthy financiers. As the recovery stalled, political battles heated up, and the country became increasingly polarized over how best to confront the aftermath of the debt crisis and how best to distribute the burden of economic adjustment among Americans.

A similar dynamic played out in Europe, with the added complication that the problem divided the eurozone, the group of EU member countries that had created a common currency in 1999. As with the world at large, eurozone countries were divided into those that borrowed heavily and those that lent heavily during the decade before 2008. The big borrowers were largely in southern Europe—Greece, Spain, Portugal, and Cyprus—but also included Ireland. They borrowed for different purposes: Greece to fund an overgrown public sector and huge budget deficits; the rest, like the United States, largely to fuel a consumption and housing boom. The big lenders were the northern Europeans, especially Germany.

Internationally too, the global financial crisis caused tension among contending interests. Governments everywhere scrambled to protect their economies, even at the expense of other countries. For example, the U.S. Congress insisted that government spending to stimulate the failing economy be used preferentially to buy American goods, but trading partners insisted that this strategy was protectionist and violated the rules of the World Trade Organization (WTO). Developing countries complained that the heavy borrowing by industrialized-country governments to deal with the crisis was making it impossible for poor nations to get the funds they needed to confront their own dire problems. The European Union was torn by conflicts among member states with widely different views as to the appropriate response to the crisis.

As the crisis unfolded, many observers wondered whether the deep recession that began in 2008 might spiral downward into a global depression similar to that of the early 1930s. It did not, in part because eventually the world's major economic powers engaged in enough macroeconomic policy cooperation to limit the damage. Nonetheless, the debt crisis in the eurozone dragged on for 10 years, with the economies of the region stagnant. And the crisis eventually fed into widespread dissatisfaction with domestic and international economic trends—dissatisfaction that had a profound impact on both domestic and international politics around the world. The global financial crisis once more demonstrated the potential for political controversy inherent in international financial affairs.

Foreign Direct Investment: The Economics and Politics of Multinational Corporations

multinational corporation (MNC)

An enterprise that operates in a number of countries, with production or service facilities outside its country of origin.

FDI is another important form of international capital movement. It differs from foreign lending because it is carried out explicitly by corporations that maintain control over the facilities they establish overseas; these corporations have come to be known as **multinational corporations (MNCs)**.[15] FDI occurs when Volkswagen sets up an auto factory in Brazil, or Telefónica de España buys the the formerly state-owned phone operator in the Czech Republic, or ExxonMobil drills for oil in Angola. In all these instances, far more than a simple transfer of capital is involved. Volkswagen could export cars to Brazil but chooses to build them there instead; individual foreign investors could buy shares in the Czech telephone company, but instead a global telecommunications corporation adds the Czech system to its network; the Angolan government could borrow money to drill for oil but instead gives a concession to an American company.

Why Do Corporations Go Multinational?

It is not easy for a corporation to set up facilities in a foreign country. But despite the inherent difficulties of doing business abroad, picking a foreign firm over a domestic one or choosing to invest abroad rather than send exports across borders can have its advantages. What makes it attractive for a corporation to establish or purchase subsidiaries across borders, and what gives the host country an interest in permitting this foreign investment?

Corporations may want to establish overseas affiliates to gain access to the local market or to take advantage of local resources—in both instances presumably because doing so through trade is less attractive or impossible. Some FDI is driven by resource location. For example, American and European oil companies, with ample experience exploring for oil, may be more effective at getting Angola's oil out of the ground than Angolan entrepreneurs could be. The case of Volkswagen in Brazil illustrates that there are often advantages to producing in the local market, such as cheaper transport costs, the ability to avoid trade barriers, or better access to market information. In the decades right after World War II, American manufacturers invested heavily in countries abroad, motivated by trade protections in Europe and developing countries. Ford, General Electric, and other big U.S. corporations faced tariffs and other restrictions imposed on their exports to Europe and the developing world, and to get around these barriers, they established local affiliates.

---

15. Some observers prefer the term *transnational corporation* to indicate that many of these firms transcend national boundaries. Most such corporations, however, maintain a clear national identity despite their global operations. In any event, both terms are commonly used and are largely interchangeable.

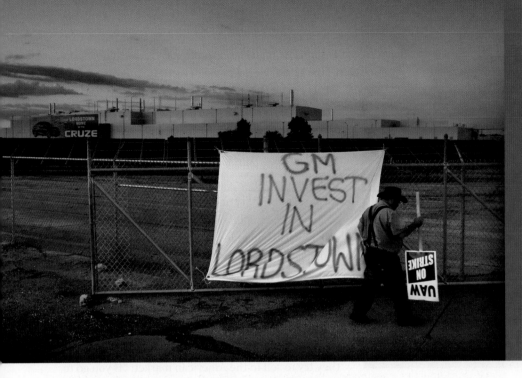

Lower labor costs in countries overseas can be lucrative for manufacturers who were once based in the United States. General Motors permanently closed its Lordstown manufacturing facility in Warren, Ohio, in 2019.

As trade barriers were reduced in Europe and, eventually, in many developing countries, other motivations for FDI surfaced. MNCs today often place different components of their production network in different countries: labor-intensive work is performed in countries with cheap labor, such as Vietnam, while work that requires a more specialized or technical skill set is sourced in countries with ample skilled labor, such as Ireland. This creates **global supply chains** that stretch around the globe and link production in one location to production elsewhere. As manufacturing has become more international, global supply chains have become longer and more intricate, sometimes involving dozens or even hundreds of corporations all over the world. Other types of FDI, such as Telefónica de España's investment in the Czech Republic, are in service sectors in which companies may have substantial experience or a famous brand name—banking or entertainment, for example. What ties all FDI together is that the corporations involved believe that overseas direct investment is profitable.[16]

Within the home countries of MNCs (that is, the countries in which they are headquartered), there is often political support for their foreign activities. After all, American corporations are constituents of American politicians, and it is part of government's job to support its constituents, corporate or otherwise. The U.S. government, like all governments, usually acts to promote and protect the interests of American corporations abroad.

However, FDI is often controversial in its countries of origin. Some in North America and western Europe, particularly labor unions, fault MNCs for not investing at home and for "outsourcing" jobs to countries with lower wages. The AFL-CIO, which represents the majority of unionized workers in the United States,

global supply chains

A network of customers and suppliers involved in the production and distribution of a product. Parts of it may be inside a multinational corporation; parts may also involve links between corporations.

---

16. For more on the economics of FDI, see Richard E. Caves, *Multinational Enterprise and Economic Analysis*, 3rd ed. (Cambridge: Cambridge University Press, 2007).

Factory workers in Shenzhen, China, sort electronic components in a manufacturing plant that produces iPhones and iPads. Abundant cheap labor in countries like China makes it profitable for foreign companies to invest in factories there.

argues: "As multinational corporations employ more of the global workforce and increase their power, workers and the labor movement face continuing attacks and challenges. . . . [G]lobal privatization leaves in its wake inequality, substantially reduced funding and resources for those who need them most, disenfranchised communities, unaccountable decision making, and a general abdication of government responsibility and accountability for the provision of vital public services."[17] Labor unions and others have demanded stricter controls on "sweatshop labor" in the developing countries, reflecting both working-class solidarity and a more prosaic desire to reduce competitive pressure.

Some politicians echo this criticism. President Donald Trump threatened American corporations that outsource with a 35 percent tax on the goods they try to sell in the American market: "If you go to another country," he told American corporate executives, "we are going to be imposing a very major border tax."[18] (Ultimately, however, this tax was not implemented.)

Some human rights activists and environmentalists also eye MNCs with apprehension. Just as corporations can move production abroad to take advantage of lower wages, they may look for pollution-friendly regimes, dictatorships that allow violations of human rights, and other ethically lax governments. In the words of a European campaign to "clean up" the world garment industry: "Incentives for foreign investors include not only low wages, but also the suspension of certain workplace and environmental regulations. If a government does attempt to strictly enforce these regulations, you can bet that many investors will quickly pack their bags for another country that is even less strict and is more accommodating."[19] And there is a cultural component to some complaints about MNCs, arguing that MNCs reduce diversity and encourage the homogenization of world culture. Nonetheless, in general, home-country governments see their interests as closely tied to those of their corporations.

Why Do Countries Let Foreign Multinationals In?

Most countries that host FDI have some interest in allowing MNCs to operate within their borders—otherwise, of course, they would keep the corporations out. Certainly, in the nineteenth century it was common for rapidly growing

---

17. AFL-CIO, "Resolution 8: Global Organizing," https://aflcio.org/sites/default/files/2017-07/Res8.pdf (accessed 1/3/21).

18. Carol E. Lee and Damian Paletta, "Donald Trump Focuses on Trade and Jobs: President Withdraws from TPP Agreement, Promises Tax on Firms that Move Operations Overseas," *Wall Street Journal*, January 23, 2017, www.wsj.com/articles/president-trump-focuses-on-trade-with-very-major-border-tax-promise-1485183598 (accessed 1/22/21)

19. From www.cleanclothes.org/intro.htm#7 (accessed 8/21/04).

nations—including the United States, Canada, Argentina, Russia, and Australia—to rely on foreign companies to build up such important industries as railroads.

Today, most governments welcome foreign corporations. This is because MNCs bring in managerial, technological, and marketing skills that might not be domestically available, as well as investment capital. Some less developed countries (LDCs) lack the trained personnel and capital necessary to access and develop their own natural resources; without foreigners, they might not be able to profit from these assets. If they allow foreign companies to pump oil or to mine copper, for example, the government can then tax some of the profits. Other poor nations with weak or small private sectors may welcome foreign corporations to provide jobs for their citizens and to gain access to world markets for their products.

Most nations are eager to attract the technological or other expertise that MNCs can mobilize. This is especially true in the case of high-tech industries, where such multinationals as IBM or Siemens may be the sole source of crucial modern technologies in their host country—that is, the country in which they've invested. For instance, when Intel opened production facilities in Costa Rica in 1997, it transformed that country's economy. The firm soon accounted for one-third of total exports, with Intel's sales alone surpassing the country's traditional banana and coffee exports. Overall, Intel invested about a billion dollars in a country of 3.5 million people, and it employed about 5,000 people directly or indirectly. It had a network of almost 500 local supplier companies, and its presence spurred the creation of a high-tech cluster with over 50 other companies. There were years when Intel's activities alone accounted for more than half of the growth of the Costa Rican economy.[20]

Yet host countries do not always have such positive views of FDI. There is always scope for disagreement over the division of the benefits. Conflict can arise, for example, over how much in taxes an oil company should pay to the local government or over the wages an automobile factory should pay to local workers. Local competitors may complain about foreign firms' presence in the domestic market. Foreign managers may be insensitive to host countries' social, cultural, and political norms. Developing-country governments have had particularly fraught interactions with MNCs. Many developing countries have gross domestic products (GDPs) smaller than the sales of the MNCs they host, which can make it difficult for them to adequately monitor the activities of these enormous corporations.

Even where there is agreement when the investment is made, views may change over time. One common pattern is that when a country is very poor, it is eager to attract FDI to bring its natural resources and other national products to market. Over time, however, as the domestic economy becomes more sophisticated, local investors become better able to undertake the activities dominated by the MNCs. As the LDC develops, its government may want its own citizens to get more of the benefits of the investment. National businesses may come to resent the

---

20. World Bank, Multilateral Investment Guarantee Agency, *The Impact of Intel in Costa Rica: Nine Years after the Decision to Invest* (Washington, DC: World Bank, 2006).

foreign competition, and local managers and technicians may feel they no longer need the MNC.

Even the case of Intel in Costa Rica is hardly clear-cut. Just as Intel's expansion spurred the country's economy, Intel's difficulties have held it back: in 2000, when the firm's growth slowed, Intel's problems depressed Costa Rican growth to half of what it would have been otherwise. And in order to attract Intel, the Costa Rican government had exempted the company from all taxes for eight years (and from half of its taxes for another four) and freed it from many regulations that apply to other domestic and foreign firms. In 2014, Intel announced that it would close its main assembly facility in Costa Rica and move these operations to Malaysia, Vietnam, and China.[21] Although Costa Rica certainly gained from having Intel invest there, the presence of this huge firm—whose total worldwide sales are larger than Costa Rica's GDP—also imposed real constraints on the small Central American nation, and the closure of its assembly plant caused job losses and economic contraction. In this context, there is plenty of scope for conflict between MNCs and host governments.

Host-Country Interactions with MNCs

Like debtors and creditors, foreign corporations and host-country governments have some common interests and some conflicting interests. This mix defines the scope of interactions between national governments and MNCs. As with foreign debt, each side has reasons to work to enable the investment. But, again as with foreign debt, each side has strong incentives to bargain for a greater share of the benefits from FDI.

This bargaining may involve negotiations over tax rates, company-sponsored training of local citizens for skilled jobs, or the MNC giving some of its business to local suppliers. The host country's weapons include its ability to regulate and tax companies within its borders, up to and including nationalizing them; essentially, it can force companies to sell out to local investors or to the government itself. The MNC's weapons include withholding its capital, technology, or expertise, which could ultimately culminate in pulling out of the local economy.

Interactions between host countries and MNCs have gone through many phases. Among the most conflictual have been relations over FDI in the raw-materials sector. Before World War I, most FDI was in mining, agriculture, or utilities. These plantation and raw-materials investments, which may have been popular at the outset, eventually became controversial, and many people in developing nations came to see them as exploitative. The case of the United Fruit Company in Central America (see Chapter 4) is a good example. Indeed, after the 1920s, more and more LDCs tended to buy out, take over, or limit foreign investment in these sectors, favoring their own investors instead. One study of forcible takings of MNCs in developing countries between 1960 and 1976, for example, found that while FDI in extractive

---

21. See "Intel Outside," *Economist*, April 19, 2014, www.economist.com/news/americas/21600985-chipmaker-shuts-factory-slicing-away-one-fifth-countrys-exports-intel-outside (accessed 1/22/21). Although the company still maintains a smaller research and development facility in Costa Rica, the country lost some 1,500 jobs.

industries (agriculture and raw materials) and utilities was just one-fifth of total FDI, these sectors accounted for more than half of the takings.[22]

Political considerations about the role of FDI have added to purely economic concerns. Especially during the 1960s, LDC governments began to argue that large foreign corporations could have a powerful and unwelcome impact on local politics. The activities of the U.S.-based International Telephone & Telegraph (ITT) Corporation in Chile demonstrated the threat. In 1970, ITT actively opposed the presidential candidacy of Socialist Salvador Allende for fear that his government would nationalize ITT's investments. After ITT's attempts to prevent Allende's victory were unsuccessful, the company participated in a series of plots to try to overthrow the president. The story ended with a coup that destroyed one of Latin America's sturdiest democracies and brought the murderous dictatorship of Augusto Pinochet to power. The notion that American companies could be complicit in such matters, long derided by Westerners as feverish imagining, was soon proved to be accurate by a congressional investigation, and this finding fueled sentiment against MNCs.[23]

For both economic and political reasons, many countries began restricting MNCs in the 1960s. This was even true of some developed nations: Canada monitored and controlled new investments, while both France and Japan limited foreign companies. But the most sweeping efforts were in the developing world, where foreign corporations were excluded from many industries and foreign ownership was strictly limited, often to a minority share. Many developing countries nationalized foreign corporations, transferring ownership to local private companies or to the government. Others allowed FDI only if the foreign company did not compete with local firms, shared ownership with local investors, or agreed to reinvest most of its profits in the host country. The turn away from MNCs in the 1960s and 1970s went hand in hand with the turn toward foreign borrowing: by borrowing, developing countries could get foreign capital without allowing foreign ownership of the projects.

But the debt crisis of the 1980s, along with the increased acceptance of global economic integration in the 1990s, eroded resistance to multinationals. Developing countries were desperate for foreign capital, especially after loans dried up. And it appeared that attracting foreign corporations was important to ensuring a nation's integration into global markets. LDCs loosened or removed their previous restrictions on FDI, and many actively encouraged foreign corporations to locate production facilities within their borders. The amounts involved were enormous: while MNCs invested about $2 billion a year in the developing world in the early 1970s, they have averaged over $500 billion a year since 2000. Even accounting for inflation, this is more than a 30-fold increase. As most developing countries have opened their economies to world markets, FDI has become less politically sensitive and more broadly desired.

22. Stephen J. Kobrin, "Foreign Enterprise and Forced Divestment in LDCs," *International Organization* 34, no. 1 (Winter 1980): 65–88.

23. Paul E. Sigmund, *Multinationals in Latin America: The Politics of Nationalization* (Madison: University of Wisconsin Press, 1980).

This does not mean that MNCs are not controversial. Indeed, many people in the developing world continue to regard foreign corporations as economically, politically, or culturally undesirable. Developing nations continue to restrict their activities. In industrialized countries too, there are continuing concerns about the exporting of jobs and, in some quarters, about the possibility that foreign investors might compromise national sovereignty. Contemporary debates over globalization are emblematic of the politically controversial nature of FDI.

Why Aren't There International Institutions Related to FDI?

There are no effective international institutions associated with FDI. This is in striking contrast to international lending, where there are both regional and global multilateral institutions: the IMF, the World Bank, the Inter-American Development Bank, and so on. One possible reason is that there are few (if any) widely accepted truly global concerns associated with FDI. In the area of international finance, it has been generally agreed for over a century that a financial crisis in one country has the potential to affect other countries. This risk incentivizes countries to find ways, including institutionalized ways, to cooperate to avoid such financial contagion, and international institutions facilitate cooperation in pursuit of these common goals. Such incentives are not as strong in the case of FDI.

Nor is there a particularly strong demand for cooperation among countries in bargaining with MNCs. Individual countries that wish to limit or regulate MNCs can do so on their own, and it is not clear that IMF-style international institutions would help with this effort. The role of international institutions in providing information or establishing standards seems less relevant in the case of FDI, where each investment has different characteristics and where host governments are often well equipped to supervise foreign companies.

There have been occasional suggestions that some international agreement or organization might help to create a common set of standards for FDI. The United Nations and other international organizations have proposed codes of conduct, and MNCs have increasingly, and voluntarily, complied with them. However, these codes of conduct fall far short of an organized intergovernmental institution. Initiatives to institutionalize and regularize relations between MNCs and host nations have made little progress. Thousands of **bilateral investment treaties** have been signed between two countries, providing protection for each other's investors, but nothing even remotely similar to the IMF has emerged.

Despite the absence of any multilateral institution, since the 1980s interactions between foreign corporations and nation-states have generally been less conflictual than they were before then. FDI today leads to much less debate than sovereign lending does. To be sure, in rich countries concerns remain about the role of MNCs in exporting jobs, while many people in developing countries worry about the economic and political impact of large foreign corporations. Nonetheless, today FDI is widely accepted as an important component of an integrated world economy and as a generally positive factor in economic development.

bilateral investment treaty

An agreement between two countries about the conditions for private investment across borders. Most of these treaties include provisions to protect an investment from government discrimination or expropriation without compensation as well as mechanisms to resolve disputes.

International Migration: Economics and Political Economy

It may seem curious to consider international migration alongside international investment. However, labor is a factor of production that moves across borders, much as capital does. In fact, international movements of labor and capital can be thought of as responding to similar economic factors and having similar economic effects. Capital can leave one country so that workers can be hired in another; this is what happens when a corporation sets up production abroad. Alternatively, labor can leave one country in order to work for capital in another; this is what happens when workers migrate to a new country to be employed by a corporation there. Whether General Motors moves a factory to Mexico to hire Mexican workers or Mexican workers move to Detroit to work for General Motors, the economic effect may be similar. It therefore makes sense to think about the economics of immigration as part of the broader pattern of global economic integration.

Of course, the movement of people raises complex social, cultural, and political issues that are typically not present with most other cross-border economic relationships. In addition, there is a substantial difference between migration for economic reasons and the movement of refugees and asylum seekers. In this section, we focus exclusively on how *economic* factors affect the politics of international migration. We will return to consider the issue from a broader perspective, including such noneconomic factors as culture and race or ethnicity, in Chapter 14. For now, we analyze the economic implications of immigration as another example of the movement of factors of production from country to country.

International migration has long been a feature of a globalized world economy. In the nineteenth and early twentieth centuries, international labor migration occurred at much higher levels than it does today. During the decades before World War I, some 100 million people left their homelands in Europe and Asia for other parts of the world. The cities of such rapidly growing countries as Canada, Australia, Argentina, and the United States were full of foreign-born workers. For the most part, before 1914 Europeans could move and work wherever they pleased, without complicated legal proceedings or documents (Asian immigration was much more heavily restricted). While international labor movements in recent years have been very large, they are proportionally smaller than those of the nineteenth and early twentieth centuries. However, labor migration has been significant—and also politically controversial.

Today, about one American resident in seven was born in a foreign country, and approximately half of this population originated in Latin America. In other developed countries, the immigrant share of the population is generally similar to that of the United States (15 percent). It is a bit lower in some countries (10 percent in Italy, 13 percent in France) and substantially higher in others (20 percent or more in

TABLE 8.1 *Countries with the Largest Number of International Migrants, 2019*

	TOTAL MIGRANTS	AS % TOTAL POPULATION
United States	50,661,100	15.4
Germany	13,132,100	15.7
Saudi Arabia	13,122,300	38.3
Russia	11,640,600	8.0
United Kingdom	9,552,100	14.1
United Arab Emirates	8,587,300	87.9
France	8,334,900	12.8
Canada	7,960,700	21.3
Australia	7,549,300	30.0
Spain	6,104,200	13.1

Source: United Nations Population Division, "International Migrant Stock 2019," Country Profiles, www .un.org/en/development/desa/population/migration/data/estimates2/estimates19.asp (accessed 1/13/21).

Canada, Australia, and Switzerland).[24] Table 8.1 shows the countries with the largest numbers of immigrants. In almost every developed country, immigration is a politically contentious issue, with some residents favoring more open borders and others wishing to limit new migrants.[25] What are the economic factors that might explain these controversies over immigration?

The economic impact of the movement of labor from one country to another is analogous in many ways to the economic impact of the movement of capital, and it can be similarly analyzed. Labor, like capital, responds to differential rates of return: higher wages in rich countries attract workers from poor countries. This is true of both unskilled labor and skilled labor, the latter of which is typically called human capital because its "owners" have invested in advanced skills. Unskilled workers from El Salvador or Morocco migrate to the United States or Germany in search of higher-paying jobs just as unskilled workers from Italy and Sweden migrated to the United States and Australia a hundred years ago. Skilled workers from India or Argentina, too, move to Europe or North America in search of higher incomes.

24. United Nations Population Division, "International Migrant Stock 2019," www.un.org/en/development /desa/population/migration/data/estimates2/estimates19.asp (accessed 12/28/20).

25. A useful resource on this highly controversial topic is the Migration Policy Institute, www.migrationpolicy .org (accessed 12/28/20).

In this sense, immigration can be explained in terms of the Heckscher-Ohlin theory discussed in Chapter 7. Countries with abundant unskilled labor will export unskilled labor; countries scarce in unskilled labor will import it. Differences across countries in labor endowments (and, consequently, wages) mean that there are economic incentives for a labor-rich country such as Mexico or China to export both labor-intensive goods and labor.

The economic impact of labor migration can also be understood using the Heckscher-Ohlin logic. An inflow of unskilled labor from abroad will tend to reduce the wages of local unskilled workers, while an inflow of skilled labor will tend to reduce the wages of local skilled workers. Thus, for example, unskilled workers in developed countries are likely to be harmed by the immigration of unskilled workers from countries with lower wages. Concerns about this labor-market competition are one source of unease about immigration in developed countries (see "How Do We Know?" on p. 400).

This is not a new phenomenon. In the century before 1914, immigration probably also exerted downward pressure on wages in migrant-receiving countries: two scholars have estimated that in such countries as the United States, Australia, and Argentina, unskilled wages were between one-eighth and one-third lower with immigration than they would have been without it.[26] While this outcome may have been bad for unskilled workers, it was probably good for the countries' economies as a whole, supplying them with much-needed labor.

Immigration benefits people in receiving countries in several ways. Employers, especially those who hire a lot of unskilled workers, gain from the lower wages they can pay; in parts of the United States, sectors such as agriculture, restaurants, and construction have come to rely on cheaper immigrant labor. The economy as a whole profits from having a larger labor force and from the reduced cost of production that lower wages can facilitate. As usual, the benefits for some are counterbalanced by costs to others: if immigration lowers the wages that employers have to pay, it also lowers the wages paid to native workers who compete with immigrants. Even for native workers, the impact of immigration can vary. Some immigrants do compete with native workers, but other immigrants complement the native workforce, providing essential labor that native workers would be reluctant to supply.

The domestic distributional effects of immigration, coupled with national political institutions, help explain changes in immigration policy over time. In the nineteenth century, there was substantial anti-immigrant sentiment among workers in such countries as the United States, Canada, and Australia. But in the 1800s, employers were far more politically powerful than labor; after all, unions were barely organized. So, while there were some restrictions on immigration, especially from Asia, most countries remained open. As the political influence of labor grew, restrictions on immigration expanded and remained stringent until the 1960s. During this decade, labor shortages began to develop in industrialized nations, and pressure grew to permit more immigration. The result was a loosening of

---

26. Kevin H. O'Rourke and Jeffrey G. Williamson, *Globalization and History: The Evolution of a Nineteenth-Century Atlantic Economy* (Cambridge, MA: MIT Press, 1999), Tables 8.1 and 8.3.

Explaining Public Opinion on Immigration

Immigration is one of the most politically controversial issues in developed countries. Both the Brexit movement in the United Kingdom and the Trump administration in the United States, along with many populist parties in Europe, emphasized concern about immigration in their campaigns, and surveys suggest that immigration policy is an important issue for many voters. How do voters decide whether they favor or oppose immigration?

To answer this question, some scholars begin with the same frameworks used to analyze international trade. The Heckscher-Ohlin model, introduced in Chapter 7, demonstrates that the relative abundance or scarcity of factors of production (land, labor, and capital) are critical for understanding trade patterns. For example, countries that have abundant labor are likely to export labor-intensive products. The related Stolper-Samuelson theorem assumes that trade protection benefits the scarce factor of production.

The same logic can explain patterns of immigration and its distributional consequences. Labor-abundant countries, such as India, the Philippines, and Mexico, are likely to experience the largest out-migration of residents, and relatively labor-scarce rich economies, such as Britain, the United States, and Saudi Arabia, are likely to experience the largest inflows of people (see Table 8.1). By the same logic, restricting immigration benefits labor in the receiving country when it is scarce.

Political scientist Kenneth Scheve and economist Matthew Slaughter used the ideas of the Heckscher-Ohlin model to explain American voters' beliefs about immigration policy.[a] They first measured voters' preferences by examining responses to a question that appeared in successive American National Election Studies nationwide surveys in 1992, 1994, and 1996: "Do you think the number of immigrants from foreign countries who are permitted to come to the United States to live should be increased a little, increased a lot, decreased a little, decreased a lot, or left the same as it is now?" The authors assumed that respondents believed that U.S. immigrant inflows increase the relative supply of low-skilled workers,

which is a reasonable assumption given that nearly one-third of U.S. immigrants lack a high school diploma or equivalent.[b] The survey also asked respondents about their wages and years of education, which serve as useful proxies for respondents' skill levels.

Scheve and Slaughter analyzed the survey data using a statistical model and found that public opinion toward immigration reflects the logic of the Heckscher-Ohlin framework: respondents with lower skills prefer a more restrictive immigration policy, whereas high-skilled respondents prefer a more open policy. In their interpretation, domestic labor competition is key: unskilled workers—who constitute a relatively scarce factor in the United States—fear that an influx of low-skilled immigrants will cause their wages to drop.

Scheve and Slaughter's findings caused considerable controversy among political economists, some of whom were skeptical that voters could correctly calculate the income effects predicted by the Heckscher-Ohlin model. Other scholars were skeptical that wages and education actually measure skill level rather than noneconomic attributes like open-mindedness and experience with foreign cultures.[c] Public opinion toward immigration remains a very active research area, with political scientists devising new experiments to determine which economic or noneconomic factors drive individual preferences toward this highly politicized issue.

a. Kenneth F. Scheve and Matthew J. Slaughter, "Labor Market Competition and Individual Preferences over Immigration Policy," *Review of Economics and Statistics* 83, no. 1 (February 2001): 133–45.

b. See Pia M. Orrenius and Madeline Zavodny, "Immigrants in the U.S. Labor Market," Working Paper 1306, Federal Reserve Bank of Dallas, September 2013, www.dallasfed.org/assets/documents/research/papers/2013/wp1306.pdf.

c. See Jens Hainmueller and Daniel J. Hopkins, "Public Attitudes toward Immigration," *Annual Review of Political Science* 17, no 1 (2014): 225–49.

Immigrant workers are an essential part of the U.S. economy. Agricultural workers in California support the production of crops that are sold domestically and internationally.

restrictions. This may also have been due to the rising influence of skilled workers in rich countries, who were less concerned about competition from unskilled immigrants.

The 1990s saw the rise of political movements that were less enthusiastic about, or downright hostile to, immigration. Concern about the economic impact of immigration rose with the financial crisis that began in 2008. In the United States and Europe, many people worried that immigrants from LDCs were taking jobs away from native workers and driving wages down. A dramatic refugee crisis that grew out of civil war in Syria and unrest elsewhere in the Middle East and North Africa compounded these anxieties. The European Union, which had received about 200,000 requests for asylum in 2009, received 1.3 million in both 2015 and 2016, and many Europeans were concerned that their countries were being, or would be, flooded with refugees.[27] Concern about immigration was central to the rise of right-wing populism in Europe, to the Brexit campaign in the United Kingdom, and to the presidential campaign of Donald Trump in the United States (for more on these developments, see Chapter 14).

The political economy of immigration involves additional economic considerations. One such concern is the potential cost of social programs that may disproportionately serve immigrants, inasmuch as they tend to be poorer than natives. However, immigrants typically pay taxes and contribute to overall economic growth. Thus, the overall (net) effect of immigrants in the United States—whether

---

27. Eurostat, "Asylum and First Time Asylum Applicants—Annual Aggregated Data (Rounded)," http://appsso.eurostat.ec.europa.eu/nui/show.do?dataset=tps00191&lang=en (accessed 1/19/21).

they cost the country more than they benefit it, or vice versa—may be hard to distinguish. Many American and European political opponents express particular concern about the fiscal effects of large-scale immigration.[28] Both supporters and opponents of immigration often raise noneconomic issues as well, which we will discuss in more detail in Chapter 14.

Certainly, immigration is one of the more prominent and visible features of contemporary globalization. Today, there are many countervailing economic interests at play that drive opposing viewpoints: workers who would compete with immigrants versus workers who would not, taxpayers concerned about the cost of immigrants versus those who see them as beneficial, employers who depend on immigrant labor versus those who do not. The topic promises to continue to be controversial.

Conclusion: The Politics of International Investment

International finance is the most globalized portion of the international economy. People and governments worldwide try mightily to attract foreign corporations and to qualify for loans from foreign lenders. There are substantial advantages to having access to the world's enormous pool of capital. This benefit gives governments powerful reasons to try to collaborate with foreign investors to smooth the path of capital as it moves from country to country.

However, international finance is not an unmitigated blessing. Foreign loans can be a boon to a developing nation, but they can also become an oppressive burden that forces the population to make huge sacrifices in order for their government to keep up interest payments. Foreign investment by MNCs can bring a country valuable technology and expertise, but it can also impose severe constraints on how much room the host nation has to maneuver in terms of investing in other services to support citizens. Governments have many interests in common with international financiers, but they also have many conflicting interests.

International finance is inherently political because powerful private actors, governments, and international institutions all come together to bargain over the terms of international financial relations. Such negotiations—over foreign loans, debt bailouts, IMF packages, the role of MNCs, and other financial issues—can be contentious. The policies associated with them are also often very controversial within nations, adding to the politicization of these problems.

---

28. For scholarship on this, see Gordon H. Hanson, Kenneth Scheve, and Matthew J. Slaughter, "Public Finance and Individual Preferences over Globalization Strategies," *Economics and Politics* 19, no. 1 (March 2007): 1–33; and Giovanni Facchini and Anna Maria Mayda, "Does the Welfare State Affect Individual Attitudes toward Immigrants? Evidence across Countries," *The Review of Economics and Statistics* 91, no. 2 (2009): 295–314.

Many countries, past and present, have used foreign capital to finance rapid economic growth and development. And many individuals, groups, and companies have benefited from their access to international finance. However, when things go wrong in the international financial system, they can go spectacularly wrong in ways that can profoundly impact international politics—and the lives of billions of people.

Study Tool Kit

Interests, Interactions, and Institutions in Context

- Within borrowing nations, there are many actors who value access to foreign funds. However, there are others who resent the constraints and burdens that foreign investments sometimes impose on debtors. Similar conflicting interests exist within lending nations.

- At the international level, both lenders and borrowers, like investors and recipients of investment, have a common interest in sustaining capital flows, which benefit both sides. Nonetheless, they may enter into conflict—especially over how the benefits from the loans or investments will be divided.

- Lenders and borrowers, and investors and recipients, bargain over the investments that tie them together. There is frequent disagreement over debt payments to foreign creditors and profit payments to foreign corporations.

- An array of important and influential international institutions structure interactions in the international financial realm. The most prominent is the IMF, which has often played a major role in managing the problems of heavily indebted countries. Like international finance generally, the role of the IMF is very controversial: some analysts think it contributes to the cooperative resolution of financial problems, while others think it takes unfair advantage of struggling debtor nations.

Key Terms

portfolio investment, p. 367

sovereign lending, p. 367

foreign direct investment (FDI), p. 367

World Bank, p. 372

recession, p. 375

depression, p. 375

default, p. 375

austerity, p. 377

Bank for International Settlements, p. 379

International Monetary Fund (IMF), p. 379

multinational corporation (MNC), p. 390

global supply chains, p. 391

bilateral investment treaty, p. 396

For Further Reading

Baldwin, Richard. *The Great Convergence: Information Technology and the New Globalization.* **Cambridge, MA: Harvard University Press, 2016.** Explains how advances in information technology have spurred the internationalization of production by multinational corporations and their global supply chains.

Blau, Francine D., and Christopher Mackie, eds. *The Economic and Fiscal Consequences of Immigration.* **Washington, DC: The National Academies Press, 2017.** Leading social scientists provide a balanced assessment of the economic implications of immigration in the United States.

Chinn, Menzie D., and Jeffry A. Frieden. *Lost Decades: The Making of America's Debt Crisis and the Long Recovery.* **New York: Norton, 2011.** Analyzes the politics and economics of the biggest financial crisis since the Great Depression.

Copelovitch, Mark S. *The International Monetary Fund in the Global Economy: Banks, Bonds and Bailouts.* **Cambridge: Cambridge University Press, 2010.** Analyzes the politics and economics of the role of the IMF in resolving international debt conflicts.

McDowell, Daniel. *Brother, Can You Spare a Billion? The United States, the IMF, and the International Lender of Last Resort.* **Oxford: Oxford University Press, 2017.** Analyzes the role of the United States and the IMF in addressing debt and financial crises.

Mosley, Layna. *Labor Rights and Multinational Production.* **Cambridge: Cambridge University Press, 2011.** Assesses the impact of FDI on the rights and opportunities available to workers in developing countries.

Pandya, Sonal S. *Trading Spaces: Foreign Direct Investment Regulation, 1970–2000.* **Cambridge: Cambridge University Press, 2014.** Analyzes the politics and economics of national responses to foreign corporations.

Tomz, Michael. *Reputation and International Cooperation: Sovereign Debt across Three Centuries.* **Princeton, NJ: Princeton University Press, 2007.** Explores the politics and economics of private lending to governments historically and in the present.

Walter, Stefanie. *Financial Crises and the Politics of Macroeconomic Adjustments.* **Cambridge: Cambridge University Press, 2013.** Explains the causes and consequences of financial crises, and government responses to them, with both historical and contemporary applications.

9

International Monetary Relations

THE PUZZLE *In the absence of global government and a global currency, how are goods and services traded among countries?*

Above: International monetary relations are often controversial. Today, the European Central Bank in Frankfurt, Germany, implements monetary policies for the entire eurozone, which comprises 19 member countries that gave up their national currencies for the euro.

On December 18, 2001, rioters swept through the cities of Argentina. They were furious about three straight years of economic stagnation and government economic policies that seemed to make matters worse. Most recently, the government had frozen bank deposits so that Argentines could take only small amounts of cash out of their bank accounts—and nothing out of the very popular accounts that many people had in U.S. dollars.

In response to the rioting, President Fernando de la Rúa declared a state of siege, but the following day the disorder spread as hundreds of thousands of middle-class Argentines joined the protests in the streets. That evening, the economy minister stepped down. A day later, violent clashes with police led to more than two dozen deaths around the country, and huge crowds surrounded the presidential palace in Buenos Aires. At the end of the day, de la Rúa resigned and was evacuated by helicopter from the presidential palace to avoid the hostile crowds.

The president of the Senate, a member of the opposition Peronist Party that controlled both houses of Congress, assumed the interim presidency. Two days later, the Peronists installed provincial governor Adolfo Rodríguez Saá as president until national elections could be held.

Rodríguez Saá declared the largest default the world had seen—on $93 billion in sovereign debt. But he too faced protests, and he resigned a week after taking office.

This time the president of the Chamber of Deputies, also a Peronist, stepped in as interim president. After further turmoil, the legislature appointed to the presidency Eduardo Duhalde, the Peronist candidate who had lost the 1999 presidential election to the now disgraced de la Rúa. Meanwhile, the country had entered full-fledged economic collapse. Argentine gross domestic product (GDP), which had declined by 8 percent over the three previous years of recession, dropped by 11 percent in 2002, and unemployment soared above 20 percent.

The ultimate reason for these extraordinary events— nationwide riots, five presidents in less than two weeks, the biggest default in history, economic disintegration— was the Argentine government's policies toward its currency. Ten years earlier, the government had set the Argentine peso as equal to one U.S. dollar and fixed it at this exchange rate. Although this policy initially led to rapid growth and many other economic achievements in Argentina, by 2001, the commitment was dragging the economy downward. It was widely blamed for general economic stagnation and for the specific banking policies that provoked popular outrage. Argentina's fortunes rose dramatically, and fell even more dramatically, thanks to its currency policies.

The events in Argentina are not alone in illustrating the importance of currencies and currency policies to economics and politics—and to people's everyday lives. Indeed, a couple of weeks after Argentine society exploded into violence over the exchange rate, another, unrelated but equally remarkable, currency development took shape halfway around the world. Twelve European countries abandoned their national monies, some of which had existed for centuries. In place of the Deutschmark, franc, lira, and other currencies, they adopted the euro (€), a common European currency. The creation of the euro dominated European politics and economics for most of the 1990s, and the early 2000s were spent consolidating, managing, and expanding the new currency.

Then, in 2008, the global financial crisis hit the eurozone. The international economic slowdown brought Europe's borrowing boom to an end and plunged the continent into recession. In the ten years that followed, the eurozone crisis dragged the entire European economy down into stagnation, threatened the existence of the euro itself, contributed to Britain's decision to exit the European Union (EU), and overall, constituted the gravest threat to European integration since the union's formation. European currency politics—the euro's rise, creation, evolution, and crisis—have been central to the continent's political economy for 40 years. Argentina and Europe are not alone: in many countries, currency policy is one of the most hotly contested economic and political issues.

Money is central to all economic transactions. A national money gives residents a common standard by which to establish prices, buy and sell, and save. But people in different countries lack a common money, so they must find a way to set prices by which they can buy, sell, and invest across borders. In this they depend on the policies of national governments, which are in charge of managing their respective national currencies.

Historically, governments have pursued very different policies toward their national currencies. Today, most governments choose among three monetary paths. One option is to give up one's national currency in favor of another money—as has occurred in a number of Caribbean and Latin American countries, which have adopted the U.S. dollar, and in most European countries, which have adopted the euro. Other governments have tied their national currency's value to that of another country,

such as the dollar or the euro (as we will discuss in more detail). Finally, many governments continue to maintain a separate national currency whose value is allowed to change in response to markets and other forces. How and why do governments choose any one of these three monetary paths?

The international monetary order has also varied enormously over the years. While national governments supply national monies, there is no international government to organize international monetary affairs. Virtually everyone has an interest in the existence of a functioning international monetary system, but different arrangements benefit some actors more than others. This disparity leads to disagreements about how such a system should be organized. How is such a quintessentially governmental function as the provision of currencies carried out at the global level in the absence of global government?

Thinking Analytically about International Monetary Relations

This chapter makes several points about the interests, interactions, and institutions associated with international monetary policy. First, within each country there are many actors who have an interest in the country's monetary affairs, which leads to conflict over the appropriate currency policy to pursue. We will see, briefly, how national currency policies are set and which groups have a stake in those policies.

In addition to individual national choices, there are important global monetary issues. Indeed, international monetary affairs—the interrelationships among national monies—are central to the international economy and thus to world politics. Stable relations among national currencies allow actors in one country to send payments to actors in other countries, making it easier for goods, people, and capital to move across borders—all important forms of international interaction. Just as it is hard to imagine national economies without national money, it is hard to see how the modern world economy could function without some cooperative arrangement guiding the use of money among countries.

What Are Exchange Rates, and Why Do They Matter?

A national monetary system allows for the convenient exchange of goods, services, and capital. Most of us probably take a reliable and stable money for granted. In its absence, however, we would be forced to barter—that is, exchange goods and services for each other. This would be extraordinarily cumbersome and inefficient, and it would pose a tremendous impediment to economic activity. Money is thus a classic public good (see Chapter 2): it benefits everyone, but because people cannot be excluded from its benefits and charged to access them, there is little incentive for private firms to provide it. This is why national governments typically determine a country's currency, print bills, mint coins, and control the money supply. It is also why governments try to instill trust in the national currency. Almost everyone in a country can agree on the desirability of a recognizable, trustworthy national money and stable prices.

But currencies exist and are used both domestically and in relation to other national currencies. For example, the U.S. dollar can be used not only to buy goods and services in the United States but also to buy euros, Canadian dollars, and Mexican pesos, among other currencies. The price of a national currency relative to other national currencies is its **exchange rate**, and like other prices, the exchange rate can go up or down. When the dollar goes up in value against some other currency—such that, for example, a dollar can buy more pesos—it is said to strengthen, or **appreciate**. When the dollar's value goes down against that of some other currency—such that, for example, a dollar can buy fewer pesos—it is said to weaken, or **depreciate**, or to be **devalued**.

When a country's currency appreciates, it is more expensive for foreigners to buy the country's goods and services; when the currency depreciates, it is cheaper to do so. The most direct experience that many people have with currency movements is as tourists or, if they live near a national border, with prices around the border. American travelers to Europe find, for example, that when the dollar is strong, local prices in Europe seem relatively low. The hotels they stay in, the restaurants they go to, and the souvenirs they purchase are relatively inexpensive. When the dollar weakens, however, local prices get much higher.

For example, in January 2020 an American staying in an Italian hotel that charged €100 a night would have paid about $110 a night, because the euro was worth $1.10; a year later, with the euro worth $1.23, the same hotel room at the same euro price would have cost $123 a night. Over the course of that year, the dollar had depreciated by about 12 percent against the euro, so goods and services in euro countries, such as Italy, cost 12 percent more. (See Figure 9.1 for an indication of how the value of the dollar has fluctuated against an average of other currencies.)

The same is true of goods bought and sold across borders. If a currency goes up or down, the prices that foreigners pay for goods priced in that currency rise or fall as well. So, a pair of Italian shoes that cost €100 in Italy in January 2020

exchange rate
The price at which one currency is exchanged for another.

appreciate
In terms of a currency, to increase in value relative to other currencies.

depreciate
In terms of a currency, to decrease in value relative to other currencies.

devalue
To reduce the value of one currency relative to other currencies.

FIGURE 9.1 *The Value of the U.S. Dollar, 1975–2019*

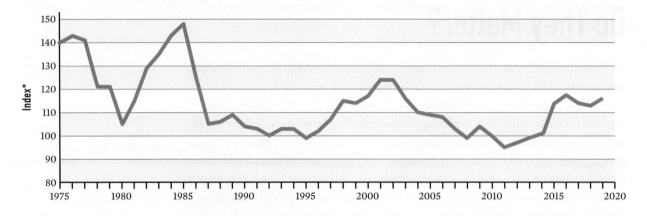

Figure source: World Bank, World Development Indicators, https://data.worldbank.org /indicator/PX.REX.REER? locations=US&view=chart (accessed 1/28/21).

*Real effective exchange-rate index. The real effective exchange-rate index is a measure of the value of the dollar against a weighted average of the currencies of the United States' major trading partners. The base year, 2010, is given the value of 100. Higher values indicate a stronger (more appreciated) dollar relative to the world's major currencies, and lower values indicate a weaker (depreciated) dollar.

could have been exported to the United States and sold for about $110 (plus shipping costs), while a year later, after the dollar had depreciated by about 12 percent, the same €100 Italian shoes would have sold for $123. When the U.S. dollar is weak against other currencies, foreign goods are expensive to Americans; however, when the U.S. dollar is strong against other currencies, foreign goods are inexpensive to Americans.

While most individuals are likely to encounter exchange rates when traveling among countries, currency values are primarily important for their impact on large-scale cross-border economic trade, investment, and finance. Indeed, although the attractiveness of a given country to foreign tourists is not particularly important to most nations, the attractiveness of that country's goods, services, and investment opportunities is crucial. Thus, the exchange rate is a very important part of a country's international economic relations.

How Are Currency Values Determined?

Like other prices, an exchange rate goes up or down in response to changes in supply and demand. Many factors affect supply and demand for a national money, but perhaps the most relevant is interest rates. As we saw in Chapter 8, foreigners considering investing in a country weigh relative interest rates; if U.S. interest rates are higher, investments in the United States promise a higher rate of return (everything else being equal).[1] But in order to invest in the United States, investors need dollars. Higher interest rates make it more profitable for people to put (or keep) their money in the country, so higher interest rates increase the demand for the currency and lead to its appreciation. Of course, the relationship works in the opposite direction as well: if people want fewer dollars, the dollar's exchange rate will go down.

---

1. For convenience, we ignore trade-related sources of currency movements. It should be clear that anything that makes a country's goods and services more attractive to foreigners will increase demand for the country's currency and lead to an appreciation (and vice versa).

Lower interest rates can lead to a depreciation of the currency, just as higher interest rates can lead to an appreciation. More generally, if foreigners want to invest in a country, they have to buy its currency; so if there is a lot of investment in an economy, demand for its currency will rise and the exchange rate will tend to appreciate. When foreigners invest heavily in the United States, all else equal, the dollar strengthens.

The relationship between interest rates and the value of the national currency is particularly important because governments routinely raise and lower interest rates as part of their **monetary policy**. Indeed, monetary policy is a powerful tool of national governments, which attempt to affect macroeconomic conditions— unemployment, inflation, overall economic growth—by manipulating monetary conditions.

In most countries, national monetary policy is implemented by a **central bank** (for example, the Federal Reserve in the United States). Central banks most commonly affect monetary conditions by raising or lowering interest rates. If the central bank wants to stimulate the economy, it lowers interest rates. Lower interest rates make it easier for people and companies to borrow, which in turn encourages the economy to expand. If the central bank wants to restrain the economy, typically because prices are rising and there is concern about inflation, it raises interest rates; this makes it harder to borrow and restrains demand.

Remember that interest rates also affect the exchange rate—higher interest rates make the currency more attractive and tend to raise its value. This means that national monetary policy can have a powerful impact on the value of a country's currency. The currency's value and movement can themselves be tools of national economic policy. For example, if a government wants to stimulate demand for its country's products in world markets, it can lower interest rates so that the currency depreciates. The weaker currency makes the country's goods cheaper to foreigners and spurs exports; it also makes foreign goods more expensive to domestic buyers and reduces imports. In this way, a monetary policy that weakens the currency can help the nation's producers. Of course, a weaker currency means that citizens can buy less with their money, so the government has to choose which effects it finds most appealing.

Allowing the Exchange Rate to Change

A national government faces other choices with respect to its currency. Among these, the most important is whether and how to let the exchange rate change relative to other exchange rates. The simplest choice is whether to "fix" the exchange rate or let it "float." A government that uses a **fixed exchange rate** promises to keep the national money at some established value in terms of another currency or in terms of a precious metal such as gold.

During the period of the classical **gold standard**, from the 1870s to 1914, a country's government "went on gold" by promising to exchange its currency for gold at an established rate (in the United States, it was one troy ounce of gold for $20.67). This move made the country's currency equivalent to gold and interchangeable at a fixed rate with the money of any other gold-standard country. Much

monetary policy
An important tool of national governments to influence broad macroeconomic conditions such as unemployment, inflation, and economic growth. Typically, governments alter their monetary policies by changing national interest rates or exchange rates.

central bank
The institution that regulates monetary conditions in a country's economy, typically by raising or lowering interest rates and the quantity of money in circulation.

fixed exchange rate
An exchange-rate policy under which a government commits itself to keeping its currency at or around a specific value relative to another currency or a commodity, such as gold.

gold standard
The monetary system that prevailed between about 1870 and 1914, in which countries tied their currencies to gold at a legally fixed price.

This pro-gold British political cartoon shows the gold standard vanquishing its opponent, the silver standard.

floating exchange rate

An exchange-rate policy under which a government permits its currency to be traded on the open market without direct government control or intervention.

Bretton Woods monetary system

The monetary order negotiated among the World War II Allies in 1944, which lasted until the 1970s and which was based on a U.S. dollar tied to gold. Other currencies were fixed to the dollar but were permitted to adjust their exchange rates.

of the world, as a result, essentially shared one currency. Gold-backed money invested by Germans in Japan, or by Belgians in Canada, would be paid back in equivalent amounts of gold-backed money. Contracted prices would not fluctuate, for exchange rates did not change.

A government that commits itself to a fixed exchange rate also commits itself to the policies necessary to maintain the set rate. For example, if the currency was poised to depreciate against other currencies, meaning the exchange rate would fall, the government might raise interest rates to encourage money to come into the country—in other words, so that foreigners would buy the country's currency. This increase in demand for the currency would make the exchange rate rise back to the set level.

At the other extreme is a **floating exchange rate**, under which a currency's value is allowed to change more or less freely, driven by markets or other factors. This is the regime currently in place for most major currencies, including the U.S. dollar, the Japanese yen, and the euro. If a government chooses this exchange-rate regime, the price of the currency moves around in line with changes in supply and demand. Map 9.1 on p. 414 indicates which countries worldwide follow fixed versus floating exchange-rate regimes.

There are intermediate steps between a fully fixed currency and a freely floating one. For instance, a government can allow its currency to vary, but only within limits, or it can fix the exchange rate for short periods, changing the currency's value as desired. This approach avoids some of the costs of each system but also forgoes some of the benefits. At the global level, the **Bretton Woods monetary system**, which followed the classical gold standard and prevailed from 1945 to 1973, was something of a compromise. It was based on a fixed rate and a gold standard for the United States and on a "fixed but adjustable rate" for other currencies on the dollar standard. This system of fixed but adjustable rates (an **adjustable peg**) required governments to keep currency values fixed for relatively long periods but permitted them to alter ("adjust") currency rates if and when they found it desirable to do so.

In practice, the Bretton Woods monetary system meant that the U.S. dollar's value could not change (it was fixed at $35 per ounce of gold). Governments of other countries also fixed their currencies against the dollar, but these governments had more flexibility: they could devalue or readjust the value of their currencies if they felt a change was necessary. Typically, such changes were infrequent, occurring once every five to seven years. The Bretton Woods monetary system was seen as a middle ground between gold-standard rigidity and complete unpredictability. As under the gold standard, exchange rates were stable enough to encourage international trade and investment. As under a more flexible system, countries could vary exchange rates as necessary, albeit rarely.

As these examples indicate, a national government's decisions about the exchange rate often depend on international monetary conditions. While national policies are important, from the standpoint of international economics and politics more generally, it is the *global* nature of international monetary relations that is most relevant. We will return to these international issues later in the chapter. First, however, we evaluate the potential for *domestic* conflicts of interest over exchange-rate policy.

adjustable peg
A monetary system of fixed but adjustable rates. Governments are expected to keep their currencies fixed for extended periods but are permitted to adjust the exchange rate from time to time as economic conditions change.

Who Cares about Exchange Rates, and Why?

Analysts often say that the exchange rate is the most important price in any economy, because the exchange rate affects all prices, directly or indirectly. A national government's currency policy has a broad and deep impact on its economy, and governments often pursue other, related policies to support their chosen currency policy. Both exchange rate policy and the economic measures needed to sustain it affect different domestic groups differently. This disparity can lead to disagreement over the appropriate currency policy to pursue.

Governments

A government deciding what to do with its currency must consider important—often conflicting—trade-offs and domestic interests. One dimension of conflict involves whether the currency should be fixed, floating, or somewhere in between. Each choice helps some domestic actors and hurts others.

Fixed exchange rates, such as the gold standard or a peg to the dollar, provide currency stability and predictability, which greatly facilitate international trade, investment, finance, migration, and travel. Under the gold standard, business people, investors, and immigrants did not have to worry about changes in exchange rates or about major impediments to moving money around the world. The stimulus to trade was substantial; being on gold in this period is estimated to have raised trade between any two countries by 30–70 percent.[2] A fixed currency also provides a monetary anchor that keeps prices stable. It is thus very much in the interests of those engaged in cross-border economic exchange as well as those who want to keep inflation low.

However, there are costs to fixing the exchange rate, so some people and governments are strongly opposed to it. By definition, a government on a fixed exchange rate is committed to maintaining its currency's value, even if economic conditions could be improved with a change. A fixed rate reduces or eliminates a

---

2. See, for example, Antoni Estevadeordal, Brian Frantz, and Alan M. Taylor, "The Rise and Fall of World Trade, 1870–1939," *Quarterly Journal of Economics* 118, no. 2 (May 2003): 359–407; and J. Ernesto López-Córdova and Christopher M. Meissner, "Exchange-Rate Regimes and International Trade: Evidence from the Classical Gold Standard Era," *American Economic Review* 93, no. 1 (March 2003): 344–53.

MAP 9.1 *Exchange-Rate Regimes, 2019*

Today, several of the world's major economies, including the United States and Japan, allow the value of their currency to float independently. However, exchange-rate regimes around the world span a wide spectrum, from those that have given up their national currency, such as countries in the eurozone, to those that peg the value of their currency to the dollar, the euro, or other currencies. Countries with a "crawling peg" or "managed floating currency" can be considered to have floating exchange rates, though with some limits on changes in the value of the currency.

FIXED RATE REGIMES

No national currency
- USES DOLLAR
- USES EURO
- USES CFA FRANC

Fixed peg arrangements
- PEGGED TO DOLLAR
- PEGGED TO EURO
- PEGGED TO "OTHER"

FLOATING RATE REGIMES
- CRAWLING PEG
- MANAGED FLOATING CURRENCY
- INDEPENDENTLY FLOATING CURRENCY

Map source: International Monetary Fund, *Annual Report on Exchange Arrangements and Exchange Restrictions 2019*, August 10, 2020, www.imf.org/en/Publications/Annual-Report-on-Exchange-Arrangements-and-Exchange-Restrictions/Issues/2020/08/10/Annual-Report-on-Exchange-Arrangements-and-Exchange-Restrictions-2019-47102 (accessed 1/29/21).

Arctic Ocean

UNITED
KINGDOM
NORWAY
SWEDEN
FINLAND
NETH.
GERMANY
IRELAND
FRANCE
BELARUS
UKRAINE
RUSSIA
KAZAKHSTAN
MONGOLIA
N. KOREA
S. KOREA
JAPAN
GEORGIA
UZBEKISTAN
KYRGYZSTAN
PORTUGAL
SPAIN
ITALY
SERBIA
GREECE
TURKEY
TURKMENISTAN
TAJIKISTAN
CHINA
MOROCCO
ISRAEL
LEB.
SYRIA
IRAQ
IRAN
NEPAL
BHUTAN
HONG KONG
Pacific Ocean
ALGERIA
LIBYA
JORDAN
KUWAIT
MYANMAR
(BURMA)
TAIWAN
SAUDI
ARABIA
EGYPT
UAE
INDIA
VIETNAM
MAURITANIA
SENEGAL
MALI
NIGER
ERITREA
OMAN
PAKISTAN
THAILAND
LAOS
PHILIPPINES
MARSHALL
ISLANDS
CHAD
SUDAN
YEMEN
AFGHANISTAN
BANGLADESH
CAMBODIA
PALAU
MICRONESIA
GUINEA
NIGERIA
CEN.
AFR.
REP.
S. SUDAN
ETHIOPIA
MALAYSIA
GHANA
CAMEROON
SRI LANKA
INDONESIA
PAPUA NEW GUINEA
IVORY COAST
D.R.
CONGO
UGANDA
KENYA
SOMALIA
MALDIVES
TANZANIA
Indian Ocean
ANGOLA
ZAMBIA
MALAWI
MADAGASCAR
NAMIBIA
MOZAMBIQUE
ZIMBABWE
AUSTRALIA
SOUTH
AFRICA
BOTSWANA
NEW
ZEALAND

A currency exchange-rate board, like this one in Tehran, Iran, is a familiar sight for foreign travelers. Travelers to foreign countries find that their money goes further when their home country's currency is strong relative to the local currency. The same is true when goods are traded across borders; buyers find that foreign goods are less expensive when their own currency is relatively stronger.

government's ability to have its own independent monetary policy, which can be costly. For example, if an economy is in recession, a common economic policy response is to lower interest rates and thereby promote borrowing to expand domestic consumption and investment. This move stimulates the economy, as mentioned earlier, and may help alleviate the recession.

But if a country is on a fixed exchange rate, its interest rates are dictated by the need to keep the currency's value constant. For example, if the exchange rate threatens to depreciate, the government will have to raise interest rates in order to encourage investors to buy its currency. This is the case even in difficult economic times, when there can be strong pressures for the government to allow the currency to depreciate so as to make the country's goods more attractive to foreign consumers. The government's commitment to a fixed exchange rate makes this impossible.

A fixed exchange rate, of course, makes the central bank—the institution charged with running domestic monetary policy—much less influential, and central bankers may have reservations about giving up their ability to control interest rates. More generally, producers of goods that compete on import or export markets might want the government to be able to change the currency's value so that it becomes easier for them to sell their products. But this is impossible with a fixed exchange rate.

Fixed-currency constraints were at work in the run-up to the 2001 Argentine crisis. In 2001, the Argentine peso had been tightly fixed to the U.S. dollar for 10 years, but the Argentine economy was in great distress. There were powerful pressures for the government to address broader economic conditions—in particular, to lower interest rates and to depreciate the currency so that Argentine goods would become more competitive on international markets. To carry out this strategy, the Argentine government needed to loosen the peso's link to the dollar. But at the same time, many Argentines did not want to see the peso's value change; among them were millions of homeowners whose mortgages were in dollars and who would have had to pay substantially more in pesos if the currency was devalued. With powerful interests on both sides, the Argentine government was paralyzed.

Members of the eurozone similarly faced the constraints of a fixed exchange rate after 2008. As the global financial crisis deepened and the European debt crisis worsened, some countries that used the euro, such as Greece, Ireland, Spain, and Portugal, faced severe economic difficulties. If those countries had their own national monies, they could have loosened monetary policy and depreciated their currencies. This action would have made their goods cheaper for other countries, increasing the amount of goods they exported and thus bringing more money back into the country. By selling more, their economies would have grown faster, and perhaps they could have exported their way out of recession. But because these nations were part of a multicountry currency union, whose monetary and exchange-rate policies were set in Frankfurt by the European Central Bank (ECB) on behalf of the entire eurozone, they simply did not have the tools of monetary and exchange-rate policy in their arsenals as they attempted to confront the crisis.

The problems that a fixed exchange rate caused for the Argentine and eurozone governments demonstrate one important advantage of a floating exchange rate: floating rates give governments more freedom to pursue their own monetary policies, as they are not hampered by the need to keep their exchange rates fixed. But this advantage is countered by the fact that floating exchange rates can move around a great deal, which can impose costs on those engaged in international trade and investment and can impede international economic exchange more generally. Volatility (that is, frequent significant shifts) in currency values almost certainly makes international trade and investment, travel, and finance more difficult.[3]

Consumers and Businesses

Depending on their position in the economy, different actors have different interests, and often conflicting views, about how the national currency should be managed. Those whose economic activities are entirely domestic are likely to favor a floating exchange rate, because they are indifferent to currency fluctuations but want the government to be able to affect the national economy as necessary. Those with international economic concerns have an interest in a fixed currency because too much volatility in exchange rates can be harmful to their activities.

Just as people, firms, and groups may have conflicting interests over whether a currency should be fixed or floating, actors' interests may also differ over a currency's desirable value (that is, whether it should be stronger or weaker). Government policy can have a powerful impact on whether a currency's value rises or falls in the short and medium run, which in turn can affect important domestic interests.

A strong exchange rate allows consumers and others to buy more of the world's products, thereby increasing national purchasing power. But there is a trade-off: a strong exchange rate makes domestic goods more expensive to foreigners, which harms national producers who compete with foreigners on local or world markets. This is why manufacturers and farmers typically complain about a strong currency: it leads to a surge of cheaper imports, and it dampens exports.

For example, the U.S. dollar appreciated by more than 50 percent between 1981 and 1985. This rise in value was associated with a big increase in Americans' purchasing power and ability to buy goods from the rest of the world and travel abroad—all of

---

3. The specific constraints on exchange-rate policy are known as the Mundell-Fleming conditions, after the two economists who pioneered the approach. They imply, simply put, that in a financially integrated country, the government must choose between a stable exchange rate and an independent monetary policy; it cannot have both. See, for example, Jeffry A. Frieden, "Invested Interests: The Politics of National Economic Policies in a World of Global Finance," *International Organization* 45, no. 4 (Autumn 1991): 425–51.

which contributed to a sense of prosperity among American consumers. However, the strong dollar led to a flood of cheaper imports into the United States and made U.S. exports more expensive to foreigners. As a result, serious problems arose in American manufacturing industries, and 1.5 million manufacturing jobs were lost.

The strong dollar was particularly damaging to firms that either sold many of their products abroad or competed with imports; it led the president of one such firm, Caterpillar Tractor, to call the strong dollar "the single most important trade issue facing the U.S." Under pressure, in 1985 the Senate passed a unanimous resolution calling on President Ronald Reagan's administration to depreciate the dollar.[4] Eventually, the dollar did decline, and complaints subsided.

A weak currency gives a big boost to national producers. This is why countries that are trying to encourage exports—such as many developing countries—typically keep their currencies weak. It is also why manufacturers and farmers, who compete with foreign producers both at home and abroad, have an interest in a relatively weak exchange rate. But there is a trade-off here too: a weak currency reduces national purchasing power, making consumers worse off. As the dollar declines, Americans can buy fewer of the world's products—and tourists cannot afford foreign vacations so easily. Declines in a currency's value and increases in prices of foreign goods can also contribute to overall price rises and inflation.

Both strong and weak currencies have advantages and disadvantages, and there is no particular reason that one or the other is better for a country. A strong currency helps consumers (and tourists) but hurts producers who compete with foreigners; a weak currency helps producers but hurts consumers. These conflicts of interest make currency policy controversial within countries and can make governments sensitive to the domestic political and economic effects of their currency arrangements.

Such conflicts are evident when the possibility arises that a government might devalue its currency. Because the devaluation makes foreign goods more expensive and domestic goods relatively cheaper, it is in the interests of national producers. But the devaluation also reduces consumers' ability to buy goods and services. In this context, it is perhaps not surprising that governments in democratic systems typically avoid currency devaluations or depreciations in the run-up to elections, for fear that the negative impact on consumers will cost them votes.[5]

A government's interest in exchange-rate policy depends on the structure of its economy, its interest groups, and its political system. In a country with many firms and individuals engaged in economic activities across borders, the government is likely to face powerful pressure to stabilize or fix the currency's value. This is why the smaller economies of Europe that were extremely open to trade with other European countries (such as the Netherlands, Belgium, Luxembourg, Austria, and Ireland) were among the strongest supporters of the creation of the euro in the 1990s. More recently, among the newer members of the European Union, it is the

---

4. Jeffry A. Frieden, "Economic Integration and the Politics of Monetary Policy in the United States," in *Internationalization and Domestic Politics*, ed. Robert O. Keohane and Helen V. Milner (Cambridge: Cambridge University Press, 1996), 127–30.

5. S. Brock Blomberg, Jeffry Frieden, and Ernesto Stein, "Sustaining Fixed Rates: The Political Economy of Currency Pegs in Latin America," *Journal of Applied Economics* 8, no. 2 (November 2005): 203–25.

smaller countries—Estonia, Latvia, Lithuania, Slovenia—that have most enthusiastically adopted the euro. During the evolution of the euro, some larger European economies that did not trade and invest as much across European borders (such as France and Italy) were less favorably inclined to currency union, although they eventually joined the eurozone. Similarly, some of the larger, newer members today, most prominently Poland, resist joining the euro.

This is also why small countries in the Western Hemisphere that are tightly tied to U.S. trade, investment, and tourism (such as many Caribbean island nations, El Salvador, and Panama) have been the most likely to adopt the U.S. dollar or to fix their currencies to it. Larger, more self-sufficient economies (like Mexico and Brazil) have typically allowed their currencies to vary.

In preparation for Lithuania's adoption of the euro on January 1, 2015, a store lists prices in litas, the former national currency, alongside prices in euros.

One currency policy that has been the source of much controversy in recent decades is the tendency of some governments to keep their currency very weak over long periods of time in order to stimulate their exports. China offers the most prominent example of this tactic. After 1979, it organized its development strategy around the promotion of manufactured goods for export, and toward this end it kept the Chinese currency, the renminbi, artificially weak. The export promotion policy was very successful, and China has become one of the world's greatest exporters.

But if the government had let the dollars its exporters earned come back into the Chinese economy, they would have been used to buy renminbi for local purchases, and the renminbi would have appreciated against the dollar. This, in turn, would have made Chinese exports less attractive on world markets. So the Chinese government used a series of measures to keep its currency depreciated. It controlled capital flows and the domestic market for foreign currency, and it held very large reserves of dollars overseas (keeping them from coming back to China to be spent).

Though the Chinese government's currency policies were successful at promoting the nation's exports, they created problems at home. Within China, the weak-currency policy effectively taxed consumers to benefit export producers. An artificially weak renminbi meant that Chinese residents had artificially low purchasing power. Chinese consumers and the country's growing middle class complained that the average Chinese person had not gotten the full benefit of the country's rapid economic growth and that disproportionate benefits had gone to the exporters.

Another set of problems was international: China's trading partners, in particular the United States, complained with increasing vehemence that the artificial weakness of the renminbi was an unfair trading practice. This dispute has threatened to break into open trade conflict between the United States and China on many occasions since 1990. (For more on recent developments, see "Controversy" on p. 420.)

Should Countries Be Allowed to Manipulate Their Currencies?

During his 2016 campaign for the presidency, Donald Trump promised that, as president, he would "label China a currency manipulator" within his first 100 days in office.[a] In April 2017, however, just before the hundredth day of his term, President Trump announced that he would not, in fact, follow through on this threat. Why had then candidate Trump been concerned about China manipulating its currency? What did his threat to label them "manipulators" imply? Why did he not carry out his promise? More generally, what is currency manipulation, and should it be discouraged, even punished, by other countries or by international institutions?

Applying the Concepts

A country may have an **interest** in "manipulating" its currency, or intervening in currency markets to alter the currency's value, in order to give its producers a competitive advantage in international markets. This policy often leads to bitter **interactions** between the country and its trading partners, who resent the policy's impact on their own producers. There are domestic and international **institutions** in place that are meant to address currency manipulation. Nonetheless, the issue remains controversial: some leaders and analysts believe that national governments should be permitted to set their currency's value as they wish.

Controversies over currency manipulation typically arise when a government sells its own currency (and buys other currencies) in order to weaken its exchange rate. A weaker (depreciated) currency reduces the price of domestic goods to foreigners and makes it more attractive for foreigners to buy the country's goods. Many developing countries purposely keep their currencies weak because they want to stimulate exports. East Asian countries, in particular, have often kept their exchange rates artificially depreciated to encourage domestic manufacturers to produce for world markets. Japan, South Korea, and Taiwan have all pursued this strategy at different points in their histories.

Most governments oppose currency manipulation by their trading partners. Although their own consumers benefit, they usually face a backlash from domestic producers who, when confronted with cheaper imports, demand that their government do something to relieve the competitive pressure on them. As a result, nations often strongly criticize countries that manipulate their currencies. In some cases, these conflicts lead to threats of retaliation and other countermeasures.

After China opened to the world economy in 1979, and especially after 1990, there were many accusations that it was manipulating its currency—the renminbi—in order to give Chinese manufacturers an advantage in world markets. Most analysts would agree that Chinese government policy did artificially weaken the renminbi. While Chinese export manufacturers benefited from this policy because it enabled them to sell more of their goods abroad, producers who competed with Chinese exports—including many European and American manufacturers—believed they were harmed by China's policy. Chinese consumers were also hurt by a weak currency because it reduced their purchasing power, and European and American consumers benefited because they could buy Chinese goods more cheaply.

In an effort to avoid conflicts over currency manipulation, the International Monetary Fund (IMF) and the

---

a. "Donald Trump's Contract with the Voter," https://assets
.donaldjtrump.com/_landings/contract/O-TRU-102316-Contractv02
.pdf (accessed 1/28/21).

World Trade Organization (WTO) have rules against it. Despite the importance of these international institutions, however, they have little enforcement power in this realm. These issues are usually dealt with in bilateral interactions between the country accused of manipulating its currency and that country's trading partners.

Interactions between the United States and countries that it considers to be currency manipulators have often been conflictual. Under then existing U.S. law, the Treasury Department declared Japan a currency manipulator in 1988, Taiwan in 1988 and 1992, and China between 1992 and 1994. In these cases, the United States put pressure on these countries to stop the practice, and eventually the Treasury Department found that the manipulation had ceased. But complaints persisted, especially as China's exports to the United States continued to grow.

A 2015 law gave the U.S. government more tools to punish alleged manipulators, including the ability to cut off some government funds to the country in question and the option to reevaluate existing trade agreements. When Donald Trump promised to label China a currency manipulator, he was threatening to impose these and potentially other sanctions on a country that he regarded as harming American economic interests.

Why didn't Trump follow through? For one thing, by the time President Trump took office, most economic analyses indicated that China was not trying to weaken its currency. In fact, the Chinese government appeared to be trying hard to prevent weakening of the renminbi. For another thing, the Trump administration felt that labeling China a currency manipulator would interfere with its own efforts to secure China's cooperation in dealing with an increasingly troubling problem: North Korea's acquisition of nuclear weapons. For both economic and diplomatic reasons, then, President Trump did not label China a currency manipulator. In 2019, though, after declaring a trade war on China, the Trump administration did in fact declare that China was manipulating its currency, only to rescind the finding a few months later as negotiations progressed.

The broader question remains: Should international institutions, or individual governments, try to punish a government for manipulating its currency? After all, many analysts believe that poor countries should have weak currencies to stimulate exports and production more generally, and consumers in rich countries benefit when they can buy more inexpensive goods from weak-currency countries. Others, however, argue that a government that artificially weakens its currency is putting unfair

China has faced accusations that it was artificially weakening the value of its currency, the renminbi.

competitive pressures on producers in other nations, thereby potentially provoking protectionist retaliation.

To some extent, currency manipulation is simply a clash of interests. It helps exporters in the country whose currency is weak, and it helps consumers in other nations. These benefits come at the expense of producers in other countries and of consumers in the manipulating country. Normally, currency manipulation might simply be the source of conflictual interactions within and between countries. However, when the country accused of manipulating its currency plays a large role in international trade—such as China, or Japan in earlier years—conflicts over currency manipulation can spill over into trade conflicts. To the extent that these disagreements become a source of friction in international trade and other economic relations, they may be of broader international importance.

Thinking Analytically

1. Which groups within the United States are most likely to be harmed by Chinese currency manipulation to lower the value of the renminbi? Why? Are there U.S. groups that benefit when the renminbi is weaker relative to the dollar?

2. Why might China have decided at a certain point that changing course and propping up the value of its currency was in its economic interest?

3. When it comes to the role of international institutions, what are some arguments for their punishing currency manipulators? What are some arguments against their doing so?

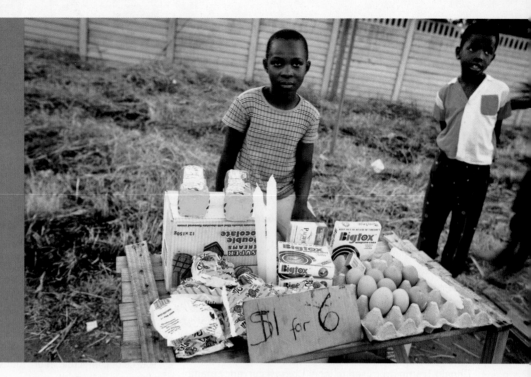

Countries with unstable economies may choose to fix their currency's value to that of a more stable currency, such as the U.S. dollar or the euro. Other countries have no national currency at all. In Zimbabwe, for example, the U.S. dollar is the most widely used of the country's legally acceptable currencies.

National currency policy implicates contending interests and complex institutions within countries. As disputes over China's currency indicate, the matter is doubly complicated because one government's exchange-rate policy inevitably affects other countries' policies. This observation takes us to the international level, where national governments interact over the structure of the international monetary system.

International Politics and International Monetary Relations

A monetary system is crucial to any modern economy; this is also true of the international economy, which requires some institutional arrangement to permit trade, investment, and other payments across borders. Each national government is responsible for a *national* monetary order that provides a trusted money with a predictable value so that prices are stable. There is no international government to arrange an *international* monetary order. However, there is certainly a need for some system to provide predictability in currency values so that firms and people can reliably compare prices across borders.

If traders, investors, tourists, and others had no idea what exchange rates would be tomorrow or next week, they would be very reluctant to engage in exchange across borders. For the international economy to work well, there must be some predictability to currency values so that people can reasonably expect that the dollar or peso they are earning today will be worth something tomorrow.

A stable and predictable monetary arrangement that allows firms and people to compare prices and transact business from one nation to another benefits almost everyone. Governments and people tend to share a desire for a general commitment to a common international monetary order. In this sense, a common regime is a Pareto improvement over a world in which there is no agreement on global monetary relations; that is, it makes all countries better off—or at least as well off—and none worse off. Agreement on a monetary regime thus has many features of a public good: everyone benefits if there is a smoothly functioning way to carry out international economic transactions.

As with most public goods, however, the provision of this monetary order is not automatic or easy. Since there is no one global institution to provide a global monetary order, a functioning order requires conscious efforts by individual national governments to alter their own policies, to contribute funds to stabilize other countries' currencies, or to otherwise help sustain the system. In the absence of a world government and a world money, many institutional arrangements have emerged to provide this global public good. Under the classical gold standard of the nineteenth and early twentieth centuries, gold was the common denominator for international transactions. Under the Bretton Woods monetary system, which prevailed from 1945 to 1973, the dollar was the centerpiece of the monetary order.

But there can be disagreements over the nature of the international monetary system and every country's place in it; the different actors in the international political economy may have conflicting interests about the kinds of international monetary institutions they would like to see in place. Governments and people often prefer different standards. During the days of the classical gold standard, for example, many people and governments—including some powerful political movements—preferred a silver standard to a gold standard.

Supporters of silver typically believed that if silver, which was plentiful, served as money, prices would be higher than they would be with gold, which was scarce. Adoption of a silver standard rather than a gold standard, they believed, would thus help raise the prices of goods they produced. By the same token, during the decades of the Bretton Woods monetary system, Americans were quite satisfied with a system that put the dollar at its center, but Europeans were less enthusiastic. International monetary relations are infused with this tension between sources of conflict and reasons for cooperation.

International Monetary Cooperation and Conflict

Just as there are conflicting interests within countries over national policy, there are conflicts of interest among countries over international monetary arrangements. It can be difficult to organize collaboration among governments to provide the public good of international monetary stability because there are powerful incentives to free ride on the efforts of others. Governments of smaller countries might reason that their contributions are too trivial to matter and thus not participate; if enough governments follow this path, cooperation will break down. For example, a global fixed-rate system such as the gold standard can facilitate international trade and investment, but the government of a small country might decide that it can benefit from the global system without fixing its own currency and tying its hands. If enough countries take this route, the system will collapse.

A successful international monetary regime depends on interactions among the governments of the world's major economies. The behavior of these governments sets the standards for the regime as a whole, and it is their responsibility to address problems involving other countries as they arise. However, governments also face major temptations to "cheat" on their international monetary commitments. In a fixed-rate regime, for example, one government might decide to devalue in order to make its producers' goods more competitive on world markets. Other countries might respond by devaluing their own currencies to allow their producers to match.

The result is akin to the undesirable outcome of a Prisoner's Dilemma game (see the "Special Topic" appendix to Chapter 2). If every nation engages in competitive devaluations, all currencies end up being devalued, and nobody gains any advantage. Meanwhile, the currency turmoil can throw international monetary relations into disorder and uncertainty, thereby interfering with normal economic activities.

Interactions among national governments, facing incentives both to cooperate and to enter into conflict, have determined the character of international monetary relations over time, including the emergence of global and regional monetary institutions. In the following section, we take a closer look at the evolution of international monetary arrangements over the past couple of centuries.

International Monetary Regimes

international monetary regime

A formal or informal arrangement shared by most countries in the world economy to govern relations among their currencies.

The decisions of individual national governments to float or to fix their currencies interact to create an **international monetary regime**—that is, an arrangement, which may be formal and institutionalized or informal, that is widely accepted to govern relations among currencies and that is shared by most countries in the world economy. There may also be regional monetary regimes that prevail in particular geographic regions, such as the eurozone in Europe.

The existence of a generally accepted international monetary regime has clear benefits for the international community in general, since it facilitates international economic exchange. It may come, however, with national-level sacrifices, as we will see. First we define the characteristics of international monetary regimes.

International monetary regimes have two principal features. The first makes clear whether currency values are expected to be fixed, floating, or a mix of both. As discussed already, the classical gold standard and the Bretton Woods monetary system were international fixed-rate regimes (although the Bretton Woods monetary system allowed for occasional adjustments). The contemporary regime is based on floating rates; there is no general agreement that national currency values should be fixed.

The second feature of an international monetary regime is agreement about whether there will be a mutually accepted benchmark against which values are measured—some common base or standard to which currencies can be compared. Three such standards have been used over time: a commodity standard, a commodity-backed paper standard, and a national paper currency standard.

A *commodity standard* uses a good with value of its own as the basic monetary unit. Typically, this good is a precious metal such as gold or silver. Under the classical gold standard that prevailed from the 1870s until 1914, for example, all major national currencies had a fixed value in terms of gold, and they could be exchanged freely on the basis of their gold equivalent. This was a fixed-rate regime based on gold as the commodity standard.

A *commodity-backed paper standard* is similar to the Bretton Woods monetary system that prevailed from 1945 to 1973. Under such a regime, national governments issue paper currency with a fixed value in terms of gold (or some other commodity). This is one step removed from a pure gold standard, as it requires that governments be able to commit credibly to stand ready to redeem the currency for gold. Nonetheless, under such a standard, national currency values are comparable because they are all expressed in terms of a common commodity: gold. Under the Bretton Woods monetary system, the U.S. dollar was fixed to gold, while all other currencies were fixed to the dollar.

Under a *national paper currency standard*, national currencies are backed only by the commitments of their issuing governments to support them. In this context, people want to know that the government will act to ensure that the national currency continues to be valuable. Although this may not mean committing to a fixed rate, it does mean committing to the currency not losing so much value as to become undesirable. Foreigners who hold dollars or euros, or who accept promises of payment in dollars or euros, do so with the expectation that even if exchange rates do change, dollars and euros will continue to be valuable national monies. Typically, only a few major currencies are used for international exchange—usually, the currencies of the world's most important trading and financial powers. This is the system that has prevailed since 1973. Today, most international exchange is measured and conducted in the dollar and the euro.

A Short History of International Monetary Systems

The modern international economy has experienced all three of these kinds of international monetary regimes.

The Gold Standard   Under the classical gold standard, most of the world's major economies had gold or gold-backed currencies tied together at exchange rates that did not change for decades. The portion of the world that was on gold—which eventually came to include every major economy except China and Persia—effectively had a common money: gold.

The stability of the classical gold standard relied on close ties among the three leading financial powers of the day—Britain, France, and Germany—along with support from smaller European nations. For example, when the 1890 collapse of Barings, a major British bank, threatened to destabilize the London markets, the central banks of France and Russia lent large sums to the Bank of England. The mere knowledge that enough money was available to address the problem helped calm investors. In 1898, the British and French helped stabilize German financial markets; a few years later, the Austrians helped calm the Berlin market. And at least seven more times between 1900 and 1914, the French stepped in to assist the British in order to stabilize the gold standard.[6]

The gold standard provided currency stability and predictability, which greatly facilitated international trade, investment, finance, migration, and travel. Most of the world's governments and many countries' citizens agreed that this common monetary standard was generally beneficial. Such a confluence of interests among the major financial centers allowed them to interact cooperatively to sustain the gold standard for many decades.

However, the costs to being on gold made some people and governments less enthusiastic. As we saw in our discussion of fixed-rate systems, governments on the gold standard gave up the ability to run their own independent monetary policy, which implied a serious loss of economic policy influence. In the United States, the gold standard was very controversial; in fact, the 1896 presidential campaign was largely fought around it. William McKinley and the Republicans ran in favor of maintaining the country's commitment to gold, but many Americans were hostile to the gold standard. The anti-gold forces, led by the Populists, wanted the government to take the dollar off gold and put it on silver at a different rate.

The move to silver would have accomplished two things: it would have devalued the dollar, making American exports more competitive, and it would have raised American prices domestically. Farmers in particular liked the idea of a devaluation, as many of them produced for export markets. They, and others, also liked the idea of raising prices, as many of them were heavily indebted, and an increase in prices could have reduced their real debt burden (the debts would have remained the same, while prices for farm products would have risen). Therefore, the Democratic Party and the Populists united around William Jennings Bryan, who famously said to gold supporters, "You shall not crucify mankind upon a cross of gold!"

Bryan lost in 1896 and again in 1900 and 1908, although the anti-gold movement he represented remained strong. (See "What Shaped Our World?" for more on this episode of U.S. history.) Nonetheless, in the major U.S. financial centers there was enough domestic political support for the international cooperation necessary to sustain the gold standard that it was solid and extensive for almost 50 years, from the 1870s until 1914.

The gold standard was suspended when World War I started in 1914, and major governments tried to restore it once the war ended. In the 1920s and 1930s, however, these attempts proved largely unsuccessful. Most countries did go on gold

---

6. For a classic account of the gold-standard era and the interwar collapse of the gold standard, see Barry Eichengreen, *Golden Fetters: The Gold Standard and the Great Depression, 1919–1939* (New York: Oxford University Press, 1992).

The Wizard of Oz and the Gold Standard

The gold standard was a central institution of the late nineteenth and early twentieth centuries. This international monetary system and the political battles over it were so prominent that one of the most famous children's stories of all time may well be a parable about the politics of exchange rates in the gold-standard era.

The book *The Wonderful Wizard of Oz* was first published in 1900; the film version was released in 1939. The story chronicles the adventures of Dorothy, a girl from Kansas whose house is swept up in a tornado and transported to a magical place populated by munchkins, witches, and other strange creatures. The Good Witch of the North counsels Dorothy to follow the yellow brick road to the Emerald City and seek the help of the Wizard of Oz to return home to Kansas. The Good Witch also gives Dorothy a pair of magic slippers. Dorothy skips along the yellow brick road and meets a brainless scarecrow, a tin man without a heart, and a cowardly lion. Together, this motley team battles the Wicked Witch of the West to gain access to the venerable wizard. At the end of the story, they realize that the wizard is a fraud, but fortunately the Good Witch reappears and informs Dorothy that she can return home simply by clicking together her magic slippers.

What does *The Wizard of Oz* have to do with exchange-rate politics? A little background on the gold standard will help to elucidate the symbolism in the story.

Institutions Starting in the 1870s, the U.S. government officially agreed to exchange dollars for gold at a fixed

rate of one ounce of gold for $20.67. This institution was intended to facilitate international trade and financial flows. However, one problem with this policy was that the domestic money supply was fixed to the availability of gold. If businesses produced more goods and services but the stock of gold remained steady, then prices would fall. This was indeed the case throughout much of the 1880s and 1890s. Because the United States was on the gold standard, it was not able to lower interest rates or allow the currency to depreciate, both of which would have boosted prices and stimulated the economy.

Interests Falling prices harmed nearly everyone, but they were especially harmful to farmers who sold their grain on world markets and borrowed money from banks to finance their operations. With the price of grain declining, farmers had difficulty earning enough to repay their debts. Industrial workers also faced tough times as unemployment increased. The dire economic conditions of the 1890s helped to fuel the Populist movement, led by Democratic presidential candidate William Jennings Bryan. He wanted to replace the gold standard with an alternative system that would help increase the money supply—in particular, a system that included silver, a much more plentiful commodity. Bryan ultimately lost the 1896 election to William McKinley, a Republican who supported the gold standard.

Interactions With this background in mind, we return to the symbolism in *The Wizard of Oz*, which was written just a few years after the 1896 election. Dorothy, representing the naive American public, believes that her problems will be solved if she simply follows a winding road paved with gold bricks. She meets a scarecrow (a farmer), a tin man (an industrial worker), and a lion whose roar masks his cowardice (Bryan). When Dorothy finally meets the Wizard (McKinley), she realizes that he is a fraud. In response, she simply clicks her slippers together to transport herself back home. In the original book, the slippers were silver.

The symbolism in *The Wizard of Oz* (note that *oz* is an abbreviation for *ounce*) reflects the political and cultural importance of different monetary systems.

again after World War I ended, but the sort of international monetary cooperation that had allowed the classical gold standard to succeed had become difficult to organize. Countries such as France and Germany were on very poor terms diplomatically, which created an atmosphere of distrust that impeded efforts to negotiate monetary collaboration. As interests diverged, interactions among the major financial players became more hostile.

This failure to cooperate in the 1920s was exacerbated by the Great Depression, which began in 1929. Faced with massive crises, governments were unwilling to forgo an economic policy that might allow them to alleviate the suffering of their citizens. After 1929, virtually all the governments that had gone on gold in the 1920s went back off it as they tried to resuscitate their failing national economies. The result was a floating-rate system based on paper national currencies. This system led to a great deal of currency volatility and instability, including many competitive devaluations, and probably contributed to the overall collapse of the international economy in the 1930s. In any case, monetary disorder was overwhelmed by the economic and military conflicts of the 1930s and 1940s.

The Bretton Woods Monetary System
As World War II drew to a close, the United States and Great Britain led the victorious Allies in designing an international monetary order that represented a fundamental reform of the gold standard. The Bretton Woods monetary system—so called because the agreements were negotiated at the Bretton Woods resort in New Hampshire—was organized around the U.S. dollar, and the dollar was tied to gold at the fixed rate of $35 per ounce.[7] Although other currencies were tied to the dollar, and thus indirectly to gold, their governments were permitted to adjust them as necessary.

This system was seen as a compromise between the inflexibility of the gold standard and the volatility of interwar currency relations. The Bretton Woods monetary order kept exchange rates stable enough to encourage international economic exchange. Unlike the gold standard, the system permitted governments other than the United States to change their currencies' values as needed, although frequent changes were frowned upon. The Bretton Woods monetary compromise kept currency values stable and currency markets open, contributing to the growth of international trade and investment while allowing national governments to pursue national policies in line with domestic conditions.

Like the gold standard, the Bretton Woods monetary system relied on collaboration among its leading members. It was sustained in large part because the Western allies after World War II saw it as an important component of their economic and military alliance structure, just as the West's willingness to undertake international trade liberalization was related to its geopolitical alliances. There was thus a confluence of both economic and noneconomic interests among Western nations that facilitated cooperation. This cooperation was reminiscent of that which

---

7. The term *Bretton Woods System* is sometimes used to describe the post–World War II international economic order more generally; we use the term *Bretton Woods monetary system* more narrowly to describe the currency order.

Representatives of 44 countries met at the Bretton Woods conference in 1944 and negotiated a new monetary system organized around the U.S. dollar. After the turbulence of the interwar years and World War II, the Bretton Woods monetary system succeeded in bringing stability to currency values.

prevailed during the classical gold standard: under Bretton Woods, as under the gold standard, for example, it was common for the world's major national central banks to lend money to each other in times of crisis.

Under the Bretton Woods monetary system, the International Monetary Fund (IMF) was established as the principal institution to monitor interstate interactions related to exchange rates. During this period, the IMF was charged with overseeing currency relations and with providing support to countries in need of short-term help to keep their exchange rates stable. The IMF made information available to members and provided currency-related standards of behavior that countries were expected to follow. The backing of the major Western financial powers, along with the institutional support of the IMF, was central to the stability of the Bretton Woods monetary system.

Eventually, however, international monetary cooperation failed because of fundamental disagreements among countries. By the early 1970s, the U.S. government was unwilling to make the sacrifices necessary to keep the dollar fixed to gold. President Richard Nixon believed that the Bretton Woods commitments constrained American economic policy more than was acceptable, and the U.S. government felt itself too restricted by the rigid link between the dollar and gold. It eventually broke that link in order to give itself more monetary independence.

Today's International Monetary System Since 1973, international monetary relations have been based on floating exchange rates among a small number of major currencies, typically those of the principal industrial and financial nations (especially the United States, Japan, Germany, and Great Britain). While today's international monetary system does not depend on explicit commitments to fixed exchange rates, its orderly functioning still requires the major national governments to work together, especially in times of crisis.

Although the IMF was originally designed to monitor and assist the functioning of a modified fixed-rate international monetary order, the fund has remained important even after the shift to floating rates. When the major governments believe that exchange rates are fluctuating too wildly, they can coordinate their monetary policies to try to reduce these wide swings; the IMF sometimes serves as the venue for these sorts of discussions. At times, currency problems in developing countries have led the major financial powers to intervene to attempt to stabilize exchange rates and keep a crisis from spreading; again, the IMF frequently participates in such attempts at crisis management and sometimes leads them.

Diverse alignments of national interests and patterns of strategic interaction among states help account for different international monetary outcomes. It is striking that both the gold standard and the Bretton Woods monetary system each relied in major ways on the leadership of one country—Great Britain and the United States, respectively. Nonetheless, the participation of other major financial and monetary powers was needed to keep the systems going, so a sense of common interests was also crucial. As the collapse of both systems indicates, such participation can be difficult to sustain. It can be impeded by fundamental disagreements over how to share the costs of stabilizing the system or by a lack of trust among governments that the commitments of others will be honored.

Today's world of floating exchange rates presents a related set of problems. While the major powers do interact, generally cooperatively, to try to avoid major monetary disturbances, exchange rates still fluctuate quite widely. Since 1980, for example, the U.S. dollar has risen and fallen by very large amounts against other major currencies. While few people in the United States seem overly worried about this volatility, in smaller countries that trade more with the rest of the world, these currency fluctuations can be widely unpopular.

The current system is not monolithic (as was the gold standard) or organized (as was Bretton Woods), but it does have some clear defining features. Countries can allow their currencies to float freely, and large countries typically do; but smaller countries appear less enthusiastic about this currency volatility, and they often link their currency to that of a larger nation or bloc. The absence of an established global monetary system has, in fact, led some countries to try to develop regional monetary systems that can at least stabilize exchange rates among groups of countries.

Regional Monetary Arrangements: The Euro

In the absence of a global agreement on stabilizing currencies, some countries have tried to work out regional arrangements. Where countries can resolve problems of cooperation, a more orderly system can be maintained regionally even as monetary cooperation disintegrates globally. This was the strategy pursued by most of the members of the European Union after the collapse of the Bretton Woods monetary system. Most EU countries trade and invest a great deal with one another—an arrangement that leads them to want to limit exchange-rate fluctuations. Starting in 1973, they committed themselves to stabilizing exchange rates among EU member countries with the goal of eventually working toward a common currency.

But the road to the euro was not an easy one, for both domestic and interstate political reasons. Within countries, some interests were often less than enthusiastic about a common monetary policy. In practice, fixing EU exchange rates meant pegging them to the German currency (the Deutschmark); at the time, Germany was the largest economy in the European Union and had a long-standing commitment to keeping its currency, as well as its prices, stable.

In countries with currencies more inflated than Germany's, pegging the currency to the Deutschmark meant that governments would have to bring inflation down. The typical approach was to raise interest rates and implement austerity measures, such as restraining wages and cutting government spending. In France and Italy, labor unions and public employees, especially, felt that their interests would be sacrificed to the currency peg. It was not until 1985 that supporters of a fixed rate won out in these two countries. In Great Britain and Sweden, there were even fewer supporters of a fixed rate, and for most of the 1979–98 period during which the German-led system prevailed, these two nations kept their distance from the growing currency union.

At the regional level, interactions among the governments of the European Union were often conflictual. Because other EU currencies were fixed to the Deutschmark, other countries had to follow Germany's monetary policy. This arrangement was satisfactory as long as they all agreed on the course of German policy. In 1991, however, in the aftermath of the reunification of the eastern and western parts of Germany, the German central bank was concerned about inflation. To restrain prices, it raised interest rates very high. This measure, taken for entirely domestic reasons, forced the rest of the currency bloc to make a difficult choice. They too could raise interest rates and drive their economies into recession; or they could keep interest rates low, in which case money would flow out of their countries, toward Germany's higher interest rates, and force them to leave the peg. The eventual result was a currency crisis (discussed in more detail shortly)—and the decision by many EU members to break the Deutschmark link.

Movement toward currency union continued, nonetheless, because of domestic consensus in most EU countries on the desirability of stabilizing currencies—even at the cost of giving up national-level control over policy and, in many cases, a powerful national symbol, the currency. The next move was to plan for a common currency, the euro, to be managed by a common ECB. This measure appealed to countries other than Germany because it meant that European monetary policy would be made by a European, rather than a German, central bank and would presumably take European conditions as a whole into account.

Germany went along for several reasons. First, the ECB was to be based in Frankfurt, and its constitution was drafted to ensure that it would be very similar to the German central bank. These facts helped allay German fears that the new institution would stray too far from the low-inflation principles that Germans preferred. Second, Germany itself wanted a reduction in currency volatility in Europe, and it was clear that other EU members would not accept a continuation of the Deutschmark-based system. Third, the creation of the euro and the ECB was connected to a broad array of cooperative ventures among EU member governments on a wide range of

MAP 9.2 *Members of the Eurozone, 2021*

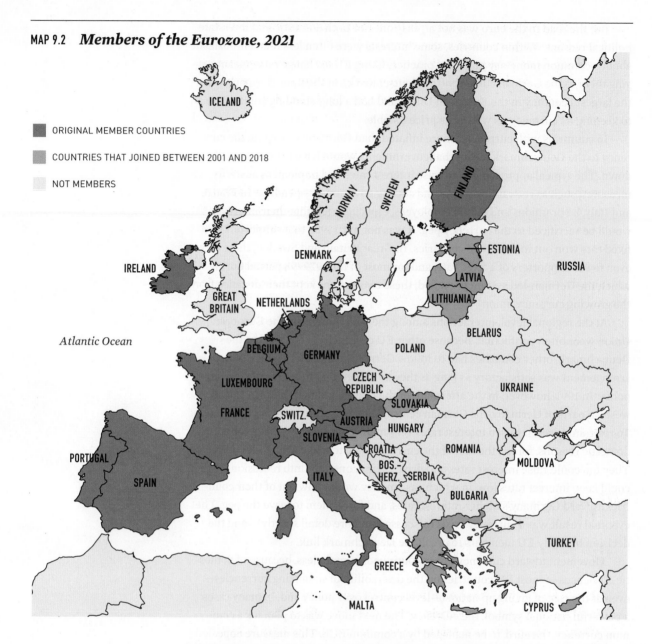

ORIGINAL MEMBER COUNTRIES

COUNTRIES THAT JOINED BETWEEN 2001 AND 2018

NOT MEMBERS

ICELAND

NORWAY

SWEDEN

FINLAND

DENMARK

ESTONIA

RUSSIA

LATVIA

LITHUANIA

IRELAND

GREAT BRITAIN

NETHERLANDS

BELARUS

Atlantic Ocean

BELGIUM

GERMANY

POLAND

LUXEMBOURG

CZECH REPUBLIC

UKRAINE

FRANCE

SWITZ.

SLOVAKIA

AUSTRIA

HUNGARY

SLOVENIA

CROATIA

ROMANIA

MOLDOVA

PORTUGAL

BOS.-HERZ.

SERBIA

SPAIN

ITALY

BULGARIA

TURKEY

GREECE

MALTA

CYPRUS

issues. Just as economic cooperation between the United States and western Europe was facilitated by their military alliance, monetary union among western European countries was facilitated by the fact that they had come to cooperate in so many other dimensions, from trade policy and antitrust law to foreign policy.

The combination of gradually emerging domestic consensus within most EU member countries and increasingly cooperative interactions among EU governments led to the adoption of the euro and its successful introduction as Europe's circulating money in 2002. As of 2021, 19 of 27 EU members share the euro, which is used by nearly 350 million people. (See Map 9.2 for members of the eurozone in 2021.)

The United Kingdom, which has since left the EU, was never a eurozone member. Denmark has not adopted the euro but has fixed its own currency against the euro very tightly. Sweden remains outside the eurozone, as do six other, newer members of the European Union in central and eastern Europe (Bulgaria, Croatia, the Czech Republic, Hungary, Poland, and Romania). Many in these countries are wary of how eurozone membership would restrict their ability to manage their own monetary policies. This wariness has been heightened by the fact that the eurozone itself was recently wracked by a crisis that threatened its very unity (which we will discuss shortly).

The creation of this regional currency union reflected the interests of many countries to stabilize their exchange rates in a time of turbulence. There are several other such regional currency arrangements. For example, 14 central and western African countries share a common currency, which is pegged to the euro; and eight Caribbean island nations and territories share the common East Caribbean dollar, pegged to the U.S. dollar.

Many other countries deal with concern over currency volatility by pursuing unilateral measures, such as adopting another currency (for example, Panama, Ecuador, El Salvador, and East Timor use the U.S. dollar as their currency) or linking their currency to that of another country. These strategies aim to achieve the desired balance between currency stability and policy independence—either on one's own or in collaboration with other national governments. While they may succeed in reducing threats to individual countries or groups of countries, these strategies do not address problems at the global monetary level, which some analysts regard as a matter for concern. Nor do they address the continuing problem of spreading currency crises, to which we turn in the next section.

What Happens When Currencies Collapse?

Even those who pay little attention to international monetary affairs notice the occasional spectacular currency crisis, such as those that affected Europe in 1992–93 and again in 2011, East Asia in 1997–98, or Argentina in 2001. Indeed, currency crises have been a frequent feature of the modern international political economy, and they are one of the more dramatic effects of national currency policy. Currency crises have been closely related to the financial and debt crises discussed in Chapter 8 and have been associated with all-encompassing economic and political upheavals.

Currency crises usually result when government exchange-rate commitments are not fully credible. In this sense they are analytically comparable to crises in military affairs that result when the threats and promises of governments are not fully credible (see Chapter 3). In the case of currency affairs, when private economic actors do not believe the promises of a government with respect to its exchange rate, they can react in ways that cause a major crisis.

Effects on Government

Up to now, we have assumed that when a government fixes its exchange rate, it stays fixed until the government decides, on its own, to alter the arrangement. But we also know that it can be economically and politically difficult for a government to sustain a fixed currency because a government with a fixed exchange rate may not be able to undertake monetary policies desirable to address national economic conditions.

This was the problem in Argentina in 2001, when the tight dollar-peso link made it virtually impossible for the Argentine government to reverse a three-year recession. It was also the problem in a number of eurozone countries in the aftermath of the crisis that began in 2008, for the fact that they had given up their national currencies made it very difficult for them to act to ease the impact of the Great Recession. In these circumstances, expectations that the government will not be able to sustain its commitment to a fixed rate or to membership in a currency union can create concern among economic actors about the future course of the currency. And this concern can feed on itself until it becomes a panic.

A typical currency crisis follows a fairly predictable trajectory. In order to reap the benefits of a fixed currency, the government commits itself to a fixed exchange rate—a peg to gold, the dollar, or the euro at a specific rate. This move presumably has all the advantages we have identified, but it also imposes costs. Over time, for some reason, the government faces economic and political difficulties in maintaining a fixed exchange rate. Perhaps the local economy is doing poorly, or exporters are clamoring for a devaluation that will make their goods more attractive abroad, or the country's main exports are losing markets to competitors.

As the government faces increasing pressures to devalue the currency, people begin to lose faith in the government's commitment to keeping the exchange rate stable. This unease gives investors strong reasons to sell the nation's currency. After all, nobody wants to hold on to an asset, in this case a currency, that is going to lose value. So, investors at home and abroad start converting the country's currency into more reliable foreign currency. The government usually continues to assure the public that the exchange rate will be maintained, in an effort to keep people from selling the currency. But as doubts about the government's credibility grow, more and more people may go to the banks to exchange their local currency for more reliable dollars or euros.

The government itself is torn. On the one hand, there are powerful domestic interests in favor of keeping the currency's exchange rate where it is. Companies and others that have borrowed in a foreign currency, for example, are anxious to make sure the national currency is not devalued. For those with foreign-currency debts, a devaluation would increase the cost of their debt by requiring more of the national currency to buy the foreign currency they must use to repay the debt. In addition, a devaluation would reduce national purchasing power—an unpopular move with consumers, who would have to pay more for many goods as a result. On the other hand, there are good reasons to allow the currency's value to drop: it might alleviate economic distress and help national farmers and manufacturers compete with foreigners. ("How Do We Know?" on p. 436 looks at the decision to devalue the currency in several European countries.)

At the same time, sustaining the fixed rate can be very difficult. The government would have to take some action to convince people to hold on to the national currency rather than buying dollars or some other foreign currency. Most commonly, a government trying to convince investors and others to hold on to the national money has to raise interest rates in order to make the local currency more attractive—and raising interest rates is likely to exacerbate the country's economic difficulties.

Eventually, the government runs out of time, money, or patience, and the currency is devalued. A drop in a currency's value may have a positive effect by helping national producers compete with foreigners. But it also usually has some very powerful negative effects. Anyone in the country with substantial foreign-currency debts, including the government, faces serious trouble. As the local currency drops in value, the burden of foreign-currency debt rises. In early 2002, for example, the Argentine peso's value dropped from one to the dollar to three to the dollar in two months, so a $1 million debt went from being a 1-million-peso debt to a 3-million-peso debt. In such circumstances, large numbers of debtors go bankrupt, which in turn leads many banks to fail because their customers cannot pay their debts. A recession almost always ensues, which can even turn into a deep financial and debt crisis. Indeed, most currency crises eventually turn into broader banking crises. This scenario has been repeated hundreds of times, from the nineteenth century through the present in developed and developing countries.

When the Argentine government devalued the peso in 2001, many homeowners whose mortgages were denominated in dollars saw the value of their debt triple compared to their salary (paid in pesos) in a span of just two months. This result fueled public anger.

International Repercussions

The international aspect of currency crises can be particularly troubling. Currency crises can be transmitted from one country to another as uncertainties about one country feed uncertainties about others. Investors looking at countries that are economically or politically similar may believe that the collapse of one country's currency portends the collapse of others like it.

Throughout the nineteenth century, currency crises (often originating in the United States, then a heavily indebted developing country) had repercussions all over the industrialized world. When, in 1931, Austria was hit by a currency and banking crisis, the resulting fears soon affected neighboring Hungary, leading to a crisis there. Then the crisis hit Germany, then the rest of central Europe, then Great Britain; eventually, most of Europe was brought down by a "contagious" currency crisis that almost certainly deepened the Great Depression.

In the past 30 years, there have been many rounds of currency crises. The first was associated with the less developed countries' sovereign debt defaults of the early and middle 1980s. In this case, the currency crises followed, rather than led,

HOW DO WE KNOW?

Devaluation or Depression in the European Union

When the global financial crisis hit in 2008, governments in central and eastern Europe had to figure out how they would respond. These nations had recently entered the European Union, and many of them were on track to adopt the euro. Most had currencies that were tightly tied to the euro.

As the world economy spiraled downward, each country faced a serious exchange-rate policy choice. On the one hand, in order to move forward toward adoption of the euro, the government could hold fast to its peg to the euro. However, doing so would restrict it from adopting an independent policy, such as devaluing its currency. And this was a major restriction; one of the typical recommendations for small open economies in crisis is to devalue in order to make national goods more attractive on world markets and stimulate exports. On the other hand, if the government chose to devalue, it would forgo the opportunity to join the eurozone.

Political scientist Stefanie Walter analyzed the political economy of this choice.[a] She focused on the interests at play in different central and eastern European societies, particularly on their citizens' debts in foreign currencies. In the Baltic states of Estonia, Latvia, and Lithuania, for example, between 60 and 90 percent of total loans were in foreign currency. A devaluation would have dramatically increased the cost of this debt. If a Latvian homeowner took out a €100,000 mortgage in 2005, this would have been equal to about 70,000 Latvian lats (at the then current exchange rate of 1.00 lat to €1.42). But if the lat were devalued by 30 percent (so that the lat and the euro

TABLE A *Foreign-Currency Debt and Currency Depreciation*

	LOANS IN FOREIGN CURRENCY[a]	MAXIMUM DEPRECIATION OF NATIONAL CURRENCY[b]	REAL GDP GROWTH RATE, 2009[b]	CHANGE IN UNEMPLOYMENT RATE, 2007–10[b]
Latvia	88.4%	1.2%	–17.7%	13.3%
Estonia	85.3%	0%	–14.3%	12.2%
Lithuania	64.0%	0%	–14.8%	13.5%
Poland	32.6%	43%	1.6%	0%
Czech Republic	13.6%	21%	–4.7%	2%

a. Martin Myant and Jan Drahokoupil, "International Integration, Varieties of Capitalism and Resilience to Crisis in Transition Economies," *Europe-Asia Studies* 64, no. 1 (2012): 1–33.
b. Stefanie Walter, *Financial Crises and the Politics of Macroeconomic Adjustments* (Cambridge: Cambridge University Press, 2013), Table 7.1.

were approximately equivalent), the mortgage would have increased in local value to about 100,000 lats.

In some other countries, citizens had not borrowed very much in foreign currency. In Poland, foreign-currency debts were barely 30 percent of total loans, and in the Czech Republic there were few foreign-currency debts. People in these countries were less vulnerable to devaluation.

Walter argues that the countries whose economic interests were most vulnerable to devaluation chose to keep their currency peg (Table A). Lithuania, Estonia, and Latvia, in fact, underwent massive recessions; unemployment approached 20 percent, and GDP dropped by over 15 percent in just one year. Nonetheless, they held on to their euro dreams, and all three countries are now in the eurozone.

Poland and the Czech Republic, whose economic interests were less vulnerable to devaluation, opted to devalue their currencies. Their exports boomed, and as a result they experienced little or no increase in unemployment. The Czech Republic had only a shallow recession, and Poland had none. On the other hand, both countries largely foreclosed their option to join the eurozone—a step they did not particularly favor in any case.

---

a. Stefanie Walter, *Financial Crises and the Politics of Macroeconomic Adjustments* (Cambridge: Cambridge University Press, 2013), 181–217; and Stefanie Walter, "Crisis Politics in Europe: Why Austerity Is Easier to Implement in Some Countries Than in Others," *Comparative Political Studies* 49, no. 7 (2016): 841–873.

the larger financial crisis. As country after country found itself unable to sustain its currency's value in the face of massive debt problems, currencies collapsed as well. Since the early 1990s, it has become more common for currency crises to be the source of broader financial and economic difficulties.

Case Study: Europe, 1992

One of the first major modern currency crises affected European countries that were moving toward currency union. In this process, most EU countries had pegged their currencies to Germany's currency, the Deutschmark. In 1991, the German central bank raised interest rates quickly and steeply to keep prices from rising after the unification of the eastern and western parts of the country.

This action presented a difficult choice for the other European countries whose currencies were tied to the Deutschmark. On the one hand, they could keep interest rates low, which would cause investors to pull their money out of these other countries in favor of Germany's higher interest rates. As investors pulled out and sold the non-German currencies, these countries would eventually have to devalue their currencies against the Deutschmark and break the peg. On the other hand, the other countries could raise interest rates along with Germany, which would shove them into a recession. In sum, German policy confronted European governments with a stark choice between continued membership in the Deutschmark bloc on the one hand and avoiding a recession on the other. The rest of Europe was already mired in slow growth and double-digit unemployment, and there was little enthusiasm for more austerity measures that would reduce wages and public spending (even though they would slow inflation).

In the summer of 1992, investors and currency traders began anticipating that Great Britain and Italy would not maintain their currencies' pegs to the Deutschmark. Investors sold off their holdings of these currencies, thus intensifying speculation that the pound and the lira would be devalued. The British and Italian governments pushed interest rates up to try to convince investors to hold on to their pounds and liras, but in the end, the cost seemed extreme, and both devalued their currencies. Foreign-exchange traders started selling off other currencies in the months that followed. Governments tried to hold on to the link to the Deutschmark (at one point, the Swedish central bank pushed interest rates to 500 percent), but the cost was too high.

Eventually, six other European nations followed Britain and Italy in devaluing their currencies. The damage to monetary unification was repaired quickly and effectively enough to move forward with plans for the euro. But it was clear that even the world's richest nations were not immune to currency crises that could force governments to devalue and change their policies. The perception began to grow that there might be a common interest in trying to limit the negative effects of currency crises, since they could be transmitted from nation to nation.

Case Study: Mexico

Within a year of the European currency crisis, the idea that currency crises could cross national borders was brought home to Mexico. With the North American Free Trade Agreement (NAFTA) in effect, the Mexican government wanted to hold the peso steady against the U.S. dollar. And in the run-up to a hotly contested presidential election campaign, the government wanted to keep the peso strong and Mexican incomes high. But in January 1994, a rebellion broke out in southern Mexico, and in March, one of the ruling party's leading presidential candidates was assassinated. These events worried investors, who came to believe that the government's position was shaky. As the election year of 1994 wore on, the government struggled to maintain its commitment to the peso, both to uphold its reputation and, through the strong peso, to increase the purchasing power of Mexican consumers.

But currency traders did not believe that the government could hold to its promises. Investors became more and more skittish, and the narrowness of the victory won by the ruling Partido Revolucionario Institucional (PRI), or Institutional Revolutionary Party, in the August 1994 presidential election was not reassuring. The PRI's secretary-general was assassinated in September, further scaring investors, who worried that the new government would be too unstable to commit credibly to the currency peg.

As the new government took office in December, currency traders sensed they could take a "one-way bet" against the peso by selling it for dollars: if the peso was devalued, they would win; if it wasn't, they wouldn't lose. As the speculators sold off the currency, the government tried desperately to keep the currency stable, but a few days before Christmas 1994, it floated the peso—which promptly sank. Yet another government had been forced to devalue its currency.

Following the common pattern of currency crises leading to financial crises, Mexico was next hit by a crippling banking crisis as a result of the currency collapse. When the peso was strong, many banks and companies borrowed heavily in dollars. The devaluation of the peso triggered mass bankruptcies as the real cost of dollar debts soared. The peso's value dropped in the space of a month from about 30¢ to about 15¢, so the real burden on a Mexican company of a $1 million foreign debt doubled from about 3.3 million pesos to 6.6 million.

Many indebted firms collapsed, followed by their domestic bankers, and within weeks the country was in the throes of a financial panic. The country's output dropped by 6 percent, and inflation soared above 50 percent. The fallout of the Mexican crisis affected all of Latin America, which was plunged into recession.

Case Study: East Asia The next round of currency and financial crises was even more dramatic. In 1997, the East Asian economies were booming: about $50 billion a year flowed into East Asia from global financial markets, with tens of billions more in direct investment from multinational corporations. The region seemed well on its way to rapid economic development. But there were a few warning signs of slowing growth and a bubble in housing and financial markets. By 1996 and early 1997, exports were lagging, inflation was rising, and banks were taking on more and more debt. Soon, investors began to anticipate devaluations and started selling off East Asian currencies.

In a now familiar spiral, the movement away from the region's currencies became a flood, then a stampede, then a panic. The sell-off spread from Thailand

and the Philippines to Indonesia and Malaysia, then to Taiwan and Korea. The size and efficiency of international financial markets seemed to facilitate the attacks by making it remarkably easy for investors to speculate against government attempts to defend their currencies. Joseph Stiglitz, then chief economist at the World Bank, gave an example of the process:

> Assume a speculator goes to a Thai bank, borrows 24 billion baht, which, at the original exchange rate, can be converted into $1 billion. A week later the exchange rate falls; instead of there being 24 baht to the dollar, there are now 40 baht to the dollar. He takes $600 million, converting it back to baht, getting 24 billion baht to repay the loan. The remaining $400 million is his profit—a tidy return for one week's work, and the investment of little of his own money. . . . As perceptions that a devaluation is imminent grow, the chance to make money becomes irresistible and speculators from around the world pile in to take advantage of the situation.[8]

As more and more investors did as Stiglitz described, expectations of devaluations grew. Since no investor wanted to hold on to currencies that would lose value, billions of dollars flooded out of the East Asian economies, and eventually governments were, in fact, forced to devalue. Within weeks of the initial attack, the currencies of Korea, the Philippines, and Malaysia dropped by 40 percent, that of Thailand by 50 percent, and that of Indonesia by 80 percent. The political fallout was also intense: the government of Thailand fell, and after more than 30 years in power, the Suharto dictatorship in Indonesia collapsed.

Case Study: Europe, 2011–2015

The most recent major currency crisis in Europe was different from the early-1990s crisis: it involved the threat that a multicountry currency union might break up. The member states of the eurozone have very different economies and have grown at different rates, but as long as the zone as a whole was growing, these differences did not cause many problems. When the global financial crisis began in 2008, however, it put major strains on the very structure of the euro.

A group of eurozone member states—especially Greece, Ireland, Portugal, and Spain—had borrowed very heavily after the euro was created. Their economies had boomed, but at the same time, these debt-financed booms raised prices and wages and made it harder for these countries to compete in the global market. Faced with the worldwide recession, the major debtor countries had trouble servicing their debts. Soon they were in full financial crisis and had to be bailed out by their EU partners, to the tune of over a trillion euros (see Chapter 8).

As the debt crisis dragged on, it appeared that it might threaten some countries' membership in the eurozone. The hardest-hit member state, Greece, certainly might have benefited from the ability to devalue its currency—except that it no longer had a currency to devalue. And it was not clear that the other members of the eurozone were enthusiastic about Greece staying in the currency union. Indeed,

---

8. Joseph E. Stiglitz, *Globalization and Its Discontents* (New York: Norton, 2002), 94–95.

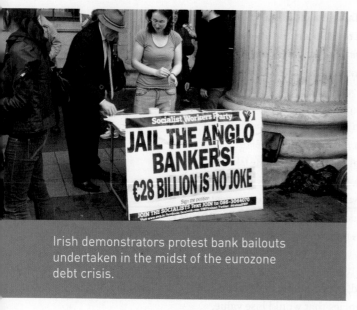

Irish demonstrators protest bank bailouts undertaken in the midst of the eurozone debt crisis.

in 2015, Greece appeared to come very close to being forced out of the eurozone because of its continuing difficulties in servicing debts to banks and governments in other eurozone member countries. Nonetheless, the threat of the breakup of the euro helped push the eurozone's leaders toward a resolution of the crisis, involving a combination of painful austerity measures in the debtor nations, bailouts from the rest of the eurozone, and a small amount of debt restructuring. Thus far, the euro's unity has been preserved, but at a very high cost.

The dramatic economic and political effects of the crises in Europe, Mexico, Argentina, and East Asia—and of others in Turkey, Russia, Brazil, Venezuela, and elsewhere—caught the world's attention. So too did the fact that currency and banking crises could spread quickly from country to country, as they did in East Asia in 1997–98. This realization led many of the world's economic leaders to see these currency crises as threats to the international monetary order and the world economy more generally. One nation's currency collapse could be transmitted to others, to an entire region, or to the whole world. Currency and financial instability had, after all, lengthened and deepened the Great Depression of the 1930s. The currency crises of the 1990s and the early 2000s led many to believe that in a globalized financial system, such attacks had the potential to destabilize the entire world economy.

Containing Currency Crises

Concern that currency crises can have broad international effects makes attempts to counter them something of an international public good. Thus, major governments have a common interest in containing such crises—although, as with all public goods, there is often conflict over how to distribute the cost of providing the service of containment. This challenge has given rise to complex interactions in which governments, private investors, and international institutions both cooperate and contend over attempts to limit the damage caused by currency crises.

Indeed, over the past 20 years, governments of the major financial centers and the leading international financial institutions have often cooperated to try to slow the spread of currency crises. The IMF, other international institutions, and creditor governments have often mobilized tens of billions of dollars to try to support governments facing currency crises. The reasons for major governments to cooperate in the face of currency crises are closely related to the reasons for cooperation to address sovereign debt crises, as discussed in Chapter 8. Cooperation among national governments can help mitigate the international impact of currency crises or help countries avoid them altogether.

However, such cooperation has not always been easy to organize and sustain. As with all public goods, there are incentives for each government to free ride and hope that other governments will pay the price of stabilizing the monetary order. What's more, many people believe that it is not a good idea to spend billions to support a failed or failing currency; such an effort may prop up undeserving governments and banks. This issue highlights the fact that currency crises can be controversial in domestic politics; governments are often blamed for allowing the crisis to take place, for not dealing with it effectively, or for inappropriately setting the currency in the first place.

Supporters of currency crisis interventions have regarded them as striking examples of efficient international cooperation to sustain the global monetary order and the global economy more generally. But critics have charged that these interventions force taxpayers to bail out foolish investors and overextended governments, encouraging a continuation of irresponsible government and private behavior. The clash has largely pitted contending interests against one another (see Chapter 8 for similar debates over financial bailouts), and these disagreements are sure to continue. The mix of common interests and contentious issues ensures that currency crises, and controversies over them, will continue to plague many currencies and globalized financial markets.

Conclusion: Currencies, Conflict, and Cooperation

Argentines and Greeks are not alone in learning from experience that currency policy can make a significant difference to economic and political life. Over the past 30 years, billions of people in dozens of countries have experienced both the positive and negative effects of national currency policies. The exchange rate is controversial within countries because its impact differs among groups, firms, regions, and individuals with competing interests. There are many who benefit if the currency is fixed, and others who are harmed. For every firm that gains as a currency depreciates, there is another that loses. This clash of interests, mediated through national political institutions, determines national attitudes toward the exchange rate.

International monetary relations too have a profound impact on international economic and political affairs. There is a reason that the classical gold standard and the Bretton Woods monetary system gave their names to entire economic eras: the ordering principles of these currency regimes were central to their respective international economies. Without functioning international monetary arrangements, global economic activity would be immensely difficult.

Governments have powerful reasons to collaborate in devising international monetary arrangements, but they also have significant interests that conflict. Inasmuch as an international monetary regime is a public good, governments have strong incentives to free ride and let others provide it; they also have strong reasons to try to make sure it is provided, and they have reasons to want the regime to be organized in ways favorable to themselves. Such a mix of incentives for cooperation and incentives to bargain hard characterizes the politics of international monetary relations today, as it has for centuries. These dueling incentives can be seen in the currency policy issues that are likely to preoccupy national governments, and the world community, over the coming years.

The first contentious issue has to do with the overall structure and functioning of the international monetary system as well as cooperation among the world's major financial and monetary powers. Many scholars believe that more organized collaboration among major governments is desirable to avoid future problems and crises. Certainly, there is a desire among many governments to collaborate in devising a new monetary order. Yet there are also powerful interests in conflict, since governments disagree about the appropriate characteristics of such an order.

In the absence of global agreement on international monetary relations, many countries continue to devise regional currency arrangements. The eurozone remains intact, and some of the European Union's newer members are still considering whether to join it. Many countries in Africa and the Middle East have already linked their currencies to the euro or plan to do so. There have been similar proposals for informal or formal currency unions in Latin America, North America, and parts of Asia.

Because many governments find these regional proposals an appealing way to reduce currency instability, some observers have suggested that we may be heading toward a world of currency blocs: an expanded eurozone eventually including much of the Middle East and Africa and parts of Asia, a dollar zone in the Western Hemisphere, and an East Asian currency area. The future of such arrangements depends both on the interests that governments have in developing them and on their interactions to pursue their monetary goals. Whether national governments come together on the global level to forge a new international monetary regime or continue to devise regional arrangements such as the euro, international monetary relations will profoundly shape the world economy.

Study Tool Kit

Interests, Interactions, and Institutions in Context

- There are many contending interests over monetary affairs within countries, which leads to domestic conflict over the appropriate currency policy to pursue.

- Although every country can set its currency policy as it wants, the fact that exchange rates value currencies relative to one another means that outcomes are the product of interactions among countries' policies. As a result, countries may have reasons to cooperate with one another to create arrangements that are mutually beneficial.

- Virtually everyone has an interest in the existence of a functioning international monetary system. But different arrangements benefit some actors more than others, which leads to disagreement about how such a system should be organized and about how the burdens and benefits should be distributed among countries.

- International monetary institutions, such as the gold standard, the Bretton Woods monetary system, or the eurozone, can create rules that facilitate cooperation in international monetary policy.

Key Terms

exchange rate, p. 409

appreciate, p. 409

depreciate, p. 409

devalue, p. 409

monetary policy, p. 411

central bank, p. 411

fixed exchange rate, p. 411

gold standard, p. 411

floating exchange rate, p. 412

Bretton Woods monetary system, p. 412

adjustable peg, p. 413

international monetary regime, p. 424

For Further Reading

Eichengreen, Barry. *Globalizing Capital: A History of the International Monetary System.* 3rd ed. Princeton, NJ: Princeton University Press, 2019. Presents a general historical survey of the economics and politics of the international monetary order.

Eichengreen, Barry. *Golden Fetters: The Gold Standard and the Great Depression, 1919–1939.* New York: Oxford University Press, 1992. A classic analysis of how the gold standard collapsed in the interwar period.

Eichengreen, Barry, Arnaud Mehl, and Livia Chiṭu. *How Global Currencies Work: Past, Present, and Future.* Princeton, NJ: Princeton University Press, 2018. Evaluates the history of global currency relations and discusses the possible future of international currencies.

Frieden, Jeffry A. *Currency Politics: The Political Economy of Exchange Rate Policy.* Princeton, NJ: Princeton University Press, 2015. Explains the politics and economics of government exchange-rate policy choices, with applications to the gold standard, European monetary integration, and Latin American currency policies and currency crises.

Schelkle, Waltraud. *The Political Economy of Monetary Solidarity: Understanding the Euro Experiment.* Oxford: Oxford University Press, 2017. Analyzes the problems and prospects of the eurozone and compares it to the creation of an American monetary union.

Steinberg, David A. *Demanding Devaluation: Exchange Rate Politics in the Developing World.* Ithaca, NY: Cornell University Press, 2015. Explores how domestic interests and institutions affect currency policy in the developing nations.

Varoufakis, Yanis. *Adults in the Room: My Battle with the European and American Deep Establishment.* New York: Farrar, Straus and Giroux, 2017. A controversial inside look at the eurozone crisis, by the equally controversial former Greek finance minister.

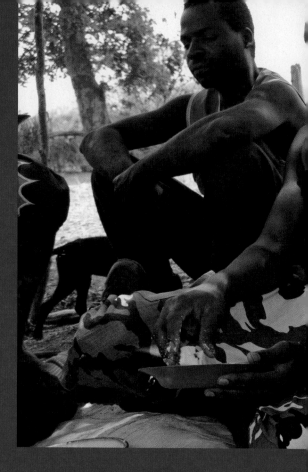

10

Development: Causes of the Wealth and Poverty of Nations

THE PUZZLE *Why are some countries rich and others poor? How do international politics and economics affect development?*

Above: Despite the overall growth of the world economy in recent decades, billions of people still live in poverty. For example, citizens of Zambia are significantly worse off today than they were when Zambia achieved independence in 1964. The average Zambian lives on the equivalent of less than $1,700 per year.

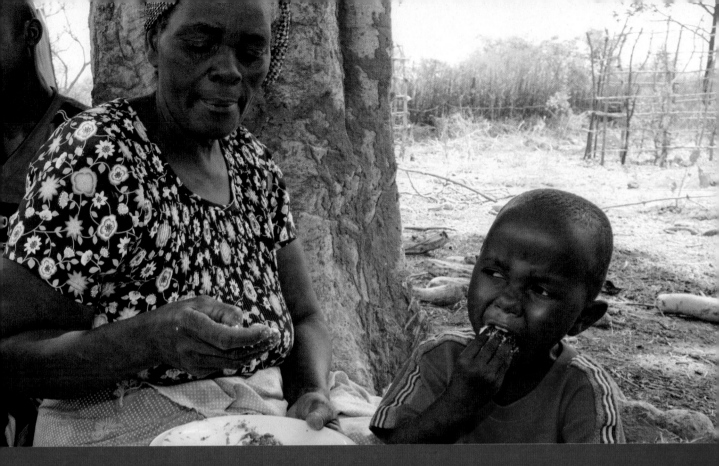

In 1964, the African nation of Zambia and the East Asian country of South Korea were at roughly equivalent levels of development. Indeed, when Zambia achieved its independence from British colonial governance in 1964, its prospects appeared far more promising than those of South Korea. Zambia was rich in copper, and its newly elected president, Kenneth Kaunda, was popular at home and respected abroad for his intelligence and seriousness of purpose. South Korea, in contrast, had no resources to speak of, was ruled by a despised and ridiculed military dictatorship, and depended heavily on American aid, which was being cut back.

Nearly six decades later, the two countries could not be more different. The economy of Zambia has failed miserably. In the 30 years after Kaunda's election, Zambian income per person fell until, by the mid-1990s, the average Zambian had barely half the income they'd had at independence. Faced with this development failure, Zambians voted Kaunda out of office amid substantial political unrest and widespread food riots. The government's struggles were compounded by the AIDS epidemic that swept Africa in the 1990s.

While conditions have improved somewhat since then, Zambia still has one of the lowest standards of living in the world. Real gross domestic product (GDP) per person is currently lower than it was at independence. Life expectancy is just 64 years; child labor rates are high, with nearly one-third of children ages 5–14 in the workforce; and almost 60 percent of the population lives below the international poverty line, on less than $1.90 a day.[1] Today, Zambia is a developmental tragedy.

Meanwhile, South Korea has become a prosperous industrial nation. In 1996, the Organisation for Economic Co-operation and Development recognized Korea's progress and made the country a member of this club of rich countries. South Korea had "graduated" from the developing to the developed world. It now has a standard of living comparable to that of France. Life expectancy is 83 years, adult literacy is practically universal, and real per capita income is over $43,000 a year. Although the two nations had similar starting points 50 years ago, today South Korea is an industrialized, developed nation, while Zambia is desperately poor.

1. UN Development Programme, "Human Development Report 2016: Human Development for Everyone," 2016, http://hdr.undp.org /en/content/human-development-report-2016 (accessed 2/2/21); World Bank, "Sub-Saharan Africa," https://data.worldbank.org /region/sub-saharan-africa (accessed 1/13/21). Comparisons of per capita income or GDP can be made on many bases. Here we use real per capita figures, which are controlled for inflation.

This comparison illustrates two realities of contemporary economic development. First, billions of people live in conditions of poverty. The average American earns more in three weeks than the average inhabitant of sub-Saharan Africa earns in a year. In the world's poor countries, every year five million children under the age of five die of malnutrition, and another five million die from curable and preventable diseases. In sub-Saharan Africa, nearly one-third of all children under age five are malnourished, barely one-third of secondary school-age children attend school, 42 percent of the population lacks a basic water supply, and 72 percent are without basic sanitation.[2]

Second, developmental experiences have varied widely. In 1960, countries such as South Korea and Taiwan were dismally poor—poorer than most of Africa. Today, these two nations are advanced industrial countries with per capita incomes comparable to those in western Europe. And the world's two most populous countries, China and India—home to over one-third of the world's people—have been growing very rapidly for 40 years. China's living standards are today 17 times higher than they were in 1990; India's are six times higher. The differences among developing nations are enormous; for example, the gap between Latin American and sub-Saharan African per capita GNI is substantially bigger than that same gap between Latin America and the industrialized nations.

In fact, the proportion of the world's population living in abject poverty has declined since the 1980s. Most international organizations use an international absolute poverty line equivalent to about $1.90 a day per person in 2021 dollars, taking into account differences in the cost of living across countries.[3]

The stark fact remains that 6 billion of the total world population of about 7.5 billion live in poor countries. While not everyone in poor countries is poor, these nations have an average income per person of just one-quarter that of the rich countries. Most of the world's people are poor.

The continued poverty of much of the world's population leads us to ask why so many countries are poor. Why have some countries developed successfully while others have stagnated? Why have the experiences of less developed countries differed so widely? Within these questions lie related issues about the relationship between developing countries and international politics: How has the international political economy affected the development of poor nations? Has it been a hindrance or a help to them?

2. Bernadeta Dadonaite, "What are Children Dying from and What Can We Do About it?" Our World In Data, August 9, 2019, www.ourworldindata.org/what-are-children-dying-from-and-what-can-we-do-about-it (accessed 3/18/21); Rolfe Eberhard, "Access to Water and Sanitation in Sub-Saharan Africa," Deutsche Gesellschaft für Internationale Zusammenarbeit, January 2019, www.oecd.org/water/GIZ_2018_Access_Study_Part%%20I_Synthesis_Report.pdf (accessed 1/13/21).

3. Branko Milanović, *Global Inequality: A New Approach for the Age of Globalization* (Cambridge, MA: Harvard University Press, 2016). The numbers cited here are from the World Bank, "Poverty," October 7, 2020, www.worldbank.org/en/topic/poverty/overview (accessed 1/13/21).

Thinking Analytically about Development

This chapter makes several points about the politics and economics of development. We note that although everyone in poor countries prefers more development to less, individuals and groups within countries may have conflicting interests with respect to how development is achieved. Powerful domestic groups that pursue policies to enrich themselves might prevent the adoption of other measures that would improve economic conditions for everyone else. Domestic social and political institutions can have a major impact on how such conflicts of interest among different domestic groups affect a country's development. Some institutional arrangements empower special interest groups, while others can overcome those who would stand in the way of development. In addition, a country's institutions can either facilitate or impede cooperation to promote policies that are conducive to economic growth.

At the international level, rich and poor nations generally have a common interest in accelerating the economic growth of the developing world. As poor nations grow, their demand for the products of rich nations grows, and they are better able to supply rich nations with goods and services they need. However, there have been many instances of rich countries supporting policies and institutions that disfavor less developed countries. For example, agricultural policies in Europe, North America, and Japan help farmers in rich countries at the expense of farmers in poor countries.

Given these conditions, successful economic growth requires that a country overcome both the domestic obstacles posed by interests and institutions that are detrimental to development and the international obstacles created by conflicts of interest with wealthy nations.

If Everyone Wants Development, Why Is It So Hard to Achieve?

Less developed countries (LDCs) want to develop, and few people would deny them the opportunity to do so.[4] However, steps to improve a nation's developmental prospects sometimes threaten the interests of certain actors at home or abroad. Recognizing this fact, we can identify three prominent approaches that explain why such a universally accepted goal as development appears to be so difficult to attain. These approaches consider geography, domestic factors such as a nation's political economy, and domestic institutions.

Geographic Location

One view is that the geographic realities of some countries impede their growth. The fact that the world's tropical regions are generally poor, while its temperate regions are generally rich, suggests that geography and climate affect development, directly or indirectly. There is little doubt that such factors play some part in explaining patterns of development.

Landlocked countries, regions with diseases that are difficult to control or cure, and areas that are very far from major markets for their goods are all at a developmental disadvantage—and this disadvantage was probably greater in an earlier era, when medical knowledge was limited and transportation and communications costs were much higher. By virtue of weather and disease, tropical environments in particular may be less conducive to urbanization and industrialization than temperate zones. Some scholars ascribe many of the developmental problems of tropical regions like sub-Saharan Africa, for example, to geography itself.[5]

But geographic factors cannot be the whole story, as there is a great deal of variation among countries within the same regions. Indeed, if we compare LDCs that have very similar geographic characteristics, we find that some have done extremely well, whereas others have done very poorly (see "What Shaped Our World?" on p. 450). While the climate and geography of a nation shape its development, they do so by way of their impact on the people, social structures, politics, and policies of the nation. Later in this chapter we return to analyses in which geography plays a part in the development process in conjunction with other socioeconomic and political factors.

> **less developed countries (LDCs)**
> Countries at a relatively low level of economic development.

---

4. Observers use a variety of terms to describe these countries. During the Cold War, it was common to refer to them as the *third world*, to distinguish them from the capitalist *first world* and the communist *second world*. Today it is more common to use the label *less developed country* or, more optimistically, *developing country*; some observers refer to the more successful of these countries as *emerging markets*. Another convention is to refer to these countries collectively as *the South* because they tend to be located geographically to the south of the richer countries. We will use some of these terms interchangeably.

5. For prominent statements on geography and development, see Jared Diamond, *Guns, Germs, and Steel: The Fates of Human Societies* (New York: Norton, 1997); David E. Bloom and Jeffrey D. Sachs, "Geography, Demography, and Economic Growth in Africa," *Brookings Papers on Economic Activity* 1998, no. 2 (1998): 207–95; and Jeffrey Sachs, Andrew Mellinger, and John Gallup, "The Geography of Poverty and Wealth," *Scientific American*, March 2001, 70–75.

Paths to Development

Why have some countries prospered, with their economies growing over time, while others have stagnated or even declined? One way to understand the interests, interactions, and institutions that lead some countries to prosper while others struggle is to compare countries that began their modern developmental experience under similar conditions, especially when they now diverge substantially.

Consider the cases of Zambia and Botswana. These two southern African countries gained their independence from Great Britain in 1964 and 1966, respectively. Both countries are landlocked and have substantial mineral wealth. At independence, Zambia was much richer than Botswana, perhaps twice as rich, but today Zambia remains very poor, while Botswana is thriving.[a] Why?

Interests The interests that dominated Zambian politics were largely urban: the business community and the urban middle and working classes, along with workers in the country's major copper mines. In contrast, the new Botswanan government presided over an economy with few initial natural resources: the main economic activity was cattle ranching, with most cattle in the hands of indigenous political leaders (the tribal chiefs). This difference meant that the Zambian government had incentives to channel its resources from the countryside and the copper belt to the cities, while the Botswanan government had incentives to develop the country's cattle-ranching economy.

Institutions Following independence, the new Zambian government created institutions that centralized power. The country's rulers institutionalized a single-party state, destroying most of the country's democratic institutions. The government also created institutions to take over the country's copper mines from private owners. The government's monopoly on power allowed it to use its copper earnings to award benefits to its core supporters. The government also

The Botswanan parliament in Gaborone.

discriminated against farmers to provide cheap food to its core urban supporters, and it raised high barriers to imports to encourage local industries. Thus, Zambian political institutions served the interests of the business community and the urban middle and working classes while leaving other domestic groups, notably farmers, in poverty.

The new Botswanan government pursued a different path. Rather than centralizing power in the hands of one political party, it maintained and strengthened democratic political institutions. It invested in public goods to promote farming, especially cattle ranching; spent heavily on education and infrastructure; provided a stable environment for private investment; and encouraged foreign investment in the country's natural resources. Eventually, rich diamond deposits were discovered, which helped speed up economic growth.

Interactions The structure of Zambia's dominant interests, and the institutions that allowed them to control political power, led the government to pursue policies that reinforced the position of Zambia's urban-dwelling minority to the detriment of the society as a whole. In contrast, the principal interests in Botswana led the government to encourage agrarian development and maintain inclusive democratic institutions. Today, Botswana is a thriving, democratic nation with a 2019 real per capita GDP of $8,093, while Zambia is an economically, politically, and socially troubled country, whose 2019 per capita GDP was $1,654—about one-fifth that of its neighbor.[b]

There are many reasons why one country develops while another does not. Whether it is divergent domestic interests, different national political institutions, or varied interactions among them, they all have a powerful impact on government policies and domestic politics.

a. Real GDP per capita here and elsewhere in this section comes from Alan Heston, Robert Summers, and Bettina Aten, Penn World Table Version 7.0, Center for International Comparisons of Production, Income, and Prices at the University of Pennsylvania, June 2011, https://www.rug.nl/ggdc/productivity/pwt/pwt-releases/pwt -7.0?lang=en (accessed 2/4/21); and World Bank, World Development Indicators, http://data.worldbank.org/country (accessed 1/13/21).

b. Expressed in purchasing power parity (PPP) terms, in 2019 Botswana's GDP per person was $18,553 while Zambia's was $3,624. World Bank, World Development Indicators, http://data.worldbank .org/country/ Zambia and https://data.worldbank.org/country/ botswana (accessed 1/13/21).

Two other approaches dominate attempts to explain patterns of development. One focuses on domestic factors, another on domestic institutions. International factors are relevant as well, and we return to them later in the chapter. However, the fact that there is so much variation among countries that are similarly situated and that face similar international conditions implies that domestic factors and institutions are crucially important.

Domestic Factors

Within developing nations, there are interests, interactions, and institutions that can speed or impede economic growth. While every country is different and every experience is unique, certain common features of national political economies help explain why some nations have been more successful than others. At the outset, it is crucial to recognize that government policies have a powerful impact on a country's economic growth, either encouraging or slowing it. In fact, almost all explanations of development and underdevelopment consider the actions (or inactions) of governments.

A very important policy that governments can undertake to boost development is to provide public goods that contribute to economic growth and prosperity. One such public good is the economic **infrastructure**, including a physical infrastructure—of roads, railroads, airports, utilities, ports, and the like, which are necessary to allow trade and exchange—and such economic institutions as financial and monetary systems, which permit people to make payments and investments easily. A social infrastructure too—public health and sanitation, education, urban planning—can encourage growth and development by allowing citizens to focus their efforts on economic activity in a productive way. In contrast, if the government does not build and maintain roads and schools, impedes normal banking operations, allows prices to spiral out of control, and fails to control disease and social problems, it is hard to imagine how the economy can develop.

Another crucial function for government is to ensure the security of property. After all, economic growth requires everyone from farmers to factory owners to invest in improving their ability to produce, and they are unlikely to make such improvements if their property rights are not safe. Secure property rights—which people in developed countries take for granted—mean that property owners can be confident that their material goods will not be seized arbitrarily.

A commitment to protect private property does not necessarily benefit only the rich; in most poor societies, the principal property owners are farmers. To take advantage of new economic opportunities, farmers must set aside time, energy, and money to improve the soil. They put their livelihood on the line in order to plant coffee trees, clear woodland, or irrigate. How can they undertake such risky investments if they cannot be sure that the benefits will come back to them? If marauders can steal their animals and torch their fields? If local government officials can extort any wealth they see being earned? If the national government taxes away all their earnings?

Long-term economic growth requires a stable and reliable environment within which people can plan for the future. A government that invests in education and

infrastructure
Basic structures necessary for social activity, such as transportation and telecommunications networks, and power and water supply.

Some countries, including the Philippines, have recently chosen to pursue a policy of infrastructure development to facilitate trade and exchange, attract foreign investment, grow their economies, and ultimately join the ranks of wealthy nations.

public health, creates an efficient economic infrastructure, and ensures stable monetary and financial systems can facilitate economic growth. People need a credible commitment that the government will abide by its promises to provide such public goods. Governments that cannot or will not credibly promise to provide important public goods inhibit their citizens' ability to take advantage of economic opportunities.

Why might a government not be willing or able to commit to creating a favorable environment for economic growth? After all, even the most selfish rulers presumably stand to benefit from a prosperous economy. And all societies have workers, farmers, and businesspeople with an interest in active and effective government policies to expand the range of economic opportunities.

Some countries' governments might simply lack the technical expertise to manage modern economic growth, in which case foreign assistance, in the form of both money and skills, may be needed. More often, the answer is not so easy.

In many societies, certain actors have interests that run counter to broad-based economic development. This is not to say that such actors consciously desire to limit growth, but that the pursuit of their interests can ultimately harm the economy. (This phenomenon is not specific to LDCs, of course; every country has actors with an interest in manipulating the economy to benefit themselves, even at the cost of slowing economic growth.)

In developing countries, such actors are often engaged in traditional economic sectors whose livelihood would be threatened by the growth of a more modern economy. For example, wealthy landowners may prefer that the property rights of poor farmers not be protected so that they can encroach on the land being farmed by the poor. Owners of labor-intensive plantations or mines may have little reason to support urbanization, industrialization, or education, because these developments would draw workers away and raise labor costs. Powerful corporations that receive generous subsidies and protections want to maintain them, even if they are a burden on taxpayers and consumers. Bureaucrats who can extort bribes in return for favors have nothing to gain from a more open and efficient administration.

The dismal experience of sub-Saharan Africa since independence provides an example of how actors whose interests are at odds with the general social interest can impede economic growth. As Map 10.1 shows, many of the world's poorest countries are found in sub-Saharan Africa. Development policy in this region has often served to benefit small groups and to harm the rest of society. For decades, governments systematically drained resources from the countryside—by taxing farmers directly, keeping farm prices artificially low, or employing other means—in order to channel funds into the cities.

While countries often justified these policies as a way of speeding urbanization and industrialization—and they may indeed have had that effect—in societies that were 80 or 90 percent rural, this process amounted to impoverishing the masses to benefit a narrow urban elite. However, the urban elite was a politically import-ant base of support for African governments. It included urban businessmen, gov-ernment employees, and the military, on which many governments relied to stay in power. As a result, many African governments pursued economic policies that depleted the farm sector, which represented most of the population and most of the meaningful economic opportunities, in the interest of catering to inefficient urban enterprises and bureaucracies.[6]

Self-serving groups whose goals conflict with those of the rest of society can significantly impede economic growth, but interests alone are insufficient to explain countries' different paths of development. After all, every country has powerful special interests, including groups whose interests may be an obstacle to broader development, but every country also has masses of farmers, workers, business-people, and others who stand to benefit from policies that promote growth. What ultimately determines the character of government policies toward development is not just the interests in play but also the nature of their interactions: how poli-ticians, social groups, and the public bargain, fight, cooperate, and negotiate their way toward an outcome.

Conditions in some societies may make it easy for actors to come together in pursuit of shared goals, but other societies may have endemic divisions that make this collaboration very difficult. Hostility and conflict among ethnic or regional groups can impede both political stability and effective national government policies if rivalries between groups overcome a concern for the common good. Because many LDCs have boundaries that were determined by colonial powers without regard to preexisting ethnic or religious features of the population, they can be very diverse, and competition among groups can complicate the making of economic policy.[7]

Generally speaking, as we saw in Chapter 2, the larger the group, the more dif-ficult collective action is. This means that, as we saw with respect to trade policies

---

6. Robert H. Bates, *Markets and States in Tropical Africa: The Political Basis of Agricultural Policies* (Berkeley: University of California Press, 1981) is the classic examination of this process.

7. For a survey, see Alberto Alesina and Eliana La Ferrara, "Ethnic Diversity and Economic Performance," *Journal of Economic Literature* 43 (September 2005): 762–800. This is not a problem only for poor countries, but it can be particularly troubling there.

MAP 10.1 *Economic Activity around the World*

This map shows that per capita gross domestic product (GDP), the most widely used measure of economic activity, varies greatly around the world. People in many African and South Asian countries live on less than $4,000 per year on average, a small fraction of the per capita GDP of North American and European countries. However, per capita GDP tells only part of the story, as it is an average. Some countries with relatively high per capita GDP, such as Brazil or South Africa, nonetheless have serious problems with poverty owing to the highly unequal distribution of income and wealth within the country.

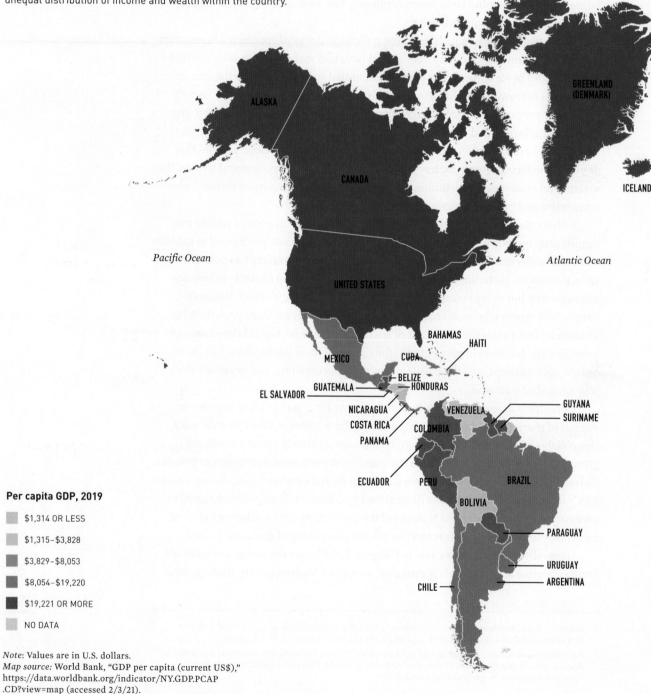

Per capita GDP, 2019

- $1,314 OR LESS
- $1,315–$3,828
- $3,829–$8,053
- $8,054–$19,220
- $19,221 OR MORE
- NO DATA

Note: Values are in U.S. dollars.
Map source: World Bank, "GDP per capita (current US$)," https://data.worldbank.org/indicator/NY.GDP.PCAP .CD?view=map (accessed 2/3/21).

Arctic Ocean

RUSSIA

UNITED
KINGDOM
SWEDEN
FINLAND
NORWAY
GERMANY
BELARUS
IRELAND
UKRAINE
KAZAKHSTAN
MONGOLIA
N. KOREA
GEORGIA
S. KOREA
FRANCE
UZBEKISTAN
KYRGYZSTAN
JAPAN
ITALY
TURKMENISTAN
TAJIKISTAN
PORTUGAL
SPAIN
TURKEY
CHINA
GREECE
SYRIA
IRAN
NEPAL
Pacific Ocean
MOROCCO
TUNISIA
ISRAEL
LEB.
IRAQ
BHUTAN
MACAU
ALGERIA
LIBYA
JORDAN
SAUDI
ARABIA
MYANMAR
(BURMA)
HONG KONG
EGYPT
UAE
TAIWAN
MAURITANIA
MALI
NIGER
CHAD
SUDAN
ERITREA
OMAN
YEMEN
PAKISTAN
INDIA
VIETNAM
PHILIPPINES
SENEGAL
AFGHANISTAN
THAILAND
GUINEA
NIGERIA
CEN.
AFR.
REP.
S. SUDAN
ETHIOPIA
BANGLADESH
LAOS
CAMBODIA
CAMEROON
SRI LANKA
MALAYSIA
GHANA
UGANDA
KENYA
SOMALIA
IVORY COAST
D.R.
CONGO
Indian Ocean
INDONESIA
PAPUA NEW GUINEA
TANZANIA
ANGOLA
MALAWI
ZAMBIA
MADAGASCAR
NAMIBIA
MOZAMBIQUE
ZIMBABWE
AUSTRALIA
SOUTH
AFRICA
BOTSWANA

NEW
ZEALAND

in Chapter 7, broad social interests are less likely than narrower special interests to be organized. Thus, special interest groups have an advantage in influencing policy. Nonetheless, sometimes the existence of a powerful common national goal (such as national unification or resistance to an external threat) can lead groups to set aside their differences and focus together on developmental requirements. For example, observers have suggested that competition with North Korea and China, respectively, partially motivated the rapid growth of South Korea and Taiwan. The economist Mancur Olson was optimistic that development could be spurred, and self-interested special interests denied, when societies were dominated by encompassing coalitions—that is, alliances that include enough of society to be concerned for broad social welfare.[8]

Whether important social actors interact in a cooperative manner to spur development also depends on domestic political institutions. These institutions affect the influence of those pressing for the public interest and those advocating for the goals of specific groups. More representative political institutions, for example, are likely to give more weight to broad public concerns about overall economic growth. Countries with more democratic political institutions appear to provide more public goods than do authoritarian political systems—more basic education, more public health, more equitable and efficient distributions of land.[9] In fact, part of the problem in postcolonial Africa has been the very undemocratic nature of most of the region's political systems, which allowed a narrow urban elite to use the government to exploit the masses of farmers and other rural dwellers.

However, the relationship between democracy and development has been contested. While some believe that democratic regimes are more conducive to development than authoritarian ones are, others argue that authoritarian regimes may be better suited to force-march their countries toward development. Still others believe that there is no clear relationship between regime type and development.[10]

Domestic Institutions

How and why have certain societies developed institutions that are conducive to economic growth, while others have not? The interests that characterize a society, the interactions among them, and the institutions that develop within the society are all interrelated. Nonetheless, some scholars emphasize how the human and material resources that societies possess give rise to interests and institutions that may be more or less favorable to development.

---

8. Mancur Olson, *The Rise and Decline of Nations: Economic Growth, Stagflation, and Social Rigidities* (New Haven, CT: Yale University Press, 1982).

9. See, for example, Matthew A. Baum and David A. Lake, "The Political Economy of Growth: Democracy and Human Capital," *American Journal of Political Science* 47, no. 2 (April 2003): 333–47; Nancy D. Lapp, *Landing Votes: Representation and Land Reform in Latin America* (New York: Palgrave Macmillan, 2004); David Stasavage, "Democracy and Education Spending in Africa," *American Journal of Political Science* 49, no. 2 (2005): 343–58; and David S. Brown and Ahmed Mushfiq Mobarak, "The Transforming Power of Democracy: Regime Type and the Distribution of Electricity," *American Political Science Review* 103, no. 2 (2009): 193–213.

10. An excellent summary of the debate and the evidence is James A. Robinson, "Economic Development and Democracy," *Annual Review of Political Science* 9, no. 1 (2006): 503–27.

Many countries that are rich in natural resources remain poor. Nigeria is one of the world's largest oil exporters, but the average Nigerian has hardly benefited from this natural wealth. Poor Nigerians frequently risk death to pilfer oil from pipelines.

This view incorporates the geographic features of different regions of the world into a broader interpretation of developmental paths. For example, societies that rely on the exploitation of rich natural resources with the use of plantation agriculture or mining are often dominated by powerful elites whose interests work against development. Elites in these societies can create political institutions that are strongly biased against popular participation and that serve to retard broad-based participation in economic growth (see "How Do We Know?" on p. 458).

This perspective helps explain the surprising fact that many regions that are extremely rich in natural resources are developmental disasters. The relationship between resource wealth and underdevelopment is strong enough to have prompted theories of a "resource curse," in which initial wealth gives rise to subsequent poverty. One idea is that the government of a country with a natural resource that can be easily and lucratively exploited may have few reasons to encourage productive activities other than those associated with that resource. Another related view is that when a country experiences massive inflows of funds, whether through the private or the public sector, there are greater incentives for people to use those funds to engage in such corrupt practices as buying favors from the government or extorting bribes from private companies.

In contrast, the government of a country with few natural resources, if it wants economic growth, has little choice but to undertake measures that will make the economy more productive. Recalling the comparison of Zambia and South Korea noted at the outset of this chapter, it may be that Zambia's copper wealth gave its rulers little incentive to invest in other areas of society—such as education, public health, and economic infrastructure—in order to increase the country's ability to

Explaining Developmental Differences: North and South America

What explains the major developmental differences among countries with similar economic starting points? One instructive comparison is between North and South America. The two regions were colonized by Europeans at roughly the same time and got their independence within a few decades of each other; since then, however, they have diverged in important ways.

Two economic historians, Stanley Engerman and Kenneth Sokoloff, have argued that the kinds of economic activities the regions undertook early in their modern history had a lasting impact on their subsequent social, political, and economic evolution. Their initial patterns of economic organization created powerful interests that could craft institutions with an enduring effect on subsequent political, social, and economic development. Engerman and Sokoloff have brought many different kinds of evidence to bear in comparing North and South American developmental paths.[a]

Many Latin American colonies and countries were drawn into the world economy on the basis of plantation agriculture (such as sugar, cotton, or coffee, as in the plantation pictured here) or labor-intensive mining (silver, gold). These economic activities created highly unequal societies made up of wealthy landowners or miners on the one hand and poorly paid workers or enslaved people on the other. Naturally, the wealthy landowners and miners were the dominant interests in these societies. These powerful interests played a major part in creating

a. A summary of their work is in Stanley Engerman and Kenneth Sokoloff, "History Lessons: Institutions, Factor Endowments, and Paths of Development in the New World," *Journal of Economic Perspectives* 14, no. 3 (2000): 217–32. Other components can be found in Stanley Engerman and Kenneth Sokoloff, "Factor Endowments, Institutions, and Differential Paths of Growth among New World Economies: A View from Economic Historians of the United States," in *How Latin America Fell Behind*, ed. Stephen Haber (Stanford, CA: Stanford University Press, 1997), 260–304; Stanley Engerman and Kenneth Sokoloff, "The Evolution of Suffrage Institutions in the New World," *Journal of Economic History* 65, no. 4 (December 2005): 891–921; and Kenneth Sokoloff and Eric Zolt, "Inequality and the Evolution of Institutions of Taxation: Evidence from the Economic History of the Americas," in *The Decline of Latin American Economies: Growth, Institutions, and Crises*, ed. Sebastian Edwards, Gerardo Esquivel, and Graciela Márquez (Chicago: University of Chicago Press, 2007), 83–136.

undemocratic political institutions, which reflected and reinforced the great inequalities in society and helped the wealthy hold on to power.

The bias in colonial and postcolonial political institutions can be seen in their rules on who was eligible to vote. All 13 original colonies that made up the United States restricted voting to those with property, sometimes substantial property. But over the decades after independence, these property ownership requirements were gradually relaxed and eventually eliminated. By 1850, White male adult Americans could vote whether or not they owned property or were literate, while every Latin American country restricted voting to those who both owned property and were literate.

As a result, at a time when 13 percent of the U.S. population voted in elections, the proportion in Latin America was at most 1 or 2 percent. To be sure, the United States at that time would not qualify as a democracy by our current standards: African Americans and women could not vote. Nonetheless, the difference in the extent to which politicians faced a broad electorate is striking. The image on the next page depicts a lively scene from the 1852 U.S. elections.

These differences in the right to vote persisted for decades, even centuries. Around 1900, 18 percent of Americans voted—although this advance was marred by the fact that the southern states, controlled by White supremacists, had imposed literacy requirements in order to restrict the voting rights of African Americans. In most Latin American countries, the proportion voting was still below 5 percent. Even in 1940, the share of Americans voting was still two to four times greater than the share of Latin Americans.

The institutions that restricted Latin Americans' access to the political system had a powerful effect on what their governments had incentives to do. Where only the wealthy could influence politics, policies reflected elite interests. In Latin America, governments dominated by these interests lacked policies to improve education, public health, or the economic opportunities of the poor. Biased institutions and the lack of developmentally oriented policies retarded economic growth.

In most of North America, however, early economic activities created fewer inequalities. Small-scale wheat farming in the United States and Canada, for example, produced a class of independent family farmers and a society that was quite equal. This equality was reflected in democratic political institutions as well as in substantial government investments in infrastructure, education, and other economically important activities. Here, the developmentally oriented institutions and policies encouraged economic growth. As early as 1850, literacy for white adults in the United States was above 90 percent—a level that many Latin American countries have reached only recently, if at all. Of

course, because literacy was actively discouraged (even prohibited) among enslaved people, literacy among African American adults in the United States was under 20 percent.

In fact, the experience of the American South underscores the argument that economic activities affect interests, which in turn affect institutions, which in turn affect developmental paths. In the southern United States, unlike in the North and Midwest, there were substantial slave plantation regions growing cotton and tobacco. In this aspect, the South was more like Latin America than like the North. Engerman and Sokoloff show that in the former plantation areas in the nineteenth and twentieth centuries, inequalities were much greater than elsewhere in the United States; the right to vote was much more restricted, and of course these restrictions persisted for a century after slavery was abolished; and there was much less spending on education and other public works. The highly unequal nature of southern American society, Engerman and Sokoloff argue, created an enduring legacy that was reflected in the South's institutions and that held back its economic growth for many decades.

The experiences of Latin America and of the American South demonstrate how domestic economic, political, and social interests and institutions created early in a region's economic history can have a long-lasting impact on its subsequent development.

produce anything more than raw materials. By contrast, South Korea's lack of any major exportable raw materials forced its government to focus on improving the productive capacities of its people.[11] The broader point is that geographic and other inherent features of a country are important for subsequent development inasmuch as they have a substantial impact on the kinds of interests and institutions that arise.

In sum, to understand why countries have developed in a certain way, we need to understand people's interests, their ability or inability to interact in ways that foster cooperation, and the political institutions that determine how these interests are translated into policy. Domestic factors, and especially national government policies, are crucial to understanding national developmental success or failure.

In addition to domestic factors, the international environment shapes the constraints and opportunities faced by developing countries in various ways. Many people in LDCs argue that international conditions have not been helpful to their prospects and, indeed, that the current poverty of much of the world is due to the structure of the international system.

How Do Rich Countries Affect the Developing World?

There is evidence that interests, interactions, and institutions at the international level are responsible for at least some of the current problems of poor nations. While developed and developing countries have many interests in common, there are also many real and potential conflicts of interest among them.

Rich and poor nations have many shared interests. Economic growth in the developing world can create enormous opportunities for wealthy countries. As we saw in Chapters 7, 8, and 9, rich-country corporations can profit from investing in and selling to developing nations, while poor countries can benefit from the capital, technology, and expertise that such corporations bring. LDCs' exports provide cheap goods for industrial-country consumers while they make money for the exporters. Banks from the industrialized world are eager to make loans to developing countries, in part because poor countries that are short of capital are willing to pay higher interest rates than can be earned elsewhere. The growth of poor countries' economies expands investment opportunities and markets for rich-country businesses. All these factors suggest why the relationship among rich and poor nations could be cooperative and the scope for mutually beneficial exchange very large.

By the same token, all countries have a common interest in the successful management of international economic affairs. Developed and developing countries alike benefit from well-functioning international trading, financial, and

---

11. See, for example, Halvor Mehlum, Karl Moene, and Ragnar Torvik, "Institutions and the Resource Curse," *Economic Journal* 116, no. 508 (2006): 1–20; Michael L. Ross, "What Have We Learned about the Resource Curse?" *Annual Review of Political Science* 18, no. 1 (2015): 239–59; and Macartan Humphreys, Jeffrey D. Sachs, and Joseph E. Stiglitz, eds., *Escaping the Resource Curse* (New York: Columbia University Press, 2007).

monetary systems. Few, if any, nations stand to gain from a breakdown of the international economy or from the transmission of financial crises from one country to another. International collaboration to smooth the operation of the world economy and to deal with problems that may arise is generally in the interest of all countries. Indeed, most international economic organizations—including the International Monetary Fund (IMF), the World Bank, and the World Trade Organization (WTO)—have both rich and poor nations as their members.

However, the interests of developed and developing countries may also clash. As we have seen in other areas of international politics, agreement over the desirability of cooperation coexists with disagreement over how to distribute the benefits of cooperation. For example, a multinational mining company and an LDC government have a common interest in getting minerals out of the ground and to market, but they are likely to disagree about the division of the profits. Similarly, LDC companies and governments may appreciate being able to borrow from international banks, but there is likely to be political controversy about making the sacrifices necessary to pay back their debts—especially in hard times. The fact that rich-country corporations can profit from low wages in the LDCs means that they may have little interest in encouraging development that will raise wages.

Such a mix of common and conflicting interests is central to the international political economy of development. It can be seen in the historical dynamics of colonialism and many contemporary examples.

Did Colonialism Hamper Development?

One aspect of the international order that is often blamed for underdevelopment is the legacy of colonialism. As we discussed in Chapter 1, from the sixteenth through the twentieth centuries colonial rule was often justified as being in the interests of

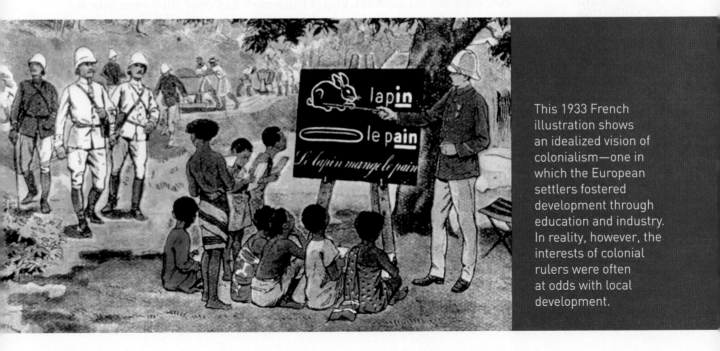

This 1933 French illustration shows an idealized vision of colonialism—one in which the European settlers fostered development through education and industry. In reality, however, the interests of colonial rulers were often at odds with local development.

both the colonial powers and the colonized. Indeed, colonialism encouraged broad-based economic growth in a number of poor countries, for sometimes the interests of the rulers and ruled were similar. Some colonial regimes supplied roads, railroads, ports, and other infrastructure both to facilitate their rule and to gain access to the colonies' resources, and this infrastructure facilitated the economic and political development of the colonial society overall. Some of today's most developed nations—the United States, Canada, Australia, New Zealand—were longtime colonies.

Nonetheless, many other colonial relationships were characterized by conflicting interests, and the enduring impact of colonialism in these former colonies has often been negative. Most imperial powers wanted to use their colonies for the mother country's benefit whether or not it was beneficial to the colonial societies. They often reserved economic advantages for their own citizens and restricted colonial subjects' access to economic opportunities. And when the colonial rulers' interests were inconsistent with local development, it was the rulers' interests that prevailed. This situation led to interactions that subordinated colonial societies and economies to the needs of the empire.

Colonialism, indeed, institutionalized a relationship in which the interests of the colonies were secondary to those of the mother country. For example, colonial policy commonly directed colonial trade toward the mother country, restricted manufacturing in the colonies, and otherwise gave trading privileges to the colonial power. (This was true of British policy toward the 13 colonies in North America; see Chapter 1.) Such preferential policies were intended in part to benefit residents of the great power and in part to deny benefits to real or potential enemies in other empires. This approach can hardly have been beneficial for development, and it may have been highly detrimental.

Colonial rule was commonly negligent at best, predatory at worst. One famous example is that of Leopold II, king of Belgium, in the Congo (the former Belgian Congo, now known as the Democratic Republic of the Congo). When the European powers colonized Africa in the late nineteenth century, they permitted Leopold to turn the Congo into his own personal possession. For decades, Leopold exploited the indigenous people mercilessly, forcing them to gather ivory, rubber, and other raw materials and turn them over to his own colonial government.[12]

In one study, three scholars analyzed how different forms of colonialism systematically affected subsequent development in the former colonies. Daron Acemoglu, Simon Johnson, and James Robinson suggest that the countries and regions of the colonial world can be divided into two types. The first includes countries where European settlers could live easily, without fear of high mortality owing to tropical diseases or other threats. In these regions, the scholars write, settlers from the colonial powers "went and settled in the colonies and set up institutions that enforced the rule of law and encouraged investment."[13] European settlers, in other words,

---

12. A classic analysis of the Congo's experience is Adam Hochschild, *King Leopold's Ghost: A Story of Greed, Terror, and Heroism in Colonial Africa* (Boston: Houghton Mifflin, 1998).

13. Daron Acemoglu, Simon Johnson, and James A. Robinson, "The Colonial Origins of Comparative Development: An Empirical Investigation," *American Economic Review* 91, no. 5 (December 2001): 1395.

LA NOUVELLE YORCK.

ué dans l'Amérique septentrionale dans l'Isle de Manahatan près l'embouchure du fleuve hudson, Les Hollandois commencerent à la bâtir en l'année ...mmerent nouvelle Amsterdam, mais en 1666, ils en furent privés par les Anglois, qui la nommerent la nouvelle Yorck,

In regions with climates hospitable to European immigrants, such as the Atlantic coast of North America, settlers moved in and established political institutions that set the stage for successful economic development.

went where they could survive, and they established social, political, and economic institutions that were conducive to economic growth. These institutions persisted, and in such countries as Canada and Australia the result was successful development.

In regions of the second type, where European settlers were much more likely to die of disease or other factors, the colonial powers engaged in predatory policies. There, the scholars say, the Europeans "set up extractive states with the intention of transferring resources rapidly to the metropole. These institutions were detrimental to investment and economic progress."[14] In other words, where large-scale European immigration and settlement were not feasible, the colonial powers simply exploited the region for their own benefit, establishing institutions that were not conducive to economic growth. These institutions too persisted and served to impede successful development.

To evaluate their argument, Acemoglu, Johnson, and Robinson looked at the death rates of early European settlers in colonial regions between the 1600s and the 1800s. There is little reason to think that these death rates would in themselves have a direct impact on modern economic growth, but in fact the settlers' mortality rates were strongly correlated with underdevelopment today. This is powerful evidence for the kind of effects the three scholars anticipated.

It seems clear that different types of colonial experiences and the different institutions put in place by colonial powers have had enduring effects on development. Where the common interests of colonial powers and people in the colonies predominated, the impact of colonialism was favorable (or at least neutral). But

---

14. Acemoglu, Johnson, and Robinson, "Colonial Origins of Comparative Development," 1395.

where the colonial powers' interests went against those of the local population and the colonialists imposed their will—for instance, by extracting labor and resources from the colony by force—the impact of colonialism was detrimental.

Although the lasting effects of colonialism explain some of the disparity between rich and poor nations, they cannot explain all of it. After all, most Latin American nations have been independent for 200 years—longer than many developed countries have been in existence—and even most former colonies in Africa, Asia, and the Caribbean have been independent for over 60 years. Some poor countries—such as China, Thailand, Iran, Liberia, and Ethiopia—have never been colonies and yet have suffered from severe developmental problems.[15] Scholars thus invoke other international factors, such as the international economy and international institutions, to explain barriers to development.

How Does the International Economy Affect LDCs?

Some analysts believe that general features of the international economy impede the development of poor nations. One prominent argument was made in the 1950s by Raúl Prebisch, an Argentine economist and for many years the head of the UN Economic Commission for Latin America (ECLA).[16] Prebisch accepted that, in principle, trade was good for both rich and poor countries. However, he noted that LDCs produced mostly raw materials and agricultural products, while rich countries produced mostly manufactured goods. He contended that this very fact meant that trade worked against the interests of the LDCs and in favor of the interests of the developed countries.

The problem, Prebisch said, was that the prices of the LDCs' products tended to decline over time relative to the prices of the industrialized countries' products. This disparity arose because LDCs sold mainly **primary products**—that is, agricultural goods and raw materials. And because markets for the LDCs' primary products were very competitive (there were millions of cocoa or coffee farmers), prices moved up and down very easily. However, markets for manufactured goods (automobiles, machinery) were controlled by a few large, **oligopolistic** firms—that is, firms that could control their markets. These firms could ensure that prices rose whenever possible and did not fall even in adverse market conditions.[17]

The result was that the **terms of trade**—the relative movement of export and import prices—of countries that specialized in primary products deteriorated: they got less for what they sold, and they paid more for what they bought. Countries that specialized in producing raw materials and farm products for world markets, Prebisch and his supporters argued, were thus at a fundamental disadvantage.

primary products
Raw materials and agricultural products, typically unprocessed or only slightly processed. The primary sectors are distinguished from secondary sectors (industry) and tertiary sectors (services).

oligopoly
A situation in which a market or industry is dominated by a few firms.

terms of trade
The relationship between a country's export prices and its import prices.

---

15. However, parts of China were occupied by foreign powers, and Ethiopia was invaded and occupied by Italy for several years.

16. For a survey and analysis, see Joseph L. Love, "Raúl Prebisch and the Origins of the Doctrine of Unequal Exchange," *Latin American Research Review* 15, no. 3 (1980): 45–72.

17. Prebisch also observed that because manufacturing was usually unionized, wages were also less flexible, which contributed to the rigidity of industrial prices.

Prebisch and his followers in ECLA concluded that the very structure of the world economy was biased against the developing world. In this view, the industrialized countries had an interest in maintaining a structure of international trade that was detrimental to the LDCs. Although many scholars were skeptical of the argument, it was very popular in the developing world. Indeed, it justified policies that many LDCs were pursuing—of protecting the home market and artificially spurring industrialization.

Are International Institutions Biased against LDCs?

Even among those who accept that the world economy can benefit LDCs, many scholars believe that international political factors are responsible for exacerbating the problems of development. They emphasize the relative powerlessness of developing nations in their interactions with richer countries. In this view, the principal obstacle facing LDCs is not global markets but the character of the international order and of international institutions whose rules are written by rich nations in order to serve their own interests.

While all countries can benefit from international economic exchange, the greater power of rich countries to influence patterns of international trade and finance can certainly work against the interests of LDCs. Indeed, rich countries often pursue their own interests in ways that harm prospects for development in poor countries. The problem is not that the industrialized nations purposefully or maliciously attempt to impoverish poor countries. Rather, it is that rich countries' policies to safeguard their own interests (or at least the interests powerful enough to matter to their governments) create problems for poor countries.

Farm trade policy is a good example. As we saw in Chapter 7, almost all industrialized countries extensively subsidize and protect their farmers. This policy has the effect of restricting the opportunities of LDC farmers, many of whom would otherwise be able to undersell farmers in North America, western Europe, and Japan. There is no intellectual or economic justification for these protectionist policies; they are simply the result of the interests of American, European, and Japanese farmers, which conflict with the interests of developing-country farmers.

American cotton policy illustrates the point. The U.S. government spends several billion dollars a year to subsidize American cotton farmers. This policy is lucrative for the recipients of the subsidies and politically attractive for U.S. politicians. The subsidy program pays farmers extra to produce cotton, which increases American output of cotton beyond what it would otherwise be; it therefore

Farmers in the developing world have a comparative advantage in providing agricultural products (like coffee beans) to world markets, but Western governments subsidize their farms so heavily that developing nations' farmers are hampered in their ability to compete.

raises the world supply of cotton and lowers its price. These effects, in turn, drive down the prices that cotton farmers in developing countries can command. While these farmers may be lower-cost producers than the American farmers, they do not have the luxury of expensive farm support programs.

The upshot is that the U.S. government has, since 1995, paid almost $2 billion a year in subsidies to American cotton farmers—almost all of which has gone to about 25,000 farmers. Cotton farmers in Texas alone have received nearly $11 billion in subsidies since 1995.[18] Meanwhile, several million cotton farmers in Africa, Asia, and Latin America have had their incomes cut by the resultant reduction in the world price of cotton.

The power disparity between rich and poor countries clearly works against LDCs. The governments of the developing world have been almost entirely unsuccessful at getting their farmers greater access to the markets of the industrialized nations. Meanwhile, the governments of rich countries have been quite successful in getting LDCs to open their markets to manufacturers, multinational corporations, and international banks from the developed world. The weakness of LDCs relative to developed nations means that they often lose out in international interactions of this sort, to the ultimate detriment of their economic prospects.[19]

The same pattern prevails within the major international economic institutions. While LDCs participate in international economic institutions—most are members of the IMF, the World Bank, and the WTO—these institutions are dominated by rich countries, and it is no surprise that their policies largely reflect the interests of their dominant members, even when these policies may be in conflict with the interests of poor nations.

We saw in Chapter 9 that many critics in the developing world regard the IMF as a tool of rich nations. Indeed, in the IMF, voting is weighted by the financial and economic size of the member states such that rich countries effectively control the institution (Figure 10.1). In fact, the United States has enough votes to veto any proposal, as do the member states of the European Union. This means that the rich countries can bend IMF policies and procedures in their favor—for example, to deal lightly with their allies or harshly with their enemies—even when such action is not generally consistent with the IMF's own rules.

International trade agreements similarly reflect the interests of the rich and powerful. Initiatives of developing countries are frequently ignored, even when they clearly would support the WTO's purported goal of trade liberalization. Many developing-country exports to industrialized nations face protectionist barriers instituted at the behest of affected industries that do not want to face such stiff competition.

Perhaps most important is the attempt by developing nations (and a few industrial countries that export farm products) to push the WTO to encourage greater openness to farm products, especially among the highly protectionist rich countries.

---

18. Full data are available at "Cotton Subsidies," Environmental Working Group, https://farm.ewg.org/progdetail.php?fips==00000&progcode==cotton&regionname==theUnitedStates (accessed 1/15/21).

19. Joseph Stiglitz discusses many such examples in *Making Globalization Work* (New York: Norton, 2006); see pp. 85–86 for the cotton example.

FIGURE 10.1 *Voting Power in the International Monetary Fund, 2020*

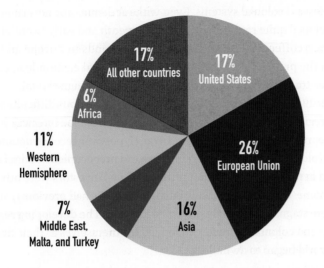

Figure source: International Monetary Fund, "IMF Members' Quotas and Voting Power, and IMF Board of Governors," February 17, 2021, www.imf.org/external/np/sec/memdir/members.aspx#E (accessed 2/17/21).

Agricultural trade liberalization would open up important new opportunities to farmers in developing countries, many of whom are low-cost agricultural producers. But because the principal losers would be farmers in developed countries, the rich nations have adamantly resisted including trade in farm products on the agenda for liberalization.

The interests of developed- and developing-country governments clash in many arenas. The power disparities between rich and poor countries typically mean that interactions among them are decided in favor of the rich. Moreover, the institutions that govern the international economy were created largely by rich and powerful countries, so their policies and decision rules reflect their own concerns. In all these ways, the alignment of interests, interactions, and institutions in the international order can limit the prospects for successful development of poor nations.

Development Policies and Development Politics

Over the past century, poor countries have experienced many changes in the domestic and international spheres that have affected their development. Conditions both at home and abroad have influenced the interests, institutions, and interactions that structure the development process. Before 1914, most developing regions—whether they were independent, as in Latin America, or colonial, as in most of the rest of the world—focused their efforts on primary products (agricultural goods and raw materials). Dominated as they were by those with interests in selling their goods abroad, they welcomed access to global markets and foreign capital as they strove to develop their mineral wealth and their farmland.

The importance of export-oriented interests was reinforced by their control over political institutions—a situation that occurred in both autocratic, independent countries and colonial systems. Even without democratic governments, many nations developed quite rapidly in the late nineteenth and early twentieth centuries, selling copper, coffee, cotton, and other primary goods to Europe and North America. In the process, they usually accepted general economic openness: relatively free trade, the gold standard, and inflows of foreign capital.

But after 1914, as the world economy experienced serious difficulties, most developing regions turned inward. World War I, the troubled interwar years and the Great Depression of the 1930s, World War II, postwar reconstruction, and the start of the Cold War all kept the developed world preoccupied—and relatively uninterested in the developing regions. International investors were otherwise engaged at home; the foreign markets into which LDCs had previously sold their products were stagnant or heavily protected, or both. The developing regions, both independent and colonial, were forced to fend for themselves as their ties to the developed world began to dwindle.

Import-Substituting Industrialization

In the context of these international trends, beginning in the 1930s a different set of interests came to the fore in many developing countries. With the collapse of foreign markets, export interests could no longer claim primacy, and initiative often shifted to economic groups interested in domestically oriented growth. Many developing countries therefore adopted policies encouraging industrial development so that domestic producers could supply goods that the countries had previously imported. Latin America led the way in practice as in theory, adopting measures to stimulate industry.

Though international events, the dislocations of the two world wars, and the Great Depression may have forced the initial turn inward, eventually it became a more conscious strategy. As domestic industrial interests grew in size and strength, they were able to push for a complex of policies known as **import-substituting industrialization (ISI)**, which had the goal of substituting local products for imports. It was in this context that Raúl Prebisch and his followers argued that such enforced self-sufficiency was desirable and should be deepened.

There were powerful domestic interests in favor of ISI. Most generally, developing-country governments wanted their economies to move away from primary production (raw materials and agricultural products) and toward industry, in line with Prebisch's theory that accelerated industrialization would aid broader development. These governments also believed that modern societies required a manufacturing base and that indigenous industrial capacity would provide a measure of national security.

At the same time, there were more specific interests in favor of the new policies. The political dominance of raw-materials producers—copper miners, oilmen, plantation owners, ranchers—had reinforced the previous emphasis on primary production for export. As foreign markets collapsed, these internationally oriented groups lost influence and were supplanted by pro-industrial groups that strongly

import-substituting industrialization (ISI)

A set of policies, pursued by most developing countries from the 1930s through the 1980s, to reduce imports and encourage domestic manufacturing, often through trade barriers, subsidies to manufacturing, and state ownership of basic industries.

supported ISI, such as the urban business and middle classes and the industrial working class. The institutional evolution of developing societies, particularly the emergence of more representative political systems (democracies, in some cases), reduced the influence of the old exporting elites and increased the power of the urban groups.

Both broad and narrower interests in ISI were also at play in the former colonies in Africa and Asia as they won their independence. Colonialism had been associated with selling primary products to the colonial power, but decolonization was associated with efforts to replace raw materials and agricultural production with urban manufacturing. And just as colonial societies were often dominated by colonial or local miners, oilmen, or farmers, postcolonial societies came to be dominated by such urban interest groups as businessmen, the middle classes, labor, and government employees.

For these reasons, after 1945 almost all the long-independent developing nations of Latin America and the newly independent ones of Africa, Asia, and the Caribbean reduced their economic ties with the rest of the world, protected and subsidized local manufacturing, and attempted to stimulate domestic industrial development. In important ways, these policies reflected the view that engagement with the world economy could impede national economic development.

For decades, most LDCs followed the broad outlines of import substitution, including:

- Trade barriers to protect domestic manufacturers from foreign competition and encourage national industrial development

- Government incentives to industry, including tax credits, cheap loans, and other subsidies to draw investors into the modern industrial sector

- Government provision of basic industrial services by public enterprises—electric power, telecommunications, transport, finance—to supplement or replace private provision that was seen as too expensive or too limited

All over the third world, government policies encouraged the development of large state sectors behind high protectionist barriers. The result was rapid industrialization in many areas of production. Between 1950 and 1970, for example, Brazil and Mexico developed large automobile industries where none had previously existed, and by the 1970s the two countries were producing a million cars a year. By the 1970s, indeed, most of the larger developing countries pursuing ISI—India, Brazil, Mexico, Argentina—were nearly self-sufficient in manufactured products.

However, ISI had weaknesses. The industries it encouraged were not efficient and had difficulty selling their goods abroad. After all, they had grown up in protected markets and were not originally expected to be competitive in international markets. Over time, the balance between exports and imports in these countries became worrisome; underperforming exports struggled to earn enough money to pay for essential imports.

As problems mounted, the inward-looking self-sufficiency of ISI began to lose support. In part, the Prebisch-ECLA view declined for intellectual reasons:

evidence accumulated that the argument might not be correct or that economic ties with developed countries might not have as negative an impact as had been suggested. There were also pragmatic and political reasons why the LDCs turned toward global integration. Many producers with previous interests in ISI came to believe that selling only to a small and poor home market restricted their potential. The insularity of protected markets left many manufacturers technically backward, making products of low quality—a fact that became increasingly troubling with the rise of modern electronics and computing.

The bias against producing for export meant that developing countries sold little in world markets. Therefore, they could not buy much abroad, which left them vulnerable to crises when, for example, oil prices skyrocketed in the 1970s. And the ISI bias against agriculture impoverished many farmers, leading to mass internal migrations that flooded the cities with the formerly rural poor. By the early 1980s, ISI was in trouble.

Export-Oriented Industrialization

export-oriented industrialization (EOI)

A set of policies, originally pursued in the mid-1960s by several East Asian countries, to spur manufacturing for export, often through subsidies and incentives for export production.

Beginning in the mid-1960s, South Korea, Taiwan, Singapore, and the British colony of Hong Kong turned toward an alternative to ISI: **export-oriented industrialization (EOI)**. These governments encouraged their manufacturers to produce for foreign, especially American, consumers. They used many techniques to push exports, including low-cost loans and tax breaks to exporters, and they maintained a very weak currency to make their products artificially cheap.

Like those countries pursuing ISI, the export-promoting governments typically used substantial state intervention in the economy to achieve their goals. Yet, while the rest of the third world used government involvement in the economy to turn industry inward in the 1960s and 1970s, the governments of export-oriented countries pushed it outward. This approach meant relying on often volatile international markets, but it had the advantage of forcing national manufacturers to produce goods that met rigorous technological, quality, and price standards.

By the late 1970s, the four EOI economies of East Asia were flooding world markets with toys, clothing, furniture, and other simple manufactures. South Korean exports skyrocketed from $385 million in 1970 to $15 billion in 1979, with 90 percent of the revenue coming from manufactured goods. On this basis, South Korea's government pursued heavy industrial development by sponsoring modern steel mills, chemical factories, and a new auto industry.

Globalization and Development

The devastating debt crisis that struck the developing world in the early 1980s (see Chapter 8) led most countries pursuing ISI to reassess their relationship to the world economy. The crisis hit the ISI economies particularly hard because they had so much trouble increasing exports and generating the money they needed to service their debts.

It did not go unnoticed that the East Asian EOI economies weathered the crisis with less trouble than the ISI economies. The East Asian businesses were used

A strategy of export-oriented industrialization led some developing countries to produce high-quality goods to be sold overseas. By the 1980s, this strategy had proved highly successful for countries like South Korea. Here, a steel mill in Pohang, South Korea, produces steel that will be provided to Iraq in exchange for oil field stakes.

to selling abroad and could increase exports rapidly to service their debts. After a couple of difficult years, the so-called Asian Tigers—South Korea, Taiwan, Singapore, and Hong Kong—resumed rapid growth. Meanwhile, the deep crisis in the ISI economies eventually drove them to turn toward world markets, and even export promotion, themselves. By the late 1980s, almost all developing countries had abandoned ISI and opted to integrate their economies into global markets.

The debt crisis also left the LDCs vulnerable to pressure from the industrialized countries—and from such international institutions as the IMF and the World Bank—to change their economic policies. In return for having their debts restructured, LDCs came under pressure to implement reforms favored by governments and institutions from the rich world.

For both domestic and international reasons, then, over the course of the 1990s many LDCs adapted to the new interest in globalization. Along with greater trade openness, most LDCs also adopted more market-oriented policies. They privatized many government enterprises, welcomed foreign investment, and pursued more restrictive monetary and fiscal policies to keep inflation low. These policies were also generally embraced by the governments of countries in eastern and central Europe and the former Soviet Union as they made their way from communist central planning toward market societies in the 1990s. The shift toward economic openness had both international and domestic sources. As the rest of the world economy grew rapidly, and as globalization advanced elsewhere, it was hard for poor nations to continue denying themselves access to the opportunities the world economy might make available. Powerful domestic actors in the developing world increasingly saw their interests as being served by tapping into global markets, global capital, and global technologies. And economic integration seems to have worked relatively well.

Perhaps the most striking such turn, with the most striking results, was made by China. In 1979, the Communist Party ruling the world's most populous nation dramatically shifted its economic strategy. The government embraced private enterprise and export promotion, encouraging both state-owned and new private enterprises to sell into world markets. The country's exports jumped from $9 billion in 1979 to $253 billion in 2000. The following year, after long negotiations, China joined the World Trade Organization. Since then, the country's exports have skyrocketed: in 2009 China became the world's largest exporter, and in 2020 Chinese exports exceeded $2.6 trillion. The domestic impact of China's turn to global markets has been even more striking, as per capita GDP increased from under $200 in 1980 to over $10,000 in 2020. Even controlling for inflation and different price levels, output per person rose more than twenty-fold in forty years—representing sustained rates of economic growth that the world had never seen before.

India, the developing world's other giant, made a similar if less dramatic transition toward the international economy and also realized rapid economic growth. So too did dozens of other LDCs. Much of the developing world has been drawn into the global supply chains that characterize modern international trade, which has increased the importance of developing countries to the developed world: much of what is consumed in the rich countries is made in poor countries. It has also, however, highlighted the fact that many developing countries are subject to economic and political trends that are outside their control—trends that are, indeed, controlled by developed countries.

Despite the success of many developing-country economies, in fact, most of them remain relatively weak in international economic organizations. This has led many actors in the developing world to resent the perceived bias of international economic institutions, and it has driven many LDC governments to attempt to counter the power imbalance with the power of numbers.

Attempts to Remedy the Bias of International Institutions

Developing countries have long attempted to address their relative international political weakness. Beginning in the 1950s, many countries in Asia, Africa, and the Caribbean that gained their independence after World War II grouped themselves into an international organization, the Non-Aligned Movement, that focused on economic and political issues of concern to developing nations and pledged to avoid alliances with either the American-led West or the Soviet-led East.

Group of 77

A coalition of developing countries in the UN, formed in 1964 with 77 members, that seeks changes to the international economic order to favor the developing world. It has grown to over 130 members but retains the original name.

The Non-Aligned Movement eventually gave rise to developing-country coalitions at the UN and in international institutions more generally. The UN variant was formed in 1964 with 77 members and has since been known as the **Group of 77** (although it currently has over 130 member countries). These developing-country-based institutions attempt to use the collective power of numbers in the world political arena to reform the economic order in favor of the developing world.

In the 1970s developing countries fought in the UN and elsewhere for what they called the New International Economic Order (NIEO). They wanted to renegotiate the international economic order so that it would be more in line with the economic needs of poor nations. They proposed curtailing the rights of foreign investors, revising trade agreements to favor the products of the developing world, and enhancing the influence of LDC governments in international economic organizations. These efforts resulted in some UN resolutions and other initiatives, but little of a concrete nature was accomplished.

The LDCs were more successful at using their control over natural resources to strengthen their bargaining position with rich nations. The most striking example came from members of the Organization of the Petroleum Exporting Countries (OPEC), a group of developing-country oil producers whose creation in 1960 had gone almost unnoticed. But in 1973, in the midst of a war between Israel and its Arab neighbors, OPEC's Arab members doubled the price of oil to more than $5 a barrel, then two months later doubled it again to nearly $12 a barrel. They did so by purposely restricting their supply of oil to world markets, a move that drove up world oil prices.

As the price increases persisted, it was clear that a small group of developing countries had dramatically changed the terms on which they sold their goods. Tens of billions of dollars flowed into the coffers of developing-country governments, and for the first time a group of developing nations appeared to have the upper hand in economic dealings with the West. In the wake of this electrifying development, other third-world commodity producers—of copper, coffee, iron ore, bauxite, and bananas—tried to emulate OPEC in creating international **commodity cartels**, organizations of producers who cooperate to restrict the supply and raise the price of their products.

Some of the other commodity cartels had an impact, but the oil sector was unique in the scale of its achievements. Oil producers were particularly successful for several reasons. There were few readily available substitutes for oil, so price increases did not reduce consumption very much. In addition, just a few OPEC members controlled a very large share of the world's oil: Saudi Arabia, Kuwait, Qatar, and the United Arab Emirates together had nearly half the world's oil reserves. They did not need to sell oil quickly and could hold it off the market to keep prices high. An additional source of power was the solidarity of OPEC's Muslim members in and around the Middle East, who shared cultural and political ties.

OPEC was able to obtain enormous amounts of money for its members. Some of this income was shared with other developing countries, although many poor countries that did not have oil themselves were harmed by the oil shocks. In addition, a few oil states were able to leverage their resources into increased influence at the IMF and World Bank. But, by the early 1980s it was clear that LDC attempts to achieve far-reaching international reforms had largely failed. Some natural resource producers had gotten richer, but the underlying institutions of the international political economy had not fundamentally changed.

The role of developing countries began to shift with the very rapid growth of some of the largest poor countries. The most striking case is that of China—which is now the world's largest exporter and its second-largest economy. China has undertaken systematic efforts to increase its international influence. Within existing

commodity cartels
Associations of producers of commodities (raw materials and agricultural products) that restrict world supply of their products and thereby cause the price of their goods to rise.

international organizations, it has argued for—and sometimes obtained—a larger say over collective decisions. In addition, China has moved, on its own and with others, to challenge the domination of the organizations created and largely run by the rich countries of the Organisation for Economic Co-operation and Development. Chinese development banks have become major lenders to other countries in Asia and Africa, and the Chinese government's Belt and Road Initiative promises a trillion dollars in infrastructure investment in Eurasia, Africa, and Oceania. China spearheaded the creation of the Asian Infrastructure Investment Bank, widely seen as a more LDC-friendly alternative to the World Bank (see Chapter 8).

China's major efforts, along with the increasing economic and political influence of such large developing countries as India and Brazil, has led to the gradual inclusion of these nations in some of the international discussions that had previously been the sole domain of rich countries. In fact, in the aftermath of the global financial crisis that began in 2008, the Group of 20 Finance Ministers and Central Bank Governors played a major role in attempting to address the crisis. The Group of 20 includes representatives of nine developing nations: Argentina, Brazil, China, India, Indonesia, Mexico, Russia, Saudi Arabia, and Turkey.

Many observers believe that this expansion of the "leadership group" in international economic affairs reflects an opening up of at least some global discussions to the concerns of developing countries. Nonetheless, the countries represented tend to be the largest and richest nations in the developing world, and on balance, LDCs still find themselves subject to international economic trends and constrained by international institutions over which they have little or no control.

Is Foreign Aid an Answer?

Many people believe that problems of development could be substantially alleviated by increased foreign aid from the rich nations of the world (see "Controversy" on p. 476). And there are certainly examples of places and projects where foreign aid has improved the quality of life for people in poor nations. However, foreign aid is unlikely to play a major role in overcoming problems of underdevelopment for at least two reasons.

First, the amounts of aid given are quite small and are unlikely to grow. In recent years, total foreign assistance has been about $150 billion a year. This may seem like a lot, but it averages out to less than $25 per person in the LDCs, and it is dwarfed by the amounts of private investments and loans that come into the developing world from abroad. Although rich countries have often expressed support for increasing aid, few countries have followed through in practice. In 1970, the rich nations set a target of 0.7 percent of their GDP as aid, but the actual number today is about one-third of that target. There is very little popular support for foreign aid in most developed nations, and there seems to be little prospect that the situation will change.

Second, and perhaps more important, there is good reason to believe that even increased levels of aid would not go very far toward solving the basic problems of developing countries. LDC governments that act in the narrow interests of themselves or their supporters are likely to use the aid they receive for similarly narrow

Humanitarian aid often provides food to people in poor countries who might otherwise be in danger of starvation. Volunteers, such as this group from USAID, help prepare and distribute meals.

purposes. There is substantial evidence that much foreign aid is misused by recipient governments. By the same token, there is evidence that much foreign aid is given by developed-country governments for geopolitical and military reasons and not to alleviate poverty.

To be sure, humanitarian assistance can make a difference in the lives of people in the developing world. However, sustained economic development provides the best hope for achieving the broader goal of lifting poor countries out of poverty. Governments that are willing and able to pursue policies aimed at stimulating growth may use aid effectively as a supplement to good policies. But aid alone, especially in the small amounts currently available, cannot go far toward satisfying the massive needs of impoverished people in developing countries.[20]

Globalization and Its Discontents

Over the past 30 years, most developing countries have committed themselves to engagement with the global economy. In this context, they may share more interests in common with developed nations. The LDCs have also tended to participate more fully in international economic institutions, reflecting a widespread acceptance of the desirability of economic integration and a broader belief that developed and developing nations can build on their common interests to create opportunities that will speed economic growth and development in Africa, Asia, and Latin America.

---

20. For two among many divergent views on aid, see Dambisa Moyo, *Dead Aid: Why Aid Is Not Working and How There Is a Better Way for Africa* (New York: Farrar, Straus, and Giroux, 2009); and Jeffrey D. Sachs, *The Age of Sustainable Development* (New York: Columbia University Press, 2015).

What Helps the Global Poor Best: Aid or Trade?

In the year 2000, HIV, malaria, and tuberculosis killed millions of people in the developing world. These diseases reached epidemic proportions in some regions of Asia and Africa and were endemic (consistently present) in many others. That year, the rich countries of the world began the process of creating the Global Fund to Fight AIDS, Tuberculosis and Malaria. Since 2002, the Global Fund has spent over $60 billion to help poor countries in the fight against these deadly diseases. At the end of 2019, it was estimated that these efforts had saved some 38 million lives, will have averted over 200 million new cases of AIDS, malaria, and tuberculosis, and will have helped dozens of poor countries formulate a more effective response to the COVID-19 pandemic.[a] The quality of life of hundreds of millions of people has been measurably improved by aid to promote global public health.

Such funds comprise only a fraction of the aid given to the developing world overall. Indeed, over the past 70 years the rich countries of the world have given over $3 trillion in aid to poor countries. While there have been some major successes in improving public health, foreign aid targeting other developmental goals has often failed to produce a lasting improvement in living conditions. More than 700 million people in the developing world still live in abject poverty, barely at or below the income level necessary to guarantee subsistence. Is aid the most effective way to help the world's poor? Might there be a better way?

Activists, policy makers, and scholars have long argued about how best to help the world's poorest people. Some emphasize how foreign aid from rich nations can have a powerful, beneficial impact on the living standards of the poor. Others downplay the potential for aid to make a difference and instead emphasize the need for economic reforms so that poor countries can take advantage of international trade. The debate is often characterized as one between aid and trade: whether it is more effective to give money to developing countries or to encourage them to pursue better economic policies.

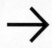

Applying the Concepts

This disagreement has to do with how aid, or trade, might affect the **interests** of people and policy makers in poor countries. And the effect on interests, in turn, depends on the social and political **institutions** of the poor countries— in particular, whether governments are set up in such a way that they are willing and able to put aid money to appropriate uses. Central to this issue is the nature of **interactions** between donors and the recipient governments, particularly whether the donors are themselves willing and able to ensure that their money is used productively to improve the lives of the poor.

Supporters of foreign aid argue that aid has important economic and political effects. Economically, they believe that the prospect of receiving aid can give policy makers in the developing world reasons to initiate efforts to alleviate poverty and spur economic development. By loosening some of the tight financial constraints that governments of poor countries face, aid may also encourage these governments to pursue policies that benefit the poor. And while policy makers may not have an interest in reducing poverty, especially if national political institutions are undemocratic or otherwise do not reflect the interests of the poor, donor countries and nongovernmental agencies can use financial incentives to encourage recipient governments to adopt better policies.[b]

Politically and socially, supporters of foreign aid also hope that aid will reduce some of the extreme pressures

Aid from the Global Fund has supported malaria prevention programs and provided mosquito nets to people in many developing countries, including the Ivory Coast.

---

a. The Global Fund, "Results & Impact," December 21, 2020, www.theglobalfund.org/en/impact (accessed 1/25/21).

b. Jeffrey D. Sachs, *The Age of Sustainable Development* (New York: Columbia University Press, 2015).

on these countries' populations so that they can more fully participate in national life. The Global Fund, in alleviating the burden of disease on developing countries, shares this goal. Jeffrey Sachs, a prominent economist and strong supporter of more generous aid, argues that "development aid, when properly designed and delivered, works, saving the lives of the poor and helping to promote economic growth."[c]

Aid skeptics question whether governments in developing nations will do the right thing with the aid they receive. They argue that many of these governments do not rely on the poor for political support and so have little interest in pro-poor policies. Aid money may go to benefit only their supporters, such as powerful interest groups or corrupt politicians. As Nobel laureate Angus Deaton writes: "Aid undermines what poor people need most: an effective government that works with them for today and tomorrow."[d]

Those who are pessimistic about the positive impact of aid may quote the old saying: "Give a man a fish, and he can eat for a day; teach him to fish, and he can eat for the rest of his life." Their general view is that it is important for developing countries to adopt policies that lead to economic growth and development—especially policies tying them to the world economy so that they can take advantage of the opportunities offered by international markets.

There is evidence to support both positions. Scholars have typically found that aid does not spur development unless the assisted governments adopt appropriate policies.[e] On the other hand, even skeptics accept that foreign aid can make a difference in the lives of the poor; Deaton writes: "Foreign aid . . . has much to its credit, particularly in terms of health care, with many people alive today who would otherwise be dead."[f]

Some economists have suggested a third position: that aid should be focused not on broad national policies

Some argue that developing countries are better served by policies that promote trade. Here, workers at a factory in Bangladesh manufacture clothing for export.

but rather on targeted interventions that affect particular aspects of the lives of the poor. Such programs might include finding more effective ways to deliver medicine or education to poor villages or developing measures to encourage poor farmers to adopt more efficient techniques.[g] While this approach seems to have achieved some success, it largely abandons attempts at thoroughgoing changes to the development process.

In light of these arguments, how can well-meaning people and governments in the rich countries of the world best help the global poor? Aid transfers money to the developing world but may not be effective in the long run. Trade—and economic reforms in general—may hold long-term promise, but the problem of poverty is pressing and unlikely to be alleviated quickly by policy change. Wherever the answer lies, the quality of life of hundreds of millions of people is at stake.

c. Jeffrey Sachs, "The Case for Aid," *Foreign Policy*, January 21, 2014, https://foreignpolicy.com/2014/01/21/the-case-for-aid/ (accessed 2/17/21).

d. Angus Deaton, "Weak States, Poor Countries," Project Syndicate, October 12, 2015, www.project-syndicate.org/commentary/economic-development-requires-effective-governments-by-angus-deaton (accessed 2/17/21).

e. Craig Burnside and David Dollar, "Aid, Policies and Growth," *American Economic Review* 90, no. 4 (2000): 847–868.

f. Deaton, "Weak States, Poor Countries."

g. Nobel laureates Abhijit Banerjee and Esther Duflo, in *Poor Economics: A Radical Rethinking of the Way to Fight Global Poverty* (New York: Public Affairs, 2011), present a prominent argument for this position.

Thinking Analytically

1. How might foreign aid affect the interests of recipient governments? Would these effects be good for the poor?

2. How might domestic political institutions affect the ways in which foreign aid would be put to use in recipient countries?

3. How do interactions between donors and recipient governments affect the ways in which foreign aid could help the poor?

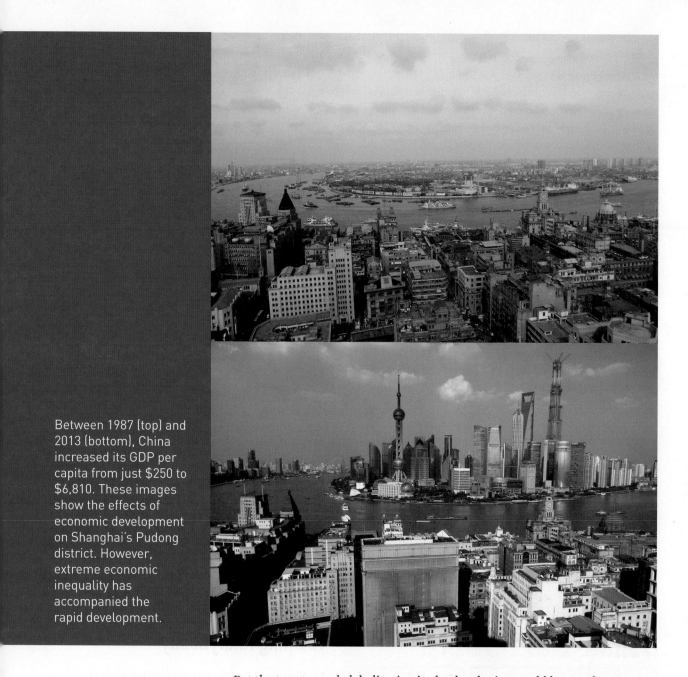

Between 1987 (top) and 2013 (bottom), China increased its GDP per capita from just $250 to $6,810. These images show the effects of economic development on Shanghai's Pudong district. However, extreme economic inequality has accompanied the rapid development.

But the turn toward globalization in the developing world has not been without difficulties and critics. One source of stress has been the financial and currency crises that have affected a score of developing countries (see Chapters 8 and 9). While such developing countries as Mexico, Thailand, and Argentina benefited from massive inflows of capital, they also suffered debilitating crises when these flows stopped. As developed countries had themselves discovered, integration into world markets has costs as well as benefits, creates losers as well as winners. The depth of these currency and financial crises led many observers to question whether the benefits of openness to international investment truly outweighed its costs.

The threat of crisis was heightened by the concern that economic openness was not delivering the kind and rate of economic growth that many analysts had anticipated. Economic reform was, in the minds of many, justified by how rapidly such countries as South Korea had rushed to modernity and how relatively equitable their societies had become in the process. This justification was attractive to people in developing countries whose economies had been stagnant and in which the gap between rich and poor had been growing.

But even after opening more to the world economy, many developing countries grew only slowly or not at all—an outcome that disappointed those who had hoped to see tangible results of the economic reforms. Even more disturbing was the increasingly unequal distribution of income in many of the reformed developing countries. Then there were true developmental disasters, countries that seemed to be sinking ever further into destitution and, in some cases, social chaos.

Although there have been success stories, the overall picture is still troubling. Many of the developing world's people remain in poverty. While the impoverished constitute a smaller share of the LDC population than they did 30 years ago, because of population growth the number of people living in poverty remains well over three billion, while some 800 million of these live in extreme poverty.[21] In addition, many developing countries—including some of the fastest growers—have become more unequal as they have grown.

Disappointment with the results of 30 years of reform-oriented development policies and outcomes has contributed to something of a backlash against the economic reforms of the 1980s and 1990s—a backlash that in some ways is similar to what many developed nations have experienced over the past decade. Some of this backlash has taken the form of electoral successes by politicians who have been critical of the current pattern of globalization. The governments of Venezuela, Bolivia, and Iran, for example, are highly critical of the trend toward economic openness and integration into international markets. Even governments that remain committed to engagement with the world economy have searched for ways to reduce the social costs of this integration and to address the political discontent that has become common in much of the developing world.

Conclusion: Toward Global Development

At the human level, the most pressing issue today is how to improve the living standards of the billions of people in the developing world who live in or near poverty. This is why so many nongovernmental organizations (which we discuss more in Chapter 11) focus on development issues. Generally, finding an effective

---

21. World Bank, "Poverty and Shared Prosperity 2020: Reversals of Fortune," 2020, https://openknowledge .worldbank.org/bitstream/handle/10986/34496/9781464816024.pdf (accessed 1/25/21).

path toward the goal of broad-based economic development requires a clear understanding of how and why countries have failed or succeeded in developing. While scholars and others continue to debate the matter heatedly, the preceding discussion points to several components of a reasonable diagnosis of the sources of underdevelopment and offers suggestions about what might be done to overcome them.

Addressing International Factors

While developed and developing countries have many interests in common, there are also important areas in which their interests conflict. And interactions between developed and developing countries almost always favor developed countries. Industrialized nations are richer and more powerful than LDCs and can usually get their way in bilateral and multilateral negotiations. Although scores of developing nations have been involved in international trade bargaining rounds, the outcomes of these interactions have been far more reflective of developed-country concerns than of developing-country preferences.

International institutions tend to reflect inherent power relations among nations, which means that they favor developed over developing nations. The principal international economic organizations—the IMF, the World Bank, the WTO—all have an implicit or explicit bias toward the interests of rich nations. Sometimes the bias is formal, as is the case in the IMF, where votes are weighted by economic size; sometimes it is informal, based only on the greater wealth and power of the industrialized world. Either way, the policy bias of these international institutions can bend outcomes in ways that are not favorable to the developmental prospects of poor nations.

Developed countries are unlikely to cede influence over international institutions or over the outcomes of international bargaining for purely humanitarian reasons. Yet rich and poor nations share a common interest in faster growth and more stability in LDCs, and there may be scope for agreement on reforming international institutions to make them more responsive to LDCs' concerns. Indeed, the IMF and World Bank have undertaken reform efforts to address some LDC criticisms of their activities. But many observers believe that reform of international institutions has to go further in order to have a substantial impact on development prospects.[22]

To the extent that these international factors impede LDC progress, addressing them might speed it up. Because both the developed and the developing world can benefit from faster growth and more stability in LDCs, there is scope for LDC and developed-country interests to emphasize shared goals over individual ones. However, a diagnosis of development failure that rests too strongly on international constraints faces the reality that the same international conditions seem to allow for strikingly different national economic outcomes—for example, as we've seen in Botswana and Zambia. While the external environment may not be as favorable

---

22. Joseph E. Stiglitz, *Globalization and Its Discontents Revisited: Anti-Globalization in the Era of Trump* (New York: Norton, 2017) is a prominent statement of the position that lays much of the blame on the structure of the international order and presents proposals for global reform.

as LDCs might like, it has permitted the emergence of some very striking success stories in addition to spectacular failures. This observation leads us back to the conclusion that domestic forces are probably the principal factors affecting economic growth and development.

Addressing Domestic Factors

As we have seen, interests within a poor country can stand in the way of its overall economic progress. Powerful groups may hamper the government's ability to improve education, social services, or the economic infrastructure. But even the most malevolent interests can impede economic progress only if they are successful in dominating society and politics. Where the impact of self-interested groups is countered by broad public pressure, the result is less likely to impede economic development. Where groups can cooperate to support the provision of public goods, rather than fighting over private benefits, all of society will be better off in the long run.

Likewise, the political institutions of developing nations have a powerful impact on whether their citizens are able to overcome obstacles to development. A well-functioning electoral democracy, for example, can reduce the impact of venal private interest groups and can serve as a brake on the activities of corrupt public employees.

The conclusion that domestic features of LDCs are key to understanding their problems is cautiously optimistic. It is optimistic because it suggests that the future of developing nations is largely in their own hands, rather than being hostage to geographic destiny or the nature of the international system. Indeed, a growing number of countries have succeeded in narrowing the development gap. But this optimism must be guarded. For where economic development has been held back for decades—even generations—by domestic interests, interactions, or institutions, it is likely to be difficult to change these conditions. Nonetheless, this would appear to be the most promising path forward in the continuing effort to reduce the enormous disparity between the world's rich minority and its poor majority.

Study Tool Kit

Interests, Interactions, and Institutions in Context

- Although everyone in poor countries prefers more development to less, individuals and groups within countries may have conflicting interests with respect to development policy. The pursuit of private interests by powerful groups can impede the adoption of measures that would spur economic growth.

- Domestic social and political institutions can have a major impact on how these conflicts of interest affect development. They can either empower or overcome special interest groups that stand in the way of development. They can either facilitate or impede the ability of actors to cooperate to promote government policies conducive to economic growth.

- At the international level, rich and poor nations generally have a common interest in accelerating the economic growth of the developing world. However, there have been many instances of rich countries supporting policies and institutions that disfavor less developed countries.

- Successful economic growth requires that a country overcome both the domestic obstacles posed by interests and institutions that are detrimental to development and the international impediments created by conflicts of interest with wealthy nations, which can draw on superior reserves of economic and political power.

Key Terms

less developed countries (LDCs), p. 449

infrastructure, p. 451

primary products, p. 464

oligopoly, p. 464

terms of trade, p. 464

import-substituting industrialization (ISI), p. 468

export-oriented industrialization (EOI), p. 470

Group of 77, p. 472

commodity cartels, p. 473

For Further Reading

Acemoglu, Daron, and James Robinson. *Why Nations Fail: The Origins of Power, Prosperity, and Poverty.* **New York: Crown, 2012.** Presents a strong theoretical argument for the importance of political institutions in affecting economic development, along with a range of empirical evidence to illustrate the theory.

Banerjee, Abhijit V., and Esther Duflo. *Good Economics for Hard Times.* **New York: Public Affairs, 2019.** The winners of the 2019 Nobel Prize in Economics develop their analyses of global problems, including poverty in developing countries, and present concrete proposals to alleviate poverty, based largely on the authors' many years of work in the field.

Engerman, Stanley L., and Kenneth L. Sokoloff. *Economic Development in the Americas since 1500: Endowments and Institutions.* **Cambridge: Cambridge University Press, 2012.** Demonstrates how differences in the underlying economic characteristics of different societies in the Americas had a profound and lasting effect on their socioeconomic and political organization and on their subsequent economic development.

Milanović, Branko. *Global Inequality: A New Approach for the Age of Globalization.* **Cambridge, MA: Harvard University Press, 2016.** Provides a data-intensive and historically informed summary of the level of and trends in international inequality.

Rodrik, Dani. *One Economics, Many Recipes: Globalization, Institutions, and Economic Growth.* **Princeton, NJ: Princeton University Press, 2007.** Presents a prominent economist's ideas about how globalization can be made more compatible with the needs of developing countries.

Stiglitz, Joseph E. *Globalization and Its Discontents Revisited: Anti-Globalization in the Era of Trump.* **New York: Norton, 2017.** Provides a critical look by the Nobel laureate and former World Bank chief economist at how the contemporary international economic order impedes economic growth and development and what might be done about it.

11

International Law and Norms

THE PUZZLE *In a world of sovereign states, how can the international community constrain states' actions? When and why do states do what is "right"?*

Above: The International Court of Justice issued an order for provisional measures in January 2020 against Myanmar to prevent the genocide of Rohingya Muslims, a crisis that international observers have been monitoring since 2016. Shown here, Rohingya refugees sit at a makeshift camp near the border, waiting to cross into Bangladesh.

Shocked by the suffering of wounded soldiers after the Battle of Solferino, fought in 1859 as part of the Italian wars of unification, Swiss social activist Henry Dunant began a campaign to reform and limit the conduct of states during wartime. The result of Dunant's efforts, and the efforts of many others mobilized to the cause, was the first Geneva Convention, on the treatment of wounded soldiers, adopted in 1864. This agreement was followed by a second convention, on the treatment of members of armed forces at sea, in 1906, and a third convention, on the treatment of prisoners of war, in 1929. These three agreements were revised in 1949 and joined by a fourth convention on the protection of civilians in wartime.

These treaties outlining the laws of war are typically referred to as the Geneva Conventions, and they form one of the most clearly articulated and respected bodies of international law in today's world. War between states might seem an unlikely interaction to be governed by such an international institution. At the same time that states are sending their soldiers into battle to kill their enemies and possibly die for their country, they generally follow international laws regulating how that killing is done and how prisoners and civilians are to be treated.

The Geneva Conventions are monitored and supervised by the International Committee of the Red Cross, part of the International Red Cross and Red Crescent Movement. The conventions have now been ratified by all 193 members of the United Nations (UN), firmly establishing their provisions as nearly universally acknowledged and respected international law.

The conventions, however, have not ended all atrocities, especially within countries. In 1994, Hutu extremists in Rwanda began a mass murder of ethnic Tutsis. Roughly 800,000 people are believed to have been killed within 100 days. The killings ended only when the Rwandan Patriotic Front, a militia of mostly Tutsi rebels who had originally started the civil war, reentered the conflict and seized control of the country.

The international community watched and condemned this unmistakable act of genocide but did little to stop it. In 1999, then UN secretary-general Kofi Annan challenged the international community to define its obligations to protect vulnerable peoples when their own governments either cannot or will not protect them. Taking the lead, Canada sponsored the International Commission on Intervention and State Sovereignty in

September 2000. In December 2001, the commission issued its report with the provocative title *The Responsibility to Protect*.[1] The report argued that the international community not only must prosecute crimes against humanity but also has a responsibility to protect at-risk populations through military means if necessary. This new obligation was quickly dubbed R2P, after the title of the report. In April 2006, the UN Security Council affirmed R2P, recognizing it as a new norm of international behavior.

Although hopes were high that R2P would help realize the lessons learned from Rwanda, it met quickly with resistance from certain members of the Security Council, reflecting a fundamental tension between state sovereignty and international law. Although R2P has been applied in a few cases, its potential to enable more effective international responses when states commit atrocities against their own citizens has so far been underwhelming. It has failed to prevent abuses against civilians during conflict in Libya and Syria, and it has not prevented what many call ongoing genocides against the Rohingya in Myanmar and the Uighurs in China.

The Geneva Conventions are international treaties in which states consent to treat armed personnel and civilians in humane ways. Though the conventions have had an important impact, they do not diminish the sovereignty of states, as the principle of sovereignty includes the right to freely enter into agreements that constrain one's actions. R2P, however, stands in stark contrast to this principle. This new international norm, championed by the UN with the consent of its member states, explicitly limits national sovereignty in cases of widespread human rights abuses and state-sponsored violence. This is important because it legitimizes the intervention of states in the internal affairs of other states whether or not the targets give their consent. The Geneva Conventions and R2P are both part of a growing collection of laws and norms, respectively, that are broadly referred to as *global governance*.

The puzzle of international law, though, is this: Why would sovereign states agree to be bound by international rules? This is especially curious in the case of norms like R2P, to which individual states have not necessarily agreed to bind themselves but on which they may be held to account. Why and how do states collectively own behavior? How are private actors, who are supposedly subject to states under the concept of sovereignty, able to alter state behavior?

Thinking Analytically about International Law and Norms

International law and norms are institutions that seek to shape how states understand their interests and that constrain the many ways in which states interact. States create and abide by international law because it facilitates cooperation. Indeed, where we observe strong international laws, the benefits of cooperation to states are generally large enough that these laws are often self-enforcing, or in the interests of states to follow willingly. International law clarifies the obligations of states, defines violations that are subject to retaliation, and sometimes provides for independent tribunals to resolve disputes. Through these mechanisms, international law helps states to understand, meet, and manage their obligations to one another.

International norms affect world politics by changing how individuals and, in turn, states conceive of their interests and appropriate actions in their interactions with other states. Norms are standards of behavior that reflect a community's beliefs about what constitutes appropriate behavior for an actor in a specified condition. Norms affect interactions because they are understood by states to be right and morally correct rules of conduct.

As we will see, international NGOs, transnational networks, and private transnational actors are also important in global governance because they can bring attention to new issues, advocate for changes in law and norms, or facilitate cooperation between states by providing information or monitoring compliance. They can influence international laws and norms though advocacy, setting rules, and even helping write international law.

1. The full report is available at https://idl-bnc-idrc.dspacedirect.org/bitstream/handle/10625/18432/IDL-18432.pdf?sequence=6&isAllowed=y (accessed 2/18/21).

What Is International Law?

International law is established by states through either custom or convention as a way to facilitate international cooperation or regulate international behavior. The Geneva Conventions are one example, but others abound. For instance, the World Trade Organization (WTO) sets rules on the exchange of goods and services and increasingly on investment and property rights; the UN Convention on the Law of the Sea (UNCLOS) governs the use of the oceans and seabed resources; and the Convention on the Prohibition of the Use, Stockpiling, Production, and Transfer of Anti-Personnel Mines and on Their Destruction, more simply known as the Ottawa Convention, outlaws the use and production of land mines and mandates the clearing of existing minefields. International human rights law, which we will examine in more detail in Chapter 12, intrudes deeply into national political practices. Precisely because the specific rules of international law matter, states often bargain intensely over these rules and their interpretation. Law does not mean the end of conflict between states but is itself the product of political interaction and struggle. Nonetheless, international law is valued and typically followed for the cooperation that it helps bring about.

International law is "a body of rules which binds states and other agents in world politics in their relations with one another and is considered to have the

international law
A body of rules that binds states and other agents in world politics and is considered to have the status of law.

Key Moments in the Development of International Law

1648—Peace of Westphalia

1807—Slave Trade Act in Britain banned the international slave trade

1863—International Committee of the Red Cross founded

1864—First "Geneva Convention for the amelioration of the condition of the wounded in armies in the field" signed

1865—International Telegraph Union established

1899 and 1907—The Hague Conventions

1920—League of Nations founded from the Paris Peace Conference

1924—Declaration of the Rights of the Child adopted by the League of Nations

1945—International Military Tribunal at Nuremberg

1945—Charter of the United Nations signed

1946—International Court of Justice established

1948—Universal Declaration of Human Rights adopted by the UN General Assembly

1963—Limited Test Ban Treaty enacted

1982—UN Convention on the Law of the Sea signed

1993—Chemical Weapons Convention signed

1997—Convention on the Prohibition of the Use, Stockpiling, Production, and Transfer of Anti-Personnel Mines and on their Destruction (Ottawa Convention) signed

1998—Rome Statute established the International Criminal Court

2005—Responsibility to Protect (R2P)

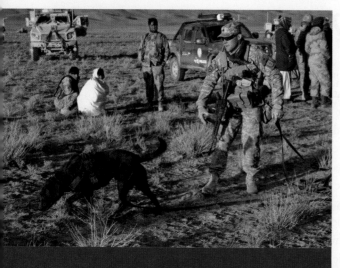

States cooperate under the Ottawa Convention to clear existing minefields. Although the treaty was ratified in 1999, there is still much work to be done. Here, a member of the U.S. military searches for mines and explosives in Afghanistan.

status of law."[2] This definition might appear circular at first, with law being constituted by rules having the status of law, but two aspects of the definition help us understand international law more precisely.

First, international law is a *body of rules* linked together in a common logical structure. Law is not simply a list of rules. Rather, to stand as law, rules must be woven together by one or more unifying principles, such as sovereignty. In contemporary international law, sovereignty stands as the primary unifying principle. Even though sovereignty is often violated in practice, it still forms the foundation on which rules governing state and nonstate behavior become international law.

Second, to have the *status of law*, a body of rules must include both primary rules, which regulate behavior, and secondary rules, which regulate how primary rules are made.[3] Primary rules can define behavior that is prohibited ("Don't do *x*") or behavior that is required ("must do *y*"). The Ottawa Convention, for instance, explicitly prohibits the use of land mines, which is an example of a law prohibiting a specific behavior. The same convention also requires certain behavior: it stipulates that states must destroy their stockpiles of land mines within four years of the treaty's coming into force, which finally happened on March 1, 1999, when Burkina Faso became the fortieth country to ratify the agreement.

To have the status of law, primary rules must be made in accordance with secondary rules. One can think of secondary rules as akin to a constitution or the rules about how rules are made. To be governed by the "rule of law" is thus to set and enforce primary rules in ways that are consistent with secondary rules. Primary rules enacted in compliance with existing secondary rules are given the status of law. In international law, the principle of sovereignty implies a secondary rule about how other rules are made: under sovereignty, only states can bind themselves to international law. In the case of the Ottawa Convention, its primary rules become law because it was negotiated and ratified by sovereign states as an international treaty.

As a body of rules, duly enacted under secondary rules, international law is distinct from international norms (taken up later in this chapter) and other international institutions. Norms are often singular rules, disconnected from any larger body of rules, and can contradict secondary rules, especially sovereignty. Thus, R2P is an emerging norm and not law, even though it was affirmed by the UN Security Council, because it explicitly violates the principle of sovereignty by calling for intervention into the internal affairs of states under some circumstances and because it has not been accepted as binding by the states most likely to be subject to those interventions.

---

2. Hedley Bull, *The Anarchical Society: A Study of Order in World Politics* (New York: Columbia University Press, 1977), 127.

3. This conception of the status of law follows from H. L. A. Hart, *The Concept of Law* (Oxford: Clarendon, 1961).

How Is International Law Made?

States establish and abide by international law, like any other institution, because it facilitates cooperation. A specific type of international law applies even amid armed conflict. **International humanitarian law** (also known as the **laws of war**) seeks to constrain states from the worst abuses during armed conflict. States may also bargain over international law, with some preferring certain rules over others. For instance, UNCLOS was enacted in 1982 after 9 years of hard negotiations, largely over rules on the exploitation of mineral resources on the ocean floor. It did not come into force until 12 years later, once it was finally ratified by the required 60 countries. Even though 165 countries have now joined the treaty, and it is widely acknowledged as international law governing the use of the seas, the United States was so opposed to some of the provisions that it has refused to sign the final document. Most of the time, however, it is the benefits of cooperation made possible by rules and adherence to those rules that lead states to create and abide by international laws. This includes cases of reciprocity, in which states abide by international law or norms because they are better off if other states do the same. The UN Charter's Article 2(4) prohibition on the use of force is an example. Although many states would be more powerful if they invaded and conquered their neighbors, the benefits of peace and stability that go along with respect for territorial integrity mean that compliance with this aspect of international law is high.

In international relations, there are two principal mechanisms for making international law.[4] The first is custom, or accepted practice. States carry out certain practices because they believe they are legally obligated to do so. Such **customary international law** usually develops slowly, over time, as states come to recognize some practices as appropriate and correct. The law of diplomatic immunity, whereby ambassadors and other embassy staff are exempt from the laws of their host nation, is a classic example. This practice became law by custom because it was in the interests of both home and host countries to continue to honor it. Diplomatic immunity permits embassy personnel to report on their host country, negotiate with host-country representatives, and generally promote the interests of their home country without fear of possibly politically motivated prosecutions for crimes invented by their host nation. It also prevents potential misunderstandings between countries over the activities of their diplomats from escalating into larger disputes. Countries have learned that rather than imprisoning and punishing diplomats, it is best just to send them home if they violate national laws. Despite occasional abuses, such as diplomats racking up large numbers of parking tickets for traffic violations, the practice of diplomatic immunity is sufficiently beneficial to home and host countries that, over time, it came to be recognized as international law.

Although diplomatic immunity has been in effect for centuries, it was codified as law in the Vienna Convention on Diplomatic Relations enacted in 1961. Freedom of the seas is another important rule that was accepted as customary international

international humanitarian law (laws of war)

A body of rules that seeks to limit the effects of armed conflict, protect noncombatants, and restrict means and methods of warfare for humanitarian reasons.

customary international law

International law that usually develops slowly, over time, as states come to recognize practices as appropriate and correct.

---

4. The sources of international law are formally defined by Article 38 of the Statute of the International Court of Justice. In addition to conventions and custom, which we discuss here, the statute allows for law to follow from "general principles of law recognized by civilized nations" and, as a subsidiary means, "the teachings of the most highly qualified publicists of the various nations." The statute is available at www.icj-cij.org/en/statute (accessed 12/18/20).

Before the concept of crimes against humanity was codified in the Rome Statute of the International Criminal Court, these crimes were first prosecuted by tribunals formed in the aftermath of World War II. The International Military Tribunal for the Far East tried the leaders of Japan for crimes committed during the war.

law long before it was codified in UNCLOS. Finally, the concept of crimes against humanity also developed largely as customary law and was finally codified in the Rome Statute of the International Criminal Court (ICC), which went into effect in 2002 (see "What Shaped Our World?" on p. 491).

Secondary rules that govern the establishment of customary international law remain vague, however. The number of countries that must recognize a practice as legitimate and the length of time before it is accepted as law are not specified by any other rule. For this reason, as the examples of diplomatic immunity, freedom of the seas, and crimes against humanity show, customary international law is increasingly being codified in formal international agreements, particularly in areas where specific rules are contentious. But overall, customary international law tends to evolve in areas where states have strong incentives to cooperate and benefit little from violating the rules that support this cooperation.

International treaties, which are negotiated and then ratified by states, represent the second mechanism for creating international law. International treaties typically originate in a convention to negotiate a new agreement involving a large number of states. It is not necessary for a treaty-drafting process to involve all states, and many important treaties were initiated by smaller groups of states. Some agreements are easily reached, such as the first Geneva Convention (though the original negotiations involved just 12 states). As in the UNCLOS negotiations, however, hard bargaining may ensue precisely because substantial gains are at stake and states seek deals more favorable to their interests.

Within global governance more generally, these two mechanisms for creating international law apply to both public international law—or the regulation of interactions among states or between states and other actors—and private international law, in which a separate body of law regulates private but transnational legal battles.

As we will explain in the next section, agreements differ in their obligations, precision, and delegation, sometimes in order to address conflicts of interests that would otherwise prevent states from reaching agreement. Once a convention is finalized by international negotiations, the agreement must then be ratified by each member state in accordance with its domestic constitutional provisions. By ratifying treaties like the Geneva Conventions, states voluntarily take on the constraints of international law, in many cases binding their own state to specific standards in the future. This type of state commitment to international law is not interpreted as a violation of the principle of sovereignty. With international conventions, the secondary rules of international law are quite clear: countries that sign an international convention are bound to respect the terms of the agreement.

Crimes against Humanity

The concept of crimes against humanity is one of the most significant developments in international law of the last century.

Institutions The Rome Statute of the ICC, adopted in 1998 and entered into force in 2002, defines crimes against humanity as any of the following acts when committed as part of a planned and systematic attack directed against any civilian population: (1) murder; (2) extermination; (3) enslavement; (4) deportation or forced population transfer; (5) imprisonment or other severe deprivation of liberty in violation of fundamental rules of international law; (6) torture; (7) rape and other forms of sexual violence; (8) persecution against any identifiable group based on political affiliation, race, nationality, culture, religion, or gender; (9) enforced disappearance of persons; and (10) apartheid. In contrast, war crimes are single, isolated instances of abuse carried out during armed conflict. Crimes against humanity are intentional, systematic violent acts against civilians.

Interests The states' interests in prosecuting crimes against humanity have evolved and grown over time. The first known use of the phrase *crimes against humanity* was in the U.S. Republican Party's 1860 platform, on which President Abraham Lincoln was elected; it described the reopening of the African slave trade as "a crime against humanity and a burning shame to our country and age." In May 1915, the Allied powers in World War I denounced the Armenian Genocide carried out by the Ottoman government as a "crime against humanity." The term, however, was first developed systematically in the London Charter of the International Military Tribunal, under which the Nuremberg trials of Nazi leaders were conducted after World War II.

A traditional understanding of war crimes did not allow for the prosecution of government officials for crimes carried out against their own citizens. The Holocaust, in which 6 million Jews were systematically exterminated by the Nazi regime, was not then illegal under international law. With an interest in punishing officials of the Nazi regime for the Holocaust and other atrocities, the drafters of the London Charter gave first real form to the doctrine of crimes against humanity.

The doctrine was carried over into the International Military Tribunal for the Far East and the so-called Tokyo trials, which prosecuted Japanese government officials for atrocities carried out during the war, especially the Nanking Massacre, in which hundreds of thousands of Chinese civilians and disarmed soldiers were murdered and tens of thousands of women were raped by the Japanese Imperial Army. As is clear from this history, the concept of crimes against humanity originated in the desires of the victors of World War II to punish the losing states for atrocities conducted in the course of the conflict and to prevent similar behaviors from recurring in the future.

Interactions Through the charters and military tribunals created after World War II, crimes against humanity became international law largely through custom and were formally codified only when the Rome Statute created the ICC. Government officials are now held responsible for widespread abuses of their own citizens, potentially subject to punishments for violations of basic rights and possibly even to armed intervention to halt abuses.

This relatively recent innovation in international law is important because, like human rights law more generally (see Chapter 12), it defines international law as resting on a common humanity that is superior to the policies of any state. This law clearly constrains the rights and, more important, the actions of states within the international community. R2P is an extension of the doctrine of crimes against humanity. It not only allows for the prosecution of such crimes after they have happened, such as at Nuremberg and Tokyo, but also calls on the international community to actively respond to stop the abuses as they are happening.

The ICC is not without controversy. Its track record reveals a disproportionate focus on African states and leaders, raising important questions about the potential for bias in investigations and prosecutions. Partly because the United States is not a state party to the Rome Statute, the ICC has limited authority to investigate its behavior, with the notable exception of cases in which a citizen of a nonmember country engages in criminal acts under ICC jurisdiction in an ICC member country. This provision allowed the ICC to open an investigation in 2020 into alleged crimes by the U.S. military and Central Intelligence Agency in Afghanistan. In early 2021, the ICC was officially investigating 13 situations of alleged war crimes and crimes against humanity, encompassing 29 cases in eight countries.

Is All International Law the Same?

Even when states have a shared interest in establishing international law to facilitate cooperation, they must still agree on what form the law will take. International law varies across several dimensions. First, international law varies in **obligation**, or the degree to which agents are legally bound by an international rule. High-obligation rules "must be performed in good faith regardless of inconsistent provisions of domestic law" or changing state interests, subject to certain exceptions, such as self-defense or necessity.[5] High-obligation laws, such as the Geneva Conventions or laws prohibiting crimes against humanity, are unconditional and require reparations to the injured party if they are breached. Low-obligation laws are merely aspirational, urging states to live up to some standard of behavior. As we will explain in Chapter 12, much early human rights law took this form.

Even high-obligation laws are often contingent or contain escape clauses. The 1994 UN Framework Convention on Climate Change (UNFCCC), which we will discuss in Chapter 13, requires parties to the agreement to reduce their greenhouse gas emissions, but only after they consider "their specific national and regional development priorities." Likewise, the Limited Test Ban Treaty enacted in 1963, which outlaws certain forms of nuclear weapons testing, permits states to withdraw from the agreement if they decide that "extraordinary events" jeopardize their "supreme interests."

A second dimension on which international law varies is in its **precision**, or the degree to which international legal obligations are fully specified. More precise laws narrow the scope for reasonable interpretation. An important aspect of precision is that "for a set of rules, precision implies not just that each rule in the set is unambiguous, but that rules are related to one another in a noncontradictory way, creating a framework within which case-by-case interpretation can be coherently carried out."[6]

Much of international law is quite precise, with international treaties running to hundreds and sometimes thousands of pages of definitions, terms, and rules. The UNCLOS treaty, for example, contains 17 parts, 320 articles, and 9 annexes, plus an additional agreement (with 9 more annexes) elaborating on Part XI of the treaty. States often seek to retain control over international law and to limit future interpretations of the law by being as precise as possible in the treaty itself.

Other agreements, however, are remarkably imprecise. Commercial treaties, for instance, typically require states to create "favorable conditions" for investment and to avoid "unreasonable regulations." Such imprecise terms are usually not the product of poor legal draftsmanship but rather reflect continuing disagreement between states over the exact nature of the obligations being specified. Vague terms ensure that settling on an agreement will not bring bargaining to a close and that states will continue to negotiate, albeit within a legalized framework.

Finally, international law also varies in its degree of **delegation** to third parties, wherein courts, arbitrators, mediators, or others are given the authority to

---

obligation

The degree to which states are legally bound by an international rule. High-obligation rules must be performed in good faith and, if breached, require reparations to the injured party.

precision

The degree to which international legal obligations are fully specified. More precise rules narrow the scope for reasonable interpretation.

delegation

The degree to which third parties, such as courts, arbitrators, or mediators, are given authority to implement, interpret, and apply international legal rules; to resolve disputes over the rules; and to make additional rules.

---

5. We owe these dimensions, and the examples used here, to Kenneth W. Abbott, Robert O. Keohane, Andrew Moravcsik, Anne-Marie Slaughter, et al., "The Concept of Legalization," in *Legalization and World Politics*, ed. Judith L. Goldstein, Miles Kahler, Robert O. Keohane, and Anne-Marie Slaughter (Cambridge, MA: MIT Press, 2001), 25.

6. Abbott et al., "Concept of Legalization," 29.

implement, interpret, and apply the rules specified; to resolve disputes over the rules; and to
make additional rules. In domestic law, courts
often have tremendous delegated powers to
interpret the law and, in so doing, to fill in legal
gaps left in the original statutes. When the degree
of delegation is high and statutes are imprecise,
courts may actually make new law through their
interpretations—a result sometimes decried by
critics as judicial activism.

In international relations, states are generally
reluctant to delegate significant legal authority to
third parties. The power to interpret law and possibly make new law has the potential to bind states
in ways they did not anticipate and would not have
approved if considered in advance. In the realm
of dispute settlement, the scope of delegation
ranges from international courts with relatively
broad jurisdiction, binding decision-making pow-

Under some international laws, states agree to
delegate extensive rulemaking powers to specialized
agencies, such as the International Civil Aviation
Organization (ICAO). The ICAO establishes rules and
standards that help states cooperate on the common
goal of safe and orderly air transport.

ers, and the ability to set legal precedents (as in the ICC in the enforcement of crimes
against humanity) to limited dispute settlement bodies with more narrow mandates
and national vetoes of decisions (as under the old General Agreement on Tariffs and
Trade, or GATT). Having even less delegated authority are various arbitrators and
mediators, who can recommend more or less binding solutions to disagreements.

In the realm of rulemaking and implementation, international law may delegate sweeping powers to administrative bodies, though these are usually found only
in specialized agencies like the International Civil Aviation Organization (ICAO).
In most cases, administrative bodies have more conditional powers subject to state
overrides, as in the International Monetary Fund (IMF) and World Bank.

By considering these three dimensions—obligation, precision, and delegation—
we can distinguish between hard and soft law.[7] Hard law is obligatory and precisely
defined, and it delegates substantial authority to third parties, particularly international courts. Soft law is aspirational and ambiguous, and it does not delegate significant powers to third parties. Countries often adopt soft law because it is easier to
achieve, is more flexible and therefore better suited to dealing with uncertain futures,
infringes less on state sovereignty, and facilitates compromise. Soft law is not a failure
of lawmaking but reflects intentional choices by states to write law appropriate to the
issue area or to the extent of cooperation that they are currently prepared to accept.

Although there is no guarantee that soft law will lead to hard law, agreements in
new issue areas often begin as soft law that sets goals for states and creates frameworks for continuing negotiations. This soft law may eventually become hard law as
states gain experience, bargain over specific issues, and write more detailed treaties.
A clear example is the UNFCCC, which was dismissed by critics as toothless when

---

7. Kenneth W. Abbott and Duncan Snidal, "Hard and Soft Law in International Governance," in
   Legalization and World Politics, ed. Goldstein et al., 37–72.

it was first signed but later led to the effective Montreal Protocol, in force since 1999, and to the Kyoto Protocol (see Chapter 13). At the extreme, soft law blends into international norms, like R2P, which we will consider later in the chapter.

Does International Law Matter?

Can international law "domesticate" international politics? That is, can international law become more like domestic law found within states? Can the use of force in international relations be tamed by international law? Perhaps no questions have vexed diplomats and scholars of international relations more.

Supporters of international law view it as an effective—perhaps essential—tool in facilitating cooperation and managing conflicts. According to international lawyer Louis Henkin, "almost all nations observe almost all principles of international law and almost all of their obligations almost all of the time."[8] Sometimes high levels of compliance result from more or less explicit enforcement mechanisms in international law. Yet states may comply with international law even without enforcement provisions.

International lawyers Abram Chayes and Antonia Chayes argue that states typically do comply with international law, and when they fail to do so, it is either because the law itself is imprecise or because they lack the capacity to fulfill their obligations.[9] In their view, states want to observe, say, the Geneva Conventions on the rules of war, but they may not have effective control over their own soldiers, who may abuse prisoners. Such was the case in the infamous Abu Ghraib scandal that shocked the world in 2004, when pictures of American soldiers abusing Iraqi prisoners surfaced online. Proponents point to the high rates of compliance as evidence of international law's potential. In this view, law can be a significant constraint on the interactions of states.

More skeptical observers see international law as unrealistic and utopian, or at least a reflection of state interests, rather than as a severe constraint on state actions. Two main problems exist. First, law is seldom precise enough to deal with every possible interaction between actors. Indeed, in domestic politics, lawyers earn their livings from and courts are clogged with cases in which the parties disagree on what the law says or requires in their specific circumstances. We should hardly expect international law to be more precise and less open to creative interpretation than domestic law is. In one telling instance, when NATO was considering intervening in Kosovo in 1999, British foreign secretary Robin Cook told U.S. secretary of state Madeleine Albright that he had "problems with our lawyers" over using force without the approval of the UN Security Council. Albright responded that he should "get new lawyers."[10] Albright's sentiment still applies today. If international law is malleable and can be interpreted to justify whatever states might want to do, it is a weak constraint, at best, on their actions.

Second, as we have seen, international law is the product of states' interests and interactions. States decide the rules by which they will constrain themselves,

---

8. Louis Henkin, *How Nations Behave: Law and Foreign Policy* (New York: Columbia University Press, 1968), 47. Italics in original omitted here.

9. Abram Chayes and Antonia Handler Chayes, "On Compliance," *International Organization* 47, no. 2 (1993): 175–205.

10. Michael J. Glennon, *Limits of Law, Prerogatives of Power: Interventionism after Kosovo* (London: Palgrave Macmillan, 2001), 178.

FIGURE 11.1 *Treaties Containing Punishment Provisions*

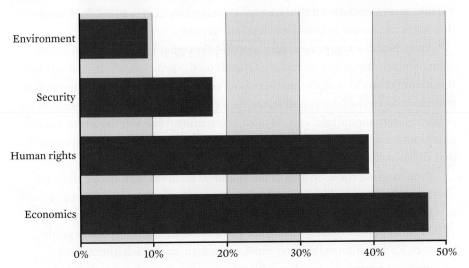

Figure source: Barbara Koremenos, *The Continent of International Law: Explaining Agreement Design* (New York: Cambridge University Press, 2016).

including the degree to which these rules are obligatory, precise, and delegated. That states therefore comply with rules they have written is, at one level, hardly surprising. This is sometimes described as the "selection problem" in international relations, in which it can be hard for scholars to tell the difference between cases in which law is effective at constraining states and cases in which states sign on to only those agreements that are consistent with how they would behave anyway.[11]

According to skeptics, therefore, international law does not constrain states, despite seemingly high levels of compliance with the law. Rather, countries only sign agreements and make laws that serve their interests and obligate them to undertake actions they would want to do anyway. With states crafting the laws that constrain them and then interpreting the meaning of those laws for their own purposes, it is very difficult for scholars to demonstrate conclusively that international law has an independent effect on state behavior over and above states' interests.

The truth likely lies somewhere between these extremes. The questions here are how, when, and why international law alters state behavior. International cooperation often requires that states subordinate their short-term interests for long-term benefits. Most forms of international cooperation must balance the incentives of smaller, weaker states with those of more powerful states. In many cases, agreements must be designed such that "weaker states can expect to benefit from cooperation" and powerful states can still exert enough informal influence in areas that are particularly important to them.[12]

Can international law constrain states to act in ways that are not in their short-term interests? Enforcement provisions in international agreements vary widely. As shown in Figure 11.1, nearly 40 percent of human rights agreements and more than 45 percent of economic agreements contain clauses empowering members to

---

11. George W. Downs, David M. Rocke, and Peter N. Barsoom, "Is the Good News about Compliance Good News about Cooperation?" *International Organization* 50, no. 3 (1996): 379–406.

12. Randall W. Stone, "The Scope of IMF Conditionality," *International Organization* 62, no. 4 (2008): 589–620.

punish the noncompliance of other members, while less than 10 percent of environmental agreements include such provisions.[13] We should note, however, that just because agreements do not contain explicit enforcement provisions does not mean that states cannot use informal mechanisms to punish noncompliance.

Even though an agreement may specify enforcement provisions, the enforcement of international law ultimately depends on the principle of national self-help. It is a truth of world politics that there is no central authority higher than the state that can enforce law between all states. As we discussed in Chapter 5, there are no police in international relations. At most, international law sets the terms and conditions under which victims can legally and legitimately retaliate against countries that violate rules of behavior.

Even in world trade, an area of international relations with strong and well-developed international laws, the WTO only permits victims of illegal trade barriers to retaliate by imposing punitive duties on goods purchased from the violator. The WTO cannot punish violators itself, nor can it mandate that other states punish violators. Each victimized country must, on its own, decide whether to seek and carry out retribution for clearly illegal acts. This dependence on self-help necessarily limits the effectiveness of international law.

At the same time, countries generally follow international law because of the very real and important benefits of the cooperation that it enables. Like all institutions, international law facilitates cooperation by setting more or less obligatory standards of behavior, helping to verify compliance by articulating more or less precise rules, lowering the costs of decision making by creating rules that do not need to be renegotiated for each interaction, and managing disputes.

To take one example, in analyzing the problem of restraints on violence during war, the political scientist James Morrow argues that cooperation depends on reciprocity.[14] A state is more likely to treat enemy prisoners of war (POWs) well if it expects its opponent to treat its captive soldiers well, and violations by one state are likely to provoke retaliation by another. The Geneva Conventions, especially when ratified by both parties, make clear that the states understand, accept, and are likely to follow international laws regulating the treatment of POWs. This makes it easier for states to presume that others will treat POWs humanely and for them to do the same for theirs, and it defines relatively clearly what constitutes a violation that could be legitimately punished through retaliation. By setting rules that help clarify expectations on both sides, the Geneva Conventions reinforce an equilibrium (treating POWs well as long as the other states treat POWs well) that might otherwise prove more fragile or tend to erode under the stress of war.

In facilitating cooperation, obligation and precision may be the most important dimensions of international law, because, as just explained, they set expectations for the behavior of others and reduce the range within which states can argue that the law does not apply to their interactions in a particular instance. Simple words

13. Barbara Koremenos, *The Continent of International Law: Explaining Agreement Design* (New York: Cambridge University Press, 2016), 229.

14. James D. Morrow, *Order within Anarchy: The Laws of War as an International Institution* (New York: Cambridge University Press, 2014).

matter here because they define which behaviors are consistent with cooperation and which are not. It is the anticipated benefits of cooperation that lead states to create international law in the first place, and it is the actual benefits of cooperation that lead them to comply with the rules once they are in place.

Widespread transgressions of law would undermine the gains from cooperation that states seek, so states generally refrain from violating laws in pursuit of their short-term interests. The greater the benefits of cooperation, and the more evenly these benefits are shared, the more likely that international law will constrain the policies of all states. The more states have to lose by not cooperating, the more likely that international law will shape their interactions and alter outcomes.

State Counsellor of Myanmar and de facto Prime Minister Aung San Suu Kyi testifies in front of the International Court of Justice in a hearing on Myanmar's genocide of the Rohingya people.

International law is also most effective when it is delegated to courts, arbitrators, and other tribunals. When states disagree on what the law says or how it should be applied in specific situations, referring the dispute to an independent decision-making body can help prevent conflicts from escalating. The international adjudication procedures of the WTO are one highly developed example of how delegations to a supranational institution can mitigate disagreements that might otherwise undermine international trade relations.[15] Delegation to courts also takes place in international humanitarian law. For example, the International Court of Justice (ICJ) responded to an application from The Gambia which alleged violations in Myanmar of the Convention on the Prevention and Punishment of the Crime of Genocide. In response, in early 2020, the ICJ issued an order requiring Myanmar to prevent genocide against the Rohingya, which many observers argue began in 2016.[16]

Domestic courts, however, are also important in the enforcement of international law. In many countries, including the United States, international treaties are superior to domestic laws; once treaties are enacted, they override domestic laws that contradict their provisions and cannot be changed by subsequent legislation. Treaties thereby become part of "domestic" law and are enforced in the same way as all other laws in the ratifying countries.

Domestic courts are also increasingly appealing to international law in interpreting domestic statutes. In *Roper v. Simmons* (2005), which overturned laws permitting death sentences for juvenile offenders in the United States, the U.S. Supreme Court cited as support the UN Convention on the Rights of the Child, which had previously been signed by the U.S. president but never ratified by the Senate. Writing for the majority, Justice Anthony Kennedy argued it was "proper that we acknowledge the overwhelming weight of international opinion against

15. Christina L. Davis, *Why Adjudicate? Enforcing Trade Rules in the WTO* (Princeton, NJ: Princeton University Press, 2012).

16. Richard C. Paddock, "U.N. Court's Order on Rohingya Is Cheered, but Will Myanmar Comply?" *New York Times*, January 24, 2020, www.nytimes.com/2020/01/24/world/asia/myanmar-rohingya-genocide.html (accessed 3/25/21).

the juvenile death penalty. . . . The opinion of the world community, while not controlling our outcome, does provide respected and significant confirmation of our own conclusions."[17] As international law is directly and indirectly incorporated into domestic law, the enforcement powers of states within their own jurisdictions are being harnessed to it.

In addition, some international law creates *compliance constituencies* within states that then have interests in ensuring that their governments follow the rules.[18] Even when some domestic groups might benefit from breaking international laws, other constituencies have a strong interest in upholding them. WTO law, for instance, opens foreign markets to trade and helps ensure nondiscriminatory treatment for goods from different countries. Although import-competing industries that favor protection might advocate policies that violate WTO rules, export industries that are dependent on foreign markets have an interest in ensuring that their governments uphold their obligations. Similarly, militaries are often staunch advocates of upholding the Geneva Conventions, especially with regard to the treatment of prisoners. Transnational advocacy networks that propagate norms that subsequently become embedded in international law, as we will discuss in the next section, are also likely to continue advocating for compliance.

Anticompliance constituencies may also exist, typically when political parties use nationalism, xenophobia, or anti-foreign rhetoric to mobilize supporters. For example, in the United States, the Trump administration targeted asylum-seeking migrants with persecution that violated international law, including forced child separation, indefinite detentions, and other human rights abuses, in part for domestic political reasons.

Thus, the benefits of cooperation, both to states as a whole and to particular groups within states, can make international law self-enforcing. Although still reliant on and limited by the principle of self-help, states have an interest in following international law when they recognize that they are better off when other states also follow the rules. In this way, international law can significantly influence and constrain the interactions of states even without any external enforcement mechanism. Nonetheless, international law is unlikely to end the bargaining failures that lead states into war or resolve other sources of conflict.

Like other institutions, international law facilitates cooperation, but it does not ensure that cooperation will always prevail. It is a useful tool for guiding the interactions of states in more constructive directions and for bringing about desirable outcomes in world politics, but it is not a panacea. The difficulty of demonstrating the independent effect of international law, however, ensures that the debate about its effectiveness will continue. As we will see in Chapter 12, the selection problem is central to debates about the usefulness of international human rights law.

---

17. Quoted in Robert J. Delahunty and John Yoo, "Against Foreign Law," *Harvard Journal of Law and Public Policy* 29, no. 1 (2005): 291–330. The trend toward citing foreign law is strongly opposed by conservatives, who see it as overturning democratic processes within the United States.

18. Miles Kahler, "Conclusion: The Causes and Consequences of Legalization," in *Legalization and World Politics*, ed. Goldstein et al., 283–84.

What Are International Norms?

International norms are another type of institution that constrains states. **Norms** are shared standards of behavior for actors with a given identity, defined in terms of rights and obligations. They rest on a community's beliefs about what behavior is appropriate for an actor under some specified condition. Norms may be codified into international law, but norms as institutions can exist and be respected by members of a community even when they are not written down in formal agreements. In our everyday life, many of our interactions are regulated by norms that have nothing to do with law. You are not required by law to hold an elevator for others, for instance. But to intentionally—or even unintentionally—allow the doors to close on someone rushing to the elevator is regarded as rude, and you may even apologize for letting the door close, even though the now excluded passenger cannot hear you.

Similarly, and with greater political importance, norms of fairness—which are not required in any way by law but reflect deep-seated social understandings—shape political appeals and policies in many countries, although exactly what is "fair" is not always clear and has varied considerably over time. In this same way, many now recognize a nuclear "taboo" in international relations—a normative prohibition against the use of nuclear weapons—even though the norm is nowhere found in international law.

Like law, international norms shape the behavior of states in important ways. Norms affect the interactions of states because they are understood by people within those states to be rules of conduct that are right and appropriate. In other words, norms define what it is we *should* do and thereby shape our understanding of our interests. In our everyday lives, of course, individuals and countries do many things they should not. Norms are often violated. They are standards of behavior, not prohibitions or straitjackets. But even if we choose to violate norms, we must then excuse our behavior, justify it, or risk being ostracized by our community.

We can group most norms into three broad categories. The first category, which we refer to as *constitutive norms*, defines what makes an actor legitimate or appropriate under given circumstances. What it means to be a state, for instance, is defined largely by norms.[19] At the level of everyday diplomacy, all states have flags, national anthems, and—even in the poorest states—ministries of science and technology. No law requires this, but there is remarkable similarity in the form and practices of states in the world today. To show that they are indeed modern states, many countries also buy advanced military equipment for which they have little use and even less ability to maintain—most notably fighter jets, which appear to have enormous symbolic value. More broadly, norms shape what it means to be sovereign at any point in history, which includes evolving ideas about when states can legitimately intervene in one another's "sovereign" areas of control, as reflected today in the new norm of R2P.

The second category, *procedural norms*, defines how decisions involving multiple actors should be made. As such, procedural norms are analogous to secondary rules

19. Statehood and sovereignty are defined as law through the UN Charter and other international agreements. The "rights" that sovereignty entails, however, have varied dramatically over time depending on how states choose to interpret the law.

norms

Standards of behavior for actors with a given identity; norms define what actions are "right" or appropriate under particular circumstances.

The possession of advanced military equipment has come to be a powerful symbol of legitimate statehood, even for countries that have little need for it. Venezuela, for instance, owns dozens of fighter jets.

in international law (rules about how to make rules). In domestic politics, procedural norms are often well established. In legislatures, for instance, ramming through a major bill late at night without due warning to the opposition, though permitted by the rules, is usually regarded as unfair and illegitimate and taints the resulting legislation. Norms are often challenged and occasionally violated. That they can be violated does not make them unimportant; rather, it often demonstrates their importance.

In international relations, procedural norms are generally less robust. Sovereignty implies that all states are formally equal and thus that each state is entitled to an equal voice in world affairs—at least in principle. These beliefs are an important justification for multilateralism, the practice of "diffuse reciprocity" in international relations in which states are expected to offer one another roughly equal benefits over time.[20] Yet, states with more power are often acknowledged to have special rights and greater responsibilities in recognition that their support is necessary for multilateralism to be effective. The United States and other major donors are often consulted, for instance, by IMF staff before loan agreements are formally presented to the executive directors for approval.[21] Such procedural norms give more powerful states a larger voice in diplomatic circles than the formal equality of sovereignty otherwise allows.

Finally, the third category, *regulative norms*, governs the behavior of actors in their interactions with other actors. R2P is one example, as is the norm of international election monitoring. The nuclear taboo is also a regulative norm.[22] Although the United States did drop two atomic bombs on Japan in 1945, ending World War II, no country since has used nuclear weapons, despite the fact that at least nine countries are now believed to possess workable bombs. Although nuclear weapons are held in reserve as the ultimate defense—a lingering threat to all enemies—political leaders are reluctant to contemplate using them, even when they are technically feasible and possibly efficient. To destroy hardened underground bunkers—whether of the type that hid Saddam Hussein during the Iraq War or those that protect the Iranian or North Korean nuclear programs—the United States has devoted considerable resources to developing large conventional "bunker-busting" bombs, even when existing tactical nuclear weapons could likely accomplish the same task more effectively.

That countries do not use nuclear weapons for fear of retaliation is undoubtedly part of the explanation for this norm. But deterrence alone cannot explain the taboo: such weapons are not used even when the target does not have nuclear weapons or the capacity to retaliate against the user directly. Leaders appear reluctant to

20. John Gerard Ruggie, ed., *Multilateralism Matters: The Theory and Praxis of an Institutional Form* (New York: Columbia University Press, 1993), 11.

21. Randall W. Stone, *Controlling Institutions: International Organizations and the Global Economy* (New York: Cambridge University Press, 2011).

22. Nina Tannenwald, "The Nuclear Taboo: The United States and the Normative Basis of Nuclear Non-Use," *International Organization* 53, no. 3 (1999): 433–68.

cross the nuclear threshold for fear of being branded as immoral, either personally or on behalf of their country. According to numerous journalistic reports, U.S. president Trump asked national security and homeland security officials repeatedly over several years why the United States could not use nuclear weapons against hurricanes—reports which Trump denied after being challenged on them. Although there are many reasons why this idea is not likely to be effective, one can also read the reactions to his questions, even among members of his own administration, as consistent with the existence of the nuclear taboo.

Norms are often difficult to identify. When they are not written down, they exist only by collective assent. In turn, when norms are deeply internalized, actors typically do not even consciously contemplate violating them, meaning that behavior consistent with norms often appears entirely voluntary or as the exercise of free will. To take an extreme example, nearly all societies have strongly internalized norms against walking up to a stranger and spitting in their face for no reason, yet this norm almost never appears to affect our conscious choices. We do not consciously debate which stranger's face to spit into while walking down the sidewalk. That we do not want to violate this norm is not evidence that it is unimportant but rather evidence that it is so deeply internalized that we are not even aware that it constrains our behavior.

The taboo against the use of nuclear weapons is an example of a regulative norm. Since the U.S. bombing of Hiroshima (above) and Nagasaki in 1945, no country has resorted to a nuclear attack, at least in part because of the international norm against the use of such weapons.

The nuclear taboo works in similar ways. That nuclear first strikes are not on the list of options considered by leaders in diplomatic disputes does not mean that the norm is not having an effect; instead, it suggests that the norm is sufficiently internalized that we are not aware of how fundamentally it shapes our interests and interactions.

Norms are more easily observed when they are violated (see "Controversy" on p. 502, discussing tensions between norms and laws of political assassination). Their presence is often revealed both by the condemnations of others and by the justifications given by the transgressing party. For example, since 1945 there has been a growing norm against changing international borders through the use of force, described as the "territorial integrity" norm.[23] When Saddam Hussein invaded and seized Kuwait in August 1990, the international community quickly denounced his actions. Although Hussein challenged the prior border as an anachronism of British colonial rule—in an attempt to reframe the issue as one of decolonization—and proclaimed Kuwait to be the long-lost nineteenth province of Iraq, his justifications for the land grab were broadly rejected by the rest of the international community. The United States and a coalition of other states fought a war to return Kuwait to sovereignty.

23. Mark W. Zacher, "The Territorial Integrity Norm: International Boundaries and the Use of Force," *International Organization* 55, no. 2 (2001): 215–50.

Extrajudicial Execution and the War on Terror

In late 2011, after several failed attempts to assassinate Anwar al-Awlaki, a member of Al Qaeda, the United States located and killed him and several of his fellow Al Qaeda members with a barrage of drone-fired Hellfire missiles. His death marked the first time that a U.S. citizen was targeted and killed by a U.S. drone strike, provoking reactions of relief and outrage around the world. Such "targeted

Applying the Concepts

killings," as U.S. policy makers call them, present a trade-off between American **interests** in eliminating potential threats to the United States and other countries and compliance with the **institution** of international law. They also raise problematic questions about reciprocity in **interactions** between states.

The legality of targeted killings remains controversial under international law. A strategy borrowed from Israeli antiterrorist practices, these killings were introduced as part of the post-9/11 war on terrorism by President George W. Bush's administration, and the Obama and Trump administrations both continued the practice. The first known U.S. case occurred in November 2002 when a U.S. Predator drone hit a car carrying six members of al Qaeda, including Qaed Sinan al-Harithi, the principal target of the attack because of his involvement in the October 2000 bombing of a U.S. naval vessel. These killings are controversial because they are extrajudicial. Any details of specific and imminent threats posed by the target individuals are often kept secret, leaving the public to trust that if the United States had not taken immediate action, a significant attack on the country would have been both imminent and inevitable.

Under international law and many domestic laws around the world, the use of lethal force outside of armed conflict is illegal unless it is used as a last resort against a specific and imminent threat. During armed conflict, the laws of war suggest that lethal force should only be used against those directly participating in the conflict (that is, against armed combatants). Thus, the debate over the legality and the normative appropriateness of the United States' targeted-killing policy centers on whether the war on terrorism is considered an active conflict, on the nature of the specific threats posed by targeted individuals, and on the viability of other means of capture or punishment, such as arrest.

This policy also raises important issues associated with the benefits of reciprocity in an era of rapidly changing military technology and prominent conflict with nonstate actors. Can the United States expect other countries to abide by international law and norms when it exempts itself from the rules?

In January 2020, a U.S. air strike ordered by President Donald Trump killed Iranian general Qasem Soleimani, moving the targeted-killing policy into even more controversial territory: Soleimani was a military leader of a country with which the United States was not in active armed conflict. The United States argued that it was acting in self-defense to prevent an imminent attack, an international legal standard with a very narrow definition. According to a 2010 UN report, in order for a targeted killing in the name of self-defense to be legitimate, the act must be perpetrated "against a real and imminent threat when the necessity of that self-defense is instant, overwhelming, and leaving no choice of means, and no moment of deliberation."[a]

---

a. Report of the Special Rapporteur on extrajudicial, summary or arbitrary executions, Philip Alston https://www2.ohchr.org/english/bodies/hrcouncil/docs/14session/A.HRC.14.24.Add6.pdf. May 28, 2010.

undermines reciprocal respect for international laws that also benefit the United States. Without full information on the nature of the threats posed by targeted individuals, it can be difficult for outsiders to assess the normative justification for or the legality of these actions. But the thousands killed over the two decades of this policy, including hundreds of civilian adults and children, as well as the degree to which the practice of targeted killing increases the United States' vulnerability to similar practices, make clear why the policy is both normatively questionable and potentially undermining of the United States' long-term interests.

Although the United States may be able to get away with flouting international law, is it in its interest to do so? Norms and laws surrounding political assassination are based in a logic of reciprocity. One could argue that all states are better off without their political and military leaders living in constant fear of assassination by foreign powers, so in this sense, the U.S. policy may increase the risk that another country will assassinate its own military and political leaders.

Targeted killing is thus an evolving international norm that is in tension with international law and that

Thinking Analytically

1. What is the difference between targeted killing and extrajudicial assassination?

2. If states get to define when a killing is a "last resort against a specific and imminent threat," how can other states be confident in that judgment?

The international community raised similar objections when Russia annexed the Crimea from Ukraine in 2014, claiming it as part of its historical territory. Although no state or coalition rose to reverse Russia's action in this case, the reactions of norm-abiding others and the justifications and excuses offered by Russia clearly displayed the territorial integrity norm at work. No actor needs to justify its behavior to others unless it is at risk of transgressing a norm held by the community to which it belongs.

Unlike law, norms need not be consistent with one another or with secondary rules. Indeed, the norm of national self-determination conflicts with sovereignty: If the state is the ultimate authority within a territory, how can a nation within that territory freely decide to secede? We have already discussed how R2P conflicts with sovereignty, and the same holds for many of the human rights norms examined in the next chapter.

Tension between norms creates opportunities for actors to interpret rules selectively to their own advantage. When faced with two morally just but conflicting rules, which one do you follow? Germans faced exactly this kind of choice in deciding whether to back NATO's intervention in Kosovo. On the one hand, many Germans were committed to a foreign policy that eschewed war and the use of force; on the other, they had pledged to never again stand idly by as a genocide unfolded. Despite contradictions such as these, however, norms—as with law—can serve as important constraints on states in their interactions.

How Are International Norms Created?

For a principle or idea to become institutionalized as a norm, the standard of behavior it specifies must be accepted as right and appropriate by a sufficiently large proportion of any given population, although how large that proportion must be is not always clear. Norms change. Where once it was acceptable in some countries to enslave people, including the practice of buying and selling humans in an open public market, we now find the practice morally repugnant. Though many people around the world are still held in various forms of bondage, not least in forced labor and sex trafficking, these markets are now illicit, and individuals found guilty of human trafficking meet not only legal consequences but also stigma.

Although norms can feel as though they are fixed permanently, international history suggests that norms can change dramatically. What does this process look like? Some norms change through the work of committed activists, some grow out of periods of norm contestation, and some evolve through intrastate competition for insider status, prestige, or international benefits.

A principle or idea is not considered an international norm until a sufficiently large or influential group of people or state leaders decides that failing to abide by the norm is wrong or objectionable. These processes can be sudden or more drawn out. For example, it took decades of domestic and international activism to end the apartheid system of racial segregation in South Africa, and although most of the apartheid laws were repealed in 1991, societal and racial tensions remain today. Similarly, colonial-era efforts to "civilize" foreign people through imperial movements were widely viewed as normal international behavior by powerful states. The normative shift that accompanied decolonization not only prioritized national self-determination but also redefined colonialism as inherently racist and grounded in white supremacy. Once this normative change began to take hold, most colonial powers moved rapidly toward granting independence to their territories.

Once people agree on new norms, in turn, practices that once might have been common become odious, or at least inappropriate, and even sometimes unimaginable. Over time, norms can develop a taken-for-granted quality, an unquestioned and perhaps unquestionable status. But all norms were originally just principles or ideas without the support of widely shared standards of appropriate behavior.

Some principles become norms simply by the force of their own inherent moral standing. The nuclear taboo may be one such example of a principle that so obviously improves human welfare that almost everyone accepts it. Other norms are propagated by powerful states or through international organizations. The Washington Consensus on economic liberalism, which held broad sway in the 1990s and early 2000s, was heavily promoted by the United States through its policies and by the IMF and World Bank. Still other norms may be championed by virtuous leaders seeking to distinguish themselves from those who are perhaps less virtuous. These leaders' efforts to signal their commitment to democracy have been a factor in spreading the norm of inviting monitors to oversee elections in new democracies (see Chapter 2).

Norms can thus begin with individuals or groups who seek to advance a principled standard of behavior for states and other actors. Transnational advocacy networks (TANs) are central to spreading norms throughout the international system. Comprising individuals and NGOs deeply committed to ethical beliefs, TANs aim to persuade other individuals and groups to share their commitment. We call these individuals and groups **norms entrepreneurs**.

The International Campaign to Ban Landmines (ICBL), for instance, provides a clear example of how a group of committed activists was able to call attention to an issue and convince many other people around the globe that existing practices were morally wrong. The ICBL is a network of hundreds of NGOs in some 100 countries working to outlaw and remove land mines, which still kill and maim over 6,000 people worldwide each year. It was the primary force behind the negotiation and adoption of the Ottawa Convention.

The convention was negotiated and signed in 1997 and entered into force in March 1999. As of March 2021, 164 countries have joined the convention, and only 32 countries remain outside the treaty entirely, including China, Egypt, India, Israel, Pakistan, Russia, and the United States.[24] In 1997, the ICBL and its coordinator, Jody

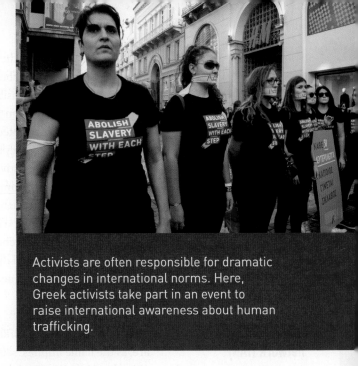

Activists are often responsible for dramatic changes in international norms. Here, Greek activists take part in an event to raise international awareness about human trafficking.

norms entrepreneurs
Individuals or groups that seek to advance principled standards of behavior for states and other actors.

---

24. See www.icbl.org/en-gb/the-treaty/treaty-status.aspx (accessed 2/18/21).

Williams, were awarded the Nobel Peace Prize for their work. In bestowing the award, the Norwegian Nobel Committee applauded the campaign for moving the ban from "a vision to a feasible reality" and acclaimed the organization as a model for international disarmament and peace.

Once norms are adopted, supporters of those norms then hold their governments accountable to acceptable standards of international behavior. Political leaders who hold deep normative commitments may decide to rule out certain policy options, deeming them immoral in the face of these international standards. Even if they are tempted to violate norms, leaders may fear that their constituents will punish them for violating widely accepted standards of behavior. Political leaders may also be held to account by citizens of other states, as in the anti-apartheid movement, which we will discuss in Chapter 12. In this way, even authoritarian governments that are not accountable to their own people can be pressed to uphold international norms.

transnational advocacy network (TAN)

A set of individuals and nongovernmental organizations acting in pursuit of a normative objective.

TANs: Changing Minds, Altering Interests

Transnational advocacy networks (TANs) are, as the name implies, sets of activists allied in pursuit of a common normative objective, including (in the contemporary era) human rights, the environment, economic and social justice, democracy, women's rights, and abortion rights or, conversely, the right to life. The actors that make up TANs may include (1) international and domestic NGOs involved in research and advocacy; (2) local social movements; (3) foundations and other philanthropic organizations; (4) the media; and (5) churches, trade unions, and consumer and other civil organizations.[25] The number of TANs has grown dramatically over the past 50 years. In 1953, there were about 100 identifiable TANs; today, they number well into the thousands—so many, in fact, that a proper count is nearly impossible.[26]

Nearly all the major issues that engage citizens within countries are now the subject of transnational advocacy efforts. For example, the Planned Parenthood Federation of America, often on the front lines of the movement to make or keep abortion legal, has 10 foreign affiliates and cooperates with hundreds of other organizations and countless individuals worldwide in the women's rights and legalized abortion movement. Heartbeat International, a network of pro-life pregnancy centers, has affiliates in more than 47 countries and works with many churches and other organizations to promote the right to life. After first gaining momentum in the United States, the struggle over abortion has become an international political issue with transnational networks on both sides of the question coordinating action, sharing information and tactics, and mobilizing new members. TANs

---

25. Margaret E. Keck and Kathryn Sikkink, *Activists beyond Borders: Advocacy Networks in International Politics* (Ithaca, NY: Cornell University Press, 1998), 9. We exclude international organizations and governments from this list, although individuals in these organizations may interact with TANs. On public transnational networks, see Anne-Marie Slaughter, *A New World Order* (Princeton, NJ: Princeton University Press, 2004).

26. For the latest available figures, see Kathryn Sikkink and Jackie Smith, "Infrastructures for Change: Transnational Organizations, 1953–93," in *Restructuring World Politics: Transnational Social Movements, Networks, and Norms*, ed. Sanjeev Khagram, James V. Riker, and Kathryn Sikkink, 30, Table 2.1 (Minneapolis: University of Minnesota Press, 2002); and Jackie Smith, "Exploring Connections between Global Integration and Political Mobilization," *Journal of World-Systems Research* 10, no. 1 (2004): 266, Table 2.

coordinate the activities of participants around the globe and initiate, lead, and actively direct collective action on issues of concern.

TANs can change how actors conceive of their interests by promoting new moral values. In essence, TANs urge actors to have preferences about certain practices—owning slaves, using land mines—rather than thinking only about the possible outcomes of those practices, such as greater wealth or victory on the battlefield. Of course, norms existed and spread throughout the world prior to the recent proliferation of TANs. After all, not all norms are connected with TANs and their activities. But one important function of TANs is to encourage and support what they deem as socially appropriate behavior and help spread norms across national borders. Martha Finnemore and Kathryn Sikkink, two leading scholars of norms in international relations, posit a three-stage **norms life cycle** that can help us understand how TANs shape norms and interests and, thus, political outcomes.[27]

In the first stage, norms entrepreneurs actively work to convince a critical mass of other individuals in other states to embrace their beliefs. During the second stage, once a new framework has taken hold, a *norms cascade* occurs: the number of adherents to the norm passes a tipping point beyond which the idea gains sufficient support that it becomes a nearly universal standard of behavior to which others can be held accountable. The tipping point is often hard to identify in advance; it is determined not only by the number of actors that adopt the new belief but also by the leadership or visibility of those actors within the international community. Conformity to the new norm can then be established through coercion (such as economic sanctions in the case of human rights norms) or through socialization (a process akin to peer pressure in which states adopt new behaviors because that is what "good" states do).

In the third stage of the cycle, norms are internalized or become so widely accepted that they acquire the taken-for-granted quality that makes conforming to them almost automatic. Indeed, even contemplating violation of the deeply internalized cultural norms against, say, eating certain foods can make some people feel ill. Norms against slavery, violence against political prisoners, or violating the rights of children—once the subjects of TAN activity—are now at least partially internalized within many countries, although violations still occur. Few norms governing interactions between states have reached this final stage, although the nuclear taboo may be close. Were North Korea to use a nuclear weapon, for instance, it would likely be

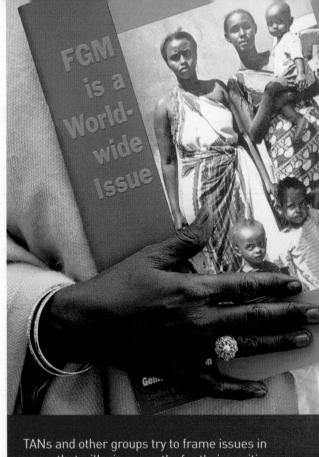

TANs and other groups try to frame issues in a way that will win sympathy for their position. Opponents of female genital mutilation/cutting have adopted this phrasing to emphasize its violence.

norms life cycle
A three-stage model of how norms diffuse within a population and achieve a taken-for-granted status.

27. Martha Finnemore and Kathryn Sikkink, "International Norm Dynamics and Political Change," *International Organization* 52, no. 4 (1998): 887–917.

strongly condemned by the international community for violating the norm, indicating the robust presence of the taboo and its role as a constraint in other cases.

Do Norms Matter?

Norms constrain states and other actors in two principal ways: first, by redefining their interests, and second, by changing their interactions. In both cases, isolating the effects of norms on policy is difficult. To the extent that norms define how individuals and states perceive their interests, the selection problem identified in the preceding discussion of international law becomes even more acute. If norms shape interests, and states act on those interests, distinguishing the independent effect of norms on action is nearly impossible. Nonetheless, there is reason to believe that the effects of norms on state action may be considerable.

Norms define interests by shaping what actors believe is right and appropriate behavior under specific circumstances. Countries as a whole may respect norms out of concern for their reputations as honorable or norm-abiding states. Such a reputation may have intrinsic value. It may also be valued because it facilitates cooperation with other countries or allows countries that possess this reputation to avoid other costs. As individuals, leaders may seek for their own egotistic reasons to be seen as moral and "upstanding." Other leaders may do the right thing simply because it is right. Even if leaders are cross-pressured by circumstances or by self-interested groups to transgress norms, they can be held to account by their own citizens, and especially by voters.

States are not the only actors bound by international norms. Nonstate actors, including multinational corporations and rebel groups, can also find themselves subject to international norms, targeted by transnational advocacy networks, or pressured by norm-supporting states. Consumer boycotts of corporations are one tactic for naming and shaming companies that violate international norms or law.

Following several failed attempts to establish global corporate social responsibility (CSR) standards in the 1970s, international norms related to global CSR took off in the late 1990s. Global CSR norms now include a number of internationally shared expectations among states and other global actors regarding the appropriate behavior of responsible multinational corporations. As shown in Figure 11.2, these expectations include the UN Global Compact, which outlines voluntary corporate commitments to "universal principles" in human rights, labor, the environment, and anti-corruption; and the Global Reporting Initiative (GRI), which was formed from an alliance of nonstate global actors and sets standards for corporations to engage in standardized reporting on their own economic, environmental, and social impacts, both positive and negative, as they relate to sustainable development.

Why Do Global Actors Comply with International Norms and Law?

In many areas of international politics, states and nonstate actors can agree on laws, norms, and standards and can even bring them into formal existence through international bodies. This is true across diverse issue areas in international politics,

FIGURE 11.2 *Global Standards for Corporate Social Responsibility: The United Nations Global Compact and the Global Reporting Initiative, 2000–2020*

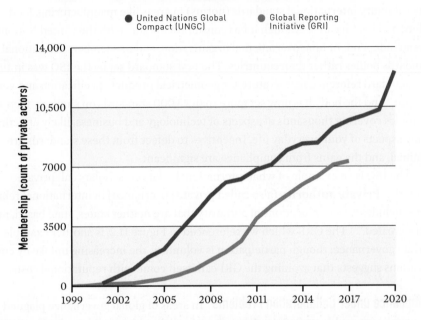

● United Nations Global Compact (UNGC) ● Global Reporting Initiative (GRI)

including trade, the laws of war, human rights, global air traffic controlling, and foreign direct investment. But for both international law and international norms, getting states and nonstate actors to comply is a perpetual problem, particularly when the short-term self-interest of international actors comes into conflict with international standards.

Figure source: Daniel Kinderman, "Corporations and Global Standards of Corporate Social Responsibility," in *Handbook of the International Political Economy of the Corporation*, ed. Andreas Nölke and Christian May, 365–83. (Cheltenham, UK: Elgar, 2018).

Compliance under Coordination Problems In some areas, compliance is straightforward for states and nonstate actors alike. When the benefits of cooperation are clear and when states simply need to agree on a standard in order to cooperate globally (like the coordination games introduced in the "Special Topic" appendix to Chapter 2), then compliance tends to be nearly universal once the norm or law has been set, and the agreement functions in mostly mundane fashion. For example, the Universal Postal Union, established in 1874, has nearly universal membership and is responsible for the Universal Postal Convention and the Postal Payment Services Agreement, which require that states make available a uniform flat rate to mail a letter to anywhere in the world and that they treat foreign and domestic mail equally. States are better off complying with these agreements, and defection occurs primarily in cases in which state capacity is very weak. (That is, states without functional governments tend to have trouble delivering foreign and domestic mail.) Norms also operate in this space without too much controversy. It is technically legal to mail a letter internationally with a postage stamp that is placed somewhere other than in the upper right-hand corner of an envelope, but because it significantly slows down the transmission of that letter and risks that it will be lost, most of us comply with the norm without thinking too much about it.

The International Organization for Standardization (ISO), created in 1947, is one of the more vitally important global organizations that few people have heard of, and it has the highest rates of norm compliance by states, multinational corporations, and other private actors. The ISO is a unique form of private governance that sets voluntary international standards (norms) in areas like manufacturing, food safety, and health care. Although it has consultative status with the United Nations, it is an independent nongovernmental organization, and its members are national standards bodies rather than countries. The first standard set by the ISO was in 1951 for "standard reference temperature for geometrical product specification and verification," and the body has now set more than 23,000 standards on similarly technical topics covering thousands of aspects of technology and business, likely affecting many aspects of your everyday life. Incentives to defect from these standards are minimal, and the gains from compliance are significant.

The ISO is an example of what international relations scholars call private authority. **Private authority** (also called private governance) in international relations includes "sites or locations of authority that are neither states, state based, nor state-created."[28] The GRI, which we referenced in Figure 11.2, is another example of private governance; though participation is voluntary, the increasing uptake by corporations suggests that avoiding the GRI can itself come with reputational costs.[29]

private authority

An expression of legitimate rulemaking by nonstate actors in international affairs, including the establishment of norms governing the behavior of private global actors such as multinational corporations and international NGOs.

Compliance under Collaboration Problems
In areas of global governance plagued by compliance problems (see the discussion of collaboration problems in Chapter 2), a number of strategies for encouraging compliance and increasing cooperation cut across issue areas, types of global actors, and international law and norms. These strategies include providing information by monitoring compliance, naming and shaming violations, and pressuring more powerful states to reward compliance or penalize noncompliance.

If it is possible to violate a standard without being detected, noncompliance becomes more likely. Therefore, monitoring compliance with international laws and norms has become an important and influential strategy for increasing international actors' compliance. By revealing information about compliance, transnational monitors allow all parties to an agreement to have greater confidence that the other stakeholders will honor present and future agreements.

Having enacted a law, reached an agreement, or recognized a norm, global actors acquire information about compliance in one of three ways. First, they can rely on the self-reports of others. Many international agreements depend on this mechanism, requiring states to report on their efforts to reduce atmospheric emissions, for instance. This system is in fact relatively weak, as states that have incentives to cheat on agreements are also likely to have incentives to lie about their cheating. Self-reports are useful only when they can be verified by one of the other mechanisms.

---

28. Rodney Bruce Hall and Thomas J. Biersteker, *The Emergence of Private Authority in Global Governance* (Cambridge: Cambridge University Press, 2002), 5.

29. Daniel Kinderman, "Corporations and Global Standards of Corporate Social Responsibility," in *Handbook of the International Political Economy of the Corporation*, ed. Andreas Nölke and Christian May, 365–83 (Cheltenham, UK: Elgar, 2018).

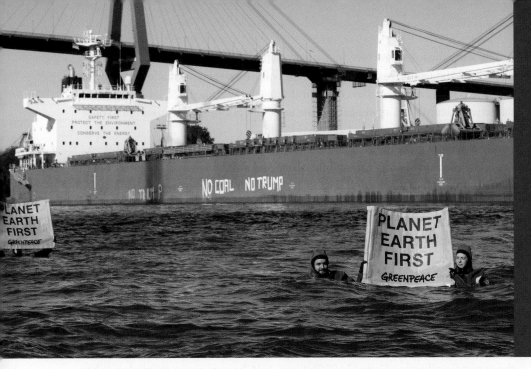

TANs may protest complex international laws to draw broader public attention to policies that they find objectionable. Greenpeace frequently stages outsize demonstrations—which it knows will attract an audience—against laws that it sees as harmful to the environment.

Second, states and nonstate actors can monitor one another's behavior directly. For example, the arms control agreements negotiated between the United States and the Soviet Union during the Cold War depended on direct monitoring. Direct monitoring is often quite expensive, however, as each state must expend resources to collect information about often hard-to-observe behaviors by others. Direct monitoring is sometimes likened to police patrols actively circulating on their "beats" looking for violations of the law.[30] This type of monitoring can be inefficient, since monitors must be in the field even when violations are not occurring. It can also be imperfect, since monitors may be occupied or distracted elsewhere when violations do occur. Nonetheless, this practice is a common means of monitoring compliance in international relations.

Third, states and nonstate actors can monitor one another indirectly by listening to the testimony of trustworthy third parties. Here, TANs, international NGOs, and intergovernmental organizations can be useful in identifying and calling attention to violations of international agreements. Having championed the ban on land mines into international law, the ICBL now monitors state compliance very closely. Indirect monitoring is common in the human rights issue area, where organizations like Amnesty International and Human Rights Watch track practices globally and issue calls to their members and states when they observe violations. Transparency International, to take another example, ranks countries annually according to their level of corruption in business and politics.

Similar practices are emerging in the issue area of the environment. Nearly 10,000 NGOs were officially permitted to participate in the 1992 Earth Summit, the largest-ever gathering of national leaders to discuss protecting the environment. Not only did these organizations conduct a parallel summit and make policy

---

30. See Mathew D. McCubbins and Thomas Schwartz, "Congressional Oversight Overlooked: Police Patrols versus Fire Alarms," *American Journal of Political Science* 28, no. 1 (February 1984): 165–79.

proposals to the interstate meeting, but through their participation they were accredited and legitimized as the watchdogs of the agreements made at the conference. With its new acceptance and prominence, this transnational environmental network has played an important role in calling international attention to poor environmental policies and practices worldwide.

Indirect monitoring is similar to school or office fire alarms: when problems arise, any concerned party can pull the alarm and alert others who respond, but the alarm is only pulled when necessary. By facilitating monitoring and reducing its costs, a variety of international actors including TANs, individual states, and private governance structures can help promote compliance with international laws and norms that states would otherwise be reluctant to follow.[31]

In some cases, the technology associated with monitoring compliance with global standards can change the efficacy of the standards dramatically. For example, illegal logging in countries with poor regulatory environments was long thought to be an intractable problem, in part because once trees were cut and processed into wood products, tracing their origin was nearly impossible. Illegally harvested timber could evade even the most reputable certification standards, like those of the Forest Certification Council (FSC). Since 2011, however, new technologies have allowed organizations like the FSC to not only document supply chains but also audit corporate reporting by using samples of wood products to validate the real (as opposed to the reported) geographic origin of harvested wood products. It is now significantly more difficult for state or market actors to try to pass off illegal harvests as meeting environmental standards.[32]

When noncompliant behavior is documented via monitoring, "naming and shaming" can play an important role in increasing compliance. Additionally, pressuring more powerful states or other influential international actors to unilaterally reward compliance or sanction noncompliance can also be effective. These strategies can be combined and used by TANs, global networks, formal international organizations, international NGOs, private governance structures, or even individual states.

States and their leaders typically value their reputations as "good" countries or individuals that respect and comply with standards of appropriate behavior. Multinational corporations also devote significant time and attention to maintaining their reputations globally. When third parties call attention to violations of norms and laws, offending actors can be castigated or shamed into altering abhorrent behavior. States or organizations that are publicly shamed for violating norms and laws may become international pariahs that other states will be reluctant to trust, collaborate with, or include in mutually beneficial cooperative arrangements. Although naming and shaming might seem like a weak tool to leverage good compliance from otherwise strong states and powerful corporations, over the long run this strategy can severely weaken a state's reputation and put potentially profitable cooperation at risk.

---

31. On the credibility of transnational NGOs, see Peter Gourevitch, David A. Lake, and Janice Gross Stein, eds., *The Credibility of Transnational NGOs: When Virtue Is Not Enough* (New York: Cambridge University Press, 2012).

32. Benjamin Cashore, Graeme Auld, and Deanna Newsom, *Governing Through Markets: Forest Certification and the Emergence of Non-State Authority*. (New Haven: Yale University Press, 2004).

Tens of thousands of farmers across India gathered for several months in 2021 to protest legislation that would prompt the deregulation of wholesale trading and undermine a decades-long policy of agricultural subsidies from the government. Their concerns were amplified when Khalsa Aid, an international NGO based in the United Kingdom, began to press for change.

"Name and shame" interactions are complicated and can take many forms. In the era of social media, any single consumer can name and shame a state, a corporation, or any globally prominent actor (for more on social media as a political force, see "How Do We Know?" on p. 514). In many cases, successful naming and shaming is most effective when it can be combined with the coercive power of other states. In the **boomerang model** proposed by Margaret Keck and Kathryn Sikkink, NGOs in one state are able to activate transnational linkages to bring pressure from other states to bear on their own governments (Figure 11.3).[33] This process is most likely to be effective when NGOs or individual citizens are blocked from influencing their own governments, as is common in many nondemocratic regimes. Unable to appeal to their own governments, these actors activate transnational networks to bring their plight to the attention of NGOs and individuals in other countries, who, in turn, press their governments or, perhaps, international organizations into action. These other governments then demand that the first state alter its behavior or remove the block on its own NGOs. In this way, foreign states can be mobilized to try to influence the offending state or nonstate actor.

The anti-apartheid movement in South Africa is a good example of the boomerang model in action (see Chapter 12). Excluded from power and influence in the White-dominated government, Black South Africans, their NGOs, and their South African allies appealed to foreign TANs in their struggle. These advocacy networks mobilized opinion and voters in other countries—mostly in Western democracies—whose governments placed sanctions on South Africa and eventually helped topple the apartheid regime. As this example suggests, the essence of the boomerang process involves domestic groups activating transnational networks to bring greater pressure to bear on their government than they would otherwise be able to exert on

boomerang model
A process through which NGOs in one state are able to activate transnational linkages to bring pressure from other states on their own governments.

33. Keck and Sikkink, *Activists beyond Borders*, 12–13.

Social Media and the Arab Spring

Starting in Tunisia in December 2010, political protests rolled across North Africa and the Middle East. In a matter of months, as the protests spread, regimes were toppled in Tunisia, Libya, and Egypt. Meanwhile, the government in Bahrain cracked down on demonstrators, deterring further protests, and civil war broke out in Syria. Many of these events played out across social media platforms, including Facebook and Twitter, where protesters posted video, provided commentary, or simply communicated with friends and family. Indeed, social media were believed to be so central at the time that the Arab Spring was also called the "Twitter revolution." Yet, some have pushed back against the importance of social media as a political force, pointing out that "Twitter cannot stop a bullet."[a] What role did social media play in the Arab Spring?

Zachary C. Steinert-Threlkeld examined the effect of tweets on protest activity in 16 countries during the Arab Spring.[b] In any protest, there is safety in numbers—especially when the government is likely to target demonstrators. In considering whether to attend a protest, each person must anticipate whether others will attend as well, making protest a highly strategic interaction with other protesters and the state. Because the stakes are so high, individuals rely on many signals about the likely behavior of others. In the past, such signals included conversations with family and friends, declarations made in coffee shops, and encouragement from local religious or union leaders. Today, social media allow for broader communication in real time. Does wider communication make a difference?

Steinert-Threlkeld begins by distinguishing between "core" members of a community—those who have numerous followers on Twitter and who are likely to be political activists working with various transnational advocacy or nongovernmental organizations—and "peripheral" members, who have few followers. Core members, he argues, tweet a lot, are highly visible, and may be essential for planning protests. The 5 percent of Twitter users in Syria

FIGURE A *Coordination on Twitter and Protest Turnout*

Figure source: Adapted from Zachary C. Steinert-Threlkeld, "Spontaneous Collective Action: Peripheral Mobilization during the Arab Spring," *American Political Science Review* 111, no. 2 (May 2017): 379–403.

with the most followers, for instance, sent out nearly 50 percent of all tweets in that country surrounding the 2011 protests. But protest turnout, he shows, is driven by peripheral individuals.

The more that peripheral members coordinate their activities, measured by the use of the same hashtags on Twitter, the more protests occur. Figure A shows that as individuals with fewer followers (the periphery) tweet using the same hashtags, representing more coordination, more protesters participate the next day. Conversely, frequent tweeters—core members—do not affect protest turnout; the corresponding graph (not shown) is essentially flat.

Frequent tweeters may be essential for planning protests, yet it's the tweets from everyday people that inspire protesters to show up. Rather than getting their information only from the local bar or market, protesters may coordinate their activities today more effectively through social media. Although we cannot know what would otherwise have happened in the Arab Spring, Twitter may have raised overall turnout—and helped to bring down several governments.

---

a. Jared Keller, "Evaluating Iran's Twitter Revolution," *The Atlantic*, June 18, 2010, www.theatlantic.com/technology/archive/2010/06/evaluating-irans-twitter-revolution/58337 (accessed 2/26/21).

b. Zachary C. Steinert-Threlkeld, "Spontaneous Collective Action: Peripheral Mobilization during the Arab Spring," *American Political Science Review* 111, no. 2 (May 2017): 379–403.

FIGURE 11.3 *The Boomerang Model*

This stylized depiction of the boomerang model shows how NGOs that are blocked from influence within their own state (State A) can appeal to other transnational NGOs, which can press their states (State B) or an international organization to press State A to change its policy.

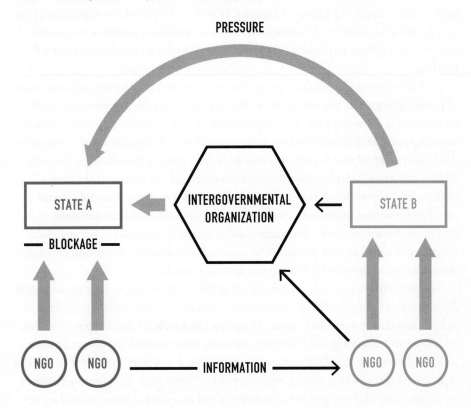

their own. The process does not require any actor to alter its perceived interests; instead, the activation of transnational ties changes the nature of the domestic actors' interactions with their government and makes socially inappropriate behavior more costly for aberrant states.

Figure source: Margaret E. Keck and Kathryn Sikkink, *Activists beyond Borders: Advocacy Networks in International Politics* (Ithaca, NY: Cornell University Press, 1998), 13.

Conclusion: Can States Be Constrained?

Can the behavior of influential global actors be changed by international law and norms? This remains a lively debate in which scholars do not have settled answers. On one side, traditionalists argue that international law binds states only to the extent that they want to be bound; in turn, other efforts to regulate behavior by nonstate actors exist only because states that might otherwise regulate, control, and limit these efforts permit them to flourish. From this perspective, international law and norms are at best soft constraints. Powerful states retain the ability to go it alone, and they face few costs associated with noncompliance with international law. When globally dominant states become weaker, are replaced, or experience significant ideological change among their national leadership, the global international law and norms in place are likely to change as well.[34] In many ways the rise of authoritarian states like China and Russia, as well as the global consequences of the Trump-led U.S. withdrawal from international cooperation, provides an ongoing test of some of these arguments, as we will discuss in the concluding chapter to this book.

On the other side, globalists argue that international law, norms, and new areas of private governance are emerging as effective forms of global governance. In this view, political authority previously exercised by states is migrating to new supranational authorities that can regulate states through international law, voluntary standards, and external monitoring, in some ways relocating responsibilities formerly fulfilled by states.[35] Here, nations respect international law because they benefit from the cooperation it facilitates and incur costs if they don't comply. A variety of global actors, including global civil society, multinational corporations, and NGOs, can hold states and others accountable for their compliance. For the globalists, international law and norms are increasingly constraining states and nonstate actors in their actions both at home and with one another.

As with all debates over supranational authority, there are no easy answers. The persistence of international law and norms does appear to be changing patterns of state interaction in some issue areas, including human rights and the environment, which we will discuss in the following chapters. International law constrains some actions of some states at least some of the time, and it punishes or at least sullies the reputations of states that violate legitimate rules. TANs make cooperation between countries more likely by serving as endorsers and monitors of international agreements. They perform essential roles in supporting and observing compliance with both the international human rights and environmental standards. And global private governance continues to play an important role of communicating standards and raising the floor on acceptable corporate behavior.

Compliance with international law may also be influenced by what's at stake, though it is still debated whether compliance is more or less likely when the stakes are higher. Compliance is also likely to be affected by who would bear the costs of noncompliance at a domestic level—and by the associated domestic politics. Additionally, as political scientist Randall Stone argues in relation to the IMF, many problems of global governance are plagued by the challenge of designing cooperative

---

34. Among other traditionalist sources, see Robert Gilpin, *Global Political Economy: Understanding the International Economic Order* (Princeton, NJ: Princeton University Press, 2001), chap. 15; and Stephen D. Krasner, "Power Politics, Institutions, and Transnational Relations," in *Bringing Transnational Relations Back In: Non-State Actors, Domestic Structures and International Institutions*, ed. Thomas Risse-Kappen, 257–79 (New York: Cambridge University Press, 1995).

35. See David Held, Anthony McGrew, David Goldblatt, and Jonathan Perraton, *Global Transformations: Politics, Economics and Culture* (Stanford, CA: Stanford University Press, 1999), esp. chap. 1; Walter Mattli, "Public and Private Governance in Setting International Standards," in *Governance in a Global Economy: Political Authority in Transition*, ed. Miles Kahler and David A. Lake, 199–225 (Princeton, NJ: Princeton University Press, 2003); and Virginia Haufler, "Globalization and Industry Self-Regulation," in *Governance in a Global Economy*, ed. Kahler and Lake, 226–52.

arrangements that include compliance incentives for both powerful states and weaker states in the international system.[36] A set of rules that is too constraining for the most powerful states will drive them out of the agreement, rendering the system less influential. But a set of rules that is too favorable to powerful states may be also increase noncompliance by the less powerful, but more numerous, states in the system.

Although the traditionalists may be correct in their view that states, in principle, still have the authority to ignore international law and control transnational groups, it is not clear that states retain the ability or political will to do so. Precisely because international law and norms are in many cases useful to states, it is often difficult for states to ignore their restraints. That China and Russia engage in norm contestation with powerful democracies also suggests the importance of international law and norms.

Globalists, however, may exaggerate the extent to which international law and norms can substitute for government at the global level. International law is still hampered by the need for self-enforcement. Many efforts to enforce international standards and values are voluntary associations that cannot legally bind their own members, much less others. Lacking the political authority of states, they must rely on voluntary compliance from their targets, which is often uneven.

Contestation over global governance structures related to the environment, human rights, corporate governance, freedom of information, and state versus individual security are likely to continue under a more contested international order. States and nonstate actors alike have a stake in international law and norms, and interests, interactions, and institutions are sure to play a central role in ongoing changes in global governance.

---

36. Randall W. Stone, "The Scope of IMF Conditionality," *International Organization*, 62, No. 4 (2008): 589–620.

Study Tool Kit

Interests, Interactions, and Institutions in Context

- International law and norms are institutions that seek to shape how states understand their interests and to constrain the ways in which they interact.

- States create and abide by international law because of the cooperation it enables. Although states are typically dependent on "self-help" for enforcement, the benefits of cooperation to states are often large enough that international laws are self-enforcing, or in the interests of states to follow apparently willingly.

- International norms affect world politics by changing how individuals and, in turn, states conceive of their interests and by defining what constitutes appropriate interactions with other states.

- Private authority emerges in areas in which private actors are pressured by other global actors to comply with new standards of behavior. When other private actors begin complying with a new standard, norm, or law, the incentives for others to comply increase.

Key Terms

international law, p. 487

international humanitarian law, p. 489

customary international law, p. 489

obligation, p. 492

precision, p. 492

delegation, p. 492

norms, p. 499

norms entrepreneurs, p. 505

transnational advocacy network (TAN), p. 506

norms life cycle, p. 507

private authority, p. 510

boomerang model, p. 513

For Further Reading

Abbott, Kenneth W., Jessica F. Green, and Robert O. Keohane. "Organizational Ecology and Institutional Change in Global Governance." *International Organization* 70, no. 2 (April 2016): 247–77. Explains the role of private transnational regulatory organizations in global environmental politics.

Adler-Nissen, Rebecca. "Stigma Management in International Relations: Transgressive Identities, Norms, and Order in International Society." *International Organization* 68, no. 1 (2014): 143–76. Demonstrates that international order is formed in part by stigmatizing nonconforming and norm-violating states.

Goldstein, Judith L., Miles Kahler, Robert O. Keohane, and Anne-Marie Slaughter, eds. *Legalization and World Politics.* Cambridge, MA: MIT Press, 2001. Some of the best contemporary research on international law by political scientists.

Guzman, Andrew T. *How International Law Works: A Rational Choice Theory.* New York: Oxford University Press, 2008. Explains how international law can succeed through reciprocity, reputation, and retaliation even in the absence of third-party enforcement.

Hathaway, Oona A., and Scott J. Shapiro. The *Internationalists: How a Radical Plan to Outlaw War Remade the World.* New York: Simon & Schuster, 2017. A lively historical account of the 1928 plan to abolish war through international law, with relevance to today.

Keck, Margaret E., and Kathryn Sikkink. *Activists beyond Borders: Advocacy Networks in International Politics.* Ithaca, NY: Cornell University Press, 1998. A classic study of the growth and role of TANs.

Morrow, James D. *Order within Anarchy: The Laws of War as an International Institution.* New York: Cambridge University Press, 2014. Examines how law conditions expectations and state behavior in the context of the Geneva Conventions.

Stroup, Sarah S., and Wendy H. Wong. *The Authority Trap: Strategic Choices of International NGOs.* Ithaca, NY: Cornell University Press, 2017. Explores how leading NGOs command deference from various powerful audiences and influence the practices of states, corporations, and other organizations.

Towns, Ann E. *Women and States: Norms and Hierarchies in International Society.* New York: Cambridge University Press, 2010. Examines the changing international norms that govern the relationships between women and the states in which they live.

12

Human Rights

THE PUZZLE *Why do states undertake costly actions to protect the human rights of people outside their borders? In light of the widespread support for the principle of human rights, why has the movement to protect those rights not been even more successful?*

Above: After beginning in the United States in response to racial injustice, the Black Lives Matter movement quickly spread across the globe. Here, protesters march through the streets of London.

For over 40 years, the White-dominated government of South Africa pursued a strict policy of racial segregation and inequality called apartheid. Distinguishing among Whites, Indians, Coloureds, and Africans or Blacks, this policy assigned everyone to a "homeland" within the territory of the state, regulated employment and movement into the cities, and created a system of racial discrimination designed to perpetuate the political and economic dominance of the White minority. Human rights abuses under apartheid were widespread. In addition to denying the political, economic, social, and cultural rights of more than three-quarters of South Africa's population, the White government engaged in arbitrary arrests and detentions without trial as well as torture and executions without judicial review. The full extent of the abuses perpetrated by the regime was revealed only by the post-apartheid Truth and Reconciliation Commission.[1]

---

1. David Black, "The Long and Winding Road: International Norms and Domestic Political Change in South Africa," in *The Power of Human Rights: International Norms and Domestic Change*, ed. Thomas Risse, Stephen C. Ropp, and Kathryn Sikkink (New York: Cambridge University Press, 1999), 80.

The transnational advocacy network (TAN; see Chapter 11) of organizations focused on human rights worked closely with South African opposition groups to bring international pressure to bear against the apartheid regime. In November 1962, the United Nations (UN) General Assembly adopted Resolution 1761 condemning apartheid and calling for all countries to terminate economic and military relations with South Africa. The UN Security Council imposed a mandatory embargo on weapons sales to the White regime in 1977.

As domestic unrest flared in 1984 following constitutional reforms that gave political rights to Indians and Coloureds but not to Africans, the government began a brutal crackdown. To signal their displeasure with the widespread human rights abuses, by 1986 all of South Africa's major trading partners—including the United States—had adopted economic sanctions.

The combination of increasing internal dissent, both nonviolent and violent, and international censure brought about the end of apartheid in 1990 and started the peaceful transition to Black-majority rule, which finally became a reality in 1994. Primary credit for apartheid's repeal goes to the brave South African men, women, and children of all backgrounds who stood up against the racist regime. Nonetheless, the anti-apartheid struggle stands out for two things it showed us about the power of the global human rights movement.

First, the national struggle played out on a global stage. Blocked at home from influencing the White regime, the Black majority appealed to allies abroad for support. By documenting and publicizing abuses and by mobilizing activists worldwide, the struggle against apartheid set a visible precedent for TAN activity and success in the broad area of human rights.

Second, the anti-apartheid struggle demonstrated that states are, at times, willing to bear costs to express their disapproval of other governments and to support the victims of widespread human rights abuses. Not all states cooperated in the movement to dismantle apartheid, and some were pushed into doing so only by vigorous pressure from activists. Nonetheless, opposing apartheid was an important turning point for states in using their influence to isolate and punish regimes that systematically abuse their own people.

Despite the global human rights movement's success in ending apartheid, efforts to promote human rights in other countries have been highly uneven. Concerns remain about human rights practices in many places, including China, Myanmar, Russia, Syria, and even the United States with regard to the death penalty and the treatment of detainees in the global war on terrorism. The Black Lives Matter movement, for example, has spread from its origins in the United States around the globe, and worldwide demonstrations have both expressed support for American protesters and called out racial injustice in other countries. Although nearly everyone supports human rights in principle, and many rights are codified in international law, disagreement continues on what constitutes a human right and when human rights should be protected.

Noninterference by others in a state's internal affairs is a defining and often highly treasured principle of national sovereignty—a principle that South Africa's apartheid regime appealed to repeatedly in an effort to insulate itself from foreign scrutiny. By condemning the human rights abuses of others, states not only violate this norm of noninterference but also risk opening themselves to foreign interference. Why do states undertake costly actions, such as sanctioning South Africa, with no immediate benefit to themselves or their own citizens?

As the example of South Africa makes clear, human rights practices around the globe are undoubtedly better than they would be without broad support for human rights, international laws governing how states treat their citizens, TANs "naming and shaming" abusers, and states occasionally punishing violators with sanctions. Yet few countries respect all human rights, and a significant number of countries violate many of these rights. Why isn't international human rights law more effective?

Thinking Analytically about Human Rights

In addressing this puzzle, our discussion considers the interests, interactions, and institutions involved in international human rights. First, we will see that international human rights law is an institution created by and largely reflecting the political norms and values of Western, liberal democracies. The norms embodied in these laws are not shared equally by all countries and have not yet been internalized by many societies and governments. Thus, even when formally codified, they remain controversial.

The interests and interactions involved in enforcing human rights help explain both why some actors work hard to promote human rights abroad and why states that violate human rights do so despite international norms. Individuals have an interest in international human rights, and this is why they sometimes encourage their leaders to take action to punish states that violate them. But, as we will see, these interests are rarely strong enough to compel states to pay the high costs to protect vulnerable individuals and groups outside their own borders.

Thus, states that violate human rights anticipate that in their interactions with other states, they probably will not face serious consequences for their behavior and, therefore, can abuse individuals and groups without significant penalties. Unfortunately, these states are most likely correct. International human rights law does indeed promote improved practices. Its full promise, however, has not yet been realized.

What Are International Human Rights?

Human rights are rights that all individuals possess by virtue of being human, regardless of their status as citizens of particular states or members of a group or organization. These rights are, by definition, universal and apply to all humans equally.

The concept of human rights has a long philosophical tradition, dating from the Enlightenment in the eighteenth century. English philosopher John Locke (1632–1704) first developed the modern notion of natural rights, the idea that people are by nature free and equal and, therefore, possess certain basic rights that are not contingent on the laws, customs, or beliefs of any particular society or government. This idea then informed the American and French Revolutions, embodied in the famous second sentence of the Declaration of Independence, which states "that all men are created equal, that they are endowed by their Creator with certain unalienable Rights, that among these are Life, Liberty and the pursuit of Happiness."

The first concrete international steps toward regulating how governments can treat their citizens were undertaken in the UN Charter, adopted in 1945. This movement was spurred by the atrocities of World War II, especially the Holocaust, in which at least 6 million Jews and other minorities were systematically "dehumanized" and killed. Article 55 of the charter states that "based on respect for the principle of equal rights and self-determination of peoples, the United Nations shall promote . . . universal respect for, and observance of, human rights and fundamental freedoms for all without distinction as to race, sex, language, or religion."

Soon after the United Nations was founded, work began on an effort to clarify which rights Article 55 embodied and which rights states would be expected to protect. The **Universal Declaration of Human Rights (UDHR)**,[2] adopted by the UN General Assembly in 1948, is the product of those deliberations. Defined as a "common standard of achievement for all peoples" and broadly accepted as the foundation of modern human rights law, its 30 articles identify a diverse set of rights. Although governed only by soft law (see Chapter 11), the UDHR is today considered to be the authoritative standard of human rights.

René Cassin, one of the main authors of the UDHR, described the document as having four pillars, supporting "dignity, liberty, equality, and brotherhood." Each of the pillars represents a different historical principle and philosophy of human rights. The first two articles of the UDHR set out a timeless human dignity shared by all individuals regardless of race, religion, nationality, or sex. Articles 3–21 of the declaration define a first generation of civil liberties and other rights founded in a Western philosophical and legal tradition that can be traced to the Enlightenment, such as freedom of speech, freedom of association, and equal protection and recognition before the law.

human rights

The rights possessed by all individuals by virtue of being human, regardless of their status as citizens of particular states or members of a group or organization.

Universal Declaration of Human Rights (UDHR)

A declaration, adopted by the UN General Assembly in 1948, that is defined as a "common standard of achievement for all peoples" and forms the foundation of modern human rights law.

---

2. See https://www.un.org/en/universal-declaration-human-rights/ (accessed 7/13/20).

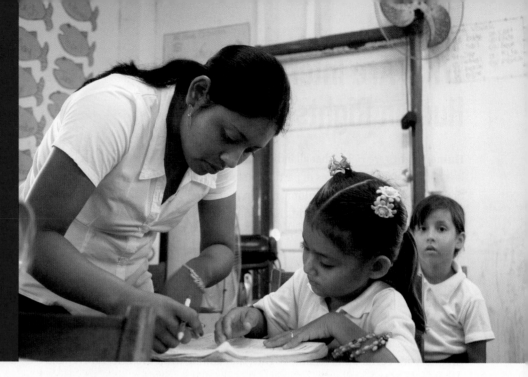

The UDHR establishes that everyone has a right to education and that elementary education shall be free. The United Nations estimates that 57 million children do not have a school to go to.

Articles 22–26 focus on political, social, and economic equality—a second generation of rights that emerged during the Industrial Revolution and that is often associated with socialist thought. This second generation includes the rights to employment, to an adequate standard of living, to the formation of trade unions, and to education.

Articles 27 and 28 address rights of communal and national solidarity, which were first developed in the late nineteenth century and championed by the states emerging from colonialism.[3] This last generation of rights, however, is far less developed in the UDHR than the first two generations are.

In tandem with the UDHR, the UN negotiated the Convention on the Prevention and Punishment of the Crime of Genocide, the first human rights treaty with clearly defined obligations and precise rules. The term *genocide* was coined by Raphael Lemkin, a Polish lawyer of Jewish descent who immigrated to the United States in 1941, to capture the essence of what happened during the Holocaust. It combines the Greek word *genos*, for "race" or "people," with the Latin word *cidere*, "to kill." The Genocide Convention, as the UN initiative is widely known, follows Lemkin closely in defining genocide as "acts committed with the intent to destroy, in whole or part, a national, ethnical, racial or religious group."

Pushed to the forefront of the human rights agenda because of the Holocaust, the Genocide Convention became the first piece of hard international human rights law. With 152 state parties to the agreement, it is also one of the most widely recognized and supported treaties ever written.[4] The United States signed the treaty

---

3. Micheline R. Ishay, *The History of Human Rights: From Ancient Times to the Globalization Era* (Berkeley: University of California Press, 2004), 3–4.

4. See https://www.un.org/en/genocideprevention/documents/atrocity-crimes/Doc.1_Convention%20 on%20the%20Prevention%20and%20Punishment%20of%20the%20Crime%20of%20Genocide.pdf (accessed 6/29/20).

in 1948 but did not ratify it until 40 years later. Senator William Proxmire (Democrat from Wisconsin), a major supporter, was well known for his speeches in favor of ratification, which he delivered on the Senate floor every day that the body was in session from 1967 to the eventual vote on the treaty in 1986 (for a total of 3,211 speeches).

After negotiating the UDHR and the Genocide Convention, the UN then began the much more difficult task of translating the UDHR into legally binding and internationally enforceable treaties. Unfolding over 18 years, the negotiations eventually produced two separate agreements: the **International Covenant on Civil and Political Rights (ICCPR)** and the **International Covenant on Economic, Social, and Cultural Rights (ICESCR)**.[5]

Although there was nearly universal agreement on the UDHR, the attempt to write hard international law protecting human rights got caught, like so many other attempts at cooperation, between the Cold War superpowers. The solution was to write two separate treaties: one focusing on the civil and political rights of liberty then favored by Western states and the other focusing on the economic, social, and cultural rights of equality and brotherhood supported by the then communist states and others in the developing world. As formal treaties completed in 1966 and in force from 1976, the twin covenants are considered legally binding for all states that have signed them.

The ICCPR details the basic rights of individuals and nations, defining in sometimes more precise terms the political and civil rights first claimed in the UDHR. The ICCPR affirms the rights to life, liberty, and the freedom of movement; the presumption of innocence; equal standing before the law; legal recourse when rights have been violated; and privacy. In addition, all individuals are guaranteed freedom of thought, conscience, and religion; freedom of opinion and expression; and freedom of assembly and association. The covenant forbids torture and inhumane or degrading punishment, slavery and involuntary servitude, and arbitrary arrest and detention. It also prohibits propaganda advocating war or hatred based on race, religion, or national origin.

The ICCPR also provides for the right of all people to choose freely whom they will marry and to found a family, and it requires that the duties and obligations of marriage and family be shared equally between partners. It guarantees the rights of children and prohibits discrimination based on race, sex, color, national origin, or language. It restricts the death penalty to the most serious of crimes, guarantees condemned people the right to appeal for commutation to a lesser penalty, and forbids the death penalty entirely for people under 18 years of age.

Currently, 173 of the UN's 193 member countries are parties to the ICCPR. The United States ratified the treaty in 1992, but only after declaring that its provisions were "not self-executing"—meaning that although the agreement is binding as a matter of international law, its provisions would not automatically become domestic law without further legislation by the U.S. Congress. Human rights practices under

International Covenant on Civil and Political Rights (ICCPR)

The agreement, completed in 1966 and in force from 1976, that details the basic civil and political rights of individuals and nations. The ICCPR and ICESCR together are known as the "twin covenants."

International Covenant on Economic, Social, and Cultural Rights (ICESCR)

The agreement, completed in 1966 and in force from 1976, that specifies the basic economic, social, and cultural rights of individuals and nations. The ICCPR and ICESCR together are known as the "twin covenants."

---

5. For more information on the covenants and their texts, see www.ohchr.org/EN/ProfessionalInterest /Pages/InternationalLaw.aspx (accessed 6/29/20).

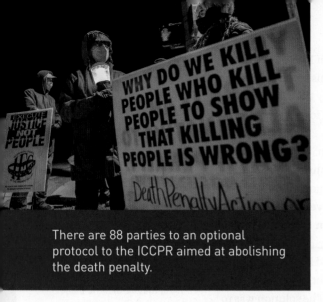

There are 88 parties to an optional protocol to the ICCPR aimed at abolishing the death penalty.

the covenant are monitored by the UN Human Rights Committee, a group of 18 experts that meets three times a year to consider interstate complaints of violations and periodic reports submitted by member states on their compliance with the treaty.

The parallel ICESCR reiterates and affirms the basic economic, social, and cultural rights of individuals and nations, including the right to earn wages sufficient to support a minimum standard of living and the right to form trade unions and strike. The ICESCR also codified rights to equal pay for equal work; equal opportunity for advancement; paid or otherwise compensated maternity leave; free primary education and accessible schools at all levels; and copyright, patent, and trademark protection for intellectual property. The treaty forbids the exploitation of children and requires all countries to cooperate to end world hunger. Each nation that has ratified this covenant is required to submit reports on its progress in providing for these rights to the secretary-general of the UN. The ICESCR currently has 171 members. The United States signed the covenant in 1977 under President Jimmy Carter, but it has never ratified it because of continuing opposition to provisions that would go substantially beyond existing domestic laws.

Together, the UDHR and the twin covenants are often referred to as the **International Bill of Rights**. Over time, additional rights have been added through supplementary conventions, as summarized in Table 12.1. The agreements listed in the table highlight the range of rights that are now more or less protected under international law, including, in certain cases, the right of individual petition through which victims of human rights abuses can seek redress directly from international courts. In short, as the list demonstrates, the international community now possesses an extensive body of international human rights law, albeit one that remains controversial and possesses varying degrees of national support for different provisions.

Why Are Human Rights Controversial?

Because of differing legal traditions, domestic political regimes and institutions, and philosophies, states often have different interests in human rights. Even though human rights are by definition universal, states do not necessarily have the same interests in promoting the same rights to the same extent. States have interests in supporting rights that they already respect domestically and in fighting against new rights that they see as costly to protect. They also have an interest in preserving their own sovereignty, and therefore they may resist the attempted imposition of certain rights within their borders by outside actors. States may also have a strategic interest in promoting rights that their adversaries will deny or find costly to implement.

Many of the rights defined in the UDHR—especially many of the economic and social rights—are drawn directly from President Franklin D. Roosevelt's New Deal, which was enacted during the Great Depression of the 1930s. Through the 1950s,

International Bill of Rights

The UDHR, ICCPR, and ICESCR collectively. Together, these three agreements form the core of the international human rights regime.

TABLE 12.1 *UN Human Rights Agreements*

TREATY	DATE SIGNED/IN FORCE	BRIEF DESCRIPTION
Universal Declaration of Human Rights (UDHR)	1948	Outlines basic human rights.
Convention on the Prevention and Punishment of the Crime of Genocide	1948/1951	Bans acts committed with the intent to destroy, in whole or part, a national, ethnic, racial, or religious group.
International Convention on the Elimination of All Forms of Racial Discrimination (ICERD)	1965/1969	Bans all racial discrimination, with particular attention to policies and practices of apartheid.
International Covenant on Economic, Social, and Cultural Rights (ICESCR)	1966/1976	Details the basic economic, social, and cultural rights of individuals and nations.
International Covenant on Civil and Political Rights (ICCPR)	1966/1976	Details the basic civil and political rights of individuals and nations. Optional protocol (1966/1976) permits petitions from individuals. Second optional protocol (1989/1991) commits state parties to abolishing the death penalty.
Convention on the Elimination of All Forms of Discrimination against Women (CEDAW)	1979/1981	Bans discrimination against women, focusing on education, employment, health, marriage, and the family. Optional protocol (1999/2000) permits petitions from individuals.
Convention against Torture and Other Cruel, Inhuman or Degrading Treatment or Punishment (CAT)	1984/1987	Bans torture under all circumstances. Optional protocol (2002/2006) establishes regular visits to monitor state practices.
Convention on the Rights of the Child (CRC)	1989/1990	Details the special rights of children. Optional protocol (2000/2002) bans children in the armed forces from participating in hostilities. Second optional protocol (2000/2002) prohibits the sale of children, child prostitution, and child pornography. Third optional protocol (2011/2014) allows the submission of complaints by individual children.
International Convention on the Protection of the Rights of All Migrant Workers and Members of Their Families (ICRMW)	1990/2003	Details the special rights of workers outside their country of origin.
Convention on the Rights of Persons with Disabilities (CRPD)	2007/2008	Mandates equal status and treatment for individuals with disabilities. Optional protocol (2007/2008) permits petitions from individuals.
International Convention for the Protection of All Persons from Enforced Disappearance (ICPPED)	2007/2010	Prohibits arrest, detention, or abduction of individuals without acknowledgment by the state.

Note: For texts and updated membership information, consult www.ohchr.org/EN/ProfessionalInterest/Pages/InternationalLaw.aspx (accessed 7/13/20).

many people in the United States and other Western countries remained supportive of these economic and social rights. As the New Deal lost popularity, however, support for enshrining many of its progressive policies into international law diminished.

Human rights also got caught up in the Cold War competition of ideas. In public forums, Western states tended to emphasize first-generation civil and political rights already enshrined in their own systems, while the countries of the Soviet bloc and many countries in the developing world trumpeted their superior progress on second-generation economic, social, and cultural rights. This Cold War division and historical legacy continues to undermine support for the ICESCR in the United States today. Many U.S. conservatives, for instance, question whether economic, social, and cultural rights are actually rights at all, since they pertain to particular classes or groups of people (for example, workers) rather than to all human beings.[6]

Critics of the rights specified in the UDHR point to their origin in a Western, liberal philosophical tradition that emphasizes first-generation individual rights over second- and third-generation collective rights. This criticism has merit—but only to a point. The modern idea of human rights is rooted in a moral vision that sees all humans as equal and autonomous individuals. Political scientist Jack Donnelly observes that "it is a relatively simple matter to derive the full list of rights in the Universal Declaration from the political principle of equal concern and respect."[7]

Although the rights founded in this tradition may now be widely accepted because of their status as international standards and law, the philosophical tradition itself is not universal. An alternative philosophy, for example, is the notion of "Asian values," which elevates the rights of families and communities and the goal of social and political stability over the rights of individuals (see "What Shaped Our World?" on p. 529). Although nearly everyone may agree that some human rights exist in principle, the debate continues over exactly which rights individuals have, underscoring the point that rights are an institution that evolves over time. International human rights are not fixed but are a product of struggle, debate, and social interests.

This continuing debate also demonstrates that human rights have not been internalized as norms in all societies and governments. Although human rights are more deeply held in Western, democratic countries, few rights have obtained the taken-for-granted quality in which violations are considered taboo or inappropriate, except in the direst circumstances. Freedom from torture is likely one of the most widely and deeply held human rights. However, the debate over the treatment of suspected terrorists that began in the United States after the attacks on September 11, 2001, suggests that torture or practices that border on torture remain acceptable instruments of government policy for some Americans.

---

6. Jack Donnelly, *Universal Human Rights in Theory and Practice*, 3rd ed. (Ithaca, NY: Cornell University Press, 2013), 40.

7. Donnelly, *Universal Human Rights in Theory and Practice*, 63.

The Asian Values Debate

Although nations around the world broadly agree that human rights are important, as is reflected in their near-universal support for the UDHR and the twin covenants, exactly which rights should be prioritized remains contested. Some of the most controversial questions about promoting human rights arose in the Asian values debate of the 1990s, a controversy that continues today in a slightly altered form.

Interests For many human rights advocates, the *Universal* Declaration of Human Rights is aptly titled. However, an alternative, "Asian values" approach to human rights was propounded by Southeast Asian leaders in the 1990s, most visibly by Mahathir Mohamad of Malaysia and Lee Kuan Yew of Singapore. As East Asian countries began to develop more rapidly, often under authoritarian governments with a notable degree of control over their economies, their leaders asserted a distinct—and in their view, superior—"Asian" approach to human rights.

Interactions The key articulation of the Asian values approach was the Bangkok Declaration of 1993. This document affirmed the commitment of signatories to the UDHR while also stressing the principles of sovereignty and noninterference. The Bangkok Declaration departed from the standard approach, however, in calling for greater attention to economic, social, and cultural rights and downplaying political rights and civil liberties. Proponents argued that Asian societies were founded on a philosophy that emphasizes the welfare of the community over individual freedoms. Rooted in Confucian thought, Asian values were said to prioritize respect for authority and social harmony.

Critics of this position charged that it was simply cover for the authoritarian rule of Mahathir, Lee, and other political leaders within the region. Lee had been in power since 1959, and though he was often described as a "benevolent dictator," he detained without trial hundreds of alleged extremists and ruthlessly crushed political opposition. Mahathir was criticized for imprisoning political activists, including his rival Anwar Ibrahim, and for undermining the independence of the judiciary.

As their countries succeeded economically, these leaders pushed back against their critics by appealing to different political principles and cultural affinities. Mahathir in 1997 called the UDHR an "oppressing" instrument by which the United States and other countries tried to impose Western values on Asians, adding that Asians needed stability and economic growth more than they needed civil liberties.[a]

Institutions The Asian values debate represented a significant attempt to alter the underlying norms of human rights, which had developed largely under the influence of Europe and the United States in the postwar period. As an institution, the UDHR was broad enough that all could see their respective priorities within it, so the controversy was really over which rights deserved to be foregrounded.

As the debate unfolded, however, Lee of Singapore went further and criticized Western individualism for the perceived decadence of Western societies, including high rates of crime, drug abuse, and family breakdown. The debate was eventually cast not just as one of cultural disagreement over human rights priorities but as one of cultural superiority. This change in focus hardened differences on both sides of the debate. Support for Asian values as a distinct approach to human rights waned after the Asian financial crisis of 1997, which called into question the economic success on which much of the movement rested.

Today, emphasis on a distinct Asian understanding of human rights is once again building under China's growing international leadership. As with the earlier Asian values campaign, appeals to Confucius—this time from China's Xi Jinping, among others—affirm party authority and subordinate political and civil rights to the need for political stability and growth. Even when nearly all countries sign on to a human rights institution like the UDHR, the specific rights that will be prioritized in practice remain contested.

---

a. Stephen Chapman, "Is Democracy Foreign to 'Asian Values'?" *Chicago Tribune*, July 31, 1997, http://articles.chicagotribune.com/1997-07-31 /news/9707310080_1_asian-values-southeast-asian-nations-human- rights (accessed 2/11/21).

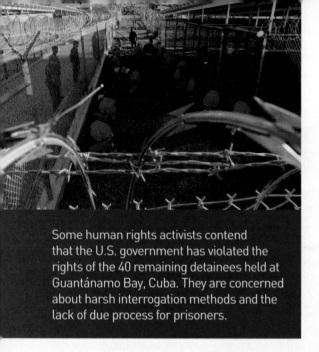

Some human rights activists contend that the U.S. government has violated the rights of the 40 remaining detainees held at Guantánamo Bay, Cuba. They are concerned about harsh interrogation methods and the lack of due process for prisoners.

The power of the anti-torture principle was evident in the President George W. Bush administration's attempts to deny that it was engaging in torture. The U.S. government went so far as to redefine some practices, such as waterboarding, as not inconsistent with international law—an interpretation not supported by most other states. President Donald J. Trump took an even more aggressive stance and publicly defended torture. "Only a stupid person would say it doesn't work," he stated. And even if torture were not effective, Trump concluded, those being tortured "deserve it anyway, for what they're doing."[8]

Actual practice suggests that the norm against torture is, in fact, ambiguous and fails to significantly constrain government behavior. That human rights norms have not yet been internalized or, at best, are only weakly internalized implies that individuals and states still act on human rights and enforce laws only when it is in their self-interest to do so.

Are Some Rights More Important than Others?

Although the UDHR specifies a wide range of rights, it appears that (to paraphrase George Orwell's *Animal Farm*) although all rights are equal, some are more equal than others. Few, if any, human rights are internalized as norms, but some rights in the UDHR and ICCPR do have a special status in international law and, along with the Genocide Convention, appear to have broader support than others.

In the ICCPR, Article 4 permits the suspension of some rights in cases of social or public emergency, but it simultaneously identifies a small number of other rights that cannot be suspended for any reason. These **nonderogable rights** include freedom from torture or cruel and degrading punishment; the right to be recognized as a person before the law; and freedom of thought, conscience, and religion.[9] In contrast, none of the rights identified in the ICESCR are nonderogable, and all can be limited by states acting under the law. Despite their special status, however, nonderogable rights are not automatically enforced more than other rights are, as the continuing practice of torture in countries around the world makes clear.

In turn, many of these nonderogable rights have gained special support within the global human rights movement. Amnesty International, generally considered the world's leading human rights organization, identifies its core mission as protecting individuals from torture; from cruel, inhuman, or degrading punishment; and from arbitrary arrest, detention, and exile. It also works to defend the freedoms of thought, conscience, religion, opinion, and expression.[10] Individuals imprisoned solely for the peaceful expression of their beliefs are what Amnesty International

nonderogable rights

Rights that cannot be suspended for any reason, including in cases of social or public emergency.

---

8. Adam Serwer, "Can Trump Bring Back Torture?" *The Atlantic*, January 26, 2017, www.theatlantic.com /politics/archive/2017/01/trump-torture/514463 (accessed 2/18/20).

9. Specifically, Article 4 prohibits the suspension of Articles 6 (inherent right to life, referring to the death penalty), 7 (torture), 8 (paragraphs 1 and 2, on slavery and servitude), 11 (imprisonment from contractual obligation), 15 (ex post facto criminal offenses), 16 (recognition before the law), and 18 (freedom of thought, conscience, and religion).

10. Articles 5, 9, 18, and 19 of the UDHR.

calls **prisoners of conscience (POCs)**. One prominent POC was the Nobel Peace Prize winner Liu Xiaobo (1955–2017), who was jailed in 2009 simply for coauthoring a proposal for political and legal reform in China.

The focus of Amnesty International, overlapping to a considerable extent with the nonderogable rights of the ICCPR, is shared by many human rights organizations. In focusing on these more limited rights and publicizing violations of only these rights, Amnesty has done much to influence notions of what human rights are today. To the extent that certain rights have become or moved toward becoming international norms, as explained in Chapter 11, Amnesty International and the other major human rights organizations that make up the TAN have had much to do with shaping this process. Building support for human rights and changing conceptions of human rights–related interests for both individuals and states has been a major achievement of the human rights TAN.

Finally, by examining when states are willing to incur costs in order to punish human rights violations in other states, we can infer something about which rights are most important to them. Economic sanctions are a common tool that states use to punish violators of human rights. For example, states may limit trade, loans, or travel to the target country in order to put pressure on the government to improve political and civil rights. Since sanctions also inflict costs on the states that impose them, these states must weigh their interest in defending certain rights against their other priorities. Indeed, many violations of human rights go entirely unpunished, sometimes even unnoticed. Actual sanctions by states against violators are relatively rare. But when states have taken steps to impose sanctions against human rights abusers, these steps have almost always been intended as punishment for unfair political detentions and torture or for the suspension of peaceful political opposition.[11]

For instance, the United States imposed sanctions on South Korea and Chile in 1973 for their unlawful detention and abuse of political prisoners, and it levied sanctions against Paraguay, Guatemala, Argentina, Nicaragua, El Salvador, and Brazil in 1977 for the same issues. Even in the case of South Africa, sanctions were not imposed against the country for its policy of apartheid in general; they were only established after insurrection commenced and the South African government began to brutally repress political opponents. States clearly act to enforce some rights more frequently than others. In practice, the rights that states appear ready to defend are narrower than the full range of rights articulated in the UDHR and may, in fact, be limited to the nonderogable rights identified in the ICCPR.

Overall, as an institution, international human rights remain a work in progress. Although codified in at least soft law, rights are themselves objects of political struggle, as they define what is and is not acceptable government behavior toward a nation's own citizens. Countries differ in their views of which rights they are bound to protect and which rights they should seek to enforce when abused by other states. Thus, to account for the politics of international human rights, we must examine not just human rights law but also the interests and interactions of states.

prisoners of conscience (POCs)
Individuals imprisoned solely for the peaceful expression of their beliefs. The term was coined by the human rights organization Amnesty International.

---

11. See David A. Lake and Wendy H. Wong, "The Politics of Networks: Interests, Power, and Human Rights Norms," in *Networked Politics: Agency, Power, and Governance*, ed. Miles Kahler (Ithaca, NY: Cornell University Press, 2009), 148.

Should Economic Sanctions Be Imposed on Governments That Violate Human Rights?

In August 2020, the United States imposed new or continuing economic sanctions on 22 countries, often for human rights violations by their governments. However, sanctions also affect the ordinary people living in the target countries. Using economic leverage to try to promote better protection of political and civil rights poses a difficult moral question: If sanctions can reduce human rights abuses by governments, but only at the cost of increased suffering by average citizens, are they justified?

Applying the Concepts

Sanctions are most often imposed when countries have opposing **interests**, whether they differ over human rights practices, the development of new weapons, or some other issue. Restricting trade, travel, or new loans is an **interaction** or, more specifically, a form of coercion, intended to raise the cost of certain actions to the target state and thereby influence it to change its behavior. Since sanctions must be imposed by many, if not all, countries to achieve their desired result—as the target can otherwise obtain needed commodities or finance from nonparticipating countries—they are most likely to be effective when coordinated through a multilateral **institution**, such as the United Nations. Because countries may not have similar interests, reaching agreement at the UN or elsewhere can be difficult.

Some of the most troubling sanctions were those imposed against Iraq after the Persian Gulf War of 1991. Four days after Iraq's invasion of Kuwait, the UN Security Council passed a resolution imposing economic sanctions on Iraq, including a trade embargo on all exports to the country other than basic food and medical supplies.[a] Although the war ended quickly, the sanctions continued for the next 12 years.

One justification for maintaining the policy was that restrictions on international trade and finance would sap Saddam Hussein's power and thereby end the human rights abuses that the autocrat had inflicted on the Iraqi people. Yet the World Health Organization reported in March 1996 that, among other detrimental effects, sanctions-related deprivations in Iraq had caused infant mortality to rise by a factor of six, equivalent to the deaths of hundreds of thousands of children under age five.[b] Denis Halliday, the UN humanitarian coordinator for Iraq, condemned the sanctions. Upon resigning in 1998 after a 34-year career with the United Nations, he described the program in Iraq as "satisfying the definition of genocide."[c]

In light of the suffering imposed on Iraqis by the sanctions, many countries now use targeted, or so-called smart, sanctions limited to specific government leaders and their supporters. Indeed, most U.S. sanctions are now imposed only on specified elites. Targeted sanctions aim to freeze assets that certain individuals hold abroad, prohibit travel, or otherwise penalize leaders for their behavior. The aim is to impose pain only on the regime's supporters, ideally motivating them to change policy to alleviate their own suffering. Even with such smart sanctions, however, it appears difficult to impose sufficient pain on the elite that they will turn against the regime, since they are its primary

Iraqi women wait in line to receive food rations in 2003 amid sanctions imposed against the country.

beneficiaries. It is also hard to limit the effects of sanctions to the elite alone. Even smart sanctions, however carefully designed they may be, will nearly always impose some costs on society as a whole.

The issue is not just whether sanctions work to bring about improved human rights practices, although the more effective they are, the stronger the case is for their use. The record on success is mixed.[d] The more perplexing moral question is: How much pain is political change worth to members of the target society? And who has the right to determine the answer to this question? In the case of South Africa, the political opposition to White-minority rule actually called for and supported sanctions. As Bishop Desmond Tutu, a South African leader in the anti-apartheid movement, wrote in the *New York Times* in June 1986: "There is no guarantee that sanctions will topple apartheid, but it is the last nonviolent option left, and it is a risk with a chance."[e]

The Iraqi case was different. The sanctions were imposed not at the request of opposition groups within Iraq (who at the time were still heavily repressed by the regime) but by the United States and its allies. In the midst of the sanctions against Iraq, then U.S. ambassador to the UN Madeleine Albright was asked in a *60 Minutes* interview about the possibility that up to half a million Iraqi children had died as a result of the trade and financial restrictions. Albright responded: "We think the price is worth it." Although she later said she had been asked a "loaded" question and regretted her answer, she did not disavow it.[f] But of course the "we" here was the United States, not necessarily the Iraqi people.

The question of the value of sanctions arises with any attempt to levy economic restrictions, including those currently directed at Syria because of the brutal civil war being waged by the Assad regime against a highly

Madeleine Albright served as U.S. Ambassador to the United Nations from 1993 to 1997.

factionalized opposition and those directed at Iran because of its nuclear program. Even if some groups in Iraq might have supported sanctions against the regime, despite some suffering by the people, who gets to decide whether it is "worth it"?

Thinking Analytically

1. Which groups within a target country are most directly affected by, say, a general trade embargo? In what ways could these impacts be expected to influence leaders' behavior?

2. Should sanctions ever be used to force governments to improve their human rights practices? If yes, when and under what conditions?

3. Does it make a difference if the conflict of interest is not over human rights but, rather, over an economic or security issue? On what issues and toward what kinds of countries might sanctions ever be an appropriate tool of diplomacy?

a. UN Security Council Resolution 661, Iraq/Kuwait, August 6, 1990.

b. World Health Organization, "The Health Conditions of the Population in Iraq since the Gulf Crisis," WHO/EHA/96.1, March 1996.

c. *Paying the Price: Killing the Children of Iraq*, written and presented by John Pilger, directed by Alan Lowery (London: Carlton Television, 2000).

d. The classic study on the effectiveness of sanctions is Gary Clyde Hufbauer, Jeffrey J. Schott, and Kimberly Ann Elliott, *Economic Sanctions Reconsidered: History and Current Policy*, vol. 1, *History and Current Policy*, 2nd ed. (Washington, DC: Institute for International Economics, 1990).

e. Desmond Tutu, "Sanctions vs. Apartheid," *New York Times*, June 16, 1986.

f. Madeleine Albright, *Madam Secretary: A Memoir* (Norwalk, CT: Easton Press, 2003), 274–75.

Why Do Individuals and States Care about the Human Rights of Others?

Proponents of improving human rights, including Amnesty International, Human Rights Watch, and hundreds of other nongovernmental organizations (NGOs), clearly suggest that individuals and states should possess and act on an interest in the human rights of others around the globe. But the puzzle still remains. Why would individuals and states care about how other states treat their citizens? Why is it in their interests to promote and potentially enforce laws governing the human rights practices of other states? In turn, as sovereign entities, why would states want to constrain their dealings with their own people and open themselves to the scrutiny of others? In answering these questions, we begin by addressing why states violate human rights in the first place.

Why Do States Violate Human Rights?

States violate human rights for many reasons. Some violations arise from a lack of state capacity. Many poor countries, for instance, may sincerely want to but simply cannot afford to provide free primary schooling to everyone, as required under the ICESCR. Other governments may not be able to control their militaries or police sufficiently to stem human rights abuses. For instance, the United States was appropriately criticized when its troops, apparently acting on their own volition and not under an official policy directive, abused prisoners at Abu Ghraib prison in Iraq during the 2003 war. Recognizing states' varying capacities to implement standards, many human rights are soft law, understood to be aspirations or goals toward which states should strive rather than strict rules to which they can and should be held accountable.[12]

In other cases, however, states violate human rights in defense of their national security. Violent or potentially violent opposition to the state is illegal everywhere, and thus it counts as criminal, not political, behavior. Amnesty International specifically excludes as POCs any individuals who use or advocate violence. Nelson Mandela, a leader of the anti-apartheid movement in South Africa, was originally designated a POC in 1962 after his arrest for organizing strikes to protest apartheid. But Mandela's status was revoked by Amnesty after he was convicted in 1964 of trying to overthrow the government violently. Yet the dividing line between criminal and political activities is often ambiguous, and some states prosecute individuals as criminals for political actions that would be considered legal elsewhere. Even when actions are clearly criminal, however, prosecution and punishment may be abusive if individuals are not given due process under the law.

When under attack or perceived attack, states are sometimes tempted to violate the rights of groups or individuals that they fear may be allied with a foreign power.

---

12. See Wade M. Cole, "Mind the Gap: State Capacity and the Implementation of Human Rights Treaties," *International Organization* 69, no. 2 (2015): 405–41.

Thus, the United States violated the civil and political rights of many of its own citizens in the infamous Red Scare of 1917–20, which followed the Bolshevik revolution in Russia. During the first Red Scare, between 3,000 and 10,000 individuals were arrested, denied due process, and sometimes beaten during questioning. The United States also violated the rights of approximately 110,000 Japanese Americans who were interned in concentration camps following the attack on Pearl Harbor and the start of World War II. And, in the second Red Scare (1947–57), the U.S. government blacklisted, jailed, and deported Americans suspected of following a communist or other left-wing ideology.

In more recent years, since the terrorist attacks of September 11, 2001, the United States has been criticized for violating the human rights of U.S. citizens or residents accused of planning additional attacks or associating with terrorist organizations abroad.[13] Especially controversial were the targeted drone attacks authorized by President Obama against U.S. citizens abroad accused of involvement in terrorist plots. Other countries have responded similarly to attacks on their own people or soil. Indeed, the existence of an interstate or civil war is strongly associated with increased human rights violations.[14] In justifying these violations, governments often claim that national security trumps the human rights of individuals.

Governments also violate the human rights of their citizens to preserve their own hold on power. This motivation differs from the national security rationale just described. In these cases, the country is not under attack, but governments abuse their political opponents in an effort to suppress internal dissent. That is, to weaken and deter opponents, governments in essence declare war on their own citizens. One of the most egregious cases of such abuse occurred in Argentina following a military coup in March 1976. The country's three-man junta, led by General Jorge Rafael Videla, immediately began a seven-year campaign known as the Dirty War against suspected political dissidents and opponents of the military regime. Some were publicly detained, but many more individuals were "disappeared."

Although it denied any official knowledge or involvement, the Argentine military eventually kidnapped, tortured, and killed nearly 10,000 perceived political opponents.[15] Many of the disappeared, we now know, were taken on "death flights" on which they were pushed out of airplanes high above the Atlantic Ocean. As many as 500 newborns were taken from their imprisoned mothers and given to childless military families because, as General Ramón Camps (head of the Buenos Aires Provincial Police) later attempted to explain, "subversive parents will raise subversive

---

13. The United States is also accused of violating international humanitarian law, specified in the Geneva Conventions, when it treats foreign detainees as "enemy combatants" supposedly outside international law. On the Geneva Conventions and laws of war, see James D. Morrow, "The Institutional Features of the Prisoners of War Treaties," *International Organization* 55, no. 4 (2001): 971–91.

14. Steven C. Poe and C. Neal Tate, "Repression of Human Rights to Personal Integrity in the 1980s: A Global Analysis," *American Political Science Review* 88, no. 4 (1994): 853–72; and Matthew Krain, "State-Sponsored Mass Murder: The Onset and Severity of Genocides and Politicides," *Journal of Conflict Resolution* 41, no. 3 (1997): 331–60.

15. The Argentine National Commission on the Disappeared provides an "official" figure of about 9,000 "disappeared" between 1976 and 1983. Internal documents from the Argentine security services suggest a figure of 22,000. Human rights organizations estimate that the total number of casualties of this Dirty War may be as high as 30,000.

Argentina's Dirty War, which began in 1976, provoked a strong response from a vast transnational human rights network. Here, the Mothers of the Plaza de Mayo in Argentina gather to protest abuses by the junta and to demand information on their "disappeared" children.

children."[16] This was government-sponsored cruelty on a dramatic scale, intended to crush and intimidate political opponents and keep the military regime in power. Like the case of apartheid in South Africa, the Dirty War in Argentina was critical in mobilizing the human rights TAN, and that network, in turn, was instrumental in bringing about political change in Argentina.

When the fear of "others" within a society who may undermine the state combines with fragile governments seeking to preserve their rule, the result can be genocide, the most extreme form of human rights abuse, in which entire identity groups are singled out for systematic persecution and murder. Genocide is one of the most extreme crimes against humanity. The Armenian Genocide in Turkey during World War I and the Holocaust perpetrated by Germany during World War II led to the concept of genocide and modern human rights law. More recently, genocides have occurred in Rwanda (see Chapters 5 and 11); in the former Yugoslavia, where perpetrators of the Srebrenica massacre were prosecuted for the crime; and in Sudan, where former president Omar Hassan al-Bashir has been indicted by the International Criminal Court (ICC) on three counts of genocide, and the ruling transitional military government has agreed to cooperate with the ICC. Recently, the government of Myanmar has been accused of carrying out a genocide against the Rohingya, a Muslim minority largely concentrated near the border with Bangladesh.

More generally, autocracies and unstable democracies are significantly more likely to violate the human rights of their citizens than are established democracies,

---

16. Translated from Nancy Berger-Levrault, *Disparus: Rapport à la Commission indépendante sur les questions humanitaires internationales* (London: Zed Books, 1986), 29. For more on Camps, see "Ramón Camps, 67, Argentine General in the 'Dirty War,'" *New York Times*, August 23, 1994, www.nytimes.com/1994/08/23/obituaries/ramon-camps-67-argentine-general-in-the-dirty-war.html (accessed 2/18/21); and Francisco Goldman, "Children of the Dirty War," *New Yorker*, March 12, 2012, www.newyorker.com/magazine/2012/03/19/children-of-the-dirty-war (accessed 2/18/21). There have been 77 documented cases of kidnapped newborns.

In early 2017, the Trump administration issued an executive order banning persons from certain largely Muslim countries from entering the United States. This so-called Muslim Ban was extremely controversial, but, as subsequently modified, it survived several court challenges.

where political competition is respected and channeled through regular elections in which incumbent governments accept defeat and leave office.[17] Overt acts of torture (and possibly other human rights abuses) are most likely to occur in multiparty dictatorships. Single-party or personalist dictatorships sufficiently repress political opponents such that fewer acts of torture are necessary. These states may use torture if they need to, and broad civil liberties are typically denied, but opponents are deterred from challenging the government; thus, the regime typically does not need to use violence against individuals to maintain its rule. In multiparty dictatorships, however, the political opposition usually remains visible and viable, and the government is tempted to use torture to suppress opponents so that it can stay in power.[18] In all cases, the weaker or less legitimate the government, the more likely it is to abuse human rights.

However, even in democratic countries like the United States, political leaders may be tempted by abusive ideas. During the 2016 presidential campaign, for instance, then candidate Trump repeatedly called for a national database of Muslims in the United States, including U.S. citizens; surveillance to be placed on mosques; and the creation of a national ID that Muslims would be forced to carry. None of these suggestions were implemented, but they show nonetheless how even democratic political leaders may be attracted to policies that would violate the human rights of their citizens.[19]

17. Christian Davenport, "Multi-Dimensional Threat Perception and State Repression: An Inquiry into Why States Apply Negative Sanctions," *American Journal of Political Science* 39, no. 3 (1995): 683–713; and Steven C. Poe, C. Neal Tate, and Linda Camp Keith, "Repression of the Human Right to Personal Integrity Revisited: A Global Cross-National Study Covering the Years 1976–1993," *International Studies Quarterly* 43, no. 2 (1999): 291–313. Todd Landman, *Protecting Human Rights: A Comparative Study* (Washington, DC: Georgetown University Press, 2005), finds that states that have more recently become democratic are more likely to engage in human rights abuses.

18. James Raymond Vreeland, "Political Institutions and Human Rights: Why Dictatorships Enter into the United Nations Convention against Torture," *International Organization* 62, no. 1 (2008): 65–101.

19. Jeremy Diamond, "Trump Doubles Down on Calls for Mosque Surveillance," CNN, June 15, 2016, www.cnn.com/2016/06/15/politics/donald-trump-muslims-mosque-surveillance/index.html (accessed 8/26/20).

There is no single explanation for why countries violate human rights. In turn, there is no single explanation for why individuals, groups, and states seek to protect human rights at home and abroad. Repressing human rights is a political strategy that states and governments employ to protect themselves from real and perceived threats. It should be no surprise, then, that protecting human rights is also a political strategy that political actors use for a variety of aims.

Why Do States Sign Human Rights Agreements?

Some states have an interest in imposing human rights law on themselves as a means of demonstrating their commitment to democracy and political liberalization. While some governments have an interest in repressing human rights to retain political power, liberal or liberalizing governments often have an interest in promoting human rights as a means of committing themselves and their successors to political reforms.

Political scientist Andrew Moravcsik argues that democratizing states that sincerely seek to shed their autocratic and possibly abusive pasts sign human rights agreements in an attempt to lock in their new institutions and improved practices.[20] By committing to international agreements that may carry some cost if they are violated—even if that cost is only a loss of international reputation—new democratic leaders and coalitions attempt to make political backsliding more costly and thus signal a credible commitment to political reform. This observation implies that the countries most eager to ratify human rights treaties should be newly democratic or democratizing states—a proposition for which Moravcsik and others find some support. In this conception, international human rights law is a tool that states use strategically to alter their own domestic political incentives.

This notion of using international human rights treaties to commit to domestic political reforms also explains the weaker tendency and sometimes outright reluctance of established democracies to ratify human rights agreements. To the extent that human rights are already secured at home through constitutional protections and the rule of law, stable democracies have less need to bind themselves through international agreements.[21] Thus, with its own Bill of Rights and stable democratic institutions, the United States, for instance, relies on its own, internal processes for protecting human rights and is reluctant to cede any authority to international treaties like the ICCPR or to international bodies like the UN Commission on Human Rights or the ICC (see the next section) to oversee its practices.

Increasingly, however, democracies are recognizing the contradiction inherent in advocating human rights for others while failing to ratify international human rights treaties themselves. Established democracies are now signing agreements they had previously rejected and shrinking the disparities in treaty ratification between new and established democracies. The United States remains a visible

---

20. Andrew Moravcsik, "The Origins of Human Rights Regimes: Democratic Delegation in Postwar Europe," *International Organization* 54, no. 2 (Spring 2000): 217–52.

21. These states will, however, also face lower costs for signing agreements that already accord with their domestic practices. See Jay Goodliffe and Darren G. Hawkins, "Explaining Commitment: States and the Convention against Torture," *Journal of Politics* 68, no. 2 (2006): 358–71.

exception to this trend, however, in its continuing reluctance to accept international human rights accords. In fact, the United States withdrew from the UN Human Rights Council in June 2018, saying that the body was "hypocritical and self-serving." Many observers, however, saw the move as retaliation against the UN for its criticisms of the Trump administration's child separation policy at the U.S.-Mexico border.[22] As one of his first acts in office, President Joe Biden announced in February 2021 that the United States would rejoin the Human Rights Council.

Finally, some states may sign international human rights treaties because they are persuaded to do so by contingent rewards provided by others—a form of linkage (see Chapter 2). Established democracies often provide inducements for new democracies to join these regimes, such as financial assistance or the promise of future membership in international organizations, such as NATO, that provide benefits on other dimensions. For instance, as a condition of acceptance into the European Union, countries applying for membership must comply with a host of human rights treaties. Turkey's human rights practices—especially its repression of the Kurds—have been one of the major stumbling blocks in its attempt to join the European Union. By imposing human rights standards as a condition for assistance or membership in international organizations, other states hope to institutionalize democracy in transitional governments. The European Union also hopes to use the threat of expulsion to persuade states to keep their promises, but this method has so far proved ineffective in the case of Hungary, where rights to free expression and, in particular, the right to asylum have been denied under the prime ministry of Viktor Orbán.[23] The European Union has so far found little consensus in putting pressure on Hungary to address these issues.

As the example of the established democracies suggests, states also ratify international human rights treaties not to bind themselves but to constrain the human rights practices of others. They accept international oversight of their own affairs in order to secure their ability to scrutinize other nations. There are both altruistic and self-interested reasons why individuals and states seek to influence human rights in other countries.

Moral and Philosophical Motivations

Many individuals identify with a common humanity and feel personally affected by the welfare and treatment of others, including those in countries other than their own. As social animals, humans possess a degree of empathy that is weaker in some, stronger in others, but present in all.[24] This sense of empathy is on display most dramatically when individuals from countries across the globe donate to natural disaster relief efforts. The hurricanes that battered the Caribbean in late summer and fall of 2017 generated outpourings of international support and donations to victims, although for months later

---

22. Abigail Williams and the Associated Press, "U.S. Withdraws from U.N. Human Rights Council," NBC News, June 19, 2018, www.nbcnews.com/politics/politics-news/u-s-withdraw-u-n-human-rights -council-n884751 (accessed 2/11/21).

23. For more information, see Human Rights Watch, "Hungary," www.hrw.org/europe/central-asia /hungary (accessed 7/2/20).

24. For more on social preferences in humans, see Samuel Bowles and Herbert Gintis, *A Cooperative Species: Human Reciprocity and Its Evolution* (Princeton, NJ: Princeton University Press, 2011).

Immigration has become especially controversial in Europe. The populist government of Hungary under Viktor Orbán has broken with the European Union on asylum policy for refugees and taken a hard-line stance against immigration.

Puerto Rico remained without many essential services and little assistance from the mainland. When others suffer, we may hurt as well; this response can be a profound motivator of political action.

Empathy produces support not only for victims of natural disasters but also for victims of human rights abuses. Indeed, many individuals deeply support the cause of human rights for all, especially for the disadvantaged, and empathy drives many of their efforts at human rights protection. Gross violations of human rights, like genocide, strongly affect and motivate individuals and states to respond.

Domestically, human rights depend on state respect for the individual. It is our status as humans that creates and sustains our rights. It follows in the views of some philosophers and human rights advocates that we cannot secure these rights in our own countries unless we also seek to promote respect for rights abroad. If it is acceptable for some governments to abuse the rights of some people, what principled defense can we give if our own government wants to abuse our rights? In this view, human rights are secure only if they are universal not merely in principle but also in practice.

Finally, we have been socialized to identify with universal human rights. Human rights NGOs and the larger human rights advocacy network have played a critical role in educating the public about human rights and human rights practices, calling attention to human rights abuses, and eventually bringing pressure to bear on states.

As discussed in Chapter 11, the human rights TAN has successfully framed the issue of international human rights in terms that resonate with the political freedoms and civil rights that already exist in established democracies. It is thus easier to persuade citizens of democratic states to actively defend these rights abroad. The international human rights TAN has vigorously promoted concern with human rights among broad publics and has emphasized to many groups and individuals the extent to which human rights practices abroad affect their daily lives. It is in framing issues and socializing individuals to see their interests in different ways that TANs may have their greatest impact on the international politics of human rights.

Self-Interest Motivations Even if people do not have altruistic interests in protecting the human rights of others, they do have self-interests in promoting peace and prosperity, which, in a globalizing world, cannot flourish domestically without flourishing abroad too. Recall that modern human rights originated in the depths of the Great Depression and World War II. Reflecting on the causes of these twin disasters, President Roosevelt and others drew the conclusion that protecting human rights against fascism and other forms of totalitarianism was essential to the maintenance of international peace. By connecting human rights to the epic struggles against totalitarianism that defined much of the twentieth century, Roosevelt laid out the case that promoting human rights abroad was in the self-interest of both Americans and the citizens of other countries. This observation may be no less true today. As the democratic peace discussed in Chapter 4 shows clearly, there is an increasing recognition that democracy and the protection of political freedom can promote peace, economic interdependence, and growth that directly benefit all countries.

More immediately, domestic political unrest and insurrection sparked by the suppression of human rights may spill into neighboring states either directly or indirectly. As a result, all states have an interest in preventing abuses in neighboring countries. The United States, for example, became involved in Haiti's internal political unrest in 1994 to stem the flow of people escaping by boat to southern Florida over treacherous waters. European countries sent troops into Bosnia to prevent political instability and ethnic violence in the former Yugoslavia from spilling over into the rest of the Balkans and possibly beyond. Much of the concern about the ongoing civil war in Syria has been driven by refugee flows into neighboring Turkey and, especially, into the European Union. In an interdependent world, political instability and repression in one country can have direct consequences for others.

In addition to general, self-interested motivations, particular interests within countries have promoted human rights law abroad for their own instrumental purposes. This is most evident in the labor movements within the United States and Europe, which now demand that human rights (and environmental) clauses be inserted into nearly all regional trade agreements (RTAs).[25] The new United States-Mexico-Canada Agreement (USMCA), for instance, includes labor provisions that guarantee the right to bargain collectively and allow expedited review and enforcement of labor rights.[26] U.S. and European labor unions promote such clauses to level the political and economic playing fields on which their own workers compete. To protect their ability to organize and strike for higher wages at

---

25. Emilie M. Hafner-Burton, "Trading Human Rights: How Preferential Trade Agreements Influence Government Repression," *International Organization* 59, no. 3 (2005): 593–629.

26. Office of the United States Trade Representative, "UNITED STATES–MEXICO–CANADA TRADE FACT SHEET: Modernizing NAFTA into a 21st Century Trade Agreement," https://ustr.gov/trade -agreements/free-trade-agreements/united-states-mexico-canada-agreement/fact-sheets/modernizing (accessed 2/11/21).

home, these unions want to ensure that workers in labor-abundant and low-wage countries have similar rights and, indeed, possess the broader political rights necessary to form effective trade unions of their own. In this way, the economic self-interest of developed-country workers can dovetail with the interests of developing-country citizens in more effective protections for human rights.

Labor demands for human rights clauses, however, may also disguise a form of trade protectionism. By pushing for the insertion of human rights clauses into RTAs, the developed-country unions may be making free-trade pacts less appealing to developing-country trading partners and, therefore, less likely to be approved. Human rights provisions open up the opportunity for future claims that the trading partner is violating the terms of the agreement and that the trade concessions made by the home country should be withdrawn. For labor in the developed countries, human rights provisions in RTAs may be "poison pills" designed to prevent further movements toward free trade.

Together, these various motivations for protecting human rights abroad show that interests are multiple and often quite complex. Each reason, however, prompts individuals or groups to press their governments to promote international human rights law. One person may be particularly motivated by a general concern for human well-being, another by a concern with protecting democracy at home, and a third by a hidden desire for trade protection, but all combine to bring pressure to bear on their governments to make international human rights a priority.

Such pressure on governments may be increasing. In today's globalized world, as human rights NGOs grow and succeed, they influence the views of more and more individuals. In turn, the same technology that facilitates the growth of TANs also brings the horror of human rights abuses to immediate public attention. The genocide in the Darfur region of Sudan was brought into homes around the world via television and the Internet. The Syrian government's use of barrel bombs and sarin gas against its own people was documented on the nightly news. In the summer of 2014 and for much of 2019 and 2020, protests of democratic activists in Hong Kong were streamed in real time around the globe. It is now much harder to ignore human rights abuses or to deny that publics around the world knew about them while they were occurring. As global awareness of human rights violations increases, individuals may demand that their governments be more aggressive in promoting international human rights. This greater awareness was an important driver of the Arab Spring protests that diffused across North Africa and the Middle East in 2010–11 (see Chapter 11).[27]

Rarely would we expect governments to promote human rights abroad to the exclusion of all other interests that they might be seeking in their relations with other states. Nonetheless, founded in the tragedy of World War II, supported by a growing transnational human rights movement, and accelerated by technologies that bring abuses to the public's immediate attention, individuals and groups now increasingly recognize international human rights as part of their nations' interests and demand that their governments act accordingly.

27. Zachary C. Steinert-Threlkeld, "Spontaneous Collective Action: Peripheral Mobilization during the Arab Spring," *American Political Science Review* 111, no. 2 (May 2017): 379–403.

Do States Observe International Human Rights Law?

Given a now extensive body of international law, broad agreement on human rights norms, and growing interests in promoting rights, do states actually protect human rights abroad? Is interest reflected in practice? In the case of human rights practices, we can view the proverbial glass as half empty or half full. Although international human rights institutions are being developed, large-scale abuses continue to occur. Maps 12.1, 12.2, and 12.3 graphically illustrate the extent of the problem. While it can be difficult to measure such rights, and some of the information in the maps may seem surprising, the data reflected in the maps are the best available and, on the whole, indicate that human rights violations still occur across the globe. (See "How Do We Know?" on p. 548 about the difficulty of measuring human rights practices.)

At the same time, however, it appears that human rights practices have improved substantially since 1980, especially in South America, which enjoyed a wave of democratization in that decade thanks to popular outrage at the human rights abuses of the prior military regimes. Improvements have also been significant

Note: The data in this map measure the extent in 2019 to which individuals and groups had the right to choose a religion, change their religion, and practice that religion in private or in public, as well as to proselytize peacefully without being subject to restrictions by public authorities.

Map source: Michael Coppedge, John Gerring, Staffan I. Lindberg, Svend-Erik Skaaning, et al., "V-Dem Codebook v10," Varieties of Democracy (V-Dem) Project, www.v-dem.net/en /data/data/v-dem-dataset (accessed 2/12/21).

MAP 12.1 *Respect for Freedom of Religion by Public Authorities, 2019*

- ■ NOT RESPECTED
- ■ WEAKLY RESPECTED
- ■ SOMEWHAT RESPECTED
- ■ MOSTLY RESPECTED
- ■ FULLY RESPECTED
- ■ NO DATA AVAILABLE

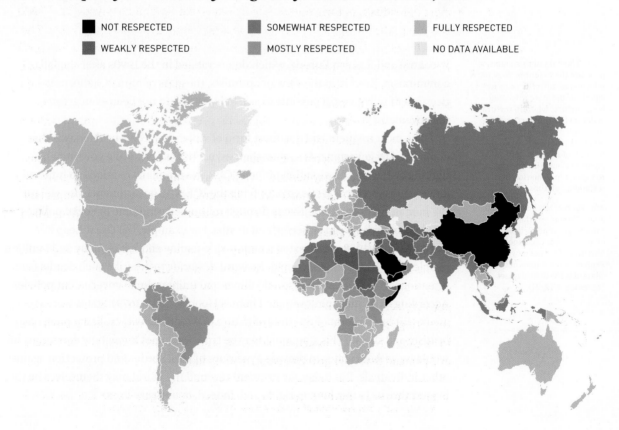

MAP 12.2 **_Respect for Norms against Torture by Public Authorities, 2019_**

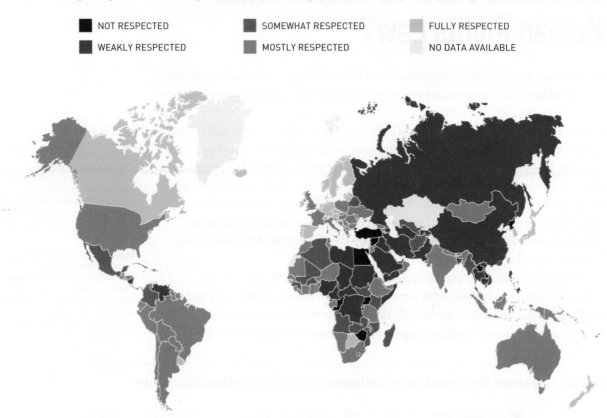

NOT RESPECTED   SOMEWHAT RESPECTED   FULLY RESPECTED

WEAKLY RESPECTED   MOSTLY RESPECTED   NO DATA AVAILABLE

Note: The data in this map measure the extent in 2019 to which state officials or other agents of the state refrained from torture, wherein torture is defined as the purposeful infliction of extreme pain, whether mental or physical, on individuals in a state of incarceration with an aim to extract information or intimidate victims.

Map source: Michael Coppedge, John Gerring, Staffan I. Lindberg, Svend-Erik Skaaning, et al., "V-Dem Codebook v10," Varieties of Democracy (V-Dem) Project, www.v-dem.net/en /data/data/v-dem-dataset (accessed 2/12/21).

in central and Eastern Europe, which democratized in the 1990s after the fall of communism. Even if, in the view of optimists, the glass of human rights practices is half full, it is still possible to ask: Why has there not been even greater improvement?

The most frequent and deadliest form of violence in the world today is that committed by governments against their own citizens (including governments fighting civil wars). In violation of the ICCPR, governments continue to inflict violence against political dissidents. Defying the ICESCR, governments also violate the human rights of their citizens through misguided economic or social policies that lead to widespread suffering and deaths. For example, the Great Leap Forward in China (1958–62) created a nationwide famine and left as many as 38 million people dead. R. J. Rummel coined the word *democide* to describe such deaths from intentional government-sponsored killings and unintentional government policies. According to political philosopher Thomas Hobbes (1588–1679), states were created to lift humans out of the state of nature in which life was "solitary, poor, nasty, brutish, and short." This statement may be true; we do not know how dangerous life would be without states to provide a measure of social order and protection against other individuals. But today, governments around the world may themselves be the biggest threats to our human rights and, indeed, to our very lives.

MAP 12.3 *Respect for Women's Freedom of Discussion by Public Authorities, 2019*

NOT RESPECTED
WEAKLY RESPECTED
SOMEWHAT RESPECTED
MOSTLY RESPECTED
FULLY RESPECTED
NO DATA AVAILABLE

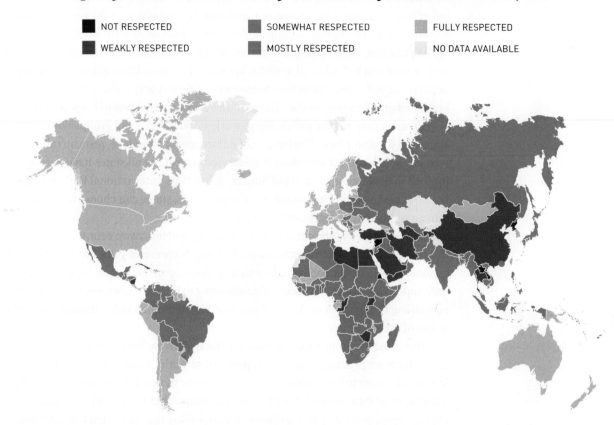

Does International Human Rights Law Make a Difference?

Given the patterns of human rights abuses depicted in Maps 12.1, 12.2, and 12.3, does international human rights law make a difference? Even if abuses continue to occur, do countries that sign human rights treaties protect the rights of their citizens better than those that have not signed the agreements? Do these human rights institutions constrain state behavior in significant ways?

The accumulating evidence on the impact of international human rights agreements on state practice is mixed. This question is, as discussed in Chapter 11, a difficult problem for researchers because the countries most likely to sign human rights agreements are also those most likely to respect human rights. If we simply examined the relationship between signing agreements and protecting human rights, we would conclude, perhaps incorrectly, that the agreements were having a huge effect on practice when, in fact, these two factors simply occur together as a reflection of some underlying trait, such as democracy and a concern for political and civil rights, that leads states both to sign agreements and to protect those rights. As a result of these difficulties, as well as the measurement problems discussed in the previous section, different analysts have found different results.

Note: The data in this map measure the extent in 2019 to which women were able to engage in private discussions, particularly on political issues, in private homes and public spaces without fear of harassment by other members of the polity or the public authorities. These data also consider restrictions by the government and its agents, as well as cultural restrictions or customary laws that are enforced by other members of the polity, sometimes in informal ways.

Map source: Michael Coppedge, John Gerring, Staffan I. Lindberg, Svend-Erik Skaaning, et al., "V-Dem Codebook v10," Varieties of Democracy (V-Dem) Project, www.v-dem.net/en /data/data/v-dem-dataset (accessed 2/12/21).

Some researchers find that international human rights agreements make no difference on practice or even have a negative effect once other factors that affect state practice (like income per capita and economic growth) are taken into account. This implies that signing agreements is associated with worse human rights practices, suggesting that international human rights law just might not matter very much.[28] After all, international law, like most international agreements, depends on self-help, and in the absence of any third-party enforcers, it places the burden of enforcement on the victims of the crime. In the case of human rights law, these victims are the politically powerless individuals and groups who are abused in the first place. The burden of enforcement, therefore, rests on others who can speak and act on behalf of these victims. Yet not all states have a strong interest in penalizing violators of human rights; thus, international human rights law is, at best, sporadically enforced. Knowing this, states can choose to violate human rights with a degree of impunity.

As described by international law scholar Oona Hathaway, countries may sign international human rights agreements for their "expressive value" rather than as a commitment to better behavior.[29] By signing these agreements, she suggests, states may hope to give the appearance of conforming to civilized norms of behavior while continuing to engage in actual practices that violate human rights behind the scenes or out of the public eye.

Our most developed explanation for the negative effect of international agreements on practice comes from political scientist James Vreeland. Focusing on the Convention against Torture and Other Cruel, Inhuman or Degrading Treatment or Punishment (CAT), Vreeland shows that the negative relationship is rooted primarily in multiparty dictatorships that both sign the CAT and use torture at higher-than-average rates. Multiparty dictatorships, he argues, are pressed by domestic political opponents, who have some influence, to ratify international conventions in hopes of changing the government's behavior over the long run. But since domestic opponents remain viable and the rule of the party in power is unstable, dictators are also most likely to abuse human rights, notably by torturing insurgents.[30] In the case of the despotic rule of Paul Biya in Cameroon, for instance, levels of torture were initially rated as "isolated" and infrequent, but once multiple parties were permitted in 1992, the practice became "common."[31] Putting these two trends together appears to explain why multiparty dictatorships sign human rights agreements and are also more likely to abuse those rights.

---

28. Linda Camp Keith, "The United Nations International Covenant on Civil and Political Rights: Does It Make a Difference in Human Rights Behavior?" *Journal of Peace Research* 36, no. 1 (1999): 95–118; Oona A. Hathaway, "Do Human Rights Treaties Make a Difference?" *Yale Law Journal* 111, no. 8 (June 2002): 1935–2042; and Daniel W. Hill Jr., "Estimating the Effects of Human Rights Treaties on State Behavior," *Journal of Politics* 72, no. 4 (2010): 1161–74.

29. Hathaway, "Do Human Rights Treaties Make a Difference?"

30. Vreeland, "Political Institutions and Human Rights."

31. See Vreeland, "Political Institutions and Human Rights," 76, for this and other examples.

By contrast, other researchers find that signing international human rights agreements actually improves practice.[32] They reach this conclusion either by modeling the selection process directly or by adjusting for the changing standards of human rights over time (see "How Do We Know?" on p. 548).

Others find that the effects of international agreements are contingent on or exist only when combined with certain other factors. Agreements "work" in essence only when they are supported by specific domestic political institutions, strong domestic courts and the rule of law, large NGO contingents, the expected tenure of political leaders, and legal standards of proof for particular rights violations.[33] Taken together, this more recent research appears to be gaining the upper hand, indicating that international human rights law is having a positive effect, but in subtle ways and only under certain limited conditions.

As reflected in these inconsistent results, however, it is very challenging to isolate the effect of international human rights agreements on state behavior. Joining human rights conventions might indeed be leading to improved protection of human rights, but at the same time, the effect on practice is overwhelmed by a number of countries signing agreements to hide their practices and insulate themselves from international pressure. Separating the impact of international institutions out from the underlying interests of states to join agreements is difficult. Although additional research is still necessary, there may be some grounds for optimism by advocates of international human rights law.

Even if international human rights institutions have only a limited effect in the short term, they may exert a more beneficial effect on human rights norms and practices in the long run.[34] Beyond simply binding states to the terms of an agreement, international human rights law also empowers social actors to conceive of their interests in new ways, provides a shared vocabulary of judgment, and emboldens societies to advocate for their own rights, sometimes leading to massive political change.

---

32. In *Protecting Human Rights*, page 157, Todd Landman uses a broader set of agreements and a longer time period than other studies do, as well as a nonrecursive model, and reports a positive effect of human rights agreements on practice. In a later survey of this debate, however, he concludes judiciously that no definitive evidence exists; see Todd Landman, *Studying Human Rights* (New York: Routledge, 2006), 103. Using his dynamic standard measure (see "How Do We Know?" on p. 548), Christopher J. Fariss, in "The Changing Standard of Accountability and the Positive Relationship between Human Rights Treaty Ratification and Compliance," *British Journal of Political Science* 48, no. 1 (2018): 239–71, finds consistent support for a positive relationship. See also Yonatan Lupu, "The Informative Power of Treaty Commitment: Using the Spatial Model to Address Selection Effects," *American Journal of Political Science* 57, no. 4 (2013): 912–25.

33. Eric Neumayer, "Do International Human Rights Treaties Improve Respect for Human Rights?" *Journal of Conflict Resolution* 49, no. 6 (2005): 925–53; Beth A. Simmons, *Mobilizing for Human Rights: International Law in Domestic Politics* (New York: Cambridge University Press, 2009); Amanda M. Murdie and David R. Davis, "Shaming and Blaming: Using Events Data to Assess the Impact of Human Rights INGOs," *International Studies Quarterly* 56, no. 1 (2012): 1–16; Courtenay R. Conrad and Emily Hencken Ritter, "Treaties, Tenure, and Torture: The Conflicting Domestic Effects of International Law," *Journal of Politics* 75, no. 2 (2013): 397–409; and Yonatan Lupu, "Best Evidence: The Role of Information in Domestic Judicial Enforcement of International Human Rights Agreements," *International Organization* 67, no. 3 (2013): 469–503.

34. The statistical evidence on long-term effects is, at best, ambiguous as well. See Emilie M. Hafner-Burton and Kiyoteru Tsutsui, "Justice Lost! The Failure of International Human Rights Law to Matter Where Needed Most," *Journal of Peace Research* 44, no. 4 (2007): 407–25.

Measuring Human Rights Practices

Observing trends in human rights practices is quite tricky. Violations of human rights are typically not advertised by governments, and some, like torture, are usually carried out in secret with few witnesses or traces of physical evidence. Even when observers suspect that governments are violating human rights on a fairly widespread and persistent basis, lawyers often lack the kinds of evidence necessary to prosecute offenders in traditional courts of law.[a]

Amnesty International and the U.S. State Department track violations as best they can, drawing on many forms of evidence, including local sources, and they issue annual reports on human rights practices for every country. Political scientists, in turn, have developed scales of human rights violations based on these reports, which then give us an approximate measure of general trends in human rights abuse and human rights respect over time and across countries.[b] In Figure A, the light-gray line represents rights practices around the globe based on the Amnesty and State Department reports. The "whiskers" around the estimates indicate the degree of uncertainty about them. This gray line is essentially flat, indicating that there has been virtually no improvement since 1946, despite the considerable efforts of the international community. Estimates such as this one have fueled controversy about the effectiveness of international human rights law.

Recently, however, political scientist Christopher Fariss has developed a new measure of human rights protection that uses the available information on actual, observed violations of human rights, and uses this to refine the traditional measure based on the Amnesty and State Department reports. He finds that the standards used by Amnesty and the State Department for assessing and including information about violations have changed in subtle ways over time, perhaps because of better

information and monitoring. For instance, it now takes fewer cases of documented torture than it did in the past for a government to be rated as a "frequent violator." It may also be the case that as practices actually have improved, the international community, as reflected in these annual reports, has become less tolerant of violators.

When rescaled to reflect these changing standards, depicted in the blue line in Figure A, we see that human rights practices have improved considerably, especially since the late 1980s. Overall, this is good news for international human rights. Even though it reminds us that human rights practices are difficult to measure accurately and consistently, this research suggests that those practices really have improved over the last generation.

FIGURE A *Estimates of Human Rights Practices around the World, 1946–2015*

● TRADITIONAL HUMAN RIGHTS MEASURE   ● FARISS'S NEW HUMAN RIGHTS MEASURE

Source: Christopher J. Fariss, "Respect for Human Rights Has Improved over Time: Modeling the Changing Standard of Accountability," *American Political Science Review* 108, no. 2 (2014): 297–318. Updated to 2015 by Christopher Fariss.

a. Yonatan Lupu, "Best Evidence: The Role of Information in Domestic Judicial Enforcement of International Human Rights Agreements," *International Organization* 67, no. 3 (2013): 469–503.

b. See David L. Cingranelli, David L. Richards, and K. Chad Clay, "The CIRI Human Rights Dataset," 2014, http://humanrightsdata.com. Version 2014.04.14 (accessed 2/11/21).

Transnational advocacy has brought international attention to China's repressive treatment of its Uighur minority. Here, protesters call out China for its human rights practices.

For instance, the Helsinki Final Act of 1975, which established the applicability of human rights in all of Europe, served as the opening wedge that allowed human rights activists to mobilize within the communist bloc countries of Eastern Europe. Three years earlier, the 35-country Conference on Security and Co-operation in Europe had convened to resolve political and territorial issues left over from World War II and to expand economic contacts between East and West. Against the wishes of the communist regimes, the countries of Western Europe insisted on the inclusion of human rights on the agenda. After trading concessions on other issues, the Western states were eventually able to gain the assent of their Eastern counterparts to the principle of "respect for human rights and other fundamental freedoms, including freedom of thought, conscience, religion or belief."[35]

Although the communist countries initially attempted to suppress publication and discussion of this principle, word soon spread, and domestic groups began to agitate for their rights and make contact with their transnational counterparts in the West. In the bright lights of public awareness, the societal groups activated by the Helsinki Accords were eventually able to mount effective challenges to the autocratic regimes that had long suppressed all dissent. Many factors contributed to the fall of the communist regimes in Eastern Europe in 1989, but the political freedom first created by the Helsinki agreement is broadly seen as a contributing cause of that political earthquake.[36]

In addition, international human rights law permits the human rights TAN to pressure governments to enforce human rights standards. The TAN, of course, has no legal standing to issue mandatory sanctions or other punishments, but the

35. Conference on Security and Co-operation in Europe, Final Act: Helsinki 1975, sec. 1a, VII, www.osce .org/helsinki-final-act?download=true (accessed 2/11/21).

36. Daniel C. Thomas, "The Helsinki Accords and Political Change in Eastern Europe," in Risse, Ropp, and Sikkink, *Power of Human Rights*, 205–33.

organizations that comprise the network do exert a significant influence by naming and shaming violators of human rights.[37] Equally if not more important, by monitoring states' human rights practices and promoting awareness of abuses, the TAN creates political pressure that may eventually force states to act. This is, at least, the aspiration of human rights activists seeking to bring world attention to the treatment of Uighurs in Xinjiang province in China and the Rohingya in Myanmar. TANs are not superseding the role of states, but they do shape the political context in which states interact with their citizens and one another. Thus, even if international human rights law does not cause governments to change their behavior in the short run, it may lead to significant political change over time by legitimizing and encouraging the mobilization of domestic political forces.

What Can Lead to Better Protection of International Human Rights?

Few human rights violators are actually punished. States do sanction one another for human rights abuses, as we have discussed already, but such penalties remain rare. Although states may be named and shamed by transnational human rights organizations, and some may modify their behavior to avoid public condemnation, most escape any significant costs for violating the rights of their citizens.

Crucially, the gains from cooperation that make international law self-enforcing, as explained in Chapter 11, are small or nonexistent when it comes to international human rights law, meaning that states have few incentives to bear high costs for enforcing the law. States that violate human rights have no interest in enforcing the law against themselves; this much is obvious. But although other states have interests in supporting human rights in principle, few gain directly from better human rights practices abroad, as we will discuss shortly. They have some interest in enforcing human rights standards, but only if the costs are not too high.

This combination of mostly empathetic interests in human rights practices abroad and few incentives to actually punish violators produces an inconsistent human rights policy for most states. Even the United States, a strong promoter of human rights, has often chosen not to act against the abusive practices of states it supports. For instance, the U.S. government failed to condemn Saddam Hussein's use of poison gas against Iraq's Kurdish minority in the late 1980s, as it was then backing Hussein in his war against Iran. The United States also did nothing to punish widespread abuses by the military junta in Chile following an American-backed coup in 1973. At the same time, the United States did press human rights concerns against the White-majority regime in South Africa, contributing to the peaceful revolution that eventually led to Black-majority rule, and spoke out in

---

37. The effectiveness of naming and shaming is open to debate. See Emilie M. Hafner-Burton, "Sticks and Stones: Naming and Shaming the Human Rights Enforcement Problem," *International Organization* 62, no. 4 (2008): 689–716.

support of the pro-democracy protesters in Egypt and Libya during the Arab Spring in 2011.

This inconsistent enforcement may explain why international human rights law is often ineffective. For some governments, the temptation to ignore human rights law to secure their hold on power may be stronger than the fear of international penalties. With regime survival as a strong core interest and the relative rarity of effective international responses to human rights violations, few leaders may feel tightly constrained by international human rights institutions or the laws that they themselves have accepted as binding.

It is costly for states to enforce international human rights laws. Naming and shaming may anger a violator whose cooperation is needed on some other diplomatic issue. Pressing the human rights provisions of the Helsinki agreement, for instance, meant that European states gave up bargaining leverage on other issues they cared about. Economic sanctions impose costs on the target state, but they also impose costs on exporters within the home state, who lose a potential market for their goods (see "Controversy" on p. 532). Businesses strongly resisted divesting from South Africa when it meant forgoing access to raw materials, cheap labor, and Africa's wealthiest consumers. Although promoting human rights always carries a price, states do sometimes act to punish human rights violations. Under what conditions is action worth it?

When Do States Take Action on Human Rights?

States are most likely to pay the costs of enforcing human rights law under three conditions. First, states act when they are faced with domestic pressure to do something to stop human rights abuses. As noted already, few governments have intrinsic interests in promoting international human rights, and most do so only in response to domestic political pressure. Governments normally weigh demands to stop abuses, however, against potential costs to business interests or other diplomatic initiatives. Domestic pressure often produces merely toothless condemnations of the abuse or loose and ineffective economic sanctions.

Nonetheless, the more outrageous the abuse, the greater the domestic pressure on governments to act. In a particularly extreme case, when President Bashar al-Assad of Syria used chemical weapons against his own civilians in April 2017, U.S. president Trump punished the Syrian regime by launching 59 cruise missiles against the Shayrat air base near Homs. Although President Trump had derided foreign military interventions during his campaign for the presidency, this use of force against Syria received broad support at home. It was not, however, followed up by any additional pressure from the United States or others. When limited action such as this is taken, it may not be effective in changing state behavior.

The boomerang effect (described in Chapter 11) employed by TANs also plays an important role in protecting human rights. Victims or other advocates in one country who are blocked from influencing their own states can bring their plight to the attention of concerned others in foreign countries, who can then press their own governments into action against the offending regime. Domestic pressure also explains why democratic states are typically the most important promoters of international human rights. Not only are such rights more consistent with the states' own practices, but these states are also more susceptible to the demands of their citizens to undertake costly efforts to advance human rights abroad.

In turn, domestic demands for action are more likely to arise when citizens are well-informed about abuses in other countries. It is here, as a monitor of practices around the globe, that the human rights TAN plays perhaps its most important role. Almost by their very nature, human rights abuses are hidden. They are typically perpetrated against individuals and groups that, though perhaps a potential threat to the regime, are nonetheless excluded from political power. Governments that violate human rights, in turn, are likely to control access to the international media and other routes by which the abused might publicize their plight. It is through the links between domestic activists, who are often the victims of abuses, and transnational activists, who largely operate out of established democracies, that human rights violations are most often brought to light.

Amnesty International's annual reports are an important vehicle for documenting state practice. Even though the U.S. State Department issues its own annual reports, many of the abuses in those reports are first uncovered and brought to public attention by the TAN. Without investigation and publicizing of abuses by human rights organizations, many more governments would be able to mistreat their citizens, confident that their odious practices would escape international scrutiny. In this issue area, the network of individuals and groups promoting new international norms and pressing their governments to make greater efforts in pursuit of those goals has had a significant effect.

The second condition under which states are more likely to act against human rights violators is when doing so serves larger geopolitical interests. Raising human rights issues as part of the Helsinki Accords was applauded by many in the West as another way to pressure the Soviet Union and its allies into political and economic reform. Saddam Hussein's human rights record only became an issue in relations between Washington and Baghdad after the Iraqi dictator invaded Kuwait in August 1990, and it later was one of several reasons given by President George W. Bush to depose Hussein in the Iraq War of 2003. Likewise, President Trump might have been more reluctant to punish Syria for using chemical weapons against its own citizens—limited though the missile strike was—if Assad's regime was not aligned with Iran. Raising human rights concerns and demanding policy change in other states can be goals in themselves, but they may also be instruments in larger political and economic struggles.

The third condition increasing the likelihood of state action against human rights violators is when the gap between the principle of sovereignty and international human rights law can be bridged. Central to the concept of sovereignty is the principle of nonintervention, which is often jealously protected by precisely those states most likely to be sanctioned by the international community for their violations of human rights law. States are, therefore, reluctant to criticize one another, except when the principle of nonintervention can be reconciled with other principles. The anti-apartheid movement was broadly supported, for instance, because it was framed not as foreign intervention but as an anticolonial struggle; thus, it fell under the right to national self-determination guaranteed in the ICCPR and ICESCR.

Although attitudes are changing slightly as various regional organizations, such as the African Union, move toward support for their own versions of the responsibility to protect (see Chapter 11), postcolonial nations remain among the states most committed to the principle of nonintervention. Under many circumstances, they would have been reluctant to intervene in the affairs of South Africa for fear of legitimizing external intervention in their own domestic politics. A key move in the anti-apartheid struggle was defining it as an anticolonial struggle against one of the last White-minority regimes on the continent.[38] With the issue framed in this way, Black-majority-rule states could not only join the sanctions against South Africa but also actively press Western states to join in the liberation struggle.

Countries do promote international human rights and punish violators, even if they do so in a weaker or more episodic way than some advocates desire. When faced with strong domestic pressures and relatively low costs, states will act to further human rights abroad. Yet states are often inconsistent in their human rights policies. Human rights are seldom the only motivation behind a state's foreign policy. The inconsistency of enforcement may make international human rights law comparatively ineffective and, thus, may explain why international human rights treaties appear to have mostly a contingent effect on human rights practices.

Will Protection of Human Rights Improve in the Future?

As with all international cooperation, promoting more effective collaboration between and among states involves building better international institutions. There are at least five ongoing innovations in international human rights institutions that may have important implications for the future.

Transitional Justice New forms of transitional justice are important innovations in international human rights practice. Following World War II, the focus of international human rights law was the criminal prosecution and punishment of individuals found to have engaged in human rights abuses. Since the 1980s and 1990s, however, emphasis has shifted to noncriminal and nonjudicial forms of reconciliation, which are believed to provide a better and more solid long-term foundation for rebuilding societies after major civil conflicts involving human rights abuses.

These new ways of seeking justice include truth and reconciliation commissions that aim to document and publicize past human rights abuses; reparations meant to repair the suffering of human rights victims; memorials that preserve evidence and commemorate victims of abuse; and institutional reforms, especially strengthening civilian control of the police and military. Also common is *lustration*,

---

38. On the construction of a norm of self-determination, see Neta C. Crawford, *Argument and Change in World Politics: Ethics, Decolonization, and Humanitarian Intervention* (New York: Cambridge University Press, 2002). On the norm of racial equality in mobilizing support for the anti-apartheid movement, see Klotz, *Norms in International Relations*.

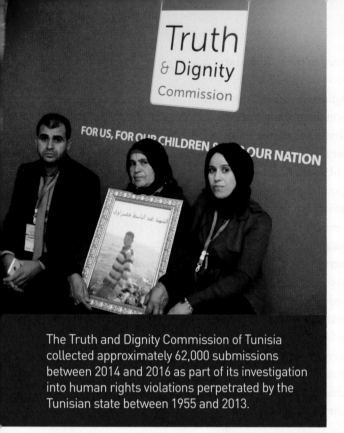

The Truth and Dignity Commission of Tunisia collected approximately 62,000 submissions between 2014 and 2016 as part of its investigation into human rights violations perpetrated by the Tunisian state between 1955 and 2013.

the government policy of preventing members of the previous regime from serving in political, bureaucratic, or sometimes even civil positions.

Advocates of transitional justice argue that it is better for a society to acknowledge and publicize past human rights abuses than to focus on criminal prosecutions. Criminal proceedings are adversarial, pitting prosecutors who may not have strong evidence of abuses that the previous government intentionally hid from public view against defendants who have no incentive to admit past wrongdoing or provide information. Criminal prosecutions may also create incentives for human rights abusers to fight longer and harder to stay in power, lest they be accused in court and likely punished.[39] To ease the transition to democracy and the rule of law, advocates suggest, revealing past abuses can heal a society and allow it to move forward rather than remain mired in prior conflicts.

The most difficult issue in transitional justice deals with amnesty, especially for the most serious crimes against humanity. Amnesties pardon individuals who committed human rights abuses or other political crimes, typically as part of an effort to put past conflicts to rest and move on. Amnesty was common in Latin American countries transitioning to democracy in the 1980s. Conditional amnesties grant forgiveness to individuals in return for their full and truthful accountings of their role and knowledge of past abuses. One of the most successful conditional amnesty–granting institutions was the South African Truth and Reconciliation Commission, which ran from 1995 to 2002, following the end of apartheid. South Africa's 1993 Interim Constitution laid out the committee's goals, stating that "there is a need for understanding but not for vengeance, a need for reparation but not retaliation, a need for ubuntu [the essence of being human] but not for victimization."[40] Lustrations frequently accompany conditional amnesties. All amnesties, however, conflict with laws proscribing crimes against humanity, which can be prosecuted internationally, and with the new ICC, which defers to national courts only when a criminal investigation has been carried out in full. The tension between international human rights law and the desire of countries to move beyond the past through transitional justice has not been resolved.

individual petition

A right that permits individuals to petition appropriate international legal bodies directly if they believe a state has violated their rights.

Individual Petition One of the most important developments in international human rights law is the right of **individual petition** to a supranational court, found

39. For a contrary view, see Kathryn Sikkink, *The Justice Cascade: How Human Rights Prosecutions Are Changing World Politics* (New York: Norton, 2011).

40. Quoted in Simon Chesterman, *You, the People: The United Nations, Transitional Administration, and State-Building* (New York: Oxford University Press, 2004), 158.

most prominently in the European Convention on Human Rights (ECHR).[41] The ECHR, adopted in 1950 by the Council of Europe and its now 47 member states, recognizes many of the same rights that were ultimately codified in the ICCPR 26 years later. It does not incorporate economic, social, or cultural rights into the corpus of rights that it protects. The ECHR's most innovative features are the European Court of Human Rights and its right of individual petition.[42] The court currently consists of 47 judges from the member states of the Council of Europe. It hears cases, offers decisions that are binding on members, and awards damages. Although there is no formal mechanism for ensuring compliance, responsibility for enforcing the decisions of the court rests with the Committee of Ministers of the Council of Europe. Enforcement is informally overseen by the European Union.

Since 1998, individuals in all member states of the Council of Europe have possessed the right to petition the court directly if they believe a state has violated their rights as specified in the ECHR. Prior to this date, an optional protocol allowed individuals to petition the European Commission of Human Rights, which could then launch cases in the court on their behalf. This measure, known as Protocol 11, is nearly unique in international law, in which states—not individuals—are normally the subjects. In the court, individuals can now bring suit against their own governments for violations of internationally recognized human rights.

In the year before the new provision took effect, 5,891 petitions were filed with the commission—already a large number. In 2001, the first full year under the new rules, 13,845 petitions were filed, representing an increase of approximately 138 percent. In 2019, the most recent year for which data are available, 44,500 applications were filed, of which 2,187 were ultimately decided by the court.[43] Today, nearly all petitions before the court are from private individuals, and the success rate is over 50 percent—that is, petitioners quite often win their cases against their own states. The ECHR is clearly having a profound effect on human rights practices in Europe, especially in the relatively new democracies of eastern Europe.

Without the right of individual petition, states can act as gatekeepers, blocking international courts from hearing cases that they might lose. Some human rights activists advocate expanding the right of individual petition to other supranational courts as a check against human rights abuses. This move would open channels to international courts now blocked by states and would likely lead to greater attention to, if not better enforcement of, human rights violations.

---

41. Rights of individual standing are also found in several optional protocols (see Table 12.1). In all cases, however, states must actively declare their willingness to allow the appropriate UN review committee to accept petitions from individuals. On how the right of individual petition can "trap" countries that sign agreements but do not intend to honor them, see Heather Smith-Cannoy, *Insincere Commitments: Human Rights Treaties, Abusive States, and Citizen Activism* (Washington, DC: Georgetown University Press, 2012).

42. On the court, see www.echr.coe.int/Pages/home.aspx?p=home (accessed 6/30/20).

43. On the court's caseload, see European Court of Human Rights, "Analysis of Statistics 2019," www.echr .coe.int/Documents/Stats_analysis_2019_ENG.pdf (accessed 6/30/20). Although the courts themselves have different rules, procedures, and roles, for comparison, the U.S. Supreme Court for the 2019 term (the most recent for which data are available) received 5,411 case filings, of which 69 were decided. See the annual report of the Supreme Court at https://www.supremecourt.gov/publicinfo/year -end/2020year-endreport.pdf (accessed 4/1/21).

The right of individual petition is now found in optional protocols to many international human rights treaties, such as the ICCPR (see Table 12.1 on p. 527). Though fewer states have ratified these protocols than have ratified the main agreements, these optional protocols are a significant step forward.

International Criminal Court (ICC)

A court of last resort for human rights cases that possesses jurisdiction only if the accused is a national of a state party, the crime took place on the territory of a state party, or the UN Security Council has referred the case to the prosecutor.

The International Criminal Court   The **International Criminal Court (ICC)** was established in 1998 and came into force in July 2002 after 60 states ratified its founding treaty. As of the end of 2020, 123 states have accepted the jurisdiction of the ICC and thus have become "state parties." The ICC possesses jurisdiction in a case only if the accused is a national of a state party, if the crime took place on the territory of a state party, or if the UN Security Council has referred the case to the prosecutor. Moreover, the ICC is a court of last resort, meaning that it cannot act if a national judicial authority has genuinely investigated or prosecuted a case—regardless of the outcome of that investigation or prosecution. The ICC can act only when a state cannot or will not act itself. As of April 2021, 30 cases have been brought before the ICC for investigation or trial.[44]

Although the ICC has prosecuted relatively few cases, this does not necessarily mean the court is ineffective. The real question is whether the existence of the court, and the possibility of prosecution, deters human rights abuses. In principle, the most effective court is one that does not need to hear any cases, because no crimes are committed, but we know this is not the case for human rights abuses. Does the ICC make any difference at all? Emerging research suggests that the ICC can deter at least the most egregious human rights violations in some circumstances. Both ratification of the ICC and prosecutions by the court have been found to reduce state-sponsored violence, while prosecutions reduce rebel group abuses.[45] These findings indicate that the court is deterring some abuses, at least at the margin.

This effect, however, may not be entirely positive. Other research finds that ICC involvement in a conflict prolongs the strife and killings, especially when the risk of prosecution at home is relatively low. Similar to the gambling-for-resurrection logic explained in Chapter 4, the risk that the leader who loses the conflict will face arrest and prosecution by the ICC creates an incentive to fight on longer than the leader otherwise would.[46] We will get a clearer picture of the ICC's effects on human rights as the court develops and investigates more cases.

The ICC remains highly controversial. As it begins to investigate and prosecute possible crimes against humanity, critics point out that nearly all the cases under consideration are from Africa, even though severe human rights violations occur

---

44. For the most recent updates, see https://www.icc-cpi.int/Pages/cases.aspx (accessed 4/1/21).

45. Hyeran Jo and Beth A. Simmons, "Can the International Criminal Court Deter Atrocity?" *International Organization* 70, no. 3 (2016): 443–75. Stephen Chaudoin, in "How Contestation Moderates the Effects of International Institutions: The International Criminal Court and Kenya," *Journal of Politics* 78, no. 2 (2016): 557–71, argues that the ICC only enhances compliance when pro- and anticompliance groups are roughly balanced within states.

46. Alyssa K. Prorok, "The (In)compatibility of Peace and Justice? The International Criminal Court and Civil Conflict Termination," *International Organization* 71, no. 2 (2017): 213–43.

elsewhere as well.[47] This pattern of prosecutorial conduct, they charge, reflects either blatant racism or, perhaps less insidiously, a willingness by the court to proceed only in regions where the major states are not significantly involved. Many African countries are quite critical of the ICC and are threatening to withdraw. Either way, the ICC risks becoming a political entity rather than a true court of last resort.

The United States, too, remains highly critical of the ICC. President Bill Clinton signed the treaty establishing the court shortly before he left office, which permitted the United States to participate in further negotiations on the court's rules of procedure. Almost immediately upon taking office, however, Clinton's successor, President George W. Bush, "unsigned" the treaty—a largely symbolic act.

In March 2012, Thomas Lubanga Dyilo (seated, back right) became the first person to be convicted by the ICC. He was sentenced to 14 years in prison for the crime of forcibly recruiting child soldiers in the Democratic Republic of the Congo.

The U.S. government raises many objections to the ICC.[48] Foremost is the fear of frivolous and politically motivated prosecutions of political leaders or American military personnel for actions taken to protect the security of the United States or as part of peacekeeping or peacemaking missions abroad. Given what is often seen as the special role of the United States in maintaining international peace and security—and in light of anti-Americanism in many countries—some skeptics of the ICC fear a string of political prosecutions in which leaders are tried not for violations of law but merely for "show" or because others disagree with their policies.

There is also concern that fears of politically motivated prosecutions in the future might constrain leaders' actions in the present. Although the United States could avoid ICC prosecution by undertaking a genuine investigation or prosecution of an action in question under its own national laws, the ICC statute is sufficiently ambiguous in defining what constitutes an adequate national-level inquiry that politically motivated prosecutions might still be possible.

The U.S. government also claims that the ICC is insufficiently accountable and lacks oversight mechanisms for both the judges and the prosecutors. On the dimensions of international law discussed in Chapter 11, critics fear that the ICC has been delegated too much power to interpret still-imprecise laws. Opponents are concerned that, without any means to remove activist judges, personnel at the ICC may escape political control and develop too much independence. In addition,

---

47 David Bosco, "Why Is the International Criminal Court Picking Only on Africa?" *Washington Post*, March 29, 2013, www.washingtonpost.com/opinions/why-is-the-international-criminal-court-picking -only-on-africa/2013/03/29/cb9bf5da-96f7-11e2-97cd-3d8c1afe4f0f_story.html (accessed 2/11/21). There is an open investigation in the country of Georgia, suggesting that a case may be filed there soon.

48 See the statement by John R. Bolton, then undersecretary for arms control and international security at the Department of State, and later U.S. ambassador to the United Nations, http://2001-2009.state.gov/r /pa/prs/ps/2002/9968.htm (accessed 7/1/20). For a review, see Jennifer K. Elsea, "U.S. Policy Regarding the International Criminal Court," Congressional Research Service, August 29, 2006, www.fas.org/sgp /crs/misc/RL31495.pdf (accessed 7/1/20).

international human rights case law and precedent are thin. Without adequate guidance from state parties on the intent of international law, the court might not just interpret, but essentially make, international law itself. Finally, critics claim that the ICC, given its prosecutorial and judicial independence, might clash with the more political and problem-solving approach of the UN Security Council. Whereas diplomacy must be flexible and aware of context, judicial proceedings that stress precedent, statutory interpretation, and equity across similar cases may conflict with the UN Security Council's charge to maintain peace and security.

After the ICC entered into force in 2002, the administration of President George W. Bush worked aggressively to exempt American nationals from the court's jurisdiction. Most important were the Article 98 agreements that were urged—some might say forced—on other countries. Article 98 of the ICC exempts a country from handing over a foreign national to the court if it is prohibited from doing so by a bilateral agreement with the national's country of origin. Under President Bush, over 100 countries signed such bilateral agreements with the United States under threat of losing all foreign and military aid or having American peacekeeping forces withdrawn. Despite sometimes significant aid cutoffs, other countries, including Barbados, Brazil, Costa Rica, Peru, Venezuela, Ecuador, Saint Vincent and the Grenadines, and South Africa, refused to sign these agreements. Although the Obama administration softened the United States' stance toward the ICC, it did not move toward becoming a state party and accepting the court's jurisdiction.

Upon the election of President Trump, there was much concern that his administration would seek to further undermine the ICC. While at first Trump did not comment on the court, in June 2020 his administration authorized sanctions against ICC employees who had investigated U.S. and allied troops and intelligence officials for possible war crimes in Afghanistan and several other Middle Eastern countries. The administration claimed that this was a move to protect U.S. sovereignty, but the sanctions drew widespread condemnation from the international community, particularly U.S. allies in Europe, for damaging the court's legitimacy and its ability to carry out independent investigations.[49] President Biden is expected to repeal the sanctions.[50]

Harnessing Material Interests   Another source for optimism is the proliferation of RTAs with human rights provisions. As we saw in Chapter 7, nearly every country in the world now belongs to at least one RTA, and nearly all RTAs contain some provisions on human rights. Some agreements are soft, or merely declarative, and appear to have no effect on behavior. Increasingly, though, RTAs contain obligatory and precise human rights provisions that bind states to international standards

49. "Trump OKs Sanctions against International Criminal Court Employees," *Los Angeles Times*, June 11, 2020, www.latimes.com/world-nation/story/2020-06-11/trump-oks-sanctions-against-international -tribunal-employees (accessed 2/11/21).

50. Colum Lynch and Robbie Gramer, "Biden Plans to Repeal Trump-Era Sanctions on ICC," *Foreign Policy*, March 31, 2021, https://foreignpolicy.com/2021/03/31/biden-remove-international-criminal -court-icc-sanctions-from-trump (accessed 4/1/21).

of behavior and threaten to withdraw trade and financial benefits if periodic reviews find substantial abuses of human rights. These hard provisions link concrete, material benefits of market access to a state's human rights practices. Unlike human rights agreements in general, and even soft RTAs, these hard provisions do have a significant, if small, effect on the extent of human rights violations.[51]

Ironically, protectionist groups looking to insulate themselves from import competition by including human rights provisions in free-trade agreements may have devised effective weapons for protecting human rights abroad—and their self-interest in seeing the agreement's benefits revoked may make threats to use these weapons credible. Human rights advocates would do well to find other ways in which they can harness instrumental, material interests to their cause of promoting better human rights practices.

One of the most important recent innovations in international human rights efforts is the Guiding Principles on Business and Human Rights, a first effort to hold international firms to account for the human rights practices of the countries in which they operate.

Guiding Principles for Business

One of the most significant human rights initiatives in recent years has been the Guiding Principles on Business and Human Rights (GPs), which were endorsed by the UN Human Rights Council in 2011.[52] Building on the International Bill of Rights, the GPs aim to establish a norm that businesses are obliged to respect human rights and that states have an equal obligation to ensure that firms operating in their territories fulfill that obligation. Faced with fundamental conflicts between human rights advocates, who want hard legal standards, and the business community, which favors voluntary "best practice" measures, the GPs aim only to establish a standard that would, if it attracted sufficient support, gain adherents over time. Norms matter, of course, but in anticipating disagreements between states, the GPs were intentionally limited to soft law. To the extent that they carry any force, it is through their adoption as standards by NGOs and TANs who then monitor and hold businesses to account. So far, such critical (typically pro-business) organizations as the International Chamber of Commerce and the International Bar Association have committed to the standards. As of August 2020, only 23 countries had adopted the recommended National Human Rights Action plans called for by the GPs.[53] Nonetheless, the GPs are significant in international human rights law, moving human rights expectations beyond states to business entities that operate within states.

---

51. Hafner-Burton, "Trading Human Rights."

52. See United Nations, "Guiding Principles on Business and Human Rights: Implementing the United Nations 'Protect, Respect and Remedy' Framework," 2011, www.ohchr.org/Documents/Publications/GuidingPrinciplesBusinessHR_EN.pdf (accessed 2/11/21).

53. See International Chamber of Commerce, "What Is the Importance of the United Nations' Guiding Principles on Business and Human Rights?" https://iccwbo.org/media-wall/news-speeches/what-is-the-importance-of-the-ruggie-framework-for-business-and-human-rights (accessed 3/14/20).

Conclusion: Why Protect Human Rights?

The puzzle of why states seek to protect the human rights of people outside their own borders is explained primarily by states' interests. Whether based on concern for the well-being of others, an understanding of common humanity and the need to preserve democracy, or purely instrumental goals, individuals, groups, and thus states do have interests in promoting human rights abroad. The human rights TAN has been critical in spreading international norms in recent decades and in activating citizens to press their governments to act more forcefully to protect human rights. The facts that human rights are an issue today in international relations and that states concern themselves with human rights abroad is testament to the activities of the human rights TAN.

International human rights law is itself an institution. Its likely positive but still-limited effectiveness in constraining abuses, in turn, follows from strategic interaction—or perhaps more precisely from the lack of real and consistent enforcement. While states have interests and are willing to pay some costs to protect human rights within other countries, rarely are they willing to make human rights a priority. As a result, states may publicly condemn abuse but impose few penalties on those who violate human rights. Knowing this, states abuse their citizens with little fear that they will be sanctioned.

The fact that the human rights clauses of RTAs do improve practice, however, suggests that institutions that link behavior to real consequences can have important effects. Current issues in international human rights law focus largely on the breadth and depth of the law itself—individual petitions, the ICC, and inclusion of obligatory human rights provisions in trade and other treaties. Given the modest effect of international human rights law on state practice, perhaps human rights advocates would do better by focusing on designing more effective enforcement institutions.

Study Tool Kit

Interests, Interactions, and Institutions in Context

- International human rights law is an institution created by—and largely reflecting the political norms of—Western, liberal democracies. The norms embodied in these laws remain controversial, are not shared equally by all countries, and have not yet been internalized in many societies and governments. Nonetheless, there is new evidence that international human rights law is improving practice in some specific contexts.

- Individuals and states have an interest in international human rights, and thus they undertake costly acts to punish states that violate the rights of their citizens. These interests are rarely strong enough, however, to compel states to pay high costs to protect vulnerable individuals and groups outside their own borders. Human rights practices, in turn, may be more affected by TANs that change how both individuals and states conceive of their interests.

- States that violate human rights reason that, in their interactions with other states, they will probably not face serious consequences for their behavior and, therefore, can freely abuse individuals and groups. Unfortunately, these states are most likely correct. Although international human rights law does appear to promote improved practices, it remains of only limited effectiveness in altering the actions of states. Despite increasing support for human rights, international law by itself is not a panacea.

Key Terms

human rights, p. 523

Universal Declaration of Human Rights (UDHR), p. 523

International Covenant on Civil and Political Rights (ICCPR), p. 525

International Covenant on Economic, Social, and Cultural Rights (ICESCR), p. 525

International Bill of Rights, p. 526

nonderogable rights, p. 530

prisoners of conscience (POCs), p. 531

individual petition, p. 554

International Criminal Court (ICC), p. 556

For Further Reading

Brysk, Alison. *Speaking Rights to Power: Constructing Political Will.* **New York: Oxford University Press, 2013.** Surveys the conditions for successful human rights campaigns by NGOs.

Donnelly, Jack. *Universal Human Rights in Theory and Practice.* **3rd ed. Ithaca, NY: Cornell University Press, 2013.** Presents a general overview of the philosophy and practice of international human rights law.

Hafner-Burton, Emilie M. *Making Human Rights a Reality.* **Princeton, NJ: Princeton University Press, 2013.** Argues against the current universalistic and legalistic approach to human rights and for an alternative model based on human rights "stewards" who focus their efforts on issues and places where progress is possible.

Hopgood, Stephen. *The Endtimes of Human Rights.* **Ithaca, NY: Cornell University Press, 2013.** A critique of the assumption that human rights are universal and of current practices of human rights promotion.

Ishay, Micheline R. *The History of Human Rights: From Ancient Times to the Globalization Era.* **Berkeley: University of California Press, 2004.** Provides a comprehensive analysis of human rights philosophy and practice from ancient Greece to the present.

Ruggie, John G. *Just Business: Multinational Corporations and Human Rights.* **New York: Norton, 2013.** Recounts the negotiations surrounding the UN Guiding Principles on Business Practices and Human Rights from the perspective of the UN Special Representative.

Sikkink, Kathryn. *The Justice Cascade: How Human Rights Prosecutions Are Changing World Politics.* **New York: Norton, 2011.** Examines the origins and consequences of international human rights prosecutions.

Simmons, Beth A. *Mobilizing for Human Rights: International Law in Domestic Politics.* **New York: Cambridge University Press, 2009.** Examines the critical role of domestic institutions in promoting effective human rights practices.

Wong, Wendy. *Internal Affairs: How the Structure of NGOs Transforms Human Rights.* **Ithaca, NY: Cornell University Press, 2012.** Demonstrates how the organizational structures and incentives of human rights NGOs shaped the transnational advocacy movement and its effectiveness.

13

The Global Environment

THE PUZZLE *Nearly everyone wants a cleaner and healthier environment. Why, then, is it so hard to cooperate internationally to protect the environment?*

Above: Though Bangladesh is responsible for only a small fraction of the carbon emissions driving global climate change, low-lying areas of the country are especially vulnerable to one of climate change's primary consequences: rising sea levels. The disproportionate effects of climate change on countries around the world, with some of the largest emitters facing fewer consequences, has hampered cooperation among members of the international community on environmental issues.

On Earth Day, April 22, 2021, President Joseph Biden committed the United States to reducing its greenhouse gas emissions by 50 percent from 2005 levels by 2030.[1] President Biden had already positioned climate change at the center of his administration's other policy initiatives, including plans for major infrastructure investments. He had also rejoined the Paris Agreement on mitigating climate change in February 2021, recommitting the United States to this first global effort to reduce carbon emissions. The Paris Agreement is part of the larger United Nations Framework Convention on Climate Change (UNFCCC). Adopted in December 2015, the Paris Agreement commits nearly all nations to undertake plans to combat climate change. The agreement also provides enhanced support for developing countries in this effort. Many analysts see the accord as a major step forward in the fight against global warming. By rejoining the agreement, the Biden administration signaled that it was placing climate change at the forefront of its agenda.

Within the United States, the Paris Agreement and climate change more generally remain controversial. Opposed to the Paris Agreement because it was perceived as placing an undue burden on the U.S. economy, former President Donald Trump had withdrawn from the accord in November 2019, a move that took effect a year later—one day after the 2020 presidential election. When President Trump announced the United States' withdrawal from the agreement, he argued both that he wanted to preserve and possibly expand jobs in coal and other carbon fuel–based industries and that other countries should bear more of the costs of addressing climate change. At the same time, a number of states, municipalities, and businesses in the United States affirmed plans to abide by the terms of the agreement. The same day that President Trump announced his withdrawal plans, the governors of California, New York, and Washington announced the formation of the United States Climate Alliance to bring together states, cities, and companies committed to meeting the nation's previous Paris commitments.

Successfully addressing environmental challenges requires coordination and cooperation at many levels. As a global agreement that relies on commitments to

1. Brad Plumer and Nadja Popovich, "The U.S. Has a New Climate Goal. How Does it Stack Up Globally?" *New York Times*, April 22, 2021, www.nytimes.com/interactive/2021/04/22/climate/new-climate-pledge.html (accessed 4/22/21).

concrete actions by each individual country, the Paris Agreement embodies this complex reality. The accord was decades in the making, having grown out of the UNFCCC, which was signed in 1992. As its name implies, the UNFCCC created only a framework for further negotiations that would address specific issues, including the reduction of greenhouse gas emissions and financing for developing countries to adapt to climate change.

The framework was followed in 1997 by the Kyoto Protocol, in force since 2005, which committed only the 24 most developed countries to reductions in greenhouse gases. Kyoto faltered after the United States withdrew in 2001. While many observers have been skeptical of the Paris Agreement because commitments are "bottom up," that is, designed by each country rather than adhering to a global formula, it may be the accord's very flexibility combined with its planned ability to adapt over time that will allow it to succeed.

In recent decades, the international community has also made substantial progress on other environmental issues. International treaties have restricted shipments of hazardous waste across borders, established protections for countless plant and animal species, banned some of the most harmful fishing practices, and protected the ozone layer. But addressing climate change remains a major challenge. NASA estimates that the earth has already warmed by an average of 1°C since 1880, that this increase is clearly attributable to human-caused emissions of greenhouse gases, and that the planet will continue to warm as greenhouse gas emissions accumulate. How much future warming we can expect is highly dependent on the rate at which countries can decrease their emissions.

The global community agreed in the Paris accord to "pursue" a limit of 1.5°C of total warming above preindustrial levels. Even though people around the world are already feeling the effects of global warming, from more typhoons in the Pacific to wildfires in California, countries have found it difficult to balance the strong measures required to address climate change with fears that such restrictions will inhibit economic growth. Even if countries meet their Paris Agreement commitments, global temperatures are still expected to rise 3°C by 2100, with serious consequences.[2] Despite this fact, most countries are not on track to meet their targets.[3] So, while the Paris Agreement, as the first universal climate accord, represents progress, it also demonstrates how difficult it is to coordinate global action.

Thinking Analytically about the Global Environment

This chapter aims to explain the sources of and impediments to international cooperation on environmental policy. First, we will see that despite widely shared interests in the quality of the environment, interactions in this realm among individuals and countries suffer from problems of collective action. Although each person and each country has an interest in a world without climate change, for instance, they also prefer to free ride on the efforts of others, saving themselves the cost of reducing emissions while benefiting from others' cutbacks. In the absence of any international authority that can mandate improved performance, free riding produces less overall environmental cooperation than individuals and countries collectively desire.

Second, individuals, groups, and countries have conflicting interests over who should bear the costs of mitigating harmful environmental practices, with rich countries typically demanding universal cuts and developing countries claiming that they should be largely exempt from costly restrictions until their economies are able to handle it. How environmental policies distribute costs affects how likely actors are to cooperate successfully on environmental issues.

Finally, international institutions facilitate environmental cooperation primarily by enhancing information and verifying compliance. Transnational advocacy networks (TANs) and other nongovernmental organizations (NGOs) now play an essential role in monitoring adherence to environmental agreements. The clearer and more easily verified the standard, the more likely states are to cooperate successfully.

2. United Nations Environment Programme, "The Emissions Gap Report 2016," November 26, 2016, https://www.unep.org/resources/publication/emissions-gap-report-2016-un-environment-synthesis-report (accessed 3/10/21).

3. Stephen Leahy, "Most Countries Aren't Hitting 2030 Climate Goals, and Everyone Will Pay the Price," *National Geographic*, November 5, 2019, www.nationalgeographic.com/science/2019/11/nations-miss-paris-targets-climate-driven-weather-events-cost-billions (accessed 2/23/21).

Why Are Good Intentions Not Good Enough?

As we have noted, international cooperation on **global climate change** has made significant progress in the past several decades—from the foundational **United Nations Framework Convention on Climate Change (UNFCCC)** signed in 1992, to the **Paris Agreement** announced in 2015. Despite broad-based interests in environmental quality, however, cooperation is sometimes thwarted by interactions in which it is difficult to coordinate large numbers of individuals or, at the international level, moderately large numbers of states.

We might personally care about the environment and want to improve the quality of the world we inhabit—that is, we have an interest in environmental cooperation—but our individual actions have little effect on the local or global ecosystem. This problem is sometimes referred to as the **tragedy of the commons**, after a famous article by the ecologist Garrett Hardin.[4]

Imagine a meadow in old England where all the villagers graze their sheep. This village "commons," as it is called, is open to all. This is the end of the Middle Ages, a long period in which nothing much seemed to change. The human population was stable, and families raised the same number of sheep for generations. But now, people have new sources of income, and some invest in sheep. There is new demand for wool and meat. Villagers choose to raise more and more lambs to adulthood and graze them on the land.

An individual farmer—let's call him Smith—is deciding whether to raise more sheep this year. He takes a look at the land. It is starting to become degraded; sheep pull grass up by the roots, so each year as there are more sheep, there is less grass in the meadow. To protect the land, Smith knows it would be better to graze fewer sheep. But even if he puts fewer sheep out to graze, he anticipates that other farmers will continue to increase the size of their flocks. In fact, he worries, if he waits until next year, there might not be enough grass for anyone. So, Smith reasons, better to raise more sheep this year and make a profit while he can. Every farmer is making the same calculation as Smith, and as a result, the once flourishing meadow further degrades, and over time the farmers can graze fewer and fewer sheep.

This dilemma, where individually rational actions lead to environmental harm, has been known for centuries. In fact, the scenario just described is exactly what happened in countless villages all over England between the end of the Middle Ages and the beginning of the Industrial Revolution. It led to a change in practice and law known as the enclosure movement, the privatizing of formerly common land. We will explain in the next section how private property is one way to resolve the tragedy of the commons.

4. Garrett Hardin, "The Tragedy of the Commons," *Science* 162, no. 3859 (1968): 1243–48.

global climate change

Human-induced change in the environment, especially from the emissions of greenhouse gases, leading to higher temperatures around the globe.

United Nations Framework Convention on Climate Change (UNFCCC)

An international agreement enacted in 1992, and entered into force in 1994, that provides an overall framework for intergovernmental efforts on climate change.

Paris Agreement

An agreement negotiated under the UNFCCC in 2015, signed by 195 countries, and entered into force in 2016. It was the first agreement to require commitments to control greenhouse gas emissions from all signatories.

tragedy of the commons

A problem that occurs when a resource is open to all, without limit. No one has an incentive to conserve, because others would use the resource in the meantime, so the resource suffers degradation.

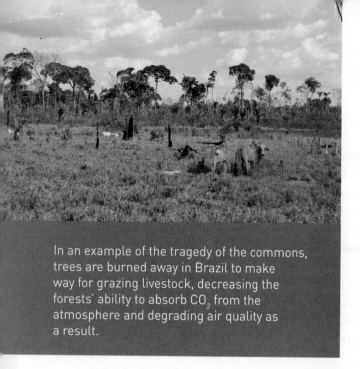

In an example of the tragedy of the commons, trees are burned away in Brazil to make way for grazing livestock, decreasing the forests' ability to absorb CO_2 from the atmosphere and degrading air quality as a result.

The tragedy of the commons is not just an interesting tale from history. It functions as a metaphor for many of our current environmental challenges. Some tragedies are local. A fishery in a lake or a forest shared by villagers can become degraded from overuse: no one has an incentive to leave the immature fish or saplings for later if others will take them today. The water in the lake itself can be subject to such a tragedy, either from overuse of the water (drawing too much for irrigation purposes) or from the dumping of pollutants into it. Each person's small amount of waste seems harmless enough, but added together, the waste can destroy the lake. The tragedy of the commons is a classic Prisoner's Dilemma (see Chapter 2).

We now face tragedies of the commons on a global scale. Take the earth's atmosphere and global climate change as one example. When only a small number of people drove automobiles, the carbon dioxide from burning gasoline did not build up significantly in the lower atmosphere or threaten the planet with global warming. But now, as more and more people own cars, the accumulation of pollution threatens the health of humans, plants, and animals, and the buildup of carbon risks causing permanent climate change (see Figure 13.1). The increasing problem of methane produced by livestock—which accounts for about 14.5 percent of all greenhouse gases produced in the world—poses a similar threat. Again, farmers have no incentive to reduce the size of their individual herds, but when all farmers make this same calculation, the global "hoofprint" of livestock production becomes a major source of emissions.

No single individual or small group can solve these problems by changing its behavior. We face similar problems with the loss of species or degradation of forests around the world. For one small town, cutting down a forest to make way for more agricultural land or a new factory might make economic sense. But globally, these individual choices have added up to a loss of forest area about the size of South Africa between 1990 and 2015.[5] Recent years have seen record-setting losses in forest cover, with Brazil accounting for about one-third of the total. This trend is especially worrying, as tropical rain forests have traditionally served as large-scale carbon "sinks," or absorbers of greenhouse gases.[6]

Because we can benefit from others' efforts to preserve the environment while having only a marginal effect ourselves, we often avoid changing our personal behaviors or incurring costs to reduce pollution. In short, even though we prefer a

---

5. Food and Agriculture Organization of the United Nations, *Global Forest Resources Assessment 2015: How Are the World's Forests Changing?* 2nd ed. (Rome: FAO, 2016), 3, www.fao.org/3/a-i4793e.pdf (accessed 3/10/21).

6. Mikaela Weisse and Elizabeth Dow Goldman, "We Lost a Football Pitch of Primary Rainforest Every 6 Seconds in 2019," World Resources Institute, June 2, 2020, www.wri.org/blog/2020/06/global-tree -cover-loss-data-2019 (accessed 8/20/20).

FIGURE 13.1 *The Greenhouse Effect*

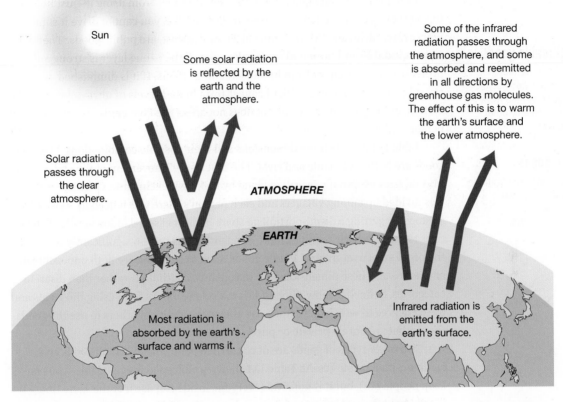

Sun

Some solar radiation
is reflected by the
earth and the
atmosphere.

Some of the infrared
radiation passes through
the atmosphere, and some
is absorbed and reemitted
in all directions by
greenhouse gas molecules.
The effect of this is to warm
the earth's surface and
the lower atmosphere.

Solar radiation
passes through
the clear
atmosphere.

ATMOSPHERE

EARTH

Most radiation is
absorbed by the earth's
surface and warms it.

Infrared radiation is
emitted from the
earth's surface.

Figure source: www.seai.ie
/images_upload/Schools
/Secondary_Schools/Subjects
/CSPE/Lesson_Plans_for
_CSPE/Climate_Change_facts
/greenhouse%20effect.jpg
(accessed 09/20/14).

cleaner environment, we nonetheless seek to free ride on the efforts of others. Since everyone makes the same calculation, we individually defect from environmental efforts and collectively produce an outcome that is less optimal for society as a whole.

The same logic applies at the international level. Most countries' efforts to conserve resources or limit pollution have only a small effect on the global environment. Even though all countries have a shared interest in protecting the environment, each also has an incentive to free ride on the efforts of others, reaping the gains of reduced emissions while not paying any of the costs. Conversely, if countries sacrifice income by imposing tighter environmental controls on themselves, they create benefits for other countries that have not paid a similarly high price. Thus, as countries free ride on the efforts of other countries, the global environment suffers as a consequence.

Collective Action and the Environment

Most of the environmental benefits we wish to gain or the harms we wish to avoid come in the form of **public goods** or **common-pool resources**. All goods, whether they are individually owned items, like your car, or goods that we can enjoy

public goods

Products that are nonexcludable and nonrival in consumption, such as clean air or water.

common-pool resources

Goods that are available to everyone, but such that one user's consumption of the good reduces the amount available for others. Common-pool resources are rival but nonexcludable.

collectively, like clean air, can be defined along two axes. First, goods are defined by whether they are excludable, or by how easily you can be kept from using them. Second, goods are classified by whether they are rival, or if your use of them precludes their use by others.

Your car is a private good. You can exclude others from using it—just hold on to your key—and if you lend it to your friend to drive, you cannot drive it somewhere else. Clean air and the ozone layer, by contrast, are public goods. They are **nonexcludable** and **nonrival** in consumption. If the ozone layer is strong and protective, we all benefit from its sunscreening effects. If it is diminished, we all are subject to an increased risk of cancer from higher levels of ultraviolet radiation. Whether you get skin cancer or not does not affect the chances that any other person will get skin cancer.

Table 13.1 depicts these dimensions and their possible combinations. Private goods are both excludable and rival. The "enclosure" movement at the end of the Middle Ages essentially privatized land by making it excludable. Once the commons was divided up among villagers and each person's share was fenced in—with the aristocracy getting a disproportionate share in most cases—landowners had incentives to manage their holdings more efficiently. This system significantly reduced the problem of overgrazing. Public goods, such as clean air, are both nonexcludable and nonrival. These dimensions are, in actuality, continuous rather than discrete categories, defined by how difficult it is to exclude others from using the goods and by the degree to which one actor's use affects the ability of others to use the goods. Goods that are purely private or purely public are rare.

Two other types of goods are of concern to policy makers: club goods and common-pool resources. As Table 13.1 shows, a club good is excludable (you can keep people out), but it is not rival (everyone inside can use it at the same time). It is called a club good because clubs—such as golf or swimming clubs—are classic examples. In the policy sphere, we can consider electricity networks, toll roads, and the Internet to be examples of club goods. Since they are nonrival, club goods tend to suffer from congestion unless some users are actively excluded ("freeways" without tolls, for instance, tend to become overcrowded, at least during rush hours).

Common-pool resources are essentially the opposite of club goods. One person's use of a common-pool resource does impinge on the ability of others to use it, so these resources are rival. But it is very difficult to exclude people from using them entirely. Goods like the old-fashioned village commons, a forest, or a fishery are common-pool resources. Global fisheries, for example, suffer greatly, with the percentage of fish stocks within biologically sustainable levels dropping from

nonexcludable goods
Goods that, if available to be consumed by one actor, cannot be prevented from being consumed by other actors as well.

nonrival goods
Goods for which consumption by one actor does not diminish the quantity available for others.

TABLE 13.1 *Private versus Public Goods, and Their Variants*

	EXCLUDABLE	NONEXCLUDABLE
RIVAL	Private goods	Common-pool resources
NONRIVAL	Club goods	Public goods

90 percent to 65.8 percent between 1974 and 2017.[7] It is difficult to exclude anyone from fishing on the high seas, but a fish caught by one boat cannot simultaneously be caught by another. Like the village commons before enclosure, common-pool resources tend to be over-exploited, often leading to environmental degradation.

Most of the environmental challenges we face today relate either to public goods or to common-pool resources. Public goods arise partly from nature. Because the earth has a single atmosphere, we all suffer from a thinner ozone layer and a warmer climate. Public goods and common-pool resources are also produced by social practice and law. The village commons described earlier is one such social practice that was altered through enclosure, a different social practice, and a new set of laws.

Similarly, the **Kyoto Protocol** created a carbon trading system that, in essence, privatized what was pre-viously a public good. Before Kyoto, the atmosphere was treated as a global commons, free for anyone to use, even when "using the atmosphere" meant emitting harmful greenhouse gas emissions into it with few restrictions. The Kyoto Protocol, however, limited the total amount of carbon pollution allowed and then divided it among the parties to the treaty through rights to pollute.

The fact that social practices and laws can change actors' incentives and, in turn, their interests is a foundation on which better environmental practices can be built: in this way, Kyoto shows the promise of rules to control environmental degra-dation. However, the treaty's limitations—that it did not cover all countries and that even signatories largely failed to live up to their commitments, especially once the United States opted out—demonstrate how difficult cooperation can be even when states have the best of intentions.

Common-pool resources like fish in the ocean or water in a lake are frequently exploited to the point of devastation because everyone benefits from using the resource but no one actor bears specific responsibility for ensuring its survival. Here, members of the activist group Sea Shepherds confront a whaling boat in an attempt to interfere with its activities.

Kyoto Protocol

An amendment to the UN Framework Convention on Climate Change, adopted in 1997 and entered into force in 2005, that established specific targets for reducing emissions of carbon and five other greenhouse gases through 2020.

Solving Collective Action Problems

Public goods are undersupplied by market forces. People want the public good, like clean air or clean water. Since they benefit from the public good, once it is supplied, there is a demand for it. The problem arises on the supply side. Because nobody can be excluded from enjoying the good if others provide it, nor does one person's use diminish the quantity of the good available to others, there is little incentive for anyone to voluntarily provide the good or to contribute to its provision by the community. People can, in short, free ride on their neighbors, their fellow citizens, or the global community.

---

7. Food and Agriculture Organization of the United Nations, *The State of World Fisheries and Aquaculture 2020* (Rome: FAO, 2020), www.fao.org/state-of-fisheries-aquaculture (accessed 6/24/20).

Resolving or at least mitigating the tragedy of the commons requires one or sometimes both of two possible strategies: actors can create private property rights, as in the enclosure movement, or actors can regulate their behavior through laws, norms, or cooperative agreements. Before doing either, however, actors must first recognize the problem and agree that action is necessary.

Five Factors in Cooperation As explained in Chapter 2, international environmental cooperation is affected by at least five factors. First, the magnitude of collective action problems typically varies by group size.[8] The larger the group of actors, the more likely they are to free ride on one another, as the contribution of each will be a proportionally smaller percentage of the total. The smaller the group, the more likely actors are to contribute to solving the problem.

This helps explain why acid rain, a problem in the 1970s, was relatively easy to address. Acid rain is produced when sulfur dioxide and nitrogen oxide are emitted into the atmosphere and subsequently absorbed by water droplets, creating a solution of sulfuric and nitric acid that eventually falls to the earth as precipitation. The highly acidic rain affects the chemical balance of soil, lakes, and streams. Indeed, acid rain killed many forests and a large amount of aquatic life in lakes before it was brought under control. Acid rain is primarily a regional phenomenon, however, falling mostly downwind of large coal-burning industrial centers. Thus, emissions from the United States fell mostly on itself and Canada; British emissions, on Scandinavia; western European emissions, on eastern Europe; and so forth. Although restricted to countries downwind of large polluters, the same problem occurs in many different regions.

The limited number of countries in each acid rain region was a key factor in facilitating negotiations for the Convention on Long-Range Transboundary Air Pollution (CLRTAP) and its optional protocol, completed in 1979 and now counting 51 members from across several acid rain regions. Together, the member states have reduced sulfur emissions by more than 60 percent below 1980 levels.[9] Small numbers do not guarantee success, however. East Asian countries were never able to copy the CLRTAP example. While air pollution in China has started to decline, it continues to cause smog problems in both Japan and Korea.

The second factor affecting international environmental cooperation is the complexity and magnitude of the problem. Some environmental problems are defined narrowly. In 1995, the Governing Council of the United Nations Environment Programme (UNEP) decided that 12 specific chemicals, the "dirty dozen," were particularly hazardous. Not only do these chemicals persist and move around in the atmosphere, but they also accumulate in animals and humans. This narrowly defined problem moved to a rapid solution. Negotiations began in 1998 on the Stockholm Convention on Persistent Organic Pollutants, which aims to protect

---

8. Mancur Olson, *The Logic of Collective Action: Public Goods and the Theory of Groups* (Cambridge, MA: Harvard University Press, 1965).

9. Keith Bull, Matti Johansson, and Michal Krzyzanowski, "Impacts of the Convention on Long-Range Transboundary Air Pollution on Air Quality in Europe," *Journal of Toxicology and Environmental Health. Part A* 71, no. 1 (2008): 51–55.

human health and the environment from chemicals that remain intact in the environment for long periods of time. The treaty was completed in 2001 and entered into force in 2004. Most countries, 184 to date, have ratified the treaty—a figure similar to the ratification numbers for more demanding treaties like the Paris Agreement and the Montreal Protocol. Similar issue-specific treaties, like the Basel Convention on the Control of Transboundary Movements of Hazardous Wastes and Their Disposal, were also negotiated quickly.

Third, as we saw in Chapter 2, groups that interact repeatedly (iteration) or frequently on other issues (linkage) will be able to induce greater contributions from one another through strategies of reciprocal punishment in which contributors sanction noncontributors by withholding future cooperation. For instance, the acid rain problem in North America and Europe was resolved with relative ease because the neighboring states interacted frequently on many dimensions (Canada and the United States are among each other's largest trading partners, for instance) and expected to interact intensely into the foreseeable future. Downwind states whose lakes were slowly dying from acid rain thus expected to have plenty of opportunities to punish their upwind neighbors if the latter did not live up to the terms of the CLRTAP.

Fourth, cooperation becomes easier when public goods come bundled with private goods for which actors are willing to pay. These bundles are called joint products.[10] Rain forests absorb significant amounts of carbon, thus helping to reduce the problem of global climate change. They are also home to many different species, thereby enhancing biodiversity. Saving acres in a rain forest to preserve a global carbon sink and promote biodiversity also provides landowners with erosion control and opportunities for ecotourism, and those landowners are free to pursue erosion control or ecotourism for their private benefit. However, such joint products may not be sufficiently large to offset the gains that farmers would accrue from clearing more forest acreage for use in commercial agriculture, as is now happening in Brazil.

In an analogous situation, in the 1980s the DuPont company saw an opportunity to increase its profits as ozone depletion came to be recognized as a global health hazard and pressure to ban chlorofluorocarbons (CFCs) began to increase. (We will discuss this in more detail later in the chapter.) DuPont was a leading producer of CFCs, accounting for nearly 50 percent of all production in the United States and 25 percent of global production. But as the leading innovator of alternatives to CFCs as well, DuPont was also well positioned to gain from a CFC ban.[11] In this case, stopping production of CFCs also provided a private profit for DuPont. For all joint products, the public good is provided as a by-product of efforts to obtain the private good. The larger the private benefits are relative to the public good, the less free riding we will observe.

Fifth and finally, when actors vary in size (as states do) or in the intensity of their preferences for public goods, a privileged group may emerge (see Chapter 2). A privileged group comprises one or a small number of actors who receive sufficient

---

10. They are also called selective incentives. See Todd Sandler, *Global Challenges: An Approach to Environmental, Political, and Economic Problems* (New York: Cambridge University Press, 1997), 45–46.

11. Karen T. Litfin, *Ozone Discourses: Science and Politics in Global Environmental Cooperation* (New York: Columbia University Press, 1994), 123–27.

benefits from the public good that they are willing to bear the cost of providing that good for everyone. The benefits of reducing ozone depletion were sufficiently large to the United States, for example, that it was willing to bear the initial costs of banning CFCs unilaterally and of leading the international fight against their use. Although the United States produced 30 percent of the world's CFCs, the savings to the country alone from reduced instances of skin cancer were sufficient to justify a major effort to limit CFC emissions. After some initial reluctance, the United States took a leadership position in the negotiations that produced the effective **Vienna Convention** and **Montreal Protocol** (see "What Shaped Our World?" on p. 576). The developed countries were then collectively motivated enough to pay for the transition to safer chemicals in developing countries.

Climate change is an especially difficult environmental problem because (1) it affects all countries around the globe, although not necessarily to the same extent, given differences in elevation, latitude, and other factors; (2) it centers on the burning of fossil fuels, the major source of energy today, and therefore affects all aspects of nearly every country's economy and society, rendering any solution enormously complex; and (3) it to date lacks sustained leadership by the world's single largest producer of greenhouse gases, the United States. On the positive side, because fossil fuels are ubiquitous, there are many joint products and opportunities for iteration and linkage. These features of the climate change problem have resulted in only tentative progress, first in the UNFCCC, then in the Kyoto Protocol, and most recently in the Paris Agreement.

Creating Property Rights: Cap-and-Trade Systems

Most economists agree that the most efficient way to overcome the collective action problems inherent in addressing climate change is to tax carbon emissions, thereby forcing polluters to pay a price for emitting carbon into the atmosphere. If taxed, the price of carbon fuels would more fully reflect the costs that they impose on society. Such carbon taxes, however, are politically unpopular with both carbon-emitting industries and consumers, who would pay higher prices for these industries' products. As with other environmental problems, efforts have focused instead on creating property rights and regulations.

In implementing the Kyoto Protocol, Europe essentially created property rights to greenhouse gas emissions. Since 2005, Europe has used an Emissions Trading Scheme (ETS) to regulate emissions. In the current phase of the program, the system includes 11,000 facilities in the electric power and industrial sectors, as well as civil aviation, and it covers some 45 percent of Europe's emissions. The ETS is what is known as a **cap-and-trade system**. Cap and trade works very well for large emitters, whose emissions can be measured. For other sources, such as individual automobiles, the European Union, like the United States, uses an efficiency standard.

In previous phases of the European Union's ETS, firms were issued free credits to emit a set amount of greenhouse gases based on their prior emissions, and the firms then could buy and sell the credits. The credits created ownership over an amount of greenhouse gases that could be released into the atmosphere in any given year—in essence creating a property right to a certain quantity of pollutants.

Vienna Convention for the Protection of the Ozone Layer

A framework convention adopted in 1985 to regulate activities, especially emissions of CFCs, that damage the ozone layer.

Montreal Protocol

An international treaty, signed in 1987, that is designed to protect the ozone layer by phasing out the production of a number of CFCs and other chemical compounds.

cap-and-trade system

A cap-and-trade system sets an overall limit on emissions, which is then lowered over time to reduce pollutants released into the atmosphere. Firms can sell "credits" when they emit less than their allocation or must buy from others when they emit more than their allocation.

The number of credits drops a bit each year to force a reduction in total emissions. In the current phase, the majority of credits will be sold at auction, although there continue to be some free credits.

Given a cap-and-trade system, economists believe that selling credits at auction is the most efficient way to allocate them. Those who find it most difficult to reduce their greenhouse gas emissions will bid for the credits. Others may find that there are less expensive alternatives to buying credits, such as improving energy efficiency or investing in renewable energy. Once the credits are issued, companies can buy and sell them if they find they need more or fewer than they originally thought. Starting from a 2005 baseline, the European Union's ETS reduced emissions from installations covered by the mechanism by about 35 percent by 2019 (Phase III), far exceeding the original target of 21 percent, and it now aims to reduce emissions by 55 percent by 2030 (Phase IV).[12] While not a party to the Kyoto Protocol, the state of California also uses a cap-and-trade system for its state-established carbon goals.

In addition to buying and selling credits within Europe, European countries can buy credits from developing countries. A similar system exists in Japan. Since developing countries do not have a carbon cap under the Kyoto Protocol, these emissions savings are documented through a program known as the Clean Development Mechanism (CDM). In order to sell credits through the CDM, a project in a developing country has to clearly document that it is reducing emissions from what would otherwise be business as usual.

Since the reduction in emissions in developing countries is offset by an increase in allowed emissions in Europe (or elsewhere within the Kyoto Protocol), the CDM does not reduce total global emissions. The real goal of the CDM is to increase investment in green energy in developing countries by incentivizing projects that would qualify for sellable emissions credits. As of 2020, almost 8,000 emissions reduction projects had been initiated. In the early years of the CDM, most credits were issued for projects in China. The majority of CDM-approved projects are still in Asia, but the European Union and the United Nations have made an effort to increase the number of projects in other countries in Asia and in other parts of the developing world. After 2012, China was no longer eligible for the CDM.

Under the Paris Agreement, the incentives for developing countries are a bit different. Now, each country makes a **nationally determined contribution (NDC)** to the goal of reducing the threat of global warming. NDCs can be achieved however each country chooses. A country might set a greenhouse gas cap, a renewable energy target, or an acreage of forests to be protected. If choosing a greenhouse gas cap, the country may implement a cap-and-trade system and even link with the European ETS so that its companies can buy and sell credits with other countries.

China is actively developing a domestic cap-and-trade system. On December 9, 2017, it formally launched a nationwide market for carbon emissions. This system is a key Chinese NDC under the Paris Agreement, and it was also a major point in a 2014 agreement between President Xi Jinping and then U.S. president Barack

nationally determined contribution (NDC)

The commitment each party to the Paris Agreement makes as to how it will contribute to reducing the threat of global warming.

---

12. See European Commission, "EU Emissions Trading System (EU ETS)," https://ec.europa.eu/clima /policies/ets_en (accessed 4/22/21).

The Montreal Protocol and the Protection of the Ozone Layer

The 1974 finding that human-made chemicals called chlorofluorocarbons (CFCs) were destroying the stratospheric ozone layer (Figure A) initiated the most rapid and successful international environmental effort in history.[a] Countries responded to this threat quickly with steps that included banning aerosol sprays in 1978. At the same time, the United States and other countries pushed for international action. As scientists' predictions became more dire, the unexpected discovery of the enormous Antarctic ozone hole in 1984 dramatically confirmed their fears. The Vienna Convention, signed in 1985, established a framework for limiting CFCs. Two years later, the Montreal Protocol established a strict global phaseout plan. And the London Amendment to the Montreal Protocol, adopted in 1990, accelerated the timeline for phasing out CFCs. Since then, as the science has progressed, more chemicals have been added to the phaseout list.

The Montreal Protocol has worked. Emissions of ozone-depleting substances (ODS) have decreased dramatically. Although ODS remain in the atmosphere for decades and continue to cause damage to the ozone layer (see Figure B), scientists have identified "fingerprints of healing" of the ozone layer and predict it will recover to its pre-1980s levels by 2070.[b]

Interactions The ozone layer is a classic example of a public good. Everyone can share equally in its benefits of protection from the sun's harmful ultraviolet light. However, once humans became capable of polluting it, the ozone layer was subject to the tragedy of the commons. Unless everyone agreed to protect the ozone layer together, no single group of people or country could enjoy its benefits.

Figuring out how much human activity needed to be curtailed required scientific input. But determining who would reduce their emissions, by how much, and who would pay for it required active bargaining among governments often concerned about companies within their borders. That the United States, the wealthiest and most powerful nation, was cutting its own emissions first made these interactions easier, forcing reluctant countries to stay at the table and enabling the global community to find solutions to these challenges.

FIGURE A *The Chemistry of Ozone Depletion*

Ultraviolet radiation strikes a CFC molecule...

...and causes a chlorine atom to break away.

The chlorine atom collides with an ozone molecule...

...and steals an oxygen atom to form chlorine monoxide and leave a molecule of ordinary oxygen.

When a free atom of oxygen collides with the chlorine monoxide...

...the two oxygen atoms form a molecule of oxygen. The chlorine atom is released and free to destroy more ozone.

Note: C: carbon; Cl: chlorine; F: fluorine; O: oxygen.

---

a. Mario J. Molina and F. Sherwood Rowland, "Stratospheric Sink for Chlorofluoromethanes: Chlorine Atom-Catalysed Destruction of Ozone," *Nature* 249, no. 5460 (1974): 810–12.

b. Susan Solomon, Diane J. Ivy, Doug Kinnison, Michael J. Mills, et al., "Emergence of Healing in the Antarctic Ozone Layer," *Science* 353, no. 6296 (2016): 269–74; and Paul A. Newman, Eric R. Nash, S. Randolph Kawa, Stephen A. Montzka, et al., "When Will the Antarctic Ozone Hole Recover?" *Geophysical Research Letters* 33, no. 12 (2006).

FIGURE B Ozone Hole on September 24, 2006

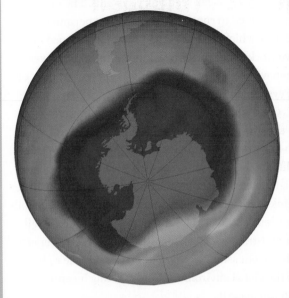

This image depicts the largest ozone hole ever observed: 11.4 million square miles. Purple and blue identify areas with the least amount of ozone; green and yellow areas have more ozone.

Figure source: www.nasa.gov/images/content/160657main _OZONE_large.jpg (accessed 7/02/20).

Interests The global community had a clear interest in protecting the ozone layer, so, accordingly, it shared an interest in reducing the emissions of ODS. However, the problem faced in any tragedy of the commons is that it is always better for you if someone else goes first. Moreover, different publics and different businesses had very different priorities. The American public was concerned about ODS by the late 1970s, and U.S. companies had developed some alternative products. By contrast, the European public was not yet focused on the issue, and manufacturers in France, Italy, and the United Kingdom still wanted to produce CFCs and related chemicals. As a result, the initial negotiations were a tough fight between the United States and Europe.

By the time of the Montreal Protocol, interests had changed again, with British prime minister Margaret Thatcher (a former chemist) and U.S. industrial leaders schooling President Ronald Reagan on the importance of the agreement. The major challenge then was how to ensure that developing countries that were not yet major manufacturers would go along with the ban instead of jumping in to take advantage of a deserted market.[c]

Institutions The Montreal Protocol is managed by the UN Environment Programme (UNEP). The cornerstone of the agreement is the phaseout of ODS, but developing countries were allowed to phase them out at a slower rate. When the parties to the treaty agreed to accelerate the phaseout in the London Amendment, they also agreed to what became known as the Multilateral Fund, a special fund designed to compensate developing countries for the cost of the phaseout and to provide technical and financial assistance with the transition to other chemicals. To date, the Multilateral Fund has spent over $3 billion.[d] The Montreal Protocol is today the only global treaty with universal membership. All 193 UN members are parties to the treaty.

The phaseout has not been without criticism. In particular, the slow phaseout of another ODS, called methyl bromide, was an issue of contention for years. The United States sought and received special protection for this substance, which made tomatoes and strawberries easier to transport over longer distances.[e] In the end, while experts had recommended a phaseout by 2001, the chemical was not fully phased out until 2015. Critics argued that the United States had used its considerable power, which earlier had pushed through the Montreal Protocol, to protect its own industry. Additionally, there have been some issues with noncompliance. In 2018, reports surfaced that new releases of carbon tetrachloride, one of the phased-out chemicals, were originating from China.[f]

Despite these challenges, the Montreal Protocol is widely viewed as successful because of its design. The agreement is flexible, dynamic, and meant to be informed by the latest scientific research. It has also relied heavily on the willingness of developed countries to pay the cost of the entire global public good. While $3 billion may sound like a lot, that figure was spread out over 26 years. Thus, the amount, while unprecedented in an international environmental agreement, was relatively modest. By contrast, the transition to a non-carbon-based global economy is estimated to cost in the trillions.

c. Richard Elliot Benedick, *Ozone Diplomacy: New Directions in Safeguarding the Planet* (Cambridge, MA: Harvard University Press, 1998).

d. Multilateral Fund for the Implementation of the Montreal Protocol, www.multilateralfund.org/default.aspx (accessed 7/20/17).

e. Brian J. Gareau, "A Critical Review of the Successful CFC Phase-out versus the Delayed Methyl Bromide Phase-out in the Montreal Protocol," *International Environmental Agreements: Politics, Law and Economics* 10, no. 3 (2010): 209–31.

f. M. F. Lunt, S. Park, S. Li, S. Henne, et al., "Continued Emissions of the Ozone-Depleting Substance Carbon Tetrachloride From Eastern Asia," *Geophysical Research Letters* 45, no. 20 (2018).

Organizations like the International Whaling Commission, which includes many nonwhaling member countries, may solve collective action problems by creating enforceable regulations.

Obama. Establishing a national market for emissions trading has been a challenge in China, a huge country with relatively weak regulatory systems. The market was expected to run essentially as an experiment until 2020, by which time government officials hoped to have worked out the kinks in the system.[13] However, the coronavirus pandemic delayed full implementation of the system until at least 2021.[14]

Once China's system is up and running, it is possible that the government will begin to work with other cap-and-trade systems, including those in Europe and California. Other countries such as Pakistan are also weighing creating domestic emissions markets in order to link them with China's system.[15] Although the details of various national plans differ and are important, all cap-and-trade mechanisms attempt to create property rights in emissions as a way of privatizing the right to use the global environment and creating incentives to better manage it.

Regulation The ban on whaling illustrates an alternative model for solving collective action problems related to the environment: a centrally set regulation.[16] Like fisheries in general, whales are a common-pool resource that has been overexploited in the past. To address this issue, the whaling industry voluntarily created the International Whaling Commission (IWC) in 1946. In an attempt to limit annual catches to sustainable yields, the governing council of the IWC assigned each country an annual quota. With the council composed almost entirely of representatives of whaling states, and with each member country lobbying to set its quota as high as possible, the IWC set the aggregate quota far higher than a cap that would allow the whale population to regenerate itself. As a result, the limits were ineffective and the number of whales plummeted.

Starting in the early 1960s, annual catches fell from approximately 15,000 to less than 5,000 whales per year—not as a result of strict quotas but because of declining whale populations. Even though the industry recognized that its long-term health required stricter quotas and lower rates of exploitation, the member states were unable to resist their incentives to catch as many whales as quickly as they could.

13. Chris Buckley, "Xi Jinping Is Set for a Big Gamble with China's Carbon Trading Market," *New York Times*, June 23, 2017, www.nytimes.com/2017/06/23/world/asia/china-cap-trade-carbon-greenhouse.html (accessed 3/10/21).

14. "China's Power Giants Prepare for World's Biggest Carbon Market," Bloomberg News, June 11, 2020, www.bloomberg.com/news/articles/2020-06-11/china-s-power-giants-prepare-for-world-s-biggest-carbon-market (accessed 2/23/21).

15. Faseeh Mangi and Mathew Carr, "Pakistan Weighs Carbon Emissions Market With a Link to China," Bloomberg News, December 18, 2019, www.bloomberg.com/news/articles/2019-12-19/pakistan-weighs-carbon-emissions-market-with-a-link-to-china (accessed 2/23/21).

16. M. J. Peterson, "Whalers, Cetologists, Environmentalists, and the International Management of Whaling," *International Organization* 46, no. 1 (Winter 1992): 147–86.

It is here that the rules of the IWC as an institution became important in finally moving toward effective regulation. Environmentalists became concerned about the whaling issue not from a sustainable catch perspective but from an interest in protecting whales. Some of their concern was about protecting biodiversity, but much of it was simply about defending whales for their beauty and perceived intelligence.

The environmental community eventually figured out that it could use the IWC rules to its advantage. Any country that pays its dues can join the IWC, so environmentalists began to pay annual membership fees for countries that might not otherwise belong to the organization as a way of diluting the voice of the whaling countries. While there are only a handful of whaling countries, today there are 88 member states in the IWC. With a growing number of anti-whaling members, some "bought" by environmentalists, the IWC finally enacted a complete ban on whaling in 1982, and it took effect in 1985. The efforts of environmentalists were aided by U.S. law, which would not allow whaling countries to purchase fishing permits within the U.S. exclusive economic zone.

The total ban within the IWC has proved effective. Even on the high seas, a ban is much easier to monitor than a numerical limit. Since the 1970s, a number of whale stocks have recovered considerably. Some, like the humpback, are thought to be near their pre-exploitation levels, while others, like the blue whale, have not recovered nearly as well.[17] Scientists are still trying to understand why some species are faring so much better than others.

In sum, the tragedy of the commons threatens public goods and common-pool resources. The interactions of large numbers of individuals or countries can produce outcomes that are undesirable for society as a whole. Even though we all value the environment, our individual actions have a marginal impact and we free ride on the efforts of others. Problems of collective action apply among individuals and states. Choices that are reasonable for any single actor sometimes create collectively tragic results. Collective action problems are easier to solve under some conditions than others. As in the ETS or the ban on whaling, however, whenever collective action problems are large, society can adopt rules and regulations that change individual incentives to better protect the local and global environment.

Why Do Polluters Usually Win?

Political struggles over the environment often involve both bargaining problems and collective action problems. Some expect the failure to mitigate climate change to exacerbate underlying political struggles within and between countries, possibly leading to higher levels of conflict and violence. The evidence to date, however, is far from clear on this prediction (see "How Do We Know?" on p. 580).

At the same time, we know that political struggles over policy can block attempts to mitigate environmental degradation. These bargaining problems

---

17. International Whaling Commission, "Population Status," https://iwc.int/status (accessed 7/07/20).

Climate Change and Conflict

The idea of climate change as a security threat has been discussed for years, but it became common wisdom after a 2007 report by 11 retired U.S. generals and admirals described climate change as a "threat multiplier."[a] In other words, in any area where conflict might be likely, floods, droughts, rising sea levels, or other changes induced by a warming climate would increase the risk of violence.

Establishing whether climate change leads to increased conflict is difficult. The arguments presented in the 2007 report and others[b] are supported by numerous "cases" of conflicts that coincided with some major weather event, such as a flood or a drought. But it is easy to think of major natural disasters that have not been associated with an increase in unrest, including the 2004 Asian tsunami, floods in places from China to India to Peru, or even the recent drought-induced wildfires in California. What do these examples tell us? Not very much.

Scholarly research into this question is difficult and relatively new. The Intergovernmental Panel on Climate Change noted in 2014 that "collectively the research does not conclude that there is a strong positive relationship between warming and armed conflict."[c] The authors of the report held that climate change would damage "human security because it undermines livelihoods, compromises culture and identity, induces migration that people would rather have avoided, and challenges the ability of states to provide the conditions necessary for human security."[d] However, their review of the available research did not support the hypothesis that climate change would lead to an increase in armed conflict. Figure A illustrates the difficulty of establishing a link between climate change and conflict. Before the mid-1980s, one might be tempted to

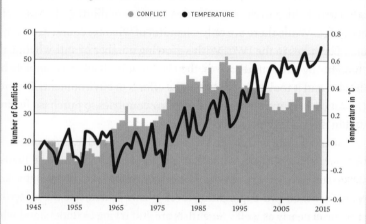

FIGURE A *Global Temperature Deviation and Conflict, 1946–2014*

● CONFLICT ● TEMPERATURE

Figure source: Halvard Buhaug, "Globalt Tempuraturavvik Og Konflikt, 1946–2014," in Nils Petter Gleditsch, *Mot en mer fredelig verden?* [Toward a more peaceful world?] (Oslo: Pax, 2016). Reprinted with permission.

Note: Conflict data are from the UCDP/PRIO database; temperature data are from https://data.giss.nasa.gov/gistemp/history/. The temperature deviations are measured for the average for the period 1951–80.

infer a positive relationship between temperature change and conflict, but more recently the trends have diverged, calling any relationship into question.

A 2019 article synthesized expert opinions on climate as a risk factor for armed conflict. Experts agreed that climate can have an effect but that it is weak relative to other possible drivers of conflict, including low socioeconomic development, low state capacity, intergroup inequality, and a recent history of violent conflict. Reflecting the difficulty of estimating the relationship, however, experts remain uncertain about the effect of climate on conflict. They estimate that climate variability and change to date have increased the risk conflict by about 5 percent. Importantly, a 2°C change in global temperature is expected to increase the risk of conflict by 13 percent, and a 4°C change is expected to increase the risk of conflict by 26 percent.[e] Though the relatively smaller increases in temperature that the planet has experienced to date may not yet have had a major impact on the incidence of conflict, climate change is expected to have larger effects on conflict in the future unless global temperature rise can be mitigated.

a. "National Security and Climate Change," CNA Corporation, 2007, www.cna.org/mab/reports (accessed 3/10/21).

b. National Intelligence Council, "Implications for US National Security of Anticipated Climate Change," September 21, 2016, www.dni.gov/files/documents/Newsroom/Reports%20and%20Pubs/Implications_for_US_National_Security_of_Anticipated_Climate_Change.pdf (accessed 3/10/21).

c. Quoted in Nils Petter Gleditsch and Ragnhild Nordås, "Conflicting Messages? The IPCC on Conflict and Human Security," *Political Geography* 43 (November 2014): 82–90.

d. Gleditsch and Nordås, "Conflicting Messages?"

e. Katharine J. Mach, Caroline M. Kraan, W. Neil Adger, Halvard Buhaug, et al., "Climate As a Risk Factor for Armed Conflict," *Nature* 571 (2019): 193–97.

typically pit a majority favoring tighter regulations against a minority of special interests that, if not actually advocating environmental degradation, aim to block costly new regulations or to shift the costs of policy change onto others. Even if most people share an interest in protecting the environment, any policy to improve environmental practices will create losers, who will have to give up activities or practices that were previously permitted, and winners, who will enjoy the benefits of a greener world.

The key concept to understand in these bargaining problems is **externalities**, which are costs or benefits resulting from an actor's decision that affect stakeholders other than that actor. When an externality exists, the decision maker does not bear all the costs or reap all the gains from a particular action. If a firm decides to dump waste into a river, others bear the costs of either using contaminated water or purifying it themselves. In this case, the firm has imposed a cost, or negative externality, on others. If a school club cleans a stretch of beach, it is not only the club's members who benefit from a litter-free and safer swimming area but also any others who might use the same spot. In this instance, the club has provided benefits, or created a positive externality, for others.

Fracking, the process of injecting liquid at high pressure into subterranean rocks so as to force open existing fissures and extract oil or gas, also harms the larger environment, causing substantial shifts in ground and groundwater levels.

Externalities represent a divergence between the individual costs or benefits of action and the broader costs or benefits to society as a whole. Typically, individuals are motivated to act by only their private costs and benefits, and they do not take into account the costs and benefits that their actions impose on others. As a result, from the point of view of society at large, people individually decide to dump too much waste or fail to clean up enough beaches. When externalities exist, the independent decisions of individual actors lead to suboptimal results. Through some form of cooperation, everyone's welfare can be improved, and each individual, in principle, can be made better off.

Externalities create problems of bargaining or redistribution in which one side's gains come as a result of another side's losses. The question is who benefits from and who pays the costs of any externality. If the actor gets all the benefits or pays all the costs—if there is no externality—that actor is likely to choose reasonably efficiently how to balance the trade-off. But when one actor receives the benefits and another must shoulder the costs, the two actors must bargain over the gains and losses and who should pay to mitigate the externality.

The dilemma raises the following questions: Why do those who stand to lose from tighter environmental restrictions so often win? Why do the special interests that oppose environmental regulations tend to succeed in blocking greater controls? To answer these questions, we must examine two sets of winners and losers in international environmental policy.

externalities

Costs or benefits resulting from an actor's decision that affect stakeholders other than that actor. When an externality exists, the decision maker does not bear all the costs or reap all the gains from the action.

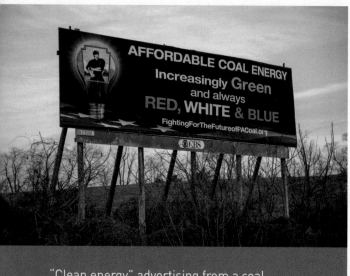

"Clean energy" advertising from a coal company. Producers of oil and coal are often accused of "greenwashing" by minimizing the environmental hazards of their methods.

Domestic Winners and Losers

Industries that create negative externalities— so-called dirty industries—enhance their profits by not paying the full costs of production, which include the harm they impose on others. Firms that can dump waste into a river avoid the expense of treating that waste or otherwise disposing of it in ways that are environmentally safe. This ability to off-load the costs onto others—who then suffer from environmental degradation—increases the firm's profits, reduces the costs of the goods it sells and makes it more competitive, or both. Firms and industries thus have an interest in opposing stiffer environmental regulations that would compel them to reduce the negative externalities they produce.

Even industries that do not directly degrade the environment with their resource extraction or production processes have interests in looser environmental laws. The oil industry, which frequently promotes its clean production methods in glossy magazine or online ads, has fought renewable energy resources that, were they widely available, would compete directly with their main product. Likewise, the auto industry has often opposed efforts to improve gasoline mileage or reduce emissions because the new technologies would raise the price of cars and, at least at the margin, reduce demand.

Competition constrains firms to reduce their costs of production as much as possible. The process of economic globalization heightens this constraint by bringing domestic firms into competition with foreign manufacturers, which may not face the same pressures for increased environmental regulations in their bases of production. By opposing new environmental regulations—and in some cases, by lobbying to remove existing regulations as competition increases—firms lower their costs of production at the expense of the environment. This competition for regulatory laxity is feared to produce a "race to the bottom" in environmental policy as countries seek to undercut one another in offering business-friendly policies to internationally mobile companies. To date, there is relatively little evidence for such a race. Producing at lower cost, however, benefits not only the firms but also consumers, who gain from cheaper prices for goods. Indeed, lax environmental regulations may lower the cost of products and thus give consumers incentives to ignore the environmental practices of their producers.

Nearly every alternative policy for protecting the global environment creates losers and winners who press their governments to change policy in their preferred direction. Nonetheless, the balance of political power typically favors entrenched or vested interests. The industries and groups that would lose from tighter environmental regulations are relatively few in comparison with the majority that would gain from a greener environment, and they suffer direct and immediate costs. In this way, polluters are similar to protectionist industries (discussed in Chapter 7) that gain concentrated benefits from import restrictions and are more motivated to enter the political arena as a result. Oil markets are dominated by just a few major firms that suffer concentrated costs of environmental regulations. Automobile manufacturers claim that increased mileage standards will require costly new research and development and raise the price of cars, thereby reducing demand. These costs give the potential losers a stronger incentive to attempt to influence government policy.

As an exception that tests the rule, CFC producers—especially DuPont, the industry leader—dug in their heels on reducing emissions until it became clear that new chemical alternatives would soon be available and might even increase their profits. When the costs of change are not large, even politically powerful industries may yield to demands for tighter environmental regulations. Once regulated, moreover, firms may then lobby hard to create international agreements that level the playing field by regulating foreign firms as well.[18]

Firms and industries may not support environmental regulations that would require them to change their manufacturing processes or reduce demand for their products. While some auto companies have started producing electric cars to comply with regulations on gas mileage or emissions, others have resisted. For example, in 2019, when the Trump administration revoked California's long-standing ability to set its own emissions standard for automobiles, four major car companies sided with California in a lawsuit, in essence declaring that they wanted to be held to a higher emissions standard, while several others sided with the Trump administration's rollback.

Conversely, the benefits of a cleaner environment are diffuse, and the beneficiaries, as we have seen, suffer from collective action problems. Because the benefits are spread across many individuals or groups, few have strong interests in lobbying their governments to alter current practices. The intensity of the losers' interests in opposing stiffer regulations typically compensates for their smaller numbers relative to the majority.

Moreover, these industries and groups have employees and stockholders who are citizens and voters. Industries can mobilize those workers and stockholders to press their case to elected politicians. Oil companies, for example, have political influence because many voters depend on the oil industry—or related industries that rely on inexpensive fossil fuels—for their livelihoods. Clean-energy industries, such as wind or solar power firms that might blossom if there were a national cap-and-trade program, are small and lack the same resources. Their future growth, and the workers and stockholders who might benefit directly from their growth, are mostly promises rather than real-life voters who can reward or punish politicians for the legislation they adopt today.

---

18. On domestic business interests, see Elizabeth R. DeSombre, *Domestic Sources of International Environmental Policy: Industry, Environmentalists, and U.S. Power* (Cambridge, MA: MIT Press, 2000).

Regions that rely on glacial meltwater, such as the Bolivian Andes, stand to suffer greatly from rapidly melting glaciers, even though they may contribute very small amounts of carbon emissions.

Over time, we can see how this calculus is changing. Today solar power employs more people in the United States than the coal industry does. Oil and gas still are the largest employers, but wind power and biofuels are growing. Different states, however, offer very different pictures. California leads the nation in solar power jobs, and it is also the leading state in support of cap-and-trade and the Paris Agreement. Wyoming and West Virginia still have many coal jobs, and their residents largely welcomed President Trump's decision to leave the Paris Agreement.[19]

International Winners and Losers

Environmental issues also divide developed and developing countries. Externalities exist both within countries, creating domestic winners and losers, and between countries. In the latter case, the costs of environmental degradation are borne not only by the country releasing pollutants into the atmosphere, for instance, but also by neighboring countries or perhaps all countries. This situation creates the vexing question of who gains from lax environmental standards and, more important, which countries should pay for creating a greener world.

Historically, the largest polluters have been the rich states in Europe and North America. Since 1850, these countries have released nearly two-thirds of cumulative carbon emissions.[20] Even today, the United States uses far more energy and emits far more pollutants per capita than any other country. With 4.3 percent of the world's population, the United States emits around 14 percent of the world's greenhouse

19. Nadja Popovich, "Today's Energy Jobs Are in Solar, Not Coal," *New York Times*, April 25, 2017, www.nytimes.com/interactive/2017/04/25/climate/todays-energy-jobs-are-in-solar-not-coal.html (accessed 2/23/21).

20. Mengpin Ge, Johannes Friedrich, and Thomas Damassa, "6 Graphs Explain the World's Top 10 Emitters," World Resources Institute, November 25, 2014, www.wri.org/blog/2014/11/6-graphs -explain-world-s-top-10-emitters (accessed 3/10/21).

FIGURE 13.2 *International Leadership and Climate Change*

This bar chart illustrates two key ideas in controlling carbon emissions. First, each bar represents total carbon emissions in each year. The green area of each pie represents the reliable leaders in reducing carbon emissions—places that year in and year out invest in decarbonization. This includes all of Europe, most of Canada, about one-third of the United States (the coastal states that have led in this area), Japan, New Zealand, Costa Rica, Chile and others. The red area is comprised of blockers who, as the label suggests, actively attempt to block initiatives to reduce carbon emissions. The blue area represents the places in the reluctant middle ground. As is obvious from the charts, reliable leaders slightly decreased their emissions over time, but this progress has been massively offset by an increase in total emissions, largely from reluctant countries.

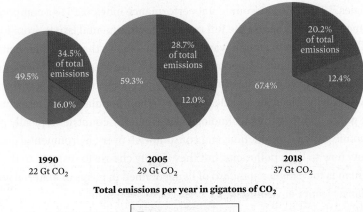

1990	2005	2018
22 Gt CO_2	29 Gt CO_2	37 Gt CO_2

Total emissions per year in gigatons of CO_2

■ Reliable leaders
■ Blockers
■ Reluctant middle ground

gases. Worldwide, the average individual produces 5.0 metric tons of greenhouse gases each year. The average American emits 16.0 tons per year, more than the average resident of any other country besides Australia, Kazakhstan, and some of the oil-rich principalities in the Middle East. By contrast, Japan, a state at a comparable level of economic development, averages 9.5 metric tons per person per year.[21] The developed countries have, by far, the largest cumulative and ongoing impact on the environment (see Figure 13.2).

The greatest source of new pollutants in the future, however, will be the developing countries. We have already seen this increase in China, where carbon emissions have grown from 15 percent of the world's total in 2001 to 30 percent today. China's emissions in 2018 totaled 11.2 billion tons, and Chinese citizens now emit 7.8 tons per capita. While that is less than the United States, it is still 16 percent more per person than the European Union average.[22] China continues to rely heavily on coal for 60 percent of its energy needs.[23] But China's carbon emissions now appear to have stabilized. In fact, its emissions decreased by 0.7 percent from 2014 to 2015,

Figure source: David G. Victor, "Is International Cooperation on Climate Policy Working?" Presentation to the Scripps Institute of Oceanography, University of California San Diego, August 2020. For a discussion of leaders and blockers, see David G. Victor, "We Have Climate Leaders. Now We Need Followers," *New York Times*, December 13, 2019, https://www.nytimes.com/2019/12/13/opinion/climate-change-madrid.html (accessed 4/23/21).

21. J. G. J. Olivier and J. A. H. W. Peters, "Trends in Global CO_2 and Total Greenhouse Gas Emissions: 2019 Report," PBL Netherlands Environmental Assessment Agency, May 2020, www.pbl.nl/sites/default/files/downloads/pbl-2020-trends-in-global-co2-and-total-greenhouse-gas-emissions-2019-report_4068.pdf (accessed 2/23/21).

22. Olivier and Peters, "Trends in Global CO_2 Emissions."

23. "Country Insight—China," BP, www.bp.com/en/global/corporate/energy-economics/energy-outlook/country-and-regional-insights/china-insights.html (accessed 2/23/21).

largely because of a decline in coal usage.[24] While this decrease has not continued, large increases have also not occurred. All this coal brings with it an enormous amount of air pollution, an issue that has increasingly concerned Chinese citizens and the Chinese government in recent years. Regulations have expanded significantly since 2005,[25] but pollution in Chinese cities is still far above healthy levels.[26] Although China's large population and growing economy put its environmental practices on the front pages of the world's newspapers, the same story could be told for virtually every other developing country.

Typically, countries increase their pollution until they reach a certain level of development, and then they start to increase pollution controls and invest in cleaner technologies.[27] The Yale environmental performance index (EPI)—a composite score of measurements across the full range of environmental issues, from forest and wildlife protection to air and water pollution—shows that wealthier countries generally have higher environmental performance (see Map 13.1). Though developing countries may have more forests and open space, they usually face real challenges in delivering clean air and clean water to their populations. These challenges are often political rather than technological; developing countries typically prioritize economic growth, production, and consumption over environmental quality. They know how to limit pollutants, but they simply choose to respond to their citizens' demands for a higher standard of living defined in terms of material goods rather than a cleaner environment.

Exactly when in its development trajectory each country chooses to address pollution varies. China has now taken on this issue, with more than half of the goals in its current "Five-Year Plan" (its major economic planning document) focused on energy and the environment. India is now seeing a rapid rise in air pollution because its coal-fired power plant capacity increased by 93 percent from 2005–14 without controls on the two main polluting gases.[28] However, the Indian government announced new pollution standards in 2015, and enforcement began at the end of 2017. In 2019, India initiated a National Clean Air Programme to reduce air pollution across the country.[29]

Some of the easiest steps to prevent further environmental degradation could be taken in the developing world. For some emissions, such as the air pollutants that plague cities in China, India, and other developing countries, the government could set the kinds of regulations that already exist in the developed world. For other pollutants, especially greenhouse gases, countries that are

24. Olivier and Peters, "Trends in Global CO_2 Emissions."

25. Jeremy J. Schreifels, Yale Fu, and Elizabeth J. Wilson, "Sulfur Dioxide Control in China: Policy Evolution during the 10th and 11th Five-Year Plans and Lessons for the Future," *Energy Policy* 48 (2012): 779–89.

26. Nickolay A. Krotkov, Chris A. McLinden, Can Li, Lok N. Lamsal, et al., "Aura OMI Observations of Regional SO_2 and NO_2 Pollution Changes from 2005 to 2015," *Atmospheric Chemistry and Physics* 16, no. 7 (2016): 4605–29.

27. Gene M. Grossman and Alan B. Krueger, "Economic Growth and the Environment," *Quarterly Journal of Economics* 110, no. 2 (1995): 353–77.

28. Krotkov et al., "Aura OMI Observations."

29. Ministry of Environment, Forest and Climate Change, "World Environment Day: 5 June, 2019," Government of India, http://moef.gov.in/wed-2019-2/national-clean-air-programme-ncap (accessed 2/23/21).

still building out their infrastructures can limit emissions more easily than can a developed country where infrastructure has already been built around fossil fuel–based power.

It is more economically advantageous to build a new wind plant in a developing city with a demand for increased power, for instance, than in a city where an existing natural gas plant already provides all the electricity the city needs. Moreover, because industries in developing countries often use older and less efficient technologies, governments and firms can undertake energy improvements at relatively low cost and result in significant greenhouse gas savings. The fact that many of the easiest steps to reduce carbon emissions could be taken in the developing world is a key rationale behind the European Union's ETS, which allows its firms, facing high costs for further reducing their emissions, to buy carbon credits from developing countries, where the costs of reducing an equivalent amount of emissions are much lower.

A similar but distinct issue arises with biodiversity. Most of the world's tropical forests, home to the earth's greatest biodiversity and important carbon sinks, are in developing countries. People concerned about greenhouse gases argue that protecting these forests should be a priority. However, groups in many developing countries note that in the process of developing, North America and Europe engaged in a great deal of deforestation.

As countries develop, land is often converted from forest cover to more economically productive uses, such as farmland, industry, and cities. The United States has converted an estimated 256 million acres of forest land to other uses since the beginning of European settlement 400 years ago. Most of that conversion occurred during the late nineteenth century, when the country's economy was growing most rapidly. In fact, U.S. forest cover has remained remarkably stable, at about one-third of the total landmass, since 1912.[30] By contrast, some countries with important tropical forest resources still have over 50 percent forest cover. Two examples are Brazil and Indonesia, but both of these countries have seen considerable declines in forested land area over the last 25 years.[31]

Thus the question arises of who should or will pay to leave these forests undeveloped. Their existence creates a positive externality for the global community, and their destruction would create a negative externality. But in the short run, the citizens of developing states might benefit significantly from exploiting this resource.

The differing interests of local, national, and international communities create tough bargaining problems in addressing global environmental issues. Even recognizing that they have a disproportionate responsibility for cleaning up the

30. U.S. Department of Agriculture, "U.S. Forest Resource Facts and Historical Trends," August 2014, www.fia.fs.fed.us/library/brochures/docs/2012/ForestFacts_1952-2012_English.pdf.

31. Brazil's forest cover has decreased from 65 to 59 percent, and Indonesia's has decreased from 61 to 50 percent. World Bank, "Forest area (% of land area)," http://data.worldbank.org/indicator/AG.LND.FRST .ZS?end=2015&locations=BR&start=1990&year_low_desc=false (accessed 2/23/21).

MAP 13.1 *Environmental Performance Index, 2019*

The Center for Environmental Law and Policy at Yale University and the Center for International Earth Science Information Network at Columbia University have developed a composite environmental performance index (EPI) for 180 countries. It provides a common way to measure countries' performance on a range of important environmental issues. The map divides countries into seven categories based on their overall performance. The United States and Canada, along with a number of other developed countries, have scores in the top category. On average, sub-Saharan Africa has the lowest scores.

Overall EPI Score by Country Quintile

- 66.6–87.7
- 53.5–66.5
- 45.2–53.4
- 36.1–45.1
- 15.5–36.0
- NO DATA

Map source: Environmental Performance Index, http://epi.yale.edu /downloads (accessed 7/07/20).

Arctic Ocean

NORWAY

UNITED
KINGDOM

SWEDEN

FINLAND

RUSSIA

IRELAND

GERMANY

BELARUS

FRANCE

UKRAINE

KAZAKHSTAN

MONGOLIA

N. KOREA

GEORGIA

S. KOREA

ITALY

SPAIN

GREECE

UZBEKISTAN

KYRGYZSTAN

JAPAN

TURKEY

TURKMENISTAN

TAJIKISTAN

MOROCCO

ISRAEL

LEB.

SYRIA

IRAQ

IRAN

CHINA

NEPAL

BHUTAN

HONG KONG

Pacific Ocean

JORDAN

KUWAIT

MYANMAR
(BURMA)

ALGERIA

LIBYA

EGYPT

SAUDI
ARABIA

UAE

TAIWAN

MAURITANIA

MALI

NIGER

CHAD

ERITREA

OMAN

PAKISTAN

INDIA

VIETNAM

SENEGAL

YEMEN

THAILAND

PHILIPPINES

GUINEA

NIGERIA

SUDAN

AFGHANISTAN

LAOS

CAMBODIA

GHANA

CAMEROON

CEN.
AFR.
REP.

S. SUDAN

ETHIOPIA

BANGLADESH

MALAYSIA

IVORY COAST

D.R.
CONGO

UGANDA

KENYA

SOMALIA

SRI LANKA

INDONESIA

PAPUA
NEW GUINEA

Indian Ocean

TANZANIA

SOLOMON
ISLANDS

ANGOLA

ZAMBIA

MALAWI

MADAGASCAR

NAMIBIA

MOZAMBIQUE

AUSTRALIA

ZIMBABWE

SOUTH
AFRICA

BOTSWANA

NEW
ZEALAND

environment, because of both their past practices and their relatively greater present wealth, some developed countries still want to link their efforts to greater contributions by developing countries (see "Controversy" on p. 592).

When industries and environmentalists or rich and poor countries bargain, the result can be political stalemate. Such was the case in the decade after the 1997 Kyoto Protocol. The United States was not willing to join Kyoto, and developing countries were unwilling to make firm commitments to control their emissions. The desire of developed countries was not that developing countries reduce their emissions immediately, because their emissions were quite low (especially in 1997, when the Kyoto Protocol was drafted) and they would need energy to develop. Rather, developed countries wanted the developing world to commit to controlling emissions with a plan to reduce them at a later date.

The impasse was ultimately broken at Copenhagen in 2009. While the Copenhagen Accord was only a one-page document, it specified for the first time that all countries, not just developed countries, would make specific commitments to mitigate climate change. Then, two years later in South Africa, countries came together again in the Durban Platform for Enhanced Action, which set out a road map for negotiating a new agreement that would commit the countries of the world to action beyond 2020. They set the deadline for completing that agreement for four years later: 2015 in Paris.

The key to success at Durban was a realignment of important developed and developing countries who now saw each other as partners. In Durban, the Europeans teamed up with the countries that emitted the fewest greenhouse gases and stood to suffer most from climate change—namely, the least developed countries and the small island states. They found a common interest in pushing the United States and the larger developing countries to commit to doing more. The Europeans, after all, had been strictly controlling greenhouse gases under the Kyoto Protocol for a number of years; for competitive reasons, their companies wanted industries in the United States, as well as in rapidly growing nations like China, to be equally bound.

At the time, the United States was interested in controlling greenhouse gases, but the Obama administration had been unable to push climate legislation through Congress. By 2014, however, President Obama had come up with a plan that could be implemented through executive action. China was also moving along with clean energy under its Five-Year Plan. As a result, the United States and China were ready to come to the table, first with bilateral agreements and then at the Paris Conference in 2015. Even if the national plans submitted under that agreement do not themselves contain significant cutbacks in carbon emissions by developing countries, the principle that all countries share in the responsibility for reducing emissions has now been firmly established.

Bargaining over the Future Environment

Alternative policy solutions create gains and losses for different groups. Industries prefer that consumers or taxpayers pay to clean up industrial environmental waste, and developing countries prefer that developed countries restrict their pollutants more severely so that the developing countries can industrialize at lower cost. Even though everyone may gain from cooperation, each actor prefers a different policy outcome. As shown in Figure 2.2 (p. 56), cooperation creates net gains through a movement toward the Pareto frontier, but actors will still bargain over where on the frontier a policy will settle. Cooperation and bargaining occur simultaneously. The political fight is not about the need for protecting the environment but about who will bear the costs of a cleaner environment.

Often, the political battle results in compromise. In the European ETS discussed earlier, economists argued that the most efficient system would be to auction emissions credits equal to total output, thereby allocating the credits to those firms that needed them the most and generating income for the governments involved. Instead, at the insistence of firms, in the first two rounds the credits were given free to existing companies and were based on current emissions levels. This arrangement allowed the firms to pass higher costs along to consumers while at the same time selling their credits in the ETS. One European NGO has estimated that the companies' profits added up to €24 billion between 2008 and 2014.[32]

While advocacy groups have an agenda that should make us skeptical of any exact estimate, the politics of why the companies would receive a windfall are relatively obvious: the European Union needed to induce them to join the plan and not wield their political influence to block its implementation. In fact, academic research on the ETS has shown that the cost of the carbon permits was passed through to consumers and that companies' stock market value went up when they were able to charge higher prices.[33] The "losers" from limits on carbon emissions, in this case, did not actually lose very much. The ETS responded to the economic problems caused by free permits, however, by beginning the transition to auctions, and in fact, the majority of permits in the current round are being auctioned.

Sometimes, though, the fight between the winners and losers created by environmental policy is sufficiently intense that it blocks movement toward greater cooperation. Paradoxically, the more we care about the future and about the future environment, the more that is at stake and the more intense this political fight will be.

For the potential winners from environmental protection, the higher value they place on the future environment mobilizes supporters into the political arena to change policy. Because they care more about the future, they are willing to exert greater effort today to promote policies to protect that environment. The farther into the future the winners look, the more likely they are to forgo agreement today in the hope of getting a better agreement that guarantees their preferred policies for a longer period. Each day that passes without significant political progress means that more carbon is accumulating in the atmosphere. But even though the immediate environment might suffer from a lack of cooperation, a better bargain over a longer period of time might make such a delay worthwhile.

---

32. Carbon Market Watch, "Industry Windfall Profits from Europe's Carbon Market," March 2016, https://carbonmarketwatch.org/wp-content/uploads/2016/03/Policy-brief_Industry-windfall-profits-from-Europe%E2%80%99s_web_final-1.pdf (accessed 2/23/21).

33. Natalia Fabra and Mar Reguant, "Pass-through of Emissions Costs in Electricity Markets," *American Economic Review* 104, no. 9 (2014): 2872–99; James B. Bushnell, Howard Chong, and Erin T. Mansur, "Profiting from Regulation: Evidence from the European Carbon Market," *American Economic Journal: Economic Policy* 5 no. 4 (2013): 78–106.

Who Should Bear the Costs of Addressing Global Climate Change?

Nepal is distinguished by snowy ranges, ancient glaciers, deep gorges, and the historic villages of the Sherpa people. It is also home to the rare snow leopard, musk deer, and red panda. But this landscape is fragile; Nepal is warming. In a development that scientists believe to be human-induced climate change, the temperature in this area has been increasing at the rate of 0.06°C per year, faster than the global average,[a] and the majority of glaciers in the Himalayas have been retreating (melting has exceeded snowfall) for decades.[b]

Global warming will eventually affect everyone, but it already affects some far more than others. Today, Nepalis face frequent floods as the glaciers melt.[c] If warming trends continue, Nepal will face many more threats. Across the globe, homes, livelihoods, and cultures are at risk; famine and disease will increase; some species will become extinct.

Applying the Concepts

Nepal is an interesting lens through which to examine the ethics of global warming. Earlier in this chapter, we noted that countries have relatively similar interests in preventing climate change but suffer from collective action problems that make mitigation difficult. In the case of Nepal, however, its **interests** are more extreme. It does not contribute heavily to global climate change but is more at risk than many countries from its effects. At the same time, as a small and relatively poor country, its **interactions** with others are limited. Indeed, it has little leverage in bargaining with other countries over carbon emissions. If Nepal is to escape from the growing consequences of climate change, it must rely on other countries, a sense of fairness and justice, and the creation of global **institutions** that regulate emissions. What sort of bargain would be fair? Who should bear the costs of change?

For Nepal, one of the main issues in climate negotiations is how to get high-carbon-emitting countries, such as the United States, to reduce their emissions. Though a majority of Americans want the United States to "take aggressive action to slow global warming,"[d] U.S. policy tends to go back and forth depending on which party controls Washington. Workers for fossil fuel companies tend to be in "red" states, while renewables have blossomed in "blue" states. The U.S. fossil fuel industry, which actively opposes domestic carbon controls, is large and politically well entrenched. In contrast, companies in the renewable sector support such controls as well as the clean-energy transition of other countries.

The Kyoto Protocol operated on the principle that because developed countries like the United States had contributed more to the problem and were wealthier, they should restrain their emissions first. This was one interpretation of the idea of "common but differentiated responsibilities," which appeared in the UNFCCC as well as the other treaties signed at the Rio de Janeiro global conference on sustainable development in 1992.

For many years, the developed countries, particularly the United States, focused on the "common" part of

a. Arun B. Shrestha and Raju Aryal, "Climate Change in Nepal and Its Impact on Himalayan Glaciers," *Regional Environmental Change* 11, no. 1 (2011): 65–77.

b. Tobias Bolch, A. Kulkarni, A. Kääb, C. Huggel, et al., "The State and Fate of Himalayan Glaciers," *Science* 336, no. 6079 (2012): 310–14.

c. Shaun D. Richardson and John M. Reynolds, "An Overview of Glacial Hazards in the Himalayas," *Quaternary International* 65 (2000): 31–47.

d. Chris Kahn, "Most Americans Want 'Aggressive' Action on Climate Change: Reuters/Ipsos Poll," Reuters, June 6, 2017, https://www.reuters.com/article/us-usa-climatechange-poll/most-americans-want-aggressive-action-on-climate-change-reuters-ipsos-poll-idUSKBN18X198 (accessed 3/10/21).

the phrase. Developing countries, however, focused on "differentiated," arguing that they could wait to address greenhouse gases. Even before President George W. Bush pulled out of the Kyoto Protocol, the U.S. Senate signaled that it would not sign on unless large developing countries also committed to serious greenhouse gas controls. Faced with this resistance from developed countries, developing countries have held together as a group known as the Group of 77. By Copenhagen, some members of this group—in particular the small island nations at risk of being swamped by sea level rise—chose to be much more forceful than other developing nations.

A new understanding of "common but differentiated responsibilities" has emerged. Under the Paris Agreement, each country makes its own nationally determined contribution that conforms to the country's preferred approach to mitigating climate change. Brazil has an economy-wide target, while China has separate targets for energy and forestry. The United States too was able to design its own commitment. The Paris Agreement allocates more funding for countries like Nepal.

Although countries have moved toward a new understanding that all have some responsibility for addressing climate change, tough bargaining is still under way over who should bear what cost. The Biden administration rejoined the Paris Agreement soon after taking office in 2021, promising to reduce U.S. carbon emissions by 50 percent from 2005 levels by 2030.

Thinking Analytically

1. What would be a "fair" bargain internationally? Should countries that already emit high levels of carbon have a right to continue to pollute? Should developing countries that have not previously contributed significantly to global emissions be permitted to emit more carbon?

2. Should people be allocated a quantity of greenhouse gases that they can emit annually? Would a Nepali have the same rights to emit a limited quantity of carbon as an American? Or should citizens of developed countries bear a higher cost to make up for their historically higher emissions already in the atmosphere?

3. Depending on your answers to the first two questions, what kind of institution is necessary and appropriate to ensure that the bargain reached is actually implemented?

In 2019, environmental activist Greta Thunberg addressed the United Nations and challenged national leaders for not addressing climate change. At age 15, Thunberg began protesting daily outside the Swedish parliament, an action that soon inspired other youth and led her to become an internationally recognized advocate for environmental justice.

For those who would stand to lose from tighter environmental regulations, the value they place on the future may also mobilize them into the political arena to try to protect the favorable policies they now enjoy. Policies that greatly reduce carbon emissions, for instance, will reduce profits in fossil fuel–dependent industries today and in the years ahead. Burning less fossil fuel will reduce both profits for oil companies and the value of the oil reserves they own. Higher costs of production not only lower incomes in developing countries in the present but also reduce growth and income in the future. As the value we place on the future increases, the environment becomes more important to the winners—but the costs of complying with greater regulations become more important to the losers as well.

Coupled with the problem of bargaining over the future is the equally difficult problem of representing future generations in current decision making. After all, no political system possesses a mechanism that represents the interests of future populations to the present generation. Given the notoriously short attention spans of politicians, often driven only by the next election, who in any political system represents future citizens and voters?

We know little about the interests of future generations. Although we can extrapolate from our current preferences, many factors can intervene. We do not know what the future rate of technological change will be, which may make various environmental problems easier or harder to solve than we expect. Assuming that wealth and incomes continue to rise, we do not know how future citizens may evaluate yet more consumption of physical goods, like cars, relative to consumption of intangible goods, like the scenic beauty of an unspoiled coastline or old-growth forest.

Even if we could estimate future interests, there is no one at present to advocate for those future generations in any systematic way. Environmental TANs often claim that they are representing future generations, but their political clout is still limited. Future generations neither vote now nor pay membership dues to TANs that can, in turn, press governments to change policy. Younger climate activists, such as Greta Thunberg, claim to speak for their generation and others in the future and are attempting to shame politicians into greater action. This new movement was gaining momentum before the COVID-19 pandemic displaced it from the political agenda. TANs and young activists can make normative arguments on behalf of future generations, but this is at best an indirect and significantly weaker form of representation than if the future citizens' votes and voices could be heard today. As a consequence, we are bargaining with ourselves on behalf of future generations—and it is perhaps not surprising that we usually let ourselves win.

How Can Institutions Promote International Environmental Cooperation?

Within countries, governments play an important role in controlling environmental degradation. Producing public goods and regulating the use of common-pool resources are fundamental roles for any government. In all but the so-called failed states, governments tax citizens and use the revenue to provide a variety of public goods, including national defense, police and fire protection, public infrastructure, public health, education, and, of course, environmental protection. Governments also impose restrictions on automobile emissions, the dumping of toxic waste, oil drilling, and so on that aim to improve environmental quality and encourage people and firms to use scarce resources more efficiently. Government is not a perfect solution. Some governments are too responsive to polluters and fail to enact sufficient environmental protections. But government's ability to allocate resources authoritatively helps mitigate collective action problems that would otherwise make environmental cooperation even more difficult.

National laws and policies are the primary means for implementing international environmental cooperation. Even if states create international institutions, most of their provisions are enforced authoritatively through national legislation and policy. For instance, the members of the Convention on International Trade in Endangered Species of Wild Fauna and Flora (CITES), one of the earliest and most successful environmental treaties, make decisions at the international level, but national governments must enforce trade restrictions on endangered species, generally through their customs authority and their equivalent of a fish and wildlife service.

Relative to authoritative government regulations on domestic externalities, international cooperation between sovereign states to mitigate transnational externalities will always be more difficult and tenuous. States free ride on one another's efforts and overexploit their shared resources. Institutions are not a panacea. Without interests in environmental cooperation and effective bargains between countries, international institutions cannot by themselves create success. Institutions can be only as strong as their members' interests in cooperation. Nonetheless, as we saw in Chapter 2, international institutions facilitate cooperation among states committed to a cleaner environment by providing information, setting standards, and verifying compliance.

As we discussed in Chapter 11, international agreements can be structured as either hard or soft law. The majority of environmental treaties, including the most successful ones, have been structured as soft law. While hard law looks attractive, because it contains penalties for noncompliance, it is often difficult to get countries to agree to it, and if countries do agree, they often make more conservative

Transnational environmental problems like climate change are primarily combated by the actions and regulations of individual national governments. Many states have passed laws setting vehicle emissions standards as part of their efforts to fight climate change.

commitments than they might otherwise make under soft law. Soft law can often be aspirational—setting goals, such as keeping global warming within 2°C and trying for 1.5°C in the Paris Agreement. What distinguishes an effective treaty like CITES is not enforcement per se but the precision of the commitments it requires. As relatively hard law, it has elaborate appendices that enumerate clear limits on the trade in thousands of specific species.

The virtue of aspirational soft law is that it encourages countries to reach for long-term, difficult solutions. It also allows them to take in new information as it arises and adapt their methods and goals accordingly. Since most environmental agreements are based on scientific determination of a problem, progress requires constantly updating policy as the science advances. Richard Benedick was the lead U.S. negotiator for the Vienna Convention and the Montreal Protocol. As he said in a speech on the protocol's twentieth anniversary, not only was the agreement about taking preventive action (negotiations began when the problem of CFCs was theorized but not proven), but "because of the still evolving science [it was] deliberately designed to be a dynamic and flexible process."[34]

The modern environmental movement began in the 1960s and is often dated from the 1962 publication of Rachel Carson's book *Silent Spring*, which warned of the effects of toxic chemicals on the environment. The movement built on a century of growing awareness about the need for conservation: organizations to protect birdlife and the first national parks date back to the nineteenth century. The first international agreement, the Ramsar Convention on Wetlands of International Importance, concerned the threat posed by habitat loss to the global migratory patterns of birds. Negotiations began with an international conference that included not just governments but also NGOs, including TANs and other experts. The decision to negotiate an agreement was informed by the advice of the International Waterfowl and Wetlands Research Bureau, a science-oriented TAN now called Wetlands International.[35]

The Ramsar negotiation and its use of scientific information to inform both the decision to draft a convention and the contents of the agreement established a pattern for future environmental agreements. CITES grew out of a similar

34. Richard E. Benedick, "Science Inspiring Diplomacy: The Improbable Montreal Protocol," in *Twenty Years of Ozone Decline: Proceedings of the Symposium for the 20th Anniversary of the Montreal Protocol*, ed. Christos Zerefos, Georgios Contopoulos, and Gregory Skalkeas, 13–19 (Dordrecht, Netherlands: Springer, 2009).

35. Ramsar, "History of the Ramsar Convention," www.ramsar.org/about/history-of-the-ramsar-convention; and Wetlands International, "Our History," www.wetlands.org/about-us/our-history (accessed 7/08/20).

meeting of the International Union for Conservation of Nature (IUCN). The IUCN has a particularly interesting structure, with a membership that includes national governments, NGOs, and individual scientists. Its scientific committees research and deliberate to determine which species are threatened, endangered, or extinct. At its 1963 meeting, the IUCN membership agreed to negotiate a treaty on trade in endangered species. The treaty was completed 10 years later, and it ultimately came into force in 1975. CITES itself has committees to determine which species should be protected, but much of the scientific work continues to be conducted by IUCN members.

Several later agreements required the formation of new international informational bodies to inform the treaty negotiations. In his detailed book on the negotiations for the Vienna and Montreal agreements, Benedick describes the need to find global scientific consensus, especially because American scientists had taken the lead in the research and were communicating much more closely with the U.S. government than with other countries. In 1977, UNEP initiated a new body for sharing scientific findings and drawing consensus conclusions called the Coordinating Committee on the Ozone Layer (CCOL). It was not until 1981 that the Governing Council of the UNEP authorized the start of negotiations, which began the following year.[36]

A similar approach was taken in addressing climate change. In 1988, UNEP and the World Meteorological Organization (WMO) established the Intergovernmental Panel on Climate Change (IPCC) to bring together scientists from around the world to analyze and evaluate what was known about climate science. The IPCC's first assessment, published in 1990, contributed directly to the negotiations of the UNFCCC, which concluded in 1992. Its second assessment, published in 1995, set the stage for the Kyoto Protocol. Each assessment, involving thousands of scientists, has contributed to the negotiations cycle.[37]

Without solid scientific data—including data from the social sciences, which the IPCC includes in its reports on mitigation and on impacts and adaptation—it is difficult to know how to adapt to change. Similarly, countries need a well-informed deliberative process to consider how to respond to changing conditions. The Paris Agreement continued this approach with a five-year review process. It is widely acknowledged that the first set of country commitments is not sufficient to reach a 2°C target, much less the 1.5°C aspiration set forth in the agreement. The hope

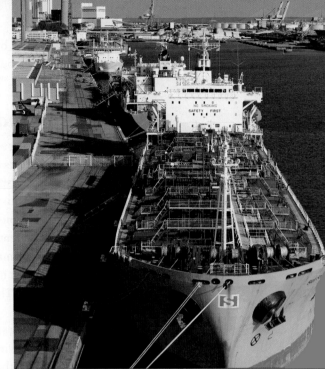

The effectiveness of environmental regulations may depend on how easy it is to verify compliance. A change in the rules related to dumping oil at sea made it much easier to check whether ship captains were adhering to the standard, and it increased compliance rates to over 98 percent.

---

36. Richard Elliot Benedick, *Ozone Diplomacy: New Directions in Safeguarding the Planet*, expanded ed. (Cambridge, MA: Harvard University Press, 1998).

37. Intergovernmental Panel on Climate Change, "History of the IPCC," www.ipcc.ch/about/history (accessed 7/08/20).

of the framers is that, by requiring a scientific review and evaluation every five years, countries will be encouraged to take on more ambitious goals through their repeated interactions.[38]

Setting Standards and Verifying Compliance

In addition to setting aspirations and providing information, international environmental institutions can also support cooperation by establishing standards of behavior to which states can be held accountable. Although each issue area and agreement has unique features and a unique history, countries often negotiate framework conventions that establish general principles on which all states can agree. The Convention on Biological Diversity (CBD), for instance, states that diversity is "a common concern of humankind" that all countries have a duty to protect, and it includes additional principles for the development and use of genetic resources. The UNFCCC, aimed at reducing carbon emissions, has a similar structure.

After establishing such frameworks, states proceed in some issue areas to negotiate more stringent environmental safeguards specifying limits on emissions, banning certain practices, or otherwise defining unacceptable behavior. The CBD, for example, has two much more specific protocols, the Cartagena Protocol (on biosafety) and the Nagoya Protocol (on genetic material), and, as we have discussed, the UNFCCC first advanced with the Kyoto Protocol and then with the Paris Agreement.[39]

Restrictions on the intentional discharge of crude oil at sea demonstrate how the clarity and transparency of the agreed-upon standards matter in supporting cooperation.[40] After a tanker delivers its cargo of crude oil, an average of 300 tons remains on board, stuck to the cargo tank walls. Before regulations were put into effect, ships would clean their tanks on the return voyage by pumping seawater into the tanks and discharging the oily slop back into the ocean. With many ships making multiple trips each year, oil tankers were intentionally discharging approximately 1 million tons of oil into the ocean annually.

In the International Convention for the Prevention of Pollution of the Sea by Oil, adopted in 1954, countries first set standards that permitted tankers to continue cleaning their tanks with seawater but mandated that discharges be no more than 100 parts oil per million parts seawater. The standard was subsequently tightened in 1969. Nonetheless, both the looser and the tighter standards were widely ignored. Oil company surveys from the 1970s show that tankers owned by the oil companies themselves averaged discharges of 3 times the legal limit and that independently owned tankers averaged discharges of 30 times the legal limit.

---

38. Joeri Rogelj, Michel den Elzen, Niklas Höhne, Taryn Fransen, et al., "Paris Agreement Climate Proposals Need a Boost to Keep Warming Well below 2° C," *Nature* 534, no. 7609 (2016): 631–39.

39. A second pattern of negotiations and agreements is simply to establish a procedural regime with a commission that makes annual decisions about regulatory rules. The IWC is an example of this type of organization. On patterns of agreement formation, see Oran R. Young, *International Governance: Protecting the Environment in a Stateless Society* (Ithaca, NY: Cornell University Press, 1994), esp. chap. 4.

40. This case is drawn from Ronald B. Mitchell, "Regime Design Matters: Intentional Oil Pollution and Treaty Compliance," *International Organization* 48, no. 3 (Summer 1994): 425–58.

In 1978, countries adopted new standards requiring all tankers to use new, more expensive technologies that minimized discharges by preventing the oil and seawater from coming into contact or by using crude oil itself to wash the tanks. These new technologies were required for all tankers built after 1982, and all existing tankers had to be retrofitted by 1985. Despite the greater cost, compliance rates rose to over 98 percent by 1991.

What explains the difference in compliance with these standards? Since cleaning the tanks with seawater usually took place on the open ocean, far from other observers, ship captains could act with impunity and ignore mandated discharge limits—and it appears that they usually did. The new technologies, in contrast, required the installation of clearly observable equipment on every ship. When a ship entered port, it could easily be verified whether the tanker met with the new standard. The ease of verification forced tanker captains to alter their behavior, virtually ending the intentional discharge of crude oil into the ocean.

For similar reasons, complete bans are easier to verify than restrictions on emissions; this fact helps account for the success of the Vienna Convention and subsequent amendments outlawing CFCs. With CFCs, as with bans on whaling and the killing of endangered wildlife, any possession or trade in prohibited substances is sufficient evidence of noncompliance. Enforcement efforts can then focus on tracking down any sales of CFCs (or elephant ivory, rhinoceros horns, and other banned goods). For example, soon after CFC bans went into effect, the black market grew to about 20 percent of prior consumption. In 1995, the illegal trade in CFCs through the Port of Miami and along the U.S.-Mexico border was second in value only to trade in illegal drugs, prompting a unilateral effort by the United States to block the smuggling. The clear rules banning CFCs enabled this crackdown.

Restrictions on carbon emissions are harder to enforce, especially when many independent agents, such as firms, are potentially contributing to the problem. Evidence of some carbon in the atmosphere is not evidence of cheating. To demonstrate that a country is failing to live up to its carbon-reduction commitments, emissions must be monitored consistently over long periods—a much more daunting task.

In addition to their roles in official monitoring and reporting, environmental TANs have been central in verifying governments' compliance with international environmental accords. Most environmental agreements depend on self-reporting of emissions. As we noted in Chapter 2, self-reporting is effective only when reports are subject to external verification. TANs often play the role of fire alarm, sounding the alert when governments violate agreements or fail to report accurately. By calling attention to failures at living up to the letter and, sometimes, the spirit of the agreements, TANs assist member states in identifying and bringing pressure to bear on noncomplying governments. The current dense network of committed environmental activists relieves governments of much of the responsibility for monitoring one another's performance, thereby facilitating and enhancing the prospects for successful cooperation.

TAN monitoring has been prominent in the whaling industry since the IWC instituted a complete ban on whaling in 1982.[41] After phasing out its commercial operations, Japan has continued to engage in scientific whaling, which aims to demonstrate that whale populations are robust enough to permit some commercial whaling. Much of the whale meat nonetheless ends up for sale in Japanese fish markets. Before the International Court of Justice (ICJ) declared that the country's scientific whaling program was illegal, Japan caught approximately 800 whales per year for self-declared scientific purposes, about the same as Norway's commercial catch and all aboriginal whaling catches combined (which are exempt from the ban). Japan has declared that it intends to continue its scientific whaling program despite the ICJ's ruling. Recently, of the three nations that still whale, Japan has left the IWC and resumed commercial whaling,[42] while Iceland has moved toward stopping whaling altogether.[43]

Although it is impossible to police the entire ocean, the limited scope of scientific whaling allows NGOs to track the whaling fleets, observe their operations, often film the killings, and catalog each whale caught. Each season, ships from Greenpeace, an international environmental action group, have shadowed the Japanese fleet, sometimes attempting to disrupt its operations by harassing the factory ships and placing themselves between the hunters and their prey. Countries report their scientific whaling activities to the IWC every year, and as a result of these efforts by the NGOs, relatively accurate independent verification of these self-reports is possible.

Facilitating Decision Making

Effective environmental agreements provide a venue for analytical deliberation and an infrastructure for reaching decisions and then carrying them out. The core decision-making structure of almost all the major environmental agreements, including the CBD, UNFCCC, and Vienna Convention, is a Conference of Parties (COP)—meetings of the member states generally held annually but more often if necessary.

Rule changes, new protocols, and other decisions under these conventions can take place only at a COP. In the run-up to the Paris Agreement, the UNFCCC held preliminary COPs four or five times a year. In addition, complex agreements, like the UNFCCC and the CBD, have numerous smaller groups and subsidiary bodies that deal with policy and technical issues and take their recommendations to the COP. Some treaties have much more specific technical committees; CITES, for

---

41. Not all opposition to whaling is conducted by international groups. There is, in fact, a steadfast group of Japanese activists who have been opposing Japanese whaling and dolphin hunting (an additional issue that raises international concern) for decades. The Japanese conservationist Sakae Hemmi founded the Elsa Nature Conservancy in Tsukuba, Japan, in 1976 to promote domestic activism aimed at protecting species from whales to elephants.

42. Fynn Holm, "After Withdrawal from the IWC: The Future of Japanese Whaling," *The Asia-Pacific Journal: Japan Focus*, February 15, 2019, www.asia-pacificresearch.com/after-withdrawal-from-the-iwc -the-future-of-japanese-whaling/5628514 (accessed 2/23/21).

43. Ariella Simke, "Iceland to Stop Killing Whales in 2020, Choosing to Watch Them Instead," *Forbes*, May 10, 2020, www.forbes.com/sites/ariellasimke/2020/05/10/iceland-to-stop-killing-whales-in-2020 -choosing-to-watch-them-instead (accessed 2/23/21).

instance, has species-focused technical bodies and a connection to the IUCN. The institution of the UNFCCC was essential to reaching the Paris Agreement; without an existing forum and a history of ongoing negotiations, it is unlikely that states would have been able to make the breakthroughs necessary to achieve this landmark accord.

In addition to COPs, most treaties have a secretariat. A secretariat provides a professional staff to administer the treaties' provisions and prepare for meetings. UNEP, for example, acts as the secretariat for a number of treaties, including the Vienna Convention/Montreal Protocol. The UNFCCC has an independent secretariat located in Bonn, Germany. Some smaller treaties have no permanent staff and operate instead with a coordinating committee. One country will also act as the repository for the treaty and is likely to carry out some coordinating functions in the absence of a secretariat.

The amount of permanent institutional infrastructure in place depends heavily on the complexity of the treaty and agreement among members. Treaties like CITES and the Montreal Protocol have among the most complex and institutionalized infrastructures of any treaties. Simple treaties like the Stockholm Convention rely on decision making at COPs, enforcement by each signatory country, and coordination among national points of contact.

Agreements vary in how they provide for rule changes and in the level of support they require from member states to enact these changes. Many conventions require consensus, which is generally defined as unanimous support, but even then conventions may leave themselves some flexibility. The UNFCCC states that "every effort" will be made to make decisions by consensus, but failing that, a three-fourths majority can approve amendments to the convention. This fail-safe has ensured in recent years that some agreements, including the Copenhagen Accord and the Paris Agreement, were not defeated by one or two holdout countries.

Environmental TANs also provide important policy input on international agreements, creating nearly unique international public-private partnerships that facilitate cooperation on environmental issues. The UN Conference on Environment and Development (the so-called Earth Summit, held in Rio de Janeiro in 1992)—which produced conventions on biodiversity, climate change, and desertification—hosted 2,400 NGO participants within the main meeting site and an additional 17,000 at a parallel conference.

Observer groups have become the norm throughout the UN system. They try to influence negotiations both through direct lobbying of delegates and through side events where they provide information, analysis, and suggested approaches to the questions under debate. They also act as observers, attending formal sessions and reporting on the results. Since Rio, organizations have preferred to be inside the negotiation hall rather than at the parallel event. This preference led to substantial crowding at Copenhagen, where the 40,000 participants (including government representatives, NGOs, business organizations, and press) exceeded the capacity of the facility.

Since then, the UNFCCC has placed quotas on NGOs (which in UN parlance include TANs and local NGOs, businesses and universities). Nevertheless, there were some 7,000 participants representing over 1,100 UN-defined NGOs at Paris,

France and other nations celebrated the Paris Agreement as a landmark of international cooperation to combat climate change. However, whether the agreement can successfully compel countries to reduce their emissions remains to be seen, and initial signs are not positive.

and many thousands more attended the separate parallel event.[44] These groups include the types of TANs and local environmental NGOs that we have discussed, but they also include business representatives, who play an important role in representing economic interests to their respective delegations.

Resolving Disputes

A critical aspect of any agreement is providing mechanisms for dealing with conflict. Governing the commons requires countries to come together to find common ground. By anticipating repeated interaction in which countries can raise concerns and seek to address them, the structure of meetings provides a venue where conflicts can be addressed over time. As we have seen in this chapter, while some of the simple environmental agreements were negotiated quickly, many have required a decade or even two to arrive at global consensus.

International environmental agreements generally lack formal dispute resolution mechanisms. Rather, most treaties depend on the good faith of the member countries themselves to work out disagreements within a multilateral setting. The Montreal Protocol to the Vienna Convention, however, was the first global environmental agreement to develop and use a noncompliance response system, located in its Implementation Committee. This mechanism remains focused on facilitating, not enforcing, compliance. During the 1990s, when it became clear that several countries from the former Soviet Union (including Belarus, Russia, and Ukraine), as well as some developing countries, were not in full compliance with their CFC emissions obligations, the Implementation Committee urged and finally approved new CFC phaseout plans. Additional financial resources from other industrialized countries, the Global Environmental Facility, and the World Bank helped facilitate compliance.

44. United Nations, "Report of the United Nations Conference on Environment and Development, 3–4 June 1992," https://undocs.org/en/A/CONF.151/26/Rev.1(vol.I); and United Nations Framework Convention on Climate Change, "Conference of the Parties, Twenty-First Session, Paris, 30 November to 11 December 2015," December 1, 2015, http://unfccc.int/resource/docs/2015/cop21/eng/misc02p01.pdf (accessed 2/23/21).

The Kyoto Protocol tried to go further with complex enforcement mechanisms, but as we have seen, that approach did not prove popular. At its root, any environmental treaty depends on the consent of the participants. There is no supranational government to enforce decisions on those who choose not to participate. Treaties like the Montreal Protocol have proved successful because the most enthusiastic member states were able to offer sufficient carrots and sticks to the more reluctant ones. The Paris Agreement relies more on normative pressure for all countries to join than on dispute resolution. It remains to be seen how effective this approach will be.

Conclusion: Can Global Environmental Cooperation Succeed?

We began this chapter by asking why international environmental cooperation is so hard to achieve. To answer that puzzle and tie the threads of our analysis together, we can compare the relative success of cooperation on ozone depletion and the much slower progress on global climate change. Ozone depletion and global climate change became issues of international concern at around the same time. The first convention on ozone depletion was negotiated in 1985, the first on global climate change in 1992.

As described in "What Shaped Our World?" on p. 576, concerns about ozone depletion were effectively addressed within a few years, as countries cooperated relatively quickly to curtail the production of CFCs. Efforts to address climate change, in contrast, still face major hurdles today. What accounts for the difference in the two outcomes? How can the analytical tools of interests, interactions, and institutions help us understand why we find successful international cooperation in the first case and only limited cooperation to date in the second?

At its root, the answer to our puzzle is quite simple. People's daily actions create significant externalities for the environment and one another. These externalities, in turn, produce severe problems of collective action. Individuals and countries would like to benefit from a cleaner environment but would also like others to bear the costs of protecting environmental quality. Both the stratospheric ozone layer and the quantity of greenhouse gases in the atmosphere are global public goods. Although everyone benefits from a thicker ozone layer and fewer greenhouse gases, and everyone is harmed by CFC and carbon emissions, the fact that we all experience these effects may be precisely the problem. Since we all share the benefits of a healthy atmosphere and we all face private costs in changing our behavior, we all attempt to free ride on one another, hoping to reap the benefits of a greener environment without having to give up our current lifestyles. In turn, even when free riding can be overcome, there is still hard bargaining between industries and countries over who should bear the costs of changes in policy.

In the case of ozone depletion, the gains from a ban far exceeded the costs of change. When the ban was implemented in 1989, the cost of transitioning to new chemical alternatives was estimated to be $27 billion by 2075. Meanwhile, the Environmental Protection Agency calculated that the reduction in skin cancer for Americans alone would save $6.5 trillion in medical costs over the same time period.[45] Some of these estimates have since changed, but the important point is that at decision time, the expected benefits far outweighed the costs.

In the case of climate change, however, there are large, immediate, and continuing costs for reducing carbon emissions, while the benefits are long-term and difficult to calculate. Changes to the global climate are complex, and impacts will vary tremendously by locality. In 2006, the British economist Nicholas Stern published an extensive review of the economics of climate change. It estimated that, even if global temperature is stabilized at no more than 2°C, climate change will cost the world 5–10 percent of its total gross domestic product (GDP) each year, with the costs being considerably higher in many poor countries. By contrast, the Stern team suggested that the transition to clean energy would cost more on the order of 1 percent of global GDP.[46] Newer research also shows that climate costs are lowest when warming is limited to below 2°C.[47]

If we just look at the numbers, mitigation still looks less expensive than the impacts. The difference is not quite as stark, however, as the several-hundred-times rate of return that the world achieved by rapidly eliminating ODS from use. In reality, the Montreal Protocol was an amazing bargain, one not likely to be repeated often. Moreover, it touched a very specific part of the economy, and the fear, particularly of skin cancer, was also specific. Climate change touches almost every part of every economy, and its impacts are diverse and diffuse. The costs of climate change are already happening. Scientists know that the probability of droughts and floods and other extreme climate events has already increased. But they are very cautious and can speak in only probabilistic terms about whether climate change "caused" any specific event.

Although both issues involve collective action problems, cooperation in addressing ozone depletion was easier to achieve because of the highly concentrated nature of the CFC industry; it included relatively few firms and countries, with most production and usage occurring in just a handful of developed states. The smaller number of parties involved lowered the costs of collective action and made effective cooperation possible. The United States enjoyed a preeminent position in the industry as both the largest producer and the largest consumer of CFCs. Its leadership on the issue was decisive.

In addition, the problem of collective action is compounded by the distributional consequences of alternative policy solutions, especially in the case of global climate change. Every policy creates winners and losers, but the benefits of eliminating CFCs were clear. In the case of climate change, hydrocarbon fuels are the lifeblood of modern economies, and the interests that would lose from any significant change in policy are large and politically powerful. As renewables producers grow in size and political power in many economies, this is starting to change. Moreover, the International Energy Agency now believes that both the United States and China

45. Litfin, *Ozone Discourses*, 128.

46. "Stern Review: The Economics of Climate Change: Summary of Conclusions," http://webarchive. nationalarchives.gov.uk/20100407163608/http://www.hm-treasury.gov.uk/d/Summary_of_Conclusions. pdf (accessed 2/23/21).

47. Nicole Glanemann, Sven N. Willner, and Anders Levermann, "Paris Climate Agreement Passes the Cost-Benefit Test," *Nature Communications* 11, no. 110 (2020). See also Julia Rosen, "The Science of Climate Change Explained: Facts, Evidence, and Proof," *New York Times*, April 23, 2021, www.nytimes.com /article/climate-change-global-warming-faq.html (accessed 4/23/21).

have decoupled their economies from energy, meaning that they can see economic growth without concomitant growth in energy consumption.[48] Yet, as seen in former president Trump's calls to rescue and preserve jobs in the U.S. coal industry, vested interests continue to play a role in setting environmental policy.

Finally, international institutions have played a role in facilitating and codifying cooperation in both ozone depletion and global climate change. Negotiations have occurred within meetings of global leaders, and the agreements reached at these meetings have been institutionalized into conventions and subsequently amended in various protocols. Accords on both issues began with conventions outlining broad principles of cooperation and then moved on in subsequent agreements to substantive cuts. Greater cooperation on ozone depletion has been helped by relatively clear rules reducing and, later, banning specific chemicals. The rules governing reductions in carbon and other greenhouse gases, in contrast, are less well articulated, perhaps because the underlying issues remain highly contested.

Without doubt, the road from the UNFCCC signing to the accord reached in Paris was very long and exceedingly winding. But despite the greater complexity of the issues, the challenges of collective action, and the potential costs of mitigation, the global community has agreed on a path forward to reduce greenhouse gases. Since rejoining the Paris Agreement, President Biden has attempted to reestablish the United States as a leader in combating global climate change and build a coalition of like-minded states to reduce carbon emissions. How successful these efforts will be, however, remains to be seen.

The past five decades have seen the development of a complex network of international environmental law and institutions. As we have discussed, these can be relatively easy to negotiate and administer, or they can be among the most complex and challenging of agreements. They involve the management of a global commons, resources that we all share and that no country or set of countries can control. This process began by looking at examples of agreements in other issue areas, but it has developed a pattern of its own, including the heavy reliance on scientific bodies to inform negotiators and the need for flexible and adaptive agreements.

Most environmental agreements cannot rely on the heavy hand of international government to enforce their rules. Countries must come willingly, perceiving that these agreements are in their own best interests. That is all the more reason to use adaptive architecture: countries' interests change over time. As we have started to experience the real costs of climate change and to realize the benefits of cleaner energy and greater forest protection, global support for the Paris Agreement has grown. We can also see real success in other agreements. The ozone hole has begun to heal. Several whale species are now back to their pre-exploitation levels. That said, the world is on a precarious course. Even if the NDCs in the Paris accord are completely implemented, global temperatures will rise at least 1.5°C. Even at that level, the effects of climate change will be substantial and potentially catastrophic. Whether countries truly rise to the challenge remains an open question.

---

48. International Energy Agency, "Decoupling of Global Emissions and Economic Growth Confirmed," March 16, 2016, www.iea.org/newsroom/news/2016/march/decoupling-of-global-emissions-and -economic-growth-confirmed.html (accessed 2/23/21).

Study Tool Kit

Interests, Interactions, and Institutions in Context

- Despite common interests in the quality of the environment, the interactions among individuals and countries suffer from problems of collective action and free riding. This is especially true for public goods (global climate) and common-pool resources (fisheries). The result is less overall environmental cooperation than individuals and even countries themselves collectively desire.

- Small groups of actors, one of whom is substantially larger than the others and all of whom interact frequently on multiple issues, are most likely to cooperate effectively on international issues relating to the environment.

- Distributional conflicts within and between countries can impede progress in mitigating harmful environmental practices. Individuals, groups, and states have conflicting interests in who should bear the costs of policy change. How environmental policies distribute these costs affects how likely actors are to cooperate successfully on issues relating to the environment.

- International institutions facilitate environmental cooperation primarily by enhancing information and verifying compliance. There is now a wide range of agreements covering many environmental problems. TANs and other NGOs now play an essential role in monitoring compliance with environmental agreements. These accords, however, can only be as effective as the underlying cooperation between countries permits.

Key Terms

global climate change, p. 567

United Nations Framework Convention on Climate Change (UNFCCC), p. 567

Paris Agreement, p. 567

tragedy of the commons, p. 567

public goods, p. 569

common-pool resources, p. 569

nonexcludable goods, p. 570

nonrival goods, p. 570

Kyoto Protocol, p. 571

Vienna Convention for the Protection of the Ozone Layer, p. 574

Montreal Protocol, p. 574

cap-and-trade system, p. 574

nationally determined contribution (NDC), p. 575

externalities, p. 581

For Further Reading

Bechtel, Michael M., Federica Genovese, and Kenneth F. Scheve. "Interests, Norms and Support for the Provision of Global Public Goods: The Case of Climate Co operation." *British Journal of Political Science* 49, no. 4 (2019): 1333–55. Examines individual support by sector of employment for environmental regulation.

Colgan, Jeff D., Jessica F. Green, and Thomas N. Hale. "Asset Revaluation and the Existential Politics of Climate Change." *International Organization* 75 (2020). Offers a dynamic theory of climate politics based on the present and future revaluation of assets as a contest between winners and losers.

Cullenward, Danny, and David G. Victor. *Making Climate Policy Work.* Cambridge: Polity, 2020. Criticizes widely touted market-based solutions to climate change and advocates for greater regulation and industrial policy.

Dietz, Thomas, Elinor Ostrom, and Paul C. Stern. "The Struggle to Govern the Commons." *Science* 302, no. 5652 (2003): 1907–12. Lays out a framework for addressing the tragedy of the commons in international agreements.

Gore, Albert. *An Inconvenient Sequel: Truth to Power.* New York: Rodale, 2017. Highlights the dangers of global warming and the technologies to address it.

Green, Jessica F. "Transnational Delegation in Global Environmental Governance: When Do Non-state Actors Govern?" *Regulation & Governance* 12, no. 2 (2018): 263–76. Provides a historical and theoretical overview of when and what governance functions are delegated to private, transnational actors.

Henson, Robert. *The Thinking Person's Guide to Climate Change.* 2nd ed. Boston: American Meteorological Society, 2019. Produced by one of the most venerable atmospheric science organizations, provides an excellent overview for nonscientists of the facts and debates around climate change.

Hickmann, Thomas. "The Reconfiguration of Authority in Global Climate Governance." *International Studies Review* 19, no. 3 (2017): 430–51. Reviews alternative governance schemes for the global environment and how they interact at the nonstate, state, and international levels.

Klein, Naomi. *This Changes Everything: Capitalism vs. the Climate.* New York: Simon and Schuster, 2014. Roots the problem of climate change deep in capitalism as an economic system.

Shellenberger, Michael. *Apocalypse Never: Why Environmental Alarmism Hurts Us All.* New York: Harper, 2020. Written by a lifelong environmentalist who acknowledges that climate change is real and challenging, offers a skeptical review of some of the more dire claims made by climate activists.

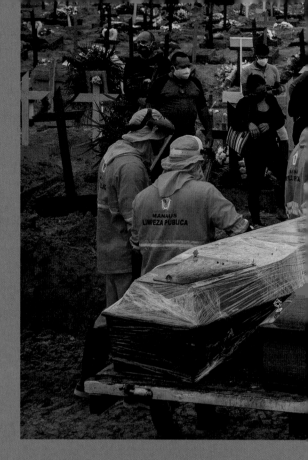

14

Challenges to the Global Order

THE PUZZLE *In the coming decades, the international system will face challenges from actors seeking weapons of mass destruction or the ability to disrupt computer networks, the rise of a new superpower in Asia, and growing opposition to economic globalization. Can political science tell us what the future will hold?*

Above: As the COVID-19 virus spread worldwide, over 2 million people perished, straining medical systems and societies around the globe. Countries responded individually to the pandemic, but international cooperation remained weak.

608

The COVID-19 virus originated in Wuhan, China, in late 2019. The virus quickly diffused around the globe and by the end of 2020 had infected over 75 million people and killed nearly 2 million. In the United States alone, the virus infected almost 18 million people and killed over 318,000 in its first year, rivaling the number of U.S. deaths sustained in all wars fought during the twentieth century.

China informed the World Health Organization (WHO) on January 3 about a cluster of pneumonia cases of unknown origin, and it released the genomic sequence of the virus on January 10.[1] The Chinese government shut down Wuhan on January 23, 2020, to limit the spread of the virus, but the disease had already begun to diffuse internationally. Within a month, cases were reported in 21 countries.[2] After initially praising China's response, U.S. president Donald Trump later criticized China for delaying and misrepresenting the extent of the virus and faulted the WHO for being too deferential to Beijing in its handling of the pandemic.[3] President Trump later declared that he was cutting U.S. funding to and terminating the United States' relationship with the organization, a decision that was reversed when President Joseph Biden came into office in January 2021.[4] Given the ongoing failure of national governments to coordinate an effective international response to the pandemic, it is not entirely clear that faster notification by China or action by the WHO would have mitigated the virus's spread.

Each country responded to the spread of the COVID-19 virus in its own way. Some, like New Zealand, shut down fast and "hard," closing their borders and restricting movement and economic activities within their own populations. Others, like Sweden, decided to rely on individual responsibility and wait for "herd immunity," which arises when enough people have gotten the virus and recovered that

---

1. World Health Organization, "Listing of WHO's Response to COVID-19," June 29, 2020, www.who.int/news/item/29-06-2020-covidtimeline (accessed 12/13/20).

2. Michelle L. Holshue, Chas DeBolt, Scott Lindquist, Kathy H. Lofy, et al., "First Case of 2019 Novel Coronavirus in the United States," *New England Journal of Medicine* 382 (2020): 929–36.

3. Javier C. Hernández, "Trump Slammed the W.H.O. over Coronavirus. He's Not Alone." *New York Times*, May 29, 2020, www.nytimes.com/2020/04/08/world/asia/trump-who-coronavirus-china.html (accessed 12/21/20). See also Jon Greenberg, "Fact-checking Donald Trump's Criticism of the World Health Organization," Politifact, April 16, 2020, www.politifact.com/article/2020/apr/16/fact-checking-donald-trumps-criticism-world-health (accessed 12/21/20).

4. Berkeley Lovelace Jr., "Trump Says the U.S. Will Cut Ties with World Health Organization," CNBC, May 29, 2020, www.cnbc.com/2020/05/29/trump-says-the-us-will-cut-ties-with-world-health-organization.html (accessed 12/21/20).

transmission to uninfected people naturally slows. Still others, including the United States, decentralized further and allowed states, provinces or even cities to formulate their own responses. With this varying patchwork of national policies, there were very few attempts at international coordination.

Countries aimed to produce vaccines against the virus at "warp speed," as the United States' vaccine development program was called, again with little international coordination. Indeed, there was more than a little competition between countries over who could get a vaccine to market first. Despite this lack of interstate coordination, transnational nongovernmental organizations such as GAVI, with funding from various international organizations, national governments, and private philanthropists, have taken a leadership role in coordinating a response in developing nations.[5]

The global pandemic brought into sharp relief the existence of global challenges that demand robust international cooperation.[6] The people of the world share interests not just in preventing the spread of deadly pathogens but also in halting catastrophic environmental changes and preventing conflicts with modern weapons that have the potential to wipe out millions of people. In some respects, the current world is a better place than ever before to address such challenges. A rich set of international institutions has developed in the 70 years since World War II, constituting what we call the postwar order. At the same time, this order faces a number of challenges that call into question whether it can continue to meet the needs of the future. In this chapter, we revisit the postwar order to understand what it entails and consider three main challenges that are likely to shape its future.

The first challenge comes from states and groups whose interests are hostile to those of the United States and its allies and who have sought to resist by developing weapons of mass destruction (WMD)—primarily nuclear but also chemical or biological weapons—and cyber weapons that can disrupt computer networks around the globe.

The second challenge comes from the rise of states that might seek to displace the United States as the global leader and alter the rules of the international order in their favor. Foremost among these states is China, whose rapid economic growth will soon make it the world's largest economy.

A third challenge comes from the backlash to globalization exemplified by the rise of populist parties. There has long been resistance to the economic aspects of globalization from people hurt by exposure to international markets, but the success of populist movements in recent years reflects concerns about threats to national identity and sovereignty.

Thinking Analytically about the Future of World Politics

As we have done throughout this book, we analyze these challenges by thinking in terms of interests, interactions, and institutions. The international institutions and patterns of interaction established after World War II benefit some actors at the expense of others. U.S. military dominance and leadership of global institutions threatens states and groups whose interests are hostile to the United States or who seek greater influence over the rules. Economic institutions that favor open markets threaten the jobs and wages of those who compete with foreign imports and the cultural interests of those who dislike foreign influences.

In each case, conflicting interests give rise to interactions between actors seeking to change the system and actors that benefit from the existing system. Efforts by states and groups to acquire WMD have brought them into conflict both with the United States and with international regimes designed to limit the spread of these technologies. The rise of China has brought it into tension with the United States and U.S. allies in East Asia, leading to a risk of war. The growing strength of groups opposed to globalization has created conflict with other parties, countries, and institutions that favor economic liberalization. Even when faced with common challenges, like climate change or a pandemic, countries insist on the right to respond in line with their own self-defined national interests. How these interactions play out will not only affect important outcomes like war and peace, the spread of nuclear weapons, and the openness of the world's major economies, but it will also shape the nature of the international order, if any, that emerges in the coming decades.

5. See www.gavi.org (accessed 12/23/20).

6. Tana Johnson, "Ordinary Patterns in an Extraordinary Crisis: How International Relations Makes Sense of the COVID-19 Pandemic," *International Organization* 74, no. S1 (2020): E148–68.

The Postwar Order and Its Challenges

What we call the *postwar order* is defined by a number of developments that took root in the aftermath of World War II and then expanded with the end of the Cold War. As outlined in Chapter 1 and then explored in subsequent chapters, the postwar order had four main sets of principles, or "pillars." Not all states embraced all principles. The order was more an à la carte than a fixed menu, allowing states to pick and choose which parts to adhere to or not. But together the pillars supported a historically unprecedented period of peace and prosperity. Whether the postwar order can be considered to persist today is a difficult issue. Many of the pillars of this order, described below, continue in largely their original institutional forms and serve at least some of their original purposes. At the same time, U.S. international leadership, the rise of new powers like China, and growing populism within the United States and Europe challenge both the principles and practices that created the postwar order. Determining when an "era" of international history is "over" is fraught, and often seen only in retrospect. There is no doubt, however, that the order that formed after World War II is increasingly fragile.

The first pillar was a near universally accepted set of norms on sovereignty and self-determination, embodied in the UN Charter. *Sovereignty* defines states as the ultimate authorities within their territories and as formally equal units under international law (see the "What Shaped Our World?" box in Chapter 2). This principle, in turn, implies that states possess rights to national *self-determination*: that is, that they are free to determine their own political status and form of government. It also supports the principle of noninterference, which holds that no state has the right to intervene in the internal politics of another. These rights, of course, were often breached in practice, leading one author to describe sovereignty as an "organized hypocrisy."[7] But this first pillar formed a set of rules that structured expectations about how states would conduct relations with one another.

The second pillar was a collective security system limited to countries in Europe and North America, which were also core actors in the third and fourth pillars. Although attempts to establish collective security at the global level foundered on the rocks of the Cold War rivalry between the United States and the Soviet Union, the Western bloc had success in building a collective security mechanism around shared interests and alliances. Looking inward, states in Europe and North America created what political scientist Karl Deutsch and his collaborators as early as 1957 presciently called a pluralistic security community (PSC), in which the use of military force between members was rendered unimaginable. This formed the heart of the democratic peace discussed in Chapter 4 and was embodied in the North Atlantic Treaty Organization (NATO) and later the European Union. With

---

7. Stephen D. Krasner, *Sovereignty: Organized Hypocrisy* (Princeton, NJ: Princeton University Press, 1999).

the United States as the linchpin, the PSC extended to parts of Asia, most notably to Japan. Looking outward, this same collective security system deterred possible expansion or aggression by the Soviet Union during the Cold War. The system rested on a "balance of terror," a term ascribed to nuclear strategist Albert Wohlstetter in 1958, in which the threat of nuclear annihilation maintained a fragile peace between the superpowers.[8]

This collective security system helped bring about a relatively peaceful period in world history. Perhaps most important, despite a number of Cold War crises and deep ideological hostility between the United States and the Soviet Union, the collective security system devised after 1945 has helped avoid war between the major powers for 75 years; it is remarkable that the superpower rivals never fought each other directly. For this reason, the decades following World War II are sometimes referred to as the "Long Peace."[9]

This second pillar was never universal, however, as it excluded much of the developing world where competition between the superpowers often played out and where conflicts within and between states were more frequent. As we saw in Chapter 6, the post-1945 period saw a large number of long and bloody civil wars, particularly in newly decolonized regions like Africa, Asia, and the Middle East, many of which were proxy wars between the United States and the Soviet Union.

As we saw in Chapter 3, however, there has been a downward trend in interstate wars since 1945. Given that the postwar era was ushered in with the detonation of two atomic bombs over Japan, the fact that the world avoided a feared nuclear holocaust is no small thing. Indeed, early concerns that nuclear technology would spread rapidly around the world turned out to be overly pessimistic, as today only nine countries (out of 193) have nuclear weapons (see "What Shaped Our World?" on p. 627).

The Bretton Woods System constituted the third pillar of the postwar order. As highlighted in Chapter 1 and explored in detail in Part Three, the set of economic institutions created during and soon after World War II facilitated efforts to lower tariffs, encourage international trade, stabilize exchange rates, and promote international investment and capital mobility. Initially limited to states in North and South America and Europe, this liberal international economy soon grew to include most of the world's countries, creating the dynamics of globalization that we experience today. Even China and Russia joined the World Trade Organization (WTO) in 2001 and 2012, respectively. As trade and investment have expanded dramatically in the postwar era—indeed, accelerating after the 1980s—the liberal international economy has created new challenges, which we will explore later in the chapter. But by some key measures, the 75-year period since the end of World War II has been quite good for the world in terms of quality of life. Over this period, the global income per capita has grown at the fastest rate in human history, and the percentage of the world's population living in extreme poverty has fallen from over

---

8. Albert Wohlstetter, *The Delicate Balance of Terror* (Santa Monica, CA: RAND Corporation, 1958).

9. See John Lewis Gaddis, "The Long Peace: Elements of Stability in the Postwar International System," *International Security* 10, no. 4 (Spring 1986): 99–142.

70 percent in 1950 to about 10 percent today. Life expectancy at birth has increased dramatically over this period as well.[10]

The fourth pillar aimed to promote human rights and, alongside those rights, greater democracy. This pillar was enshrined in the UN Charter and subsequent human rights conventions (Chapter 12). Though intended to be universal, human rights have been most clearly honored and promoted by the same core countries in Europe and North America that were central to the other pillars. Indeed, as we have seen, the very idea of human rights has proved to be controversial, and those rights have been protected unevenly across countries.

Beyond the substance of the postwar order as embodied in these four pillars, two other elements are noteworthy. First, leadership by the United States was crucial for setting the direction and creating the institutions of the order. No order, however, can be the result of only one country's actions. Great Britain was an essential partner in creating the Bretton Woods institutions as well as NATO. Countries in Latin America were critical in promoting notions of sovereignty and nonintervention.[11] A leader without followers is not a leader. Yet, the United States was a catalyst for many innovations underpinning the postwar order. As a large country, in turn, it often formed a privileged group, as defined in Chapter 2, that benefited sufficiently from providing public goods that it was willing to pay a disproportionate share of their costs. At the same time, it was able to ensure that the order and its supporting institutions reflected U.S. interests. As we explained in Chapter 2, rules are rarely neutral: they reflect the needs and desires of powerful countries. While the postwar order certainly benefited other countries, it perhaps benefited the United States most of all.

Second, the order was embedded in a series of multilateral institutions that were formed shortly after World War II. Creating a set of global institutions in which all or nearly all countries are members was at the time historically unprecedented. We have encountered a number of the key postwar institutions throughout this book, including the United Nations, NATO, the General Agreement on Tariffs and Trade (GATT, which later became the WTO), the International Monetary Fund (IMF), the World Bank, and the European Union. But these well-known organizations are just the tip of the iceberg. Figure 14.1 shows the number of intergovernmental organizations—defined as organizations with at least three member states—in existence from 1815 to 2014. The explosive growth of these institutions since the end of World War II is particularly pronounced. These organizations deal with an array of issues discussed in this book, including security, trade and finance, development assistance, human rights, and the environment.

Not all countries have an equal voice in these institutions, however. The UN Security Council gives a veto to its five permanent members—all great powers on the Allied side of World War II. The weighted voting scheme of the IMF privileges the developed economies. But these multilateral institutions reflect a

---

10. A wealth of data about economic development, poverty, inequality, and living standards is compiled and summarized by Our World in Data, https://ourworldindata.org (accessed 3/10/21).

11. Marcos Tourinho, "The Co-Constitution of Order," *International Organization* 75, no. 2 (2021).

FIGURE 14.1 *Number of Intergovernmental Organizations, 1815–2014*

Figure sources: Jon C. Pevehouse, Timothy Nordstrom, and Kevin Warnke, "The COW-2 International Organizations Dataset Version 2.0," *Conflict Management and Peace Science* 21, no. 2 (2004): 101–19. Updated to 2014 from data provided by Pevehouse.

shared social purpose and give smaller countries a voice in setting international rules and norms.[12]

With the collapse of the Soviet Union in 1991, the United States emerged as the world's lone superpower. In the ensuing decade, the institutions of the postwar order expanded in terms of both their membership and the depth of their activities. Freed from the constraints of the Cold War rivalry, the United Nations became much more active in managing both international and civil conflicts, as we saw in Chapter 5.

The WTO and IMF not only accepted new members but also took on new functions. World trading rules, which had originally focused on manufactured goods, were broadened to cover other sectors, such as services and agricultural products. The IMF, which had been founded to help stabilize exchange rates and international payments, expanded its mandate to monitor all financial issues that affect global stability.

NATO, rather than withering after its mission to contain the Soviet Union was complete, expanded its membership to the east and took on new "out of area" missions (see the "What Shaped Our World?" box in Chapter 5). Other regional security organizations, such as the African Union and the Association of Southeast Asian Nations (ASEAN), also became more active in managing conflicts.

The process of building institutional order from the ruins of World War II—and then expanding it after the Cold War—was especially pronounced in Europe. The process of European integration started in 1951 as a modest effort to cooperate in the production of coal and steel, two heavy industries that were strategically

---

12. John Gerard Ruggie, ed., *Multilateralism Matters: The Theory and Praxis of an Institutional Form* (New York: Columbia University Press, 1993).

important in the emerging Cold War with the Soviet bloc. Economically, this project was intended to promote growth and improve living standards; politically, it would cement alliances among countries that only six years earlier had been deadly enemies. In the ensuing decades, the integration project expanded dramatically. In 1957, growing economic and political ties led to the creation of a customs union—that is, a union of states with low internal tariffs and a common external tariff when trading with the rest of the world. In 1992, this organization became the European Union, which created a single market among its members and thus eliminated all internal barriers to trade. After the end of the Cold War, the European project, like other institutions from this period, took on new members and new roles. The organization has grown from 6 original members to 27 at present, and 16 of these countries have joined since 1990. In 1995, 26 EU members abolished passport and other border controls, greatly facilitating the movement of people within the region. In 1999, 11 EU members adopted the euro as a common currency and phased out their national currencies; by 2015, 8 additional countries had followed suit, creating the 19 member states using the euro as of 2021. Thus, a century that began with Germany and France fighting two major wars against each other ended with those countries using the same money.

In the coming years, the United States may face challenges to its leadership on the world stage from states that are rapidly growing in economic and military power, such as China.

Given this generally good news, why are the coming decades likely to be defined by challenges to this system? Although the postwar order created benefits for the world as a whole, the benefits were not evenly distributed: the system created losers as well as winners. Like any set of institutions and rules, the postwar order gave some states, particularly the United States and its allies, more influence than others and a larger share of the gains. Some countries, groups, and individuals were left with very little power and therefore see the existing order as indifferent or even hostile to their interests.

Three sets of actors, in particular, have incentives to challenge the postwar order. The first consists of states and groups whose interests conflict with those of the United States and its allies and who see U.S. military dominance as a core threat to their interests. During the 1990s, the term *rogue states* was coined to refer to a group of countries that were determined to confront the United States and the U.S.-led order: North Korea, Iran, Iraq (before the U.S. invasion in 2003), and Libya (before the ouster of Mu'ammar Qaddafi in 2011). These countries have sought to expand their regional influence at the expense of the United States and its allies, and they see U.S. military power and influence as standing in their way.

Over the last two decades, these states have been joined by a potent set of nonstate actors, most prominently terrorist organizations like Al Qaeda and the Islamic State (IS). Although terrorism long predates September 11, 2001, the attack on that day reflected a major escalation in efforts by some groups to push the United States out of the Middle East and Asia. Groups like Al Qaeda and the Islamic State have seen eradicating Western political and cultural influences in those regions as central to their quest to establish an Islamic state, and they use terrorism to circumvent U.S. military power by attacking civilian targets (see the "What Shaped Our World?" box in Chapter 6).

Another strategy that dissatisfied actors may use in an effort to neutralize U.S. military dominance, which we consider in detail in this chapter, is the acquisition of weapons of mass destruction (WMD)—nuclear, chemical, and biological weapons. Since these weapons are both extraordinarily destructive and hard to defend against, possessing them can rapidly increase an actor's ability to impose costs even on the most powerful states. Cyber weapons have also recently come into play, promoting concerns about cybersecurity. As countries become more dependent on integrated computer networks, opponents can hack or penetrate these systems and thereby gain access to information or create havoc on military and civilian assets. Like WMD, cyberattacks are hard to identify and defend against, and they can be carried out by a wide variety of actors, including both rogue states and terrorist groups. The proliferation of WMD and cyberattacks thus presents significant challenges to the United States, its allies, and international agreements designed to slow the spread of these weapons.

A second set of challengers consists of states that were relatively weak when the postwar order was constructed and that now want to use their increasing power to alter existing bargains and institutions. Dramatic economic growth has propelled some previously poor states into the upper ranks of the world economy, and most forecasters predict a significant reshuffling of the largest economies in the coming decades. Figure 14.2 shows the 10 largest economies in 1960 and compares them to projected rankings for 2050. China is expected to overtake the United States as the world's largest economy within the next decade or two. The center of economic power will also shift from the West and North to the East and South, as India, Indonesia, and Brazil join China in the upper ranks.

These shifts present challenges to the existing order, since countries with increased economic power are now pursuing increased political power. India and Brazil, for example, have sought greater influence within international institutions. The two are part of an effort—joint with Japan and Germany—to obtain permanent seats on the UN Security Council, thereby breaking the monopoly held by the victors of World War II.[13]

A newly empowered Russia has also challenged the U.S.-led order. After the Soviet Union collapsed, Russia experienced a decade of economic stagnation and internal instability. During this period, Western institutions like the European Union and NATO extended their reach to include former Soviet allies and the former Soviet republics of Latvia, Lithuania, and Estonia. Starting at the turn of the twenty-first century, the Russian economy rebounded primarily because of higher

---

13. For a discussion of UN Security Council reform efforts in the context of a larger study of whether and how international institutions respond to changes in the power of their members, see Phillip Y. Lipscy, *Renegotiating the World Order: Institutional Change in International Relations* (Cambridge: Cambridge University Press, 2017), esp. chap. 8.

FIGURE 14.2 *The 10 Largest Economies, 1960–2050*

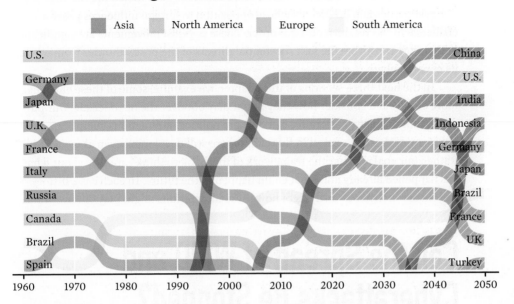

Asia   North America   Europe   South America

1960									2050
U.S.									China
Germany									U.S.
Japan									India
U.K.									Indonesia
France									Germany
Italy									Japan
Russia									Brazil
Canada									France
Brazil									UK
Spain									Turkey

1960   1970   1980   1990   2000   2010   2020   2030   2040   2050

oil prices, and a resurgent Russia, under the leadership of Vladimir Putin, began pushing back against Western institutions. Russian invasions of Georgia in 2008 and Ukraine in 2014 were both motivated by Putin's interest in preventing those states from entering the Western orbit.

Foremost among this set of challenges, though, is the one posed by China's growing economic and military power. As we will discuss later in this chapter, periods when a rising state threatens to surpass the power of the current leader are fraught with uncertainty, and in some cases they have been associated with major wars. The rise of China thus raises the pressing question of whether there will be a struggle over leadership of the international system.

The third set of challengers consists of those that see their interests as harmed by globalization—the dramatic expansion of global markets and economic flows— that has been encouraged by the United States and Western economic institutions. Although globalization has generated a great deal of wealth overall, its effects are uneven, and for some groups and individuals it has generated both economic and noneconomic costs. We saw in Chapter 10 that many people in poorer countries see the global economic system as a cause of their underdevelopment and have at times sought to shut themselves off from its effects. In the developed world, some workers who have been exposed to global markets have experienced economic insecurity in the form of job losses, downward wage pressure, or greater income volatility. These harmful outcomes have inspired efforts by labor unions and political parties to slow or reverse globalization.

At the same time, economic opposition to globalization has been joined by resistance to cross-border flows of people, including economic migrants and refugees fleeing civil war and instability. In addition to exacerbating domestic concerns about job losses, these flows have sparked opposition from those who see

Figure source: Tom Orlik and Bjorn Van Roye, "An Economist's Guide to the World in 2050," Bloomberg Business, November 11, 2020, www .bloomberg.com/graphics/2020 -global-economic-forecast-2050 (accessed 3/10/21).

Note: GDP is compared using market exchange rates.

migrants as weakening their country's national identity and sovereignty. Particularly in Europe and the United States, these concerns have fueled the rise of populist parties and politicians whose opposition to foreign influences poses a challenge to the Western postwar order. These populist movements are significant in that they constitute the first substantial threats to the postwar order from within its core members.

In the next three sections of this chapter, we examine some of these challenges more closely and consider how they might play out over the next decade. Our purpose is not to make predictions. Not only are political interactions complicated, but many of those discussed in this chapter are still developing even as we write. Rather, our goal is to use the framework of this book to think carefully about what has happened already and what could happen in the future. In each case, history and theory inform our analysis of how these interactions might play out over time.

Can the Spread of WMD and Cyberattacks Be Stopped?

On July 28, 2017, North Korea launched a missile from an arms production facility in the north of the country. The missile stayed aloft for about 47 minutes, following a trajectory that took it 2,300 miles into space, before arcing steeply downward and landing in the sea west of Japan, about 620 miles from its launch site. The test was one of several that North Korea conducted in 2017, but it marked an important milestone. Based on the size and velocity of the missile, experts estimated that it had a maximum range of about 6,000 miles—far enough to hit the western United States, including cities as distant as Chicago. The launch demonstrated for the first time that North Korea had the ability to hit the United States with a missile that could one day carry a nuclear warhead. Just over a month later, North Korea detonated a nuclear explosive much more powerful than anything it had tested before.

The two tests marked North Korea's entry into an exclusive club of states that have the technology to impose enormous costs on the United States in spite of its overwhelming military power. Though not the first U.S. adversary to acquire this capability—Russia and China have had it for decades—North Korea is the most successful of a group of challengers that have sought to develop or acquire WMD in recent years. This group includes a number of states that are or have been hostile to the United States and its allies, particularly Iraq, Iran, North Korea, and Libya, but it also includes nonstate actors like the transnational terrorist groups Al Qaeda and the Islamic State. All these actors, although diverse, have two key features in common: interests that put them in conflict with the United States and an inability to defeat the United States' conventional military power. Thus, these actors have incentives to seek WMD as a relatively easy way to shift the military balance in their favor.

The pursuit of WMD by these actors creates conflict not only with the United States but also with U.S. allies in Asia, Europe, and the Middle East who might also be targeted by these weapons. It also poses problems for international institutions that seek to stop the proliferation of these technologies. The interactions between those who want to acquire WMD and those who want to stop the spread of these weapons have presented significant international challenges in recent decades, and they will continue to be a central feature of world politics in the coming years.

The Colonial Pipeline, one of the largest pipelines in the United States carrying refined gasoline to the East Coast, was hit by a ransomware attack in May 2021. The cyberattack caused massive disruptions, including gas shortages, as the company preemptively shut down the pipeline to prevent further attacks.

In addition, a new type of weapon is emerging on the international scene: cyber weapons. As countries become ever more reliant on computers for managing everyday governmental and business tasks as well as critical infrastructure, such as electricity grids and water systems, the security of these networks becomes of paramount importance. This concern extends beyond allegations of hacking into election systems—which, though they have received significant attention in the media, have not been proved. Rather, the worry is that cyberattackers may steal the intellectual property of businesses and top secret information stored on government computers and cripple countries by shutting down vital infrastructure.

What implications does the spread of such weapons and cyber threats have? What, if anything, can be done to prevent hostile actors from acquiring them or using them to threaten others?

What Do Theory and History Tell Us?

Stopping the spread of nuclear, chemical, and biological weapons—collectively known as WMD—has been a pressing item on the international agenda for as long as these weapons have existed. Cybersecurity is a relatively new but no less pressing concern. As of this writing, nine states are known to possess nuclear weapons (the United States, Russia, Great Britain, France, China, India, Pakistan, Israel, and North Korea). Iran has pursued uranium enrichment, raising suspicions that it is seeking nuclear weapons. In addition, about 20 states possess the technology and knowledge to produce nuclear weapons in a very short time frame if they choose to do so. Fewer states are known to have chemical and/or biological weapons—the production and use of which are outlawed by international treaties—but a handful of states are suspected of having illicit stocks or programs under way to develop them.[14] The ability to penetrate computer systems may be more widespread, although among the states that might threaten the United States and its allies, only Russia, China, and North Korea appear to have devoted major resources to this effort. The United States, Israel, and perhaps some European states have made

---

14. See, for example, Arms Control Association, "Chemical and Biological Weapons Status at a Glance," April 2020, www.armscontrol.org/factsheets/cbwprolif (accessed 3/24/21).

significant efforts of their own that allow them to penetrate computer systems elsewhere, as occurred in the Stuxnet attacks on Iran's nuclear infrastructure in 2010.

Given the horrendous killing power of WMD, it may seem obvious that their spread is undesirable. The lessons of theory and history, however, are more complicated. Particularly in the case of nuclear weapons, one can make a strong argument that their overwhelming destructive power has made them a force for peace. This argument hinges on the idea that nuclear war jeopardizes the overriding interest of most actors: survival. Whatever other interests states or individuals may have, those goals are meaningless if attaining them leads to the actor's destruction.[15] Thus, a war involving nuclear weapons threatens to impose costs that far exceed the value of whatever good might be at stake in a dispute.

The massive costs of nuclear war mean that the bargaining range of deals that both sides prefer over war generally includes any possible division of the good; a state should prefer any deal, even one in which it gets nothing, over starting a nuclear war, in which the risk of its complete destruction is high. At the very least, the enormous destructive potential of any war between states with nuclear weapons should encourage caution and a greater willingness to compromise. In short, possession of highly destructive weapons should create a condition of mutual deterrence in which neither side would contemplate an attack on the other, forcing them to resolve their disputes in other ways. During the Cold War, this condition was referred to as one of *mutually assured destruction*, with the colorful acronym MAD.

To work, mutual nuclear deterrence has very few requirements.[16] The first is that each side must possess a survivable second-strike force; that is, each state must possess enough weapons that its arsenal could survive a first strike by the other state and still be formidable enough to cause unacceptable levels of damage for the initiator. Why is this necessary? If one state's nuclear arsenal is relatively easy to destroy with a crippling first strike, then a commitment problem arises that could generate incentives on both sides to initiate preemptive war. In the event of a crisis, the stronger state would be tempted to deliver a knockout blow that would deprive the other state of any ability to retaliate. In the absence of a credible commitment by the stronger state not to strike first, the vulnerable state would face a temptation to "use them or lose them"—to launch its weapons first in order to ensure that they would not be destroyed on the ground. Only when both states have enough weapons to ride out a first strike and still deliver a crippling blow of their own would neither state have a destabilizing temptation to launch preemptively. In practice, this means that each side must have not only a large number of weapons but also a means of protecting them, such as by hardening missile sites against attack or by making the weapons mobile (on vehicles, airplanes, or submarines) so that they are hard to eliminate.

The second requirement for mutual deterrence to work is that the leaders must be rational, at least in the very limited sense that they care about their

---

15. Obviously, individuals who engage in suicide terrorism may have different priorities, as we saw in Chapter 6.

16. See Scott D. Sagan and Kenneth N. Waltz, *The Spread of Nuclear Weapons: An Enduring Debate*, 3rd ed. (New York: Norton, 2012), chap. 1.

survival. The deterrent effect of nuclear weapons depends on the assumption that they will inspire caution by making the costs of war loom large relative to the potential benefits. For this to happen, those whose fingers are on the triggers must value their own survival and the survival of their nation enough to consider war unacceptably costly. In addition, the weapons must not be easily subject to accidental launch.

Finally, mutual deterrence assumes that in the event of an attack, each side will be able to reliably verify where that attack originated. Deterrence hinges on the expectation that anyone who initiates an attack will face a devastating counter-attack. Hence, the actor that strikes first must expect that the target will be able to identify it. If it were impossible to know where the attack came from, then a potential initiator might think it could escape retaliation.

What does the evidence suggest? Although the logic of mutual deterrence may seem overly optimistic, the historical track record is encouraging. There has never been a nuclear war. Indeed, the only actual use of nuclear weapons—the bombings of Hiroshima and Nagasaki, Japan, by the United States in 1945—occurred when a nuclear country attacked a non-nuclear one. This observation suggests that what is dangerous about nuclear weapons is not their spread, per se, but their *uneven* spread, which leaves haves and have-nots. Even conventional war between states possessing nuclear weapons is extremely rare; the only such case is the 1999 Kargil War between India and Pakistan (see the "What Shaped Our World?" box in Chapter 4).

The deterrent effect of mutually assured destruction is most prominently evident in the absence of war between the United States and the Soviet Union from 1945 to 1990, which we referred to earlier as the Long Peace.[17] Although several factors contribute to this observation (including the collective security pillar of the postwar order), the fact that both states had enormous nuclear arsenals that gave them second-strike capabilities induced a level of caution and pragmatism in their relationship that allowed them to avoid direct warfare and to make compromises when necessary.

If the logic and historical track record of nuclear deterrence is so solid, why has there been such an effort to stop the proliferation of nuclear weapons and other WMD? Why might some states have an interest in preventing the spread of these weapons? There are three main reasons. First, even if nuclear weapons may reduce the danger of war in some circumstances, they nonetheless influence the distribution of power among states. A state whose power increases—such as by acquiring a potent new weapon—may seek to revise the status quo in its favor. This development could harm the interests of other states even if it never leads to war.

For example, if Iran were to acquire nuclear weapons, its power and influence in the Middle East would increase to the detriment of the United States, Israel, Saudi Arabia, and any other country with which Iran has disputes. North Korea's nuclear weapons threaten to make it very costly for the United States or Japan to help South Korea in the event of another war on the Korean peninsula. Hence, states may have an interest in stopping the spread of WMD in order to protect

---

17. See Gaddis, "The Long Peace."

A Pakistani soldier stands guard over missiles that could deliver nuclear weapons. The security of Pakistan's nuclear arsenal is of great concern, since a number of militant groups are active in that country.

other interests that would be jeopardized by the emergence of an enemy with such capabilities.

Second, the states that have recently obtained or may soon obtain these weapons may be unable to meet all the requirements for mutual deterrence noted earlier. Unlike the United States and the Soviet Union during the Cold War, many of these states are relatively poor and domestically unstable. They may not have the resources to build and protect an adequate second-strike force, and they may not have the technology or resources to safeguard their weapons against theft or accidental launch.

The case of Pakistan, which acquired nuclear weapons in the late 1980s, illustrates some of these concerns.[18] As we saw in Chapter 4, Pakistan's military has considerable independence from the country's civilian leadership, and evidence suggests that the military has handled its nuclear weapons in a risky manner during several crises with India, thereby raising the danger of unintentional use. In addition, influential elements of the regime, particularly the intelligence services, have close ties to militant groups in the region, thereby raising concerns about a transfer of nuclear technology to extremists. Moreover, Pakistan seems to have exercised loose control over its nuclear scientists. A. Q. Khan, the "father" of Pakistan's bomb, is suspected of running a network that sold key technologies to Iran, Libya, and North Korea.[19] If new proliferators resemble Pakistan rather than a more stable state such as, say, Great Britain, then there is reason for concern.

The third concern, one that has come to the fore since the 9/11 terrorist attacks, is that the spread of WMD may make it more likely that these weapons will fall into the hands of terrorist organizations. This could happen intentionally (such as if a hostile state were to give or sell a weapon to a terrorist) or unintentionally (through theft or the complicity of extremist elements within the state).

There is reason to doubt whether the logic of deterrence could prevent the use of WMD by terrorist organizations in the same way that it does with states. While terrorists may act in rational ways (as we discussed in Chapter 6), at least some have demonstrated their willingness to commit suicide for their cause, suggesting that the threat of retaliation may not dissuade them. Moreover, unlike states, terrorist networks do not constitute a geographically defined target, so it can be especially hard to identify the perpetrators and their base. And even if the responsible organization can be found, it can be difficult to carry out retaliatory strikes without also

---

18. For a discussion of these concerns, see Sagan and Waltz, *Spread of Nuclear Weapons*, chap. 3; and Scott D. Sagan, "How to Keep the Bomb from Iran," *Foreign Affairs* 85 (September–October 2006): 45–59.

19. The status of these allegations is contested. Although the Pakistani government admitted Khan's involvement—and pardoned him after he confessed—Khan later retracted his confession.

killing innocent people, since terrorists embed themselves within civilian populations that may or may not share their goals. While it might have been credible during the Cold War for the United States to threaten the Soviet Union with massive retaliation in the event of a Soviet nuclear strike, it is harder to make the same threat today against, say, Pakistan for the activities of a small number of terrorists operating within its borders. Hence, a terrorist organization may expect to be able to escape retaliation, and/or it may consider the risks of retaliation acceptable, given terrorists' extreme preferences.

Other types of WMD and cyber warfare share some characteristics of new nuclear proliferators that make nonconventional attacks using chemical, biological, or cyber weapons hard to deter. For the most part, chemical weapons meant to be used on a large scale are relatively easy to identify. The chemical ingredients necessary to make chemical weapons are both somewhat rare and must be stored in large quantities. This suggests that actors that plan to use chemical weapons could potentially be identified, if necessary, with some confidence. The world knew relatively quickly when Iraqi president Saddam Hussein used chemical weapons, first in the Iran-Iraq War in the 1980s and again against his Shiite opponents in Iraq following the Persian Gulf War of 1991. Likewise, strong evidence quickly emerged when President Bashar al-Assad used chemical weapons against his domestic opponents in Syria in 2012 and 2013, even though the United States did not retaliate after President Barack Obama famously declared that the deployment of chemical weapons was a "red line" that Assad should not cross. At the same time, small batches of chemical weapons can be manufactured relatively easily. Sarin gas, for example, was used in a chemical weapons attack by a religious cult in the Tokyo subway in 1995.

Biological weapons and cyber warfare capabilities are much harder to identify and trace. Biological weapons can in principle be developed in almost any biology lab. Computer hacks can also, in principle, be carried out from anywhere. As then candidate Trump declared in 2016 in reference to recent cyberattacks on the Democratic National Committee (DNC), "I don't think anybody knows it was Russia that broke into the DNC. . . . I mean, it could be Russia, but it could also be China. It could also be lots of other people. It also could be somebody sitting on their bed that weigh 400 pounds, OK?"[20]

The different technologies involved with biological and cyber warfare render deterrence extremely unstable. Without the ability to confidently identify perpetrators of attacks, retaliation is difficult. Whom do you strike back against—and with what weapon? As these technologies develop, how do states ensure the "chain of control" over the potential weapons? If someone in a college biology lab or in their basement can carry out a biological attack or cyberattack, how does any government retain control over the technology without completely stifling innovation in the civilian arena? And perhaps most important, how can these weapons be kept out of the hands of terrorists?

---

20. Linda Qiu, "Trump Falsely Claims, 'I Never Said Russia Did Not Meddle,'" *New York Times*, February 18, 2020, www.nytimes.com/2018/02/18/us/politics/fact-check-trump-russian-meddling-election.html (accessed 3/10/21).

Preventing the Spread of WMD and Cyber Warfare

How can the proliferation of WMD and cyber weapons be prevented? The answer depends in part on whether the potential proliferator is a state or a nonstate actor, such as a terrorist group. In general, there are two ways to prevent an actor from acquiring a new weapon: (1) by altering the actor's incentives so that abstention becomes a better course of action, or (2) by preventing the actor from getting the necessary technology and material, such as the fissile material required to fuel a nuclear explosion. These strategies are not mutually exclusive, but they are likely to meet different levels of success depending on the actor in question.

As we saw in Chapter 6, terrorists have extreme interests that make them particularly willing to kill and be killed for their cause. Efforts to alter a cost-benefit analysis are less likely to succeed with such actors; it is unclear what promises or threats would induce them to alter their behavior voluntarily. As a result, preventing terrorists from acquiring WMD or cyberattack capabilities requires a focus on denying them technology—that is, ensuring that they do not get their hands on highly enriched uranium or plutonium for nuclear weapons or on chemical or biological agents that can be weaponized. Since nuclear and chemical facilities are large and obvious, most clandestine terrorist organizations cannot pursue this route to developing weapons; they are more likely to buy or steal the components they need. The task of denial therefore primarily entails securing nuclear and laboratory facilities against theft and policing efforts to buy or sell these materials on the black market. In the case of cyber weapons, this task may be almost impossible.

Most states share an interest in preventing nuclear fuel from falling into the wrong hands, so there is a strong basis for international cooperation to secure stockpiles of uranium and plutonium and to police theft and smuggling. Indeed, the United States and Russia, the two largest and most experienced nuclear powers, cooperated extensively in this area in the 25 years after the end of the Cold War. Although these efforts were successful, tensions over Russian support for separatists in Ukraine in 2014—and worsening relations between the United States and Russia since then—have led to a suspension and further unraveling of nuclear security cooperation.[21] Thus, despite states' strong shared interest in preventing nuclear terrorism, joint efforts in this area can fall prey to conflicts over other issues.

Preventing the spread of WMD to states may also entail the denial of nuclear, biological, and chemical ingredients. Given the current diffusion of scientific knowledge and technology, however, most reasonably advanced states already have the resources to develop a WMD program. As a result, efforts to slow proliferation among states focus primarily on shaping their interests. States that contemplate developing or acquiring WMD or cyber warfare tools do so because they believe there will be some benefit to having them: enhanced security from an outside

---

21. For a summary and timeline, see Mariana Budjeryn, Simon Saradzhyan, and William Tobey, "25 Years of Nuclear Security Cooperation by the U.S., Russia and Other Newly Independent States: A Timeline," Russia Matters, June 16, 2017, www.russiamatters.org/analysis/25-years-nuclear-security-cooperation-us-russia-and-other-newly-independent-states (accessed 3/24/21).

threat, greater prestige and influence regionally or globally, or access to additional technologies.[22] Strategies for preventing the spread of WMD and cyber warfare tools must alter these incentives by increasing either the costs of proliferation or the benefits of abstention.

The main strategies that have been used to this end coincide with the three core concepts of our framework: finding alternative ways to address the security interests of potential proliferators, cooperating through international institutions to establish and enforce rules against proliferation, and engaging in coercive interactions designed to forcibly disarm hostile states.

Guaranteeing the Security Interests of Potential Proliferators

One approach to preventing the spread of nuclear weapons is to address the underlying reasons why a state may want such technology in the first place. The most common motive is fear of attack by another nuclear-armed state.[23] This motive is evident in the historical pattern of proliferation. The United States developed nuclear weapons during World War II amid a fear that Nazi Germany would acquire them first. The Soviet Union responded to the onset of the Cold War with a nuclear program of its own, achieving a nuclear capability in 1949. This development sparked concerns in Great Britain and France, which then sought their own nuclear deterrents. In the early 1960s, a growing rift between the Soviet Union and China led the latter to seek its own nuclear arsenal, which it achieved in the mid-1960s. China's nuclear capabilities induced fear in neighboring India, which had already clashed with China over their disputed border. The Indian nuclear program produced a usable weapon in the 1980s, with the result that India's longtime enemy, Pakistan, embarked on a program of its own. Hence, the spread of nuclear weapons has been driven largely by security concerns, with each new proliferator sparking fears in its rivals and leading them to seek a bomb of their own.

It follows that proliferation of new weapons can be halted by finding ways to address the security interests that lead states to proliferate. Indeed, the historical record suggests a number of cases in which this strategy has worked—when states that faced stronger and/or nuclear-armed rivals and had the technological and scientific ability to develop nuclear weapons nonetheless abstained from doing so. For example, why did China's acquisition of nuclear weapons lead to a response in kind from India but not from other states in the region that also had reason to fear China (particularly Japan, Taiwan, and South Korea)? The answer lies in the fact that these states found other ways to redress their insecurity. In particular, all three had defensive alliances with the United States, which meant that even though they did not have a nuclear deterrent of their own, they were protected by the "nuclear umbrella" of the United States. Evidence suggests that the Soviet Union induced

---

22. For a discussion of the motives behind nuclear proliferation, see Scott D. Sagan, "Why Do States Build Nuclear Weapons? Three Models in Search of a Bomb," *International Security* 21, no. 3 (Winter 1996–97): 54–86.

23. For a careful analysis of how security interests lead to proliferation, see Alexandre Debs and Nuno P. Monteiro, *Nuclear Politics: The Strategic Causes of Proliferation* (New York: Cambridge University Press, 2017).

similar restraint in its ally Syria, which was tempted to develop nuclear weapons in response to Israel.[24] By extending security guarantees to friendly states, the superpowers helped to dampen those states' incentives to seek their own arsenals.

Of course, for such guarantees to work, the promise of protection has to be sufficiently credible that states are willing to entrust their security to another party rather than build their own arsenal. For countries that have no nuclear-armed patron willing to defend them, such as North Korea and Iran, this strategy will not work.[25] Even among close allies, there may be doubts in this regard. Concerns that the United States would not "risk New York to save London or Paris" led Britain and France to acquire nuclear weapons in the 1950s. North Korea's ability to reach U.S. territory with nuclear-armed missiles could induce similar fears in South Korea and Japan. If South Korea believes that the United States will not "risk San Francisco to save Seoul," its government could decide to end its nuclear abstention and acquire its own deterrent against the threat from the North.

This also implies that the umbrellas that were relatively effective in preventing the proliferation of nuclear weapons will be less effective in encouraging states not to develop biological and cyber weapons. If one state's possession of biological or nuclear weapons fails to deter other states from initiating conflict, then it stands to reason that this state cannot effectively extend a deterrent umbrella over other states. A nuclear umbrella is not easily reshaped into a biological or cyber umbrella.

International Institutions: The Nuclear Non-Proliferation Treaty An alternative mechanism for preventing proliferation relies on an international institution to foster cooperation among states with a shared interest in this goal. The primary institutional mechanism for this purpose is embodied in the nuclear Non-Proliferation Treaty (NPT), the origins and main provisions of which are described in "What Shaped Our World?" on p. 627. This treaty prohibits all but five states—the United States, Russia, Great Britain, France, and China—from possessing nuclear weapons, and thus provides the legal framework for preventing their further spread.

As with many international institutions, the strength of the NPT lies in setting out standards of acceptable behavior and providing mechanisms for monitoring compliance through the International Atomic Energy Agency (IAEA). The NPT is weaker when it comes to enforcement, which is left to the states themselves. IAEA inspections uncovered evidence of plutonium diversion by North Korea in the early 1990s, and they documented numerous instances of noncompliance by Iran going back several decades. Once cheating is discovered, however, the IAEA has no authority to impose sanctions. Instead, it must submit charges of noncompliance to the UN Security Council, which has the ability to authorize economic or military sanctions. As we saw in Chapter 5, however, the Security Council is not a neutral body; rather, it is dominated by five permanent members (the P5), each of which

---

24. Benjamin Frankel, "The Brooding Shadow: Systemic Incentives and Nuclear Weapons Proliferation," *Security Studies* 2, no. 3–4 (Spring–Summer 1993): 47–51.

25. North Korea has a defensive alliance with China, but China has never suggested that it would be willing to extend a nuclear umbrella over North Korea.

WHAT SHAPED OUR WORLD?
The Nuclear Non-Proliferation Treaty

In 1963, U.S. president John F. Kennedy predicted that by 1975, some 20–25 countries might possess nuclear weapons—a prospect that he considered "the greatest possible danger" facing humanity.[a] At the time, only the United States, the Soviet Union, Great Britain, and France had developed nuclear bombs. China was on the verge, and a number of other countries were exploring the possibility. Yet Kennedy's prediction was far off the mark. By 1975, only two new nuclear states had joined the original five: Israel and India. The next 40 years saw only two more: Pakistan and North Korea. Four states—South Africa, Ukraine, Kazakhstan, and Belarus—possessed nuclear weapons but gave them up. Twenty-three other states started nuclear weapons programs but eventually gave them up, and still others have the technology to produce a bomb but have chosen not to.[b]

There are a number of reasons why nuclear weapons have not spread as widely as originally feared. Some of the credit goes to the nuclear Non-Proliferation Treaty (NPT). Concluded in 1968, the treaty has increased from 61 signatories in 1970 to 190 today. How did the NPT come about, and what does it do?

Interests Underlying the NPT was the concern that a world of many nuclear states would be a dangerous place for everyone. In addition to the risk of nuclear war, radioactive fallout from such an event would harm even those not directly involved. Still, this common interest alone was not enough to guarantee a deal. The primary interest of states that already had nuclear weapons was to prevent other countries from eroding their nuclear monopoly.

Most non-nuclear states had two interests at stake. In addition to their security interest in limiting their non-nuclear rivals' access to these weapons, they wanted to protect their ability to develop civilian nuclear energy programs. The fissile material that makes nuclear weapons go bang—plutonium and enriched uranium—is part of the fuel cycle of a nuclear reactor. Restrictions on the ability to possess or produce these fuels could hamper these countries' ability to harness nuclear energy. Finally, some states that did not yet have nuclear weapons wanted to hold open the option of developing or acquiring them and thus had no interest in a treaty.

Interactions The NPT reflects a bargain between the five countries that had tested a bomb by the time the treaty was concluded, on the one hand, and everybody else, on the other. The former, recognized as nuclear weapons states, promise to refrain from giving non-nuclear states any of their weapons, to make good-faith efforts to reduce and eventually eliminate their own nuclear stockpiles, and to assist non-nuclear states in the development of peaceful nuclear energy programs. In return, the other states promise not to develop nuclear weapons, either by purchasing them or by diverting nuclear material from their reactors. As we saw in Chapter 2, however, efforts to control arms can give rise to a Prisoner's Dilemma in which each state fears that its own restraint will be exploited by others. The solution to this problem required not just a deal, but an institution.

Institutions In addition to laying out standards of acceptable behavior, the NPT provided a mechanism for monitoring compliance in the form of the International Atomic Energy Agency (IAEA).[c] In exchange for assistance, states must sign "safeguard agreements" with the IAEA that impose restrictions on their activities and provide for inspections to ensure that no material is diverted. In the event that a violation of the treaty is detected, enforcement is left to the UN Security Council, which can impose sanctions, as it did in the case of Iran.

Instances of cheating by NPT members are rare, but this observation obscures some weaknesses of the institution. Most of the states that developed nuclear weapons after 1968—India, Pakistan, and Israel—never signed the agreement; South Africa signed in 1991 only after it decided to give up its nuclear arsenal. Moreover, the treaty permits states to withdraw with only six months' notice. This is what North Korea did in 2003 after being confronted with evidence that it had been illicitly enriching uranium. There is also no mechanism for enforcing the provision that nuclear states must work toward dismantling their arsenals, a promise that they have been slow to fulfill.

a. "Text of President Kennedy's News Conference on Foreign and Domestic Affairs," *New York Times*, March 22, 1963, www.nytimes.com/1963/03/07/archives/text-of-president-kennedys-news-conference-on-foreign-and-domestic.html (accessed 3/24/21).

b. See Rupal N. Mehta, *Delaying Doomsday: The Politics of Nuclear Reversal* (New York: Oxford University Press, 2020), esp. Table 1.1, 63.

c. The IAEA, in fact, predates the NPT, having been created in 1957.

can veto any enforcement action it does not like. Sanctions against North Korea, for example, have at times been blocked or watered down by China, the country's main trading partner. Hence, enforcement of the NPT requires consensus in the Security Council—something that may not occur if the noncompliant state has backers within that body.

How well has the NPT fared in preventing the spread of nuclear weapons? Its track record is mixed. From one perspective, the NPT regime has seen some notable successes. Several countries that once had active nuclear programs and previously refused to sign, such as South Africa, Brazil, and Argentina, abandoned their nuclear ambitions and signed the treaty. In the cases of Brazil and Argentina, the NPT played a role in helping these two former rivals shed their nuclear programs in a transparent manner.

The NPT regime also played a productive role in defusing a potential crisis caused by the breakup of the Soviet Union. A number of the 15 new, formerly Soviet states were "born nuclear" because Soviet-era weapons were present in their territory. Since there was general agreement that Russia, the largest of these states, would inherit the former Soviet Union's designation as a nuclear-armed state, the other three states—Ukraine, Belarus, and Kazakhstan—all came under pressure to give up their weapons and sign the NPT as non-nuclear states.

Because of long-standing fears of Russia, some policy makers in Ukraine thought that the arsenal they had inherited would serve as a useful deterrent against their larger, nuclear-armed neighbor. However, the other nuclear powers insisted that Ukraine could join the NPT only as a non-nuclear state and that the alternative was to be ostracized by the international community, threatening the new country's standing and access to economic aid.[26] Ukraine signed the NPT as a non-nuclear power in 1994; Belarus and Kazakhstan followed suit. In this example, the international institution performed exactly as one would hope: by setting a clear standard for acceptable behavior and raising the expected costs of noncompliance.

The NPT regime has also had notable weaknesses, however. Since the treaty recognizes the right of non-nuclear states to develop civilian nuclear energy programs, there is danger that proliferators will use these programs to conceal illicit activity and evade punishment. Iran, for example, revealed in 2002 that it was enriching uranium and argued, correctly, that it had the right to generate fuel for nuclear reactors (though it did not have the right to conceal those activities from the IAEA). The concern is that the same enrichment process can also be used to make highly enriched uranium for a nuclear weapon.

While IAEA inspections seek to prevent this kind of diversion, several states have managed to cheat on their obligations and escape detection for some time. North Korea, Iraq, Libya, and Iran were all NPT signatories, and all managed to have active or nascent nuclear programs at some point after signing. There is also no mechanism to force states to sign the NPT or to prevent them from backing out after they have signed. Hence, the NPT does not provide foolproof protection against determined proliferators.

---

26. Sagan, "Why Do States Build Nuclear Weapons?" 80–82.

約3,700km

今回

NHKG

北朝鮮

約2,700km

先月29日

北朝鮮

11:02

In the summer of 2017, North Korean tests of ballistic missiles, which could someday be used to carry nuclear weapons, had residents of South Korea and Japan on edge. What can be done to stop or reverse the nuclear programs of hostile actors like North Korea?

A key question is whether something like the NPT can be adapted to chemical, biological, and cyber weapons. The Chemical Weapons Convention (CWC), an arms control agreement similar in intent to the NPT, entered into force in April 1997 and now has 193 state members, including the United States.[27] The CWC prohibits the development, production, acquisition, stockpiling, and use of chemical weapons, and it charges states with the responsibility to enforce these bans within their territories. The CWC also includes a verification system, including the right of any member to demand a surprise inspection of facilities in other countries.

The Biological Weapons Convention (BWC) has operated since 1975 and is similar to the CWC in scope: it bans the production, storage, and use of all biological weapons. As of early 2021, 183 countries belong to the BWC.[28] Despite years of negotiations, however, the convention lacks any verification mechanism. A proposed protocol was abandoned in 2001 after U.S. president George W. Bush decided it was against the national interests of the United States. Central to this de facto veto of any verification regime were concerns that it would be too intrusive, giving foreign powers the right to inspect a wide variety of facilities, including those belonging to private firms, within the United States. In the same way, although states are beginning to consider and discuss limiting cyber warfare technologies, there has been little formal progress to date.[29] Issues of verification and inspection seem to be intractable, and the highly decentralized nature of biological and cyber technologies appear likely to limit the scope for international agreements.

---

27. See Organisation for the Prohibition of Chemical Weapons, "Chemical Weapons Convention," www.opcw.org/chemical-weapons-convention (accessed 12/12/20).

28. See United Nations, "Biological Weapons Convention," www.un.org/disarmament/biological-weapons (accessed 12/12/20).

29. See Anna-Maria Talihärm, "Towards Cyberpeace: Managing Cyberwar Through International Cooperation," UN Chronicle, www.un.org/en/chronicle/article/towards-cyberpeace-managing-cyberwar-through-international-cooperation (accessed 12/12/20).

Coercive Disarmament What, then, can be done about states like North Korea, Iran, or Iraq under Saddam Hussein—states that have actively sought or, in the case of North Korea, actually acquired nuclear weapons and other technologies? These states' actions show that they do not fear the international disapproval that comes with being in noncompliance with the NPT or with using chemical weapons. Moreover, these states' interests in nuclear weapons may be rooted in more than just insecurity that can be assuaged through security guarantees (and anyway, they do not have strong protectors willing to cover them with a nuclear umbrella). Iran has aspirations for greater regional influence, and North Korea has long harbored the goal of unifying the Korean peninsula under its rule.

The ultimate tool for stopping or reversing nuclear proliferation is *coercive disarmament*: the threat or use of military force. A state can issue a compellent threat against a would-be proliferator, directing it to dismantle its program or face attack. The United States issued veiled threats to this effect against North Korea during a 1994 crisis over the latter's nuclear program, and it made such threats explicit during the crisis that led to the invasion of Iraq in 2003 (though it was later determined that Iraq had already halted its WMD programs).

If threats alone are not enough to induce disarmament, the final option is to use military force to eliminate a foe's nuclear program altogether. A classic example of this strategy is Israel's attack on an Iraqi nuclear reactor in 1981. Without warning, Israeli planes entered Iraqi airspace and bombed a reactor at Osirak that had been part of Iraq's nascent nuclear program. Widely criticized at the time, the attack successfully set back Iraq's program for at least a decade. In September 2007, Israeli planes launched a similar attack on an alleged nuclear site in Syria. Although there is uncertainty about what exactly the Israelis destroyed—and Syria denied that the site was part of a nuclear program—subsequent investigations by the IAEA found evidence consistent with undeclared nuclear activities.[30] During negotiations over Iran's nuclear program, Israel hinted that it might also strike that country's nuclear facilities.

Coercive disarmament faces several major obstacles. First, the threat of force alone is unlikely to work, because disarmament generates a potentially dramatic power shift: the state that gives up its weapons makes itself weaker and, thus, vulnerable to further demands. To frame this point in the language of Chapter 3, coercive disarmament generates a commitment problem: the threatening state must credibly commit that if the target gives in to its demands and disarms, it will not exploit the target's weakness by making further demands. If such a commitment cannot be made credibly, then the target has good reason to resist the threat.

In actual cases that the United States has confronted, a credible commitment along these lines has been hard to achieve because of underlying conflicts of interest. As we noted in Chapter 3, the United States' conflicts with North Korea and Iran were not caused by those countries' nuclear programs. In fact, the causal arrow runs in the opposite direction: the United States has had long-standing

---

30. IAEA Board of Governors, "Implementation of the NPT Safeguards Agreement in the Syrian Arab Republic: Report by the Director General," November 19, 2008, www.isis-online.org/publications/syria/IAEA_Report_Syria_19Nov2008.pdf (accessed 3/10/21).

conflicts with those countries, and the conflicts contributed to those countries' desire to acquire nuclear weapons. Thus, it would not be unreasonable for Iran and North Korea to fear that if they gave in to U.S. demands to dismantle their weapons programs, they would essentially be making themselves more vulnerable to further demands.

This fear is not hypothetical. In 2003, Libya agreed to a disarmament deal with an assurance that the United States would not seek to oust Libyan leader Mu'ammar Qaddafi.[31] Eight years later, the United States intervened in a rebellion against Qaddafi, leading to his ouster, capture, and death (see the "Controversy" box in Chapter 5). The North Korean government routinely cites this episode as a reason to oppose any deal with the United States.[32] To enhance the chances that threats of force will succeed, they must be matched with some effort to reassure the target that its newfound weakness will not be exploited. Given the United States' underlying conflicts with these countries, it is not always obvious how to make such a commitment believable.

If threats alone do not work, then force may be the last resort, as in the case of Israel's attack on the Osirak reactor and the U.S.-led war on Iraq.[33] A central difficulty with replicating Israel's approach, besides the costs associated with using force, is that states seeking to develop nuclear weapons have learned from this example. Proliferators have taken steps to harden and disperse their nuclear sites so that they are less vulnerable to attack.

North Korea, for example, makes extensive use of tunnels and underground bunkers to hide and protect key elements of its nuclear program. As a result, it is hard to ensure that air attacks will succeed. North Korea also has an enormous arsenal of conventional artillery within range of Seoul and could inflict horrific losses on South Korea in response to an attack. The alternative approach of invading and occupying a country, as in the case of Iraq, increases the chances of verifiably eliminating a program, but the costs associated with such a venture are much higher. Even talking about this possibility has risks. If North Korea feared an invasion and interpreted U.S. military moves as a prelude to an attack, it might decide to launch its weapons preemptively—that is, to use them rather than lose them. The difficulties of coercive disarmament of any nuclear program are only magnified in the case of biological and cyber weapons. It would be virtually impossible to identify and destroy sites where these weapons are being developed or stored.

What policy makers are left with in these tough cases is making a decision from among several alternatives, each of which has drawbacks. Military force is costly and of questionable effectiveness, particularly in the long term and for biological and cyber weapons. Economic sanctions, to be effective, require viable international

---

31. For a discussion of factors leading to this deal, see Bruce W. Jentleson and Christopher A. Whytock, "Who 'Won' Libya?: The Force-Diplomacy Debate and Its Implications for Theory and Policy," *International Security* 30, no. 3 (2005): 47–86.

32. See, for example, Mark McDonald, "North Korea Suggests Libya Should Have Kept Nuclear Program," *New York Times*, March 24, 2011, www.nytimes.com/2011/03/25/world/asia/25korea.html (accessed 3/10/21).

33. For a discussion of the effectiveness of military strikes to stop proliferation, see Sarah E. Kreps and Matthew Fuhrmann, "Attacking the Atom: Does Bombing Nuclear Facilities Affect Proliferation?" *Journal of Strategic Studies* 34, no. 2 (April 2011): 161–87.

cooperation, which in some cases is lacking. The international community could, of course, let the state acquire nuclear or other new weapons and rely on deterrence to render those weapons harmless. Deterrence has been the de facto policy toward North Korea since it acquired nuclear weapons a decade ago.[34] This strategy has a good track record historically, but one cost of this approach is that each case of proliferation generates incentives for neighboring states to follow suit. The probable chain reaction increases the risks of accidents or of weapons falling into the wrong hands. And as noted, deterrence is much harder to achieve for biological and cyber weapons.

The alternative is for the United States and its allies to strike bargains with states such as North Korea and Iran to address some of the underlying conflicts that led them to seek WMD in the first place. Such deals would attempt to convince these states to relinquish their weapons in exchange for economic aid, an end to diplomatic isolation, some kind of security guarantees, and perhaps substantive compromises on some of the regional issues that are sources of hostility. As we saw in Chapter 3, efforts to reach such a deal with North Korea have been frustrating and so far unsuccessful. President Trump's outreach to President Kim Jong-Un, including two summits and even a step across the demilitarized zone into the North, failed to thaw relations between the United States and North Korea. President Kim is unlikely to bargain away his capability to hit the U.S. mainland, but it might be possible to negotiate limits on North Korea's nuclear arsenal.

As explained in Chapter 3 (see that chapter's "Controversy" box), negotiations between the United States, other major states, and Iran led to the Joint Comprehensive Plan of Action (JCPOA) in 2015, a deal that sought to restrict Iran's nuclear program for 10–15 years in exchange for an easing of economic sanctions and the unfreezing of some assets held in the United States.[35] Although the JCPOA froze Iran's nuclear program and rolled back its enrichment activities, the concessions made to Iran provoked opposition in the United States. President Trump in fact called the accord "the worst deal ever negotiated."[36] In October 2017, President Trump announced that he would no longer certify the JCPOA as being in the United States' national interest, and the United States formally withdrew from the agreement in May 2018.

Iran announced in May 2019 that it would suspend implementation of some aspects of the agreement, and several months later it began to increase its uranium enrichment activities beyond agreed-upon limits. As of early 2021, the new administration of President Biden appears to be negotiating indirectly with Iran, through the other signatories to the agreement, regarding whether to restart talks about the

---

34. For an argument that deterrence is the best option with respect to North Korea, see Scott D. Sagan, "The Korean Missile Crisis: Why Deterrence Is Still the Best Option," *Foreign Affairs* 96 (November /December 2017): 72–82.

35. For a balanced assessment of the deal, see Gary Samore, "The Iran Nuclear Deal: A Definitive Guide," Belfer Center for Science and International Affairs, August 2015, www.belfercenter.org/sites/default /files/legacy/files/IranDealDefinitiveGuide.pdf (accessed 3/10/21).

36. Steve Holland and Yara Bayoumy, "Trump Expected to Decertify Iran Nuclear Deal, Official Says," Reuters, October 5, 2017, www.reuters.com/article/us-iran-nuclear-usa/trump-expected-to-decertify -iran-nuclear-deal-official-says-idUSKBN1CA2ID (accessed 3/10/21).

JCPOA. Whether President Biden decides to reenter the Iran agreement, renegotiate its terms, or adopt a wholly new approach, the continuing nuclear programs in both North Korea and Iran demonstrate how hard it is to contain proliferation in the face of states determined to acquire nuclear weapons. The challenges are even greater, and the options fewer, in attempting to limit the proliferation of other WMD, especially cyber weapons. Nonetheless, the deep penetration of an organized team of what are almost certainly Russian hackers into the computer systems of many U.S. government agencies and possibly U.S. firms, revealed in December 2020, demonstrates just how vulnerable we may be.

Will China and the United States Fight for Global Leadership?

When representatives of 46 countries gathered in San Francisco in June 1945 to sign the UN Charter, the honor of being the first to sign went to China, in recognition of its enormous suffering and efforts during World War II. As the world's most populous country and a major presence in Asia, China was expected to play a significant role in the postwar order, holding one of the coveted permanent seats on the newly created UN Security Council. However, more than a decade of warfare and occupation at the hands of Japan and two decades of civil war had left China in little position to be a world power at the time. Indeed, Chinese people now refer to the prior years as "the century of humiliation," when internal political decay led Western powers as well as Japan to take advantage of China's weakness to demand a variety of territorial and economic concessions.

In 1949, when the Communists finally prevailed over the Nationalists in the civil war, the latter fled to the island of Taiwan, leading to a split between the communist People's Republic of China (PRC) on the mainland and the pro-Western Republic of China (ROC) offshore. At the insistence of the United States, China's seat in the United Nations went to the ROC, and the most populous country in the world no longer had a role in the most important postwar institution. As the United States and its allies built the institutions that would govern the global economy—the GATT, the IMF, and the World Bank—the PRC, like other communist countries, was not at the table.

China's exclusion from global institutions lasted two decades. In the early 1970s, a growing rift between China and the Soviet Union created an opportunity for the United States to seek closer relations with the PRC. As part of this process, the PRC replaced the ROC in most international institutions. In 1971, the PRC took over China's permanent seat on the UN Security Council; in 1980, the PRC replaced Taiwan in the IMF and the World Bank.[37] Even so, China had relatively little

---

37. For a discussion of the process by which China replaced Taiwan in international institutions, see Lipscy, *Renegotiating the World Order*, chap. 9.

China's growing wealth has translated into increased military power that will likely match that of the United States in the future. As part of its effort to modernize its military, China has built aircraft carriers capable of transporting fleets of fighter jets.

influence in these institutions, where voting power rested overwhelmingly with the United States, Europe, and Japan. China would have to wait another two decades before entering the WTO.

China's limited role in the creation of the postwar order is striking in view of projections that it will surpass the United States as the world's largest economy in the next decade. By some measures, it already has. Since it enacted major reforms in 1979, China's economy has grown on average almost 10 percent per year, compared to about 2.6 percent for the United States over the same period. China's growth rate has begun to slow recently, down to about 6 percent in 2019, and its per capita income remains less than a quarter of that of high-income countries. Economists predict an eventual convergence of growth rates as China completes its current phase of extensive growth, in which it is mobilizing underutilized resources, largely in rural areas, and exploiting existing technologies. Whether China will be able to successfully manage the transition to "intensive growth"—that is, growth that relies on indigenous innovation—remains an open question. China is certainly investing significant capital in programs like "Made in China 2025," a 10-year plan to develop 10 high tech industries.[38] How this top-down model of state-capitalist innovation will compare to the advanced economies' bottom-up model of market capitalism will determine relative growth rates in the future.

China's development has increased not only its wealth but also its military power. Although figures on China's military spending are uncertain and controversial, it is estimated that the country's defense budget has grown at an average rate of 8 percent per year over the last decade.[39] China has long possessed the largest army

38. James McBride and Andrew Chatzky, "Is 'Made in China 2025' a Threat to Global Trade?" Council on Foreign Relations, May 13, 2019, www.cfr.org/backgrounder/made-china-2025-threat-global-trade (accessed 12/30/20).

39. U.S. Department of Defense, *Annual Report to Congress: Military and Security Developments Involving the People's Republic of China 2020*, 139, https://media.defense.gov/2020/Sep/01/2002488689/-1/-1/1/2020-DOD-CHINA-MILITARY-POWER-REPORT-FINAL.PDF (accessed 12/30/20).

in terms of personnel, but its increases in military spending have helped modernize the Chinese military with advanced technology. In the process, China has enhanced its power projection capabilities—that is, its ability to project military force beyond its borders—through investments in aircraft carriers and midair refueling technologies. Moreover, China also possesses a modest arsenal of nuclear weapons, with an estimated stockpile of nuclear warheads in the low 200s with 75–100 intercontinental ballistic missiles capable of hitting Europe or the United States, though both are expected to double in the next decade.[40]

In 2015, China launched a national strategic plan to develop 10 high tech industries within 10 years. The ambition is to develop autonomous technologically intensive industries able to compete globally with Western manufacturers.

To be sure, the United States will continue to be the world's dominant military power for some time. In recent years, U.S. defense spending has accounted for 35–40 percent of the world's total. The United States also enjoys a large technological lead, and its nuclear arsenal dwarfs China's many times over (Table 14.1). Nonetheless, although U.S. military power is spread more widely across the globe, including in Europe and the Middle East, the gap between U.S. and Chinese relative military power in Asia is shrinking.

China's rise is part of a recurring pattern in world politics. Over the long run, the cast of major actors on the world stage is in flux as states and empires rise and fall. The underlying mechanism usually revolves around technology and economic growth.[41] States that discover and adopt new technologies and economic models tend to experience rapid growth in resources and power, thereby extending their influence in world politics. As other states catch up or make their own innovations, previous leaders can be challenged and even usurped, allowing a new set of players to take center stage. This process not only changes the identity of the main actors in international politics but also creates dynamics that are themselves important.

What are the implications of China's rise? Will China seek to use its growing power to reshape global institutions from which it was initially excluded? Will conflicts between the United States and China increase the risk of war? To answer these questions, we need to identify how rising power affects interactions between the rising state and the current world leader. We also need to examine the role that institutions, both international and domestic, might play in containing potential conflict between the two.

---

40. U.S. Department of Defense, *Annual Report to Congress*, 55, 87, 166.

41. See, for example, Paul Kennedy, *The Rise and Fall of the Great Powers: Economic Change and Military Conflict from 1500 to 2000* (New York: Random House, 1987); and Robert Gilpin, *War and Change in World Politics* (Cambridge: Cambridge University Press, 1981).

TABLE 14.1 *Comparing the Military Capabilities of China and the United States, 2019*

CAPABILITY	UNITED STATES	CHINA
Total military spending	$684.6 billion	$181.1 billion
Percentage of world military spending	39.1%	10.3%
Active military personnel	1,379,800	2,035,000
Nuclear warheads	6,185	290
Intercontinental ballistic missiles	400	98
Nuclear submarines	14	4
Aircraft carriers	11	2
Cruisers, destroyers, and frigates	110	83
Bombers	157	211
Heavy/medium transport aircraft	675	88
Fighter aircraft	3,311	1,976
Main battle tanks	2,836	5,850
Artillery pieces	6,916	9,196

Note: All figures are 2019 estimates.

Sources: International Institute for Strategic Studies, *The Military Balance 2020* (London: Routledge, 2020), chap. 2. Nuclear warhead data from the Stockholm International Peace Research Institute (SIPRI), www.sipri.org/research/armament-and-disarmament/biological-chemical-and-nuclear-weapons/world -nuclear-forces (accessed 12/30/20). China recently commissioned a second aircraft carrier. See Benjamin Brimelow, "China is getting ready to field its 3rd aircraft carrier—here's why it's no match for US flattops," *Business Insider*, October 7, 2020, https://www.businessinsider.com/how-chinas-aircraft-carriers-compare -to-us-navy-flattops-2020-10 (accessed 7/3/2021).

What Do Theory and History Tell Us?

Both theory and history tell us that the rise of a new major power is potentially danger-ous because of its effect on international bargaining. We saw in Chapter 3 that a large shift in the relative military power of two states has several effects. As a state becomes more powerful, it expects to do better in the event of a war. As a result, it will be more willing to threaten force to change the status quo. Bargains that were acceptable when the state was relatively weak will no longer be satisfactory. Hence, a rising state has an interest in using its newfound power to renegotiate preexisting arrangements. Of course, this development alone does not make war inevitable, since the costs of war ensure that a bargaining range exists. It is possible that the demands of the rising state can be defused peacefully through negotiated changes that reflect the new power distribution. Nonetheless, opportunities for crises will increase—along with the attendant danger of war—because of information and commitment problems.

One such problem is particularly dangerous in this context: because the rising state cannot commit *not* to revise deals in the future, the declining state may have an incentive to wage preventive war. As we saw in Chapter 3, the declining state may decide that war now is preferable to some future bargain that favors the rising state. An anticipated decline creates a temporary window of opportunity to try to secure one's military advantage by fighting and defeating the rising challenger. Theory tells us, then, that a change in relative power influences both interests and interactions in a way that makes conflict more likely: the rising state acquires an interest in revising the status quo, and the declining state faces a strategic environment that encourages preventive war.

Does the historical record confirm this fear? The argument that rising power increases the danger of war can be traced to one of the earliest known scholars of war, the Greek historian Thucydides. Writing in the fifth century B.C.E., Thucydides sought to explain the Peloponnesian Wars between two Greek city-states: Athens and Sparta. In his view, the wars arose because Sparta, which had once dominated the region, sought to contain the growing power and ambition of Athens, which was increasingly challenging Sparta's predominance. Thucydides's oft -quoted conclusion reads: "What made war inevitable was the growth of Athenian power and the fear which this caused in Sparta."[42]

More recently, scholars have seen echoes of this logic in other major wars; indeed, a recent popular book refers to the risk of war during periods of power transition as "Thucydides's trap."[43] As discussed in Chapter 5, a key dynamic underlying both world wars was Germany's growing ambition following its unification and rapid industrial and population growth in the late nineteenth century. Before World War I, Germany assertively strove to acquire more territory, expand its colonial holdings, and wield influence in world politics commensurate with its power. The settlement that followed World War I—which stripped Germany of territory, colonies, and influence—only exacerbated the discrepancy between what Germany possessed and what it believed it could possess, given its resources. Although Germany's fanatical, genocidal goals in World War II were due largely to Hitler's extreme ideology, the country's feeling that it was entitled to more ensured that it would seek to revise the restrictive terms of the postwar settlement at some point.[44] Hence, the connection between rising power and an assertive foreign policy is borne out in the case of Germany.

---

42. Thucydides, *History of the Peloponnesian War*, trans. Rex Warner (London: Penguin, 1954), 49.

43. Graham Allison, *Destined for War: Can America and China Escape Thucydides's Trap?* (Boston: Houghton Mifflin Harcourt, 2017). For earlier scholarship suggesting that Thucydides's logic is central to understanding major wars in the modern era, see Robert Gilpin, "The Theory of Hegemonic War," *Journal of Interdisciplinary History* 18, no. 4 (Spring 1988): 591–613. For a sophisticated and nuanced analysis of power transitions, see Robert Powell, *In the Shadow of Power: States and Strategies in International Politics* (Princeton, NJ: Princeton University Press, 1999).

44. This case is famously made by A. J. P. Taylor, *The Origins of the Second World War* (New York: Atheneum, 1961), esp. 24.

It is crucial, however, not to overgeneralize from this case, notwithstanding its obvious importance. There are also cases in which rising power did not lead to war. For example, the United States overtook Great Britain by most measures of power around the dawn of the twentieth century. The transition took place relatively peacefully, with Britain acquiescing to U.S. dominance in the Western Hemisphere in a series of crises over Venezuela and the boundary with Canada. The handover of world leadership from Britain to the United States proceeded over the next several decades, aided by their common effort against Germany. By the 1950s, Britain was clearly a junior partner of its former colony.[45]

At that point, the United States faced a strong challenge from the Soviet Union, which built a massive conventional force and attained nuclear parity with the United States by the 1970s. Although the Cold War was a tense and dangerous time, the U.S.-Soviet rivalry also ended without direct warfare between the two superpowers. The combination of American alliances and nuclear weapons helped contain and deter the Soviet threat, and the Soviet Union eventually collapsed as a result of economic exhaustion. Finally, as the Cold War waned, there were concerns about an emerging struggle for power between the United States and either Germany, a powerhouse economy at the center of Europe, or Japan, whose dynamic economic growth in the 1980s led to warnings of a "coming war with Japan."[46] Neither of these predictions came true. Although the United States in some ways accommodated the rising influence of these states, the process was peaceful and never escalated to threats of military conflict.

Why does the interaction between a rising power and the current leader sometimes end peacefully? A large part of the answer lies in the states' interests: how severely their interests conflict and how costly it is to use military power to force change. Consider Figure 14.3, which revisits the simple bargaining framework introduced in Chapter 3. As before, the horizontal bar represents all possible divisions of the good in dispute, and the relative military power of the states involved is captured by the line labeled *War outcome* that divides the bar into shares that each state expects to obtain in the event of war.

Both the upper and the lower parts of this figure illustrate a power shift in favor of State A. Initially, State B is the stronger state, and the expected war outcome is close to its ideal point (the left end of the bar). We then assume that after a period of relative growth, State A will be stronger, so the war outcome after this power shift will be closer to State A's ideal point (the right end of the bar). The difference between the upper and the lower scenarios is the costs of war for each side. In the upper part, the costs of war are small relative to the shift in power, whereas in the lower part, the costs of war are relatively large.

The situation in the upper scenario of Figure 14.3 is obviously quite dangerous, as we saw in Chapter 3. The declining State B expects to get more through war in

---

45. For a discussion of the transition of world leadership from Britain to the United States, see Kori Schake, *Safe Passage: The Transition from British to American Hegemony* (Cambridge, MA: Harvard University Press, 2017).

46. See, for example, George Friedman and Meredith Lebard, *The Coming War with Japan* (New York: St. Martin's Press, 1991).

FIGURE 14.3 *When Are Power Shifts Dangerous?*

Initially, State B is the stronger state, but as power shifts in favor of State A, the expected outcome of war shifts to the right, reducing the value of war for State B. Here, the costs of war are low compared to the size of the power shift, and the best possible deal that State B can get in the future is worse than its value for war now. Hence, the declining State B may have an incentive to wage preventive war.

However, if the costs of war are large enough, then a deal may be found that States A and B prefer over war both now and after the power shift. Here, the possible deal gives both states more than their current and future values for war.

the initial period (the portion of the bar to the right of the blue dotted line) than it expects to get from any deal that is in the bargaining range after the power shift; that is, any feasible bargain in the second period is farther from State B's ideal point than what it can achieve by fighting now. Hence, the danger of preventive war is quite real.

This is not the case in the lower scenario, however. Here the bargaining range that will hold after the power shift includes deals that the declining State B prefers over fighting a war now. If the states were to reach a deal at, say, the line labeled *Possible deal*, then State A could credibly commit not to use force to revise the deal in the future. Such a deal gives State A more than it can expect to get through war, even after it has grown stronger. As a result, State B has no incentive to wage a preventive war in the initial period. The danger of war is much lower in this second scenario because the costs of war loom large relative to the shift in power. These costs make it harder for the rising State A to take advantage of its newfound capabilities.

Recall that the costs of war in this model are measured relative to the value of whatever good is in dispute. Hence, the interaction between a rising and a declining state is more likely to look like the lower scenario if either the material costs of war are very high or the value of the good in dispute is low. In short, a power shift is not particularly dangerous if war is too costly to contemplate or if the conflicts of interest in the relationship are so small that there is little worth fighting over.

This logic helps explain the relatively peaceful power shifts mentioned earlier. The Cold War challenge by the Soviet Union coincided with an enormous increase in the costs of war due to the advent of nuclear weapons. As we just saw, the United States and the Soviet Union avoided war in large part because of the threat of mutually assured destruction in the event of a nuclear exchange. In the cases of Germany and Japan in the late twentieth century, there was little threat of a military confrontation with the United States because of the common interests that bound them together—common interests stemming from a shared strategic threat during the Cold War, strong commercial and financial ties, shared democratic values, and a history of beneficial cooperation.

A Coming Showdown or Peaceful Engagement?

We thus have three kinds of historical precedents for thinking about the implications of China's rise: (1) the rise of Germany in the first half of the twentieth century witnessed a series of major wars, (2) the Soviet challenge during the Cold War was contained until the country collapsed, and (3) the rises of Germany and Japan in the last decades of the twentieth century were peacefully accommodated. How then is the rise of China in the twenty-first century likely to play out?

A key debate among scholars and policy makers is over what China's interests will be as its power grows in the future. Simplifying very complex questions, it is possible to identify two general schools of thought. Pessimists view the rise of China as inherently dangerous. They argue that China's interests are different from those of the United States and that its demands for status, recognition, and influence will inevitably transform world politics into more of a zero-sum contest. In this view, China's current policies—however moderate they may be—are not a good predictor of what a more powerful China is likely to demand in the future. The pessimists conclude that the United States ought to prepare for more intense competition with China now, while the United States is still the more powerful of the two countries.

At the most general level, pessimists fear that China's political and economic systems are incompatible with a U.S.-led international order that values democracy and capitalism. Politically, China is a single-party autocracy (see Map 4.1, p. 178) that does not permit any competitors of the Communist Party and suppresses individual rights to expression, association, and religion. The Chinese regime's strong interest in retaining this system puts it into conflict with the increasing emphasis on democracy and human rights among international institutions and nongovernmental organizations (see Chapter 12). China has resisted pressure to improve its human rights practices, and it has been loath to approve actions by the United Nations to intervene in purely domestic political struggles anywhere for fear of legitimating international involvement in its own political system, arguing that state sovereignty takes precedence over other norms. Although China has liberalized its economy in recent decades and embraced many aspects of the liberal international trading system, it has resisted efforts to open key state-dominated sectors to international competition. This suggests that China is exploiting the rules of the open international economy rather than genuinely integrating itself into that system.

More specifically, pessimists extrapolate from the theory and history that we just reviewed that because China was relatively weak as key elements of the postwar order were constructed, it will inevitably use its growing power to revise the system in its favor.[47] After World War II, the United States built a network of alliances in Asia that enabled it to project power into the region in an effort to contain what was then called "Red" China—the communist PRC. Agreements with Japan, South Korea, Taiwan, and the Philippines created an extensive U.S. military presence that allowed it to prosecute wars (in Korea and Vietnam, for example) and to patrol vital shipping lanes. Although American foreign policy shifted away from the containment of communism after the end of the Cold War, the United States' alliance network and military presence in Asia remained in place, albeit somewhat diminished in size.

As a result, U.S. military power continues to stand in the way of several Chinese interests in the region. Foremost among these is China's long-standing desire to bring the island of Taiwan back under its rule. China does not recognize Taiwan as an independent country, considering it instead to be a breakaway province. In the 1970s the PRC convinced the United States and other countries to accept this "One China" view; as a result, Taiwan was officially ousted from international institutions, and the U.S. alliance with Taiwan was terminated. Nevertheless, the United States continues to sell arms to the island and has made it clear that it would resist any effort by China to reunify by force (see Chapter 5 for more on the complex

---

47. See, for example, Aaron L. Friedberg, "The Struggle for Mastery in Asia," *Commentary* 110, no. 4 (November 2000): 17–26.

MAP 14.1 *U.S. Military Bases in the Eastern Hemisphere*

As China seeks to expand its influence in Asia, it encounters a ring of U.S. military bases in the Pacific, Southeast Asia, the Persian Gulf, and East Africa that were constructed during the Cold War and after. China not unreasonably feels contained by the United States' established presence in the region.

● U.S. BASES (25+)   ● U.S. BASE(S)   ● U.S. SMALL BASE(S) ONLY   *U.S. COLONIES

strategic interaction here). Thus, although China is much more powerful than Taiwan by any measure, U.S. military power deters China from wielding the threat of force against the island.

The U.S. presence in the region also frustrates other Chinese territorial interests (Map 14.1). China has disputes with a number of countries—including key American allies and security partners like Japan, the Philippines, Malaysia, and Vietnam—over their maritime boundaries and small islands in the South and East China Seas (see Map 2.1). The disputed waters are rich in fish, oil, and natural gas, and some of the islands have strategic value for projecting power and controlling shipping lanes. By maintaining bases that "contain" China and promising military aid to U.S. allies in the event of a conflict, the United States makes it harder for China to expand its power beyond its territorial borders.

All of these considerations suggest that China has significant conflicts with the existing international order. Therefore, we might expect China to look for opportunities to weaken the U.S. alliance system in Asia, thereby reducing the United States' presence and influence in the region. It might also seek to weaken institutions and actors that promote democracy or support intervention in domestic conflicts and to sponsor alternative institutions that do not have these priorities.

In the pessimists' view, then, China, unlike Japan, cannot be accommodated in the existing U.S.-led international system, and it will ultimately seek to overturn that order and institute its own. Just as Germany sought mastery of Europe in the first half of the twentieth century, China will use its new power to seek mastery in Asia, pushing out American influence. If so, the dangers of China's assertiveness and the preventive incentives of the United States loom large. President Xi Jinping's more nationalist style of leadership and foreign policy assertiveness reinforce fears that U.S. and Chinese interests are simply incompatible.

Optimists, on the other hand, argue that China largely benefits from the existing international order and is likely to be a "responsible stakeholder" within that order. While China's rise will inevitably require some adjustment to the major postwar institutions and their rules, as explained above, optimists see few fundamental conflicts of interest between Washington and Beijing. Optimists recommend continuing engagement with China until it shows definitively that it will not accept the current international order.

In lieu of cooperation within the existing international order, China may choose to develop and invest in new institutions that operate under its own rules. For example, China spearheaded the development of the Asian Infrastructure Investment Bank in 2016, in which it is the largest vote holder.

Optimists argue that even though China wielded little power when the postwar order was being built, it currently benefits a great deal from those rules and institutions and therefore has no serious incentive to disrupt them. The openness of the international trading system has been a boon to Chinese exporters and contributed significantly to China's remarkable economic growth in recent decades. China's top export markets in recent years have been the United States, Japan, Vietnam, South Korea, and Germany; the top sources of foreign direct investment into the country are Singapore, South Korea, Japan, Germany, and the United States (excluding several offshore financial centers). Thus, China is deeply economically integrated with the United States and U.S. allies in Asia and Europe. As a result, the benefits of the system and the potential costs of conflict are both quite high from China's perspective.

Proponents of this view also put a good deal of faith in the role of institutions, both international and domestic, to peacefully accommodate China's rise and mitigate the risk of war. Already, key international organizations have adjusted to take into account China's growing economic and political power. As we saw earlier, this process began in 1971, when the PRC took over China's permanent seat in the UN Security Council from Taiwan. In 1999, China joined the WTO. And reforms to the voting rules in the World Bank and IMF have increased China's clout in those institutions. For example, China's share of voting power in the IMF increased from

2.6 percent in 1990 to 6.1 percent in 2020, making it the third-most-influential country after the United States and Japan.[48]

In the long run, optimists also suggest that economic growth will eventually push China's domestic institutions toward greater political freedom and democracy. The underlying idea is that wealth and trade will give rise to a potent middle class of businesspeople and merchants who will demand greater political liberalization, just as the development of a vibrant and politically active middle class contributed to the emergence of democracy in western Europe. If prosperity leads to political liberalization, then China's growing power can be rendered harmless through democracy, which will weaken the influence of its military and sensitize its leaders to the costs of military conflict. In this case, the rise of China could be as benign as the rise of the United States in the late nineteenth century or the rises of western Europe and Japan in the late twentieth century.

Neither pessimism nor optimism suggests that war between the United States and China is inevitable or even likely. Even if China's interests are incompatible with the existing international order, war between major powers with nuclear weapons would be enormously costly, and it is not clear that either Washington or Beijing would be willing to risk war over their differences—however large or small they may be. If circumstances are close to the bottom scenario in Figure 14.3, mutually acceptable compromises may be possible.

What Will the United States Do?

How to respond to the rise of China has been a core question of U.S. foreign policy for much of the last three decades. The terms of the policy debate can be framed by the two views—optimistic and pessimistic—that we just summarized.

According to pessimists, the best way to respond is to contain China in the same way that the West contained the Soviet Union during the Cold War.[49] Such a containment strategy would have two main prongs. The first would be an effort to slow down China's amazing economic growth by denying it access to the large U.S. market. Since a good deal of China's growth is based on exports to the West, advocates of containment argue that allowing these exports to have free access to Western markets serves only to strengthen an inevitable adversary.

The second prong of the containment strategy would be to strengthen and build alliances with China's neighbors in order to create an effective counterweight to its growing power. This would mean maintaining U.S. military bases in the region, particularly in Japan, South Korea, and the Philippines, and strengthening ties with other states that have reason to fear China's growing might, such as India and Vietnam, both of which have territorial conflicts and regional rivalries with China. By adding the power of these countries to that of the United States, such alliances

---

48. Information on current voting shares in the IMF comes from International Monetary Fund, "IMF Members' Quotas and Voting Power, and IMF Board of Governors," March 24, 2021, www.imf.org /external/np/sec/memdir/members.aspx (accessed 3/24/21). Information on past shares was provided by Phillip Lipscy; see Lipscy, *Renegotiating the World Order*, chap. 3.

49. See, for example, Gideon Rachman, "Containing China," *Washington Quarterly* 19, no. 1 (Winter 1996): 126–39.

would blunt the impact of China's growth on the balance of military capabilities and increase the costs of war. In short, the containment strategy would seek to prevent China from becoming more aggressive by slowing the rise of its power and making war less attractive.

Optimists advocate a strategy of continued engagement that seeks to encourage positive institutional changes.[50] At the international level, the engagement strategy involves promoting Chinese membership in a web of institutions dealing with security, trade, and finance. Supporters of engagement successfully pushed for China to (1) be admitted into the WTO; (2) play a larger role in the Association of Southeast Asian Nations (ASEAN), which deals with regional security issues; and (3) be granted a larger say in the decisions of the IMF and the World Bank.

Such efforts seek to increase the benefits that China derives from the existing set of international institutions and thereby diminish its incentives to upend that order. These reforms not only move the status quo in China's favor but also increase the costs of war relative to the benefits that can be won. The hope is that if China is enmeshed in a web of existing institutions, its leaders will find a belligerent foreign policy—and the threat of exclusion from those institutions—to be too costly.[51]

Before 2017, U.S. policy combined elements of both strategies but prioritized economic engagement. On the military side, the United States maintained its bases in East Asia while pursuing closer partnerships with India and Vietnam. Over the past decade it also spoke of a "pivot to Asia," which meant, among other things, a reorientation of military and diplomatic resources away from Europe and the Middle East to Asia.[52] There was, however, no effort to pursue defensive alliances equivalent to an East Asian NATO nor any serious talk of preventive war.[53]

On the economic side, the United States followed the strategy of engagement, pushing for expanded trade and economic integration. The United States supported China's admission into the WTO, guaranteeing favorable treatment of Chinese exports, and promoted China's active participation in a variety of regional and global organizations.

This policy mix—limited military containment plus economic engagement—reflected interests at both the international and domestic levels. Many East Asian countries profit from trade ties with China, and they are reluctant to jeopardize those ties by taking a more confrontational approach. Moreover, the enormous

---

50. See, for example, James Shinn, ed., *Weaving the Net: Conditional Engagement with China* (New York: Council on Foreign Relations, 1996); Audrey Kurth Cronin and Patrick M. Cronin, "The Realistic Engagement of China," *Washington Quarterly* 19, no. 1 (Winter 1996): 141–69; and Kenneth Lieberthal, "A New China Strategy: The Challenge," *Foreign Affairs* 74 (November–December 1995): 35–49.

51. For an argument that membership in security institutions can change the way China's foreign policy makers see their security interests, see Alastair Iain Johnston, *Social States: China in International Institutions, 1980-2000* (Princeton, NJ: Princeton University Press, 2008).

52. Although this process started under the administration of President George W. Bush, the term "pivot to Asia" became popularized under the Obama administration because of the efforts of Secretary of State Hillary Clinton; see Hillary Clinton, "America's Pacific Century," *Foreign Policy*, no. 189 (November 2011): 56–63.

53. Unlike NATO, in which all of the allies are committed to defending one another, U.S. alliances in Asia are bilateral: U.S.–Japan, U.S.–South Korea, and U.S.–Philippines. There are no security commitments between U.S. allies in the region. For a discussion of this difference, see Christopher Hemmer and Peter J. Katzenstein, "Why Is There No NATO in Asia? Collective Identity, Regionalism, and the Origins of Multilateralism," *International Organization* 56, no. 3 (Summer 2002): 575–607.

potential costs of a military conflict with China mean that it would be extremely unattractive, and hence unlikely, for the United States to engage China in a preventive war. Although its nuclear arsenal is currently rather small and vulnerable, China is developing more survivable capabilities, including submarine-launched ballistic missiles, which would give it a second-strike force. Thus, nuclear deterrence plays a role in U.S.-China relations similar to the role it played during the Cold War.

In addition to these international considerations, policy toward China is heavily influenced by domestic interests within the United States. China's impressive economic development not only inspired concerns about its military power but also led businesses in the United States and around the world to eagerly contemplate the prospects of selling into the vast Chinese market. As over a billion Chinese consumers became wealthy enough to buy cell phones and cars, the potential profits were expected to be enormous. American businesses thus lobbied hard to improve relations between the two countries. Over time, however, international business has grown increasingly disillusioned with China's restrictions on trade and investment—and especially with what many American firms regard as intellectual property theft and forced technology sharing. The lure of China's market has diminished, weakening this once important constituency that favored better relations with China.

In addition, although low-cost imports from China are a boon to American consumers, certain sectors of the American economy have experienced wage and job pressures from the "China shock" that began when that country entered the WTO. Indeed, one study estimated that the United States' dramatic increase in Chinese imports since 1990 was responsible for about one-quarter of the concurrent decline in American manufacturing employment.[54] U.S. voters who have experienced job and wage losses and trade unions representing workers who compete with Chinese imports have thus been vocal in protesting China's trading practices. Although they are not large in raw numbers, the fact that these voters are concentrated in closely contested states in the Midwest made their views politically salient in both the 2016 and 2020 presidential elections (see Chapter 7).[55]

The balance of interests within the United States toward China was upended in 2016 with the election of President Trump. Trump catalyzed a reevaluation of U.S.-China policy during his campaign, calling the PRC an "economic enemy" and promising to stop China from taking American jobs.[56] Once in office,

---

54. David H. Autor, David Dorn, and Gordon H. Hanson, "The China Syndrome: Local Labor Market Effects of Import Competition in the United States," *American Economic Review* 103, no. 6 (October 2013): 2121–68.

55. David Autor, David Dorn, Gordon Hanson, and Kaveh Majlesi, "A Note on the Effect of Rising Trade Exposure on the 2016 Presidential Election" (unpublished manuscript, January 6, 2017), www.ddorn.net/papers/ADHM-President2016.pdf (accessed 3/10/21). For more evidence that trade can affect voting in U.S. presidential elections, see J. Bradford Jensen, Dennis P. Quinn, and Stephen Weymouth, "Winners and Losers in International Trade: The Effects on U.S. Presidential Voting," *International Organization* 71, no. 3 (2017): 423–57.

56. For a sample of rhetoric that Trump used against China during the campaign, see Veronica Stracqualursi, "10 Times Trump Attacked China and Its Trade Relations with the U.S.," ABC News, November 9, 2017, http://abcnews.go.com/Politics/10-times-trump-attacked-china-trade-relations-us/story?id=46572567 (accessed 3/10/21).

Trump signaled the end of engagement in his *National Security Strategy of the United States of America*, released in December 2017. Referring to the challenge posed by rising competitors like China, the document declares as "false" the premise "that engagement with rivals and their inclusion in international institutions and global commerce would turn them into benign actors and trustworthy partners."[57]

Although President Trump claimed to have warm personal relations with President Xi, the United States and China entered into a trade war beginning in March 2018, when Trump announced that he would impose tariffs on Chinese imports in response to the country's "unfair" trade practices. This set off a retaliatory cycle of punishing trade restrictions (see Figure 14.4). By the end of 2019, the United States and China had imposed new tariffs on many of the goods traded between the two countries. A "phase one" trade agreement signed in January 2020 essentially constituted a ceasefire in the trade war, holding the higher tariffs at their current levels without resolving any of the underlying issues.

U.S. restrictions on sales of semiconductor chips to China also proved to be significant. In 2018, the United States banned the sale of semiconductors to ZTE, a leading telecommunications equipment manufacturer in China, following a dispute over the company's illegal export of U.S. technology to Iran and North Korea. Although the ban was later lifted, many Chinese interpreted this move as political and an indication that the United States would be an unreliable supplier in the future; China quickly realized that it needed to become more self-sufficient in the production of high tech goods. China has also interpreted the United States' ongoing efforts to prevent other countries from buying telecommunications company Huawei's 5G network equipment as a hostile act. These controversies have seriously deteriorated relations between Washington and Beijing.

President Biden has promised to review U.S. relations with China, but in many ways he has also called for a hard-line approach to Beijing.[58] There are now few voices in the United States arguing for a return to the pre-trade-war status quo. In a departure from the unilateral trade war initiated by President Trump, however, the Biden administration will likely try to recruit additional allies to bring pressure to bear on China at the negotiating table. Indeed, it appears that China is anticipating such a move and attempting to cut deals with U.S. allies to preempt such a strategy.[59] U.S.-China relations will likely remain quite tense in the years ahead.

---

57. Office of the President of the United States, *National Security Strategy of the United States of America*, December 2017, 3, https://trumpwhitehouse.archives.gov/wp-content/uploads/2017/12/NSS-Final-12-18-2017-0905.pdf (accessed 3/10/21).

58. James Traub, "Biden is Now a China Hawk—With Limits," *Foreign Policy*, September 3, 2020, https://foreignpolicy.com/2020/09/03/biden-is-now-a-china-hawk-with-limits (accessed 12/31/20).

59. Steven Lee Meyers, "With Concessions and Deals, China's Leader Tries to Box Out Biden," January 24, 2021, www.nytimes.com/2021/01/03/world/asia/china-eu-investment-biden.html (accessed 3/24/21).

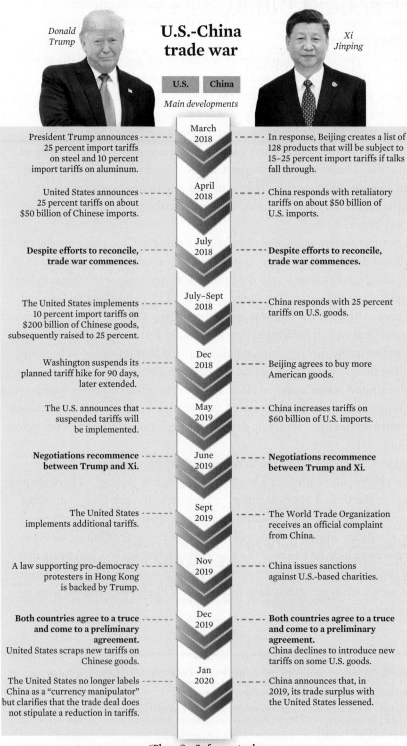

FIGURE 14.4 *Timeline of the Trade War between the United States and China*

U.S.-China trade war

| U.S. | China |

Main developments

March 2018

President Trump announces 25 percent import tariffs on steel and 10 percent import tariffs on aluminum.

In response, Beijing creates a list of 128 products that will be subject to 15–25 percent import tariffs if talks fall through.

April 2018

United States announces 25 percent tariffs on about $50 billion of Chinese imports.

China responds with retaliatory tariffs on about $50 billion of U.S. imports.

July 2018

Despite efforts to reconcile, trade war commences.

Despite efforts to reconcile, trade war commences.

July–Sept 2018

The United States implements 10 percent import tariffs on $200 billion of Chinese goods, subsequently raised to 25 percent.

China responds with 25 percent tariffs on U.S. goods.

Dec 2018

Washington suspends its planned tariff hike for 90 days, later extended.

Beijing agrees to buy more American goods.

May 2019

The U.S. announces that suspended tariffs will be implemented.

China increases tariffs on $60 billion of U.S. imports.

June 2019

Negotiations recommence between Trump and Xi.

Negotiations recommence between Trump and Xi.

Sept 2019

The United States implements additional tariffs.

The World Trade Organization receives an official complaint from China.

Nov 2019

A law supporting pro-democracy protesters in Hong Kong is backed by Trump.

China issues sanctions against U.S.-based charities.

Dec 2019

Both countries agree to a truce and come to a preliminary agreement.
United States scraps new tariffs on Chinese goods.

Both countries agree to a truce and come to a preliminary agreement.
China declines to introduce new tariffs on some U.S. goods.

Jan 2020

The United States no longer labels China as a "currency manipulator" but clarifies that the trade deal does not stipulate a reduction in tariffs.

China announces that, in 2019, its trade surplus with the United States lessened.

"Phase One" of a new trade agreement is signed on January 15, 2020.

Source: Beiyi Seow, "China Trade Surplus With US Dropped 8.5% To $296 Bn In 2019," *International Business Times*, January 14, 2020, www.ibtimes.com/china-trade-surplus-us-dropped-85-296-bn-2019-2901938 (accessed 3/10/21).

Will Globalization Survive the Populist Backlash?

China's impressive economic growth over the past few decades is part of a much larger process that has had important consequences throughout the world: economic globalization. The term *globalization* refers to the spread of activities and ideas across the globe. As applied to economics, globalization involves increasing integration of national economies through the movement of goods, services, money, and people across borders. This process took off in the last decades of the twentieth century, owing to improvements in technology, particularly transportation, communication, and information technologies. The advent of the Internet, in particular, reduced the effects of distance, making it possible to transmit information anywhere in the world instantaneously.

But globalization was not simply a result of technological change; it was also a product of decisions made by governments to facilitate the flow of cross-border economic exchanges, as we saw in Chapters 7 and 8. This process has been aided by a series of global institutions and regional trade agreements such as the WTO, the North American Free Trade Agreement (NAFTA, now recast as the United States-Mexico-Canada Agreement or USMCA), and the European Union. These agreements not only lowered barriers to the movement of goods, capital, and (in the case of the European Union) people; they also created mechanisms to outlaw and punish certain kinds of restrictions.

Thus, these international institutions enshrined the dominance of the liberal economic view that states should respect private property and that economic exchanges should be determined by the choices of private actors—in short, that markets, rather than governments, should be the primary drivers of economic outcomes. While this view has been influential since the eighteenth century, it became the consensus view in the West after World War II. It ascended globally with the end of the Cold War in what came to be known as the "Washington Consensus." The result has been an explosion of world trade over the last 50 years and a dramatic increase in the flow of capital across borders (see Figure 1.2).

While globalization may seem an inexorable trend, there are also strong forces pushing in the opposite direction. As we saw in Chapters 7–10, freer flows of trade, capital, and people create losers as well as winners, and the former have interests in slowing or reversing these processes. Those who see unrestrained trade as endangering their economic livelihoods have long resisted globalization. More recently, the resistance to globalization in the developed world has been fueled by concerns about immigration, which people see as posing both economic and cultural threats. The growing success of populist parties and politicians in Europe and the Americas has shown the power of appeals to reassert national identity and sovereignty against the forces of globalization.

Will globalization continue, pushed forward by the incessant march of technology? Or will the turbulence associated with globalization engender a political

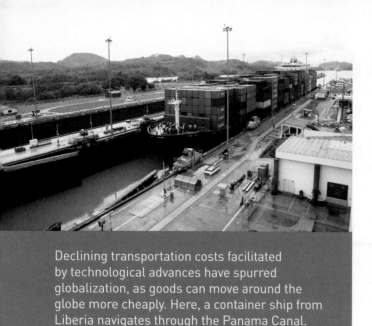

Declining transportation costs facilitated by technological advances have spurred globalization, as goods can move around the globe more cheaply. Here, a container ship from Liberia navigates through the Panama Canal.

backlash significant enough to grind it to a halt? Thinking through these questions requires that we understand the interests generated by globalization, how the interactions between the winners and losers will play out, and whether existing institutions can survive this conflict.

What Do Theory and History Tell Us?

Changes in technology influence how economic actors pursue their interests, particularly their interests in maximizing income. Lowered transportation and communication costs create strong incentives to overcome boundaries and increase the scope of markets so that they are global, rather than national or regional. As transportation costs decline, proximity to the consumer becomes less important. A company trying to decide where to build a production facility can focus on other criteria, such as labor costs and tax or regulatory policies. Improved transportation technologies thus allow companies to look around the world to find a location that will allow them to maximize profits.

This is true whether the company produces a physical good, such as a toy or an article of clothing, or a service, such as accounting or insurance. Indeed, the decline of communication costs brought about by the Internet has allowed companies to move many services offshore that were traditionally handled domestically, such as customer support services. Some hospitals in the United States have even sent patients' X-rays to India to be read by radiologists there—radiologists who demand a much lower wage than do their American counterparts.[60]

As companies find it profitable to increase the scope of their markets, they pressure governments to lower barriers to the movement of goods, services, and money across borders. A company that wants to locate a production facility in China but sell its wares to the United States will lobby the United States to allow free entry of Chinese-made products. Otherwise, trade barriers may nullify the advantages of making the goods in China. Multinational companies also have an interest in ensuring that they can move their capital around the globe freely so that they can transfer profits made in one country to another and make direct investment decisions without having to worry about barriers. Furthermore, these companies have an interest in strong property rights protections so that they can open facilities in any country without fear that their property or profits will be seized. As we have seen, there are a number of reasons why these multinational companies wield substantial influence on government policy and, hence, why they are a potent force in pushing globalization forward.

---

60. Frank Levy and Kyoung-Hee Yu, "Offshoring Radiology Services to India," Working Paper MIT-IPC-06-005, Industrial Performance Center, Massachusetts Institute of Technology, Cambridge, MA, September 2006.

History also tells us, however, that globalization is neither inevitable nor irreversible. People living in 1913 could look back at similarly impressive global flows of goods, capital, and people. In the preceding century, trade had grown from 2 percent of world income to 18 percent. International capital flows were also increasing impressively, as foreign-held assets grew from about 7 percent of world GDP in 1870 to 17.5 percent in 1913. And people were crossing borders at a scale that dwarfs the migration rates of today: between 1870 and 1910, about 10 percent of the world's population relocated permanently from one country to another; the comparable figure for the past three decades is no more than 2 percent.[61]

World War I and the economic dislocations that followed brought this period of globalization crashing to a halt, and during the period between the world wars, new national barriers were erected against the flow of goods and money. Although economic integration is today much wider and deeper than it was in 1913, this case offers a stark reminder that political conflict can slow or even reverse seemingly inevitable economic processes.

Indeed, globalization in its contemporary form has generated no shortage of conflicts, both among and within states, because it creates losers as well as winners. As we have seen, among the winners are economic actors who can take advantage of increased opportunities to move money and goods throughout the world—particularly, multinational companies and investors. Increased efficiency has also benefited consumers in the form of lower prices on imported goods. Who are the losers?

Economic Costs of Globalization

The main resistance to globalization comes from actors who see the lower barriers to trade and capital flows as threatening to their economic interests. Recall from Chapter 7 that there are different theories for thinking about who wins and who loses from trade liberalization. The Ricardo-Viner, or specific-factors, model holds that trade interests are determined by the sector one works in: those in sectors that compete with imports want protection, while those in sectors that rely on exports want liberalization. The alternative theory, Stolper-Samuelson, holds that trade interests are determined by the factor of production—capital, labor, or land—that provides one's income. In this view, free trade benefits those factors that are relatively abundant in a country at the expense of those factors that are relatively scarce.

In the developed world, where capital is relatively abundant and labor (particularly unskilled labor) is scarce, capital wins from free trade while unskilled labor loses. In the developing world, where unskilled labor is abundant, holders of capital lose from free trade while labor benefits. It is generally thought that while the predictions of Ricardo-Viner hold in the short term, long-term patterns of conflict follow the predictions of Stolper-Samuelson.[62] In other words, as globalization persists

---

61. These figures are from David Dollar and Aart Kraay, "Spreading the Wealth," *Foreign Affairs* 8, no. 1 (January–February 2002): 122–23; and Nicholas Crafts, "Globalisation and Economic Growth: A Historical Perspective," *World Economy* 27, no. 1 (2004): 46.

62. Michael Mussa, "Tariffs and the Distribution of Income: The Importance of Factor Specificity, Substitutability, and Intensity in the Short and Long Run," *Journal of Political Economy* 82, no. 6 (November–December 1974): 1191–203.

and deepens, conflicts will increasingly crystallize along class lines: capital versus labor, with the positions of each determined by whether they are in the developing or developed world.

Economic Insecurity in the Developed World

In developed countries, the group most negatively affected by globalization is workers—especially unskilled workers. As rich countries become more closely integrated with developing countries, workers in the former face increasing competition from unskilled workers in the latter. A company that makes toys or clothing can find workers in China or Vietnam willing to accept much lower wages than workers would accept in the United States. As a result, the production of labor-intensive goods has moved away from developed countries to the developing world, causing job losses in the former. For example, from 1970 to 2000, the textile and clothing industries in the five richest developed countries shed more than 4 million jobs—that is, over 62 percent of their labor force—a trend that has only continued now that China is a member of the WTO.[63] Workers in affected sectors who have not lost their jobs have experienced stagnant or falling wages and have suffered from job insecurity.

Given this situation, it is not surprising that labor unions in rich countries have been at the forefront of a backlash against globalization. What may be surprising is how broadly based the opposition to globalization among labor unions has been. Consider, for example, what happened in 1999 when the United States approved a treaty admitting China into the WTO, thereby giving China permanent most-favored-nation trading status. Unions representing textile and clothing workers voiced their full-throated opposition to the pact, which would increase international competition for this beleaguered sector.

They were joined by some apparently strange partners.[64] For example, the Teamsters Union, which represents truckers, lobbied against the treaty. This stance was curious because at the same time, one of the teamsters' largest employers, United Parcel Service, was lobbying for a coveted new air route for landing cargo planes in China. One U.S. official summed up the contradiction like this: "It seems that the Teamsters want us to have more cargo flights to China, but no cargo." Even stranger was the opposition by the United Auto Workers. Until China's admission into the WTO, virtually no U.S.-made cars could be sold in China; after the treaty passed, U.S. automakers would have freer access to the Chinese market.

Stranger yet was the opposition by a major dockworkers' union, the International Longshore and Warehouse Union. These workers make their living loading and unloading ships engaged in international trade. One would think that expanding trade with China would have been in their interests. Yet opposition to the pact came not only from workers in sectors that directly competed with Chinese imports

---

63. Organisation for Economic Co-operation and Development, "A New World Map in Textiles and Clothing: Adjusting to Change," Table 3.1, www.oecd-ilibrary.org/trade/a-new-world-map-in-textiles-and-clothing_9789264018556-en (accessed 1/22/21).

64 The following is based on Thomas L. Friedman, "America's Labor Pains," *New York Times*, May 9, 2000, www.nytimes.com/2000/05/09/opinion/foreign-affairs-america-s-labor-pains.html (accessed 3/24/21).

but also from workers in sectors that thrived on exports and might, therefore, have been expected to support the deal.

This kind of class-based, rather than sector-based, opposition is exactly what the Stolper-Samuelson theorem predicts. The insecurities that globalization has created for workers in sectors that compete with imports is rippling outward and affecting the attitudes of workers in other sectors as well, generating political cleavages along class lines. Their fears are based on a number of concerns that include, but also go beyond, issues of job losses.

One fear is that globalization is exacerbating inequality, with workers increasingly left behind. Indeed, there is evidence of increasing income inequality in many countries, although economists debate how much of this trend is due to international trade. After all, other developments over the last several decades, including the weakening of labor unions and the increasing importance of technology, account for much of the gap. Regardless of the actual role of trade in exacerbating inequality, the perception of a strong effect is widespread and politically potent.[65]

In addition, there is an asymmetry between labor and investment capital that derives from the fact that capital can move around the globe in search of higher profits much more easily than workers can move around looking for jobs and better wages. Companies can threaten to close up shop and move, and this threat gives managers (who represent capital) bargaining leverage over workers to lower their wages and benefits. It also leads to more job insecurity.

Unions have also expressed concerns about a "race to the bottom" in labor standards. In the developed world, unions fought hard for a number of protections that most people now take for granted: minimum wage laws, prohibitions on child labor, limits on the length of the workweek, and worker safety regulations. These protections either do not exist or are much weaker in developing countries. Unions fear that the increased mobility of investment capital means that companies can move around the world looking for places with fewer worker protections. If countries compete for capital by weakening or resisting demands for these protections, hard-fought gains in labor standards could wither away.

Economic Insecurity in the Developing World
People in poorer countries have also experienced insecurity as a result of globalization. Though the Stolper-Samuelson theorem predicts that trade liberalization will raise the incomes of unskilled workers in developing countries in the long run, there are several reasons why people in poor countries approach globalization with fear and resistance.

One reason has to do with the relatively weak social safety nets that exist in developing countries. In the developed world, growing exposure to international trade after World War II coincided with the expansion of government assistance designed to protect workers from economic hard times, such as unemployment benefits, poverty alleviation programs, and government-subsidized health insurance. These initiatives had the effect of cushioning workers from the hard edges of

---

65. Thomas M. Flaherty and Ronald Rogowski, "Rising Inequality as a Threat to the Liberal International Order," *International Organization* 75, no. 2 (2021).

international competition. In poorer countries, however, these safety nets are generally not as strong, so workers face economic dislocations with greater insecurity.

Workers in the developing world may also have less access to institutions that give them clout in political and economic decision making. Representative democracy, for example, is still more common in rich countries than in poor ones. As a result, workers in the latter have a harder time translating their numbers into political power to demand greater redistribution. Similarly, the right to form labor unions is not as strong in many developing states as it is in the developed world. These institutions enable workers to pool their efforts and resources and to act collectively in pursuit of wage and benefit demands from employers. Even if globalization creates a larger pie of profits, weak or nonexistent unions make it harder for workers to get a larger slice of that pie.

Finally, increasing capital mobility has exacerbated the volatility of poor economies, since large sums of foreign money can enter or leave at a moment's notice. As we saw in Chapters 8 and 10, countries that lose the faith of international capital markets can suffer devastating punishments. In a very short time, capital flight can cause inflation and unemployment to spike. And while international institutions like the IMF may come to a country's rescue, their assistance often requires that governments cut back spending and subsidies that benefit the poor. Given all this, it is easy to see why many people in the developing world do not perceive what economic theory tells us is their long-term interest in globalization.

The Rise of the Populists

The backlash against globalization has grown even more potent as opposition based on traditional economic concerns has combined with other, noneconomic sources of resistance. Discontent with economic integration has always rested to some degree on its social and cultural effects—that is, on the fear of importing foreign influences and diluting national identity.[66]

This fear has been exacerbated in recent years not by the cross-border movement of goods and capital but by the movement of people. For many years, Europe has seen a steady flow of migrants, primarily from northern Africa and the Middle East, seeking economic opportunity. Starting in 2015, the influx became a flood: more than a million people arrived in that year alone, either by boat across the Mediterranean Sea or on foot through southeastern Europe. The majority of these newcomers came from Syria, Iraq, and Afghanistan, fleeing long-running civil wars in those countries (see Chapter 6). In the United States, immigration from Mexico has long been a contentious issue, and deciding what to do about the approximately 11 million undocumented people in the country has been politically vexing. In recent years, the salience of the issue has increased, as more and more refugees from the Syrian Civil War and people fleeing crime and violence in Central America have sought entry into Europe and the United States, respectively. Although President Biden has promised comprehensive immigration reform, the United States has

---

66. Yotam Margalit, "Lost in Globalization: International Economic Integration and the Sources of Popular Discontent," *International Studies Quarterly* 56, no. 3 (September 2012): 484–500.

Recent populist movements in Europe have been fueled by opposition to the flow of migrants entering the continent from Syria and other countries in the Middle East.

been wrestling with changes in policy since the late 1970s without significant consensus, and efforts to revise rules on immigration are likely to remain fraught.

Opposition to accepting migrants and refugees stems from a variety of considerations. As we saw in the "How Do We Know?" box in Chapter 8, one factor is economic. For workers in recipient countries, the influx of generally low-skilled labor from abroad is seen as a threat to jobs and wages.[67] There is considerable disagreement among economists about the magnitude of net job losses due to immigration, and the fact that newcomers also purchase goods and services means that there can be positive economic effects as well.[68] Nonetheless, the perception that immigrants are "taking our jobs" has proved to be politically potent.

Opposition to immigrants can also stem from a perception that they are a drain on the country's budget because of their alleged dependence on welfare and unemployment benefits. Once again, there is limited evidence that immigrants disproportionately draw on social spending, and most pay taxes into the system. These facts have not prevented politicians from promoting the image of lazy immigrants (presumably not the same ones who "took our jobs") who come to their country to live on its generous dole.

Beyond these economic concerns, opposition to accepting foreign migrants can also rest on perceptions that they pose a cultural threat because they come with different customs, religious beliefs, languages, or skin colors. Indeed, the far-right Alternative for Germany (AfD) party has explicitly depicted migration as a foreign invasion and made no secret of the fact that Muslim migrants were the

67. Kenneth F. Scheve and Matthew J. Slaughter, "Labor Market Competition and Individual Preferences over Immigration Policy," *Review of Economics and Statistics* 83, no. 1 (February 2001): 133–45.

68. See, for example, Francine D. Blau and Christopher Mackie, eds., *The Economic and Fiscal Consequences of Immigration* (Washington, DC: National Academies Press, 2017), www.nap.edu/catalog/23550/the-economic-and-fiscal-consequences-of-immigration (accessed 3/10/21).

primary target of its opposition. In the same fashion, U.S. president Trump referred to migrants as "invaders" and singled out Muslims in the travel ban enacted by his administration in early 2017—a ban that the Biden administration repealed as one of its first acts. Indeed, studies of attitudes toward immigration show that the religious and ethnic backgrounds of prospective newcomers play a significant role in the degree to which people in recipient countries are willing to accept them.[69]

At a minimum, cultural concerns are expressed in terms of assimilation: recipient-country residents may see the perceived unwillingness of migrants to adapt to local customs and speak the local language as a threat to their national identity and unity. In more extreme rhetoric, cultural concerns emerge in terms of threats to law and order. In Germany, for example, widely shared—and often wildly overstated or fabricated—stories of Muslim refugees raping Western women epitomize the view that the newcomers are defiling the nation.[70]

To a large extent, flows of people to the United States and Europe are not a result of globalization. Nor do they reflect rules or decisions of liberal economic institutions, none of which mandate openness to migration (though there are international agreements that require states to accept people seeking asylum from political threats). Rather, the movement of people is rooted—as it always has been—in persistent underdevelopment, political instability, and civil war. The geographic proximity of wealthy countries, like the United States and Germany, to poor regions, like Central America and northern Africa, makes migration an attractive option for people seeking better circumstances. Nevertheless, opposition to migration intersects with and has given greater potency to opposition to globalization and its institutions by fueling the rise of populism.

Populism describes a broad array of political movements that claim to speak on behalf of "the people" in opposition to corrupt elites, both domestic and foreign.[71] Populism can take a variety of different forms depending on the local context, and it can arise on either the left or the right of the political spectrum. Populists on the left tend to emphasize radical redistribution of wealth, nationalization of property, and anti-imperialism; those on the right tend to stress nationalism, traditional cultural values, and a rejection of foreign influences.

Populist movements have a long history in Latin America, where they tend to be on the left. Recent populist movements in Europe and the United States have grown predominantly on the right, mobilizing voters opposed to immigration, trade, and international institutions. In doing so, they have drawn support from those who fear wage and job losses because of foreign trade or competition with migrant labor, those who fear cultural and demographic changes because of the influx of people

---

69. For a recent review of the literature, see Jens Hainmueller and Daniel J. Hopkins, "Public Attitudes Toward Immigration," *Annual Review of Political Science* 17 (2014): 225–49.

70. See, for example, Melissa Eddy, "Bild Apologizes for False Article on Sexual Assaults in Frankfurt by Migrants," *New York Times*, February 16, 2017, www.nytimes.com/2017/02/16/world/europe/bild-fake -story.html (accessed 3/10/21).

71. There is an enormous literature on populism and its rise. An important effort to define populism is Cas Mudde, "The Populist Zeitgeist," *Government and Opposition* 39, no. 4 (2004): 541–63. For a succinct discussion of the recent rise of populism in Europe, see Anna Grzymala-Busse, "Global Populisms and Their Impact," *Slavic Review* 76, no. S1 (2017): S3–S8.

FIGURE 14.5   *Share of Votes for Populist Parties in EU Member States, 1990–2019*

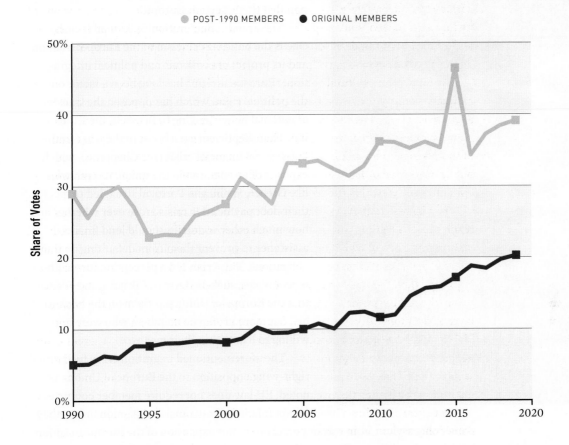

● POST-1990 MEMBERS   ● ORIGINAL MEMBERS

from foreign cultures, and those who resent the influence that international institutions have on national policy making.[72] Opposition to changes in traditional gender and racial hierarchies has also been important. In short, the populist coalition brings together traditional economic foes of globalization and people motivated by noneconomic interests in protecting cultural identity and national sovereignty.

It is no surprise that this kind of populism is on the rise in Europe, where populism had, by 2017, scored electoral victories by the Law and Justice Party in Poland and the Hungarian Civic Union in Hungary; led to strong showings by the AfD in Germany, the National Front in France, and the Freedom Party of Austria; and fueled the Brexit vote in Great Britain. Figure 14.5 shows vote shares for populist parties in EU member states since 1990. Although populist vote shares have been highest in the central and eastern European countries that joined the European

Note: The figure shows the share of votes for populist parties for each year. For the purposes of this figure, populist parties were defined as parties whose platform claimed (1) that the party represented the interests of the "people" or "the nation" as opposed to particular groups, classes, or sectors; and (2) that the establishment elite had acted against this popular interest.

Figure source: Anna Grzymala-Busse, "Populist Party Support," Database, Stanford University, 2020.

72. For some recent studies showing the effects of economic shocks and migration on voting for right-wing, nationalist parties in Europe, see Italo Colantone and Piero Stanig, "The Trade Origins of Economic Nationalism: Import Competition and Voting Behavior in Western Europe," *American Journal of Political Science* 62, no. 4 (2018): 936–53; and Sascha O. Becker and Thiemo Fetzer, "Does Migration Cause Extreme Voting?" Working Paper 306, Center for Competitive Advantage in the Global Economy, University of Warwick, October 2016.

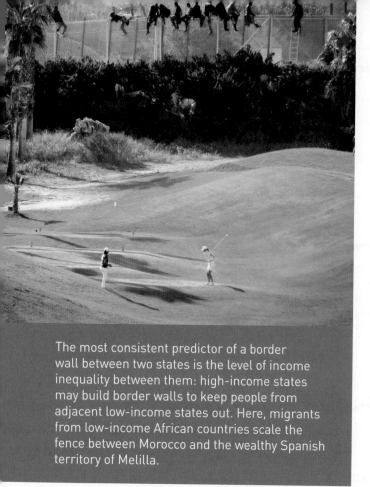

The most consistent predictor of a border wall between two states is the level of income inequality between them: high-income states may build border walls to keep people from adjacent low-income states out. Here, migrants from low-income African countries scale the fence between Morocco and the wealthy Spanish territory of Melilla.

Union after the end of the Cold War, since 1990, there has been a steady growth in support for populist parties across Europe.

This trend reflects a combination of factors. One is the building criticism of the European Union and its project of economic and political integration. "Euroskepticism" has long been a factor on the political right, which has opposed the transfer of national policy making to Brussels, the EU capital. That skepticism got a boost in the wake of the 2008 global financial crisis (see Chapter 8), which exposed deep rifts within the union. As countries like Greece, Spain, and Portugal struggled to meet their debt payments, a crisis arose over whether and how much other countries should lend financial assistance to prevent them from defaulting on their obligations. This crisis fed a perception in wealthier countries, such as Germany, Britain, and France, that the European Union put them on the hook to bail out more profligate members who were not willing to live within their means.

The aforementioned migration crisis further fed right-wing opposition to the European Union. As noted, EU law does not require member countries to accept migrants from outside the union unless they are seeking asylum from war or persecution. But expansion of the European Union into central and eastern Europe after the end of the Cold War created large flows of people from the new member states, which tended to be poorer, into wealthier EU countries. The enormous influx of people into the region starting in 2015 then created a new problem that EU institutions struggled to manage. Countries on the front lines of the migrant flow, especially Greece, Italy, and Hungary, were unable and unwilling to absorb the influx, and many migrants hoped to move on to wealthier states in northern Europe, such as Germany and Sweden.

Recognizing the need to spread the burden of absorbing the migrants, the EU developed a resettlement plan whereby each country would commit to accepting a certain number of people. The plan provoked resistance in a number of countries, particularly those with populist governments or strong populist movements. As a result of the crisis, Euroskeptics could add another charge against the institution: it was forcing their countries to take in foreign migrants.

Thus, both old and new complaints came together to fuel populist opposition to migration, EU institutions, and the overall project of European integration. All these trends converged in Britain's decision to withdraw from the European Union, popularly known as "Brexit." In a popular referendum in 2016, Britain narrowly voted to leave the union, which it finally did on December 31, 2020, after extended and difficult negotiations.

Populism came to the United States with the election of President Trump in 2016.[73] Trump's campaign drew heavily on populist themes, as he voiced strong opposition to immigration, free trade, and the ease of international investment (which helps U.S. companies move facilities abroad). As a result, he drew crucial support from voters in regions of the country where the loss of manufacturing jobs was particularly acute. He came into office promising both to build a wall on the United States' southern border with Mexico—a potent symbol of defending national sovereignty—and to withdraw from or renegotiate prior trade deals, including NAFTA. (For more on the issue of border walls, see "How Do We Know?" on p. 660.)

Populism has now spread globally. India's prime minister, Narendra Modi, has been accused of using Hindu nationalism to mobilize his political supporters.

Trump also took aim at another key institution of the postwar order: NATO. Trump criticized NATO allies for failing to spend enough money on defense (see the "What Shaped Our World?" box in Chapter 5). Although this criticism is not new (it was made by Presidents Bush and Obama before him), Trump seemed to imply that the United States' commitment to defending NATO allies would be contingent on their increasing defense spending—something that no previous president had suggested.[74]

The future of populism in the United States is somewhat uncertain after the election of President Biden. The Republican Party as a whole was never as populist as the former president, and it continues to draw significant support from businesses that benefit from globalization, free trade, and low-wage immigrant labor. Most Republicans also have continued to support NATO. Nonetheless, Trump had broad support from Republican voters, and his populist message resonated with many even after he lost reelection—demonstrated by the large numbers of people, and notably elected officials, who supported his claims that the 2020 election was stolen from him. Regardless of President Trump's future within the Republican Party, it is clear that populism will remain an appealing platform for many voters and candidates for office.

Beyond Europe and the United States, populism is also growing in developing countries. Prominent populist movements swept Indian prime minister Narendra Modi into office in 2014 and Brazilian president Jair Bolsonaro into office in 2018. Populism is thus not just a "first world" trend; it has a transnational dimension that

73. For evidence of the role of populism in the 2016 U.S. election, see J. Eric Oliver and Wendy M. Rahn, "Rise of the *Trumpenvolk*: Populism in the 2016 Election," *Annals of the American Academy of Political and Social Science* 667, no. 1 (2016): 189–206.

74. See, for example, David E. Sanger and Maggie Haberman, "Donald Trump Sets Conditions for Defending NATO Allies against Attack," *New York Times*, July 20, 2016, www.nytimes.com/2016/07/21/us/politics/donald-trump-issues.html (accessed 3/10/21). After Trump became president, he refused to confirm the United States' commitment to defending NATO allies on his first visit to Europe in May 2017, though he did later confirm this commitment.

Why Do States Build Border Walls?

On November 9, 1989, thousands of people in Berlin, East Germany, used hammers, picks, and shovels to tear down one of the world's most famous walls: the fortified barrier between East and West Berlin that had solidified the Cold War division of the city. The images of people dancing on the rubble seemed to symbolize the triumph of democracy, liberalism, and open borders.

In retrospect, the period of falling walls ushered in by that event was short-lived. Figure A shows the number of borders around the globe that had a human-made barrier in the period 1945–2016. Within 10 years of the fall of the Berlin Wall, the number of fortified borders started to increase dramatically. The growth is particularly pronounced in the Middle East, northern Africa, and Asia; in Europe, border walls vanished entirely after 1989 but went up again in 2015 at the height of the migration crisis. And on November 8, 2016—almost exactly 27 years after the fall of the Berlin Wall—the United States elected a president whose most prominent campaign promise was to build a wall along the entire U.S.-Mexico border.

Why do states build walls along their borders? The Berlin Wall was built to keep citizens in: to stem the flow of East Berliners trying to flee to the West. More commonly, walls are intended to keep foreigners out—specifically, armies and migrants. This observation suggests two broad interests that motivate wall building: interstate *security concerns* would lead to walls built for defensive purposes, while *opposition to migration* would prompt states to build walls to make it harder for people to cross the border.

To understand the relative importance of these considerations, David Carter and Paul Poast collected data on all human-made border barriers over the last two centuries and examined the factors that determined whether any given pair of neighboring states had a wall.[a] They found that the strongest and most consistent predictor is income inequality: as the difference in GDP between the states increases, so does the likelihood that a wall will be built by the wealthier country. There is also evidence that border walls are more likely to separate democratic from non-democratic countries. Both of these findings suggest that the main purpose for wall building is to impede the flow of migrants from poorer and less democratic neighbors.

Carter and Poast found less evidence that conventional security concerns lead to walls. Whether the states had a territorial dispute or had recently engaged in a militarized dispute did not appear to have a strong, consistent effect on whether there was a wall between them. While border fortifications historically served a defensive purpose, modern weaponry has rendered them less effective. Castle walls crumbled with the advent of the cannon. In the 1930s, the French built a series of fortifications and obstacles to prevent a repeat of the German invasion that occurred in World War I, but in World War II, German tanks swept around that line.

This is not to imply that border walls have no security rationale. The surge of wall construction following the September 11, 2001, terrorist attacks suggests that fears of infiltration by extremists provided additional justification for barriers. In today's world, walls are built to keep out people, not armies.

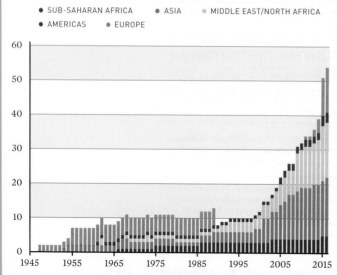

FIGURE A *Interstate Borders with Walls, 1945–2016*

- SUB-SAHARAN AFRICA
- ASIA
- MIDDLE EAST/NORTH AFRICA
- AMERICAS
- EUROPE

a. David B. Carter and Paul Poast, "Why Do States Build Walls? Political Economy, Security, and Border Stability," *Journal of Conflict Resolution* 61, no. 2 (2017): 239–70.

Figure source: David B. Carter and Paul Poast, "Why Do States Build Walls? Political Economy, Security, and Border Stability," *Journal of Conflict Resolution* 61, no. 2 (2017): 239–70. Updated to 2016 with information from Samuel Granados, Zoeann Murphy, Kevin Schaul, Anthony Faiola, et al., "Raising Barriers: A New Age of Walls," *Washington Post*, October 12, 2016, www.washingtonpost.com/graphics /world/border-barriers/global-illegal-immigration-prevention.

is ironic given its nationalist orientation.[75] Populist parties have given one another support and encouragement, seeing each other as natural allies in their opposition to prevailing institutions. Their rise has also created opportunities for another adversary of the U.S.-led postwar order: Russia. Russia has seen its foreign policy interests harmed by the extension of the European Union and NATO into central and eastern Europe. Thus, while Russian president Vladimir Putin is no populist himself, he shares common interests with people elsewhere who are similarly skeptical of those international institutions and of democracy at home.[76] As a result, Russia has in recent years supported populist politicians and parties. Most prominently, it interfered in the 2016 U.S. presidential election by spreading online messages that benefited Trump.[77]

Backlash and the International Trading System

In sum, the last decade has seen the dramatic growth of a broad set of actors motivated by economic, cultural, and foreign policy interests to oppose globalization and the institutions that have propelled it forward. The resulting political backlash has created conflicts both within and among states. Just as those who stand to gain from globalization pushed governments to lower barriers to trade and money flows and to construct institutions to facilitate economic integration, those who stand to lose have sought to influence policy in the other direction. The economic losers have incentives to seek protection from foreign competition in the form of trade barriers or restrictions on capital flows.

Economic insecurity has also increased demand for social welfare programs designed to cushion workers from the shocks of competition, such as unemployment insurance, health insurance, and job retraining programs. As we saw in Chapter 7, free trade generally creates economic benefits that exceed the costs to those whose jobs may be lost. Hence, in principle, everyone could be made better off as long as some of those benefits were redistributed. Redistribution would naturally come at the expense of the winners, however, who may or may not accommodate those demands.

Those who see globalization in terms of noneconomic costs to cultural identity or national sovereignty have also sought to stem its effects. Unlike economic losses, these losses cannot be compensated through a redistribution of resources; rather, they propel efforts to elevate the traditional national culture and restrict the expression of foreign cultural influences.

---

75. For a discussion of the relationship between populism and nationalism, as well as a consideration of populism's transnational aspects, see Benjamin de Cleen, "Populism and Nationalism," in Cristobal Rovira Kaltwasser, Paul Taggart, Paulina Ochoa Espejo, and Pierry Ostiguy, eds., *The Oxford Handbook of Populism*, 342–62, esp. 355–58 (New York: Oxford University Press, 2017). On transnational ties, see Katrin Bennhold and Michael Schwirtz, "Capitol Riot Puts Spotlight on 'Apocalyptically Minded' Global Far Right," *New York Times*, January 26, 2021, www.nytimes.com/2021/01/24/world/europe/capitol -far-right-global.html (accessed 3/24/21).

76. See, for example, Yulia Netesova and Torrey Taussig, "Trump and Putin: Populists of a Feather?" *National Interest*, March 28, 2017, http://nationalinterest.org/feature/trump-putin-populists -feather-19933 (accessed 3/24/21).

77. A declassified summary of the U.S. intelligence community's findings with respect to Russian actions can be found in Office of the Director of National Intelligence, "Assessing Russian Activities and Intentions in Recent U.S. Elections," January 6, 2017, www.dni.gov/files/documents/ICA_2017_01.pdf. At the time of this writing, additional investigations by the intelligence community, Congress, and the U.S. Department of Justice continued to explore the extent of Russian interference.

The demands of those who stand to lose from globalization seem likely to prevent further liberalization in the near future. Prospects for further liberalization within the WTO have been poor for some time. The WTO's most recent round of global talks, launched in 2001, ended in 2016 after 15 years of fruitless negotiations. The deadlock resulted primarily from the divergent interests of rich and poor countries. The trade war between the United States and China has further challenged the international trade regime. Even with the change in the U.S. presidency, there appears to be little support for reversing this trend.

If global liberalization continues to stagnate, what comes next? One possibility is that other states will take over the United States' role in sustaining and propelling further liberalization. The Trans-Pacific Partnership (TPP), negotiated by but ultimately rejected by the United States as a counterweight to Chinese influence, may survive in part because other TPP signatories, particularly Japan and Canada, are still interested in expanding trade within the Asia-Pacific region. The United States' withdrawal from the TPP may also create an opening for China to play a larger role in setting trade rules through an alternative agreement known as the Regional Comprehensive Economic Partnership. In Europe, the European Union faces immediate challenges from populist governments and parties as well as the departure of its second-largest economy, Great Britain. Will China, Japan, and what remains of the European Union cooperate to lead a global system? Or will they at least maintain economic openness in their respective regions?

The alternative is an unraveling of the global system, which would likely lead to a reduction in international economic activity. In constructing the postwar economic institutions, policy makers hoped to avoid a repeat of the 1930s, when the Great Depression led countries to impose tit-for-tat restrictions on trade, exacerbating economic contraction and increasing political tensions that ultimately culminated in world war. The system was successful in many respects, including its ability to contain some of the effects of the 2008 global financial crisis.[78]

Such benefits, however, are abstract and intangible. For those who feel harmed by globalization, the benefits derived from large-scale crises that were avoided—or crises that happened but were not as bad as they could have been—are immaterial relative to the local, concrete costs. Weakening political support in the very countries that constructed the postwar system poses the most serious threat to its survival.

Conclusion: Can Common Interests Prevail?

The globe is becoming increasingly integrated—not only by globalization but also by technology, the movement of people, and transnational externalities like climate change. As the COVID-19 pandemic has made clear, countries now face generalized

---

78. See, for example, Daniel W. Drezner, *The System Worked: How the World Stopped Another Great Depression* (Oxford: Oxford University Press, 2014).

threats to human well-being. A communicable disease anywhere is a disease everywhere. Global climate change threatens people and livelihoods around the world. The current system of global governance is highly decentralized, with each state remaining sovereign and cooperation dependent on an overlying network of international and nongovernmental organizations. Whether or not this system can meet the challenges of the twenty-first century is an open question—and one on which the future of humankind may rest.

Every case considered in this chapter tells a similar story: the institutions and patterns of interaction that took hold after World War II have created winners and losers. Some states and groups see the current system as hostile to their interests and seek to increase their power by acquiring new weapons. Other states, like China, are growing in power and have an interest in changing current bargains and rules in their favor. Finally, some groups see the process of globalization, and the institutions that have promoted it, as threatening to both economic and noneconomic interests.

The resulting clashes of interests will color future interactions, leading to political, economic, and possibly military conflict. The acquisition of WMD by hostile states or terrorist organizations and the growing power of China pose potential threats to the United States and its allies, raising the danger of preventive war. The backlash against globalization and the rise of populism have created political conflict within and between states, undermining political support for the postwar economic system and the institutions that upheld it. At stake is not just the flow of goods and capital across borders but the ability of people fleeing poverty and violence to find opportunity and security in other countries.

Set against these gloomy observations is the recognition that these challenges—and others, like a global pandemic or climate change—also generate common interests. The destructive potential of today's weapons means that a common interest in peace looms large relative to whatever gains could be won through war. As a result, states have an incentive to manage the rise of new powers and the spread of WMD in a peaceful manner. The wealth that can be created by globalization means that everyone can potentially gain, as long as the process is governed in a way that redistributes some of the gain to those actors that stand to lose. Inflows of people from different backgrounds can create discomfort and fear, but they can also be sources of vitality and innovation. In short, many of the challenges posed by the changing world can be met if the gains from cooperation can be spread in a satisfactory way.

The COVID-19 pandemic illustrates the problems and challenges of managing common interests. While different national responses to the spread of the virus allowed for a degree of experimentation to see which policies worked and which did not, and as pharmaceutical companies and countries competed against one another and perhaps brought vaccines to market faster than otherwise might have been possible, it also became clear that any solution to the pandemic required a coordinated international response. A hot spot anywhere could cause the virus to spread everywhere. And it also became immediately clear that not all countries were equally capable of responding to the pandemic; many lacked the resources

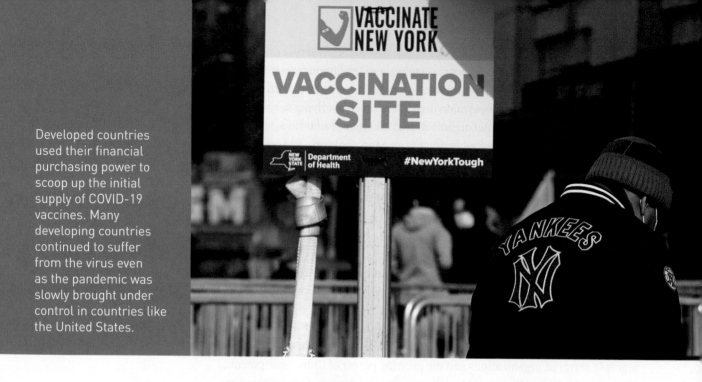

Developed countries used their financial purchasing power to scoop up the initial supply of COVID-19 vaccines. Many developing countries continued to suffer from the virus even as the pandemic was slowly brought under control in countries like the United States.

to promote safe behaviors, the ability to acquire personal protective equipment for first responders, or even adequate hospitals to treat sick patients. Highlighting these disparities, the rich nations of the North that developed vaccines also purchased the vast majority of the initial doses, leaving countries in the global South unable to secure supplies, at least at first. In the end, the countries least able to deal with the pandemic may suffer the most from it.

Faced with common challenges, countries may eventually be forced to consider new and more effective ways to cooperate internationally. Disease, pollution, and people forced to leave their homes due to government abuse, famine, violence, or terrorism do not respect national borders. To deal with these modern plagues, governments will eventually have to coordinate their responses or suffer the consequences. Yet, as we have seen throughout this text, problems of collective action can thwart the best of intentions, with each country attempting to free ride on the efforts of others. Distributional concerns are also important, especially when the costs and benefits of various solutions affect countries and powerful groups within countries differently. We also lack appropriate institutions at the global level to facilitate cooperation in many issue areas. There are very real challenges before us if we are to cope with the transnational problems now confronting humankind.

The history of international relations warns us not to be overly optimistic. There are real hatreds in the world, and people do not always act on the basis of an enlightened self-interest. World politics will never be free of conflicting interests or hostile interactions, and institutions will never entirely eliminate these conflicts through rules and redistribution. Some threats cannot be eliminated, only managed.

Yet we have also seen unmistakable signs of progress. Interstate war is not obsolete, but it is less frequent today than it was in the past. Although many people around the world still live in poverty, there have been tremendous advances in wealth and living standards. Democracy, considered a pernicious and destabilizing political form only two centuries ago, has spread to every continent, giving individuals greater say in the decisions that affect their lives. International cooperation to stop civil conflict and genocide, to protect human rights, and to safeguard the global environment has advanced significantly, even if these efforts fall short of the ideal.

We opened this book with the story of how a lone man defused violence between Arabs and Jews in 1921 by appealing to their shared interest in peace and prosperity. Although the peace of that day did not last, the man's efforts were still worthwhile. Progress is possible, even if perfection is not. Though conflicts will always remain, we have not yet exhausted all the opportunities to recognize and act on humanity's common interests.

Study Tool Kit

Interests, Interactions, and Institutions in Context

- The postwar order—the institutions and patterns of interaction that developed after World War II—generated a number of benefits, including economic development, increased trade and financial flows, the spread of democracy, and the decline of interstate war. Actors that see this order as hostile to their interests or that seek greater power within it will pose significant challenges in the coming decade.

- States and terrorist organizations that are hostile to the United States and its allies see weapons of mass destruction—nuclear, chemical, cyber, and biological weapons—as a way to counter U.S. military superiority. As a result, there will be growing conflict between actors who want WMD and those who would be harmed by proliferation. Whether the spread of WMD can be slowed depends on whether the latter actors can find a way—through cooperation, coercion, or institutions—to alter the interests of potential proliferators.

- The rise of China as a global power may lead to increased conflict between that country and the current world leader, the United States. Whether this dynamic will lead to war depends on the interests that prevail in both countries and on whether international and domestic institutions can make China a partner, rather than a rival, of the United States.

- Globalization creates winners and losers and increases the potential for political conflict within and among countries. Those who have experienced economic and noneconomic losses from the cross-border movement of goods, capital, and people form a potent opposition to globalization and the economic institutions that have promoted it. The rise of populist resistance in the United States and Europe presents a direct challenge to the postwar order from within the very states that constructed it.

For Further Reading

Debs, Alexandre, and Nuno P. Monteiro. *Nuclear Politics: The Strategic Causes of Proliferation*. New York: Cambridge University Press, 2017. Rigorously analyzes how strategic incentives influence whether states decide to acquire nuclear weapons.

Flaherty, Thomas M., and Ronald Rogowski. "Rising Inequality as a Threat to the Liberal International Order." *International Organization* 75, no. 2 (2021): 495–523. Examines the causes and consequences of income inequality for international politics.

Frieden, Jeffry A. *Global Capitalism: Its Fall and Rise in the Twentieth Century, and Its Stumbles in the Twenty-First*. New York: Norton, 2020. Explains the development of the global economy since 1900.

Gilpin, Robert. *War and Change in World Politics*. Cambridge: Cambridge University Press, 1981. Develops a general theory of the rise and fall of global leaders and argues that this theory explains major wars over the last several centuries.

Goldstein, Avery. "China's Grand Strategy under Xi Jinping: Reassurance, Reform, and Resistance," *International Security* 45, no. 1 (Summer 2020): 164–201. Summarizes China's grand strategy from 1992 to the present and argues that President Xi is not breaking with past policy but more boldly pursuing the nation's aims.

Lake, David A., Lisa L. Martin, and Thomas Risse. "Challenges to the Liberal Order: Reflections on International Organization." *International Organization* 75, no. 2 (2021): 225–257. Surveys the pillars of the liberal international order, the emerging challenges to that order, and implications for the study of world politics.

Lipscy, Phillip Y. *Renegotiating the World Order: Institutional Change in International Relations*. Cambridge: Cambridge University Press, 2017. Examines whether and how international institutions respond to changes in the relative power of their members.

Mudde, Cas, and Cristobal Rovira Kaltwasser. *Populism: A Very Short Introduction*. New York: Oxford University Press, 2017. Examines the causes and consequences of the success of populist parties around the world.

Sagan, Scott D., and Kenneth N. Waltz. *The Spread of Nuclear Weapons: An Enduring Debate*. 3rd ed. New York: Norton, 2012. Presents a debate between two scholars over whether the spread of nuclear weapons is good or bad for the world.

Shirk, Susan L. *China: Fragile Superpower*. New York: Oxford University Press, 2007. Examines how domestic politics within China will determine whether its rise as a global power takes place peacefully.

Valeriano, Brandon, Benjamin Jensen, and Ryan C. Maness. *Cyber Strategy: The Evolving Character of Power and Coercion*. New York: Oxford University Press, 2018. Understanding cyber strategies as coercion, finds that though cyber threats are potentially disruptive, they rarely produce concessions.

Glossary

absolute advantage The ability of a country or firm to produce more of a particular good or service than other countries or firms can produce with the same amount of effort and resources. Compare *comparative advantage*.

accountability The ability to punish or reward leaders for the decisions they make, as when frequent, fair elections enable voters to hold elected officials responsible for their actions by granting or withholding access to political office.

actors The basic unit for the analysis of international politics; can be either individuals or groups of people with common interests.

adjustable peg A monetary system of fixed but adjustable rates. Governments are expected to keep their currencies fixed for extended periods but are permitted to adjust the exchange rate from time to time as economic conditions change.

agenda setting Actions taken before or during bargaining that make the reversion outcome more favorable for one party.

alliances Institutions that help their members cooperate militarily in the event of a war. Compare *collective security organizations*.

anarchy The absence of a central authority with the ability to make and enforce laws that bind all actors.

appreciate In terms of a currency, to increase in value relative to other currencies. Compare *depreciate*.

asymmetrical warfare Armed conflict between actors with highly unequal military capabilities, such as when rebel groups or terrorists fight strong states.

audience costs Negative repercussions for failing to follow through on a threat or to honor a commitment.

austerity The application of policies to reduce consumption, typically by cutting government spending, raising taxes, and restricting wages.

autocracy A political system in which an individual or small group exercises power with few constraints and no meaningful competition or participation by the general public. Compare *democracy*.

balance of power A situation in which the military capabilities of two states or groups of states are roughly equal.

bandwagoning A strategy in which states join forces with the stronger side in a conflict.

Bank for International Settlements One of the oldest international financial organizations, created in 1930. Its members include the world's principal central banks, and under its auspices they attempt to cooperate in the financial realm.

bargaining An interaction in which two or more actors must decide how to distribute something of value. In bargaining, increasing one actor's share of the good decreases the share available to others. Compare *cooperation*.

bargaining range The set of deals that both parties in a bargaining interaction prefer over the reversion outcome. When the reversion outcome is war, the bargaining range is the set of deals that both sides prefer over war.

bilateral investment treaty An agreement between two countries about the conditions for private investment across borders. Most of these treaties include provisions to protect an investment from government discrimination or expropriation without compensation as well as mechanisms to resolve disputes.

boomerang model A process through which NGOs in one state are able to activate transnational linkages to bring pressure from other states on their own governments.

Bretton Woods monetary system The monetary order negotiated among the World War II Allies in 1944, which lasted until the 1970s and which was based on a U.S. dollar tied to gold. Other currencies were fixed to the dollar but were permitted to adjust their exchange rates.

Bretton Woods System The economic order negotiated among allied nations at Bretton Woods, New Hampshire, in 1944, which led to a series of cooperative arrangements involving a commitment to relatively low barriers to international trade and investment.

brinksmanship A strategy in which adversaries take actions that increase the risk of accidental war, with the hope that the other will "blink" (lose its nerve) first and make concessions.

bureaucracy The collection of organizations—including the military, diplomatic corps, and intelligence agencies—that carry out most tasks of governance within a state.

cap-and-trade system A cap-and-trade system sets an overall limit on emissions, which is then lowered over time to reduce pollutants released into the atmosphere. Firms can sell "credits" when they emit less than their allocation or must buy from others when they emit more than their allocation.

central bank The institution that regulates monetary conditions in a country's economy, typically by raising or lowering interest rates and the quantity of money in circulation.

civil war A war in which the main participants are within the same state, such as the government and a rebel group. Compare *interstate war* and *terrorism*.

coercion A strategy of imposing or threatening to impose costs on other actors in order to induce a change in their behavior.

coercive diplomacy The use of threats to advance specific demands in a bargaining interaction. Compare *crisis bargaining*.

collaboration A type of cooperative interaction in which actors gain from working together but nonetheless have incentives not to comply with any agreement. Compare *coordination*.

collective action problems Obstacles to cooperation that occur when actors have incentives to collaborate but each acts with the expectation that others will pay the costs of cooperation.

collective security organizations Broad-based institutions that promote peace and security among their members. Examples include the League of Nations and the United Nations. Compare *alliances*.

commodity cartels Associations of producers of commodities (raw materials and agricultural products) that restrict world supply of their products and thereby cause the price of their goods to rise.

common-pool resources Goods that are available to everyone, but such that one user's consumption of the good reduces the amount available for others. Common-pool resources are rival but nonexcludable. Compare *public goods*.

comparative advantage The ability of a country or firm to produce a particular good or service more efficiently than it can produce other goods or services, such that its resources are most efficiently employed in this activity. The comparison is to the efficiency of other economic activities that the actor might undertake given all the products it can produce—not to the efficiency of other countries or firms. Compare *absolute advantage*.

compellence An effort to change the status quo through the threat of force. Compare *deterrence*.

cooperation An interaction in which two or more actors adopt policies that make at least one actor better off relative to the status quo without making others worse off. Compare *bargaining*.

coordination A type of cooperative interaction in which actors benefit from all making the same choices and subsequently have no incentive not to comply. Compare *collaboration*.

credibility Believability. A credible threat is a threat that the target believes will be carried out. A credible commitment is a commitment or promise that the recipient believes will be honored.

crisis bargaining A bargaining interaction in which at least one actor threatens to use force in the event that its demands are not met. Compare *coercive diplomacy*.

customary international law International law that usually develops slowly, over time, as states come to recognize practices as appropriate and correct.

decolonization The process of colonial possessions winning independence, especially during the rapid end of the European empires in Africa, Asia, and the Caribbean between the 1940s and the 1960s.

default To fail to make payments on a debt.

delegation The degree to which third parties, such as courts, arbitrators, or mediators, are given authority to implement, interpret, and apply international legal rules; to resolve disputes over the rules; and to make additional rules.

democracy A political system in which candidates compete for political office through frequent, fair elections in which a sizable portion of the adult population can vote. Compare *autocracy*.

democratic peace The observation that there are few, if any, clear cases of war between mature democratic states.

depreciate In terms of a currency, to decrease in value relative to other currencies. Compare *appreciate*.

depression A severe downturn in the business cycle, typically associated with major declines in economic activity, production, and investment; a severe contraction of credit; and sustained high unemployment. Compare *recession*.

deterrence An effort to preserve the status quo through the threat of force. Compare *compellence*.

devalue To reduce the value of one currency relative to other currencies.

diversionary incentive The temptation that state leaders have to start international crises in order to rally public support at home.

entrapment The condition of being dragged into an unwanted war because of the opportunistic actions of an ally.

EOI See **export-oriented industrialization**.

exchange rate The price at which one currency is exchanged for another.

export-oriented industrialization (EOI) A set of policies, originally pursued in the mid-1960s by several East Asian countries, to spur manufacturing for export, often through subsidies and incentives for export production. Compare *import-substituting industrialization*.

externalities Costs or benefits resulting from an actor's decision that affect stakeholders other than that actor. When an externality exists, the decision maker does not bear all the costs or reap all the gains from the action.

extremists Actors whose interests are not widely shared by others; individuals or groups that are politically weak relative to the demands they make.

FDI See **foreign direct investment**.

first-strike advantage The situation that arises when military technology, military strategies, and/or geography give a significant advantage to whichever state attacks first in a war.

fixed exchange rate An exchange-rate policy under which a government commits itself to keeping its currency at or around a specific value relative to another currency or a commodity, such as gold. Compare *floating exchange rate*.

floating exchange rate An exchange-rate policy under which a government permits its currency to be traded on the open market without direct government control or intervention. Compare *fixed exchange rate*.

foreign direct investment (FDI) Investment in a foreign country via the acquisition of a local facility or the establishment of a new facility. Direct investors maintain managerial control of the foreign operation. Compare *portfolio investment*.

free ride To fail to contribute to a public good while benefiting from the contributions of others.

GATT See **General Agreement on Tariffs and Trade**.

General Agreement on Tariffs and Trade (GATT) An international institution created in 1947 in which member countries committed to reducing barriers to trade and providing similar trading conditions to all other members.

In 1995, the GATT was replaced by the WTO. Compare *World Trade Organization*.

genocide Intentional and systematic killing aimed at eliminating an identifiable group of people, such as an ethnic or religious group.

global climate change Human-induced change in the environment, especially from the emissions of greenhouse gases, leading to higher temperatures around the globe.

global supply chains A network of customers and suppliers involved in the production and distribution of a product. Parts of it may be inside a multinational corporation; parts may also involve links between corporations.

gold standard The monetary system that prevailed between about 1870 and 1914, in which countries tied their currencies to gold at a legally fixed price.

Group of 77 A coalition of developing countries in the UN, formed in 1964 with 77 members, that seeks changes to the economic order to favor the developing world. It has grown to over 130 members but retains the original name.

Heckscher-Ohlin trade theory The theory that a country will export goods that make intensive use of the factors of production in which it is well endowed. For example, a labor-rich country will export goods that make intensive use of labor.

hegemony The predominance of one nation-state over others.

human rights The rights possessed by all individuals by virtue of being human, regardless of their status as citizens of particular states or members of a group or organization.

humanitarian interventions Interventions designed to relieve humanitarian crises stemming from civil conflicts or large-scale human rights abuses, including genocide.

ICC See **International Criminal Court**.

ICCPR See **International Covenant on Civil and Political Rights**.

ICESCR See **International Covenant on Economic, Social, and Cultural Rights**.

IMF See **International Monetary Fund**.

import-substituting industrialization (ISI) A set of policies, pursued by most developing countries from the 1930s through the 1980s, to reduce imports and encourage domestic manufacturing, often through trade barriers, subsidies to manufacturing, and state ownership of basic industries. Compare *export-oriented industrialization*.

incomplete information A situation in which actors in a strategic interaction lack information about other actors' interests and/or capabilities.

individual petition A right that permits individuals to petition appropriate international legal bodies directly if they believe a state has violated their rights.

indivisible good A good that cannot be divided without destroying its value.

infrastructure Basic structures necessary for social activity, such as transportation and telecommunications networks, and power and water supply.

institutions Sets of rules (known and shared by the relevant community) that structure interactions in specific ways.

insurgency A military strategy in which small, often lightly armed units engage in hit-and-run attacks against military, government, and civilian targets.

interactions The ways in which the choices of two or more actors combine to produce political outcomes.

interest groups Groups of individuals with common interests that organize to influence public policy in a manner that benefits their members.

interests What actors want to achieve through political action; their preferences among the possible outcomes that might result from their political choices.

International Bill of Rights The UDHR, ICCPR, and ICESCR collectively. Together, these three agreements form the core of the international human rights regime.

International Covenant on Civil and Political Rights (ICCPR) The agreement, completed in 1966 and in force from 1976, that details the basic civil and political rights of individuals and nations. The ICCPR and ICESCR together are known as the "twin covenants."

International Covenant on Economic, Social, and Cultural Rights (ICESCR) The agreement, completed in 1966 and in force from 1976, that specifies the basic economic, social, and cultural rights of individuals and nations. The ICCPR and ICESCR together are known as the "twin covenants."

International Criminal Court (ICC) A court of last resort for human rights cases that possesses jurisdiction only if the accused is a national of a state party, the crime took place on the territory of a state party, or the UN Security Council has referred the case to the prosecutor.

international law A body of rules that binds states and other agents in world politics and is considered to have the status of law.

international humanitarian law (laws of war) A body of rules that seeks to limit the effects of armed conflict, protect noncombatants, and restrict means and methods of warfare for humanitarian reasons.

International Monetary Fund (IMF) A major international economic institution established in 1944 to manage international monetary relations. It has gradually reoriented itself to focus on the international financial system, especially debt and currency crises.

international monetary regime A formal or informal arrangement shared by most countries in the world economy to govern relations among their currencies.

interstate war A war in which the main participants are states. Compare *civil war*.

irredentist An actor that seeks to detach a region from one country and attach it to another, usually because of shared ethnic or religious ties. Compare *separatist*.

ISI See **import-substituting industrialization**.

iteration Repeated interactions with the same partners.

Kyoto Protocol An amendment to the UN Framework Convention on Climate Change, adopted in 1997 and entered into force in 2005, that established specific targets for reducing emissions of carbon and five other greenhouse gases through 2020.

laws of war See **international humanitarian law**.

LDCs See **less developed countries**.

League of Nations A collective security organization founded in 1919 after World War I. The League ended in 1946 and was replaced by the *United Nations*.

less developed countries (LDCs) Countries at a relatively low level of economic development.

linkage The linking of cooperation on one issue to interactions on a second issue.

mercantilism An economic doctrine based on a belief that military power and economic influence complemented each other; applied especially to colonial empires in the sixteenth through eighteenth centuries. Mercantilist policies favored the mother country over its colonies and over its competitors.

MFN status See **most-favored-nation status**.

military-industrial complex An alliance between military leaders and the industries that benefit from international conflict, such as arms manufacturers.

MNC See **multinational corporation**.

monetary policy An important tool of national governments to influence broad macroeconomic conditions such as unemployment, inflation, and economic growth. Typically, governments alter their monetary policies by changing national interest rates or exchange rates.

Montreal Protocol An international treaty, signed in 1989, that is designed to protect the ozone layer by phasing out the production of a number of CFCs and other chemical compounds.

most-favored-nation (MFN) status A status established by most modern trade agreements guaranteeing that the signatories will extend to each other any favorable trading terms offered in agreements with third parties.

multinational corporation (MNC) An enterprise that operates in a number of countries, with production or service facilities outside its country of origin.

national interests Interests attributed to the state itself, usually security and power.

nationalism A political ideology that prioritizes attachment to one's nation, where nations are groups defined by common origin, ethnicity, language, or cultural ties.

nationally determined contribution (NDC) The commitment each party to the Paris Agreement makes as to how it will contribute to reducing the threat of global warming.

NATO See **North Atlantic Treaty Organization**.

NDC See **nationally determined contribution**.

neo-mercantilism A belief that national economic policy should encourage exports and discourage imports, and that the country should aim to run a trade surplus. So called in relationship to the classical mercantilism of the colonial powers, which aimed at running trade surpluses with their colonies.

nonderogable rights Rights that cannot be suspended for any reason, including in cases of social or public emergency.

nonexcludable goods Goods that, if available to be consumed by one actor, cannot be prevented from being consumed by other actors as well. Compare *nonrival goods*.

nonrival goods Goods for which consumption by one actor does not diminish the quantity available for others. Compare *nonexcludable goods*.

nontariff barriers to trade Obstacles to imports other than tariffs (trade taxes). Examples include restrictions on the number of products that can be imported (quantitative restrictions, or quotas); regulations that favor domestic over imported products; and other measures that discriminate against foreign goods or services. "Buy American" laws that govern what state and local governments can buy, for example, are an implicit—but nontariff—obstacle to the purchase of imports.

norms Standards of behavior for actors with a given identity; norms define what actions are "right" or appropriate under particular circumstances.

norms entrepreneurs Individuals or groups that seek to advance principled standards of behavior for states and other actors.

norms life cycle A three-stage model of how norms diffuse within a population and achieve a taken-for-granted status.

North Atlantic Treaty Organization (NATO) An alliance formed in 1949 among the United States, Canada, and most of the states of Western Europe in response to the threat posed by the Soviet Union. The alliance requires its members to consider an attack on any one of them as an attack on all. Compare *Warsaw Pact*.

obligation The degree to which states are legally bound by an international rule. High-obligation rules must be performed in good faith and, if breached, require reparations to the injured party.

oligopoly A situation in which a market or industry is dominated by a few firms.

outbidding A strategy of terrorist attacks designed to demonstrate superior capability and commitment relative to other groups devoted to the same cause.

outside options The alternatives to bargaining with a specific actor.

P5 See **permanent five**.

Paris Agreement An agreement negotiated under the UNFCCC in 2015, signed by 195 countries, and entered into force in 2016. It was the first agreement to require commitments to control greenhouse gas emissions from all signatories.

Pax Britannica "British Peace," a century-long period, beginning with Napoleon's defeat at Waterloo in 1815 and ending with the outbreak of World War I in 1914, during which Britain's economic and diplomatic influence contributed to economic openness and relative peace.

peace-enforcement operation A military operation in which force is used to make and/or enforce peace among warring parties that have not agreed to end their fighting. Compare *peacekeeping operation*.

Peace of Westphalia The settlement that ended the Thirty Years' War in 1648; often said to have created the modern state system because it included a general recognition of the principles of sovereignty and nonintervention.

peacekeeping operation An operation in which troops and observers are deployed to monitor a cease-fire or peace agreement. Compare *peace-enforcement operation*.

permanent five (P5) The five permanent members of the UN Security Council: the United States, Great Britain, France, Russia (formerly the Soviet Union), and China.

POCs See **prisoners of conscience**.

portfolio investment Investment in a foreign country via the purchase of stocks (equities), bonds, or other financial instruments. Portfolio investors do not exercise managerial control of the foreign operation. Compare *foreign direct investment*.

power The ability of Actor A to get Actor B to do something that B would otherwise not do; the ability to get the other side to make concessions and to avoid having to make concessions oneself.

precision The degree to which international legal obligations are fully specified. More precise rules narrow the scope for reasonable interpretation.

preemptive war A war fought with the anticipation that an attack by the other side is imminent. Compare *preventive war*.

preventive war A war fought with the intention of preventing an adversary from becoming stronger in the future. Preventive wars arise because a state whose power is increasing cannot commit not to exploit that power in future bargaining interactions. Compare *preemptive war*.

primary products Raw materials and agricultural products, typically unprocessed or only slightly processed. The primary sectors are distinguished from secondary sectors (industry) and tertiary sectors (services).

prisoners of conscience (POCs) Individuals imprisoned solely for the peaceful expression of their beliefs. The term was coined by the human rights organization Amnesty International.

private authority An expression of legitimate rulemaking by nonstate actors in international affairs, including the establishment of norms governing the behavior of private global actors such as multinational corporations and international NGOs.

protectionism The imposition of barriers to restrict imports.

provocation A strategy of terrorist attacks intended to provoke the target government into making a disproportionate response that alienates moderates in the terrorists' home society or in other sympathetic audiences.

proxy wars Conflicts in which two opposing states "fight" by supporting opposite sides in a war, such as the government and rebels in a third state.

public goods Products that are nonexcludable and nonrival in consumption, such as national defense or clean air or water. Compare *common-pool resources*.

quantitative restriction (quota) A limit placed on the amount of a particular good that is allowed to be imported and sold domestically.

quota See **quantitative restriction**.

rally effect People's tendency to become more supportive of their country's government in times of dramatic international events, such as crises or wars.

recession A sharp slowdown in the rate of economic growth and economic activity. Compare *depression*.

reciprocity In international trade relations, a mutual agreement to lower tariffs and other barriers to trade. Reciprocity involves an implicit or explicit arrangement for one government to exchange trade-policy concessions with another.

regional trade agreements (RTAs) Agreements among three or more countries in a region to reduce barriers to trade among themselves.

resolve The willingness of an actor to endure costs in order to acquire a particular good.

Ricardo-Viner (specific-factors) model A model of trade relations that emphasizes the sector in which factors of production are employed rather than the nature of the factor itself. This differentiates it from the Heckscher-Ohlin theory, in which the nature of the factor—labor, land, capital—is the principal consideration.

risk-return trade-off In crisis bargaining, the trade-off between trying to get a better deal and trying to avoid a war.

RTAs See **regional trade agreements**.

security dilemma A dilemma that arises when efforts that states make to defend themselves cause other states to feel less secure; can lead to arms races and war because of the fear of being attacked.

separatist An actor that seeks to create an independent state on territory carved from an existing state. Compare *irredentist*.

sovereign lending Loans from private financial institutions in one country to sovereign governments of other countries.

sovereignty The expectation that states have legal and political supremacy—or ultimate authority—within their territorial boundaries.

specific-factors model See **Ricardo-Viner model**.

spoiling A strategy of terrorist attacks intended to sabotage a prospective peace between the target and moderate leadership from the terrorists' home society.

state A central authority that has the ability to make and enforce laws, rules, and decisions within a specified territory.

Stolper-Samuelson theorem The theorem that trade protection benefits the scarce factor of production. This view flows from the Heckscher-Ohlin theory: if a country imports goods that make intensive use of its scarce factor, then limiting imports will help that factor. So in a labor-scarce country, labor benefits from protection and loses from trade liberalization.

TAN See **transnational advocacy network**.

tariff A tax imposed on imports. Tariffs raise the domestic price of the imported good and may be applied for the purpose of protecting domestic producers from foreign competition.

terms of trade The relationship between a country's export prices and its import prices.

terrorism The use or threatened use of violence against noncombatant targets by individuals or nonstate groups for political ends. Compare *civil war*.

theory A logically consistent set of statements that explains a phenomenon of interest.

trade barriers Government limitations on the international exchange of goods. Examples include tariffs, quantitative restrictions (quotas), import licenses, requirements that governments buy only domestically produced goods, and health and safety standards that discriminate against foreign goods.

tragedy of the commons A problem that occurs when a resource is open to all, without limit. No one has an incentive to conserve, because others would use the resource in the meantime, so the resource suffers degradation.

transnational advocacy network (TAN) A set of individuals and nongovernmental organizations acting in pursuit of a normative objective.

Treaty of Versailles The peace treaty between the Allies and Germany that formally ended World War I on June 28, 1919.

UDHR See **Universal Declaration of Human Rights**.

UN See **United Nations**.

UNFCCC See **United Nations Framework Convention on Climate Change**.

United Nations (UN) A collective security organization founded in 1945 after World War II. With over 190 members,

the UN includes all recognized states. Compare *League of Nations*.

United Nations Framework Convention on Climate Change (UNFCCC) An international agreement enacted in 1992, and entered into force in 1994, that provides an overall framework for intergovernmental efforts on climate change.

United Nations Security Council (UNSC) The main governing body of the UN, which has the authority to identify threats to international peace and security and to prescribe the organization's response, including military and/or economic sanctions.

Universal Declaration of Human Rights (UDHR) A declaration, adopted by the UN General Assembly in 1948, that is defined as a "common standard of achievement for all peoples" and forms the foundation of modern human rights law.

UNSC See **United Nations Security Council**.

veto power The ability to prevent the passage of a measure through a unilateral act, such as a single negative vote.

Vienna Convention on the Protection of the Ozone Layer A framework convention adopted in 1985 to regulate activities, especially emissions of CFCs, that damage the ozone layer.

war An event involving the organized use of military force by at least two parties that reaches a minimum threshold of severity.

Warsaw Pact A military alliance formed in 1955 to bring together the Soviet Union and its Cold War allies in Eastern Europe and elsewhere; dissolved on March 31, 1991, as the Cold War ended. Compare *North Atlantic Treaty Organization*.

World Bank An important international institution that provides loans at below-market interest rates to developing countries, typically to enable them to carry out development projects.

World Trade Organization (WTO) An institution created in 1995 to succeed the GATT and to govern international trade relations. The WTO encourages and polices the multilateral reduction of barriers to trade, and it oversees the resolution of trade disputes. Compare *General Agreement on Tariffs and Trade*.

WTO See **World Trade Organization**.

Credits

Alamy Stock Photo; **p. 422:** Kate Holt/Bloomberg via Getty Images; **p. 427:** Everett Collection; **p. 429:** Everett/Shutterstock; **p. 435:** STR/REUTERS/Newscom; **p. 440:** Brendan Donnelly/Alamy Stock Photo.

CHAPTER 10 Pages 446-447: ImageBROKER/Shutterstock; **p. 450:** Jonathan ORourke/Alamy Stock Photo; **p. 452:** Xinhua/Alamy Stock Photo; **p. 457:** STR/REUTERS/Newscom; **p. 458:** Sarin Images/GRANGER; **p. 459:** GRANGER; **p. 461:** GRANGER; **p. 463:** De Agostini Picture Library/G. Dagli Orti/Bridgeman Images; **p. 465:** Cavan Images/Alamy Stock Photo; **p. 471:** REUTERS/Alamy Stock Photo; **p. 475:** REUTERS/Alamy Stock Photo; **p. 476:** Sia Kambou/AFP via Getty Images; **p. 477:** Sheikh Rajibul Islam/Alamy Stock Photo; **p. 478:** Carlos Barria-China Stringer Net/REUTERS/Newscom.

CHAPTER 11 Pages 484-485: Hein Htet/EPA-EFE/Shutterstock; **p. 488:** 615 Collection/Alamy Stock Photo; **p. 490:** Everett Collection Historical/Alamy Stock Photo; **p. 493:** Peter Carey/Alamy Stock Photo; **p. 497:** AP Photo/Peter Dejong; **p. 500:** AP Photo/Juan Carlos Hernandez; **p. 501:** National Archives; **p. 502:** Abaca Press/Balkis Press/Sipa USA/Newscom; **p. 503:** SOPA Images Limited/Alamy Stock Photo; **p. 505:** Pacific Press Media Production Corp./Alamy Stock Photo; **p. 507:** Graeme Robertson/Getty Images; **p. 509 Fig. 11.2:** Figure courtesy of Daniel Kinderman. Based on Daniel Kinderman, "Corporations and Global Standards of Corporate Social Responsibility," in Handbook of the International Political Economy of the Corporation, ed. Andreas Nölke and Christian May, 365–83. (Cheltenham, UK: Elgar, 2018); **p. 511:** Dpa Picture Alliance/Alamy Stock Photo; **p. 513:** Pradeep Gaur/Shutterstock.

CHAPTER 12 Pages 520-521: Simon Chapman/LNP/Shutterstock; **p. 524:** Jim West/Alamy Stock Photo; **p. 526:** Jeremy Hogan/SOPA Images/Shutterstock; **p. 530:** Shutterstock; **p. 532:** Karim Sahib/AFP/Getty Images; **p. 533:** Richard Ellis/Alamy Stock Photo;

p. 536: AP Photo/Eduardo Di Baia, File; **p. 537:** John Cetrino/EPA/Shutterstock; **p. 540:** Vadim Pacajev/Alamy Stock Photo; **p. 549:** Dursun Aydemir/Anadolu Agency via Getty Images; **p. 554:** Mohamed Hammi/SIPA/Newscom; **p. 557:** REUTERS/Alamy Stock Photo; **p. 559:** Ryan Mearns.

CHAPTER 13 Pages 564-565: Raihan Hasan/Zeppelin/SIPA/Shutterstock; **p. 568:** Shay Levy/Alamy Stock Photo; **p. 571:** Collet Guillaume/SIPA/Newscom; **p. 578:** International Whaling Commission; **p. 580 How Do We Know?:** Halvard Buhaug, "Globalt Tempuraturavvik Og Konflikt, 1946–2014,"in Nils Petter Gleditsch, Mot en mer fredelig verden? [Toward a more peacefulworld?] (Oslo: Pax, 2016). Reprinted with permission; **p. 581:** Roberto Nistri/Alamy Stock Photo; **p. 582:** Jim West/Alamy Stock Photo; **p. 583:** REUTERS/Norihiko Shirouzu/Newscom; **p. 584:** Ashley Cooper/Alamy Stock Photo; **p. 592:** Hans Blossey/imageBROKER/Shutterstock; **p. 593:** Peter de Clercq/Alamy Stock Photo; **p. 594:** J J Guillen/EPA-EFE/Shutterstock; **p. 596:** Luong Thai Linh/EPA/REX/Shutterstock; **p. 597:** Richard Cummins/Alamy Stock Photo; **p. 602:** Romuald Meigneux/Sipa/Shutterstock.

Chapter 14 Pages 608-609: Raphael Alves/EPA-EFE/Shutterstock; **p. 615:** Li Xueren/Xinhua News Agency/Newscom; **p. 617 Fig. 14.2:** From "An Economist's Guide to the World in 2050, by Tom Orlik and Bjorn Van Roye. Bloomberg.com, November 11, 2020. Used with permission of Bloomberg L.P. Copyright ©2020. All rights reserved; **p. 619:** SIPA USA/Alamy Stock Photo; **p. 622:** Rizwan Tabassum/AFP via Getty Images; **p. 629:** Kyodo via AP Images; **p. 634:** ITAR-TASS News Agency/Alamy Stock Photo; **p. 635:** AP Photo/Ng Han Guan, File; **p. 643:** Xinhua/Alamy Stock Photo; **p. 648:** Xinhua/Alamy Stock Photo; **p. 650:** Glow Images/Alamy Stock Photo; **p. 655:** REUTERS/Alamy Stock Photo; **p. 658:** Jose Palazon/REUTERS/Newscom; **p. 659:** REUTERS/Alamy Stock Photo; **p. 664:** Anthony Behar/Sipa USA)(Sipa via AP Images).

Index

entrapment, 207

enumeration, 7

environment, 564–607. *See also* climate change

  bargaining over future, 590–94

  collective action and, 569–71, *570*, 604–5

  common goods and common-pool resources and, 569–71, *570*, *571*

  cooperation by institutions on, 566, 595–603, 605

  creating property rights (cap-and-trade system) for, 574–78

  domestic winners and losers over, 582–84

  externalities and, 581

  facilitating decision making on, 600–602

  five factors in cooperation for, 572–74

  good intentions and, 567–69

  international winners and losers over, 584–90, *585*, *588–89*

  Montreal Protocol and, 494, 574, *576*, 576–77, *577*

  nationally determined contribution (NDC) for, 575, 605

  nonexcludable goods and, 570, *570*

  nonrival goods and, 570, *570*

  political struggles over, 579–81

  protection of ozone layer for, 570, 573–74, *576*, 576–77, *577*

  public goods and, 569–71, *570*

  regulations for, 578–79, 582–83, *583*

  resolving disputes over, 602–3

  and responsibility for bearing cost of global climate change, 592–94

  setting standards and verifying compliance for, *597*, *598–600*

  solving collective action problems and, 571–79

  success of cooperation for, 603–5

  thinking analytically about, 566

  and tragedy of the commons, 567–69, *568*, *569*, 572

environmental activists, 594, *594*, 596

environmental agreements, *495*, 496

environmental issues, international norms for, 511–12

environmentalists, and multinational corporations, 392

environmental movement, 594, *594*, 596

environmental performance index (EPI), 586, *588–89*

Environmental Protection Agency, 603–4

environmental treaties, 595–97, 600–603, 605

EOI (export-oriented industrialization), 470–71

equilibrium, 87

equity investment, 367, 367n2, 368

Eritrea, 256, 265

escape clauses, in international law, 492

Estonia, 419, 436, *436*

ETA (Euskadi Ta Azkatasuna), *287*, 287–88, 291

Ethiopia, 256, 265

ethnic differences, civil war from, 256–57, 258–59, 261–62, 265

ethnic lobbies, 167–68

ETS (Emissions Trading Scheme), 574, 575, 587, 591

EU. *See* European Union

EUFOR (European Union force) Althea, 237n40

euro, 408, 418–19, 430–33, *432*, 436, 615

Europe

  leading up to World War I, 15–18, *18*

  populism in, 654, *657*, 657–58, 662

  after World War I, 19–22, *20*

  after World War II, 614–15

  in World War II, 22–23

European alliances, 208–15

  in Cold War, 211–13

  leading up to World War II, 210–11

  NATO as, 212–15

  pre–World War I, 209–10

  Warsaw Pact as, 212

European Central Bank (ECB), 338, 417, 431

European Commission of Human Rights, 555

European Convention on Human Rights (ECHR), 555

European Court of Human Rights, 555

European Economic Community (EEC), 338

European sovereign debt crisis, 365–66

European Union (EU)

  and adoption of euro, 408, 418–19

  devaluation or depression in, 436, *436*

  Emissions Trading Scheme of, 574, 575, 587, 591

  and euro, 408, 418–19, 430–33, *432*

  and eurozone debt crisis, 364–66, 378, 389, 408, 416–17, 439–40

  and global financial crisis, 376

  and globalization, 31, 32, 36–37, 38, 39, 649, 64939

  and human rights, 539, *540*, 541

  and immigration, 401

  international finance and, 366

  and International Monetary Fund, 380, 381

  populism and, *657*, 657–58, 661, 662

  in postwar order, 611–12, 613, 614–15

and trade, 308, 317–18, 333, *334*, 337, 338, *349*

  withdrawal of Britain from, 299, *299*, 338, 366, 400, 401

European Union force (EUFOR) Althea, 237n40

"Euroskepticism," 658

Eurozone

  debt crisis of, 364–66, 378, 389, 408, 416–17, 439–40

  members of, 432, *432*

Euskadi Ta Azkatasuna (ETA), *287*, 287–88, 291

exchange rate(s), 409–22

  and appreciation, 409

  Bretton Woods monetary system and, 412

  and central bank, 411, 416

  consumers and businesses and, 417–22

  and currency manipulation, 419–22

  defined, 409

  and depreciation or devaluation, 409

  determination of currency values, 410–11

  fixed, 407–8, 411–12, 413–17, *414–15*

  fixed but adjustable (adjustable peg), 412, 413, *414–15*, 431

  floating, 412, *414–15*, 417, 430

  gold standard and, 411–12, *412*

  governments and, 413–17

  importance of, 409–10, *410*

  interest rates and, 411

  regime for, 411–13, *414–15*

  specific constraints on, 417, 417n3

  in today's international monetary system, 429–30

exchange-rate regime, 411–13, *414–15*

execution, extrajudicial, 296, 502–3

export-oriented industrialization (EOI), 470–71

extended deterrence, 106

extermination, 491

externalities, 581

extrajudicial killings, 296, 502–3

extremists

  and civil war, 269

  and terrorism, 282, *283*, 285

ExxonMobil, 390

F

Facebook, and Arab Spring, 514

"factor endowments," 312

factors of production, and trade, *51*, 311–13, 323–24, 325

fait accompli, 68–69

Fakhrizadeh, Mohsen, *106*

Falkland Islands, 152–54, *153*, *154*, 156, *157*, 161, 182

nuclear energy programs, civilian, 627

nuclear non-proliferation treaties, 626–29

nuclear power facilities, on-site inspections of, 72, *72*

nuclear stockpiles, 627

nuclear taboo, 499, 500–501, *501*, 505

"nuclear umbrella," 625–26

nuclear weapons. *See* weapons of mass destruction

Nuremberg trials, 491

O

Obama, Barack
  and Afghanistan, 275
  on chemical weapons attacks by Syria, 118, 623
  and China, 36, 645*n*52
  and climate change, 575–78, 590
  and Cuba, 167–68
  and Egypt, 189
  and International Criminal Court, 558
  and international investment, 373
  on peace and democracy, 176
  targeted killings by, 502, 535

obligation, in international law, 492, 496

observer groups, 601

ODS (ozone-depleting substances), 576, 577, 604

offense-defense balance, 127, 127*n*31

offensive alliances, 197–98, 206*n*17

offshore services, 650

Ohlin, Bertil, 311

oil industry, and environment, 582, *582*, 583, 598–99

oil interests, 172

oil prices, 473

oil sales, and civil war, 266

oil shocks, 30, 31, 483

oil tankers, discharge at sea of crude oil by, 598–99

oligopolistic firms, 464

one country–one vote rule, 77

on-site inspections, of nuclear power facilities, 72, *72*

ONUSAL (UN Observer Mission in El Salvador), 237

OPEC (Organization of Petroleum Exporting Countries), 30, 31, 473

"Operation Enduring Freedom," 295

opportunity cost of production, 359, *359*

Orbán, Viktor, 539, *540*

organic pollutants, 572–73

Organisation for Economic Co-operation and Development, 447

Organization of Petroleum Exporting Countries (OPEC), 30, 31, 473

Ottawa Convention, 487, 488, *488*

Ottoman Empire, 11
  and Armenian Genocide, 491
  leading up to World War I, 18
  after World War I, 19, 21

outbidding, 293–94

outcome, reversion, 65–66, 67–69

outside options, 67–68

"outsourcing" jobs, 391–92

ozone-depleting substances (ODS), 576, 577, 604

ozone hole, 576, *577*

ozone layer, 570, 573–74, *576*, 576–77, *577*, 603–4

P

P5 (permanent 5), 221, 222, 225, *225*

Pacific Islands Forum (PARTA), *349*

Pact of Steel, 197

Pakistan
  drone attacks in, 296
  and Kashmir region, 98, *98*, 166, 191, *257*
  killing of bin Laden in, 298
  United Nations and, *231*, 240
  and weapons of mass destruction, 619, 621, 622, *622*, 622*n*19, 625, 627

Palestinian(s), 133, *133*, 134, 265, 293

Palestinian terrorist groups, 281, 284, 285, 288

Panama, 433

Paracel Islands (Vietnam), 43

Paraguay, 531

Pareto, Vilfredo, 56

Pareto frontier, 56, *56*, 57, *57*

Pareto improvement, in national trade policies, 334

Paris Agreement
  defined, 567
  effectiveness of, *602*, 603
  and fossil fuels, 574
  global support for, 605
  and global warming, 566, 596, 597–98
  and nationally determined contribution, 575, 593
  Barack Obama and, 590
  and Donald Trump, 565, 584
  UN Framework Convention on Climate Change and, 600, 601

PARTA (Pacific Islands Forum), *349*

Partido Revolucionario Institucional (PRI), 438

partisan politics, trade and, 330–31, *331*, 332–33

Pax Britannica, 10–12

PCA (Permanent Court of Arbitration), 75–76

peace
  "at any price," 111
  democratic, 176, 182, 183, 186–87
  long, 137, 211–13
  peacekeeping and, 238, *238*

peace-enforcement operation, 224

peacekeeping forces
  and civil war, 275–77
  contributors to, 225, *225*
  defined, 217–18, *218*
  deployment of, 224–26
  effectiveness of, 238
  examples of, 226, *226*
  free-rider problem with, 220
  for Israel and Syria, 219
  number of active, 228, *230–31*

Peace of Westphalia, 8, 49

Pearl Harbor, 22, 183, 535

Peloponnesian War (431-401 BC), 637

People's Republic of China (PRC), 633. *See also* China

per capita gross domestic product, 453, *454–55*

Pérez, Carlos Andrés, 382

permanent 5 (P5), 221, 222, 225, *225*

Permanent Court of Arbitration (PCA), 75–76

persecution, 491

Persian Gulf War (1991)
  allied troop contributions to, 228, *229*
  bargaining and, 203
  deterrent threats and, 182–83
  economic development and, 32
  hand-tying and, 120
  and "new world order," 228–32
  United Nations and, 240

Peru, 281, 293

petition, individual, 554–56, 555*n*41

Philippines
  currency crisis in, 439
  development in, *452*
  financial crisis in, 385
  and maritime disputes with China, 43, 44, 45
  military bases in, 644
  out-migration from, 400
  United States defense pact with, 198

philosophical motivations, to sign human rights agreements, 539–41

Pinochet, Augusto, 395

"pivot to Asia," 645, 645*n*52

Planned Parenthood Federation of America, 506

plantation agriculture, 458, 459

Plehve, Vladimir, 157*n*16

pluralistic security community (PSC), 611–12

Universal Postal Union, 509

UNMIK (UN Interim Administration Mission in Kosovo), *230*

UNMISS (UN Mission in the Republic of South Sudan), *231*

UNMOGIP (UN Military Observer Group in India and Pakistan), *231*

UNPROFOR (UN Protection Force), 233

unskilled workers

    effect of globalization on, 652–54

    effect of migrants and refugees on, 655

    migration of, 398–401

UNTSO (UN Truce Supervision Organization), *231*

uranium, highly enriched, 624, 627, 628

U.S. Defense Department, 164

U.S. dollar

    adoption by countries of, 408, 419, 433

    in Bretton Woods monetary system, 412, 428

    and exchange rate, 409, *410*, 417–18

U.S. House of Representatives, 77

U.S. Senate, 77

U.S. State Department, 163, 164

U.S. Treasury Department, 421

USMCA (United States–Mexico–Canada Agreement), 308, *321*, 337, 346–47, *348*, 541, 649

U.S Supreme Court, on juvenile death penalty, 497–98

V

vaccines, 610, *663*

Vandenberg, Arthur, 147n2

vehicle emissions standards, 583, *583*, *596*

Venezuela, 382, *383*, 479, *500*

veto power, *220*, 222, 224–25, *225*, 239–40, 613

Videla, Jorge Rafael, 535

Vienna Convention for the Protection of the Ozone Layer

    and chlorofluorocarbon bans, 599

    decision-making structure of, 600

    defined, 574

    dispute resolution by, 602

    and Montreal Protocol, 576

    negotiation of, 596

    secretariat of, 601

    and sharing of scientific findings, 597

Vienna Convention on Diplomatic Relations, 489

Vietnam

    and China, 35, 43, 44, 45, 46, 644

    and France, 67

    and globalization, 32

    multinational corporations in, 395

Vietnam War (1955-1975), 44, 95n6, 99–100

Volkswagen, 390

voting rights, and development, 458–59

voting rules, 77–79

Vreeland, James, 546

W

wage reduction, 335

    from "China shock," 646, 652

"wagging the dog," 158–61

Wales, 264

Walter, Stephanie, 436

Wani, Burhan, *257*

war, 92–143

    and anarchy, 95–96

    bargaining and duration of, 129, *129*

    bargaining model of, 96, 100–103, *104*, 105

    bargaining over goods as source of future bargaining power and, 121–23

    brinksmanship ("slippery slope") and, 115–17

    civil, 95, 253–78

    from commitment problems, 120–32

    communicating resolve and, 114–20

    compellence and deterrence in, 103–6, *107*

    compromise and, 132–35

    costs of, 93–94, 101, 102, 104, 105, 137–38, 190

    and declining conflict over territory, 136–37

    defined, 95

    and democracy and international organizations, 138–39

    and dispute resolution, 100, 100n14

    domestic politics and, 144–93

    expected outcome of, 101, 104, 105

    frequency of, 94, *95*, 135

    incentives to represent and problems of credibility and, 111–14

    from incomplete information (misperceptions or mistakes), 96–97, 107–20, *108*

    from indivisibility, 132–35

    interests at, 97–100, *98*

    from interests of influential groups within states, 97

    international institutions and, 194–244

    interstate, 95

    limited, 111

    and military interests, 148, 162–66

    and nuclear deal between United States and Iran, 124–25

    as obsolete, 135–39

    over goods, 97–100

    over policies, 98–99

    over regime type, 99–100

    over territory, 97–98, *98*

    paying for power and, 119–20

    political costs of, *161*, 161–62

    power shifts and, 636–40, *639*

    preemptive, 127–32, *128*, 130n32, 209, 620

    preventive, 96, 123–27, 130, 131, 209

    proxy, 27, 265–66

    purpose of, 95–107

    and realism, 95–96, 147

    reasons for, 94, 135, 139–40

    in response to changing power, 123–26, *125*

    in response to fear of attack, 127–32, *128*

    and security dilemma, 96

    on terrorism, 502–3

    thinking analytically about, 94, *95*

    total, 111

    trade and, 137–38

    tying hands and, 117–18

    women leaders and, 155, *155*

war crimes, 491

war debts, after World War I, 21

warfare

    asymmetrical, 252

    guerrilla, 252, 267, 271–75, *274*

Warsaw Pact, 25, *26*, 31, 212, 213, 214

Washington, George, 73

"Washington Consensus," 505, 649

waterboarding, 530

wealth

    and civil war, 263, 278

    and trade, 308

The Wealth of Nations (Smith), 309

weapons, 9

weapons of mass destruction (WMD), 618–33. *See also* nuclear weapons

    bargaining over, 121–23

    brinksmanship and, 115–17, 119

    China and, 618, 619, 625, 626, 627, 628, 635

    and coercive disarmament, 630–33

    during Cold War, 60–61, *61*, 137, 621, 625, 638, 640

    Cuban Missile Crisis and, 26–27, *117*

    defined, 619

    deterrence of, 106, *106*, 295

    and distribution of power among states, 621–22

    guaranteeing security interests of potential proliferators of, 625–26

    in Hiroshima and Nagasaki, 23, *501*, 621

    international institutions and, 626–29

    Iran and, 121–22, 124–25, 618, 619, 621, 622, 626, 628, 630–33

    Iraq and, 33–34, 618, 627, 628, 630

    lessons of history on, 619–23